American Journal of International Law

VOLUME 77
1983

Published by

American Society of International Law

AMERICAN JOURNAL OF INTERNATIONAL LAW

VOLUME 77 CONTENTS 1983

[No. 1, January 1983, pp. 1–218; No. 2, April 1983, pp. 219–412; No. 3, July 1983, pp. 413–738; No. 4, October 1983, pp. 739–1025.]

PAGE

Power Sharing in the Law of the Sea — *Philip Allott* 1
Recognition of Governments Should Not Be Abolished — *M. J. Peterson* 31
The GATT and Multilateral Treaty Making: The Tokyo Round — *D. M. McRae & J. C. Thomas* 51
The Strait of Tiran, the Gulf of Aqaba, and the 1979 Treaty of Peace between Egypt and Israel — *Ruth Lapidoth* 84
The Tunisia-Libya Continental Shelf Case: Geographic Justice or Judicial Compromise? — *Mark B. Feldman* 219
The Legal Validity of Ultra Vires Decisions of International Organizations — *Ebere Osieke* 239
The Senate Role in Treaty Ratification — *Michael J. Glennon* 257
Towards Relative Normativity in International Law? — *Prosper Weil* 413
Strengthening the Soft International Law of Exchange Arrangements — *Joseph Gold* 443
Freedom of the Air and the Convention on the Law of the Sea — *Kay Hailbronner* 490
Choice of Law under the International Sales Convention: A U.S. Perspective — *Isaak I. Dore* 521
The Law of the Sea Convention and Third States — *Luke T. Lee* 541
Fisheries under the United Nations Convention on the Law of the Sea — *Shigeru Oda* 739
The Extraterritorial Application of the German Antitrust Laws — *David J. Gerber* 756
ICSID Arbitration and the Courts — *Georges R. Delaume* 784
The General Admission of Aliens under International Law — *James A. R. Nafziger* 804

Editorial Comments

Dulce et Decorum Est: The Strategic Role of Legal Principles in the Falklands War — *Thomas M. Franck* 109
Broadening the Advisory Jurisdiction of the International Court of Justice — *Louis B. Sohn* 124

An Alternative to the Law of the Sea Convention — *Anthony D'Amato* 281
Alwyn Freeman (1910–1983) — *Oscar Schachter* 285
On the Degradation of the Constitutional Environment of the United Nations — *Leo Gross* 569
Israel's Air Strike upon the Iraqi Nuclear Reactor — *Anthony D'Amato* 584
Human Dignity as a Normative Concept — *Oscar Schachter* 848

Notes and Comments

Review Essay: Good Faith in Public International Law — *Michel Virally* 130
Current Attempts to Revise International Law—A Comparative Analysis — *F. V. García-Amador* 286
On the Inadequate Reach of Humanitarian and Human Rights Law and the Need for a New Instrument — *Theodor Meron* 589
The Francis Deák Prize 615
The Teaching of International Human Rights Law in U.S. Law Schools — *Richard B. Lillich* 855
Soviet Theory of International Law for the Seventies — *Kazimierz Grzybowski* 862

Correspondence 134, 295, 404, 606, 727, 872, 982

Contemporary Practice of the United States Relating to International Law — *Marian Nash Leich* 135, 298, 616, 875

Judicial Decisions — *Monroe Leigh* 144, 308, 624, 878

Current Developments

The Proposed Iran Claims Act of the United States — *Marian Nash Leich* 166
The Panama Canal Treaty and Jurisdiction of U.S. Courts — *Marian Nash Leich* 167
The Thirty-fourth Session of the International Law Commission — *Stephen C. McCaffrey* 323
House Approves Proposal Permitting ICJ to Advise Domestic Courts — *Jack M. Goldklang* 338
Proposed Amendment of the Foreign Corrupt Practices Act of 1977 — *Peter D. Trooboff* 340
The 1982 Session of the UN Sub-Commission on Prevention of Discrimination and Protection of Minorities — *Jeanette Hantke* 651
Model American Convention on the Prevention and Punishment of Serious Forms of Violence — *Richard B. Lillich* 662
Discovery of Documentary and Other Evidence in a Foreign Country — *Robert B. von Mehren* 896
The African Charter on Human and Peoples' Rights — *U. O. Umozurike* 902
The Iran-United States Claims Tribunal — *Marian Nash Leich* 913

Book Reviews and Notes — *Edited by Leo Gross* 169, 345, 669, 915

Books Received 212, 407, 728, 986

Official Documents

United Nations General Assembly. Resolution on Principles Governing the Use by States of Artificial Earth Satellites for International Direct Television Broadcasting 733

International Legal Materials. Contents, Vol. XXI, Nos. 5–6 (1982); Vol. XXII, Nos. 1–4 (1983) 216, 411, 737, 990

Table of Cases 993

Index 996

The views expressed in the articles, editorial comments, book reviews and notes, and other contributions which appear in AJIL are those of the individual authors and are not to be taken as representing the views of the Board of Editors or the American Society of International Law.

Manuscripts in triplicate may be sent to the Editors-in-Chief of AJIL, Professors Oscar Schachter and Louis Henkin, Columbia University School of Law, New York, N.Y. 10027. Subscriptions, orders for back numbers, correspondence with reference to AJIL and books for review should be sent to the AMERICAN JOURNAL OF INTERNATIONAL LAW (ISSN 0002-9300), 2223 Massachusetts Avenue, N.W., Washington, D.C. 20008.

AJIL is published in January, April, July, and October and is supplied to all members of the American Society of International Law. The annual subscription to nonmembers of ASIL is $52.00, plus $2.50 for all foreign subscriptions (including ASIL Proceedings). Available back numbers of AJIL will be supplied at $11.00 each. ($21 of membership fee is allotted to AJIL subscription.)

EDITORIAL OFFICE:
BOX 44
COLUMBIA UNIVERSITY SCHOOL OF LAW
NEW YORK, N.Y. 10027

BUSINESS OFFICE:
2223 MASSACHUSETTS AVENUE, N.W.
WASHINGTON, D.C. 20008

STATEMENT OF OWNERSHIP, MANAGEMENT AND CIRCULATION

(Act of August 12, 1970; Sec. 3685, Title 39, U.S. Code)

Filed November 1983, *American Journal of International Law* (issued quarterly, January, April, July, October), Prince & Lemon Streets, Lancaster, Pennsylvania 17603. Published by American Society of International Law, 2223 Massachusetts Avenue, N.W., Washington, D.C. 20008. Editors-in-Chief, Louis Henkin and Oscar Schachter, Columbia University School of Law, New York, N.Y. 10027. Owner, American Society of International Law. *Average* number of copies per issue, last 12 months: total printed, 7,968; paid circulation, 6,673; mail subscriptions, 6,673; total paid circulation, 6,673; free distribution, 128; total distribution, 6,801; office use, left over, unaccounted, spoiled after printing, 1,167. For *single* issue nearest to filing date: total printed, 7,984; paid circulation, 6,611; mail subscriptions, 6,611; total paid circulation, 6,611; free distribution, 128; total distribution, 6,739; office use, left over, unaccounted, spoiled after printing, 1,245.

American Journal of International Law

January 1983
Vol. 77 No. 1

Published by
American Society of International Law

PATRONS OF THE SOCIETY

Honorable ARTHUR H. DEAN
Honorable HERMAN PHLEGER
GENEVIEVE E. TILLAR (deceased)
W. ROBERT MORGAN
BRUNSON MACCHESNEY (deceased)
ALONA E. EVANS (deceased)
JOHN N. HAZARD
Honorable JOHN R. STEVENSON
ARTHUR R. ALBRECHT

In Memoriam

DR. JAMES BROWN SCOTT
HENRY C. MORRIS
ARTHUR K. KUHN
ALEXANDER FREEMAN
STANLEY P. SMITH

PATRONAGE, GIFTS AND BEQUESTS

Upon donation to the Society of $5,000 or more by gift or bequest, any member of the Society or individual eligible for membership may be elected a Patron of the Society. Upon donation of at least $5,000 in the name of a deceased person, such person may be elected a Patron posthumously.

Gifts and bequests may be made in the name of the American Society of International Law, Washington, D.C. Such contributions are deductible from federal returns for income, estate and gift tax purposes. The Society is incorporated by Act of Congress approved September 20, 1950 (64 Stat. 869).

MANLEY O. HUDSON MEDAL

The American Society of International Law bestows from time to time without regard to nationality a gold medal to commemorate the life work of Manley O. Hudson. Such awards are made for preeminent scholarship and achievement in international law and in the promotion of the establishment and maintenance of international relations on the basis of law and justice. Medals have been awarded to Manley O. Hudson (1956), Lord McNair (1959), Philip C. Jessup (1964), Charles De Visscher (1966), Paul Guggenheim (1970), Myres S. McDougal (1976), Eduardo Jiménez de Aréchega (1978), Richard Reeve Baxter (1981), Oscar Schachter (1981), and Hardy Cross Dillard (1982).

Second-class postage paid at Washington, D.C. and additional mailing office

Postmaster: If undeliverable, send notice on Form 3579 to: American Journal of International Law
2223 Massachusetts Ave., N.W. Washington, D.C. 20008

Printed by Lancaster Press, Lancaster, Pa. 17604

AMERICAN JOURNAL OF INTERNATIONAL LAW

VOL. 77 January 1983 NO. 1

CONTENTS

PAGE

Power Sharing in the Law of the Sea *Philip Allott* 1
Recognition of Governments Should Not Be Abolished *M. J. Peterson* 31
The GATT and Multilateral Treaty Making: The Tokyo Round *D. M. McRae & J. C. Thomas* 51
The Strait of Tiran, the Gulf of Aqaba, and the 1979 Treaty of Peace between Egypt and Israel *Ruth Lapidoth* 84

Editorial Comments
Dulce et Decorum Est: The Strategic Role of Legal Principles in the Falklands War *Thomas M. Franck* 109
Broadening the Advisory Jurisdiction of the International Court of Justice *Louis B. Sohn* 124

Notes and Comments
Review Essay: Good Faith in Public International Law *Michel Virally* 130
Correspondence 134

Contemporary Practice of the United States Relating to International Law *Marian Nash Leich* 135

Judicial Decisions *Monroe Leigh* 144

Current Developments
The Proposed Iran Claims Act of the United States *Marian Nash Leich* 166
The Panama Canal Treaty and Jurisdiction of U.S. Courts *Marian Nash Leich* 167

Book Reviews and Notes *Edited by Leo Gross*
Lachs, Manfred. *The Teacher in International Law (Teachings and Teaching)* (Thomas M. Franck) 169
Mukherjee, Sakti, and Indrani Mukherjee. *Major Issues in International Law* (John N. Hazard) 171
Jütte, Rudiger, and Annemarie Grosse-Jütte (eds.). *The Future of International Organization* (John Gerard Ruggie) 172
Lillich, Richard B. (ed.). *International Aspects of Criminal Law: Enforcing United States Law in the World Community* (Bruce Zagaris) 173
Van den Wijngaert, Christine. *The Political Offence Exception to Extradition: The Delicate Problem of Balancing the Right of the Individual and the Public International Order* (Valerie Epps) 175
Singh, Elen C. *The Spitsbergen (Svalbard) Question: United States Foreign Policy, 1907–1935* (Edward Gordon) 177
Auburn, F. M. *Antarctic Law and Politics* (Christopher C. Joyner) 180
Boisson, Philippe. *La Sécurité en Mer* (Elisabeth Mann Borgese) 182
Dam, Kenneth W. *The Rules of the Game: Reform and Evolution in the International Monetary System* (Robert E. Litan) 185
Olson, Robert K. *U.S. Foreign Policy and the New International Economic Order: Negotiating Global Problems, 1974–1981* (Robert F. Meagher) 186

Wyatt, Derrick, and Alan Dashwood. *The Substantive Law of the EEC* (Robert B. von Mehren) 188
Canenbley, Cornelis (ed.). *Enforcing Antitrust against Foreign Enterprises* (Ronald C. Griffin) 189
Kerse, C. S. *EEC Antitrust Procedure* (Joseph P. Griffin) 191
Sauvant, Karl P. *The Group of 77. Evolution, Structure, Organization* (Marcia A. Wiss) 192
Sauvant, Karl P. (ed.). *The Collected Documents of the Group of 77.* 6 vols. (Marcia A. Wiss) 192
Bulajić, Milan. *Međunarodno pravo ekonomskog razvoja: Pravni aspekti novog medunarodnog ekonomskog poretka* (Peter B. Maggs) 193
Proceedings of the Twenty-Third Colloquium on the Law of Outer Space (Ivan A. Vlasic) 194
Kneifel, J. L. *Fluggesellschaften und Luftverkehrssysteme der sozialistischen Staaten UdSSR, Polen, CSSR, Ungarn, Bulgarien, Rumänien, Kuba, Jugoslawien und der VR China* (Boleslaw A. Boczek) 196
Kneifel, J. L. *Staatliches und internationales Luftverkehrsrecht der sozialistischen Staaten UdSSR, DDR, Polen, CSSR, Ungarn, Bulgarien, Rumänien, Kuba, Jugoslawien und der VR China* (Boleslaw A. Boczek) 196
Weber, Ludwig. *Die Zivilluftfahrt im Europäischen Gemeinschaftsrecht* (Boleslaw A. Boczek) 196
Byrne, Edward M. *Military Law* (3d ed.) (J. Ashley Roach) 198
Maneli, Mieczyslaw. *Juridical Positivism and Human Rights* (S. Prakash Sinha) 199
Rights and Responsibilities. International, Social, and Individual Dimensions (Laurent Marcoux, Jr.) 201
Lillich, Richard B. (ed.). *The Family in International Law: Some Emerging Problems* (Luke T. Lee) 202
Soviet Year-Book of International Law, 1980 (John N. Hazard) 203
Polish Yearbook of International Law, Vol. X, 1979–1980 (K. Grzybowski) 205
Briefer Notices: Finger and Harbert (eds.), 207; Rumpf, 208; Rowles, 208; Dreyfus, 209; Katō, Kumamoto, and Matthews (eds.), 210; Hingorani, 211; Fischer (ed./ann.), with Wälde, 211.
Books Received 212
International Legal Materials. Contents, Vol. XXI, No. 5 (September 1982) and No. 6 (November 1982) 216

Manuscripts in triplicate may be sent to the Editors-in-Chief of AJIL, Professors Oscar Schachter and Louis Henkin, Columbia University School of Law, New York, N.Y. 10027. Subscriptions, orders for back numbers, correspondence with reference to AJIL and books for review should be sent to the AMERICAN JOURNAL OF INTERNATIONAL LAW (ISSN 0002-9300), 2223 Massachusetts Avenue, N.W., Washington, D.C. 20008.

AJIL is published in January, April, July, and October and is supplied to all members of the American Society of International Law. The annual subscription to nonmembers of ASIL is $52.00, plus $2.50 for all foreign subscriptions (including ASIL Proceedings). Available back numbers of AJIL will be supplied at $11.00 each. ($21 of membership fee is allotted to AJIL subscription.)

EDITORIAL OFFICE:
BOX 44
COLUMBIA UNIVERSITY SCHOOL OF LAW
NEW YORK, N.Y. 10027

BUSINESS OFFICE:
2223 MASSACHUSETTS AVENUE, N.W.
WASHINGTON, D.C. 20008

The American Society of International Law

The American Society of International Law was organized in 1906 "to foster the study of international law and to promote the establishment and maintenance of international relations on the basis of law and justice."

The Society serves as a meeting place and forum for scholars, teachers, officials, lawyers, and others, from some one hundred countries. In April, it holds a three-day Annual Meeting at which current problems of international law are discussed. The Society also sponsors regional meetings outside of Washington in cooperation with other institutions. Salient questions of international law and relations are considered in depth by panels and study groups organized by the Society's Board of Review and Development. Works of scholarship are often published under the Society's auspices in connection with studies sponsored by the Board, many in the Society's series of *Studies in Transnational Legal Policy*.

The Society periodically issues four publications:

The American Journal of International Law, the leading journal in the field of international law, has been published since 1907. The *Proceedings of the American Society of International Law* carries the papers and discussion of the annual meeting of the Society.

International Legal Materials, a bimonthly, is a unique international collection of texts of current official documents, including legislation, treaties, court decisions, and reports. Subscription rates are $30 a year for members of the Society, $65 for others.

The quarterly *Newsletter* provides members with news of the Society and other organizations in the field.

Society membership is open to all persons of whatever nationality and profession who are interested in its objectives. Dues are: regular, $55; special category, $30 for persons *not* resident in a member country of the Organisation for Economic Co-operation and Development; intermediate, $25; student, $15. Membership application form is printed at the back of each issue of AJIL.

POWER SHARING IN THE LAW OF THE SEA

*By Philip Allott**

The United Nations Convention on the Law of the Sea is a fact. It exists. Whether or not it becomes a fully operational treaty–signed, ratified, in force, widely supported, generally followed–it is and will be the cause of significant effects. Its very existence modifies political, economic, and legal relationships in countless ways whose direction and intensity we can predict only in a most speculative way. What we can say in advance is that the effect of the Convention—its own fate as a treaty and its impact on international relations—will substantially depend on how it is perceived. It is itself the product of mental processes. It will in its turn intrude into the mental processes of those involved in any way in the activities to which it relates. The purpose of the present article is to suggest a particular and unified structure of ideas within which the significance of the Convention may be perceived as a whole—a structure that, when grasped as a whole, facilitates the task of determining the significance of its individual provisions and has implications for our general perception of contemporary international law and society.

The problem of determining the significance of facts of social behavior (including legal acts) is at least as old as Western philosophy itself. From the beginning it has seemed that social facts participate in two worlds, the natural or physical world of cause and effect and the mental world of ideas.[1] Ideas have the peculiar characteristic that they are what they are about. Ideas about ideas are ideas. The physical sciences, on the other hand, have proceeded, at least until recently and still today for almost all everyday science, on the assumption that scientific ideas are about an external world different in kind from ideas. The scientific observer could and can, for almost all practical purposes, claim to be merely an observer. At one point in the 18th century (under the seductive influence of Hume), and for some in the 19th century (the positivists and their followers), and now more recently with the rise, first, of behaviorism and, lately, of socio-biology, there have been those for whom the study of social facts need be no different in principle and, sooner or later, in method from the study of all other phenomena.[2]

* Fellow of Trinity College, Cambridge. This article is based on a paper given at a meeting of the International Law Association (British branch) held in Cambridge on May 15, 1982. Mr. Allott was a member of the United Kingdom delegation to the Third United Nations Conference on the Law of the Sea. The views expressed are personal.

[1] Now the reason why man is more of a political animal than bees or any other gregarious animals is evident. Nature, as we often say, makes nothing in vain, and man is the only animal whom she has endowed with the gift of speech. And whereas mere sound is but an indication of pleasure or pain, . . . the power of speech is intended to set forth the expedient and inexpedient, and likewise the just and the unjust. And it is a characteristic of man that he alone has any sense of good and evil, of just and unjust, and the association of living beings who have this sense makes a family and a state.

ARISTOTLE, POLITICS, bk. I, at 10–12 (tr. Jowett).

[2] There is nothing chimerical in the hope that general laws, sufficient to enable us to answer these various questions [prediction and control of social events] for any country or time with

There has been a powerful and continuing tradition to the contrary effect, asserting or assuming the specific nature of mental phenomena. It is a tradition that has been reinforced from many different philosophical directions since the 18th century, by forms of philosophy that may be mutually inconsistent and even antagonistic in all other respects: Kant and Hegel and the idea of the autonomy of mental structures,[3] Marx and the powerful concept of *ideology*,[4] the hermeneutic tradition and the elusive concept of *interpretation*,[5] linguistics and structuralism and the concepts of *meaning and significance*.[6] Within this tradition, every perceived social fact—a soap powder, a poem, a form of food, a social institution, a historical event[7]—acts through a mental

---

> the individual circumstances of which we are well acquainted, do really admit of being ascertained; and moreover, that the other branches of human knowledge, which this undertaking presupposes, are so far advanced that the time is ripe for its commencement. Such is the object of the Social Science.

2 J. S. MILL, A SYSTEM OF LOGIC 536 (1843). *See also* E. O. WILSON, SOCIOBIOLOGY: THE NEW SYNTHESIS (1975), and ON HUMAN NATURE (1978). Wilson has said elsewhere:

> The question that science is now in a position to approach is the very origin and meaning of human values, from which all ethical pronouncements and much of political practice flow. Philosophers themselves have not explored the problem; traditional ethical philosophy begins with premises that are examined with reference to their consequences but not their origins.

Academic Vigilance and the Political Significance of Sociobiology, BIOSCIENCE, March 1976, at 183, 189.

3 Kant and Hegel both considered that the process of thought is not merely a product of the world outside the mind. Either thought creates the world as we know it (Kant) or thought and the world are not essentially different (Hegel). *Cf.* the correction by Leibniz of the empiricist axiom: "nothing in the intellect which was not before in the senses; *nothing but the intellect itself.*" G. W. VON LEIBNIZ, NEW ESSAYS ON THE UNDERSTANDING, bk. II, §2 (1704) (trans. and emphasis added by present author).

4 *See especially* K. MARX & F. ENGELS, THE GERMAN IDEOLOGY (English tr., Moscow 1964). The leading modern work is K. MANNHEIM, IDEOLOGY AND UTOPIA (1936). *See also* M. OAKESHOTT, RATIONALISM IN POLITICS AND OTHER ESSAYS (1962); J. PLAMENATZ, IDEOLOGY (1971); FRANKFURT INSTITUTE FOR SOCIAL RESEARCH, ASPECTS OF SOCIOLOGY, esp. ch. XII (tr. Viertel 1973). On the Marxian concept in neo-Marxian contexts, see C. SUMNER, READING IDEOLOGIES (1979).

5 "Interpretation is the work of thought which consists in deciphering the hidden meaning in the apparent meaning, in unfolding the levels of meaning implied in the literal meaning." P. RICOEUR, THE CONFLICT OF INTERPRETATIONS—ESSAYS IN HERMENEUTICS 13 (1974). *See also* R. A. MAKKREEL, DILTHEY, PHILOSOPHER OF THE HUMAN STUDIES (1975); Z. BAUMAN, HERMENEUTICS AND SOCIAL SCIENCE—APPROACHES TO UNDERSTANDING (1978).

6 Modern linguistics, pioneered by Saussure, has sought to move one focus of philosophical attention from the problem of truth (logic and epistemology) to the problem of the functioning and function of language itself (including all kinds of signs and symbols) as a phenomenon in its own right. Language is seen not merely as a neutral vehicle for conveying ideas but as a substantive human activity in itself, itself the cause of psychological and social effects. Structuralism, especially as developed by Lévi-Strauss, has carried further a similar orientation to cover the whole field traditionally claimed by anthropology. For the structuralist, all human and social phenomena (including rule making and rule following) are interrelated structures of meaning to those who participate in them and they may be studied as such by those who observe them systematically.

7 *See, e.g.*, R. BARTHES, *Soap-powders and detergents*, in MYTHOLOGIES (English ed. 1972); Jakobson, *Linguistics and poetics*, in STYLE IN LANGUAGE (Sebeok ed. 1960); C. LÉVI-STRAUSS, MYTHOLOGIQUES I: LE CRU ET LE CUIT (1964), and TOTEMISM (tr. Poole 1963); J.-P. SARTRE, CRITIQUE DE LA RAISON DIALECTIQUE, ch. II, "Du groupe à l'histoire" (the French Revolution) (1960).

complex that rests as a superstructure on a real-world material basis. In that mentalized form the social fact participates in the mental processes of the members of society and it is through modification of the mental complex, among other means, that the real-world facts may be modified in their turn. The real-world fact and the mental complex of the social fact interact with each other. But each has its own history and its own potentialities for further development. The correspondence that may exist between them at any given time does not mean that either is exclusively the cause of the other. As between the power of the idea of the thing and the power of the thing itself, neither is necessarily the master of the other.

Positive law seems to fit uncomfortably within such a notion of social fact. Positive law has a spurious autonomy. It seems to be separate both from the real-world substratum that underlies it and from the mental complexes through which it is perceived. As a mental fact, it seems nevertheless not to have, or to have any need for, any actual thinking subject. As a social fact, it nevertheless seems to be abstracted from every actual and particular real-life situation, to be beyond the real, metaphysical. It lacks the power of subjectivity that energizes mental fact. It lacks the concreteness of actuality that energizes social fact. And yet positive law is one of the most powerful manifestations of real-world forces and one of the most powerful determinants of social behavior. For all its disembodied objectivity, positive law is a leading cause and effect of social fact. Its spurious autonomy is the cunning of the law. For the critic of the law who places himself in the idealist tradition, it is precisely this consideration which creates the challenge. To seek to understand positive law only in terms of the real-world forces that have caused it and the real-world effects that it causes is to ignore and subvert its great ideological power. To seek to understand positive law only in its own terms, to discount the illusion, to be loyal exclusively to the texts as self-contained structures of ideas is to abandon hope of rational control over the law as a leading cause of real-world effects. The attitudes of lawyers themselves, especially those within the common law tradition, tend to oscillate between these poles.

The concept of *significance* is designed to square this analytical circle, to grasp what a social fact means, but not what it means only for the empirical observer looking in from outside and not what it means only to the insider for whom participation in the social fact is the living of a part of his life. Significance means a significance that combines in a single structure the perspectives of the outsider and the insider and that both the outsider and the insider can recognize as a representation of the real social fact they respectively observe and experience. The method of finding such significance assumes that the social fact in question (in the present case, a set of treaty texts) is surrounded by layer-upon-layer of *contexts* and participates in a network of interlocking *relationships*. Each social fact is a complex of such contexts and relationships. The method seeks to assemble an orderly pattern of such contexts and relationships, bringing into a single focus a field of vision that extends from a single word of text to the phenomenon of social organization as a whole. The more complete and orderly the integrated structure within which we place a given social fact, the more completely do we know the power we have over it and it has over us.

It is thus possible to look at the Law of the Sea Convention as a specific phenomenon, the center of its own structure of significance. It happens to take the form of a written text, highly wrought in structure and formulation, so that the structural method of analysis must treat the text of the Convention as the central focus of analysis. The method moves in towards the text through its surrounding layers of significance and then moves out from the text to resituate it in relation to other structural phenomena of international society. Such a critical method, as applied here to the Law of the Sea Convention, should be regarded as appropriate for establishing the significance of any other important legal act in written form.

* * * *

The Law of the Sea Convention takes its place in the long history of international relations. It is already a major event in that history. As a self-standing fact, the Convention meets other objects in the field of international relations: the Geneva Conventions of 1958, customary international law, prenormative state practice, the international constitutional structure, the international class struggle, the New International Economic Order, the world balances of power. These great ideological structures, leviathans in the contemporary international sea, must make room for the newcomer, and countless lesser structures (regional, bilateral, local, temporary) must accept its existence. They are, first and foremost, structures of relationships, the latest transient product of countless international and social interactions over long periods of time, constantly in the process of further development, developing internally and developing in relation to each other. The LOS Convention, already on the move as its significance is modified by the attitudes and behavior of governments and others, must take up station in formation with a fleet itself in a state of rapid and complex movement. Itself an effect of such causes, the Convention now becomes a cause among such effects.

This most general international context of the Convention enters into every word of every provision. There is nothing in the Convention that does not have a relationship with these general structural relationships of international society. This is not to say that there are not other contexts of a still more general character, up to and including, as we shall see, the thought-structures known as Justice, Equity, Law, society, the state system—ideas without which such a far-reaching legal structure could not be articulated. They are the *causae sine qua non* of the Convention. But the *causa causans* of the structure of the whole Convention and of particular relationships within the Convention is to be found in the general structures of the same level of generality in the specific field of international relations.

It is these general structures of contemporary international society that have made possible the particular form in which the Convention has emerged as a social fact. These structures have, through a particular configuration of their interaction over a particular period of time, generated a *legislative* act. The Convention is a legislative act, not in the attenuated form represented by the hallowed formula of "lawmaking treaty," but in the fullest and most literal sense. The Convention has the two defining characteristics of legislation:

—it transforms social policy into legal rules;

—that transformation is effected by an autonomous process.

The process of the Third United Nations Conference on the Law of the Sea (UNCLOS III) was consensus, a fascinating and complex phenomenon in its own right.[8] Consensus is an "invisible hand" process, in the sense indicated by Adam Smith: "[The individual] intends only his own gain, and he is in this, as in many other cases, led by an invisible hand to promote an end which was no part of his intention."[9] Adam Smith's concept was developed at much the same time that Rousseau was developing his concept of the "general will," which is a very similar concept, also based upon a principle of cumulative causation:

> But when the whole people decrees for the whole people, it is considering only itself; and if a relation is then formed, it is between two aspects of the entire object, without there being any division of the whole. In that case the matter about which the decree is made is, like the decreeing will, general. This act is what I call a law.[10]

There is a fine piece of continental European legal terminology that is not used in the common law systems but that reflects the same concept to this day. Continental lawyers speak of "the legislator" as the source of law: *le législateur, der Gesetzgeber, il legislatore*. They would say, "the legislator apparently did not provide for such-and-such a situation." In an international consensus situation, the law is not made by one state or two, not by the majority of states, not even by the unanimous assent of all states. It is made by the disembodied hand of the international legislator, his hand pushed this way and that by the pressures of debate, interests, power. The *ratio legis* is to be found in the real-world forces whose ideological interaction is resolved, on this occasion, in the text of the Convention mediated through the decision-making process of the conference. Precisely the same may be said of modern political systems at the national level. In Britain the legislator is not Parliament but the political process in general, acting through the occasional mediation of, among other things, Parliament. Constitutional theory at the national level must constantly develop to take account of such changing phenomena. Constitutional theory at the international level must do no less.

[8] *See* Jenks, *Unanimity, the Veto, Weighted Voting, Special and Simple Majorities and Consensus as Modes of Decision in International Organisations*, in CAMBRIDGE ESSAYS IN INTERNATIONAL LAW: ESSAYS IN HONOUR OF LORD MCNAIR 48 (1965); Casson, *Le Consensus dans la pratique des Nations Unies*, 1974 ANNUAIRE FRANÇAIS DE DROIT INTERNATIONAL 456; Sohn, *Voting Procedures in United Nations Conferences for the Codification of International Law*, 69 AJIL 310, 333 (1975); Vignes, *Will the Third Conference on the Law of the Sea Work According to the Consensus Rule?*, *id.* at 119; Buzan, *Negotiating by Consensus: Developments in Technique at the United Nations Conference on the Law of the Sea*, 75 *id.* at 324 (1981).

[9] A. SMITH, AN INQUIRY INTO THE NATURE AND CAUSES OF THE WEALTH OF NATIONS, bk. IV, ch. II, at 456 (Glasgow 1976) (1776).

[10] J.-J. ROUSSEAU, THE SOCIAL CONTRACT, bk. IV, ch. VI, at 192 (tr. Cole 1913, rev. 1973) (1762).

The forces participating in such a process obviously cannot be identified definitively. But in multilateral international diplomacy, a practice has developed—a sort of constitutional convention—under which states assemble in ad hoc political groups or political parties. Without surrendering their separate identities, they recognize shared interests with other states and seek to maximize their power and influence by acting in concert. In the international political system the groups are fluid, temporary, overlapping in membership, sometimes only weakly coherent, sometimes notably monolithic. But, whatever their individual characters, they are now crucial to the process and they were crucial in UNCLOS: the coastal states, the maritime states, the broad-margin states, the principal fishing states, the landlocked and geographically disadvantaged states, the marine scientific research states, the nuclear weapons states, the land-based producers of minerals, the like-minded states, the median line states, the equitable principles states, the Arab states, the European Community states, the Soviet and East European states, the Group of 77.

Such more or less formal and structured, more or less publicly acknowledged combinations of states can only be the result of a process in which states first *identify* their interest, then *recognize* others who share the interest, and finally *combine* with others to promote that interest. Such a process—identify, recognize, combine—has long been an important characteristic of political systems. In modern political systems it has become a primary structural feature.[11] Such groups are mediating structures in the relationship between the Many and the One, the essential struggle of political systems which has taken on a particularly problematic character in modern mass democracies, at least in those which may be classed as open societies.[12] They involve a partial loss of autonomy on the part of the members of the group in exchange for a share in the enhanced power of the group as a group and a possibility for each member of the group to influence disproportionately the exercise of that power, that is, the possibility of a marginal advantage over the other members in benefiting from membership in the group. Once again, therefore, there is a principle of cumulative causation at work in such groups, as each member seeks to promote its own interest and thereby contributes to the communal benefit of the group. Once again also, the behavior involved is a universalizing behavior, intermediate universalizing between the self-government of the individual and the unified self-government of society as a whole.

The genesis and development of legal texts through such a consensus process is exceptionally obscure. It is very difficult to unravel the story of how a text came to acquire its final form, especially, as at UNCLOS, when all substantive discussion was off the record. Instead of the will of a majority opposed to the will of the minority, there is the interaction of many wills within the groups and among the groups, interacting not merely in relation

[11] *See* "Interest Groups," in 7 INTERNATIONAL ENCYCLOPEDIA OF THE SOCIAL SCIENCES 486, and "Political Group Analysis," in 12 *id.* at 241 (Sills ed. 1968); D. TRUMAN, THE GOVERNMENTAL PROCESS: POLITICAL INTERESTS AND PUBLIC OPINION (1951); P. LOVEDAY & I. CAMPBELL, GROUPS IN THEORY AND PRACTICE (1962).

[12] In the sense of the term especially associated with 1 K. POPPER, THE OPEN SOCIETY AND ITS ENEMIES 173 (5th ed. 1966).

to a draft text and a limited number of proposed amendments but in relation to an infinite number of possible alternative textual formulations, as various as the ingenuity and the patience of the negotiators will allow. A brief conversation on a social occasion may generate a new solution or a new will to agree where more formal methods have failed, and the promotion of a given solution may involve many kinds of interpersonal social behavior, going far beyond the simple dialectic of debate and decision. UNCLOS itself was dazzlingly prolific in creating ad hoc negotiating procedures, spawned by hope out of necessity: working groups (restricted and open-ended), negotiating groups, confrontations between interest groups, "friends of the chairman" of a committee, the President's bureau, appointed and self-appointed mediators in smoke-filled rooms. It is to be hoped that someone will in due course write the natural history of UNCLOS as a decision-making system.

The nature of the consensus process raises special problems in relation to *travaux préparatoires*. In the case of the LOS Convention the problem is exceptionally acute. The Convention is not quite in the happy position of the Treaty Establishing the European Economic Community, for example, which has no effective *travaux* at all and whose interpretation and application has been much assisted by their absence. Nor is it in the familiar position of leading codification treaties, such as the Vienna Convention on the Law of Treaties, where the four-stage *travaux* (ILC rapporteur's reports, ILC debates, ILC draft articles, conference papers and debates) are well known and their relevance well understood.

Instead, in the case of the LOS Convention, there is already and there will increasingly accumulate an amorphous mass of material, including very miscellaneous conference documents, together with contemporaneous and retrospective accounts purporting to describe the evolution of the texts. It should be understood here and now (before misunderstanding develops) that such material cannot be regarded as *travaux préparatoires* in the traditional sense (as used, for example, in Article 32 of the Vienna Convention on the Law of Treaties). With the possible exception of the successive published texts of the Convention, they do not have the objective character of *negotiating facts*, the actual material chain of causation of the resulting instrument, which is the essence of traditional *travaux*. The random and disorderly character of some of them and the partisan character of much of the rest mean that it would be wiser to regard them as a new kind of phenomenon, a physical manifestation of the decision-making process of consensus.

It is intrinsic to the kind of process the present study seeks to identify that its frontiers in place and time are not sharply defined. The process is focused in the sessions of the conference itself but is as extensive as the field of forces that impinge on the conference, that is to say, as extensive as the whole political system of international society. It began before the opening session of the conference and it continues after the conference is formally closed. We are all participating in it, seeking to influence the formulation of the texts, seeking to influence the attitude of governments to the adopted texts, seeking to influence the interpretation and application of the texts, their real-world effect. The so-called preparatory work of an instrument such as the LOS Convention is thus in reality part of the continuing *work* of the Convention, not merely its *preparatory* work.

The legislative view of the consensus process as outlined above throws an especially clear light on the position of those states which repudiate the consensus product at whatever stage of its organic existence. Through the metamorphic process of consensus, the product undergoes constant changes in form and vitality. It develops in response to the pressures that are applied to it. At a particular moment of metamorphosis (say, the final conference vote on a treaty, signature, or ratification), a participant may repudiate the consensus product, may seek to reform it or to destroy it. Whether the product is strong enough to resist such pressures and whether it is able to adapt itself in response to the pressures are contingent questions, not in the sole control of the repudiating party, not capable of being predetermined by legal rules or principles. The will of the repudiating party meets the combined will embodied in the consensus product. In the case of the LOS Convention, it remains to be seen whether the negative attitude of certain states at the latest stages of the process will destroy, cripple, or transform the product or whether the will of the Convention will be strong enough to cause them to change their attitude or to enable it to become a powerful formative source of general international law for all states, including those which do not choose to be contracting parties to it.

Beyond the outermost structural context (the general structures of international relations) and the second structural layer (the Convention as the fruit of a specific legislative process), the third contextual layer is that of the Convention itself as an organized structural whole.

The Convention's main structural feature is its comprehensiveness. It is comprehensive in dealing with the whole nonland area of the world. It is also legally comprehensive. It has a rule for everything. The rule may be a permissive rule. It may be an obligation. It may confer an explicit freedom or leave a residual liberty by not specifying a right or a duty. But a Flying Dutchman wandering the sea areas of the world, carrying his copy of the Convention, would always be able to answer in legal terms the questions: who am I? who is that over there? where am I? what may I do now? what must I do now? The Convention would never fail him.

The first paragraph of the Preamble to the Convention provides: "Desiring to settle *all issues* relating to the law of the sea" (emphasis added).[13] The last paragraph adds a belt to the braces: "Affirming that *matters not regulated* by this Convention continue to be governed by the rules and principles of general international law" (emphasis added).

The way the Convention makes its rules is the way all legislation makes rules: by the process of legal classification. It recognizes persons by classifying them as legal persons. It establishes relationships between legal persons by applying jural relations to them. It specifies the content of the jural relations by classifying places, things, and activities. That is the transforming process

[13] Texts from the Law of the Sea Convention are taken from the Draft Convention, UN Doc. A/CONF.62/L.78, of Aug. 28, 1981.

of all legislation; there is no other way that social policy can be transformed into legal rules.

On one possible analysis of the Convention, one might say that it recognizes 57 kinds of legal person (Annex A below) to answer the questions: who am I? who is that over there? One might similarly say that the Convention recognizes 58 legal sea areas (Annex B below) to answer the question: where am I? The legal situation varies intrinsically as the legal persons participating in the situation vary and as the legal sea area in which activity occurs varies.

Needless to say, the Convention makes constant use of the eight fundamental Hohfeldian forms of jural relation.[14] But the Convention, at the textual level, makes use of a very large number of set formulas for establishing relations between legal persons in respect of places, things, and activities (Annex C below) to answer the questions: what may I do? what must I do?

It is worth recalling the way such structural mechanisms operate in lawmaking.

There is a classic and apparently unpromising topic in university jurisprudence courses that is introduced by the injunction, "distinguish ownership and possession." The subject turns out to be very enlightening for the student. He gradually sees that ownership and possession are in fact areas situated on a broad *spectrum* of possible relationships between persons and all kinds of things: ownership of many different degrees, possession, constructive possession, custody, control, and so on. Then he comes to see that each of these relationships is itself a *bundle* of rights: right to exclude, right to possess, right to alienate, right to profit, right to manage, right to bequeath, and so on. He then sees that what the law does is to transform social policy into legal rules by an endless process of manipulating and permuting such possible legal elements, switching them on and off, aligning them in this direction or that. From this it finally becomes clear that the prelegislative stage, before the moment when policy becomes law, consists of a complex dialectical struggle among interested parties, all seeking to have the disembodied legislator do various quite specific things:

—recognize my *group* as fit to be abstracted into a *legal person*, subject or object of a given legal relation;

—recognize a given *place, thing, or activity* in which my group is interested as fit to be abstracted into the *material legal base* of a legal relation;

—recognize an *interest* of my group as fit to be abstracted into the *primary legal objective* of a legal relation, consecrated as a right or protected by a duty.

The long saga of the negotiation of the LOS Convention was nothing other than such a prelegislative process. But there are two other fundamental features of the general legislative process that are of particular importance in

[14] Right, privilege, power, immunity; no-right, duty, disability, liability. *Cf.* Kocourek's revised list: claim, immunity, privilege, power; duty, disability, inability, liability. Hohfeld, *Some Fundamental Legal Conceptions as Applied in Judicial Reasoning*, 23 YALE L.J. 16 (1913); A. KOCOUREK, JURAL RELATIONS (1927). For a review of post-Hohfeldian developments, see Pound, *Fifty Years of Jurisprudence*, 50 HARV. L.R. 557, 571 *ff.* (1937).

understanding the nature of the LOS Convention, what may be called the "layering of legal relations" and the "delegation of power."

The layering of legal relations refers to the fact that the legislator may *superimpose* legal relations on each other, so that the same area, the same interest, the same activity may be the focus of any number of overlapping legal relations. There is the familiar example of a chattel, one and the same chattel, which may be subject to the ownership of *A*, the right to possession of *B*, the possession of *C*, the constructive possession of *D*, the bailee's possession of *E*, the custody of *F*, the control of *G*, and may be subject to overriding powers of any number of power holders up to and including the powers of local, state, and national public authorities. To resolve the prelegislative dialectical struggle, the legislator may involve the interested parties in a structural complex of legal relations, complementing each other, mutually dependent, so that the legal fact corresponding to the social fact may be a network of abstract relationships whose significance is as much potential as actual, contingent upon the way the abstractions are interpreted and applied in practice.

Of such potential legal relations, one is of outstanding importance in the structure of the LOS Convention: that of *power*. The Convention is a massive structure of powers. We tend to overlook the extent to which treaties confer powers, as opposed to more static forms of right. It seems that treaties are more and more conferring powers, but the LOS Convention is without parallel or precedent in the scale of its delegation of power. Powers obviously give rise to special problems for international law. Powers are a sort of delegated legislative function. The law allows me to choose at some later date to alter someone else's legal position with impunity and to my advantage. Powers may also be regarded as a form of *licensed wrong*. I may do what in other circumstances would be a wrong and the existence of the power confers on me an immunity from the normal legal consequences. But the license is always a limited license. The area of the immunity is legally and strictly circumscribed by what in administrative law is known as the concept of *vires*. Within the area of the power there is an infinite number of possible discretionary choices of action and inaction. Outside that area, action or inaction may be unlawful.

A great problem of modern international law is accordingly how to make sense of the large-scale conferring of powers within a system that does not have a regular court system to enforce *vires* or a body of administrative law to provide the principles used to identify the limits and to confer a *locus standi* on those who may challenge unlawful acts. Nor does the international system have an organized structure of political accountability to check on the application of powers from day to day and to review the discretionary choices made within the limits of powers, the *intra vires* decisions that are not in any case within the jurisdiction of courts, except to the extent that the administrative law deems them to be the misuse of a power (*détournement de pouvoir*).

Both the layering of legal relations and the delegation of powers are *boundary phenomena*. My right may begin where someone else's right ends. The more extensive my power, the more limited someone else's freedom. The boundaries between powers are expressed by power modifiers, what in English administrative law is called the "fettering" of powers. The fixing of these power modifiers is a major part of the process of negotiation and compromise at international conferences. All the participants at UNCLOS spent countless hours with their attention concentrated on a number of subtle distinctions such as:

generally accepted / applicable / relevant;
taking account of / on the basis of;
necessary steps / all necessary steps;
due notice / due publicity;
due regard / reasonable regard;
prevail / supersede;
without discrimination / on a footing of equality;
have the right to / shall be entitled to;
endeavor / make every effort;
in conformity with / in accordance with;
compatible with / not incompatible with;
where appropriate / as appropriate;
subject to / without prejudice to.

Those who have not taken part in international negotiations tend to underestimate the significance of these boundary concepts within jural relations. Those who take part in international negotiations tend to become obsessed with such distinctions—and may forget a few weeks later what all the excitement was about and why one particular formula or another was a major national interest. But, whatever the actual rationality of the negotiating process at any given time, the outcome is a text that depends on such modifiers to express the substance of a specific legal relationship.

The powerishness of the LOS Convention and the luxuriance of its layering of legal relations account for the vast dispute settlement system created in part XV (together with section 5 of part XI). There was a very general feeling that it would be pointless to create a legal structure of such complexity, containing thousands of subtle legal relationships, if there were no secure means of resolving disputes of interpretation and application. The dispute settlement provisions, in all their own subtlety and complexity, should be regarded as a gloss on every substantive provision of the Convention, integrated into the very functioning of every provision. They are a caution and a guarantee attached to each provision,[15] whose benefit, however, is only available to those states which become parties and not to those which seek to profit from what is advantageous to them in the Convention without becoming parties to it.

The place of the dispute settlement provisions in the Convention is one example of the obsessive concern of UNCLOS with the concept of "the package," another fundamental structural feature of the Convention as a whole.

[15] *See* Adede, *Law of the Sea: The Scope of Third-Party, Compulsory Procedures for the Settlement of Disputes*, 71 AJIL 305 (1977); Adede, *Law of the Sea—The Integration of the System of Settlement of Disputes under the Draft Convention as a Whole*, 72 *id.* at 84 (1978); Rosenne, *Settlement of Fisheries Disputes in the Exclusive Economic Zone*, 73 *id.* at 89 (1979).

The Preamble refers to the concept: "Conscious that the problems of ocean space are closely interrelated and need to be considered as a whole. . . ." Article 309 prohibits reservations, largely on package grounds. The *travaux préparatoires,* such as they are, will be found to contain countless affirmations of the package concept. If the concept does survive and is used by courts and tribunals in applying the Convention, it could have an important effect, especially, oddly enough, if the Convention does not enter into force as a treaty and has to be applied as a formative source of customary international law.

It is not possible to list here all the package aspects of the Convention. Among the most important is the all-embracing package that incorporates the subject matter of all four of the Geneva Conventions into a single Convention, with the addition and integration within that one Convention of what is in effect a major pollution convention and a major piece of international economic legislation (the deep seabed regime). The three main parts of the Convention (general law of the sea, deep seabed, pollution and marine scientific research) should also be regarded as subordinate integrated packages.

Beyond these there are some more recherché packages:

> —the links between and among the 12-mile territorial sea, the 200-mile exclusive economic zone (EEZ), and transit passage through straits used for international navigation;
>
> —the link between Article 55 (on the legal regime of the EEZ) and Article 86 (virtually a definition of the high seas);
>
> —the link between the delimitation articles (15, 74, and 83) and Article 298 (optional exception for delimitation disputes);
>
> —the links among Article 76 (definition of the continental shelf), Article 134(4) (limits of the international seabed area), and Annex II (Commission on the Limits of the Continental Shelf).

Of course, there are also countless special links within articles and between neighboring articles where compromises were arrived at by balancing one text against another.

One particular extrinsic relationship presents exceptional problems: the relationship with corresponding provisions of the Geneva Conventions of 1958. Those Conventions are a brooding omnipresence that haunts many of the UNCLOS texts. The second paragraph of the Preamble to the LOS Convention is as follows: "*Noting* that the developments that have occurred since the United Nations Conferences on the Law of the Sea held at Geneva in 1958 and 1960 have accentuated the need for a new and generally acceptable Convention on the law of the sea." Article 311(1) provides: "This Convention shall prevail, as between States Parties, over the Geneva Conventions on the Law of the Sea of 1958."

It is important to realize the tension between these two texts whose significance may be gathered if four points are borne in mind. (1) In UNCLOS there was a strong sentiment among nonparties to the Geneva Conventions (and even, perhaps, among some parties) that those Conventions were outdated, no longer corresponded to the real forces of the world. (2) There was universal agreement that prenormative state practice and even customary international law had developed in certain significant respects since Geneva. (3) At the same time, the Geneva Conventions remained valid treaties among the parties to them and a major formative source of customary international law for all states; as a matter of fact, very many of the general law of the sea articles in the LOS Convention are based directly and literally on Geneva texts. (4) Finally, even if and when the Convention enters into force, the Article 311 rule is a narrow technical rule of displacement among parties to the new Convention. The Convention contains no provision creating a general supersession of the Geneva Conventions, excluding them as a formative source of customary international law or excluding their application among parties to the Geneva Conventions who do not become parties to the LOS Convention.

The structure of the main legal sea areas is an instructive illustration of the relationship of continuity and discontinuity between the new Convention and the Geneva Conventions. Geneva law was based on five main legal sea areas (internal waters, territorial sea, contiguous zone, continental shelf, high seas). Several more arose in subsequent state practice and established themselves with more or less legal finality. UNCLOS adds a further four main legal sea areas to the Geneva five (archipelagic waters, EEZ, straits used for international navigation, deep seabed).

Superficially, the legal basis of the Geneva five remains the same, epitomized by the key words *sovereignty* (internal and territorial waters), *control, sovereign rights, freedoms*. But important changes have taken place within those structures.

The territorial sea sovereignty is to be exercised "subject to this Convention and to other rules of international law" (Article 2). The other relevant provisions of the Convention are articulated in terms of rights and duties conferred and imposed now on one party to the territorial sea relationship (coastal state), now on the other (other states, foreign ship), as the different holders are permuted from provision to provision. The rights are mainly in the form of powers and freedoms.[16] The right of innocent passage is "subject to this Convention" (Article 17). Passage is defined in a slightly more elaborate way than in Geneva (Article 18). Passage must take place "in conformity with this Convention and with other rules of international law" (Article 19). The coastal state must not hamper innocent passage "except in accordance with this Convention." The coastal state may adopt laws and regulations "in conformity with the provisions of this Convention and other rules of international law" (Article 21).

[16] In the Hohfeldian sense of such terms (*see* note 13 *supra*). For Hohfeld, a privilege (or liberty) is the opposite of a duty and a power is the correlative of a liability. *Cf.* Kocourek:

> Since freedom is the base from which and for which legal transactions are entered into, the significance of the idea of jural relationship becomes apparent—a jural relation is a situation of fact upon which one may affect (through the existence and exercise of a power) or may claim to affect (because of the existence of a duty), the freedom of another with legal consequences.

A. Kocourek, Jural Relations 16 (2d ed. 1928).

This network of rather obsessively interconnected rights, each delicately balanced against others, contains at its core two new lengthy specifications that are not found in the Geneva texts:

—the long list in Article 19 of activities that are to be considered prejudicial to the peace, good order, or security of the coastal state, which thus becomes an important part of the legal content of the relevant rights (powers) and duties of the parties to the territorial sea relationship; and

—the long list in Article 21 of matters in respect of which the coastal state may adopt laws and regulations, which similarly becomes an important part of the legal content of the rights (powers) and liabilities of the parties to the territorial sea relationship.

These lists are important evidence of a new balance of power in the territorial sea. It would not be difficult to analyze the real-world forces that generated them. But they symbolize and emphasize the true character of the territorial sea as a legal area. The facile formula of "sovereignty—subject to the right of innocent passage" is not adequate. The complex layering of superimposed legal relations and the intricate interaction of delegated powers mean that the territorial sea is properly regarded as *an area of legal mutuality* and *an area of legal potentiality*. The statuses of the interested parties are intrinsically interdependent. The Convention creates the possibility of an infinite number of derived legal situations as the parties exercise their powers within a framework the Convention provides but the parties must complete by their day-to-day actions.

Superficially, the legal status of the continental shelf (Articles 77 to 81) is also remarkably similar to that created by Geneva: epitomized in the concept of functional sovereign rights. But the appearance is deceptive. The status is transformed by the fact that the superjacent waters, up to a distance of 200 nautical miles, are EEZ, no longer straightforward high seas. In addition, Article 56 gives functional sovereign rights in respect of the seabed and subsoil of the EEZ. Where the EEZ and continental shelf overlap—up to a distance of 200 nautical miles—the two sets of sovereign rights overlap. Presumably in that area, the EEZ generally trumps the continental shelf, at least for all practical purposes. But there are important differences: the *inherent* nature of the continental shelf rights in what is perceived as a natural prolongation of the land territory (Article 77(3), read with Article 76(1)), and the emphasis on the *exclusivity* of the continental shelf rights (Article 77(2)). For example, these differences might continue to have a bearing on the delimitation of the continental shelf between neighboring states.

The mystery of the relationship between the continental shelf and the EEZ is aggravated by the problematic relationship between the EEZ and the high seas. Where do the high seas begin? Under Geneva, they begin at the outer edge of the territorial sea. The position is not so straightforward under the LOS Convention.

The UNCLOS high seas legal status is essentially the classical high seas status, epitomized in a nonexhaustive ("*inter alia*") list of freedoms (Article

87). The list is different from the Geneva list in significant ways and the article does not contain the catch-all reference found in Article 2 of the High Seas Convention to other freedoms "which are recognized by the general principles of international law." However, there are five grounds for thinking that that omission does not have a straightforwardly negative effect. The Article 87 list is expressly nonexhaustive. It is slightly wider than the Geneva list. The article contains a reference to "other rules of international law" (in relation to the exercise of the freedoms). There are references in other articles to "other internationally lawful uses of the sea" (referring in the given contexts to the high seas: for example, Article 58). There is the reference in the Preamble to the continued effect of general international law.

But the relevance of the precise status of the high seas for present purposes is that it seeps back, as it were, into the EEZ status. It is not quite right to say simply that the EEZ ends at 200 nautical miles and the high seas begin at that point. Article 58 gives all states a certain status in the EEZ: they have the high seas freedoms of Article 87. And Article 58(2) applies the remainder of the high seas articles (Articles 88 to 115) to the EEZ. It also applies to the EEZ "other pertinent rules of international law . . . in so far as they are not incompatible with" the Convention provisions on the EEZ.

In other words, it is not at first sight clear whether the EEZ is essentially the high seas with a special EEZ regime superimposed upon it (the "high seas minus" view) or whether the EEZ is a new sui generis zone of the coastal state in which the high seas freedoms are the equivalent of the right of innocent passage in the territorial sea (the "EEZ minus" view).

A preferable view is that the EEZ should be regarded as a *horizontally shared zone* between the coastal state and other states. This view is supported by the extraordinarily balanced drafting of the fundamental EEZ article (55), entitled "specific legal regime of the EEZ":

> The exclusive economic zone is an area beyond and adjacent to the territorial sea, subject to the specific legal régime established in this Part, under which the *rights and jurisdictions* of the coastal State and the *rights and freedoms* of other States are governed by the relevant provisions of this Convention [emphasis added].

The view is supported further by the parallel provisions in Articles 56 and 58(3) under which the coastal state, in exercising its rights and performing its duties in the EEZ, must have *due regard* to the rights and duties of other states (56), and other states, in exercising their rights and performing their duties in the EEZ, must have *due regard* to the rights and duties of the coastal state (58(3)). It is reinforced still further by the remarkable wording of Article 59, a perfect example of the administrative lawism of the Convention:

> *Basis for the resolution of conflicts regarding the attribution of rights and jurisdiction in the exclusive economic zone*
>
> In cases where this Convention does not attribute rights or jurisdiction to the coastal State or to other States within the exclusive economic zone, and a conflict arises between the interests of the coastal State and any other State or States, the conflict should be resolved on the basis of

equity and in the light of all the relevant circumstances, taking into account the respective importance of the interests involved to the parties as well as to the international community as a whole.

Whatever may be regarded as the essence of the relationship of the EEZ to the high seas, there is another fundamental difference in the status of the high seas as compared with the Geneva Conventions. The deep seabed area beyond the limits of national jurisdiction (that is, beyond the EEZ and the continental shelf), called in the Convention "the Area," is subject to the special regime created by part XI of the Convention. Part VII (on the high seas) contains a reference to part XI in Article 87(2), which provides that the high seas freedoms shall be exercised "with due regard for the rights under this Convention with respect to activities in the Area." Article 89 also provides that "no State may validly purport to subject any part of the high seas to its sovereignty" (which might or might not apply to the seabed of the high seas). Part XI itself contains a whole array of provisions on the legal status of the Area and its mineral resources. They are "the common heritage of mankind" (136). No state may claim or exercise sovereignty or sovereign rights over any part of them. No state or natural or juridical person may appropriate any part of them (Article 137). All rights in the resources of the Area are vested in mankind as a whole, on whose behalf the International Sea-Bed Authority (ISA) is to act (Article 137(2)). The general conduct and responsibility of states in the Area are controlled by Articles 138 and 139. Activities in the Area are to be carried out for the benefit of mankind as a whole (Article 140). Under Article 3 of Annex III, the Authority may confer power to explore in the Area and exploit its resources on the Enterprise (the organ of the Authority that carries out activities in the Area on behalf of the Authority), states parties to the Convention, and other entities (including companies). Part XI, read with Annexes III and IV, in fact creates a complex system covering every aspect of conducting "activities" in the Area. And part XI itself contains a provision (Article 135) to the effect that "neither this Part nor any rights granted or exercised pursuant thereto shall affect the legal status of the waters superjacent to the Area or that of the air space above those waters."

In short, therefore, it may be said that, under the LOS Convention, the high seas proper are also a *horizontally shared area.* That area is shared between, on the one hand, mankind and all states and the ISA and legal persons with derived rights and, on the other hand, all states as the holders of the general high seas freedoms. It is accordingly, once again, an area of legal mutuality. And the deep seabed, under the LOS Convention, may be regarded as the *ne plus ultra* of legal potentiality. The deep seabed governmental system (legislative, executive, judicial) waits upon its implementation by countless subordinate decisions taken within the framework of the Convention structure, going to the fourth generation of concretization[17] and beyond: Convention,

[17] In the sense in which Kelsen used the word. Concretization (or individualization) is the process by which "the general norm which, to certain abstractly determined conditions, attaches certain abstractly determined consequences, [is] individualized and concretized in order to come in contact with social life, to be applied in reality." H. KELSEN, GENERAL THEORY OF LAW AND STATE 135 (tr. Wedberg 1945/49).

implementing legislation, executive decisions thereunder, application of decisions, resolution of disputes, and enforcement (judicial and otherwise).

It is apparent that one could demonstrate by a similar analysis that the other UNCLOS main legal sea areas (straits used for international navigation, archipelagic waters, contiguous zone) had the same structural character, and the same applies a fortiori to the numerous minor legal sea areas (safety zones, suspension zones, marine scientific research zones, and so on). In all these cases, boundaries between superimposed legal relations are fixed by critical power modifiers that create an area of interaction of powers among interested states; their legal effect is essentially an administrative law effect, depending on postlegislative activity to extrapolate from, and to interpolate into, the texts, and to extend and to intend the texts—through cascades of derived legal action (prescribing, deciding, enforcing).

The *vertical* boundaries between different legal sea areas and between the legal sea areas of different states are of the same intrinsic nature. Their establishment is the subject of a power conferred on the coastal state or states concerned. That power is in each case subject to critical power modifiers.

One vertical sea boundary has taken on a completely new significance as compared with the Geneva regime: the outer edge of the continental shelf. Under the LOS Convention it gives rise to an opposite states situation between the coastal state and mankind as a whole. The international deep seabed regime begins where the continental shelf (and, in some cases, the EEZ) ends. The legislation of a new outer limit became a matter of universal concern at UNCLOS. It was clear that, within the Convention structure, the second part of the Geneva formula (exploitability: Continental Shelf Convention, Article 1) would not be sufficiently precise or definitive to serve as a general boundary rule. The states with wide continental shelves were determined not to lose too much of what was apparently theirs under the Geneva formula. Other states were determined that the wide-margin states should not profit unreasonably at the expense of mankind as a whole.

The problem was resolved with very great difficulty[18] and in Article 76 the international legislator has wrought a work of exceptional complexity. It is of particular interest and relevance in forming any overall view of the legislative significance of the Convention. The Article 76 system consists of two phases. The first is the *identification* of the outer limits of the continental shelf by reference to geographical and, especially, geological concepts. The second is the *establishment* of the outer limits as legally final and binding by the coastal state, in some cases in conjunction with the Commission on the Limits of the Continental Shelf (CLCS).

The identification of the outer limits makes use of five concepts that are technical in origin but that become legal terms of art by reason of the way they are used in Article 76: natural prolongation of land territory (paragraph 1); continental margin (paragraph 2); outer edge of the continental margin

[18] For an account of the later stages of the negotiation, see Oxman, *The Third United Nations Conference on the Law of the Sea: The Eighth Session (1979)*, 74 AJIL 1, 19–23 (1980), and —*The Ninth Session (1980)*, 75 *id.* at 211, 227–31 (1981).

(paragraph 4(a)); foot of the continental slope (paragraph 4(b)); and submarine ridges (paragraph 6). The outer limits of the continental shelf are in principle at the edge of the continental margin, as defined, unless that outer edge does not extend as far as 200 nautical miles from the baselines of the territorial sea (in which case the outer limit is at 200 nautical miles); the outer limits are also subject to a general cut-off point (paragraph 5) at 350 nautical miles from the territorial sea baselines or else, except on submarine ridges, 100 nautical miles from the 2,500-meter isobath.

It follows that there are in principle four possible outer limits to the continental shelf: 200 nautical miles, the outer edge of the continental margin, 350 nautical miles, and 100 miles from the 2,500-meter isobath.

Because of the complexity of these provisions, because they involve questions of sophisticated technical judgment, and because of the new interest of all states in the resulting boundaries, it was agreed to set up an administrative law type of procedure to help to settle particular boundaries. The coastal state first *delineates* the outer limits on the basis of the Convention provisions. It then *submits* information on the limits to the CLCS, a permanent international body of 21 experts. The CLCS follows the procedure set out in Annex II to the Convention. By a two-thirds majority the CLCS approves *recommendations* "on matters related to the establishment" of the outer limits and *submits* them to the coastal state. If the coastal state disagrees with the recommendations, it makes a revised or new submission to the Commission. The coastal state then *establishes* the outer limits *on the basis of* the recommendations of the Commission.

The key sentence is in a form that will bring a sparkle to the eye of any administrative lawyer: "The limits of the shelf established by a coastal State on the basis of these recommendations shall be final and binding."

Each of the critical power modifiers in Article 76 was keenly considered, disputed, and negotiated. The outcome is not only a complex structure of technical and legal elements but also a sophisticated balance of powers and responsibilities. In particular, it raises the archetypal problem of administrative law: who has the last word? Is it the coastal state, the CLCS, or some putative third-party settlement instance under part XV of the Convention?

The outer limit of the continental shelf is thus a boundary for whose determination the international community has delegated intricate powers to the coastal state and others. The international community has also, in one respect, made the continental shelf itself into a partially shared area, where the coastal state acts as an agent of the international community or at least as its statutable benefactor. Under Article 82 the coastal state must surrender a percentage of the value of production from the continental shelf sites located more than 200 nautical miles from the baselines. The percentage eventually reaches a ceiling of 7 percent. It is paid to the International Sea-Bed Authority, which is to distribute the revenues equitably by taking into account the interests and needs of the developing countries. The implementation of these provisions depends on a distribution of powers among the coastal state, the ISA and, to the extent that they might be held applicable, the Convention's dispute settlement procedures. Under Article 160(2)(f)(i), the ISA's task is divided, on a classic constitutional law pattern, between two bodies: the Council, which recommends rules, regulations, and procedures for the equitable distribution; and the Assembly, which considers and approves. Disputes relating to the ISA's role under Article 82 would appear not to be within the contentious jurisdiction of the Sea-Bed Disputes Chamber of the International Tribunal on the Law of the Sea under Article 187, but some matters arising under Article 82 might in some circumstances be the subject of a request for an advisory opinion under Article 191 or (if they involved a "dispute" between states, in the technical sense) of proceedings under the general provisions of part XV.

So far as the other vertical boundaries, between neighboring states, are concerned, the Geneva Conventions contain three slightly differently formulated rules for three cases: territorial sea, continental shelf (opposite coasts), and continental shelf (adjacent coasts). But the structure of the three rules was the same: failing agreement, the median or equidistance line, subject to special circumstances. Those were the three classical elements in the light of which many sea boundaries were settled. On the basis of those provisions, states could delimit the sea areas unilaterally using the residual rule; but the provisions provide the conceptual framework for negotiation and settlement, resulting in an agreed settlement containing any appropriate variation of the median or equidistance line and taking account of such special circumstances as the parties wished to treat as relevant. In the case of a dispute that could not be resolved by agreement, third-party settlement procedures could be used and the Convention provisions could be applied (subject to any reservation made under Article 12 of the Continental Shelf Convention) as governing rules of law.

In post-Geneva state practice, three significant developments occurred:

—most actual delimitation settlements were accomplished on the basis of a median or equidistance line adjusted to fit the circumstances of the case;[19]

—the International Court of Justice told us that the Geneva rule, at least so far as the continental shelf was concerned, was a contractual rule and did not adequately reflect the position under customary international law;[20]

—the internal balance of the Geneva rule itself was adjusted by state practice and judicial decisions and was brought closer to the International Court's view of customary international law by the displacement of the

[19] For inter-state sea boundary agreements, see the series published by the U.S. DEP'T OF STATE, OFFICE OF THE GEOGRAPHER, LIMITS IN THE SEAS; N. PAPADAKIS, INTERNATIONAL LAW OF THE SEA: A BIBLIOGRAPHY 116–23 (1980).

[20] North Sea Continental Shelf Cases (Federal Republic of Germany/Denmark; Federal Republic of Germany/Netherlands), 1969 ICJ REP. 3 (Judgment of Feb. 20). *See* Friedmann, *The North Sea Continental Shelf Cases—A Critique*, 64 AJIL 229 (1970); Grisel, *Lateral Boundaries and the ICJ Judgment*, *id.* at 562 (1970); Blecher, *Equitable Delimitation of Continental Shelf*, 73 *id.* at 60 (1979); Rhee, *Equitable Solutions to the Maritime Boundary Dispute between the United States and Canada in the Gulf of Maine*, 75 *id.* at 590 (1981). For further references, see N. PAPADAKIS, *supra* note 18, at 120–22.

median or equidistance line as the cornerstone of the rule in favor of "equitable principles."[21]

When UNCLOS came to work on the corresponding provisions, these three factors had to be taken into account in deciding how far to reproduce the Geneva texts. But a fourth factor of fundamental significance also dominated the legislative process: the real-world fact that 50 and more of the states participating in the conference had unresolved sea boundary problems with neighboring states. In formulating rules that might apply to or affect their own situation, they had to temper their natural loyalty to the Geneva Conventions and court decisions with a realistic appreciation of where their interests lay. What happened was that more or less half of the specially interested states decided that their interests would be best served by the apparently more "equitable" approach of the judicial decisions (and they became known as the "Equitable Principles Group"). The rest thought that the original spirit of Geneva had been sound, that (respecting also the Aristotelian tradition) equality was the ultimate equity (and they became known as the "Median Line Group").

During session after session, debates and pseudo-debates and stylized indirect negotiation took place between the two groups. The process by which the final texts of Articles 15, 73, 84, and 298(1)(a) were settled is thus an unusually exposed example of a legislative process. In particular, the growing impatience of the rest of the conference and the threat of a third-party intrusion into their relationship made the groups feel ever less assured as masters of their own fate. In the later stages they suffered like Damocles as one person or another—the independent chairman of the relevant negotiating group, the President of the conference, an influential delegation not a member of either group—threatened to personify the otherwise disembodied international legislator and provide a solution. The choices available were to have no rules on the subject in the Convention, to have rules but permit reservations to them, or to find a form of words, a philosopher's stone combining the uncombinable and producing something that, if not pure gold, could at least be accepted as worthwhile by all concerned.

The solution adopted for the territorial sea (Article 15) is the Geneva text (Article 12, Territorial Sea Convention) with minor linguistic changes: failing agreement, median or equidistance line, special circumstances. A completely different solution—and one and the same solution—was adopted for the EEZ and continental shelf (Articles 74 and 83).[22] Judged only by the standards of alchemy could it be said to be anything but bizarre.

[21] THE UNITED KINGDOM AND THE FRENCH REPUBLIC DELIMITATION OF THE CONTINENTAL SHELF DECISION OF 30 JUNE 1977, CMND. 7438 (1978), *reprinted in* 18 ILM 397 (1979). *See* Bowett, *The Arbitration between the United Kingdom and France concerning the Continental Shelf*, 49 BRIT. Y.B. INT'L L. 1 (1978); McRae, *Delimitation of the continental shelf between the United Kingdom and France*, 15 CAN. Y.B. INT'L L. 173 (1977); Colson, *The United Kingdom-France Continental Shelf Arbitration*, 72 AJIL 95 (1978), and —*Interpretive Decision of March 1978*, 73 *id.* at 112 (1979); Quéneudec, *L'Affaire de la délimitation du plateau continental entre la France et le Royaume-Uni*, 83 REV. GÉNÉRALE DROIT INT'L PUBLIC 53 (1979).

[22] The text of Article 74 is as follows (the text of Article 83 being the same with the substitution of references to the continental shelf):

The delimitation rule in Articles 74 and 83 has a three-part structure containing a *process*, a *principle*, and a *purpose*:

process = agreement: if agreement is not reached within a reasonable period of time, resort to the dispute settlement procedures of part XV;

principle = international law, as referred to in Article 38 of the Statute of the International Court of Justice;

purpose = to achieve an equitable solution.

The *process* sets the procedural *vires* of the powers of the states concerned. But they are subject to an important qualification introduced by Article 298(1)(a)(i). There is a right for a state to exclude sea boundary delimitation disputes from the compulsory third-party settlement procedures of part XV. Thus, the reference in Article 74(2) and Article 83(2) to part XV, although it is in an obligatory form ("shall resort to"), does not itself necessarily amount to an acceptance of compulsory jurisdiction. However, Article 298(1)(a)(i) does go on to require a state that has excluded such disputes to accept submission of the dispute to conciliation under Annex V, section 2, if agreement is not reached "within a reasonable period of time." The compulsory conciliation system is closely modeled on that contained in the Vienna Convention on the Law of Treaties and its annex. This substitute obligation to submit to conciliation is itself subject to an exception for disputes "necessarily involving the concurrent consideration of any unsettled dispute concerning sovereignty or other rights over continental or insular land territory."

If a dispute is submitted to conciliation under Annex V, section 2, the parties must *negotiate on the basis of* the conciliation commission report. If those negotiations do not result in agreement, there is one last possibility at the end of the road: "the parties shall, *by mutual consent*, submit the question to one of the procedures provided for in section 2, *unless the parties otherwise agree*" (Article 298(1)(a)(ii)) (emphasis added). It is a rare sort of obligation ("shall") that depends on the mutual consent of those subject to it and is subject to their not agreeing otherwise. Sense can only be made of such an apparent contradiction if it is analyzed as a duty coupled with a power rather than a

---

Delimitation of the exclusive economic zone between States with opposite or adjacent coasts

1. The delimitation of the exclusive economic zone between States with opposite or adjacent coasts shall be effected by agreement on the basis of international law, as referred to in Article 38 of the Statute of the International Court of Justice, in order to achieve an equitable solution.

2. If no agreement can be reached within a reasonable period of time, the States concerned shall resort to the procedures provided for in Part XV.

3. Pending agreement as provided for in paragraph 1, the States concerned, in a spirit of understanding and co-operation, shall make every effort to enter into provisional arrangements of a practical nature and, during this transitional period, not to jeopardize or hamper the reaching of the final agreement. Such arrangements shall be without prejudice to the final delimitation.

4. Where there is an agreement in force between the States concerned, questions relating to the delimitation of the exclusive economic zone shall be determined in accordance with the provisions of that agreement.

duty coupled with a freedom. That is to say, at the moment when the provision becomes applicable, the parties do not have unfettered discretion to do what they will as if there were no provision at all. The provision contains the policy desideratum of the international community speaking through the international legislator. That desideratum is that the unresolved dispute should not be allowed, merely because it has not been resolved by the procedures followed theretofore and especially because it has not been so resolved, to remain indefinitely unresolved or to become a source of extralegal conflict or the subject of self-help.

Following through this long process chain, we find that Articles 74 and 83 do not contain a substantive default provision, applicable in the case of an absence of agreement; nor do they contain a fully constraining third-party settlement system. The overall change from the corresponding Geneva structure is illuminating. The process aspect of the UNCLOS text is concerned, in what may be seen as a more realistic and sophisticated approach, rather with constraining the *behavior* of the states concerned in relation to their unresolved sea boundaries than with predeciding their dispute by edict.

The same may be said of the mysterious *principle* in Articles 74 and 83. At first sight, it is nonsensical to require states to reach agreement *on the basis of international law*, when that obligation is contained within an instrument that is to be the highest and most authoritative possible source of international law. The apparent nonsense is made worse by the reference to Article 38 of the Statute of the International Court of Justice, which, as has long been recognized, is emphatically not an apt list of either the formal or the material sources of international law.

This formulation of the text replaced a series of earlier attempts to epitomize the current state of customary international law on the matter or at least to find a mutually agreeable substantive formula inspired by the current law. An especially ingenious attempt to do so was made in a previous draft of the Convention (known as the ICNT/Rev.1): "in accordance with equitable principles, employing, where appropriate, the median or equidistance line, and taking account of all the relevant circumstances."

"Equitable principles" was the key phrase, originating in the Truman Proclamation of 1945; it had been brought into prominence by the International Court of Justice. The reference to the median or equidistance line and relevant circumstances reflected the prominence that Geneva, state practice, and the International Court had given to that method as the natural point of departure for sea boundary delimitations. The fact that neither of these now traditional elements is mentioned in the final text of Articles 74 and 83 is another of the apparent foibles of that text. But the reference to international law and to Article 38 of the Statute must be given some meaning. It must be taken to be legislation by means of a symbolic formula. It is saying that the process of delimitation must be conducted in the light of the principles that have been evolved by international law and that, for this purpose, international law must be understood in a special extended sense to include not only fully formed international law but also the material found in formative sources of international law (such as prenormative state practice, judicial decisions, general principles of law). The vital point to understand about such a symbolic formula is that it does *not* transform all these heterogeneous materials into international law by the legislative act of the Convention. It is *not* merely legislation by reference. The complete ragbag of such materials does *not* together constitute the "UNCLOS substantive rule" on delimitation. What the Convention does is to set the parameters of the delimitation *process*. Those parameters are finite in number and kind but not wholly specific. They are not wholly specific, but they are exclusive.

So far as the *purpose* of the process is concerned, the third element of the structure of Articles 74 and 83—"in order to achieve an equitable solution"—similar considerations apply. If one did not firmly believe in the ultimate rationality of the general will and the inevitability of the invisible hand, it might at first seem that the use of this expression is a disaster. It cuts across and short-circuits the subtle concept of "equitable principles," which is also imported, as noted above, by the reference to "international law." Both the International Court of Justice in the *North Sea Continental Shelf* cases and the court of arbitration in the *Anglo-French* case took pains to make it clear that their task was not simply to roam freely in search of equity.

> [I]t is not a question of applying equity simply as a matter of abstract justice, but of applying a rule of law which itself requires the application of equitable principles, in accordance with the ideas which have always underlain the development of the legal régime of the continental shelf in this field. . . .[23]

This excellent dictum accords closely with the general theme of the present study. We may say that the reference in the UNCLOS text to an "equitable solution"—which is a phrase that has also been used by the International Court—was designed as an avoidance tactic, so that, in the interest of fairness between the two parties most concerned (the Median Line Group and the Equitable Principles Group), references to *both* the shibboleth concepts could be omitted from the final text.

But the underlying intention of the legislator would seem to be the same as that indicated by the International Court in the passage quoted above. The concepts of "equitable principles" and "equitable solution" are playing in this context a role analogous to that played by "reasonableness" in English law. They are high-level power modifiers whose referent is a subtle amalgam of an attitude or approach (fairness, common sense) and evolved artificial legal principles. Those principles are both abstract and situational. In the case of the continental shelf, they may include the concepts of natural prolongation, general direction of the coast, proportionality, equidistance, other sea boundaries, natural resource distribution—or, in a given case, one or more of such concepts may not be relevant or may only be subsidiarily relevant. In any event, their application to a given case depends strictly on the precise situation of the case. And, of course, different principles might apply, or the same principles might apply differently, in the case of EEZ delimitation. Articles 74

[23] North Sea Continental Shelf Cases, 1969 ICJ REP. at 47.

and 83 are separate provisions and it would be possible to establish different EEZ and continental shelf boundaries between the same states.

So, finally, in reassembling the elements of Articles 74 and 83, it is necessary to recall that the essential power that is modified in these complex ways is a power to *agree*. What sense can there be in a legal provision's conferring a power to agree and, hence necessarily, a power that has *vires* limits? States, it might seem, have (subject to the principle of *jus cogens* and the constraints of existing agreements) an inherent power or freedom to agree at any time on any terms. Or, if Articles 74 and 83 are taken at their face value and are regarded as containing the obligation that the use of the word "shall" would naturally imply, what sense can there be in a legal provision's imposing a duty to *agree* on the basis of certain principles? A duty to negotiate in good faith would be comprehensible. A duty to negotiate with a certain objective in view would be comprehensible. But a duty to agree on a certain basis seems difficult to reconcile with the essence of freedom of contract and with the fact that negotiation is intrinsically a two-party affair that could hardly be made the subject of substantive duties owed either reciprocally between the two parties or to third parties.

The answer to this puzzle is to be found in the structure of ideas that it has been the purpose of the present study to propose. Articles 74 and 83—and countless other provisions in the LOS Convention—are not simply contractual terms; nor do they lay down rules of law in the classical sense. *They delegate decision-making powers.* The current structural development of international law is involving states more and more not only in the mystical composite personage of the international legislator but also in performing the function of the executive branch of their own *self-government.*

In the mainstream of the Western democratic tradition (exemplified in Locke and in Marx), all government aspires to the condition of self-government. Whether the ideal is articulated by reference to a hypothetical pregovernmental state of affairs (Locke and the state of nature) or to a hypothetical postgovernmental state of affairs (Marx and the "administration of things" in the poststate world), that ideal acts as a constant critical force drawing social arrangements into their future, forever competing with the natural forces of anarchy and disintegration. The ideal or myth (golden age or millennial) of self-government is the ideological force that causes social arrangements to cohere and to persist, the social anti-entropy force. In sustaining social arrangements, it legitimizes their repressive aspect, the subjection of the individual to the collectivity. In the name of freedom it requires obedience. And, indeed, in the present state of the development of social arrangements, somewhere between the golden age and the millennium, the ideal manifests itself as, and morally sustains, a vast structure of subjection of the individual to the power structure of government, of the "state" (in the internal sense of that word). Government by consent is, for the time being, as much government as it is consent.

The development of the international constitutional structure since the 18th century has proceeded on a different basis. International society has seemed to lack, at least since the 18th century and especially since the Russian

Revolution of 1917, a single coherent and distinctive ideological structure (ideal or myth) to sustain and condition its social arrangements, and it has seemed to lack the real-world instruments of organized physical force that, in national society, confer de facto legitimacy on social arrangements through their efficiency and inevitability. These notorious disadvantages may be more apparent than real. From the natural law ethos of early modern international law to the rationalistic naturalism of some modern international law theory,[24] there may be more of a coherent underlying ideological structure, however dimly perceived by the participants in international society, than is normally supposed. But what matters for present purposes is that such apparent inadequacies of the international system have led most participants and observers to import the notion of "consent" wholesale into international theory as the all-purpose solvent of theoretical mysteries and as the validating, sustaining, and conditioning force in the development of international social arrangements.

It is important to realize the particular character of the notion of consent as it is used in modern international theory. It has been derived in part as a deduction from the principle of the sovereign equality of states, partly from a loose analogy with the long established municipal law institution of contract, and partly from the timeless anthropological phenomenon of the sanctity of the promise. It is emphatically not "consent" in the sophisticated sense of the mainstream Western democratic tradition (of Locke and Marx). National society, in its scale and its complexity and its repressive intensity, would not have been able to survive and progress if its ideological basis had been nothing more than "consent" in this direct, literal, contractual sense. The LOS Convention causes us, once again, to realize that such a notion of consent is no longer able to contain and sustain the reality of the post-1945 development of international self-government. In the present study we have considered four aspects of the Convention that illustrate the new reality:

(1) *consensus* as the generator of autonomous law, created *by* the subjects of the law but also created *for* them;

(2) *powers* delegated en masse and leading to a cascade of derived activity (legislative, decision making, enforcing);

(3) *administrative law procedures* integrated in the substantive provisions (as dispute settlement mechanisms and other forms of third-party intervention and, although not the subject of the present study, in the form of international organizational structures, especially the International Sea-Bed Authority);

(4) and, finally, the puzzle with which we are presently concerned: the delegation of what seems to be a *power/duty to agree* on the basis of certain substantive principles.

The accidents of litigation have led the International Court of Justice on two recent occasions to consider the phenomenon of a fettered power/duty

[24] It would be invidious to mention any particular names among those who have contributed to such an approach to international law beyond acknowledging the leading role of Myres S. McDougal.

to negotiate. In the *North Sea Continental Shelf* cases and in the *Fisheries Jurisdiction* case the Court's decisions laid down a series of matters that the parties were to take into account in the negotiation they were obliged by international law to undertake. The individual and dissenting opinions of Members of the Court expressed more clearly than the Court itself the theoretical anguish such a decision engenders: the tension between a freedom and a duty, between the judicial function of the Court to declare the law and/or to decide legal disputes and the responsibility of the parties to settle their dispute by peaceful means. The Court itself hovered between two underlying conceptual structures to explain the form of its decisions: the duty to settle such a dispute by negotiation and the "regime" character of the thing the parties had to establish by agreement. But it also came close to a more novel and fruitful idea.

> The legal situation therefore is that the Parties are under no obligation to apply either the 1958 Convention, which is not opposable to the Federal Republic, or the equidistance method as a mandatory rule of customary law, which it is not. But as between States faced with an issue concerning the lateral delimitation of adjacent continental shelves, there are still rules and principles of law to be applied; and in the present case it is not the fact either that rules are lacking, or that the situation is one for the *unfettered appreciation of the Parties* [emphasis added].[25]

> It is one of the advances in maritime international law, resulting from the intensification of fishing, that the former *laissez-faire* treatment of the living resources of the sea in the high seas has been replaced by a recognition of a *duty to have regard* to the rights of other States and the needs of conservation for the benefit of all [emphasis added].[26]

The idea that is here struggling to reach the surface of international consciousness is the distinction between a freedom and a power. The story of the development of international society since 1945 is the story of a progression from legal freedoms to legal powers. A freedom implies the absence of legal control. A power implies the absence of unfettered discretion. The development of modern national society was also the development of powers. The way that national society responded to that development was by extending the notion of self-government from legislation to executive action by means of the concepts of constitutionalism, the Rule of Law, government under the law. The constitutional struggles of centuries culminated in the late 17th and 18th centuries in the great Rule of Law achievements which provided the theoretical basis for the spectacular development of the powers of government in the 19th and 20th centuries.[27] The essence of the Rule of Law concept lies in the idea of Law as the actualization of the general interest. Each holder of a power under the law must act as an agent of all society. In subjecting itself

[25] North Sea Continental Shelf Cases, 1969 ICJ REP. at 46.

[26] Fisheries Jurisdiction Case (UK v. Iceland), 1974 ICJ REP. 3, 31 (Judgment of July 25).

[27] Especially the (British) Bill of Rights (1689), the great decided case of *Entick v. Carrington* (1765), the (United States) Declaration of Independence (1776) and (federal) Constitution (1789, with the Bill of Rights amendments of 1791), and the (French) Declaration of the Rights of Man and of the Citizen (1789). For Entick v. Carrington, see (1765) 19 State Trials 1029.

to legal powers, society is appointing agents to whom it delegates the function of acting on its behalf. Especially in advanced societies, society governs itself through the law, which is created by and for it and through the decision making that is carried out in its name and as a series of limits on its natural freedoms. Natural freedom is limited by law and powers under the law. Law and powers under the law are limited by their function of serving the interests of society.

To say that international society has now also reached such an "advanced" state of development is to say nothing new or surprising. To ask that the rights and duties of states, under both customary and treaty international law, be perceived in what has in the present study been called an "administrative law" perspective is to ask for a general and far-reaching change of attitude. But such a change of attitude at once enables us to grasp the true significance of much of the LOS Convention. It might also enable us to face with more equanimity certain areas of modern international law and practice that are otherwise a cause of serious concern, areas in which a discretionary power of states seems to be uncontrollable and yet in which its uncontrolled exercise is able gravely to prejudice the general interest of international society: the recognition of states and governments, the right of self-defense, the imposition of trade and other sanctions not under Security Council authority, the expropriation of foreign property and investments, the transnational protection of industrial property rights, interstate weapons supplies, the determination of matters within the domestic jurisdiction of a state, the military use of outer space, the application of the principle of *jus cogens* to treaties, the determination of so-called international crimes (including aggression) otherwise than by decision of the Security Council, the exercise of criminal jurisdiction (including the so-called effects doctrine and extradition, political offenses, and political asylum).

A change of perspective is required to see that all such rights (and the countless other comparable rights in the LOS Convention) are in reality *shared powers*, shared between the holder of the power and the community of states, in which regard for the interests of other states and of all states is of the essence. There are no freedoms from the law. There are no freedoms apart from the law. Freedoms are powers conferred by and under the law. The sovereign of modern international society is the same as the sovereign of the modern Western democratic tradition: *systemic authority*, the authority which flows from participation in the system. It flows from the *subjects* of the system whose participation legitimizes the system. It flows from the *system* whose benefits the subject may not claim if he does not accept its burdens. The benefit of a power is the discretionary choices that it protects. The burden of a power is respect for the interests of society as a whole, which confers the power on the holder as the agent of all its members.

Consideration of certain aspects of the LOS Convention has thus led us to see that states are not only representatives of the people who are their nationals. States are also appointed as representatives of the international community as a whole by the international legislator who confers powers on them and thereby organizes the world's self-government.

Annex A

Subjects of Rights and Duties

1. All states / every state / a state
2. Foreign states (foreign ships)
3. Developing states
4. States parties to the Convention
5. Third states (and their nationals)
6. Peoples who have not obtained full independence
7. Coastal state
8. Archipelagic state
9. States bordering straits
10. States with opposite or adjacent coasts
11. State bordering an enclosed or semi-enclosed sea
12. Landlocked state
13. Geographically disadvantaged state
14. Developing landlocked state
15. Developed landlocked state
16. States with special geographical characteristics (sgc's)
17. Developing state with sgc's
18. Developed state with sgc's
19. Coastal state with overwhelming dependence on living resources of the sea
20. Neighboring state of archipelagic state
21. Neighboring landlocked or geographically disadvantaged state to marine scientific research state
22. Transit state (between landlocked state and the sea)
23. Flag state
24. State of registry of an aircraft
25. State of which a ship's officer is a national
26. State that issued a master's certificate
27. State of origin of archaeological or historical objects
28. User state (of straits)
29. Other fishing states in the region
30. State of origin of anadromous fish
31. Catadromous fish state
32. Port state
33. Large investment state (in seabed mining)
34. Large consumer state (of seabed minerals)
35. Exporter state (of seabed minerals)
36. Developing state with special interests
37. States from certain geographical regions
38. State party to a dispute
39. Member of the International Sea-Bed Authority (and its organs and subordinate bodies)
40. International Tribunal on the Law of the Sea
41. International Court of Justice
42. Court / tribunal
43. Competent international organization / diplomatic conference
44. UN / specialized agencies / UN Secretary-General
45. Commission on the Limits of the Continental Shelf
46. Mankind / mankind as a whole
47. Persons in control of a pirate ship
48. Persons doing unauthorized broadcasting
49. Slave
50. Owner of a submarine cable or pipeline
51. Any person
52. Master / officer / crew (of a ship)
53. Diplomatic agent / consular officer
54. Local authorities (of a coastal state)
55. Nationals of other states
56. Operator / prospective contractor
57. State enterprises, state entities, natural or juridical persons (sponsored by a state party)

Annex B

Legal Sea Areas

1. Internal waters
2. Territorial sea
3. Bay (single state)
4. Bay (more than one state)
5. Historic bay
6. River mouth / delta
7. Port / foreign port
8. Ports and roadsteads
9. Port or offshore terminal
10. Sea lane / air routes over them
11. Low-tide elevation
12. Island / fringe of islands
13. Rocks that cannot sustain human habitation or economic life of their own
14. Archipelago (and connecting waters)
15. Archipelagic waters

16. Land area (Article 47(7))
17. Contiguous zone
18. Straits used for international navigation
19. Straits subject to long-standing international conventions
20. Article 36 straits
21. Article 38(1) and 45(1)(b) straits
22. Straits between high seas (or EEZ) and high seas (or EEZ)
23. Internal waters within a strait
24. Enclosed or semi-enclosed sea
25. Ice-covered area
26. Exclusive economic zone
27. Continental shelf
28. Continental shelf beyond 200 nautical miles
29. Superjacent waters of continental shelf
30. Artificial islands in EEZ
31. Artificial islands over continental shelf
32. Installations and structures in EEZ
33. Installations and structures over continental shelf
34. Other installations and structures
35. Platforms
36. Scientific research installations and equipment
37. Safety zones around installations and structures
38. Safety zones around marine scientific research (MSR) installations and equipment
39. MSR-designated areas
40. Areas of suspended passage in territorial sea
41. Areas of suspended passage in archipelagic waters
42. Fishing conservation area in EEZ
43. Fish stock adjacent to EEZ
44. Stationary and mobile structures and installations for activities in the (deep seabed) Area
45. High seas
46. All parts of the sea that are not included in the EEZ, in the territorial sea, or in the internal waters of a state or in the archipelagic waters of an archipelagic state
47. The area of seabed and ocean floor beyond the limits of national jurisdiction (the Area)
48. Seabed and subsoil under other sea areas
49. The bed of the high seas beyond the continental shelf
50. Waters superjacent to the Area / airspace above those waters
51. Water column beyond the limits of the EEZ
52. (Any area of) the marine environment
53. (Area) beyond the territorial sea
54. Airspace / airspace under the sovereignty of a coastal state
55. Any place outside the jurisdiction of any state
56. Area where the adoption of special pollution measures is necessary
57. Vessels
58. Aircraft

Annex C

Legal Relations

1. May / may not
2. Shall / shall not
3. Right
4. Exclusive right
5. Sovereign right / sovereign right for the purpose of, etc.
6. Rights and facilities
7. Rights and benefits
8. Legitimate interests
9. Rights and legitimate interests
10. Interests
11. Existing rights and legitimate interests
12. Traditional rights and other legitimate activities
13. Interests and needs
14. Special needs and interests
15. Special consideration
16. Preference
17. Equal treatment
18. Sovereign equality
19. Most-favored nation
20. Common heritage (of mankind)
21. Sovereignty
22. Full sovereignty
23. Sovereignty, territorial integrity, and political independence
24. Duty / obligation
25. Freedom
26. Power
27. Powers and functions
28. Discretion
29. Jurisdiction / national jurisdiction
30. Exclusive jurisdiction
31. Control

32. Jurisdiction and/or control
33. International legal personality
34. Legal capacity
35. Immunity
36. Privileges and immunities
37. Inviolability
38. Responsibility and liability
39. Final / binding / binding force
40. Principle
41. Policy
42. Claim
43. Nonrecognition
44. Validly purport to subject
45. Not prejudice / not affect / not entail any abridgment
46. Consent / implied consent
47. Regime / legal regime / international regime
48. Legal status / status
49. International lawful (uses)
50. Internationally agreed
51. Generally accepted
52. Applicable
53. Laws, regulations, measures, rules, guidelines, criteria, standards, recommended practices and procedures
54. Recommendation
55. Decision
56. Agreement / establish by agreement
57. Good faith
58. Abuse of right
59. Consensus

RECOGNITION OF GOVERNMENTS SHOULD NOT BE ABOLISHED

*By M. J. Peterson**

Recognition of governments serves three functions in the international legal system: ensuring that only regimes clearly deserving such status are accepted as governments of states, assuring new governments that others will respect their status, and informing courts, government agencies, and nationals of recognizing states that a particular regime is in fact the government of another state. Lately, some statesmen and a respectable number of legal scholars have come to view recognition of governments as causing more difficulties than it is worth as it is now used. In particular, they suspect that decisions whether to recognize a new regime often depend more on its character or policy than on its ability to meet the objective test of effectively ruling its state, and they believe that current doctrine on the effects of recognition or nonrecognition creates unnecessary confusion. As the late Judge Baxter wrote in 1978:

> [A]n institution of law that causes more problems than it solves must be rejected and replaced by working arrangements that are flexible and realistic. The partial withdrawal of law from this area of international relations will facilitate the maintenance of relations with states in which extraconstitutional changes of government are taking place, and that in itself is a good thing.[1]

Recognition of states is not at issue here. Those who advocate abolishing recognition of governments agree that recognition of new states will remain necessary as long as the international system lacks central institutions capable of determining for all when a new state has emerged. In fact, most of the arguments for abolishing recognition of governments rest on the assumption that recognition of states will remain and provide the framework within which changes of government can be handled without resort to recognition.

To assess the validity of arguments in favor of abolishing recognition of governments, it is necessary to understand why that legal institution has fallen into such disrepute, and to determine whether other "working arrangements" would perform the three functions mentioned above at least as well as does recognition of governments.

I. The Roots of Disrepute

International law on recognition of governments has always dealt with two main topics: (1) the circumstances necessitating and the conditions permitting

* Assistant Professor of Government, Harvard University, and Associate at the Harvard Center for International Affairs. The author wishes to thank Henry Steiner, Oscar Schachter, and the anonymous readers to whom the manuscript was referred by the *Journal* for their comments on earlier drafts.

[1] Baxter, *Foreword* to L. T. GALLOWAY, RECOGNIZING FOREIGN GOVERNMENTS: THE PRACTICE OF THE UNITED STATES, at xi (1978).

recognition of a new government, and (2) the effects of granting or withholding recognition for the new government, the deciding government, their respective states and nationals, and third parties. Developments in both areas have brought the legal institution into question. The narrowing of effects has encouraged the belief that recognition of governments no longer performs any useful functions in the international system. The apparent arbitrariness of many recognition decisions has made it seem a political game that creates more confusion than its useful functions are worth.

The Changing Effects of Recognition

Although 19th-century state practice maintained great distinctions between recognized and unrecognized governments, legal doctrine contained principles that could be used to criticize their extent. First, it was universally accepted that the legal personality of the state remains undisturbed by any change in government, no matter how legal or illegal in domestic law. Thus, changes of government did not affect the state's rights and duties under international law. Nineteenth-century discrimination against unrecognized governments meant, however, that a state could have difficulties fulfilling its duties or (more frequently) exercising its rights. Yet as early as 1896, legal scholars were arguing that this creates an anomalous situation that should be corrected either by abolishing recognition of governments or by narrowing its effects so that state rights and duties would not be disturbed.[2] Second, except among the members of the Quadruple Alliance in the years 1815–1830, and among certain Western Hemisphere governments later in the century, it was generally conceded that each state (or, in the more democratic formulations, the people of each state) has the right to establish whatever government it wishes. This doctrine, though often ignored, gave powerful impetus to arguments that the origins of a government were far less important than its ability to control the state effectively and to win or extract obedience from the people. Since recognition became an issue only when regimes came to power in ways contrary to the constitution, laws, or customs of the country affected, this was a powerful argument against it. Though a legal succession could be interpreted to mean that the recognition granted to one government was handed to its successor along with the rest of its legitimate claims to power, the idea that origins should be irrelevant won wider acceptance as the principles of self-determination and nonintervention gained adherents.

Three 20th-century developments gave impetus to basing practice on these 19th-century arguments. First, as nonrecognition came to be used to express ideological dislike for particular new governments, periods of nonrecognition lengthened. The maximum length increased from 3 years in the 19th century to 16 years during the interwar period, and 30 or more in the postwar period (the record being the Portuguese refusal to recognize the Soviet Government from 1917 until the Portuguese Government itself was overthrown in 1974). The number of ideologically based nonrecognitions also increased dramatically after 1917. Once begun, these ideological nonrecognitions were often

[2] 1 A. Rivier, Principes de Droit des gens 283 (1896).

hard to reverse. Large or important segments of opinion in the nonrecognizing state—and even in the target state—came to view any change in attitude toward the new regime as highly significant. Governments would be tempted, therefore, to deal with particular issues or crises that arose on an ad hoc basis, expanding the content of "informal" or indirect contact to do so.

This tendency was reinforced by a second development. In the late 19th and early 20th centuries, governmental activity expanded into such fields as transport, regulation of economic activity, direction of all or some economic enterprises, health, scientific research, and social services heretofore left largely to private initiative. It soon became apparent that international cooperation in these fields, as in more traditional fields of government concerns like regulation of international trade and financial transactions or suppression of crime, meant that governments had to stay in more constant and more varied contact with one another. The need to maintain contact encouraged the definition of many activities as routine or administrative matters separate from political decisions like entering into formal diplomatic relations with another government. This alone, but even more so when combined with protracted nonrecognition of a new government, widened the range of low-level contacts.

Third, there was a great expansion of multilateral relations, whether in the form of conferences or of standing intergovernmental organizations. This expansion, which stemmed in part from the need to heighten cooperation in nonpolitical fields and in part from efforts to prevent a repetition of World War I by creating new mechanisms of political cooperation, reinforced the effects of the second trend, and made avoidance of political contact with unrecognized governments more difficult. In most multilateral undertakings, decisions about who could participate were made by a simple or (more often) qualified majority of the members. This meant that a government might be forced to consider political matters with another it did not recognize, unless it could get enough other members to agree that the latter ought not to be allowed to participate.[3] In most cases, it could not, which would put it in a position where political discussions could not be avoided and bilateral relations could not always be kept separate from multilateral ones. Though some legal scholars have advocated ending the confusion by requiring all members of an organization to recognize a new government once its delegates are admitted to participation,[4] governments have been reluctant to hand recognition decisions over to others.

[3] The United States succeeded in maintaining such a majority against seating delegates of the People's Republic of China (PRC) in the United Nations General Assembly from 1949 until 1971; between October 1971 and January 1979 it had to deal with the PRC as a fellow member of the United Nations though refusing to recognize it.

[4] Such a solution has been advocated by H. LAUTERPACHT, RECOGNITION IN INTERNATIONAL LAW 166–69 (1947); T. CHEN, THE INTERNATIONAL LAW OF RECOGNITION 222–23 (1951); J. CHARPENTIER, LA RECONNAISSANCE INTERNATIONALE ET L'EVOLUTION DU DROIT DES GENS 317–18 (1956); S. PATEL, RECOGNITION IN THE LAW OF NATIONS 79 (1959); Chatelain, *La Reconnaissance internationale,* in 2 LA TECHNIQUE ET LES PRINCIPES DE DROIT PUBLIC 707, 710 (C. Rousseau ed. 1950); Q. Wright, *Some Thoughts about Recognition,* 44 AJIL 548, 558–59 (1950); Tabata, *Admission to the U.N. and Recognition of States,* 5 JAPANESE ANNUAL OF INTERNATIONAL LAW 1, 1 (1961); and P. CORBETT, THE GROWTH OF WORLD LAW 67 (1971).

The result of these three developments is a striking change in legal doctrine on the effects of recognition in bilateral relations. In, to pick a date at random, 1890, a government would treat another it did not recognize with great reserve. Diplomats and consuls remained in place, but were instructed to avoid all but the most necessary and informal contact with officials of the new regime. Thus, communications were confined to oral discussion, third person *notes verbales*, or letters addressed to the official by name rather than title. Official ceremonies and receptions were also avoided. Negotiations were usually, though not always, confined to matters affecting the diplomatic or consular missions themselves, the protection of nationals' lives and property, or emergencies requiring immediate action. Though governments differed in the extent of their caution, none concluded the most formal types of agreements with unrecognized regimes, or included political clauses in other agreements. Some even avoided making trade agreements or armistices (using cease-fire agreements between military commanders instead). Even so, heads of diplomatic missions would usually remain at their posts, particularly when the interval of nonrecognition was expected to be short, and did not present new credentials when their government recognized the regime they had been dealing with informally.[5]

By the 1970's, restraint was more an option than a requirement in many areas. An unrecognized government participating in a multilateral organization or conference could not be ignored there. Diplomats and consuls now pursued a wider variety of negotiations and had wider freedom to conclude agreements. Armistices no longer raised any problems. Long-term trade agreements were possible, some made directly with the regime, but more with state-owned enterprises or private associations acting with government approval. Far-reaching political agreements were possible if expressed informally; the 1972 U.S.-China Shanghai Communiqué, a press statement that laid out understandings on a variety of issues—such as the future of Taiwan—and formed the basis of the two Governments' relations until U.S. recognition in January 1979, is the most notable recent example. State visits, such as that of Chinese Premier Zhou Enlai to Ethiopia in 1973 or of U.S. President Nixon to China in January 1972, were not impossible despite all the public ceremony they entail. In fact, the only forms of bilateral contact universally avoided were conclusion of a formal bilateral treaty on political matters; conclusion of a comprehensive commerce, friendship, and navigation treaty (where one had lapsed or never existed between the states concerned); final settlements of claims; and establishment of formal diplomatic relations.[6] U.S.-China relations reflect these developments: the liaison offices were turned into embassies effective with recognition, a claims settlement was reached in May 1979, and the United States extended most-favored-nation status to the Peo-

[5] A change of the sending government would require new credentials even if the new government decided to retain the diplomatic representative sent by its predecessor. *See* 1 P. PRADIER-FODÉRÉ, COURS DE DROIT DIPLOMATIQUE 388–89 (1881).

[6] *See, e.g.*, 1 J. VERHOEVEN, LA RECONNAISSANCE INTERNATIONALE DANS LA PRATIQUE CONTEMPORAIN 355–415 (1975).

ple's Republic (PRC) in their Trade Agreement of July 1979.[7] If the interval of nonrecognition was short, diplomats still remained at their posts. They would leave if the interval of nonrecognition was extended, if their government recognized a rival claimant as the government of the affected state, or if the new government insisted. Again, new credentials are not issued at recognition; a recognizing government's intent to leave the same diplomats at their posts is assumed when it replies to the new regime's note announcing that it has taken power and wishes to continue diplomatic relations with other governments.[8]

In the 19th century, national courts tended to treat unrecognized regimes as legally nonexistent. The longer nonrecognitions of the 20th century, coupled with the faster pace and greater number of international transactions, pushed courts away from these ideas. The courts in civil law states, which asserted greater independence from the executive in this regard, were the first to break with tradition. They began to treat the acts of an unrecognized regime in clear control of its state as acts of state to be given full legal effect if they regulated the activities of persons on their own territory, nationalized property there, involved tasks of routine administration and taxation, provided legal authenticity to documents (as by notarization), or granted nationality to ships, aircraft, corporations, or persons. Courts in common law states adopted similar views somewhat later. In the United States, they changed their views during the long nonrecognition of the Soviet Government in 1917–1933; British courts slowly followed after World War II.[9] Giving full effect to the internal acts of an unrecognized regime that ruled the whole state received specific international endorsement in the *Tinoco* claims arbitration of 1923.[10]

Similarly, courts in civil law states began the modern shift towards granting immunity from suit to regimes controlling the whole state. Again, the courts of common law states did likewise after some delay. Changes in opinion, reinforced in some countries by the adoption of legislation defining the conditions under which sovereign immunity should be granted and leaving courts to decide these matters without guidance from the executive in each case, have now resulted in the extension of the same immunity from suit to unrecognized governments controlling the whole state as to recognized governments.[11] It

[7] U.S.-PRC Agreement on the Settlement of Claims of May 11, 1979, 18 ILM 551 (1979); Art. II of the U.S.-PRC Agreement on Trade Relations of July 7, 1979, *id.* at 1041.

[8] E. SATOW, GUIDE TO DIPLOMATIC PRACTICE sec. 21.1–3 (Gore-Booth 5th ed. 1979). If diplomatic relations had been interrupted or a new head of mission sent, then new credentials would be necessary.

[9] On European courts, see 1 J. SPIROPOULOS, DIE DE FACTO REGIERUNG IM VÖLKERRECHT 123–71 (1926); NOEL-HENRY, LE GOUVERNEMENT DE FAIT DEVANT LE JUGE (1927); and P. STIERLIN, DIE RECHTSSTELLUNG DER NICHTANERKANNTEN REGIERUNGEN IM VÖLKERRECHT (1940). On U.S. courts, see 2 M. WHITEMAN, DIGEST OF INTERNATIONAL LAW 604–55 (1963); and RESTATEMENT (SECOND) OF THE FOREIGN RELATIONS LAW OF THE UNITED STATES §113 (1962). On British courts, see Merrils, *Recognition and Construction*, 20 INT'L & COMP. L.Q. 476 (1971).

[10] Tinoco Case (UK v. Costa Rica), 1 R. Int'l Arb. Awards 370 (1923).

[11] On the general question of sovereign immunity for unrecognized governments, see T. CHEN, *supra* note 4, at 140–45; RESTATEMENT (SECOND), *supra* note 9, §65; Lord Atkin's opinion in

should be noted, though, that the general sovereign immunity these regimes and governments enjoy is less broad than that prevalent in the 19th century. Today, sovereign immunity is generally held not to cover suits arising from private acts and commercial dealings undertaken by governments, whereas in the 19th century it covered suits arising from almost any governmental act.

Differences of treatment persist in three fields: a new government's ability to sue in foreign courts, suits involving governmental acts having extraterritorial effect, and possession of state property located abroad. Nonrecognition is no longer considered an absolute bar to the new regime's suing in foreign courts, but most courts remain somewhat reluctant to entertain such suits.[12] Courts are far less ready to give extraterritorial effect to the acts of unrecognized governments than to those of recognized governments,[13] and generally insist that there be recognition before the return of state property acquired by a previous government (embassy buildings and bank accounts are the most frequent objects of dispute).[14]

At present, therefore, because the effects of nonrecognition are relatively narrow, many observers believe that recognition of governments seems to make little difference. Advocates of abolition have been quick to argue that its remaining functions could now be performed, perhaps more slowly but no less effectively, in other ways. New governments could have their status accepted bit by bit as the need arose. In multilateral relations they would receive assurance that their status would be respected, at least in large part, by all governments participating in the same organizations and conferences. With the widening of intergovernmental and transnational contacts and the improvement of communications, individual nationals of foreign states and particular organs or agencies of foreign governments could determine for themselves who rules where and act accordingly. Though sometimes advanced simply as a cure for legal confusion, arguments that the few remaining dif-

---

The *Arantzazu Mendi*, 1939 Crim. App. 256 (H.L.), 9 Ann. Dig. 60; and Wulfsohn v. Russian Socialist Federated Soviet Republic, 234 N.Y. 372 (1923), 2 Ann. Dig. 39. Recent legislation includes the U.S. Foreign Sovereign Immunities Act of 1976, 28 U.S.C. §§1602–1611, 71 AJIL 595 (1977), 15 ILM 1388 (1976); and the UK State Immunity Act of 1978, 17 *id.* at 1123 (1978). Similar rules appear in the European Convention on State Immunity, 11 *id.* at 470 (1972).

[12] In the 1930's, a number of European scholars argued that there is no general obstacle to admitting such suits. *See* J. SPIROPOULOS, *supra* note 9, at 130; and E. VON LIVONIUS, DER VÖLKERRECHTLICHER ANERKENNUNG 15 (1934). European legal codes permit unrecognized governments to sue. British and American courts remain reluctant to entertain their suits. On U.S. attitudes, see Russian Socialist Federated Soviet Republic v. Cibrario, 239 N.Y. 158 (1924), 2 Ann. Dig. 41; Republic of Vietnam v. Pfizer, Inc., 556 F.2d 892 (8th Cir. 1977), *summarized in* 72 AJIL 152 (1978); and RESTATEMENT OF THE FOREIGN RELATIONS LAW OF THE UNITED STATES (REVISED) §205 (Tentative Draft No. 2, 1981).

[13] *See* T. CHEN, *supra* note 4, at 145–66; J. CHARPENTIER, *supra* note 4, at 22–39; RESTATEMENT (SECOND), *supra* note 9, §113; and RESTATEMENT (REVISED), *supra* note 11, §205. The extraterritorial acts of recognized governments are not given automatic effect; their effects are limited by rules on conflict of laws.

[14] *See* RESTATEMENT (SECOND), *supra* note 9, §111; P. JESSUP, A MODERN LAW OF NATIONS 45 (1950); R. DHOKALIA, INTERNATIONAL LAW 230–33 (1963); and S. MOOKERJEA, INTERNATIONAL LAW 130 (1968).

ferences could be treated better without the notion of recognition have received the most attention from those who feel that the way recognition decisions are made is unnecessarily arbitrary.

The Changing Rules of Decision

There has been only one rule governing decisions on whether to grant or refuse recognition to a new government: the necessary, but not sufficient, criterion is whether a government effectively controls its state. Within the limits of this rule, which forbids recognizing before control is shown or continuing to recognize after control is lost, governments are free to adopt any one of a number of rules for decision. To add to the confusion, most governments have asserted several at once, choosing among them as circumstances warrant.

Between 1830 and 1914, most recognition decisions were based on the effectivist rule: that is, recognition was granted once the foreign government was satisfied that the new government did in fact control its state.[15] There were, however, instances of refusal to recognize because the new government had come to power by using extreme violence,[16] or because it was receiving too much foreign help to be considered a truly indigenous government.[17] More frequent were delays of recognition until the population had given its express approval of the new government in an election or referendum,[18] or until the new government had made assurances that it would respect international agreements made by its predecessor.[19]

In doctrinal terms, the most striking moves away from effectivism were monarchical and democratic legitimism. In both, new governments that departed from the preferred form were refused recognition. Monarchical legitimism found some use in Europe during the Quadruple Alliance era (1815–1830), but declined and then disappeared rapidly from recognition decisions. Democratic legitimism was invoked in the Americas late in the century. The

[15] This is usually called a "defactoist" rule in the literature on recognition. That term distinguishes decisions based solely on whether the new regime controls the state only from decisions based on ideological beliefs about the relative acceptability of different forms of government. The term "effectivist" is meant to provide a distinction between decisions based on control and those based on all other considerations.

[16] British, Dutch, French, Italian, and United States nonrecognition of the Karageorgevich dynasty in Serbia, which was brought to power in 1903 by a coup resulting in the deaths of the former King and Queen, several of her relatives, and several ministers of the Government. *See* 1 H. SMITH, GREAT BRITAIN AND THE LAW OF NATIONS 229–33 (1932).

[17] British, French, and United States nonrecognition of the Rivas Government of Nicaragua (1854–1856), which came to power with the aid of American adventurers led by William Walker, and U.S. nonrecognition of the French-aided Imperial Government of Mexico under Maximilian (1854–1867). *See* 1 J. MOORE, DIGEST OF INTERNATIONAL LAW 141 and 147 (1906).

[18] Swiss and United States delay in recognizing the Second French Empire (J. MOORE, *supra* note 17, at 125–126); Austrian, British, German, and Russian delay in recognizing the Third French Republic (FONTES JURIS GENTIUM, Series B: Digest of the Diplomatic Correspondence of the European States, sec. 1, vol. 1, pt. 1, at 164–70); general delay in recognizing the Portuguese Republic in 1910–1911 (1 H. ACCIOLY, TRAITÉ DE DROIT INTERNATIONAL PUBLIC 182–83 (1940)).

[19] *See* p. 39 *infra*.

United States had occasionally invoked popular support as a separate criterion for recognition, but the move to democratic legitimism was made first by the five Central American Republics of Costa Rica, El Salvador, Guatemala, Honduras, and Nicaragua in an additional protocol to their 1907 Treaty of Peace and Amity. They undertook "not [to] recognize any other Government which may come into power in any of the five Republics as a consequence of a *coup d'état*, or of a revolution against the recognized Government, so long as the freely elected representatives of the people thereof, have not constitutionally reorganized the country."[20] This agreement hardly discouraged coups, but the parties applied it among themselves with little controversy. Problems arose when the United States Government, which with Mexico had brought the five Republics to the conference producing the Treaty, cited it to justify its own policy in the area, a policy that combined nonrecognition with armed intervention and other forms of interference.[21] U.S. policy took on particularly strong tones of constitutional legitimism under the presidency of Woodrow Wilson, who began U.S. nonrecognition of the Carranza Government of Mexico on these grounds in 1913.

After 1918, recognition and nonrecognition were used frequently to express sympathy for or hostility to a new government. Many of the traditional doctrines defining circumstances in which governments could delay recognition came to be used to cover decisions taken for arbitrary reasons. Constitutional legitimism was again attempted by treaty in Central America between 1923 and 1931,[22] and was occasionally asserted by other Western Hemisphere governments. Interest in constitutional legitimism or in insisting upon express popular acceptance has continued to wax and wane in the Western Hemisphere. Such ideas were not as popular in the rest of the world, though the Soviet "Brezhnev Doctrine" can be read to include the idea that non-Communist governments coming to power in states previously ruled by Communists should not be recognized.[23] Similar reasoning often lay, at least in part, behind the long, ideologically based nonrecognitions of the PRC Government. The fact of foreign assistance has been used to explain other nonrecognitions, such as those of the Lon Nol or Heng Samrin Governments of Cambodia in 1970 and 1979, respectively.

Under prolonged nonrecognition, legal assertion diverges from reality. As the number and length of prolonged nonrecognitions increased, many legal scholars and some statesmen came to feel strongly that legal assertion must follow reality by being based solely on the fact of who rules rather than on the nature of their rule or how it came about. Governments like the British and Swiss that had been following effectivist policies for some years found themselves joined by an increasing number of others.

[20] Text in 2 AJIL, Supp. 229, 229–30 (1908).

[21] For fuller discussion, see R. SHARP, NONRECOGNITION AS A LEGAL OBLIGATION 43–47 (1934).

[22] Text of the 1923 Treaty in 17 AJIL, Supp. 117 (1923). This Treaty included the 1907 provisions plus clauses aimed at preventing the organizers of a coup from attaining high office in the Government formed by the postcoup elections.

[23] English translation in 7 ILM 1323 (1968).

Recognition of governments was also discredited in many minds by the frequent use by stronger states of a new government's need for recognition to extract from it promises about its general policy or specific actions. This practice was quite common in the 19th century in those parts of the world where colonization had not occurred or had already ended. Thus, the United States Government used recognition for this purpose quite frequently in the Caribbean and Central America. Acting together, the European great powers traded recognition for a long series of promises from the new Sultan of Morocco in 1908, and for the Chinese Republic's continued adherence to the treaties providing extraterritoriality for foreign nationals and various privileges for the great powers in 1911.[24] This practice continued in the interwar era, though some of the intended victims were strong or clever enough to resist. Attempts to impose stipulations on the Soviet Union were abandoned quite early. Efforts to impose them on the Turkish and later Chinese Governments ended in favor of the intended victim. Mexican Governments resisted U.S. attempts to secure guarantees of prerevolutionary grants of oil rights. In the postwar period, use of threats not to recognize in order to extract concessions has disappeared, in part because the costs of the policy (the resentment created in the target state) came to outweigh the gains, and in part because more efficacious means to the same end were found. The anti-imperialist cast of postwar discourse has meant, though, that the practice is still criticized as if its revival were likely.[25]

II. The Alternative

Governments disturbed by these practices have reacted in two ways. Some have sought to de-emphasize recognition of governments by lessening the difference in treating legal and extralegal changes; others have sought to end the difference by abolishing recognition of governments altogether. De-emphasis can take two forms: adopting an effectivist recognition policy, or avoiding the question of recognition by defining specific changes of government as "legal" whenever possible.

The first form, adopting effectivist policies, is an old remedy and need not be treated at length here. It does not abolish the distinction between legal and extralegal changes of government, but does specify that reaction to the extralegal changes should be kept within rather narrow bounds. If the new government has control, its status should be acknowledged; if it does not, it should not be given status it does not deserve. Strict adherence to this rule would end the various political uses of recognition and the abuses stemming from them. It would not of itself clarify doctrine on the effects of recognition but, by encouraging governments to abandon lengthy nonrecognitions of gov-

[24] *See* 1908 FOREIGN RELATIONS OF THE UNITED STATES [hereinafter cited as FRUS] 648–49; 1912 FRUS 68–86, *passim*; and 1913 FRUS 84–115, *passim*.

[25] On the particular instances, see 1 G. HACKWORTH, DIGEST OF INTERNATIONAL LAW 250–52, 257–63, 280–81, and 305–07 (1944); S. MACCORKLE, AMERICAN POLICY OF RECOGNITION TOWARDS MEXICO 82–100 (1933); and H. LAUTERPACHT, *supra* note 4, at 33–36. For a discussion of why using recognition as a bargaining tool is unlikely to recur, see M. Peterson, *Political Use of Recognition*, 34 WORLD POL. 324, 347–98 (1982).

ernments clearly in control of their states, it would avoid the problems that arise when prolonged nonrecognition has to be combined with contacts of various sorts.

The second form, reclassifying as "legal" a number of changes formerly deemed "extralegal," has been practiced since World War I. In the 19th century, the line between "legal" and "extralegal" was usually assumed to be the same as that between "violent" and "peaceful." Even then, however, it was possible to arrange a partly violent and partly peaceful takeover. In a number of Latin American republics this became a fine art: a group seeking to take over without putting the armed forces in the streets would first persuade (with threats if necessary) the vice-president, or whoever stood to succeed to the presidency, to resign. This official would be replaced by the person the group wished to see in power. After a suitable, but fairly short, interval, the president would be induced to resign, and the new vice-president would succeed. The government would have been changed according to constitutional procedures and without overt violence.[26] In countries where the head of state was a ceremonial figure and the real power was exercised by the head of government, a "legal" takeover could be arranged by persuading the head of state to appoint a new head of government, whether elections had been held or not.[27] A number of Latin American coups even inspired a doctrine that coups could be ignored for recognition purposes if the newly installed group was a faction of a movement that had previously taken over the country.[28]

None of these doctrines, not even that assuming a change is legal if the head of state grants formal approval, has won general acceptance or been used in all the actual cases.[29] Though there was some interest in creating general rules during the interwar years, governments today have preferred to be vague and to confine their comments to "the question of recognition does not arise" in doubtful cases, without specifying the basis for defining a change as "legal." This second method, too, does not abolish recognition of governments. It does not end the distinction between "legal" and "extralegal" changes; it only moves the line a bit and makes it fuzzier. It does not necessarily

[26] *E.g.*, the 1931 coups bringing Ureña to power in the Dominican Republic, Montero in Chile, and the "Acción Communal" group in Panama, as well as two changes of president in Portugal during 1926. 1 G. HACKWORTH, *supra* note 25, at 231, 243, 269, and 293–95.

[27] Mussolini's takeover in Italy, Hitler's appointment as Chancellor of Germany, and changes of premier in Thailand in 1932 and 1935. 2 M. WHITEMAN, *supra* note 9, at 463–64. Also the 1948 Communist coup in Czechoslovakia, the 1957 Thai coup, U Nu's forced resignation as Premier of Burma in 1958, and the Greek colonels' coup of 1967. *Id.* at 466 and 548; [1948] 4 FRUS 733–55; 56 DEP'T STATE BULL. 750 (1967).

[28] *E.g.*, the 1931 accession of the Ocampo junta in Peru, which was drawn from a faction of the "August 1930" movement that had been in power. [1931] 2 FRUS 918–21. President Obregón of Mexico tried to persuade U.S. President Harding to recognize his Government with the same argument in 1921. *See* his letter dated June 11, 1921, in [1921] 2 FRUS 419.

[29] Exceptions noted, *inter alia*, in 1 G. HACKWORTH, *supra* note 25, at 306–07; 2 M. WHITEMAN, *supra* note 9, at 265; Hsiung, *China's Recognition Practice*, in CHINA'S PRACTICE OF INTERNATIONAL LAW 14, 43 (J. Cohen ed. 1972); and AUSTRALIAN MINISTRY OF EXTERNAL AFFAIRS, CURRENT NOTES ON INTERNATIONAL AFFAIRS 660 (1971).

end political abuse in recognition decisions because the possibility of considering a change "extralegal" remains. It also has no effect on the confusion about effects of recognition, except as it actually reduces the number of nonrecognitions.

A few governments, believing that de-emphasis in any form will not solve the problem, have opted to abolish recognition of governments completely. They propose confining recognition to states and indicating their readiness to deal with any regime that comes to power in another state by maintaining formal diplomatic relations with it.

The elements of a doctrinal argument for this position have been present a long time, but they have been assembled only recently. In the late 1890's, the Swiss legal scholar Alphonse Rivier argued:

> It results from the principle of the permanence or identity of the nation, which subsists and remains the same regardless of the changes occurring in the form of its government, that a recognition of the new state of affairs, of the transformation of the constitution, by other nations does not appear at all necessary.[30]

Another form of Rivier's argument is that since having a government is a necessary attribute of statehood, questioning the status of the government means questioning the continued existence of the state itself.[31] A somewhat different approach insists that failure to accept a new government denies the state its right to participate in international affairs because such participation is only possible through a government.[32] The long-standing tradition that recognition need not be indicated by formal note or public statement, but could be inferred from the establishment of formal diplomatic relations with the new regime,[33] was also useful to the abolitionists. They could point out that legal doctrine already included a relatively quiet way to indicate acceptance of a new regime's status, and thus could claim that their ideas were less of a break with past practice than they might have seemed at first glance.

The new doctrine sought to fulfill the functions traditionally performed by recognition of governments by equating formal diplomatic relations with acceptance of the new government's existence and status, rather than using the traditional formula that having diplomatic relations is an act equivalent to recognition and recognition means acceptance of the new government's existence and status. Its advocates were quick to adopt and extend an argument first raised by Mexican Foreign Minister Genaro Estrada in 1930:

> After a very careful study of the subject, the Government of Mexico has transmitted instructions to its Ministers or Chargés d'Affaires in the

[30] 1 A. RIVIER, *supra* note 2, at 293.

[31] Huess, *Zum Problem juristischer Unterscheidung völkerrechtlicher Anerkennungsarten*, 19 ZEITSCHRIFT FÜR VÖLKERRECHT 1, 4–5 (1935); 1 J. DE LOUTER, LE DROIT INTERNATIONAL PUBLIC POSITIF 245 (1920); and Brown, *The Legal Effects of Recognition*, 44 AJIL 617, 630–33 (1950).

[32] Charvin, *La République démocratique allemande et le droit international*, 75 REV. GÉNÉRALE DROIT INT'L PUBLIC [RGDIP] 1014, 1022 (1971); N. Ulanova, *Recognition of States and Governments and Participation in Multilateral Treaties*, 1961 SOVIET Y.B. INT'L L. 321.

[33] One of the few points of general agreement among statesmen and legal scholars in both the 19th and 20th centuries.

> countries affected [by coups in 1930 and 1931], informing them that the Mexican Government is issuing no declarations in the sense of grants of recognition, since that nation considers that such a course is an insulting practice and one which, in addition to the fact that it offends the sovereignty of other nations, implies that judgment of some sort may be passed upon the internal affairs of those nations by other governments, inasmuch as the latter assume, in effect, an attitude of criticism, when they decide, favorably or unfavorably, as to the legal qualifications of foreign régimes.
>
> Therefore, the Government of Mexico confines itself to the maintenance or withdrawal, as it may deem advisable, of its diplomatic agents, and to the continued acceptance, also when it may deem advisable, of such similar accredited diplomatic agents as the respective nations may have in Mexico; and in so doing, it does not pronounce judgment, either precipitately or *a posteriori*, regarding the right of foreign nations to accept, maintain or replace their governments or authorities.[34]

The precise meaning of the "Estrada Doctrine" was unclear from the start, and the Mexican Government has never fully explained it. Some of its early supporters claimed that it meant to abolish recognition of governments.[35] Others argued that it amounted to combining tacit forms of recognition and an effectivist rule for decision.[36] Mexican behavior, notably the long refusal to recognize the Franco Government of Spain[37] and a few delays in signaling acceptance of coup-born Western Hemisphere governments, supports the latter view. In any event, the Estrada Doctrine is not prominent in the current discussions. Many states outside the Western Hemisphere have admitted ignorance of it,[38] and it has not been mentioned in the arguments of those most interested in abolishing recognition of governments.

The new doctrine—that recognition applies only to states, that all effective regimes are to be accepted as governments, and that this acceptance is to be indicated by continuing formal diplomatic relations with the new regime—was first applied by France and Belgium in the mid-1960's.[39] Their initial uses were hesitant. In a 1965 Senate debate, the Belgian Foreign Minister ended up having to explain that the policy advocated using tacit recognition, not abolishing it.[40] The French note to the Boumédienne Government of Algeria

[34] Press statement of Sept. 27, 1930, *translated in* 25 AJIL, Supp. 203 (1931).

[35] *See* many of the early Latin American reactions in INSTITUTO AMERICANO DE DERECHO Y LEGISLACIÓN COMPARADA, LA OPINIÓN UNIVERSAL SOBRE LA DOCTRINA ESTRADA (1931).

[36] Jessup, *The Estrada Doctrine*, 25 AJIL 719 (1931); and the Mexican diplomat M. Nervo, *La Doctrine Estrada et la reconnaissance des gouvernements "de facto,"* 4 SÉANCES ET TRAVAUX DE L'ACADÉMIE DIPLOMATIQUE INTERNATIONALE 84–88 (1931). A later acceptance of this interpretation appears in 1 J. VERHOEVEN, *supra* note 6, at 91.

[37] The Mexicans went even farther, continuing to recognize the Republicans as the Government of Spain from 1939 until 1977. *See* New York Times, March 19, 1977, at 4, col. 3.

[38] *See* responses from the Burundi, Danish, Dutch, and Libyan Governments in L. T. GALLOWAY, *supra* note 1, App. A. The Finns view it as a Western Hemisphere doctrine inapplicable to their policy (*id.*,n.28), while the Swiss say it applies only in certain circumstances and cite the Spanish and Angolan civil wars as examples (*id.*, n.33).

[39] 1 J. VERHOEVEN, *supra* note 6, at 90, credits France with the first use.

[40] Exchange between Senator Rolin and Foreign Minister Spaak on Dec. 14, 1965, *quoted in* 4 REV. BELGE DROIT INT'L 541–42 (1968).

in 1965 and the Belgian note to the Qaddafi Government of Libya in 1969 stated both that the sending state recognized only states, not governments, and that the note or the continuation of formal diplomatic relations should be deemed the equivalent of recognition.[41] These may have been simply explanations given for the benefit of legislators, the public, and foreign governments unfamiliar with the new doctrine rather than retreats from it. Recent French statements indicate that abolition is the goal. The statement on the 1979 change of government in Iran is typical:

> The practice of the French government consists, moreover—is it necessary to recall?—of recognizing States and not governments. France is ready to pursue cooperation with Iran in respect of the mutual interests of the two countries. Its ambassador in Teheran has made contact with Mr. Bazargan. The French government earnestly hopes that the process of normalization will lead to the reestablishment of civil peace and security throughout Iran.[42]

Belgium's express recognition of the PRC Government was not a retreat from abolition. It was clearly motivated by special circumstances, both the need to disavow relations with a rival regime and Chinese insistence on a statement ending a long nonrecognition that had begun before Belgium adopted its new doctrine.

Today, Belgium and France are the most consistent users of the new doctrine, but it has also been applied at times by the West German, Soviet, Kenyan, Swiss, Italian, and Spanish Governments.[43] The Austrian, Finnish, Irish, Ivory Coast, Portuguese, and Saudi Arabian Governments have professed adherence to it,[44] and some Francophone African states have also used it.[45] However, most governments continue to treat recognition of governments as a separate legal institution even if they are giving it less prominence.

III. The Alternative Evaluated

Those who advocate abolition argue that the traditional functions of recognition would be equally well fulfilled by maintenance or severance of diplomatic relations as the situation required. Their objections to recognition can be summarized under four headings: (1) most changes of government occur so quickly that the question who rules the state is answered almost before it can be asked; (2) the speed and intensity of modern communications allows government agencies, courts, and foreign nationals to determine accurately on their own who actually does rule any state; (3) any attempt to use recognition for influencing a new government's fate or policy will be ineffective; and (4) political uses of recognition cause more practical difficulties than they

[41] 1966 Annuaire Français de Droit International 918; 7 Rev. Belge Droit Int'l 319 (1971).

[42] 83 RGDIP 808 (1979).

[43] R. Yakemtchouk, L'Afrique en droit international 51–53 (1971); 4 Africa Contemporary Record C64–65 and C79 (1971–72); 75 RGDIP 158–59 (1971); 1974 Annuaire Français de Droit International 1065; 79 RGDIP 525 (1975); Washington Post, May 1, 1975, at A36; 1976 Italian Y.B. Int'l L. 412.

[44] L. T. Galloway, *supra* note 1, App. A and notes thereto.

[45] 1 J. Verhoeven, *supra* note 6, at 91, notes that Senegal and Madagascar follow it.

are worth by ignoring reality. All of these arguments have received sympathetic responses from governments, many of which have adopted effectivist policies or reduced the publicity they give to questions of recognition.

There are, however, circumstances and considerations that make outright abolition undesirable. In two sets of circumstances, first, the relatively uncommon one of an extended civil war and second, the quite common one of a lack of diplomatic relations between two countries, there is need for a mechanism allowing explicit statements about a new government's status. The need for consistency and clarity in legal doctrine also makes outright abolition less desirable than it appears at first glance.

To begin with the rarer situation, although most changes of government are accomplished relatively quickly, some are not. They may be prolonged because a group unable to accomplish a coup chooses the more lengthy tactic of beginning its antigovernment struggle in the countryside, because a group that thought it could accomplish a coup does not succeed and turns instead to waging a wider struggle, because a government widens the struggle to maintain its position against challengers, or because a coalition that overthrows a government falls apart and rival factions contend for power. In any of these situations, there may be periods when two or more groups have equally plausible claims to be the government of the state. Traditionally, international law has dealt with this problem by resolving doubts in favor of the previously established government for as long as possible.

There often comes a time, however, when this delaying tactic cannot be used any longer. Government agencies, courts, and nationals acting on their own might decide at about the same time which government deserves acceptance, but there is a potential for confusion and contradictory decisions that can be avoided if all follow foreign ministry guidance. If the former government has disappeared and the struggle is between rival factions, the likelihood of divergent conclusions is greater and coordination therefore more important. Admittedly, such situations are infrequent, and it can be legitimately objected that legal doctrine should not be made on the basis of rare cases. However, they have occurred often enough that, given the rise of mass participation in politics and of heated ideological contention, they can be expected to recur in the future. Thus, legal doctrine must take them into account. Even L. Thomas Galloway admits as much when he notes that should questions of status arise that a court cannot resolve on its own, it will seek guidance from the State Department.[46] Though he uses this point as an argument for abolishing recognition of governments, one could as easily view it as an argument for retaining it.

The more common circumstance is lack of diplomatic relations between two governments. Most governments cannot afford to maintain diplomatic missions in the capitals of all 170 independent states of the world. Instead, they send missions to neighbors and to more distant states of particular importance to them, and deal with other states through these missions or through missions to international organizations. Diplomatic relations may also be lack-

[46] L. T. GALLOWAY, *supra* note 1, at 152.

ing because they were severed before the new government came to power. In the past, severance of diplomatic relations was uncommon except in case of war between two states. Displeasure might be indicated by recalling the head of the mission for extended "consultations," but only rarely would the whole mission be withdrawn. Today, however, severance of diplomatic relations is more common; many governments find it an effective gesture because it appeals to excited populaces and is not very hard or costly to make.[47] In either situation, acceptance of a new government cannot be indicated by continuing what does not exist; the foreign government has to indicate its attitude by some statement.

Several examples will indicate the complications attendant on the alternative to recognition when diplomatic relations are absent. The Mexican Government caused great confusion when it recalled its ambassador to Brazil a few weeks after the military coup that ousted João Goulart in March 1964. The recall was part of a routine personnel change in the Foreign Ministry, but Mexican statements on the matter were so confusing that neither the Brazilians nor third governments were certain of Mexico's attitude until the following September.[48] Most African governments had to comment on the 1974 Portuguese coup because they had earlier severed diplomatic relations with Portugal in response to an OAU resolution that called for such action until Portugal conceded independence to its African colonies. They did not reestablish diplomatic relations until the new Portuguese Government showed that it would accept decolonization.[49] In 1975, the Khmer Rouge Government of Cambodia insisted that France (among other powers) close its Embassy in Phnom Penh. When the Vietnamese imposed a Government of their own in 1979, the French had to explain their attitude toward the new regime:

> Recent events have complicated the situation. The establishment of diplomatic relations could possibly be envisioned only if there clearly existed a Khmer government effectively exercising power over the whole country, and that apparently is not the case. Moreover, it is noteworthy that neighboring countries, especially the members of the Association of Southeast Asian Nations, have not shown any haste in this regard. In these conditions, a French initiative at the present time could only be premature.[50]

In such situations, a government wishing to make its position clear has to make some statement—even if only to representatives of the new government. The statement might take the form of a joint communiqué announcing the establishment of diplomatic relations, or it might be a public statement that the new government is the effective ruler of its state.

In addressing the matter of precision in legal doctrine, it must be admitted that the current state of affairs regarding relations with unrecognized governments is not satisfactory. Advocates of abolishing recognition of govern-

[47] *Compare* the number discussed in the Chronique section of the RGDIP in 1930 and 1976.

[48] R. McChesney, International Law and Mexican Foreign Policy 57–61 (PhD diss., University of Virginia, 1969).

[49] 79 RGDIP 525 (1975).

[50] 1979 Annuaire Français de Droit International 983.

ments argue that the only way to cure the confusion is to get rid of the institution permitting it, and they would seem to have a good case. The state of United States-China and United States-Cuba relations in 1974 was such that it was hard to remember that the United States had recognized the Cuban Government in 1959, but had yet to recognize the Chinese Government.[51] Diplomatic relations with the Cuban Government, which had been severed in January 1961, were conducted through third states, Czechoslovakia representing Cuba in Washington and Switzerland representing the United States in Havana; at the same time, the United States and China conducted their relations through "liaison offices" given diplomatic status by both sides.[52] High United States officials visited China and conferred with the Chinese on many issues, including the great political questions of the day, while direct Cuba-United States contacts were limited to UN headquarters and secret sessions at airports.[53] Agreements with China, though made by the very informal methods of joint communiqués or government-encouraged understandings between Chinese state corporations and foreign private companies, touched on the future of Taiwan, policies in Asia, and trade; new agreements with Cuba included only an exchange of notes on refugees in 1965, an antihijacking pact in 1973, and a maritime boundary agreement provisionally in force since 1978.[54] Both trade and travel contacts with Cuba remained prohibited, while with China limited trade and travel were allowed.[55] The only sure indication of the two Governments' respective positions came in the courts. Being recognized, the Cuban Government and its agencies were able to sue in U.S. courts; being unrecognized, the Chinese Government could not.[56]

It is true that abolishing recognition would end the sort of confusion that occurs when relations with an unrecognized government become friendlier than those with a recognized one, but the same could be accomplished by basing recognition decisions solely on control. Any time such confusion has arisen, recognition has been withheld for political reasons. If recognition had been granted when control was shown, confusion about who was or was not recognized would not have arisen. Abolishing recognition would not end the expression of different degrees of friendship or hostility among governments. Recognition was never a guarantee of friendly relations; it simply indicated

[51] A number of scholars and officials who ought to know better have been confused on this point. *See, e.g.*, Stepan, *U.S.-Latin American Relations*, 58 FOREIGN AFF. 659, 689–90 (1980); L. Silberman (former U.S. Ambassador to Yugoslavia), *No Recognition for Cuba and Vietnam Now*, New York Times, April 25, 1977, at 31; and (at least with the headings supplied in the published version) then Deputy Secretary of State Warren Christopher's address, "Normalization of Diplomatic Relations," Dep't of State Press Release No. 269, June 10, 1977.

[52] The text of the communiqué establishing the liaison offices appears in 67 AJIL 536 (1973). In the United States, the grant of diplomatic status required special legislation, which can be found in *id.* at 762.

[53] On the limits to contacts with Cuba, see Binder, *US and Cuba Discussed Links in Talks in 1975*, New York Times, March 29, 1977, at 8.

[54] DEP'T OF STATE, TREATIES IN FORCE ON JANUARY 1, 1981, at 45–46.

[55] *Compare* regulations governing trade, financial transactions, and travel in Title 22, pt. 52.72 *with* those in Title 33, pts. 500, 505, 515, and 520 in the 1975 Code of Federal Regulations.

[56] *E.g.*, Republic of Cuba v. Mayan Lines, S.A., 145 So.2d 679 (4th Cir. 1961); and Banco Nacional de Cuba v. Sabbatino, 376 U.S. 398 (1964).

that no doubts about the other government's status stood in the way. In fact, it is possible to combine recognition with an absence of virtually all relations. The British recognized the Hoxha Government of Albania in 1945, but have never established diplomatic relations or carried on much trade with it.[57]

In certain respects abolition would create more confusion than it would cure. The idea that recognition applies only to states[58] rests in part on a notion that recognition should apply only to subjects of international law, and not to their agents. However, the term "recognition" has a much broader meaning in international law. As in domestic law, "recognition" means taking formal cognizance of and giving legal effect to the existence of any number of situations, whether the emergence of a new entity (a state, a rebel group deserving belligerent status), a particular circumstance (war, foreign military occupation of a given territory), or a potentially controversial fact (claim to sovereignty over territory, existence of a foreign court ruling relevant to some case). If viewed in this broader perspective, there is nothing objectionable about applying recognition to the emergence of new governments.

Questions about the status of, communication with, and approval of new regimes are logically separate, but have tended to become intertwined. Advocates of abolition argue that current doctrines allowing governments great discretion about whether to recognize permit, if not encourage, identification of acknowledging status with approval, while communication is treated separately in all the informal ways previously discussed. They propose breaking the status-approval link by forming a link between status and communication. Under their alternative, status would be assumed once a government entered into formal communication (established diplomatic relations) with the new regime. Questions of approval would be left aside. This whole proposal rests on beliefs that governments must remain in as constant formal contact as possible and that the need for communication will overcome any disapproval of the new regime. Certainly, the expansion of "informal," "nonpolitical," and indirect forms of intergovernmental communication in the course of the 20th century supports their ideas.

Yet, on reflection, the situation seems far less simple. Creating a link between formal communications and the granting of status does not banish the possibility that questions of status will get mixed up with approval or disapproval of the new regime. Governments have long used severance of diplomatic relations to express strong disapproval of the current policies or postaccession political evolution of other governments. As noted earlier, this practice has become more common in recent years. It seems unlikely that such connections between communications and approval will be given up. Yet separating them will be necessary if linking status to formal communications is to break all links between approval and acceptance of status.

[57] 1 M. WHITEMAN, *supra* note 9, at 226; the 1980 EUROPA YEARBOOK includes no Albanian mission in London or British mission in Tirana in its lists of diplomatic missions accredited to each Government.

[58] This is not a new idea; several supporters of the Estrada Doctrine advanced it in 1931. *See* Jessup, *supra* note 36, at 721.

Then, too, the link between formal communications and acceptance of status rests on an inaccurate assumption and creates unnecessary complications. Such a link assumes that governments communicate mainly through diplomatic missions and cannot get along without them for long. This was largely true in the 19th century, but is not true today. Multilateral organizations, transgovernmental channels between agencies charged with similar tasks, contacts with state-owned enterprises or trade bodies, and various sorts of informal envoys all provide alternatives to diplomatic missions, as do the services of third parties. Many of these methods are cumbersome and ill-adapted to the discussion of important political issues, but they mean that governments are not faced with a choice between formal diplomatic relations and no contact at all. Moreover, the formal communications-status link does not work when diplomatic relations are absent. Finally and most seriously, a link between communications and status means that any failure to communicate during the early days of a regime's existence will be viewed as a sign of doubt about its status—regardless of the reason for the failure.

For all these reasons it is clear that separation of status and approval occurs only if all three questions are separated from one another. Total separation can best be realized by reforming the rules on recognition to require that decisions about status be guided by the effectivist rule. Nations could then base their decisions about communication on their relations with the other country or their ability to support a diplomatic mission without having to worry whether the lack of diplomatic relations suggests doubts about the new regime's status. Approval or disapproval can be indicated in many ways that have no relation to status or formal diplomatic relations, such as increasing or decreasing aid, encouraging or discouraging contacts between nationals, or commenting publicly on events in the other country.

Even if governments continue to insist upon links, the effectivist rule will still provide the best solution. A link between approval and communications creates some inconvenience, but it raises far fewer complications than a link between approval and status. An effectivist recognition rule would guide governments towards using the less inconvenient form of linkage.

Many advocates of abolition create more logical confusion when they support their ideas by saying that states maintain diplomatic relations with states rather than with governments. States do not maintain diplomatic relations with anyone, though writers often personalize them for brevity's sake. States are abstract entities capable of acting only through some human agent, and the government is that agent. A state communicates, fulfills its obligations, and asserts its rights through its government. It is thus through the contact between one government acting on behalf of its state and another government acting on behalf of its state that international relations are carried out. If states could act on their own, recognition of governments would never have raised any problems because governments would have had no international significance. This need for and reliance on human agents is expressed in the traditional diplomatic practice, still followed even by governments flirting with the notion that diplomatic relations are undertaken between states, of accrediting diplomats from the head or government of the sending state to the head or government of the receiving one.[59]

Worse, any confusion of recognition with maintenance of diplomatic relations could threaten the almost universally accepted rule that recognition ends only with the demise of the recognized government and may not be withdrawn at the will of the recognizing government.[60] In the past, this rule has provided an important protection against the worst sort of possible political abuses, and is a powerful reinforcement for the idea that according status should depend on the fact of control rather than on emotional reactions or political calculations. Were recognition of governments abolished, some statesmen might be tempted to view severance of diplomatic relations as a method for challenging status as well.

Those who believe that the international community should refuse to accept regimes that come to power by means violating international law (for example, as a result of foreign imposition) have an additional reason to retain recognition of governments.[61] Though refusal to continue diplomatic relations with the new regime might serve to indicate severe disapproval, its symbolic effectiveness is greatly reduced since there are many reasons for not having diplomatic relations that have no connection to the international legality or illegality of the new regime's origins. Particularly in a world where recognition normally followed an effectivist rule, nonrecognition would be an indication of severe disapproval. The danger that individual states might use such decisions as a new form of political response could be decreased by requiring that they be made collectively, as through the United Nations.[62]

Thus, for both practical and doctrinal reasons, abolishing recognition of governments would be a mistake. This is not to argue that the existing institution is perfect. Far from it. Advocates of abolition are correct in their basic

[59] As codified in Art. 14 of the Vienna Convention on Diplomatic Relations, TIAS No. 7502, 23 UST 3227, 500 UNTS 95.

[60] The RESTATEMENT (REVISED), *supra* note 12, §203, appears to endorse the idea of withdrawing recognition from a government still in control of its state, using the "de-recognition" of the Teipeh Government as an example. In strict legal terms, however, this was the ending of an illegal prolonged recognition of a regime that had lost control of its state 29 years before, not a withdrawal of recognition from an effective government. The only way it could be taken to be the latter is by assuming that Taiwan is a state independent of China, something neither the Teipeh nor the United States Government has ever done.

[61] Though it has been proposed that recognition be denied to regimes that are imposed by foreign intervention, depend for their continued existence on foreign support, base themselves on policies of racial discrimination, represent counterrevolutionary movements, or commit massive violations of human rights in the course of consolidating power, none of these ideas has won general support. In the absence of such support and, equally important, relatively objective and agreed criteria for determining whether a new regime falls into any of the agreed categories, this author believes such proposals are simply excuses for continuing to play political games with recognition regardless of whether decisions are made by individual states or some UN body.

[62] Collective decisions could form the basis for severe discrimination against any such regime. The International Court of Justice suggested various possibilities in its advisory opinion on *Legal Consequences for States of the Continued Presence of South Africa in Namibia (South West Africa) notwithstanding Security Council Resolution 276 (1970).* 1971 ICJ REP. 16, 55–56.

criticisms of recognition as it has been practiced, and in their insistence that any government in effective control of its state should have its status acknowledged and respected. If recognition of governments is to perform its proper functions, and confusion among acknowledgment of status, communication, and approval is to be avoided, recognition decisions must be based solely on whether the new government has control of its state. This effectivist rule would secure the advantages sought by advocates of abolition without causing the disadvantages attendant upon abolition.

THE GATT AND MULTILATERAL TREATY MAKING: THE TOKYO ROUND

*By D. M. McRae and J. C. Thomas**

Introduction

Multilateral treaty making, sometimes called the "international legislative process,"[1] occurs in a variety of forms and under the auspices of many international organizations. Concern that insufficient information is available about the way treaties are negotiated in different forums and that the process is haphazard led to a proposal for its review in the Sixth Committee at the 32d session of the United Nations General Assembly.[2] Acting upon this initiative, the General Assembly adopted Resolution 32/48, which called upon the Secretary-General to report on the techniques and procedures used in the elaboration of multilateral treaties. In order to assist in the preparation of this report, comments were requested from states, specialized agencies and other intergovernmental organizations, and the offices of the United Nations.

The report of the Secretary-General,[3] while pointing to the diversity of activities involved in treaty making through international organizations, confirms the lack of detailed information about the process. The responses of many international organizations showed in outline the procedures by which treaties are concluded, but in few cases was substantial detail or any analysis of the process provided.[4] It was clear that a better understanding of the international legislative process would require a detailed investigation into all aspects of the treaty-making techniques of particular organizations. The advantage of such an investigation is that it can both explain the work of those organizations and offer insights into the treaty-making process in the international community generally. Methods and techniques that are utilized in one forum may be unique; on the other hand, they may be readily applied to treaty making elsewhere. It was with these considerations in mind that this study of the treaty-making process of the Tokyo Round of Multilateral Trade

* Professor of Law, University of British Columbia, and BA, LLB (U.B.C.), MA (Sussex), respectively.

Some of the material in this paper is based upon interviews and correspondence with government and international organization officials. The authors are grateful for this assistance but remain responsible for any views expressed. Research for this paper was supported by a grant from The Donner Canadian Foundation.

[1] Suy, *Innovations in International Law-Making Processes*, in THE INTERNATIONAL LAW OF HUMAN WELFARE 187 (Macdonald, Johnston, & Morris eds. 1978).

[2] UN Doc. A/32/143 (1977).

[3] Review of the Multilateral Treaty-Making Process, Report of the Secretary-General, UN Doc. A/35/312 (1980).

[4] An exception is the report of the International Law Commission. *See id.*, Add. 2.

Negotiations (MTN), conducted under the auspices of the General Agreement on Tariffs and Trade (GATT) from 1973 to 1979, was undertaken.[5]

The Secretary-General's report surveys the procedures that have been adopted by various international bodies and for this purpose divides the stages of the treaty-making process into: the initiation of treaty making, the formulation of treaties (negotiations), the adoption of treaties, postadoption concerns, and the supplementing and updating of treaties. In this article a similar classification has been adopted, although less emphasis will be given to the postadoption concerns, and to supplementing and updating. The article will focus on the initiation of, and negotiations within, the Tokyo Round and the adoption of the MTN codes.

I. GATT AND THE MTN

GATT is one of the principal international organizations concerned with the substantive issues of international trade policy. Since 1947 it has overseen a series of rounds of negotiations aimed initially at reducing tariff barriers to trade and, more recently, dealing with the reduction or elimination of nontariff measures as well. While GATT has received the attention of a number of scholars and detailed studies of its operation have been undertaken,[6] there has been little concern with the process of GATT negotiations. Indeed, due to its rather different beginnings, GATT appears to have been treated by many observers as a unique creature that does not stand up to traditional legal analysis.

The unlikely beginnings of GATT, and the fact that it survived and indeed thrived, have been noted by virtually all observers. GATT was an interim agreement of provisional application, pending the coming into force of the Havana Charter and the establishment of the International Trade Organization (ITO).[7] It is not surprising, therefore, that no provision was made within the General Agreement for the subsequent conduct of tariff negotiations: "The General Agreement was conceived as a *product* of the negotiations, not as a framework for conducting them."[8] In view of this lack of provisions for negotiations, in the first rounds reference was had to the rules of Article 17 of the Havana Charter. The parties would simply adopt those rules with minor changes for each conference.[9]

[5] A brief report on the GATT treaty-making process was provided to the Secretary-General in response to Resolution 32/48. *See id.*, Annex. A copy of this report was provided to the authors by the GATT secretariat.

[6] *See* G. CURZON, MULTILATERAL COMMERCIAL DIPLOMACY (1965) [hereinafter cited as G. CURZON]; K. KOCK, INTERNATIONAL TRADE POLICY AND THE GATT: 1947–67 (1969); J. JACKSON, WORLD TRADE AND THE LAW OF GATT (1969); K. DAM, THE GATT-LAW AND INTERNATIONAL ECONOMIC ORGANIZATION (1970); J. EVANS, THE KENNEDY ROUND AND AMERICAN TRADE POLICY: THE TWILIGHT OF THE GATT? (1971); R. HUDEC, THE GATT LEGAL SYSTEM AND WORLD TRADE DIPLOMACY (1975); and G. & V. Curzon, *The Management of Trade Relations in the GATT*, in A. SHONFIELD, G. CURZON, V. CURZON, T. WARLEY, & G. RAY, INTERNATIONAL ECONOMIC RELATIONS OF THE WESTERN WORLD 1959–1971, VOL. I: POLITICS AND TRADE (1976).

[7] J. JACKSON, *supra* note 6, at 36–37.

[8] *Id.* at 220–21.

[9] K. DAM, *supra* note 6, at 57.

These first rounds of tariff negotiations were conducted essentially bilaterally. States drew up detailed lists of requests addressed to the states from which tariff concessions were sought, and states that were prepared to make concessions drew up lists of offers of tariff reductions. Substantive negotiations would then take place between pairs of states or small groupings of interested states on a selected product-by-product basis. This emphasis on bilateral negotiations stemmed mainly from the preeminence of the United States in international trade and economic matters in the postwar period. United States domestic law demanded that U.S. negotiators achieve strict reciprocity and implied that negotiations could take place only with the "principal supplier" of a particular good to the United States.[10] At the same time, the results of bilateral negotiations were multilateral in that concessions were extended to all contracting parties by virtue of the General Agreement's nondiscrimination or "most-favored-nation" provision, Article I.[11]

For many years there was general dissatisfaction among GATT members about the unwieldiness of selective product-by-product negotiations, the lack of prospects for involvement by the developing states, and the difficulty of reconciling the interests of low-tariff states with those of high-tariff states. Thus, almost from the beginning, proposals were made periodically for the reform of GATT negotiations. A compromise solution to these problems—or to at least some of them—was found at the 1963 GATT ministerial meeting initiating the Kennedy Round. There, agreement on the employment of an automatic formula was forthcoming. This was possible in large part because the U.S. Executive, in obtaining its grant of negotiating authority from Congress, had been able to secure a mandate to negotiate broad categories of goods rather than having to continue the previous cumbersome and extremely detailed, selective product-by-product method.[12] The ministerial meeting adopted a resolution stating: "in view of the limited results obtained in recent years from item-by-item negotiations, the tariff negotiations . . . shall be based upon a plan of substantial linear tariff reductions with a bare minimum of exceptions which shall be subject to confrontation and justification."[13] The adoption of this resolution meant that in the Kennedy Round, rather than negotiating each product separately, most participants negotiated from their short lists; that is, all tariffs would be reduced automatically except for those withdrawn by states or placed on their lists of exceptions, and those exceptions would have to be justified in discussions with trading partners.[14] Notwithstanding this innovation, the tariff negotiations remained largely bilateral because the process of justifying exceptions and seeking concessions from the

[10] J. JACKSON, *supra* note 6, at 243; K. KOCK, *supra* note 6, at 100.

[11] Article I provides that "any advantage, favour, privilege or immunity granted by any contracting Party to any product originating in or destined for any other country shall be accorded immediately and unconditionally to the like product originating in or destined for the territories of all other contracting Parties."

[12] G. CURZON, *supra* note 6, at 102.

[13] Ministerial Meeting, May 1963, Conclusions and Resolutions Adopted on 21 May 1963, GENERAL AGREEMENT ON TARIFFS AND TRADE, BASIC INSTRUMENTS AND SELECTED DOCUMENTS [hereinafter cited as BISD], 12th Supp. 47 (1964).

[14] K. DAM, *supra* note 6, at 69–70.

lists of exceptions took place bilaterally or in some cases amongst small groups of states.

Little in the preceding rounds of GATT negotiations prepared the participants for the ambitious undertaking of the Tokyo Round; unlike its predecessors, the Tokyo Round covered a number of issues that had not previously been the subject of GATT negotiations. By the late 1960's it was recognized that the main barriers to international trade were no longer tariffs; nontariff measures taken by states, such as the granting of export subsidies or the levying of countervailing duties to assist domestic producers, the establishment of quota programs, and the use of different methods of valuing goods for customs purposes, represented greater threats to trade liberalization than tariffs. Thus, the participants in the Tokyo Round were presented with the task of negotiating multilateral instruments through which the use of nontariff measures could be controlled. Although an Anti-Dumping Code had been negotiated in the Kennedy Round (proving that nontariff measures could be the subject of successful negotiations), the idea of placing tariff negotiations within a greatly expanded agenda of trade concerns was a novel one.

The MTN therefore represents a more complex series of negotiations than had previously been attempted under GATT auspices. It provides a good basis for viewing both the treaty-making techniques adopted in GATT-sponsored negotiations in the past and the ability of the participating states to adapt procedures to deal with new problems. To understand the GATT treaty-making process it will be necessary to recount the conduct of the MTN[15] and to analyze the principal features of the negotiating process. The implications of the Tokyo Round for the multilateral treaty-making process in general can then be considered.

II. The Initiation of the Tokyo Round

BACKGROUND

Although the "Tokyo Declaration"[16] is commonly taken to signify the start of the Tokyo Round of multilateral trade negotiations, its antecedents go back some years. The previous Kennedy Round had left unfinished business, which was recognized in the adoption of the GATT Programme of Work in November 1967.[17] The directions taken there—trade in industrial products, agriculture, and the trade of developing countries—were inevitably to lead to a new round of multilateral trade negotiations. In addition, efforts had been made at various sessions of the contracting parties to push for greater

[15] For collections of articles discussing the results of the Tokyo Round, see 11 L. & POL'Y INT'L BUS. 1257 (1979); and 13 CORNELL INT'L L.J. 145 (1980). *See also* Finlayson & Zacher, *The GATT and the Regulation of Trade Barriers: Regime Dynamics and Effects*, 35 INT'L ORG. 561 (1981), for an analysis of the evolution of the GATT system.

[16] Declaration of Ministers Approved at Tokyo on 14 September 1973, GATT Doc. MIN (73) 1, BISD, 20th Supp. 19 (1972–73).

[17] BISD, 15th Supp. 67–72 (1966–67). The Council established a Committee on Trade in Industrial Products and an Agriculture Committee, and reactivated the Committee on Trade and Development's Special Group on Tropical Products.

trade liberalization. The last of the annual reductions under the Geneva Protocol of 1967 were due to be applied on January 1, 1972, and many parties believed that the momentum of trade liberalization had to be maintained.[18] This need was recognized by the Director-General of GATT in his statement to the 26th annual session of the contracting parties:

> It is my view that 1971 should see the contracting parties at the negotiating table, engaged in a concerted effort to secure the further reduction of barriers to trade; this, after all, is the prime purpose and business of this organization and the objective of the painstaking work on which the contracting parties have been engaged over the past two years.[19]

Though the contracting parties concluded the 26th session without a formal call for a new round of negotiations, they did reaffirm the need for continued trade liberalization and to that end directed the Committee on Trade in Industrial Products to explore the possibilities for concrete action in reducing barriers to trade in that sector. The Agriculture Committee was directed to seek mutually acceptable solutions to the problems peculiar to international trade in agricultural products.[20]

The following year, at the 27th session of the contracting parties, a decision was taken in principle to pursue a new round of multilateral trade negotiations. Though it did not formally initiate negotiations, the desirability of doing so was recognized. Thus, in summing up the Programme of Work of the contracting parties, the Chairman of the session noted that there had been a consensus on a number of issues. On trade policy it was said that the "CONTRACTING PARTIES further agree that, looking to the longer term, it is their intention, as a principal objective, to pursue in the GATT a new major initiative for dealing with the longer-term trade problems as soon as this is feasible."[21] There was disagreement over the next steps to be taken. Some parties favored resolving those problems that were susceptible to prompt action, and postponing others for the time being. Others favored giving the committees more time "to examine various techniques and modalities"[22] that would provide the necessary impetus for multilateral action under the GATT.

The signal that the major trading nations were ready to begin multilateral trade negotiations came less than 3 months after the conclusion of the 27th session, with the announcement in February 1972 of two similar declarations on international economic relations: one by the United States and Japan, and the other by the United States and the European Economic Community (EEC). The signatories undertook "to initiate and actively support multilateral and comprehensive negotiations in the framework of GATT."[23] These declarations were welcomed at the meeting of the GATT Council in March 1972, and at the 28th session of the contracting parties in November 1972 the formal decision to begin preparations for multilateral trade negotiations was

[18] GATT Doc. W.26/5 (1970).

[19] GATT Doc. L/3348 (1970).

[20] GATT Doc. L/3366 (1970), BISD, 17th Supp. 18–19 (1968–70).

[21] GATT Doc. L/3641 (1971), BISD, 18th Supp. 37 (1970–71).

[22] *Id.* at 40.

[23] THE TOKYO ROUND OF MULTILATERAL TRADE NEGOTIATIONS: REPORT BY THE DIRECTOR-GENERAL 49 (1979) [hereinafter cited as DIRECTOR-GENERAL'S REPORT].

taken. At the suggestion of the Japanese delegation, the parties decided to hold a special meeting[24] at the ministerial level the following year in Tokyo to set guidelines for the negotiations.[25] They also decided to establish a Preparatory Committee for the Tokyo meeting to develop "methods and procedures for the negotiations" by drawing upon the work of the three existing committees established under the 1967 Programme of Work of the contracting parties.

The Preparatory Committee, chaired by the Director-General, was established in early 1973. It discussed the whole range of issues to be dealt with in the ministerial meeting and in the subsequent trade negotiations, and it adopted a report and a draft declaration.[26] The declaration set forth the issues to be considered in the multilateral trade negotiations and the general principles to govern the negotiations, and made provision for the establishment of a Trade Negotiations Committee that would elaborate the detailed negotiating procedures. Two issues could not be resolved by the Preparatory Committee and were left for discussion in the ministerial meeting. These were the extent of special and differential treatment to be accorded to the developing states, and the relationship between trade negotiations and international monetary reform, a matter of dispute between the United States and the EEC.

THE TOKYO DECLARATION

The meeting of ministers took place in Tokyo in September 1973. Apart from dealing with the two issues left open by the Preparatory Committee, the Ministers adopted the declaration prepared by the committee as the "Tokyo Declaration of GATT Ministers"[27] and it became the basic constitutional document for the MTN. The objectives of the negotiations, as described in the declaration, were to "achieve the expansion and ever-greater liberalization of world trade" and to "achieve benefits for the international trade of developing countries."[28] Six subjects were identified:[29] (1) negotiations on tariffs, (2) reduction or elimination of nontariff measures, (3) reduction or elimination of barriers to trade in selected sectors, (4) the adequacy of the multilateral safeguard system, (5) agriculture, and (6) tropical products. The declaration also provided for the establishment of a Trade Negotiations Committee (TNC) to "elaborate and put into effect detailed trade negotiation plans and to establish appropriate negotiating procedures," and to "supervise the progress of the negotiations."[30]

Other provisions of the declaration stated that the negotiations were to be conducted on "the basis of the principles of mutual advantage, mutual commitment and reciprocity" in accordance with the normal principles applicable under the GATT.[31] It was also stipulated that the developed countries did

[24] GATT Doc. S.R.28/8, at 112 (1972).

[25] GATT Doc. L/3773/Rev.1, BISD, 19th Supp. 12 (1971–72).

[26] GATT Doc. MIN (73) W/2.

[27] *Supra* note 16 [hereinafter cited as Tokyo Declaration].

[28] Tokyo Declaration, para. 2.

[29] *Id.*, para. 3.

[30] *Id.*, para. 10.

[31] *Id.*, paras. 5 and 9. The most significant of these is the most-favored-nation status accorded to all GATT contracting parties under Article I.

not expect strict reciprocity from the developing countries and that the least developed countries should receive special attention.[32] A difference of opinion between certain states over the link between monetary reform and trade was resolved by paragraph 7, which recognized that the relationship between the two must be kept in mind throughout the negotiations. Paragraph 8 embodied an important principle by providing that the negotiations were to be "considered as one undertaking, the various elements of which shall move forward together."

THE INITIATION OF THE TOKYO ROUND IN PERSPECTIVE

The above account of the origins of the Tokyo Round shows that the initiation of multilateral trade negotiations differs from the initiation of other multilateral treaty-making endeavors. This is evident, first, in the way the round was convened. The Tokyo Declaration was not the result of a single act or initiative; rather, there were a variety of factors and pressures that led to the decision to conduct trade negotiations. These included the unfinished work of the Kennedy Round, the general desire for trade liberalization, a fear of creeping protectionism, and the progress made in the GATT committees set up as a result of the 1967 Programme of Work. The specific actions that led to the drafting of the Tokyo Declaration were the joint statements by the major trading nations that they were prepared to enter into trade negotiations.

A consequence of the way the Tokyo Round began is that there was no formal preparatory work comparable, for example, to that prepared by the International Law Commission for the first United Nations Conference on the Law of the Sea, or the conferences on diplomatic and consular relations and on the law of treaties. The preparatory work that did exist for the Tokyo Round consisted mostly of technical studies prepared pursuant to the 1967 GATT Programme of Work, among them a report and an inventory of nontariff barriers affecting international trade prepared by the Committee on Trade in Industrial Products, and a report by the Committee on Trade and Development's Special Group on Tropical Products. Working Group 3 of the Committee on Trade in Industrial Products had prepared a draft "Code for Preventing Technical Barriers to Trade" (the "Standards Code"), which became the basis for negotiations on that subject; and a "Draft Instrument on Government Purchasing Policies, Procedures and Practices" prepared by the Organisation for Economic Co-operation and Development (OECD) was used as the starting point for negotiations on government procurement. The work of the Preparatory Committee itself was of a procedural nature, including such matters as formulating agenda items for the negotiations and considering the principles upon which negotiations would take place. The committee made no attempt to formulate texts that would provide a basis for the drafting of codes.

The origins of the Tokyo Round also illustrate the relationship between events that occurred within the formal structure of GATT and events that took place outside GATT and the formal negotiations. Although the mo-

[32] Tokyo Declaration, paras. 5 and 6.

mentum for multilateral trade negotiations grew within the GATT Council and the sessions of the contracting parties, it was the independent declarations by the major trading states that ensured that such negotiations would proceed. These declarations were of particular importance because they demonstrated a commitment to multilateral trade negotiations that was more than a formal concurrence with decisions taken within GATT. The actual initiation of the Tokyo Round took place in a ministerial meeting of states at Tokyo rather than within a GATT organ.

III. The Negotiation of Multilateral Trade Agreements

PARTICIPANTS

States

Among the states participating in the Tokyo Round, two groups can be readily identified: the major trading states (the United States, the EEC, Japan) and the developing states. However, many of the participants did not fit into either group, and some of the newly industrialized developing states[33] shared characteristics with states not in the developing group.

The impact of the major trading states, or group of states, on multilateral trade negotiations is self-evident. Two-thirds of the world's trade is carried on between the United States, the European Economic Community, and Japan.[34] Their needs and interests, particularly those of the former two, have traditionally dominated multilateral trade negotiations. The United States has held a preeminent position in GATT; substantively, the General Agreement very much mirrors American views of international trade liberalization in the immediate postwar period. Earlier rounds of tariff negotiations were convened on the initiative of the United States, negotiating procedures were mandated by the requirements of U.S. domestic law, and the timing and schedule of GATT negotiations depended upon the authority to negotiate trade agreements granted by Congress to the United States Executive.[35] Though the United States was to maintain this position of dominance, the Tokyo Round also saw the EEC, and to a lesser extent Japan, having a major impact upon trade negotiations.

The developing states, on the other hand, share only a minor portion of world trade. Their particular interest, the question of special and differential treatment to be accorded them, which was a major issue before both the Preparatory Committee and the ministerial meeting, runs counter to the fundamental GATT principle of nondiscrimination. The Tokyo Declaration contained numerous references to developing countries, stating that there was no need for strict reciprocity in trade commitments between developed and developing countries, that special and differential treatment might be needed

[33] *E.g.*, Brazil, Argentina, India.

[34] 1 DIRECTOR-GENERAL'S REPORT, *supra* note 23, at 16.

[35] *See generally* Jackson, *The General Agreement on Tariffs and Trade in United States Domestic Law*, 66 MICH. L. REV. 249 (1967).

for developing countries in particular areas, and that the problems of the least developed states should receive special attention. Yet the views or approaches of the developing countries could not be described as monolithic. The Tokyo Declaration recognized this variation in interest, mentioning specifically the problems of the least developed countries. Moreover, the "newly industrialized countries" had interests akin to those of the traditional trading states. In fact, they were to play an important role in the Tokyo Round, bridging the gap between industrialized states and developing countries.

The remaining states in the Tokyo Round can barely be classified into a single group. Some of them, like Canada, Switzerland, and the Nordic states, share a significant portion of world trade and thus their interests were indistinguishable from those of the major trading states. Two-thirds of Canada's trade is with the United States, and Canada is the second largest trading partner of the United States. Hence, on some issues Canada was able to exert an influence equivalent to that of Japan or the EEC. On the other hand, the interests of countries like Australia and New Zealand were concentrated in certain areas (in particular, agriculture) and did not necessarily range over the whole agenda of the MTN.

Secretariat

Although it was not directly involved in the negotiating process, the secretariat of GATT was to play an important role in the Tokyo Round. In part, it performed the secretarial functions usually provided by an international organization for an international conference, such as the preparation of background studies and the servicing of meetings. However, its role went beyond this, partly as a result of the technique of negotiations traditionally employed in GATT tariff negotiating rounds. In addition, the secretariat was called upon to chair the groups set up for negotiating the various items on the agenda, while the Director-General chaired the steering committee for negotiations, the Trade Negotiations Committee.

A further task assumed by the secretariat, apparently without explicit mandate, was to provide special assistance to developing countries. Prior to the round the secretariat had concluded that in view of the complexity and technical nature of the issues, developing countries would require assistance[36] in the form of summaries, country studies, analyses of the impact of tariff proposals, and advice on the preparation and submission of request lists. The secretariat would provide the kind of logistical support for developing countries that the developed states were able to provide for themselves. The GATT secretariat was not alone in actively helping developing countries. By Resolution 82 (III) the Trade and Development Board of the United Nations Conference on Trade and Development (UNCTAD) had decided that the UNCTAD secretariat should also provide assistance to developing countries involved in the MTN,[37] and representatives of the Commonwealth secretariat

[36] 1 DIRECTOR-GENERAL'S REPORT, *supra* note 23, at 109.
[37] UN Doc. TD/B/455, at 5 (1973).

were also present in Geneva to support developing country participants in the MTN.

THE INSTITUTIONAL STRUCTURE FOR NEGOTIATIONS

The Trade Negotiations Committee

The membership of the TNC included all governments participating in the Tokyo Round.[38] The work of the committee, which met for the first time in October 1973 and elected the Director-General of GATT as its Chairman, can be divided into three phases. In the initial phase the committee had to complete any outstanding preparatory work and prepare the way for negotiations. Not surprisingly, some disagreement emerged over what should be priority matters and how negotiations should proceed.

The view of some delegations that different negotiating techniques should be analyzed was regarded by other delegations as premature. However, it was suggested that the committee would avoid controversy in organizing the work if the terms of paragraph 3 of the Tokyo Declaration (which identified the various subjects of the negotiations) were adhered to. Accordingly, it was argued, six groups should be created to deal with the six topics listed in paragraph 3.[39]

Though this proposal received a wide measure of support, there was still uncertainty over whether more detailed terms of reference would be needed for the groups, whether the groups should engage in further technical work before negotiations started, and whether some groups should begin working before others. It was suggested that fact-finding and analytical work preparatory to negotiations might be undertaken by meetings of experts convened by the Chairman of the TNC, or that the TNC itself might meet at the technical level to undertake such work. No consensus could be reached on either proposal and it was left to the Chairman to continue the consultations on the matter.[40]

At the second meeting of the TNC in February 1974,[41] the Director-General presented a draft program of work for the groups based on consultations with members of the committee. This program was adopted[42] and the groups proposed at the previous meeting, and identified by the letters (a) to (f) from paragraph 3 of the Tokyo Declaration, were set up. They were to be chaired in the first instance by members of the GATT secretariat and dates for the first meetings of four of them were set: Group 3(a), tariffs; Group 3(b), nontariff measures; Group 3(e), agriculture; and Group 3(f) tropical products.[43] The tasks envisaged for these groups amounted to data collection and analysis rather than substantive negotiations, and they took as their starting point the work that had been carried out since 1967 in the committees of the GATT

[38] In the Tokyo Round, unlike previous rounds, participation was open to noncontracting parties to GATT.

[39] MTN/P/1, para. 19, at 4 (1973).

[40] *Id.* at 6.

[41] MTN/P/2 (1974).

[42] MTN/2 (1974).

[43] Groups 3(c) (sector), and (d) (safeguards) did not meet until after October 1974.

Council. Thus, Group 3(a) (tariffs) was provided with a note prepared by the secretariat summarizing the work of the Committee on Trade in Industrial Products,[44] and Group 3(e) (agriculture) concerned itself with bringing up to date the analytical and statistical documentation assembled under the 1967 Programme of Work of GATT.[45]

When the groups reported to the next session of the TNC in July 1974, it was noted that though they had undertaken most of the work assigned to them, there were still specific points to be dealt with before "effective negotiations" could begin.[46] The impediment to "effective negotiations" was that some states had not yet obtained appropriate legislative or other authority to enable them to engage in negotiations, despite the expectations created first by the declarations of early 1972, and more importantly by the Tokyo Declaration.[47] Therefore, an important impetus for the start of negotiations was the statement by the representative of the United States at the July 1974 meeting of the TNC that the U.S. Trade Bill would soon receive congressional approval. The Chairman of the TNC urged other states to follow the U.S. example by ensuring that they had the necessary authority to begin substantive negotiations as quickly as possible.[48] To help delegates focus on the particular issues for negotiations, the Chairman circulated an "illustrative list . . . of substantive points which would confront delegations when effective negotiations began."[49] However, it was emphasized in discussions that the list was unofficial and did not modify the Tokyo Declaration, "which remained the sole basis for negotiations."

The nature and function of these "groups" changed following the signal for the start of substantive negotiations, namely, enactment of the U.S. Trade Act by Congress in January 1975. The following month the TNC formally constituted the groups as forums for the negotiations and so concluded the initial phase of its own work.

The second phase of the TNC's activities began once negotiations in the groups were under way. Its function was less to direct and coordinate activity than to meet when necessary to deal with specific issues as they arose. Thus, it was convened in November 1976 to deal with a Brazilian proposal to establish a group concerned with "framework" issues. In July 1978, the TNC met ostensibly to review progress in the negotiations. In fact, the major issue to be addressed was a complaint by developing states that the institutional structure and the method of negotiating were excluding them from effective participation in the round. The TNC served as a forum for the airing of this complaint, although the matter was never really resolved.

The third phase of the work of the TNC encompassed the final stages of the round. At this time, reports and draft texts were submitted by the Chairmen of the various groups and subgroups. No real negotiations took place in the TNC over the substance of these draft texts. The committee considered

[44] MTN/4 (1974).

[45] MTN/5 (1974).

[46] MTN/P/3, at 2 (1974).

[47] 1 DIRECTOR-GENERAL'S REPORT, *supra* note 23, at 8.

[48] MTN/P/3, at 2 (1974).

[49] *Ibid.*

the relationship of the drafts to existing GATT provisions and the "final clauses" to be attached to each text, and decided whether the texts presented to the TNC would be put to a vote.

Though the TNC had the responsibility of monitoring the progress of the negotiations, there was little need for any active role in this regard. Paragraph 8 of the Tokyo Declaration had provided that the negotiations were to be "considered as one undertaking, the various elements of which shall move forward together." The Chairmen of the groups were conscious of this requirement and endeavored to ensure that other groups were informed of issues that could have implications for their work. Thus, an attempt was made to achieve a rough "parallel forward movement" in the negotiations without recourse to coordination by the TNC. In the final stages of drafting, texts prepared by one group were often scrutinized by another. For example, at its meeting in December 1978, Group "Agriculture" reviewed the draft "Standards Code" prepared by Sub-Group "Technical Barriers to Trade" to determine the applicability of the code to agriculture.[50] This type of consultation diminished the need for the TNC to play a coordinating role.

Thus, although it was an essential part of the formal structure of the MTN, the TNC was not really central to the actual negotiations. It provided a focus for the negotiations but, like the plenary session of a multilateral conference, its sessions were devoted to advancing the negotiations, or signaled the beginning and end of the process. The TNC was not the real forum for bargaining.

The Groups

Following their formal constitution by the TNC in February 1975, the groups were known by their subjects rather than by subparagraphs of paragraph 3 of the Tokyo Declaration; hence, they became Group "Tropical Products," Group "Tariffs," Group "Non-Tariff Measures," Group "Agriculture," Group "Sector Approach," and Group "Safeguards."

Apart from the principles enunciated in the Tokyo Declaration, little formal guidance was given to the groups on how they were to operate: Group Tropical Products was asked to "organize and conduct negotiations in this sector"; Group Tariffs, to "draw up a tariff negotiating plan of as general application as possible"; Group Non-Tariff Measures, to "initiate negotiations . . . on as wide a basis as possible"; Group Agriculture, to "decide itself how to organize its work"; Group Sector Approach, to "carry out an examination of the possibilities for the co-ordinated reduction or elimination of all barriers to trade in selected sectors"; and Group Safeguards, to "carry out an examination of the adequacy of the multilateral safeguard system."[51] Thus, wide discretion was vested in each group to determine its own work program and method of operation. At its initial meeting, Group Non-Tariff Measures established four subgroups to deal with quantitative restrictions, technical barriers to trade, customs matters, and subsidies and countervailing duties. Later, a fifth subgroup on government procurement was set up. Group Agriculture also

[50] MTN/AG/9 (1978).

[51] MTN/W/10 (1975).

organized itself in this way, setting up subgroups on grains, meat, and dairy products.

In November 1976, the TNC approved the Brazilian proposal and created the Framework Group pursuant to paragraph 9 of the Tokyo Declaration, which provided that consideration should be given to improvements in the international framework for the conduct of world trade. The group was to seek to negotiate improvements in the framework of world trade, "particularly with respect to trade between developed and developing countries and differential and more favourable treatment to be adopted in such trade."[52]

Any participant state in the Tokyo Round was entitled to take part in the work of the various groups. Some states participated in all; others limited their activities to those of particular interest to them. The level of representation in the groups varied from ambassadorial to technical. Though some groups were successful in negotiating tariff or nontariff concessions or codes, others were not. It is useful, therefore, to consider briefly the work of each group.

Group Tropical Products. Initially, this group continued the work of the Special Group on Trade in Tropical Products of the Committee on Trade and Development. It involved defining tropical products and seeking to provide members with a full understanding of the trade in this sector.

The Tokyo Declaration had provided that "tropical products" was to be treated as "a special and priority sector," and it was seen as symbolically important in demonstrating the good will of the developed states and their desire to ensure that the Tokyo Round would bring benefits to the developing countries. Thus, substantive negotiations began as early as May 1975, and 10 of the 11 states asked to make tariff reductions implemented their concessions in 1976 or early 1977, well in advance of the conclusion of the MTN.[53] However, though the Tokyo Declaration may have envisaged negotiations on other matters affecting tropical products, the negotiations were limited to offers and requests for the reduction or elimination of tariff and nontariff measures.

Group Tariffs. The TNC had charged Group Tariffs with drawing up a "tariff negotiating plan of as general application as possible." The group asked the secretariat to suggest elements that might be included in a negotiating plan and the resultant checklist[54] was considered by the group in July 1975. It included several alternative techniques for tariff negotiation (linear reduction technique, harmonization technique, item-by-item technique) and canvassed a series of related issues such as the depth of reduction, the basis for the reduction, tariff disparities, and the staging of cuts. The checklist also referred to exceptions and exemptions to a tariff reduction formula. However, although the group considered the potential economic impact of various reduction formulas, it was unable to reach agreement on an appropriate formula. Progress was achieved on base dates, base rates, and special and differential

[52] MTN/17 (1976).

[53] 1 DIRECTOR-GENERAL'S REPORT, *supra* note 23, at 38–39.

[54] MTN/TAR/W/4 (1975). The checklist was revised by the secretariat following the group's July meeting; *see* MTN/TAR/W/4/Rev.1 (1975).

treatment for developing countries,[55] some of which was based on work that had been undertaken in earlier GATT committees, in particular the Tariff Study made by the Committee on Trade in Industrial Products, which had been continuously kept up to date.[56]

Various tariff negotiating proposals were made in Group Tariffs, but no agreement on a particular formula was reached and the impasse was resolved independently of the group at a meeting of U.S. Special Trade Representative Strauss and EEC Commissioner for External Relations Haferkamp in July 1977. The tariff negotiating formula endorsed at that meeting was not even put before Group Tariffs for discussion or approval. In fact, the group had its last meeting in December 1976, some 6 months before the Strauss-Haferkamp meeting, and it did not meet again. Substantive negotiations on tariffs took place completely outside Group Tariffs.

Group Non-Tariff Measures. The work of Group Non-Tariff Measures covered such a wide area that the group divided itself into five subgroups, which meant that the work of the group itself was largely of a supervisory nature. However, it did begin exploring ways to deal with nontariff measures that were not the subject of negotiation in the subgroups.[57]

Between the years 1975 and 1977, with the exception of Sub-Group Technical Barriers to Trade, work in the subgroups was mainly of a preparatory nature, continuing the work of previous committees and working parties of GATT. For example, Sub-Group Subsidies and Countervailing Duties finished compiling an inventory of prohibited export subsidies without prejudice to the future negotiating positions of members. This work was begun by a GATT working party in 1960.

Negotiations were undertaken at an early stage in Sub-Group Technical Barriers to Trade, which had the advantage of the relatively advanced draft "Standards Code" before it. The subgroup concentrated on achieving agreement on the technical definitions in the code. The Sub-Group Government Procurement, which was set up in July 1976, used the OECD draft mentioned above to help it identify the issues that might be amenable to negotiation.

Not all of the subgroups were successful in drafting codes, but agreements on technical barriers to trade, government procurement, subsidies and countervailing duties, customs valuation, import licensing procedures, and antidumping did result from the work of Group Non-Tariff Measures.

Group Agriculture. The work of Group Agriculture was hampered by a dispute between the United States and the EEC over its competence. The EEC preferred that agriculture be dealt with as a separate issue; the United States, on the other hand, wished to have issues relating to agriculture dealt with in the groups to which they were most closely related. The EEC had made its position clear at the February 1974 meeting of the TNC,[58] and the creation of Group Agriculture might be seen to have supported that position. However, disagreement continued within the group, manifesting itself in con-

[55] 1 DIRECTOR-GENERAL'S REPORT, *supra* note 23, at 45.

[56] *Id.* at 42.

[57] MTN/NTM/W/4 (1975).

[58] MTN/P/2 (1974).

troversy over whether particular issues were within its competence or within the competence of other groups. By the end of 1975, there was concern that this dispute not only had brought the work of Group Agriculture to a standstill but also had affected the work of the other groups.[59] It was suggested, therefore, that rather than let the group's work be completely stalemated, states would engage in consultations and negotiations outside the group, and in fact it did not meet between December 1975 and December 1977.[60]

Following the Strauss-Haferkamp meeting in July 1977, negotiations on agriculture did get under way, but in the key sectors for which subgroups had been established, grains, meat, and dairy products, progress was slow. The work of Sub-Group Grains was rendered redundant by the negotiations, under the auspices of UNCTAD, of a successor to the International Wheat Agreement. Thus, no code resulted from the work of that subgroup.[61] However, an "arrangement regarding bovine meat" and competing texts of an "international dairy arrangement" were included in the final documents of the Tokyo Round.

Group Sector Approach. The creation of this group, though favored by certain states such as those with a resource-based export trade, was received with skepticism by states that believed better results could be achieved through negotiations within the other groups. The philosophy behind the creation of this group was that tariff and nontariff measures in respect of particular areas or commodities should be dealt with together, and not be left to the other groups as part of general tariff or nontariff measure negotiations. The group met on a number of occasions, but negotiating plans were not devised nor were substantive negotiations entered into.[62] However, an agreement on trade in civil aircraft, though not directly resulting from the deliberations of the group, arose out of negotiations inspired by the "sector" approach.

Group Safeguards. The purpose of this group was to examine the adequacy of the safeguard system deriving from Article XIX of the GATT. The initial meetings were concerned with identifying the issues that should be negotiated, and in July of 1976 a group of states placed a set of principles relating to safeguards before the group.[63] However, these principles did not find favor with many of the developing countries which, in turn, tabled their own guidelines. Some discussions on these alternative drafts were held within the group and informally outside it; however, this group was also affected by the general inertia that plagued the round until mid-July 1977, and it was not until June 1978 that a draft integrated text was placed before Group Safeguards. This draft became the subject of further negotiations.

The question of safeguards, involving as it does the right of a state to derogate from its GATT obligations in emergency or other circumstances, was, not surprisingly, a contentious matter and difficult to resolve. In fact, all that Group Safeguards was able to achieve was a recommendation to the TNC

59 MTN/12, at 2 (1975).

60 It was agreed, however, that the participants would send summary notes of their meetings to the secretariat, which in turn would distribute them to other participants. MTN/AG/5 (1976).

61 1 DIRECTOR-GENERAL'S REPORT, *supra* note 23, at 26.

62 *Id.* at 88–89.

63 *Id.* at 93.

that the work be continued in an effort to achieve an agreed safeguard system. The negotiations both inside and outside the group were ultimately unsuccessful in achieving a code.

Group Framework. Group Framework, promoted vigorously by developing countries led by Brazil, was viewed less enthusiastically by the major developed states out of concern that it might become a vehicle for the rhetoric of the "New International Economic Order." The group's purpose was to consider the reform of the GATT system, particularly as it affected developing countries. A program of work for the group had been prepared prior to its formal constitution by the TNC,[64] and the initial meetings focused on the points in that program. In 1977 Brazil put a comprehensive proposal before the group building upon the original work program, which became the basis for substantive negotiations in 1978. The GATT secretariat also tabled draft texts and made proposals both at the request of states and on its own initiative.[65] Four texts ultimately were presented by the group to the TNC as final documents.

THE NEGOTIATIONS

Background

The mechanics of negotiations in the Tokyo Round can only be understood against the background of previous tariff negotiating rounds conducted under the auspices of GATT. The early negotiating rounds, it must be emphasized, were concerned almost exclusively with tariffs. The technique adopted in these rounds was that of "request and offer," based on bilateral negotiations between the "principal supplier" of a commodity and the state from which a tariff reduction was sought. The procedure operated as follows. Prior to the negotiating round, the principal suppliers would draw up "Lists of Requests" for tariff reductions addressed to their trading partners. These lists would be sent to the countries from which the concessions were sought and copies would be sent to the GATT secretariat for distribution to all other GATT contracting parties.

The contracting parties to whom requests were addressed would then respond with "Lists of Offers" for tariff reductions, or "Lists of Responses to Requests," which would be forwarded to the principal supplier, again with copies to the GATT secretariat. The secretariat would forward copies of these "Lists of Offers" to all states who had also made offers.[66] The substantive negotiations, once the round commenced, were between the principal supplier that had made a request for a tariff reduction and the state that had made an offer for a tariff concession. Thus, negotiations were essentially bilateral,[67] although in Curzon's view, the use of the secretariat introduced an important

[64] MTN/17 (1976).

[65] 1 DIRECTOR-GENERAL'S REPORT, *supra* note 23, at 98.

[66] According to Curzon, in this way "no country can receive offers of concessions unless it itself has made such offers." G. CURZON, *supra* note 6, at 72–73.

[67] K. DAM, *supra* note 6, at 61.

multilateral element into the negotiations.[68] Once an agreement on concessions was reached, it was embodied in a "consolidated document" and deposited with the GATT secretariat.[69] At the conclusion of the round, the concessions granted on the basis of bilateral negotiations would, in effect, be "multilateralized" by virtue of the most-favored-nation provision of the General Agreement.[70]

Criticism of this country-by-country, product-by-product approach to negotiations led to proposals for reform, which resulted in the addition in 1955 of Article XXVIII *bis* to the General Agreement contemplating negotiations on either a selective "product-by-product" basis or "by the application of such multilateral procedures as may be accepted by the contracting parties concerned."[71] Following the Dillon Round attempts were made to devise a negotiating technique that would move away from item-by-item negotiations, and prior to the Kennedy Round it was agreed that tariff negotiations would be based upon "a plan of substantial linear tariff reductions with a base minimum of exceptions which shall be subject to confrontation and justification."[72]

This approach had the effect of changing the initial focus of negotiations into a multilateral mode, for it required initial agreement upon a tariff negotiating plan. This was done in the Trade Negotiations Committee set up for the Kennedy Round; in the absence of firm agreement on a negotiating plan, it was agreed there that a 50 percent reduction rule would be employed as a "working hypothesis" for the linear tariff reduction.[73] However, this new approach, as far as negotiating techniques are concerned, amounted to a difference in form rather than substance. The focus of negotiations shifted away from tariff concessions to exceptions to the linear tariff reduction, and these exceptions were negotiated precisely by the request-and-offer procedure.[74]

The Tokyo Round inherited the approach of the Kennedy Round to tariff negotiations. Essentially, it involved general agreement on a tariff negotiating formula, a matter on which there could be multilateral negotiations, with the possibility of resort to the bilateral request-and-offer procedure for dealing

[68] G. CURZON, *supra* note 6, at 73, states:

> Before negotiations begin, each contracting party knows what all its partners are willing to offer. If the offer of an individual country is not enough in itself, the knowledge that a second or third country is willing to pay something too for a given concession allows the negotiations to open under more propitious auspices than might have been the case in a classical bilateral situation.

[69] No agreement was considered final until the round was concluded, in order to allow for subsequent reopening in the light of other concessions.

[70] In view of this extension of benefits to other states, there would be a period at the end of each round "during which requests and offers previously made were reshuffled." K. DAM, *supra* note 6, at 63. Dam regards this as the "only truly multilateral element of the negotiations." *Ibid. See also* Finlayson & Zacher, *supra* note 15, at 586.

[71] General Agreement on Tariffs and Trade, TIAS No. 1700, 55 UNTS 194, *amended* March 10, 1955, 8 UST 1767, TIAS No. 3930, 278 UNTS 168, Art. XVIII *bis*, para. 2(a).

[72] Conclusions and Resolutions, *supra* note 13, BISD, 12th Supp. 47 (1964).

[73] BISD, 13th Supp. 109 (1964).

[74] Some countries were expressly excluded from the linear tariff reduction formula, and were allowed to negotiate on a product-by-product basis. *Id.* at 112.

with exceptions to the agreed formula. The tariff negotiating formula was not stipulated in the Tokyo Declaration, nor was it agreed to in the TNC. The task assigned to Group Tariffs, therefore, was to devise the appropriate formula.

The Tokyo Round, it has been noted, differed from previous negotiating rounds in that a primary concern was with nontariff impediments to trade. Reduction or elimination of nontariff barriers was something with which the GATT contracting parties had had little experience, apart from the Anti-Dumping Code in the Kennedy Round, and hence there was no clear negotiating procedure to be followed. The Director-General of GATT noted that nontariff measures were more diversified than tariffs and that "similar negotiating techniques could not be applied to them."[75] It is instructive, therefore, to see how states responded to this new type of negotiation.

Formal Negotiations

No formal substantive negotiations took place in the TNC and it is to the groups that attention must be turned. Group Tariffs attempted to devise a tariff negotiating formula through traditional multilateral negotiations, and specific proposals were introduced by Canada, the United States, the EEC, Japan, and Switzerland. However, no agreement was reached within the group, and the formula was determined independently.[76] The group did not meet after December 1976, and exceptions to the formula were negotiated by the request-and-offer technique. Some states did not employ the formula and engaged in request and offer on a product-by-product basis. This technique was also utilized for tropical products in accordance with a decision made at an early meeting of that group.[77] As a result, Group Tropical Products as such had a small role in providing a forum for formal negotiations.

The third group that was concerned, in part at least, with tariffs was Group Agriculture. As has been seen, its work was hampered by a dispute between the United States and the EEC, but following the resolution of their differences, again reached independently of the group, negotiations on tariffs in agriculture also took place on the request-and-offer basis. The procedure was formally endorsed by the group in July 1977, and this, too, had the effect of removing negotiations from the group itself.

The groups on nontariff measures, sector, safeguard, and framework were to draw up agreements or codes setting standards for behavior. Two subgroups of Group Non-Tariff Measures worked from draft texts prepared by GATT or by the OECD. In Group Non-Tariff Measures itself it was agreed[78] that

[75] 1 DIRECTOR-GENERAL'S REPORT, *supra* note 23, at 49.

[76] The formula that resulted from meetings between U.S. Special Trade Representative Robert Strauss and EEC Commissioner for External Relations Haferkamp in Brussels in July and September 1977 was based on a Swiss proposal that had been placed before Group Tariffs. The formula was agreed to as a "working hypothesis" and was generally acquiesced in by the major trading participants in the Tokyo Round. The procedure agreed to at that time was that there would be a general tariff plan based on the tariff-cutting formula, followed by a tabling of requests for specific tariff reductions. *Id.* at 47.

[77] *Id.* at 38–39.

[78] MTN/NTM/35 (1977).

matters that were not within the purview of any subgroup would be dealt with by the request-and-offer procedure. Although the parties intended that the procedure not apply to "measures with respect to which multilateral solutions were being sought in the Sub-Groups,"[79] in November 1977 it was noted in Sub-Group Customs Matters that requests had been received on matters falling within its competence. Thus, it too adopted the request-and-offer technique and bilateral negotiations ensued. The same occurred in Sub-Group Government Procurement, which had been engaged in negotiations on a draft code placed before it in March 1978. When the question arose of the procedure to be followed to determine the governmental entities to which the code should be applied, support was overwhelming for the request-and-offer procedure, which was accordingly adopted. The result was that the subgroup adjourned while the necessary bilateral negotiations took place. Group Quantitative Restrictions also resorted to request and offer and abandoned the attempt to formulate a code.

In the remaining groups and subgroups of Group Non-Tariff Measures negotiations proceeded more traditionally. The lack of a draft text upon which discussion could be based meant that greater reliance was placed on those states with a particular interest in the subject to produce texts that could form the basis of discussion. In effect, resort had to be had to informal negotiations outside the groups or subgroups. The meetings of the groups themselves tended to be characterized by a degree of formality, and although in the subgroups less formality was evident and some drafting took place, informal negotiations outside the groups and subgroups were felt to promise the most progress. In Sub-Group Technical Barriers to Trade, for example, the Chairman suggested in September 1977 that members resort to informal consultations and negotiations on specific proposals that had been placed before it.[80]

Informal Negotiations

Three categories of informal negotiations were held in connection with the Tokyo Round. The first is the bilateral negotiation that is essential to the request-and-offer procedure. There is, of course, a degree of formality about this procedure, and while it has multilateral implications, it involves the negotiation by individual states of their own arrangements with other states. The technique has a well-established place in tariff negotiations, but one of the significant factors of the Tokyo Round was that states resorted to request and offer to resolve nontariff issues as well.

The second type of informal negotiation was resort to "bilateral and plurilateral" consultations and discussions outside the framework of the groups and subgroups. In part, these were simply the informal negotiations and consultations that take place in any international conference where the chairman of a committee consults informally with committee members in order to resolve an impasse, or where members meet informally to try to present a united front. However, in Sub-Groups Customs Matters[81] and Technical Barriers to

[79] *Id.* at 3.
[80] MTN/NTM/36 (1977).
[81] MTN/NTM/40 (1978).

Trade,[82] active consultations on the outside were specifically encouraged by the subgroups themselves. In the former, the Chairman noted at the meeting of February 13, 1978 that it had been agreed that while a draft valuation code constituted a basis for future work, "bilateral and plurilateral consultations involving as many members of the Sub-Group as possible should begin shortly with the aim of producing a revised draft." This draft was to be brought back to the subgroup for further consideration.

These outside negotiations and consultations, although unofficial, often had a significant effect on the formal negotiations, both directly and indirectly. Positions agreed to in informal consultations would be brought back to the group for adoption or for further discussion. The value of these informal negotiations was noted by the Chairman of the TNC at its meeting of December 1975:

> It seems to me that both multilateral and bilateral consultations are really essential to ultimate success of the negotiations. I think that what is important is not that consultations take place under the auspices of one Group or another but that information regarding consultations is immediately communicated to all Groups.[83]

The comment reflected the desire to have "transparency" in the negotiations and to promote the parallel development of the negotiations on the various sectors called for in paragraph 8 of the Tokyo Declaration.

In some instances, however, the informal consultations did not serve merely to facilitate the work of the groups. Positions circulated as information papers espousing the views of some delegations were not under the auspices of any group, but in fact they reflected a general consensus. For example, the agreement reached by the United States and the EEC and acquiesced in by other states was circulated as a "working hypothesis for tariff reductions" and was said to be "circulated at the request of certain delegations."[84] The "working hypothesis" was stated in mandatory terms and reflected an agreed formula, agreement having been reached totally outside the formal institutional structure. In effect, Group Tariffs, which had been asked to determine the negotiating formula, had been bypassed.

As negotiations progressed, recourse to informal consultations increased. In 1977 the informal negotiations were to a degree formalized with the emergence of an unofficial body that came to be known as the "seven plus seven" committee. The name derived from the committee's initial composition of seven developed and seven developing states, but the number of participants varied depending upon the subject under discussion.[85] Its functions were those of an unofficial steering committee for the negotiations, advising the Chairman of the TNC whether that committee should be convened and what it should discuss. Thus, through this committee it could be anticipated whether issues would be contentious in the TNC, and conflict in the plenary body was thereby minimized. Though the committee was never formally constituted, had no

[82] MTN/NTM/41 (1978).

[83] MTN/W/24 (1975).

[84] MTN/INF/11 (1977).

[85] Some of the initial participants were the United States, the EEC, Japan, Canada, the Nordic countries, Austria, Switzerland, Mexico, Argentina, Brazil, and India.

defined mandate, and did not keep records of its meetings, its existence has been seen as critical to the development of the negotiations. It could be used as a forum for considering proposals that states did not want to put before the groups, and it often reviewed "information" documents before their circulation to participating states as the work of "certain delegations."

The third type of informal negotiation associated with the Tokyo Round took place outside the auspices of the MTN altogether. The principal example was the bilateral consultation between the United States and the EEC in Brussels in July 1977,[86] the Strauss-Haferkamp meeting. The meeting was quite critical because it came at a time that negotiations were moving very slowly, and its resolution of the dispute over agriculture and the agreement on a tariff formula provided an impetus for negotiations. The impact of this meeting illustrates both the dominance of the United States and the EEC in multilateral trade negotiations and the effect of outside factors upon the negotiations. Other examples of such "external influence" are the passage of the U.S. Trade Act in 1975, which allowed serious negotiations to get under way, and the Bonn Economic Summit of 1978. The participants at Bonn charged their GATT negotiators with the task of bringing the trade negotiations to a successful conclusion by the end of that year. This clear indication of political commitment by the developed states gave further momentum to the negotiations.

IV. The Conclusion of the Tokyo Round

In April 1979, the groups and subgroups submitted their texts to the TNC. Though the responsibility of the TNC was the rather formal one of giving a final endorsement to those texts, the task was one of substance because issues that had not been resolved in the groups were left for determination by the committee. Two major issues were dealt with. The first was the question of accession to the MTN instruments by noncontracting parties to GATT. This was resolved in the April meeting of the TNC with the assumption that those non-GATT states which became parties to the MTN agreements would not act in a way that would nullify or impair advantages to GATT contracting parties under the General Agreement itself.[87]

The second issue was more difficult. In the latter stages of negotiations within the groups,[88] it had been proposed that decisions on the adoption of final texts and on the number of ratifications needed to bring them into force should be taken by a two-thirds majority. The Chairmen of the groups deferred the matter by passing it on to the Chairman of the TNC, who placed it before the April meeting of that body. The proposal for a two-thirds majority, which originated with the developing states, met with considerable opposition from those most closely involved in the drafting of the texts. Given the number of countries involved in the Tokyo Round, a two-thirds majority rule would have given developing states a veto over the adoption of instruments. It was argued by the opponents of the proposal that the MTN was not

[86] The two officials met in Brussels on several occasions during the Tokyo Round.

[87] MTN/P/5, at 2 (1979).

[88] MTN/NTM/65–69 (1979).

a general diplomatic conference and that the TNC could not by vote prevent countries from entering into agreements if they wished to. Since the TNC operated by consensus, the proposal for a two-thirds majority rule failed to be endorsed by the committee.

This result led to intensive negotiations during the summer and fall of 1979. Parallel texts had been presented by developed and developing states to the TNC on antidumping, dairy products, and customs valuation, and in the absence of a two-thirds majority voting rule for the adoption of the MTN instruments, the competing texts remained.[89] The negotiations were successful in producing a "protocol" for the Customs Valuation Code and at least certain "understandings" on the Anti-Dumping Code. The developing countries thereupon withdrew their competing texts on antidumping and customs valuation, but alternative texts on dairy products remained till the meeting of the contracting parties in November 1979, and were subsequently opened for signature.

The meeting of the TNC on April 12, 1979 resulted in a *Procès-Verbal*[90] under which the participating states would by their signatures authenticate the annexed texts and indicate their intention of submitting the relevant texts to their governments for ratification. Signature of the Procès-Verbal could also indicate that only some of the texts were thereby authenticated and it was recognized that some states, in particular the least developed states, might wish to study the texts further before signing. The Procès-Verbal also noted that work on "safeguards" should be continued.

Up to this point, the MTN had taken place outside of the formal GATT structure[91] and in November 1979 the contracting parties met to bring the results of the round within the GATT system. It was important, as the Director-General of GATT subsequently noted, to integrate the results "in such a way as not to detract from the authority of the GATT rules . . . and from the unity and consistency of the GATT trading system."[92] The action of the contracting parties at this meeting took the form of a decision[93] in which they reaffirmed "their intention to ensure the unity and consistency of the GATT system" and stated that they would "oversee the operation of the system as a whole and take action as appropriate." The decision also took note of the agreements negotiated in the Tokyo Round and indicated that rights of GATT members not parties to these agreements would not be impaired.[94] In effect, the contracting parties were asserting a supervisory role over the agreements that emerged from the Tokyo Round.

The contracting parties also decided to establish a committee to continue work on safeguards, and they adopted a Work Programme for GATT that

[89] MTN/P/5, at 5 (1979).

[90] BISD, 26th Supp. 189–91 (1980).

[91] As noted previously, the round had been convened by a meeting of Ministers in Tokyo, and not by the decision of a GATT organ.

[92] 2 DIRECTOR-GENERAL'S REPORT, *supra* note 23, at 20.

[93] Decision of Nov. 28, 1979 (L/4905), BISD, 26th Supp. 201 (1980).

[94] It was also provided that the committees set up under the agreements would send reports to the GATT contracting parties and provision was made for GATT contracting parties that were not parties to the agreements to attend meetings of committees as observers.

would both implement the results of the Tokyo Round and identify further areas for cooperation in international trade matters. Other actions by the contracting parties at this time included: according to developing countries "differential and more favourable treatment, reciprocity and fuller participation";[95] a declaration of trade measures taken for balance-of-payment purposes;[96] a decision on safeguard action for developing countries;[97] an understanding regarding notification, consultation, dispute settlement, and surveillance;[98] and a decision to establish a subcommittee of the Committee on Trade and Development to examine protective measures affecting imports from developing countries.[99]

This meeting of the contracting parties marked the conclusion of the Tokyo Round.

V. The Tokyo Round as Multilateral Treaty Making

In the light of the above description, is it possible to make some assessment of the Tokyo Round as an exercise in multilateral treaty making? Obviously, the round must be considered a success, at least in some respects, for although the benefits may not have been as great as some might have anticipated at the outset, tariff concessions were obtained, nontariff barriers were reduced or eliminated, and agreements or codes on the reduction of nontariff barriers were drawn up. On the other hand, it is still too early to tell to what extent these agreements will receive widespread acceptance. The purpose here, however, is not to assess the substance of the agreements reached but rather the process of negotiation that emerged from the Tokyo Round. This will be done in three ways. First, the specific features of the treaty making of the Tokyo Round will be outlined and discussed. Second, the extent to which the states involved expressed dissatisfaction with the negotiations will be considered. Third, the compatibility of the agreements resulting from the Tokyo Round with existing international trading arrangements will be assessed. In other words, do the agreements promote consistency and coherence in the structure of the international trade system?

THE TREATY-MAKING PROCESS

Formulation

The most significant feature of the preparatory phase of the Tokyo Round was the lack of formal preparation for the multilateral trade negotiations. There was an element of continuity from the earlier Kennedy Round and the Work Programme of GATT organs in the intervening years can be seen as providing background for the negotiations. However, only one draft text was available as a result of earlier GATT work (it has been seen that a draft OECD text on government purchasing policies also was used as a basis for negotiations). As a result, heavy reliance was placed upon initiatives by individual

[95] Decision of Nov. 28, 1979 (L/4903).
[96] Adopted on Nov. 28, 1979 (L/4904).
[97] Adopted on Nov. 28, 1979 (L/4897).
[98] Decision of Nov. 28, 1979 (L/4907).
[99] Decision of Nov. 28, 1979 (L/4899).

delegations, and in some cases upon the GATT secretariat, for the formulation of draft texts. While this lack of preparation contrasts with the more formalized multilateral treaty making at some United Nations-sponsored conferences that have relied on preparatory work by the International Law Commission, it finds some parallel in the Third United Nations Conference on the Law of the Sea (UNCLOS III). Nevertheless, as will be seen, the institutional structure of the MTN left the Tokyo Round less able to remedy the consequences of lack of preparatory work than other multilateral treaty-making conferences.

The way that the round was initiated made formal preparation more difficult. It was the action of the major trading states, outside of GATT, that enabled negotiations to get under way, not a decision by a GATT organ for which there had been considerable background work. Trade negotiations depend upon the willingness of the major trading nations to discuss concessions, and insofar as tariff negotiations are concerned, there is little formal preparatory work in the nature of draft texts that could have been undertaken in advance.[100] On the other hand, the negotiation of nontariff measures, particularly in the form of codes, could be the subject of extensive preparatory work prior to the initiation of a negotiating round, and draft texts could have been prepared. In this respect the Tokyo Round did not get off to as good a start as it might have.

A consequence of this lack of preparatory work was that there was no agreement at the outset on the form of the final instruments. The participants had in mind a negotiating process whose objective was the reduction of tariffs, the elimination or reduction of the effect of nontariff barriers, and more generally the liberalization of trade. They did not have the specific objective of producing a multilateral agreement. The Tokyo Declaration was concerned with subjects for negotiations, the principles upon which negotiations should proceed, and the special problems of developing countries, but it did not indicate what kinds of instruments should ensue. Still, although there was no formal commitment to the conclusion of treaties, protocols, rules of practice, or an annex to the General Agreement itself, it was assumed by many states that the results of the round in the case of tariffs would be new protocols to the General Agreement, and in the case of nontariff measures would be a series of agreements similar in form to the Anti-Dumping Code that had resulted from the Kennedy Round. Thus, the negotiation of "codes," though not formally stipulated, was implicit.

Nevertheless, this lack of defined objectives may well have contributed to the difficulties of reconciling the results of the Tokyo Round (the "codes") with existing international trade legislation.

Negotiations

Two features of the Tokyo Round distinguish it from other multilateral treaty-making negotiations. The first is the use of the request-and-offer tech-

[100] The type of preparatory work that was undertaken involved the study of different approaches to tariff negotiating formulas. The exchange of lists of requests and lists of offers prior to the earlier rounds can also be seen as a form of preparatory work.

nique in which the states that are principally concerned engage in bilateral negotiations whose results are then extended multilaterally to the other participants. As has been seen, this technique was developed for tariff negotiations, and although it was criticized for involving a country-by-country, product-by-product form of negotiation and was modified in form at least in the Kennedy and Tokyo Rounds by the adoption of linear reduction and harmonization formulas for tariff negotiations, request and offer has endured. Indeed, in the Tokyo Round the technique was applied outside the tariff negotiations to nontariff measures as well. The utility of request and offer for multilateral treaty making generally will be considered later. Suffice it to say here that its particular attraction in tariff negotiations, and trade negotiations generally, is that it focuses on the states with the greatest interest in the matter being negotiated. States that will be affected by the outcome, but with a less substantive interest, play a subsidiary role.

The second feature of the Tokyo Round is the predominance of informal negotiations outside the groups and subgroups. In part, such informality is a concomitant of the bilateral negotiations that take place under the request-and-offer technique, but even the Tokyo Round negotiations on nontariff measures, which were designed to draw up various codes and were therefore multilateral in scope, were characterized by a high degree of informality. Negotiations not only were conducted outside the groups and subgroups, but also were held on a bilateral basis, and on occasion informal negotiations were mandated by the subgroup itself. Though these informal negotiations generally took place among the various delegations in Geneva, they also occurred elsewhere, *e.g.*, the negotiations between the United States and the EEC in July 1977 that were critical to the round as a whole. The outside informal negotiations were highly dependent upon both the personalities of the leading participants and political events outside the Tokyo Round. The American Trade Representative, Robert Strauss, was a pivotal figure in the negotiations.

Resort to informal negotiations outside the formal conference arena is a characteristic of many international negotiations for the conclusion of multilateral treaties. The Tokyo Round, however, placed informal negotiations on a much higher level of importance, to the extent that the formal negotiating groups were largely irrelevant to the actual negotiation of the instruments. Little drafting took place in these groups; in fact, there was no formal mechanism for drafting agreements at all. This reliance on informal negotiating bodies and consensus procedures at the MTN finds some parallel in UNCLOS III which, Buzan has pointed out,[101] both formalized negotiating by consensus and adopted an "active consensus" procedure. The law of the sea negotiations initially moved to consensus procedures within the formal negotiating bodies, but subsequently negotiations were moved into informal groups. Later still, special negotiating groups were set up within the overall framework of the conference. By contrast, in the MTN informal negotiations commenced almost from the outset.

[101] Buzan, *Negotiating by Consensus: Developments in Technique at the United Nations Conference on the Law of the Sea*, 75 AJIL 324 (1981).

However, not even in the MTN could negotiations be totally informal. It has been seen that an informal steering committee, the "seven plus seven" group, came into existence[102] to monitor negotiations and to ensure that progress was being made. This occurred in spite of the fact that the task might well have fallen within the responsibility of the TNC; but the "seven plus seven" committee performed the important role of ensuring that difficulties were identified and major points of controversy minimized before a matter was formalized in the TNC. The committee conferred a degree of "premanagement" on the round that some participants saw as essential.

In both the request-and-offer negotiations and the informal "multilateral-type" negotiations of the Tokyo Round, the GATT secretariat played a central role. Its "clearinghouse" function was vital to the success of the bilateral negotiations because states could act with full knowledge of what had resulted from other bilateral negotiations. In the informal negotiations, too, the secretariat had the important task of gauging progress, and of circulating positions of states, often under its own name, in order to assess responses. Confidence in key secretariat officials was essential and the GATT secretariat by and large enjoys such confidence.

It is difficult to determine precisely why the GATT secretariat enjoys so much confidence amongst the contracting parties. The secretariat was originally the staff of the Interim Commission for the International Trade Organization (ICITO), and though a separate body, it generally follows the regulations and practices of the United Nations Secretariat.[103] The expertise of individual members of the GATT secretariat is recognized and sought after, and the Director-General has generally maintained a relatively high profile. The prestige and stature of the secretariat may in part result from its recognized role in the complaints panel procedure; Hudec notes that the panel format "put the secretariat more into the center of things" and that within 5 years after GATT came into being "the secretariat was well on its way to becoming a voice of considerable authority on all GATT affairs."[104]

This recognition of the authority of the secretariat is manifested in the acceptance of secretariat officials as chairmen of groups and subgroups in the Tokyo Round.[105] It also helps explain the acceptance by the developed states of an active role by the secretariat on behalf of the developing states at the round, the most striking example of which occurred in Group Framework

[102] Some observers have suggested that the lower profile of the Director-General of GATT in the Tokyo Round (as compared with that of his predecessor in the Kennedy Round) may have contributed to the need for the creation of an informal steering committee. On the other hand, there was some precedent in GATT for such an informal body. In 1975 the "Consultative Group of 18," which was a committee of high-level officials of member states, was set up on a provisional basis to discuss sensitive issues of international trade. The success of the Consultative Group resulted in its being constituted as a permanent GATT body in November 1979. BISD, 25th Supp. 289–90 (1977–78).

[103] J. JACKSON, *supra* note 6, at 145–48.

[104] R. HUDEC, *supra* note 6, at 76–77.

[105] However, the choice of secretariat officials resulted from the inability of the participants to choose chairmen from the representatives of states.

where the secretariat took initiatives, formulated proposals, and presented draft texts to the group.[106]

Adoption of Agreements

It has been noted already that there was no formal mechanism in the Tokyo Round for the drafting of agreements. At best, the process can be described as ad hoc. Individual states would put their own drafts forward, subsequent drafts would be compilations of the earlier drafts of a number of states, and often the final drafting would be the responsibility of a particular state or group of states, or of a secretariat official. In this respect the Tokyo Round negotiations differ from other multilateral treaty-making endeavors where a drafting committee is a standard organ of the negotiating process. Even in the TNC, which marked the final stage prior to adoption of the texts, no attempt was made to scrutinize the drafting of the agreements. The TNC was concerned with how the instruments were to be adopted (by vote or by consensus) and whether nonmembers of GATT could participate.

A further feature of the Tokyo Round was that although the objective was to produce single texts for each of the codes, in some cases competing texts were produced and presented as alternatives to the TNC. The scope for handling competing texts adhered to by different groups of states is limited where there is a general multilateral interest at stake, but it is feasible in the field of trade where separate obligations can be undertaken bilaterally.

DISSATISFACTION WITH THE NEGOTIATIONS

Few would claim that the negotiations in the Tokyo Round, which have been described as "frighteningly cumbersome,"[107] were regarded as an unqualified success by any state. They were complex and diffuse and, not surprisingly, the developing states expressed considerable dissatisfaction with them. This reaction deserves some attention, for the special concerns of developing states in international trade was one of the principal planks of the Tokyo Declaration. The Tokyo Round, more than any of the previous rounds, was intended to take heed of these special needs, and developing countries demonstrated their interest in the negotiations by attending in large numbers.[108]

At the first meeting of the TNC, these countries indicated that they wished to "take part in all areas of the negotiations at all stages of the work."[109] It

[106] On the one hand, this action by the secretariat may be seen as a further aspect of its assistance to developing countries. On the other hand, by taking an active role and directing the course of negotiations the secretariat ensured that the developing countries would not turn Group Framework into a forum for debate on the New International Economic Order.

[107] Jackson, *The Crumbling Institutions of the Liberal Trade System*, 12 J. WORLD TRADE L. 93, 96 (1978).

[108] No more than 20–30 states participated in the early rounds. In the Tokyo Round there were over 100 participants, the increase being attributable to greater participation by developing states.

[109] MTN/P.1, at 1 (1973).

was decided at that meeting that no separate group should be established to deal with the special concerns of developing countries; they were to be dealt with in each group.[110] The wish of developed states to be seen to be responding to the needs of developing countries was manifested in Group Tropical Products, a sector of particular interest to some developing countries, where negotiations moved quickly and the implementation of concessions granted in the negotiations soon followed.

In the formal meetings of the groups and subgroups, the developing countries were generally active in proposing drafts, and it was on their initiative that Sub-Group Government Procurement and Group Framework were established. Nevertheless, the developing states were not satisfied with the way negotiations proceeded. In the July 1978 meeting of the TNC, they issued a statement stressing the need for their full participation in all of the negotiations, and not just in those concerned with the special and differential treatment to be accorded to them. The complaint made to the TNC was that the style of negotiations had isolated them and prevented them from participating effectively in the round. In their view, "major decisions should be taken at meetings in which all countries, including developing countries, were able to participate." They argued further that a negotiating document should not be adopted "unless the large majority of participants declared themselves in favour of it."[111] However, although representatives of the developed states indicated that they welcomed the "constructive suggestions" of the developing states, no measures were taken to give them effect. In fact, within 2 weeks of the July 1978 meeting of the TNC, a "Framework of Understanding" was circulated by the major trading states and other developed countries,[112] which was said to contain "the necessary elements . . . to ensure a successful conclusion of the negotiations in accordance with the Tokyo Declaration."[113] Not surprisingly, the developing countries were angered. They had not participated in the drafting of the "Understanding," nor did they consider that issues of major concern to them were being addressed.[114] They drew attention to the fact that in spite of their objections at the TNC meeting only 2 weeks previously, they were once again being excluded from important negotiations.

The final attempt by the less-developed states to exercise a major influence on the negotiations came with their unsuccessful proposal to the TNC in the latter stages of the round that decisions on the adoption of final texts and on the number of ratifications necessary to bring the texts into effect be taken by a two-thirds majority. This proposal would have given the developing states a veto over the instruments to emerge from the Tokyo Round.

It would be a mistake to ignore the political implications of the developing countries' protest at the method of negotiation and the consensus rule in the TNC. GATT and the tariff rounds have traditionally been dominated by the major trading states and some protest against this dominance, symbolic or otherwise, was to be expected. What is perhaps more surprising is that the

[110] *Id.* at 4.

[111] MTN/P.4, at 2 (1978).

[112] The group included the United States, the EEC, Japan, Switzerland, Canada, New Zealand, the Nordic countries, Australia, and Austria.

[113] MTN/INF/33 (1978).

[114] MTN/INF/38 (1978).

call for a New International Economic Order did not emerge more obviously in the negotiations and that the issue of a two-thirds majority in the TNC was not pushed further than it was. This restraint implies some recognition by the developing states of the frailty of the MTN, and of their interest in not spoiling the gains that had been made by forcing the issue of majority control in the TNC.[115]

CONTRIBUTION OF THE AGREEMENTS TO THE INTERNATIONAL TRADE SYSTEM

The final basis on which to evaluate the Tokyo Round is to determine to what extent the agreements negotiated further rationalize international trade legislation, or whether in spite of substantive gains, they contribute to more complexity, confusion, and incoherence in the obligations of states in international trade. It is here that some serious questions can be raised about the agreements that resulted from the MTN. Again, it must be emphasized, concern is not with the new substantive obligations undertaken under these agreements, but rather with the relationship of these agreements to existing international trade legislation and, in particular, to the GATT itself. The formal documents emerging from the Tokyo Round[116] were two protocols to the General Agreement dealing with tariff reductions, and nine "codes," some of which are referred to as "agreements" and others as "arrangements." The protocols to the General Agreement were in the form usually adopted for bringing the results of the rounds within the GATT system.[117] The agreements and arrangements[118] are not formally connected to the General Agreement in the same way. On their face they stand alone as international agreements, but it is clear from their provisions that they are inextricably related to the GATT. They are open to signature by GATT contracting parties, or by states that have provisionally acceded to GATT, or by other states approved by the GATT contracting parties. The Director-General of GATT is the depositary for the agreements and the GATT secretariat is called on to perform a variety of secretarial functions under them.

The relationship between the MTN agreements and the GATT itself was considered by the contracting parties in their November 1979 meeting and their action taken at that time may be seen as an effort to assert the primacy of the existing GATT system over the new agreements. This position is not clear, however, and it is further complicated by the fact that some of the agreements contain provisions that purport to take precedence over provisions of the General Agreement. For example, it is provided in the Agreement on Technical Barriers to Trade that disputes arising between the parties relating to rights and obligations under that Agreement should be referred to the dispute settlement procedures under the Agreement before the parties avail

[115] It is the view of some participants that a two-thirds majority voting rule in the TNC would have led to the collapse of the Tokyo Round and perhaps put GATT's future in doubt.

[116] The documents are found in BISD, 26th Supp. (1980).

[117] For the protocol to the GATT following the Kennedy Round, see BISD, 15th Supp. 4–5 (1966–67).

[118] The term "agreement" will be used to cover both "agreements" and "arrangements."

themselves "of any rights which they have under the GATT."[119] Other agreements set up dispute settlement mechanisms but make no statement about the relationship between these procedures and the GATT dispute settlement procedures.[120] Still others simply adopt the GATT dispute settlement procedure.[121] Both the creation of separate committees under the agreements and the provision of separate dispute settlement procedures have led to the suggestion that what might develop is a series of "mini-GATTS,"[122] which may weaken the GATT system itself or lead to the development of a new GATT-MTN system.[123] It is clear, however, that the agreements resulting from the Tokyo Round raise many legal questions about their relationship with the GATT system and their compatibility with existing GATT obligations.

It must be asked whether the process of negotiations in the MTN can in any way be regarded as responsible for the lack of congruence between the systems set up in the MTN agreements and the GATT system, and for the lack of congruence between the agreements themselves. Two factors already identified may well have contributed to this. First, the lack of background or preparatory work heightens the opportunity for such conflict. Questions of the relationship between the proposed treaty and existing agreements can well be raised during the preparatory phase, but during the period of actual negotiations they are more likely to be overlooked. Second, even in the absence of preparatory work, problems of consistency between agreements in language, procedures, and institutions can be dealt with in a formal drafting committee during negotiations. It is here that one of the major deficiencies of the MTN as a process leading to the conclusion of a multilateral treaty becomes clear. The method of drafting referred to earlier left no real opportunity for the perusal of different texts so as to obtain consistency in language, or the common use of procedures or institutions. Nor was there any real opportunity to consider the relationship of the new provisions to existing GATT procedures and obligations. Other multilateral treaty-making conferences have been able, to some extent, to remedy the deficiencies deriving from inadequate preparatory work by establishing a drafting committee whose role, albeit restricted, has allowed it to endeavor to achieve consistency throughout the text being negotiated.

This aspect of the negotiation of the MTN agreements leaves much to be desired, and it supports the conclusion of Professor Jackson that "very little was accomplished [in the MTN] in dealing with the long-term (and very real)

[119] Art. 14(23). A similar provision is found in the Agreement on the Implementation of Article VII of the GATT (Customs Valuation), Art. 20(11). *See* BISD, 26th Supp. 116 (1980).

[120] Agreement on the Interpretation and Application of Articles VI, XVI and XXIII of GATT (Subsidies and Countervailing Duties), Art. 18. *See* BISD, 26th Supp. 171 (1980). For the view that provisions of this nature oust the GATT dispute settlement procedure completely, see Bourgeois, *The Tokyo Round Agreements on Technical Barriers and on Government Procurement in International and EEC Perspective*, 19 Common Mkt. L.R. 5, 17 (1982).

[121] Agreement on Import Licensing Procedures, Art. 4(2). *See* BISD, 26th Supp. 154 (1980).

[122] Jackson, *The Birth of the GATT-MTN System: A Constitutional Appraisal*, 12 L. & POL'Y INT'L BUS. 21, 52 (1980).

[123] *Id.* at 56.

problems of the institutional-legal structure of a workable and effective international system for economic relations."[124]

VI. Conclusions

Any conclusions to be drawn about multilateral treaty making in the Tokyo Round must be tempered with caution. GATT, it has often been emphasized, is a unique institution that operates in a less formalized and more ad hoc way than many international organizations. Moreover, the traditional objective of GATT negotiations has been the reduction or elimination of tariffs, which may result in highly specialized techniques that cannot be transferred elsewhere. Nevertheless, the techniques of treaty making employed in the Tokyo Round can be considered to determine whether they may be of more general application.

MULTILATERAL TRADE NEGOTIATIONS

Two major difficulties may be identified for future multilateral trade negotiations. The first is the dissatisfaction of the developing states, not only with the substantive benefits received from the negotiations, but also with a method of negotiating that they felt excluded them.[125] Despite the emphasis in the Tokyo Declaration on special and differential treatment for developing countries and the considerable assistance given them by the GATT secretariat, they still felt that decisions were made without their participation and that the technique of negotiating operated to minimize their influence. These concerns obviously cannot be taken too far; this was the first round in which many developing countries participated, and a lack of familiarity with the process was to be expected. Moreover, in the final analysis they were not prepared to push their complaints in the TNC to force the issue of voting. By comparison with the proceedings of other international organizations, or of other multilateral treaty-making endeavors, GATT and the MTN have been relatively free from North-South confrontation. But if calls for a complete restructuring of the international trading system[126] are to be avoided, some attention will have to be directed in GATT to the concerns of developing states with the techniques of negotiation.

The second difficulty with the Tokyo Round negotiations is the inadequacy of the end results, the various agreements and arrangements on nontariff matters, as endeavors in international lawmaking. Bilateral and informal negotiations may well have been effective in producing the compromises that seemed necessary to bring the round to a conclusion, but the agreements that

[124] *Ibid.*

[125] The delegate of Yugoslavia, speaking to the TNC on behalf of the developing countries, made clear that the concerns of those countries were both substantive and procedural: "In spite of the fact that at some stages of the negotiations the developing countries were not invited, and that transparencies were often absent, we could not assume that proposals and requests submitted by the developing countries were not known. It is regrettable that many of them were ignored. . . ." MTN/P/5, at 36 (1979).

[126] *See* UNCTAD, Monthly Bull., No. 179, December 1981.

emerged may well contribute to a good deal of confusion in the "institutional-legal" structure of the GATT system. The creation of a variety of supervisory committees, and of separate conciliation and dispute settlement procedures, paralleling existing mechanisms in GATT, raises the probability of legal conflict between the new mechanisms and GATT. The decision of the contracting parties to exert some supervisory role over the system does not clear up the ambiguity; what is needed is an initiative to rationalize the procedures that have been developed and to attempt to secure some agreement on the common use of institutions among the new instruments and GATT.

It has been suggested already that some of these difficulties might have been avoided if the participants in the Tokyo Round had provided for a drafting committee, which could have reviewed each text and made proposals for the common use of language in the various agreements and for ensuring their compatibility with GATT procedures. This measure would not necessarily have solved the difficulties that are now apparent between the MTN Agreements and the General Agreement, but it might have prevented unintended conflict and have reduced the scope for subsequent dispute and debate over the meaning of inconsistent terminology and incompatible procedures.

MULTILATERAL TREATY MAKING

The two significant features of treaty making in the Tokyo Round were the request-and-offer technique and the substantial resort to informal negotiations. Can either of these be applied to multilateral treaty making in other fields? Initially, some caution must be expressed, for though the techniques of the Tokyo Round may be regarded as relatively effective as negotiating tools (*i.e.*, in securing the compromises necessary for agreement), they manifest significant deficiencies as a process of lawmaking or of law reform.[127] They must be seen, then, as contributions to negotiating technique, as opposed to the process of actually drafting and concluding treaties.

The Tokyo Round itself showed that the request-and-offer technique can be applied beyond the area of tariff negotiations. The attraction of the technique for multilateral treaty making generally is that it places emphasis upon negotiations between the states principally concerned with the subject and minimizes the role of those states whose concern is more incidental. However, it is dependent upon some agreement or understanding that other states will accept the results of these bilateral negotiations as applicable to them as well.[128] Moreover, as has been seen, a large number of states, admittedly those with a substantially smaller share of world trade, felt at the Tokyo Round that the technique excluded them from real participation in negotiations. The request-and-offer technique was developed in GATT because it accorded with the requirements of the U.S. negotiating authority and it suited the interests of

[127] R. HUDEC, *supra* note 6, at 265, makes the point that the Tokyo Round was concerned with "trade negotiations," not "law reform negotiations." But the various agreements that resulted from the round are, in fact, exercises in law reform.

[128] The most-favored-nation provision of Article I of GATT has this effect.

the major trading states that traditionally have dominated the organization. It flourished because the technique was well suited to the negotiation of tariffs over a wide range of goods. Nevertheless, by focusing on the states predominantly affected by the outcome of the negotiations, request and offer might well be useful for negotiations on other matters.

Resort to informal negotiations outside the formal negotiating structure is not novel, nor is it confined to GATT negotiations. What is significant about the Tokyo Round is the extent to which informal negotiations became the principal focus, to the point where the formal institutions had a very secondary role to play. Thus, the round was very dependent upon initiatives taken by individual states, upon the personalities of the participants, and upon events occurring independently of the round. In fact, because control over the negotiations was not exercised centrally by the formal negotiating organs, the round became particularly vulnerable to and dependent upon external events, in particular the independent actions of the principal trading states.

For informal negotiations to work successfully, it seems that two important conditions must be present. The first is the existence of a body that will keep track of negotiations and seek to resolve difficulties informally. At the Tokyo Round such a body, the "seven plus seven" committee, was formed to respond to that need. Its role could have been performed by the TNC, but to move matters into a formal body might well have prejudiced the informal nature of the negotiations. The key to these negotiations was that they could be kept informal until substantial agreement was reached.

The second element necessary to informal negotiations, and also to request-and-offer negotiations, is that the secretariat must play an active and central role. In request-and-offer negotiations its "clearinghouse" role is crucial because it ensures "transparency," but in the informal negotiations of the Tokyo Round as well the secretariat was actively involved in monitoring negotiations, seeking to move them forward, and circulating the positions of states under its own name to preserve anonymity. Such a role demands a degree of confidence in the secretariat which has developed in GATT but may not be present in other international organizations.

It has already been pointed out that the techniques and procedures developed in negotiations of GATT must be considered in the light of its unique nature as an institution. This applies both to the origins and to the structure of the institution and to the questions that the GATT contracting parties address. Though it is concerned with the development of a global international regime for international trade, the approach of the contracting parties to trade questions is not based on a "grand design." The negotiating rounds are concerned with pragmatic issues of commercial policy between individual states. Traditionally, the question has been whether a particular tariff in one state ought to apply to a particular good from another state. This type of issue is specific and amenable to negotiation and contrasts with the issues faced by many international lawmaking forums that attempt to resolve general questions of the jurisdiction or authority of states. This reduction of issues to particular questions that can be easily managed may well be one of the reasons for the relative success of GATT as an international negotiating forum.

THE STRAIT OF TIRAN, THE GULF OF AQABA, AND THE 1979 TREATY OF PEACE BETWEEN EGYPT AND ISRAEL

*By Ruth Lapidoth**

The July 1982 issue of this *Journal* (pp. 532–54) published an article written by Professor Mohamed ElBaradei, *The Egyptian-Israeli Peace Treaty and Access to the Gulf of Aqaba: A New Legal Regime*, in which he gives a contextual interpretation and evaluation of the regime laid down by Article V(2) of the Treaty of Peace. Article V(2) reads:

> The Parties consider the Strait of Tiran and the Gulf of Aqaba to be international waterways open to all nations for unimpeded and non-suspendable freedom of navigation and overflight. The Parties will respect each other's right to navigation and overflight for access to either country through the Strait of Tiran and the Gulf of Aqaba.[1]

A study of the historical development of customary and treaty law relevant to "inland seas" (*i.e.*, bays) and to straits at their entrance leads ElBaradei to the conclusion that, while certain inland seas surrounded by one state are included in that state's internal waters, the regime of bays bordered by several states is uncertain. As to straits leading to such inland seas enclosed by more than one state, their regime was dealt with by Article 16(4) of the 1958 Geneva Convention on the Territorial Sea and the Contiguous Zone, which foresaw nonsuspendable innocent passage for such straits as well, *i.e.*, straits "used for international navigation between one part of the high seas and . . . the territorial sea of a foreign State." But in ElBaradei's opinion, this provision was an innovation of the Convention and hence not binding upon states that have not become parties to it (in particular, the Arab states). Moreover, he considers that this regime applied only to the strait leading to the inland sea, and not to passage through the inland sea itself (*i.e.*, the Gulf of Aqaba).

In his analysis of the provision on freedom of navigation included in Security Council Resolution 242, ElBaradei expresses the opinion that the term "freedom of navigation" should be understood as a reference to the general, underlying principle, and should not be interpreted as indicating the applicability of the high seas freedom of navigation.

ElBaradei further believes that under the new 1982 Convention on the Law of the Sea, straits leading to inland seas surrounded by several states are subject to nonsuspendable innocent passage, while rights of navigation in the

* Professor of Public International Law, The Hebrew University, Jerusalem. This article was completed while the author was David Ben Gurion Visiting Professor of Law at the Law Center, University of Southern California. It is partly based on research done for her book on *The Red Sea and the Gulf of Aden*, published in 1982 in the series International Straits of the World (General Editor, Prof. Gerard J. Mangone).

[1] Treaty of Peace, Egypt-Israel, Mar. 26, 1979, *reprinted in* 18 ILM 362, 365 (1979).

inland seas themselves are not dealt with, although the Convention does contain certain provisions dealing with other aspects of such seas (*i.e.*, enclosed and semi-enclosed seas).

He welcomes the application to the Gulf of Aqaba of the regime foreseen by the Peace Treaty for the Strait of Tiran and expresses the opinion that this provision may contribute towards the affirmation of a right of nonsuspendable and unimpeded right of passage between all the coastal states of inland seas and the high seas. Since the regime of the Peace Treaty does not automatically apply to third states, such as Jordan and Saudi Arabia (the other coastal states of the Gulf of Aqaba), for them the Strait and the Gulf will continue to be regulated by the general law as outlined above.

ElBaradei considers that the "freedom of navigation" foreseen by the Peace Treaty should be a regime analogous to unimpeded transit passage and not to freedom of navigation as it applies to the high seas, and he recommends that Egypt and Israel supplement the Peace Treaty provisions with a detailed regulation of the rights and duties of ships and aircraft in the Strait and in the Gulf.

ElBaradei's learned analysis will certainly contribute to a better understanding of the general law and the special provisions of the Peace Treaty. However, as outlined in the following pages, the present author has reached somewhat different conclusions with regard to both the general law on straits and bays surrounded by several states and the interpretation of the Peace Treaty. This author also intends to examine some other relevant matters with which ElBaradei did not deal in detail, *e.g.*, the relation between the Peace Treaty provision and the 1982 Convention on the Law of the Sea,[2] the limitation of forces foreseen by the Peace Treaty, the question of ensuring implementation, and the U.S. commitments.

I. The Regime of Bays and the Gulf of Aqaba

International law distinguishes among three categories of bays (or gulfs): those enclosed by the territory of a single state, those that wash the shores of several states, and historic bays.[3] Only the rules concerning the first category were codified by the 1958 Geneva Convention on the Territorial Sea and the Contiguous Zone: a bay for the purposes of international law is a well-marked indentation, *i.e.*, the indented area is as large as, or larger than, that of the semi-circle whose diameter is a line drawn across the mouth of the indentation. If the distance between the low-water marks of the natural entrance points does not exceed 24 miles, a closing line may be drawn between the low-water marks, and the waters thus enclosed are considered as internal waters. If the breadth of the natural entrance exceeds 24 miles, a straight baseline of 24

[2] As this article goes to press, the final text of the Convention is not yet available to the author. Reference will be made to the last available draft, Working Paper 1 of the Drafting Committee, dated June 7, 1982, No. 82-16124. The Convention will be cited hereinafter as the 1982 Convention on the Law of the Sea.

[3] On bays, see mainly L. Bouchez, The Regime of Bays in International Law (1964); and M. Strohl, The International Law of Bays (1963).

miles may be drawn within the bay so as to enclose as much water area as possible with a line of that length.[4]

Some authors, *e.g.*, Professors L. J. Bouchez and ElBaradei, have distinguished between bays on the one hand, and "inland seas connected with the high seas by means of a strait" on the other. In their opinion, "[f]rom the geographical point of view, the difference between bays and inland seas . . . is that the bay itself is directly connected with the high seas, while between the inland sea and the high seas a strait or arm of the sea is situated."[5] From the legal point of view, however, there is no difference between these two categories of sea space, and Bouchez has dealt with many "inland seas" in the context of the regime of bays. The present writer prefers to use the term "bay" since the expression "inland sea" may easily be confounded with internal waters or internal seas.

No specific rule on territorial sovereignty over bays within the littoral of two or more states is included either in the 1958 Convention or in the 1982 text. Opinions among authors on this subject are divided, a minority considering that the coastal states may, by common agreement among all of them, acquire sovereignty over such waters, either *pro diviso* or *pro indiviso*, and hence that the territorial sea should be measured from straight baselines;[6] while the majority reject the appropriation of the bay by the surrounding states.[7] Consequently, Bouchez has concluded that "a strong tendency has manifested itself according to which the territorial sea is to be measured from low-water mark in the case of bays enclosed by more than one State."[8] This rule is based on the need to ensure freedom of access to the high seas for those coastal states not situated at the entrance to the bay.[9] In the words of Eric Suy:

> Un tel système [of closing the bay by a straight baseline] n'est pas approprié aux baies dont plusieurs Etats sont riverains puisque l'Etat se trouvant au fond de la baie a le droit de libre navigation sur la haute mer, droit qu'il peut faire valoir contre l'Etat qui domine l'entrée de la baie. Le droit de libre navigation présuppose pour chaque Etat riverain le droit selon lequel les voies d'accès naturels à la haute mer doivent rester ouvertes.[10]

[4] Art. 7 of the 1958 Convention on the Territorial Sea and the Contiguous Zone, 15 UST 1606, TIAS No. 5639, 516 UNTS 205 [hereinafter cited as the 1958 Convention on the Territorial Sea]; Art. 10 of the 1982 Convention on the Law of the Sea.

[5] L. BOUCHEZ, note 3 *supra*, at 20, *quoted in* ElBaradei, *The Egyptian-Israeli Peace Treaty and Access to the Gulf of Aqaba: A New Legal Regime*, 76 AJIL 532, 534 (1982).

[6] *See* references in L. BOUCHEZ, note 3 *supra*, at 172 n.159. To this list may be added 3 J. VERZIJL, INTERNATIONAL LAW IN HISTORICAL PERSPECTIVE 294, 592 (1970).

[7] *See* references in L. BOUCHEZ, note 3 *supra*, at 171 nn.157 and 158. To this list should be added 4 C. ROUSSEAU, DROIT INTERNATIONAL PUBLIC 395, 397 (1980); Gross, *The Geneva Conference on the Law of the Sea and the Right of Innocent Passage through the Gulf of Aqaba*, 53 AJIL 564, 576 (1959).

[8] L. BOUCHEZ, note 3 *supra*, at 173.

[9] 3 G. GIDEL, LE DROIT INTERNATIONAL PUBLIC DE LA MER 595–96 (1934); C. ROUSSEAU, note 7 *supra*, at 395.

[10] Suy, *Les Golfes et les baies en droit international public*, 54 DIE FRIEDENSWARTE 101, 112 (1957/58).

Bouchez has concluded that "if, as formulated in Article 3 of the Convention on the High Seas, land-locked nations are entitled to free communication with the sea, then *a fortiori* States which are situated at the sea must have such a right."[11] He is therefore of the opinion that a right of nonsuspendable innocent passage applies not only to straits by virtue of Article 16(4) of the Territorial Sea Convention (see *infra* p. 91), but also to a bay surrounded by several states: "If it is not permitted to suspend the right of passage in the case of straits, it is *a fortiori* prohibited to suspend that right in the case of bays."[12]

Historic bays are "waters over which the coastal State, contrary to the generally applicable rules of international law, clearly, effectively and continuously, and over a substantial period of time, exercises sovereign rights with the acquiescence of the community of States."[13] Historic bays are under the sovereignty of the coastal state, although they do not fulfill the geographical criteria applicable to ordinary bays. It is not quite clear whether or when historic bays are part of the territorial sea or of internal waters.[14]

Several authors have maintained that a historic title may be acquired not only over bays within the littoral of one state, but also over a bay enclosed by the territory of two or more states,[15] as was demonstrated by the judgment of the Central American Court of Justice in the case of the Gulf of Fonseca, which is enclosed by Nicaragua, El Salvador, and Honduras.[16] However, the weight of the case as a precedent on this special issue is somewhat limited because the Court stated that "the parties are agreed that the Gulf is a closed sea."[17] In other words, the closed sea status of the gulf was not in dispute, but the parties disagreed over the consequences of this status: Nicaragua maintained that the waters should be divided among the littoral states, whereas El Salvador regarded them as belonging to all of them in co-ownership.[18] Moreover, as ElBaradei pointed out, the Court considered that a right of innocent passage applied in the bay.[19]

All bays are subject to two important general rules: according to the 1958 Convention on the Territorial Sea and the Contiguous Zone, "the system of straight baselines may not be applied by a State in such a manner as to cut off from the high seas the territorial sea of another State."[20] This rule, when applied to bays enclosed by several states, whether historic or not, prevents the

[11] L. Bouchez, note 3 *supra*, at 179. [12] *Id.* at 181.

[13] *Id.* at 281. *See also* Y. Blum, Historic Titles in International Law (1965). For a different theory on historic waters, see Hashem, *Rationale of the Theory of Historic Bays with Special Reference to the International Status of the Gulf of Aqaba*, 25 Rev. Egyptienne Droit Int'l 1 (1969).

[14] *See* Historic Bays, Memorandum by the Secretariat of the United Nations, UN Doc. A/CONF.13/1 (1957), in 1 [First] United Nations Conference on the Law of the Sea, Official Records 21–28, paras. 94–136; Y. Blum, note 13 *supra*, at 296 *et seq.*; Malek, *La Théorie dite des baies historiques*, 1957 Rev. Droit Int'l pour le Moyen-Orient 129.

[15] *E.g.*, L. Bouchez, note 3 *supra*, at 199; Hashem, note 13 *supra*.

[16] English translation in 11 AJIL 674 (1917).

[17] *Id.* at 693. [18] *Id.* at 693–94 and 709–11.

[19] ElBaradei, note 5 *supra*, at 538.

[20] Art. 4(5) of the 1958 Convention on the Territorial Sea; Art. 7(6) of the 1982 Convention on the Law of the Sea.

closing of the bay as internal waters in those cases where not all of the coastal states are also littoral states at the entrance to the bay. In addition, it was laid down that "where the establishment of a straight baseline . . . has the effect of enclosing as internal waters areas which previously had been considered as part of the territorial sea or of the high seas, a right of innocent passage . . . shall exist in those waters."[21] These two rules were enunciated in the context of the general straight baseline system, but they should also be applicable to bays, for the delimitation of bays may be regarded as a specific application of the straight baseline system.

The 1982 Convention on the Law of the Sea does not introduce any considerable changes into the regime of bays. However, it does introduce the notion of "enclosed or semi-enclosed seas," which also includes bays within the littoral of two or more states (Articles 122 and 123). There is no mention of any right to close semi-enclosed seas as internal waters.[22] Moreover, several delegations have stressed the need to guarantee freedom of navigation in such seas.[23] This idea was also included in a formal amendment presented at the 11th and final session of the Conference on the Law of the Sea,[24] but as happened to most amendments presented at that session, its sponsor responded to an appeal by the President of the conference and renounced pressing it to a vote.[25]

In conclusion, two categories of bays may be subjected to the complete sovereignty of the littoral state: (1) bays indenting a single state and that fulfill certain geographical conditions; and (2) historic bays. In these situations the territorial sea is measured beyond those bays. However, a state may not apply the straight baseline system in such a manner as to cut off from the high seas the territorial sea of another state, and in waters that have been transformed from high seas or territorial sea into internal waters by virtue of that same system, a right of innocent passage shall prevail. Bays that are surrounded by several states and not subject to a historic title may not be considered as internal waters, particularly if not all of the littoral states have a coast at the entrance. Thus, the present writer cannot agree with ElBaradei that the regime of bays surrounded by several states is uncertain.[26] Moreover, to the extent that there is disagreement among writers on the subject of such bays, it concerns the question whether the littoral states may, by agreement among all of them, determine their general status, but all agree that a right of access to the high seas must prevail.

Until the conclusion of the Egypt-Israel Treaty of Peace in 1979, the Gulf of Aqaba was subject to the rules of general international law applicable to bays bordered by several states, not all of which are situated at the entrance.

[21] Art. 5(2) of the 1958 Convention; Art. 8(2) of the 1982 Convention.

[22] *See* ElBaradei, note 5 *supra*, at 548.

[23] *See, e.g.*, the statement by the delegates from Thailand, 2 THIRD UNITED NATIONS CONFERENCE ON THE LAW OF THE SEA, OFFICIAL RECORDS 275 (1975); Iran, at 273; German Democratic Republic, at 276; and Israel, at 274.

[24] UN Doc. A/CONF.62/L.110 (1982).

[25] UN Press Release No. SEA/494, Apr. 30, 1982, at 9.

[26] ElBaradei, note 5 *supra*, at 544 and 553; *but see* p. 549.

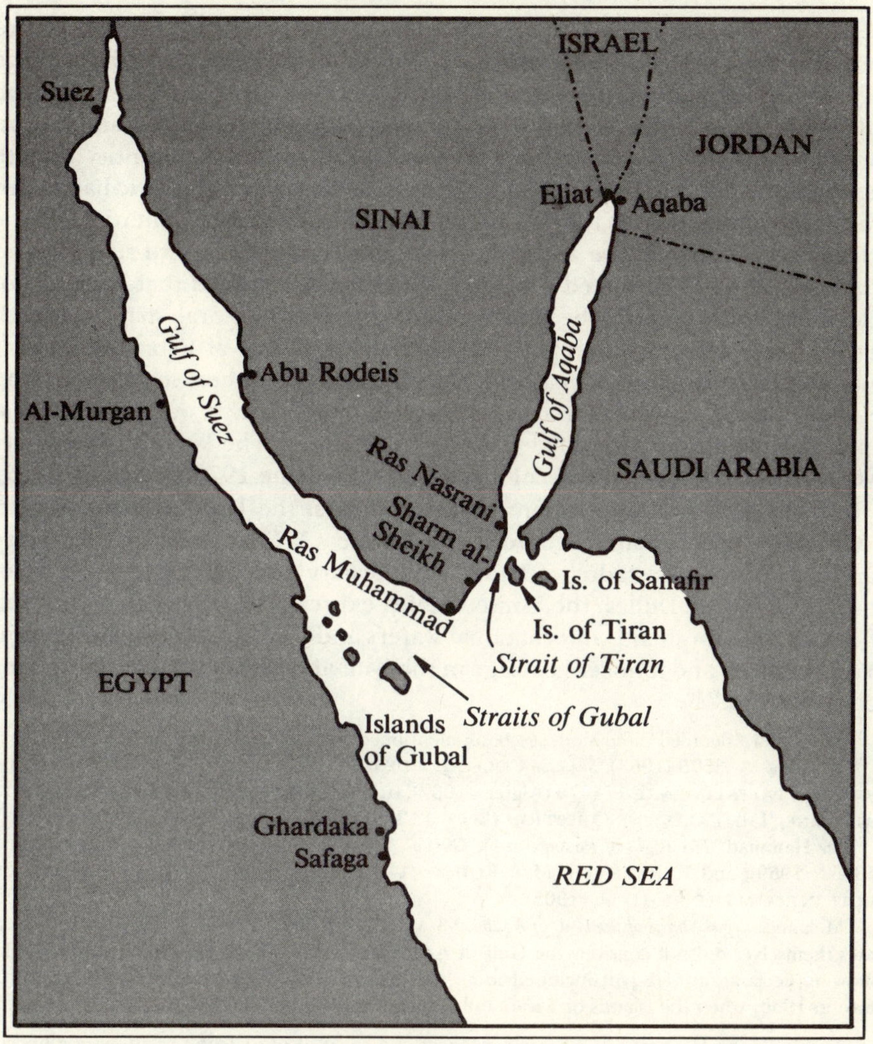

MAP 1
THE GULF OF AQABA AND THE STRAIT OF TIRAN

This meant that according to the majority of authorities, most of the waters of the Gulf were part of the territorial sea of the littoral states subject to the regime of innocent passage, and probably even to nonsuspendable innocent passage, like the Strait at its entrance. Even in the opinion of those writers who would permit the inclusion of such gulfs in the internal waters of the littoral states, such inclusion would depend on the agreement of all the coastal states, which did not exist in the case of the Gulf of Aqaba, and freedom of access for all would have to be respected.

In connection with the dispute over Israel's right to sail in the Gulf of Aqaba and through its entrance, several jurists, mostly Arab, have raised questions about the legal status of the Gulf and the rights of the littoral states.

ElBaradei only mentioned those questions, and they will be discussed here very cursorily.[27] (1) The Government of Saudi Arabia has argued that despite the number of states by which it is bordered, the Gulf is a "closed Arab gulf."[28] But the Gulf is surrounded by four independent states, and Egypt, Jordan, and Saudi Arabia cannot be considered as one legal entity despite their cultural affinity. (2) The Gulf of Aqaba is said to be a historic bay.[29] But it appears that neither of the two conditions for the establishment of a historic title are fulfilled (effective and continued control by the littoral states,[30] and acquiescence by the affected states).[31] (3) It has been argued that Israel is not a legitimate coastal state because Israel occupied its littoral strip in March 1949, after the conclusion of the Egypt-Israel armistice of February 1949.[32] But this armistice did not deal with the Eilat area;[33] rather, it was left to be settled by the Israel-Jordan armistice agreement,[34] which was concluded in April 1949 and which clearly left the area to Israel. The latter's sovereignty over the Eilat area was also recognized by Egypt in the 1979 Treaty of Peace.

In several official declarations and documents, the United States has described the Gulf of Aqaba as "international waters." Thus, in an aide-mémoire handed to the Ambassador of Israel on February 11, 1957, by Secretary of State John Foster Dulles, the United States expressed its belief that the Gulf of Aqaba "comprehends international waters and that no nation has the right to prevent free and innocent passage in the Gulf and through the Straits giving access thereto."[35]

[27] For a more detailed discussion, see book mentioned in note * *supra*, at pp. 121–24.

[28] UN Doc. A/3575 (1957). *See also* COLLOQUE DE JURISTES ARABES SUR LA PALESTINE, LA QUESTION PALESTINIENNE 174–76 (Algiers, 1967), translated as SEMINAR OF ARAB JURISTS ON PALESTINE, THE PALESTINE QUESTION (Beirut, 1968).

[29] *See* Hammad, *The Right of Passage in the Gulf of Aqaba*, 15 REV. EGYPTIENNE DROIT INT'L 118–51 (1959); and E. RABBATH, MER ROUGE ET GOLFE D'AQABA DANS L'ÉVOLUTION DU DROIT INTERNATIONAL 41–55 (1965).

[30] Melamid, *Legal Status of the Gulf of Aqaba*, 53 AJIL 412 (1959). Indeed, in the past the littoral states themselves did not consider the Gulf of Aqaba as historic waters, as demonstrated by the following declaration of Egypt included in an aide-mémoire presented to the U.S. Embassy in Cairo in 1950, when the islands of Tiran and Sanafir came under Egyptian control:

> [T]his occupation being in no way conceived in a spirit of obstructing in any way innocent passage through the stretch of water separating these two islands from the Egyptian coast of Sinai, it follows that this passage, the only practicable one, will remain free as in the past, in conformity with international practices and recognized principles of the law of nations.

Quoted in 9 UN SCOR (659th mtg.), para. 103 (1954). The declaration was originally given in French.

[31] *See* statements by the United States, France, Costa Rica, the United Kingdom, Italy, the Netherlands, New Zealand, Australia, Belgium, Canada, Norway, Sweden, Denmark, and Iceland before the General Assembly, 11 UN GAOR (666th, 667th, and 668th mtgs.) at 1275 *et seq.*, UN Docs. A/PV.666–68 (1957).

[32] *See* COLLOQUE DE JURISTES ARABES, note 28 *supra*, at 170–74; and Hammad, note 29 *supra*, at 140–51.

[33] *See* Art. 7 of the Egyptian-Israeli General Armistice Agreement of Feb. 24, 1949, UN Doc. S/1264/Rev.1, 42 UNTS 252.

[34] *See* Hashemite Kingdom of Jordan-Israel General Armistice Agreement, Apr. 3, 1949, UN Doc. S/1302/Rev.1, Ann. I, Map I, pt. 2, 42 UNTS 304 (map not reproduced in UNTS).

[35] 36 DEP'T STATE BULL. 392–93 (1957). This passage was also cited by Henry Cabot Lodge, U.S. representative to the General Assembly, on March 1, 1957, 11 UN GAOR (666th mtg.) at

The term "international waters" has no specific legal meaning, but probably the authors of the statements intended to express the idea that these sea spaces must be open to international navigation, no matter what their specific legal status.[36] The same expression was used again in 1975 in a Memorandum of Agreement between the United States and Israel.[37] Article 14 dealt with passage through international straits in general and through the straits of Bab el Mandeb and Gibraltar in particular. This text invoked "the principle of freedom of navigation on the high seas and free and unimpeded passage through and over straits connecting international waters."[38] Again it would seem that the authors envisaged sea spaces in which a right of passage should apply, whatever their legal status might be for other purposes.

Finally, the notion of semi-enclosed seas must be recalled. The Gulf of Aqaba apparently falls within the definition of such sea spaces, and hence the 1982 Convention on the Law of the Sea recommends that the littoral states cooperate in matters of conservation and exploitation of resources and in scientific research.

II. The Regime of Straits and the Strait of Tiran

Unlike bays enclosed by several states, straits in recent decades have been the subject of extensive scholarly research[39] and of diplomatic negotiations at the First (1958) and Third (1973–1982) Conferences on the Law of the Sea. In the wake of their crytallization and application by the International Court of Justice in the *Corfu Channel* case (1949),[40] the general rules of international law on straits were codified by Article 16(4) of the 1958 Geneva Convention on the Territorial Sea and the Contiguous Zone: "There shall be no suspension of the innocent passage of foreign ships through straits which are used for international navigation between one part of the high seas and another part of the high seas or the territorial sea of a foreign state." This

---

1277–78, and in a statement delivered to the Heads of Mission of the Arab states in Washington on June 27, 1957. *See* 3 The Arab-Israeli Conflict 668 (J. N. Moore ed. 1974). *See also* 4 M. Whiteman, Digest of International Law 465–80 (1965). President Dwight D. Eisenhower again referred to this statement in an address on Feb. 20, 1957, when he said that the Gulf of Aqaba constituted international waters and no nation had the right to prevent free and innocent passage in the Gulf. He added, "the United States was prepared to exercise this right itself and to join with others to secure general recognition of this right." 36 Dep't State Bull. 387–91 (1957). For additional statements to this effect, see Gross, note 7 *supra*, at 576 n.52. For declarations by other states on the right of passage, see references in note 31 *supra*.

[36] J. Verzijl, note 6 *supra*, at 602.

[37] 14 ILM 1468 (1975).

[38] This provision was not terminated by the new 1979 Memorandum of Agreement between the United States and Israel. *See* Art. 8 of the 1979 text, 18 ILM 537 (1979).

[39] *See, e.g.*, E. Brüel, International Straits: A Treatise on International Law, 2 vols. (1947); R. Lapidoth, Les Détroits en droit international (1972); W. Butler, Northeast Arctic Passage (1978); M. Leifer, Malacca, Singapore and Indonesia (1978); R. Ramazani, The Persian Gulf and the Strait of Hormuz (1979); S. Truver, The Strait of Gibraltar and the Mediterranean (1980); S. Alexandersson, The Baltic Straits (1982) (the last six volumes were published in the series International Straits of the World under the general direction of G. Mangone).

[40] Corfu Channel case (United Kingdom v. Albania), 1949 ICJ Rep. 4 (Judgment of Apr. 9).

text deals with two questions: what categories of waterway qualify as international straits to which the straits regime applies, and what is that regime?

The definition of straits, according to the Convention, is based upon two elements: their geographical situation, and their function. From the geographical point of view there are two groups of passages that are "legal" straits: (1) those that link two parts of the high seas, and (2) those that communicate between one part of the high seas and the territorial sea of a foreign state. Opinions have differed over whether the latter group is subject to the international straits regime only by virtue of the Convention, or also under customary law. ElBaradei seems to accept the view that this half of the definition "was not part of customary international law and could only be binding upon ratification,"[41] while Professor Leo Gross has stated that "the debates at the Conference would seem to give substance to the view that the rule was part of international law."[42] The second point of view is supported by the fact that these straits in fact lead to bays bordered by several states—a category of straits in which the right of passage has long been recognized by customary law.[43] Thus, Gilbert Gidel wrote:

> [L]a situation paraît comparable, à la grandeur près des espaces dont il s'agit, à celle d'une mer qui ne communique avec le reste des mers que par une entrée extrêmement resserrée, dont l'une et l'autre rive sont placées sous la souveraineté du même Etat. . . . A partir du moment où plusieurs riverains se partagent les côtes de cette mer, celui qui détient l'entrée a, en vertu du droit international, et à moins de l'institution de régimes conventionnels spéciaux, l'obligation de laisser les Etats tiers passer par cette entrée. Il paraît devoir en être de même dans le cas d'une baie.[44]

The second element of the definition of straits under Article 16(4) of the 1958 Convention concerns their use: they have to be "used for international navigation." This condition would exclude from the straits regime those passages that have not been used for navigation, as well as those that have only served national coastal navigation. ElBaradei, when dealing with a somewhat similar term—international waterways—defined international navigation as "between two states other than the coastal state, in contradistinction to [navigation in] waterways used exclusively for local navigation and leading to internal waters of the coastal state."[45] This definition of international navigation is too narrow and this writer believes that the term also includes navigation between the coastal state and a foreign state.[46]

[41] ElBaradei, note 5 *supra*, at 545. *See also* Djamchid, *Du droit de passage dans le détroit de Tiran*, 30 REV. EGYPTIENNE DROIT INT'L 28 (1974); Murti, *The Legal Status of the Gulf of Aqaba*, 7 INDIAN J. INT'L L. 203 (1967); and A. EL-HAKIM, THE MIDDLE EASTERN STATES AND THE LAW OF THE SEA 155–61 (1979).

[42] Gross, note 7 *supra*, at 594. *See also* P. MARTIN, LE CONFLIT ISRAÉLO-ARABE, RECHERCHES SUR L'EMPLOI DE LA FORCE EN DROIT INTERNATIONAL PUBLIC POSITIF 110 (1973).

[43] Gross, note 7 *supra*, at 594.

[44] G. GIDEL, note 9 *supra*, at 603.

[45] ElBaradei, note 5 *supra*, at 546.

[46] In this respect an analogy with the term "international flights" may be interesting.

It is difficult to establish a criterion for the frequency of use required in order that the passage may be considered as "used" for international shipping.[47] Moreover, it is not easy to get precise and reliable information on the movement of ships through straits.[48] In the *Corfu Channel* case, the International Court declared that passage need not be necessary or indispensable for international navigation for a strait to qualify as an "international strait."[49]

Straits included in the territorial sea of the states bordering them are subject to a regime of reinforced innocent passage.[50] First, while the coastal state may temporarily suspend innocent passage in its ordinary territorial sea, it may not do so in international straits, as laid down by Article 16(4). Second, whereas the right of innocent passage by warships in the ordinary territorial sea is controversial,[51] it is a well-established right for international straits, as demonstrated by the *Corfu Channel* case.[52] Third, while there may be differing views on the criterion that determines whether the passage in the territorial sea is innocent or not, it is certain that with regard to passage through straits only the behavior of the ship at the time of passage (*i.e.*, an objective test) is determining. This conclusion, too, is based on the *Corfu Channel* Judgment where the Court recognized as innocent the passage of British men-of-war, though the passage had a political aim and was accompanied by a manifestation of power.[53]

The reinforced right of nonsuspendable innocent passage prevails also in an intermediary state between war and peace, which according to some authors can exist not only de facto but also legally.[54] In the *Corfu Channel* case, the Court noted the very strained relations between Albania and Greece and

[47] *See, e.g.*, R. BAXTER & J. TRISKA, THE LAW OF INTERNATIONAL WATERWAYS WITH PARTICULAR REGARD TO INTEROCEANIC CANALS 9 (1964): and M. MCDOUGAL & W. BURKE, THE PUBLIC ORDER OF THE OCEANS—A CONTEMPORARY INTERNATIONAL LAW OF THE SEA 212 (1962); Pharand, *International Straits*, in THESAURUS ACROASIUM, VOL. VII: THE LAW OF THE SEA 64, 67–71 (Thessaloniki 1977).

[48] *See* Hodgson & McIntyre, *Maritime Commerce in Selected Areas of High Concentration*, in HAZARDS OF MARITIME TRANSIT 1, 3 (T. Clingan & L. Alexander eds. 1973).

[49] 1949 ICJ REP. at 28.

[50] On innocent passage, see Arts. 14–23 of the 1958 Convention on the Territorial Sea, and Arts. 17–32 of the 1982 Convention on the Law of the Sea. *See also* G. GIDEL, note 9 *supra*, at 193–291; 4 M. WHITEMAN, note 35 *supra*, at 343–80; Slonim, *The Right of Innocent Passage and the 1958 Geneva Conference on the Law of the Sea*, 5 COLUM. J. TRANSNAT'L L. 96 (1966).

[51] In April 1982, two amendments were submitted to the Law of the Sea Conference in order to authorize states to limit the right of innocent passage of warships in their territorial sea: UN Docs. A/CONF.62/L.97 (1982), and A/CONF.62/L.117 (1982). In response to appeals by the President of the conference, Mr. Koh, the amendments were not pressed to the vote, but he read out a statement saying that the sponsors' agreement to renounce the vote was "without prejudice to the right of coastal States to safeguard their security interests in accordance with articles 19 and 25 of the Convention." *See* UN Press Release No. SEA/494, Apr. 30, 1982, at 37.

[52] 1949 ICJ REP. at 28. It has been maintained, however, that the passage of warships in straits may be subjected to stricter regulations than the passage of merchant ships. *See* Note, *Peacetime Passage by Warships Through Territorial Straits*, 50 COLUM. L. REV. 220 (1950).

[53] On this point, see Sir Gerald Fitzmaurice, *The Law and Procedure of the International Court of Justice: General Principles and Substantive Law*, 27 BRIT. Y.B. INT'L L. 1, 28–29 (1950).

[54] G. SCHWARZENBERGER, *The Law of Armed Conflict*, in 2 INTERNATIONAL LAW AS APPLIED BY INTERNATIONAL COURTS AND TRIBUNALS 40 (1968); Jessup, *Should International Law Recognize an Intermediate Status Between Peace and War?*, 48 AJIL 98 (1954).

found that "Albania, in view of these exceptional circumstances, would have been justified in issuing regulations in respect of the passage of warships through the Strait, but not in prohibiting such passage or in subjecting it to the requirement of special authorization."[55]

In summary, it seems to follow from state practice, case law, and the 1958 Convention on the Territorial Sea with regard to international straits, that freedom of navigation applies without restriction to the high seas spaces that may be encompassed in the strait, and that in areas of territorial sea the regime of nonsuspendable innocent passage applies. However, in three respects the right of innocent passage in straits has apparently been greater than in the territorial sea: the test of "innocence" has depended upon objective criteria or ship behavior; the right of such passage has been applied to both merchant vessels and warships; and suspension of this right has been denied both in time of peace and in times of "cold war." During an actual war the right of innocent passage in international straits may be restricted.

Until the conclusion of the 1979 Treaty of Peace between Egypt and Israel, the Strait of Tiran was subject to the general rules on straits. It qualifies for the regime of international straits since it fulfills the two conditions analyzed above. (1) Until an extension of the territorial sea to at least 7½ miles is generally recognized and opposable to other states, the Gulf of Aqaba contains some small areas of high seas, and hence the Strait of Tiran links the high seas of the Red Sea to those pockets of high seas in the Gulf of Aqaba, in accordance with the first-mentioned alternative of the geographical element of international straits. When a 12-mile territorial sea is generally accepted, the Gulf of Aqaba will be entirely included in the territorial seas of the littoral states, but the Strait of Tiran will still be an international strait because it conforms to the second alternative of the geographical criterion, namely, it connects the high seas of the Red Sea to the territorial sea of states that do not border the strait, Israel and Jordan. (2) The Strait of Tiran is considerably used for international navigation by vessels going to and from the ports of Aqaba and Eilat.[56]

Several arguments have been raised against the applicability of nonsuspendable innocent passage to ships going through the Strait to Eilat. ElBaradei has maintained[57] that the application of this regime to straits linking high seas to the territorial sea of a foreign state does not concern the Arab states who have refrained from becoming a party to the 1958 Convention, since this rule is allegedly an innovation of the Convention and therefore binding only upon the parties to it. As has been shown above, this is apparently an erroneous assumption. Other arguments against passage through Tiran have already been discussed in the context of the rules applicable to the Gulf of Aqaba, namely, the claim that the Strait of Tiran leads to internal waters, or to a historic bay, and that Israel may not enjoy rights of a littoral state of the Gulf.

[55] 1949 ICJ REP. at 29.

[56] For a different opinion, see A. EL-HAKIM, note 41 *supra*, at 162–66 and 167.

[57] ElBaradei, note 5 *supra*, at 545. *See also* the authors referred to in note 41 *supra*.

Another argument raised in the context of this controversy and mentioned by ElBaradei concerns the state of belligerency:[58] it has been maintained that free passage through the Strait must be granted only in time of peace, whereas a state of war existed between the states bordering the Strait and Israel. However, the widely held view is that according to the United Nations Charter, member states may not declare or maintain a state of war with each other, and therefore they cannot validly claim special rights deriving from an alleged belligerency, particularly not after the cessation of active hostilities.[59] Moreover, the right of nonsuspendable innocent passage also prevails in an intermediary state between war and peace, which would exclude any right to close the Strait after the cessation of active hostilities.

It remains to be asked what bearing the 1982 Convention on the Law of the Sea would have on the Strait of Tiran. The new Convention deals with passage through straits independently of the regime of the territorial sea, and it distinguishes among several categories of straits, subject to different regimes.[60] Among these categories, four are of relevance to our discussion. First, there is a "right of transit passage, which shall not be impeded" or suspended for all ships and aircraft in straits that are used for international navigation between two areas of high seas or exclusive economic zones. Transit passage is defined as the exercise of the freedom of navigation and overflight solely for the purpose of continuous and expeditious transit of the strait.[61] The Convention defines the rights and obligations of the transiting vehicle on the one hand, and of the coastal state on the other hand.

Second, a more limited right of nonsuspendable innocent passage would apply to ships (1) in a strait used for international navigation where the strait separates an island of a certain state from its mainland and where a route of similar convenience exists seaward of the island, and (2) in straits between an area of the high seas or an exclusive economic zone and the territorial sea of a foreign state.[62]

These two regimes, unimpeded transit passage and nonsuspendable innocent passage, would differ mainly in three respects: under the second regime the coastal state has a wider power to regulate passage, aircraft enjoy only such rights of passage as apply to the land territory, and submarines must

[58] H. CATTAN, PALESTINE AND INTERNATIONAL LAW: THE LEGAL ASPECTS OF THE ARAB-ISRAELI CONFLICT 174 (2d ed. 1976); Hartwig, *Der israelisch-ägyptische Streit um den Golf van Akaba*, 9 ARCHIV DES VÖLKERRECHTS 42 (1961–62).

[59] R. HIGGINS, DEVELOPMENT OF INTERNATIONAL LAW THROUGH THE POLITICAL ORGANS OF THE UNITED NATIONS 214–15 (1963); Moore, *The Arab-Israeli Conflict and the Obligation to Pursue Peaceful Settlement of International Disputes*, 19 KAN. L. REV. 403, 422–23 (1971); N. FEINBERG, THE LEGALITY OF A 'STATE OF WAR' AFTER THE CESSATION OF HOSTILITIES UNDER THE CHARTER OF THE UNITED NATIONS AND THE COVENANT OF THE LEAGUE OF NATIONS 42 (Jerusalem, 1961).

[60] Among the proliferous literature on the new regime, see in particular Reisman, *The Regime of Straits and National Security: An Appraisal of International Lawmaking*, 74 AJIL 48 (1980); Moore, *The Regime of Straits and the Third United Nations Conference on the Law of the Sea*, *id.* at 77; Burke, *Submerged Passage Through Straits: Interpretations of the Proposed Law of the Sea Treaty Text*, 52 WASH. L. REV. 193 (1977).

[61] Arts. 36–44 of the 1982 Convention on the Law of the Sea.

[62] Art. 45 of the 1982 Convention.

travel on the surface showing their flag; whereas in the case of transit passage, the discretion of the coastal state is more restricted, aircraft have a right of passage, and submarines may navigate submerged.[63]

It is doubtful whether the differentiation between these two categories of straits is fortunate. Until the Caracas session (1974) of the Law of the Sea Conference, the basic accepted principle was that a single legal regime should apply to passage through almost all straits.[64] The distinction was introduced as a compromise;[65] it has no logical justification and may lead to unnecessary complications and misunderstandings.[66]

The third regime mentioned in the 1982 Convention concerns those straits "in which passage is regulated in whole or in part by long-standing international conventions in force specifically relating to such straits" (Article 35(c)). Apparently, the drafters had in mind primarily the Turkish Straits, the Danish Straits, and the Strait of Magellan.[67]

A fourth category of straits are those for which a particular international agreement has laid down different rules that are compatible with the regime foreseen by the 1982 Convention.[68]

It seems that the two last-mentioned categories differ from each other in two respects: on the question of longevity and on the compatibility with the general Convention. A long-standing convention may subsist even if it is not compatible with the regime laid down by the 1982 Convention, while an agreement that is not "long-standing" would survive only if it is compatible with it. For instance, an agreement purporting to restrict the rights of navigation laid down by the general Convention would not be considered as compatible with the latter. The conditions for the validity of the non-long-standing agreement are somewhat different according to whether it is an existing agreement or one that is concluded after the respective parties have joined the 1982 general Convention.[69]

As we shall see later, the Strait of Tiran falls into the fourth category as a result of the 1979 Treaty of Peace. But the question may be asked, what would the regime of the Strait be under the 1982 Convention, without the Peace Treaty? Professor John Norton Moore included the Strait of Tiran among those passages which would be subject to nonsuspendable innocent passage,[70] and Professor ElBaradei apparently assumes the same.[71] However,

[63] Opinions differ somewhat on whether submerged passage has actually been authorized by the Convention. *See* the articles referred to in note 60 *supra*.

[64] *See* the U.S. proposal, submitted to the UN Sea-bed Committee, UN Doc. A/AC.138/SC.II/L.4 (1971). For comments, see Knight, *The 1971 United States Proposals on the Breadth of the Territorial Sea and Passage Through International Straits*, 51 OR. L. REV. 759 (1972). *Compare* the draft submitted by the Soviet Union to the Sea-bed Committee, UN Doc. A/AC.138/SC.II/L.7 (1972), and by the Communist bloc to the Caracas session of the Third Law of the Sea Conference, UN Doc. A/CONF.62/C.2/L.11 (1974), in 3 OFFICIAL RECORDS 189.

[65] United Kingdom draft submitted to the Caracas session, UN Doc. A/CONF.62/C.2/L.3 (1974), 3 OFFICIAL RECORDS 183.

[66] For criticism of this distinction, see Reisman, note 60 *supra*, at 66–67.

[67] *See* Moore, note 60 *supra*, at 111.

[68] Art. 311 of the 1982 Convention on the Law of the Sea.

[69] *Compare* Art. 311(2) *with* 311(3).

[70] Moore, note 60 *supra*, at 112.

[71] *See* ElBaradei, note 5 *supra*, at 550.

the littoral states of the Gulf of Aqaba that do not border the Strait could claim a reinforced right of transit through the Strait on several grounds. For purposes of navigation, a bay enclosed by several states has been assimilated to the open sea:

> *Détroits faisant communiquer deux mers libres.* — On doit considérer comme tels non seulement les détroits qui conduisent à l'océan ou à une mer grand'ouverte, mais aussi ceux qui aboutissent à une mer intérieure dont le littoral appartient à plusieurs souverains car une pareille mer est réputée libre.[72]

If a bay enclosed by the territory of more than one state "est réputée libre," then the strait leading to it is linking the high seas to a sea space that is considered open sea, and hence unimpeded transit passage would apply. Although this legal interpretation applies to all bays and seas surrounded by several states, it seems to be of particular relevance where not all the littoral states of the bay also border the strait, as in the case of the Strait of Tiran.[73]

The application of a strengthened regime of free passage through the Strait of Tiran may also be implied in the classification of the Gulf of Aqaba as "international waters." As mentioned earlier, President Eisenhower and Secretary of State Dulles used this expression in relation to the waters of the Gulf, which implied that they should be open to international navigation, whatever the specific legal status of the waters for other purposes might be.[74] A fortiori the passage from the high seas to these "international waters" should be free.

III. The 1979 Treaty of Peace

The Gulf of Aqaba and the Strait of Tiran have been a central issue in the relations between Egypt and Israel, and therefore it is not surprising that this subject was dealt with extensively in the peace settlement. Our analysis will center on (1) the limitation of forces, (2) the international character of the Gulf and the Strait, (3) the nature of the foreseen rights of navigation and overflight, (4) the question of ensuring implementation, (5) U.S. commitments, and (6) the relation of the regime laid down by the Treaty of Peace to general international law.

The Limitation of Forces

In the wake of the Camp David Framework,[75] the Peace Treaty contains certain security arrangements based on limitation of forces. The Sinai peninsula is divided into three zones (A, B, C), the amount of forces permitted in each of them decreasing from west to east. (See map 2.) In addition, Israel undertook to limit its forces in a zone of the Negev adjacent to and east of

[72] 1 P. Fauchille, Traité de droit international public, pt. 2, "Paix," at 250, para. 506 (1925).

[73] According to L. Bouchez, note 3 *supra*, at 179: "obviously the State which is not situated at the entrance nevertheless is entitled to free communication with the high seas" even if the sovereignty of the littoral states over the waters of the bay should be recognized.

[74] *See* note 36 *supra* and accompanying text. [75] 17 ILM 1470 (1978).

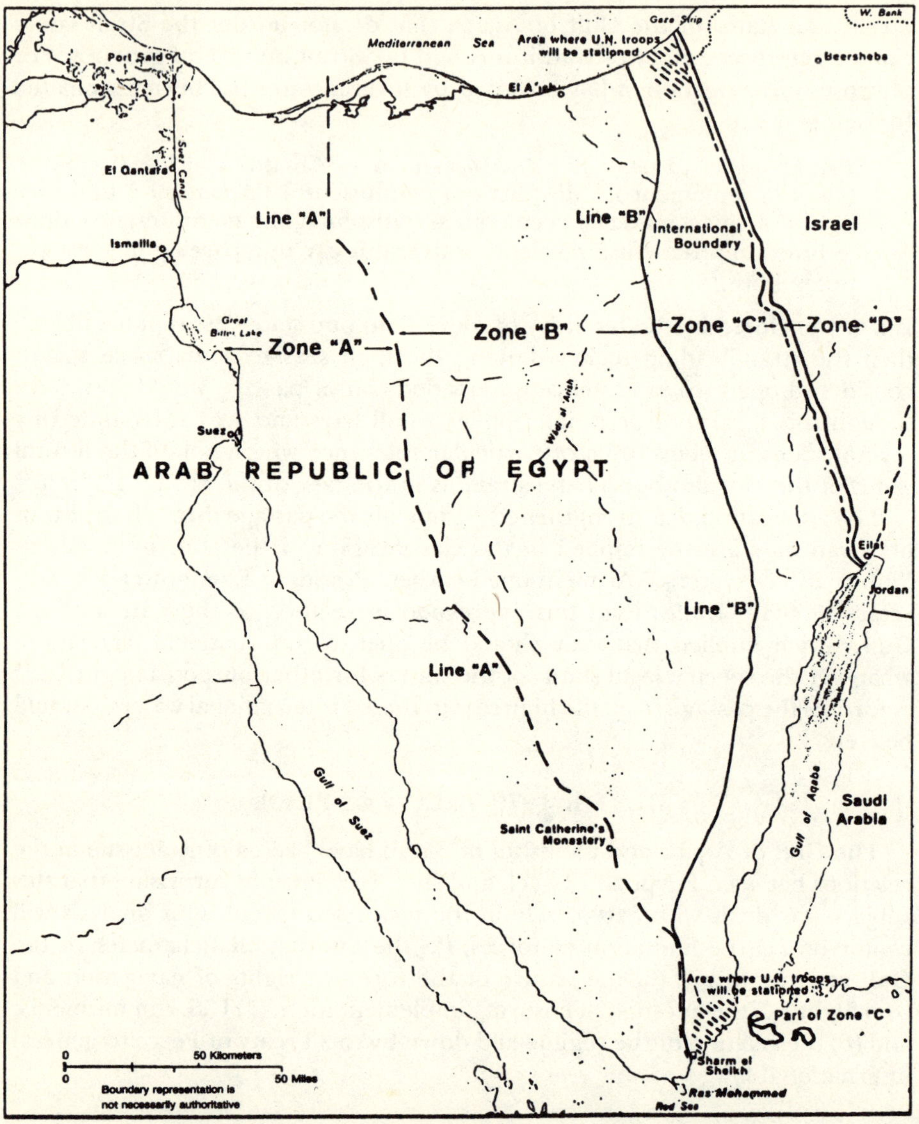

MAP 2

DIVISION OF THE SINAI PENINSULA UNDER THE PEACE TREATY

the international border (Zone D). The Egyptian coast of the Gulf of Aqaba and of the Strait of Tiran, as well as the islands of Tiran and Sanafir, are included in Zone C, *i.e.*, an area where Egyptian forces are limited to civil police armed with light weapons and equipped with unarmed police helicopters and light boats lightly armed.[76] The Multinational Force and Observers (MFO), which are entrusted with the responsibility of supervising the limitation of forces in the zones and ensuring freedom of navigation in the Strait

[76] Arts. II(1)(c), III(4), and IV(3) of Ann. I to the Treaty of Peace, *supra* note 1.

of Tiran, are also stationed in Zone C (for details, see *infra*). A narrow strip—the southern sector of Israel's coast at the northern end of the Gulf—is part of Zone D, in which Israel is limited to four infantry batallions (about 4,000 persons), and their military installations and field fortifications. No tanks, artillery, and anti-aircraft missiles, except individual surface-to-air missiles, are permitted in Zone D. The aerial and naval regime for Israel in Zone D is similar to the one foreseen for Egypt in Zone A, *i.e.*, along the Suez Canal and the Gulf of Suez: flights of combat aircraft and reconnaissance flights of Israel may take place over Zone D, but only unarmed, noncombat aircraft may be stationed there. Israel may operate naval vessels along the coast, but, as in all the "zones," only civilian airfields and civilian maritime ports and installations may be built there.[77] The northern sector of Israel's coast, *i.e.*, the area of the port of Eilat itself, is not subjected to limitation of forces.

Thus, the western coast of the Gulf of Aqaba is subjected to three different sets of rules: along the larger part of the coast, from the south to the north, and on the islands of Tiran and Sanafir, there will be only light Egyptian police forces and multinational forces; in a narrow adjoining strip, in the north, Israeli activity will be restricted; and at the northern tip, no limitation is specified.

The International Character of the Gulf and the Strait

The conclusion of the Treaty of Peace was preceded by the adoption of the 1978 Camp David Framework, which stated that the Strait of Tiran and the Gulf of Aqaba were "international waterways to be open to all nations for unimpeded and nonsuspendable freedom of navigation and overflight." Professor W. Michael Reisman compared this language with the relevant provisions of the negotiating text of the UN Law of the Sea Conference (which in 1982 became the text of the Convention):

> With this sort of formula, tortured, casuistic interpretations are not necessary. Indeed, Camp David is redundant in emphasizing precisely what the ICNT [Informal Composite Negotiating Text] overlooks. The waterways are characterized as "international" and any hint of a territorial competence with regard to passage is repeatedly excluded; there is no "right of transit" characterizable by the coastal state, but instead and only the traditional freedom of navigation, and that right may not be impeded or suspended. Interpreted logically or teleologically, Camp David produces freedom of navigation and, were it necessary, even a right of submerged transit. The ICNT achieves nothing approaching that clarity.[78]

The provisions of the Camp David Framework were later incorporated in and supplemented by the 1979 Treaty of Peace, quoted at the beginning of this study. The second sentence, which deals with the rights of access of the parties, was added by the Treaty, while the first sentence, which grants freedom of navigation to all nations, was already included in the Camp David

[77] *Id.*, Arts. II(1)(d), III(1), (2), and (5), and IV(1) and (5) of Ann. I.

[78] Reisman, note 60 *supra*, at 76.

text. In order to avoid any restrictive interpretation of the first sentence under the impact of the second one, the parties included in the "Agreed Minutes," signed simultaneously with the Treaty of Peace, a provision saying that "[t]he second sentence of paragraph 2 of Article V shall not be construed as limiting the first sentence of that paragraph."[79] It was added, however, that "[t]he foregoing is not to be construed as contravening the second sentence of paragraph 2 of Article V" concerning the parties' obligation to respect each other's right of access.

The text of the article clearly gives a positive answer to the preliminary question whether Tiran is an international strait: the parties consider it to be an "international waterway," and thus any doubt or disagreement over whether it fulfills the conditions of an international strait has been settled. Moreover, the Peace Treaty assimilates the Gulf of Aqaba to the Strait of Tiran in this respect, as well as with regard to the applicable regime of navigation and overflight, which confirms the legal theory described above that the passage through a gulf enclosed by several states, not all of which border on its entrance, should be subject to the regime of straits.[80]

Foreseen Rights of Navigation and Overflight

The Treaty foresees an objective regime ensuring freedom of navigation and overflight to all members of the international community, in line with the principle of equality and nondiscrimination,[81] and it particularly emphasizes the rights of the Treaty parties. As Reisman stated in the above quotation, "there is no 'right of transit' characterizable by the coastal state, but instead and only the traditional freedom of navigation, and that right may not be impeded or suspended." The question of course arises, what does freedom of navigation include? In Professor W. T. Burke's opinion, "the term 'freedom of navigation' in traditional international law refers to vessels on the high seas and authorizes a broad freedom of operation and maneuver, including military activities and practices, as well as freedom to stop or move slowly in a particular area." He sees the term "navigation" as including, *inter alia*, surveillance and inspection, military maneuvers, the testing of equipment, refueling operations, and the placing and retrieving of objects and buoys.[82]

Nevertheless, like other freedoms of the high seas, freedom of navigation "is exercised under the conditions laid down by these articles and by the other rules of international law . . . [and] with reasonable regard to the interests of other States in their exercise of the freedom of the high seas."[83] Those ships and aircraft which will exercise the right of freedom of navigation and overflight granted by the Treaty of Peace will have to take into consideration the configuration of the Gulf of Aqaba and the Strait of Tiran and accordingly limit their activities in these sea spaces.

[79] 18 ILM 392, 392 (1979).

[80] *See* note 12 *supra* and accompanying text.

[81] *See, e.g.*, Arts. 24(1)(b), 25(3), and 42(2) of the 1982 Convention on the Law of the Sea.

[82] Burke, note 60 *supra*, at 201 & n.28.

[83] Art. 2 of the 1958 Convention on the High Seas, 13 UST 2312, TIAS No. 5200, 420 UNTS 82.

These and other considerations led Professor ElBaradei to the conclusion that "the objective of the parties thus seemed to be the establishment of a regime analogous in content to the UNCLOS regime of transit passage," and not freedom of navigation.[84] This conclusion does not seem warranted. He bases his opinion on several facts. Thus, he relies on the assumption of the parties that the waters along the coast of the Gulf of Aqaba continue to be territorial seas, which is implied by Article IV(3) of Annex I to the Peace Treaty.[85] However, there is no contradiction between the notion of territorial sea and freedom of navigation. The latter is an activity, while the former is a legal regime. With the ascent of the functional approach to the law of the sea, it should not be surprising that a function usually linked to the regime of the high seas may by agreement be exercised in a certain area that is part of the territorial sea. An analogous phenomenon may be observed under the 1958 and 1982 Conventions with regard to certain sea spaces that are part of internal waters, yet a right of innocent passage, usually linked to the regime of the territorial sea, applies to them.[86] Moreover, the 1982 Convention has now separated the regime of passage through international straits from the nature and regime of the relevant waters, and it expressly states that the "régime of passage through straits used for international navigation established in this Part shall not in other respects affect the status of the waters forming such straits."[87]

Another point raised by ElBaradei in order to show that the parties to the Treaty intended to establish a regime similar to transit passage rather than freedom of navigation concerns the limitation of naval and aerial activities in the "zones." It should be remembered, however, that the two articles in the Annex that deal with these limitations expressly include the proviso "without prejudice to the provisions of this Treaty";[88] thus, the freedom of navigation and overflight laid down by Article V(2) of the Treaty prevails despite the limitation of forces and of activities in the zones. ElBaradei nevertheless thinks that the provisions on limitation of forces show that the parties were very security-conscious; hence, it would not seem reasonable that they intended to grant to all nations rights involving security risks, which are inherent in several activities included in freedom of navigation. Yet the clear language of Article V, paragraph 2 of the Treaty and the express recognition of the predominance of this provision by the proviso in the articles dealing with limitation of forces seem to indicate that the parties favored freedom of navigation for all nations and therefore did not consider it a security risk. They may have believed that freedom of navigation rather than free passage was needed in order to provide for the security needs of Israel, as demonstrated by the Israeli interception in September 1978 in the Gulf of Aqaba of a ship, the *Argios Dimitrios*, that

[84] ElBaradei, note 5 *supra*, at 551.

[85] "Egyptian civil police equipped with light boats, lightly armed, shall perform normal police functions within the territorial waters of Zone C."

[86] Art. 5(2) of the 1958 Convention on the Territorial Sea; Art. 8(2) of the 1982 Convention on the Law of the Sea.

[87] Art. 34(1) of the 1982 Convention.

[88] Arts. III(6) and IV(6) of Ann. I, Treaty of Peace, *supra* note 1.

was full of explosives and had been sent to Eilat in order to seriously harm the town and its inhabitants. The prevention of such incidents probably necessitates freedom of navigation. Israeli security needs have also to be seen in light of the fact that two of the littoral states of the Gulf of Aqaba, Jordan and Saudi Arabia, still claim to be in a state of war with Israel.

Several facts indicate that the parties actually meant freedom of navigation when they used this expression in the Treaty of Peace. The term appears consistently in all the relevant texts—first, in Security Council Resolution 242 of 1967 to which the Preamble of the Peace Treaty refers. In that resolution, which was adopted unanimously and accepted by both Egypt and Israel, the Security Council affirmed "the necessity (a) for guaranteeing freedom of navigation through international waterways in the area." This text, too, was given a restrictive interpretation by ElBaradei, which does not seem justified.[89] Second, the expression occurred in the relevant provision of the Camp David Framework cited above. Third, it appears in Article V(2) of the Peace Treaty, which states the existence of the "freedom." Fourth, it is found in the provisions of Annex I that deal with implementing that freedom: "With respect to these United Nations forces and observers, as appropriate, the Parties agree to request the following arrangements: . . . d. Ensuring the freedom of navigation through the Strait of Tiran in accordance with Article V of the Treaty of Peace."[90] Fifth, a similar expression was used again in 1981, when the parties agreed on the establishment of the Multinational Force and Observers.[91] The consistent repetition of the term "freedom of navigation" seems to indicate that this is really what the parties had in mind. The same conclusion follows from a comparison of the two paragraphs of Article V of the Treaty of Peace: the first, which deals with the Suez Canal and the Gulf of Suez, speaks of "the right of free passage," while the second recognizes "freedom of navigation and overflight." This comparison shows that the parties were well aware of the difference between freedom of navigation and free passage, and that they consciously chose the first for the Strait of Tiran and the Gulf of Aqaba, while the second was applied to the Suez complex.

ElBaradei's reliance on the UNCLOS text as a guide to the intentions of the parties to the Treaty of Peace is probably subject to doubt also from a historical point of view. The forerunner of the Peace Treaty, the Camp David Framework, was concluded in September 1978. At that time, and even when the Peace Treaty itself was signed (March 1979), it was far from certain that the United Nations conference would eventually be able to agree on a new Convention on the Law of the Sea. Moreover, the delegation of Israel at the conference has on several occasions expressed its disapproval of some aspects of the straits regime proposed in the UNCLOS texts.[92] For these reasons, it is most probable that the parties to the Treaty of Peace intended to establish

[89] ElBaradei, note 5 *supra*, at 546.

[90] Art. VI(2)(d) of Ann. I, Treaty of Peace, *supra* note 1.

[91] Art. 10(d) of the Annex to the Protocol (on the establishment of the MFO), 20 ILM 1190, 1191 (1981).

[92] *See, e.g.*, statement by the Head of the Israel Delegation, Ambassador S. Rosenne, on March 31, 1982 (not yet published in the *Official Records*).

a regime for Tiran and the Gulf of Aqaba without reference or reliance on the proposals and negotiating texts of the conference.

To conclude, the Treaty of Peace recognizes the Strait of Tiran and the Gulf of Aqaba as international waterways and foresees for them a very liberal regime of freedom of navigation and overflight. Several textual as well as teleological reasons seem to indicate that the parties had in mind freedom of navigation in its traditional meaning, subject, of course, to the limitations imposed by the rules of international law and those that reasonably follow from the special configuration of the Strait and the Gulf. The freedom envisaged is not limited to a right of passage.

Machinery of Implementation

The Camp David Framework and the Treaty of Peace set forth machinery for the implementation of the two sets of rules described above, namely, those concerning the limitation of forces in the various zones, and those recognizing freedom of navigation in the Strait of Tiran: the parties agreed to "request the United Nations to provide forces and observers to supervise the implementation of this Annex [*inter alia*, establishing the zones] and employ their best efforts to prevent any violation of its terms."[93] Thus, the parties intended to empower the force not only to supervise, but also to prevent violations. In addition, as already mentioned, the force would also be responsible for "ensuring the freedom of navigation through the Strait of Tiran in accordance with Article V of the Treaty of Peace."[94] The term "ensuring" is quite strong and indicates that the force was not simply to supervise the application of free navigation, but actively to ensure its implementation.

As early as July 1979, it became clear that the Security Council would not fulfill the tasks foreseen for it by the Treaty of Peace, since at that time the mandate of the United Nations Emergency Force (UNEF II), which had been in the Sinai since 1973, came to an end, and the Security Council did not renew the mandate.[95]

In 1981, as the date of the final withdrawal of Israel to the international boundary between Egypt and Israel drew nearer, Egypt and Israel, with the help of the United States, reached agreement on the establishment of the MFO. The relevant documents include a Protocol (the main agreement), an Annex (which deals with military matters), an Appendix (which lays down what facilities and immunities should be granted to the MFO), and several exchanges of letters concerning the involvement of the United States.[96] The MFO certainly deserves a thorough analysis, but here it will be discussed only insofar as it is relevant to the subject of this article.

[93] Art. VI(1) of Ann. I, Treaty of Peace, *supra* note 1.

[94] *Id.*, Art. VI(2)(d).

[95] *See* Bar Yaacov, *Keeping the Peace Between Egypt and Israel, 1973–1980*, 15 ISRAEL L. REV. 197, 198 (1980).

[96] *See* reference in note 91 *supra*. The exchanges of letters were not published in ILM, but have been published in various publications of Congress, *e.g.*, *Creation of the Multinational Force and Observers (MFO) for the Sinai: Hearings and Markup Before the House Comm. on Foreign Affairs*, 97th Cong., 1st Sess. 161–73 (1981).

The MFO will fulfill all the tasks foreseen by the Peace Treaty for the United Nations force, namely, supervising the limitation of forces and ensuring the freedom of navigation in the Strait of Tiran.[97] It will consist of "a headquarters, three infantry batallions totalling not more than 2,000 troops, a coastal patrol unit and an observer unit, an aviation element and logistics, and signal units" (Article 19 of the Annex). The force will operate in the Sinai, including Zone C along the Egyptian coast of the Gulf of Aqaba and the islands of Tiran and Sanafir, while the observers will supervise Zone D (within Israel), including a narrow strip on the shores of the Gulf. The MFO is deployed in Zone C and fulfills its functions in all four zones. It is stationed mainly in camps located near the Mediterranean coast in the north, and in the Sharm el-Sheikh area, near the Strait of Tiran.[98] In fact, freedom of navigation is to be ensured by a contingent located at Sharm el-Sheikh, and by an observation post established on the island of Tiran.[99] The texts specify how the limitation of forces will be supervised, *i.e.*, by the operation of checkpoints, reconnaissance patrols, and observation posts in Zone C, and by periodic verification in all zones;[100] but the means and measures for ensuring freedom of navigation are not specified, which apparently leaves their choice to the Director-General and the Commander of the force. Last, it has to be mentioned that the MFO will not be abolished unless both parties so agree (Article 3 of the Protocol).

The U.S. Involvement

The Camp David Frameworks and the Treaty of Peace were negotiated with the active participation of the United States, and the involvement of Washington in the process was demonstrated by the fact that President Carter signed the documents as a witness. But the United States went further and to a certain extent committed itself to ensuring the implementation of the Peace Treaty and to preventing violations. In a letter addressed to the parties and bearing the date of the signing of the Treaty of Peace, the President confirmed that in case of an actual or threatened violation of the Treaty, the United States would consult with the parties and would take measures that it deemed appropriate to achieve compliance with the Treaty.[101] In addition, the United States has undertaken several commitments related to specific matters dealt with in the Treaty, *inter alia*, the question of navigation and overflight in the Strait of Tiran and the Gulf of Aqaba. Thus, it is said in a Memorandum of Agreement between the Governments of the United States

[97] Art. 5 of the Protocol, Arts. 8–10 of the Annex, note 91 *supra*.

[98] Art. II(1)(c)(5) of Ann. I, Treaty of Peace, note 1 *supra*.

[99] Apparently, the islands are under Egyptian sovereignty, as stated by the representative of Egypt in the Security Council on Feb. 15, 1954, 9 UN SCOR (659th mtg.) at 19 (para. 102) and 25 (paras. 123–25). Similarly, in a press conference Minister of State Boutros Ghali said on Apr. 25, 1982, that "the two islands are now part of Zone C in Sinai under Egyptian sovereignty."

[100] Art. VI of Ann. I, Treaty of Peace, note 1 *supra*; Art. 10 of the Annex to the Protocol on the establishment of the MFO, note 91 *supra*.

[101] 18 ILM 532–33 (1979).

and Israel[102] that "the United States will support the parties' rights to navigation and overflight for access to either country through and over the Strait of Tiran and the Gulf of Aqaba pursuant to the Treaty of Peace" (Article 4). This promise of support is limited to the implementation of the rights of access of the parties themselves, *i.e.*, Egypt and Israel, to their respective countries, mentioned in the second sentence of Article V(2) of the Treaty. The regime of freedom of navigation and overflight for all nations recognized in the first sentence will thus benefit only from the general commitment of the United States mentioned earlier, while the right of access of the parties will enjoy its more active support. By the way, the text does not specify by what means this support will be given.

The Memorandum of Agreement also contains another, more general provision on rights of navigation, which provides that if a violation of the Treaty of Peace should threaten the security of Israel, including, *inter alia*, a blockade of Israel's use of international waterways, "the United States will be prepared to consider, on an urgent basis, such measures as the strengthening of the United States presence in the area, the providing of emergency supplies to Israel, and the exercise of maritime rights in order to put an end to the violation" (Article 3).

The expression "international waterways" could refer to all the relevant passages: the Suez Canal, the Strait of Gubal, the Gulf of Suez, the Strait of Tiran, the Gulf of Aqaba, and probably even the Strait of Bab el Mandeb. A blockade of any of these waterways would be considered not only a violation of the Treaty of Peace, but also a threat to the security of Israel, in which case the United States would consider what measures it should take. The Memorandum even mentions several possible measures to be taken, like strengthening the U.S. presence in the area, providing emergency supplies to Israel, and exercising maritime rights in order to put an end to the violation. In another provision (Article 2), the remedial measures that the United States would consider taking in case of a violation or threat of violation of the Treaty of Peace are said to include "diplomatic, economic and military measures." The "maritime rights" to be exercised by the United States are not specified, bu they could include sending convoys through the blockaded waterways.

The Treaty of Peace and General International Law

The first part of this article examined the rules applicable to the Gulf of Aqaba and the Strait of Tiran under general international law including the 1958 Geneva Conventions, as well as the relevant innovations of the 1982 Convention on the Law of the Sea. The question now arises, what is the relation of these various rules to the Treaty of Peace? With regard to the relation between the general *lex lata* and the regime of the Peace Treaty, it seems clear that between the parties the latter should supplement the former

[102] *Id.* at 537–39. It should be mentioned that Egypt frowned on the conclusion of the Memorandum of Agreement between the United States and Israel, and was not interested in concluding a similar agreement with the United States. *See id.*, letters from Egypt, at 536–37.

and prevail since it is a positive and special law that grants more liberal rights of navigation on a basis of nondiscrimination.

When the 1982 Convention enters into force, its relevant provisions may become binding also upon the parties to the Treaty of Peace, either because they formally become parties to it or because some of its rules may develop into customary law.[103] With regard to the Gulf of Aqaba, no question arises on the relation between the Peace Treaty and the 1982 Convention, since the latter does not deal specifically with navigation and overflight in bays enclosed by several states. The provisions of the Peace Treaty would thus continue to prevail over the *lex lata* left intact by the new Convention.

The law of straits, on the other hand, has been considerably modified by the new text. The relation between these new rules and other agreements is expressly regulated by the new Convention itself; as was mentioned above, long-standing conventions specifically relating to certain straits will prevail (Article 35(c)). It could be argued that by the time the 1982 Convention enters into force, the Treaty of Peace will already be "long-standing," especially if Resolution 242 of 1967 (which affirmed "the necessity (a) for guaranteeing freedom of navigation through international waterways in the area") is considered as the starting point of the regime confirmed by the Treaty.[104]

If, however, the date of the adoption of Resolution 242 is not considered as determining, then it is doubtful whether the Treaty of Peace will already be seen as "long-standing" when the new Convention enters into force. Therefore, the relation between the two would have to be examined in the light of the general provision dealing with the relation between the new Convention and other existing conventions and international agreements (Article 311): "(2) This Convention shall not alter the rights and obligations of States Parties which arise from other agreements compatible with this Convention and which do not affect the enjoyment by other States Parties of their rights or the performance of their obligations under this Convention." This text lays down two conditions for the continued validity of special agreements: that they be compatible with the new Convention and that they preserve other states' rights and obligations. Both conditions are fulfilled by the Treaty of Peace. It certainly is compatible with the new Convention since it establishes liberal rights of navigation and overflight, which is in line with one of the main objectives of the new text: to "facilitate international communication," as laid down in the Preamble. Again, no rights or obligations of other states are impaired; there is only an offer of additional rights to third states.

The continued validity of the relevant provisions of the Peace Treaty was also officially recognized by the United States, in a statement of Assistant Secretary of State James Malone, the President's Special Representative and

[103] Moore, note 60 *supra*, at 121: "With or without a new convention . . . the UNCLOS straits regime seems destined to serve as a powerful model for the development of a new customary law of straits transit." However, according to conference President Koh, and other participants, states may not "pick what they like and disregard what they do not like" in the Convention. *See* Press Release SEA/514, Dec. 10, 1982, at 8.

[104] On the relationship between Resolution 242 and the Treaty of Peace in the context of the rules applicable to the Strait of Tiran and the Gulf of Aqaba, see also *id.* at 113.

Chairman of the U.S. Delegation to UNCLOS III, made on January 29, 1982, and included in the *Congressional Record*:

> The U.S. fully supports the continuing applicability and force of freedom of navigation and overflight for the Strait of Tiran and the Gulf of Aqaba as set out in the peace treaty between Egypt and Israel. In the U.S. view, the treaty of peace is fully compatible with the LOS convention and will continue to prevail. The conclusion of the LOS convention will not affect these provisions in any way.[105]

It follows that the provisions of the Peace Treaty concerning freedom of navigation and overflight in the Strait of Tiran and the Gulf of Aqaba will prevail after the entry into force of the new 1982 Convention on the Law of the Sea. If this were not the case, Egypt and Israel would be precluded from becoming parties to the new Convention, since they undertook, by Article VI of the Treaty of Peace, to fulfill the Treaty in good faith, without regard to other instruments, and not to enter into any obligations in conflict with it.

Conclusion

The Treaty of Peace between Egypt and Israel foresees rules on navigation and overflight in the Gulf of Aqaba and the Strait of Tiran that are in line with the general trend of enhancing freedom of communication, and that in turn may also strengthen this trend. The most interesting features of these rules are, first, that the Treaty subjects the Gulf and the Strait leading to it to the same rules; second, following to some extent the example of certain other international waterways,[106] a limitation of forces has been agreed upon; third, again in line with the tradition of certain other waterways,[107] the rights of navigation and overflight are defined irrespective of the legal status these sea spaces may have for other purposes—a functional rather than a jurisdictional approach; fourth, in accordance with the rules applicable to most international waterways, the rights of navigation and overflight are granted to all nations; and last, the Treaty grants freedom of navigation and overflight, and not merely free passage as suggested by ElBaradei. Of course this freedom is not absolute, and it is limited by the parallel rights of other states as well as by restrictions flowing from the geopolitical configuration of the Gulf and the Strait, but it certainly is much wider than transit passage.

In actual practice, the Strait and the Gulf are plied by vessels belonging to many countries, Western and Communist, developed and developing. As pointed out by ElBaradei, the provision recognizing freedom of navigation and overflight to all nations is of a declaratory nature.[108]

Professor ElBaradei recommended[109] that the Peace Treaty be supple-

[105] 128 Cong. Rec. S4089 (daily ed. Apr. 27, 1982).

[106] *See, e.g.*, Art. 5 of the Treaty between Argentina and Chile, *signed* at Buenos Aires on July 23, 1881: "Magellan's Straits are neutralized for ever, and free navigation is guaranteed to the flags of all nations. To insure this liberty and neutrality no fortifications or military defences shall be erected that could interfere with this object." 72 Brit. & Foreign St. Papers 1103, 1104.

[107] *Ibid.*

[108] *See also* Akehurst, *The Peace Treaty Between Egypt and Israel*, 7 Int'l Rel. 1035, 1048 (1981).

[109] ElBaradei, note 5 *supra*, at 554.

mented by an additional agreement between Egypt and Israel stating in detail the rights and duties of the coastal states and those of the ships and aircraft enjoying rights of navigation and overflight. This is a sound proposal, but the rules should be defined in the context of freedom of navigation and overflight, and not by analogy to mere transit passage. However, the validity and applicability of the rules laid down by the Treaty of Peace do not depend on the conclusion of such an additional text. These provisions are self-executing and foresee a liberal regime of freedom of navigation and overflight which, as between the parties, supplements and prevails over the traditional law of international straits and the rules laid down by the 1982 Convention as well.

EDITORIAL COMMENTS

Dulce et Decorum Est: The Strategic Role of Legal Principles in the Falklands War

Introduction

Since 1945, Britain has relinquished 5,200,000 square miles of colonial possessions with some 800 million inhabitants. Many of these ex-colonies, such as Malaya, Zambia, and Jamaica, contain inestimable billions of dollars' worth of natural resources. Around the globe, from the Caribbean to Fiji, the thin, red line has by and large responded rather gracefully to the recessional; hardly a shot has been fired in anger.

Then came the Argentine invasion of the Malvinas. To hold those barren, forlorn Falkland Islands, inhabited by a mere 1,800 agoraphiles, the British expended the lives of about 250 of their countrymen and killed nearly 1,000 Argentinians.[1] The cost of the operation to Britain has been put at $2.6 billion, including the replacement cost of seven ships.[2]

What is to be made of all this by the international lawyer concerned with world order? Was it a selfless, necessary defense of principles that are the pillars of civilized conduct among states? Or was it a declining world power's sclerotic delusion of Thermopylae? Are we to derive from the Falklands war the moral that principles do matter? Or only, as Samuel Johnson said after the 1770 Falklands war, that an exaggerated sense of patriotism "is the last refuge of scoundrels"?[3]

These questions matter, because, on the one hand, small wars are becoming endemic in a world brittle as a tinderbox. On the other, the erosion of principled conduct by states is equally alarming, since a decent concern for principle is the cohesive force in building a society. Without it, social interaction is purely random and social evolution directionless. The meaning of the Falklands war thus affords an insight into the state of the international system.

Observing the unfolding of the Falklands crisis, in Britain and at the United Nations, the author became convinced that principles of international law directly affected strategic outcomes and had a dramatic mobilizing effect on public opinion, particularly in Britain and Western Europe. Principled legal thinking by governments also had significant consequences at the United Nations. Ignoring strategic, geographic, ethnic, social, and economic factors, nations reacted to the crisis by asking, "What precedential effect would an Argentine victory have on us?" In a rather dramatic fashion, political-strategic

[1] N.Y. Times, June 16, 1982, at A24. [2] *Id.*, June 20, 1982, §4, at E1.

[3] Professor Hugh Trevor-Roper's brief, illuminating note on Johnson's inquiry into the 1770–1771 Falklands crisis, including this quotation, is found in *id.*, May 29, 1982, at 23.

concerns were subordinated to considerations of principle; or, more precisely, principle became a dominant factor in the political-strategic equation.

The Falklands crisis thus provides a case study of the potential role of international legal principles in the conduct of world politics. It also illustrates the dangers that arise when principles are neglected or applied selectively.

THE ABILITY OF PRINCIPLE TO RALLY THE PUBLIC

Why Britain Fought

The bloody little conflict in the southwest Atlantic was patently a war of inconvenience for Britain, whose participation cannot be explained in conventional terms of self-interest. To study the rallying of Britons to the war is to confront the dynamic power of legal principles to mobilize the polity. This is no everyday phenomenon. War on behalf of abstract principle, common in the era of the Crusades, is nowadays quite rare. We in the West do not live in an era of "*dulce et decorum est, pro patria mori.*"[4] If asked to die for our country, we must be primed by credible reasons bigger than life itself. Yet the British marines did not believe—indeed, were not asked to believe—that the Falklands were the doorstep to Dover. Rumors of oil discoveries offshore were painstakingly denied. Prime Minister Margaret Thatcher's reason was, simply, that "Britain . . . has a duty to the whole world to show that aggression will not succeed and to uphold the cause of freedom."[5] It was reason enough.

In a London pub of a May afternoon,[6] to the tune of World War II Vera Lynn records,[7] the talk was not of avenging a national insult or even of recapturing useful real estate, but of protecting the world from the contemporary moral equivalent of Neville Chamberlain's "peace in our time." Poor little Czechoslovakia had become poor little Falkland "kelpers." An *Economist* poll showed that 76 percent of the British public backed their Government's response to the Argentine aggression.[8]

The Western European Attitude

This response, in varying degrees of intensity, seemed to predominate throughout that part of the European community which had been invaded by Germany in the Second World War. Mlle. Edmonde Dever, the Belgian Ambassador to the United Nations, early captured that feeling:

> If the use of force were to be rewarded, this would encourage any state with territorial ambitions to follow suit. Peace in the world would become even more precarious and many countries, no matter what group they

[4] HORACE, ODES, III, ii, 13.

[5] N.Y. Times, May 21, 1982, at A10.

[6] The author was in Britain for the United Nations during part of the events herein described, although only occasionally in pubs.

[7] Dame Vera Lynn, perhaps best known for her World War II rendition of "White Cliffs of Dover," had resurfaced for the occasion with a new recording called "I Love This Land," which became an instant hit in Britain.

[8] The Economist, May 1, 1982, at 12.

> belonged to, would feel threatened. The reaction of many small countries in the world to the Argentine invasion demonstrates, furthermore, that this danger has been understood.[9]

This perception ensured the early passage—over the opposition only of Panama—of Security Council Resolution 502 calling on Argentine troops to withdraw from the islands.[10] It also facilitated severe Western European economic and military sanctions against Argentina.[11]

The United States: Principle Skepticism

In the United States, however, the response to the unfurling of the banner of principle was much more mixed. As might be expected, the "Eastern Establishment" rallied to Britain. The *New York Times* columnist Flora Lewis had no doubt that "Britain has gone to war for no special national interest, neither conquest nor security, but in defense of a general principle against military seizure of land."[12] New York Senator Daniel Patrick Moynihan, himself a former U.S. Ambassador to the United Nations, called for Argentine withdrawal and submission of the issue to a special chamber of the International Court.[13] But many ordinary Americans seemed to agree with Ambassador to the United Nations Jeane Kirkpatrick, who had difficulty discerning the principle at issue. In the seizure by Argentina of land it believed to be rightfully its own, she thought, there could be no question of aggression. Kirkpatrick also believed that, even if there was a principle at stake, it ought to give way to practical considerations of U.S. self-interest in maintaining friendly relations with the major anti-Communist Government in Latin America. Asserting that "there aren't very many people in our Government who take an interest in Latin America,"[14] she held a flurry of meetings with Argentinian officials, such as Brigadier José Miret, the Secretary of State Planning, in an effort to keep the United States from tilting towards Britain. A small band of "Latin Americanists" in the State Department cheered her on, while leaking to the media horror stories of the costs to U.S. interests that would follow any overt tilt towards imperial England.[15]

These voices of geopolitical pragmatism were joined by intellectual adherents of the American "death of principle" school. With aggression everywhere richly rewarded, or at least condoned—China's against Vietnam, Vietnam's against Cambodia, India's against East Pakistan, Russia's against Afghanistan, Iraq's against Iran, Israel's against Iraq and Lebanon, Tanzania's against Uganda, to mention but a few instances of mounting global unilateral "quick

[9] Amb. Edmonde Dever, UN Doc. S/PV.2363, at 48–50 (1982).

[10] UNSC Res. 502 (Apr. 3, 1982).

[11] The European Economic Community unanimously voted to impose economic and military sanctions on Argentina on Apr. 10, 1982. N.Y. Times, Apr. 11, 1982, §1, at 1, 12.

[12] N.Y. Times, May 23, 1982, §4, at E23.

[13] 128 CONG. REC. S3366–68 (daily ed. Apr. 13, 1982).

[14] N.Y. Times, May 31, 1982, at A5.

[15] For coverage of the Haig-Kirkpatrick *contretemps*, see *id.*, May 31, 1982, at A5, and June 1, 1982, at A8.

fixes"—it was surely at best a churlish self-delusion to sacrifice one jot or tittle of coolly appraised self-interest for the chimera of "principle."

The man who was then Secretary of State, Alexander Haig, probably shared none of these views, but during April and most of May, he spearheaded the effort to remain pragmatically evenhanded. He could do little else, so long as the President still vacillated between the combatants. In April, after the invasion, Reagan used the occasion of Argentina's Independence Day to tell an astounded President Galtieri that it "has never been more important to reaffirm the common interests and values of Argentina and the United States."[16] Not until his address to the British Parliament of June 8 did President Reagan publicly align the United States with the principle for which Britain was fighting, by noting "that armed aggression must not be allowed to succeed, and that people must participate in the decisions of government under the rule of law."[17]

Although Prime Minister Thatcher has confided that "in her heart of hearts" she believed that the United States "knew and always knew that there could never be any neutrality between the military junta and democracy,"[18] this is more gracious than true. The United States was divided. As late as May 31, Ambassador Kirkpatrick was still making an end run to President Reagan to reverse the new policy of siding openly with London.[19]

Why was the United States so late in choosing sides?

Some, in the administration, saw neutrality as essential to playing the cherished game of shuttle diplomacy. Washington's incurable need to be the global mediator has the same origin as the urge to be a global policeman. In 1945, at the San Francisco founding of the United Nations, Secretary of State Edward Stettinius announced that, UN or no UN, we would continue not only to "protect our interests, which extend to the whole world," but equally, to "play the role of mediator between our major Allies whenever their interests conflict."[20] The Secretary was not thinking of General Galtieri and Mrs. Thatcher, of course, but of Joseph Stalin and Winston Churchill. Although neither then nor now were our mediations exactly a *succès fou*, the urge dies hard. And so long as it persists, we must at least seem neutral ("like a fire department neutral between house and fire," one British MP remarked dourly to the author).

Unfortunately, neutrality has costs to strategy as well as to principle. Arguably, our abstemiousness made a negotiated settlement more difficult. In April and early May, Argentina's obduracy fed on U.S. evenhandedness. Had Buenos Aires been certain that we were ready to provide all necessary military aid to the British forces, various proposed compromises might not have foundered. Then, too, neutrality eventually got us into more trouble with Argentina than necessary, because it was seen as a trick, a betrayal, when we at last sided

[16] For this quote and the comment thereon by Carlos Fuentes, see Anthony Lewis, *id.*, May 31, 1982, at A13.

[17] *Id.*, June 9, 1982, at A1.

[18] *Id.*, June 3, 1982, at A14.

[19] *Id.*, June 1, 1982, at A8.

[20] *Id.*, May 29, 1945, at 8. The text is slightly different in the official State Department version. 12 DEP'T STATE BULL. 1007, 1013 (1945).

with England. Such mixing and changing of signals, inducing cognitive dissonance in Argentina, was the natural consequence of Washington's need to mediate. It would have been more prudent to have left mediation to UN Secretary-General Javier Pérez de Cuéllar, who eventually landed the job, anyway. The new Secretary-General had just been chosen precisely for his ability to perform this sort of task. Also, as a new man in an underrated role, his prestige could not but have been enhanced by being invited to try, whether or not he succeeded.

In April, however, it was still inconceivable to our Department of State that a quarrel between two of our "major allies" should be mediated by anyone but us, least of all by the Secretary-General of that dangerous organization. The State Department's neutral stance was thus tactical, rather than deeply felt. But, as we have already noted, it fitted nicely with the world view of two other groups of Americans: those who, like Ambassador Kirkpatrick, opposed a tilt towards Britain for reasons of geopolitical strategy, and those who simply exhibited the national penchant for skepticism when faced with any summons to defend higher principles.

The latter is almost a native American trait. We may fight to defend our ships against Barbary pirates and German U-boats. We will probably defend access to distant but essential oilfields. But we do not follow the flag to war for abstract concepts. For us, war is an instrument of pragmatic self-defense, not a way to teach first principles to the heathen. America's reluctance to ratify even the most basic international treaties, even one prohibiting genocide, reflects a national preference for keeping our pragmatic options free of normative entanglements.

In this respect, British and American recent history is illustrative of two somewhat disparate views of the role of norms and principles in world affairs. Britain, with France, entered the Second World War at enormous cost to honor a commitment to principle.[21] The challenge to that principle happened to occur in Poland, a country with an unpalatable government that was neither strategically essential to the two Western European democracies nor defensible logistically. Yet the principle had to be upheld. The United States, by contrast, entered the war only after the Japanese had obligingly met the requirements of our strategic geopolitical pragmatism by mauling the Pacific fleet at Pearl Harbor.

The U.S. attitude changed briefly after the San Francisco Conference, where we sponsored a UN Charter that bound states to work collectively in defense of normative principles. Temporarily believing in this new order, we found ourselves fighting at Pusan to defend the principle of nonaggression, even though Secretary of State Dean Acheson, shortly before, had told us that South Korea was not within our strategic ambit.[22] That war was not a

[21] On March 31, 1939, British Prime Minister Neville Chamberlain, speaking for his country and for France, pledged help if Poland's independence was threatened by Germany. On Aug. 25, a British-Polish treaty of alliance was signed in London. Agreement of Mutual Assistance between the United Kingdom and Poland, 143 BRIT. & FOREIGN ST. PAPERS 301–03 (1939).

[22] This may have been an inadvertence. *See* Acheson, *Crisis in Asia—An Examination of U.S. Policy*, 22 DEP'T STATE BULL. 111, 116 (1950).

great success, in part because other members of the United Nations provided little support. The next war, in Vietnam, was also fought on principles, some of which were disguised as the "domino theory." That venture proved a disaster, compounded by the dawn of a public suspicion that the principles being asserted were only rather tenuously coupled to the facts. After it was over, many of those who had convincingly used legal and moral principles to argue against U.S. intervention in Vietnam fell silent when the Pol Pot regime turned genocidally against its own population and when the victors in Hanoi invaded Kampuchea and established dominion over Laos. Principles, to many Americans, evidently served no—or purely operational—purposes.

The British thus have had a different recent experience than Americans with committing their national honor and future to causes that, seen as discrete events unconnected to "tides of history" or the social *willen*, are likely to appear quixotic to many Americans. Significantly, it was American liberals, not British Social Democrats, who whispered that the Falklands war was provoked to buttress Mrs. Thatcher's standing with the electorate.

The *Economist* poll does illustrate the continuing power of principle in mobilizing British society for action, even for costly and painful sacrifice. Britons demonstrated their belief in the importance of principles in general and of the particular principle at stake. They were willing to share their leaders' belief that the asserted principle was genuinely threatened. To state this to Americans risks making the British—perhaps with some Western Europeans—seem rather culturally exotic.

The Strategic Power of Principle to Rally Governments: The "Third World"

The Falklands crisis is illustrative of the role of principles not only in mobilizing the British public but also in affecting the operation of the international system.

What happened at UN headquarters in May and June illustrates the residual power of principles to shape policies and behavior of members of the international community. In the corridors of the General Assembly building, the junta found itself almost without support, except from a few states with interests and ambitions similar to Argentina's. In speeches at the Security Council, there were pro forma invocations of colonialism's evils.[23] But in the delegates' lounge even most Latin Americans distanced themselves from the military "adventurists." Ambassador Muñoz Ledo of Mexico—a country with a better claim to Texas than Argentina's to the Falklands—stated publicly: "We reject the use of force to settle this or any other conflict."[24] His Foreign

[23] For example, Amb. Javier Chamorro Mora of Nicaragua was particularly strident in his denunciation of British colonialism and support for its "victim," Argentina, despite Nicaragua's well-known aversion to the "fascists" of Buenos Aires who were believed to be sending troops to act as U.S. proxies in Central America. UN Doc. S/PV.2363, at 16–25 (1982). *See also* N.Y. Times, May 23, 1982, §1, at 16.

[24] Amb. Muñoz Ledo, UN Doc. S/PV.2362, at 41, 46 (1982).

Ministry condemned the invasion outright.[25] The Bogotá delegation was nicknamed "British Colombians" for their perceived posture.

After the Security Council ordered Argentina to leave the Malvinas, over the lonely opposition of Panama, Flora Lewis wrote approvingly in the *New York Times*, "The United Nations has never been able to prevent or reverse these challenges to principle. But it has broadened a sense of the value of asserting it in a world where so many are weak and so few are mighty."[26] This reassertion in the Security Council could not have happened had there been a conventional split between Third World "victims" and First World "exploiters." But there was no such knee-jerk reaction. Clearly, among many Third Worlders, even Latin Americans, principle took precedent over hemispheric solidarity. Rio de Janeiro's leading newspaper, *Jornal do Brasil*, echoing the sentiments of its Government, asked, "why must Argentina's neighbors adopt a continental position as a bloc when the Government of Argentina has demonstrated such little appreciation for what peace on this continent means to them?"[27] Lamenting the demise of the inter-American system for preserving the power of law over force, São Paulo's leading newspaper, *O Estado*, concluded: "It was one of its own members, and an influential one at that, that hastened its demise."[28]

This new deviation from Third World solidarity could not be explained solely in terms of the Argentine junta's global unpopularity, although this did play a part. There were many things the Group of 77 could have done, beginning with convening the General Assembly, that were omitted because Argentina just could not collect the necessary votes. Aside from the action of Venezuelan dockworkers in refusing to unload Scotch whiskey,[29] the junta got very little tangible help, only some watered-down resolutions of the OAS and the Havana meeting of the nonaligned. Even these did not condone the use of force.[30]

The Principles at Stake

The principles that moved so many nations during the Falkland crisis are both clear and basic to the system established by the UN Charter. Article 2(3) obliges members to "settle their international disputes by peaceful means," while 2(4) prohibits "the threat or use of force" against a state. These concepts are further embroidered in the landmark Declaration on Principles of International Law concerning Friendly Relations and Co-operation among States, adopted by the General Assembly in 1970.[31] It "solemnly proclaims" that

[25] N.Y. Times, May 23, 1982, §1, at 16.

[26] *Id.*, §4, at E23.

[27] *Id.*, §1, at 14.

[28] *Ibid.*

[29] *Id.*, June 3, 1982, at A14.

[30] Draft Final Communiqué, Political Section, Ministerial Meeting of the Coordinating Bureau of the Non-Aligned Countries, May 31–June 5, 1982, Doc. NOAL/CONF.6/BUR.3/DOC.1/REV.2, at 40–42. The nonaligned, while aligned with Argentina in respect of its claim of sovereignty over the Malvinas, reiterated the call for "peaceful settlement of disputes between states and non-use of force in international relations." *Id.* at 40.

[31] GA Res. 2625 (XXV), 25 UN GAOR Supp. (No. 28) at 121, UN Doc. A/8028 (1970).

every state "has the duty to refrain from the threat or use of force to violate the existing international boundaries of another State or as a means of solving international disputes, including territorial disputes."[32] Argentina, of course, joined in supporting that declaration, which also requires states to settle disputes by "negotiation, inquiry, mediation, conciliation, arbitration, judicial settlement, resort to regional agencies, or arrangements or other peaceful means of their choice," but never by resort to military force.[33]

Another, more controversial, set of principles evoked by the Falklands crisis has to do with the disposition of the islands, which are a British colony. Under Article 73 of the UN Charter, the colonial power is obliged to recognize that "the interests of the inhabitants of these territories are paramount" and to promote, within the UN system, "the well-being of the inhabitants" including the right "to develop self-government, to take due account of the political aspirations of the peoples, and to assist them in the progressive development of their free political institutions." The Declaration on Friendly Relations also purports to give the people of each colony the right freely to choose the "establishment of a sovereign and independent State, the free association or integration with an independent State or the emergence into any other political status freely determined by a people."[34] This is important because it makes clear that the decolonization of a territory need not lead to independence or merger with a neighboring state, but that self-determination can take the form of free association with the "mother country," the direction preferred by the Falkland inhabitants.

Not every nation at the United Nations thought these principles were worth defending in this specific instance. Each did its own cost-benefit analysis. Ambassador Noel Dorr of Ireland said that "though the principles at stake are none the less important, the area in dispute is small and geographically isolated [and] the population of the islands is tiny."[35] He called, unsuccessfully, for a cease-fire that would have left the Argentinian forces in control.[36]

Diplomatic action at the United Nations in May and June showed that Dorr was in the minority. To most, preponderant weight was given to the principle factor. Principles matter in two related senses. First, principles like Article 2(4) are perceived to lay down the basic rules of the game. Most states, if they are not themselves parties to the dispute, tend to "vote for the rules" because they perceive themselves to have a greater national interest in protecting them from erosion than in supporting either side. Of course, in many instances, it is difficult to tell who violated the rules: which state "started" the crisis. But when that is clear, as it was in the Falklands invasion, then states tend to lean on the violator, as did Mexico, Colombia, Brazil, and Chile, even while occasionally genuflecting to the cherished icons of hemispheric solidarity.

[32] *Ibid.* The provisions of the declarations are not numbered.

[33] *Ibid.*

[34] *Ibid.*

[35] Amb. Noel Dorr, UN Doc. S/PV.2360, at 56 (1982).

[36] Ireland: draft resolution, UN Doc. S/15106 (1982). The resolution called on both parties to suspend hostilities for 72 hours, while the Secretary-General renewed his good offices efforts. The resolution was not adopted.

There is a second sense in which principles matter. They are, after all, the fragile strands of extrapolative logic that link one situation with others. Many at the United Nations with no direct stake in the disposition of the Falklands chose up sides because a key issue—may historic titles be used to force changes in established national boundaries?—reminded them of another situation in which they did have a strong interest. Of course, this works both ways. Venezuela supported Argentina,[37] while Guyana strongly supported Britain,[38] because Venezuela has a claim based on historic title against Guyana. Guatemala and Belize saw the issue as similar to their own boundary dispute.[39] Kenya, a large part of its territory still claimed by Somalia on the basis of historic title, was outspoken in Britain's cause. Ambassador Maina made it clear that

> whether or not the [Argentine] claims are valid . . . they should not be settled at the expense of people who now live on the Falkland Islands. They are paramount, and in our view their interests are paramount. Whatever claims Argentina may have against the British, based on history and the imperialism of the past, may be settled without treating the people of the Falkland Islands like chattels in real estate. . . . If we bend the principle of decolonization of peoples to look like the redistribution of territories, this Organization is in real trouble. One has only to look at any map of one's choice to see why. . . . [A]ny attempt to redraw the map of the world would lead this planet to endless war and destruction.[40]

Maina addressed Argentina as "a violent member of the United Nations committing naked aggression against its neighbours."[41]

The lack of African support for Argentina is also understandable in another sense which illustrates the role of reciprocal principles in a slightly different fashion. As Ambassador Maina pointed out, as recently as September 1981, at the meeting of nonaligned foreign ministers, Argentina had dissociated itself from a resolution calling for support to southern African liberation movements insofar as that implied aid to armed struggle. The stated ground was that "resorting to force is incompatible with the Charter of the United Nations." Wryly, Maina asked: "what happened between September 1981 and April 1982 . . . to transform Argentina . . .?"[42]

The direct connection made by governments between the events in the South Atlantic and matters close to their own national interest was apparent to anyone following the proceedings in the Security Council. Of the 15 current

[37] Amb. Zambrano Velasco, UN Doc. S/PV.2362, at 21–35 (1982).

[38] Informally, as in the Havana meeting of the nonaligned. *See* note 30 *supra*.

[39] Amb. Delpree-Crespo of Guatemala told the Security Council:

> It is inconceivable that the colonialist system, which is fortunately in its death throes throughout the world, including our continent, should have sprung to life, allowing a colonialist empire to impose its interests upon our America to the detriment of a Latin American country, whose right to sovereignty over the full extent of its territory has been internationally recognized.

UN Doc. S/PV.2362, at 97, 98–100 (1982). He clearly indicated that Guatemala, in respect of Belize, had suffered "similar treatment" in "similar circumstances." *Ibid.*

[40] Amb. C. G. Maina, UN Doc. S/PV.2364, at 21, 23–26 (1982).

[41] *Id.* at 26.

[42] *Ibid.*

members of the Council, 11 are states on one side or another of problems very similar to that of the Falklands. France has a network of little bits and pieces of empire, many in the category of "*départements d'outre mer*" that wish to remain French. In May, the deputy representing one of these overseas departments, St. Pierre et Miquelon in the Gulf of St. Lawrence, made a panicky prediction of an imminent Canadian invasion of his homeland. Guyana, equally nervous about an oil-rich neighbor that claims two-thirds of its territory, on May 11 notified the United Nations that it had been the subject of a "threatening" incursion by Venezuelan soldiers.[43] Both jeremiads proved, at the least, premature. But they reflected the understandable fear that one thing leads to another, an operational view of principle. Even the United States has ties with Puerto Rico, and expects soon to establish links with the distant Northern Marianas, comparable to those of Britain with the Falklands. "Historic title" forms the basis of claims by Ireland to Northern Ireland, Japan to the Southern Kurile Islands currently in Russia's keep, Togo to British Togoland which was annexed to Ghana, Spain to Gibraltar, and China to those parts of the British Hong Kong colony ceded by China in 1842 and 1860.[44] As Panamanian Foreign Minister Jorge Illueca told the Security Council, the Gibraltar case is indistinguishable from the Falklands issue: "these colonial enclaves," he said, "have no justification; they are inadmissible, reprehensible, and stand condemned by the world conscience."[45]

The Panamanian position, too, illustrated the role of a sort of principled thinking. As the voice of this world conscience, Panama—the only Hispanic Latin American country then on the Security Council—provided most of the ardent, if eccentric, support for Argentina. Delegates were startled by the temper of Illueca's outbursts, which attributed Prime Minister Thatcher's intractability to "the glandular system of women" and called on the United Nations to deprive the British Ambassador, Sir Anthony Parsons, of the use of his knighthood since, in the world organization, "we do not have any monarchial system."[46] The Panamanians privately admitted that what occasioned all this verbal excess was not the Malvinas so much as thoughts of the Panama Canal. Here, again, the power of principles—extrapolative thinking—was at work. Illueca surprised delegates with the theory that the Falkland Islanders deserved no right of self-determination because, he contended (wrongly), they are all "employees of a colonial company who are of the same nationality as the oppressor nation."[47] The bigger game he was really stalking, however, was the Panama Canal company and its resident U.S. "zonians."

This author asked one Panamanian representative whether he had considered that, if Argentina had succeeded in asserting its historic title, the Gov-

[43] Letter dated May 11, 1982, from the Permanent Representative of Guyana to the United Nations addressed to the President of the Security Council, UN Doc. S/15072 (1982).

[44] Treaty between Great Britain and China, *signed* at Nanking, Aug. 29, 1842, 30 BRIT. & FOREIGN ST. PAPERS 389–92 (1842); Convention of Friendship between Great Britain and China, *signed* at Pekin (*sic*), Oct. 24, 1860, 50 *id.* at 10–12 (1860).

[45] Foreign Minister Jorge Illueca, UN Doc. S/PV.2362, at 63, 81 (1982).

[46] Illueca, UN Doc. S/PV.2363, at 76, 92 (1982).

[47] Illueca, UN Doc. S/PV.2362, at 71 (1982).

ernment of Colombia might have revived its old claim to its isthmus province. "Oh, but they wouldn't," the Panamanian replied, somewhat uncertainly. But how could he be sure? Panama, after all, had been "stolen" from Colombia by the same two colonial powers, Britain and the United States, that 70 years earlier had relieved Buenos Aires of the Malvinas.

For most countries, not being the subject of claims based on historic title, the principles at stake in the Falklands were not quite so specifically relevant. Yet they were perceived as no less important. As British historian Hugh Trevor-Roper wrote to the *New York Times*, "if Argentina had kept its spoil today, the rule of law would have been replaced by that of force, and no undefended island would have been secure."[48] Ambassador Jacobs of Antigua and Barbuda said, "as a small island State whose only defence against the aggression of those larger and more powerful than ourselves is the Charter of the United Nations and the resolutions of this Security Council, we must deplore Argentina's illegal use of force."[49] In a world where 62 states have populations of fewer than a million, and 32 have fewer than 200,000, Jacobs spoke for a significant constituency. Most of these vulnerable nations agreed with Shridath Ramphal, the Secretary General of the Commonwealth, who said bluntly: "in making a firm and unambiguous response to Argentina's aggression, Britain is rendering a service to the international community as a whole. . . . Commonwealth countries, including in particular Commonwealth countries in Latin America, have stood full square behind Britain in this matter."[50]

This was far from public posturing. Nations and territories felt themselves threatened by the ripple effect an Argentine victory would have had. Worried senior officials of the Netherlands Antilles rushed to New York in May to request UN technical assistance in constructing a status that would permit their constitutional link with the Netherlands to continue in peace. "We do not wish to follow Suriname's disastrous experience with premature independence," their representative said. On the other hand, the Antilles did not want the link with Holland to provide an excuse for "liberation" from "colonialism" by a powerful Latin American neighbor. (When it was suggested that the islands might escape the "colonial" label by constructing a relationship with the Netherlands that either could terminate on notice, one of the visitors replied, "Oh no. We cannot give the Netherlands the power to rid themselves of us so easily.")[51]

When Principles Are Not Principles

But what does all this activity prove about the utility of principles in the international system? Perhaps only that nations, like the citizenry of Britain, may still be moved—or manipulated—by appeals to principle. Reflecting Americans' traditional reserve towards such appeals, Ronald Steel pointed out

[48] N.Y. Times, May 29, 1982, at 23.

[49] Amb. Lloydston Jacobs, UN Doc. S/PV.2360, at 83 (1982).

[50] S. S. Ramphal, "International Collective Security: Precondition for Peace and Security," Statement to Parliamentary Mass Lobby, Central Hall, Westminster (Apr. 27, 1982).

[51] The author participated in these unrecorded discussions.

in an op-ed piece for the *New York Times*[52] that what the Argentine junta tried to do in the Falklands follows quite logically from similar acts the international community has tolerated with a mere wink. The geopolitically pragmatic practice, he argued, long ago obliterated the principles. India's seizure of the Portuguese colony of Goa, in 1961, was benevolently overlooked by the UN system. Although the Portuguese fascist dictatorship made it impossible to demonstrate the political preference of the Goans, it is probable that the inhabitants of the enclave had no desire, after 450 years as part of Portugal, to be "liberated" by India. When the Goan invasion came to the notice of the Security Council, Ambassador Adlai Stevenson charged that India had violated the Charter principles.[53] But nothing was done, except that U.S. Ambassadors to New Delhi are still instructed not to visit the area in order to avoid legitimizing its annexation.

In a similar case, the United States and the United Nations actually helped take the western half of the vast island of Papua New Guinea (West Irian) away from Holland and, without the consent of the inhabitants, handed it to Indonesia.[54] During the transfer, the UN flag flew over the territory for 8 months. In 1963, after assuming control, Indonesia conducted a rigged "consultation" which a shamefaced international community accepted as a *fait accompli*.[55]

More recent examples are the Indonesian seizure of Portuguese East Timor and the Moroccan taking of the Spanish (Western) Sahara, both in 1975. In each instance, the preferences of the local inhabitants for independence were clearly evidenced and blatantly ignored. In Timor, there was bitter resistance to the invaders, which was brutally suppressed. The General Assembly passed a toothless resolution.[56] In the Western Sahara, a visiting UN fact-finding mission reported the overwhelming desire of the indigenous population for independence,[57] and the International Court of Justice in its advisory opinion on the legal status of that territory reiterated its assertion that "the subsequent development of international law in regard to non-self-governing territories, as enshrined in the Charter of the United Nations, made the principle of self-determination applicable to all of them." The "right of self-determination requires a free and genuine expression of the will of the peoples concerned."[58]

[52] Steel, *Self-Interest*, N.Y. Times, May 28, 1982, at A27.

[53] 16 UN SCOR (987th mtg.) at 15–18, UN Doc. S/PV.987 (1961).

[54] Agreement between the Republic of Indonesia and the Kingdom of the Netherlands concerning West New Guinea (West Irian), 18 UN GAOR Annex 1 (Agenda Item 20), UN Doc. A/5578 (1963).

[55] GA Res. 2504 (XXIV), 24 UN GAOR Supp. (No. 30) at 3, UN Doc. A/7630 (1969).

[56] GA Res. 3485 (XXX), 30 UN GAOR Supp. (No. 34) at 118, UN Doc. A/10034 (1975).

[57] The mission was authorized by GA Res. 3292 (XXIX), 29 UN GAOR Supp. (No. 31) at 103, UN Doc. A/9631 (1974). *See* Report of the United Nations Visiting Mission to Spanish Sahara, in the Report of the Special Committee, UN Doc. A/10023/Add.5, Annex, at 26–27 (1975).

[58] Advisory Opinion on Western Sahara, 1975 ICJ Rep. 12, 31–32 (in part quoting with approval its Advisory Opinion on The Legal Consequences for States of the Continued Presence of South Africa in Namibia (South West Africa) notwithstanding Security Council Resolution 276 (1970), 1971 *id.* at 16, 31).

When all this was ignored by the invading Moroccan army, the General Assembly passed two contradictory resolutions, one recognizing the right of the Saharawis to independence and the other ratifying the *fait accompli*.[59]

Both times, the United Nations ineffectually criticized the usurping government but did nothing more concrete. The British Government certainly did not identify with the Timorese, some 50,000 of whom died defending the same right Britain now claims for the Falkland kelpers. As for the United States, it has tut-tutted, made a short shadow play of restricting military sales to Morocco and Indonesia, but staunchly supported and supplied both aggressor regimes.[60]

These are dramatic instances of national policy based not on principle but on pragmatic geopolitical strategy. In East Timor and the Western Sahara, the West supported its surrogates, the legions of General Suharto and King Hassan, without much thought for cost to the credibility and deterrent power of the principles at stake. Who could blame Galtieri's anger and confusion at being treated so differently from Suharto and Hassan?

The junta's confusion was further compounded by the unprincipled way that the Third World had previously dealt with the Falklands issue in the General Assembly and in the councils of the nonaligned. In both settings, the Argentine claim has essentially been recognized since 1965 by resolutions that called for negotiations between Argentina and Britain to terminate the "colonial" presence.[61] In 1973 the Assembly explicitly determined that "the way to put an end to this colonial situation is the peaceful solution of the conflict of sovereignty."[62] This was tantamount to a call for Britain to negotiate the islands' transfer to Argentina, while somehow "bearing in mind" the interests of the inhabitants.

That line of resolutions on the Falklands, paralleling others on Gibraltar,[63] while not sanctioning Argentina's use of force, did implicitly reject the inhabitants' claim to self-determination. It is the most egregious instance of abandonment by the Third World of the very principle to which its member states owe their existence. True, the population of Gibraltar (about 30,000) is small, and of the Falklands, even smaller. However, the UN debates show absolutely no attempt to make the distinction on that basis, if only because there are other Third World countries with comparably minute populations. Such a line would have been impossible to draw without intense internal squabbling within the Third World bloc. The dirty little truth of the matter is that the Falklanders and the people of Gibraltar were not thought worthy

[59] GA Res. 3458A (XXX) and GA Res. 3458B (XXX), 30 UN GAOR Supp. (No. 34) at 116–17, UN Doc. A/10034 (1975).

[60] *See The Question of Self-Determination in Western Sahara: Hearing Before the Subcomms. on International Organizations and on Africa of the House Comm. on International Relations*, 95th Cong., 1st Sess. (1977); *Human Rights in East Timor: Hearings Before the Subcomm. on International Organizations of the House Comm. on International Relations*, 95th Cong., 1st Sess. (1977).

[61] GA Res. 2065 (XX), 20 UN GAOR Supp. (No. 14) at 57, UN Doc. A/6014 (1965).

[62] GA Res. 3160 (XXVIII), 28 UN GAOR Supp. (No. 30) at 108–09, UN Doc. A/9030 (1973).

[63] *See, e.g.*, GA Res. 2429 (XXIII), 23 UN GAOR Supp. (No. 18) at 64, UN Doc. A/7218 (1968), which asks Britain "to terminate the colonial situation in Gibraltar."

of the right to self-determination because they are not about to self-determine themselves *into* the Third World, but wish to remain linked with the "mother country," an example of the unsurprising fact that the Third World, too, sometimes sacrifices principles for geopolitical pragmatism.

A senior Indian diplomat explained it a little differently:

> Before the non-aligned meet, various special interest resolutions are drafted within the regional sub-group concerned. The rest of us rarely get a look at the texts until a week or so before the vote. Anyway, we really don't care, since it's all cut and dried and doesn't affect us much. Among the Third World, each region goes along with every other region's agenda. That's how we manage to stay a group.[64]

This attitude may change, however, when a First World country feels really strongly about one of the items and applies bilateral pressure—the way the United States has done when resolutions about Puerto Rico were under consideration. But, the Indian representative indicated, the British "never really lobbied us about the Falklands or Gibraltar resolutions. They seemed to feel that those resolutions were just a lot of hot air. And we rather felt the same."[65] Unfortunately, the Argentines took them at face value, as a hunting license.

Caring for Principles

From all this, one might conclude that the principles for which Britain purported to fight in the South Atlantic are bunk, to be trotted out when convenient, then forgotten when not. Every law student knows that, for every principle, there is a countervailing one. International law is an illusion created by lawyers to gull the naive into serving somebody else's self-interest. Always, in international affairs, ahead of principle comes praxis, which is highly selective, pragmatic, strategic, and indifferent to rules.

Well, as T. S. Eliot would say, that is a way of putting it.[66] But let us try another. The Falklands crisis points to a social phenomenon: principles evidently can rally both people and nations, even overcome countervailing perceptions of self-interest. This rallying has strategic consequences. There is no doubt that Argentina's diplomatic isolation sapped its will to fight and its ability to secure weapons, replacement parts, and credits as well. Principles, in the Falklands war, were effective *because they were credible* to those asked to defend them.

But, besides their capacity to rally, principles have another strategic capability. They can deter. Principles that are regularly implemented over a long period tend to make certain conduct "unthinkable." The idea that something "just isn't done" is both descriptive and proscriptive. However, once a principle is violated with impunity—the previously unthinkable seizure of

[64] Interview conducted by author, New York, June 2, 1982.

[65] *Ibid.*

[66] "That was a way of putting it—not very satisfactory," T. S. Eliot, "East Coker," from *Four Quartets*, in THE COMPLETE POEMS AND PLAYS 123, 125 (1952).

an embassy in Tehran, for example—it loses part of its credibility and thus its capacity to deter. It is no longer unthinkable. Restoring its unthinkability is rather like putting toothpaste back in a tube.

A government that sees others successfully ignore principles will not give them much weight when calculating its own strategic self-interest. After Goa, West Irian, East Timor, the Western Sahara, Afghanistan, Cambodia, the Iran-Iraq and Mideast wars, it is hardly surprising that Buenos Aires believed it could invade the Falklands without stirring up a hornet's nest.[67] The principles for which Britain fought in the Falklands had lost their capacity to deter violators, even if they still retained a lingering ability to rally defenders.

Unfortunately, a principle with just enough life to rally defenders but not enough to deter violators is not just another compromise. It is a particular danger to world stability, leading to unpredictability and potentially lethal miscalculations.

The sad truth is that the international community has not very ardently tended even its most basic principles. Yet social scientists tell us that rule building is a universal social imperative, that a sense of shared, generally obeyed principles gives definition to a society and distinguishes it from a random rabble.[68] The international system does, indeed, maintain many of the trappings of a society: a fixed population (of states), repetitious patterns of interactions, an agreed system of communications, and elaborate, if politically rudimentary, institutions. Yet, when it comes to principles, the states in the system remain careless about going consistently to their defense.

Tending principles only once in a while is probably worse than abandoning them altogether. Yet that is precisely what happened in the Falklands. The British military action in the Falkland Islands—costly, prolonged, perhaps quixotic—was senseless in cost-benefit terms if it was fought merely to reclaim real estate. It is equally indefensible in Benthamite terms, for the relative happiness of the 1,800 islanders would have been purchased by the greater unhappiness of an equal or larger number of battle casualties.

The campaign can be justified only as a reinforcement of basic principles crucial to peace. These are surely worth fighting for, if states are thereby persuaded to adhere to them. But a principle asserted occasionally may not be worth defending if only because it is already incapacitated, having lost its power to deter.

In his June address to the British Parliament, President Reagan emphasized that armed aggression must not be allowed to succeed and that people must

[67] Carlos Fuentes made a somewhat different connection:

> If Mrs. Kirkpatrick was sent down to Buenos Aires to say, "What wonderful people you are, you are not totalitarians, you are simply authoritarians, we love you," and Mr. Enders went down there, and Secretary Haig, when asked what the United States had in common with the Argentine military regime, said, "We both believe in God"—naturally the junta felt they had the green light from the United States to go forward with this adventure.

Quoted by Anthony Lewis, N.Y. Times, May 31, 1982, at A13.

[68] *See, e.g.*, S. Hoffmann, *International Systems and International Law*, 14 WORLD POL. 205, 207 (1961).

participate in the decisions of government under the rule of law. "If there had been firmer support for that principle some 45 years ago," he added, "perhaps our generation wouldn't have suffered the bloodletting of World War II."[69] But so, too, the Argentine invasion of the Falklands and resultant bloodshed would probably have been unthinkable if the international community had defended those principles more vigorously in inconvenient settings like the Middle East, Afghanistan, East Timor, and the Western Sahara.

One must assume, perhaps naively, that Britain and all those who supported it at the United Nations have made a bond in blood that commits them, not to the kelpers, but to uphold in future—regardless of pragmatic strategic and geopolitical considerations—the important rules of civilized conduct for which the Falkland war was fought.

THOMAS M. FRANCK

BROADENING THE ADVISORY JURISDICTION OF THE INTERNATIONAL COURT OF JUSTICE

The adoption of the Manila Declaration on the Peaceful Settlement of International Disputes by the General Assembly on November 15, 1982, has focused attention again on the need to improve means for the settlement of international disputes. Among existing means that might be improved is use of the International Court of Justice. While states have shown great reluctance to increase the jurisdiction of the International Court of Justice to render binding decisions, it might be possible to broaden the Court's advisory jurisdiction, if it can be done without revising the Charter of the United Nations or the Statute of the Court.

Under the Charter of the United Nations, the General Assembly and the Security Council were granted broad power to request that the Court give an advisory opinion on "any legal question."[1] The General Assembly was also empowered to authorize other organs of the United Nations and specialized agencies to request advisory opinions of the Court, but only with respect to "legal questions arising within the scope of their activities."[2] The General Assembly gave such authorization to several organs of the United Nations and to more than a dozen of the specialized agencies.[3] By 1982, 15 requests for advisory opinions had been made by United Nations organs, and 3 by specialized agencies.[4]

Proposals for broadening the advisory jurisdiction of the Court have envisaged in particular the following possibilities:

[69] N.Y. Times, June 9, 1982, at A16.

[1] UN CHARTER art. 96(1).

[2] *Id.* art. 96(2).

[3] For a list, see the latest Y.B. ICJ, ch. III, sec. II.

[4] 1981 *id.* at 46 nn.2–4, and 47 nn.1–3.

1. The most common has been the proposal that the General Assembly should authorize, in addition to the specialized agencies, other public international organizations, general or regional, to request advisory opinions of the Court.[5]

2. More controversial has been the proposal that two or more states should be permitted to submit a dispute between them to the Court for an advisory opinion, especially when they cannot agree to submit it to the Court for a binding decision.[6] It has been contended that it would discredit the Court if states were free to treat as only advisory an opinion that they had voluntarily solicited.[7]

3. Some objections have also been raised to the proposal that a national tribunal that has to decide a complex issue of international law might find it useful to refer that issue to the Court for an advisory opinion.[8]

All these proposals have run into the basic difficulty that both the United States and the Soviet Union are reluctant to allow a revision of the Charter of the United Nations or of the Statute of the International Court of Justice, which would be necessary to provide direct access to the Court in the cases contemplated. In the search for a way around this objection, the idea has emerged to use the solution adopted by the General Assembly with respect to references to the Court of cases considered by the Administrative Tribunal of the United Nations.

When faced with various challenges to the judgments of that Tribunal, the General Assembly in 1955 established a Committee on Applications for Review of Administrative Tribunal's Judgments. Its sole purpose is to present requests to the International Court of Justice for an advisory opinion whenever

[5] See the 1971 Report of the Secretary-General summarizing the views of various governments concerning the role of the International Court of Justice, UN Doc. A/8382, paras. 263–305, at 90–101 (1971) (proposals by Argentina, Austria, Canada, Cyprus, Denmark, Finland, Guatemala, Iraq, Italy, Madagascar, Mexico, the Netherlands, Sweden, Switzerland, the United States, and Yugoslavia). For a discussion of these proposals, see *Report on steps that might be taken by the General Assembly to enhance the effectiveness of the International Court of Justice,* in AMERICAN BRANCH, INTERNATIONAL LAW ASSOCIATION, 1971–72 PROC. & COMMITTEE REPORTS 142, 156–58; Golsong, *Role and Functioning of the International Court of Justice: Proposals Recently Made on the Subject,* 31 ZEITSCHRIFT FÜR AUSLÄNDISCHES ÖFFENTLICHES RECHT UND VÖLKERRECHT 673, 681–82 (1971). *See also* Szasz, *Enhancing the Advisory Competence of the World Court,* in 2 THE FUTURE OF THE INTERNATIONAL COURT OF JUSTICE 499, 514–16 (L. Gross ed. 1976). The question was revived in 1977 in the Special Committee on the Charter of the United Nations and on the Strengthening of the Role of the Organization. *See* the report of the committee, 32 GAOR Supp. (No. 33) at 61–62, 147–48, UN Doc. A/32/33 (1977).

[6] UN Doc. A/8382, *supra* note 5, para. 274, at 92–93 (United States).

[7] *Id.*, para. 284, at 95 (Switzerland); UN Doc. A/C.6/SR.1212, at 3–5 (1970) (Soviet Union).

[8] *See* C. W. JENKS, THE PROCESS OF INTERNATIONAL ADJUDICATION 161, 166–68 (1964); P. JESSUP, THE PRICE OF INTERNATIONAL JUSTICE 67–71 (1971) (citing earlier suggestions by W. R. Bisschop and Sir Hersch Lauterpacht); Gross, *The International Court of Justice: Consideration of Requirements for Enhancing its Role in the International Legal Order,* 65 AJIL 253, 275–76, 308–13 (1971). For a detailed discussion of problems created by this proposal, see Caflisch, *Reference Procedures and the International Court of Justice,* in 2 THE FUTURE OF THE INTERNATIONAL COURT, *supra* note 5, at 572–609.

the committee finds that there is a substantial basis for an objection to the judgment of the Tribunal made by a member state, the Secretary-General, or the person in respect of whom the judgment of the Administrative Tribunal was rendered.[9] When necessary, the Tribunal is obliged to revise its judgment "in conformity with the opinion of the Court."[10] Thus, this procedure has two novel features: it allows a de facto appeal from the judgment of the Tribunal, and it gives individuals indirect access to the International Court of Justice. In the two opinions requested in this manner, the Court carefully examined the legitimacy of the procedure and found it acceptable.[11] Building on this precedent, a suggestion has been made that the General Assembly create "an organ of the United Nations specially for the purpose of requesting advisory opinions in defined circumstances" and subject to specified conditions.[12] This suggestion was revived recently by the American Bar Association (ABA), which recommended the "approval by the United States of expansion of the advisory opinion jurisdiction of the International Court of Justice to include questions of international law referred by national courts."[13]

The ABA proposal deals only with the reference by a national court of difficult questions of international law to the Court for an advisory opinion, but it can be easily extended to presentation of questions to the Court by an international organization or a pair of states. Of these three proposals, it might be useful to discuss in more detail the reference by a national court, which is more complex but at the same time might be more fruitful; after a slow start, a similar procedure before the Court of Justice of the European Communities is now used in more than 60 cases per year.[14]

The adoption of a reference procedure from national courts would require coordinated measures by international and national authorities: the adoption by the General Assembly of an appropriate resolution establishing a Special Committee on Advisory Opinions and determining the modalities of such reference; the approval of an authorizing statute by each national legislature willing to accept this procedure; and appropriate action by state or provincial legislatures in the United States and other federal states.

[9] GA Res. 957 (X), Nov. 8, 1955, 10 GAOR Supp. (No. 19) at 30–31, UN Doc. A/3116 (1955). For the text of the revised Statute of the Administrative Tribunal of the United Nations, Art. 11, see UN Doc. AT/11/Rev.4 (1972) (UN Pub. Sales No. E.73.X.1).

[10] Statute of the UN Administrative Tribunal, *supra* note 9, Art. 11(3).

[11] Application for the Review of Judgment No. 158 of the United Nations Administrative Tribunal, 1973 ICJ REP. 166, 171–75; and Application for the Review of Judgment No. 273 of the United Nations Administrative Tribunal, 1982 *id.* at 325, 331–40.

[12] C. W. JENKS, *supra* note 8, at 160–61.

[13] AMERICAN BAR ASSOCIATION, SUMMARY OF ACTION OF THE HOUSE OF DELEGATES, 1982 MIDYEAR MEETING 12 (Chicago 1982). The report of the Committee on International Courts of the Section of International Law and Practice, of Oct. 14, 1981, on which this resolution was based, was prepared by the Chairman of the Committee, L. B. Sohn, with the assistance of an Ad Hoc Committee composed of David E. Birenbaum, Edison W. Dick, Anthony F. Essaye, Alan Kashdan, Stuart Lemle, Arthur Rovine, George Spina, and Leonard Theberge.

[14] *See, e.g.*, SYNOPSIS OF THE WORK OF THE COURT OF JUSTICE OF THE EUROPEAN COMMUNITIES IN 1978, at 7, 14 (1979) (62 decisions in 1978 in cases referred to the Court; 495 such cases decided by the end of 1978).

The ABA proposal envisages referral to the International Court of Justice early in the proceedings, as soon as it has become evident that a complex issue of international law is involved. Once the parties to the dispute have agreed to the referral, the national tribunal would formulate the question to the Court and forward it to the Special Committee of the General Assembly, together with the briefs prepared by the litigants. The Special Committee would submit the question to the Court only after deciding that it satisfied the criteria for referral established by the General Assembly.

The procedure proposed by the ABA does not establish a hierarchy of courts. It is not an appeal procedure that would allow the International Court of Justice to revise a national decision. Instead, the proposal would establish a system of cooperation, allowing the Court to help national tribunals deal with difficult problems relating to the interpretation of international law, especially a treaty. The opinions of the Court would thus make it possible for tribunals of different countries to apply a particular rule of international law in a uniform fashion, and even would be of assistance when different tribunals in the same country disagree on the interpretation of an international agreement, as has been happening recently in the United States.

There would be no interference by the International Court of Justice in the interpretation of domestic law, which would remain within the unfettered competence of the national tribunal that referred the question to the Court. Should a rule of international law as interpreted by the International Court of Justice conflict with a rule of domestic law, the national tribunal would be free to decide—in accordance with national constitutional law—how that conflict should be resolved. For instance, in the United States the rule is that a domestic law is to be construed, as far as possible, so as not to bring it into conflict with international law.[15]

While the International Court of Justice would provide a uniform interpretation of an international rule, the national tribunal would decide how that rule should be applied, if at all, to the case before it.

Originally, the ABA considered that any question of international law might be referable to the Court, but in view of the current uncertainty about some important questions of international law, exemplifed by several important disputes between the developed and developing countries, it has been suggested that United States acceptance be limited to questions involving the interpretation or application of bilateral and multilateral treaties. These treaties contain the rules of law agreed by the parties to them; consequently, the controversy can relate only to the meaning of the rule and not to its very existence. Moreover, since the United States has already accepted the jurisdiction of the International Court of Justice in more than 40 international agreements, treaty interpretation is an area in which the United States might be willing to accept additional jurisdiction.

[15] As Chief Justice Marshall stated, "an Act of Congress ought never to be construed to violate the law of nations, if any other possible construction remains." Murray v. Schooner *Charming Betsy*, 6 U.S. (2 Cranch) 64, 118 (1804). This early principle was confirmed not too long ago in Lauritzen v. Larsen, 345 U.S. 571, 578 (1953).

United States courts are not strangers to this kind of reference procedure. They engage in a similar system of "certification," as federal courts faced with a difficult question of state law have found it useful to gain the views on that question of the highest court of the state concerned.[16] The Supreme Court has pointed out that the certification procedure "does, of course, in the long run save time, energy, and resources and helps build a cooperative federalism"; it also can be depended upon to produce the correct determination of the state law in question.[17]

As was already noted, in the European Communities the reference system has been adopted on the international level in the form of "preliminary rulings" concerning, *inter alia*, the interpretation of the Community Treaty of 1957. This procedure is optional for lower national tribunals, but obligatory for tribunals of last instance.[18] The Community Court has carefully avoided decisions on the merits of a case, and when necessary has rephrased the questions to enable it to give an abstract interpretation, "without interfering with the competence of national courts to decide controversies."[19]

The novel feature of the procedure proposed by the ABA is that requests from national courts would not go directly to the International Court of Justice but would be filtered through the Special Committee of the General Assembly. While entitled to submit the questions to the Court, the Special Committee would not be obliged to do so in every case. It does not seem desirable to give unrestricted access to the Court to possibly hundreds or even thousands of national courts, as such access might overwhelm the Court with "trivial, inappropriate, needlessly involved, unripe and politically sensitive cases."[20] The Special Committee may be authorized by the General Assembly to limit the cases to those which seem to raise important issues: *e.g.*, when there have already been conflicting interpretations of a particular rule by tribunals of different countries. The Special Committee may also be authorized to adjust the number of questions forwarded to the Court in the light of the Court's docket, either by submitting fewer requests when the Court has many cases between governments before it, or by submitting more requests when—as at present—the Court has few cases before it.

While the proposal has been approved by the ABA, it still faces many obstacles. Although the idea was endorsed in principle by the U.S. Govern-

[16] *See* Note, *Inter-Jurisdictional Certification: Beyond Abstention Toward Cooperative Judicial Federalism*, 111 U. PA. L. REV. 344 (1963); Lillich & Mundy, *Federal Court Certification of Doubtful State Law Questions*, 18 U.C.L.A. L. REV. 888 (1971).

[17] Lehman Bros. v. Schein, 416 U.S. 386, 391 (1974).

[18] European Economic Community Treaty, 298 UNTS 11, Art. 177. There are similar provisions in other Community treaties and in the 1965 Treaty Establishing the Benelux Court of Justice. *See* L. BRINKHORST & H. SCHERMERS, JUDICIAL REMEDIES IN THE EUROPEAN COMMUNITIES 250 (2d ed. 1977) ("the preliminary ruling has become the most important function of the Court of Justice"); J. W. Schneider, *The Benelux Court*, 4 NETH. Y.B. INT'L L. 193 (1973).

[19] M. Waelbroeck, *The Application of EEC Law by National Courts*, 19 STAN. L. REV. 1248, 1255 (1967).

[20] Szasz, *supra* note 5, at 517.

ment during the Carter administration,[21] the Department of State was not enthusiastic about it. At first, the Department believed that an amendment to the United Nations Charter would be required and it stated that the United States was opposed to any Charter amendment.[22] When confronted with the idea that amending the Charter could be avoided by establishing a Special Committee to act as an intermediary to the Court, the Department expressed doubts about the compatibility of such device with the Charter. As a compromise, it has been suggested that the United States might ask the General Assembly to study the matter, and if necessary request an advisory opinion of the Court on the very question whether implementation of the Special Committee proposal would be compatible with the Charter.

The various issues raised by the ABA proposal are being explored now in Congress[23] and at the United Nations. Although there are obstacles to be overcome before this proposal is realized, the task is not impossible; it may, however, take a while.

LOUIS B. SOHN*

[21] DEP'T OF STATE, REFORM AND RESTRUCTURING OF THE UNITED NATIONS SYSTEM 7 (Selected Documents No. 8, 1978) (statement by the President: "we would support a national appellate court, before rendering its own judgment in a case, having recourse to the International Court of Justice for an advisory 'preliminary opinion' on issues of international law").

[22] *Id.* at 16–17. *See also Department of State Study on Widening Access to the International Court of Justice*, 16 ILM 187, 190–91, 204–06 (1977).

[23] On Dec. 17, 1982, the House of Representatives adopted a resolution presented by the Committee on Foreign Affairs (H.R. Con. Res. 86, as revised), urging the President "to consider the feasibility of pursuing, through the United Nations," the idea of expanding the advisory jurisdiction of the International Court of Justice, and in particular to:

> explore the appropriateness of the establishment of a special committee, under United Nations auspices, authorized to seek an advisory opinion of the International Court of Justice, upon request by a national court or tribunal which is duly authorized by national legislation to make such a request, regarding any question of international law of which such court or tribunal has jurisdiction.

128 CONG. REC. H10198 (daily ed. Dec. 17, 1982).

* This comment is based on a statement made on Nov. 6, 1982, at the meeting of the International Studies Association-South, held in Atlanta, Georgia.

NOTES AND COMMENTS

REVIEW ESSAY: GOOD FAITH IN PUBLIC INTERNATIONAL LAW

It is commonly understood by international lawyers that a requirement of good faith in various contexts is a well-established principle of international law and even one of the most fundamental ones. Article 2(2) of the Charter of the United Nations, supported by General Assembly Resolution 2625 (XXV) on the principles governing friendly relations and cooperation among states, and Articles 26 and 31(1) of the Vienna Convention on the Law of Treaties, are relied upon to demonstrate the acknowledgment of this principle in state practice. According to these articles (of which, incidentally, Articles 26 and 31 of the Vienna Convention are declaratory of customary rules), all obligations deriving from treaties (and from the Charter in the first instance) are to be interpreted and implemented in good faith. Moreover, in the *Nuclear Tests* cases, the International Court of Justice proclaimed that "[o]ne of the basic principles governing the creation and performance of legal obligations, *whatever* their source, is the principle of good faith."[1]

So far, so good. But if one persists and asks exactly what that means and precisely how good faith functions in the creation and performance of international obligations, one will obtain only vague explanations. In the cases just mentioned, the Court merely drew the conclusion that the declarations by the French authorities that they did not intend to make further atmospheric nuclear tests were binding upon France; the Court scarcely elaborated on why good faith was operative in such a case.

Strangely enough, this so often invoked principle has rarely been studied in depth, and it is very difficult to find satisfactory answers to these questions in the legal literature. More exactly, it *was* difficult before the publication a few years ago of the book *Good Faith in Public International Law* by Elisabeth Zoller,[2] which seems not to have received the attention it deserves in English-speaking countries.

This study can be considered as comprehensive; it is impossible nowadays to discuss good faith in international law without referring to it. Indeed, the author tries to trace the imprints left by good faith on every aspect of international law. The book is divided into two parts: recourse to good faith, and the effects of good faith. In the first, she successively studies good faith and the law of treaties (conclusion and performance); good faith and international customary law (acquisition of rights, abuse of rights, and proceedings before international tribunals); and good faith in the law of international organizations (as applied internally under the rules established by the organizations and as regards their powers). The second part is devoted to questions of interpretation (subjective and objective), international responsibility (breach

[1] 1974 ICJ REP. 253, 268 (emphasis added).

[2] E. ZOLLER, LA BONNE FOI EN DROIT INTERNATIONAL PUBLIC. (Paris: Editions A. Pedone, 1977. Pp. xxvii, 392. English summary precedes French text.)

of law and injury), and nullity (admission of nullity and consequences of a claim in nullity).

In all these fields the author has subjected international legal practice to a careful and rigorous analysis, which shows how frequently the concept of good faith is used and how important it is to the functioning of legal mechanisms. However, this learned study ends with disconcerting and disappointing conclusions. The author claims that good faith is not an autonomous source of legal rights and duties, but can only, in a very limited hypothesis, be used to defend against excusable error. Estoppel itself can be explained without the help of good faith. The role of good faith in the performance of international obligations is just as elusive. In every case, legal rules or concepts more precise than good faith suffice to explain the legal effects that are produced (*e.g.*, the rule *pacta sunt servanda*, the concept of the unlawful act).

Consequently, no general obligation to behave in good faith exists in public international law. Good faith is no more than an ethical principle. Moreover, it is well known that it does not always inspire state conduct in international affairs, even though states resent as a slur on their honor the slightest doubt about their good faith. Whence, in order to avoid diplomatic complications, the habit of resorting to other concepts when criticizing their behavior.

As surprising as they are, conclusions deriving from such a large and rigorous inquiry are to be taken seriously. Do they require a complete revision of traditional conceptions about the matter? If they are true in every respect, we should admit that the references to good faith in texts as important as the Charter of the United Nations or the Vienna Convention are devoid of legal meaning, that those references are legal niceties or allusions to the need to moralize international relations. Such far-reaching assertions cannot be accepted without hesitation.

On several occasions, the author underlines the social importance of good faith, even its social necessity, already alluded to by the International Court of Justice (p. 344). She recognizes that "the principle of good faith refers to a rule of social conduct obvious in the sight of everybody" in the last paragraph of her book. Elsewhere, she finds good faith "an institution immanent in every legal order" (p. 12). That is quite good. Why, then, and by what inconsistency, would international law not yet have integrated these realities into its system of rules and concepts, since they directly involve its functioning?

Ultimately, the very concept of good faith has to be reexamined. Although in its introductory chapter the book lists many different meanings of good faith, this concept is persistently considered by the author as a subjective one, resting upon individual psychology (p. 10). From such a point of departure, it is hardly surprising that good faith will always be seen as a purely moral concept.

Good faith is certainly that, but not only that. It refers also, as the author admits, to rules of behavior. In particular, good faith requires that the expressed will be consistent with the real will and, more generally, that the legal reality be consistent with what it seems to be (that is, consistent with the appearances created by the declarations or the behavior of legal actors). Good faith excludes any separation between reality and appearances.

So conceived, good faith is indeed one of the main conditions for the functioning of any legal order, as Zoller, following the International Court of Justice, acknowledges. More particularly, however, it is essential to a nonformalistic order, which allows the most room for the creation and performance of law by the will of those who are submitted to it, and does not possess any system of enforcement independent of their will. It is therefore of fundamental importance to the international legal order, which is marked by all these characteristics. In many respects, it constitutes the postulate on which this order rests in its entirety. The effects attached to the expressed will and, more broadly, to the behavior of international actors are conceivable only because it is assumed that they act in good faith and that what is apparent is in conformity with their real will. If this postulate is not taken for granted, the whole fabric of international law will collapse.

To contend that good faith has no room in international law because governments very often behave in bad faith is a poor argument. In fact, the argument runs the other way. If international actors really act in bad faith, if they think and will other than what they say, if they have no intention of being bound when they pretend to commit themselves, then it is absolutely necessary to deprive this bad faith of any efficacy. This can be done only if the actors are taken at their word, whatever their true will may be: that is, if they are presumed to be acting in good faith.

To sum up, good faith fulfills in international law three significant functions, which are closely related.

First, as we have seen, good faith is always presumed of actors in international legal life; this makes it possible to ascertain the legal meaning of their behavior. Good faith is at the foundation of *pacta sunt servanda*, since when states enter into a contract, they are always assumed to have willingly committed themselves to its terms. Thus, their will must produce the effects it has openly sought, and they must be considered effectively bound, in accordance with their declarations.

The same reasoning is equally appropriate to unilateral acts that convey a state's intent to be bound, which is what the International Court of Justice found in the *Nuclear Tests* cases. (One can question whether the expression of a will to be bound was discernible in the declarations cited by the Court, but this is an issue of fact that leaves the reasoning intact.)

Similarly, when, by its behavior, a state makes clear in a concrete case that it intends to apply a rule of law, it must be deemed to be acting in good faith and its behavior accordingly deserves to be considered as a customary precedent.

A second function of good faith is that it furnishes a measure—or pattern—for determining the extent of the legal obligations assumed by states or other subjects of international law. This is why good faith is not only the basis, but also an integral part of *pacta sunt servanda*. It also explains Article 31(1) of the Vienna Convention and other like texts. That a legal obligation must be interpreted and performed in good faith means that it prescribes all that good faith implies, but only what good faith implies. This is true of every conventional obligation and can be extended to every legal obligation, whatever its source, as the Court recognized in the judgment quoted above.

From a practical point of view, one will probably have to resort to more precise criteria (like the rules of interpretation in Articles 31–33 of the Vienna Convention, or the concept of reasonableness) in order to ascertain concretely what good faith actually prescribes, but it is good faith that determines the goal to be attained.

Last, good faith protects those who trust, reasonably, the appearances created by the behavior of other international legal actors (who have confidence in the good faith of those actors), or who have truly fallen into error: the innocent victims, in all good faith, of appearances.

Thus, good faith presents itself as an absolutely necessary ingredient to the operation of the whole international legal order, namely, to the creation and performance of law. Moreover, this quality is very well shown in the various chapters of Zoller's book. She herself describes it evocatively when she says that good faith is like "oil in the engine." In my view, oil, in this case, would mean gasoline.

Ultimately, the difference between Zoller's position and the thesis that I am advocating could be said to belong to the realm of philosophy rather than to legal science. I could agree, perhaps, if it is understood as legal philosophy, but I would be happier with legal epistemology, even if this phrase has a pronounced touch of pedantry. The real question is whether we consider law in isolation from all the social factors (including ideological and ethical ones) that have an effect on its functioning (beginning with its making)—Kelsen's celebrated first precept for a pure science of law—or whether we admit that these factors have to be taken into consideration in order to discover the foundations of the rules, usually buried under their overt meaning, but essential to understanding their very bearing in difficult cases.

From the standpoint of Kelsen's criteria, Zoller's conclusions would probably be right. If, on the contrary, we take the broader view, I think that we cannot escape recognizing that good faith is really a principle of international law, and that all the actors in the international legal order are subjected to it and must endure its consequences, since good faith will serve to determine both the legal effects of their declarations and behavior and the extent of their duties. It is not a simple ethical principle, when applied to law, even though it is *also* an ethical principle and was borrowed by law from the ethical realm.

On the other hand, it is true that, in practice, this general principle of law has only marginal value as an autonomous source of rights and duties. On this point, Zoller's conclusions cannot be faulted. But does this finding imply that the role of good faith is a minor one? Is the only conceivable test of the legal nature of a concept that it be an autonomous source of legal rights and duties? Is that the most suitable one in this case? The point is debatable. Even apart from its function in helping measure the extent of the obligation undertaken, which is far from negligible, good faith plays, *mutatis mutandis*, a role in international law comparable to that of a catalyst in a chemical reaction. Alone, the catalyst is completely passive. It must be added to other elements for a reaction to occur; without it, nothing will happen, even if all the necessary components are present in sufficient quantities. It is a bit the same with good faith. It is never taken into consideration by law in the abstract, as a purely psychological disposition. It is always related to specific behavior or declarations and it invests them with legal significance and legal effects. Furthermore, like many general principles of law, good faith is often hidden by the more precise rules it has generated (*e.g., pacta sunt servanda*), so that it becomes no longer necessary to rely upon it expressly for ordinary practical purposes. But even in such instances, general principles retain their full value as the *ratio legis* to which one may profitably turn in difficult cases. Nobody can ignore them without running the risk of not understanding the real meaning of the rules. Nobody can ignore that good faith forms part of the foundation of the whole international legal structure without running the risk of reducing international law to a set of hollow legal formulas.

MICHEL VIRALLY*

CORRESPONDENCE

TO THE EDITORS-IN-CHIEF:

September 21, 1982

The case note on *United States v. Whiting*, which appears in the Judicial Decisions section of your July 1982 issue, reflects a serious misunderstanding of the law of search and seizure in the armed forces. At the bottom of page 625, the note states that in *Whiting* the U.S. Court of Military Appeals "did not consider Whiting's constitutional rights, the application of which might have led to a contrary result." It then goes on to argue that the Fourth Amendment should apply to searches conducted by military officials abroad.

Your readers should be made aware that searches by military officials have, in fact, been subject to the Fourth Amendment, including the requirement for "probable cause," since at least 1959 when *United States v. Brown* (10 CMA 482, 28 CMR 48) was decided. The Fourth Amendment requirements have recently been codified in the Military Rules of Evidence, Executive Order 12198, March 12, 1980, which closely follow the Federal Rules of Evidence in form and substance.

The search in *Whiting* was conducted only after the appropriate commander had determined that probable cause existed; this determination was subject to judicial review at Sergeant Whiting's trial and on appeal. The only issue before the Court of Military Appeals was whether the NATO Status of Forces Agreement granted Whiting any rights in relation to search and seizure *beyond* those given him by the Fourth Amendment. This question the court answered, correctly, in the negative.

Judge Fletcher's dissent was not over whether the Fourth Amendment should apply to overseas searches. Rather, he argued that a search conducted in violation of the Status of Forces Agreement was, by that fact alone, "unreasonable" under the Fourth Amendment. This novel approach goes far beyond existing Fourth Amendment jurisprudence, and would allow individuals indirectly to gain rights under an international agreement, even if the contracting parties did not intend to create any individual rights. The majority rejected Judge Fletcher's approach, again correctly.

BURRUS M. CARNAHAN, Lt. Col., USAF
Staff Judge Advocate

* Professor, University of Law, Economics and Social Sciences, Paris, and Graduate Institute of International Studies, Geneva.

CONTEMPORARY PRACTICE OF THE UNITED STATES RELATING TO INTERNATIONAL LAW

MARIAN NASH LEICH*

The material in this section is arranged according to the system employed in the annual *Digest of United States Practice in International Law*, published by the Department of State.

ALIENS

(U.S. *Digest*, Ch. 3, §3)

Federal Diversity Jurisdiction

Congressman Robert W. Kastenmeier, Chairman of the Subcommittee on Courts, Civil Liberties and the Administration of Justice of the House Committee on the Judiciary, asked for the views of the Department of State on H.R. 6691, a bill that would abolish federal court jurisdiction based upon diversity of citizenship but would retain similar jurisdiction based upon alienage. The Department's reply, by a letter from Powell A. Moore, Assistant Secretary for Congressional Relations, to Congressman Kastenmeier, dated August 9, 1982, read in part:

> The Federal courts have exercised jurisdiction in cases involving aliens since the first Judiciary Act in 1789. The Department of State welcomes the continuation of Federal jurisdiction in these cases.
>
> The United States is responsible under international law to provide aliens fair and impartial justice and access to the United States court system. In some cases treaties provide specific standards of access to the judicial process, but even without a treaty, an alien is entitled to certain internationally recognized minimum standards of justice. Under international law, moreover, the Federal government is responsible for any denial of justice by a State court, even though the Federal government has no direct authority over those tribunals. Thus, while the Department has great confidence in the competence, integrity and impartiality of the State court systems, the availability of civil jurisdiction in Federal courts under a single nationwide system of rules tends to provide a useful reassurance to foreign governments and their citizens.
>
> It is worth noting that, for these reasons, the American Law Institute endorsed retention of alienage jurisdiction in its study of Federal jurisdiction. That report stated:
>
> > Whether the state courts in fact generally render full, fair, and speedy justice to alien litigants is largely beside the point. It is important in the relations of this country with other nations that any possible appearance of injustice or tenable ground for resentment be avoided.

* Office of the Legal Adviser, Department of State.

> This objective can best be achieved by giving the foreigner the assurance that he can have his cases tried in a court with the best procedures the federal government can supply and with the dignity and prestige of the United States behind it.

(The American Law Institute, *Study of the Division of Jurisdiction between State and Federal Courts*, p. 108.)[1]

Diplomatic Missions

(U.S. *Digest*, Ch. 4, §1)

Communications to Courts

A letter dated August 18, 1982 and addressed to District Judge Walter T. McGovern, U.S. District Court for the Western District of Washington, by William F. Baxter, Assistant Attorney General of the United States, constituted a formal statement of interest by the United States in *Washington Public Power Supply System v. Western Nuclear, Inc.* (No. C81-1362M), with specific reference to a motion of the Government of the United Kingdom for leave to file a brief amicus. The brief was expected to support the defendants' motion to dismiss for want of jurisdiction under *Timberlane Lumber Co. v. Bank of America* (549 F.2d 597 (9th Cir. 1976)). The United States expressed no views on the jurisdictional question but urged that the United Kingdom be afforded an opportunity to present its views as amicus on the issue of dismissal and that they be afforded due consideration.

The case was related to the treble damage action initiated by Westinghouse Electric Corporation in October 1976 against 12 foreign and 17 domestic corporations, alleging a conspiracy by a worldwide cartel to rig bids, fix prices, and divide portions of the world uranium market.[1] The suit was settled in 1980.

Subsequently, in December 1981, the Washington Public Power Supply System brought a new treble damage action against a number of the Westinghouse defendants, alleging that it paid inflated fuel prices because of the defendants' manipulation of the uranium market through the cartel.

The U.S. statement of interest read in part:

> As the court is aware, the Government of the United Kingdom (as well as a number of other foreign governments) in recent years have expressed serious concern over United States antitrust litigation, including litigation over international uranium marketing arrangements, which they perceive as threatening to their sovereign interests. The intensity and authenticity of the concern of the Government of the United King-

[1] Dept. of State File No. P82 0127-0417.

The Department had made a similar recommendation in 1977 in regard to H.R. 9622, 95th Cong., 1st Sess. (1977). *See* H.R. Rep. No. 95-893, 95th Cong., 2d Sess. (1978).

[1] *See In re* Uranium Antitrust Litigation. Westinghouse Electric Corp. v. Rio Algom Ltd., 617 F.2d 1248 (7th Cir. 1980).

dom is reflected in its enactment in 1980 of legislation at least partially in response to the uranium litigation then pending in the United States District Court in Chicago.

The Court of Appeals for this Circuit has held, in the *Timberlane* case, that considerations of international comity must be taken into account in considering whether jurisdiction should be asserted in an antitrust case challenging conduct which occurred outside the United States. *Timberlane Lumber Co. v. Bank of America*, 549 F.2d 597 (9th Cir. 1976). Where litigation is perceived by a foreign government as potentially affecting its sovereign interests, and where considerations of international comity are relevant as a matter of law to the issue before the court, the views and representations of the foreign government should be afforded appropriate deference and weight.

The filing by a foreign government of an *amicus curiae* brief is the appropriate mechanism for foreign governments to communicate their views to United States courts in which litigation is pending which they consider may affect their interests. Prior to 1978, it was customary for foreign governments to communicate such concerns by delivering diplomatic notes to the Department of State, which the Department of State would in turn deliver to the federal courts. In that year, however, the Clerk of the United States Supreme Court notified the Solicitor General that a foreign government wishing to present views to a federal court in a pending case should do so by submitting a brief *amicus curiae*. Accordingly, since that time both the Department of Justice and the Department of State have consistently encouraged interested foreign governments to do so.

We believe that such presentations may assist the courts in their consideration of the views of foreign governments and in making appropriate accommodations between the laws and policies of the various sovereign nations. Indeed, in a context in which foreign government interests may be relevant as a matter of law, serious foreign relations concerns could arise if those governments were denied a means of communicating their views to the judiciary.[2]

Treaties and Other International Agreements

(U.S. *Digest*, Ch. 5, §1)

Reservations—American Convention on Human Rights

Following a request to the Inter-American Court of Human Rights from the Inter-American Commission on Human Rights for an advisory opinion interpreting Articles 74(2) (ratification and entry into force) and 75 (reservations) of the American Convention on Human Rights, the Court invited

[2] Dept. of State File No. P82 0147-0738.

On Aug. 23, 1982, Judge McGovern directed that an order be entered in the minutes granting the motion of the Government of the United Kingdom to file an amicus curiae brief and for access to the pleadings, access to be permitted for the attorneys only and under the terms of the protective orders in the case.

interested states and organs of the Organization of American States to submit observations.

The Commission formulated its request in the following terms:

> [F]rom what moment is a state deemed to have become a party to the American Convention on Human Rights when it ratifies or adheres to the Convention with one or more reservations: from the date of the deposit of [the] instrument of ratification or adhesion or upon the termination of the period specified in Article 20 of the Vienna Convention on the Law of Treaties?

The written observations of the United States, transmitted in a letter dated September 3, 1982, from Acting Legal Adviser James H. Michel to Charles Moyer, Secretary of the Inter-American Court of Human Rights, follow in major part:[1]

> The United States considers that Articles 74(2) and 75 of the American Convention and Article 20 of the Vienna Convention on the Law of Treaties are not in conflict.[2] Rather, they act in concert to fix the point in time at which a State ratifying or adhering to the American Convention with a reservation becomes a Party. That point in time occurs as soon as any State Party accepts the reservation, and if no State Party has acted to accept or object to the reservation within a twelve-month period, it occurs at the end of that period.
>
> Article 74(2) of the American Convention provides that ratification of or adherence to the American Convention is "made by the deposit of an instrument of ratification or adherence with the General Secretariat," and that the American Convention enters into force for each new State ratifying or adhering to it "on the date of the deposit of its instrument of ratification or adherence." Thus a State becomes Party to the American Convention, and assumes the legal responsibilities contained therein, on the date of the deposit of its instrument of ratification or adherence. Article 74(2) is thus consistent with Article 16 of the Vienna Convention, which provides that

[1] The headings to the quoted portion of the letter and most of the footnotes are omitted here.

[2] The *travaux préparatoires* of the American Convention do not address the relationship of Articles 74(2) and 75. The draft Convention which was prepared by the Commission for consideration at San Jose would have permitted reservations only if a constitutional provision were contrary to a provision of the Convention. *Draft Inter-American Convention on Protection of Human Rights*, OEA/Ser.K/XVI/1.1 (Sept. 22, 1969), at 22. In the written observations submitted on this draft, both Argentina and the Dominican Republic objected that it was inconsistent with the Vienna Convention on the Law of Treaties. *Conferencia Especializada Interamericana sobre Derechos Humanos*, OEA/Ser.K/XVI/1.2 (1973), at 48, 51. Similarly, the United States proposed eliminating Article 66 on the grounds that it restricted the customary scope of reservations, which included inconsistency with legislation and judicial decisions as well as constitutional provisions. *Id.*, at 89. The working group which considered this article amended the Commission draft to refer to "constitutional or legal provisions," but, at the committee level, the words "or legal" were removed. The committee decision was based on Article II(1) of the Convention which obligated States Parties to adopt the necessary legislative measures to implement the rights conferred by the Convention. A U.S. proposal to substitute an article referring to the Vienna Convention failed in committee. *Id.*, at 379. However, at the plenary session, an extended debate took place on the system to be adopted concerning reservations. Unfortunately, the record merely notes that the final outcome was the adoption of a proposal by Uruguay which referred to the Vienna Convention. *Id.*, at 459.

"Unless the treaty otherwise provides, instruments of ratification, acceptance, approval or accession establish the consent of a State to be bound by a treaty upon:

. . .

"(b) their deposit with the depositary. . . ."

In executing its responsibility to deposit instruments of ratification and accession, the depositary must determine when an instrument of ratification or accession which has been presented by a State subject to one or more reservations should be accepted for deposit.

There is a distinction between tender or receipt of an instrument of ratification or adherence which contains reservations and the actual deposit of that instrument.

The distinction between the tender or receipt and the deposit of an instrument of ratification or adherence was addressed in a report on depositary practice in relation to reservations prepared in 1964 by the Secretary-General of the United Nations. The report compiled the observations of States and international organizations on depositary practice. In that study the following question was posed:

"When an instrument of ratification, accession or acceptance is accompanied by a reservation which is not expressly permitted or prohibited by the text of the convention and not otherwise already accepted:

"(a) Do you receive the instrument for definitive deposit; or

"(b) Do you treat the instrument as having been tendered for deposit pending consultation with interested States regarding the reservation?"

Both the Organization of American States (OAS) and the United States responded that their practice was to follow alternative (b). The OAS responded simply that "[t]he answer is (b)." The United States took the opportunity to elaborate on its understanding of depositary practice with respect to reservations, saying:

"The United States Government as depositary ordinarily considers that it cannot immediately accept the instrument for definitive deposit. It may, of course, receive the document, deferring a determination with respect to definitive deposit until appropriate steps have been taken to resolve any question concerning the acceptability of the reservation. In general, the instrument in such a case is treated as having been tendered for deposit pending consultation with the interested States regarding the reservation."

When the distinction between the tender or receipt and the deposit of instruments of ratification is kept in mind, it is clear that the purported inconsistency between Article 74 and the Vienna Convention does not exist.

Article 20, paragraph 4 of the Vienna Convention provides that, unless the treaty in question stipulates otherwise,

"(a) acceptance by another contracting State of a reservation constitutes the reserving State a party to the treaty in relation to that other State if or when the treaty is in force for those States;

. . .

"(c) an act expressing a State's consent to be bound by the treaty and containing a reservation is effective as soon as at least one other contracting State has accepted the reservation."

These provisions, incorporated by reference in Article 75 of the American Convention, provide the applicable standards for the General Secretariat to apply in serving as depositary for the American Convention. The Secretariat may thus not deposit an instrument of ratification or adherence containing a reservation unless and until the requirements set forth in Article 20, paragraph 4 of the Vienna Convention have been met. When those conditions have been met, the State's instrument of ratification or adherence is deposited, and, in accordance with Article 74(2) of the American Convention, the American Convention enters into force for the ratifying State on that date.

The practice and procedure specified in the American Convention and, by reference, the Vienna Convention, are consonant with the underlying legal significance of the reservation and ratification process. The act of ratification or of accession "establishes on the international plane" a State's "consent to be bound by a treaty." Vienna Convention, Art. 2, paragraph 1(b). When a State proposes to ratify a treaty with a reservation, it in effect proposes a unilateral modification of "the legal effect of certain provisions of the treaty in their application to that State." Vienna Convention, Art. 2, paragraph 1(d). While such modification does not *prima facie* invalidate the attempt at treaty adherence, see *The Genocide Convention Case*, [1951] I.C.J. 25, unless the reservation made is provided for in the treaty, the principle of reciprocity requires that other Parties to the treaty have the opportunity to consider, and to accept or reject, the proposed unilateral modification before the ratifying State acquires treaty rights.

Under the Vienna Convention, an instrument of ratification or accession presented for deposit with a reservation "is effective as soon as at least one other contracting State has accepted the reservation." Vienna Convention, Art. 20, paragraph 4(c). *See, id.*, Art. 2, paragraph 1(b) (concerning the definition of "ratification" and "accession"). The ratifying State is then bound by the terms of the treaty, as modified by its reservation. *Id.*, Art. 20, paragraph 4(c), Art. 21, paragraph 1.

Acceptance by one Party of another State's reservation does not, of course, in any way impinge upon the right of other Parties to consider independently the proposed reservation. While there is little international practice on this point, since the acceptance of reservations to multilateral treaties is usually tacit, it appears that an explicit acceptance by another contracting State of a reservation constitutes the reserving State a Party to the treaty in relation to the accepting State, but not in relation to all States Parties. *See* Vienna Convention, Art. 20, paragraph 4(a).[3]

[3] From the point of view of the jurisdiction of the Inter-American Commission on Human Rights, once a ratifying or adhering State becomes a Party to the American Convention in relation to one other State, the ratifying or adhering State is bound under international law to respect the terms of the American Convention. As such, it is a State Party to the American Convention for

The procedures which govern the acceptance of reservations to the American Convention are set forth in Articles 20 and 23 of the Vienna Convention. American Convention, Art. 75. Reservations may be accepted expressly or tacitly.

An express acceptance of a reservation must be formulated in writing and communicated to the contracting States and to the other States entitled to become Parties to the treaty. Vienna Convention, Art. 23, paragraph 1. The General Secretariat, as depositary, has the responsibility for communicating the receipt of a written notice of acceptance. *Cf.* Standards on Reservations to Inter-American Multilateral Treaties, sec. D(4).

Tacit acceptance of a reservation is considered to have occurred "if [a State] shall have raised no objection to the reservation by the end of a period of twelve months after it was notified of the reservation or by the date on which it expressed its consent to be bound by the treaty, whichever is later." Vienna Convention, Art. 20, paragraph 5.

The instrument of ratification or adherence of a reserving State is deposited, and the reserving State thus becomes a Party to the American Convention, when its instrument of ratification has been tendered to the General Secretariat for deposit *and* at least one State Party has accepted the proposed reservation, either expressly at any time or tacitly by not objecting within the twelve-month period specified in the Vienna Convention.[4]

Act of State Doctrine

(U.S. *Digest*, Ch. 6, §8)

Treaty Provisions for Compensation in Expropriations, and Judicial Abstention

In a letter to the Solicitor General of the United States, Rex E. Lee, dated November 19, 1982, the Legal Adviser of the Department of State, Davis R. Robinson, set out the Department's views: (1) that the 1951 Treaty of Amity

---

the purposes of Articles 33–51 of the American Convention and of Article 1, paragraph 2(a), and Articles 19 and 23 of the Statute of the Inter-American Commission on Human Rights. Statute of the Inter-American Commission on Human Rights, approved by OAS G.A. Res. 447 (Oct. 1979), *reprinted in* Organization of American States, *Handbook of Existing Rules Pertaining to Human Rights* 95, OEA/Ser.L/V/II.50 doc. 6 (1980). Presumably, such State would also be a State Party within the meaning of all provisions relevant to the operation of the Court.

To be sure, there may be instances when it will be relevant that certain Parties to the American Convention are not Parties in relation to each other. For example, it would seem that a State Party could allege pursuant to Article 45 that another State Party has committed a violation of the Convention only if the two States involved were Parties in relation to each other. This issue could arise if one or more States were to oppose the entry into force of the Convention between themselves and the reserving State. *Cf.* Vienna Convention, Art. 20, paragraph 4(b). In such cases there would be a group of States, all of which would be Parties to the American Convention. However, they would not all be Parties in relation to one another. Presumably, the Commission will address issues of this kind, as they may arise, on a case-by-case basis.

[4] Dept. of State File Nos. P82 0104-1309, 0151-1361, and 0151-1362.

and Economic Relations between the United States and Ethiopia[1] specifies a "controlling legal" principle, as called for in the Supreme Court's decision in *Banco Nacional de Cuba v. Sabbatino*,[2] for compensation in the event of expropriation; and (2) that where such a controlling legal principle is present, U.S. courts may presume that adjudication would not be inconsistent with U.S. foreign policy interests under the act of state doctrine. The Legal Adviser expressed the Department's anticipation that courts would not rely upon silence by the Executive in expropriation cases where a controlling legal principle for compensation exists as a basis for abstention under the act of state doctrine. He also indicated that in such circumstances the Department of State would not, as a general rule, plan to inform the courts of the absence of foreign policy objections to adjudication.

Mr. Robinson's letter was written in conjunction with a brief amicus for the United States in *Kalamazoo Spice Extraction Company v. The Provisional Military Government of Socialist Ethiopia.*[3] The letter states in material part:

> As expressed in *Banco Nacional de Cuba v. Sabbatino*, 376 U.S. 398 (1964), the presumption that the courts should abstain from considering the expropriatory acts of foreign states appears to have reflected two major concerns of the Supreme Court. The first was that articulation by United States courts of an applicable international law standard for compensation would pose special difficulties, including a perceived risk of conflict with the Executive Branch's assertion of a governing legal standard in the conduct of foreign relations. The second of the Court's principal concerns was that adjudication could complicate the conduct of bilateral relations with the expropriating state—for example, by frustrating ongoing claims settlement negotiations between the two governments.
>
> Where, as in the present case, there is an applicable treaty standard, the first of these concerns falls away. The second concern—potential interference with ongoing claims negotiations or other foreign relations interests—does not, in our view, warrant automatic abstention by the courts on Act of State grounds. As Legal Adviser Monroe Leigh wrote to the Solicitor General concerning foreign expropriations in 1975:
>
>> In general this Department's experience provides little support for a presumption that adjudication of acts of foreign states in accordance with relevant principles of international law would embarrass the conduct of foreign policy. [Letter of November 25, 1975, *reprinted at* Appendix I to *Alfred Dunhill of London, Inc. v. Cuba*, 425 U.S. 682, 706 (1976).]
>
> The experience of the past seven years has reinforced this conclusion. Accordingly, we believe that a broad, inflexible rule of abstention in expropriation cases is not necessary to safeguard our foreign policy interests. When, as in this case, there is a controlling legal standard for compensation, we believe that the presumption should be that adjudi-

[1] *Signed* Sept. 7, 1951, 4 UST 2134, TIAS No. 2864.

[2] 376 U.S. 398, 428 (1964).

[3] No. 82-1521 (6th Cir. filed Nov. 19, 1982). For the district court's opinion, which is summarized *infra* at p. 144, see 543 F.Supp. 1224 (W.D. Mich. 1982).

cation would not be inconsistent with foreign policy interests under the Act of State doctrine.

If, however, the Department of State determines in a given case that judicial abstention is necessary for foreign policy reasons, it will request the Department of Justice to communicate that determination to the appropriate court. Such a communication could be either in response to an inquiry from a court concerned about the foreign policy implications of the case before it or on the initiative of the Executive Branch. (Private litigants and foreign governments frequently bring cases to the attention of the Department of State which they believe raise Act of State concerns.) If we indicate that adjudication would be inconsistent with foreign policy interests of the United States, we trust that the court will give appropriate weight to our views. As a general rule, however, where there is a controlling legal standard for compensation, we would not plan to inform the courts of the absence of foreign policy objections to adjudication of expropriation claims. Therefore, we would anticipate that silence on the part of the Executive in such cases would not be relied upon as a basis for judicial abstention under the Act of State doctrine.[4]

[4] Dept. of State File No. P82 0168-0262.

The brief amicus for the United States argued that, contrary to the district court's ruling, U.S. treaty provisions calling for "prompt payment of just and effective compensation" in expropriations incorporate a precise, controlling legal principle of international law. Referring to the Legal Adviser's letter, the brief also stated the Department's policy on communications to courts in expropriation cases involving the act of state defense where a treaty or other agreement provides such a controlling legal principle. The brief stated that the Executive would, generally, plan to communicate with the courts in such circumstances only where it had discerned an inconsistency between domestic adjudication and the foreign policy interests of the United States.

JUDICIAL DECISIONS

MONROE LEIGH

Act of state doctrine—expropriation of foreign assets—compensation terms in Treaty of Amity and Economic Relations not a bar to the application of act of state

ETHIOPIAN SPICE EXTRACTION SHARE CO. v. KALAMAZOO SPICE EXTRACTION CO., ET AL.; KALAMAZOO SPICE EXTRACTION CO. v. THE PROVISIONAL MILITARY GOVERNMENT OF SOCIALIST ETHIOPIA. 543 F.Supp. 1224.
U.S. District Court, W.D. Mich., July 6, 1982.

This litigation, consisting of two related actions, arises out of an expropriation by the Provisional Military Government of Socialist Ethiopia (PMGSE). In 1966, the Kalamazoo Spice Extraction Company (Kal-Spice), a U.S. corporation, established the Ethiopian Spice Extraction Share Company (ESESCO) under the laws of Ethiopia, with Kal-Spice owning approximately 80 percent of ESESCO's shares. Kal-Spice arranged financing and built a production facility with the alleged understanding that ESESCO would sell Kal-Spice its entire output of oleoresin spices each year. The operation was profitable until 1975, when PMGSE expropriated a majority of ESESCO's shares.

In one of the two actions,[1] plaintiff Kal-Spice sought damages for PMGSE's expropriation, and PMGSE moved to dismiss on the ground, *inter alia*, that the action was barred by the act of state doctrine.[2] Despite the existence of a 1953 treaty between the United States and Ethiopia providing for "prompt payment of just and effective compensation" in cases of expropriation, the U.S. District Court for the Western District of Michigan (per Gibson, J.) held that the act of state doctrine barred the plaintiff's claim.

In reaching this conclusion, the court addressed three central issues. The first related to the Treaty of Amity and Economic Relations between the United States and Ethiopia of 1951. Article VIII, paragraph 2 of the Treaty provides:

> Property of nationals and companies of either High Contracting Party, including interests in property, shall receive the most constant protection and security within the territories of the other High Contracting Party. Such property shall not be taken except for a public purpose, nor shall it be taken without the *prompt payment of just and effective compensation.*[3]

[1] The other action in this case was brought by ESESCO, which sought to recover the purchase price of an order of oleoresin received by Kal-Spice prior to the expropriation. ESESCO moved for summary judgment on its claim. However, the court held that there remained unresolved issues of material fact. As of the date of this writing, ESESCO's claim is still being litigated.

[2] PMGSE also moved to dismiss Kal-Spice's claim on the grounds that it was immune under the Foreign Sovereign Immunities Act, that there were no contacts with the state of Michigan sufficient to establish personal jurisdiction, and that venue would be proper only in the District of Columbia. The court, however, did not address these sovereign immunity issues in view of its disposition of the action on act of state grounds.

[3] *Signed* Sept. 7, 1951, 4 UST 2134, TIAS No. 2864 (emphasis added).

In evaluating the effect of the Treaty on the act of state doctrine, the court focused its analysis on the following language of the Supreme Court in *Banco Nacional de Cuba v. Sabbatino*:

> [T]he Judicial Branch will not examine the validity of a *taking of property within its own territory* by a foreign sovereign government, extant and recognized by this country at the time of suit, *in the absence of a treaty or other unambiguous agreement regarding controlling legal principles*, even if the complaint alleges that the taking violates customary international law.[4]

PMGSE argued that because the Treaty contained no definitions of the terms "prompt," "just," or "effective," it was not the type of "treaty or other unambiguous agreement regarding controlling legal principles" contemplated by the Supreme Court in *Sabbatino*. The court agreed, holding that the terms of the Treaty were so "inherently general, doubtful, and susceptible of multiple interpretation that in the absence of an established body of law to clarify their meaning a court cannot reasonably be asked to apply them to a particular set of facts."[5] Although the court acknowledged that the terms of the Treaty could be clarified by resort to the definitions in sections 187–190 of the *Restatement (Second) of Foreign Relations Law of the United States* (1965), the court held that it would be unwarranted to rely on this authority as accurately expressing the meaning intended by the Government of Ethiopia in its Treaty agreement.

The court found further support for its conclusion by reference to the underlying policy of the act of state doctrine, which it characterized as that of foreclosing judicial examination of acts of foreign states where such adjudication might conflict with or embarrass the executive branch in its conduct of foreign relations. Thus, the court reasoned, an "exception for 'a treaty or other unambiguous agreement . . .' seems to address a formal and binding statement of agreement upon principles which removes the danger of judicial misconstruction of the foreign policy of the Executive Branch."[6] Under this rationale, the court concluded that the Treaty of Amity and Economic Relations did not provide sufficient controlling legal standards to remove the danger of conflict with the executive branch.

The second issue addressed by the court was whether the Hickenlooper Amendment,[7] which in certain cases bars the application of the act of state doctrine to confiscations in violation of international law, could be invoked under the facts of this case. The court held that it could not, relying for this conclusion on the reasoning of the U.S. Court of Appeals for the Second Circuit in *Banco Nacional de Cuba v. First National City Bank*.[8] Under the Second Circuit's rationale, the Hickenlooper Amendment was intended to prevent the United States from becoming a thieves' market for expropriated property. It did not give U.S. corporations the right to apply assets under their control in the United States to recoup losses suffered by reason of an expropriation

[4] 376 U.S. 398, 428 (1964) (emphasis added).
[5] 543 F.Supp. 1224, 1230.
[6] *Ibid.*
[7] 22 U.S.C. §2370(e)(2).
[8] 431 F.2d 394 (2d Cir. 1970), *rev'd on other grounds*, 406 U.S. 759 (1972).

of their properties in a foreign territory. Applying this rationale, the court reasoned that since there had been no attempt by some other entity to market the expropriated interest in ESESCO in the United States, the exception provided by the Hickenlooper Amendment was not applicable.

The final issue was whether the expropriation by PMGSE constituted "a taking of property within its own territory." Where the site of the property taken is outside the territory of the foreign state, the court observed, the act of state doctrine does not apply.[9] Kal-Spice argued that the nationalized shares of ESESCO's stock were located in the United States and that the seizure of Kal-Spice's interest in ESESCO therefore did not occur within Ethiopian territory. PMGSE contended that the legal situs of the shares in ESESCO was in Ethiopia as the place of incorporation, regardless of the location of the stock certificates and the residence of the shareholders. The court agreed with PMGSE, holding that the shares of stock had their situs in Ethiopia at the time of the taking since all of the physical assets for which the stock certificates were evidence of an ownership interest were located in the place of incorporation, Ethiopia.[10]

Comment. As far as this reviewer is aware, this decision represents the most extreme application of the act of state doctrine since *Banco Nacional de Cuba v. Sabbatino.* Even those critics of the Supreme Court's judgment in that case found a modicum of comfort in the fact that the Court had reserved its position as to whether the act of state doctrine should apply if there existed a "treaty or other unambiguous agreement regarding controlling legal principles." Some critics went further and, relying on the negative implications of the Harlan reservation, drew the conclusion that the act of state doctrine could not be applied to defeat application of international law in a federal court if the controlling legal principles had been embodied in a treaty. The present judgment, if sustained on appeal,[11] will undermine these hopes and once again illustrate the stultifying effects on the progressive development of international law of the legal principles laid down by Justice Harlan in *Sabbatino.*

Foreign Sovereign Immunities Act—liability of People's Republic of China for defaulted 1911 railway bonds—state succession

RUSSELL JACKSON, ET AL. v. THE PEOPLE'S REPUBLIC OF CHINA. 550 F.Supp. 869.
U.S. District Court, N.D. Ala., September 2, 1982.

Plaintiffs filed a class action suit against the People's Republic of China (PRC) to obtain payment on certain Hukuang Railways Sinking Fund Gold Bonds issued by the Imperial Chinese Government in 1911. The bonds were

[9] *See, e.g.,* United Bank Ltd. v. Cosmic Int'l, Inc., 542 F.2d 868 (2d Cir. 1976).

[10] *See, e.g.,* Jellenik v. Huron Copper Mining Co., 177 U.S. 1, 13 (1900) (property represented by certificates of stock may be deemed to be held by the company within the state that created it).

[11] Kalamazoo Spice Extraction Co. v. The Provisional Military Gov't of Socialist Ethiopia, No. 82-1521 (6th Cir. filed Nov. 19, 1982). For the views of the Department of State on the issues raised in the case, see *supra* pp. 141–43.

issued to finance the construction of the Hukuang Railway, still in operation as an integral part of China's transportation system. The bonds entitled the bearer to a principal sum and an annual payment of 5 percent interest.

In 1912, the Imperial Chinese Government was replaced by the Government of the Republic of China. The new Government made timely interest payments on the bonds until December 15, 1930. Two partial payments of interest were made in 1937–1938. In 1947, the Nationalist Government, then led by Chiang Kai-shek, formally pledged to honor the bonds as soon as internal economic conditions permitted. The Communist Party, however, seized control of China in 1949, and the former Nationalist Government withdrew to Taiwan. Neither the authorities on Taiwan nor the PRC has made payments on the bonds.

Upon filing of suit, proper service was made on the PRC through the U.S. Department of State. The Chinese Government, however, failed to respond, and the U.S. District Court for the Northern District of Alabama (per Clemon, J.) entered a default judgment in accordance with Rule 55(e) of the Federal Rules of Civil Procedure. Based on expert testimony, the court awarded damages in the amount of $41.3 million plus interest.

In determining whether the PRC was liable for payment, the district court faced two principal legal questions: (1) the liability of a successor government for financial obligations incurred by a prior regime, and (2) the immunity of a foreign sovereign to suit in a U.S. court. The district court answered the first question by observing that under an established principle of international law, changes in the government of a state do not usually affect preexisting rights and obligations.[1] The court ruled that since the Communist Government succeeded both the Imperial and the Nationalist Governments, it was bound to honor the financial obligations that they had incurred.

As for the second question, the court relied on the Foreign Sovereign Immunities Act of 1976 (28 U.S.C. §§1330, 1391, 1602–1611) (FSIA). Section 1605(a)(2) of the Act provides that a foreign state will not be immune to suits based upon a commercial activity carried on in the United States by the foreign state; section 1603(d) states that the commercial character of an activity is determined by reference to the nature of the particular transaction or act, rather than by reference to its purpose. Relying on two cases involving foreign airlines operating in the United States,[2] the court concluded that authorizing the sale of bonds in the United States constituted a "commercial activity" for which the Chinese Government did not enjoy immunity.

Comment. Although several nations are in default on dollar bonds previously issued to U.S. investors, this is the first instance in which a federal court has found a foreign government liable for such defaulted loans. For that reason, the present case may set a significant precedent for other U.S. bondholders.[3]

[1] 550 F.Supp. 869, 872 (citing Lehigh Valley R. Co. v. State of Russia, 21 F.2d 396, 401 (2d Cir. 1927)).

[2] 550 F.Supp. at 873 (relying on Sugarman v. Aeromexico, Inc., 626 F.2d 270 (3d Cir. 1980), and Behring Int'l, Inc. v. Imperial Iranian Air Force, 475 F.Supp. 383 (D.N.J. 1979)).

[3] Class actions seeking $619 million from the Soviet Union have already been filed to recover on bonds that were issued by the Imperial Russian Government in 1916 and then repudiated by

Of more immediate concern, the Chinese Government has warned that any action to attach Chinese property based on the district court's judgment could lead to corresponding measures against American property in China. Although the U.S. State Department has thus far remained aloof, it has been reported that the Department may eventually become involved to try to prevent the case from hindering U.S.-Chinese relations.[4]

A point at issue in this decision is the court's evaluation of the international law of state succession. There appears to be no universal rule of international law concerning the debt obligations of successor governments,[5] although the majority of international scholars seems to agree that a successor government is liable for the acts and obligations of prior governments, despite peaceful or revolutionary political changes over time.[6] In addition, since the Hukuang Railroad continues to operate to the PRC's benefit, the Chinese Government may owe a greater obligation to its creditors than it might otherwise.[7]

The fact remains, however, that the bonds had been in default long before the Communist Party assumed power. Unlike the typical situation in which the prior government ceases to exist when replaced by its successor, the Nationalist Government (which, it should be remembered, pledged to honor the bonds) continues to exist, albeit as the sovereign authority of Taiwan. This raises the question whether it could be held liable, perhaps as a joint obligor, for part of the debt obligation.

Another question arising from this decision is whether and how plaintiffs will collect their $41.3 million judgment. Section 1610 of the FSIA provides that foreign property located in the United States can be subject to attachment and execution if "the foreign state has waived its immunity . . . either explicitly or by implication." The PRC did not enter an appearance in this case, nor did it recognize the jurisdiction of the court. Furthermore, there is no indication that the PRC has waived its immunity from attachment and execution by treaty.[8]

---

the Bolshevik Government. Other nations in default in dollar bonds include Cuba, Czechoslovakia, Romania, Hungary, Bulgaria, and Bolivia. Wall St. J., Sept. 9, 1982, at 44. *See also* N.Y. Times, Sept. 9, 1982, at D10.

[4] Wall St. J., *supra* note 3.

[5] 1 G. HACKWORTH, DIGEST OF INTERNATIONAL LAW 539 (1940).

[6] *See generally* G. HACKWORTH, *supra* note 5; D. P. O'CONNELL, STATE SUCCESSION IN MUNICIPAL LAW AND INTERNATIONAL LAW 239 (1967); 1 G. SCHWARZENBERGER, INTERNATIONAL LAW 164 (1957); 1 J. B. MOORE, DIGEST OF INTERNATIONAL LAW 249 (1906). *See also* German Settlers in Poland, 1923 PCIJ, ser. B, No. 6.

[7] *Cf.* Vilas v. City of Manila, 220 U.S. 345 (1911) (if municipal government enjoys the property rights of the former government, it also is subject to any liabilities associated with these rights).

[8] *Cf.* the Agreement between the Government of the United States of America and the Government of the People's Republic of China concerning the Settlement of Claims, *signed* May 11, 1979, 30 UST 1957, TIAS No. 9306, which provides that the PRC will pay $80.5 million as the "full and final settlement" of the claims of U.S. nationals "against the PRC arising from any nationalization, expropriation, intervention, and other taking of, or special measures directed against, property of nationals of the USA on or after October 1, 1949."

Sovereign immunity—Foreign Sovereign Immunities Act—commercial activity and tortious conduct exceptions not applicable to support jurisdiction over defendant in oil spill disaster

MATTER OF SEDCO, INC. 543 F.Supp. 561.
U.S. District Court, S.D. Texas, March 30, 1982.

Petróleos Mexicanos (Pemex), the national oil company of Mexico, and Permargo, a privately owned Mexican drilling company, were defendants in litigation arising out of the 1979 oil well drilling disaster in the Bay of Campeche, off the coast of Mexico. Both defendants moved to have the action dismissed, alleging that the court lacked jurisdiction over them. In the present action, the U.S. District Court for the Southern District of Texas granted Pemex's motion on the basis of sovereign immunity, finding that the commercial activity and the noncommercial tort exceptions to the Foreign Sovereign Immunities Act (28 U.S.C. §§1330, 1391, 1602–1611) (FSIA) were inapplicable. Applying the Texas long-arm statute to Permargo, the court found that it was "doing business" in Texas and that the exercise of jurisdiction over it would not be a denial of due process. The court therefore denied Permargo's motion to dismiss for lack of in personam jurisdiction.

With respect to Pemex, the court's first inquiry was whether the company was an agency or instrumentality of a foreign state and thus entitled to invoke the protection of the FSIA. The court observed that the Government of Mexico, unlike that of the United States, owns its country's natural resources and that Pemex was a decentralized governmental agency charged with the exploration and development of Mexico's hydrocarbon resources. Emphasizing that Pemex is governed by a council of presidential appointees that makes decisions in furtherance of Mexican national policy, the court had no difficulty in finding Pemex to be a "foreign state" within the meaning of section 1603(a) of the FSIA.

Having determined that Pemex was an agency of Mexico, the court focused its inquiry on two of the exceptions to sovereign immunity found in the FSIA. First, the court applied the third clause of section 1605(a)(2), which denies a foreign state immunity in a lawsuit based upon acts of the foreign state in connection with commercial activity performed outside the United States that has direct effects in the United States. The court held that Pemex's act of drilling an exploratory oil well in its patrimonial waters was not commercial activity, but was uniquely sovereign in nature. A basic attribute of sovereignty, the court held, is control over the state's mineral resources. The data derived from Pemex's exploration were to be integral to the Mexican Government's long-range planning and policy making. Moreover, Pemex had not entered into a contract with anyone for the oil and gas produced, nor had it contracted with a United States business to drill the well. The court observed in this regard that while the existence of a contractual relationship is not essential to the finding of commercial activity by a foreign state, it is often indicative of conduct of such character.

The court next turned to the applicability of section 1605(a)(5), which denies immunity to foreign states sued for tortious conduct that causes, *inter alia*, damage to or loss of property in the United States. While this provision is silent with respect to where the tort must occur, the court concluded from the legislative history of the FSIA that the tortious act must occur wholly within the jurisdiction of the United States. Because the acts that were the basis of the lawsuit all took place in Mexico or its territorial waters, the court determined that section 1605(a)(5) was also inapplicable.

In addition, the court found that even if the tort had not occurred outside the United States, the acts complained of were discretionary in nature and therefore specifically immunized from suit. Section 1605(a)(5)(A) provides that the tortious act exception shall not apply to any claim based upon the performance of "a discretionary function regardless of whether the discretion be abused." The court relied on cases decided under the Federal Tort Claims Act (28 U.S.C. §2680(a)), which contains a parallel discretionary act exception, and held that the execution by Pemex of a national plan to explore for Mexico's natural resources was discretionary within the meaning of the FSIA. To deny immunity to a foreign state for implementation of its domestic economic policies, the court held, would be to "completely abrogate the doctrine of foreign sovereign immunity by allowing an exception to swallow the grant of immunity."[1]

In contrast, because the other Mexican defendant, Permargo, was not a government instrumentality, its motion to dismiss for lack of in personam jurisdiction failed by a simple application of the Texas long-arm statute. This statute provides that the Secretary of State of Texas is the designated agent for service of process where nonresident corporations are "doing business" within the state and where the lawsuit arises from these transactions.[2] "Doing business" is defined by the statute to include committing a tort, in whole or in part, within the state. The court found that the tort requirement was met in that the cause of action arose out of Permargo's alleged negligence in its capacity as the drilling contractor on the well at the time of the blowout. In addition, the court held that because the oil slicks released by the well harmed the Texas coast, the alleged maritime tort occurred in part in Texas. Accordingly, the court held that the "doing business" definition applied to Permargo.

The court next examined Permargo's contacts with Texas to ensure that the requirements of due process, as established by the Supreme Court, were met.[3] Basing its decision on facts obtained through jurisdictional discovery, the court found that Permargo had had a systematic business presence in Texas as exemplified by the following activities: negotiating leases and purchasing drilling rigs in Texas; maintaining bank accounts in Texas through which it made payments to its suppliers; and keeping a general business agent in Texas authorized to conduct business for Permargo. The court concluded

[1] 543 F.Supp. 561, 567.

[2] Tex. Rev. Civ. Stat. Ann. art. 2031b (Vernon 1964).

[3] *See, e.g.*, Hanson v. Denckla, 357 U.S. 235 (1958); World-Wide Volkswagen Corp. v. Woodson, 444 U.S. 286 (1980).

that Permargo had purposely availed itself of the benefits and protection of the laws of Texas in such a way as to satisfy the requirements of due process.

Comment. This decision represents the resolution of an initial jurisdictional skirmish in what the court termed "a tangle of litigation."[4] As of this writing, the decision has not been certified for an interlocutory appeal, and apparently no decisions on the merits of the case have yet been rendered. However, as offshore drilling increases in frequency and oil spills inevitably occur, the jurisdictional holdings in this case may supply important precedent to future litigants.

U.S. Constitution—equal protection—deprivation of education to illegal alien schoolchildren not justified by substantial state goal

PLYLER v. DOE. 102 S.Ct. 2382.
U.S. Supreme Court, June 15, 1982.

A Texas statute withheld from local school districts any state funds for the education of children who were not "legally admitted" to the United States. The statute also authorized local school districts to deny enrollment to such children.[1] Plaintiffs, Mexican school-age children who had entered the United States illegally and resided in Texas, sought injunctive and declaratory relief against exclusion from the state's public schools. The U.S. District Court for the Eastern District of Texas permanently enjoined the defendants from denying a free education to members of the plaintiff class, and the U.S. Court of Appeals for the Fifth Circuit affirmed. The Supreme Court (per Brennan, J.) affirmed by five to four the decision of the court of appeals. For the first time, the Court held that illegal aliens are "persons" entitled to the protection of the Equal Protection Clause of the Fourteenth Amendment to the Constitution.

The Fourteenth Amendment provides: "No state shall . . . deprive any person of life, liberty, or property, without due process of law; nor deny to any *person within its jurisdiction* the equal protection of the laws." (Emphasis added.) The defendants argued that persons who have entered the United States illegally are not "within the jurisdiction" of a state even if they are present within the state's boundaries and subject to its laws. On this ground, they attempted to distinguish prior due process cases; they emphasized that, unlike the Equal Protection Clause, the Due Process Clause contains no jurisdictional limitation. The Court, however, rejected this argument. Regardless of his immigration status, the Court reasoned, "an alien is surely a 'person' in any ordinary sense of that term."[2] Moreover, the Court clarified that it has

> never suggested that the class of persons who might avail themselves of the equal protection guarantee is less than coextensive with that entitled to due process. To the contrary, we have recognized that both provisions were fashioned to protect an individual class of persons, and to reach every exercise of State authority.[3]

[4] 543 F.Supp. at 564.

[1] TEX. EDUC. CODE ANN. §21.031 (Vernon Cum. Supp. 1981).

[2] 102 S.Ct. 2382, 2391. *See also id.* at 2409 (dissenting opinion).

[3] *Id.* at 2392 (citing Yick Wo v. Hopkins, 118 U.S. 356, 369 (1886)).

In determining the appropriate level of judicial scrutiny of the permissibility of the discrimination against the illegal aliens, the Court recognized that undocumented resident aliens cannot be regarded as a "suspect class" and that education is not a "fundamental right," which would require the state to justify its statutory classification by showing that it served a "compelling government interest." Nevertheless, the Court held, because the Texas statute imposed a lifetime hardship on a discrete class of children not accountable for their status, the discrimination engendered by the statute had to further some "substantial" state goal in order for the statute to be considered rational.

The Court found no support for the discrimination in any congressional policy.

The Court rejected the defendants' contention that the statutory classification should be sustained on the ground that it furthered the state's interest in the "preservation of the state's limited resources for the education of its lawful residents."[4] Although the state may have an interest in mitigating potentially harsh economic effects resulting from an influx of illegal immigrants, the statute did not constitute an effective method of dealing with the problem. Even assuming that the flow of illegal aliens has a net impact on a state's economy, the Court reasoned that charging tuition to undocumented children was an ineffectual attempt to stem the tide of illegal immigration. Moreover, the Court found no merit to the assertion that undocumented alien children were appropriately denied an education because of the special burdens they imposed on the state's ability to provide high-quality public education.

Chief Justice Burger filed a dissenting opinion, in which he was joined by Justices White, Rehnquist, and O'Connor, objecting to the heightened level of scrutiny applied by the majority. The Chief Justice pointed out that in *San Antonio School District v. Rodriguez*,[5] the Court had expressly rejected the proposition that state laws concerning public education are subject to special scrutiny under the Equal Protection Clause. The issue, as framed by the Chief Justice, is simply whether, for purposes of allocating its finite resources, a state has a legitimate reason to differentiate between persons who are lawfully within the state and those whose presence is unlawful.

Three of the four members of the Court who joined Justice Brennan's opinion also filed separate concurring opinions. Justice Marshall reiterated his belief that an individual's interest in education is fundamental and that "a class-based denial of public education is utterly incompatible" with the Equal Protection Clause.[6] Justice Blackmun maintained that when a state offers an education to some but denies it to others, it creates classifications that "strike at the heart of equal protection values by involving the State in the creation of permanent class distinctions."[7] Justice Powell, emphasizing the appropriateness of the Court's heightened review in this case, concluded: "A legislative classification that threatens the creation of an underclass of future citizens

[4] 102 S.Ct. at 2400.

[5] 411 U.S. 1 (1973).

[6] 102 S.Ct. at 2402 (citing San Antonio School Dist. v. Rodriguez, 411 U.S. at 70–133 (Marshall, J., dissenting)).

[7] 102 S.Ct. at 2404.

and residents cannot be reconciled with one of the fundamental purposes of the Fourteenth Amendment."[8]

Treaties—Warsaw Convention preempts California law regarding limitation of liability—constitutionality of Warsaw Convention

IN RE AIRCRASH IN BALI, INDONESIA ON APRIL 22, 1974. 684 F.2d 1301. U.S. Court of Appeals, 9th Cir., August 24, 1982.

Following a 1974 air crash in Indonesia, in which plaintiffs' decedents and 104 other persons died, a jury found defendant Pan American World Airways, Inc. (Pam Am) negligent and awarded damages in the amount of $300,000 to one set of plaintiffs and $651,500 to another. The U.S. District Court for the Central District of California declined to reduce these verdicts to the limits imposed by the Warsaw Convention, ruling that under California law a decedent cannot by contract compromise his survivor's right to wrongful death recovery and that therefore the contractual limitations imposed by the Warsaw Convention and related international agreements were inapplicable.[1]

The U.S. Court of Appeals for the Ninth Circuit (per Fletcher, J.) reversed, holding that California law is preempted by the Warsaw Convention and that the Warsaw Convention is not unconstitutional since the plaintiffs would have a remedy against the United States for any "taking" of property that resulted.

The Warsaw Convention,[2] a multilateral treaty ratified for the United States by the President with the consent of the Senate in 1934, *inter alia*, limits the liability of air carriers in the event of accident or loss (Article 22), except where injury or death is caused by the carrier's "wilful misconduct" (Article 25). Article 22 also permits the passenger and the carrier to contract for a higher limit on liability. Because of dissatisfaction with certain provisions of the Convention, particularly its liability limitation, it was amended by the Hague Protocol in 1955,[3] and the Montreal Agreement in 1966.[4] The Montreal Agreement, a private agreement by the airlines that has the status of a special contract under Article 22 of the Warsaw Convention, provides that the signatory airlines accept absolute liability for injury up to a limit of $75,000 per passenger.

In holding that California law was preempted by the Warsaw Convention, the court observed that the district court had based its decision in part on a finding that the Convention's low liability limitation was no longer justified by virtue of changes that had occurred in the airline industry since 1934. The court of appeals did not dispute that such changes may have occurred, but considered them to be irrelevant as a matter of law: "Unfortunately, we know of no doctrine that would allow us to examine congressional enactments to see if they still serve the purpose for which they were designed. . . . [W]e may not avoid preemption by substituting our judgment for that of Congress

[8] *Id.* at 2406.

[1] 462 F.Supp. 1114 (C.D. Cal. 1978).

[2] *Concluded* Oct. 12, 1929, 49 Stat. 3000 (1934), TS No. 876, 137 LNTS 11.

[3] *Done* Sept. 28, 1955, 478 UNTS 371. The United States did not adhere to the Hague Protocol, at least in part because its increased limit on liability was regarded as being too low.

[4] CAB Order No. E-23680, 31 Fed. Reg. 7302 (1966).

to hold that the Convention has outlived its usefulness."[5] The court observed that if California law could be invoked to circumvent the application of the Convention's limitation, neither uniformity nor an effective limitation of the airlines' liability could be achieved. Thus, California law necessarily conflicted with the congressional scheme and, the court held, was preempted by the Convention.

Concerning the Convention's constitutionality, plaintiffs argued that the limitation on liability was so arbitrary and unreasonable as to deprive them of substantive due process and equal protection and that it impermissibly burdened their decedents' constitutional right to international travel.[6] In support of this argument, they asserted that the Convention's limitation was no longer rationally justified by existing industry conditions. The United States (defendant-intervenor), while not asserting a national interest in limiting liability *per se*, responded that concessions, particularly as to limitations of liability, were necessary to gain the cooperation of foreign countries in international air travel negotiations and that the Convention's liability and venue provisions could in some cases significantly benefit U.S. plaintiffs.

The court held that plaintiffs' constitutional arguments, while substantial, would fail if another remedy were available to provide full compensation to them. It found that such a remedy could be available under the Tucker Act (28 U.S.C. §1491), provided that the Convention's liability limitation constituted a "taking" under the just compensation clause of the Fifth Amendment.[7]

The court emphasized that it did not by this resolution imply that substantive due process and just compensation are completely complementary protections. Generally, however, if the loss claimed is compensable, the regulation at issue will not be found unconstitutional.[8] As to application of the Tucker Act, the court held that the "treaty exception" to jurisdiction of the Court of Claims under the Tucker Act (28 U.S.C. §1502) was inapplicable to plaintiffs because their rights arose under California law, not a treaty. Further, the court held that plaintiffs' wrongful death claims were "property" within the meaning of the Fifth Amendment, since the plaintiffs had a right under California law to recover damages caused by the wrongful deaths of their decedents. However, because the case had to be remanded to the district court for the admission of new evidence on the issue of willful misconduct, which might render the limitations of the Warsaw Convention inapplicable, the court declined to decide whether the Convention's liability limitation could effect

[5] 684 F.2d 1301, 1308.

[6] The court noted that this may be a case where the constitutional rights can be protected only if interested third parties are permitted to raise them. *See, e.g.*, Griswold v. Connecticut, 381 U.S. 479, 481 (1965).

[7] Defendants' argument that those plaintiffs who were residents of Australia had no standing, or limited standing, to raise constitutional objections was rejected. The court held that while not all constitutional protections are available to nonresident aliens, "the fifth amendment surely does not permit . . . the application of different rules of decision to residents and nonresidents suing on the same cause of action in the same court." 684 F.2d at 1308 n.6.

[8] Thus, the Supreme Court held in Dames & Moore v. Regan, 453 U.S. 654, 689–90 (1981), that if the executive agreement entered into with Iran to secure the release of the American hostages effected a taking of the claimants' property, the Tucker Act remedy would be available.

a taking, reserving that question for determination by the United States Court of Claims should the Convention's limitation ever be applied to these plaintiffs.

Comment. A point of interest in this case is the court's conclusion that "excessive exercise of the government's law-making powers may constitute a 'taking' under the fifth amendment."[9] The court noted that while the plurality opinion of the Supreme Court in *San Diego Gas & Electric Co. v. San Diego*[10] left this question open, a majority of the Justices supported that conclusion.[11]

If the Court of Claims holds that the Convention's limitations do not constitute a "taking," the constitutionality of the Convention will need to be determined independently of the Tucker Act. Moreover, a resolution of the constitutional issue is likely to appear more pressing if the Senate approves a pending treaty, the Montreal Aviation Protocols, that would remove the "wilful misconduct" exception from the Convention's liability limitation.[12]

Decisions of Foreign Courts

UNITED KINGDOM

Letters of credit—documentary misstatement not material to enforcement—illegal collateral agreement renders credit unenforceable under IMF Agreement

UNITED CITY MERCHANTS (INVESTMENTS) LTD. v. ROYAL BANK OF CANADA. [1982] 2 W.L.R. 1039.
House of Lords, May 20, 1982.

In this case the House of Lords resolved two points of English law involving the enforceability of a confirmed irrevocable letter of credit.[1] The first point related to the mutual rights and obligations of the confirming bank and the beneficiary under the terms of a documentary credit. The second point involved the effect on the credit transaction of a collateral exchange contract violative of Article VIII, section 2(b) of the Bretton Woods Agreement.

Plaintiff, Glass Fibres and Equipment Ltd. (the Sellers), agreed to sell a plant for the manufacture of glass fibers (the goods) to a Peruvian company, Vitrorefuerzos S.A. (the Buyers). The Buyers arranged for payment through a confirmed irrevocable letter of credit issued by their Peruvian bank, Banco Continental S.A. (the Issuing Bank). The Issuing Bank appointed defendant, the Royal Bank of Canada (the Confirming Bank), to advise and confirm the credit to the Sellers (the beneficiaries of the credit).

An initial payment of 20 percent of the invoice price of the goods was made by the Confirming Bank to the Sellers. As to the bulk of the remaining pay-

[9] 684 F.2d at 1311 n.7.

[10] 450 U.S. 621, 623 (1981).

[11] 684 F.2d at 1311 n.7 (relying on 450 U.S. at 633 (Rehnquist, J., concurring); *id.* at 1301 (Brennan, J., dissenting)).

[12] The Montreal Aviation Protocols Nos. 3 and 4 (not to be confused with the Montreal Agreement) would also increase the liability limitation to approximately $117,000 and allow an additional $200,000 in payments under a mandatory insurance program. *See* S. REP. NO. 45, 97th Cong., 1st Sess. (1981). *See also* Leich, Current Developments Note, 76 AJIL 412 (1982).

[1] The decision of the English Court of Appeal in this case is reported in [1981] 3 W.L.R. 242. For a discussion of this decision, see 76 AJIL 627 (1982).

ments, the letter of credit provided that such payments were contingent, *inter alia*, upon the loading of the goods on board a vessel in London for shipment to the Buyers by December 15, 1976. In fact, the goods were not loaded on board the vessel until the following day. However, in order to comply with the terms of the credit, the carrier's freight brokers issued a bill of lading falsely stating that the goods were on board the vessel by December 15.

On presentation of the shipping documents, the Confirming Bank refused to make payment on the ground that it had information in its possession that suggested that shipment was not effected as it appeared in the bill of lading. As a result, the Sellers sued on their contract with the Confirming Bank.[2] The Confirming Bank contested liability on two grounds: (1) that a material misrepresentation of fact on the face of the bill of lading relieved it of its obligation to make payment to the Sellers, and (2) that a collateral exchange contract between the Buyers and the Sellers rendered the contract unenforceable.

With regard to the first defense, the House of Lords (per Lord Diplock) reversed the Court of Appeal and held that the inaccurate notation on the bill of lading did not relieve the Confirming Bank of its contractual obligation to pay the Sellers. The Court observed that it is "trite law" that in a confirmed letter of credit transaction the seller and the confirming bank "deal in documents and not in goods."[3] Indeed, the Court stated, the "whole commercial purpose" for which the system of confirmed documentary letters of credit has been developed in international trade is to give to the seller an assured right to be paid before he parts with control of the goods, regardless of any claims that the buyer may have against the seller as to performance under the contract of sale. Therefore, if the documents presented by the seller to the confirming bank conform on their face with the requirements of the credit, the bank is under a contractual obligation to make payment. This principle, the Court noted, holds true notwithstanding that the bank may have knowledge that the seller has already committed a breach of the sales contract that would entitle the buyer to rescind the contract of sale and to refuse to pay for the goods.

The Court acknowledged that there is one established exception to this contractual obligation, which arises when the seller fraudulently presents the confirming bank with documents that contain material representations of fact that the seller knows to be untrue. The Court held, however, that the instant case did not fall within this fraud exception for two reasons: (1) because the Sellers were not aware that the bill of lading had been misdated, and (2) because the inaccuracy of the notation was not material. A misstatement in a stipulated document in a confirmed letter of credit transaction is only material, the Court ruled, if it causes a reduction in "the price which the goods to which the documents relate would fetch on sale if, failing reimbursement by the buyer, the bank should be driven to realise its security."[4] The Court held that the 1-day delay in placing the goods on board the vessel did not

[2] United City Merchants (Investments) Ltd., to whom the Sellers transferred the credit as security for advances, appeared as coplaintiff.

[3] [1982] 2 W.L.R. 1039, 1045.

[4] *Id.* at 1047.

affect the price that the goods would have brought and therefore concluded that the misstatement of fact on the bill of lading was not material within the meaning of the fraud exception.

The second principal issue concerned an agreement between the Buyers and the Sellers that was collateral to the contract of sale and that enabled the Buyers to convert Peruvian currency to U.S. dollars. The Sellers agreed to invoice the Buyers in U.S. dollars at double the true sale price of the goods and to remit one-half of each installment payment to the Buyers' dollar account in Miami, Florida.

The Confirming Bank argued that this transaction was in violation of Peru's exchange control regulations and therefore unenforceable in England by virtue of the Bretton Woods Agreement Order-in-Council 1946, which gave the force of law to Article VIII, section 2(b) of the Bretton Woods Agreement, establishing the International Monetary Fund. Article VIII, section 2(b) states that "[e]xchange contracts which involve the currency of any member and which are contrary to the exchange control regulations of that member maintained or imposed consistently with this agreement shall be unenforceable in the territories of any member. . . ."[5]

With regard to this second defense, the House of Lords affirmed the decision of the Court of Appeal and held that the collateral agreement was not a contract entered into solely in connection with the sale of the goods, but rather an exchange contract "in disguise." Accordingly, the agreement violated the exchange control regulations of Peru and was unenforceable under the Bretton Woods Agreement. The Court ruled, however, that the unenforceability of the collateral agreement did not render unenforceable the entire contract for the sale of goods and that the Confirming Bank remained liable for that half of the purchase price that corresponded to the uninflated price of the goods.

Finally, the Court refused to rescind the payment already paid by the Confirming Bank to the Sellers under the first 20 percent installment. The Court reasoned that the violation in question merely rendered the contract unenforceable, not null and void. Had the Confirming Bank known of the collateral agreement at the time of the first installment, it could have resisted payment of one-half of that installment. However, even if the Confirming Bank had possessed such knowledge, nothing in English law would have prevented it from voluntarily paying the unenforceable half as well. Therefore, the Court concluded, the Confirming Bank could not rescind any portion of its "voluntary" payment of the first installment.

Comment. By this decision, the House of Lords preserves the strength of the letter of credit as an instrument of international trade financing. In requiring actual fraud on the part of the seller and by applying a narrow test of materiality, the Court avoids what would otherwise have resulted in a weakening of the independence of confirmed letter of credit transactions.

[5] *Id.* at 1050. At the time of these transactions, both England and Peru were signatories to the Bretton Woods Agreement.

NEW ZEALAND*

Sovereign immunity—whether doctrine applies to Government of the Marshall Islands—recovery of claim

MARINE STEEL LTD. v. GOVERNMENT OF THE MARSHALL ISLANDS. [1981] 2 NZLR 1.
High Court of New Zealand, July 29, 1981.

Marine Steel Ltd., a registered New Zealand company, had entered into a contract to repair a ship owned by the Government of the Marshall Islands. All the work was carried out in New Zealand and, although the contract contained an arbitration clause providing for settlement of disputes "by arbitration at a judicial Court in the Marshall Islands," when a dispute arose over payment, the arbitration clause was not invoked by the defendant. Instead, the parties negotiated a settlement agreement in place of the original contract. Settlement, however, was not forthcoming, and the plaintiff sought leave to institute proceedings in the High Court of New Zealand.

The case was heard in Auckland before Barker J. He adverted immediately to the questions of sovereign immunity that were raised by the plaintiff's application and undertook a detailed consideration of the present state of the doctrine of sovereign immunity.

The initial difficulty with which the Court was faced was the judgment, binding in New Zealand, of the Privy Council in *The Philippine Admiral*.[1] The Judicial Committee had ruled that actions in rem, but not actions in personam, could be maintained against a foreign sovereign in normal commercial transactions. After canvassing several other English decisions, Barker J. referred to the decision of the House of Lords in *I Congreso del Partido*,[2] in which Their Lordships could see no reason for distinguishing actions in rem from actions in personam when a sovereign power engages in commercial activity. He then held that, since the comments on actions in personam in *The Philippine Admiral* were obiter, he was not bound by them, particularly in view of the fact that they were out of line with a later House of Lords decision, which, however, did not bind the New Zealand Court.

Barker J., however, chose not to found his judgment on this ground, since he doubted whether even the restrictive view of sovereign immunity could apply to the Government of the Marshall Islands. He noted the historical facts surrounding the Marshall Islands and referred to a decision of the United States Court of Appeals for the Second Circuit, showing that the islands are not regarded, for the purposes of the Federal Tort Claims Act, as part of the United States.[3] He then proceeded to consider where sovereignty lies in United Nations Trust Territories such as the Marshall Islands. After citing various academic authorities, he fastened onto Francis B. Sayre's conclusion that there is general concurrence that sovereignty in trust territories does not

* Prepared by Rupert Granville Glover, Lecturer in International Law, University of Canterbury, New Zealand.

[1] 1977 A.C. 373.

[2] [1981] 3 W.L.R. 328, *summarized in* 76 AJIL 402 (1982).

[3] Callas v. United States, 253 F.2d 838 (1958).

lie with the administering power.[4] Barker J. pointed out that this was accepted by one of the majority judges in the *Callas* case, where it was held that the United States did not exercise the incidents of sovereignty over the Marshall Islands. He concluded that, although the Marshall Islands are probably nearer full sovereignty than they were in 1958 when the *Callas* case was decided, they have nevertheless not yet achieved the status of a sovereign state, and that, accordingly, the doctrine of sovereign immunity does not apply to the present Government of the Marshall Islands. The Court therefore granted leave to serve a notice of writ under the rules of the New Zealand Code of Civil Procedure.

Comment. Barker J.'s judgment in this case is an interesting one. He acknowledged that it is unusual for a New Zealand court to be faced with difficult points of international law. However, he showed himself to be willing to address these points in a manner that is largely free from the judicial conservatism that has often marked British decisions in this area. His survey of recent decisions, British and American, led him to seek to abandon the only one that was technically binding on him, and although he did not base his judgment on this ground, he nevertheless set up a valuable dictum endorsing the more restricted view of sovereign immunity. Indeed, he concluded his judgment with an observation that the New Zealand authorities should consider enacting a statute comparable to the United Kingdom State Immunity Act, 1978 and the United States Foreign Sovereign Immunities Act of 1976.

As well, Barker J. was prepared to conclude that, for the purposes of the *ex parte* motion before him, the state of international law concerning the location of sovereignty in United Nations Trust Territories was not sufficiently clear to require him to hold that the issuance and service of proceedings against the Government of the Marshall Islands amounted to a potential breach of the rule of sovereign immunity. He did state, however, that this position might change if sufficient evidence to the contrary were to be adduced.

The *Marine Steel* case is likely to be cited in future Commonwealth decisions in this area of law.

FEDERAL REPUBLIC OF GERMANY*

Instrumentality of foreign state engaged in commercial activity—no immunity from prejudgment garnishment

IN RE PREJUDGMENT GARNISHMENT AGAINST NATIONAL IRANIAN OIL CO. 1981 *Wertpapier-Mitteilungen* 661. 27 *Recht der Internationalen Wirtschaft* 484 (1981).

Court of Appeals of Frankfurt, May 11, 1981.

Plaintiffs obtained orders of prejudgment garnishment against the National Iranian Oil Company (NIOC), attaching debts allegedly owed to NIOC by 19 banks, and NIOC appealed. On appeal, the attachment defendant contended that the accounts were not subject to attachment since it had sovereign im-

[4] Sayre, *Legal Problems Arising from the United Nations Trusteeship System*, 42 AJIL 263 (1948).

* Prepared by Stefan A. Riesenfeld, of the Board of Editors.

munity and because plaintiffs had obtained attachments in the United States to secure the same claims. The Frankfurt Court of Appeals rejected defendant's contentions and upheld the levy.

The court prefaced its opinion with the observation that a foreign state's immunity from German jurisdiction had to be determined separately for jurisdiction to adjudicate (process of cognition) and enforcement jurisdiction (process of execution). As to the latter, assets of a foreign state are immune if they serve activities that pertain to governmental functions. The court held that this was not the case with respect to the claims by NIOC against the banks since the defendant was a government-owned corporation with separate legal personality and special capitalization. The order of garnishment authorized a levy on property only of defendant, not of the state of Iran itself, even if Iran were the real owner of the accounts and the proceeds would be transferred ultimately to the Iranian treasury to be used for governmental functions. In view of the decision of the Federal Constitutional Court in the case of the *Philippine Republic*,[1] no preliminary question had to be submitted to that Court. The fact that attachment plaintiffs had also obtained attachments in the United States did not invalidate the orders of garnishment issued in Germany and could be considered only in separate proceedings.

In a subsequent case[2] involving a suit against the same defendant, based on an alleged breach of contract for the construction of pipelines, and a prejudgment attachment of claims arising out of letters of credit for the payment of oil sales, another panel of the same Court of Appeals stayed all further proceedings because defendant had brought the issue of immunity of its assets from attachment before the Federal Constitutional Court by independent proceedings.[3]

Creation of a new state—requirements under international law—effect of acquisition of nationality of new state purportedly established on man-made island

IN RE CITIZENSHIP OF X. 1978 *Deutsches Verwaltungsblatt* 510.
Administrative Court of Cologne, May 3, 1978.

Plaintiff, a German citizen by birth, obtained a document, issued on August 26, 1975, conferring upon him citizenship of the "Duchy of Sealand." The so-called Duchy consists of a former anti-aircraft platform, erected by the United Kingdom approximately 8 nautical miles off its southern coast, outside its territorial waters. The platform rests on strong pillars connecting it with the seabed, and it has an area of approximately 1,300 square meters. The British forces abandoned the installation after the end of World War II, and

[1] *Reported in* 73 AJIL 305 (1979). The holding of that case as there printed should have included the words "are not subject to execution" following the words "forum state" in line 4.

[2] Court of Appeals Frankfurt a. M., Order of May 4, 1982, 28 RECHT DER INTERNATIONALEN WIRTSCHAFT 439 (1982).

[3] For a discussion of that procedure, see Riesenfeld, Book Review, 74 AJIL 473, 475 and 476, text to nn.15 and 16 (1980) (reviewing FONTES JURIS GENTIUM. SERIES A, SECTIO II. Tomus 5 and Tomus 6 (1978 and 1979)).

in 1967 a British army officer, Major R.B., took possession and proclaimed it the Duchy of Sealand. Major R.B. issued a constitution for his territory, assuming the title of Roy of Sealand. At present, 106 persons are citizens of the Duchy of Sealand, and 40 persons reside on it. Plaintiff occupies the office of Minister of Foreign Affairs and President of the State Council.

Plaintiff instituted proceedings for a declaratory judgment establishing loss of his German nationality by virtue of his having acquired the citizenship of a foreign nation. The court dismissed the action for the reason that the Duchy of Sealand did not qualify as a foreign state under international law and therefore could not confer foreign nationality so as to warrant loss of German citizenship in accordance with the German Law on Nationality of 1913.

The court held that to constitute a state under international law three essential attributes had to be present: territory, population, and government. The Duchy of Sealand lacked at least two of these. First, territory must consist of a naturally created portion of the earth's surface and not of a man-made island. Second, population denotes a group of persons leading a common life and forming a living-community, a bond that did not exist among the citizens of the Duchy of Sealand, not even among the 40 persons staying on the platform.

This case is another unsuccessful attempt to establish a new state on an artificial island in order to escape the laws of the coastal state. Similar efforts in Italy[1] and the United States[2] have also failed.

FRENCH REPUBLIC*

Supremacy of treaty over prior statute—effect of lack of reciprocity—exclusive jurisdiction of Minister of Foreign Affairs to determine presence or absence of reciprocity

IN RE REKHOU. 1982 Dalloz-Sirey, *Jurisprudence* 137.
Conseil d'Etat (en banc), May 29, 1981.

The case involves the jurisdiction of the Conseil d'Etat (Council of State), the supreme administrative court of France, to determine the presence or absence of reciprocity in the application of a treaty, and the effect of the lack thereof. The French Constitution provides in Article 55: "Treaties or agreements that are properly ratified or approved possess, upon their publication, authority superior to statutes, subject to the condition that each agreement or treaty is applied by the other party." This provision has precipitated many controversies and resulted in conflicting holdings of the two highest courts of France, the Cour de Cassation (Court of Cassation) and the Conseil d'Etat.

[1] For the "Isola delle Rose" off the coast of Rimini and its ultimate abatement, see the judgment of the Italian Council of State in the case of Chierici e Rosa c. Ministero Marina mercantile e Capitaneria di porto di Rimini, Nov. 14, 1969, 55 RIVISTA DIRITTO INTERNAZIONALE 728 (1972).

[2] The attempts to create "Atlantis" on Triumph Reef, United States v. Ray, 423 F.2d 16 (5th Cir. 1970), and "Abalonia" and "Taluga" on Cortes Bank, are discussed in Stang, *Wet Land: The Unavailable Resource of the Outer Continental Shelf*, 2 J.L. & ECON. 153 (1968).

* Prepared by Stefan A. Riesenfeld, of the Board of Editors.

Thus, while the Cour de Cassation has held that a treaty prevails even over a subsequent inconsistent statute,[1] the Conseil d'Etat accords a treaty supremacy only over a prior inconsistent statute.[2]

The present controversy involved the application of the so-called Accords of Evian of March 19, 1962, establishing new relations between Algeria and France.[3] The Accords were approved by popular referendum on April 8, 1962, and their implementation was authorized by a statute of April 13, 1962.[4] Article 15 of the Declaration on the Principles Concerning Economic and Financial Cooperation between Algeria and France[5] (one of the Accords) guaranteed on the part of France the rights to retirement and disability pensions acquired in the service of French governmental agencies and on the part of Algeria such rights acquired in the service of Algerian governmental agencies prior to the exercise of self-determination, *i.e.*, July 3, 1962.

Mr. Rekhou, a resident of Algeria, had served as director of a school under French administration. In 1964 the French authorities ruled that pursuant to a statute of 1959, the amount of his retirement pension was subject to be frozen as of July 3, 1962. Despite Rekhou's request, this decision was not reversed by the Minister of Education. Rekhou sought relief from the administrative ruling and the Minister's inaction, claiming that these decisions violated his rights under said Article 15, as construed by the Minister of Foreign Affairs in an opinion given on December 14, 1971 in another case, and that the Accords of 1962 superseded the statute of 1959. In opposition to Rekhou's complaint, the French Minister of Finance denied the applicability of Article 15 because Algeria had failed to comply with that article. The Conseil d'Etat considered reciprocity to be crucial to deciding the issue, but held that an administrative judge lacked the power to determine "whether and to what extent the mode of execution of a treaty or accord by the other party is such as to divest the provisions of that treaty or accord of the authority which is conferred upon them by the constitution." As a result, the Court stayed further proceedings until the Minister of Foreign Affairs determined whether reciprocity existed in 1964.

Comment. Apparently, the judgment of the Conseil d'Etat goes no further than to hold that lack of reciprocity deprives a treaty provision of its superiority over an inconsistent statute, without passing on its applicability in general. At any rate, as to administrative proceedings, the judgment establishes the exclusive jurisdiction of the Minister of Foreign Affairs to make a finding on reciprocity, although ordinary courts of justice have asserted such power.[6]

[1] Administration des Douanes c. Soc. des Cafés Jacques Vabre, 1975 Bull. Civ. (ch. mixte, en banc), Case No. 4, *discussed by* Riesenfeld, Comment, 74 AJIL 892, 899, text to n.37 (1980).

[2] *In re* Union démocratique du travail, 1980 REV. DROIT PUBLIC 531 (Oct. 22, 1979).

[3] For the text of the Governmental Declarations of March 19, 1962, see 1962 J.O. 3024. English excerpts are published in U.S. DEP'T OF STATE, AMERICAN FOREIGN POLICY, CURRENT DOCUMENTS 796–808 (1962).

[4] Law No. 61-421, 1962 J.O. 3843.

[5] *Id.* at 3026.

[6] *See* Calonec, Note, 1982 D.S. Jur. 138.

Direct applicability of Council regulations in courts of the member states of the European Economic Community—ineffectiveness of domestic decrees reenacting such regulations

SYNDICAT UNIQUE DES VIGNERONS DE L'AUDE. 1981 *Revue Trimestrielle de Droit Européen* 363.
Conseil d'Etat (Litigation Section, 2d and 6th Subsections), June 21, 1981.

According to the case law of the Court of Justice of the European Communities, EEC Council regulations are directly applicable in the courts of the member states, and domestic legislation duplicating or reenacting such regulations are without effect and may be illegal.[1] The instant case presents an interesting application of that rule by the French Conseil d'Etat.

According to long established case law of the Conseil d'Etat, a private person may demand the modification or repeal of a general administrative regulation on the ground that the legal or factual conditions existing at the time of its enactment have changed. In 1970 the EEC Council adopted a regulation prohibiting the addition of sugar to wine during fermentation except in certain geographic areas, excluding the southern regions of France. On April 21, 1972, France enacted a decree conforming its domestic legislation to the Community regulation. Complainant, an association of winegrowers in a southern region, considered the decree to be discriminatory and no longer justified because of a change in climatic conditions. Accordingly, it asked the Prime Minister to repeal the provision excluding the southern regions from the area permitted to add sugar. The Prime Minister took no action, and complainant sought annulment of the denial of its request implied by the Prime Minister's inaction. The Conseil d'Etat rejected the complaint on the ground that the direct applicability of EEC Council regulations barred the Government from acting on the request for modification of a domestic decree that merely reenacted a Community regulation still in force.

ITALIAN REPUBLIC*

Act of state—foreign expropriation in violation of international law—lack of jurisdiction over the subject matter

S.P.A. IMPRESE MARITTIME FRASSINETTI E S.P.A. ITALIANA LAVORI MARITTIMI E TERRESTRI c. REPUBBLICA ARABA DI LIBIA. 64 *Rivista di Diritto Internazionale* 169 (1981).
Corte di Cassazione (Combined Sections), May 26, 1979.

In 1967, plaintiffs, Italian construction firms with head offices in Geneva, concluded a contract with the Port and Lights Authorities of Tripoli for the construction of a pier in that harbor. In 1969, the Government of Libya was overthrown and the new authorities expelled the Italian construction crew

[1] Amsterdam Bulb B.V. v. Produktschap voor Siergewassen, Case 50/76, Feb. 2, 1977, 1977 ECR 137.

* Prepared by Stefan A. Riesenfeld, of the Board of Editors.

and seized all construction equipment. Efforts to obtain return of the property failed. As a result, plaintiffs instituted suit against Libya for restitution of their property or, alternatively, for damages. The Government of Libya failed to appear and suffered a default judgment. On petition for relief from that judgment to the Italian Supreme Court (the Court of Cassation), Libya claimed that the Italian courts lacked in personam jurisdiction over Libya, that Libya was immune from suit by reason of the act of state doctrine, and that it was not the proper party defendant.

The Italian Court of Cassation held that the proceedings were in the nature of a writ of prohibition, which precluded the third objection. The Court viewed the act of state defense as an assertion of lack of jurisdiction over the subject matter. Finding that the acts of the Libyan authorities amounted to an expropriation, the Court held that by reason of a universally accepted principle of international law, forming part of the Italian legal system by virtue of Article 10, paragraph 1 of the Constitution, acts of a foreign state performed in the exercise of a public function are not cognizable in Italian courts, even to consider their conformity with rules of international law. The Court concluded that because the confiscation in issue was a political measure and not a commercial activity, the plaintiffs' complaint must be dismissed.

Jurisdiction over felonies committed by citizens abroad—admissibility of evidence taken abroad by investigating magistrate

Case against BUSCETTA. 64 *Rivista di Diritto Internazionale* 174 (1981).
Corte di Cassazione (Criminal Section), February 19, 1979.

Buscetta, an Italian national, was convicted by the court of first instance in Salerno of trafficking in narcotics in the United States and the conviction was affirmed by the court of appeals in Salerno. On writ of error to the Italian Court of Cassation, Buscetta assigned as error that the Minister of Justice had not requested the prosecution as required by law and that the conviction was based, *inter alia*, on evidence illegally obtained by the investigating magistrate by way of interrogation of witnesses in the United States.

The Court held that the Italian Penal Code, section 9, paragraph 1 extended to felonies committed by citizens abroad and did not require that prosecution be based on a request by the Minister of Justice. It held further that evidence taken by an Italian magistrate abroad without violation of international law was admissible. Although the use of letters rogatory was the ordinary method of gathering proof abroad, modern international law had developed other forms of judicial cooperation. Therefore, it was proper to conclude that, with the consent of a foreign state, Italian judicial authorities had the power to obtain directly, in the territory of the consenting state, all evidence that would normally have been obtained by means of letters rogatory, and that such evidence was admissible in an Italian trial.

Current Developments Regarding Judicial Decisions Reported in the Journal, 1981–1982

Cabell v. Chavez-Salido, 102 S.Ct. 735, 76 AJIL 616; *reported at* 454 U.S. 432.

Dames & Moore v. Regan, 101 S.Ct. 2972, 75 AJIL 954; *reported at* 453 U.S. 654.

Haig v. Agee, 101 S.Ct. 2766, 75 AJIL 962; *reported at* 453 U.S. 280.

Immigration and Naturalization Service v. Wang, 101 S.Ct. 1027, 75 AJIL 952; *reported at* 450 U.S. 139; *reh'g denied*, 451 U.S. 964.

International Association of Machinists and Aerospace Workers v. Organization of Petroleum Exporting Countries, 649 F.2d 1354, 76 AJIL 160; *cert. denied*, 102 S.Ct. 1036.

Perez v. The Bahamas, 652 F.2d 186, 76 AJIL 173; *cert. denied*, 454 U.S. 865.

Piper Aircraft Co. v. Reyno; Hartzell Propeller, Inc. v. Reyno, 102 S.Ct. 252, 76 AJIL 394; *reported at* 454 U.S. 235.

Rex v. Cia. Pervana de Vapores, S.A., 660 F.2d 61, 76 AJIL 393; *cert. denied*, 102 S.Ct. 2306.

Speiss v. C. Itoh & Co. (America), 643 F.2d 353, 75 AJIL 972; *cert. dismissed*, 102 S.Ct. 984; *vacated and remanded*, 102 S.Ct. 2951 (in light of *Sumitomo Shoji America, Inc. v. Avagliano*, 102 S.Ct. 2374, 76 AJIL 845).

Texas Trading & Milling Corp. v. Federal Republic of Nigeria, 647 F.2d 300, 75 AJIL 968; *cert. denied*, 102 S.Ct. 1012.

United City Merchants (Investments) Ltd. v. Royal Bank of Canada, 3 W.L.R. 242, 76 AJIL 627; *aff'd in part and rev'd in part*, [1981] 2 W.L.R. 1039, 77 AJIL 155.

United States v. McRary, 665 F.2d 674, 76 AJIL 619; *cert. denied*, 102 S.Ct. 2306.

Verlinden B.V. v. Central Bank of Nigeria, 647 F.2d 320, 75 AJIL 965; *cert. granted*, 102 S.Ct. 997.

CURRENT DEVELOPMENTS

The Proposed Iran Claims Act of the United States

On September 14, 1982, the Department of State submitted proposed legislation (S. 2967) to Congress that would authorize the Foreign Claims Settlement Commission to adjudicate "small" claims of U.S. nationals against Iran, *i.e.*, those for less than $250,000, in the event of an agreement between the United States and Iran for an *en bloc* settlement to cover such claims. The Commission's adjudications would be made in accordance with the provisions and procedures of the International Claims Settlement Act of 1949, as amended, subject to the provisions of the relevant claims settlement agreements (the Claims Settlement Agreement of the Algiers Accords and any lump sum settlement agreement negotiated with Iran).

The proposed bill would also permit the Federal Reserve Bank of New York to recover certain costs incurred by the U.S. Government in connection with the arbitration of other claims before the Iran-United States Claims Tribunal at The Hague. Further, it would authorize the Secretary of the Treasury to reimburse the bank for its expenses as fiscal agent of the United States in the implementation of the hostage release agreements.

A portion of the Department's letter of transmittal describing other provisions of the proposed legislation follows:

> In addition to United States contributions to the Tribunal, providing a forum for hearing and deciding the claims of United States nationals, the United States Government provides many valuable services to United States claimants, such as the service of documents and the presentation of positions and supporting legal arguments on major issues of common interest. The proposed legislation would require successful claimants to help bear the costs of these Government services to or on behalf of the claimants.
>
> The bill would permit the Government to recover a portion of its expenses by authorizing the Federal Reserve Bank of New York to deduct an amount equal to two percent of any payment from the Security Account in satisfaction of an award of the Tribunal in favor of a U.S. national. The amounts thus deducted will be covered into the miscellaneous receipts of the Treasury as reimbursement to the Government of the expenses it has incurred in connection with the operations of the Tribunal. The agencies incurring those expenses will not directly benefit from the deduction, but will continue to be responsible for justifying to the Congress appropriations necessary to pay their expenses. The reimbursement will be collected only from those U.S. claimants who avail themselves of the Tribunal, receive a favorable award, and are paid from the Security Account. Claimants who do not benefit from both the Tribunal and the Security Account would not be required to contribute to the reimbursement of the Government. The bill also provides that once the deduction has been made, payments to U.S. claimants will be made directly without further delay or any additional deductions. Pursuant to

a directive license issued by the Treasury Department on June 7, the Federal Reserve Bank of New York has been making deductions, and depositing the proceeds into miscellaneous receipts, from accounts received to date in satisfaction of awards of the Tribunal. The bill would ratify this action retroactively.

Finally, the bill includes two technical sections intended (a) to preclude duplicate deductions from payments to claimants with "small" claims which are adjudicated by the Foreign Claims Settlement Commission and (b) to authorize the Secretary of the Treasury to reimburse the Federal Reserve Bank of New York for expenses it has incurred as fiscal agent of the United States in implementation of the Algiers Accords.[1]

MARIAN NASH LEICH*

THE PANAMA CANAL TREATY AND JURISDICTION OF U.S. COURTS

In *Egle v. Egle*,[1] an action for child custody, the U.S. Court of Appeals for the Fifth Circuit on June 17, 1982 requested that the Legal Adviser of the Department of State file by letter or amicus curiae brief the executive branch's view as to whether the court retained jurisdiction to consider an application for rehearing of an appeal in which it had affirmed the former District Court for the District of the Canal Zone on March 31, 1982, the last day of that court's existence.

A further question from the court asked about the applicability of the "'nationality' principle of international jurisdiction" to any further disposition of the case (since neither the defendant nor the minor children in his custody, as residents of the former Canal Zone, were any longer subject to the territorial jurisdiction of the United States).

On August 9, 1982, a memorandum for the United States as amicus curiae was filed, expressing the views of both the U.S. Department of Justice and the Office of the Legal Adviser of the Department of State. It discussed the court's questions in part as follows:

> 1. The first question posed by the Court relates exclusively to the Court's federal appellate jurisdiction as a matter of domestic United States law.
>
> In response to this question, it is the position of the executive branch (1) that 28 U.S.C. 1291–92 expressly accord this Court jurisdiction to hear appeals from the former United States District Court for the District of the Canal Zone, and (2) that neither the [Panama Canal] Treaty nor any subsequent Act of Congress has repealed such jurisdiction.
>
> 2. In response to the Court's second question, it is the position of the executive branch that the United States cannot order Mr. Egle to return his minor children to this country on the basis of the so-called "nationality" principle of jurisdiction since no treaty or federal statute authorizes such action.

[1] Dept. of State File No. P82 0141-1322, 132 CONG. REC. S12662 (daily ed. Sept. 29, 1982).

* Office of the Legal Adviser, Department of State.

[1] 673 F.2d 1326, 679 F.2d 380 (5th Cir. 1982).

3. It follows from our response to the Court's first question, however, that the Court remains free—by virtue of its 28 U.S.C. 1291–92 jurisdiction, and without reference to the nationality principle—to apply the full range of its 28 U.S.C. 2106 remedial powers to the disposition of this case, subject only to the *de facto* limitations which necessarily stem from Article XI of the Treaty.

4. Notwithstanding our conclusion that this Court retains jurisdiction effectively to require Mr. Egle to return the children, such obligation would not be *directly* enforceable in Panama. See, *e.g., Restatement (Second) of the Foreign Relations Law of the United States*, §§6, 7. In our view, therefore, the central issue presented here relates not to the existence of the Court's power to order Mr. Egle to return the children but rather to the Court's power to enforce such an order.[2]

MARIAN NASH LEICH*

[2] Dept. of State File No. P82 0147-1440 (footnotes omitted).

* Office of the Legal Adviser, Department of State.

BOOK REVIEWS AND NOTES

EDITED BY LEO GROSS

The Teacher in International Law (Teachings and Teaching). By Manfred Lachs. The Hague, Boston, London: Martinus Nijhoff Publishers, 1982. Pp. 236. Indexes. $47.50; Dfl.110.

Some judges write great decisions. A few write felicitously. Judge Manfred Lachs of the International Court of Justice is to be counted among the small, happy breed that is abundantly endowed with both skills. Known equally for writing judicious compacts (on peaceful uses of outer space, for example) and compact judgments, Lachs has here produced a graceful *pensée* on the interaction between concepts and teachers, and their impact on the "real world."

In the author's words, he is dealing with "human thinking, the influence of ideas on man, the power of thought on human action." He seeks to demonstrate that a "thought, born of others within specific dimensions of time and place is given expression, radiates, is appropriated, is eventually found malleable and is transmuted, becoming almost a new thought, and at any stage may act with great power to transform the lives of men." We have, here, a rather Mendelian botany of ideas, and it is highly convincing.

It is also encouraging. The idea that ideas matter, and can transform social realities, provides the rationale and guiding light for those of us who have dedicated our lives to teaching, sometimes at the cost of direct involvement in action. While some can play both roles—that of thinker and of doer—others find the roles antithetical. Lachs absolves cloistered scholars from guilt about their nonutility by demonstrating, again and again, that ideas, teachings, and writings directly affect outcomes in the real world, whether or not the scholar ever sets foot beyond the high wall. And he attests to the scholar's importance to the judge, for example, in helping him formulate principled responses to real conflicts.

This book, then, is a graceful compliment to those who live and labor in the world of ideas. It is also likely to encourage and strengthen whatever residual intellectual tendencies lie largely dormant in the young law student of the utilitarian 1980's.

The book is not only a call, in its nonhortatory fashion, to the life of the mind. It is also a delight to one's literary sensibilities, demonstrating that subtle and complex concepts need not be purveyed in a fashion suggesting translation from the German. Referring to the 17th century, to take one of many examples, Lachs writes thus of the continuing effect of a way of thought the rationalists had hoped to extirpate:

> The natural-law element continued in the teachings of theorists no less than the positivistic, for we must not forget that, even if canon law no

> longer held sway, the belief in a universal order working for the good of men was profoundly anchored in the troubled consciences of the late 17th century. Indeed, with no other dogmatic support, that age was to cling to it as to a rock from which the necessary spring of optimism must gush forth for the secular redemption of mankind [p. 55].

Not that the book is a bouquet of roses. There are thistles, too, but they are every bit as delightful. Emer de Vattel is described as "the wearer, like Gentilis, of a truly motley thinking cap." Stroynowski is a "teacher and guide . . . though not an original thinker." Sir Thomas Erskine Holland "played an important part in the period before World War I," but "his views have since been largely overtaken."

As one would expect of a respecter of concepts, Lachs rejects the popular contemporary notion that the tradition of "Western" jurisprudence has been rendered obsolete by the rebirth of the "Third World." While he acknowledges that international law, in the course of this century, has experienced a profound transformation from being the prerogative of "civilized nations" to being a global social imperative, he notes that this "does not, however, mean that an entirely new structure of law is needed." While there are new challenges, new technologies, and new ideas all around us, there is no intellectual mandate for

> a rejection of "yesterday," for not everything from the past is outdated: it is much more by building upon, transmuting and enriching some of the progressive achievements epitomized in the teachings I have touched upon that the teachings of international law may live up to the great expectations of our day [p. 90].

Although Lachs evidently admires the initiator of the seminal thought, he is also generous to those, like his former colleagues of the International Law Commission, who do their conceptualizing in a corporate fashion. "Why do we nowadays need committees for what used to be accomplished by heroic individuals?" he asks. "Might we not expect that all the Pegasuses they design will turn out to be flightless camels?" Yes, but then camels, he notes, are not without virtue as a means of getting from here to there over shifting sands. Corporate legal conceptualizing may be "perhaps lacking in brilliance and fancy," but "nearer the mark than an individual compilation . . . because no one mind can be expected to be equally adept in the different facets of codification, namely: consolidation, harmonization and discipline. It is obvious that different kinds of mind will be better equipped to tackle each."

The author's own multi-dexterity seems an exception to this observation. The reader has reason to be grateful that Renaissance Man has not been wholly replaced by corporate man, for it is the former who has given us the most complete, entertaining, and edifying chronicle of international legal teachers and teaching attempted in this century.

THOMAS M. FRANCK
Board of Editors

Major Issues in International Law. By Sakti Mukherjee and Indrani Mukherjee. Calcutta: The World Press Private Ltd., 1981. Pp. xiii, 302. Index. $8.50; £3.25; Rs.50.

Is the gap between First and Third World conceptions of international law widening? Western jurists will scrutinize this volume, said to be one of the first student texts prepared in the Third World, to find an answer to this question. The conclusion that there is no radical difference in conceptions is impelling, although in their concluding chapter the authors express disappointment, if not anger, at the reluctance of rich countries to perceive the needs of poor countries for a new international economic law.

The presentation is balanced, for the authors have read widely and present not only the practice of states, including, of course, India, and the judgments and awards of international tribunals, but also a profusion of views of traditionalists and modernists of the West. If there is a favored position adopted by the authors, it is closer to that of Wolfgang Friedmann, on whom there is heavy reliance, than to that of the radical revisionists.

As Westerners might expect, the authors urge recognition in international law of the equality of states and, especially, of measures that will enhance economic equality. They perceive numerous contributions to the corpus of international law by the Third World: in developing a law of self-determination, sovereignty over natural resources, racial equality, nondiscrimination among peoples, and more equitable rules on rights and obligations of successor states after liberation from colonial status.

This is not a text supporting Soviet positions. Indeed, many Soviet positions are criticized: the continuing espousal of traditionalist attitudes toward state sovereignty (including the immunity of states for acts *jure gestionis*) and exclusion of individuals from subject status in international law, and the adherence to a restrictive interpretation of the functions of the United Nations and of its organs. By implication, in their chapter on recognition of states, the authors disapprove of the Soviet practice of recognizing left-wing aspirants to power over their established governments. Also, the authors give no support to the arguments of Soviet professors that General Assembly resolutions, when adopted by large majorities including representatives from each group perceived by the Soviet side to be contending camps, may be taken as evidence of "crystallized custom." The authors are orthodox; they indicate that resolutions cannot be accepted as a source of law, not only because the Charter denies them that status, but also because "the international political situation indicates that member nations are not prepared to provide such sweeping power to the Assembly" (p. 63). Like many Western jurists, the authors limit themselves to arguing that "there is no denying the fact that opinions and demands of a vast majority of humanity should not be brushed aside" (p. 50).

Indian practice is featured under several topics, and as knowledge of it is not readily available to Westerners, these paragraphs will prove useful. Would that there were fuller treatment of that practice! Fortunately, the chapter on the history of international law includes not only the traditional Western events, but Indian experience in ancient times when law was developed to regulate the acquisition of territory, to define jurisdiction, and to establish alliances, treaties, and the rules of diplomatic intercourse, warfare, and the administration of occupied territories.

If this text is widely adopted in the Third World's law faculties, it can help to instill sound principles contributing to stability of law, while indicating to students the plausible arguments that may be effective in advancing Third World positions.

JOHN N. HAZARD
Board of Editors

The Future of International Organization. Edited by Rudiger Jütte and Annemarie Grosse-Jütte. New York: St. Martin's Press, 1981. Pp. 228. Index. $22.50.

Reading this book reminded me of a poster I saw some years ago at the University of California, Berkeley. It said: "Nobody can have two good ideas until everybody has had one." There are some good ideas in this collection of papers. But they are severely rationed. And they are interspersed with such tired clichés as "IGOs cannot exist without member states, but nation-states can and do function without IGOs" (p. 33). Moreover, despite the promise implied by its title, this is not a book that deals with the future at all. Rather, it describes and in some instances attempts to explain the recent past. Lastly, though most of the contributors to the volume are Europeans, there is little sign that their thinking has been influenced by the exciting intellectual currents that have swept through European social science in the past two decades, from structuralism and neo-Marxism to phenomenology and hermeneutics. Instead, with few and only partial exceptions, we find discussions cast in the institutionalist mold, and in one case even the obligatory roll-call voting analysis, that prevailed in this country in the 1950's and 1960's. The result is desultory—much like the NIEO negotiations out of which several of the authors try to squeeze whatever juice remains.

The book is divided into four parts under the following headings: "Growth and Change of International Organization," "Changing Issues and Structures," "Adjusting Normative Standards for International Behaviour," and "Management and Resolution of Conflicts."

The first part consists of a brief analytical overview of contemporary international organization, and of a head count of IGO's established since 1945. The former, by R. Jütte, makes the provocative observation that international organization should no longer be viewed as "an international structure of cooperation, but rather an institutional framework to carry out conflicts," but it does not take that point very far. In addition, the piece is difficult to follow because in several instances the German sentence structure remains virtually intact and the choice of concepts often is an unhappy one (*e.g.*, confrontative, instrumentalization, effectivity). The chapter detailing the growth of IGO's comes to the less-than-startling conclusion that "those who were, or are, optimistic about the role of IGOs as locomotives for change into a better world are likely to be disappointed" (p. 35).

The second part consists of six chapters that address aspects of North-South relations, primarily the NIEO. It contains an interesting socialist critique of the NIEO by Jan Bielawski, a Pole, which, however, is marred by its being embedded in an apologia for the role of the socialist countries in the North-South dialogue. There is nothing else in the section that is not well known and readily available elsewhere.

Part 3 is supposed to elucidate changing norms in international relations that stem from recent processes of international organization, but its two chapters have a tough time pinpointing effective, as opposed to rhetorical, innovations. And they have nothing whatever to say about how existing norms lose legitimacy and new norms are established.

The last part of the book is a mixed bag. One chapter, if it can be called that (less than nine printed pages, including footnotes), reanalyzes some of the data contained in Robert Butterworth's casebook of international conflicts that have been referred to international organizations,[1] but it comes to no new conclusions. The remaining two chapters, both perfectly respectable but neither adding a great deal to the stock of knowledge about the issues they address, are a narrative piece on Namibia and an empirical overview of the role of the OAU in conflict resolution in Africa.

There can be no conclusion to this review because there is no conclusion to the book under review, nor is there an attempt in the book to relate individual chapters to the introduction or vice versa. In the end, it all looks like another international boondoggle that required publication to justify itself to a funding agency.

JOHN GERARD RUGGIE
Columbia University

International Aspects of Criminal Law: Enforcing United States Law in the World Community (Fourth Sokol Colloquium). Edited by Richard B. Lillich. Charlottesville: The Michie Company, 1981. Pp. ix, 245. Index. $19.50.

Since the publication of *International Criminal Law*[1] in 1965 and the two-volume *A Treatise on International Criminal Law*[2] in 1973, international criminal

[1] R. BUTTERWORTH, MANAGING INTERSTATE CONFLICT, 1945–74: DATA WITH SYNOPSES (1976).

[1] INTERNATIONAL CRIMINAL LAW (G. Mueller & E. Wise eds. 1965).

[2] A TREATISE ON INTERNATIONAL CRIMINAL LAW, 2 vols. (M. C. Bassiouni & V. Nanda eds. 1973). Reviewed in 68 AJIL 150–52 (1974).

law has experienced significant growth.[3] This latest contribution, the product of the Fourth Sokol Colloquium of the University of Virginia School of Law, contains stimulating analytical articles on both classical (*e.g.*, jurisdiction and extradition) and new (*e.g.*, prison exchange treaties) areas of U.S. application of international criminal law.

The book is divided into three chapters: "Obtaining People and Evidence from Abroad through Formal Legal Processes"; "Direct United States Enforcement on the Seas and Abroad"; and "Protecting United States Citizens Abroad Through Treaties." Chapter 1 is subdivided into "Obtaining People" and "Obtaining Evidence." Alona E. Evans, now deceased, provides a strong, concise, and comprehensive discussion of the legal, policy, and practical aspects of extradition and rendition. She deftly explains that a government's usual choice of exclusion, expulsion, or other forms of rendition instead of extradition suggests that many governments believe that extradition places too many procedural restrictions on the requesting state. Louis G. Fields, Jr., an Assistant Legal Adviser in the Department of State, examines recent jurisprudence of U.S. courts on the political offense exception and accurately captures the U.S. and international trend toward limiting that exception, especially when terrorists or violent crimes are involved. Thomas E. Carbonneau of Tulane University School of Law, in *French Judicial Perspectives on the Extradition of Transnational Terrorists and the Political Offense Exception*, traces the evolution in the French courts from a liberal interpretation of the political offense exception to a restrictive test in which complicity in terrorist activities and participation in violent acts are considered common criminal activities. Paul B. Stephan, III, of the University of Virginia School of Law, in *Constitutional Limits on International Rendition of Criminal Suspects*, discusses three questions: why U.S. constitutional rights should not apply to aliens abroad; whether conduct that does not amount to a constitutional violation may be considered unconstitutional if it is contrary to a treaty obligation or norm of international law; and the extent to which U.S. officials must participate directly in the allegedly unlawful conduct that is challenged. Professor Stephan bases his discussion on a strong conceptual framework by applying Hohfeldian analysis to constitutional issues. Sigmund Timberg, who now practices law in Washington, D.C., traces the growth of foreign governments' irritation at the extraterritorial application of U.S. criminal law in antitrust cases, and the concomitant difficulties of obtaining discovery abroad in the *Uranium Cartel* case.

Chapter 2 contains two incisive articles that overlap somewhat with each other as well as with Stephan's article. Stephan's colleague, Stephen A. Saltzburg, in his examination of the extraterritorial application of the U.S. Bill of Rights, presents an excellent analysis of many recent cases. Saltzburg argues

[3] For background on the existence, meaning, and development of international criminal law, see Schwarzenberger, *The Problem of an International Criminal Law*, 3 CURRENT LEGAL PROBS. 263 (1950), and the essays in chs. 1 and 2 of 1 A TREATISE ON INTERNATIONAL CRIMINAL LAW, *supra* note 2.

that, especially insofar as searches by U.S. officials on the high seas and the interrogation of passengers are concerned, the protections of the Bill of Rights do apply. The article takes the position that foreign officials not acting pursuant to a U.S. request for assistance are not limited by the Constitution, and it sets forth a framework for defining the degree of U.S. participation that invokes constitutional protections and the types of protections required by the Bill of Rights. Ved P. Nanda, of the University of Denver College of Law, also discusses the extraterritorial application of U.S. constitutional protections in intercepting drug traffic at sea and in the enforcement at sea of the Fishery Conservation and Management Act. Nanda concludes that "random and subterfuge searches" without probable cause by the Coast Guard, although justified by courts under the major exception of an administrative search (not requiring a warrant), are in essence designed to seek evidence of a crime, and, hence, not yet justified by U.S. constitutional law.

Chapter 3 contains two contrasting views on U.S. prisoner exchange treaties. Robert E. Dalton, an Assistant Legal Adviser in the Department of State, contributes an excellent overview of the history of legislation to implement prisoner exchange treaties, and then a commentary on the judicial decisions upholding the exchanges of U.S. prisoners, especially from Mexico. However, Jordan J. Paust, of The University of Houston College of Law, argues that the prisoner exchange treaties are unconstitutional because no federal power exists pursuant to the U.S. Constitution to incarcerate an individual within the United States who was prosecuted for violation of a foreign law pursuant to foreign procedures. He also argues that by incarcerating U.S. citizens who have been victims of procedures that are contrary to U.S. criminal and constitutional procedures and human rights laws, the U.S. Government itself becomes an accomplice in the deprivation of constitutional rights and in the violation of fundamental human rights as well. Paust questions the validity of waivers of the right to raise constitutional objections made by U.S. citizens prior to their transfer to the United States.

Though the index is an abbreviated subject matter index and is of only marginal value, practitioners, policy makers, and academicians with an interest in international criminal law will all find this a valuable book. These highly readable articles are strongly recommended to persons working in the field.

BRUCE ZAGARIS
Of the District of Columbia Bar

The Political Offence Exception to Extradition: The Delicate Problem of Balancing the Right of the Individual and the Public International Order. By Christine Van den Wijngaert. Deventer: Kluwer, 1980. Pp. xxi, 263. Selected bibliography, indexes. Dfl.108.

Dr. Van den Wijngaert has undertaken an extensive and thorough review of the political offense exception to extradition. The topic is one of much interest partly because of the worldwide impact of terrorism and partly because of the ease of travel for perpetrators of crime. In American courts the recent cases[1] of IRA members who claimed the protection of the political offense exception to prevent their extradition have caused much controversy. The courts have always had difficulty in applying the exception and have evoked considerable criticism for frequently managing to find it applicable to those defendants whose political stance is found acceptable, while denying its application to those whose aspirations are deemed anathema. This difficulty has persuaded the current administration to negotiate a number of treaties and to propose legislation permitting the Executive, rather than the judiciary, to determine whether an offense is political.[2] Such an approach may well compound the problem.

The book is divided into five chapters. First comes a historical introduction. The author then distinguishes the political offender from other criminals and explores the variety of legal alternatives available for dealing with him. An attempt is made to define the political offense, bringing to bear the differing juristic approaches of the Western world, and the exceptions to the exception are carefully detailed. Next, a review of the Belgian approach is undertaken, together with some proposals *de lege ferenda* that seek to balance the rights of the defendant with the necessity of maintaining world order. The author then provides a critical analysis of the exception. She raises the question whether it is now an anachronism and decides that it is only partly so. Finally, she proposes an alternative solution to the problem.

The solution provides that the requested state would not be permitted to extradite to a state where the offender would be liable to "persecution" or unfair trial. Indeed, a state has no obligation to extradite if it prefers to remain neutral with respect to a particular political dispute, but any state refusing extradition has the obligation to prosecute the offender in its own courts: *aut dedere aut judicare*. The proposed solution stems from the underlying theme of the book: the attempt to balance the rights of the individual with the need for international order, but the solution itself creates a number of problems.

A determination not to extradite because the offender would suffer persecution or an unfair trial requires some sort of a political judgment that courts are ill-equipped to make and that would, presumably, embarrass the executive at least as much as denying extradition because of the political offense exception. However, if the requested state refuses extradition because of a declared neutrality with respect to the internal politics of the requester, it may suffer the accusation of failing its international obligations.

[1] *See, e.g.*, McMullen v. Immigration & Naturalization Service, 658 F.2d 1312 (9th Cir. 1981), 76 AJIL 386 (1982); United States v. Mackin, 668 F.2d 122 (2d Cir. 1981), 76 AJIL 391 (1982). *See also* Eain v. Wilkes, 641 F.2d 504 (7th Cir.), *cert. denied*, 102 S.Ct. 390 (1981), 75 AJIL 662 (1981).

[2] *See, e.g.*, Extradition Treaty, Sept. 14, 1979, United States-Colombia, Art. 4, para. 3, 97th Cong., 1st Sess., TREATY DOC. NO. 97–8 (*entered into force* Mar. 4, 1982); Extradition Treaty, June 24, 1980, United States-Netherlands, Art. 4, para. 4, 97th Cong., 1st Sess., TREATY DOC. NO. 97–7 (not yet in force); and S. 1639, 97th Cong., 1st Sess. (1981).

Perhaps the most difficult part of the author's solution is the requirement of prosecution in domestic courts when extradition is denied. The evidentiary difficulties alone are enough to pose major obstacles and relying on the requesting state to supply most of the evidence does not comport with the reasons for refusal to extradite. Persecutory states or those with unfair trial systems presumably provide questionable evidence. Taking the evidence as given by the requesting state hardly demonstrates a neutral stance with respect to the requester's internal politics. The prospect of asking domestic juries to pass judgment in such cases is also not pleasing from either the defendant's or the prosecutor's position.

Despite such difficulties, this book is worthy of careful consideration. It is well written and copiously documented. Its strength is that the author has clearly perceived the competing forces at work regarding the political offense exception and has offered a solution aimed at balancing the inherent tensions.

VALERIE EPPS
Suffolk University Law School

The Spitsbergen (Svalbard) Question: United States Foreign Policy, 1907–1935. By Elen C. Singh. Oslo: Universitetsforlaget, 1980. Pp. iv, 244. Index. Appendixes. $23.

The Svalbard Archipelago, several hundred miles north of the Norwegian mainland, is part of Norwegian sovereign territory by virtue of an international treaty that has been in effect since 1925.[1] In recent years Svalbard has attracted international attention primarily because of its strategic location opposite the Soviet Union's militarily important Kola peninsula, and because of related disagreements between Norway and the Soviet Union over the scope of rights enjoyed by the latter under the treaty and the delimitation of the Barents Sea. But earlier in the century, "the Spitsbergen question," as it was called,[2] was of interest primarily to international lawyers for whom an intriguing technical problem was posed by the palpable need to restore order and resolve conflicting mining claims on Svalbard at a time when its status under international law was that of *terra nullius*—*i.e.*, when there was no territorial sovereign available to do so.

The relevant political history begins in the early 1900's. Although the islands were discovered in the late 12th century and were visited seasonally

[1] Under the treaty, the island group includes Bear Island, which lies about halfway between the Norwegian mainland and Spitsbergen; *see* note 2 *infra*.

[2] The name *Svalbard* is of old Norse origin, meaning "land with cold coasts." The name *Spitsbergen* was in general use from 1596, when the Dutch explorer William Barents sighted the islands and named them after their pointed mountains. After Norway assumed sovereignty over the islands in 1925, Svalbard became the official name of the island group and West Spitsbergen was, until 1969, the name of the largest island. Since 1969 the name of that island has been simply Spitsbergen.

by hunters, whalers, and fishermen from at least the 17th century onward, their forbidding climate and inaccessibility to navigation during most of the year discouraged permanent settlement until the turn of the century. Change came with the discovery of large deposits of coal of commercial quality and its subsequent exploitation by miners of several nationalities. From that time the islands' status as *terra nullius* became problematical.

U.S. interest in the status of Svalbard began virtually at the outset of the coal boom. The first successful commercial exploitation of Svalbard's coal was carried out by two American citizens, Boston businessmen Frederick Ayer and John M. Longyear. In 1906, they bought a large tract of coal-bearing land on Advent Bay from a Norwegian firm. Seeking to avoid Norwegian and other taxes and regulations, they incorporated the Arctic Coal Company in West Virginia. They then wrote to Secretary of State Elihu Root requesting that evidence of their mining claims, which they included with their letter, be placed on file with the State Department as proof of the priority of their claims, so that they could "invoke and obtain the intervention and protection of the Government of the United States in respect of their rights and interests" in case these should become a matter of dispute. They soon did.

From the perspective of overall U.S. foreign policy, the Spitsbergen question represented a minor issue, since the islands themselves were not then of direct importance to the United States for military, economic, or political reasons. Such interest as the American Government could be said to have had in the matter consisted entirely in the economic interests of the two Bostonians, who were, however, men of seemingly infinite resourcefulness and political influence. At that, U.S. interest might have been expected to wane following Ayer and Longyear's sale of control of their Svalbard properties to Norwegian businessmen in 1916. In fact, however, the State Department's interest continued more or less in full force until the early 1930's. Singh's short but informative book tells why the Department ever got involved in the matter and why that involvement survived the commercial exit of the two Americans.

Singh asks first why the State Department's initial response to Ayer and Longyear's request was not simply that the question of property rights in Svalbard was outside the accepted sphere of U.S. influence and that, as a matter of principle, the Department did not involve itself in European political questions. The answer she gives—*all* her answers, however brief, smack of an authority I shall explain below—is that Ayer and Longyear were the beneficiaries of persistent high-level lobbying in their behalf by Massachusetts Senator Henry Cabot Lodge and Washington attorney Nathaniel Wilson. In addition, but apparently as something of an afterthought, the Department hoped that the Americans' venture would lead to U.S. penetration of European economic markets.

Why did the Department's interest outlast the Americans' sale of the properties in 1916? Because certain Department officials, principally Secretary of State Robert Lansing and departmental counsel Fred Nielsen, had by then become fascinated with the legal problems presented by international efforts to resolve conflicting land claims, yet retain the islands' status under international law as *terra nullius* (as was initially the plan).[3]

Following the conclusion of World War I, sentiment shifted away from retaining this awkward status, in part in recognition of Norway's wartime efforts, which were felt to have benefited the Allied forces in subtle ways that Norway's official neutrality belied. Accordingly, at the Paris Peace Conference, a treaty was drafted and adopted recognizing Norwegian sovereignty over Svalbard, subject to a right of nationals of the signatory states to exploit Svalbard's resources. Why did U.S. interest in Svalbard not end, finally, with the coming into effect of this treaty in 1925? Because the treaty contained an unusual provision permitting the Soviet Union to accede to it on the same basis as the original signatory states once its domestic political situation stabilized sufficiently to permit the new Soviet Government to turn its attention to international questions such as Svalbard. The approval of the other signatories was required as a condition of Soviet accession. The U.S. Government, adamantly opposed to any action that might be interpreted as implying international recognition of the new Soviet state, succeeded in preventing approval of Soviet accession until, in 1933, it too formally recognized the Soviet Union, which acceded to the treaty shortly thereafter.

I noted earlier that Singh's study has an authoritative ring to it. Though written during the years 1973 to 1975 as a doctoral dissertation at the University of Denver's Graduate School of International Studies, it was published only recently, in Norway, with a grant from the Norwegian Research Council for Science and the Humanities. (It is available in the United States through Columbia University Press.) What renders it unique and unquestionably worthy of even belated publication is that its author had privileged access to the archives of both the State Department and the Norwegian Foreign Ministry, as well as to the unpublished personal papers of Longyear and Scott Turner, the manager of the Arctic Coal Company's operations in Svalbard from 1906 to 1916. Thus, although at times one wishes that Singh had analyzed the materials to which she had unique access at greater length and in greater depth than she has done, her study is nonetheless well-nigh indispensable to anyone who needs firsthand details about the diplomatic history of Norwegian sovereignty over the islands, the terms under which that sovereignty has been maintained, and of course, the story of the U.S. Government's interest in the question from 1907 to 1935.

A number of points she makes could themselves be the subject of a dissertation. For example, she concludes that at the very time Ayer and Longyear were the sole beneficiaries of whatever policy the State Department adopted, they were also its sole source of information about conditions on Svalbard and the coal mining operations there. "The assumption that State Department policy would thus reflect the Company suggestions," she says (in something

[3] *See, e.g.*, Lansing, *A Unique International Problem*, 11 AJIL 763 (1917); and Nielsen, *The Solution of the Spitsbergen Question*, 14 *id.* at 232 (1920).

of an understatement), "was partly borne out by the documentation examined" (p. 4).

The published version of Singh's dissertation contains an epilogue, apparently written just prior to publication, in which she briefly traces developments in and regarding Svalbard since 1935. Its purpose, one supposes, is to address the question of why a study of diplomatic events early in the century is timely now. The answer lies in the persistent campaign undertaken by the Soviet Union in recent years to effect a de facto condominium over Svalbard, despite its explicit treaty commitment to recognize Norwegian sovereignty over the entire archipelago. This campaign, in turn, appears to be related to Svalbard's strategic location and to prospects for further discoveries of valuable natural resources on the islands and on their extensive continental shelf. These factors are only alluded to in Singh's work, however, since they lie outside its principal focus of inquiry.

EDWARD GORDON
Albany Law School

Antarctic Law and Politics. By F. M. Auburn. Bloomington: Indiana University Press, 1982. Pp. xx, 361. Index. $32.50.

Antarctica is a barren frontier of extremes. It is at once the coldest, windiest, highest, most isolated, and most desolate region on earth.[1] Approximately 98 percent of the continent lies under a mantle of ice averaging more than 1 mile in thickness.[2] At the same time, because annual precipitation there rarely exceeds 5 centimeters, Antarctica quite accurately can be designated one of the world's largest and driest deserts.[3]

Notwithstanding these profoundly inhospitable climatic and environmental features, Antarctica today is attracting increasing political and economic attention because of the bountiful living resources found in the circumpolar seas and the suspected presence of hydrocarbon deposits trapped within the continental shelf. Given these circumstances, publication of Auburn's volume comes at a most propitious time, and it should be received as a distinctly welcome contribution by international law practitioners, scholars, and governmental policy makers.

Thematically, this work is divided into two general parts. The initial two-thirds of the study examines the multifaceted notion of sovereignty as applied to Antarctica; sets out various national interests and priority concerns there; assesses the purpose, functions, and legal ramifications of the 1959 Antarctic

[1] *See generally* International Institute for Environment and Development, *The Future of Antarctica* (Earthscan Press Briefing Doc. No. 5, 1978), *reprinted in Exploitation of Antarctic Resources: Hearing Before the Subcomm. on Arms Control, Oceans, and the International Environment of the Senate Comm. on Foreign Relations*, 95th Cong., 2d Sess. 189–95 (1978).

[2] *Id.* at 192.

[3] *Id.* at 193. *See also* Rubin, *Antarctic Meteorology*, in FROZEN FUTURE 146, 162 (R. Lewis & P. Smith eds. 1973).

Treaty;[4] explains and evaluates the operation and procedures of the "Antarctic System" (*i.e.*, the Consultative Party arrangement) vis-à-vis the formal Treaty regime;[5] and considers the legal and jurisdictional implications of criminal acts, marriages, tort proceedings, property rights, and behavioral standards for governments that have personnel on the continent.

The concluding third of the book deals with the natural resource potential of the continent and the requisite need for preserving and protecting its environment. Auburn discusses the critical role of krill in the Antarctic food chain, as well as its conceivably great potential as a source of world protein,[6] and the likelihood of exploiting oil and gas in the offshore Antarctic environs. In regard to the former, insightful analyses are provided of both the Sealing Convention[7] and the Convention for the Conservation of Antarctic Marine Living Resources,[8] especially insofar as they supply conservation principles absent in the Antarctic Treaty.[9] Concerning hard minerals and hydrocarbons, Auburn devotes considerable space to stressing the need for a special regime to regulate nonliving resources in the area. To do otherwise, he rightly avers, would invite political confrontation and very likely unmitigated, albeit incalculable, environmental depredation in the future.

In the main, *Antarctic Law and Politics* constitutes a thoughtful, sophisticated assessment of how and why the current Consultative Party framework operates, the contentious political, legal, and economic issues that must be addressed in forthcoming years, and the *Realpolitik* obstacles impeding international accommodation. A paragraph evaluating the Marine Living Resources Convention could quite logically be read as an appraisal of how Auburn actually feels about the entire Antarctic regime framework today:

> The Antarctic system is the source of complicated freezing clauses, consensus in decision-making, absence of effective dispute settlement, lack of provision for open meetings, and a privileged position for members of the [Convention's] Commission [comprised of the Consultative Parties]. Monopolisation of negotiation of the Convention by the Consultative Parties is difficult to justify. The objection procedure for conser-

[4] Antarctic Treaty, Dec. 1, 1959, 12 UST 794, TIAS No. 4780, 402 UNTS 71 (*entered into force* June 23, 1961).

[5] The Consultative Parties include the 12 original Treaty members (*viz.*, Argentina, Australia, Belgium, Chile, France, Japan, New Zealand, Norway, South Africa, the Soviet Union, the United Kingdom, and the United States). Since 1959, three other nations—Poland, East Germany, and West Germany—have been accorded Consultative Party status. Nonconsultative parties to the Treaty include Czechoslovakia, Denmark, the Netherlands, Bulgaria, Romania, and Brazil.

[6] A tiny, shrimplike crustacean, krill conceivably could supply annual sustainable yields of 150 million tons in additional protein. TETRA TECH, THE ANTARCTIC KRILL RESOURCE: PROSPECTS FOR COMMERCIAL EXPLOITATION 121 (1978). *See also* K. A. GREEN, ROLE OF KRILL IN THE ANTARCTIC MARINE ECOSYSTEM (1977); and G. GRANTHAM, THE UTILIZATION OF KRILL (1977).

[7] Convention for the Conservation of Antarctic Seals, *done* June 1, 1972, 29 UST 441, TIAS No. 8826 (*entered into force* for the United States Mar. 11, 1978).

[8] *Opened for signature* May 20, 1980, *entered into force* April 7, 1982, *reprinted in* 19 ILM 841 (1980).

[9] Article IX(f) of the Antarctic Treaty contains the only reference to "resources," and designates "preservation and conservation of living resources in Antarctica" to be an apt measure for discussion at Consultative Party meetings.

vation measures and agreement not to consider national quota allocation comes from the Whaling Convention and practice. In these important matters little seems to have been learnt from past experience [p. 238].

In short, Auburn has provided the interested legal scholar and government official with an intelligent, balanced, admirably well-documented presentation of an issue in international law that is bound to assume ever-increasing global salience during the next two decades. It is fortunate indeed that such a timely, ambitious, and authoritative study has become available: not only does it lucidly set out the ways Antarctic activities are "governed," but also it furnishes the reader with an objective appraisal of various problems and flaws within that process. This in itself is a noteworthy accomplishment.

In conclusion, this reviewer would be remiss if he failed to mention five appendixes of pertinent documentation,[10] as well as four maps and an impressive 20-page bibliography of Antarctic-related literature. Thus, while *Antarctic Law and Politics* has obvious value for its detailed information and legal treatment, it also holds special utility as a research tool. It should serve as an excellent companion to the Society's recently published book, *The New Nationalism and the Use of Common Spaces: Issues in Marine Pollution and the Exploitation of Antarctica* (1982), edited by Jonathan I. Charney.

CHRISTOPHER C. JOYNER
The George Washington University

La Sécurité en Mer. By Philippe Boisson. Dunkerque: Grafic Foto Edition, 1981. Pp. 369. Indexes. F.250.

The author is fortunate to have his PhD thesis printed in this handsome and beautifully illustrated (black and white), almost coffee-table format, edition. But he has earned his good fortune: for his work is thorough, well organized, well written, and very timely; and he has managed to distill from his ocean of facts a number of insights that can be broadly applied.

Boisson deals with all aspects of safety at sea, which, as he rightly points out, are inextricably linked. "The problems of the marine environment are closely related to the concept of safety at sea, in the sense that this latter expression covers both the safeguarding of human life and the protection of the ecological balance in the marine environment."

After a historical introduction, tracing legislation on the safety of navigation back through the Middle Ages to antiquity, the book is divided into three main parts. Part I, "The Promoters of Safety at Sea," examines structures, both national and international, together with institutions, laws, and conventions that over the past 150 years have served to protect human lives and the environment and to safeguard navigation, fisheries, and offshore industries. Due importance is given to the history, the changing structure, and the

[10] Included among these are texts of the Antarctic Treaty (1959), the Agreed Measures for the Conservation of Antarctic Fauna and Flora (1964), the Antarctic Seals Convention (1972), and the Convention on the Conservation of Antarctic Marine Living Resources (1980).

achievements of the Inter-Governmental Maritime Consultative Organization, as well as to its internal "democratization" and the expansion of its activities (ch. 1).

An interesting point the author draws attention to is that the fears of the industrialized states that this process of "democratization," especially in its application to the Maritime Safety Committee, might *decrease efficiency* remained unfounded: for the developing countries, lacking qualified personnel, simply failed to make use of their right to participate in the activities of the technical committees—and things remained pretty much the way they were before. This experience should provide a lesson for both developed and developing countries concerned with the implementation of the Convention on the Law of the Sea as a whole, and with the establishment of the International Sea-Bed Authority in particular.

But the network of international organizations that are concerned with safety at sea has other components as well: the International Labour Organisation (ILO), the International Telecommunication Union (ITU), the World Meteorological Organization (WMO), and the International Hydrographic Organization (IHO). All provide important norms, standards, and services that enhance safety at sea. To complete the picture, the author mentions a number of relevant nongovernmental organizations (ch. 2).

Chapter 3 deals with national legislation regarding safety at sea, with particular emphasis on the U.S. and Canadian experience. Also, the history of the regulation of navigation in the Straits of Malacca makes very timely and interesting reading.

Chapter 4 deals with national structures charged with the responsibility of regulating navigation and offshore industries, surveillance of their activities, and enforcement of laws, standards, and regulations. Here the author draws largely on the French experience.

The final chapters of part I deal with the role of seamen's organizations (the principal classification organizations), such as the Bureau Veritas, Lloyd's Register of Shipping, and the American Bureau of Shipping, and conclude with an assessment of how local, national, and international measures interact.

The fundamental question that arises is whether the rules and regulations for the safety of life at sea are adapted to the realities of today. Are they not outdated or obsolete—unable to cope with the momentous changes upsetting maritime activities at this time?

The author concludes that the new law of the sea, emerging from the Third UN Conference on the Law of the Sea, will affect, in important ways, the traditional principle of the freedom of navigation, by extending the powers of preventive regulation of coastal states. "This law, however, remains incomplete, and contingent rather than legally inhibiting."

Part II presents a "General Study of the Norms for the Prevention of Accidents at Sea," against the background of the dramatic, quantitative as well as qualitative, transformation of navigation over the past 50 years. Suffice it to mention that seaborne traffic has increased sixteenfold between 1937 and 1974, and that there are 31,000 collisions at sea every year! This part of the book deals with ship construction and equipment, for general merchant shipping as well as for specialized vessels (tankers, carriers of noxious cargoes, liquefied gas carriers, nuclear-powered ships). It examines international conventions and national legislation, and comments on the role of "flags of convenience" or "free registration" states. IMCO's long-drawn battle to rid the oceans of substandard vessels is recalled in this connection. "The struggle against flags of convenience over the past two or three decades has given meager results," the author concludes,

> even in the matter of substandard vessels. . . . During the first year of application of the Boarding Program enacted by the U.S. Coast Guard, the number of defects noted on ships registered in Panama and Singapore was clearly above average. The results of the program of inspection of foreign tankers in American ports in 1977–1978 have confirmed the same tendencies. On account of the timidity of the actions undertaken by the international community, most of the flags-of-convenience States have not bothered to change their attitude with regard to substandard vessels.

Citing human error as one of the chief causes of maritime accidents, the author points out the importance of training and the need to control the number of hours worked at one stretch. He deals with systems of navigational aids, traffic regulations, and traffic separation schemes. The concluding chapters of this part are devoted to the particular safety needs of ships, instruments, and personnel engaged in scientific research, recreation (yachting), fisheries, and offshore industries.

Finally, part III of the book covers surveillance and enforcement, without which any regulation "remains dead letter." The powers and responsibilities of the flag state, the coastal state, and the port state are elucidated. Particular attention is given, again, to the French experience. The work of the U.S. Coast Guard is pointed to as a particularly successful example of surveillance and enforcement.

One cannot but agree with the author, however, that police action, while necessary, cannot entirely solve the problem of enforcement, and that it must be complemented by voluntary action and self-enforcement. "It would appear that respect for technical rules and regulations depends essentially on the valor and conscience of the seamen: Considering the immensity of the oceans and the difficulties of controlling them, the fear of the policeman remains ineffective." One might mention, in this connection, that the Greek shipowners and seamen have just formed a voluntary association—the first in existence—for the enhancement of safety at sea as proposed here.

While the author remains somewhat skeptical about whether UNCLOS III will make a decisive contribution to the improvement of safety at sea, he sets his hopes on regional cooperation. The establishment of a European "Agency for the Protection of the Sea," or "European Sea-Guard," or "European Maritime Agency," with adequate powers for monitoring, surveillance, and enforcement of norms and regulations agreed on at the level of the EEC, might go a long way toward solving the problems of safety at sea: but even this, he fears, is utopian at present and would require a change of heart and the awakening of a spirit of true cooperation among the nations of Europe, still entrenched, each of them, in its own particularism.

The law on safety at sea is part and parcel of the law of the sea in general, which exhibits the same problems Boisson reveals with regard to safety at sea. Many of these problems arise from the peculiar mixture of public and private, national and international sources of law, both in the narrower and in the wider domain. "One of the characteristics of the law on maritime safety is that it is based both on international law and on internal provisions," the author comments. Unilateral action by states and the action of international organizations play an equally important part in the making of this law. International action is needed because unilateral action, on matters of safety (and security!), is handicapped by the competitive structure of the nation-state system. National action and implementation are needed to give effect to internationally agreed standards, norms, and regulations.

Essential as this interaction is, in many cases it does not function properly. As Boisson points out, many years are often needed to internalize international conventions through internal legislation. And when it happens, differences—and conflicts—may arise due to variances in national interpretations—with no international court in place to settle such issues. A third difficulty, as Boisson sees it, is the fragmentary nature of both national and international law. Although *harmonization* is of the utmost practical importance, "the regime of maritime safety is characterized by its extreme diversity: diversity of national and international sources, variety of rules, imperatives, interpretations, exhortations, plurality of objects, each of which has to respond to specific norms of construction and use."

Boisson's book is of great and direct interest to anybody concerned with the dangers and risks at sea, which, as he points out, will remain more severe than those on land, no matter how much we may do to improve both law and practice. It is of particular interest at a time when the whole law of the sea, as it emerges from the Third UN Conference on the Law of the Sea, has to go through the process of implementation through national legislation. Both the international civil servant and the national legislator can learn a great deal from Boisson's study.

ELISABETH MANN BORGESE
Dalhousie University

The Rules of the Game: Reform and Evolution in the International Monetary System. By Kenneth W. Dam. Chicago and London: The University of Chicago Press, 1982. Pp. xviii, 382. Index. $27.

Following his earlier scholarly study of the rules of international trade, *The GATT: Law and International Economic Organization* (1970),[1] Kenneth Dam (recently appointed as Deputy Secretary of State) has now provided an excellent history and analysis of the international monetary system.

The author uses both his economic and his legal talents to examine the rules that have governed nations' international monetary affairs over four distinct periods: (1) the "international gold standard," which ended as World War I began (ch. 2); (2) the "gold exchange standard," which prevailed in

[1] Reviewed in 65 AJIL 853–56 (1971).

the period between the two world wars (ch. 3); (3) the Bretton Woods fixed exchange rate regime, which ended in the early 1970's (ch. 4); and the current semi-floating exchange rate system (ch. 6). Given the reawakened interest in various forms of the "gold standard," chapters 2 and 3 are particularly worthwhile—not only to lawyers interested in international trade but to general readers who want a sophisticated, but nevertheless highly readable, guide to the often misunderstood issues surrounding that subject. The same is true of chapter 6, which, although written at a somewhat more technical level, clearly traces the causes of the decline of the dollar as the anchor of the fixed exchange rate system established by the Bretton Woods Agreement.

The rest of the book (chs. 5 and 7–9), which concentrates on the intricacies of the International Monetary Fund and the various monetary reform efforts it has sponsored or closely been involved with, is of less general interest. At the same time, it is these chapters that best illustrate the "legal" features of the international monetary system through the complex rules that govern a country's access to IMF assistance. In addition, Dam's extensive analysis of various "reform" proposals that have recently circulated in the international community also gives the international lawyer an excellent grounding in the difficulties of drafting any international monetary agreement that would purport to replace the now defunct Bretton Woods Agreement.

This same analysis is used by the author to argue that "evolution," rather than an internationally agreed-upon "reform" document, will characterize international monetary developments in the near future. In particular, Dam makes a persuasive case that the system will evolve toward one that makes use of several "reserve" currencies, including not only the dollar, but perhaps the German mark, the Japanese yen, and the SDR. Moreover, the author highlights the fact that the growth of commercial bank lending of foreign exchange, coupled with the rise of such regional monetary confederations as the European Monetary System, has eroded the importance of the IMF as an international monetary policeman and has pushed it toward a role of operating primarily for the benefit of less-developed countries.

This book is certain to be regarded as a landmark contribution to the international legal and economic literature and its more general chapters should be of interest to any reader who wants to understand what is commonly believed to be an arcane and difficult subject.

ROBERT E. LITAN
Of the District of Columbia Bar

U.S. Foreign Policy and the New International Economic Order: Negotiating Global Problems, 1974–1981. By Robert K. Olson. Boulder: Westview Press; London: Frances Pinter Ltd., 1981. Pp. xviii, 168. Selected bibliography. Index. $22.50.

Those interested in updating their knowledge of North-South discussions for the period from 1975 through 1980 will find a good summary of the major negotiations in this small volume by Olson, a retired U.S. Foreign

Service officer and a former official of the U.S. Department of State. Written primarily from official sources and conversations with U.S. officials, it provides a succinct summary of underlying conflicts between the United States and the developing countries in "New International Economic Order" (NIEO) discussions.

Olson opens his book by linking NIEO discussions to three central U.S. foreign policy interests in the post-World War II era: "maintenance of the open, free market international economic order, resistance to communist political and military intervention throughout the free world, and support for the newly emerging nations and assistance for their introduction into the international system." He argues that all three of these basic interests must be kept in mind if one is to understand the U.S. response to the NIEO.

He poses two questions: Does U.S. policy, as carried out, support basic U.S. interests? Have negotiations in the NIEO been an effective process for global problem solving? He answers with a guarded yes to the first and a strong no to the second.

The approach is chronological and descriptive, with a short introduction to the 1974 meetings setting forth the framework for the NIEO. Most of the international negotiations from 1975 through the 11th special session of the General Assembly, August 1980, are touched on and a few major international events such as the Soviet invasion of Afghanistan are woven in. The centerpiece of his discussion is UNCTAD V, held in Manila in May and June of 1979.

UNCTAD V was, in the view of most observers, a failure, as were most of the other negotiations covered by this book. Why? Olson argues that neither the NIEO nor the present international economic order is negotiable. He argues that the United States could not negotiate away the free enterprise system and the developing countries cannot accept a basic needs program or a series of ad hoc measures in lieu of the NIEO. He discusses the major agenda items of UNCTAD V to establish his thesis. He concludes his volume with a recommendation that "a new initiative, appropriate to the realities ahead and to the gravity of the issues be undertaken." This is not elaborated on, and in light of his earlier comments it is hard to see why the new initiative would succeed.

Olson is unduly pessimistic and, in this reviewer's mind, too static in his theory of change and faulty in his analysis. After all, the Third World has made enormous progress over the past 35 years. Virtually all of the developing countries have achieved political independence. They have also changed the questions being asked about development, organized themselves in the Group of 77, the nonaligned nations, and have an international organization that is used for research, UNCTAD. They have used international forums to pursue their ideas and have forced the developed world to take seriously their complaints about transnational corporations, restrictive business practices, the transfer of technology, fluctuating commodity prices, etc. They have laid the groundwork for fundamental modifications in the international economic order. Finally, the United States does not disagree with most of the proposed institutional changes on the basis of principle. The Common Fund and the

Integrated Commodity Programme are derived from institutional structures such as the U.S. Commodity Credit Corporation and its farm subsidies. The U.S. concern is a fear that the majority rule of various institutional structures will diminish U.S. influence and power. The fundamental issue is who will gain and who will lose if there is an international redistribution of wealth and power.

ROBERT F. MEAGHER
The Fletcher School of Law and Diplomacy

The Substantive Law of the EEC. By Derrick Wyatt and Alan Dashwood. London: Sweet and Maxwell, 1980. Pp. xxvi, 386. Index. $65.75, cloth; $44, paper.

As the European Economic Community (EEC) has expanded in recent years (Great Britain, Denmark, and Ireland joined the original six members in 1973, Greece joined in 1981, and Spain and Portugal may become members soon), knowledge of the law governing trade within the Community, and between the Community and other nations, has grown increasingly more important. Authors Wyatt and Dashwood have provided a valuable aid to understanding the developing law within this recently created legal structure.

This book is intended to be both a textbook for study and a source book for the practitioner. It is a detailed compilation of much of the substantive law that has developed since the signing of the Treaty of Rome, which established the EEC, on March 25, 1957. The authors first review the origins and development of the EEC within the movement for European federation after World War II, knowledge of which is essential to understand fully the broad scope and purposes of the Community. They then discuss a number of important areas of substantive law: the law concerning the free movement of goods and persons across international borders, agricultural policy, competition policy, industrial property, and public undertakings. Community law derives from a variety of sources, and in each subject area the authors consider the relevant terms of the Treaty, the regulations of the Commission, directives of the Council of Ministers, and decisions of the European Court of Justice. Dashwood is Legal Secretary to the European Court of Justice and he frequently draws on examples from cases before the Court. These cases are helpful in demonstrating both the terms of the substantive law and the types of problems that arise as a result of the grafting of Community law onto the preexisting national law of the individual member states.

The impact of Community law upon the municipal law of its members has been one of the most important effects of the EEC. Because of the far-reaching nature of the economic integration achieved by the EEC, Community law has substantially limited the freedom of its member states to regulate economic activity—and even to act in some spheres not directly tied to economic policy. The provisions of the Treaty that promote the free movement of workers across national borders, for example, have restricted the nations' ability to set their own immigration policies. This subjection of local activities to dual and sometimes conflicting sets of legal rules—a problem that the United States of America has experienced through its federal system of government—has raised many complex legal problems. When, for example, does imposing certain taxes become the equivalent of charging a customs duty, which is prohibited by the Treaty? The growth of EEC law has thus provided a new source of rights for individuals against the member states and among themselves. Other aspects of Community law, such as the competition policy which is similar to American antitrust laws, impose greater obligations on persons doing business in the Community. This book should be a useful reference source for analyzing these new rights and obligations.

As complete as is the treatment of each topic addressed, several areas of Community law, such as transportation policy and international investment, are not covered in this book. These omissions do not, however, detract from the usefulness of this volume, which should be a welcome addition to the literature on the law of the EEC in both the law office and the law school library.

ROBERT B. VON MEHREN
Board of Editors

Enforcing Antitrust against Foreign Enterprises. Edited by Cornelis Canenbley. Deventer: Kluwer, 1981. Pp. xiii, 125. Dfl.74; $37.

American capitalism is faltering.[1] Traditional remedies designed to revive the economy have not worked.[2] The problem lies in our inability to diagnose current maladies properly or resolve procedural problems prompted by the application of special laws. This book is a welcome addition to a growing body of literature devoted to procedural problems. It is a primer for practitioners seeking solutions to knotty international questions.

The book lists the conditions under which a state might apply its antitrust laws extraterritorially (pp. 7–11). It offers the reader a way to assess when such action is imminent. The book's editor recommends that a practitioner do the following:

> (1) examine the relevant principles of international law;
>
> (2) analyze the text of the antitrust law to see whether it applies to the entity under investigation; and
>
> (3) survey and catalog the conditions under which the state might apply its law extraterritorially.

The reader is invited to list the ways a state might acquire jurisdiction over

[1] *Jobless Rate Hits 41-Year High: U.S. Total Soars Past 10 Million,* Chicago Tribune, May 8, 1982, at 1, col. 4. *Economic Scene: A Step Slide Into Recession,* N.Y. Times, Nov. 11, 1981, at 32, col. 1.

[2] Carl Rowan hints at this in a syndicated article appearing in the South Bend (Indiana) Tribune. Rowan, *U.S. Voters Didn't Grasp How Well Off They Were,* South Bend Tribune, May 6, 1982, at 14, col. 5. *See Reagan, Thatcher and Liberalism,* N.Y. Times, Nov. 19, 1981, at 27, col. 1.

a foreign entity; to survey and neutralize the affirmative defenses the entity might employ; and to evaluate the remedies should the entity refuse to comply with extraterritorial orders.

Under international law states have jurisdiction over people within their borders. A state may acquire jurisdiction over nonresidents if their behavior abroad is linked with miscreant domestic behavior (p. 12). Yet state jurisdiction over nonresidents on antitrust questions will vary (*ibid.*). In the absence of an international consensus that abusive economic behavior is a crime all nations condemn, the laws of the state devoted to competition must be consulted to determine whether a nation will seek jurisdiction. In chapter 2, the book lists legal doctrines and tests nations employ as a rationalization for applying their laws extraterritorially (pp. 7–12).

The book deals with items frequently sought by everyone: testimony and documents. It reports on the rules of protocol to be followed (pp. 19–40, 41–49), the willingness of one nation to assist another in retrieving information (pp. 73–76), and providing remedies (pp. 50–57). Under the "civil investigation demand," for example, the U.S. Department of Justice may obtain documents and testimony pertinent to antitrust investigations (p. 20).[3] If the information is abroad, Rule 4(i) of the Federal Rules of Civil Procedure provides for service on persons in foreign countries. Apart from such proceedings, courts have authority to compel the production of documents and testimony abroad. If the court has in personam jurisdiction over a person in possession of needed information, it may order its production in a private suit.[4]

Persons abroad who are ordered to do something may react, it is suggested, in two ways. They may appear *specially* (emphasis added) to contest the jurisdiction of the court (pp. 65–66). They may enlist the aid of their state to overcome assertions of extraterritorial authority (pp. 72–80). The book lists blocking statutes promulgated by various nations to deprive people of the capacity to comply with foreign orders. It also lists plaintiffs' remedies (pp. 50–57) where these statutes pose no obstacle and nonresidents persist in their refusal to submit to questioning or to surrender documents. In West Germany, for example, cartel authorities have the capacity to impose fines upon foreign undertakings or persons for noncompliance with requests for information (p. 52). The decision to fine may be executed by seizing the property of the foreign undertaking or person within West Germany.

This is a good book. Its shortcoming is that it covers too many countries in insufficient depth. A thoroughgoing examination of the law of Great Britain, the European Economic Community, West Germany, and the United States

[3] *See* Antitrust Civil Process Act (1962), 15 U.S.C. §§1311–1314.

[4] Foreign law may pose an obstacle to the production of documents abroad. Application of Chase Manhattan Bank, 192 F.Supp. 817 (1961), *aff'd*, 297 F.2d 611 (2d Cir. 1962); United States v. First Nat'l Bank, 396 F.2d 897 (2d Cir. 1968). A summary of these cases appears in the book at pp. 21 and 22.

would have been quite enough. On balance, however, the book is worth reading. The text and appendix will prove to be invaluable research tools.

RONALD C. GRIFFIN
Washburn University of Topeka School of Law

EEC Antitrust Procedure. By C. S. Kerse. London: European Law Centre Ltd., 1981. Pp. xxxvi, 337. Index. $102.

Since the accession of the United Kingdom and the Republic of Ireland to the European Economic Community (EEC) nearly 10 years ago, the number of high-quality English-language analyses of the substantive antitrust provisions of the Treaty of Rome (the "constitution" of the EEC) has increased steadily. However, until the publication of this remarkable book, there has been no comprehensive analysis of the EEC's antitrust procedure. In his preface, Kerse states that he has attempted "to describe and explain in detail the procedures of the Commission and Court of Justice of the European Communities in antitrust cases under Articles 85 and 86 of the Rome Treaty." After an introductory chapter describing the EEC rules on competition and outlining the functions of the various entities involved in enforcing those rules, Kerse examines various phases of procedure in six chapters, entitled "Starting the Machinery," "Fact-finding," "Rights of the Defence," "Involvement of National Authorities," "Commission Decisions," and "Fines and Penalties." The final three chapters deal with "General Legal Rules," "Judicial Review by the European Court of Justice," and "National Courts and National Law." The book concludes with 40 pages of very useful appendixes and a very good index. There are also tables of legislation and cases, and numerous, very thorough footnotes. The law is stated as of April 20, 1981.

Kerse's goal was to write "a useful practical handbook . . . primarily for lawyers, . . . that others, businessmen, students, etc. may also find helpful and instructive." He has achieved this goal in an outstanding manner. Those involved in the enforcement of the EEC competition rules and those who seek an informative comparative explanation of EEC procedure should find the book invaluable. Objective and insightful analyses are skillfully combined with constructive criticism. Moreover, the book contains many details of procedure that are unavailable to all but the handful who monitor EEC developments as a full-time occupation. At several key points Kerse compares EEC and U.S. antitrust procedure. There are three discussions of particular interest to Americans. First, Kerse traces the development and status of the EEC's rules on subject matter jurisdiction over entities located outside the EEC. His discussion carefully explains the difference between the approaches of the Commission and the Court of Justice, and between the "effects" and "enterprise entity" theories of jurisdiction. Second, there is an informative discussion of the Commission's powers to obtain information from entities located outside the EEC and the effect of foreign laws designed to "block" such extraterritorial discovery. Third, a very helpful section analyzes the unsettled issue of whether an injured party can sue for damages for breach of Articles 85 and 86. Kerse discusses several theories under which such a private action might be successful in the national courts of the 10 member states of the EEC.

This reviewer understands that Kerse is preparing a supplement to this book that will cover developments through midsummer 1982. The commitment to keep this very useful book up to date further enhances its value and strengthens its position as an essential addition to any library that purports to be serious about EEC antitrust law.

JOSEPH P. GRIFFIN
Of the District of Columbia Bar

The Group of 77. Evolution, Structure, Organization. By Karl P. Sauvant. New York, London, Rome: Oceana Publications, Inc., 1981. Pp. xv, 232. Index. $22.50.

The Collected Documents of the Group of 77. 6 vols. (The Third World Without Superpowers, 2d series.) Edited by Karl P. Sauvant. Dobbs Ferry: Oceana Publications, Inc. Vol. 1, 1981: pp. lii, 592; vol. 2, 1981: pp. vii, 607; vol. 3, 1981: pp. vi, 554; vol. 4, 1981: pp. viii, 588; vol. 5, 1982: pp. xii, 572; vol. 6, 1982: pp. x, 576. $50/vol.

When a group is ad hoc, as is the Group of 77, forming itself only whenever the need arises for a particular set of negotiations, understanding it requires access to far more documents than are needed for a more institutionalized entity, which typically would have only a few documents setting forth its rules of operation. Sauvant has provided the reader of his six-volume compilation of the documents of the Group of 77 with just such a comprehensive source of the group's major documents, agendas, proposals, reports, declarations, rules of procedure, and plans. His shorter work offers a clear and concise monograph on the group's evolution, structure, and organization.

Stimulated by Raúl Prebisch, UNCTAD's first Secretary-General, the Group of 77 was formed at the first session of UNCTAD in 1964. Since then it has expanded to encompass more than 130 nation-states from the Third and Fourth Worlds. These states have formed a flexible, informal, multi-centered group that has no permanent institutions, no headquarters, no regular staff, no secretariat, and no constitution. It is dedicated to decision by consensus to protect the sovereign rights of each member and their common interests.

The Group of 77 is the economic counterpart of the nonaligned countries, which played a major role in placing the development agenda before the world community. Within the UN framework it has become the principal organ for Third and Fourth World negotiations for the establishment of the "New International Economic Order" and related structural changes in the world economy. Its organization is based upon the UN's and UNCTAD's regional group model, categorizing all members as African, Asian, or Latin American and giving equal representation to each region. It is multi-centered, with main focuses in Geneva (UNCTAD), Vienna (UNIDO), New York (UN), and Washington (IBRD and IMF). But it has also constituted itself in Paris and Mexico for particular negotiations.

The supreme organ of the Group of 77 is the Ministerial Meeting, which sets policy for the group until the next Ministerial Meeting. The principal product of the Ministerial Meeting is the program of action or declaration, which embodies the consensus of the Group of 77 on all substantive items to be discussed at the next UNCTAD meeting. In the opinion of this reviewer, the procedure for arriving at a consensus, which has been defined as "the absence of any formal objection,"[1] could profitably be subjected to Fisher and Ury's "getting to yes" one-text system for negotiation.

Sauvant's monograph cites the evolution toward New York as the central forum and the decline of Geneva, which he describes as being relegated to the preparation of legal and quasi-legal documents, not to policy formulation. While this may be an accurate characterization of some observers' perceptions, this reviewer would argue for another viewpoint: that both the United Nations and UNCTAD are being pushed offstage in favor of GATT, the IMF, and the World Bank in the real development agenda for the '80's and '90's. The legal and quasi-legal documents coming out of Geneva from GATT have more importance to economic development than do the Charter of Economic Rights and Duties of States or the New International Economic Order, which originated in New York. Protectionism, conditionality, reciprocity, and graduation are being debated in Geneva and Washington, not in New York. These are the real issues of interdependence which must be resolved before Global 2000.

MARCIA A. WISS
Of the District of Columbia Bar

Međunarodno pravo ekonomskog razvoja: Pravni aspekti novog međunarodnog ekonomskog poretka (The International Law of Economic Development: Legal Aspects of the New International Economic Order). By Milan Bulajić. Belgrade: Servis Saveza udruženja pravnika Jugoslavije, 1980. Pp. xi, 279.

The author is a Yugoslav diplomat and legal scholar who has been an active participant in numerous international conferences on economic issues in international law. The present book is the combination of a survey of the legal issues in the North-South dialogue and a proposal of a course of action by the developing countries to protect their interests.

After several introductory historical chapters the author moves to a topic-by-topic analysis of the key issues and documents in the effort by the developing countries to create a new international economic order. There are chapters devoted to the right to self-determination and permanent sovereignty over natural resources, maritime conferences, transnational corporations, the

[1] Informal Composite Negotiating Text of the Convention on the Law of the Sea, UN Doc. A/CONF.62/WP.10/Rev.3 (1980), Art. 161.

revision of the Paris Convention for the Protection of Industrial Property, transfer of technology, and restrictive practices. In each chapter the author outlines the history of negotiations toward the achievement of a code or convention that would reflect the interests of the developing countries and the particular reasons for the success or failure of these negotiations.

The author argues that the developing countries cannot create a new international order merely by using their voting majority in the United Nations to push through resolutions, but must achieve a consensus that will attract the votes of the developed countries and their adherence to international codes of conduct. In many cases, the author argues, rules that lack binding force but that gain widespread acceptance as international customary law and by incorporation into national constitutions may be more effective than a convention ratified by a few nations. He points out in particular the importance for developing countries of creating cadres of highly qualified jurists to represent their interests in international bodies. He calls for the creation of new mechanisms in the United Nations with the broad participation of legal specialists from the developing countries to further the development of the new international legal order.

Bulajić's long years of experience as a diplomat are reflected in the overall tone of the book, which counsels negotiation, persistence, and technical competence rather than radical action as the best way to achieve the goals of the southern half of the North-South dialogue. The book as a whole is a most welcome addition to this dialogue.

PETER B. MAGGS
University of Illinois at Urbana-Champaign

Proceedings of the Twenty-Third Colloquium on the Law of Outer Space. International Institute of Space Law of the International Astronautical Federation. New York: American Institute of Aeronautics and Astronautics, 1981. Pp. 287. Index.

The bulk of this volume consists of 40 separate reports (223 pages, large format, with two columns per page), many of them in abstract form, presented at the 23d annual meeting of the International Institute of Space Law, a subsidiary body of the International Astronautical Federation. The volume also includes a summary of discussions and a history of the Institute, as well as six annexes and a useful catalog of topics explored at previous symposiums.

In common with its predecessors, this symposium, held in Tokyo, was truly international, with contributing participants including nationals of the United States (a dozen), the USSR (seven), Brazil, Canada, Chile, the Federal Republic of Germany, Japan, and the Netherlands, plus officials of the United Nations, the European Space Agency, and the COMSAT Corporation. Many of the pioneers of space law are herein represented: C. Q. Christol, E. Galloway, S. Gorove, M. Menter (of the United States); Y. M. Kolossov, V. S. Vereshchetin, G. P. Zhukov (of the Soviet Union); I. H. Ph. Diederiks-Verschoor (of the

Netherlands); K.-H. Böckstiegel (of the Federal Republic of Germany); and the ubiquitous N. Jasentuliyana of the UN Secretariat. Whereas the Agreement Governing the Activities of States on the Moon and Other Celestial Bodies (opened for signature on December 18, 1979) was clearly the central topic of the symposium, contributions in this volume cover a vast array of additional subjects, such as remote sensing of the earth by satellite, the allocation of radio frequencies by the ITU, environmental protection of outer space, the legal status of the European Space Agency, solar- and nuclear-powered satellites, registration of spacecraft, the delimitation of outer space, export control of space technology, private space law, and even a proposal for an international "code of offenses against the peace and security of mankind," the latter being one of the longest contributions (pp. 211–19), with only a tenuous connection to space law.

In contrast to most other topics discussed, the Moon Treaty receives a sustained analysis, with maximum attention focused upon Article XI. The article enunciates the application of the concept of the "common heritage of mankind" to the moon and its natural resources and subjects future exploitation of these resources to an "international regime." The Treaty does not define the common heritage and postpones the elaboration of an international regime until such time when the exploitation of lunar resources becomes feasible. These potentially crippling imperfections in the Treaty, while noted, apparently were not regarded by the participants in the colloquium as being too serious, for the majority found the Agreement as a whole a valuable addition to the corpus of space law. In a noteworthy departure from the general feeling that the Treaty is a step in the right direction, Professor S. B. Rosenfield of the New England School of Law concluded that because of the weakness in Article XI, "there is no justification for this treaty" at all (p. 71). It may be added that the present text of this article is responsible for the U.S. refusal to sign and ratify the Treaty.

In view of the relative scarcity of Soviet writings in Western legal periodicals, one looks forward with particular interest to reading contributions by Soviet scholars. Regrettably, their contributions to these *Proceedings* are far too short (an average of two to three pages) and closely follow the already familiar official position of the Soviet Government. Perhaps worth noting is a report that suggests a continuing lukewarm attitude on the part of the Soviet Union toward the concept of common heritage (*e.g.*, R. V. Dekanozov, p. 7) and the assertion of "the right of space objects of States to fly over the territory of other States at altitudes lower than 100/110 km above sea level for the purpose of reaching outer space and celestial bodies or for returning to the Earth" (G. P. Zhukov, p. 222; V. S. Vereshchetin, p. 210).

Overall, this is a useful publication, primarily for its analysis of the Moon Treaty. Its quality would have been enhanced had the organizers limited the *Proceedings* to that single topic and insisted on fewer but more elaborate reports.

Ivan A. Vlasic
McGill University

Fluggesellschaften und Luftverkehrssysteme der sozialistischen Staaten UdSSR, Polen, CSSR, Ungarn, Bulgarien, Rumänien, Kuba, Jugoslawien und der VR China. By J. L. Kneifel. Nördlingen: Verlag F. Steinmeier, 1980. Pp. 318. DM 98.

Staatliches und internationales Luftverkehrsrecht der sozialistischen Staaten UdSSR, DDR, Polen, CSSR, Ungarn, Bulgarien, Rumänien, Kuba, Jugoslawien und der VR China. By J. L. Kneifel. Nördlingen: Verlag F. Steinmeier, 1980. Pp. 220. DM 98.

Die Zivilluftfahrt im Europäischen Gemeinschaftsrecht. By Ludwig Weber. Berlin, Heidelberg, New York: Springer-Verlag, 1981. Pp. xxviii, 428. Index. DM 114; $51.90.

The first two of these volumes, dealing with civil aviation and air law of the "socialist" states, are authored by a West German jurist who has written extensively on public international and comparative aeronautical law, focusing in particular on the civil aviation of the Soviet bloc and other Communist countries. His two monographs represent a logical whole and complement one another.

The first book describes the development and the present (mid-1970's) state of the airline companies and air transportation systems of the member countries of the Council of Mutual Economic Aid (CMEA or COMECON) and Yugoslavia and China. The German Democratic Republic and Vietnam are not included, but the civil aviation of the former was the subject of a separate study by the same author. Whereas the first study is concerned primarily with economic aspects of the subject, the other book by Kneifel focuses on the legal dimensions of air transport of the COMECON countries, including the German Democratic Republic. Despite difficulties in obtaining reliable data, especially for the first monograph, the author was able to present an impressive comparative picture of civil aviation in these countries, having gained much insight from sources available at IATA, ICAO, and the U.S. Civil Aeronautics Board, as well as from original materials from the countries concerned.

The first monograph consists of four parts. The introductory sections place the air transportation systems of the Communist countries within the context of the integrative scheme and objectives of the Council of Mutual Economic Aid. The second part gives a detailed country-by-country account of the development and promotion of civil aviation in the COMECON countries, dealing, *inter alia,* with such topics as aircraft industry, airports, flight safety, personnel training, and the organization and management of the airlines. The bulk of the book is devoted to a detailed analysis of the air transport networks and routes of each national airline. The Soviet AEROFLOT stands out as the world's largest airline; the other COMECON airlines compare only with minor West European air transport companies. In his conclusions Kneifel notes what has become particularly obvious in recent years: that the COMECON countries' need to modernize their airlines' technological infrastructure has coincided with an acute shortage of the necessary hard currency which these airlines themselves—like the shipping lines—are designed to supply.

In his second monograph Kneifel approaches the legal dimensions of the topic from three perspectives. First, the major part of his analysis deals with public aeronautical law, both domestic and international. He examines the national air laws of the individual countries, both in historical perspective and in their present status, delving into such subjects as registry, flight safety, airports, aircraft commander and crew, aircrafts in distress, and violation of airspace. The author notes that despite a continued trend toward harmonization there are still significant differences among the national regulations of the COMECON countries. The analysis of international air law focuses on the many bilateral air traffic agreements concluded by the Communist countries with each other and with other states. A section describing the procedures before the U.S. Civil Aeronautics Board that govern the granting of landing rights to selected Communist countries in the United States is of particular interest to American readers. Another section examines the participation of these countries in ICAO and other international (not "supranational," as claimed by Kneifel) organizations and arrangements.

The second legal dimension examined by the author deals with relations between the airlines of the countries concerned. These are governed either by IATA, of which some of the airlines are members, or by intrabloc agreements. In the third legal perspective Kneifel addresses himself to relations between the airlines and their customers, including in particular problems of liability and compensation for damage.

Kneifel's monographs do not provide much theoretical insight or synthesis but are a rich source of information on the economic and legal aspects of civil aviation in the Soviet bloc and some other Communist countries. This makes them a unique reference source on a subject that has not, so far, been treated in such a detailed and comprehensive manner. Both studies are richly documented by scores of tables and figures and contain extraordinary amounts of bibliographical references in several languages, but no index. Each book contains an English summary but they are, unfortunately, of such poor linguistic quality as to make them virtually incomprehensible to the reader.

Weber's book on civil aviation in the European Community is another massive study on international air law, but of a much more complex legal nature, resulting from certain ambiguities found in the fundamental law of the Community. As in other areas involving the issue of the Community's "common policy," such as fisheries and shipping, the question is whether and to what extent the Community's common policy can be applicable to such a unique field as civil aviation. The purpose of Weber's book is to explore the legal dimensions of the problem and suggest a legal framework within which the national air transport laws could be coordinated and eventually integrated into a common civil aviation policy of the European Community.

Weber's study is divided into two parts. The first presents a historical review of attempts to integrate European civil aviation dating back to French and British "internationalization" plans of the early 1930's; reviews the legal, economic, and organizational structures of civil aviation in the EEC; and explains in detail the major legal issues involved. Briefly, the transportation provisions of the Treaty of Rome, designed to adjust the national regulations to a Community-wide transportation system, apply to transportation by rail, by road, and on inland waterways, but not to maritime and air transport. However, the Council has the power to adopt rules regulating these two transportation systems. Furthermore, for a long time it was not clear whether the general provisions of the EEC Treaty were applicable to these systems. The question was finally settled in 1974 by the European Court of Justice in its leading *French Seamen* decision (involving the general provision on the right of settlement). The Court held that the general provisions were indeed applicable insofar as this would promote the attainment of the Treaty's objectives, in this case the common transportation policy. One must add, however, that all this does not prejudice the power of the Council to transfer the competences with regard to air transport policy gradually from the member states to the Community.

The ramifications of the Court's decision and many other legal issues of national, Community, and international aeronautical law are scrutinized in depth in the second major part of Weber's work. The applicability of the general Treaty provisions (*e.g.*, the rule of nondiscrimination, the right of establishment, the antitrust provisions), the division of competences between the Community and the member countries, the EEC Treaty and the rules of international air law (Chicago Convention and bilateral agreements), and the EEC Treaty and domestic legislation of the members are among the topics discussed. The contribution of the Community's organs to the development of a common air transport policy is also examined.

In his conclusions Weber suggests three levels on which a common civil aviation policy of the EEC could be realized in accordance with the Treaty of Rome: adopting measures designed to remove incompatibilities between Community law, on the one hand, and international agreements and domestic law, on the other; harmonizing the domestic laws of the member countries; and finally, developing a common air transportation policy through gradual integrative measures in the strict sense of the word. A good English-language summary, four annexes, an abundant multilingual bibliography, and a subject index complete this very well-done volume, which will certainly remain a standard work on the subject for years to come.

The three books reviewed here are primarily legal analyses that do not take account of developments in regional integration theory, an area so intensively explored by American political scientists. Still, these three regional studies of civil aviation should be welcomed by political scientists desiring new and relatively unknown materials for their regional integration study, by area scholars with an interest in Eastern and Western Europe, and, of course, by jurists, both theoreticians and practitioners, specializing in public aeronautical law.

BOLESLAW A. BOCZEK
Kent State University

Military Law (3d ed.). By Edward M. Byrne. Annapolis: Naval Institute Press, 1981. Pp. xxiii, 790. Table of abbreviations, 47 appendixes, self-quizzes with answers, glossary, bibliography, table of cases cited, and index. $22.95.

Violations of the law of armed conflict are generally handled in the military criminal justice system of the offender, although the jurisdiction of military law encompasses foreign nationals who violate the laws of war. Civilian criminal systems also have assumed jurisdiction of such offenders. This third edition of *Military Law* clearly, yet comprehensively, describes the U.S. military justice system by which violations of the law of armed conflict are dealt with as breaches either of the Uniform Code of Military Justice (UCMJ)[1] or of the law and customs of war. Although *Military Law* makes no attempt to deal with violations of the law of war, most violations of that law by members of the U.S. armed forces would also violate the UCMJ, either as a substantive crime of violence or as disobedience of orders.[2]

Captain Byrne, a respected teacher, advocate, and military judge, has again revised his most useful textbook, which is also suitable for self-instruction by civilian and military lawyers alike, as well as interested nonlawyers. *Military Law* presents a comprehensive, yet lively, picture of the system by which discipline is maintained in the U.S. armed forces and adherence by them to the law of armed conflict is enforced.[3] It does not, however, reflect the latest changes to the UCMJ brought about by the Military Justice Amendments of 1981,[4] but they and subsequent changes will undoubtedly be incorporated in the fourth edition.

J. ASHLEY ROACH
Judge Advocate General's Corps, U.S. Navy

Juridical Positivism and Human Rights. By Mieczyslaw Maneli. New York: Hippocrene Books, 1981. Pp. 406. Index.

Maneli's book is a welcome contribution for more than the reason that there has been a paucity of philosophical writings on human rights in recent years. In it he restates the tradition of legal positivism, clarifies the distortions

[1] 10 U.S.C. §§801–940.

[2] For example, the Secretary of the Navy has issued a general order, SECNAV Instruction 3300.1A of May 3, 1980, which requires the reporting to higher authority by each member of the Department of the Navy who has knowledge of or receives a report of an apparent violation of the law of armed conflict suspected of having been committed by or against members of, or persons accompanying or serving with, the armed forces of the United States, or their property, as well as violations of the law of armed conflict suspected to have been committed by or against allied military or civilian personnel or against allied military or civilian property. Failure to do so is punishable by confinement at hard labor for 2 years and a dishonorable discharge or dismissal, even if the accused did not know he was required to report such violations to higher authority. This aspect of the order is designed to make punishable any cover-ups like those associated with the My Lai incident.

[3] It is the policy of the U.S. Department of Defense that all military operations and related activities in armed conflict shall be conducted in compliance with the law of war. Dep't of Defense Directive No. 5100.77 of July 10, 1979, Subject: DoD Law of War Program.

[4] Pub. L. No. 97–81, Nov. 20, 1981, 95 Stat. 1085 (amending 10 U.S.C. §§701, 813, 832, 838, 867, and 869, and adding §§706, 707, and 876a). Nor does the book reflect the minor technical corrections to the UCMJ made by Pub. L. No. 96–513, Title V, §511(24 & 25), Dec. 12, 1980.

suffered by it, and advances his "Positivist Realism" as a theory adjusted to the social realities at the end of the 20th century. Thus he shows that Bentham was distrustful of the ruling few and sought the greatest happiness of the greatest number through his principle of utility, that Austin did not abandon human freedom to the caprice of the legislator, and that Ihering maintained that society cannot interfere in private rights. Maneli does not regard Kelsen as representative of juridical positivism but, rather, a travesty of it, since Kelsen reduced the entire juridical system to a formal structure devoid of content, whereas provisions of law in juridical positivism have definite content and are a source of rights. The hostility of natural law theorists to the positivist theory of interpretation of law was politically motivated, for in rejecting autocratic legal systems they also rejected the precepts for interpreting the law under the positivist theory, and the historical school opposed it because it tried to justify its own convictions. Recent Soviet jurists, as opposed to those who prevailed during Stalin's rule, have recognized man's rights, not because of any influence of natural law but because of the utilitarian realization that governing increasingly requires, even in the Soviet Union, the consent of the governed. The "tremendous step forward" made by American realists (Dewey, Llewellyn, Holmes, Cardozo, *et al.*) went beyond the formalistic logic of syllogisms in its search for a methodology to preserve valued ideals in modern times. They started the search but, Maneli says, they never found the answer. The answer, he claims, is provided by Chaim Perelman's "New Rhetoric." The result is Maneli's Positivist Realism, which is "a philosophical amalgam of juridical positivism and American jurisprudence, international and municipal norms on human rights, and the philosophy and methodology of the New Rhetoric."

And this is where my troubles with Maneli begin. Although I wish he had coined a more adequate term to do justice to his position, since he does add a new element to the realists' position, it is his uncritical and wholesale endorsement of the New Rhetoric that is fraught with difficulties. For one thing, it makes the same mistake that Holmes made earlier ("Life of law is not logic, but experience") by positing the data of positivistic facts and historical experience in opposition to the technique of logic. Furthermore, under its "New Theory of Argumentation," plurality of minds operates through dialogue whereby individuals should seek accommodation and compromise. However, the New Rhetoric's open-ended pluralism cannot be capable of resolving conflicts, or even of defining them with any clarity, without being bound by the prevalence of a system providing the contours of the circumscribing values. Moreover, as we lawyers well know, argumentation alone is not sufficient to resolve disputes. There comes a point when it has to be stopped and capped with authoritative decision. Also, genuine and abiding conflicts of values and interests exist in which the New Rhetoric's mandate that "individuals should not push their interests and convictions too far" (p. 183) is no more useful than pious preaching and just as ineffective in resolving the conflict. Again, there seems to be a naive conviction in it that people are reasonable, or only reasonable people count, and that differences can be resolved by dialogue. Finally, there are problems with the concept of audience in the New Rhetoric.

Perelman, in his own works, has set up a "universal audience" to which a number of acceptable theses can be presented in order to make the argumentation rational. Does, however, such an audience exist that shares common values?

As to human rights, Maneli maintains, upon evidence, that the positivist theory of human rights is based on social and political realities and that human rights have become a part of positive international law. To the extent his argument, unlike that of natural law, is that a valid theory of human rights cannot ignore the historicity of man, I agree with him, an agreement that he has so kindly mentioned in his thought-provoking book.

S. PRAKASH SINHA
Pace University School of Law

Rights and Responsibilities. International, Social, and Individual Dimensions. Proceedings of a conference sponsored by the Center for Study of the American Experience. Los Angeles: University of Southern California Press, 1980. Pp. 298. $18.

This book contains a disparate collection of papers and comments that do not succeed in binding together under the intended theme of "rights and responsibilities." The contributions vary from a broad comparative study of the individual in Eastern and Western societies to an article on the rights and responsibilities of the newsman. There is also a thoughtful, albeit brief, examination of the concepts of individual freedom and social responsibility in the United States by Professor Barbara C. Jordon. The majority of the papers, however, focus upon issues related to human rights and American foreign policy, and the book will be of particular interest to persons concerned with foreign affairs and the international protection of human rights.

Most of the foreign policy papers, which were written during the Carter administration, criticize the former President's human rights policy. While some of the criticisms are valid, the papers and comments are more interesting for their unintentional insights into the current administration's approach to human rights and foreign policy. Many of the Reagan administration's principal themes, such as the notion that there is an important difference between totalitarian and authoritarian regimes, are to be found here. Ernest Lefever, President Reagan's original nominee for the position of Assistant Secretary of State for Human Rights and Humanitarian Affairs, dwells at length on the notion that "zealots" have focused on the small sins of U.S. allies and have overlooked the massive sins of its adversaries. A careful reading of these papers will reveal not only the broad underpinnings of current American policies on human rights, but also many of the serious conceptual flaws in those policies.

The essay of greatest interest to international lawyers will be Kenneth Thompson's, entitled *Tensions Between Human Rights and National Sovereign Rights.* Thompson identifies three basic perspectives on world politics: the traditional diplomatic perspective, the legal perspective, and the theological perspective. These three different viewpoints lead to three very different approaches to international human rights policies. In Thompson's view, respect for domestic jurisdiction is the essential element of the diplomatic approach, while proponents of the theological position advocate most forcefully the active pursuit of a human rights policy. International lawyers take a middle position and argue that human rights are no longer matters of exclusive domestic jurisdiction because the protection of human rights and fundamental freedoms is now the subject of a number of important international treaties, such as the Covenants on human rights. An increasing number of jurists would add that the Universal Declaration of Human Rights has now become part of customary international law. Thompson stresses, however, that the jurists' ultimate conclusion qualifies the invocation of any international legal principle as a matter of policy judgment, which must take into consideration all of the potential risks and advantages.

Apart from the interesting legal debate over human rights and domestic jurisdiction, there is little in this book that will be of interest to international lawyers. Rather, the book will appeal to those persons who have a specific interest in human rights and American foreign policy.

LAURENT MARCOUX, JR.
Canadian Human Rights Foundation

The Family in International Law: Some Emerging Problems (Third Sokol Colloquium). Edited by Richard B. Lillich. Charlottesville: The Michie Company, 1981. Pp. xii, 164. Index. $17.50.

This volume is a collection of four essays published under the Gustave Sokol Program in Private International Law of the University of Virginia School of Law. Its raison d'être, as stated in Walter J. Wadlington's foreword, was to introduce an international dimension to "one of the most dynamic areas of law reform in the United States during the past two decades": namely, family law. The International Year of the Child in 1979 provided the setting for blending family law scholars with those of international law to explore international solutions to family law problems, particularly those affecting children. Thus, with the exception of the lead article by Willis L. M. Reese on the Hague Convention on Celebration and Recognition of the Validity of Marriages, the rest of the papers deal with various aspects of children's rights: child custody controversies arising from "Operation Babylift," by Thomas E. Carbonneau; a critique of the Draft Convention on the Rights of the Child, by Harvey Schweitzer; and an assessment of the role of the 1959 Declaration on the Rights of the Child and the Draft Convention in light of the current status of children's rights in the United States, by Richard E. Crouch. The latter raises a larger issue of the appropriateness of the federal Government's participation in a multilateral treaty dealing with a subject matter hitherto reserved to the various states. He poses the question:

> how best to establish the rights of the child on our own shores before we irrevocably commit ourselves internationally to a view that will close off all meaningful alternative domestic options. It is at once fascinating and distressing to contemplate that expedient considerations of current international politics might force us to take a position internally as to the

> rights of persons within, and the power of the state over, the nuclear family, that we cannot live with at home. The problems presented by federalism itself are obvious, and the powerful federal presence in what is almost the last remaining area of exclusively state law is quite a change to contemplate [p. 20].

In other words, we have the specter of *Holland v. Missouri* revisited, albeit on a multilateral scale.

Notwithstanding its title, the volume under review deals with the subject mainly from the U.S. perspective. To readers who expect a broader, comparative approach, this may come somewhat as a disappointment.

Since the publication of this volume, controversies surrounding the rights of the child in the United States have, if anything, intensified as well as expanded in scope. Do the rights attach as of conception or birth, or somewhere in between? Do children have the right or duty to be bused to schools? What about school prayers, tax credit for tuition, school lunch, or even the right of teenage employment? We can also expect an influx of Amerasian children fathered by American servicemen in Korea and Southeast Asia—claiming, perhaps rightfully so, their right to U.S. citizenship.[1] Along with refugees resettled in the United States, many of them children, these Amerasians will face a multitude of legal problems—adoption, sponsorship, custody, support, etc.—in comparison to which the problems generated by Operation Babylift would pale into insignificance. And, finally, how do all of these tie into the 1959 Declaration on the Rights of the Child or the proposed convention?

Perhaps one of the next Sokol Colloquiums can once again be devoted to these intricate, as well as practical, legal problems under the same able editorship.

LUKE T. LEE

Soviet Year-Book of International Law, 1980. Moscow: Izdatel'stvo "Nauka," 1981. Pp. 405. 4 rubles, 90 kopecks.

What legal questions have arisen during COMECON's 30 years? What are the relationships between international and municipal law and international

[1] The bases for such a claim may be briefly summarized: section 301(g) of the Immigration and Nationality Act confers U.S. citizenship "at birth" upon a person born abroad, one of whose parents is an American citizen. This is qualified, however, by section 309(a), which states that, if only the father was a U.S. citizen, the child would be denied U.S. citizenship unless "the paternity of such child is established while such child is under the age of 21 years by legitimation" (no such restriction is placed on the mother). According to recent Supreme Court decisions, section 309 might be challenged as violating the Equal Protection Clause of the 14th Amendment in two major aspects: discrimination based on sex (Caban v. Mohammed *et ux*, 441 U.S. 380 (1978)) and discrimination against illegitimate children (Trimber v. Gordon, 430 U.S. 762 (1976)).

The above view appears to be supported by the Department of Justice. Thus, in the *Attorney General's Report to the President on Women's Equality* (128 CONG. REC. H5369, 5376 (daily ed. Aug. 5, 1982)), the following immigration and naturalization laws are listed under "Uncorrected Sex Bias in Federal Statutes":

> 8 U.S.C. §1101(b)(1)(D)—Defines "child" for purposes of obtaining a status, benefit, or privilege by virtue of the child's relationship to its "natural mother" [and] 8 U.S.C. §1409—Child born out of wedlock "shall be held to have acquired at birth the nationality status of his mother . . ." (if mother is a U.S. citizen).

public and private law? These were the major agenda items for the 1979 and 1980 annual meetings of the Soviet Association of International Law. Thanks to more detailed reporting than that of the 1978 meeting, and publication of one of the key papers, foreign readers can savor the varied thoughts currently emerging among Soviet jurists.

I. I. Lukashuk of Kiev, in his key report on COMECON, contrasts interparty agreements and interstate norms. He castigates Boris Meissner of Cologne for calling the declarations and agreements of Communist Parties of member states of COMECON "quasi-legal" in character (p. 30). Lukashuk argues that as early as the 1974 textbook on international law, it was said that declarations and communiqués issued by meetings of representatives of Communist and workers' parties are not in law international treaties, although they have great importance in the formation of socialist international legal principles and norms. They are to be seen as an inspiration to the formulation of law through treaties but not as legal norms themselves.

The papers on the other prime topics presented at the meetings are not published, but the rather full report of the secretary provides readers with a basis for guessing at least the outlines of the arguments. Debate was heated over when and how treaty norms enter into municipal law. The Association's President, G. I. Tunkin, summed it up in his final comment, saying that he opposed the view of several speakers that a treaty binds the USSR and its citizens only if ratified. He declared that states are free in international law to utilize whatever means they wish to give effect to an international law norm. When ratification is required by the terms of the treaty, of course, it must be ratified, but otherwise it need not be under any rule of international law. Tunkin also opposed the use by some speakers of the noun "transformation" instead of "implementation" to describe what happens when an international law norm is incorporated in municipal law.

Tunkin, in closing the discussion, found it necessary to correct the confusion that had developed over the relationship between public and private international law, especially as to the proper classification of the precedents accumulating in the work of the administrative tribunals of the various international organizations. To Tunkin, it must be recognized that private international law is composed in part of national statutes and in part of international norms, but the latter are not part of international public law. The norms arising from the precedents of the administrative tribunals settling disputes over tenure in international organizations are international norms but no part of the corpus of international public law. Thus, international private law is composed of both national and international norms, although there is a tendency to strengthen the international element.

Tunkin found it necessary at the meeting's end to dress down a Bulgarian scholar who argued that international laws of three kinds exist today: the law of peaceful coexistence (universal law); socialist international law; and the international law of the world imperialist system (p. 295). Those who have followed Tunkin's long-standing effort to gain recognition that there is but one general international law binding upon all will appreciate his annoyance. There can be no separate international law for imperialist powers. He is even reluctant to accept the argument of his colleagues, Judge Kozhevnikov and others, that a socialist international law has emerged from the practice of socialist states among themselves. Tunkin's tactic is to place every state under the same system of norms and to revise the general system over the years by the infusion increasingly of norms acceptable to the socialist states. One of the ways to do this is through recognition of socialist views as *jus cogens.* A paper in the *Year-Book* goes into detail on this process.

The meetings ended with statements by the authors of papers that they had been aided by the discussion. Those with long memories will be able to contrast this amicable ending with what happened when E. B. Pashukanis and A. Y. Vyshinsky had the final say. Those they criticized often found their careers ruined. Today the speakers express a variety of views and leave with their careers intact, although it is to be noted that on one issue, that of Afghanistan, there was unanimous adoption of a resolution in 1980 criticizing "the imperialist states and the Peking hegemonists for their attack on the sovereignty of independent Afghanistan" (p. 293). The mavericks so frequently heard in meetings of the American Society of International Law have no counterparts in Moscow when the issue is of high national politics.

JOHN N. HAZARD
Board of Editors

Polish Yearbook of International Law, Vol. X, 1979–1980. Warsaw: Polish Academy of Sciences, Institute of State and Law, 1981. Pp. 345. Bibliography. Zl.130.

The 10th volume of the *Yearbook* follows the well-established pattern. The doctrinal part (12 contributions) is followed by the review of the Supreme Court decisions in international civil law cases (Tomaszewski) and of arbitral awards of the Polish Chamber of Commerce (Wiśniewski). Court decisions deal with collateral liability and recognition of foreign judgments, while arbitral awards deal with disputes arising from international business transactions. The book review section, the list of treaties (made or denounced by Poland) (Kranz), and the bibliography of Polish writings of the period (1978–80) (Czeczot-Gawrakowa) complete the volume. It must be noted that commercial and economic agreements represent the largest category of listed treaties, including a significant number of agreements on fisheries, navigation, and commerce.

It is of course impossible to review in detail all the contributions included in the volume. It opens with an important ideological article by the editor-in-chief, and is followed by an investigation into the meaning of military détente (Multan) and a very interesting article (de Fiumel) on the judicial relations between the EEC and COMECON. De Fiumel indicates that owing to the organizational differences, the EEC is able to act as a unit, while the international relations of COMECON, including the making of commercial agreements, still fall within the competence of individual countries.

In the next group of articles, two pieces on the succession of treaties precede contributions on the law of the sea. Of those, the article by Góralczyk—*The New Law of the Sea*—deserves special attention. Written before the last session of the Conference on the Law of the Sea, it points to some basic objections to the developments in this area of international law. Góralczyk admits that although opposed by the socialist states, fishery or economic zones have become a part of the new customary law of the sea. Unilateral extension of national jurisdiction over the vast areas of adjacent coastal waters by the majority of members of the international community has forced the United States, the USSR, Japan, and other seafaring nations to follow suit, and has thus restricted the traditional freedom of the sea. He insists, however, that another proposed innovation in this area of international law, the creation of special regimes for the exploitation of seabed and other resources outside national jurisdiction, requires adoption in a formal treaty, approved by the three segments of international society: capitalist states, the socialist system, and the Third World. The "common heritage of mankind" is a new concept and, although approved by the resolution of the UN General Assembly, is not binding on the members of the United Nations. The resolution "could not alter the actual situation" (pp. 141–42).

The second half of the volume is devoted to studies in the area of conflicts of law (private international law). It includes articles on liability for damages in maritime shipping (Łopuski), on the influence of international commercial transactions on the development of the theory of obligations (Rajski), and on sexual equality in the socialist system of private international law (Sośniak and Skapski), including the important question of public policy (*ordre public*).

The volume ends with a very interesting article on the status of observers in international organizations of a universal character (Grabowska), restricted to the situation in the United Nations. However, it may be noted that observers also occur in other international organizations, some of them of universal character (GATT).

Studies on the equality of the sexes are thematically linked to the introductory article by Symonides, *The Polish Initiative on the Preparation of Societies for Life in Peace*. Articles on the equality of the sexes are linked to the international instruments of human rights to which socialist countries wholeheartedly adhered. It is the thesis of Professor Symonides that the Polish initiative follows ancient Polish tradition going back to the 15th century and was a constant theme developed by Polish publicists and promoted by Polish foreign policy, down to the present day. In the post-World War II period, Polish peace initiatives were reflected in various disarmament schemes and in the struggle for international protection of human rights. He admits that disarmament initiatives have never aimed at changing the existing balance of forces. Curiously enough, the present Soviet position in the Geneva negotiations is the same as the Polish position. Regarding international protection of human rights, he is of the opinion that it is a "necessary guarantee of peace and . . . a bulwark against the possible resurgence of fascism," a position confirmed by the Helsinki Declaration.

One may wonder, however, whether Polish initiatives aimed at establishing a regime of peace and protection of human rights are little more than propaganda. In Soviet opinion (and practice) international intervention to protect human rights in the Soviet Union is steadfastly opposed as intervention into matters within its exclusive domestic jurisdiction. That position has been maintained even after the Helsinki Declaration, which made protection of human rights a cornerstone of the regime of détente and relaxation of tensions. That Polish diplomacy adheres in practice to the Soviet line seems to be proved by the fact that in the Madrid discussions (1982), following the imposition of the martial law regime in Poland, the Polish delegation rejected a probe into the denial of human rights in Poland and into the total suppression of political opposition.

A final observation may seem somewhat picayune compared to the gravity of the problems raised above. Symonides, an expert in many areas of international law, suggests that Polish canonists (Skarbimierz and Włodkowic) knew in the beginning of the 15th century the concept of the law of nations. With somewhat reckless abandon he asserts that Włodkowic invoked the law of nations (p. 9). Had he read carefully the magnificent studies of the late Professor Ehrlich of the Jagiellonian University (which he quotes), he would have known that Polish canonists referred to canon law, the law of nature, and divine law. It is true that they developed notions that were fundamental to the future doctrines of international law, but the notion of international law, or the law of nations, is of a much later date.

K. Grzybowski
Duke University

BRIEFER NOTICES

U.S. Policy in International Institutions: Defining Reasonable Options in an Unreasonable World. Special student edition, updated and revised. Edited by Seymour Maxwell Finger and Joseph R. Harbert. (Boulder: Westview Press, 1982. Pp. xv, 217. Index. $24, cloth; $12, paper.) This book is designed, as stated in the preface, as an aid to teaching an undergraduate course in U.S. foreign policy and to provide at least "supplementary material" on international economic and resource issues, and on U.S. policy in international organizations. It is an "updated and revised" special student edition. The copyright date is 1982.

Despite the merit of several of the essays in this volume, this reviewer found that the book falls short of its aspirations. No volume of this sort can be up to the minute; publishing delays generally guarantee that it will be out-of-date in at least some respects. But more could be done in "updating" than is here reflected. In the first place, though the table of contents is an outline of a good course, the contents themselves are often short and elementary discussions. Second, one wonders what the "updating" consisted of: on Africa, the main items are an article by Julius Nyerere for *Foreign Affairs* (July 1977) and excerpts from "remarks by U.S. Secretary of State Cyrus Vance" before the NAACP, made on July 1, 1972. The understandable result is that neither piece speaks to the issues of the 1980's in Africa; the Rhodesia of Ian Smith has long disappeared to be replaced by the problem of (as I write) Mugabe's Zimbabwe. It is unclear when the brief article on the law of the sea was written, but it is also seriously out-of-date as a teaching tool.

On the other hand, there are several thoughtful pieces, such as Karl Sauvant's on the "New International Economic Order," which Sauvant views (to what will be the stupefaction of many) as essentially a conservative and reformist set of principles. His prescriptions do not seem likely to achieve much acceptance, but at least they are provocative.

SEYMOUR J. RUBIN
Board of Editors

Der internationale Schutz der Menschenrechte und das Interventionsverbot. By Helmut Rumpf. (Baden-Baden: Nomos Verlagsgesellschaft, 1981. Pp. 106. DM 39.) Rumpf's essays explore the relationship between two principles in international law: nonintervention and international enforcement of human rights.

His point of departure is the assumption that a violation of international law occurs whenever a state's sovereignty is intruded upon by a foreign state or international organization in the absence of a treaty or a universally recognized justification for intervention.

Rumpf reviews the development of the nonintervention principle from its classical origins (Vattel, Kant) to the postwar era. He notes with alarm the modern tendency to subordinate nonintervention to competing political impulses (*e.g.*, decolonization, termination of racial discrimination). Thus, despite frequent inclusion of nonintervention clauses in multilateral agreements, there has been an ever expanding catalog of "universal" human rights whose violation is purportedly subject to vindication through intervention.

Rumpf analyzes several modern examples of intervention. In each case the intervening party relied upon some "universal humanitarian" principle (self-serving phrases like "protect democracy" and "fraternal assistance"). He notes that this so-called humanitarian intervention is not a creation of 20th-century relationships. His discussion of the French Revolution is an excellent case study.

Throughout, Rumpf's underlying theme is that nonintervention must be the fundamental basis of international law. He concludes that in the absence of preexisting agreements voluntarily entered into by all parties authorizing intervention, it cannot be justified unless the state whose sovereignty is to be compromised has wantonly violated a basic human right.

BRUCE M. BOTELHO

El Conflicto Honduras-El Salvador y el orden jurídico internacional. By James Rowles. (San José: EDUCA, 1980. Pp. 303.) The short, but bloody, conflict between Honduras and El Salvador in July of 1969 spawned a series of treatises by Honduran and Salvadoran jurists on various aspects of the war. Inspired more by patriotic fervor than by any apparent interest in objective research or analysis, these works did little to clarify the facts of this emotionally charged incident.

It has been left for an American legal scholar to produce the first carefully documented and thoroughly researched review of the causes and facts of this tragic occurrence. Rowles, in eight incisive chapters, covers the historical background of both countries, their participation in and frustration with the Central American Common Market, the immediate antecedents of the dispute, and, in particular detail, the OAS's efforts to prevent the outbreak of hostilities, and later, its ultimately successful actions in terminating the shooting war and starting the long process leading to the signing of a peace treaty. Unfortunately, this Spanish version of Rowles's work went to press before the signing of the peace treaty, negotiated under the guidance of a distinguished Peruvian statesman and signed in Lima in late 1980. A planned English edition of the work is scheduled to include this treaty and, I hope, a discussion of its interesting legal complexities and meticulously drafted ambiguities.

Rowles's careful scholarship and broad-ranging research have produced a valuable description and analysis of the international legal aspects of the only open conflict between Western Hemisphere states in the second half of the present century. Especially interesting is his chronicle of the arduous labor of Ambassador Sevilla-Sacasa and the OAS "Group of Seven" who, often at considerable personal risk, contributed substantially to the prompt cessation of hostilities. Also worthy of particular attention is the description and analysis of the human rights elements involved.

This is a good, detailed case study of the actual negotiations involved in the management and resolution of a thorny international dispute.

HEWSON A. RYAN
The Fletcher School of Law and Diplomacy

Droit des relations internationales (2d ed.). By Simone Dreyfus. (Paris: Cujas, 1981. Pp. 417.) International lawyers from common law countries cannot fail to be impressed by the caliber of international lawyers from France and the substantial contribution made by them to the body of international law. This book is worthy of the tradition of teachers of law from the French universities.

The volume is intended as an introduction to international law for students of international relations, for as the author observes in her preface,

> everything which touches upon international relations must be seen from a double point of view, the political point of view and the legal point of view. No analysis could be complete without reference to the rules of law applicable to relations between States. Whether or not it is followed . . . international law is an essential element in every international question.

The book is divided into two main parts. The first deals with the characteristics of international society: its historical evolution, the subjects of international law, the sources, and peaceful and hostile relations among the members of contemporary international societies.

In the second part, the author deals with the mechanisms of association adopted in international society: the League of Nations, and the United Nations and the specialized agencies (the ILO, the World Bank, and UNESCO); and finally, certain regional organizations (the Council of Europe, the European Communities, and COMECON).

After each section, there is an "*annexe pédagogique*," which is meant to assist study of the principal themes of the book. It includes a brief bibliography, a list of basic concepts, key words and useful expressions, and certain general questions and themes for consideration, as well as practical exercises. The latter are supplemented at the back of the book by an outline of the history of a mythological country, "La République Azuréenne," a republic that frequently needs advice from the legal adviser in its Foreign Ministry.

The author in her preface indicates that she aimed to achieve clarity and simplicity, while at the same time illustrating the theoretical questions of international law by reference to concrete examples taken from actual practice.

The author has achieved her aims. The principles of international law are expressed clearly and the historical details, as well as those taken from current events, should ensure that the student will understand the relevance of international law to the relations between members of the international community.

DAVID FLINT
The New South Wales Institute of Technology

Environmental Law and Policy in the Pacific Basin Area. Edited by Ichirō Katō, Nobuo Kumamoto, and William H. Matthews. (Tokyo: University of Tokyo Press, 1981. Pp. ix, 229. Index. ¥ 5400.) This volume is composed of papers presented at the first Asian-American Conference on Environmental Protection in Sapporo, Japan, in August 1978. The ambitious undertaking suggested by the title is examined in three sections, entitled "Southeast Asia," "Japan," and "The United States and International Cooperation." Owing to the book's dependence on the conference materials, there is no comprehensive review of the subject. The study is so limited in scope that Korea is the subject of only one paragraph in the introduction and China is dealt with in less than four pages. The articles follow no unified theme and are of varying quality.

The section covering Southeast Asia contains an article by Peter S. J. Chen on *Development and Environmental Planning in Singapore* that is well organized and highly informative. For purposes of a general review the reader will be disappointed to find that the paper on Indonesia examines only water pollution and purposely excludes questions related to air and soil pollution. The selection on Thailand is excellent, but it only focuses on lead poisoning. Other papers in the section are either too rudimentary, as is the one on Malaysia, or too concerned with procedural systems, as is the one on the Philippines.

The book's best section is on Japan and it gives the reader a splendid overview of that nation's environmental issues. Particularly noteworthy are the essays by Nobuo Kumamoto, *Recent Tendencies and Problems of Court Cases on Environmental Pollution* and Yasuta Abe, *Land Reclamation and the Protection of the Sea and Seashore Surrounding Japan*.

Future editions might be improved if the final section, "The United States and International Cooperation," were separated into two parts. Each subject is worthy of more thorough examination. The paper by Matthews and Carpenter presents an adequate analysis of the problems related to the requirement of Environmental Impact Statements for Agency for International Development assistance under the National Environmental Protection Act. The article by Bosselman concerning the historical development of public parks in the United States appears somewhat out of place.

The editors have saved the best for last. *Regional Cooperation for the Protection of the Environment in the East Asian Seas and the Pacific* by Tsutomu Fuse and Toru Iwama is informative and a pleasure to read and leaves one with an appreciation of the dynamic nature of environmental law and policy in the Pacific Basin area. The editors would be well advised to exercise more editorial control at the outset of future Asian-American Conferences on Environmental Protection if the papers presented are to be published.

ALAN D. WIENER
University of Miami

Prisoners of War (2d ed.). By R. C. Hingorani. (Dobbs Ferry: Oceana Publications, Inc., 1982. Pp. xvii, 315. Index. $30.) The first edition of this work appeared in 1963. In the second edition, Hingorani pays some attention—though not as much as one might desire—to such post-1963 developments as Protocol I Additional to the 1949 Geneva Conventions and the delayed repatriation of Pakistani prisoners of war at the end of the 1971 India-Pakistan-Bangladesh war.

This book is more an informed, yet personal, commentary on the proper status, maintenance, and release of prisoners of war than a systematic legal analysis of the relevant customary and conventional rules. Although there are some citations to the third Geneva Convention and to Protocol I, they are not always complete or precise. Very little attempt is made to interpret specific provisions of the Convention or Protocol. In some instances, only a reader already conversant with the existing law will readily be able to distinguish Hingorani's personal preferences from his exposition of the law.

In general, Hingorani argues the case for expanding the class of persons eligible for prisoner-of-war treatment, and for making prison camp conditions more humane than they often have been. He does this without being rigid or doctrinaire. He has an eye for what is practical and realistic, as well as for what is humane. Thus he is able to propose reforms in a number of areas (for example, regarding assessment of the expense of maintaining prisoners of war) that make good sense. His tone tends to be didactic at times.

As an Indian scholar, Hingorani expresses the Third World viewpoint on such matters as inclusion of wars of self-determination in the definition of international wars covered by Protocol I. The book's Third World outlook should enhance its interest to Western readers. However, Hingorani's espousal of the Third World position leads him into an untenable distinction between World War II-style resistance movements, which, in his view, must meet the four conditions of Article 4(A)(2) of the third Geneva Convention to qualify for prisoner-of-war status, and post-World War II national liberation movements, which, he says, need only satisfy the conditions of Protocol I, Article 44.

The book has three appendixes: the third Geneva Convention, the (Indian) Geneva Conventions Act (1960), and excerpts from Protocol I. The Geneva Conventions Act is noteworthy for its assertion of jurisdiction over any person of any nationality who commits or attempts to commit anywhere a grave breach of any of the four Geneva Conventions.

FREDERIC L. KIRGIS, JR.
Washington and Lee University

A Collection of International Concessions and Related Instruments. Vol. I. Edited and annotated by Peter Fischer, with Thomas W. Wälde. (London, Rome, New York: Oceana Publications, Inc., 1981. Pp. vi, 505. Index. $50.) Since

1976, when the first two volumes of this series (dealing with medieval documents) were published,[1] research has revealed that the amount of historical material is more voluminous than anticipated. Hence it was decided to begin publication of the current agreements in a separate Contemporary Series, of which this is the first volume. It contains eight documents relating to timber in Sierra Leone, asbestos in Colombia, metallurgy in Mauritania, iron and steel in Liberia, oil in Egypt, electric power and aluminum in Indonesia, lead and zinc in Chile, and ore in the same country. The contemporary documentation begins with January 1, 1975, the year after the world energy crisis began to have a significant impact. The definition of an international concession (p. v) used in the earlier series (vol. I, p. xviii) is followed in the Contemporary Series:

> a synallagmatic act by which a State transfers the exercise of rights or functions proper to itself to a foreign private person which, in turn, participates in the performance of public functions and thus gains a privileged position vis-à-vis other private law subjects within the jurisdiction of the State concerned.

More simply, transactions between sovereigns and foreign private persons.

As in the medieval series, the documents are reproduced from the sources from which they are extracted (mostly English, but including the parallel Arab text of the Egyptian agreement). Each item is preceded by an editorial note identifying the source and briefly summarizing the document. This collection should be highly useful, as a repository of current practice, to lawyers engaged in negotiating and drafting agreements of this type.

EDWARD DUMBAULD
U.S. Senior District Judge

[1] Reviewed by this reviewer in 71 AJIL 190–91 (1977).

BOOKS RECEIVED*

International Law—General

Bernhardt, Rudolf (ed.). *Encyclopedia of Public International Law. Instalment 2: Decisions of International Courts and Tribunals and International Arbitrations.* Published under the auspices of the Max Planck Institute for Comparative Public Law and International Law. Amsterdam and New York: North-Holland Publishing Co., 1981. Pp. xvii, 309.

Conforti, Benedetto. *Lezioni di Diritto Internazionale* (2d ed.). Naples: Editoriale Scientifica, 1982. Pp. xi, 289. Index. L.18.000.

Lleonart y Amsélem, A. J. *Investigación científica y derecho internacional.* Madrid: Instituto de Ciencias Jurídicas, 1981. Pp. 269, including an English summary (pp. 21–52). Indexes.

Oda, Shigeru, and Hisashi Owada (eds.), with the assistance of Kazuya Hirobe. *The Practice of Japan in International Law, 1961–1970.* Tokyo: University of Tokyo Press, 1982. Pp. xxxii, 471. Index. $55. Distributed by Columbia University Press.

International Economic Law & Relations

Gold, Joseph. *The Fund Agreement in the Courts: Volume II. Further Jurisprudence Involving the Articles of Agreement of the International Monetary Fund.* Washington: International Monetary Fund, 1982. Pp. xii, 499. Indexes. $17.50.

* Mention here neither assures nor precludes later review.

Khan, Kabir-ur-Rahman. *The Law and Organisation of International Commodity Agreements.* The Hague, Boston, London: Martinus Nijhoff Publishers, 1982. Pp. xxv, 416. Indexes. Dfl.170; $74.

Sanders, Pieter (ed.). *Yearbook Commercial Arbitration.* Volume VII–1982. Deventer: Kluwer, 1982. Pp. xx, 445. Dfl.75; $37.

Law of the Sea & Maritime Law

Jenisch, Uwe. *Bibliographie des deutschen Schrifttums zum Internationalen Seerecht 1945–1981.* Frankfurt am Main: Alfred Metzner Verlag, 1982. Pp. xxix, 141. Index.

Temas Maritimos. (Ciclo de Conferencias organizado en conmemoración del Día del Mar, 25 a 29 de febrero de 1980.) Santiago: Universidad de Santiago de Compostela, 1981. Pp. 70.

Shusterich, Kurt Michael. *Resource Management and the Oceans: The Political Economy of Deep Seabed Mining.* Boulder: Westview Press, 1982. Pp. xx, 344. Index. $22.50.

Soons, Alfred H. A. *Marine Scientific Research and the Law of the Sea.* Deventer: Kluwer, 1982. Pp. xix, 383. Index. Dfl.95; $38.

Use of Force & Law of War

Bothe, Michael, Karl Josef Partsch, and Waldemar A. Solf. *New Rules for Victims of Armed Conflicts: Commentary on the Two 1977 Protocols Additional to the Geneva Conventions of 1949.* The Hague, Boston, London: Martinus Nijhoff Publishers, 1982. Pp. xxi, 746. Index. Dfl.340; $145.

Terrorism

Alexander, Yonah, and Charles K. Ebinger (eds.). *Political Terrorism and Energy: The Threat and Response.* New York: Praeger Publishers, 1982. Pp. xiii, 258. $29.95.

Alexander, Yonah, and Kenneth Myers (eds.). *Terrorism in Europe.* New York: St. Martin's Press, 1982. Pp. 216. Index. $25.

Farrell, William Regis. *The U.S. Government Response to Terrorism: In Search of an Effective Strategy.* Boulder: Westview Press, 1982. Pp. x, 142. Index. $20.

Human Rights

Marie, Jean-Bernard. *Glossary of Human Rights: Basic terms in universal and regional instruments.* Paris: Editions de la Maison des sciences de l'homme, 1981. Pp. 339. In English and French.

Papacostas, Alkis-B. N. *The Helsinki Final Act.* Athens, 1980. Pp. 111. In Greek.

Zuijdwijk, Ton J. M. *Petitioning the United Nations: A Study in Human Rights.* Hampshire: Gower Publishing Co., Ltd.; New York: St. Martin's Press, 1982. Pp. xv, 397. Index. $35.

International Criminal Law

Leu, Hans-Joachim. *Introducción al derecho internacional penal.* Caracas: Ministerio de Relaciones Exteriores, 1982. Pp. 174. Index.

Willis, James F. *Prologue to Nuremberg: The Politics and Diplomacy of Punishing War Criminals of the First World War.* Westport and London: Greenwood Press, 1982. Pp. xiii, 292. Index. $29.95.

Environment & Natural Resources

Bartels, Martin, Michael Fritzsche, Wolfgang Hauser, Christian Kirchner, Erich Schanze, Fabian G. v. Schlabrendorff, and Albrecht Stockmayer. *Bibliography on Transnational Law of Natural Resources.* Deventer: Kluwer; Frankfurt am Main: Alfred Metzner Verlag, 1981. Pp. 227. DM 58.

Diaz, Luis Miguel. *Responsabilidad del estado y contaminación: aspectos jurídicos.* Mexico: Editorial Porrua, S. A., 1982. Pp. 163. Index.

Skala, Astrid K. *Internationale technische Regeln und Standards zum Umweltschutz: Ihre Entstehungsarten und rechtlichen Wirkungen.* Cologne: Carl Heymanns Verlag KG, 1982. Pp. 251. Index. DM 48.

Young, Oran R. *Resource Regimes: Natural Resources and Social Institutions.* Berkeley, Los Angeles, London: University of California Press, 1982. Pp. x, 276. Index. $25.

International Organizations

Chatterjee, S. K. *Legal Aspects of International Drug Control.* The Hague, Boston, London: Martinus Nijhoff Publishers, 1981. Pp. xxiv, 587. Index. Dfl.285; $124.

Duffar, Jean. *Contribution à l'étude des privilèges et immunités des organisations internationales.* Paris: Librairie Générale de Droit et de Jurisprudence, 1982. Pp. 391. Index. F.280.

Kapteyn, P. J. G., P. H. Kooijmans, R. H. Lauwaars, H. G. Schermers, and M. van Leeuwen Boomkamp (eds.). *International Organization and Integration: Annotated Basic Documents and Descriptive Directory of International Organizations and Arrangements.* Vol. II.A (2d rev. ed.). The Hague, Boston, London: Martinus Nijhoff Publishers, 1982. Pp. xxiv + 640. Index. Dfl.235; $99.

Luard, Evan. *A History of the United Nations. Volume 1: The Years of Western Domination, 1945–1955.* New York: St. Martin's Press, 1982. Pp. viii, 404. Index. $27.50.

Moskowitz, Moses. *The Roots and Reaches of United Nations Actions and Decisions.* Alphen aan den Rijn: Sijthoff & Noordhoff, 1980. Pp. 210. Index.

Pomerance, Michla. *Self-Determination in Law and Practice: The New Doctrine in the United Nations.* The Hague, Boston, London: Martinus Nijhoff Publishers, 1982. Pp. xi, 154. Index. Dfl.90; $39.50.

Puchala, Donald J. (ed.). *Issues Before the 37th General Assembly of the United Nations 1982–1983.* New York: United Nations Association of the United States of America, 1982. Pp. 156. Index.

European Community Law

Borrmann, Axel, Christine Borrmann, and Manfred Stegger. *The EC's Generalized System of Preferences.* The Hague, Boston, London: Martinus Nijhoff Publishers, 1981. Pp. 276. Dfl.145; $59.50.

Hilf, Meinhard. *Die Organisationsstruktur der Europäischen Gemeinschaften: Rechtliche Gestaltungsmöglichkeiten und Grenzen.* Berlin, Heidelberg, New York: Springer-Verlag, 1982. Pp. xviii, 442. Index. DM 98; $43.60.

North, P. M. (ed.). *Contract Conflicts. The E.E.C. Convention on the Law Applicable to Contractual Obligations: A Comparative Study.* Amsterdam and New York: North-Holland Publishing Company, 1982. Pp. xviii, 401. Dfl.115; $53.50.

La Politica Mediterranea della CEE. Under the direction of Antonio Tizzano. Naples: Editoriale Scientifica, 1981. Pp. 522. Indexes.

Private International Law

Bryde, Brun-Otto. *Internationale Verhaltensregeln für Private—Völkerrechtliche und verfassungsrechtliche Aspekte.* Frankfurt am Main: Alfred Metzner Verlag, 1981. Pp. xi, 125. DM 32.

Collection of Conventions (1951–1980). Edited by the Permanent Bureau of the Hague Conference on Private International Law. Pp. 313. Distributed by Maarten Kluwer. Dfl.40; $25.

Lipstein, K. *Principles of the Conflict of Laws, National and International.* The Hague, Boston, London: Martinus Nijhoff Publishers, 1981. Pp. xii, 144. Index. Dfl.75; $33.

Pålsson, Lennart. *Marriage in Comparative Conflict of Laws: Substantive Conditions.* The Hague, Boston, London: Martinus Nijhoff Publishers, 1981. Pp. lxxvi, 388. Index. Dfl.200; $87.

U.S. Foreign Relations: Law & Policy

Bartell, Joyce J. (ed.). *The Yankee Mariner and Sea Power: America's Challenge of Ocean Space.* Los Angeles: University of Southern California Press, 1982. Pp. 299. $20. Distributed by Transaction Books.

Chiswick, Barry R. (ed.). *The Gateway: U.S. Immigration Issues and Policies.* Washington and London: American Enterprise Institute for Public Policy Research, 1982. Pp. 476. $22.95, cloth; $12.95, paper.

Pastor, Robert A. *Congress and the Politics of U.S. Foreign Economic Policy, 1929–1976.* Berkeley, Los Angeles, London: University of California Press, 1980. Pp. xiii, 366. Index. $28.50, cloth; $8.95, paper.

Sanford, Jonathan E. *U.S. Foreign Policy and Multilateral Development Banks.* Boulder: Westview Press, 1982. Pp. xiv, 279. Index. $22.

Tahir-Kheli, Shirin (ed.). *U.S. Strategic Interests in Southwest Asia.* New York: Praeger Publishers, 1982. Pp. x, 230. $26.95.

Arms Control & Disarmament

Burt, Richard (ed.). *Arms Control and Defense Postures in the 1980s.* Boulder: Westview Press; London: Croom Helm, 1982. Pp. x, 230. Index. $25.

Foreign & Comparative Law

Aaron, Henry (ed.). *VAT: Experiences of some European Countries.* Deventer: Kluwer, 1982. Pp. 278. Dfl.140; $70.

Alcock, Pete, and Phil Harris. *Welfare Law and Order: A Critical Introduction to Law for Social Workers.* London: The MacMillan Press, Ltd., 1982. Pp. xvi, 219. Index. $27.25. Distributed by Humanities Press.

Chang, Luke T. *China's Boundary Treaties and Frontier Disputes.* London, Rome, New York: Oceana Publications, Inc., 1982. Pp. xii, 443. Index. $45.

Crawford, James. *Australian Courts of Law.* New York: Oxford University Press, 1982. Pp. xv, 297. Index. $42.50.

Ellis, Maarten J., and Paul M. Storm (eds.). *Business Law in Europe: Legal, tax and labour aspects of business operations in the ten European Community countries and Switzerland.* Deventer: Kluwer, 1982. Pp. xvi, 606. Dfl.230; $92.

Freymond, Jacques, Isabelle Graf-Junod, and Alison Browning. *Diplomatische Dokumente der Schweiz 1848–1945.* Vol. 6 (1914–1918). Bern: Benteli Verlag, 1981. Pp. lxxiv, 902. Indexes.

Schoenblum, Jeffrey A. *Multistate and Multinational Estate Planning.* Vols. I and II. Boston and Toronto: Little, Brown and Company, 1982. Vol. I: pp. xxxvii, 809; vol. II: pp. xxxvii, 721. Index. $125 for 2-vol. set.

International Relations & Politics

Craig, Gordon A., and Alexander L. George. *Force and Statecraft: Diplomatic Problems of Our Time.* New York: Oxford University Press, 1983. Pp. xiv, 288. Index. $19.95.

Falk, Richard, Samuel S. Kim, and Saul H. Mendlovitz (eds.). *Toward a Just World Order* (Vol. I of *Studies on a Just World Order*). Boulder: Westview Press, 1982. Pp. x, 652. $35, cloth; $16.50, paper.

Leu, Hans-Joachim. *La Doctrina de las relaciones internacionales.* Caracas: Editorial Jurídica Venezolana, 1980. Pp. 153. Bs. 35.

Quigg, Philip W. *A Pole Apart: The Emerging Issue of Antarctica.* A Twentieth Century Fund Report. New York: New Press (McGraw-Hill Book Company), 1983. Pp. xiv, 299. Index. $19.95.

INTERNATIONAL LEGAL MATERIALS*

CONTENTS

VOL. XXI, NO. 5 (September 1982)

PAGE

TREATIES AND AGREEMENTS

Egypt-United States: Treaty concerning the *Reciprocal Encouragement and Protection of Investments* 927

France-Federal Republic of Germany-United Kingdom-United States: Agreement concerning Interim *Arrangements relating to Polymetallic Nodules of the Deep Sea Bed* ... 950

Japan-Sri Lanka: Agreement concerning the *Promotion and Protection of Investment* ... 963

Libya-Malta: Special Agreement for the *Submission to the International Court of Justice of a Continental Shelf Dispute* 971

JUDICIAL AND SIMILAR PROCEEDINGS

Arbitration Tribunal: Award in the Matter of an *Arbitration between Kuwait and the American Independent Oil Company (AMINOIL)* 976

United Kingdom: Court of Appeal Judgment in Abu Dhabi Gas Liquefaction Company *v.* Eastern Bechtel Corporation and Chiyoda Chemical Engineering & Construction Company and Eastern Bechtel Corporation and Chiyoda Chemical Engineering & Construction Company *v.* Ishikawajima-Harima Heavy Industries Co. *(Consolidation of Arbitration Proceedings; Appointment of Same Arbitrator in Separate Arbitrations)* 1054

United States:

Court of Appeals for the Second Circuit Decision in Sperry International Trade *v.* Israel *(Enforcement of Arbitral Award; Prejudgment Attachment under U.S. Foreign Sovereign Immunities Act)* 1066

District Court for the District of Delaware Opinion in Transportes Aereos de Angola *v.* Ronair, Inc. and Jet Traders Investment Corporation *(Diplomatic Recognition; Standing to Pursue Claim in U.S. Courts)* 1081

International Trade Administration, Department of Commerce, Orders to U.S. Foreign Subsidiaries in France, Italy, the Federal Republic of Germany and the United Kingdom concerning the *Denial of Export Privileges for Soviet Gas Pipeline Equipment* 1098

LEGISLATION AND REGULATIONS

Cuba: Legislative Decree on *Economic Association between Cuban and Foreign Entities* .. 1106

United States:

Department of Commerce International Trade Administration, Office of Export Administration

Foreign Policy Export Controls with Specific Regulations concerning Trade with the U.S.S.R. 1115

Revisions to the *Reporting Requirements on Restrictive Trade Practices or Boycotts* 1121

Foreign Missions Act and Excerpts from the Congressional Conference Report .. 1125

REPORTS

United Nations: Report of the Secretary-General on the *Work of the Organization* 1136

* ILM subscription, $65; concessionary rate to ASIL members, $30. Address orders to ILM, 2223 Massachusetts Ave., NW, Wash., D.C. 20008. Outside U.S., please add $5.

PAGE

OTHER DOCUMENTS

Arab Summit: Fez Declaration concerning *Agreed Principles for Achieving Peace in the Middle East* 1144

China-United States: Joint Communique on *Taiwan* and Statements before the U.S. Senate Committee on the Judiciary concerning the Communique 1147

Israel: Statement by the Foreign Minister on the *U.S. Policy for Peace in the Middle East* 1158

United Nations: Documents concerning the *U.N. Interim Force in Lebanon and the Israeli Incursion of Lebanon* 1165

United States:

Department of State Fact Sheet on the *Plan for the P.L.O. Evacuation from West Beirut* 1193

Presidential Statement on *U.S. Policy for Peace in the Middle East* 1199

RECENT ACTIONS REGARDING TREATIES TO WHICH THE UNITED STATES IS A PARTY 1203

RECENT ACTIONS REGARDING TREATIES TO WHICH THE UNITED STATES IS NOT A PARTY 1208

NOTICE OF OTHER RECENT DOCUMENTS (not reprinted) 1210

VOL. XXI, NO. 6 (November 1982)

TREATIES AND AGREEMENTS

European Atomic Energy Community-United States Department of Energy: Agreement for Exchange of Information concerning a *Cooperative Program in Radioactive Waste Management* 1211

Iceland-Norway: Agreement on the *Continental Shelf between Iceland and Jan Mayen* .. 1222

Panama-United States: Treaty concerning the *Treatment and Protection of Investments* 1227

Third United Nations Conference on the *Law of the Sea*:

Final Act 1245

United Nations Convention on the Law of the Sea 1261

JUDICIAL AND SIMILAR PROCEEDINGS

United States:

Court of Appeals for the District of Columbia Circuit Decision in the Matter of the Arbitration between Maritime International Nominees Establishment *v.* Guinea and United States (Intervenor) (*Foreign Sovereign Immunities Act; ICSID Arbitration; Waiver of Immunity* 1355

United States *Decisions concerning Carbon Steel Imports:*

Introductory Note 1374

International Trade Administration *Preliminary Determination of Sales at Less than Fair Value:* Certain Steel Products from Belgium 1378

International Trade Administration *Final Affirmative Countervailing Duty Determination:* Certain Steel Products from Belgium 1383

International Trade Administration *Suspension of Investigations:*

Re Carbon Steel Wire Rod from Brazil 1411

Re Carbon Steel Wire Rod from Argentina 1416

Re Carbon Steel Wire Rod from Venezuela 1420

International Trade Administration *Termination of Countervailing Duty and Antidumping Investigations:* Certain Steel Products from Belgium, et al.

Press Briefing by Secretary of Commerce 1422

Termination of Investigations 1427

Appendix on Petitions Withdrawn 1428

Appendix on Product Definitions 1429

Appendix on Arrangement between ECSC and US 1429

PAGE

Court of International Trade Decision in Republic Steel Corporation *v.* United States (*Price Supports for Coking Coal*) 1435
International Trade Administration *Amended Affirmative Preliminary Determination:* Certain Steel Products from West Germany 1435
Court of International Trade Decisions in Sacilor, Acieres et Laminoirs de Lorraine *v.* United States (*Confidential Information Furnished by Foreign Steel Producers in Antidumping Proceedings*) 1437

OTHER DOCUMENTS
International Centre for Settlement of Investment Disputes *Additional Facility for the Administration of Conciliation, Arbitration and Fact-Finding Proceedings*
Introductory Notes 1443
Rules Governing the Additional Facility for the Administration of Proceedings by the Secretariat of the International Centre for Settlement of Investment Disputes 1445
Administrative and Financial Rules 1447
Conciliation Rules 1449
Arbitration Rules 1458
Fact-Finding Rules 1469

RECENT ACTIONS REGARDING TREATIES TO WHICH THE UNITED STATES IS A PARTY 1473
RECENT ACTIONS REGARDING TREATIES TO WHICH THE UNITED STATES IS NOT A PARTY 1477
NOTICE OF OTHER RECENT DOCUMENTS (not reprinted) 1478
INDEX TO VOLUME XXI 0000

Join—

THE AMERICAN SOCIETY OF INTERNATIONAL LAW

Society membership includes:

- four issues each year of the most distinguished journal in the field, *THE AMERICAN JOURNAL OF INTERNATIONAL LAW.*
- the Society's *NEWSLETTER.*
- the opportunity to buy other Society publications at reduced prices, such as the valuable bimonthly documentary, *INTERNATIONAL LEGAL MATERIALS*, the *PROCEEDINGS* of the Society's Annual Meeting, and books published under Society auspices such as *LEGAL ASPECTS OF INTERNATIONAL TERRORISM.*
- the opportunity to participate in significant, Society-sponsored meetings (the Annual Meeting, regional meetings, study panels).
- occasion to join with others in contributing to the development of international law through the Society's wide-ranging studies and publications.

If you wish to join the Society, please clip out this page, fill out the application on the reverse side, and mail it, together with your check, to the Membership Secretary, American Society of International Law, 2223 Massachusetts Avenue, N.W., Washington, D. C. 20008. You will receive the *AJIL* and *Newsletter* for the current year.

If your institution wishes to subscribe to *AJIL*, please so indicate on the reverse side.

The American Society of International Law

2223 Massachusetts Ave., N.W., Washington, D.C. 20008 (202) 265-4313 CABLES "AMINTLAW"

Oxford

The International Law of Human Rights

PAUL SIEGHART. This is the first self-contained text of the substantive international law of human rights. It explains the subject; sets out, right by right and with full cross-references, the relevant texts of the eight major international instruments; presents their interpretation by competent independent international institutions and by the superior courts of thirty countries in nearly 1,000 decided cases; summarizes twenty-four subsidiary conventions; and presents the twenty-three established international procedures for the supervision, interpretation, and application of the substantive law.

February 1983 600 pp. $77.00

The International Law of the Sea
Volume I

D. P. O'CONNELL; *edited by* I. A. SHEARER, *University of New South Wales.* To be published in two volumes, this comprehensive exposition of the principles and doctrines developed by jurists, law-making institutions and diplomats during the past 400 years surveys the evolution of the freedom of the seas, and the growth of claims to national jurisdiction over territorial waters, the sea bed, and ocean resources. Critically analyzing the results of the United Nations Third Conference on the Law of the Sea, convened in 1973, this study assesses the prospects for orderly change in light of the questions raised by the conference.

1982 666 pp.; maps $74.00

Courts and Free Markets
Perspectives from the United States and Europe
Volumes 1 & 2

TERRANCE SANDALOW, *Dean of the Michigan Law School, and* ERIC STEIN, *University of Michigan Law School.* This two volume work explores the parallels and contrasts in the constitutional history and practice of the American and European systems of law; much of the discussion centers on the role of the U.S. Supreme Court and that of the Court of the European Communities. Of particular interest are the various legislative solutions which have sought to ensure the free movement of goods and persons across the boundaries of state or local jurisdiction.

Volume 1: 1982 271 pp. $39.50
Volume 2: 1982 329 pp. $39.50

Basic Documents in International Law
Third Edition

IAN BROWNLIE, *University of Oxford.* This collection of basic texts has become an established aid both to the practicing lawyer and to the student of international law. Major additions are the *Convention on the Law of the Sea* and the *Charter of Economic Rights and Duties of States. On the first edition:* "This is an invaluable collection of material which should be at the hand of every student of international law and affairs."–*Canadian Bar Review*

March 1983 336 pp. cloth $32.50 paper $12.95

Prices and publication dates are subject to change.

OXFORD UNIVERSITY PRESS
200 Madison Avenue, New York, New York 10016

0802

American Journal of International Law

April 1983
Vol. 77 No. 2

Published by

American Society of International Law

PATRONS OF THE SOCIETY

Honorable ARTHUR H. DEAN
Honorable HERMAN PHLEGER
GENEVIEVE E. TILLAR (deceased)
W. ROBERT MORGAN
BRUNSON MACCHESNEY (deceased)
ALONA E. EVANS (deceased)
JOHN N. HAZARD
Honorable JOHN R. STEVENSON
ARTHUR R. ALBRECHT

In Memoriam

DR. JAMES BROWN SCOTT
HENRY C. MORRIS
ARTHUR K. KUHN
ALEXANDER FREEMAN
STANLEY P. SMITH

PATRONAGE, GIFTS AND BEQUESTS

Upon donation to the Society of $5,000 or more by gift or bequest, any member of the Society or individual eligible for membership may be elected a Patron of the Society. Upon donation of at least $5,000 in the name of a deceased person, such person may be elected a Patron posthumously.

Gifts and bequests may be made in the name of the American Society of International Law, Washington, D.C. Such contributions are deductible from federal returns for income, estate and gift tax purposes. The Society is incorporated by Act of Congress approved September 20, 1950 (64 Stat. 869).

MANLEY O. HUDSON MEDAL

The American Society of International Law bestows from time to time without regard to nationality a gold medal to commemorate the life work of Manley O. Hudson. Such awards are made for preeminent scholarship and achievement in international law and in the promotion of the establishment and maintenance of international relations on the basis of law and justice. Medals have been awarded to Manley O. Hudson (1956), Lord McNair (1959), Philip C. Jessup (1964), Charles De Visscher (1966), Paul Guggenheim (1970), Myres S. McDougal (1976), Eduardo Jiménez de Aréchaga (1978), Richard Reeve Baxter (1981), Oscar Schachter (1981), and Hardy Cross Dillard (1982).

Second-class postage paid at Washington, D.C. and additional mailing office

Postmaster: If undeliverable, send notice on Form 3579 to: American Journal of International Law
2223 Massachusetts Ave., N.W. Washington, D.C. 20008

Printed by Lancaster Press, Lancaster, Pa. 17604

AMERICAN JOURNAL OF INTERNATIONAL LAW

VOL. 77 **April 1983** **NO. 2**

CONTENTS

PAGE

The Tunisia-Libya Continental Shelf Case: Geographic Justice or Judicial Compromise? *Mark B. Feldman* 219
The Legal Validity of Ultra Vires Decisions of International Organizations *Ebere Osieke* 239
The Senate Role in Treaty Ratification *Michael J. Glennon* 257

Editorial Comments
An Alternative to the Law of the Sea Convention *Anthony D'Amato* 281
Alwyn Freeman (1910–1983) *Oscar Schachter* 285

Notes and Comments
Current Attempts to Revise International Law—A Comparative Analysis *F. V. García-Amador* 286
Correspondence 295
Contemporary Practice of the United States Relating to International Law *Marian Nash Leich* 298
Judicial Decisions *Monroe Leigh* 308

Current Developments
The Thirty-fourth Session of the International Law Commission *Stephen C. McCaffrey* 323
House Approves Proposal Permitting ICJ to Advise Domestic Courts *Jack M. Goldklang* 338
Proposed Amendment of the Foreign Corrupt Practices Act of 1977 *Peter D. Trooboff* 340

Book Reviews and Notes *Edited by Leo Gross*
Morrisson, Clovis C., Jr. *The Dynamics of Development in the European Human Rights Convention System* (W. M. Reisman) 345
Henkin, Louis (ed.). *The International Bill of Rights: The Covenant on Civil and Political Rights* (Torkel Opsahl) 347
Tay, Alice Erh-Soon (ed.), in collaboration with Graeme Connelly and Roger Wilkins. *Teaching Human Rights* (Roger S. Clark) 349
Weston, Burns H., Richard A. Falk, and Anthony A. D'Amato. *International Law and World Order: A Problem-Oriented Coursebook* (James A. R. Nafziger) 350
Recueil des Cours de l'Académie de droit international de La Haye, 1979. 3 vols. (Alfred P. Rubin) 353
Akehurst, Michael. *A Modern Introduction to International Law* (4th ed.) (Richard W. Nelson) 357
Kapteyn, P. J. G., P. H. Kooijmans, R. H. Lauwaars, H. G. Schermers, and M. van Leeuwen Boomkamp (eds.). *International Organization and Integration: Annotated Basic Documents and Descriptive Directory of International Organizations and Arrangements*. Vols. I.A and II.A (2d rev. ed.) (Eric Stein) 359
Guy, Diana, and Guy I. F. Leigh. *The EEC and Intellectual Property* (Thad W. Simons, Jr.) 360

Higgins, Rosalyn. *United Nations Peacekeeping. Documents and Commentary. Vol. IV: Europe 1946–1979* (Richard W. Nelson) 361

Rajan, M. S. *The Expanding Jurisdiction of the United Nations* (Mahnoush H. Arsanjani) 365

Halderman, John W. *The Political Role of the United Nations: Advancing the World Community* (Mahnoush H. Arsanjani) 366

Reinhard, Hans. *Rechtsgleichheit und Selbstbestimmung der Völker in wirtschaftlicher Hinsicht* (C. Rüdiger Wolfrum) 368

Gorove, Stephen (ed.). *United States Space Law: National and International Regulation.* Binders I and II (Paul G. Dembling) 369

Quigg, Philip W. *A Pole Apart: The Emerging Issue of Antarctica* (M. J. Peterson) 372

Jaenicke, Günther, Erich Schanze, and Wolfgang Hauser. *A Joint Venture Agreement for Seabed Mining* (Christopher C. Joyner) 373

Barston, R. P., and Patricia Birnie (eds.). *The Maritime Dimension* (Christopher C. Joyner) 373

Hollick, Ann L. *U.S. Foreign Policy and the Law of the Sea* (Christopher C. Joyner) 373

Hill, Christopher. *Maritime Law* (Peter A. Thomas) 376

Bothe, Michael, Karl Josef Partsch, and Waldemar A. Solf. *New Rules for Victims of Armed Conflicts: Commentary on the Two 1977 Protocols Additional to the Geneva Conventions of 1949* (Howard S. Levie) 377

Roberts, Adam, and Richard Guelff (eds.). *Documents on the Laws of War* (Howard S. Levie) 383

Smith, Bradley F. *The American Road to Nuremberg: The Documentary Record, 1944–1945* (John M. Rogers) 385

Horn, Norbert, Hein Kötz, and Hans G. Leser. *German Private and Commercial Law: An Introduction* (Detlev F. Vagts) 386

Golbert, Albert S., and Yenny Nun. *Latin American Laws and Institutions* (Isidoro Zanotti) 388

Odle, Maurice A. *Multinational Banks and Underdevelopment* (Michael P. Malloy) 390

Dinstein, Yoram (ed.). *Israel Yearbook on Human Rights. Vol. 11* (L. C. Green) 391

South African Yearbook of International Law, Volume 6, 1980 (Natalie K. Hevener) 393

Foreign Relations of the United States, 1950, Volume IV: Central and Eastern Europe; The Soviet Union (Elmer Plischke) 394

Foreign Relations of the United States, 1951, Volume III: European Security and the German Question. Parts 1 and 2 (Elmer Plischke) 397

Freymond, Jacques, Isabelle Graf-Junod, and Alison Browning. *Diplomatische Dokumente der Schweiz 1848–1945.* Volume 6 (1914–1918) (Forest L. Grieves) 400

Fleury, Antoine, and Gabriel Imboden. *Diplomatische Dokumente der Schweiz 1848–1945.* Volume 7-I (1918–1919) (Forest L. Grieves) 400

Hofer, Walther, and Beatrix Mesmer, in collaboration with Peter Hurni, Martin Lüdi, and Peter Martig. *Diplomatische Dokumente der Schweiz 1848–1945.* Volume 9 (1925–1929) (Forest L. Grieves) 400

Cavelier, Germán. *Documentos para la Historia Diplomática de Colombia. Textos. Vol. I: 1820–1830. Vol. II: 1830–1860* (Isidoro Zanotti) 401

Cavelier, Germán. *El Régimen Jurídico de los Tratados Internacionales en Colombia* (Isidoro Zanotti) 401

Briefer Notices: Wood, 403; Cavelier, 404. Correspondence, 404.

Books Received 407

International Legal Materials. Contents, Vol. XXII, No. 1 (January 1983) 411

The American Society of International Law

The American Society of International Law was organized in 1906 "to foster the study of international law and to promote the establishment and maintenance of international relations on the basis of law and justice."

The Society serves as a meeting place and forum for scholars, teachers, officials, lawyers, and others, from some one hundred countries. In April, it holds a three-day Annual Meeting at which current problems of international law are discussed. The Society also sponsors regional meetings outside of Washington in cooperation with other institutions. Salient questions of international law and relations are considered in depth by panels and study groups organized by the Society's Board of Review and Development. Works of scholarship are often published under the Society's auspices in connection with studies sponsored by the Board, many in the Society's series of *Studies in Transnational Legal Policy*.

The Society periodically issues four publications:

The American Journal of International Law, the leading journal in the field of international law, has been published since 1907. The *Proceedings of the American Society of International Law* carries the papers and discussion of the annual meeting of the Society.

International Legal Materials, a bimonthly, is a unique international collection of texts of current official documents, including legislation, treaties, court decisions, and reports. Subscription rates are $30 a year for members of the Society, $65 for others.

The quarterly *Newsletter* provides members with news of the Society and other organizations in the field.

Society membership is open to all persons of whatever nationality and profession who are interested in its objectives. Dues are: regular, $55; special category, $30 for persons *not* resident in a member country of the Organisation for Economic Co-operation and Development; intermediate, $25; student, $15. Membership application form is printed at the back of each issue of AJIL.

THE TUNISIA-LIBYA CONTINENTAL SHELF CASE: GEOGRAPHIC JUSTICE OR JUDICIAL COMPROMISE?

*By Mark B. Feldman**

> The result of the application of equitable principles must be equitable. . . . It is . . . the result which is predominant; the principles are subordinate to the goal.[1]

Introduction

On February 24, 1982, the International Court of Justice delivered a Judgment in the *Case Concerning the Continental Shelf (Tunisia/Libyan Arab Jamahiriya)* that entails a significant restatement of the law of maritime boundary delimitation as set forth in the Court's 1969 Judgment in the *North Sea Continental Shelf* cases.[2] Although both Libya and Tunisia based their cases primarily on the principle of natural prolongation in its physical dimension, the Court found that concept inapplicable in the case before it. At the same time, the majority of the Court declined to consider the equidistance method as a possible means of effecting a delimitation in accordance with equitable principles. Rather, the Court laid down the general rule that "delimitation is to be effected in accordance with equitable principles, and taking account of all relevant circumstances,"[3] and it undertook "to balance up the various considerations which it regards as relevant in order to produce an equitable result."[4]

The Judgment has been criticized by the four dissenting judges,[5] and by some commentators,[6] as lacking in legal principle, verging on an unauthorized determination *ex aequo et bono*, and providing little guidance for the delimi-

* Mr. Feldman is now in private practice in Washington, D.C. Previously, he was Deputy Legal Adviser of the Department of State and responsible for the U.S. maritime boundary program.

[1] Case Concerning the Continental Shelf (Tunisia/Libyan Arab Jamahiriya), 1982 ICJ Rep. 18, 50, para. 70 (Judgment of Feb. 24), *reprinted in* 21 ILM 225 (1982) [hereinafter cited as Continental Shelf].

[2] North Sea Continental Shelf Cases (Federal Republic of Germany/Denmark; Federal Republic of Germany/Netherlands), 1969 ICJ Rep. 3 (Judgment of Feb. 20) [hereinafter cited as North Sea].

[3] Continental Shelf, 1982 ICJ Rep. at 92, para. 133(A)(1).

[4] *Id.* at 60, para. 71.

[5] *Id.*, Dissenting Opinion of Judge Gros [hereinafter cited as Gros Dissent] at 129, 153, para. 19; Dissenting Opinion of Judge Oda [hereinafter cited as Oda Dissent] at 157, 157, para. 1; Dissenting Opinion of Judge Evensen at 278, 296, para. 14.

[6] J. Charney, A Preliminary Evaluation of the Judgment by the International Court of Justice in the *Case Concerning the Continental Shelf (Tunisia/Libyan Arab Jamahiriya)* (presented at the annual meeting of the American Society of International Law, Apr. 23, 1982) [hereinafter cited as Charney]; *compare* T. Stein, The Libyan-Tunisian Continental Shelf Case; The Impact of New Trends in the Law of the Sea on the Delimitation of Maritime Boundaries 5 (also presented at the 1982 ASIL annual meeting, Apr. 23, 1982) [hereinafter cited as Stein].

tation of maritime boundaries in other disputes. While recognizing some merit in these concerns, the author believes the Court has taken a significant step towards the formulation of integrated principles that can be applied to the delimitation of unitary maritime boundaries governing both the continental shelf and the exclusive economic zone. The Court has reconfirmed its decision in the *North Sea* cases that delimitation does not entail an equitable distribution (or sharing out) of the resources of the shelf. The Court has also reconfirmed the principle that "the land dominates the sea";[7] a delimitation must not encroach upon areas in front of the coasts of the parties. Generally, geology will not be a significant factor in maritime delimitation, but a delimitation will be expected to effect a reasonable degree of proportionality between the areas appertaining to the coastal states and the length of their relevant coasts.

BACKGROUND

Tunisia and Libya are neighbors on the African continent and the Mediterranean Sea. They share a land frontier extending 285 miles from Bur al Hattabah to Ras Ajdir on the North African coast. The most striking feature of the boundary area is a radical change in the direction of the Tunisian coast some 97 miles northwest of the terminus of the international boundary line. (See map 1.) The Libyan coast in the area is relatively smooth and follows a general direction west-northwest/east-southeast. The Tunisian coastline follows the same general direction towards the Gulf of Gabes, but its coastal front is interrupted, 45 miles west of Ras Ajdir, by the bulge of the large Tunisian island of Jerba. Fifty-two miles further west, the coast doubles back in a northeastward direction creating the concavity of the Gulf of Gabes.

The second significant geographical feature of the area is a group of Tunisian islands, the Kerkennah, which lie 11 miles off the Tunisian coast south of Ras Kaboudia. The Kerkennah archipelago consists of two main islands and several smaller isles, which have an area of approximately 180 square kilometers. The Kerkennah are surrounded by an extensive belt of low-tide elevations and shoals 9–27 miles in width. The waters separating the islands from the mainland are too shallow for general navigation.

A significant amount of hydrocarbon exploration and drilling has occurred in the boundary area since the first offshore oil concession was granted by Tunisia in 1964. The Tunisian concession line of October 21, 1966 was bounded on the east by a stepped line running at a bearing of approximately 26°, roughly perpendicular to the general direction of the coast in the vicinity of Ras Ajdir. In 1968 Libya granted a concession up to the Tunisian line and subsequent Libyan concessions followed the same 26° line. The concessions granted by Tunisia in 1974 extended further east up to an equidistance line. Both parties claimed larger areas before the Court.

THE ISSUE

The dispute was submitted to the Court by Special Agreement pursuant to Article 40 of the Statute of the Court on December 1, 1978. The parties

[7] Continental Shelf, 1982 ICJ Rep. at 61, para. 73 (quoting North Sea, 1969 ICJ Rep. at 51, para. 96).

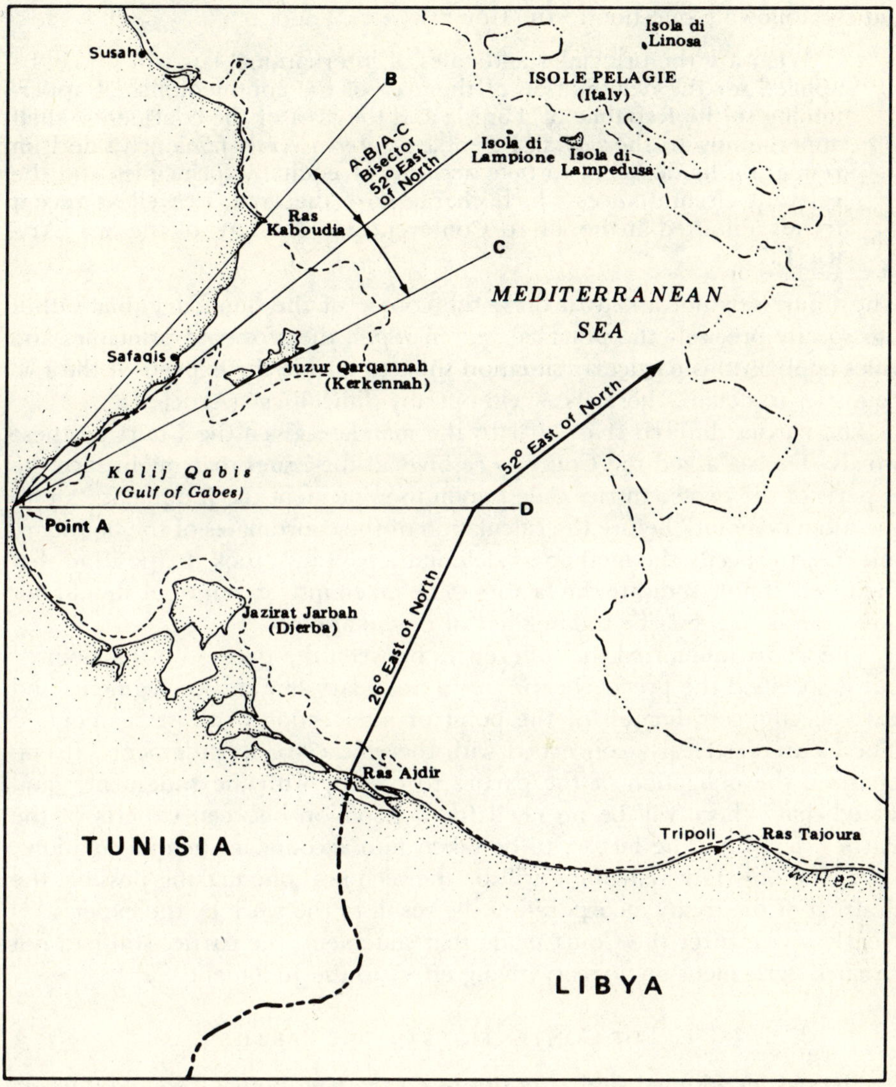

ICJ AWARD:
Libya-Tunisia Maritime Boundary Dispute

Point A	Most westerly point on the low water line of the Gulf of Gabes
A-B	Construction line drawn from Point A past the seaward tip of Ras Kaboudia
A-C	Construction line drawn from Point A along the seaward coast of the Juzur Qarqannah
A-D	Parallel of latitude of the most westerly point on the low water line of the Gulf of Gabes
——-——-	International boundary
———	ICJ "Award Line"
----------	20 meter bathymetric contour
—···—···	100 meter bathymetric contour

MAP 1

put the following question to the Court:

> What are the principles and rules of international law which may be applied for the delimitation of the area of the continental shelf appertaining to the Republic of Tunisia and the area of the continental shelf appertaining to the Socialist People's Libyan Arab Jamahiriya and, in rendering its decision, to take account of equitable principles and the relevant circumstances which characterize the area, as well as recent trends admitted at the Third Conference on the Law of the Sea [Article I].[8]

The Court was not asked to draw the course of the boundary, but rather "to specify precisely the practical way in which the aforesaid principles and rules apply in this particular situation so as to enable the experts of the two countries to delimit those areas without any difficulties" (Article I).

The parties differed sharply as to the mandate given the Court by these words. Tunisia asked the Court to resolve all the issues that might face the experts of the two countries called upon to implement the Judgment, "up to the ultimate point" before the calculation of the coordinates of the boundary line, *i.e.*, to specify the method of delimitation.[9] Libya took the position that the Court should indicate the factors to be taken into account but should not go so far as to prescribe the method of delimitation.[10]

The Court minimized the differences between the parties on this point,[11] but it specified the precise bearing of a boundary line in two segments and gave specific coordinates for the point of intersection of those segments.[12] The Court was clearly concerned with the efficacy of its judgments. It emphasized the obligation of the parties to comply with the Judgment[13] and stated that "there will be no need for negotiation between experts of the Parties regarding the factors to be taken into account in their calculations. . . . The only task remaining will be the technical one making possible the drafting of the treaty incorporating the result of the work by the experts."[14] Nearly a year after the Court made that statement, the parties still had not reached agreement on a treaty giving effect to the Judgment.

I. The Contentions of the Parties

The parties adopted similar positions on the law. Both Libya and Tunisia relied on natural prolongation. Each eschewed equidistance. However, they disagreed about both the facts and the application of the law to the facts.

[8] Special Agreement between the Republic of Tunisia and the Socialist People's Libyan Arab Jamahiriya, *signed* June 10, 1977, *quoted in* Continental Shelf, 1982 ICJ Rep. at 21, para. 2. Neither state was party to the 1958 Geneva Convention on the Continental Shelf, 15 UST 471, TIAS No. 5578, 499 UNTS 311.

[9] Continental Shelf, 1982 ICJ Rep. at 39, para. 27.

[10] *Ibid.*, para. 28.

[11] *Id.* at 39–40, paras. 29–30.

[12] *Id.* at 93–94, para. 133(C)(2).

[13] *Id.* at 40, para. 30; Judge Gros was concerned that Libya did not recognize fully the authority of the Court and felt the Court did not go far enough to make clear that "apart from the drawing upon a map of the line already determined, nothing was negotiable in the Judgment." *Id.*, Gros Dissent at 146, para. 5.

[14] *Id.* at 40, para. 30.

LIBYA

Libya relied primarily on the assertion that the "continental shelf off the coast of North Africa is a prolongation to the north of the continental landmass,"[15] and it argued that a boundary due north from Ras Ajdir would reflect this prolongation. However, in its Counter-Memorial Libya recognized the equity of an adjustment of such a line to the northeast opposite the point of significant change in the general direction of the Tunisian coast.[16]

The Libyan position was based on (1) the broad geographical relationship of the two states as neighbors to the east and west of each other facing north on the Mediterranean; (2) the geological unity of the African landmass and the submerged shelf as part of the same tectonic plate, "the African platform"; and (3) the projection seaward of the terminal point of the land boundary. Libya argued that the general direction of the North African coast is east-west and that the east-facing Tunisian coast in the Sahel area is an anomaly, an "incidental special feature" that should be discounted in any delimitation.[17] A substantial portion of the Libyan Memorial was devoted to demonstrating that a delimitation based on the equidistance method would be inequitable because of the distorting effect of the bulge of the Sahel coast and the Tunisian islands.[18] The Libyan Reply laid the foundations for the argument that France and Italy had agreed to a fisheries modus vivendi along the 26° line in the early 1900's.[19]

TUNISIA

Contrary to expectations, Tunisia did not propose an equidistance boundary. Rather, it supported a delimitation much further to the east.[20] Relying primarily on geomorphology and historic fisheries, Tunisia argued that the natural prolongation of the continent in the boundary area is eastward and that the continental shelf at issue is "submerged Tunisia."[21] Among other points, Tunisia made the following arguments:

> (1) The physical contours of the seabed, which parallel the contours of the Tunisian coast, demonstrate that the continental shelf is a veritable submerged Tunisia; the natural prolongation of the shelf, slope, and rise trends northeast towards the abyssal deeps.[22]

[15] Memorial of the Socialist People's Libyan Arab Jamahiriya, *Continental Shelf (Tunisia / Libyan Arab Jamahiriya)* 70, Submission 5 (Memorial of May 30, 1980) [hereinafter cited as Libyan Memorial], *quoted in* Continental Shelf, 1982 ICJ REP. at 29, para. 15.

[16] 1 Counter-memorial of the Socialist People's Libyan Arab Jamahiriya, *Continental Shelf (Tunisia / Libyan Arab Jamahiriya)* 218, Submission 7 (Counter-memorial of Feb. 2, 1981) [hereinafter cited as Libyan Counter-memorial], *quoted in* Continental Shelf, 1982 ICJ REP. at 31, para. 15.

[17] Libyan Memorial, *supra* note 15, at 48, 55, 62, and 65; Libyan Counter-memorial, *supra* note 16, at 198 and 199.

[18] Libyan Memorial, *supra* note 15, pt. III, ch. II, at 53–66.

[19] Reply of the Socialist People's Libyan Arab Jamahiriya, *Continental Shelf (Tunisia / Libyan Arab Jamahiriya)* 21–22 (Reply of July 15, 1981) [hereinafter cited as Libyan Reply].

[20] 1 Memorial of Tunisia, *Continental Shelf (Tunisia / Libyan Arab Jamahiriya)* 210–11 (Memorial of May 30, 1980) [hereinafter cited as Tunisian Memorial].

[21] *See, e.g.,* Continental Shelf, 1982 ICJ REP. at 73, para. 99.

[22] Tunisian Memorial, *supra* note 20, at 115, 125–27.

(2) The marine areas in front of the Tunisian coast, consisting of shoals and islets and seas dedicated to marine agriculture, "are the natural prolongation of the land upon which man has settled."[23]

(3) Tunisia has established sovereignty over maritime areas out to the 50-meter isobath and east as far as the ZV-45° line, where Tunisian fishermen have exploited fixed fisheries for sponge and octopus from time immemorial.[24]

Tunisia suggested a sheaf of lines, based on geomorphological and geometric factors, trending at approximately 60–63°, which it believed reflected the natural prolongation of the two states.[25]

II. The Judgment

The Court reviewed and rejected the lines proposed by the parties. It held that a delimitation based on equitable principles, taking into account the relevant circumstances, called for the boundary area to be treated as two sectors, and it indicated a line of delimitation in two segments. The first segment, closer to the coast, began at the outer limits of the territorial sea and ran at a bearing of 26° east of north (measured from Ras Ajdir) to a point on the parallel of latitude drawn from the most westerly point of the Tunisian coastline between Ras Kaboudia and Ras Ajdir.[26] That segment corresponded to the concession lines utilized by Tunisia (1966) and Libya (1968), to a fisheries modus vivendi observed by France and Italy since 1919, and to the perpendicular to the coast at the terminus of the land boundary.

The second segment of the maritime boundary, more seaward of the coast, veered to the east to take account of the radical change in direction of the Tunisian coast. (For the Court's award line, see map 1, p. 221.) However, the Court concluded that the Kerkennah Islands should not be given full effect in determining the direction of the coast.[27] Therefore, this segment of the line ran "parallel to a line drawn from the most westerly point of the Gulf of Gabes bisecting the angle formed by a line from that point to Ras Kaboudia and a line drawn from that same point along the seaward coast of the Kerkennah Islands," *i.e.*, at a bearing of 52°.[28] Judges Forster, Gros, and Oda and Judge *ad hoc* Evensen (Tunisia) dissented.

The Court began its analysis with a discussion of the principle of natural prolongation. It then examined the concept of equitable principles. Finally, the Judgment reviewed the relevant circumstances of the area and the method or methods of delimitation that would take account of such circumstances. This article will follow the same procedure.

Natural Prolongation

Tunisia and Libya agreed that the governing principle of delimitation was that stated by the ICJ in the *North Sea Continental Shelf* cases:

[23] *Id.* at 72.

[24] *Id.* at 187.

[25] *Id.* at 199–200, 205–08.

[26] Continental Shelf, 1982 ICJ Rep. at 93–94, para. 133(C)(2).

[27] *Id.* at 89, para. 129.

[28] *Id.* at 94, para. 133(C)(3).

> [D]elimitation is to be effected by agreement in accordance with equitable principles, and taking account of all the relevant circumstances, in such a way as to leave as much as possible to each Party all those parts of the continental shelf that constitute a natural prolongation of its land territory into and under the sea, without encroachment on the natural prolongation of the land territory of the other.[29]

Indeed, Libya contended that a delimitation giving effect to the principle of natural prolongation is ipso facto in accordance with equitable principles because it respects the inherent sovereign rights of each state over its appurtenant continental shelf.[30] According to the Libyan view, natural prolongation is to be determined solely on the basis of geological criteria. Tunisia agreed that natural prolongation is the controlling principle, but it argued that " 'the satisfying of equitable principles in a particular geographical situation' is part of the process of 'the identification of the natural prolongation'."[31]

The Court did not confirm the preeminence of natural prolongation. Rather, it held that the "satisfaction of equitable principles" is of "cardinal importance" in the delimitation process; "identification of natural prolongation may, where the geographical circumstances are appropriate, have an important role to play in defining an equitable delimitation, . . . but . . . the satisfying of equitable principles and the identification of the natural prolongation . . . are not to be placed on a plane of equality."[32]

The significance of natural prolongation, in the Court's view, is that it is the basis for the sovereign rights of the coastal state over its appurtenant continental shelf. But "the appurtenance of a given area, considered as an entity, in no way governs the precise delimitation of its boundaries."[33] The "idea of the natural prolongation of the land territory . . . would not necessarily be sufficient, or even appropriate, in itself to determine the precise extent of the rights of one State in relation to those of a neighbouring State."[34] Thus, the Court was "unable to accept the contention of Libya that 'once the natural prolongation of a State is determined, delimitation becomes a simple matter of complying with the dictates of nature'."[35]

The Court was not persuaded by the scientific arguments of either side. It concluded that since "Libya and Tunisia both derive continental shelf title from a natural prolongation common to both territories, the ascertainment of the extent of the areas of shelf appertaining to each State must be governed by criteria of international law other than those taken from physical features."[36] While the Court rejected the relevance of both geology and geomorphology in the case before it, it made a significant distinction between the two. "Deep" or "historical" geology was dismissed (at least where the data do not clearly demonstrate the existence of two distinct continental shelves) as having no bearing on the human interests affected by maritime delimitation:

[29] North Sea, 1969 ICJ REP. at 53, para. 101(C)(1).

[30] Continental Shelf, 1982 ICJ REP. at 44, para. 39.

[31] *Ibid.*

[32] *Id.* at 47, para. 44.

[33] *Ibid.* (quoting North Sea, 1969 ICJ REP. at 32, para. 46).

[34] Continental Shelf, 1982 ICJ REP. at 46, para. 43.

[35] *Id.* at 47, para. 44.

[36] *Id.* at 58, para. 67.

> [F]or legal purposes it is not possible to define the areas of continental shelf . . . by reference solely or mainly to geological considerations. . . . [W]hat must be taken into account in the delimitation of shelf areas are the physical circumstances as they are today; that just as it is the geographical configuration of the present-day coasts, so also it is the present-day sea-bed, which must be considered. It is the outcome, not the evolution in the long-distant past, which is of importance.[37]

Similarly, the Court did not accept any of the features cited by Tunisia as involving "such a marked disruption or discontinuance of the sea-bed as to constitute an indisputable indication of the limits of two separate continental shelves, or two separate natural prolongations."[38] However, the Court did not exclude the possibility

> that certain geomorphological configurations of the sea-bed, which do not amount to such an interruption of the natural prolongation of one Party with regard to that of the other, may be taken into account for the delimitation, as relevant circumstances characterizing the area. . . . In such a situation, however, the physical factor constituting the natural prolongation is not taken as a legal title, but as one of several circumstances considered to be the elements of an equitable solution.[39]

In the Court's view, no such features were present in the *Tunisia-Libya* case.

So far, the Court's reasoning can be said to be a clarification of the doctrine of natural prolongation as set forth in the *North Sea* cases. However, other passages in the Judgment appear to depart from the *North Sea* cases by implying that "natural prolongation" is relevant to delimitation only in cases where there are controlling physical features of the seabed. For example, the Court stated in the *dispositif* that the "area relevant for the delimitation constitutes a single continental shelf as the natural prolongation of the land territory of both Parties, so that in the present case, no criterion for delimitation of shelf areas can be derived from the principle of natural prolongation as such."[40] It is also significant that the Court did not reiterate the central provision of its 1969 Judgment, which had been relied upon by both parties.[41]

Presumably, the arguments adopted by Libya and Tunisia convinced the Court that the 1969 Judgment confused the issue by overemphasizing the physical aspects of prolongation and by appearing to make prolongation more fundamental than equitable principles. It is clear that the scientific arguments presented to the Court in the *Tunisia-Libya* case were speculative, contradictory, difficult to understand, and hard to relate to the interests involved in the delimitation of maritime boundaries. Judge *ad hoc* Jiménez de Aréchaga (Libya) noted in his concurring opinion that "the criticism by each Party of the scientific arguments presented by the other was far stronger and more

[37] *Id.* at 53–54, para. 61.

[38] *Id.* at 57, para. 66. Tunisia argued that the Tripolitanian Furrow off the Libyan coast marked the seaward limit of Libya's natural prolongation. The Court was not impressed with this argument because "that submarine valley does not display any really marked relief until it has run considerably further to the east than the area relevant to the delimitation." *Ibid.*

[39] *Id.* at 58, para. 68.

[40] *Id.* at 92, para. 133(A)(2).

[41] North Sea, 1969 ICJ Rep. at 53, para. 101(C).

convincing than their affirmative contentions." The theory of plate tectonics advanced by Libya was described by one expert as an "essay in geopoetry."[42]

The Court was right to try to put a stop to this time-consuming, expensive and, ultimately, futile line of argument. However, to the extent the Judgment appears to equate "natural prolongation" exclusively with a physical division of the shelf, it ignores the legal dimension of the concept of "natural prolongation" and does not do justice to the Judgment in the *North Sea* cases. Indeed, the continental shelf underlying the North Sea is continuous and relatively uniform. The references to geology and to features of the seabed in the 1969 Judgment are *obiter dicta.*

As Judge Jiménez de Aréchaga explains in his concurring opinion in the *Tunisia-Libya* case, the real meaning of "natural prolongation" in the 1969 Judgment is the "continuation or extension seawards of each State's *coastal front*" (emphasis added).[43] He agrees with the Court's conclusions that "natural prolongation" is not determined by geological or geomorphological facts, and that "continental shelf delimitation is not governed in an unqualified and exclusive manner by such a notion of 'natural prolongation'."[44] It does not follow, however, that natural prolongation is irrelevant when the continental shelf is continuous. Natural prolongation is useful in explaining the relationship of the coastal fronts of the parties to the shelf area to be delimited, and "the basic corollary of 'natural prolongation' is the need to avoid the 'cutting-off' of areas 'situated directly before that front'."[45]

Jiménez de Aréchaga states that "the 'most natural prolongation' is that which continues or extends more directly into the sea and is not 'cut off' by the extension or prolongation of the coastal front of another State." In his view, the corresponding principle, the other side of the coin of natural prolongation, is "the principle of 'non-encroachment', a fundamental principle of equity."[46]

This is a sound view of the 1969 Judgment, where the Court was clearly preoccupied with the cutoff effect of an equidistance line in the context of a concave coastline:

> [T]he use of the equidistance method would frequently cause areas which are the natural prolongation *or extension* of the territory of one State to be attributed to another, when the configuration of the latter's coast makes the equidistance line swing out laterally across the former's *coastal front,* cutting it off from areas situated directly before that *front* [emphasis added].[47]

The Court was also conscious of this concern in the *Tunisia-Libya* case. Tunisia raised the point, and the Court recognized that the "cut-off" effect

[42] Continental Shelf, Separate Opinion of Judge Jiménez de Aréchaga, 1982 ICJ REP. at 100, 110, para. 38 [hereinafter cited as Jiménez de Aréchaga Sep. Op.].

[43] *Id.*, Jiménez de Aréchaga Sep. Op. at 116, para. 58.

[44] *Id.*, Jiménez de Aréchaga Sep. Op. at 110, para. 39.

[45] *Id.*, Jiménez de Aréchaga Sep. Op. at 116, para. 58.

[46] *Id.*, Jiménez de Aréchaga Sep. Op. at 117, para. 59.

[47] North Sea, 1969 ICJ REP. at 31–32, para. 44.

could be an objection to an equidistance line and to the northward line proposed by Libya.[48] The Court sought to avoid a cutoff effect in this case by utilizing the perpendicular to the coastline as the boundary in the first sector and by adjusting the line in the second sector to take account of the change in the general direction of the coast. However, the Court did not expressly connect this concern to the principle of natural prolongation.

The Judgment in the *Tunisia-Libya* case might have been more useful if, instead of implying that natural prolongation applies only in two-shelf situations, it had redefined the doctrine to minimize its geological/geomorphological content. That approach has the advantage of maintaining continuity in the Judgments of the Court on maritime delimitation. Further, a Judgment so expressed would have been more firmly grounded in legal principle and would have provided clearer guidance for the resolution of other maritime boundary disputes.[49] As it stands, the Judgment can be criticized for diminishing unduly the meaning of natural prolongation—an understandable, but unfortunate, overreaction to the tactics of Tunisia and Libya before the Court.

EQUITABLE PRINCIPLES

By this time, it is beyond dispute that "equitable principles" form the foundation of the law of maritime boundary delimitation. The doctrine that maritime boundaries are to be determined by mutual agreement and in accordance with equitable principles derives from the Truman Proclamation on the Continental Shelf of September 28, 1945.[50] The Truman Proclamation is regarded as the cornerstone of continental shelf law, and its criterion of equitable principles was adopted by the ICJ in the *North Sea* cases[51] and by the court of arbitration in the *Anglo-French Continental Shelf* case.[52] Moreover, the concept was carried forward in the reference to "special circumstances" in Article 6 of the Geneva Convention on the Continental Shelf.[53]

The *North Sea* cases and the *Anglo-French* case recognized the close relationship between equitable principles and natural prolongation.[54] In *Tunisia-Libya,* however, the Court determined that it was bound to decide the case on the basis of equitable principles, "divorced from the concept of natural prolongation."[55] Thus, the Court's idea of the applicable equitable principles

[48] Continental Shelf, 1982 ICJ REP. at 62, para. 76. *See also id.* at 82–83, para. 115.

[49] Judge Gros in his dissent argued that the Court should identify not only the goal—delimitation in accordance with equitable principles—but also the rules and means for reaching it. Among the rules and factors he mentions is "that of not encroaching upon any other State's area of continental shelf." *Id.,* Gros Dissent at 148, para. 10.

[50] Proclamation No. 2667, 3 C.F.R. §67 (1943–48), 13 DEP'T STATE BULL. 485 (1945).

[51] North Sea, 1969 ICJ REP. at 32–33, 47, 53, paras. 47, 86, 101(C).

[52] THE UNITED KINGDOM OF GREAT BRITAIN AND NORTHERN IRELAND AND THE FRENCH REPUBLIC DELIMITATION OF THE CONTINENTAL SHELF DECISION OF 30 JUNE 1977, CMND. 7438 (1978), paras. 97 and 195, *reprinted in* 18 ILM 397 (1979) [hereinafter cited as Anglo-French].

[53] Continental Shelf Convention, *supra* note 8. *See* North Sea, 1969 ICJ REP. at 36, para. 55; Anglo-French, *supra* note 50, para. 70.

[54] North Sea, 1969 ICJ REP. at 53, para. 101(C)(1); Anglo-French, *supra* note 50, para. 195.

[55] Continental Shelf, 1982 ICJ REP. at 59, para. 70.

becomes decisive. However, the Judgment does not identify any equitable principles as such. It merely affirms in its operative part that "the delimitation is to be effected in accordance with equitable principles, and taking account of all relevant circumstances."[56] Indeed, the Court states that "[i]t is . . . the result which is predominant; the principles are subordinate to the goal." The "term 'equitable principles' cannot be interpreted in the abstract."[57] The equity of any principle depends on whether it produces a just result in the circumstances of the particular case. "The task of the Court . . . [is to] balance up the various considerations which it regards as relevant in order to produce an equitable result."[58]

This approach is consistent with, and no doubt influenced by, the emerging law of the sea. Article 83(1) of the Convention on the Law of the Sea adopted by the Third United Nations Conference on the Law of the Sea stipulates: "The delimitation of the continental shelf between States with opposite or adjacent coasts shall be effected by agreement on the basis of international law, as referred to in Article 38 of the Statute of the International Court of Justice, *in order to achieve an equitable solution*" (emphasis added).[59] The Court noted that "any indication of a specific criterion [in Article 83(1)] which could give guidance to the interested States in their effort to achieve an equitable solution has been excluded,"[60] but it did not hesitate to adopt the formula as its rule of decision.

It should be noted in this connection that the Special Agreement requests that the Court take into account, *inter alia,* "recent trends admitted at the Third Conference on the Law of the Sea" (*supra* p. 222). The Court interpreted this mandate as referring to trends "accepted" by the conference through their incorporation in provisions of the Draft Convention on the Law of the Sea. The parties apparently wanted these "trends" to be considered even if they did not yet enjoy the status of customary international law, although the Court did not believe the parties had adopted the "trends" as applicable between them in this case as *lex specialis.* Tunisia suggested the Court take these "trends" into account as factors in its interpretation of existing law.[61]

The Court reviewed the provisions of Articles 76 and 83 of the Draft Convention—the one defining the extent of the continental shelf, the other dealing with the delimitation of the continental shelf between states with opposite or adjacent coasts—but it found no help for the case before it other than the emphasis in Article 83(1) on the equitable solution that has to be achieved. In the words of the Court, "[t]he principles and rules applicable to

[56] *Id.* at 92, para. 133(A)(1).

[57] *Id.* at 59, para. 70.

[58] *Id.* at 60, para. 71.

[59] United Nations Convention on the Law of the Sea, Working Paper 1 of the Drafting Committee, June 7, 1982, No. 82-16124.

[60] Continental Shelf, 1982 ICJ REP. at 49, para. 50.

[61] *Id.* at 37–38, 47–48, paras. 23–24, 46. As Stein points out, it is very difficult to determine the effect on customary law of an unratified treaty, which represents a consensus *de lege ferenda.* To determine the influence of treaty provisions not having that status on the interpretation of existing law is like "shadows on shadows." Stein, *supra* note 6, at 2–3.

the delimitation of continental shelf areas are those which are appropriate to bring about an equitable result. . . ."[62]

The Court's reluctance to define the equitable principles that may apply to maritime delimitation has been criticized as deepening the uncertainty of this area of the law.[63] Such criticism may be warranted, but the Judgment does provide several significant indications of the meaning of equitable principles in the context of maritime boundary delimitation.

1. No Equitable Sharing of Resources

First, the Court took pains to emphasize the difference between equity as "a general principle directly applicable as law" and a decision *ex aequo et bono,* which would not be based on legal rules.[64] Absent agreement of the parties,[65] the Court was required

> to apply equitable principles as part of international law, and to balance up the various considerations which it regards as relevant in order to produce an equitable result. While it is clear that no rigid rules exist as to the exact weight to be attached to each element in the case, this is very far from being an exercise of discretion or conciliation; nor is it an operation of distributive justice.[66]

In this respect, the Court followed its Judgment in the *North Sea* cases where it rejected the argument of the Federal Republic of Germany that delimitation should effect an equitable sharing of the resources of the shelf.[67]

In this case, Tunisia urged the Court to consider its relative poverty in natural resources, particularly oil and gas, and its dependence on fisheries, not to refashion nature, but to avoid "widening the disparities created by nature."[68] The Court was firm, however, in holding that "these economic considerations cannot be taken into account" in the delimitation. "They are virtually extraneous factors since they are variables which unpredictable national fortune or calamity . . . might at any time cause to tilt the scale one way or the other."[69]

2. The Land Dominates the Sea

Second, a delimitation in accordance with equitable principles must take into account the relationship between the maritime areas to be delimited and

[62] Continental Shelf, 1982 ICJ REP. at 49, para. 50. In a brief aside, the Court stated that the exclusive economic zone is "part of modern international law," but it did not find that development relevant to the case before it. *Id.* at 74, para. 100.

[63] Charney, *supra* note 6, at 7; Stein, *supra* note 6, at 5.

[64] Continental Shelf, 1982 ICJ REP. at 60, para. 71; *but see id.*, Gros Dissent at 153, para. 19; *id.*, Oda Dissent at 157, para. 1.

[65] Art. 38(2), Statute of the International Court of Justice.

[66] Continental Shelf, 1982 ICJ REP. at 60, para. 71.

[67] North Sea, 1969 ICJ REP. at 22, 29, paras. 19, 39.

[68] Tunisian Memorial, *supra* note 20, at 196; *see also* Continental Shelf, 1982 ICJ REP. at 77, para. 106.

[69] Continental Shelf, 1982 ICJ REP. at 77, para. 107.

the coasts of the parties, as indicated by the general configuration of the coasts and taking account of any particular features that might cause a boundary line to cut off a state from shelf areas lying in front of its coast.[70] Among the relevant circumstances to be taken into account in achieving an equitable delimitation, the Court said, is "the element of a reasonable degree of proportionality . . . between the extent of the continental shelf areas appertaining to the coastal State and the length of the relevant part of its coast, measured in the general direction of the coastlines."[71]

Coastal Fronts. The Court began its discussion of relevant circumstances by stating that the "geographic correlation between coast and submerged areas off the coast is the basis of the coastal State's legal title," and it reiterated its characterization in the *North Sea* cases of the continental shelf as a legal concept in which "the principle is applied that the land dominates the sea."[72] Thus, the coast of each party is the starting point for every delimitation.[73] The identification of the relevant coastal fronts is critical to the projection of the general direction of the coasts, calculations of proportionality as between the length of the relevant coasts and the area attributed to each coastal state, and selection of those geographic features that should be discounted to allow for a delimitation that reflects the broad geographic relationship of the parties.

The Court observed that the areas relevant to the dispute would include only those areas "off the coast" of one of the parties, and that the area in dispute, "where one claim encroaches on the other," was that part of these areas that could be considered to lie off the coasts of both parties.[74] It is clear from the context that the Court considers an area to lie "off" the coast of a party if it is situated "in front of the coast of that Party." In the case before it, the Court determined that the seabed areas beyond Ras Kaboudia on the Tunisian coast and Ras Tajoura on the Libyan coast should not be taken into account because they "cannot overlap with the extension of the coast of the other."[75] Undoubtedly, the Court was influenced in the selection of these points by the presence of third states in the area with coasts opposite the coasts of one or both parties.[76]

The importance attached to the coastal fronts of the parties is also evident in the Court's stipulation that "a line which does have a bearing" on the delimitation is "the line designed to be 'normal' or 'perpendicular' to that section of the coast where the land frontier begins." "[T]he factor of per-

[70] *Id.* at 61 and 62–63, paras. 74 and 76. The Court concluded that the cutoff effect was not a "relevant circumstance" in this case.

[71] *Id.* at 93, para. 133(B)(5).

[72] *Id.* at 61, para. 73 (quoting North Sea, 1969 ICJ REP. at 51, para. 96).

[73] Continental Shelf, 1982 ICJ REP. at 61, para. 74.

[74] *Ibid.*

[75] *Ibid.*, para. 75.

[76] *Id.* at 62, 91, paras. 75, 130; *see also* Map No. 1, *id.* at 22. It is also significant that these points were mentioned by the parties in the course of the pleadings and the oral proceedings. Libyan Memorial, *supra* note 15, at 59; Libyan Counter-memorial, *supra* note 16, at 145; Libyan Reply, *supra* note 19, at 55; *Case Concerning the Continental Shelf (Tunisia/Libyan Arab Jamahiriya)*, Reply to Question Put to Tunisia by Judge Mosler 2 (Oct. 21, 1981). Further, these points may have been the furthest points from the international boundary controlling an equidistance line.

pendicularity to the coast and the concept of prolongation of the general direction of the land boundary are . . . relevant criteria to be taken into account in selecting a line of delimitation calculated to ensure an equitable solution."[77] In the *Tunisia-Libya* case, the Court concluded that these factors should be applied in that part of the delimited area closer to the coasts of the parties. It appeared to the Court that a line drawn on this basis would coincide with the 26° line used by the parties and their predecessor regimes for resource management purposes.[78]

Proportionality. The Court tested the method of delimitation adopted by considering whether it effected the requisite element of proportionality. The Court agreed with the parties "that that element is indeed required by the fundamental principle of ensuring an equitable delimitation between the States concerned."[79] This formulation is consistent with the approach followed in the *Anglo-French Continental Shelf* case where the arbitral tribunal emphasized that "it is disproportion rather than any general principle of proportionality which is the relevant criterion or factor."[80]

The parties differed as to which coasts should be considered and as to whether large areas of Tunisian-claimed internal waters should be included in the proportionality calculation. This issue was complicated by a dispute over the validity of straight baselines drawn by Tunisia across the Gulf of Gabes. The Court concluded that there is no general rule indicating which areas of seabed should be included. The comparison could be more or less restricted depending on the relevant circumstances; "the only absolute requirement of equity is that one should compare like with like."[81]

On the facts of this case, the Court found that a comparison of all "shelf areas" below the low-water mark would be necessary to determine the equitable character of a line of delimitation. In so doing, the Court was careful to disclaim any judgment on the validity of the Tunisian straight baselines. It emphasized that the legal status of the superjacent waters was not controlling as regards determination of the areas to be compared.

To make any proportionality calculation, it was also necessary for the Court to establish the seaward limits of the area to be delimited. This determination was complicated by the presence of third parties with actual or potential claims to the areas disputed by Libya and Tunisia. The Court concluded that it had no alternative but to treat the whole area within the lines of latitude and

[77] Continental Shelf, 1982 ICJ REP. at 70 and 85, paras. 93 and 120.

[78]

> Ras Ajdir is also the point of departure of the line perpendicular to the coast proposed by Italy in 1914, and of the line of 26° north-east which had been followed by the two Parties in the granting of concessions for the exploration and exploitation of mineral resources during the period 1964–1972.

Id. at 66, para. 86.

[79] *Id.* at 75, para. 103.

[80] Anglo-French, *supra* note 50, paras. 100–102, at para. 101. Judge Gros was of the view that the Court went further than the 1969 Judgment and used proportionality more as a method of delimitation than as a verifying factor. Continental Shelf, Gros Dissent, 1982 ICJ REP. at 152, para. 17.

[81] Continental Shelf, 1982 ICJ REP. at 76, para. 104.

longitude joining Ras Kaboudia and Ras Tajoura as appertaining to the parties before the Court, and that it could do so without prejudice to the claims of other states.[82]

Having established the area to be used for the calculation, the Court computed the proportion of the relative lengths of the relevant coastlines as Libya:Tunisia equals 31:69 (sinuosities of the coast) or 34:66 (straight lines corresponding to the general direction of the coastlines). It then calculated the ratio of the seabed area attributable to each party by the boundary method indicated by the Court as Libya, 40:Tunisia, 60. In the words of the Judgment, "This result, taking into account all the relevant circumstances, seems to the Court to meet the requirements of the test of proportionality as an aspect of equity."[83]

3. Conduct of the Parties

Third, an equitable delimitation must take into account the conduct of the parties in the boundary area, particularly where there are historical circumstances that establish a high degree of consensus for various boundary purposes. In this connection, the Court found that Italy and France had accepted the perpendicular to the coast as a tacit modus vivendi for fisheries enforcement purposes since 1919. Because France's consent was based only on silence and lack of protest, the majority did not join Judge Ago's conclusion that this line had been adopted as a maritime boundary *per se.*[84] The majority held, however, that the absence of protest,

> throughout a long period of time, could warrant its acceptance as a historical justification for the choice of the method of delimitation of the continental shelf between the two States, to the extent that the historic rights claimed by Tunisia could not in any event be opposable to Libya east of the *modus vivendi* line.[85]

The Court also noted the existence of another de facto line from Ras Ajdir at an angle of 26° east of north, *i.e.,* perpendicular to the coast, arising out of the oil and gas concessions granted by the two sides. Indeed, the Court pointedly stated that the parties had not given sufficient weight to this consideration, "which the Court finds to be highly relevant to the determination of the method of delimitation."[86]

A serious question can be raised whether the Court was justified in placing such reliance on a de facto situation that had endured, at the most, for only 8 years. Indeed, the Court was careful to explain that it was not making a finding of "tacit agreement" or of "estoppel." Rather, the Court invoked this concession line as evidence "of the line or lines which the Parties themselves may have considered equitable or acted upon as such—if only as an interim solution affecting part only of the area to be delimited." The critical factor

[82] *Id.* at 91, para. 130.

[83] *Ibid.,* para. 131.

[84] Judge Ago believed the facts established acquiescence by the French authorities. *Id.,* Separate Opinion of Judge Ago at 95, 97, para. 4. Judge Gros disputed the relevance of "the unilateral claim of one State to surveillance of its sedentary fisheries." *Id.,* Gros Dissent at 154, para. 20.

[85] *Id.* at 71, para. 95.

[86] *Id.* at 83, para. 117.

in the Court's eyes appears to have been that the same line was drawn by both parties separately, and that Tunisia was the first to do so.[87]

Even so, this aspect of the parties' conduct standing alone would not justify the method of delimitation adopted by the Court. It would be contrary to the public interest in the peaceful resolution of international disputes if a state that exercised restraint in its activities in an area claimed by another state were punished by implying it had consented to that claim. Nothing could be more inflammatory than drilling on the continental shelf claimed by another state. In this case, both Libya and Tunisia had authorized drilling in the boundary areas under concession, and there was a serious risk that hostilities might result. That risk would have been sharply increased if Tunisia had drilled even further to the east.

However, the Court found further justification for use of the 26° line: (1) it corresponded with the line perpendicular to the coast at the point of the terminus of the land frontier; and (2) approximately the same line had been used in fisheries relations between the parties for many years.[88]

THE RELEVANT CIRCUMSTANCES

As the above discussion demonstrates, consideration of equitable principles cannot be divorced from the relevant circumstances. Inasmuch as the Court did not elaborate equitable principles as such, its analysis focused primarily on identifying and balancing up the relevant circumstances.

After defining the area relevant to the delimitation, the Court turned its attention to the configuration of the coasts and other geographic circumstances. Not surprisingly, the first circumstance it identified as relevant was the change in direction of the Tunisian coast where it doubles back in a southwest-northeast direction.[89] The second was the Tunisian islands. The nongeographical circumstances deemed relevant by the Court were (1) the existing and potential delimitations with other states in the area, (2) the point of intersection of the land frontier with the coastline at Ras Ajdir, and (3) the prior conduct of the parties. These considerations are discussed elsewhere in this article.

Among other points rejected by the Court were a 45° line and a due north line asserted by Tunisia and Libya, respectively, at different times in the past. Tunisia claimed that its fisheries regulations had adopted a 45° boundary with Libya out to the 50-meter isobath from as far back as 1904. However, the Court concluded that the 45° line had been specified in Tunisian regulations only during the period 1951–1963; that it represented a unilateral assertion not accepted by Libya; and that "[t]aking all the stages of the Tunisian-Libyan

[87] *Id.* at 84, para. 118. As the Court noted, Libya brought the 26° line to the Court's attention as a line that might have been acceptable in the context of an agreed delimitation. *Ibid.*

[88] *Id.* at 84–85, para. 119.

[89] *Id.* at 63, para. 78. Tunisia argued that its eastern coast follows a "general north-south direction," Tunisian Memorial, *supra* note 20, at 195; Counter-memorial of Tunisia, *Continental Shelf (Tunisia / Libyan Arab Jamahiriya)* 47 (Counter-memorial of Dec. 1, 1980); and that its coastal front should be represented by a line drawn from Ras Ajdir to Al-Maebla, a low-tide elevation east of the Kerkennah Islands. Tunisian Memorial, *supra* note 20, at 207.

relations into account," it was not opposable to Libya.[90] This conclusion followed from the Court's finding that France and Italy had maintained a tacit modus vivendi for fisheries purposes at the 26° line since at least 1919.[91]

Similarly, the Court dismissed a due north line published by Libya on a map attached to its Petroleum Regulation of June 15, 1955 as a unilateral act not opposable to Tunisia. The "mere indication on the map of the line in question is not sufficient even for the mere purpose of defining a formal claim at the level of international relations to a maritime or continental shelf boundary."[92]

Tunisia's claim to historic title over the seabed and superjacent waters, based on fixed fisheries for mobile species on the shallow inshore banks and exploitation of sedentary species on the deeper banks, raised the fascinating question whether a state can acquire historic title by occupation and exploitation of continental shelf areas that may appertain to another state ipso facto and ab initio. The Court discussed this issue in general terms that imply a negative answer.[93] However, it found it unnecessary to pass upon Tunisia's claims, as the boundary line indicated by the Judgment did not encroach on the area claimed by Tunisia on the basis of historic title—except for the part between the 45° and 26° lines out to the 50-meter isobath. As indicated earlier, the Court determined that the latter claim was not opposable to Libya.

THE METHOD OF DELIMITATION

The Court began its examination of methods with a brief discussion of equidistance. It referred to the holding in the *North Sea Continental Shelf* cases that the equidistance method is not prescribed by a mandatory rule of customary law, and it noted that both state practice and the history of Article 83 of the Draft Convention on the Law of the Sea support the conclusion "that equidistance may be applied if it leads to an equitable solution; if not, other methods should be employed."[94] Further, the Court rejected the notion that it was required to examine the effects of applying the equidistance method as a first step, "since equidistance is not, in the view of the Court, either a mandatory legal principle, or a method having some privileged status in relation to other methods."[95]

This position was criticized sharply by the dissenting judges. Judge Gros believed that the Court had an obligation to test the equidistance method, as well as other methods, and he found it suitable in this case. Indeed, Gros objected to the "subjective" approach taken by the Court, which he regarded as "a compromise sought at one and the same time between the claims of the Parties and the opinions held within the Court."[96]

Judge Oda made a similar point by describing the Judgment as appearing, to his eyes, "simply as one appropriate to a case *ex aequo et bono* such as might

[90] Continental Shelf, 1982 ICJ REP. at 66–68, paras. 86–90, at 90.
[91] *Id.* at 70–71, paras. 93–95.
[92] *Id.* at 69, para. 92.
[93] *Id.* at 73–74, para. 100.
[94] *Id.* at 79, para. 109.
[95] *Ibid.*, para. 110.
[96] *Id.*, Gros Dissent at 148–49 and 153, paras. 11 and 18, at 18.

have been decided, if the Parties so agreed."[97] In a long, scholarly dissent, which reviews the history of the subject in detail, Judge Oda argued that the recent trends in the law of the sea give new life to the proximity principle as a basis for delimitation of maritime boundaries. His argument relies in large measure on the introduction of the 200-mile distance criterion into the definition of the continental shelf and the exclusive economic zone in Articles 76(1) and 57 of the Draft Convention. There is not space here to do justice to Judge Oda's argument, but two problems must be mentioned. First, his analysis disregards the continued significance of the concept of natural prolongation in the definition of the continental shelf, particularly when the shelf, slope, and rise extend beyond 200 miles. Second, it does not acknowledge that both the text and the history of the delimitation provisions of the Convention, Articles 83 (shelf) and 74 (exclusive economic zone), demonstrate the conference's intention to eliminate the emphasis on equidistance in Article 6 of the 1958 Convention on the Continental Shelf in light of the Court's Judgment in the *North Sea* cases. This point is alluded to in the Judgment of the Court.[98]

It should be said, however, that Judge Oda fully understands the importance of equitable principles, and the role of "special circumstances" in Article 6, in moderating the inequitable effects that can flow from application of the equidistance method in a delimitation between adjacent states. He wrote long ago that an equidistance line is only equitable in a lateral delimitation when it conforms to a perpendicular to a common coastline.[99]

In his opinion in the *Tunisia-Libya* case, Judge Oda emphasized "that delimitation of the continental shelf (or of the exclusive economic zone) should be effected in accordance with the geography of the area concerned, i.e., so as to secure reasonable proportionality between lengths of coastline and the expanses allocated." To achieve that result, he proposed adoption of "the qualified equidistance method," which he regarded as the "equitable method *par excellence*" to be tried before all others.[100]

The Court did not accept this point of view. Its methodology flows from its appreciation of the relevant circumstances. Since the perpendicular to the coast, the 26° line, "reflects all appropriate factors," the delimitation should follow that line in its initial stage. However, the Court recognized that at a certain point such a line would require adjustment to take account of the radical change in direction of the Tunisian coast.[101] In general terms, it noted that in cases of delimitation over a broad area, the use of one method to

[97] *Id.*, Oda Dissent at 157, para. 1.

[98] *Id.* at 78–79, para. 109.

[99]

> [T]he median line of the continental shelf may be acceptable where two states face each other, because, as a general rule, it would undoubtedly divide the continental shelf on an equitable basis. But if the equidistant line for two adjacent states is to be reasonable, it must be drawn perpendicularly to the common coastline.

Oda, *Proposals for Revising the Convention on the Continental Shelf,* 7 COLUM. J. TRANSNAT'L L. 1, 26 (1968).

[100] Continental Shelf, Oda Dissent, 1982 ICJ REP. at 270, para. 181.

[101] This point was conceded by Libya. Libyan Counter-memorial, *supra* note 16, at 200–03.

determine the whole course of the boundary may be inequitable. A multiplicity of methods may be necessary to minimize the distorting effects of particular features that, while tolerable close to shore, may be exaggerated to unreasonable proportions at a greater distance.[102]

In the situation before it, the Court took the view that the perpendicular to the coastline was less suitable as a basis for delimitation further from the coast, because the configuration of the coasts was such that the relationship progressed from one of "adjacency" at Ras Ajdir to one approaching "opposite" as between Ras Kaboudia and Ras Tajoura. Further, the Court did not believe that the parties, in adopting the 26° line for resource management purposes comparatively close to shore, "would both necessarily accept as equitable its effects further out to sea."[103]

The angle of the seaward segment of the line was based on the general direction of the Tunisian coast from the point of deepest concavity of the Gulf of Gabes. In the process of determining that direction, the Court was required to address the weight to be given to the Kerkennah Islands and the low-tide elevations surrounding them. Without much explanation, the Court determined that full effect "would, in the circumstances of the case, amount to giving excessive weight to the Kerkennahs."[104] Instead, it allowed half effect, following the precedent of the *Anglo-French* case where the court of arbitration allowed only half effect to the Scilly Islands. This adjustment was effected by making the line of delimitation parallel to a line bisecting the angle formed by a line drawn along the Tunisian coast and one drawn along the seaward coast of the Kerkennah Islands. As the angle of the former was 42° and the latter 62°, the angle of the bisector was 52°. (See map 1, p. 221.) The seaward extension of the line was left open, as that question implicates the interests of third states.

The effect to be given the Kerkennah Islands was a troublesome issue for the Court. Judge Schwebel wrote a brief concurring opinion to make the single point that "the Court has not carried the burden of demonstrating why granting full effect to the Kerkennahs would result in giving them 'excessive weight'." Schwebel pointed out that these islands are substantial, "close to the Tunisian mainland, divided from it by shallow waters in whose banks fisheries are fixed; the considerable population has an ancient and sustained fishing and maritime tradition."[105]

For similar reasons, Judge Gros argued that the Kerkennah Islands are entitled to full effect.[106] Judge Oda, on the other hand, would not give the Kerkennahs any effect in developing his preferred modified equidistance line. He observed that the islands are 11 miles off the mainland and, "being elongated and far from parallel to the coast, project far out to sea."[107] In his view, this projection would be particularly significant if the equidistance method were used, because a feature of that sort at a considerable distance from the

[102] Continental Shelf, 1982 ICJ Rep. at 82, para. 115.

[103] *Id.* at 87, para. 125.

[104] *Id.* at 89, para. 128.

[105] *Id.*, Separate Opinion of Judge Schwebel at 99, 99.

[106] *Id.*, Gros Dissent at 150, para. 14.

[107] *Id.*, Oda Dissent at 271, para. 183(2).

frontier point may have a disproportionate effect on an equidistance line. It may well be that the Court had similar considerations in mind when it concluded that a delimitation line veering east at an angle of 62° would give "excessive weight" to the Kerkennahs.

CONCLUSION

Although the *Tunisia-Libya* case only involved the delimitation of the continental shelf, the general principles stated by the Court and its mode of analysis appear well suited to the delimitation of the exclusive economic zone and of unitary maritime boundaries marking the continental shelf and other maritime zones. In this connection, the following points stand out:

(1) The general rule that delimitation is to be effected in accordance with equitable principles, and taking account of all relevant circumstances, is a fundamental norm that is applicable to every maritime delimitation. Although this formula is too general in itself to provide much guidance for future cases, the Court has given other indications of the principles and circumstances that are relevant to maritime delimitation.

(2) A delimitation in accordance with equitable principles will respect the extension (or natural prolongation) of the coastal fronts of the parties into and under the sea. Such a delimitation will correspond to the general geographic relationship of the coasts of the parties, and will not give such effect to particular features as will result in a line that cuts off the coast of a party from the maritime areas situated in front of that coast. The principle of nonencroachment appears relevant both to the shelf and to the superjacent waters.

(3) The equitable character of a delimitation will be tested by the principle of proportionality as stipulated by the Court in the *North Sea* cases.

(4) Finally, the Court will give considerable weight to the prior conduct of the parties where that conduct demonstrates that both parties accepted the same line as a boundary for significant purposes over a long period of time.

These criteria may not be sufficient in themselves to resolve a particular maritime boundary dispute, but they establish a helpful framework for analysis. It remains to be seen how the Court will integrate these criteria and any other considerations relevant to the delimitation of fisheries jurisdiction and the exclusive economic zone.

THE LEGAL VALIDITY OF ULTRA VIRES DECISIONS OF INTERNATIONAL ORGANIZATIONS

*By Ebere Osieke**

I. Introduction

The question of the legal validity of the acts and decisions adopted by international organizations in excess of their authority has attracted the attention of international lawyers,[1] as well as international courts and tribunals,[2] in recent years. However, no general principles or criteria for determining such validity have as yet been formulated by the international community. In the meantime, the question has continued to give rise to controversy within and outside international organizations and to gain in importance, because of persistent procedural irregularities and the increasing tendency of some of the organizations to take measures that are not expressly provided for in their constitutive instruments but that they consider necessary or essential for the effective discharge of their mandates.

The present article will examine the legal status of these acts and decisions on the basis of the writings of international lawyers, the opinions of international courts and tribunals, and the law and practice of certain international organizations, with a view to determining whether any general principles have now emerged. However, an inquiry of this sort will necessarily involve consideration of two other issues on which there are still some differences of opinion among legal commentators, namely, the right of member states to

* Reader in Law, and Ag. Head of the Department of Public and Private Law, University of Jos, Nigeria. Formerly, member of the Legal Advisory Staff, International Labour Office, Geneva, Switzerland.

[1] Osieke, *'Ultra-Vires' Acts in International Organizations—The Experience of the International Labour Organization,* 48 Brit. Y.B. Int'l L. 259 (1976–77); Osieke, *Unconstitutional Acts in International Organisations: The Law and Practice of the International Civil Aviation Organisation (ICAO),* 28 Int'l & Comp. L.Q. 1 (1979); Osieke, *Admission to Membership in International Organizations: The Case of Namibia,* 51 Brit. Y.B. Int'l L. 189, 220–22 (1980); Morgenstern, *Legality in International Organizations,* 48 *id.* at 24 (1976–77); Jennings, *Nullity and Effectiveness in International Law,* in Cambridge Essays in International Law 64 (1965); Lauterpacht, *The Legal Effect of Illegal Acts of International Organizations,* in *id.* at 88; Cahier, *La Nullité en droit international,* 76 Rev. Générale Droit Int'l Public 645 (1972); D. Ciobanu, Preliminary Objections: Related to the Jurisdiction of the United Nations Political Organs (1975); and C. Leben, Les Sanctions privatives de droits ou de qualité dans les organisations internationales spécialisées (1979).

[2] *See, e.g.,* the Advisory Opinions of the International Court of Justice on Constitution of the Maritime Safety Committee of the Inter-Governmental Maritime Consultative Organization, 1960 ICJ Rep. 150 (June 8); Certain Expenses of the United Nations (Article 17, paragraph 2 of the Charter), 1962 ICJ Rep. 151 (July 20); Legal Consequences for States of the Continued Presence of South Africa in Namibia (South West Africa) notwithstanding Security Council Resolution 276 (1970), 1971 ICJ Rep. 16 (June 21); and the Judgment on the Appeal Relating to the Jurisdiction of the ICAO Council, 1972 ICJ Rep. 46 (Oct. 18).

challenge the legal validity of the acts and decisions of international organizations and the competence of these bodies to rule on such challenges. It would therefore seem appropriate to deal with these two questions before examining the legal validity of the acts and decisions adopted in excess of authority.

The Right of Member States to Challenge the Decisions

The constitutions of most international organizations generally do not contain express provisions authorizing challenges of their acts and decisions by the member states, on grounds of excess of authority or procedural irregularity. In practice, however, member states have consistently made such challenges, and their right to do so has mostly been accepted within and outside the international organizations.[3]

The right of member states in these cases appears to derive from the consensual nature of the constitutions concerned. Because they are international treaties, each party possesses an inherent right to supervise their implementation to ensure that the organizations do not adopt decisions that would be incompatible with their objects and purposes, or that would be detrimental to the interests of the member states in excess of what they had accepted as the basis for membership.

In practice, member states have often been reluctant, for political or other reasons, to challenge the legal validity of the acts and decisions of international organizations.[4] However, the availability of the right has helped put the organizations on their guard, and its exercise by some member states has in many cases resulted in the defeat of proposals that would have constituted

[3] This right was emphasized by Judge Bustamante in his dissenting opinion in the *Certain Expenses* case:

> [W]hen, in the opinion of one of the Member States, a mistake of interpretation has been made or there has even been an infringement of the Charter, there is a right to challenge the resolution in which the error has been noted for the purpose of determining whether or not it departed from the Charter.

1962 ICJ REP. at 304.

[4] The cases of reluctance to raise objections for political reasons may be illustrated by the various resolutions concerning the apartheid policy of the Government of South Africa. Some member states from the industrialized countries refrain from raising objections on the ground of illegality because they do not wish to be seen as supporting the Government of South Africa on apartheid. One good example in recent years is the admission of nonindependent Namibia to full membership in international organizations. Many members considered that the admission might not be compatible with the law and practice of the organizations concerned, but some of them refrained from raising any formal objections and some even voted for it. *See* Osieke, *Admission to Membership, supra* note 1, at 213–16.

It has also been pointed out that member states are restricted from contesting the decisions of international organizations because these bodies do not always indicate the sources of their authority and, consequently, members do not often have the criteria they need to evaluate the "improper" decisions. *See* Wright, *The Strengthening of International Law*, 98 RECUEIL DES COURS 1, 121 (1959 III); and D. CIOBANU, *supra* note 1, at 73–74.

flagrant departures from the functions and powers of the organizations as laid down in their constitutions and other fundamental laws.[5]

The Competence of the Organizations to Decide the Challenges

The constitutions of most international organizations do not contain any provisions on their competence to determine claims concerning the legal validity of their acts and decisions. This silence has led some writers to conclude that these bodies have no competence to make such determinations, and that for them to do so would be to act as "judges in their own cases," contrary to the general legal principle *nemo debet esse judex in propria causa.* In his dissenting opinion in the *Namibia* case (1971), Judge Sir Gerald Fitzmaurice put the issue thus:

> In the institutional field, the justification for the act of some organ or body may turn upon considerations of a political or technical character, or of professional conduct or discipline, and if so, the political, technical or professional organ or body concerned will, in principle, be competent to make the necessary determinations. But where the matter turns, and turns exclusively, on considerations of a legal character, a political organ, even if it is competent to take any resulting action, is not itself competent to make the necessary legal determinations on which the justification for such action must rest. This can only be done by a legal organ competent to make such determinations.[6]

This position has not been generally accepted by writers. Indeed, the more general view, supported by pronouncements of the International Court of Justice and the consistent practice of the organs of international organizations, is that these bodies are competent to deal with claims against their competence and jurisdiction.[7] The attitude of the Court on this issue is discernible from its Advisory Opinion in the *Certain Expenses* case (1962), where it stated:

> In the legal systems of States, there is often some procedure for determining the validity of even a legislative or governmental act, but no analogous procedure is to be found in the structure of the United Nations. Proposals made during the drafting of the Charter to place the ultimate authority to interpret the Charter in the International Court of Justice were not accepted;[8] the opinion which the Court is in course

[5] *See, e.g.,* the defeat at the International Labour Conference in 1973 of the resolution concerning "the policy of discrimination, racism and violation of trade union freedoms practised by the Israeli authorities in Palestine and the occupied territories," discussed by the present writer in *Ultra-Vires Acts, supra* note 1, at 269–70; *see also* Osieke, *Unconstitutional Acts, supra* note 1, at 24–25.

[6] 1971 ICJ REP. at 299.

[7] *See* I. DETTER, LAW MAKING BY INTERNATIONAL ORGANIZATIONS 23 (1965); and D. CIOBANU, *supra* note 1, at 163–73.

[8] For the proposals made in this respect by the Belgian delegation, see Doc. 2, G/7(k)(1), 3 UNCIO Docs. 335, 336 (1945).

> of rendering is an *advisory* opinion. As anticipated in 1945, therefore, each organ must, in the first place at least, determine its own jurisdiction.[9]

According to some commentators, the competence of international organizations to determine claims against their jurisdiction is derived from their inherent power to interpret their constitutions in order to ascertain the nature and extent of their functions and powers.[10] It is difficult, however, to reconcile this assertion with reality. The interpretation of their constitutive instruments by international organizations in order to ascertain the extent of their functions and powers is not the exercise of a judicial function because there is no question or dispute involved. On the other hand, the determination of jurisdictional claims raised by member states could be characterized as the exercise of a judicial function because it involves a question or dispute necessitating considerations of a legal character. It follows, therefore, that the inherent powers of international organizations to exercise a nonjudicial function cannot be the proper basis for the performance of functions of a judicial character.

The main justification for the attribution of competence to international organizations to determine claims against their jurisdiction, or the legal validity of their acts and decisions, is the absence of review bodies with original or appellate jurisdiction to deal with these cases. To deny international organizations competence in these circumstances would create a lacuna; and it could seriously impede the effective attainment of their objects and purposes because all that a member state would have to do to create an impasse or prevent the adoption of a decision is to challenge the competence of the organ or the organization, or indeed the legal validity of the decision.

[9] 1962 ICJ REP. at 168. Again, when it considered the objection raised in the *Namibia* case that General Assembly Resolution 2145 (XXI) made pronouncements that the Assembly, not being a judicial organ and not having previously referred the matter to any such organ, was not competent to make, the Court stated:

> To deny to a political organ of the United Nations which is a successor of the League in this respect the right to act, on the argument that it lacks competence to render what is described as a judicial decision, would not only be inconsistent but would amount to a complete denial of the remedies available against fundamental breaches of an international undertaking.

The Court concluded, therefore, that it was "unable to appreciate the view that the General Assembly acted unilaterally as party and judge in its own cause." 1971 ICJ REP. at 49. Although the Court was dealing in this case with Resolution 2145, in which the General Assembly derived competence from the mandate for South West Africa, the foregoing statements constitute some indication of its approach on the question of "*compétence de la compétence*" of international organizations.

[10] This approach is normally supported by the following statement in the Report of Committee IV/2 of the San Francisco Conference:

> In the course of the operations from day to day of the various organs of the Organization, it is inevitable that each organ will interpret such parts of the Charter as are applicable to its particular functions. This process is inherent in the functioning of any body which operates under an instrument defining its functions and powers. It will be manifested in the functioning of such a body as the General Assembly, the Security Council, or the International Court of Justice. Accordingly, it is not necessary to include in the Charter a provision either authorizing or approving the normal operation of this principle.

Doc. 933, IV/2/42(2), 13 UNCIO Docs. 703, 709 (1945). *See also* I. DETTER, *supra* note 7, at 23.

It appears, therefore, that the determination of jurisdictional claims by international organizations, though perhaps not as satisfactory as a judicial determination, is necessary at the present time. Furthermore, the apparent legal defects of the present practice seem to be mitigated by the fact that in the proceedings of many international organizations, claims as to jurisdiction, or the legal validity of acts and decisions, are not often seen in their purely legal contexts by member states, but rather as political devices or manipulations by opponents to defeat a proposal. For instance, a claim that an international organization has no competence to adopt a resolution condemning the apartheid policies of the Government of South Africa will be seen by many member states as a political ploy by the opposing members to defeat the resolution. Hence, the supporters of the resolution will see its adoption as a political victory, rather than a legal triumph—and its opponents will take the opposite view.

II. The Legal Status of Reviewable Acts and Decisions

The legal status of an act or decision adopted by an international organization in excess of its authority will depend to a large extent on whether there is the possibility for review. Thus, the present section will examine the legal status of reviewable acts and decisions, while the nonreviewable cases will be dealt with in the next section.

Although there is no general review machinery in international organizations, in some of them certain acts and decisions may be reviewed if an objection or appeal has been made.[11] Such a review could be by a judicial organ, as with certain decisions of the Council of the International Civil Aviation Organization (ICAO) which are appealable to the International Court of Justice,[12] or by a political organ, normally the main or plenary body of the organization.[13]

As a general rule, all review bodies possess the power to invalidate an impugned act or decision that they find to be in excess of authority or illegal; but in determining the question of legal effects, they seem to make a distinction between substantive and procedural acts. These two categories of cases will therefore be considered separately.

Substantive Ultra Vires *Acts*

The word "substantive" is a generic term normally employed to designate certain acts and decisions that are not procedural. Stated simply, a substantive act or decision is one that is not procedural. But this definition does not get one very far in the context of international organizations because questions

[11] *Cf.* the separate opinion of Judge Sir Percy Spender in the Certain Expenses case, 1962 ICJ Rep. at 196. *See also* 3 G. Schwarzenberger, International Law as Applied by International Courts and Tribunals 53–54 (1976).

[12] *See* Art. 84 of the Chicago Convention, 61 Stat. 1180, TIAS No. 1591, 15 UNTS 295.

[13] *Cf.* Art. 7(3) of the Constitution of the International Labour Organisation, which authorizes ILO members to appeal to the International Labour Conference a decision of the Governing Body as to which are the members of the Organisation that are of chief industrial importance.

of substance are very often intertwined with those of procedure. The best approach would be to categorize as substantive all the decisions that affect the policies of an organization, such as those relating to budget, allocation of functions and powers, appointment of the executive head, amendments to the constitution, conclusion of treaties, admission to and termination of membership, and many others. The list is not exhaustive. A possible guide to what constitutes substantive acts and decisions would be the requirement of a voting majority of two-thirds and above, but this is not always determinative because some substantive decisions may be adopted by simple majorities.

With respect to the legal effects of substantive *ultra vires* acts, opinion is divided among legal commentators on whether they are *void ab initio* or voidable.[14] However, it appears from the jurisprudence of the International Court of Justice and the law and practice of international organizations that, unless there are express provisions to the contrary, substantive *ultra vires* acts and decisions of international organizations are not void ab initio, but only cease to give rise to binding legal obligations with effect from the date of their invalidation. For instance, after the International Court of Justice concluded in its Advisory Opinion on the *Maritime Safety Committee of the Inter-Governmental Maritime Consultative Organization* (*IMCO*) that the committee, which was elected on January 15, 1959, was not constituted in accordance with the Constitution of the Organization,[15] the second Assembly of IMCO, which met in 1961, decided to dissolve the committee and to constitute a new one in accordance with Article 28 of the Convention as interpreted by the Court.[16] At the same time, the Assembly confirmed and adopted the measures that had been taken by the improperly constituted committee during the period 1959 to 1961, *i.e.*, before its dissolution.[17]

The confirmation of these measures by the IMCO Assembly shows that it did not regard them as without legal validity from their inception. In other words, the Assembly did not consider them as void ab initio.

Further light may be thrown on the approach of international organizations to this question by Article 7(3) of the Constitution of the International Labour Organisation (ILO), which stipulates that an appeal to the Conference against the declaration of the Governing Body as to which members of the Organisation are of chief industrial importance "shall not suspend the application of the declaration until such time as the Conference decides the appeal." Thus, even if the declaration of the Governing Body is eventually invalidated, legal effect will be attributed to actions or measures taken on the basis of the declaration before the determination of the appeal by the Conference. The

[14] *See* D. CIOBANU, *supra* note 1, at 75; Lauterpacht, *supra* note 1, at 111; Osieke, *Ultra-Vires Acts*, *supra* note 1, at 276–77; Osieke, *Unconstitutional Acts*, *supra* note 1, at 21–22. *See also* H. Lauterpacht, *The Legal Remedy in Case of Excess of Jurisdiction*, 9 BRIT. Y.B. INT'L L. 117 (1928); Castberg, *L'Excés du pouvoir dans la justice internationale*, 35 RECUEIL DES COURS 353, 361 (1931 I); Guggenheim, *La Validité et la nullité des actes juridiques internationaux*, 74 *id.* at 195 (1949 I); and Jennings, *supra* note 1, at 83–84.

[15] 1960 ICJ REP. at 171.

[16] IMCO Res. A.21 (II) (Apr. 6, 1961); *see also* IMCO Doc. A.11/S.R.3, at 6–11 (1961).

[17] IMCO Res. A.21 (II), *supra* note 16.

justification for this interpretation is that if the invalidated declaration were regarded as void ab initio, all the decisions adopted by the improperly constituted Governing Body before the appeal is determined would be null and void, and without legal effects. Since a period of up to 10 or 11 months could elapse before the appeal is decided by the Conference, this could give rise to serious consequences in the Organisation.

Similar considerations would seem to apply to the provisions of Article 86 of the Chicago Convention that unless the Council of ICAO decides otherwise, any of its decisions on whether an international airline is operating in conformity with the provisions of the Convention "shall remain in effect unless reversed on appeal."

The nonattribution of absolute nullity to the substantive *ultra vires* acts of international organizations—although different from the position in many municipal systems—would appear to be justified by the special character of the decisions of these organizations. Many of their decisions, such as those relating to the admission of new members or the creation of committees or subsidiary organs, very often become effective immediately after adoption,[18] and it would be unrealistic to maintain that all the actions taken by the organization and its organs, as well as third parties, should be considered as absolute nullities on the basis of the subsequent invalidation of the substantive decision by a review body. The fact that these acts are only voidable may not be entirely satisfactory, but the alternative would lead to uncertainties and chaos, which would weaken the effectiveness of international organizations. A possible solution may be to suspend the implementation of decisions against which objections or appeals have been made until the matter is decided by the review body.[19]

Procedural Ultra Vires *Acts*

Where the constitution or other instrument of an international organization authorizes a certain function or power to be exercised in accordance with a specified procedure, failure to observe the procedure could constitute a ground for a review body to invalidate the resulting act or decision. It is not possible—nor indeed necessary—to draw up a list of all the procedural defects that may occur in an international organization, but these would include adoption of decisions by a method of voting other than that prescribed in the rules, *e.g.*, voting by show of hands instead of by record vote or secret ballot; failure to appoint a committee whose recommendation is required for a decision by a superior organ; adoption of a decision on a matter that was not placed on the agenda of an organ in accordance with the prescribed procedure; adoption of a decision by the wrong organ or by a smaller majority than that laid down in the rules. The list is not exhaustive.

[18] On the self-executing nature of certain decisions of international organizations, see Osieke, *Admission to Membership*, *supra* note 1, at 220–21.

[19] *See, e.g.*, Article 86 of the Chicago Convention, *supra* note 12, which stipulates that certain decisions of the ICAO Council, if appealed, shall be suspended until the appeal is decided.

The attitude of review bodies to procedural irregularities appears to be somewhat cautious. The International Court of Justice has been reluctant to admit that such irregularities could constitute the basis for invalidating a decision of an international organization. In its Advisory Opinion in the *Certain Expenses* case, the Court stated:

> If it is agreed that the action in question is within the scope of the functions of the Organization but it is alleged that it has been initiated or carried out in a manner not in conformity with the division of functions among the several organs which the Charter prescribes, one moves to the internal plane, to the internal structure of the Organization. If the action was taken by the wrong organ, it was irregular as a matter of that internal structure, but this would not necessarily mean that the expense incurred was not an expense of the Organization. Both national and international law contemplate cases in which the body corporate or politic may be bound, as to third parties, by an *ultra vires* act of an agent.[20]

Again, during the proceedings before the International Court of Justice in 1971 concerning the *Appeal Relating to the Jurisdiction of the ICAO Council,* the Government of India contended, *inter alia,* that the impugned decisions of the Council were vitiated by procedural irregularities. The Court made the following statement on the matter:

> The Court however does not deem it necessary or even appropriate to go into this matter, particularly as the alleged irregularities do not prejudice in any fundamental way the requirements of a just procedure. The Court's task in the present proceedings is to give a ruling as to whether the Council has jurisdiction in the case. This is an objective question of law, the answer to which cannot depend on what occurred before the Council. Since the Court holds that the Council did and does have jurisdiction, then, if there were in fact procedural irregularities, the position would be that the Council would have reached the right conclusion in the wrong way. Nevertheless it would have reached the right conclusion. If, on the other hand, the Court had held that there was and is no jurisdiction, then, even in the absence of any irregularities, the Council's decision to assume it would have stood reversed.[21]

It would appear, therefore, that procedural irregularities would not normally constitute a ground for invalidating the acts or decisions of an international organization by a review body, unless such irregularities result in the adoption of a wrong decision or in a miscarriage of justice. Judge Dillard emphasized this latter point in his separate opinion in the *ICAO* case: "It is, of course, not impossible to contemplate a situation of gross abuse of procedural requirements leading to a miscarriage of justice. In such a situation the validity of the decision adopted by a subordinate adjudicating body may be legitimately challenged on appeal."[22]

What amounts to a wrong decision or miscarriage of justice in this respect will depend upon the special circumstances of each case, but one clear example is where the rules stipulate that a particular decision should be adopted by a

[20] 1962 ICJ REP. at 168.

[21] 1972 ICJ REP. at 69–70.

[22] *Id.* at 100; *see also* the separate opinion of Judge Jiménez de Aréchaga, *id.* at 153.

two-thirds majority and the organ concerned adopts it by a simple majority, which derogates from the constitutional rights of some members.

As in the case of substantive *ultra vires,* the acts and decisions that are invalidated by review organs on the basis of procedural irregularities would not be void ab initio, but would merely cease to give rise to binding legal obligations after their invalidation.

Limitations to Review

The power of review bodies to invalidate the acts and decisions of international organizations would appear to be limited, as in municipal systems of law, by the operation of a number of rules, such as acquiescence, estoppel, severability, and lapse of time *ex tempore.*[23] In addition, review bodies appear to be unwilling to interfere with the exercise of discretionary power by an international organization, or to substitute their discretion for that of an organ, unless there has been a miscarriage of justice.[24] It is also doubtful whether a review body would interfere with rules, regulations, or procedures adopted by the organs of international organizations in the exercise of their constitutional powers.

The recent Draft Convention on the Law of the Sea (Informal Text) contains some provisions that may reveal the attitude of the international community on this question. Article 187 grants jurisdiction to the Sea-Bed Disputes Chamber to determine disputes between a state party and the Sea-Bed Authority concerning acts or omissions of the Authority alleged to be in violation of part XI of the Convention or its Annexes, or of rules, regulations, or procedures promulgated in accordance therewith; "or acts of the Authority alleged to be in excess of jurisdiction or a misuse of power."

At the same time, Article 190 of the Convention, which deals with limitations on the jurisdiction of the Sea-Bed Disputes Chamber with regard to decisions of the Authority, stipulates that the Chamber "shall have no jurisdiction with regard to the exercise by the Authority of its discretionary powers in accordance with this Part; in no case shall it substitute its discretion for that of the Authority"; and that "in exercising its jurisdiction pursuant to Article 187, the Sea-Bed Disputes Chamber shall not pronounce itself on the question whether the application of any rules, regulations or procedures adopted by

[23] *Cf.* J. Garner, Administrative Law 175–92 (5th ed. 1979); S. De Smith, Constitutional and Administrative Law 550–59 (3d ed. 1977); S. De Smith, Judicial Review of Administrative Action 314 (3d ed. 1973); and E. Wade & G. Phillips, Constitutional and Administrative Law 587–97 (9th ed. 1977). *See also* the interesting discussion on these limitations with respect to the acts and decisions of international organizations by Lauterpacht, *supra* note 1, at 116–21.

[24] C. W. Jenks, The Proper Law of International Organisations 85–101 (1962); also 3 G. Schwarzenberger, *supra* note 11; and the Judgments of the Administrative Tribunal of the ILO in Meyer v. International Atomic Energy Agency, Judgment No. 245 (Oct. 21, 1974); Djoehana v. Food and Agriculture Organization of the United Nations, Judgment No. 359 (Nov. 13, 1978); and Sita Ram v. World Health Organization, Judgment No. 367 (Nov. 13, 1978). *See also* the recent Judgment of the United Nations Administrative Tribunal in Adler v. United Nations, Judgment No. 267, UN Doc. AT/DEC/267, at 38 (Nov. 21, 1980).

the Authority are in conformity with the provisions of this Convention, nor declare any such rule, regulations or procedure invalid."[25]

These provisions clearly limit the review powers of the Sea-Bed Disputes Chamber over the activities of the Sea-Bed Authority when the exercise of its discretionary powers or the application of rules, regulations, and procedures it has adopted are involved.

Another limitation to the review of acts of international organizations is that review bodies do not normally have the jurisdiction to interfere on their own motions, *ex moro motu,* but may exercise their review functions only if the matter has been referred to them by a member state or an organ of the organization. Consequently, a presumption of validity, *omnia praesumuntur rite et solemniter esse acta,* will be made with respect to all the acts and decisions of international organizations to which no objections have been raised.

III. The Legal Status of Nonreviewable Acts and Decisions

One of the complexities of the law and practice of international organizations is that many of their acts and decisions, particularly those of the plenary bodies, are not subject to appeal or review by any other organ, judicial or political, within or outside the organization. Some examples of these "final" acts and decisions are those relating to the admission of a new member or the appointment of the executive head of the organization or a committee and those against which no appeal is permitted under the constitution.

The practice of international organizations shows that objections are sometimes raised against these acts and decisions,[26] but opinion is divided among international lawyers as to their legal validity if the objections are overruled by the organ concerned. Some writers consider that the acts and decisions cannot be regarded as automatically void if it is not possible to appeal them and no machinery exists for determining the objections raised against them.[27] Some other writers maintain, however, that even in the absence of compulsory jurisdiction or review machinery, the final acts and decisions that are manifestly outside the scope of the powers of an international organization, or that are based on irrelevant political considerations, should be regarded as *ultra vires* and without legal effect.[28] Thus, in the opinion of these writers, the attribution of *ultra vires* status to such acts and decisions does not depend on

[25] Draft Convention on the Law of the Sea (Informal Text), UN Doc. A/CONF.62/WP.10/Rev.3, at 78–80 (1980).

[26] Osieke, *Ultra-Vires Acts, supra* note 1, at 264–73.

[27] *Id.* at 278–79.

[28] *See* the separate opinion of Judge Morelli in the Certain Expenses case, 1962 ICJ Rep. at 222, and the dissenting opinion of Judge Bustamante in the same case, *id.* at 304. *See also* Duke Pollard, who maintains:

> [T]he status of an act by an international organisation is intrinsically independent of the existence of machinery for authoritatively appreciating it as a prelude to its enforcement or nullification as the case may be. The determinations of competent review machinery in appreciating the quality of an act in municipal systems are not constitutive; they are merely declaratory and are normally expressed to be so.

Pollard, *Conflict Resolution in Producers' Associations,* 31 Int'l & Comp. L.Q. 99, 120 (1982).

a determination or declaration by a review body.[29] This argument raises a number of important points that should be considered further.

Manifestly Ultra Vires *Acts*

The concept of "manifest *ultra vires,*" which appears to have received a measure of acceptance with respect to the improper awards of arbitration tribunals,[30] has not received the same approbation as regards the acts and decisions of international organizations. However, during the oral proceedings in the *Certain Expenses* case, the representative of the Government of the United Kingdom submitted that there was no power to apportion the expenditure arising out of *ultra vires* acts that were "manifestly invalid."[31] And according to the United States representative, *ultra vires* acts could give rise to lawful expenditure unless they were "manifestly invalid."[32]

In its Advisory Opinion in the case, the International Court of Justice also made a statement that suggests that the presumption of validity only attaches to an action pertinent to the stated purposes of an organization: "when the Organization takes action which warrants the assertion that it was appropriate for the fulfilment of one of the stated purposes of the United Nations, the presumption is that such action is not *ultra vires* the Organization."[33]

Obviously, the rather unsettled state of the law and practice of international organizations on questions of nullity and invalidity makes the concept of manifest *ultra vires* very attractive, but its practical application would give rise to considerable difficulties. It might not be easy to establish the category of acts and decisions that could be characterized as manifestly *ultra vires.* Perhaps all the acts and decisions that are contrary to the objects and purposes of an international organization should be considered as manifestly *ultra vires.* But what if no objections have been raised against them? Should they still be presumed to be *ultra vires* and nonexistent? Who decides whether an act or decision is manifestly *ultra vires?* The organ whose acts have been impugned? Or should the matter be left to the unilateral decision of a member state?

Another difficulty stems from the nature of the decision-making process in international organizations. A decision of an international organization is consensual in character and must be approved by a majority of the member states. This means that any such decision constitutes some form of understanding or agreement among the sovereign states that participated in its adoption. Therefore, it would seem difficult to maintain that a decision accepted by a majority of states in the proper exercise of their rights of membership in an international organization should be considered as *ultra vires* and nonexistent *per se, i.e.,* in the absence of a declaration to that effect by a competent review body.

[29] *Ibid.*

[30] 3 E. DE VATTEL, THE LAW OF NATIONS, bk. II, ch. XVIII, §329 (Carnegie ed. 1916). *See also* H. Lauterpacht, *supra* note 14; Jennings, *supra* note 1, at 83–84; Castberg, *supra* note 14, at 361; and Guggenheim, *supra* note 14, at 195–263.

[31] 1962 ICJ Pleadings (Certain Expenses of the United Nations) 337 (statement of May 17, 1962).

[32] *Id.* at 416.

[33] 1962 ICJ REP. at 168.

Acts and Decisions Based on Irrelevant Political Considerations

Many of the decisions of plenary organs of international organizations to which objections are often raised relate primarily to political questions, such as the apartheid policies of the Government of South Africa and the policies of the Government of Israel in the occupied territories. Invariably, the decisions on these matters are motivated on the whole by political considerations, and on many occasions, many member states, particularly those belonging to the Group of 77 and the socialist countries of Eastern Europe, vote together—a situation generally characterized as "bloc voting."

These developments have given rise to serious criticisms by the member states from the industrialized market economy countries, as well as by legal commentators. More significantly, doubt has been raised as regards the legal validity of the politically motivated decisions adopted by international organizations with the support of the "automatic" majority. One eminent jurist, Professor Eagleton, considered that if a political action taken by a majority vote were to be regarded as proof that the organ was competent under its constitution to take the action, the result would be anarchy from a constitutional or legal viewpoint.[34]

Writing about events in the United Nations, particularly the role played by the majority relating to the adoption of certain decisions, Professor Leo Gross concluded that the minority members could have prevented the spread of majoritarianism in the Organization:

> One would have been justified in expecting that the United States and other minority members, particularly those which are permanent members of the Security Council, would have been on their toes to prevent the contagion of unbridled majoritarianism from infecting that principal organ of the United Nations. This, regrettably, has not been the case.[35]

In a recent study, Professor Elihu Lauterpacht emphasized the extent to which the adoption of decisions by the majority is controlled by the legal system of international organizations:

> What conclusion is to be drawn from references to situations in which majorities in international organizations have shown their unconcern for the constitutional rights of States which can muster only minority support? It could, of course, be argued that what may appear to be illegal acts are in truth not so; that adoption by sizable majorities demonstrates the general acceptability of the line of conduct in question; and that the very fact of general acceptability excludes the possibility of illegality. But the answer to such an argument is clear. The extent to which acceptability determines legality is controlled by the legal system surrounding the conduct in question. Since it is axiomatic that international organizations operate within some legal system . . . one must look to see whether in the international constitutional system there is any such instant assimi-

[34] Statement by Professor Eagleton during the discussion in the International Law Association on review of the UN Charter. ILA, REPORT OF THE 46TH CONFERENCE 80 (1954).

[35] Gross, *Voting in the Security Council and the PLO,* 70 AJIL 470, 471 (1976).

lation of acceptability to legality. And the answer is emphatically negative.[36]

The contention that majority decisions motivated by political considerations are *ultra vires* has not been generally accepted by commentators. Speaking on the subject, the Prime Minister of Luxembourg, Gaston Thorn, stated:

> We should not complain about the intrusion of politics into the United Nations—we created the organization for political reasons, in order to apply our strategy there. What has happened recently are the accidents and setbacks of a former majority. So they should play the game! In the United Nations the problem is every bit as much one of the new minority that has not accepted its new position.[37]

According to Amadou-Mahtar M'Bow, the Director-General of the United Nations Educational, Scientific and Cultural Organization (UNESCO):

> [T]he record of the former majority is catastrophic in every field. One must not forget that it was the former majority which prevented the admission of the People's Republic of China into UNESCO for more than twenty years. Was it a technical vote or a political vote in an international institution whose purpose is to deal with science and culture? It can hardly be claimed that the 800 million Chinese had nothing to contribute to the world in the way of education, science and culture! Yet they were kept away. Solely for political reasons![38]

Recently, Ambassador Mohammed Bedjaoui, now judge of the International Court of Justice, wrote:

> [T]he process of elaborating international legal norms is much more complex than the critics of the supposed "automatic majority" would have one believe. It reflects complex power balances. When such diverse countries as Algeria, Chile and India vote together, thereby contributing to the creation of that "automatic majority" in order to try to promote the new international economic order, one loses sight somewhat too conveniently of the fact that the power of decision-making remains the prerogative of a small group of States which are "more equal than others".[39]

According to Ambassador Bedjaoui, the consequence of the emergence of the new majority is that "for the first time, the real political and economic power in the world, still held by the West, no longer finds its juridical expression embodied in the same way as it still was a few years ago, for example, in the resolutions of the United Nations, ILO, UNCTAD, or Unesco."[40]

[36] Lauterpacht, *The Development of the Law of International Organization by the Decisions of International Tribunals,* 152 RECUEIL DES COURS 381, 393–94 (1976 IV).

[37] Statement made during a broadcast debate, in E. LAURENT, UN MONDE À REFAIRE. DÉBATS DE FRANCE CULTURE. TROIS JOURS POUR LA PLANÈTE 120–21 (Paris: Editions Mengès, 1977).

[38] Statement made in the debate, *id.* at 129.

[39] M. BEDJAOUI, TOWARDS A NEW INTERNATIONAL ECONOMIC ORDER 147 (UNESCO 1979).

[40] *Id.* at 142.

These statements indicate that many commentators see the question of the "automatic majority" and "politicization" in international organizations as a political, rather than a legal, issue. It is true, of course, from a purely legal standpoint, that national review bodies normally invalidate the decisions of national administrative organs on the ground of improper considerations or motive.[41] But the situation appears to be different with respect to decisions of international organizations.

Apart from the absence of review machinery, and the consensual nature of decisions in international organizations to which reference has already been made, many of the political decisions adopted by the plenary organs of international organizations, particularly on such questions as the apartheid policy of the Government of South Africa, are symbolic in character and are, in most cases, self-executing. Their primary objective is normally to condemn the member state concerned, and that objective is fulfilled once a resolution is adopted and published. This does not mean that the question of the legal validity of the resolution is not relevant, but that question loses its significance because the primary objective of the resolution, namely, condemnation of the member state, has been attained.

Again, the political decisions of many international organizations, which are adopted in the form of resolutions, do not normally give rise to binding legal obligations for the member states. The resolutions often ask the members not to collaborate with the policies of the condemned government or to give it assistance in the implementation of its policies. Thus, any member that strongly opposes adoption of the nonbinding resolution is not under a legal obligation to implement its provisions—a factor that reduces the legal significance of political decisions in international organizations.

Finally, it is evident from the practice of international organizations that the controversy concerning "automatic majorities" normally arises when the decision concerned is of a political nature or when certain member states consider that their interests would be affected or at stake. It is important, therefore, that efforts be made to reconcile the divergent points of view and to ensure that the decisions reflect a sufficiently wide consensus of the general membership.[42] This is all the more important because quite often the decision of an international organization, especially on political issues, is the beginning of a process aimed at the attainment of certain objectives on the basis of prescribed actions and measures to be taken subsequently by the members individually or collectively. Thus, the adoption of decisions of international organizations by consensus constitutes an important element in their effective implementation.

One cannot argue on this basis, however, that majority decisions of inter-

[41] *See, e.g.,* the following British cases: Roberts v. Hopwood, 1925 A.C. 578; Chertsey U.D.C. v. Mixnam's Properties, Ltd., [1964] 2 All E.R. 627; and R. v. Hullingdon London Borough Council, *ex parte* Royco Homes, Ltd., [1974] 2 All E.R. 643. *See also* J. GARNER, *supra* note 23, at 158–59.

[42] *See* Jenks, *Unanimity, the Veto, Weighted Voting, Special and Simple Majorities and Consensus as Modes of Decision in International Organisations,* in CAMBRIDGE ESSAYS, *supra* note 1, at 48, 48.

national organizations are illegal or invalid because they were adopted against the wishes of the minority. From a purely legal point of view, what is necessary is that the decision be adopted in accordance with the prescribed rules and procedure, and once the required conditions have been fulfilled, the legal validity of the decision will not depend on the wishes or the desires of the minority of the members of the organization. To accept otherwise would be to undermine the principle of "majority rule" on which the operations of contemporary international organizations are predicated.

The Right of Member States to Reject Ultra Vires *Acts*

The contention that the acts and decisions of international organizations that are manifestly outside the scope of their functions and powers, or that are based on irrelevant political considerations, are *ultra vires* even in the absence of review machinery has led some international lawyers to assert that member states possess the right to reject them. In his dissenting opinion in the *Certain Expenses* case, Judge Winiarski, the President of the Court, rejected the contention that the nullity of a legal instrument can be relied upon only where there has been a finding of nullity by a competent tribunal. He concluded that, in the international legal system where there is no tribunal competent to make a finding of nullity,

> [i]t is the state which regards itself as the injured party which itself rejects a legal instrument vitiated, in its opinion, by such defects as to render it a nullity. . . .
>
> A refusal to pay, as in the case before the Court, may be regarded by a Member State, loyal and indeed devoted to the Organization, as the only means of protesting against a resolution of the majority which, in its opinion, disregards the true meaning of the Charter and adopts in connection with it a decision which is legally invalid. . . .[43]

Similarly, in his separate opinion in the recent case of the *Interpretation of the Agreement of 25 March 1951 between the WHO and Egypt,* Judge Gros stated:

> A decision of the WHO which is contrary to international law does not become lawful because a majority of States has voted in favour of it. The WHO and, in particular, its Assembly were created by the member States in order to carry out that which they had decided to do together, and that alone; member States are not bound to implement an unlawful act if that is what they hold it to be, and the practice of international organizations has shown that recourse is had in such circumstances to a refusal to carry out such act. Consequently nothing is settled by a decision taken by a majority of member States in matters in which a specialized agency over-steps its competence. Numbers cannot cure a lack of constitutional competence.[44]

[43] 1962 ICJ REP. at 232.

[44] 1980 ICJ REP. 73, 104 (Advisory Opinion of Dec. 20). *See also* the Report of the Special Committee on Reference to the International Court of Justice of Questions of United Nations Competence, which states that "a Member may now refuse to execute a decision of the Organization, if he feels strongly that the decision is unconstitutional," *quoted by* D. CIOBANU, *supra* note 1, at 174.

According to some writers, the right of member states to reject the actions and decisions of international organizations that they consider to be *ultra vires* is derived from their inherent right to interpret the law if they are not satisfied with the interpretation given by an international organ.[45] This right entitles member states to claim that their interpretation of the constitutions of international organizations is the correct one, and they could therefore refuse to comply with the decisions of the political organs that they claim to be unconstitutional.[46] Professor Gross has endeavored to explain the meaning and scope of the right of auto-interpretation:

> It is generally recognized that the root of the unsatisfactory situation in international law and relations is the absence of an authority generally competent to declare what the law is at any given time, how it applies to a given situation or dispute, and what the appropriate sanction may be. In the absence of such an authority, and failing agreement between the states at variance on these points, each state has a right to interpret the law, the right of autointerpretation, as it might be called. The interpretation, however, is not a "decision" and is neither final nor binding upon the other parties. In consequence of the technical insufficiency prevailing in general international law, we may never know, or, in some cases, we may not know for a time, which autointerpretation was correct. . . . This is, for better or worse, the situation resulting from the organizational insufficiency of international law.[47]

The right of member states to reject decisions they consider unconstitutional in the absence of a legal determination by a review body to that effect has not been generally accepted by international lawyers. In his separate opinion in the *Certain Expenses* case, Judge Morelli stated:

> In my view it is not possible to suppose that the Charter leaves it open to any State Member to claim at any time that an Assembly resolution authorizing a particular expense has never had any legal effect whatever, on the ground that the resolution is based on a wrong interpretation of the Charter or an incorrect ascertainment of situations of fact or of law. It must on the contrary be supposed that the Charter confers finality on the Assembly's resolution irrespective of the reasons, whether they are correct or not, on which the resolution is based; and this must be so even in a field in which the Assembly does not have true discretionary power.[48]

[45] *See* D. CIOBANU, *supra* note 1, at 174; and the discussion in Gross, *States as Organs of International Law and the Problem of Autointerpretation*, in LAW AND POLITICS IN THE WORLD COMMUNITY 59, 77–78 (G. A. Lipsky ed. 1953). *See also* Tammes, *Decisions of International Organs as a Source of International Law*, 94 RECUEIL DES COURS 261, 338 (1958 II); Waldock, *General Course on Public International Law*, 106 *id.* at 1, 108 (1962 II); and Watson, *Autointerpretation, Competence, and the Continuing Validity of Article 2(7) of the Charter*, 71 AJIL 60 (1977).

[46] This right is sometimes referred to as "the right of last resort." Thus, Professor Ciobanu has stated that "the States possess, under the law of the United Nations as it stands at present, the so-called 'right of last resort'," and in exercising such right, "a State itself corrects any defects which it may have found in the application by the relevant organ of the provisions pertaining to its competence or in the substance of the decision." He then justifies some of the refusals of UN members to implement certain contested resolutions of the main organs of the United Nations on the basis of the "right of last resort." D. CIOBANU, *supra* note 1, at 174–79.

[47] Gross, *supra* note 45, at 76–77.

[48] 1962 ICJ REP. at 224.

According to Pollux, the "easiest, the most primitive, and the most unsatisfactory solution is to say that each individual Member has the right to decide for itself how to interpret the Charter";[49] and in the opinion of Professor Quincy Wright, "the suggestion, occasionally made, that the States themselves should interpret the Charter, would tend toward nullification and a hopeless incapacity of the United Nations to function."[50] Professor Oscar Schachter has also emphasized that even if the dominant motive of a government was its own advantage, "the essential point is that this motive cannot be the *justification* to others of an interpretation which is claimed to have legal effect."[51]

Because of the divergencies of opinion that still exist on the matter, it is clear that the right of member states to reject decisions of international organizations that they consider to be *ultra vires,* or indeed the right of auto-interpretation, cannot be regarded as a generally accepted principle of international law or of the law and practice of international organizations. There is no doubt that in the course of the proceedings of international organizations, member states are continuously interpreting the constitutions of these bodies to determine the basis of the proposed acts or decisions and the nature and extent of their obligations, and to contest any proposals that appear to them to be incompatible with the express provisions of the constitutions. But to arrogate to the member states a general right to reject a properly adopted decision on the basis of a unilateral determination that it is *ultra vires* would be tantamount to making the members judges in their own cases—a situation that would be similar to the much criticized principle of *compétence de la compétence* of international organizations.[52]

IV. General Conclusions

The present study has shown that some principles have emerged concerning the legal validity of acts and decisions adopted by international organizations in excess of their authority. It has been established that member states have an inherent right to challenge the legal validity of acts and decisions; that the organizations possess the competence to determine the claims that arise; that the possibility exists in certain cases for review; and that, as a general rule, the invalidated acts and decisions are voidable rather than void ab initio.

It is also clear that many acts and decisions of international organizations, particularly those of the plenary organs, are not subject to appeal or review, and that, at present, determining the validity of some of them poses considerable difficulties. The increasing importance of international organizations and the need for effectiveness in the attainment of their objects and purposes through the full cooperation and collaboration of all the member states make it imperative to establish some form of procedure for review.

[49] Pollux, *The Interpretation of the Charter,* 23 Brit. Y.B. Int'l L. 54, 56 (1946).

[50] Wright, *supra* note 4, at 125.

[51] Schachter, *The Relation of Law, Politics and Action in the United Nations,* 109 Recueil des Cours 165, 198 (1963 II).

[52] *See* note 9 *supra* and accompanying text.

Several suggestions have already been put forward, including the creation of an ad hoc body of jurists,[53] the creation of a body made up of the senior legal officers of the international organizations,[54] and applications by member states to the International Court of Justice for binding advisory opinions. In his report to the International Symposium of the Max Planck Institute in 1974, Professor R. Y. Jennings presented the latter idea as follows:

> The Court should attain a position of greater power and importance if its advisory jurisdiction could more often be used to test the legality of the acts or omissions of international organizations. Such cases will hardly come from international organizations themselves, but a government might be enabled to move for an advisory opinion through some such device as a General Assembly Committee.[55]

An appeal to the International Court of Justice for a binding advisory opinion may constitute the best procedure for determining the legal validity of acts and decisions that are claimed to be illegal or unconstitutional. One major drawback here is that reference to the Court, even in the form of a request for an advisory opinion, is not free from practical problems[56] and could even result in protracted debates and long delays—which could further undermine the activities of the organization concerned.

Another possible approach would be to establish machinery within the international organizations themselves, on the lines of the Sea-Bed Disputes Chamber, to deal with claims relating to the legality of their acts and decisions.

[53] Suggested by Sir Gerald Fitzmaurice in his dissenting opinion in the Namibia case, 1971 ICJ REP. at 300.

[54] Suggestion by Professor Louis Sohn in *Due Process in the United Nations,* 69 AJIL 620, 621 (1975).

[55] Jennings, *Report,* in MAX-PLANCK-INSTITUT FÜR AUSLÄNDISCHES ÖFFENTLICHES RECHT UND VÖLKERRECHT, JUDICIAL SETTLEMENT OF INTERNATIONAL DISPUTES: AN INTERNATIONAL SYMPOSIUM 35, 48 (1974). *See also* Farukowa, *La Controle de la Cour internationale de Justice sur les organisations internationales—les actes ultra-vires des organisations internationales,* 78 JAPAN. J. INT'L L. & DIPL. 133 (July 1979). Also the resolution in [47] 2 INSTITUT DE DROIT INTERNATIONAL, ANNUAIRE 274 (1957).

[56] *See* I. BROWNLIE, GENERAL PRINCIPLES OF INTERNATIONAL LAW 730–32 (3d ed. 1979); and Rosenne, *The Non-Use of the Advisory Competence of the International Court of Justice,* 39 BRIT. Y.B. INT'L L. 1 (1963).

THE SENATE ROLE IN TREATY RATIFICATION

*By Michael J. Glennon**

> Others, though content that treaties should be made in the mode proposed, are averse to their being the supreme law of the land. They insist, and profess to believe, that treaties like acts of assembly, should be repealable at pleasure. This idea seems to be new and peculiar to this country, but new errors, as well as new truths, often appear. These gentlemen would do well to reflect that a treaty is only another name for a bargain, and that it would be impossible to find a nation who would make any bargain with us, which should be binding on them absolutely, but on us only so long and so far as we may think proper to be bound by it.
>
> *The Federalist* No. 64 (Jay)

INTRODUCTION

The aim of diplomacy, Sir Edward Grey said, is to enlarge the area of confidence between governments.[1] Absent that confidence, international order breaks down; as international discord increases, nations become more isolated and wary of cooperation, more willing to "go it alone" and to resort to guile and coercion as means of achieving foreign policy objectives. On the other hand, the gradual growth of a body of reciprocally held assumptions alleviates fears of diplomatic deception and generates a measure of predictability ultimately conducive to international harmony.[2]

The pursuit of stronger and clearer, mutually shared expectations is complicated, however, by legislative involvement in foreign policy formulation.[3] Multi-branch participation in that process may help form or strengthen a national consensus, and it may also lessen the likelihood of unpopular policies.[4] But a nation with more than one governmental hand at the foreign policy helm can incur costs in credibility. The hand that signs is not the hand that delivers; what looks like a good bargain to diplomats at the negotiating table

* Associate Professor of Law, University of Cincinnati College of Law. Former Legal Counsel, Senate Foreign Relations Committee. The author wishes to acknowledge the assistance of Bruce C. Johnson, a student at the College of Law.

[1] Richard, *Foreign Perspective: With Whom Do You Deal? Whom Can You Trust?*, in THE TETHERED PRESIDENCY 21 (T. Franck ed. 1981) (quoting Sir Harold Nicolson as having quoted Sir Edward Grey).

[2] *See generally* H. NICOLSON, DIPLOMACY (1963); T. FRANCK & E. WEISBAND, WORD POLITICS: VERBAL STRATEGY AMONG THE SUPERPOWERS (1971); L. HENKIN, HOW NATIONS BEHAVE (2d ed. 1979).

[3] For a comparative survey of constitutional provisions and national practices concerning legislative participation in the treaty-making process, see L. WILDHABER, TREATY-MAKING POWER AND CONSTITUTION (1971).

[4] *See generally* T. FRANCK & E. WEISBAND, FOREIGN POLICY BY CONGRESS (1979); Bennet, *Congress in Foreign Policy: Who Needs It?*, 57 FOREIGN AFF. 40 (1978).

may look altogether different to legislators in the cold light of constituents' mail. The domestic value of pluralistic governmental decision making thus competes with the international value of reciprocal expectations.[5]

The tension between these values is particularly evident in the making of the foreign policy of the United States, a nation whose Constitution mandates a fairly strict separation of powers. The recent revival of congressional involvement in international agreement making—perhaps the most important diplomatic tool for clarifying shared expectations—has further highlighted that tension. Generated principally by Watergate and Vietnam, the reassertion by Congress of its foreign policy prerogatives has raised new questions concerning the respective scope of legislative and executive powers in the making of international agreements. This article analyzes several newly arisen issues that reflect the heightened "value tension" described above, and it suggests resolutions consistent with the vindication of both values.

I. CONDITIONING SENATE CONSENT TO TREATIES

The Disputed Annex to the Spanish Bases Treaty

The authority of the Senate to condition its consent to treaties, although not set forth expressly in the Constitution,[6] is now well settled.[7] Recently, however, concern has arisen in the Senate about the continued viability of that power. That concern traces to a little-noticed dispute that followed the Senate's consent in 1976 to the Treaty of Friendship and Cooperation with Spain.[8]

After transmittal of that Treaty to the Senate on February 18, 1976[9] and hearings by the Foreign Relations Committee, which evidenced serious concern about Spanish progress towards democracy,[10] the committee appended a five-part "declaration" to the resolution of ratification it reported.[11] Among other things, the declaration stated that the Senate "hopes and intends that this Treaty will serve to support and foster Spain's progress toward free in-

[5] *See generally* Christopher, *Ceasefire Between the Branches: A Compact in Foreign Affairs,* 60 FOREIGN AFF. 989 (1982); Richard, *supra* note 1; Tower, *Congress Versus the President: The Formulation and Implementation of American Foreign Policy,* 60 FOREIGN AFF. 229 (1981/82).

[6] The Constitution merely provides that the making of a treaty requires the advice and consent of the Senate. U.S. CONST. art. II, §2, cl. 2.

[7] *See, e.g.,* RESTATEMENT OF THE FOREIGN RELATIONS LAW OF THE UNITED STATES (REVISED) §305, Comment *d* (Tentative Draft No. 1, 1980) [hereinafter cited as DRAFT RESTATEMENT] (stating that the Senate may condition its consent to a treaty, provided the condition has a plausible relation to the treaty's content or implementation); L. HENKIN, FOREIGN AFFAIRS AND THE CONSTITUTION 133–34 (1972) (stating that the Senate's constitutional right to impose reservations as a condition for consent is universally accepted); 14 M. WHITEMAN, DIGEST OF INTERNATIONAL LAW 138 (1970); Note, *The Reservation Power and the Connally Amendment,* 11 N.Y.U. J. INT'L L. & POL. 323, 327 (1978) (tracing the Senate practice of adding reservations to treaties to 1794).

[8] Jan. 24, 1976, United States-Spain, 27 UST 3005, TIAS No. 8630.

[9] S. EXEC. DOC. E, 94th Cong., 2d Sess. (1976).

[10] *Spanish Base Treaty: Hearings on Executive E Before the Senate Comm. on Foreign Relations,* 94th Cong., 2d Sess. (1976).

[11] S. EXEC. REP. NO. 5, 94th Cong., 2d Sess. 11 (1976).

stitutions."[12] The resolution of ratification, as reported by the committee, was approved by the Senate on June 21, 1976.[13]

Several weeks thereafter, the Department of State reported strong opposition within the Cortes (the Spanish parliament) to the Senate declaration, and indicated to the Senate Foreign Relations Committee that the Government of Spain would not ratify the Treaty were the Senate declaration included in the U.S. instrument of ratification. During consultation with various members of the committee, the State Department proposed inclusion of the declaration in an annex to the Treaty, to be incorporated by reference in the instrument of ratification and transmitted simultaneously.[14] "Attaching the Senate resolution to the instrument by means of an annex referred to in the instrument of ratification," the Department said, "is the equivalent of incorporating the resolution in the instrument."[15] The Senators approved, and the Treaty was ratified by the President.

Effect on the Panama Canal Treaties

It was with fresh memories of this episode that the Senate Foreign Relations Committee took up the Panama Canal Treaties.[16] The committee appended to each resolution of ratification an "understanding" that "[t]he President shall include all amendments, conditions, reservations, and understandings incorporated by the Senate in this resolution of ratification in the instrument of ratification to be exchanged with the Government of the Republic of Panama."[17] The concern in the Senate that the material it had added might be transmitted separately from the instrument of ratification is understandable: the requirements of international law concerning treaty ratification, in light of U.S. ratification practice, raise serious doubts whether a separately transmitted Senate condition would be binding on the other party. International law, at least as interpreted by the U.S. Government, requires that all reservations and other terms and conditions attached to a nation's ratification of a treaty be formulated in writing and communicated to the other party or parties to the treaty.[18] Traditionally, the United States has communicated

[12] *Ibid.*

[13] S. Res. 401, 94th Cong., 2d Sess. (1976); *see also* 122 CONG. REC. 19,390 (1976) (ratification vote).

[14] For a general discussion of the diplomatic *contretemps,* see Meron, *The Treaty War: The International Legal Effect of Changes in Obligations Initiated by the Congress,* in THE TETHERED PRESIDENCY, *supra* note 1; *Panama Canal Treaties: Hearings Before the Senate Comm. on Foreign Relations,* 95th Cong., 2d Sess. 122–23 (1978) [hereinafter cited as *Panama Canal Hearings*].

[15] Letter from Robert J. McCloskey, Assistant Secretary of State for Congressional Relations, to John J. Sparkman, Senate Foreign Relations Committee Chairman (undated) (on file with the author).

[16] *See* S. EXEC. REP. NO. 12, 95th Cong., 2d Sess. 10–11 (1978) (alluding to concern over the Spanish Treaty incident).

[17] *Id.* at 10.

[18] *See, e.g.,* letter from Douglas J. Bennet, Jr., Assistant Secretary of State for Congressional Relations, to John J. Sparkman, Chairman of the Senate Foreign Relations Committee (Jan. 26, 1978), *reprinted in Panama Canal Hearings, supra* note 14, at 49.

such Senate conditions as a part of the instrument of ratification,[19] and other nations might presumably rely on this practice. Given the requirement that the President make the Senate's qualifications on consent effective if he wishes to bring the treaty into force,[20] it is most sensible that a Senate condition be incorporated in the instrument of ratification.[21]

Rule of the Draft Restatement

The draft *Restatement of Foreign Relations Law of the United States (Revised),* however, would impose a less rigorous requirement. Section 323 provides in relevant part as follows:

> (1) When the Senate of the United States gives its advice and consent to a treaty subject to the United States entering a reservation, the President, if he makes the treaty, must include the reservation in the instrument of ratification or accession, or otherwise make it clear that the adherence of the United States is subject to the reservation.
>
> (2) When the Senate gives its advice and consent to a treaty on the basis of a particular understanding of its meaning, the President, if he makes the treaty, must respect the Senate's understanding.[22]

Comment *b* recognizes the authority of the Senate to "indicate that it will consent only if certain changes are made in the treaty or if the United States enters reservations to it"[23] and notes, accordingly, that the President "generally includes a verbatim recitation of any statement of understanding, declaration or reservation contained in the Senate resolution of consent (i) in the instrument notifying the other state or the depositary of U.S. ratification and (ii) in the proclamation of the treaty."[24] Without explanation or elaboration,

[19] *See* letter from Herbert J. Hansell, Legal Adviser to the Department of State, to Michael J. Glennon, Legal Counsel to the Senate Foreign Relations Committee (June 8, 1979), *reprinted in* 2 UNITED STATES FOREIGN RELATIONS LAW 199 (M. Glennon & T. Franck eds. 1980) [hereinafter cited as FOREIGN RELATIONS LAW].

[20] RESTATEMENT (SECOND) OF THE FOREIGN RELATIONS LAW OF THE UNITED STATES §133, Comment *c* (1965); DRAFT RESTATEMENT, *supra* note 7, §323, Comment *b.*

[21] 14 M. WHITEMAN, *supra* note 7, at 138–39. *See also* Memorandum from the Office of the Legal Adviser of the Department of State, March 22, 1971, to J. W. Fulbright, Chairman of the Senate Foreign Relations Committee, *reprinted in* S. EXEC. REP. NO. 5, 93d Cong., 1st Sess. 15–16 (1973):

> In United States law a condition placed by the Senate on its approval of a treaty—whether by reservation or by understanding—and included by the President in the instrument of ratification takes effect as domestic law along with the treaty itself. This is a necessary result of the shared constitutional role of the President and the Senate in the treaty-making process.
>
> An instrument of ratification or adherence executed by the President of the United States sets forth the text of the reservation, understanding, or other instrument as given in the Senate resolution. . . .
>
> Reservations, understandings, or declarations of intent or interpretation, in order to have international effect, are incorporated in the case of a bilateral treaty. . . .

Ibid.

[22] DRAFT RESTATEMENT, *supra* note 7, §323, paras. 1–2.

[23] *Id.*, §323, Comment *b.* [24] *Ibid.*

however, the comment then states flatly that "[t]he President may also communicate a Senate qualification separately from the ratification."[25]

The *Restatement,* now being revised by the American Law Institute, should not recognize such discretion. An absolute requirement of inclusion in the instrument of ratification is necessary to ensure an identity of expectations by both nations concerning rights and obligations imposed by the treaty. Authority to transmit material included by the Senate in its resolution of ratification by means of an "annex" not incorporated by reference or a diplomatic note only increases the possibility of misunderstanding. This applies even more to provisions that expressly or implicitly alter provisions of a treaty.

If broader presidential discretion is to be recognized, however, it should be limited to the authority to exclude from the instrument of ratification only material added by the Senate that does not genuinely represent a "condition" to its consent. For example, a "statement" or "declaration" merely expressing the sense of the Senate and not altering rights or obligations under the treaty might be viewed as within the power of the President to transmit separately from the instrument of ratification. Such authority would arguably derive from the President's power as "sole organ of the United States"[26] for the purpose of communicating with foreign governments, a power long recognized by the Senate.[27] The draft *Restatement* takes the position that the Senate could not condition its consent upon the firing of a cabinet officer,[28] presumably on the notion that dismissal is a plenary presidential power; the same might be said of the power to communicate with foreign governments.[29]

The difficulty with this argument is that it either would cause presidential power to turn on an empty semantic distinction or would make the President the sole judge of the Senate's substantive intent. It is established that the legal effect of any matter added by the Senate depends upon its substance, not its denomination.[30] But the President, under this analysis, would be empowered to exclude from the instrument of ratification material intended by the Senate to be included[31] and, conversely, would be required to include material that

[25] *Ibid.*

[26] *See infra* note 29.

[27] *See, e.g.,* S. EXEC. REP. NO. 12, *supra* note 16, at 9–10. The President's power in this regard seems settled. "As 'sole organ,' " Professor Henkin has written, "the President determines . . . how, when, where and by whom the United States should make or receive communications, and there is nothing to suggest that he is limited to time, place, or forum." L. HENKIN, *supra* note 7, at 47.

[28] DRAFT RESTATEMENT, *supra* note 7, §305, Comment *d.*

[29] In 1800, John Marshall (then a congressman) described the President as "the sole organ of the nation in its foreign relations." 10 ANNALS OF CONGRESS 613 (1800). Justice Sutherland quoted this phrase to support his theory of extensive presidential power over the conduct of foreign policy. United States v. Curtiss-Wright Export Corp., 299 U.S. 304, 319 (1936). However, as Professor Berger has pointed out, it is unlikely that Marshall had such a theory in mind, since he stated that Congress "may unquestionably prescribe the mode" of treaty compliance in the very speech in which he called the President the "sole organ." Berger, *The President's Unilateral Termination of the Taiwan Treaty,* 75 NW. U.L. REV. 577, 590 (1980).

[30] 14 M. WHITEMAN, *supra* note 7, at 140.

[31] *See supra* notes 12–17 and accompanying text.

the Senate might not have intended to be transmitted.[32] The alternative—allowing the President to look to the substance of the added material—creates equally great difficulties in that it increases executive discretion to the point of authorizing the separate transmittal of material that in the President's exclusive judgment was falsely labeled a "reservation," a formulation of authority that would not comport with traditional U.S. ratification practice.[33] The better view is that the President is required to communicate a Senate condition as a part of the instrument of ratification—unless, of course, the Senate expressly waives the requirement.

The revised *Restatement*, regardless of the position taken on the scope of presidential authority in the face of Senate "silence," should make clear that presidential discretion is diminished if the Senate consents to a treaty on the express condition that specified material be transmitted with the instrument of ratification, as it did—without objection by the executive branch—in approving the Panama Canal Treaties.[34] Such a condition (subject to the possible implication of the President's "communication" power[35]) would rest upon approximately the same constitutional footing as a condition providing that the Senate or Congress participate in the termination process.[36] If the Senate

[32] The so-called Niagara Reservation could be viewed as such a condition. In 1950, the United States and Canada reached an agreement governing the use of the Niagara River, designed to protect the scenic beauty of Niagara Falls and to allow diversion of waters from the river for generation of hydroelectric power. Convention on Uses of the Waters of the Niagara River, Feb. 27, 1950, United States-Canada, 1 UST 694, TIAS No. 2130. The U.S. Senate, uncertain as to how the U.S. share of the waters should be utilized, adopted a "reservation" to the treaty providing that the question would be resolved by an act of Congress, and that the water would not be utilized in the interim. The Government of Canada accepted the reservation, and the treaty entered into force. Henkin, *The Treaty Makers and the Law Makers: The Niagara Reservation,* 56 COLUM. L. REV. 1151, 1155–58 (1956). Congress then failed to take action on the issue over the next 5 years, a delay that proved too much for "the energetic Mr. [Robert] Moses of the New York Power Authority," who brought suit to have the reservation declared null and to have a license for hydroelectric development issued to the authority. *Id.* at 1159. The United States Court of Appeals for the District of Columbia Circuit held that the reservation was not really part of the treaty, as it dealt with a matter of purely domestic concern, and therefore was not legally enforceable; the Supreme Court, however, vacated the appeals court's judgment. Power Auth. v. Federal Power Comm'n, 247 F.2d 538 (D.C. Cir.), *vacated as moot sub nom.* American Pub. Power Ass'n v. Power Auth., 355 U.S. 64 (1957).

[33] *See* 14 M. WHITEMAN, *supra* note 7, at 138–39.

[34] *See supra* note 17 and accompanying text.

[35] *See supra* note 29.

[36] The question whether the Senate may condition its consent to a treaty by prescribing the procedure the President must follow in terminating it gave rise to considerable controversy in the aftermath of President Carter's unilateral termination effective January 1, 1980, of the Mutual Defense Treaty between the United States and the Nationalist Chinese on Taiwan (Treaty of Mutual Defense, Dec. 2, 1954, United States-China, 6 UST 433, TIAS No. 3178). The Department of Justice, relying upon the President's position as the nation's "sole representative in foreign affairs," argued that the President alone can determine whether a treaty should be terminated. The Department cited in support the dictum of Justice Sutherland in United States v. Curtiss-Wright Export Corp., 299 U.S. at 319, that the President is the "sole organ" of the United States in foreign policy. *See infra* note 131.

can validly accomplish the latter by conditioning its consent to a treaty, as the draft *Restatement* concludes it "presumably" can,[37] then presumably it can thus accomplish the former as well. Each condition would be "applicable to the treaty before it" and have a "plausible relation to its adoption."[38]

Effect of Senate Conditions

The legal effect of the inclusion of Senate conditions in the U.S. instrument of ratification depends on the response of the other signatory. The United States is effectively placed in the position of making a "counteroffer,"[39] and U.S. practice is, accordingly, to place the other signatory on notice of such conditions prior to the exchange of instruments of ratification.[40] Refusal of the other state to exchange instruments of ratification constitutes rejection of the treaty.[41] Under such circumstances, the treaty and the Senate's conditions are therefore without effect, both domestically and internationally. If, on the other hand, the other signatory expressly accepts the Senate's conditions upon exchange of the instruments of ratification, both the text of the treaty and the Senate's conditions take effect internationally and, if the treaty is self-executing, become the law of the land.[42]

Is the other signatory to the treaty, upon exchanging instruments of ratification with U.S. representatives, nonetheless bound by those conditions if it makes no comment regarding the Senate's conditions? The question gave rise to some debate during consideration of the SALT II Treaty by the Senate Foreign Relations Committee. The author advised the committee that "[i]f

---

The Senate Foreign Relations Committee did not accept this view, believing that either the Senate acting alone (by attaching a condition to a treaty) or the Congress as a whole (by statute) could constitutionally limit the President's authority to terminate a treaty. The committee based its reasoning on the separation of powers analysis in Justice Jackson's concurring opinion in the *Steel Seizure Case.* Jackson argued that independent presidential authority is at its height when Congress expressly authorizes or approves an action, is at its nadir when Congress manifests its disapproval, and is in a middle, "twilight" zone when Congress is silent. Youngstown Sheet & Tube Co. v. Sawyer, 343 U.S. 579, 635–38 (1952) (Jackson, J., concurring). When Congress disapproves of a presidential action, the Justice said, the President may act only if Congress is without power over the subject. *Ibid. See generally* Glennon, *Treaty Process Reform: Saving Constitutionalism without Destroying Diplomacy,* 52 U. CIN. L. REV. (forthcoming, 1983).

The reporters of the American Law Institute support the Senate's position in the proposed text of the new *Restatement.* DRAFT RESTATEMENT, *supra* note 7, §352, Reporters' Note 3.

37 DRAFT RESTATEMENT, *supra* note 7, §352, Reporters' Note 3.

38 *Ibid.*

39 *See, e.g.,* T. ELIAS, THE MODERN LAW OF TREATIES 28 (1974).

40 14 M. WHITEMAN, *supra* note 7, at 138.

41 T. ELIAS, *supra* note 39, at 28–29; 14 M. WHITEMAN, *supra* note 7, at 140–41.

42 As the "supreme law of the land," U.S. treaties enjoy equal status with federal statutes. U.S. CONST. art. VI, cl. 2. The Supreme Court has held, however, that insofar as a treaty is a contract, its duties must be carried out by a political branch of the Government and not by the judiciary. Foster v. Neilson, 27 U.S. (2 Pet.) 253, 314 (1829). Thus, treaty terms requiring legislative action are not enforced by the courts until Congress has enacted the appropriate legislation.

There is some controversy as to whether a treaty becomes law for domestic purposes on the date it enters into force or on the date the President formally proclaims it. DRAFT RESTATEMENT, *supra* note 7, §316, Comment *b.* The question is of minor importance, as Presidents are generally swift to issue such proclamations. *See ibid.*

the Soviet Union proceeds with the exchange of instruments of ratification, its silence constitutes assent to the treaties as modified by the United States."[43] Eugene V. Rostow,[44] however, sharply disagreed in testimony before the committee[45] and in a subsequent letter.[46] "[A] reservation has the same legal effect as a letter from my mother," he said.[47] Elaborating, Professor Rostow suggested that an amendment to the text of a treaty is of greater legal force than a reservation,[48] and that, in any event, "silence would not be acceptance."[49]

Rostow is mistaken in his conclusion that the legal effect of treaty reservations is different from that of amendments. The mistake may derive from the confusing interface between principles of domestic ratification law and those of international law. In domestic law, the Senate may condition its consent to treaties in either of two ways. It may amend its resolution of ratification by adding material (normally called a reservation, understanding, interpretation, declaration, or statement), or it may amend the resolution of ratification by inserting a condition that the text of the treaty be amended. Strictly speaking, the Senate does not "amend" the treaty text; it consents to ratification by the President on the condition that *he* amend the text upon ratification.[50] Each form of alteration is equally binding on the President, however, if he chooses to exchange instruments of ratification.[51] International law, similarly,

[43] Memorandum from Michael J. Glennon and Frederick S. Tipson to members of the Senate Foreign Relations Committee (June 25, 1979), *reprinted in* 4 *SALT II Treaty: Hearings on Ex. Y Before the Senate Comm. on Foreign Relations,* 96th Cong., 1st Sess. 18, 23 (1979) [hereinafter cited as *SALT II Hearings*].

[44] Professor Rostow appeared as chairman of the Committee on the Present Danger, a group opposed to ratification of the SALT II Treaty.

[45] 4 *SALT II Hearings, supra* note 43, at 1–15.

[46] *Id.* at 15–17. The letter was also signed by Professor Rostow's Yale Law School colleagues, Joseph W. Bishop, Robert H. Bork, Leon Lipson, Myres S. McDougal, and William M. Reisman.

[47] *Id.* at 13; *see also* 2 *SALT II Hearings, supra* note 43, at 393–94.

[48] Professor Rostow engaged in the following colloquy with Senator Joseph Biden:

> Senator BIDEN. . . . If the reservation is adopted by the U.S. Senate, and the Soviets go forward with the treaty accepting our stated interpretation—
>
> Mr. ROSTOW. That is the same drama we had in 1972. That is exactly the problem of the unilateral interpretations in 1972, which were sold to you and the Senate as grounds for abrogating the treaty. The Soviets paid no attention to our unilateral interpretations, and we did nothing about it when they were violated.
>
> Senator BIDEN. I am told by counsel that a reservation becomes a full part of the treaty. Assume that counsel is right that it does, would you then have a problem?
>
> . . . .
>
> Mr. ROSTOW. I made a list of other problems on which we think amendments or reservations are necessary and I certainly should prefer amendments. I am happy to know that your counsel thinks that a reservation becomes part of the treaty, and I will be glad to talk with him about it afterward.

2 *SALT II Hearings, supra* note 43, at 393–94.

[49] 4 *id.* at 14.

[50] *See infra* note 51.

[51] As noted above, the label used by the Senate is legally irrelevant. 14 M. WHITEMAN, *supra* note 7, at 140. Thus, a Senate amendment to its resolution of ratification providing that a given article of the treaty is without force and effect would be every bit as effective as an actual "amendment to the text" of that treaty striking the article in question.

regards a reservation to a bilateral treaty as tantamount to a proposed amendment.[52] The principal reason that the Senate sometimes prefers the "reservation" mode to the "amendment" mode is diplomatic: domestic political considerations in the nonreserving state may make it easier for its government to accept a treaty alteration that is cosmetically less glaring.[53]

The question whether nonobjection constitutes tacit acceptance of a reservation to a bilateral treaty is more difficult. While tacit acceptance of reservations to multilateral treaties has received considerable attention,[54] that of reservations to bilateral treaties has not. Given the universal acceptance of reference to contract law for the principle that a reservation to a bilateral treaty puts the reserving state in the position of rejecting the treaty and proposing a counteroffer,[55] it is not unreasonable to refer to contract law for answers to ancillary questions, such as when a counteroffer has been accepted. Principles of contract law would suggest that if the other state proceeds to the affirmative act of exchanging instruments of ratification after having been placed on notice that an alteration is demanded, it has accepted the counteroffer. Because of the dearth of authority among traditional sources of customary international law, however, it cannot be asserted that the matter is free from doubt.

In any event, the question is largely academic because the United States generally obtains the express acceptance of Senate conditions by the other

[52] The use of the terms "amendment" and "reservation" is thus somewhat confusing. As pointed out above, the Senate cannot itself amend a treaty. *See supra* text at note 50. Nor can it really enter a reservation; rather, it can impose, as a condition for its advice and consent, the requirement that the President enter a reservation. DRAFT RESTATEMENT, *supra* note 7, §305, Reporters' Note 3. In either event, the President must, *under international law,* return to the other signatory to ask consent to a new treaty. *See supra* notes 39–41 and accompanying text; *see also* 1 L. OPPENHEIM, INTERNATIONAL LAW 914 (H. Lauterpacht 8th ed. 1955) (calling a reservation "the refusal of an offer and the making of a fresh offer"); Parry, *The Law of Treaties,* in MANUAL OF PUBLIC INTERNATIONAL LAW 175, 194 (M. Sørensen ed. 1968) (stating flatly that "[a] reservation constitutes a proposal of an amendment of the treaty text").

The Vienna Convention on the Law of Treaties uses the term "reservation" to encompass both types of Senate conditions, providing in Article 2(1)(d) that " 'reservation' means a unilateral statement, *however phrased or named,* made by a State, when signing, ratifying, accepting, approving or acceding to a treaty, whereby it purports to exclude or to modify the legal effect of certain provisions of the treaty in their application to that State." Vienna Convention on the Law of Treaties, May 23, 1969, UN Doc. A/CONF.39/27, *reprinted in* 63 AJIL 875 (1969), 8 ILM 679 (1969) (emphasis added) [hereinafter cited as Vienna Convention].

[53] To cite one example, the Senate Foreign Relations Committee recommended to the Senate that changes to the Panama Canal Treaties other than those recommended by the committee itself not take the form of amendments. S. EXEC. REP. NO. 12, *supra* note 16, at 13.

[54] Brazil, *Some Reflections on the Vienna Convention on the Law of Treaties,* 6 FED. L. REV. 223 (1975); Comment, *Reservations to Multilateral Treaties: How International Doctrine Reflects World Vision,* 23 HARV. INT'L L.J. 71 (1982); *see generally* the Vienna Convention, *supra* note 52. While section II of the Vienna Convention is entitled simply "Reservations"—a shortening of the title "Reservations to Multilateral Treaties" used in an earlier draft—the President of the Vienna Conference, Professor Ago, said that the change should be understood as reflecting the fact that all reservations are, by definition, to multilateral treaties, since, strictly speaking, a so-called reservation to a bilateral treaty constitutes a proposal for a new treaty and not a true reservation at all. Brazil, *supra,* at 230–31.

[55] *See, e.g.,* Parry, *supra* note 52, at 194.

party, at least with respect to major bilateral treaties. Both sides sign a protocol of exchange of the instruments of ratification, which spells out the legal effect to be accorded all material in those instruments and thus effectively binds each party explicitly to any conditions entered by the other.[56]

The practice of executing a protocol of exchange, hitherto a relatively obscure stage in the process of treaty ratification, can be expected to gain greater prominence as attention focuses increasingly on the need for clarity and precision in treaty commitments. The evolution of the practice was hastened greatly during the Senate's consideration of the Panama Canal Treaties[57] and the SALT II Treaty.[58] A condition added to the so-called Neutrality Treaty required, apparently for the first time, that a protocol of exchange be executed and that it include one particular condition.[59] Curiously, however, the "inclusion" requirement applied only to that one condition, and not to other material added by the Senate to the instrument of ratification.[60]

The Senate Foreign Relations Committee took a great step towards clarifying this increasingly confused situation in its resolution of ratification concerning the SALT II Treaty.[61] The resolution dispensed with the outmoded lexicon of ratification law and, instead of using such labels as "amendments," "reservations," and "understandings," it set forth three explicit categories of conditions: (1) those that need not be formally communicated to or agreed to by the Soviet Union; (2) those to be formally communicated to the Soviet Union, but need not necessarily be agreed to by it; and (3) those that would require the explicit agreement of the Soviet Union.[62] This tripartite structure, the committee noted, "should avoid the ambiguities and potential misunderstandings inherent in the traditional designation."[63] It continued:

> Those designations may still be useful as indicators of a sponsor's intent. But as to whether Soviet involvement is required either through formal notice or agreement, the designations themselves would not have to carry the entire weight indicating the Senate's intentions. Placement in a particular section of the Resolution of Ratification should leave no doubt on this score.[64]

[56] *See* S. EXEC. REP. NO. 14, 96th Cong., 1st Sess. 33 (1979); DRAFT RESTATEMENT, *supra* note 7, §323, Comment *b;* 14 M. WHITEMAN, *supra* note 7, at 139. *See generally id.* at 138. *See also* discussion *supra* note 17 and accompanying text.

[57] Treaty concerning the Permanent Neutrality and Operation of the Panama Canal, Sept. 7, 1977, United States-Panama, TIAS No. 10,029; Treaty on the Panama Canal, Sept. 7, 1977, United States-Panama, TIAS No. 10,030.

[58] S. EXEC. DOC. Y, 96th Cong., 1st Sess. (1979).

[59] *See* 124 CONG. REC. 7187 (1978).

[60] *Senate Additions to the Panama Canal Treaties,* DEP'T ST. BULL., No. 2014, May 1978, at 52, 53.

[61] S. EXEC. REP. NO. 14, *supra* note 56, at 72–78.

[62] *Ibid.* The committee's chairman, Senator Frank Church, and ranking minority member, Senator Jacob Javits, previously had received assurances in an exchange of letters with Secretary of State Cyrus Vance that the President would respect the Senate's wishes on this matter, as expressed in the resolution. *Id.* at 31–32.

[63] *Id.* at 35.

[64] *Ibid.*

II. Executive Treaty-making Powers

Nonbinding Adherence to a Treaty

This article has thus far discussed specific aspects of the treaty-making process in which participation by the Senate is constitutionally appropriate. Participation by the Senate (or Congress) in certain other aspects of that process is not constitutionally mandated. A prime example of authority properly regarded as exclusively executive is the articulation of policy intentions not rising to the level of international obligations.

The most prominent recent example of such a declaration is that made by the Carter administration with respect to the so-called Interim Agreement, part of the SALT I Treaty package.[65] Immediately prior to the expiration date of the Interim Agreement and with no hope of reaching prompt agreement on a successor instrument, the United States and the Soviet Union indicated their intent to continue to adhere to its terms. Secretary of State Cyrus Vance, on September 23, 1977, issued the following statement:

> In order to maintain the status quo while SALT II negotiations are being completed, the United States declares its intention not to take any action inconsistent with the provisions of the Interim Agreement on Certain Measures with Respect to the Limitations of Strategic Offensive Arms which expires October 3, 1977, and with the goals of these ongoing negotiations, provided that the Soviet Union exercises similar restraint.[66]

The next day, September 24, the official Soviet news agency, Tass, reported in English from Moscow that the Soviet Government had made the following statement:

> In accordance with the readiness expressed by both sides to complete within the near future the work on a new agreement limiting strategic offensive arms and in the interests of maintaining the status quo while the talks on the new agreement are being concluded, the Soviet Union expresses its intention to keep from any actions incompatible with the provisions of the Interim Agreement [on] some measures pertaining to the limitations of strategic offensive arms which expired on October 3, 1977, and ending with the goals of the talks that are being conducted provided that the United States of America shows the same restraint.[67]

Such unilateral declarations, under certain circumstances, can constitute binding international obligations. Declarations made in 1905 by Chinese diplomats concerning future railway construction in Manchuria were later held by the League of Nations Commission of Inquiry to constitute a binding commitment with the force and effect of "a formal agreement."[68] In the *Eastern*

[65] Interim Agreement on the Limitation of Strategic Offensive Arms, May 26, 1972, United States-Soviet Union, 23 UST 3462, TIAS No. 7504.

[66] *Statement by Secretary Vance, September 23,* 77 Dep't St. Bull. 642 (1977).

[67] 1 Foreign Relations Law, *supra* note 19, at 34.

[68] Garner, *The International Binding Force of Unilateral Oral Declarations,* 27 AJIL 493, 497 (1933) (quoting the League of Nations Commission of Inquiry).

Greenland case of 1933, declarations of the Minister of Foreign Affairs of Norway made to his Danish counterpart were held by the Permanent Court of International Justice to be binding upon Norway.[69] Most recently, the International Court of Justice, in the 1974 *Nuclear Tests* cases,[70] held that a series of public statements by the President of France, the French Ambassador to New Zealand, the French Foreign Minister, and the French Minister of Defense constituted legally binding commitments by France to refrain from atmospheric nuclear testing.[71]

Objective or Subjective Intent?

Under the Court's analysis, the sine qua non of a binding unilateral declaration is intent. Unless "it is the intention of the State making the declaration that it should become bound," the Court said, no legal obligation obtains.[72] On the other hand, "if given publicly"—"even though not made within the context of international negotiations"—an understanding "with an intent to be bound" does confer a legal obligation.[73]

It is not readily apparent that intent to make an agreement was absent with respect to the simultaneous statements of the United States and the Soviet Union regarding the Interim Agreement.[74] The concept of "objective" intent is a commonplace in U.S. law.[75] "Conscious parallelism" between two parties' actions can be evidence of objective intent,[76] and it takes little imagination to find "conscious parallelism" in the statements of the United States and the Soviet Union. Indeed, as a domestic legal matter, it would be disturbing if a

[69] Legal Status of Eastern Greenland (Den. v. Nor.), 1933 PCIJ, ser. A/B, No. 53.

[70] Nuclear Tests (Austl. v. Fr.), 1974 ICJ REP. 253; Nuclear Tests (N.Z. v. Fr.), 1974 ICJ REP. 457 (Judgments of Dec. 20).

[71] *Id.* at 474–75. *Compare* Franck, *Word Made Law: The Decision of the ICJ in the Nuclear Test Cases,* 69 AJIL 612 (1975) (viewing the cases as legitimately extending a principle developed in an earlier line of cases and as providing a useful new vehicle for international commitments), *with* A. Rubin, *The International Legal Effects of Unilateral Declarations,* 71 *id.* at 1 (1977) (criticizing the cases as contrary to existing law and as likely to inhibit world leaders in communicating their intentions).

[72] Nuclear Tests (N.Z. v. Fr.), 1974 ICJ REP. at 472.

[73] *Ibid.*

[74] *See supra* notes 66–67 and accompanying text.

[75] In contract law, an objective standard is virtually always used to determine intent. Judge Learned Hand said that the law will not depart from the objective measure of intent even "if it were proved by twenty bishops" that a party's intent was different from that suggested by the objective standard. Hotchkiss v. National City Bank, 200 F.Supp. 287, 293 (S.D.N.Y. 1911). The law of torts deems a person to have intended the effects a reasonably prudent person would have foreseen as inevitable from his actions. Thus, a bicyclist who runs down a pedestrian on a wide, nearly empty sidewalk is liable for the intentional tort of battery, despite his insistence that the collision was an accident. Mercer v. Corbin, 117 Ind. 450, 20 N.E. 132 (1889). Even criminal law, which usually insists on proof of intent, deems a killing to have been in "a heat of passion" only if an ordinary person would have been provoked to homicide by the circumstances. The leading English case is Bedder v. Director of Public Prosecutions, [1954] 2 All E.R. 801 (H.L.), in which the Court refused to consider the special susceptibility of an impotent man.

[76] *See* United States v. Paramount Pictures, Inc., 334 U.S. 131 (1948); Interstate Circuit, Inc. v. United States, 306 U.S. 208 (1939).

President could escape altogether the constitutional consequences of concluding a binding international agreement simply by calling it something else.[77]

To assume that an agreement existed, however, does not dispose of the issue. United States jurisprudence notwithstanding, it seems clear that international law, at least at this point in its development, looks only to subjective intent. The International Court of Justice strongly implied in the *Nuclear Tests* cases[78] that a nation's own characterization of its act is controlling. It emphasized that a state is "legally required to follow a course of conduct *consistent with the declaration.*"[79] The United States declared that its statement concerning the Interim Agreement is "non-binding and non-obligatory,"[80] so it seems

[77] Professor Phillip Kurland has protested against "the executive usurpation of Congressional authority in working out secret—or at least unapproved—agreements with foreign countries," and questioned why it is that "for some reason or other we are always reminded that because it is a Constitution we are expounding we need not be concerned with what it says." Kurland, *The Impotence of Reticence,* 1968 DUKE L.J. 619, 626.

Kurland feared that the "disease" afflicting the separation of powers doctrine "appeared to be terminal." *Id.* at 261. Since 1968, however, despite much talk in Congress, nothing substantial has been done. *See Treaties and Executive Agreements,* 71 ASIL PROC. 235 (1977). For the principal congressional proposals, see H.R. 4438, 94th Cong., 1st Sess. (1975) (Morgan-Zablocki); *Congressional Review of International Agreements: Hearings on H.R. 4438 Before the Subcomm. on International Security and Scientific Affairs of the House Comm. on International Relations,* 94th Cong., 2d Sess. (1976); S. Res. 24, 95th Cong., 1st Sess. (1977) (Clark Treaty Powers Resolution); *Treaty Powers Resolution: Hearings Before the Senate Comm. on Foreign Relations,* 94th Cong., 2d. Sess. (1976) (hearings on earlier version of Clark Resolution); *Treaty Termination: Hearings on S. Res. 15 Before the Senate Comm. on Foreign Relations,* 96th Cong., 1st Sess. (1979). During this period, Congress did pass the Case Act, 1 U.S.C. §1126 (1976), requiring the Executive to transmit all executive agreements to the Senate Foreign Relations Committee. Had the joint Soviet-American statements on SALT I constituted an international agreement, it would have been required, of course, that they be transmitted under the provisions of the Case Act.

[78] 1974 ICJ REP. 253; 1974 ICJ REP. 457. *See also* the opinions of Senators Dick Clark and George McGovern that the United States had not entered into an agreement with the Soviet Government by virtue of the parallel unilateral policy declarations by the two Governments (text at notes 66–67 *supra*):

> The arguments are made that under American antitrust law an agreement would be found to exist, as it would under American contract law. This may be, but we would point out that international law, perhaps shortsightedly, has not adopted the test applied by our antitrust statutes, and that no court in this country has ever found a contract where no party intended one to exist and where all parties *ab initio* expressly refused to be bound.

S. REP. NO. 499, 95th Cong., 1st Sess. 13–14 (1977).

[79] 1974 ICJ REP. at 267 (emphasis added). The instructions of the U.S. Department of State to U.S. diplomatic personnel on the criteria to be used in determining what constitutes an international agreement provide in part as follows: "The central requirement is that the parties intend their undertaking to be of legal, and not merely political or personal, effect. Documents intended to have political or moral weight, but not intended to be legally binding, are not international agreements." Airgram from the Department of State to all U.S. diplomatic posts, Mar. 9, 1976 (State Dep't reference No. A-1394), *reprinted in* 1 FOREIGN RELATIONS LAW, *supra* note 19, at 15.

[80] *See* letter from Herbert J. Hansell, State Department Legal Adviser, to John J. Sparkman, Chairman, Senate Foreign Relations Committee, Sept. 28, 1977, *reprinted in* S. REP. NO. 499, *supra* note 78, at 9–10 (quoting Paul Warnke, *id.* at 9 n.2).

clear that the element of subjective intent was lacking. This is true whether the statement is regarded as part of an agreement or as a unilateral declaration. Either can, under international law, be binding or nonbinding, depending apparently on the nation's own characterization of its intent.

The draft *Restatement* does not address the question whether objective intent will be sufficient to render a statement obligatory. It simply states that "[s]ince an international agreement is one intended to be legally binding and having legal consequences,"[81] the pertinent draft provisions do "not apply to agreements not intended to have such legal character or consequences."[82] But it observes that "non-binding agreements" have been "made at various times in American history" and notes the 1977 U.S.-Soviet action without suggesting that it may have constituted a binding agreement.[83]

The draft *Restatement*'s benign treatment of nonbinding international actions is justified. To be sure, there is a danger that nonbinding agreements or unilateral declarations will be used to circumvent constitutionally required procedures for making agreements. But this problem is not truly analogous to the problem some have seen in the circumvention of the treaty process by executive agreement.[84] A President who circumvents the requirement of Senate advice and consent by making a sole executive agreement with another nation generally achieves, at least on the international level, the same result—a binding agreement.[85] But a President who sidesteps the Senate by issuing a nonbinding declaration parallel to a declaration issued by another nation pays a price: in the event of "noncompliance," he cannot accuse the other state of a *legal* violation.[86] Nevertheless, nonbinding international statements do serve a purpose.

The flexibility to employ such diplomatic tools is an important ingredient in the process of forming stronger and clearer reciprocal international expectations. The Final Act of the Helsinki Conference,[87] for example, has served an extraordinarily useful purpose as a nonbinding statement of principle concerning future conduct, and though nonobligatory, its authority has suffered little. Yet its existence would be doubtful had ratification as a multilateral agreement been required, and principles of constitutionalism would have derived little strength from such a complication.

[81] DRAFT RESTATEMENT, *supra* note 7, §301, Comment *e*.

[82] *Ibid.*

[83] *Id.*, §301, Reporters' Note 2.

[84] *See supra* note 77.

[85] *Compare* DRAFT RESTATEMENT, *supra* note 7, §308 (describing such presidential actions as international agreements) *with id.*, §324 (stating that all international agreements are binding on the parties).

[86] Professor Schachter has commented that nonbinding agreements do remove the matters dealt with from domestic jurisdiction and give rise to a right of the parties to raise questions of noncompliance. *See* Schachter, *The Twilight Existence of Nonbinding International Agreements,* 71 AJIL 296 (1977).

[87] Final Act of the Conference on Security and Cooperation in Europe, Aug. 1, 1975, 73 DEP'T ST. BULL. 323 (1975). *See generally* R. BILDER, MANAGING THE RISKS OF INTERNATIONAL AGREEMENT (1981).

The Need for Clarity

It is extremely important, however, that executive branch officials promulgating such a declaration make clear that it is not intended to be binding.[88] It should not be necessary—and it may not always be possible—to clarify intentions retrospectively. After the *Nuclear Test* cases,[89] nations can no longer afford—from the standpoint of their own self-interest—to make statements that leave the question of obligation unclear. The recurrent need to sift through equivocal diplomatic undertakings for indicia of intent (or lack of intent) could lead, ultimately, to the use of objective intent in determining whether an agreement exists. It would be regrettable if the articulation of public policy were chilled by the fear that even an express disclaimer might be ineffective in negating an inference of intent to be bound.[90] Clearer reciprocal international expectations require more public discussion, not less, and they also require confidence on the part of the "speaking" nation that it can control the legal consequences of its speech. Doubt induces silence, and silence, confusion. Nonbinding unilateral declarations are useful diplomatic tools in counteracting that doubt, and can form the base for a "track record" on matters of high suspicion. That track record may lead, in the end, to a formal agreement. But no such evolution of confidence is possible without a starting point of precision, and no such precision is possible without a new diplomatic will to clarity.[91]

[88] The Chairman of the Senate Foreign Relations Committee expressed concern, for example, about the apparent breadth of international commitments entered into at the economic summit meeting in Bonn on July 17, 1978. The Assistant Secretary of State for Congressional Relations responded in part as follows: "While the declaration issued in Bonn is an important political commitment, it is not an international agreement within the meaning of the United States law or international law since the parties did not evidence an intent to be legally bound." *See* 73 AJIL 130 (1979).

[89] 1974 ICJ REP. 253; 1974 ICJ REP. 457.

[90] *See* Rubin, *supra* note 71. *But see* Franck, *supra* note 71.

[91] An example of the exactness for which diplomats should strive is the statement of Soviet President Leonid Brezhnev delivered by Soviet Foreign Minister Andrei Gromyko before the United Nations General Assembly on June 15, 1982, concerning Soviet policy with respect to the first use of nuclear weapons. President Brezhnev said, "The Soviet Union assumes an obligation not to be the first to use nuclear weapons. This obligation shall become effective immediately, on the moment it is made public from the rostrum of the General Assembly." Nossiter, *Soviet Forswears Using A-Arms First,* N.Y. Times, June 16, 1982, at A1, col. 3.

An example of the ambiguity that diplomats must avoid is the statement of Foreign Minister Gromyko to the Supreme Soviet on July 6, 1978. In the process of awarding credit to the Soviet Union "for a whole number" of arms control treaties, Gromyko made reference to the Interim Agreement, "which in 1977 was extended and continues to be in force in conformity with the existing arrangement for the period of talks now in progress on concluding a new agreement." Gromyko, *On the Draft Law to Govern the Procedure for Conclusion, Execution and Denunciation of International Treaties of the USSR,* INT'L AFF. (Moscow), September 1978, at 6. Did the Soviet Foreign Minister intend to indicate that the Soviets continue to regard themselves as legally obligated by the terms of the Interim Agreement? Did the Soviets misunderstand U.S. intentions at the time the Agreement expired? Or is this merely an inaccurate "shorthand" method of summarizing a more complex legal situation? Soviet acceptance of an asymmetrical legal structure

To return to the constitutional question: if the President can "make an international agreement dealing with any matter that falls within his independent powers under the Constitution," as the draft *Restatement* says he can,[92] then he surely can exercise those same powers in a manner that results in no binding international agreement.

III. Congressional Limitations on Executive Powers

Duties of a Signatory: The Vienna Convention

A somewhat different issue is raised by U.S. adherence to the terms of the SALT II Treaty. The Treaty, submitted to the Senate on June 22, 1979,[93] has remained before it since that date, with no floor consideration thus far. A resolution of ratification was reported by the Committee on Foreign Relations on November 9, 1979.[94] In the absence of Senate action, however, under Rule XXXVII of the Standing Rules of the Senate,[95] the Treaty was taken off the Executive Calendar at the beginning of the 97th Congress in January 1981, and returned to the Committee on Foreign Relations.

Nonetheless, President Ronald Reagan, who during the 1980 campaign referred to the Treaty as "fatally flawed,"[96] indicated on May 31, 1982: "As for existing agreements, we will refrain from actions which undercut them so long as the Soviet Union shows equal restraint."[97]

If the Chief Executive, as a matter of nonbinding policy, can adhere to the terms of an agreement no longer in effect—as President Carter did[98] with respect to the Interim Agreement[99]—then it would seem that, a fortiori, he can also adhere as a matter of policy to the terms of an agreement that has not yet taken effect. The President would in both instances be acting pursuant to whatever independent authority he might bring to bear. Indeed, with respect to a signed but unratified agreement, an additional source of authority

---

concerning the Interim Agreement would be surprising, but if Gromyko's words are taken literally, a binding intent might reasonably be inferred from them. Unfortunately, Soviet leaders have not been alone in the imprecision of their legal references. *See supra* text accompanying note 53.

92 Draft Restatement, *supra* note 7, §308. The statement seems a truism: it is self-evident that the President can act within the scope of his independent powers. The debate has centered on the scope of those powers—where his end and those of Congress or the Senate begin. *Id.*, §308, Reporters' Note 1; *see supra* note 77. In the case of arms control declarations, the ultimate issue may be an impoundment question: whether the President, as Commander-in-Chief, can refuse to spend certain funds Congress has directed him to spend. *See generally* L. Tribe, American Constitutional Law 193–98 (1978).

93 S. Exec. Doc. Y, *supra* note 58.

94 S. Exec. Rep. No. 14, *supra* note 56, at 26.

95 Rule XXXVII, Standing Rules of the United States Senate, *reprinted in* Senate Comm. on Rules and Administration, 95th Cong., 1st Sess., Standing Rules of the United States Senate and Provisions of the Legislative Reorganization Acts of 1946 and 1970 and the Budget Control Act Relating to the Operation of the Senate 65–67 (Comm. Print 1977).

96 Lindsey, *Reagan Urges Ban on Arms Pact Unless Soviet Withdraws Troops,* N.Y. Times, Jan, 26, 1980, at 10, col. 5.

97 Memorial Day, 1982, 18 Weekly Comp. Pres. Doc. 730 (May 31, 1982).

98 *Statement by Vance, supra* note 66, at 642. (The Secretary of State made the actual statement.)

99 Interim Agreement on the Limitation of Strategic Offensive Arms, *supra* note 65.

arguably exists: no event has occurred that has diminished whatever authority flows from the President's signature. In contrast, the President's signature to a treaty (or agreement) that has been ratified—but has since expired—no longer confers any authority.[100] But what power, if any, actually flows from the mere act of signature?

The question is addressed by Article 18 of the Vienna Convention on the Law of Treaties,[101] which provides as follows:

> A State is obliged to refrain from acts which would defeat the object and purpose of a treaty when:
>
> (a) it has signed the treaty or has exchanged instruments constituting the treaty subject to ratification, acceptance, or approval, until it shall have made its intention clear not to become a party to the treaty; or
>
> (b) it has expressed a consent to be bound by the treaty, pending the entry into force of the treaty and provided that such entry into force is not unduly delayed.[102]

The Treaty Clause of the Constitution provides, however, that the "President . . . shall have power, by and with the advice and consent of the Senate, to make treaties provided two thirds of the Senators present concur. . . ."[103] Would Article 18 of the Convention, by its requirement that a signatory to a treaty "refrain from acts which would defeat the object and purpose" of the treaty, undermine the constitutional role of the Senate by allowing the President to incur treaty obligations without the Senate's approval?

The answer depends upon what rule would apply in the absence of that stated by Article 18. If the rule of Article 18 would effect no change in the status quo, it would represent no threat to the constitutional order. On the other hand, if the rule of Article 18 embodies a precept of customary international law that has emerged only recently, the constitutional and international legal systems may not be in harmony.

The Convention,[104] though not ratified by the United States, has been said to represent merely a codification of customary international law with respect to treaties.[105] That view may be oversimplified, however; other authorities have pointed out that while some provisions of the Convention merely set forth the existing international legal principles, other provisions represent an effort at law reform, reflecting the notions of the draftsmen as to what "progressive development" ought to take place.[106] Into which category does Article 18 fall?

[100] According to Justice Jackson's analysis of presidential powers in the *Steel Seizure Case*, the President's power is most restricted where he acts contrary to the will of Congress. Youngstown Sheet & Tube Co. v. Sawyer, 343 U.S. at 637 (Jackson, J., concurring). Where Congress—or the body charged with approving treaties, the Senate—has approved a treaty to be effective a given length of time and no longer, it might be presumed that it is contrary to the Senate's expressed will that the treaty remain in effect past the expiration date, unless the termination date is to be regarded as mere surplusage.

[101] Vienna Convention, *supra* note 52, Art. 18.

[102] *Ibid.*

[103] U.S. CONST. art. 2, §2, cl. 2.

[104] Vienna Convention, *supra* note 52.

[105] 3 *Panama Canal Treaties: Hearings Before the Senate Comm. on Foreign Relations*, 95th Cong., 1st Sess. 520 (1977) (statement of Professor Dean Rusk).

[106] Professor Rusk would appear to be in the distinct minority in applying this view to the treaty

Several commentators conclude that "[w]hether Article 18 as it now stands is declaratory of prior customary international law is uncertain. There is some authority for that conclusion, but the matter is not free from doubt."[107] In fact, however, the better view would appear to be that Article 18 codified international law as it existed at the time the Vienna Convention was adopted. The question gave rise to considerable controversy during the long process of drafting the Convention.[108] Some scholars, it is true, do believe that the

---

as a whole rather than to certain sections of it. Professor Holloway quotes with approval the statement of Sir Hersch Lauterpacht, who as special rapporteur played a major part in preparing the Convention, that the International Law Commission "is not limited to registering uniform practice. If that were its purpose, its work would be partly nominal and partly redundant." K. HOLLOWAY, MODERN TRENDS IN TREATY LAW 58 (1967). *See also* Goldie, *The International Law Commission and Progressive Development of International Law,* 28 FED. B.J. 25, 26 (1968); Jacobs, *Innovation and Continuity in the Law of Treaties,* 33 MOD. L. REV. 502, 509 (1970); Sinclair, *Vienna Conference on the Law of Treaties,* 19 INT'L & COMP. L.Q. 47, 49–50 (1970).

[107] L. HENKIN, R. PUGH, O. SCHACHTER, & H. SMIT, INTERNATIONAL LAW 604 (1980).

[108] The authors of the first tentative draft convention on the law of treaties (a group of American scholars under the auspices of Harvard Law School) regarded the obligation not to frustrate the terms of treaties pending ratification as one merely of "good faith" and not as legally binding. Draft Convention on the Law of Treaties, 29 AJIL, Supp. 657, 787 (1935).

Professor Brierly, the International Law Commission's first special rapporteur on the law of treaties, agreed with the position of the Harvard Draft Law of Treaties, [1951] 2 Y.B. INT'L L. COMM'N 70, 73, UN Doc. A/CN.4/SER.A/1951/Add.1. Sir Hersch Lauterpacht, Brierly's successor, disagreed, stressing that the obligation is a legal one, and strongly implying that "good faith" is itself a legally binding obligation in international law. Law of Treaties, [1953] *id.* at 90, 110–11, UN Doc. A/CN.4/SER.A/1953/Add.1. Sir Hersch's position was supported by the next two special rapporteurs, Sir Gerald Fitzmaurice and Sir Humphrey Waldock. Law of Treaties, [1956] 2 *id.* at 104, 113, UN Doc. A/CN.4/SER.A/1956/Add.1; Law of Treaties, [1962] 2 *id.* at 27, 46, UN Doc. A/CN.4/SER.A/1962/Add.1.

In 1966, the ILC reported the draft of the Convention on the Law of Treaties, incorporating the position that signatories of treaties have an obligation not to take actions, pending ratification, that would frustrate the purposes of the treaty. Reports of the Commission to the General Assembly, [1966] 2 *id.* at 169, 202, UN Doc. A/6309/Rev.1 [hereinafter cited as Reports]. In so doing, the Commission stated that the proposition was "generally accepted." *Ibid.* The Commission cited the Case Concerning Certain German Interests in Polish Upper Silesia, 1926 PCIJ, ser. A, No. 7, at 30, as authority. Reports, *supra,* at 202. At the same time, the Commission drafted a provision that would have imposed a similar obligation not to frustrate a treaty's terms on states that simply entered into *negotiations* for a treaty, without signing. *Ibid.* The latter provision, as governments commenting on the draft pointed out, would have represented an innovation in international law. *See id.* at 279, 291, 315, 323, 338, 344. The Vienna Conference's Committee of the Whole ultimately deleted the provision; accordingly, it did not become a part of the Convention. S. ROSENNE, THE VIENNA CONVENTION ON THE LAW OF TREATIES 172–73 (1970).

It is important to note that the governmental criticisms were directed at the application of the rule to negotiating parties—a position not incorporated in the Vienna Convention as adopted—and *not* at its application to signatories. The Vienna Conference, of course, retained the obligation of states not to frustrate, pending ratification, the purposes of treaties they have signed. Delegates to the conference seemed generally satisfied that this principle codified existing international law. For the comments of the delegates of Switzerland, India, and the Ukrainian Soviet Socialist Republic, respectively, see UNITED NATIONS CONFERENCE ON THE LAW OF TREATIES, OFFICIAL RECORDS OF THE FIRST SESSION 97, UN Doc. A/CONF.39/11 (comments of M. Bindschendler); *id.* at 98 (comments of Mr. Jagota); *id.* at 100 (comments of Mr. Lukashuk). The application to negotiating states had also given rise to considerable controversy during the deliberations of the ILC. Summary Records of the 788th Meeting, [1965] 1 Y.B. INT'L L. COMM'N 87, 88–94, UN Doc. A/CN.4/SER.A/1965. However, the members of the Commission were generally satisfied with the remainder of the rule although certain members, notably Mssrs. Tabibi and Yasseen, argued that it did represent progressive development. *Ibid.*

article represents progressive development.[109] Others, however, believe that the article represents codification,[110] and there is impressive support for their view. The International Law Commission, in preparing the draft of the Convention, appeared to take this view.[111] International tribunals recognized a signatory's obligation to refrain from acts that would frustrate a treaty's purpose pending ratification long before the Vienna Convention was adopted.[112] The United States,[113] the United Kingdom,[114] and other nations have long recognized such an obligation.[115]

For general background on the Vienna Convention, and the work on Article 18 in particular, see S. ROSENNE, *supra* (providing a guide to the "legislative history" of the Convention); I. SINCLAIR, THE VIENNA CONVENTION ON THE LAW OF TREATIES (1973) (general overview by the Senior Legal Advisor to Her Britannic Majesty's Foreign and Commonwealth Office); Rogoff, *The International Legal Obligations of Signatories to an Unratified Treaty*, 32 ME. L. REV. 263 (1980) (discussing evolution of Article 18, the legal rationales therefor, and its application to certain then pending treaties).

[109] *See* 2 C. HYDE, INTERNATIONAL LAW 1432–33 n.13 (2d. rev. ed. 1945); I. BROWNLIE, PRINCIPLES OF PUBLIC INTERNATIONAL LAW 489 (1966); I. SINCLAIR, *supra* note 108, at 39; Nisot, *L'Article 18 de la Convention de Vienne sur le droit des traités*, 6 REV. BELGE DROIT INT'L 498 (1970–71); D. O'CONNELL, INTERNATIONAL LAW 223 (1970); *cf.* J. MERVYN JONES, RATIFICATION AND FULL POWERS 81 (1949) (submitting that the rule may be somewhat overstated); Morvay, *The Obligation of a State Not to Frustrate the Object of a Treaty Prior to its Entry into Force*, 27 ZEITSCHRIFT FÜR AUSLÄNDISCHES ÖFFENTLICHES RECHT UND VÖLKERRECHT 451, 458 (1967) (stating that the rule formulated by the Vienna Convention either goes beyond customary law or states it in the broadest possible way).

[110] *See* DRAFT RESTATEMENT, *supra* note 7, §314; 1 D. ANZILOTTI, COURS DE DROIT INTERNATIONAL 372–73 (G. Gidel trans. 1929); S. CRANDALL, TREATIES, THEIR MAKING AND ENFORCEMENT 343–44 (2d ed. 1916); T. ELIAS, *supra* note 39, at 26; 3 P. FAUCHILLE, TRAITÉ DE DROIT INTERNATIONAL PUBLIC 319–20 (1926); 1 O. HOIJER, LES TRAITÉS INTERNATIONAUX 136 (1928); K. HOLLOWAY, *supra* note 106, at 28; 1 L. OPPENHEIM, *supra* note 52, at 909; Cavagliere, *Règles générales du droit de la paix*, RECUEIL DES COURS 311, 520 (1929 I); Hassan, *Good Faith in Treaty Formation*, 21 VA. J. INT'L L. 443, 452 (1981); Rogoff, *supra* note 108, at 271–72; *cf.* A. MCNAIR, LAW OF TREATIES 199 (1961) (suggesting that the signing of a treaty may limit freedom of action pending the entry into force of the treaty, but expressing reservations as to the conclusiveness of evidence for the proposition).

[111] "That an obligation of good faith to refrain from acts calculated to frustrate the object of the treaty attaches to a State which has signed a treaty subject to ratification appears to be generally accepted." Reports, *supra* note 108, at 202.

[112] Case Concerning Certain German Interests in Polish Upper Silesia, 1926 PCIJ, ser. A, No. 7, at 30; Megalidis v. Etat turc, 8 Trib. Arb. Mixtes 386, 395 (1929) (holding that "il est de principe que déjà avec la signature d'un Traité et avant sa mise en vigueur, il existe pour les parties contractantes une obligation de ne rien faire qui puisse nuire au Traité en diminuant la portée de ses clauses").

[113] U.S. Secretary of State John Hay, expressing his dissatisfaction over Colombian failure to act in accordance with the U.S.-Colombia Panama Canal Treaty, which Colombia had signed but not ratified, asserted that in signing a treaty states "bind themselves, pending its ratification, . . . to do nothing in contravention of its terms." 2 C. HYDE, *supra* note 109, at 1432–33 n.13.

[114] In 1857, Great Britain's Law Officers advised the Foreign Office that "[n]o act can be properly done by Her Majesty whilst the ratification of the Treaty is under consideration, which may at all affect any of the stipulations of the Treaty." Report by J. D. Harding, Attorney General, and R. Bethell, Queen's Advocate, to the Secretary of State for Foreign Affairs, May 15, 1857 (original on file in the Public Record Office in London, Law Officers' Reports Section, F.O. 83 2242), *reprinted in* A. MCNAIR, *supra* note 110, at 200.

[115] The Final Act of Berlin of Feb. 26, 1885—which provided that "en attendant la ratification, les Puissances signatoires de cet Acte général s'obligent à n'adopter aucune mesure qui serait contraire aux dispositions dudit Acte"—was, according to Sir Hersch Lauterpacht, "no more than

Accordingly, it seems clear that if the United States subscribes to Article 18 through ratification of the Vienna Convention, it would not undermine the role of the Senate in the treaty-making process. The constitutional allocation of power is consistent with a structure appropriate for carrying out the rule set forth in Article 18. The President clearly possesses the authority to sign treaties and, in view of the effect accorded signature by international law, he may constitutionally infer from that signature the further authority to act so as not to defeat the object or purpose of a signed treaty. "The rule of constitutional interpretation announced in *McCulloch* v. *Maryland*," the Supreme Court has said, "that that which was reasonably appropriate and relevant to the exercise of a granted power was to be considered as accompanying the grant, has been so universally applied that it suffices merely to state it."[116] A contrary rule in this context would undermine the ability of the United States to participate in the community of nations, at least to the extent that the ability to make treaties facilitates such participation.

But this does not mean that presidential power is unlimited in either scope or duration. It is important to distinguish between the President's *obligation* to observe the provisions of signed treaties awaiting ratification and his *authority* to do so. Customary international law imposes certain duties upon the United States, and therefore upon the President as its agent in matters of foreign affairs. But international law, of course, can confer no power on the President; only the United States Constitution can do so.[117] It is the Constitution that authorizes him to carry out certain international obligations of the United States. He thus cannot, in refraining from acts that would defeat the object and purpose of a signed treaty, exceed his own independent powers—although those powers are properly viewed, again, as encompassing the authority to carry out obligations incurred by the United States by virtue of its

---

declaratory of an existing principle." Lauterpacht, *Law of Treaties,* [1953] 2 Y.B. INT'L L. COMM'N 90, 110, UN Doc. A/CN.4/SER.A/1953/Add.1.

Professor Holloway states that the Latin American states follow the same principle. *See* K. HOLLOWAY, *supra* note 106, at 46 n.28.

Prior to the time of the French and American Revolutions, ambassadors were regarded as personal agents of their sovereigns, acting with full power to bind their royal clients—who were not free to disavow commitments their ambassadors made in pursuance of their delegated authority. The concept that a state might refuse to ratify a treaty signed on its behalf evolved gradually during the 19th century. *See generally* J. MERVYN JONES, *supra* note 109, at 12, 74–78. Given the existence of authority as early as 1857 for the rule eventually embodied in Article 18, and the lack of early authority for a contrary rule, it seems that the first commentators and practitioners to address the question reached the conclusion of the Vienna Convention. *See supra* notes 110–114.

[116] Marshall v. Gordon, 243 U.S. 521, 537 (1917).

[117] *But see* United States v. Curtiss-Wright Export Corp., 299 U.S. 304 (1936). *Curtiss-Wright* suggests in dictum that the United States Government, in its conduct of foreign policy, possesses not only those powers given, explicitly or implicitly, by the Constitution, but additional, extra-constitutional powers supposedly inherent in the notion of sovereignty. *Id.* at 318. The author of the opinion, Justice Sutherland, rested his argument in part on the idea that the authority of the Crown to bind British subjects in the 13 colonies as to external affairs passed directly, upon independence, not to the governments of the states, but to the Continental Congress. *Id.* at 316–17. Sutherland's historical analysis has been sharply criticized. Levitan, *The Foreign Relations Power: An Analysis of Mr. Justice Sutherland's Theory,* 55 YALE L.J. 467 (1946); Lofgren, *United States v. Curtiss-Wright Export Corp.: An Historical Reassessment,* 83 *id.* at 1 (1973).

status as treaty signatory. Similarly, if the treaty is rejected by the Senate, the President's signature is no longer available as a source of authority, and any adherence, binding or nonbinding, must thereafter flow from his independent powers.

A thornier question arises if the Senate effectively rejects the treaty through inaction; it is unclear at what point authority may no longer flow from signature. It may be that signature diminishes as a source of authority for Article 18 purposes the longer a treaty remains before the Senate, in that inaction can constitute effective rejection. After all, Article 18(a) provides that obligations flow from signature only until a state "shall have made its intention clear not to become a party to the treaty."[118]

Precisely when a state's intention becomes clear, however, is not readily determinable. Given this uncertainty, the Senate is best advised, if it wishes to signal a definite end to obligations under Article 18, simply to return the treaty in question to the President. As this normally is achieved by the adoption of a resolution,[119] the debate on such a resolution would represent an effective referendum on whether authority under Article 18 should be continued. If such a resolution were defeated, the President's political position in declining to act so as to undermine the treaty would surely be bolstered. In addition, defeat could remove any doubt about his legal position in the event that a long period of time had elapsed since the transmittal of the treaty to the Senate.[120] Similarly, should it be the President who wishes to signal a definite

[118] *See* text accompanying notes 101–102.

[119] Orders and unanimous consent requests also have been used for this purpose. The Senate has returned treaties to the Executive at the request of the Executive, but also on its own initiative. Given the President's authority to decline to ratify a treaty approved by the Senate, it might nonetheless be argued that he thus possesses, a fortiori, the lesser authority to forestall Senate approval by withdrawing a treaty. No instance has been identified in which an executive request for the return of a treaty has been rejected, however, or in which the Executive "withdrew" a treaty from the Senate without its consent. Memorandum from Congressional Research Service, Library of Congress, to Senate Foreign Relations Committee, Mar. 23, 1977, *reprinted in* 1 FOREIGN RELATIONS LAW, *supra* note 19, at 60–64; Senate Practice with Respect to Withdrawal of Treaties, Staff Memorandum, Senate Foreign Relations Committee, June 18, 1963 (on file with author); *accord* F. RIDDICK, SENATE PROCEDURE: PRECEDENTS AND PRACTICES, U.S. SENATE 829 (1973); 14 M. WHITEMAN, *supra* note 7, at 61–62. The question seems primarily political rather than legal; if a President indicates an intent not to ratify, the Senate will seldom, if ever, go through the legally feckless act of according its consent.

[120] Under such circumstances, the President might claim that he was following the express will of Congress. *See supra* note 36. The argument might be made that to observe the terms of a treaty until the defeat of a "resolution of return" would effectively change the fraction of the Senate required for approval from two-thirds to one-half. The answer, of course, is that international law as embodied in Article 18 of the Vienna Convention does not place the treaty in force; it simply proscribes action that would defeat the object and purpose of the treaty. The difference is critical. Thus, for example, if President Reagan were to sign a strategic arms reduction treaty but face a reluctant Senate, Article 18 would not give him authority to scrap prohibited missiles pending ratification, as their temporarily continued existence would not defeat the purpose of the treaty. "Failing to dismantle a weapon scheduled to be dismantled under the treaty," write the reporters of the draft *Restatement*, "might not defeat its object since the dismantling could be effected later." DRAFT RESTATEMENT, *supra* note 7, §314, Reporters' Note. The test, they suggest, is whether the consequences of the action in question "might be irreversible." *Ibid.* Thus, "[t]esting a new weapon in contravention of a clause prohibiting such a test would presumably violate the purpose of the agreement." *Ibid.*

end to obligations called for by Article 18 under a signed treaty,[121] he would be best advised to request its return from the Senate and to indicate, in a formal message to the Senate, that he does not intend to cause the United States to become a party. In the alternative, in the case of a bilateral treaty, the President might simply notify the other signatory that the United States does not intend to pursue ratification.

Status of the SALT Agreements

The latter course was taken by the Reagan administration with regard to the SALT II Treaty. "The proposal has been abandoned by this administration," Secretary of State Alexander Haig testified before the Senate Foreign Relations Committee. "We have so informed the Soviet Union. . . ."[122] A new administration might conceivably take a different view of SALT II, or the Reagan administration might change its mind, but to the extent that the United States can ever make clear its intention not to become a party to a treaty, it would thus appear to have done so with respect to SALT II. The United States is therefore not bound under the rule of Article 18 to refrain from acts that would defeat the object or purpose of SALT II, although the President may of course do so voluntarily.

This course apparently was chosen by President Reagan in his Memorial Day declaration that the United States would "refrain from actions which would undercut . . . [existing agreements] so long as the Soviet Union shows equal restraint."[123] Ironically, however, the President may inadvertently have gone beyond a mere statement of nonbinding policy. Unlike Secretary of State Cyrus Vance's similar statement concerning U.S. adherence to the terms of the SALT I Interim Agreement,[124] President Reagan's Memorial Day declaration was not made with the caveat that it was not intended to be binding. Consequently, under the rule of the *Nuclear Tests* cases,[125] the President's statement may well have created a binding obligation under international law.[126]

If so, the measure reported by the Senate Foreign Relations Committee—stating as a matter of law that the United States "shall continue to refrain from actions which would undercut the SALT I and SALT II agreements,

[121] *See supra* note 102 and accompanying text.

[122] *Nuclear Arms Reduction Proposals: Hearings Before the Senate Comm. on Foreign Relations,* 97th Cong., 2d Sess. 121 (1982) (statement of Alexander Haig, Secretary of State).

[123] *See supra* note 97.

[124] *Statement by Vance, supra* note 66, at 642.

[125] 1974 ICJ REP. 253; 1974 ICJ REP. 457.

[126] Perhaps even more troubling, in this context, is the remark of President Carter with regard to SALT II: "I consider it *binding* on our two countries." The President's News Conference of March 14, 1980, 16 WEEKLY COMP. PRES. DOC. 484, 488 (Mar. 14, 1980) (emphasis added). President Carter, of course, did not say whether he regarded the obligation as *legally* or *morally* binding; still, his statement was arguably no more equivocal than those that were held to give rise to legal obligations on the part of France in the *Nuclear Tests* cases and of Norway in *Eastern Greenland. See supra* notes 68–79 and accompanying text.

provided the Soviet Union shows equal restraint"[127]—would, if enacted, merely have caused the President's obligations under domestic law to correspond to those imposed by international law.[128] It would not have interfered with the President's foreign affairs powers because a binding commitment would already have existed as a result of his own declaration. To the contrary, the real issue is whether the issuance of such a declaration is within the scope of the President's independent powers.[129]

If, on the other hand, his declaration is viewed as a nonobligatory policy statement, the matter becomes more difficult. Clearly, Congress can prohibit the President by law from taking those steps that he would have been prohibited from taking under the SALT I and SALT II agreements. The committee's proposal might thus be seen merely as a statutory limitation on the President's authority to take certain steps not falling within his independent powers.[130] The problem is that the committee's formulation, like the President's, contained no qualification that it was not intended to be binding. The statement that the United States *shall* take or not take certain steps in the international arena, when solemnly enshrined in law, may thus itself give rise to binding international undertakings. The establishment of such undertakings by Congress would naturally raise the gravest constitutional questions. As a Senate Judiciary subcommittee pointed out, "To attempt to bind the United States to international obligations through the form of a joint resolution makes possible in principle what the Constitution and subsequent cases and commentary most certainly reject."[131]

CONCLUSION

Critics of the American brand of constitutionalism argue that, at least in the realm of international agreement making, a unitary decisional authority

[127] S.J. Res. 212, cl. 3, 97th Cong., 2d Sess. (1982), *reprinted in* SUBCOMM. ON SEPARATION OF POWERS OF SENATE COMM. ON THE JUDICIARY, 97TH CONG., 2D SESS., JOINT RESOLUTION WITH RESPECT TO NUCLEAR ARMS REDUCTIONS: REPORT ON S.J. RES. 212 at 7 (Comm. Print 1982) [hereinafter cited as JOINT RESOLUTION].

[128] This analysis assumes that both SALT I and SALT II are "existing agreements" within the meaning of the President's declaration, a proposition disputed by Senator Jesse Helms. *See* S. REP. NO. 493, 97th Cong., 2d Sess. 30 (1982) (additional views of Mr. Helms).

[129] *See Treaties and Executive Agreements, supra* note 77, and text of note 77.

[130] *See generally supra* notes 36 and 100 (discussing the power of Congress to limit the President's foreign policy power in light of the concurring opinion of Justice Jackson in Youngstown Sheet & Tube Co. v. Sawyer, 343 U.S. 579 (1952)).

[131] JOINT RESOLUTION, *supra* note 127, at 7. The subcommittee quoted from the 1816 Senate Foreign Relations Committee report noted by the Supreme Court in *Curtiss-Wright,* 299 U.S. at 319:

> The President is the constitutional representative of the United States with regard to foreign nations. He manages our concerns with foreign nations and must necessarily be most competent to determine when, how, and upon what subjects negotiation may be urged with the greatest prospect of success. . . . 8 U.S. Senate, Reports, Committee on Foreign Relations, vol. 8, p. 24.

JOINT RESOLUTION, *supra* note 127, at 6.

would be more effective internationally. One voice, they argue, can command respect; many disparate voices, however, generate confusion.

The answer, of course, is that they are correct. The United States pays a price for its system. It is a price paid consciously,[132] but a price nonetheless.

Critics of the international legal order contend, on the other hand, that its rules hinder the ability of states, however enlightened, to structure their domestic legal systems as they deem best. The international order, they argue in particular, provides disincentives to the maintenance of a system of separated power.

They, too, are correct. While international law has no compulsory enforcement organs, at least none analogous to those of domestic legal systems, it does define norms of acceptable diplomatic conduct, and in so doing it obviously discourages the establishment of governmental structures that, through diplomatic maladroitness, are more likely to transgress those norms. Indeed, it could hardly do otherwise while remaining true to the objective of facilitating international intercourse within a juridical framework.

But both sets of critics are wrong—seriously wrong—in assuming that neither system can achieve its ends without undercutting the other. The United States Constitution does not demand the abandonment of diplomacy, any more than international law mandates a surrender of sovereignty. The question is simple: how mutual confidence among nations can be strengthened most effectively. Building the reciprocal expectations at the core of that confidence, this article has suggested, depends on assuring other states that bargains with the United States will be binding on both. Because the Constitution prescribes a procedure for making such bargains, no such assurance is possible unless that procedure is honored.

While constitutional and international law do not always harmonize, they are thus, in another sense, mutually reinforcing. It is the task of both the diplomat and the constitutionalist to further that reinforcement. Neither can succeed by frustrating the work of the other.

[132] *See* Mr. Justice Brandeis's explanation of the principle underlying the separation of powers doctrine:

> The doctrine of the separation of powers was adopted by the Convention of 1787, not to promote efficiency but to preclude the exercise of arbitrary power. The purpose was, not to avoid friction, but, by means of the inevitable friction incidental to the distribution of the governmental powers among three departments, to save the people from autocracy.

Myers v. United States, 272 U.S. 52, 293 (1926) (Brandeis, J., dissenting).

EDITORIAL COMMENTS

AN ALTERNATIVE TO THE LAW OF THE SEA CONVENTION

Concomitant with its decision not to sign the Law of the Sea Convention in December 1982, the Reagan administration has proposed to some of the other 22 nonsignatory countries, including Great Britain and West Germany, a "mini-treaty" regarding deep seabed mining. The mini-treaty presumably would omit the controversial provisions of the Convention that create an international regime with powers to regulate seabed mining and independently exploit suboceanic resources.

The mini-treaty only makes sense if it will enhance the international legal position of the nonsignatories to the LOS Convention. Let us consider their position first with respect to the nonseabed mining provisions of the Convention and second with respect to its seabed mining provisions.

On the first question, if the mini-treaty contains provisions only regarding deep seabed mining, then the LOS Convention will have "third-party" effects upon the parties to the mini-treaty according to the general principles of international law. Further study on these principles would certainly be welcome. Since some of these third-party effects are controversial under present international customary law, and since the nonsignatories to the Convention presumably wish to have most of its nonseabed mining provisions apply generally, there may be a better way to ensure the universality of desirable Convention norms such as those relating to navigation through international straits, limits of the territorial sea and economic zone, and marine environmental safeguards. Accordingly, I have proposed that the mini-treaty be expanded to include provisions similar, if not identical, to those desirable provisions contained in the Convention.[1]

Such an alternate treaty (it probably would not continue to be referred to as a "mini" treaty) will ensure that nearly every nation in the world will have signed one of two treaties, each containing equivalent provisions regarding the nonseabed issues. Those provisions will therefore constitute an almost universal conventional law, and it would follow that general customary law would be similarly thus constituted. To be sure, parties to the Convention may argue that its benefits (nonseabed provisions) are available only to themselves because they have accepted its burdens (seabed provisions): this is the "package deal" theory. As I have earlier argued, the intention of parties to a treaty to retain as exclusive some or all of the norms of a treaty is irrelevant to the use the international community wishes to make of the effect of those norms upon general custom.[2] As I have tried to show, historically, and without significant exception, the international community has accepted a constitutive

[1] D'Amato, letter to the editor, N.Y. Times, Dec. 29, 1982, at A28, col. 3.

[2] *See* A. D'AMATO, THE CONCEPT OF CUSTOM IN INTERNATIONAL LAW 150–60 (1971).

rule to the effect that generalizable norms in treaties generate equivalent norms of customary law.[3]

The second question deals with the relation of the seabed mining provisions of the LOS Convention to the legal position of nonsignatories. Let us begin by considering their position if they do not enter into an alternate or mini-treaty.

If the International Court of Justice were asked to give an advisory opinion on whether nonsignatories may legally engage in deep seabed mining activities without contributing to the regulatory regime set up by the Convention, the Court would have to consider whether the Convention contains generalizable norms relating to the deep seabed that can have an impact upon customary international law.[4] Of course, one can only speculate about the factors the Court would take into account, but several lines of argument seem discernible at present. One approach would be to contend that the Convention sets up a generalizable international norm to the effect that no nation may take for itself the mineral resources of the ocean floor. Under this interpretation, that generalizable norm would transmute into a customary norm to the same effect. However, the position is easily countered by the observation that the Convention does not quite bar national exploitation of the deep seabed, but rather makes such exploitation subject to specified contributions to the Convention's regulatory regime, which regime in turn may restrict the monetary value of the minerals mined in any given period of time.

The question then presents itself: is mining-subject-to-Convention-regulation a generalizable norm that is capable of becoming a customary norm binding upon all nations? In one sense it is, because all nations are free to become a party to the LOS Convention if they wish to engage in mining on the same terms as every other nation that is a party to it. On the other hand, if a nation exercises its prerogative *not* to join the Convention, then that nation would in effect have to pay a tariff to the nations that are party to it and control its regulatory regime. Looked at in this light, the regulatory regime set up by the Convention does not appear to be assimilable to a norm of law that can be generalizable and hence can become part of customary law. For customary law is by definition universally binding; yet the nation that wants to go it alone would have a lesser legal position with respect to the regulatory regime set up by the Convention than would the nations party to it. Hence, it would follow from this argument that mining-subject-to-Convention-regulation is not a generalizable norm.

A different argument that might be made to the International Court is that the Convention establishes the principle that deep seabed minerals are the common heritage of mankind, and that proceeds from their exploitation should be shared by all nations, including those that do not engage in mining activities. This principle, I believe, states a generalizable norm. More than

[3] *See* D'Amato, *The Concept of Human Rights in International Law,* 82 COLUM. L. REV. 1110, 1130–46 (1982).

[4] *See* A. D'AMATO, *supra* note 2, at 105–07; North Sea Continental Shelf Cases, 1969 ICJ REP. 3, 43 (test is whether the provision "should, at all events potentially, be of a fundamentally norm-creating character such as could be regarded as forming the basis of a general rule of law").

that, I think it already is a norm of customary law, to judge by the consensus on the "common heritage" concept in the long negotiations leading to the Convention as well as in those on mining activities in outer space. Partial confirmation of this norm is found in the Deep Seabed Hard Mineral Resources Act of 1980,[5] which sets up a tax of 3.75 percent of the imputed value of mineral resources mined from the deep seabed.[6] This tax is to be transferred to a trust fund called the Deep Seabed Revenue Sharing Trust Fund, which would be paid into any law of the sea treaty ratified by the United States prior to June 28, 1990, "for the purposes of the sharing among nations of the revenues from deep seabed mining."[7] However, if the United States does not enter into such a treaty within the allotted time, the amounts in the trust fund "shall be available for such purposes as Congress may hereafter provide by law."[8] While the Act of course does not say that other nations are entitled to the amounts in the trust fund in the absence of a treaty, the Act at least recognizes and gives material content to the notion of sharing. Certainly, a later Congress could make the trust fund available to other nations if it believed that that was a requirement of international law.

Thus, in the absence of an alternate treaty, a nonsignatory to the LOS Convention should expect at minimum that the International Court of Justice might advise that the Convention either confirms or generates a norm of customary law requiring some sharing of the proceeds from deep seabed mining. At worst, the nonsignatory might face exclusion from mining on the ground that the regulatory regime set up by the Convention is somehow generalizable into a customary norm.

A separate and distinct possibility is that the Court might find that the Convention has no impact upon the customary law of deep seabed mining, in which case the international community would be relegated to the underlying customary rule. That rule may either prevent all mining activities or allow them subject to some reasonable provision for the "common heritage." Which of these two positions reflects customary law requires a vast historical and legal determination beyond the scope of the present essay. Good arguments can be made for either view.

It would clearly be in the interests of nonsignatories to the Law of the Sea Convention to set up an alternate treaty of their own. Then, if an international tribunal were called upon to assess the legal consequences of two conflicting multilateral treaties on the law of deep seabed mining, at least the parties to the alternate treaty would have a valid international instrument of their own to cite against the Convention. Moreover, they would argue that there is no principle of majority rule in international law that would make the Convention more significant than their own alternate treaty. And they would add that there is no principle of priority in time that would favor the Convention because it was concluded first. Finally, in the event that a tribunal might hold that the provisions of the Convention relating to seabed mining are not gen-

[5] 94 Stat. 553, 30 U.S.C. §§1401–1473 (1980).

[6] 94 Stat. 582, 26 U.S.C. §4495 (1980).

[7] *Supra* note 5, §1472(d).

[8] *Supra* note 5, §1472(e). *See* Moore, *Progress of U.S. Deep Seabed Mineral Resources Bill,* 73 AJIL 525 (1979).

eralizable norms, the new alternate treaty—by carefully couching its seabed mining provisions so as to be generalizable—might actually have an impact upon customary law that would even apply to the parties to the Convention irrespective of the Convention.

What, then, would the international law on the seabed be if an alternate treaty were concluded that conflicted with the Law of the Sea Convention? How, for example, would the International Court of Justice decide a case where the complaining state or states cite one treaty and the responding state the other?

It is too early, of course, to predict with any reasonable assurance how such a case would be decided, but some speculations may be ventured.

First, the Court or other tribunal might place considerable weight on the practice of states under the two treaties. If, for example, an American firm engaged in deep seabed mining according to the alternate treaty I have described, and there were no other mining activities by any of the countries party to the Convention, the very practice of such a firm would tend to reinforce the norms of the alternate treaty. Conversely, if deep seabed mining activities were first begun by states party to the Convention, then it would tend to be reinforced by the practice. Naturally, the Court would be greatly influenced by the reaction of states to the early mining activities. The firms engaging in the mining would be able to cite either the Convention or the alternate treaty as legal support for their activities, so that the mining would be carried out under a claim of right. In this respect, therefore, mere protest would not carry much weight.[9] Moreover, to the extent that the mining activities were protected by the host states, the "burden of proof" mechanism of the *Anglo-Norwegian Fisheries* case[10] might serve to create a presumption in favor of the international legality of the activities of the pioneer mining firms.[11]

A future tribunal, therefore, might accord great weight to whichever treaty is first implemented by actual mining practice. More conservatively, and perhaps more foreseeably, the tribunal may simply recognize two competing regimes for seabed mining. It may hold that mining activities may be carried on under either treaty, perhaps with a prohibition on staking out any seabed claim for exploration; or the mining companies may be confined to a reasonable radius of mines or mining activities actually in place.

Second, however, the way a future tribunal will decide any of the preceding considerations may be a function of the substantive provisions of the proposed alternate treaty. If the alternate treaty did not contain any provisions for sharing, or contained provisions that required sharing at such a low level as to be nearly frivolous, the International Court of Justice in a future case might look on the alternate treaty as a mere cover for self-interested exploitation rather than as a legitimate treaty giving effect to the interests of the "common

[9] Indeed, protest might serve to call attention to, and thus help articulate, the norm being protested. *See* A. D'AMATO, *supra* note 2, at 101–02.

[10] 1951 ICJ REP. 116.

[11] *See* A. D'AMATO, *supra* note 2, at 180–86; D'Amato, *Judicial Legislation*, 1 CARDOZO L. REV. 63, 78–80 (1979).

heritage of mankind." The "sharing" level would probably have to be somewhere between the 3.75 percent set up by the U.S. Congress and a figure constituting a rough average of the percentages usually paid to a private owner of mineral resources where there is a very substantial investment in exploitation technology. In addition, the figure should not act as a disincentive to potential mining companies. Therefore, the percentage might start low and increase over time after exploitation investments are recouped and later mining companies have cheaper entry. Since the signatories to the alternate treaty would presumably include the nations best equipped to be the first to engage in deep seabed mining, it would be interesting to see how they would resolve the competing interests of exploiter motivation and "common heritage" in attempting to fashion a credible alternative to the Law of the Sea Convention.

ANTHONY D'AMATO

ALWYN FREEMAN (1910–1983)

The editors of the *Journal* note with deep regret the untimely death of Alwyn Freeman on March 1, 1983. Mr. Freeman's association with the *Journal* as contributor and editor extended for almost half a century. He was a member of the Board of Editors from 1955 to 1972, an honorary editor since 1976. His career in international law was richly diversified. He had an active role in international claims cases while in the State Department, and served in the Army Judge Advocate General's Office in World War II, on the staff of the Senate Committee on Foreign Relations, and as an official of the International Atomic Energy Agency. He represented the United States in 1949–1950 on the Inter-American Juridical Commission and twice was a U.S. delegate to the Inter-American Council of Jurists. Mr. Freeman taught international law in several law schools, lectured at the Hague Academy, and was the editor of *International Lawyer* from 1975 to 1978.

While Alwyn Freeman had a wide knowledge of international law, he had a special and, one might say, passionate interest in the subject of state responsibility. His comprehensive work, *The International Responsibility of States for Denial of Justice,* begun while a graduate student in Geneva, appeared in 1938 and was widely praised. After his wartime service, he wrote authoritatively on responsibility of military personnel and on war crimes. His interest in these subjects was marked by both scholarly thoroughness and a strong commitment to the maintenance of international standards of law and justice. He took international law seriously and did not hesitate to express his strong feelings when he considered that it was ignored or abused for political reasons. His many friends in the international law community remember fondly his personal warmth and generous spirit. He will be greatly missed.

OSCAR SCHACHTER

NOTES AND COMMENTS

CURRENT ATTEMPTS TO REVISE INTERNATIONAL LAW—A COMPARATIVE ANALYSIS

The thrust of the present Note is to examine those current efforts to revise international law which have an impact on the principles of traditional international law governing state responsibility for the treatment of aliens, in particular their property rights—a prime aspect of the emerging law of the proposed New International Economic Order (NIEO). This aim, however, cannot be properly realized without first reviewing the current pursuit of a new international legal order as a whole, as well as previous efforts to the same end. To that extent, therefore, the Note will also consist of a comparative analysis of the past and current efforts to revise international law.

REVISION OF INTERNATIONAL LAW, AN OLD AND CONSTANT CONCERN

As with states now emerging from decolonization, the Latin American nations demonstrated concern for the revision of international law as soon as they became independent. Some of their efforts to achieve such a revision have particular relevance to the principles governing state responsibility for the treatment of aliens' property rights. The famous Calvo Doctrine, embodying the Latin American version of the principle of equality between nationals and aliens, is an outstanding example.[1] The Drago Doctrine was also enunciated in response to the abusive exercise of diplomatic protection in the form of threats and, at times, the actual use of armed force in Latin America.[2] The Calvo Clause is another noteworthy Latin American contribution to the development of international law and its revision. As compared to the Calvo and Drago Doctrines, the clause is intended not merely to prevent abuse of the right of diplomatic protection of nationals abroad, but to bar the exercise of such a right altogether.[3]

These doctrines, along with others—such as those repudiating the "right" of conquest, territorial acquisitions by force, and any other forms of intervention—are unequivocal expressions of the philosophy behind Latin American efforts to develop international law and to revise some of its principles and institutions.[4] Certain principles, doctrines, and institutions of international

[1] The Calvo Doctrine has received a number of multilateral endorsements, including by inter-American treaties such as the 1933 Convention on Rights and Duties of States. *See* Art. 9 of the Convention in 28 AJIL, Supp. 76 (1934).

[2] For the content and reasoning of the Drago Doctrine, see the Note transmitted to the U.S. Department of State by the then Argentinian Foreign Minister, Luis M. Drago, in 1903 FOREIGN RELATIONS OF THE UNITED STATES 1–5.

[3] For the various aspects of the Calvo Clause, see D. R. SHEA, THE CALVO CLAUSE, esp. 27–32 (1955)—still the most thorough and balanced study of the clause.

[4] The Latin American contribution to the development of international law and its revision goes far beyond the three aforementioned doctrines, but they are the most relevant for the

law still prevailing in the 19th century were rejected explicitly on occasion, as in the Preamble to the Treaty of Alliance and Confederation signed in 1856 by some Latin American countries, which spoke of the "subversive doctrines of international law that have been extended to this part of the world." What specifically was repudiated? The European balance of power system, within which colonialism, conquest, and intervention were legitimate.[5] This, in short, was the philosophy that inspired the first phase of the pursuit of a new international legal order.

In the League of Nations, the question of revision was raised at an early stage of the work of the Committee of Experts for the Progressive Codification of International Law. The constructive attitude of the committee was explicitly endorsed by the League Assembly itself when it called the Codification Conference to meet at The Hague in 1930. The Assembly declared that the codification of international law "should not confine itself to the mere registration of the existing rules, but should aim at adapting them as far as possible to the contemporary conditions of international life."[6]

Besides the "codification" of international law, the San Francisco Conference of 1945 contemplated the "progressive development" of that law. The assignment of this additional function to the United Nations General Assembly obviously has special significance for the purpose of this Note. The legislative history of the Charter provisions clearly shows that by coupling the term "progressive development" with the word "codification," the Charter explicitly charged the Assembly with encouraging changes or revisions in international law. In contrast to the League of Nations, where such a function emerged from a liberal approach to "codification," in the postwar Organization the encouragement to change or revise became a distinct and separate function.[7] Another conclusion that can be derived from the same legislative

---

purposes of the present Note. For an overall review of the regional contribution, see THE INTER-AMERICAN SYSTEM: TREATIES, CONVENTIONS AND OTHER DOCUMENTS, vol. I: LEGAL-POLITICAL AFFAIRS, pt. I, especially the Historical Introduction (a compilation annotated by F. V. García-Amador 1983).

[5] *Id.* at 59.

[6] *See* Res. of Sept. 27, 1927, LEAGUE OF NATIONS O.J., Spec. Supp. 53, at 9 (1927). For the views of members of the Committee of Experts, see *id.*, Spec. Supp. 54, at 7, 8, 14, 15, and 17 (1925).

[7] During the discussion in Committee II/2 of the amendments submitted to the Dumbarton Oaks Proposals by several delegations, a large majority voted in favor on the question whether the General Assembly should "be empowered to initiate studies and make recommendations *for promoting the revision* of the rules and principles of international law" (emphasis added). *See* Doc. 507, II/2/22, at 69, 70, 9 UN CIO Docs. 70 (1945).

In light of the decisive position taken by the San Francisco Conference, the attitude assumed by the General Assembly and other competent organs in interpreting and applying Article 13(1)(a) of the Charter was perfectly understandable. The discussion in the Committee on the Progressive Development of International Law and its Codification and the views expressed in its final report are very illuminating with regard to the point under consideration. The position taken by the Sixth (Legal) Committee of the General Assembly when it drafted the Statute of the International Law Commission also leaves no room for doubt. For a brief review of that position, see Survey of International Law in Relation to the Work of Codification, etc., Memorandum submitted by the Secretary-General, UN Doc. A/CN.4/1, at 4 (1948); and also THE WORK OF THE INTERNATIONAL LAW COMMISSION 11 (UN Pub. Sales No. E.80.V.11, 3d ed. 1980).

history is that neither of these functions is restricted to particular areas of international law.

The latter conclusion is particularly important in view of the assertion that is being made that under the Charter provision, progressive development of international law and its codification were contemplated "only in connection with international co-operation in the political field," and that there is a need "to repair its [the Charter's] omission by bringing about a *rapprochement* between economic development and the progressive development of international law."[8] A thorough review of the legislative history of the Charter does not reveal any authority to warrant such an assertion; what it does reveal is that the intention was merely to enumerate the various purposes for which the General Assembly could initiate studies and make recommendations, as is clearly reflected in both subparagraphs (a) and (b) of Article 13. No condition or limitation of the kind invoked was attached to the realization of either of those purposes.[9]

Nevertheless, neither at the League of Nations nor at the United Nations in the two and a half decades following the San Francisco Conference were the development of international law and its codification viewed as means to achieve specific goals. While the Latin American endeavors pursued a new international legal order based on principles that would guarantee the political independence and territorial integrity of nations regardless of their size or power, the experience of the two general international organizations does not exhibit any particular inspiration. Notwithstanding the amount and quality of the work done, especially within the framework of the United Nations during its first 25 years, the revision aimed at no specified goal and was merely to be made "in the light of new developments." In short, a philosophy was lacking. *A contrario*, as will be seen, like the Latin American endeavors, the current pursuit of a new international legal order is motivated by well-defined purposes and aims at specific goals.

Rationale of the Current Approach

Shortly after World War II, Judge Philip C. Jessup explored some of the possible bases for a modern law of nations. In his view, "It was a time for the burgeoning of a new international legal order."[10] In these early postwar years, he singled out, in particular, two points as keynotes of a revised international

[8] *See* M. Bedjaoui, Towards a New International Economic Order 115 (1979). In Judge Bedjaoui's opinion, the reparation of this omission in the Charter "is what the Organization is attempting to do in its efforts to replace an old order, doomed because of its injustices, by a new order inspired by more reason and more equity." *Ibid.*

[9] Early commentators on the Charter noted that in paragraph 1(a) of Article 13 the word "'political' is apparently used in contradistinction to 'legal' since section [subparagraph] *a* goes on to speak of the development and codification of international law as distinct from the promotion of international political cooperation." L. Goodrich & E. Hambro, Charter of the United Nations; Commentary and Documents 102 (1946). See in the same sense the study prepared by the UN Secretariat on Arts. 11(1) and 13(1)(a), UN Doc. A/AC.18/33, at 9 (1948), *cited in id.* at 134–35 (3d rev. ed. 1969).

[10] Jessup, *Revisions of the International Legal Order*, 10 Den. J. Int'l L. 1 (1980).

legal order: namely, that international law "must be directly applicable to the individual" and that "there must be basic recognition of the interest which the whole international society has in the observance of its law."[11] The recognition and protection of the interest of the individual as such and of the society of nations would be the aim of the revision of traditional international law.[12] Thus, as occurred after World War I, scholars were fully aware of the need to develop and revise international law in light of changing conditions and new legal developments that had already taken place in international life and that were affecting traditional principles and institutions.[13]

Post-World War II initiatives and proposals for revision eventually started to show a somewhat different face as a result of the emergence of a new rationale for revising international law. Its point of departure was the "universal" and "multicultural" character of the international community: this community or society had become worldwide, and consequently its composition had ceased to be "European" or predominantly "Occidental" in character.[14] Spokesmen for the current approach further raise two closely connected questions, one of which is the "European" or "Western"—sometimes also the "Christian"—origin of international law. Indeed, their statements on this question also carry a particular connotation.[15] As stated by Professor Röling, "The deciding point is whether present-day 'European' international law can meet with respect, accord and intrinsic acceptance in the expanded world."[16] Thus, the idea is conveyed that international law, given its "European" origin, cannot be an appropriate legal order for the present universal and multicultural society of nations.[17] The other point is whether the newly

[11] P. JESSUP, A MODERN LAW OF NATIONS 2 (1948).

[12] Some of Judge Jessup's revisionary suggestions had to do with a subject of direct concern to the revision of the traditional law of international claims. In addition to chapter V of the book cited in note 11 *supra*, see his article *Responsibility of States for Injuries to Individuals*, 46 COLUM. L. REV. 903 (1946). Among others, Professor H. Rolin also was of the view that state responsibility should be reexamined and reassessed on new bases and in light of postwar legal developments. *See Les Principes de droit international public*, 77 RECUEIL DES COURS 305, 441 (1950 II).

[13] As to the post-World War I period, see, *e.g.*, O. NIPPOLD, THE DEVELOPMENT OF INTERNATIONAL LAW AFTER THE WORLD WAR (1923), especially the introduction and pt. I, sec. II.

[14] Perhaps the first to raise the point was Professor J. L. BRIERLY, in his THE LAW OF NATIONS 44 (1949). Sometime later other scholars put special emphasis on the point and elaborated it much further. *See* especially C. W. JENKS, THE COMMON LAW OF MANKIND 62 (1958); and B. RÖLING, INTERNATIONAL LAW IN AN EXPANDED WORLD 5 (1960). The point was soon taken up by spokesmen from the newly independent states, as well as from the non-Western world as a whole. *See, e.g.*, Anand, *Attitude of the Asian-African States toward Certain Problems of International Law*, 15 INT'L & COMP. L.Q. 55 (1966).

[15] Traditional statements regarding the European role in the creation of international law have been mere assertions of a historical fact. For illustrations of assertions of this character, see C. W. JENKS, *supra* note 14, at 69–70.

[16] B. RÖLING, *supra* note 14, at 11. An even earlier illustration of the modern approach to the "European" origin of international law is found in Q. Wright, *The Influence of the New Nations of Asia and Africa upon International Law*, 7 FOREIGN AFF. REP. 33 (New Delhi 1958).

[17] As the late Professor W. Friedmann stated, "The emergence of many new states . . . is of more than quantitative significance." Friedmann, *The Changing Dimensions of International Law*, 62 COLUM. L. REV. 1147, 1150 (1962). *See also* Fenwick, *International Law: The Old and the New*, 60 AJIL 475 (1966).

emerged states "can reasonably be said to be bound in all respects by a law in the formation of which they had no part."[18] It is only natural that African and Asian spokesmen for the new approach have insisted on questioning the validity of a legal order in whose establishment their states did not participate.[19]

Apart from the above considerations, specific reasons are mentioned to explain the attitude of the newly independent states towards traditional international law. The basic complaint, as Judge Jessup described it, is "that the rules of law were developed by the exploiting imperialistic powers to promote their interests at the expense of countries which in earlier centuries were either colonies or politically and militarily weak and provided important sources of raw materials and perhaps labor to the exploiting powers."[20] In addition to their anticolonialist attitude,[21] the newly independent states resent traditional principles such as those governing state succession[22] and maritime jurisdiction.[23] In a sense, this resentment is particularly noticeable with respect to the traditional principles and institutions relating to the treatment of aliens, especially their property rights. Some of the current criticisms on this subject are of a general character, and are based on the same reasons invoked for attacking international law as a whole.[24] Most of them, however, are based on the basic complaint mentioned above. Thus, Professor Richard Falk has asserted that the institution of diplomatic protection of nationals abroad has

[18] Jennings, *The Progress of International Law,* 34 BRIT. Y.B. INT'L L. 334, 350 (1958). Ever since, the point has often been raised by European scholars. *See, e.g.,* Chaumont, *Cours général de droit international,* 129 RECUEIL DES COURS 333, 439 (1970 I). Sometimes the point is raised in a broader context that includes both the newly emerged states and those small and/or weak states in existence during the formative era, *i.e.,* the 19th century. *See* Castañeda, *The Underdeveloped Nations and the Development of International Law,* 15 INT'L ORG. 38, 39 (1961).

[19] *See, inter alia,* Judge T. O. Elias, *Modern Sources of International Law,* in TRANSNATIONAL LAW IN A CHANGING SOCIETY: ESSAYS IN HONOR OF PHILIP C. JESSUP 34, 49 (W. Friedmann, L. Henkin, & O. Lissitzyn eds. 1972); and Judge R. Pal, *Future Role of the International Law Commission in the Changing World,* UN REV., Sept. 1962, at 31; and his statement in the International Law Commission, [1957] 1 Y.B. INT'L L. COMM'N 158, UN Doc. A/CN.4/SER.A/1957.

[20] Jessup, *Non-Universal International Law,* 12 COLUM. J. TRANSNAT'L L. 415, 419 (1973).

[21] In this respect, see, *inter alia,* J. SYATAUW, SOME NEWLY ESTABLISHED ASIAN STATES AND THE DEVELOPMENT OF INTERNATIONAL LAW 230 (1961).

[22] For strong criticisms of the traditional rules governing the matter, see, *inter alia,* M. Bedjaoui's second report on Succession of States and Governments: Succession in Respect of Matters other than Treaties, [1969] 2 Y.B. INT'L L. COMM'N 69 *ff.,* UN Doc. A/CN.4/SER.A/1969/Add.l.

[23] "For example, the law of the sea, which was codified in 1958, is mainly based on customs and usages observed by the European maritime powers." N. REMBE, AFRICA AND THE INTERNATIONAL LAW OF THE SEA 8 (1980). In this respect, a French professor had previously remarked that the 1958 and 1960 Law of the Sea Conferences "had done nothing but to codify the practice of an era previous to decolonization." *See* M. FLORY, DROIT INTERNATIONAL DU DÉVELOPPEMENT 283–84 (1977).

[24] Judge S. N. Guha Roy, for instance, questions whether the law of state responsibility is part of "universal international law" on the ground that "[i]ts sole foundation is custom, which is binding only among States where it either grew up or came to be adopted." *See Is the Law of Responsibility of States for Injuries to Aliens a Part of Universal International Law?,* 55 AJIL 863, 889 (1961).

been used "as a means to impose the external will of [the] richer and more powerful nations."[25]

In view of this rationale for the current critical attitude toward traditional international law, one must wonder whether the explanation based on the present universal and multicultural character of the international community continues to be valid. It has been repeatedly said that the alien origin of the rules of international law is not the real reason behind the critical attitude of the newly emerged nations; rather, it "derives more from the fact that the structure of social relations and the interest for which these rules were developed are different from those of the newly independent states."[26] In light of this proposition, the argument based on "European" origin would be valid only if understood in the sense that the incompatibility between traditional international law and the interests of the newly emerged nations derives in turn from the alien origin of that legal order.

In concluding this rather cursory review of the rationale for the current approach to the revision of international law, it is also worth noting the following assertion:

> Far from rejecting the tenets of international law, the new states claim to be scrupulous adherents of those principles and *are quite conservative and traditionalist* in their attitude. Most of the recent suggestions for radical, structural legal changes *have come from Western scholars* rather than from the so-called "revolutionary" states which appear to be conservative [emphasis added].[27]

Such an assertion requires thorough consideration, which cannot be attempted in the confines of the present Note. Actually, whether or not "the new states . . . are quite conservative and traditionalist in their attitude" vis-à-vis the international law in existence when they became independent, and whether

[25] Falk, *Historical Tendencies, Modernizing and Revolutionary Nations, and the International Legal Order,* 8 How. L.R. 128, 133 (1962). *See also* his lectures at the Hague Academy, *The New States and International Legal Order,* 118 RECUEIL DES COURS 1, 94 (1966 II). Other statements along the same lines will be quoted in due course.

[26] Abi-Saab, *The Newly Independent States and the Rules of International Law: An Outline,* 8 How. L.J. 95, 99 (1962). *See also* S. SINHA, NEW NATIONS AND THE LAW OF NATIONS 26–27 (1967); and R. P. ANAND, NEW STATES AND INTERNATIONAL LAW 52 (1972). More recently, Professor Abi-Saab has reiterated that the newly emerged states, "instead of rejecting the system [of international law] as a whole, . . . claimed the right to re-examine its rules and to retain only those which are compatible with their interests." Abi-Saab, *The Third World and the Future of International Law,* 29 REV. EGYPTIENNE DROIT INT'L L. 27, 38 (1973). *See also* R. C. HINGORANI, MODERN INTERNATIONAL LAW 2 (1979).

[27] R. P. ANAND, *supra* note 26, at 65. With regard to the assertion quoted in the text, one might well recall the remarks made by an Egyptian Foreign Minister, Professor Boutros Ghali:

> [T]he claim that new countries have a new approach to international law is exaggerated. For example during the various African Conferences, African States in their attitude towards International Law showed that they are traditionalists. It appears that Western scholars are more enthusiastic to see a "new approach" on the part of the Afro-Asians than the Afro-Asians themselves.

See ROUND TABLE ON THE TEACHING OF INTERNATIONAL LAW AND RELATIONS, FINAL REPORT 56 (Singapore 1964).

or not "suggestions for radical, structural legal changes" come not so much from those states but from Western scholars are questions that must be evaluated in light of the positions now advanced in pursuit of a new international legal order.[28]

Further Observations and Conclusions on the Current Movement

These further observations and conclusions on the current approach to revising international law will be designed to determine whether criticisms leveled at the traditional law of international claims are *always* warranted, and whether such criticisms are always based on objective, correct perceptions of the traditional principles and institutions. Even if the answer to both questions is no, it will still be necessary to determine in which respect revision is warranted, and the spirit in which such a revision must be undertaken.

Are Criticisms of the Traditional Law of International Claims Always Warranted?

As will be recalled, spokesmen for the current approach to the revision of international law believe that the institution of state responsibility, *i.e.*, the traditional law of international claims, has served as a tool of the more powerful nations[29] or, as another Western advocate stated more bluntly, "was merely a garb that served to cloak and protect the imperialistic interests of the international oligarchy."[30] However, is this general criticism *always* warranted? The answer is no.

The history of the institution of responsibility, comprising both inter-state practice and international jurisprudence (including that of the World Court), decisively shows that the same legal principles have been applied regardless of the size and/or power of the defendant state. A mere glance at the voluminous body of international case law, in particular, will reveal that arbitral claims commissions and other international courts and tribunals have not been guided by a kind of "double standard," *i.e.*, by two sets of principles and rules of state responsibility.[31] In making this observation, we do not intend to present traditional international law as a flawless legal order; any attempt to hide its obvious shortcomings will be futile and unjustifiable. At the same time, most of the criticisms leveled nowadays at the law of international claims cannot be endorsed without serious reservations. Surprisingly enough, except for Judge Jessup and, more recently, Professor R. B. Lillich, to this author's knowledge, scholars have abstained from systematically responding to the current criticisms.[32]

[28] We will return to this point in due course. *See infra* note 35 and corresponding text.

[29] *See* Falk, *supra* note 25 and corresponding text. See in the same sense Professor F. Okoye, International Law and the New African States 176–77 (1972).

[30] Castañeda, *supra* note 18, at 39.

[31] For a very persuasive elaboration of the point, see Jessup, *supra* note 20, at 420–21.

[32] *See id.* at 415 *ff.*; and Lillich, *Duties of States Regarding the Civil Rights of Aliens,* 161 Recueil des Cours 329, 363–68 (1978 III). *See also* Professor Lillich's chapter 1, *The Development and Challenges to the International Law of State Responsibility for Injuries to Aliens,* in International Law of State Responsibility for Injuries to Aliens: Selected Contemporary Problems (R. Lillich ed., forthcoming in 1983).

As to those charges specifically concerning the traditional principles governing the treatment of aliens' property, are they really justified? In this matter, the role played by the history of foreign investments—some chapters of which reveal excessive and unwarranted demands by the capital-exporting countries and their nationals and corporations—should be neither overlooked nor underestimated. However, another factor seems to be playing a role of no less importance in generating the current criticisms and attacks: namely, a degree of misunderstanding of the true meaning of the traditional principles governing the matter. Since the point is crucial, the causes of this misunderstanding deserve to be explored.

The Chairman of the UNCTAD working group that prepared the draft Charter of Economic Rights and Duties of States has alluded to "the insufficient juridical preparation of a certain number of participants."[33] However, can this insufficient juridical preparation be attributed to a mere lack of knowledge, or rather to an inexact knowledge of certain principles and institutions of our discipline? The correct answer seems to be that the problem frequently stems from the latter. But to respond thoroughly it should be added that the inaccuracy of knowledge may well originate in erroneous or distorted images of the traditional principles and institutions, especially when such images are projected by the publications of authorities in the field. In short, whatever the real cause of the misunderstanding, the current revisionist movement is not always based upon an accurate grasp of the principles and institutions concerned. Unfortunately, space limitations prevent us from providing some examples of those misconceptions to illustrate our point.[34]

Some Revision of the Traditional Law Is Warranted

The foregoing observations should not be construed as constituting opposition to the current revisionary movement. Far from it. For, in sharp contrast to the negative feature that has just been discussed, a definitely positive aspect also characterizes the current revisionist movement: it again pursues a new international legal order that will assure protection of the interests of small and/or weak states. In this respect, however, the objectives of the current

[33] On the basis of the unique experience he acquired during the long process of elaborating the NIEO Charter, Ambassador Castañeda admitted that "[e]n bonne partie, la confusion était due à la préparation juridique insuffisante d'un certain nombre de participants, qui par ailleurs tendaient à souligner seulement l'aspect politique du document." *See* Castañeda, *La Charte des Droits et Devoirs Economiques des Etats: Note sur son processus d'élaboration,* 20 ANNUAIRE FRANÇAIS DROIT INT'L 31, 55 (1974).

[34] The point is illustrated to a rather limited extent in this author's essay, *The Proposed New International Economic Order: A New Approach to the Law Governing Nationalization and Compensation,* 12 LAW. AM. 1, 44–48 (1980). For some relevant examples of erroneous or distorted images, see J. KUUSI, THE HOST STATE AND THE TRANSNATIONAL CORPORATION: AN ANALYSIS OF LEGAL RELATIONSHIPS 54 (1979); Jiménez de Aréchaga, *State Responsibility for Nationalization of Foreign-Owned Property,* 11 N.Y.U. J. INT'L L. & POL. 179 (1978), concerning traditional principles governing breaches of state contracts and other measures affecting aliens' property rights; Hossain, *Permanent Sovereignty over Natural Resources,* in LEGAL ASPECTS OF THE NEW INTERNATIONAL ECONOMIC ORDER 36 (K. Hossain ed. 1980); and M. FLORY, *supra* note 23, at 282–83, concerning the traditional concept of national sovereignty as compared with the contemporary doctrine of "permanent sovereignty."

movement differ in a fundamental way from those of the former Latin American movement. While the latter was primarily concerned with preventing abuses of sovereignty against the states in the area by proscribing intervention and other uses of or threats to use force, the current movement is concerned, as well, with seeing that the international community and its more developed members assume obligations in favor of the developing countries. The gradual strengthening and consecration of these obligations will assure the protection of the interests of said countries.

For a long time we have been strongly persuaded of the necessity and advisability of revising the traditional law of international claims in some important respects. But it is one thing to favor revision to the extent it is really needed or advisable, *i.e.*, when the revision has become justifiable, and quite another to propose changes in the traditional law on the basis of erroneous or distorted images of its principles and institutions, as referred to above. Such images are responsible not only for the current misunderstanding and misperceptions, but also, to a large extent, for the radicalism that the current revisionary movement reflects at times.[35] Nevertheless, changes are needed in the field of international claims as much as in other areas of the law of nations. What remains to be determined is which changes are required or advisable, that is to say, where and to what extent is the currently proposed revision justifiable?

A first conclusion that seems to be in order, therefore, is that the current pursuit of a new international legal order is fully justified. It should not be doubted. Why? Is it because of postwar conditions—that is, the "universal" and "multicultural" character of the contemporary international community—that traditional international law has been found inadequate to deal with the world community, particularly with the needs of its developing members? Yes and no. Yes, because the postwar awareness of the tremendous problems posed by underdevelopment generated such concepts as preferential treatment of the developing countries in a number of fields, as well as the correlative duties and responsibilities of the international community, especially its developed members. There is no question that these realities belong exclusively to the postwar period.

The answer to our question is no, however, if the current revisionary movement is looked at from a different perspective, that of the legitimate concerns of the developing world to prevent intervention and other abuses of sovereignty by the developed countries, as well as its logical demands for the full use and control of its natural resources. In this respect, the current pursuit of a new international legal order is justified for the same reasons that the Latin American movement was justified in the past—long before the present, post-World War II conditions emerged. Then, the revisionary efforts did not gain the enthusiastic support that the same—and in some respects more far-

[35] This feature of the current revisionary movement sometimes raises objections even among non-Western scholars. For instance, Professor Anand has characterized as "excessive and perhaps unreasonable" those positions that the new and developing countries sometimes take against the colonial powers. For the position of Western scholars in this regard, see the quotation in note 27 *supra* and corresponding text.

reaching—proposals have received all over the world today, though this is another matter. The point is that the rationale behind both sets of proposals is the same; that rationale therefore did not spring from the aforementioned postwar conditions.

Whether the current pursuit of a new international legal order is justified is but one side of the problem. The other side concerns the spirit or criteria that must guide the revisionary efforts and proposals. In this regard, what must be avoided from the outset is radical positions, especially when such positions are taken with a view to favoring, unjustifiably, a particular class of countries. Ethical reasons and reasons of any other kind for revising a legal order, whether international or domestic, will never justify drastic, one-sided revisions. Moderate, well-balanced revisions must be considered, as they were in the past, a sine qua non in the current pursuit of a new international legal order. All legitimate interests, regardless of the particular categories of countries, must merit recognition and adequate protection under such a proposed legal order.[36]

F. V. GARCÍA-AMADOR*

CORRESPONDENCE

TO THE EDITORS-IN-CHIEF:

December 16, 1982

In their article, *The Plaintiff's Dilemma: Illegally Obtained Evidence and Admissibility in International Adjudication* (76 AJIL 737 (1982)), Reisman and Freedman make the valid, but unsurprising, point that the exclusion of illegally seized evidence must be justified by community policies relating to deterrence of the conduct resulting in the seizure. Just as in the domestic context, the decision of an international tribunal on whether to exclude illegally obtained evidence must involve a balancing of the community's interest in making determinations on the fullest factual base against its interest in deterring the illegal conduct resulting in the seizure of the evidence.

In discussing the *Hostages* case, the authors focus on a question that the International Court of Justice neither faced nor expressly decided, *i.e.*, whether Iran might have made use of documents illegally seized from the Embassy files (at pp. 748–51). Although I agree with the authors' conclusion on the Court's likely response to a proffer of such evidence, I believe they have overlooked the strongest argument for their conclusion. As Reisman and Freedman point out, the *dispositif* in the Court's May 24 Judgment obligated Iran to return to the United States (or its protecting power) all of the Embassy

[36] This author hopes to be excused for recalling that the same belief was expressed by him to the International Law Commission more than two decades ago, in connection with his work on the subject of state responsibility. *See* Addendum to the sixth report, [1961] 2 Y.B. INT'L L. COMM'N 46, UN Doc. A/CN.4/SER.A/1961/Add.l.

* Professor of Law, University of Miami. The present Note abstracts pertinent parts of a forthcoming book, *The Changing Law of International Claims*, now being prepared for publication by the author.

archives and documents.[1] What they fail to recognize, however, is that under the terms of the Court's Judgment there were to be further proceedings in which the evidence contained in the Embassy documents could be directly relevant. Paragraph 6 of the *dispositif* envisioned proceedings before the Court to determine the form and amount of reparations due from Iran to the United States.[2] Although the Court had held that U.S. interference in Iranian internal affairs would not constitute a legal justification for Iran's violation of diplomatic immunities, the Court did leave open the possibility that "some of the circumstances alleged, if duly established, may later be found to have some relevance in determining the consequences of the responsibility incurred by the Iranian State."[3] By requiring Iran to return the documents and archives, however, the Court denied Iran the material crucial to establishing the facts that the Court itself had characterized as possibly material. Such a requirement is consistent only with the conclusion that evidence derived from these documents could not be admitted.

One further point. Readers of the *Journal* may be interested to know that the United Nations Commission of Inquiry apparently also faced the question of whether to consider "evidence" taken from U.S. Embassy files. Although a case could be made that the commission's political function could best be served by providing Iranian militants with the broadest possible opportunity for venting their grievances, the commission did not quite see it that way. In fact it apparently rejected a "proffer" of evidence taken from Embassy files. As commission members left Tehran, their mission unfulfilled, they were pursued "by students on motorcycles who tried to stuff what looked like pizza boxes full of pasted and reassembled embassy documents into their limousine windows."[4] The pizza boxes may be comic opera; the commission's refusal to accept the documents emphatically was not. As later stated by the U.S. Agent in response to a question by Judge Gros, the commission's function was "to hear whatever grievance Iran may wish to bring before it. That is to say, the Commission would receive whatever *lawfully obtained information* the Iranians wanted to present . . . and, . . . would report on the basis of that information."[5]

In sum, both of the bodies to whom illegally seized evidence might have been presented excluded it. The Court did so in advance of any actual attempt to introduce such material; the commission did so after having had such material offered to it. The record of the hostages crisis taken as a whole thus offers even stronger support for the authors' conclusion than they seem to realize.

TED L. STEIN
University of Washington School of Law

[1] Case concerning United States Diplomatic and Consular Staff in Tehran, 1980 ICJ REP. 3, 45 (Judgment of May 24).

[2] *Ibid.*

[3] *Id.* at 41.

[4] Kifner, *How a Sit-in Turned Into a Siege,* N.Y. Times Magazine, May 18, 1981, at 54, 70.

[5] *U.S. Presses Case in World Court on American Hostages in Iran,* DEP'T STATE BULL., No. 2038, May 1980, at 36, 58 (emphasis added).

TO THE EDITORS-IN-CHIEF:

December 15, 1982

Further to the comments by John Norton Moore, *The Inter-American System Snarls in Falklands War* (76 AJIL 830 (1982)), I confess I am perplexed at the absence of serious appraisal among members of the international legal community of the respective legal issues at stake in that "obscure little war."

Moore identified the overriding concern when he noted that the dispute "is representative of many international conflicts concerning disputed sovereignty." For the international legal community the tragedy is that the machinery for peaceful resolution of such conflicts appears to have ground to a dismal halt. Given the variety of other outstanding, equally obscure, territorial claims, what does this apparent failure portend for stability in international affairs and the prevalence of international law?

Equally disturbing in the Falklands case was the absence of much in the way of serious legal argument by either party to the dispute. Argentina was notoriously vague in the substance of its claims. Yet, on the basis of some opaque claim, the OAS approved a resolution on May 29, 1982, essentially supporting Argentina. Security Council Resolution 502 was much more akin to the requirements of international law, yet it was ignored. My impression is that the OAS bottomed out as a credible international legal entity in May 1982. I am still waiting for a clear statement by Argentina of the basis for its claim to the Falklands, or is law immaterial to Argentina and the OAS?

Indeed, it has been suggested that the province of Québec in Canada has a more substantial claim to the "Malvinas Islands" than does Argentina, and its interests were never raised before the OAS.

As I understand the "facts," Bougainville landed a group of Québecois on the islands in the mid-17th century. These Québecois had originated, before settling in Québec, in the port of St. Malo and were known variously as "Maloians," hence the Spanish derivation, "Malvinians."

Naturally, I'm sure there is a "British" case which can be argued although I've not seen that done either.

Given the range of issues that arise from the conflicting claims for the Falklands, Gibraltar, Essequibo, Belize, and a myriad of others, what re-evaluations are international lawyers and the legal community making in their respective assessments of what constitutes a valid territorial claim in international law? Indeed, I've argued elsewhere that if the basis for valid territorial claims is now becoming fluid and uncertain, what is to prevent hordes of additional ostensibly valid territorial claims from being made? I submit, for argument's sake, that the United States claim to San Juan Island may be questionable given that it was ruthlessly torn from Canada after the "Pig War."

Perhaps it is time for the international legal community to seriously consider the future of international legal processes that appear to arrive at decisions in the absence of legal substance and to assess the state of the law applicable for territorial claims that appear to challenge conventional law.

C. LLOYD BROWN-JOHN
University of Windsor

CONTEMPORARY PRACTICE OF THE UNITED STATES RELATING TO INTERNATIONAL LAW

MARIAN NASH LEICH*

The material in this section is arranged according to the system employed in the annual *Digest of United States Practice in International Law*, published by the Department of State.

LOSS OF NATIONALITY

(U.S. *Digest*, Ch. 3, §1)

Appeals Procedures and Administrative Relief—Time Limitations

The Legal Adviser of the Department of State, Davis R. Robinson, was asked for an opinion on the Department's authority to take further administrative action in a loss of nationality case, specifically, to vacate the certificate of loss of nationality that had been issued. The individual concerned had failed to make a timely appeal to the Department's Board of Appellate Review and the board considered in consequence that it had no further jurisdiction over the case, not even to remand it upon request from the Office of Passport Services.

The Department's regulations governing the Board of Appellate Review provide that "merits of appeals or decisions of the Board [for administrative purposes, a part of the Office of the Legal Adviser] shall not be subject to review by the Legal Adviser or any other Department official."[1] On this basis, the Office of Passport Services considered that a determination by the board that a time limitation barring an appeal effectively precluded the Department from giving the case further administrative consideration. The board, on the other hand, considered that even if it lacked jurisdiction to consider an appeal, further action could be taken at an administrative level, as appropriate, as if the case had never been before it. The board's view was that only decisions in which it had adjudicated the merits of the appeal were final, within the meaning of the regulations.

The Legal Adviser concurred in the board's position, subject to "certain necessary limitations upon the further exercise of administrative authority." Excerpts from Mr. Robinson's memorandum to the Chairman of the Board of Appellate Review, Alan G. James, dated December 22, 1982, follow:[2]

> There is no express provision in the regulations for remanding cases which are on appeal before the Board for the purpose of vacating certificates of loss of nationality. Rather, the regulations provide generally that "[t]he Board shall take any action it considers appropriate and nec-

* Office of the Legal Adviser, Department of State.

[1] 22 C.F.R. §7.2(b).

[2] The footnotes to the memorandum are renumbered here and some are omitted.

essary to the disposition of cases appealed to it." Pursuant to this authority, the remand procedure was developed as a result of a 1976–77 understanding between the Board and the Passport Office, in order to alleviate concern over the Passport Office practice of reviewing and reversing holdings of loss of nationality after an appeal had been taken to the Board. The Board felt this practice undermined its appellate jurisdiction, as provided for in the Department's regulations. Subsequently, the Board and the Passport Office agreed that where an appeal has been filed, and the Passport Office concludes it is unable to meet the government's burden of proof, then:

> . . . the Passport Office should promptly inform the Board of its views on the appeal, forward the case record for the Board's consideration, and request the Board to remand the case to the Passport Office for further proceedings.
>
> . . . .

According to the general rule of bar, a valid and final personal judgment rendered in favor of the defendant bars another action by the plaintiff on the same claim. Traditionally, this rule has meant that only a judgment rendered "on the merits" would bar another action on the same claim. By statute, rule, or court decision, certain judgments not passing directly on the substance of claims have come to be regarded as "operating as an adjudication on the merits." The *Second Restatement of the Law of Judgments* has dropped the terminology "on the merits," as being possibly misleading, in favor of a delineation of specific "exceptions" to the general rule of bar.[3] Significantly, the *Restatement* provides that:

> A personal judgment for the defendant, although valid and final, does not bar another action by the plaintiff on the same claim:
>
> (a) *When the judgment is one of dismissal for lack of jurisdiction. . . .*[4]

The "exception" to the rule of bar set forth in the *Restatement* is consistent with the position taken in the Federal Rules of Civil Procedure regarding the effects of an involuntary dismissal. Rule 41(b) provides that, unless the court in its order specifies otherwise, an involuntary dismissal operates as an adjudication upon the merits. There are certain exceptions to this rule, however, including a *dismissal for lack of jurisdiction,* which shall not serve as an adjudication on the merits.

The U.S. Supreme Court considered this rule in *Costello* v. *United States,* 365 U.S. 265 (1961), a denaturalization proceeding. An earlier proceeding against the same petitioner had been dismissed by the district court, because the government had failed to file the requisite affidavit of good cause. The Court determined that the earlier dismissal would not bar the second proceeding. . . . The Court viewed Rule 41(b) as reaffirming the common-law principle that, in order to bar another suit, judgment must be rendered on the merits of a controversy. The dismissals which operate as a bar under Rule 41(b), e.g., failure to prosecute a claim, primarily involve situations where the defendant must prepare to defend a case on the merits because there is no initial bar to the

[3] Restatement 2d, Judgments §19, Comment a.
[4] *Id.*, at §20.

Court's reaching them. Dismissal on threshold grounds, however, would not put the defendant to such a test and, therefore, need not operate as a bar to subsequent proceedings.

Thus, a determination by the Board that it lacked jurisdiction because an appeal was time barred would not fall within the meaning of "the merits of appeals or decisions of the Board," which are final and not subject to review, under the Department's regulations. . . .

Passport Services urges that, as an alternative to dismissal, the Board should have remanded the case for further administrative proceedings. Once the Board has determined that it lacks jurisdiction to consider the merits of an appeal, however, it has no power to remand a case for further proceedings, and can only dismiss the appeal. Passport Service's request for remand cannot confer jurisdiction over an appeal where it does not otherwise exist. The U.S. Supreme Court has held that unless an appeal is timely taken, under the Federal Rules of Appellate Procedure, the reviewing court lacks jurisdiction to hear it.[5] In *United States* v. *Robinson,* 361 U.S. 220, 224 (1960), the Court described the need for timely filing of an appeal as "mandatory and jurisdictional." . . . [*See also* 9 *Moore's Federal Practice* §204.02[2]].

. . . .

. . . [W]here the Board has determined that it lacks jurisdiction over the merits of an appeal as time barred, "as distinguished from the authority to consider the threshold question of appellate jurisdiction," then the Board was at all times without power to remand the case to the Department, even though Passport Services requested that it do so.

. . . .

Where the Board has dismissed an appeal as time barred, however, that fact standing alone does not necessarily preclude the Department from taking further administrative action, under certain limited conditions, to correct manifest errors of law or fact. Professor Davis notes in his *Administrative Law Treatise* that "[e]very tribunal, judicial or administrative, has some power to correct its own errors or otherwise appropriately to modify its judgment, decree, or order."[6] . . .

. . . .

Accordingly, the fact that the Board of Appellate Review has dismissed an appeal as time barred would not act *per se* as a bar or estoppel against further administrative action. Nevertheless, the *timeliness* of any request for administrative relief properly would be considered as one of the equities affecting the reopening or reconsideration of a case, depending upon the circumstances.

The *Foreign Affairs Manual*[7] sets forth three sets of circumstances under which persons may apply for administrative reconsideration of previous holdings of loss of nationality:

(a) claims under the *Schneider* decision (1964);
(b) claims under the *Afroyim* decision (voting cases) (1967); and
(c) claims under the Attorney General's Interpretation of *Afroyim* ("intent" cases) (1969).

[5] Berman v. United States, 378 U.S. 530 (1964); 9 *Moore's Federal Practice* §204.02[1].

[6] 2 Davis at 606.

[7] 8 FAM 225.13–225.16 (1970).

The effects of the "timeliness" issue will vary among these three types of cases, depending upon the particular circumstances thought to justify vacating the certificate of loss.

In *Schneider* v. *Rusk,* 377 U.S. 163 (1964), the U.S. Supreme Court held unconstitutional section 352(a)(1) of the Immigration and Nationality Act, whereby naturalized citizens lost their citizenship by continuous residence for three years in the country of origin. The decision also effectively invalidated subsection (a)(2) providing for loss of citizenship by continuous residence for five years in any foreign country.

In *Afroyim* v. *Rusk,* 387 U.S. 253 (1967), the Court invalidated section 401(e) of the Nationality Act of 1940, which provided for loss of citizenship by voting in a foreign political election. In effect, the decision also invalidated section 349(a)(5) of the INA, the successor provision to section 401(e). The Court stated that every citizen has ". . . a constitutional right to remain a citizen in a free country unless he voluntarily relinquishes that citizenship."[8] In other decisions, e.g., *Kennedy* v. *Mendoza-Martinez,* 372 U.S. 144 (1963) (draft evasion), the Court also declared unconstitutional specific statutory provisions providing for the loss of citizenship as a result of committing certain acts.

Where the Supreme Court has declared unconstitutional the specific statutory provision under which a person previously was held to have lost his citizenship, that person would be entitled to have the certificate of loss vacated, without regard to the timeliness of his application for administrative relief. This is so because an unconstitutional statute is void *ab initio.*[9] No evidentiary question is involved. The Department's ability to investigate the circumstances surrounding the purported expatriating act has not been prejudiced, since the act concerned *could not work an expatriation,* whether or not it was done "voluntarily" or with the necessary "intent to relinquish." Under the circumstances, the Department would be able to exercise its continuing jurisdiction to provide administrative relief to an applicant, even though an appeal to the Board of Appellate Review may not be available as time barred.

Claims for reconsideration under the Attorney General's interpretation of *Afroyim* (1969)[10] or the Supreme Court's decision in *Vance* v. *Terrazas,* 444 U.S. 252 (1980), are another matter altogether. Such claims squarely raise the issue of "intent to relinquish." Prior to *Afroyim* (1967), "intent to relinquish" was not thought to be a necessary element of the expatriating act. In addition to invalidating the specific statutory provision at issue in that case (voting in a foreign political election), the Supreme Court's decision had the effect of making "intent" an element of every expatriating act.[11] In *Terrazas,* the Supreme Court reaffirmed that "intent" is a *necessary* element of *all* expatriating acts, "whether the

[8] 387 U.S. at 268.

[9] Chicago, Indianapolis & Louisville Ry. v. Hackett, 228 U.S. 559, 566–67 (1913). *See also* Norton v. Shelby County, 118 U.S. 425 (1886), wherein the U.S. Supreme Court observed that: "An unconstitutional act is not a law; it confers no rights; it imposes no duties; it affords no protection; it creates no office; it is, in legal contemplation, as inoperative as though it had never been passed." 118 U.S. at 442.

[10] Attorney General's Statement of Interpretation Concerning Expatriation of United States Citizens, 42 Op. Atty. Gen. 397 (Jan. 18, 1969).

[11] 42 Op. Atty. Gen. at 398–401.

intent is expressed in words or is found as a fair inference from proven conduct."[12] The problem, of course, is that the records of pre-1967 cases may be ambiguous or silent on the issue of intent, and the passage of many years effectively may have rendered the facts and circumstances unknowable.

Accordingly, where "intent" is placed in issue, the timeliness of an applicant's request for administrative reconsideration properly may affect the availability of such relief. An unexplained and unreasonable delay by the applicant effectively may prejudice the Department's ability to establish "intent." Where the elements of laches are present, the equities weigh against the applicant and administrative reconsideration should be denied. This is also the case where the issue in question is the "voluntariness" of the purported expatriating act, and the passage of many years has prevented the gathering of evidence. In such circumstances, it will not do to weigh only those equities which favor the applicant, because that will lead to the constant reopening of stale cases, undermining the dignity and finality of the Department's decisions.

For the foregoing reasons, I conclude that where the Board of Appellate Review has dismissed an appeal in a citizenship case as time barred, that fact standing alone does not preclude the Department from taking further administrative action to vacate a holding of loss of nationality. This continuing jurisdiction should be exercised, however, only under certain limited conditions to correct manifest errors of law or fact, where the circumstances favoring reconsideration clearly outweigh the normal interests in the repose, stability and finality of prior decisions. Such circumstances usually would involve cases where the Supreme Court has declared unconstitutional the particular section of law under which a loss was thought to have occurred. In other circumstances, where evidentiary questions of "voluntariness" or "intent" are raised, an applicant's unreasonable delay in seeking relief generally will impair the Department's ability clearly to establish the facts and circumstances necessary to resolve those questions. In such cases, further administrative consideration should be denied under the doctrine of laches.[13]

Diplomatic Privileges and Immunities

(U.S. *Digest,* Ch. 4, §2)

Most-Favored-Nation Status

In a note to the Department of State, dated December 2, 1982, the Embassy of the Philippines, taking note of Article 13 of the 1972 Consular Convention between the United States and Poland (immunity from jurisdiction of judicial and administrative authorities of the receiving state),[1] requested that in accor-

[12] 444 U.S. at 260.

[13] Dept. of State File Nos. P83 0013-0749, 0013-0750.

[1] The Convention, with protocols and exchanges of notes, was *signed* at Warsaw, May 31, 1972, and *entered into force* July 6, 1973, TIAS No. 7642, 24 UST 1231. Article 13 provides in part:

> 1. Consular officers and members of their families forming part of their households shall enjoy immunity from the jurisdiction of the judicial and administrative authorities of the receiving State.

dance with the terms of Article I, paragraph 2 of the 1947 Consular Convention between the United States of America and the Republic of the Philippines (most-favored-nation status, conditioned upon reciprocity),[2] Philippine consular officers in the United States be accorded rights, privileges, exemptions, and immunities no less favorable than those enjoyed by Polish consular officers in the United States. The Government of the Republic of the Philippines confirmed that consular officers of the United States enjoyed reciprocally in the Philippines rights, privileges, exemptions, and immunities no less favorable in any respect than those enjoyed by Polish consular officers in the United States pursuant to the 1972 United States-Polish Consular Convention.

The Department of State replied on December 6, 1982 that the request of the Republic of the Philippines was granted upon the basis of the representations and guarantee of reciprocity set forth in the Embassy's note, and that, accordingly, consular officers of the Philippines would thenceforth enjoy reciprocally in the United States rights, privileges, exemptions, and immunities no less favorable in any respect than those enjoyed by Polish consular officers in the United States pursuant to the 1972 Consular Convention between the United States and Poland.[3]

State Territory and Territorial Jurisdiction

(U.S. *Digest,* Ch. 6, §1)

Antitrust Laws—Foreign States

Public Law 97-393, approved December 29, 1982, further amended the treble damages provision (section 4, as amended) of the Clayton Act[1] by lim-

---

2. Employees of a consular establishment shall enjoy immunity from the jurisdiction of the judicial and administrative authorities of the receiving State in respect of acts performed by them within the scope of their official duties.

3. The provisions of paragraphs 1 and 2 shall not, however, apply in respect of civil action:

(a) arising out of a contract concluded by a consular officer or an employee of a consular establishment in which he did not contract expressly or impliedly as an agent of the sending State;

(b) by a third party for damage arising from an accident in the receiving State caused by a vehicle, vessel or aircraft;

(c) arising out of acts performed under Article 31 as provided in paragraph 5 of that Article.

[2] *Signed* at Manila, Mar. 14, 1947, *entered into force* Nov. 18, 1948, 62 Stat. 1593, TIAS No. 1741. Article I, paragraph 2 provides in part:

2. Consular officers of each High Contracting Party shall, after entering upon their duties, enjoy reciprocally in the territories of the other High Contracting Party rights, privileges, exemptions and immunities no less favorable in any respect than the rights, privileges, exemptions and immunities which are enjoyed by consular officers of the same grade of any third country and in conformity with modern international usage.

[3] Dept. of State File Nos. P82 0178-1847 and 0173-1062.

[1] 15 U.S.C. §15.

iting recovery of damages by a foreign state plaintiff in an antitrust action to actual damages sustained by it and the cost of suit, including a reasonable attorney's fee (section 4(b)(1)), except in cases, specified in new section 4(b)(2), where:

> "(A) such foreign state would be denied, under section 1605(a)(2) of title 28 of the United States Code, immunity in a case in which the action is based upon a commercial activity, or an act, that is the subject matter of its claim under this section;
>
> "(B) such foreign state waives all defenses based upon or arising out of its status as a foreign state, to any claims brought against it in the same action;
>
> "(C) such foreign state engages primarily in commercial activities; and
>
> "(D) such foreign state does not function, with respect to the commercial activity, or the act, that is the subject matter of its claim under this section[,] as a procurement entity for itself or for another foreign state."[2]

The Department of State, asked for its views and recommendations after enactment of the legislation and prior to action by the President, recommended that President Reagan sign the bill (S. 816) into law. In a letter from Powell A. Moore, Assistant Secretary of State for Congressional Relations, to David A. Stockman, Director of the Office of Management and Budget, dated December 20, 1982, the Department discussed the bill, as follows:

> S. 816 amends the treble damage provisions of the Clayton Act to limit foreign states to recovery of actual damages in successful antitrust suits. The possibility of treble damages relief for a foreign state enterprise is expressly authorized, however, subject to limiting conditions to assure that the enterprise may not at the same time claim or benefit in U.S. courts from any sovereign status.
>
> The bill is a legislative response to the questions raised by the Supreme Court's decision in *Pfizer* v. *Government of India,* 434 U.S. 308 (1978). In that case several governments, including the Federal Republic of Germany, India, Colombia and the Philippines, sued Pfizer and four other major U.S. pharmaceutical companies for treble damages under antitrust laws. The Supreme Court ruled that the foreign governments could properly bring such action.
>
> The Department of State initially had serious reservations about S. 816 as originally drafted and passed in the Senate, including reservations regarding a requirement of reciprocity. One criticism of the *Pfizer* decision was that it afforded a remedy to a foreign state without requiring that reciprocal rights be given to the United States by the foreign state. This criticism resulted in a provision in the original bill requiring reciprocity as a condition to recovery of any damages by a foreign state under American antitrust laws. The Department of State's position was that such a reciprocity test would be virtually impossible for other countries to meet, given differences in concept and approach to competition

[2] 96 Stat. 1964. Under new section 4(c), "commercial activity" has the meaning given it in section 1603(d), and "foreign state" has the meaning given it in section 1603(a), of Title 28, United States Code (the Foreign Sovereign Immunities Act).

laws, that determining whether reciprocal rights existed would be difficult and costly, and that such limitations to the right of access by foreign states to U.S. courts would undercut principles of nondiscrimination and national treatment. The Department was also concerned that the bill was primarily intended to cut off a single lawsuit by friendly governments, growing out of their commercial dealings in the U.S. market for which they could be sued in turn.

The new S. 816, the result of a Senate-House conference, is a much improved document. Most importantly, it eliminates the reciprocity provision, and provides that, at a minimum, foreign states may recover actual damages in successful antitrust suits. Thus, foreign governments will have at least the same remedies under the U.S. antitrust laws as does the Government of the United States, a fair outcome and one which is consistent with our foreign relations interests. The conditions which foreign state enterprises engaged in commercial activity must meet to be able to sue for treble damages are strict, but they do provide a window, albeit small, for injured parties to sue for treble damages.[3]

SOVEREIGN IMMUNITY

(U.S. *Digest,* Ch. 6, §7)

Heads of State and Their Spouses

On December 6, 1982, at the direction of the Attorney General of the United States, the United States Attorney for the Western District of Washington, Gene S. Anderson, submitted a suggestion of immunity for President Ferdinand E. Marcos, the Head of State of the Republic of the Philippines, and for Mrs. Imelda Marcos, the First Lady of the Republic of the Philippines, both of whom had been named as defendants in an action for damages and injunctive relief in the U.S. District Court for the Western District of Washington, entitled *Estate of Silme G. Domingo et al. v. Ferdinand E. Marcos, et al.* (Civil Action No. C82 1055 V).

The substantive portion of the suggestion of immunity follows:

> 1. The United States of America has an interest and concern in the subject matter and outcome of this action insofar as it involves the question of immunity from the Court's jurisdiction of representatives of a friendly foreign state. That issue arises in connection with a determination reached by the Executive Branch of the Government of the United States in the implementation of its foreign policy and in the conduct of its international relations, which determination must be given effect by the Court.
>
> 2. The Attorney General has been informed by the Acting Legal Adviser of the United States Department of State that the Government of the Republic of the Philippines has formally asked the Government of the United States to suggest the immunity of President and Mrs. Marcos from this suit. The Attorney General has been further informed by the Legal Adviser that
>
>> [t]he Department of State recognizes the immunity of President Marcos as the Head of State of the Republic of the Philippines.

[3] Dept. of State File No. P83 0001-0441.

. . .

Mrs. Marcos is a member of the immediate family of President Marcos and, therefore, partakes of his immunity. In addition, she has been notified to and accepted by the United States Government since March 6, 1979, as Special Envoy Extraordinary and Minister Plenipotentiary of the Republic of the Philippines. By virtue of this diplomatic accreditation, Mrs. Marcos is entitled to immunity in accordance with Article 31 of the 1961 Vienna Convention on Diplomatic Relations, 23 U.S.T. 3227, T.I.A.S. 7502.[1]

. . . .

3. Under customary rules of international law, recognized and applied in the United States, the head of a foreign government, its foreign ministers, and those designated by the head of state or members of his official party are immune from the jurisdiction of the United States federal and state courts. *Restatement (Second), Foreign Relations Law of the United States,* §66. The Supreme Court has mandated that the courts of the United States are bound by suggestions of immunity, such as this, which are submitted to the courts by the Executive Branch. *Ex Parte Republic of Peru,* 318 U.S. 578, 588–89 (1942); *Republic of Mexico* v. *Hoffman,* 324 U.S. 30, 36 (1945). Thus, in *Peru, supra,* the Supreme Court, without further review of the Executive's determination, declared that the suggestion of immunity must be accepted by the Judiciary as a "conclusive determination by the political arm of the Government" that the continued retention of jurisdiction would jeopardize the conduct of foreign relations. *Id.,* 318 U.S. at 589; *see Spacil* v. *Crowe,* 489 F.2d 6143, 6171 (5th Cir. 1974). Accordingly, upon the filing of a suggestion of immunity such as this, it becomes the "[C]ourt's duty" to surrender jurisdiction for which immunity has been recognized. *Peru, supra,* 318 U.S. at 588; *Hoffman, supra,* 324 U.S. at 35.

4. That the courts of the United States are mindful of the Supreme Court's teachings with respect to Executive Branch suggestions of immunity is evidenced by such recent cases as *Psinakis* v. *Marcos,* No. C-75-1725 (N.D. Cal. 1975), *result reported in* [1975] *Digest of United States Practice in International Law,* pp. 344–45 (dismissing libel action against President Ferdinand E. Marcos pursuant to suggestion of immunity), and *Kilroy* v. *Prince of Wales,* No. C 78-291 (N.D. Ohio 1978) (dismissing civil rights conspiracy action against Prince of Wales and ordering all allegations directed against Prince of Wales deemed stricken from complaint upon submission of suggestion of immunity). . . .[2]

5. The unquestioned deference of the Judiciary to Executive Branch suggestions of immunity is predicated on "compelling" considerations arising out of the conduct of our foreign relations. *Spacil* v. *Crowe, supra,* 489 F.2d at 619. First,

[1] Letter from Acting Legal Adviser James H. Michel to Attorney General William French Smith, Dec. 2, 1982, Dept. of State File No. P83 0013-0925.

[2] *See* in regard to *Kilroy* the 1978 DIGEST OF U.S. PRACTICE IN INTERNATIONAL LAW 641–43. The memorandum opinion and order of District Judge Thomas D. Lambros, dismissing the complaint against the Prince of Wales, on Dec. 7, 1978, may be found at Dept. of State File No. P83 0014-1782.

> [s]eparation-of-powers principles impel a reluctance in the judiciary to interfere with or embarrass the executive in its constitutional role as the nation's primary organ of international policy.

Ibid., citing *United States* v. *Lee,* 106 U.S. 196, 209 (1882); *Peru, supra,* 318 U.S. at 588. Second, in comparison with the Executive's institutional resources and extensive experience in the day-to-day conduct of the Country's foreign affairs, the Judiciary is ill-equipped to second-guess Department of State determinations which may affect such interests. *Spacil, supra,* 489 F.2d at 619. Finally, as the Court of Appeals for the Fifth Circuit also observed in *Spacil,* "[p]erhaps more importantly, in the chess game that is diplomacy, only the executive has a view of the entire board and an understanding of the relationship between isolated moves." *Ibid.*

6. This suggestion of immunity does not constitute an appearance on behalf of any agency of the United States or any person currently or formerly employed by the United States and named as a defendant in this action. Accordingly, this suggestion of immunity does not constitute a waiver of any objections or defenses that any such defendant might have under Rule 12 of the Federal Rules of Civil Procedure or otherwise.[3]

[3] Dept. of State File No. P83 0013-0918, 0920-0924.

On Dec. 23, 1982, District Judge Donald S. Voorhees dismissed the action against the Marcos defendants, pursuant to this "conclusive determination" of the executive branch. The plaintiffs moved to set aside and vacate the judgment and order, and for reconsideration of the question of the immunity of President and Mrs. Marcos.

JUDICIAL DECISIONS

Monroe Leigh

Arbitration—enforcement of arbitral awards—New York Convention

Bergesen v. Joseph Muller Corporation. 548 F.Supp. 650.
U.S. District Court, S.D.N.Y., October 7, 1982.

Petitioner Bergesen, the Norwegian owner of three cargo vessels, entered into certain ocean carriage charter agreements with Joseph Muller Corporation (Muller), a Swiss corporation. Pursuant to arbitration clauses in the agreements, a dispute between the parties was submitted to arbitration in New York. In due course, an arbitral award was rendered in New York in favor of Bergesen. Bergesen sought enforcement of the award in the U.S. District Court for the Southern District of New York, invoking the court's jurisdiction under the UN Convention on the Recognition and Enforcement of Foreign Arbitral Awards (the Convention),[1] as implemented by U.S. law. The court (per Haight, J.) *held,* as a matter of first impression, that the Convention requires the enforcement in the United States of arbitral awards involving entirely foreign interests even though the awards were rendered in the United States. Accordingly, the court confirmed the award and entered judgment in favor of Bergesen.[2]

Article I(1) of the Convention provides as follows:

> This Convention shall apply to the recognition and enforcement of arbitral awards made in the territory of a State other than the State where the recognition and enforcement of such awards are sought, and arising out of differences between persons, whether physical or legal. It shall also apply to arbitral awards *not considered as domestic awards in the State where their recognition and enforcement are sought* [emphasis added].

Muller opposed confirmation of the award on the ground that it did not fall under the Convention and that the court therefore lacked subject matter jurisdiction. The question before the court was whether the award at issue—which adjudicated the rights of two foreign parties and was rendered in the United States—would be considered "domestic" or "nondomestic" under U.S. law.[3]

[1] June 10, 1958, 330 UNTS 3, 21 UST 2517, TIAS No. 6997 (entered into force for the United States, Dec. 29, 1970).

[2] Bergesen initially sought enforcement of the award in Switzerland in 1979. Muller resisted the Swiss action on the grounds that the award did not fall under the Convention and was unenforceable in Switzerland because it had not been confirmed under New York law. As of the date of the court's decision in the present case, the Swiss action was still pending.

[3] The court noted that if the arbitral award was considered "domestic," it would fall under chapter 1 of the Federal Arbitration Act (9 U.S.C. §§201–208), which contains a 1-year statute of limitations with respect to enforcement. 9 U.S.C. §9. If, however, the award was considered "nondomestic," it would fall under chapter 2 of the Act, which implements the Convention and provides for enforcement within 3 years of the date of the award. 9 U.S.C. §207. Bergesen brought

The court turned first to the legislation implementing the Convention, which is contained in chapter 2 of the Federal Arbitration Act (9 U.S.C. §§201–208) (FAA). The court noted that in section 202 of the Act, Congress expressly excluded from the reach of the Convention only a single category of awards, those arising out of a relationship "which is entirely between citizens of the United States" and lacks some clear nexus with one or more foreign states. The court reasoned that if Congress, in delineating the coverage of the enforcement provisions of the Convention, had desired to exclude other types of awards, such as the one before the court, it would "undoubtedly have made that exclusion explicit."[4] Furthermore, other sections of the FAA dictated the same result. Section 203 of the Act provides that a "proceeding falling under the Convention shall be deemed to arise under the laws and treaties of the United States." Section 204 provides for alternative venue in the place of the arbitration if, under the agreement to arbitrate, that place is within the United States. And section 206 empowers the district court to compel arbitration in accordance with the agreement either "within or without the United States."[5] Thus, the court concluded, Congress specifically contemplated that arbitration agreements falling under the Convention could provide for arbitration in the United States; and "[n]o logical reason is suggested why a United States District Court, specifically granted jurisdiction and venue over such an agreement, and given the power to compel arbitration, should be denied the power to enforce the subsequent award."[6]

In further support of its enforcement jurisdiction, the court found that the legislative history of the FAA militated in favor of a broad construction of the Convention's remedies. The court observed that the congressional intent underlying U.S. implementation of the Convention was to foster U.S. business interests abroad "by encouraging them to submit their commercial disputes to impartial arbitration for awards which can be enforced in both U.S. and foreign courts."[7] In the court's view, Muller's narrower construction of the Convention would clearly thwart this intent.

Finally, the court addressed Muller's argument that the Convention "by its own terms" excluded enforcement of the award in the United States. Muller argued that the award at issue should be characterized as "domestic" because it was rendered in New York, in an arbitration conducted by the American Arbitration Association, with New York counsel appearing for the parties, and with damages payable in U.S. dollars. In response to this argument, the court turned to the *travaux préparatoires* of the Convention. The court ob-

---

his enforcement proceeding after 1 year but before the end of 3 years following the award. Thus, it was crucial to Bergesen's success to establish that the award was nondomestic.

[4] 548 F.Supp. 650, 653.

[5] Thus, the court noted, in Sumitomo Corp. v. Parakopi Compania Maritima, S.A., 447 F.Supp. 737 (S.D.N.Y. 1979), *aff'd*, 620 F.2d 286 (2d Cir. 1980), the court had held that where entirely foreign interests agree to arbitrate in New York disputes arising out of their commercial relationship, U.S. courts have jurisdiction under the Convention to compel arbitration and, if need be, to appoint an arbitrator.

[6] 548 F.Supp. at 653.

[7] *Id.* at 654 (quoting H.R. REP. NO. 1181, 91st Cong., 2d Sess. 2 (1970)).

served that the original draft of Article I(1) contained, in substance, only the first sentence (the territorial criterion) of Article I(1) as it finally emerged. The addition of the second sentence (importing the concept of "domestic" awards) was advocated by delegates of certain nations who took the position that the solely territorial criterion was not adequate to establish the true nationality of an award, which also depended on such factors as the nationalities of the parties, the object of the dispute, and the rules of procedure followed by the arbitrators. Moreover, the court noted that Article I(3) of the Convention specifically permits a state party to limit recognition and enforcement (on the basis of reciprocity) to "awards made only in the territory of another Contracting State": *i.e.*, it allows state parties to subscribe to only the first sentence of Article I(1) if they so choose. Thus, Congress could have used the power of reservation in Article I(3) to limit enforcement in the United States to awards rendered in other contracting states. However, "by refraining from such limiting action, Congress manifested its intention 'to extend as far as possible the variety of eligible awards' under the Convention."[8]

Comment. In construing perhaps the most controversial clause in the New York Convention, the court has interpreted Article I(1) and its implementing legislation in accordance with the original purposes of both the drafting nations and the Congress. As stated by the Supreme Court, the goal of the Convention, as well as the principal purpose underlying American adoption, "was to encourage the recognition and enforcement of commercial arbitration agreements in international contracts and to unify the standards by which agreements to arbitrate are observed and arbitral awards are enforced in the signatory countries."[9] In addition, this decision, if followed by other courts, will help to create an increasingly hospitable climate for both the rendering and the enforcement of arbitral awards in the United States, and thus serve the best interests of the American and international business communities.

Export controls—Arab boycott—validity of federal laws respecting boycott-related questionnaires

BRIGGS & STRATTON CORPORATION v. BALDRIGE. 539 F.Supp. 1307. U.S. District Court, E.D. Wis., May 10, 1982.

Plaintiff, Briggs and Stratton Corporation (Briggs), a United States manufacturing company that had been blacklisted by several Arab countries, brought suit challenging the constitutionality of the U.S. antiboycott laws contained in the Export Administration Act of 1979 (50 U.S.C. app. §2401 *et seq.* (Supp. III 1979)) (EAA). Briggs alleged that it was blacklisted because it had failed to respond properly to a questionnaire of the League of Arab States designed to further the League's boycott of Israel. Briggs maintained that it had not responded properly because it was prohibited from doing so by the EAA and its implementing regulations, which make it unlawful to support a boycott fostered or imposed by a foreign country against a country that is friendly to the United States. Violations of the boycott provisions are

[8] 548 F.Supp. at 657.

[9] Scherk v. Alberto-Culver Co., 417 U.S. 506, 520 n.15 (1974).

punishable by both civil and criminal penalties.[1] The U.S. District Court for the Eastern District of Wisconsin (per Gordon, J.) rejected each of Briggs's arguments, holding that the statute and regulations constitute a rational regulatory scheme, that they do not abridge the plaintiff's rights under the First, Fifth, or Ninth Amendments, and that the regulations do not interpret the statute in a manner contrary to congressional intent.

The plaintiff's principal attack was directed against Commerce Department regulations implementing the EAA with respect to the statutory element of "boycott intent." The EAA makes boycott-related conduct punishable only when it is undertaken with the "intent to comply with, further, or support [the] boycott."[2] The implementing regulations provide that boycott intent exists when one of the reasons for a person's conduct is the existence of the boycott,[3] and that such intent "does not mean that one has to agree with the boycott . . . or desire that it succeed or that it be furthered or supported."[4] In addition, the regulations allow boycott intent to be inferred from circumstantial evidence.[5] Plaintiff objected to these regulations on three grounds.

First, plaintiff alleged that the regulations read the "boycott intent" requirement out of the statute to the extent that they provide that such intent is established when a person who does not in fact support the Arab boycott of Israel or intend to abide by it answers a boycott questionnaire. The court rejected this challenge, citing legislative history showing that Congress specifically contemplated application of the EAA to such persons.

Second, plaintiff argued that the effect of the regulations on intent is at odds with the premises of the EAA, which, Briggs claimed, was designed to promote the export of American goods. The court also rejected this argument, noting that while export promotion is certainly one goal of the EAA, it is not the only one. Thus, Congress included a detailed "declaration of policy" in the Act, which states that portions of the EAA were specifically enacted to require U.S. persons "to refuse to take actions, including furnishing information . . . , which have the effect of furthering" a boycott against a nation friendly to the United States.[6]

Third, plaintiff argued that the regulations allowing boycott intent to be inferred from circumstantial evidence—that is, knowingly supplying information on a boycott questionnaire—violate the right of potential defendants to have every element of a criminal offense proved beyond a reasonable doubt. Finding that such a presumption is not unlike other presumptions found in federal jury instructions, the court held that the regulations do not place an improper burden on one charged with violating the Act.

Plaintiff also claimed that the regulations prohibiting it from answering boycott questionnaires were an irrational implementation of the EAA and therefore violated the Due Process Clause of the Fifth Amendment. The court, in rejecting this claim, cited legislative history showing that, by prohibiting the furnishing of boycott-related information, Congress intended to

[1] 50 U.S.C. app. §2410 (Supp. III 1979).

[2] *Id.*, §2407(a)(1).

[3] 15 C.F.R. §369.1(e)(2).

[4] *Id.*, §369.1(e)(4).

[5] *Id.*, §369.1(e)(5).

[6] 50 U.S.C. app. §2402(5)(B).

reinforce the more substantive provisions of the EAA that prohibit U.S. persons from refusing to do business with boycotted countries or with entities blacklisted by boycotting countries.

Plaintiff also challenged on First Amendment grounds provisions of the EAA and its implementing regulations prohibiting truthful answers to boycott questionnaires. Applying the First Amendment standard applicable to restrictions of commercial speech, the court found that the governmental interest furthered by the challenged restrictions is "substantial and more than sufficient to outweigh the marginal applicability of the first amendment."[7]

Finally, Briggs argued that because the regulations caused it to be blacklisted, and thus had affected its worldwide sales, the Government had destroyed Briggs's rights to foreign trade and had thereby effected an unconstitutional taking of property without due compensation. The court rejected this Fifth Amendment challenge, noting that the regulations apply equally to all U.S. companies, and that while "Briggs has lost some profits because it has lost some sales, . . . its property has not been seized or restrained by the government."[8]

Comment. This decision is significant as the first judicial pronouncement on the validity of a regulatory system that has been the focus of substantial litigation. *Briggs & Stratton* is the first decision rendered of six independent suits filed since 1978 challenging the constitutionality of the EAA antiboycott provisions.[9] The sweeping nature of the *Briggs & Stratton* decision, rejecting on summary judgment a wide range of challenges to the U.S. antiboycott provisions, indicates the relative invulnerability of these laws to successful legal attack and may well suggest the likely outcome of the related cases.

Iranian hostage crisis—Executive Order No. 12283—jurisdiction exists to decide former hostage's claims—President may extinguish former hostage's claims

PERSINGER v. ISLAMIC REPUBLIC OF IRAN. 690 F.2d 1010.
U.S. Court of Appeals, D.D.C., October 8, 1982.

In November 1979, Iranian militants seized the U.S. Embassy in Iran, thus precipitating the U.S.-Iran hostage crisis. In January 1981, President Carter, in order to secure the release of the hostages, entered into an executive agreement with Iran by which the United States agreed to terminate all litigation pending in U.S. courts involving claims of U.S. persons against Iran and to

[7] 539 F.Supp. 1307, 1319.

[8] *Id.* at 1320. In reaching this conclusion, the court relied upon the Supreme Court's analysis in Andrus v. Allard, 444 U.S. 51 (1979). In *Andrus,* the Court had reasoned that a loss of future profits, without any physical property restraint, is a slim basis for a taking claim.

Plaintiff also asserted that, should the court rule against its Fifth Amendment claim, "Briggs' right to pursue its trade and profit from it is worthy of ninth amendment protection." 539 F.Supp. at 1317. The court found no merit to this "barebones assertion." *Ibid.*

[9] Magic Chef, Inc. v. Baldrige, No. C82-653A (N.D. Ga. filed Mar. 30, 1982); Trane Co. v. Baldrige, No. 78 C 413 (D. Del. filed Sept. 5, 1978); Monsanto Co. v. Baldrige, No. 82-134-A (S.D. Iowa filed Mar. 1, 1982); Lone Star Steel Co. v. Baldrige, No. 832-0337H (N.D. Tex. filed Mar. 5, 1982); R. J. Reynolds, Inc. v. Baldrige, No. 82-242 (D. Del. filed May 14, 1982).

prohibit further litigation.[1] This agreement was subsequently implemented by Executive Order No. 12283.[2]

In February 1981, appellant Gregory Allen Persinger, a U.S. marine and former hostage released pursuant to the executive agreement, brought suit against Iran alleging numerous violations of treaties as well as international, constitutional, and common law. In accordance with its obligations under the executive agreement, the U.S. Government intervened and moved to dismiss the complaint. The district court, relying on *Dames & Moore v. Regan* (453 U.S. 654 (1981)), granted the motion, holding that the President could lawfully dispose of private claims against foreign governments in order to resolve an international crisis. The court also found that Iran was immune from suit under the Foreign Sovereign Immunities Act (28 U.S.C. §§1330, 1602–1611) (FSIA). On appeal, the U.S. Court of Appeals for the District of Columbia Circuit (per Bork, J.) affirmed the district court's dismissal.

At the outset, the court of appeals decided that neither the executive order nor the FSIA deprived it of subject matter jurisdiction. The court observed that if the executive order were construed as an attempt to limit jurisdiction, it would raise serious constitutional problems. Moreover, since the relevant language was addressed to claimants and not to the courts, the order was an "index of a legal change rather than a jurisdiction divestiture." Accordingly, the court concluded that "the Executive Order . . . [is] best understood as defining a rule of law to be applied by courts when faced with certain types of claims."[3]

The court then turned to the question of immunity under the FSIA. Focusing on the language of section 1605(a)(5),[4] the court identified two critical issues: (1) whether Iran's allegedly illegal actions occurred "in the United States," and (2) whether these actions were "discretionary." If the actions did

[1] Since the United States had severed diplomatic relations with Iran, the agreement was embodied in two Declarations of the Government of Algeria.

[2] 46 Fed. Reg. 7927 (1981). Executive Order No. 12283 reads, in relevant part:

> The Secretary of the Treasury shall promulgate regulations: [a] prohibiting any person subject to U.S. jurisdiction from prosecuting . . . any claim against the Government of Iran . . . ; [b] prohibiting any person not a U.S. national from prosecuting any such claim . . . ; [c] ordering the termination of any previously instituted judicial proceedings . . . ; and [d] prohibiting the enforcement of any judicial order issued in the course of such proceedings.

The court noted that subsections [c] and [d] did not apply to Persinger's case since his lawsuit was initiated after the executive order had been issued. 690 F.2d 1010, 1015.

[3] *Id.* at 1016.

[4] Section 1605(a)(5) reads in part:

> A foreign state shall not be immune from the jurisdiction of courts of the United States . . . in any case—
>
> . . .
>
> . . . in which money damages are sought against a foreign state for personal injury or death, or damage to or loss of property, occurring in the United States and covered by the tortious act or omission of that foreign state . . . ; except this paragraph shall not apply to—
>
> (A) any claim based upon the exercise or performance or the failure to exercise or perform a discretionary function regardless of whether the discretion be abused. . . .

not occur in the United States or if they were discretionary, then immunity would attach.

The first issue required a determination as to whether the U.S. Embassy in Iran was United States territory. Finding no guidance in the legislative history of the FSIA and no binding precedent under international law, the court, relying on the language of section 1603(c) of the FSIA, interpreted the term "United States" to include all territory under the concurrent jurisdiction of the U.S. Government. The court held that "American embassies abroad meet that criterion, for they are subject to the broad authority of Congress to enact legislation . . . , and of the State Department to establish rules governing consular affairs."[5]

In deciding whether the seizure was discretionary, the court looked to the Federal Tort Claims Act (28 U.S.C. §2680 (1976)), which provides that a patently illegal act is not discretionary. Assuming without deciding that the Embassy seizure was an act of the Government of Iran,[6] the court determined that the seizure was patently illegal, citing various international conventions and a decision of the International Court of Justice.[7] Therefore, Iran was not immune from suit under the FSIA and the court's subject matter jurisdiction over the dispute was established.

The next issue was whether the President could lawfully extinguish the hostages' legal claims against Iran. As framed by the court, the question was whether the President had the power to "direct the courts to apply one rule of law rather than another to a particular class of claims."[8] Referring to Justice Jackson's analysis in *Youngstown Sheet & Tube Co. v. Sawyer* (343 U.S. 579 (1952)), the court characterized this power as falling within the " 'zone of twilight in which [the President] and Congress may have concurrent authority, or in which its distribution is uncertain.' "[9] Thus, the issue was one of separation of powers; and the validity of the President's action hinged on "the views of the Legislative Branch toward such action, including 'congressional inertia, indifference or quiescence.' "[10] Following the analysis in *Dames & Moore,* the court examined the activities of Congress in this area and found that it had acquiesced in the presidential power asserted.[11] True, *Dames & Moore* and past claim settlements were distinguishable, since in these cases the issue was one of settling claims by providing alternative compensation or remedies. Nevertheless, the court found that over the years, Congress had approved "[s]trong presidential authority in the field of claim disposal, when

[5] 690 F.2d at 1017 (citations omitted).

[6] Since the district court had dismissed Persinger's complaint without taking evidence on this point, the court of appeals assumed the allegations to be true.

[7] *See* 690 F.2d at 1018–19.

[8] *Id.* at 1019.

[9] *Id.* at 1020 (quoting *Dames & Moore,* 453 U.S. at 668, in turn quoting *Youngstown,* 343 U.S. at 637).

[10] 690 F.2d at 1020 (quoting *Dames & Moore,* 453 U.S. at 668–69, in turn quoting *Youngstown,* 343 U.S. at 637).

[11] The court noted the long history of executive branch activity in settling foreign claims and continued congressional acquiescence therein. The court also emphasized that the executive order had been in existence for 1½ years without any sign of congressional disapproval.

necessary to the imperative interests of the Nation. . . ."[12] Thus, "the President need not obtain a sum of money or an alternative tribunal but may extinguish claims altogether when 'the imperatives of events' make that necessary to resolve an international crisis."[13]

Comment. The opinion of the court of appeals is significant in two respects. First, unlike *Dames & Moore,* this case involved presidential action that may fairly be characterized as extinguishing, rather than merely suspending or settling, legal claims of U.S. citizens. Therefore, much of the analysis contained in the Supreme Court decision was not applicable in this case.[14] On the other hand, the legislative history of the Hostage Act of 1868 (22 U.S.C. §1732 (1976)), combined with Congress's implicit approval of the U.S.-Iran Agreement, would suggest that the President's actions taken to resolve this particular international crisis did not violate the separation of powers doctrine. Second, unlike *Dames & Moore,* where the Supreme Court took great pain to narrow its decision,[15] the court of appeals laid down a general rule of law which authorized the President to extinguish legal claims "when 'the imperatives of events' make that necessary to resolve an international crisis."[16]

People's Republic of China—reciprocity—evidence of reciprocal Chinese legal remedies fulfills requirement of U.S. Public Vessels Act

CHINA NATIONAL TECHNICAL IMPORT CORPORATION, ET AL. v. UNITED STATES. 82 Civ. 2205 (PNL).
U.S. District Court, S.D.N.Y., December 3, 1982.

In this, the first case brought by Chinese nationals in U.S. courts since the 1949 revolution,[1] the U.S. District Court for the Southern District of New York (per Leval, J.) determined that Chinese plaintiffs were entitled to payment of an uncontested claim of $4.5 million against the U.S. Government. In so deciding, the court declared itself satisfied that a private American

[12] 690 F.2d at 1022.

[13] *Id.* at 1022–23 (quoting *Youngstown,* 343 U.S. at 637). The court declined to address Persinger's Fifth Amendment taking claim because it did not afford a basis for invalidating the executive order and because it could presumably be pursued in the Court of Claims under the Tucker Act, 28 U.S.C. §1491 (1976). In this regard, it is interesting to note Justice Powell's concurrence in *Dames & Moore,* in which he stated that the Government must compensate individuals whose claims are bargained away in order to further U.S. foreign policy objectives. *But see* Chas. T. Main Int'l, Inc. v. Khuzestan Water & Power Auth., 651 F.2d 800, 809 n.13 (1st Cir. 1981), where the court, in discussing the International Emergency Economic Powers Act, questioned whether an unliquidated claim could be considered either a "right" with respect to property or an "acquisition" of property.

[14] For example, the Supreme Court in *Dames & Moore* looked to the International Claims Settlement Act of 1949, 22 U.S.C. §1621 *et seq.* as amended (1980), as evidence of Congress's implicit approval of President Carter's action to suspend claims of U.S. nationals. As Justice Rehnquist acknowledged, the purposes of the Act were to allocate funds received from the foreign government to the claimants and to establish procedures for distributing these funds. Yet, no such alternative remedies are available to Persinger.

[15] *See* 453 U.S. at 658–62.

[16] The court of appeals has granted Persinger a rehearing, and as of this writing the case has not been resolved.

[1] *See* N.Y. Times, Nov. 2, 1982, §D, at 5.

plaintiff would have a reciprocal remedy in Chinese courts against the People's Republic of China (PRC) under similar circumstances.

The claim arose as a result of a collision in April 1981 in the South China Sea between a U.S. nuclear submarine and a Japanese merchant vessel. Plaintiffs are business entities of the PRC who sought recovery against the United States for the value of cargo lost in the collision on the ground that the loss was caused solely by the fault of the U.S. vessel. The United States did not contest the plaintiffs' allegation of fault.[2] However, it invoked section 5 of the Public Vessels Act (46 U.S.C. §785), which provides as follows: "No suit may be brought under this chapter by a national of any foreign government unless it shall appear to the satisfaction of the court in which suit is brought that said government, under similar circumstances, allows nationals of the United States to sue in its courts." Thus, the issue before the court was whether Chinese law would provide U.S. nationals with access to Chinese courts under circumstances similar to (but the reverse of) those presented in this case.

Plaintiffs alleged the existence of the requisite reciprocity and offered the court evidentiary support in two forms. First, plaintiffs offered a legal opinion by the Legal Counsel Office of a Chinese governmental organization, the China Council for the Promotion of International Trade (CCPIT).[3] The opinion stated, in relevant part:

> According to the principle of law of the People's Republic of China, the People's Court of China allows a foreign citizen, enterprise or organization to bring civil suit in it *on the basis of reciprocity.* Therefore *if the court of the United States accepts suit* brought in it by the Chinese injured party of the present case . . . , the People's Court of China, under corresponding circumstances, will accept suit brought to it by the American injured party [*sic*] [emphasis added].

Second, plaintiffs offered the court an affidavit by an American specialist in Chinese law, Professor R. Randle Edwards of Columbia Law School. The affidavit addressed the PRC's sovereign immunity, the existence of substantive and procedural remedies under Chinese law with respect to suits by Chinese citizens against the state, and the availability of such remedies to aliens. According to the affidavit, there has been "no reported instance of any foreign national being unable to bring suit in the Courts of the PRC against a [Chinese] government agency, nor is there any evidence of any attempts to bring such a suit being frustrated by substantive or procedural inadequacies of Chinese law."[4] Professor Edwards concluded that the reciprocity called for under the

[2] Indeed, by the time this case arose, the United States had admitted liability for the accident and had compensated Japanese victims of the collision. *See ibid.*

[3] The opinion, dated Jan. 20, 1982, was accompanied by a letter of Feb. 16, 1982 from the Embassy of the PRC attesting to the CCPIT's competence and qualifications. According to the affidavit of R. Randle Edwards (*see* note 4 *infra,* and accompanying text), the CCPIT plays a major role in the development of China's foreign trade. Its work includes mediation and arbitration in maritime and foreign trade disputes, and its Legal Counsel Office provides legal advice to Chinese and foreign clients.

[4] Affidavit of R. Randle Edwards, July 9, 1982, at 4. Professor Edwards noted, however, that court records are not the best source of Chinese legal principles because the Chinese traditionally

Public Vessels Act exists with respect to a cause of action in tort brought by an American citizen in PRC courts against a representative or agency of the Chinese Government, and that "[t]he defense of sovereign immunity would not be raised in such an action. . . ."[5]

In its initial response to the court, the United States denied that the reciprocity required by the Public Vessels Act existed. Following the filing of the Edwards affidavit, however, the United States withdrew its defense and stipulated that it would rely on the evidentiary representations of the plaintiffs. Despite this concession, however, the court asked the parties for additional evidence of reciprocity.

Plaintiffs responded by filing a second affidavit by Professor Edwards. This affidavit emphasized that the PRC State Constitution contains a provision similar to the provisions found in the U.S. Federal Tort Claims Act and in the Public Vessels Act providing for the waiver of sovereign immunity in cases of torts committed by the state, and that the PRC Civil Procedure Law provides foreign nationals with rights equal to those of Chinese citizens when bringing suit in the courts of the PRC. Professor Edwards concluded that a trial of similar issues in the PRC "would proceed from the filing of a complaint to the execution of a judgment with due consideration to those concepts of fair play and justice that underlie American jurisprudence."[6]

In a one-page order, the court held that the "uncontested evidence submitted by the plaintiff establishes that the reciprocity requirement of 46 U.S.C. §785 has been satisfied."

Comment. While the court's disposition of this case would appear to be correct, it is interesting to note that the legal opinion of the CCPIT does not attest to Chinese reciprocity as such, but—like the Public Vessels Act—conditions such reciprocity on the existence of reciprocal treatment for its own nationals under the laws of the alien's home state. There is no indication in the record that this issue of circularity was raised by the court or by the United States. It is certainly arguable, however, that the willingness of the United States to accept the PRC's assurances of reciprocity should not have been frustrated on this ground. Indeed, under closely similar circumstances, the U.S. Court of Appeals for the Second Circuit has held that the willingness of two governments to allow suits by nationals of the other should not "be frustrated by any such Gaston-Alphonse approach."[7]

The significance of this case, however, is more far-reaching. Since most business entities of the PRC are government-related, the prospective ability of Americans to sue the PRC, even under narrow circumstances such as those presented here, is encouraging. Equally encouraging is the evidence presented by the plaintiffs that foreign nationals can utilize the courts of China and rely on the application of a predictable system of legal principles.

---

have preferred to resolve disputes through conciliation or mediation and because China is essentially a civil law jurisdiction. *Id.* at 11.

[5] *Id.* at 19.

[6] Affidavit of R. Randle Edwards, Dec. 1, 1982, at 4.

[7] Nicholas E. Vernicos Shipping Co. v. United States, 349 F.2d 465, 470 (2d Cir. 1965) (also involving application of the Public Vessels Act).

Sovereign immunity—arbitration—agreement to arbitrate not contemplating role for U.S. courts held not to waive immunity

MARITIME INTERNATIONAL NOMINEES ESTABLISHMENT v. REPUBLIC OF GUINEA. 693 F.2d 1094.
U.S. Court of Appeals, D.C. Cir., November 12, 1982.

Maritime International Nominees Establishment (MINE), a Liechtenstein corporation, and the Republic of Guinea entered into a contract in 1971 to form a mixed economy company under the law of Guinea for the purpose of shipping Guinean bauxite to foreign markets. Under the terms of the contract, disputes were to be resolved by binding arbitration conducted by arbitrators selected by the President of the International Centre for the Settlement of Investment Disputes (ICSID). The agreement did not designate a location for arbitration proceedings.

A rift developed between the parties, and in 1975 they executed a consent form in order to invoke the arbitration services of ICSID. For reasons that were later disputed, no valid consent form was ever presented to ICSID. Asserting that it was unable to proceed to arbitration by ICSID without Guinea's consent, MINE sought an order from the U.S. District Court for the District of Columbia compelling arbitration before the American Arbitration Association (AAA). MINE asserted subject matter jurisdiction under the Foreign Sovereign Immunities Act of 1976 (28 U.S.C. §§1330, 1602–1611) (FSIA), and the Federal Arbitration Act (9 U.S.C. §4). Although Guinea did not appear in response to the petition, the court entered an order compelling arbitration. Following extensive AAA arbitration proceedings, which also took place in Guinea's absence, an award in excess of $25 million was rendered in favor of MINE.

MINE returned to the district court to confirm the arbitration award. Guinea responded by moving to dismiss for lack of subject matter jurisdiction. The district court confirmed the award, holding that Guinea had waived its immunity by agreeing to an arbitration that could be expected to be held in the United States and by engaging in commercial activities in the United States.[1]

On appeal, Guinea argued that the district court lacked subject matter jurisdiction because (1) Guinea had not waived its immunity under the FSIA, (2) the signing by both parties of the ICSID consent form committed them to an ICSID arbitration and precluded the exercise of jurisdiction to compel arbitration under the Federal Arbitration Act, and (3) the FSIA does not and cannot constitutionally confer subject matter jurisdiction over suits between foreign plaintiffs and foreign states. The United States intervened, supporting Guinea on the claim that it had not waived immunity, but disagreeing with Guinea on the constitutional claim. The U.S. Court of Appeals for the District of Columbia Circuit (per McGowan, J.) reversed, holding that the district court lacked subject matter jurisdiction on the ground that Guinea had not waived immunity. The court did not reach the other arguments raised by Guinea.

[1] 505 F.Supp. 141 (D.D.C. 1981), *summarized in* 75 AJIL 963 (1981).

Under the FSIA, both subject matter jurisdiction and personal jurisdiction are conditioned on the absence of immunity (28 U.S.C. §1330(a), (b)). The court of appeals first addressed the district court's conclusion that Guinea had implicitly waived immunity under section 1605(a)(1) of the Act[2] by agreeing to arbitrate before ICSID without designating a location other than the seat of ICSID, Washington, D.C. Because ICSID rules provide that arbitrations will take place in Washington unless otherwise specified by the parties, the lower court found that Guinea had contemplated that the arbitration would take place in the United States. The court of appeals stated that a "key reason why pre-FSIA cases found that an agreement to arbitrate in the United States waived immunity from suit was that such agreements could only be effective if deemed to contemplate a role for United States *courts* in compelling arbitration."[3] The court of appeals pointed out that MINE had asserted in the district court that U.S. courts were powerless to compel an ICSID arbitration under the arbitration agreement concluded between MINE and Guinea. MINE had so argued in order to persuade the district court to compel arbitration before the AAA. The court of appeals ruled that MINE was estopped from denying this original assertion. As a result, the court held, the contract could not be viewed as an implicit agreement to submit to the jurisdiction of U.S. courts. Because the contract, according to MINE's argument below, did not foresee a role for U.S. courts, it did not waive Guinea's sovereign immunity—even though the agreed-to arbitration would probably take place on U.S. soil.[4]

The court next considered and rejected the district court's finding that Guinea had waived immunity under the standards set forth in section 1605(a)(2) of the FSIA, *i.e.*, (1) by engaging in commercial activities in the United States, and (2) by engaging in commercial activities elsewhere that caused a "direct effect" in the United States.

First, the court held that there must at least be an agency relationship between the foreign state and an American actor in order to find that activity by the latter was conducted "by the foreign state" within the meaning of the first clause of section 1605(a)(2). The court concluded that Guinea's direction of an American shipping firm to provide certain services in connection with the contract did not meet the agency standard, since there was insufficient evidence to find that Guinea had authorized the American firm to act on its behalf. In addition, activities performed directly by the foreign state must, under the Act, have "substantial contact"[5] with the United States. Distinguishing the lesser standard of "minimum contacts" employed in due process analysis for purposes of personal jurisdiction, the court concluded that two

[2] Section 1605(a)(1) states that a foreign state shall not be immune in any case "in which the foreign state has waived its immunity either explicitly or by implication."

[3] 693 F.2d 1094, 1103 (emphasis added).

[4] By ruling on this narrow ground, the court of appeals expressly declined to rule on such issues as (1) whether a waiver of immunity for ICSID enforcement proceedings would also constitute a waiver for suits to compel an ICSID arbitration, and (2) whether the Federal Arbitration Act precludes lawsuits in U.S. courts to compel arbitration before ICSID. *Id.* at 1102 n.14.

[5] 28 U.S.C. §1603(e).

meetings in the United States of uncertain scope and importance that were attended by Guinean representatives did not constitute the required "substantial contact."

Second, the court analyzed the "direct effect" standard of the third clause of section 1605(a)(2) and held that an effect in the United States could not be direct unless it was reasonably foreseeable. The court held that an alleged loss of profits suffered by an American shipping firm employed by MINE, even if such loss were a result of a breach of contract by Guinea, was not reasonably foreseeable because the firm's involvement was not contemplated by Guinea when it entered the contract and because the loss was a loss of anticipated profits.

Comment. This opinion may be considered less significant for its holdings than for the numerous issues that it did not decide. By virtue of MINE's self-limiting arguments in the district court, the appeals court decision on the issue of implied waiver of immunity is, of necessity, a narrow one, skirting important questions concerning the relationship between sovereign immunity and agreements to arbitrate before international bodies located in the United States. In addition, the court's ruling on commercial activities by a foreign state breaks no new ground. Finally, by reversing the lower court on statutory grounds, the court of appeals avoided the more substantial question of whether a federal court may constitutionally hear a dispute between a foreign citizen and a foreign state. This question was answered in the negative by the U.S. Court of Appeals for the Second Circuit in *Verlinden, B.V. v. Central Bank of Nigeria,*[6] a case that, as of this writing, is pending before the Supreme Court.

Treaties—Warsaw Convention—conversion of liability limitations from gold standard to dollars

FRANKLIN MINT CORPORATION v. TRANS WORLD AIRLINES, INC. 690 F.2d 303.

U.S. Court of Appeals, 2d Cir., September 28, 1982.

This case involves a claim for damages by a shipper against an air carrier for loss of cargo, and the carrier's attempt to limit its liability under the Warsaw Convention.[1] In March 1979, plaintiffs, Franklin Mint Corporation (Franklin Mint) and others, contracted with defendant Trans World Airlines, Inc. (TWA) for the transportation by air of certain valuable coins from the United States to England. While the coins were allegedly worth $250,000, Franklin Mint made no special declaration of value at the time it delivered the coins to TWA. The coins were later lost or destroyed, and suit for damages was brought by the shipper against the airline. It was undisputed that TWA was liable to plaintiffs under Article 18 of the Warsaw Convention.[2] At issue,

[6] 647 F.2d 320 (2d Cir. 1981), *cert. granted,* 454 U.S. 1140 (1982), *summarized in* 75 AJIL 965 (1981).

[1] Oct. 12, 1929, 49 Stat. 3000 (1934), TS No. 876, 137 LNTS 11. The Convention, which the United States ratified in 1934, is a multilateral treaty governing a number of issues concerning civil aviation.

[2] Article 18(1) of the Convention provides: "The carrier shall be liable for damage sustained in the event of the destruction or loss of, or of damage to, any checked baggage or any goods,

however, was the extent of TWA's liability as defined by Article 22 of the Convention.

Article 22 limits a carrier's liability in the transportation of passengers, checked baggage, and goods. It defines the respective limits in terms of French gold or "Poincaré" francs, a unit of account consisting of a specified weight of gold. Absent a special declaration of value, a carrier's liability for baggage and goods is limited under Article 22 to 250 Poincaré francs per kilogram. The dollar value of that limit is then computed by converting the Poincaré francs into United States dollars.

The issue before the court was what unit of account should be used to convert judgments under the Convention into United States dollars in light of the fact that gold no longer has an official price. The U.S. District Court for the Southern District of New York held that such conversion should be based on the last official price of gold in the United States, thereby limiting TWA's liability in this case to approximately $6,500.[3] Franklin Mint, challenging the district court's method of conversion, appealed. The U.S. Court of Appeals for the Second Circuit (per Winter, J.) agreed with the lower court that the last official price of gold in the United States should be used to limit TWA's liability in the present case. It recognized, however, that the substitution of a unit of conversion was not a proper matter for judicial determination and therefore stated that the Convention's liability limitations should be considered prospectively unenforceable by U.S. courts for liability-creating events occurring more than 60 days from the issuance of the court's mandate.

Judge Winter began his analysis by observing that when the Warsaw Convention was drafted in the late 1920's, gold served official monetary functions and had an official price. Subsequently, the certainty of the gold standard progressively deteriorated. In 1978 members of the International Monetary Fund (IMF), including the United States, agreed to abolish the official price of gold. Since that time, the court noted, member states of the Warsaw Convention have utilized a variety of units of conversion; and the parties in this case offered the court four of these alternatives: (1) the last official price of gold in the United States; (2) the free market price of gold; (3) the Special Drawing Right (SDR), a unit of account established by the IMF; and (4) the exchange value of the current French franc.

The Second Circuit analyzed, seriatim, the four alternatives and determined that there were "powerful arguments" against each.[4] Despite this conclusion, however, the court felt compelled to choose a unit of conversion for purposes of the present dispute and settled, as had the district court, on the last official

---

if the occurrence which caused the damage so sustained took place during the transportation by air."

[3] 525 F.Supp. 1288 (S.D.N.Y. 1981).

[4] The court determined that Congress explicitly repealed the last official U.S. price of gold, and it therefore lacks any status in law or relationship to contemporary currency values; that the free market price of gold is highly volatile and fluctuates daily based, in part, on nonmonetary considerations of supply and demand; that the SDR can be modified or eliminated at the will of the IMF and has no basis in the Convention; and that the current French franc is simply one domestic currency whose value the French Government could unilaterally change at any time. 690 F.2d 303, 305–06.

price of gold in the United States. This choice was based, *inter alia,* on the fact that this standard was espoused by the Civil Aeronautics Board, the government agency most intimately concerned with the transaction at hand.

Although choosing a unit of conversion for purposes of the case before it, the court also concluded by way of dictum that it did not have the authority to select a unit of conversion for purposes of future judgments. Such selection was plainly a matter to be negotiated by the parties to the Convention, and, for domestic purposes, required treaty approval by the Senate or legislation passing both Houses of Congress. "Substitution of a new term is a political question, unfit for judicial resolution."[5] Accordingly, the court stated that "the Convention's limits on liability for loss of cargo are [prospectively] unenforceable in United States Courts"[6] with respect to events creating liability that occur 60 days from the issuance of the court's mandate. As to events occurring before that date, the court stated that the last official price of gold in the United States should be used to calculate the Article 22 limitations.

Comment. In assessing the court's holding, it is significant to note that Article 22's limitations apply not only to baggage and goods but also to passengers. While the amounts of the limits for passengers are different from those for baggage and goods, Article 22 defines all of the respective limits in terms of Poincaré francs. Therefore, despite a specific reference in its holding to the "loss of cargo," the court's decision would appear to affect equally the limits on a carrier's liability for injuries to passengers.

[5] *Id.* at 311.

[6] *Ibid.*

CURRENT DEVELOPMENTS

THE THIRTY-FOURTH SESSION OF THE INTERNATIONAL LAW COMMISSION

The 34th session of the International Law Commission was held in Geneva from May 3 to July 23, 1982, and was chaired by the Commission's dean, Professor Paul Reuter of France. This was the first meeting of the Commission in its new and enlarged composition. Its composition was new in the sense that all of its members were beginning a new 5-year term of office, the term of the former Commission having expired at the end of 1981. It was enlarged as a result of a decision taken by the General Assembly at its session in the fall of 1981 to expand the membership of the ILC from 25 to 34.[1]

The size of the Commission had been enlarged from its original 15 members twice before: first in 1956 to 21, then in 1961 to 25. The reasons given for the 1981 expansion were that the number of member states of the United Nations had been augmented considerably since the Commission's size was set at 25 in 1961, and that interest in the work of the Commission had increased substantially, particularly among the member states admitted since 1961.

It is difficult for this writer as a new member to determine what impact, if any, the enlargement of the Commission has had on its work. Plenary discussion of agenda items was doubtless somewhat more protracted, but probably not unduly so in most cases. Average attendance of plenary sessions over the entire 12-week period was perhaps in the low twenties (which probably reflects, on a percentage basis, about the same attendance rate as that of the Commission in its previous size and composition). The same general observations apply to the Drafting Committee, whose membership was increased proportionately, except that it seems doubtful that discussion there was significantly lengthier than in prior years.

Thus, while it is too early to tell what effect the increased size of the Commission will have on its output, preliminary indications appear to be that the pace of work will not be significantly retarded. Some representatives in the Sixth (Legal) Committee had in fact argued that expanding the membership of the Commission would increase its output. While this seems doubtful, the Commission's new, more broadly representative composition may well have the beneficial effect of enhancing the acceptability of its ultimate product.[2]

[1] UNGA Res. 36/39 (Nov. 18, 1981).

[2] This sentiment was echoed in the Sixth Committee. *See, e.g.,* the summary of the statement of Mr. Jagota of India:

> With its recently increased membership, the Commission reflected a wider range of experience and expertise and was more representative of the different regions of the world and the principal legal systems. The quality of its work was sure to improve and the compromises at which it arrived to become more widely acceptable as a result.

UN Doc. A/C.6/37/SR.46, at 18 (1982).

The Commission's first task in its 1982 session was to fill the casual vacancy created by the resignation of Ambassador, now Judge, Mohammed Bedjaoui upon his election to the International Court of Justice on March 19, 1982. Pursuant to Article 11 of its statute, the Commission elected Professor Ahmed Mahiou of Algeria to fill this vacancy.

The Commission held plenary discussions on five substantive topics during the course of the 34th session, none of which was new to its agenda.[3] Work was completed on treaties between states and international organizations or between two or more international organizations, and the Commission adopted the final text of its draft articles on this subject for submission to the General Assembly. The Commission continued its work on the following four topics: state responsibility, international liability for injurious consequences arising out of acts not prohibited by international law, jurisdictional immunities of states and their property, and the status of the diplomatic courier and the diplomatic bag not accompanied by diplomatic courier.

Also on the Commission's agenda but not discussed in plenary were the following three topics: the law of the nonnavigational uses of international watercourses, the Draft Code of Offences against the Peace and Security of Mankind, and relations between states and international organizations (second part of the topic). The work on watercourses had been delayed following the resignation of the previous special rapporteur, now Judge Stephen M. Schwebel, upon his election to the International Court of Justice in January 1981, prior to the 33d session of the Commission. The Commission failed to fill this special rapporteurship in that session, in part because some members desired to allow the newly elected Commission to choose a successor to Judge Schwebel in 1982, which it did in the 34th session by appointing Ambassador Jens Evensen of Norway. Judge Schwebel had begun to prepare a third report on the nonnavigational uses of international watercourses prior to his resignation and, with a view to facilitating the Commission's work, had submitted this report for consideration by the Commission in its 1982 session. However, both because Judge Schwebel was no longer a member of the Commission and thus was unable to present the report, and because the new special rapporteur was not appointed until late in the 1982 session, the topic was not discussed at that session.

The Draft Code of Offences had been placed on the Commission's agenda for the 1982 session in response to a resolution passed in the 36th (1981–1982) session of the General Assembly inviting the Commission to resume its work on that subject.[4] The Commission appointed Minister Doudou Thiam of Senegal special rapporteur and established a working group on the topic to be chaired by Minister Thiam. The working group met and held a preliminary exchange of views. On the basis of its recommendation, the Commission

[3] For summaries of the work of the 32d and 33d sessions, see the Current Developments Notes by Stephen M. Schwebel and George H. Aldrich in 74 AJIL 961 (1980), and 75 *id.* at 992 (1981), respectively.

[4] UNGA Res. 36/106, para. 1 (Dec. 10, 1981). For background, see Ferencz, Current Developments Note, 75 AJIL 674 (1981).

decided to proceed, in its 1983 session, with a general debate on the topic in plenary on the basis of a first report to be submitted by the special rapporteur.

Treaties between States and International Organizations

The most noteworthy accomplishment of the 1982 session, and one that launched the current quinquennium on an auspicious note, was the completion of work that had begun in 1970 on treaties between states and international organizations or between two or more international organizations. This topic had been referred to the Commission by the General Assembly in response to a recommendation made by the United Nations Conference on the Law of Treaties in 1969. Under the leadership of the special rapporteur, Professor Paul Reuter, the Commission prepared a set of draft articles that correspond largely to the provisions of the Vienna Convention on the Law of Treaties. The Commission had provisionally approved the entire set of draft articles and had adopted Articles 1 to 26 in a second reading prior to the 1982 session. The Commission's task in that session, therefore, was to complete the second reading, or final approval, of the remaining draft articles and the annex. While most members spoke on all of the remaining articles, the discussion in plenary focused principally upon two issues, both of which represented departures from the Vienna Convention: Article 36 *bis;* and the procedures for arbitration and conciliation of disputes concerning the invalidity, termination, and suspension of the operation of treaties.

Article 36 *bis,* "Obligations and rights arising for States members of an international organization from a treaty to which it is a party," obviously does not have a counterpart in the Vienna Convention. Its basic object is to provide for the circumstances under which states members of an international organization acquire rights and obligations under a treaty entered into by that organization. Examples of situations to which such an article might apply are given in the final commentary to the article:

> [A] customs union, in the case where it takes the form of an international organization, normally concludes tariff agreements to which its members are not parties. Such tariff agreements would be pointless unless they were to be immediately binding on member States. . . . [Or] an international organization, before concluding a headquarters agreement with a State, may wish its member States to agree among themselves, and with the organization itself, *beforehand* so as to establish, at least in part, some of the provisions of the headquarters agreement.[5]

The European Economic Community strongly favored the inclusion of such an article in the draft for the reasons stated in the above excerpt. The article drew opposition, however, from some representatives in the Sixth Committee as well as some members of the Commission, who viewed it as having been designed solely for the benefit of the EEC. They therefore objected to it on

[5] Report of the International Law Commission on the Work of its Thirty-fourth Session, 37 UN GAOR Supp. (No. 10) at 88–89, UN Doc. A/37/10 (1982) (emphasis in original) [hereinafter referred to as 1982 Report].

the ground that as a general principle the Commission should not draft articles to deal with exceptional and specific situations.

Two other concerns about Article 36 *bis* can perhaps be best understood in light of the version of the article that was initially presented to the Commission in its 1982 session:[6]

> The assent of States members of an international organization to obligations arising from a treaty concluded by that organization shall derive from:
>
> (a) the relevant rules of the organization applicable at the moment of the conclusion of the treaty which provide that States members of the organization are bound by such a treaty; or
> (b) the acknowledgment by the States and organizations participating in the negotiation of the treaty as well as the States members of the organizations that the application of the treaty necessarily entails such effects.[7]

The first of these other concerns was that this version of the article might not give sufficient notice to states entering into a treaty with an international organization of the circumstances under which the treaty would create rights in the member states of the organization. The second concern was that this version might not afford adequate protection to the states members of an international organization against becoming bound by obligations to which they had never expressly assented. This latter objection derived partly from the definition of "rules of the organization" to include not only the constituent instrument of the organization but also its "relevant decisions and resolutions."[8]

In the end, the Commission decided to include in the draft an article that would accomplish the basic purpose of the version most recently proposed by the special rapporteur but that was formulated so as to avoid these last two concerns. The final version, however, does nothing more than any previous version to meet the objection that it was tailored specifically and solely for the EEC; but like those versions, it contains nothing in its wording that would limit its applicability to the EEC and, indeed, many members noted that its benefits would extend to a wide variety of international organizations. Article 36 *bis,* in its final form, reads as follows:

[6] This version had actually been prepared during the previous session. After discussion in plenary, it had been referred to the Drafting Committee, but that body unfortunately did not have time to consider it. In view of the new and enlarged composition of the Commission in its 1982 session, the special rapporteur considered it fitting to "re-submit" this version in order to give new members an opportunity to comment upon it in plenary.

[7] P. Reuter, Eleventh Report on the Question of Treaties Concluded between States and International Organizations or between Two or More International Organizations, UN Doc. A/CN.4/353, at 12 (1982).

[8] Draft articles on the law of treaties between States and international organizations or between international organizations, Art. 2, para. 1(j), 1982 Report, *supra* note 5, at 27.

Article 36 bis

Obligations and rights arising for States members of an international organization from a treaty to which it is a party

Obligations and rights arise for States members of an international organization from the provisions of a treaty to which that organization is a party when the parties to the treaty intend those provisions to be the means of establishing such obligations and according such rights and have defined their conditions and effects in the treaty or have otherwise agreed thereon, and if:

(a) the States members of the organization, by virtue of the constituent instrument of that organization or otherwise, have unanimously agreed to be bound by the said provisions of the treaty; and

(b) the assent of the States members of the organization to be bound by the relevant provisions of the treaty has been duly brought to the knowledge of the negotiating States and negotiating organizations.[9]

The dispute settlement provisions of the draft articles on treaties between states and international organizations also represent a departure from the Vienna Convention on the Law of Treaties and were a second focal point of discussion in the Commission's 1982 session. Article 66 of the Vienna Convention provides separate means for the settlement of each of two categories of disputes: those concerning the application or interpretation of either of the two articles concerning norms of *jus cogens* are to be submitted to the International Court of Justice unless the parties agree to submit them to arbitration; and those concerning the application or interpretation of any of the other articles in part V of the Convention (which deals with the invalidity, termination, and suspension of the operation of treaties) may be submitted to the Conciliation Commission provided for in the Annex to the Convention.[10]

The Commission could not duplicate both parts of this system for the present topic because international organizations cannot be parties to cases before the International Court of Justice. The solution finally adopted by the Commission, over the dissents of members from socialist countries, therefore provides for the compulsory arbitration of disputes concerning the *jus cogens* articles in lieu of settlement by the ICJ. This solution was inspired by the relevant provisions of the Convention on the Law of the Sea.[11] The machinery for establishing the arbitral tribunal is set forth in the annex to the draft articles and is designed to guarantee that the tribunal will be established whenever the arbitration procedures of Article 66 are invoked. The provision of

[9] 1982 Report, *supra* note 5, at 87.

[10] As explained in the Commission's 1982 Report, this difference in treatment of the two classes of disputes was "justified purely by the fact that the notion of peremptory norms appeared to certain States to call for specially effective procedural safeguards owing to the radical nature of its consequences, the relative scarcity of fully conclusive precedents and the developments that article 64 [which provides that any treaty that conflicts with a newly emerged peremptory norm of international law becomes void] appeared to foreshadow." *Id.* at 137.

[11] *See* Annexes V and VII, Convention on the Law of the Sea, Working Paper 1 of the Drafting Committee, June 7, 1982, No. 82-16124, at 194 and 211.

the Vienna Convention for the compulsory conciliation of disputes concerning the other articles in part V was incorporated in the draft without substantial change since it was equally applicable to disputes involving international organizations.

Jurisdictional Immunities of States and Their Property

The second subject discussed by the Commission in its 34th session was jurisdictional immunities of states and their property. As long ago as 1949, the Commission had included this topic in its provisional list of subjects suitable for codification. In 1977 the General Assembly agreed with the Commission's recommendation that the topic was ripe for active consideration and placed it on the Commission's agenda. It is still, however, in the preliminary stages of development. The rather slow rate of progress on this topic is in no way due to lack of effort on the part of the special rapporteur, Ambassador Sompong Sucharitkul of Thailand, who has presented the Commission with four meticulously researched reports containing a total of 12 draft articles. The delay is due rather to the sensitivity of the topic and the inability of the members of the Commission to agree on points as fundamental as whether the draft articles should follow the "absolute" or the "restrictive" theory of state immunity.

During its 1982 session, the Commission provisionally adopted Article 1 (defining the scope of the set of articles), paragraph 1(a) of Article 2 (defining "court"), and Articles 7 ("Modalities for giving effect to State immunity"), 8 ("Express consent to the exercise of jurisdiction"), and 9 ("Effect of participation in a proceeding before a court"). Conspicuously absent from this list are the two articles that generated the most discussion: Articles 6 (stating the principle of state immunity) and 12 (stating the "trading or commercial activity" exception to state immunity).

One might wonder why the Commission finds it so difficult to state the principle of state immunity in Article 6. The Commission's difficulty is traceable to the nature of its product: to the extent that the set of draft articles on jurisdictional immunity purports to be a codification of general international law on that subject, a statement of the principle of immunity along the lines of that in the U.S. Foreign Sovereign Immunities Act[12] could be taken

12

> Subject to existing international agreements to which the United States is a party at the time of enactment of this Act *a foreign state shall be immune* from the jurisdiction of the courts of the United States and of the States *except as provided in* sections 1605 to 1607 of [the Act].

Foreign Sovereign Immunities Act of 1976, 28 U.S.C. §1604 (emphasis added). *See also* sec. 1, para. 1 of the UK State Immunity Act of 1978, ch. 33, *reprinted in* 17 ILM 1123 (1978) ("A State is immune from the jurisdiction of the courts of the United Kingdom except as provided in the following provisions of . . . this Act"); sec. 3, para. 1 of the Act to Provide for State Immunity in Canadian Courts, 1982, ch. 95, *reprinted in* 21 ILM 798 (1982) ("Except as provided by this Act, a foreign state is immune from the jurisdiction of any court in Canada"); and Art. 15 of the 1972 European Convention on State Immunity, 1972 ETS 74 ("A Contracting State shall be entitled to immunity from the jurisdiction of the courts of another Contracting State if the proceedings do not fall within Articles 1 to 14. . .").

to mean that states were absolutely immune from the jurisdiction of other states under general international law, and that the only exceptions were those carved out in the draft articles. (Should the draft articles ultimately take the form of a convention, states would, of course, be free to agree to the exceptions to jurisdictional immunity specified in them even if absolute jurisdictional immunity of states were a rule of general international law.[13]) For this reason, some members of the Commission were hesitant to support language such as, "A state is immune from the jurisdiction of another state except as provided in the present articles."

In fact, the Commission had provisionally adopted an Article 6 in 1980. This formulation, which took no position as to whether general international law supports the absolute or the restrictive theory, read as follows:

> 1. A State is immune from the jurisdiction of another State in accordance with the provisions of the present articles.
>
> 2. Effect shall be given to State immunity in accordance with the provisions of the present articles.[14]

Debate was reopened on Article 6 in the 1982 session to afford new members an opportunity to state their views. Concern was expressed in plenary discussion that the formulation adopted provisionally in 1980 did not state a rule. And to some members, the reason for the second paragraph was not clear. Accordingly, the article was sent back to the Drafting Committee for reexamination in light of the plenary discussion despite the fact that it had already been provisionally approved. It is to be hoped that the Commission will be able to agree upon Article 6, the cornerstone of the set of draft articles, in its 1983 session.

Article 12 was first before the Commission in the 1982 session, having been proposed by the special rapporteur in his fourth report.[15] It is the first substantive provision in part III of the draft, which is entitled "Exceptions to State Immunities," and the only exception proposed as a draft article in the fourth report. The special rapporteur offered an indication of what is to come in future reports, however, by including in his fourth report a tentative list of the exceptions to be contained in part III. That list is as follows:

(a) trading or commercial activity;
(b) contracts of employment;
(c) personal injuries and damage to property;
(d) ownership, possession and use of property;
(e) patents, trade marks and other intellectual properties;
(f) fiscal liabilities and customs duties;

[13] This, notwithstanding the rather astonishing claim made in the Sixth Committee during the discussion of the Commission's Report on its 34th Session that absolute jurisdictional immunity was a rule of *jus cogens. See* statement of Mr. Lukyanovich of the USSR, UN Doc. A/C.6/37/SR.39, at 9–10 (1982). *See* the response of the special rapporteur, speaking in his capacity as representative of Thailand, UN Doc. A/C.6/37/SR.44, at 4–5 (1982).

[14] 1982 Report, *supra* note 5, at 222 n.231. *See also* Schwebel, *supra* note 3, at 967.

[15] S. Sucharitkul, Fourth Report on Jurisdictional Immunities of States and their Property, UN Doc. A/CN.4/357 and Corr.1 (1982).

(g) share-holdings and membership of bodies corporate;
(h) ships employed in commercial service; and
(i) arbitration.[16]

Article 12 deals with the first exception on the list:

Article 12. Trading or commercial activity

1. In the absence of agreement to the contrary, a State is not immune from the jurisdiction of another State in respect of proceedings relating to any trading or commercial activity conducted by it, partly or wholly in the territory of that other State, being an activity in which private persons or entities may there engage.

2. Paragraph 1 does not apply to transactions concluded between States, nor to contracts concluded on a government-to-government basis.[17]

Article 12 drew mixed reviews in the Commission. Reactions ranged from complete rejection of the possibility of any exception to state immunity to warm reception of the article and the restrictive theory it represents as a reflection of contemporary international reality. The special rapporteur explained that Article 12 dealt with the exception to state immunity that he had concluded, on the basis of his empirical research, was "least open to dispute."[18] Yet several members of the Commission, most notably Professor Nikolai Ushakov of the Soviet Union, questioned the entire restrictive approach. Professor Ushakov's basic position was that because of the sovereign equality of states, the only "exception" to state immunity was express consent.

Other members agreed with the substantive thrust of Article 12 but expressed concerns about such matters as the phrase, "being an activity in which private persons or entities may there engage," and the definition of "trading or commercial activity." It was observed that the former phrase could have the effect of insulating activities in, *e.g.*, states with socialist systems that would not be immune in states having other political or economic systems. As to what constitutes a "trading or commercial activity," the special rapporteur has proposed, in an article that will be submitted to the Commission for its consideration at a later date,[19] that the nature of the activity, rather than its purpose, should be emphasized. This is in line with the U.S. Foreign Sovereign Immunities Act but caused concern on the part of some members. They took the position that it may be necessary in some cases to refer to the purpose of a particular act, as when the act is directed toward such public functions as relieving famine or assuring the welfare of the inhabitants of a particular country. While the Commission achieved no consensus on Article 12 in plenary, it did agree to refer it to the Drafting Committee, which at the 1983 session of the ILC will have the unenviable task of charting a course through the shoals of these conflicting positions.

[16] This list is *reprinted in* 1982 Report, *supra* note 5, at 213.
[17] This article is *reprinted in id.* at 209 n.210.
[18] *Id.* at 218.
[19] This is Article 3, "Interpretative Provisions," which is set forth in *id.* at 210–11 n.214.

State Responsibility

Progress on state responsibility has been painfully slow since the Commission identified it as suitable for codification at its very first session in 1949 and began work on it in 1955. The subject is obviously of fundamental importance to the entire field of public international law and it is thus unfortunate that work on it has not been completed. Yet its very centrality is undoubtedly the chief reason for the Commission's historical difficulties with the topic. Happily, work does appear to have ground ahead at a rather steady, if ponderously slow, pace since Professor, now Judge, Roberto Ago assumed the special rapporteurship in 1963. In that year, and under his leadership, the Commission recognized it had reached a deadlock, scrapped its previous work on the topic—which, indeed, had yielded meager results—and initiated a new approach. This new approach has enabled the Commission to complete the first reading of part 1 of the topic, consisting of 35 draft articles, and to begin work on part 2.

The approach embarked upon by the Commission in 1963 is succinctly described in its 1970 *Yearbook:*

> The Commission agreed on the need to concentrate its study on the determination of the principles which govern the responsibility of States for internationally wrongful acts, maintaining a strict distinction between this task and the task of defining the rules that place obligations on States, the violation of which may generate responsibility. . . . [I]t is one thing to define a rule and the content of the obligation it imposes and another to determine whether that obligation has been violated and what should be the consequences of the violation. Only the second aspect comes within the sphere of responsibility proper. . . .[20]

State responsibility has been divided into three parts. Part 1, which has been completed in first reading as noted above, deals with the origin of international responsibility and contains chapters on "General Principles," "The 'Act of the State' under International Law," "Breach of an International Obligation," "Implication of a State in the Internationally Wrongful Act of Another State," and "Circumstances Precluding Wrongfulness." Part 2 will deal with the content, forms, and degrees of international responsibility, *i.e.*, with the reparative and punitive consequences of an internationally wrongful act of a state. Part 3 (whose inclusion is not yet definite) would deal with the implementation ("*mise en oeuvre*") of international responsibility and dispute settlement.

While the Commission has decided to eschew formulation of "primary" rules imposing obligations,[21] some consideration of the different kinds of ob-

[20] [1970] 2 Y.B. INT'L L. COMM'N 178, UN DOC. A/CN.4/SER.A/1970/Add.1.

[21] The Commission stated in 1970 that the articles on state responsibility would not undertake to define

> the rules of international law which . . . impose particular obligations on States, and which may, in a certain sense, be termed "primary", as opposed to the other rules—precisely those covering the field of responsibility—which may be termed "secondary", inasmuch as they are concerned with determining the consequences of failure to fulfil obligations established by the primary rules.

Id. at 179.

ligations that can be breached will almost inevitably have to occur in the context of elaborating the rules in part 2 concerning the content, forms, and degrees of state responsibility.[22] This follows, for example, from the fact that "the content, and the object and purpose of an obligation cannot but influence the legal consequences entailed by its breach ('qualitative proportionality')."[23] Thus, it seems that the content of a given obligation will have to be taken into account in part 2 in the course of determining the consequences of its breach. Primary rules may in this way come into play through the back door during the drafting of part 2; and, in fact, what may be taken as a variety of primary rules has already cropped up in Article 19 of part 1 of the draft articles, which is entitled "International crimes and international delicts."[24]

Professor Willem Riphagen became special rapporteur for the topic of state responsibility in 1979 upon Professor Ago's elevation to the International Court of Justice. The timing of this change was convenient since it allowed the Commission to complete part 1 under the rapporteurship of then Professor Ago and begin part 2 under that of Professor Riphagen. In his second report in 1981, Professor Riphagen proposed the first five articles of part 2.[25] After discussion in plenary, these articles were referred to the Drafting Committee, which unfortunately did not have time to consider them during that session.

[22] This was spelled out in the Third Report of the Special Rapporteur, Professor Willem Riphagen, UN Docs. A/CN.4/354 and Corr.1 and A/CN.4/354/Add.1 and Add.1/Corr.1 (Chinese only) and Corr.2. *See also* 1982 Report, *supra* note 5, at 172, paras. 81 and 82.

[23] 1982 Report, *supra* note 5, at 172.

[24] Article 19 reads as follows:

> 1. An act of a State which constitutes a breach of an international obligation is an internationally wrongful act, regardless of the subject-matter of the obligation breached.
>
> 2. An internationally wrongful act which results from the breach by a State of an international obligation so essential for the protection of fundamental interests of the international community that its breach is recognized as a crime by that community as a whole, constitutes an international crime.
>
> 3. Subject to paragraph 2, and on the basis of the rules of international law in force, an international crime may result, *inter alia*, from:
>
> (*a*) a serious breach of an international obligation of essential importance for the maintenance of international peace and security, such as that prohibiting aggression;
> (*b*) a serious breach of an international obligation of essential importance for safeguarding the right of self-determination of peoples, such as that prohibiting the establishment or maintenance by force of colonial domination;
> (*c*) a serious breach on a widespread scale of an international obligation of essential importance for safeguarding the human being, such as those prohibiting slavery, genocide and *apartheid*;
> (*d*) a serious breach of an international obligation of essential importance for the safeguarding and preservation of the human environment, such as those prohibiting massive pollution of the atmosphere or of the seas.
>
> 4. Any internationally wrongful act which is not an international crime in accordance with paragraph 2 constitutes an international delict.

Report of the International Law Commission on the Work of its Thirty-first Session, UN Doc. A/34/10 (1979), *reprinted in* [1979] 2 Y.B. INT'L L. COMM'N 1, 92, UN Doc. A/CN.4/SER.A/1979/Add.1(pt. 2).

[25] These articles are *reprinted in* 1982 Report, *supra* note 5, at 168–69.

In his third report in 1982, the special rapporteur presented a new set of six articles[26] that had been formulated in light of the discussion in the previous session, and that were proposed in place of the original five articles. The Commission decided in its 1982 session to refer Articles 1 to 6 as proposed in the third report to the Drafting Committee and to confirm the referral to that committee of Articles 1 to 3 as proposed in the second report. Regrettably, the Drafting Committee once again was unable to report out any articles.

The new set of articles is designed to provide a foundation for the remainder of part 2. After an initial article linking parts 1 and 2, it consists of an article embodying the principle of quantitative proportionality (Article 2), a statement that the rules in the remainder of part 2 are of a residual nature (Article 3), and three provisions on what the special rapporteur refers to as the "peremptory sub-systems": *jus cogens* (Article 4), the United Nations system (Article 5), and international crimes (Article 6).

In the 1982 session, members discussed not only the six articles proposed in the third report, but some of those presented in the second report as well. There were many comments concerning not only the substance of the articles, but also such matters as the order in which they were presented and whether a "linkage" provision was at all necessary. Only a few highlights of the substantive comments can be mentioned here. First, there was some disagreement on whether self-defense fell within the scope of the legal consequences of an internationally wrongful act or whether it was a primary right, falling outside the scope of the topic. The view was also expressed that the Commission had no mandate to interpret the provisions of the UN Charter on self-defense and that this subject should therefore not be covered at all in the draft articles on state responsibility. Finally, a number of members suggested that the subject of international crimes should be dealt with in a separate chapter rather than in the foundational provisions of part 2.

As to what the remainder of part 2 is likely to hold in store, the special rapporteur set forth in his third report three categories, or "parameters," of legal consequences of an internationally wrongful act: self-enforcement by the author state, enforcement by the injured state, and international enforcement. There was general support in plenary discussion for the notion that part 2 should contain a catalog of legal consequences based on these three parameters, and the elaboration of such a catalog will likely occupy the Commission's attention once it has provisionally adopted the foundational articles.

International Liability for Injurious Consequences Arising out of Acts Not Prohibited by International Law

When the Commission adopted its plan for future work on state responsibility in 1970, it decided to set aside for separate treatment "questions relating to responsibility arising out of the performance of certain lawful activities—such as spatial and nuclear activities. . . . [o]wing to the entirely different basis of the so-called responsibility for risk."[27] Thus, a basic distinction

[26] These articles are *reprinted in id.* at 173–74.
[27] [1970] 2 Y.B. INT'L L. COMM'N, *supra* note 20, at 178.

was made between state "responsibility" for internationally *wrongful* acts and international "liability" for the injurious consequences of an activity that is itself *lawful.*

The Commission first took up international liability in 1978 and appointed Professor Robert Q. Quentin-Baxter as special rapporteur. The working group set up by the Commission that year to consider the scope and nature of the topic defined it as concerning "the way in which States use, or manage the use of, their physical environment, either within their own territory or in areas not subject to the sovereignty of any State."[28] Thus, it seems rather clear that the topic was originally conceived of as dealing with (strict?) liability for "ultrahazardous," but socially desirable, activities affecting the physical environment (such as nuclear reactors and space objects) that involve a substantial and unavoidable, though foreseeable, risk of harming states with no control or right to control over them. Yet in the intervening years some representatives in the Sixth Committee, as well as some members of the Commission, have resisted restricting the scope of the topic in this way, and have suggested that it could be applied to such different problems as those in the field of international economic law.

At the Commission's 1982 session, the special rapporteur presented a very helpful "Schematic Outline" of the topic as he then saw it. The "scope" section of the Schematic Outline reflects the present identity crisis:

> *Section 1*
>
> 1. *Scope*
>
> Activities within the territory or control of a State which give rise or may give rise to loss or injury to persons or things within the territory or control of another State.
>
> . . . .
>
> 2. *Definitions*
>
> . . . .
>
> "Activity" includes any human activity.
>
> . . . .
>
> "Loss or injury" means any loss or injury, whether to the property of a State, or to any person or thing within the territory or control of a State.
>
> "Territory or control" includes, in relation to places not within the territory of the acting State—
>
> any activity which takes place within the substantial control of that State. . . .[29]

The special rapporteur indicated his recognition of the unease felt in some quarters with the amorphous nature of the topic when he summarized concerns expressed in the Commission and in the Sixth Committee in his third (1982) report:

[28] *Quoted in* Report of the International Law Commission on the Work of its Thirty-second Session, 35 UN GAOR Supp. (No. 10) at 365, UN Doc. A/35/10 (1980).

[29] *Reprinted in* 1982 Report, *supra* note 5, at 179–80.

> What unexpected consequences might arise from a failure to restrict [the topic's] application to the areas in which practice is most developed? In particular, might the topic become either a rogue elephant or a useful beast of burden in connection with international economic issues—especially those relating to the adumbration of the new international economic order?[30]

Indeed, Professor Quentin-Baxter had twice before proposed limiting the scope of the topic to dangers arising out of the physical use of the environment. On the basis of comments in the Commission, however, he concluded in his 1982 report that such a limitation "would have been far too arbitrary—a judgment of Solomon that would require the baby to be cut in half."[31] The special rapporteur read the net effect of the comments in the Commission and the Sixth Committee to be:

> The best course was to suspend judgment about the unresolved questions of scope, until the content of the topic had been more fully explored. Meanwhile, it should be recognized that the materials on which the Special Rapporteur must rely would largely be found in the area of the use of the physical environment.[32]

Unfortunately, this course provided little comfort to a number of representatives to the Sixth Committee. During the course of that body's discussion of the Commission's 1982 report, it was observed, for example, that the phrase "loss or injury" could conceivably encompass injury caused to a person in one state by a newspaper story published in another,

> loss of profits by a company because a competitor in a foreign State had taken a perfectly legal action which had increased its sales at the expense of that company, or even losses caused by currency devaluation. Without a drastic narrowing of the concept of "loss or injury", virtually any individual or company would at some time or other be able to formulate a claim for reparation from, or a demand for regulation by, the State where the action had occurred.[33]

It was also pointed out in the same session of the Sixth Committee that whereas part 1 of the draft articles on state responsibility carefully limits the circumstances under which conduct is attributable to a state under international law, the special rapporteur had thus far suggested no such limitation in relation to the regime of liability for injurious consequences arising out of acts not prohibited by international law. "On the contrary, the rules of liability [cover] all activities within the territory or control of a State and the notion of control of the acting State [is defined very expansively]."[34] Similar fears about the problem of attribution had been expressed in the Commission's 1982 session. Finally, more than one representative to the Sixth Committee

[30] R. Quentin-Baxter, Third Report on International Liability for Injurious Consequences Arising out of Acts Not Prohibited by International Law, UN Doc. A/CN.4/360, at 20 (1982).

[31] *Id.* at 21.

[32] *Ibid.*

[33] UN Doc. A/C.6/37/SR.52, at 8 (1982) (summary of the statement of Ms. Schwab of the United States).

[34] UN Doc. A/C.6/37/SR.46, at 12 (1982) (summary of the statement of Mr. Siblesz of the Netherlands).

observed that the effect of the regime as currently envisioned would be to force states "to bring under their effective control internally the activities of private individuals."[35]

Thus, while the future of this topic is not at all clear, it appears that its scope will have to be narrowed considerably if it is to result in a broadly acceptable product. The topic is a naturally controversial one, involving as it does the portent of liability without fault and the appearance, at least, that the Commission is engaging in "progressive development" to a greater extent than "codification" of international law. However, at least as originally envisioned, it is an area in which there is a crying need for some sort of normative order—whether such an order takes the form of a procedural framework or a body of "primary" rules[36]—and it is to be hoped that the Commission will be able to agree upon a scope that is both manageable and sensible in light of contemporary international realities.

The Diplomatic Courier and Bag

The final topic considered by the Commission at its 34th session was the status of the diplomatic courier and the diplomatic bag not accompanied by diplomatic courier. The Commission first took up this topic in 1977 at the request of the General Assembly. In 1979 the Commission appointed Professor Alexander Yankov of Bulgaria as special rapporteur and decided to proceed with the preparation of a set of draft articles on the topic.

The special rapporteur submitted six draft articles in 1981, which were referred to the Drafting Committee after discussion in plenary. These six articles were not considered by the Drafting Committee for lack of time, however, and were redrafted and reintroduced along with eight additional articles in 1982. After discussion in plenary, all 14 draft articles were referred to the Drafting Committee. Again, this topic was the last to be considered in plenary, and there was insufficient time for the Drafting Committee to examine any of the 14 draft articles. They will presumably be taken up by the Drafting Committee in the Commission's 1983 session.

[35] *Ibid. Cf.* the statement of the U.S. representative:

> The effect of the regime contained in the schematic outline would be to compel every State to exercise supervision and control over activities of private individuals, even in areas where it had not previously done so and where it was precluded from exercising control by its own domestic constitution.

Summary of the statement of Ms. Schwab, *supra* note 32.

[36]

> In a way one might say that, in dealing with "state responsibility", we are in search of "secondary" rules fitting the great variety of "primary" rules, which are taken for granted, whereas, in dealing with the other topic [*i.e.*, liability for acts not prohibited by international law], we take the "secondary" rule of liability for injurious consequences for granted, and are in search of "primary" rules of prevention and of procedure, which fit the great variety of "transboundary" situations.

Text of statement of Mr. Siblesz of the Netherlands in the Sixth Committee, Nov. 16, 1982, at 2 (copy supplied by the Netherlands delegation).

In view of the fact that this topic is already regulated in four Conventions,[37] it is somewhat of a mystery that it is on the Commission's agenda at all. Indeed, many members began their statements on the topic by expressing this same general sentiment, and it was voiced in the Sixth Committee's discussion of the Commission's 1982 report, as it has been in prior years.[38]

In the eyes of some, however, the beauty of the topic is that precisely because the pertinent law is fairly well settled, it is one item that the Commission might be able to complete within the current quinquennium. Such progress, it is said, would help to answer allegations that the Commission takes too long to finish work on the topics referred to it;[39] but others have pointed out that giving this topic high priority in order to complete work on it would further delay work on other topics that are far more important to the nations of the world today.[40] While the Commission has not assigned specific priorities to the topics on its agenda, it has adopted a general plan of work for the current 5-year term, which is summarized below. This plan indicates that the diplomatic courier and bag will remain on the agenda but retain its present rather low level of priority.

Outlook

The general plan of work adopted by the Commission in its 1982 session for the 5-year term ending in 1987[41] indicates the progress the Commission hopes to make on each of the items remaining on its agenda. As noted above,

[37] The 1961 Vienna Convention on Diplomatic Relations, 500 UNTS 95, 23 UST 3227, TIAS No. 7502, *entered into force* Apr. 24, 1964; the 1963 Vienna Convention on Consular Relations, 596 UNTS 261, 21 UST 77, TIAS No. 6820, *entered into force* Mar. 19, 1967; the 1969 Convention on Special Missions, UNGA Res. 2530 (XXIV) (Dec. 8, 1969), annex; and the 1975 Convention on the Representation of States in Their Relations with International Organizations of a Universal Character, *done* at Vienna, Mar. 14, 1975.

[38] *See, e.g.*, the summary of the statement of the U.S. representative, *supra* note 32, at 10:

> [T]he status of the diplomatic courier and the diplomatic bag not accompanied by diplomatic courier, seemed to be one of the areas of international law least in need of immediate attention or codification. Relatively few legal questions had arisen regarding the status of the diplomatic bag or of diplomatic couriers. The law in that regard was already reasonably settled and understood. The time devoted to that topic would be more productively expended on other topics.

[39] This and other charges have been most recently expressed in a study conducted under the auspices of UNITAR. "The one problem which is cited most often as a reason for bypassing the Commission is the slow pace of its work. . . . There has been an average of seven to ten years between the ILC's investigation of a topic and the production of a final set of draft articles." M. ElBaradei, T. Franck, & R. Trachtenberg, The International Law Commission: The Need for a New Direction 15 (UNITAR 1981) [hereinafter cited as UNITAR Study]. *See also* the summary of this study by two of its authors, Franck & ElBaradei, as a Current Developments Note, 76 AJIL 630 (1982).

[40] *E.g.*, state immunity, state responsibility, and international watercourses. And this is to say nothing of the fact that allowing this topic to take precedence over others would only add fuel to the fire of another criticism leveled at the Commission, to wit, that it currently deals only with topics that are relatively insignificant and noncontroversial. *See* UNITAR Study, *supra* note 38, at 4–15, *passim*.

[41] *See* paragraph 263 of the Commission's 1982 Report, *supra* note 5, for a general discussion of the work it hopes to accomplish by the end of the 5-year term that began in 1982.

this plan does not set specific priorities; it does, however, afford a general idea of the order of importance the Commission has given to these topics. According to the plan, the Commission will endeavor to accomplish the following work within the current quinquennium: complete the first reading of part 2 of state responsibility and possibly undertake the second reading of part 1; complete the first reading of jurisdictional immunities of states and their property; "make substantial progress" on the first reading of the nonnavigational uses of international watercourses; complete the first reading of the status of the diplomatic courier and the diplomatic bag not accompanied by diplomatic courier; "advance its work" on international liability for injurious consequences arising out of acts not prohibited by international law; "continue its study" of the second part of the relations between states and international organizations; and "accord the necessary priority . . . within its five-year programme"[42] to the Draft Code of Offences Against the Peace and Security of Mankind. The provisional agenda for the 1983 session of the Commission includes all of these topics but arranges them in somewhat different order: although state responsibility and jurisdictional immunities remain at the head of the list, they are followed by the courier and bag and the Draft Code. International watercourses, international liability, and relations between states and international organizations complete the list of substantive agenda items.

This summary of the highlights of the 34th session of the International Law Commission and the prospects for the 1983 session has, of necessity, been quite general. Those interested in a more detailed account of the 1982 session are encouraged to refer to the Commission's official report.[43]

STEPHEN C. MCCAFFREY*

HOUSE APPROVES PROPOSAL PERMITTING ICJ TO ADVISE DOMESTIC COURTS

On December 17, 1982, the House of Representatives adopted a resolution supporting an expansion of the advisory opinion jurisdiction of the International Court of Justice. The resolution (H.R. Con. Res. 86) urges the President to explore the appropriateness of establishing a United Nations committee to seek advisory opinions from the ICJ. The committee would act when asked by a national court seeking advice regarding any international law question under the national court's jurisdiction.[1]

The House's vote was the latest step in considering an idea that has been a perennial subject of discussion by international law specialists beginning as early as the 1920's.[2] In the last few years, the proposal has attracted a wider

[42] *Id.*, para. 255.

[43] *See* note 4 *supra*.

* U.S. member, International Law Commission; Professor of Law, University of the Pacific, McGeorge School of Law.

[1] 128 CONG. REC. H10195–98 (daily ed. Dec. 17, 1982).

[2] Bisschop, *International Interpretation of National Case Law*, 4 BRIT. Y.B. INT'L L. 131 (1923–24); Lauterpacht, *Decisions of Municipal Courts As a Source of International Law*, 10 *id.* at 65, 94–95

audience, including the Congress. Although similar resolutions had been introduced in earlier Congresses, this was the first time a committee had given the subject serious consideration.

Hearings were held on the resolution by the Subcommittee on Human Rights and International Organizations of the House Committee on Foreign Affairs in September 1981.[3] As introduced, the resolution expressed the sense of the Congress that "the President should direct" the U.S. representative at the United Nations to propose adoption of a General Assembly resolution establishing a special committee authorized to seek advisory opinions of the ICJ regarding questions of international law. The committee would act upon request by a national tribunal when the tribunal had been authorized by domestic legislation to make such a request. The resolution, as introduced, also stated that the President should propose legislation to Congress that would authorize federal courts to request such advisory opinions and establish procedures for such requests.[4]

Clear differences of opinion were expressed in the hearings about the merits of the proposal. The sponsor of the resolution, Jonathan B. Bingham of New York, said that its purpose was to encourage use of the ICJ. In his view, an advisory opinion of the ICJ would have the same effect as an amicus brief; a domestic court would be free to accept or dismiss it.[5] Several members of the practicing bar appeared in support of the resolution. They cited the additional expertise that an ICJ opinion might provide, which would make a domestic court decision more credible in other countries. They also pointed out that domestic courts sometimes differed over the interpretation of treaties. An ICJ opinion would contribute to greater uniformity among lower courts and would encourage resolution of differences at an early stage rather than allow them to develop into conflicts that would have to be resolved by the Supreme Court.[6] Other practicing lawyers, however, stated that a need for the procedure from the point of view of U.S. litigants in the U.S. judicial system had not been demonstrated, and they suggested that the proposal might present constitutional difficulties.[7]

Administration presentations differed somewhat in approach. The Department of State stressed its support for the ICJ but suggested that the proposal needed further study, particularly as to whether authority now existed

(1929); Jessup, *The International Judicial Process,* 52 JUDICATURE 140, 142 (1968); Gross, *The International Court of Justice: Consideration of Requirements for Enhancing its Role in the International Legal Order,* 65 AJIL 253, 308–13 (1971). And for a recent discussion, see Sohn, *Broadening the Advisory Jurisdiction of the International Court of Justice,* 77 *id.* at 124 (1983).

[3] *Calling for the Establishment of a Special Committee on Advisory Opinions from the International Court of Justice: Hearing Before the Subcomm. on Human Rights and International Organizations of the House Comm. on Foreign Affairs,* 97th Cong., 1st Sess. (1981).

[4] *Id.* at 68–69; H.R. Con. Res. 86, March 4, 1981.

[5] *House Hearing, supra* note 3, at 2, 5.

[6] *Id.* at 25, 39–40. The ABA took no formal position at the hearings, but in January 1982 the ABA House of Delegates urged approval of the proposal. CONG. REC. *supra* note 1, at H10196.

[7] *House Hearing, supra* note 3, at 55–67.

for the Court to provide such advisory opinions. It also noted that the idea lacked support in other countries.[8]

The Department of Justice, in a letter submitted after the hearings, opposed the resolution for a variety of reasons.[9] It noted that a significant number of cases in which international law issues were raised involved the Government as a party; as litigator for the Government in domestic courts, the Department feared that the proposed procedure was "potentially cumbersome." In order to justify such a procedure, the Department said, there should first be evidence that domestic courts were not doing an adequate job of interpreting international law and that the ICJ was likely to do a better one. It pointed out that most international law questions arising in domestic litigation involved treaty interpretation and that the basis for construction of treaties "is not markedly different from the construction of contracts or statutes." The growing influence of international law was seen as a reason for keeping the subject in domestic courts:

> Treaties have come to govern . . . an increasing number of matters that were once wholly domestic; we should thus attempt to demystify them . . . rather than assume that our legal system is not adequate to interpret them. As the I.C.J. itself said in the *Interhandel Case,* "[T]he decisions of the United States courts bear witness to the fact that United States courts are competent to apply international law in their decisions when necessary."[10]

After approval by the House of Representatives,[11] the resolution was referred to the Senate Foreign Relations Committee. As of March 1983, no action had been taken on the resolution in the Senate and no action is planned at this time.

JACK M. GOLDKLANG*

PROPOSED AMENDMENT OF THE FOREIGN CORRUPT PRACTICES ACT OF 1977

On February 3, 1983, Senator John Heinz (R., Pa.) introduced in the 98th Congress, with Senator John Chafee (R., R.I.) as principal cosponsor, a proposal to amend the Foreign Corrupt Practices Act (FCPA) of 1977.[1] The bill had been approved by the Senate on November 23, 1981,[2] after the Com-

[8] *Id.* at 7–22. In 1976 the State Department had prepared a study, *Widening Access to the International Court of Justice,* which favored in principle amendment of the ICJ Statute and the UN Charter to permit advisory opinions by the ICJ to national courts. 1976 DIGEST OF U.S. PRACTICE IN INTERNATIONAL LAW 650 *ff.*

[9] *House Hearing, supra* note 3, at 72–74.

[10] 1959 ICJ REP. 5, 28.

[11] The House Foreign Affairs Committee approved the resolution by unanimous consent on Dec. 14, 1982. No committee report was issued.

* Office of Legal Counsel, Department of Justice.

[1] S. 414, 98th Cong., 1st Sess. (1983), 128 CONG. REC. S981 (daily ed. Feb. 3, 1983).

[2] S. 708, 97th Cong., 1st Sess. (Nov. 23, 1981), S. REP. NO. 209, 97th Cong., 1st Sess. (1981).

mittee on Banking, Housing and Urban Affairs had made certain changes in the amendments originally proposed by Senator Chafee.[3] Although a subcommittee of the House Committee on Energy and Commerce held extensive hearings on the FCPA,[4] it never reported the proposed legislation, and the 97th Congress adjourned in December 1982 without completing action on the proposal.

In the summer and fall of 1982, the key senators and congressmen, including Senator Chafee and Congressman Timothy Wirth (D., Col.),[5] and their staffs had engaged in an extensive dialogue to attempt to identify a compromise that both Houses of Congress would support. On some issues, these discussions led to a narrowing of the differences, while little progress was made on others. Enactment of S. 414 will be possible only if a compromise can be reached on the outstanding differences.

The principal points at issue at the close of the 97th Congress and the competing views on them were the following:

Liability for Third-Party Misconduct. In S. 708, Senator Chafee had proposed modifying the FCPA provision that imposes liability on U.S. companies for payments to third parties while "knowing or having reason to know" that the recipient will make an improper payment to a foreign government official. The bill would have substituted a new and more precise standard under which liability would arise only if the U.S. company sought to evade the basic statutory proscription against bribery by directing or authorizing a third party to make the payment. The bill reported by the Senate committee and approved by the Senate holds the U.S. company liable if it corruptly directed or authorized "expressly or by a course of conduct" such a payment. The committee report and floor debate elaborated on the meaning of this concept.

In the House subcommittee hearings and subsequent dialogue, Congressman Wirth made clear that he did not agree with the criticism focused on the "know or reason to know" provision. Specifically, he maintained that the phrase was not as unfamiliar in U.S. statutes as the critics argued and that the prosecution's burden in an FCPA bribery case, even with this provision, was quite heavy. Congressman Wirth was prepared to substitute a recklessness standard for the current statutory language on third-party liability or to create a bifurcated standard of "knowing" for criminal responsibility and recklessness for civil liability. In the latter instance, however, he wished to add a provision to the FCPA protecting employees of corporations who reported incidences of bribery to federal government officials.

Limitations on Scope of FCPA. Senator Chafee in S. 708 proposed redefining the provision of the FCPA that excepts from the statute's coverage so-called grease or facilitating payments. The Senator's approach focuses on the

[3] S. 708, 97th Cong., 1st Sess. (March 12, 1981).

[4] The House companion bill was introduced by Congressman Rinaldo, H.R. 2530, 97th Cong., 1st Sess. (March 17, 1981).

[5] Congressman Wirth is Chairman of the Subcommittee on Telecommunications, Consumer Protection, and Finance, which held the House hearings on the bill.

purpose of the payment rather than, as is the case under the 1977 statute, on the type of governmental responsibilities that the recipient of the payment performs. In addition, Senator Chafee proposed changes to clarify the statute's inapplicability to certain types of gifts for hospitality and the like and to certain ordinary business expenses incurred in developing sales opportunities and executing contracts. He also proposed establishing a new exception from the FCPA for a payment to a foreign government official that is lawful under the laws and regulations of his country. With some changes in language and clarifying report language and floor debate, the Senate approved each of these proposals.

Congressman Wirth objected that the Senate-approved redefinition of "grease" payments was too broad and that the provision should expressly exclude payments of this kind to "senior level officials" or some equivalent phrase covering high-level officials. The subcommittee Chairman took issue with the gifts exception because he feared that it might allow bribes to be disguised as "gifts." Finally, he was prepared to accept the lawful payment limitation, provided that it was an affirmative defense that would be unavailable when an employment relationship was used as a mere subterfuge for bribery.

Exclusivity of FCPA. Because the Justice Department maintained that foreign payments cases could be brought under the mail and wire fraud statutes[6] as well as under the FCPA, Senator Chafee proposed making the FCPA the exclusive U.S. statute governing overseas bribery. The Senate committee reported a bill that would have removed only a part of the potential application of these other criminal statutes to foreign governmental bribery. Specifically, the committee's bill would have precluded prosecution for depriving another nation of the lawful services of its officials but would allow prosecution under the other U.S. statutes for defrauding the foreign government. During the floor debate, the full Senate broadened this so-called exclusivity provision to cover both situations. Congressman Wirth objected to removing the potential use of the mail and wire fraud statutes to prosecute U.S. companies for defrauding foreign governments.

Accounting Provisions. S. 708 would have introduced a standard of financial materiality into the record-keeping and internal accounting control requirements imposed on U.S. issuers under the FCPA. In addition, Senator Chafee's bill would have added a scienter (willful misconduct) provision to these requirements so that liability would arise, for example, only for knowing falsification of corporate accounts or knowing circumvention of corporate controls. The bill would incorporate an express definition of key terms in the controls provisions to make explicit that a cost/benefit evaluation is permissible in keeping corporate books and designing an internal accounting control system. Finally, Senator Chafee sought to specify that an issuer has only a good faith obligation to attempt to cause its 50 percent or less owned domestic

[6] 18 U.S.C. §§1341 and 1343.

or foreign affiliates to comply with the FCPA's record-keeping and accounting provisions.

The Senate committee refused to accept the materiality approach. Rather, the committee eliminated the separate section imposing record-keeping requirements and included that requirement among the objectives for satisfying the other purposes of an internal accounting control system. The committee modified the scienter provision so that it would eliminate criminal liability for failure to establish the required internal accounting controls and would create a good faith exception for a civil injunctive action for failure to maintain such controls. Circumvention of internal accounting controls would, under the Senate bill, still lead to criminal liability. The Senate agreed to express statement of the cost/benefit standard and to the good faith provision for 50 percent or less owned affiliates with some textual revision.

Congressman Wirth was prepared to accept the addition of the cost/benefit test and to ameliorate the record-keeping and accounting controls provisions, which could possibly be interpreted as imposing liability for unintended errors despite an issuer's good faith efforts at compliance. However, he would not agree to eliminating the separate books and records provision or to including a broader scienter requirement. In addition, Congressman Wirth wanted the statute or its legislative history to clarify what constitutes a good faith defense in these provisions. The subcommittee Chairman also sought to have the legislative history set out the particular benefits to be weighed in applying the cost/benefit test. Finally, he believed that the amendment dealing with affiliates should allow a presumption of nonresponsibility only if the issuer holds less than 20 percent of the affiliate's voting stock and should make clear that control of an affiliate necessarily presumes control over its accounting practices. No presumption would exist for affiliates in which issuers own between 20 percent and 50 percent of the voting stock.

Consolidation of Enforcement Jurisdiction. Senator Chafee proposed and the Senate agreed to the consolidation of enforcement of the FCPA in the Justice Department. At present, the Justice Department shares enforcement responsibilities with the Securities and Exchange Commission, which investigates and initiates civil actions against issuers for noncompliance with the FCPA. The Justice Department has criminal enforcement authority for issuers and other U.S. entities and individuals subject to the statute, as well as civil enforcement responsibility against U.S. entities that are not issuers.

Congressman Wirth refused to modify his view that this bifurcated jurisdiction should continue. In the closing days of the 97th Congress, Senator Chafee appeared to have decided not to pursue this point further if a compromise on other outstanding issues could be found.

Conforming FCPA and Tax Law. Finally, S. 708 proposed to amend section 162(c) of the Internal Revenue Code, which has since the 1960's disallowed deductions for any payment to a foreign official by a U.S. taxpayer that would be illegal if U.S. law applied to the payment.[7] This meant that U.S. taxpayers

[7] Section 1065 of the Tax Reform Act of 1976 provided for other adverse tax consequences in relation to Subpart F income, Earnings and Profits calculations and DISC distributions.

would be denied a deduction for expenditures that are entirely lawful under the FCPA such as facilitating payments. Senator Chafee proposed that the FCPA serve as the applicable standard for all adverse tax consequences.

During the Senate floor debate on S. 708, this proposal was dropped from the Senate bill because of concern about the House's constitutional prerogative to initiate tax legislation. However, the provision reappeared as section 294 of the tax bill (H.R. 4961) that the Senate approved on July 23, 1982.[8] The provision gained acceptance in the conference on the tax bill and appears as section 288 of the Tax Equity and Fiscal Responsibility Act of 1982 (Pub. L. No. 97-248).

PETER D. TROOBOFF*

[8] S. REP. NO. 494, 97th Cong., 1st Sess. 164 (1982).

* Of the Board of Editors.

BOOK REVIEWS AND NOTES

EDITED BY LEO GROSS

The Dynamics of Development in the European Human Rights Convention System. By Clovis C. Morrisson, Jr. The Hague, Boston, London: Martinus Nijhoff Publishers, 1981. Pp. xii, 176. Dfl.100; $39.50.

In democratic polities, an important part of a constitution is the compact of restraint on the use of official power. Where a constitution is drafted in general terms and the system in which it is to be implemented includes a Judiciary with supervisory functions, the constitution essentially transfers the competence to maintain and change those restraints from the Executive or Legislature to the Judiciary. Constitutions, thus, install the judiciary in a central *political* role. That role is accomplished within a frame of reference provided by legal texts, but its performance is always toned by the attention necessarily given to the fundamental goals of the polity as it changes through time, the political predilections of the judges charged with the task and, inevitably, the environment of political support or restraint in the entire system. Not surprisingly, scholars and practitioners in such systems, as they seek to understand the past and assay the future, study not only the language of the texts and the formal decisions of the courts endowed with competence, but the judges themselves, their personalities, predilections, personal alignments, and past performances.

Clovis Morrisson's book is composed of six papers focusing centrally on the judges of the European Court of Human Rights and their participation in the constitutive process of the European human rights system. The first two chapters, done in the American legal realist mode, examine the attitudes both of the members of the European Commission of Human Rights and of the Judges in terms of predilections for judicial activism or judicial self-restraint and in terms of predilections for or against governments. In the first study, Morrisson chose 13 Judges, sitting between 1959 and 1978, selected because they had sat in at least five separate cases and voted on at least eight different issues. The Judges were ranked on an activism-self-restraint scale. The author conducted a comparable study of 22 Commissioners who had sat in five different cases and had at least eight votes on issues there. The results of the inquiry, summarized in tables, indicate that the Commission has been somewhat more activist than the Court, but Professor Morrisson opines that this trend may not endure.

In the second study, Morrisson tabulated all the votes cast by Commissioners, if they could be identified, in admitted cases. Commissioners were then ranked in terms of the percentage of their votes for applicants. The same test was applied to Judges on the Court. While individual scores varied widely, as would be expected, there was little institutional variation between Court and

Commission. Though the Commission appears to have been more favorable to applicants in the early years, the current trend, according to Morrisson, seems to be toward a greater homogeneity of response in both institutions.

The second part of the book is composed of four papers that review in more conventional legal fashion trends of decision by the Court and Commission with regard to abuse of the right of petition under Article 27(2); torture and inhuman and degrading treatment and punishment under Article 3; freedom of expression under Article 10; and determination of civil rights and obligations under Article 6(1). Each of these papers is balanced and tolerant, but the genre is conventional and available elsewhere.

The jurimetrical studies in the first two chapters are an imaginative application of parts of a technique used in the United States but rarely applied internationally.[1] One of the reasons may be its tendency to underestimate the *national* link of an international judge and the extent to which his decisions are not insensitive (one seeks the most euphemistic formulation possible) to his government and/or his perception of its continuing interests. That may be a less important factor in the Commission and the Court of Human Rights than it is, let us say, in the European Court or in the International Court of Justice; but it seems wrong to ignore it completely in any case with interstate political implications. (Curiously, Morrisson indicates the nationalities of Commissioners but does not do so for Judges.)

There would appear to be certain more fundamental difficulties in seeking to explain judicial performance in the European human rights context solely by the criteria of role perceptions of judicial activism or self-restraint or a scaling of judge and commissioner performance in terms of predilections for applicants or governments. These role perceptions may, indeed, be significant factors, but given the fluidity of legal formulation and the complementarity of norms, in which contradictory norms often appear in sets, other factors such as political values and their relation to the content of decisions may be as important as, if not more important than, role perceptions of appropriate judicial behavior. Nor should speculation about the personality variable exclude inquiry and insights available from depth psychology. Without expanding the range of factors, it will be most difficult to explain the apparent contradiction in a single judge's performance, the judge being "activist" in one case but "restrained" in another. In assessing performance, role perceptions should be crosscut with value preferences and the extent to which they are at stake in particular cases. Nor should we be formalistic in identifying the role players. One cannot ignore, in bureaucracies such as those of the European human rights system, the critical role of permanent clerks and administrative officials, those faceless bureaucrats who may sometimes play determinative roles by their characterization of claims, formulation of issues, and advice.

[1] An interesting exception is the two-volume study by Liacouras on judges of the International Court of Justice. P. LIACOURAS, THE INTERNATIONAL COURT OF JUSTICE: MATERIALS ON THE RECORD OF THE INTERNATIONAL COURT OF JUSTICE IN CONTENTIOUS PROCEEDINGS, 2 vols. (preliminary ed. 1962).

While jurimetrical studies such as those of Morrisson make it possible to project provisional alignments of Commission or Court for certain cases, they must be used prudently and cautiously. Morrisson would be among the first to admit that many other factors must be considered when making such projections, not the least of them being political identity, personality variables, the content of particular decisions, and the impact alternative options will have on public order throughout Europe. Nonetheless, Morrisson's study is important in forcing scholars to study actors rather than abstractions and in confirming the general trend of decision in the bodies he studies and some of their institutional implications. This is a clearly written and useful book.

W. M. REISMAN
Board of Editors

The International Bill of Rights: The Covenant on Civil and Political Rights. Edited by Louis Henkin. New York: Columbia University Press, 1981. Pp. x, 523. Index. $35.

Since the International Covenant on Civil and Political Rights of 1966 came into force in 1976, the number of states parties has doubled from 35 to 70 (August 1982). They now include most of the important members of the United Nations except the United States and China. All regions and groupings, from the most to the least developed countries, are represented. States parties have to report regularly to the Human Rights Committee on how they are implementing the Covenant. The Committee was created as an independent body under the Covenant and since 1977 has questioned the representatives of states parties in public meetings and reported back to these states as well as to the General Assembly (as discussed by Dana D. Fischer in 76 AJIL 142 (1982)). Since 1981 the Committee has added "general comments" on this experience to its reports. In addition, 27 of the states parties, including many developing countries, have now accepted the Optional Protocol under which the Committee examines "communications" (*i.e.*, complaints) from individuals claiming to be victims of violations of the Covenant. Many "views" by the Committee on the merits of such cases have been published, beginning in 1979. A third function of the Committee, also optional, is to consider interstate communications. Though resort to this procedure is in force for 14 states parties, it has not been used thus far.

During the formative years of this new global system, members of the Committee have been assisted by a variety of official and unofficial sources. In turn, its own work and documents are inspiring a growing literature. Until recently, however, the principles and provisions of the Covenant itself had not been the subject of any comprehensive account. Such an undertaking would have been too ambitious for any one individual. The volume edited by Professor Louis Henkin of Columbia University has achieved the task as well as anyone could reasonably expect at this stage, and thus is particularly important and welcome.

The book is composed of 14 essays by different authors. Seven of them discuss the system by which the observance of civil and political rights of individuals is to be ensured. Seven others deal with the substance of these rights as set out in part III, Articles 6–27 of the Covenant. This substance spans a broad array of subjects: from the right to life, physical integrity, and liberty (Dinstein), via due process (Noor Muhammad), freedom of movement (Jägerskiöld), personality, privacy, and family (Volio), freedom of conscience, expression, and political freedoms (Partsch), and equality and nondiscrimination (Ramcharan), to the rights of minorities (Sohn). However, the essays are naturally interlocking. Two of the others come particularly close to these seven: an examination of peoples' right to self-determination under Article 1 of the Covenant (Cassese), which advances the sympathetic, but quite controversial, thesis that this right embodies the civil and political rights of individuals; and the discussion of permissible limitations on those rights (Kiss, assisted by Di Ferrante). The other essays on the system include a general introduction (Henkin), one on the legislative history (Pechota), and one on the basic obligations of states and permissible derogations (Buergenthal). The discussions conclude with essays on implementation of the Covenant in domestic law (Schachter) and by international measures (Robertson). The basic instruments are appended, followed by careful and detailed notes and a useful index.

This layout makes the volume not only easy to use, but also more interesting to read than an article-by-article commentary would have been. Moreover, it is so well planned and edited that the result is a fairly coherent treatise on practically all aspects of the Covenant as a distinct system of law. To a remarkable degree Louis Henkin has succeeded in bringing the essays together despite the varying backgrounds, approaches, and styles of the authors.

All the authors discuss their subjects in a scholarly manner, most of them making at the same time an effort to read into the Covenant as much as possible, contrary to the tendency shown by governments in practice. The preface expresses justified concern that the Covenant "machinery" is, *inter alia,* too "diplomatic" to provide a comprehensive guide to interpretation. The reviewer can confirm this point from his personal experience.

Yet it must be observed that the quickly developing practice of states parties and of the Human Rights Committee soon will become a more important source than this book could possibly reflect. Most of the essays rely generally more on the roots of the Covenant, including the *travaux préparatoires,* than on the facts of its growth as a living system. They refer to the recent developments as far as possible, but one cannot take for granted that their interpretations will prevail. Having himself advocated similar ones in the Committee and sympathizing warmly with many points made in the book, the reviewer must still express doubts as to whether they will stand the test of experience.

Space here does not allow comments essay by essay as one might have wished. Certain points made in them are particularly interesting in the light of the evolving practice. The divisions and sometimes narrow votes that shaped the Covenant prior to 1966 lead Pechota to suggest that consensus might have been a better method. Indeed, since 1977 the Human Rights Committee has worked on that basis, and it is not at all likely that it would have been more effective had it resorted to majority vote as the Covenant envisages.

Several of the authors, *e.g.*, Henkin, Pechota, and Robertson, seem to hold that the Covenant may be invoked as part of universal international law both by and against states that have not ratified it, and then presumably may be upheld by any lawful remedy, bilateral or otherwise. This may be so. But the credibility and value of such a practice would certainly be increased if the Committee were at least to be kept informed about it, under the reporting system or otherwise. The fact that most states have not adopted the optional interstate clause is perhaps no obstacle to the notification of such situations, but these notifications must then be distinguished from "communications." The Committee is not a center of power, but the Covenant may become more influential if that organ becomes a center of information.

The book is also a suitable point of departure for discussing many other themes, such as the merits of various strategies for further developing Covenant rights. Among those which have already occupied some UN organs are the issuance of a declaration elaborating on norms implied by the Covenant (*e.g.*, minority rights under Article 27, as reported by Sohn), and even of another convention (*e.g.*, on torture). New alternatives have arisen as part of the implementation process in the Human Rights Committee. Apart from its case law on communications, possibilities are offered by the reporting system itself, at present in particular the "general comments" under Article 40(4). Those adopted after the book was prepared, in 1981 and 1982, are a modest beginning. Enlightened doctrine, as contained in this book, is also a useful instrument in this respect. Theory and practice must interact.

The international selection of contributors to this volume is excellent, but nevertheless predominantly Western. There was every reason to produce it as it is, and the whole world should be grateful to Louis Henkin and his fellow contributors for having so well brought forward much that would otherwise have been too easily forgotten in a busy practice. Let us hope that its emanation from the academic circles of a superpower not party to the Covenant will not be used against the authors or theses of this book. Nevertheless, for reasons suggested above, while the book as a whole deserves much more praise than criticism, one cannot predict a very long life for it as an authoritative source on the Covenant. Its successors will be greatly indebted to it. But in due course later undertakings of this kind will have to be based on more truly global teamwork and on all the new material that will become available in the meantime.

TORKEL OPSAHL
University of Oslo
Human Rights Committee, Member

Teaching Human Rights. Edited by Alice Erh-Soon Tay in collaboration with Graeme Connelly and Roger Wilkins. Canberra: Australian National Commission for UNESCO, 1981. Pp. vi, 216. Index. $A8.80.

There is a ferment on the human rights front in Australia. In 1980 the federal Government ratified the International Covenant on Civil and Political

Rights, albeit with numerous reservations to accommodate the states. A federal Human Rights Commission, with powers largely on the promotional rather than the protective end of the spectrum, was established in 1981. On May 11 of 1982, in *Koowarta v. Bjelke-Petersen,* the High Court of Australia opted, by a slim 4–3 majority, for a broad interpretation of federal power in the human rights area pursuant to the "external affairs" provision of the Constitution.

This very interesting set of essays is a part of this ferment. It consists of papers delivered at a 1980 conference organized by the Australian National Commission for UNESCO. The title perhaps suggests that the papers are concerned with the "how to" of teaching human rights, but in fact most of them address particular substantive or policy areas.

The collection is organized in four parts. The first is entitled "Human Rights and the Australian Polity." I found particularly thought-provoking the introduction by Eugene Kamenka and Alice Erh-Soon Tay on *Human rights and "the" Australian tradition.* The second part is on "Foreign Policy and International Affairs." The highlight here is C. G. Weeramantry's chapter, *National and international systems as denigrators of human rights,* a very cogent Third World critique of human rights doctrine. Part 3 is on "Teaching Human Rights: The Philosophical Problem." It addresses primarily the question of what are human rights and what is their jurisprudential origin. Part 4 is called "Looking at Special Cases." It deals mainly with questions of race and ethnicity. Its examples are drawn from the Australian experience—particularly non-British immigrants and aborigines. The American-based reader is struck by the similarities of the problems there and here. This last part concludes with a cryptic and unconvincing chapter by Peter Singer on animal rights.

The overall quality of this collection is consistently high. Like any symposium with multiple authors, it hardly adds up to a coherent whole, but it is essential reading for anyone teaching in the human rights area. It probably has a future also as a set text for courses in Australian universities and those elsewhere which emphasize comparative material.

ROGER S. CLARK
Rutgers Law School

International Law and World Order: A Problem-Oriented Coursebook. By Burns H. Weston, Richard A. Falk, and Anthony A. D'Amato.* St. Paul: West Publishing Co., 1980. Pp. lxxi, 1195. Index. Documentary supplement. $23.95.

In many schools, the changing times have prompted public international law curricula to take account of significant developments: the emerging role of individuals, corporations, international organizations, and other nonsovereign actors in the international legal system; the gradual restructuring of

* Recipients, American Society of International Law Certificate of Merit (1982) for a work "which exhibits high technical craftsmanship and is of high utility to practicing lawyers and scholars."

the global order to accommodate Third World appeals for transfers of technology, economic self-determination, reallocations of resources, and the like; a growing unwillingness of the public to tolerate excessive armament and militarism; the growth of a workable body of human rights laws; and some shift of focus from diplomatic intercourse to the satisfaction of basic human needs. The discipline of international law is ever more concerned with all the ways in which human beings regulate and allocate values that touch upon more than one country or society.

Taking full account of these and other developments, *International Law and World Order* provides a superb means of getting students to think creatively about the basic professional lore, *lex lata* and *ferenda,* by involving them directly in the solution of transnational problems and by stimulating their imaginations and consciences to improve world order. Having used the materials since they appeared in an unpublished first edition by Burns Weston, this reviewer wishes to express his warmest gratitude to Professor Weston and his coauthors and to report the enthusiasm of students for the materials. Students have told the reviewer that the heated classroom discussion often continues afterward.

The opening words in this course book alert students to what lies ahead:

> Had you been a young lawyer serving in the United States Army at the end of World War II, you might have found yourself arriving in London on June 20, 1945 as a member of a large staff ordered to prepare for a trial of leading Nazis captured as criminals of war [p. 1].

The stage is set for the beginning section of the book, a full discussion of the international legal process—concepts of international law, its sources, its force and effect, its history, and its scope—within the context of the Nuremberg experience. A concluding section of the book reconsiders fundamental presumptions from a future-oriented, reformist perspective.

The core of *International Law and World Order* consists of eight hypothetical problems, which are carefully crafted to engage student participation. Armchair scholasticism will not do. To this reviewer, the book's problem orientation can realistically make a significant contribution to education in world order. If, to quote Martin Buber, in the beginning is relation and life is dialogue, the curriculum of global studies should involve future decision makers and civic leaders in problem solving and the articulation of personal accountability and authenticity. With such training, educated elites can more effectively join in the mutual hallowing of life, certainly a compelling goal of existence, by responding to basic human needs.

Each of the problems includes a fact statement, a set of pertinent readings, notes, questions, and an extensive bibliography. The presentation of materials is syncretic and impressively organized so as to stimulate the reader to develop those same characteristics. Rather than dwelling on infinite regressions of doctrine or case law, the course book addresses eight hypothetical problems involving basic human needs of war prevention, sociopolitical justice, economic well-being, and environmental protection. This framework is comparable to others, such as that of Roger Fisher and William Ury, who have identified five basic human needs: security, economic well-being, a sense of belonging, recognition, and control over one's life. In the reviewer's judgment, several concerns of global order merit greater technical treatment than the book provides: treaty interpretation, global disarmament, territoriality/sovereignty, and human migration. All in all, however, the problems in this course book expose most current world-order concerns, doctrines, approaches, and legal issues in a way that commends the book for undergraduate, graduate, or professional education.

The book's functionalist approach takes creditable account of nongovernmental dynamics. Although the nation-state understandably remains the centerpiece, the authors clearly understand that today's international legal framework is complex. In a sense, the more things change, the more they stay the same. Before the theories about sovereignty of Jean Bodin and King James I and the origins of the modern consensual system at Westphalia in 1648, such nongovernmental institutions as medieval trade fairs, the Hanseatic League of Merchants, the church, and overseas charter companies were highly visible in international affairs. Today, once again, nonsovereign actors are reemerging as respectable subjects for international legal inquiry. Thus, international organizations within the UN family, multinational corporations, individual petitioners for human rights, and nongovernmental entities such as the Red Cross and the International Law Association are helping scholars, including the coauthors of *International Law and World Order,* to map a legal system that is still incomplete.

Students using this course book come to understand, or at least some of them do, that international law *works,* despite a primitive enforcement machinery and sanctions that rely on mutual expectations and reciprocity in the absence of a global version of the corner cop. The book also assists students in understanding the limitations of international law and in appreciating that rules and adjudication, though important, are not the sine qua non. Thus, students learn to explore the vast underbrush of principles, norms, rules of etiquette, technical standards, and alternative modes of dispute settlement that more fully constitute the international legal process. Problems in this course book can be used, for example, to develop negotiating skills. Principles and techniques of negotiation, despite their presumably ancient origins, are only now becoming a subject of serious study on both theoretical and practical levels. It is becoming important to train students of international law in those principles of negotiation and other modes of nonadjudicative dispute settlement that may be applicable to family and global disputes alike. Side-by-side problem solving, rather than face-to-face confrontation, offers an innovative mode of teaching. Using problems in the course book, a class examining a Latin American maritime dispute, for example, might be divided into two groups, each of which would employ the method devised by Fisher and Ury for effective negotiation: separate the people from the problem; focus on interests, not positions; invent options for mutual gain; and insist on objective criteria as the basis for a final resolution of a dispute.

Whatever the mode of teaching, the most basic tools of the trade, with which this course book competently equips students, include a working knowledge of the process of claim and counterclaim that characterizes international law, and a familiarity with its salient institutions, channels of communication, and vocabulary. Just finding one's way around the international system and effectively using the distinctive vocabulary and syntax of international law are critical skills in helping the world to talk things out. With these skills, students trained in problem solving can help keep the planet in one piece, whether they emerge as practitioners or civic leaders. *International Law and World Order* is a pioneering course book for these changing times.

JAMES A. R. NAFZIGER
Willamette University College of Law

Recueil des Cours de l'Académie de droit international de La Haye, 1979. 3 vols. (Vols. 162, 163, and 164 of the collection.) Alphen aan den Rijn: Sijthoff & Noordhoff, 1980. Vol. I, pp. 449; vol. II, pp. 445; vol. III, pp. 423.*

Three courses at the Hague Academy in 1979 were inspired by the conclusion in 1977 of two Protocols to the four 1949 Geneva Conventions on the protection of the victims of armed conflict. Dietrich Schindler (University of Zurich) examines the basic legal classifications in *The Different Types of Armed Conflicts According to the Geneva Conventions and Protocols.* His short analysis reveals the great complexity of the classification system introduced by the 1949 Geneva Conventions, which divides "armed conflict" (a slippery concept itself) into "international" and "not of an international character," and establishes different legal regimes for each. Schindler dismisses as unrealistic proposals to unify the law that applies in international and noninternational armed conflicts. But he does not seem to notice that his arguments against those proposals, based on the unwillingness of states to agree on rules that inhibit their military responses to rebels, speak equally against further entrenching the current classification system. Other alternatives are not mentioned, such as abandoning attempts at treaty drafting for a while, and publicizing the actual practice of states in applying humanitarian rules of war while they deny that there is a war. Even within Schindler's technical approach, it is hard to understand his discussion of "regional organizations" as if they might play a role in recognizing the appropriate legal status for some insurgent groups. He does not consider that South Africa is not a member of the OAU or that Israel is not a member of the Arab League or Conference of Islamic States or any other regional group that might claim this authority in the Middle East. To ameliorate the problems in the existing texts he seems to urge negotiation of additional texts. In sum, this short course seems to reflect the thinking in Geneva and among experts in the laws of war who, dealing with the complexity of the treaty framework and current negotiations, have lost sight of the larger framework of the law.

* A letter from the Hague Secretariat to this reviewer in February 1981 indicated that a fourth volume for the 1979 course, which would be 165 of the collection, was expected in due course. It had not been received by the end of 1982. In fairness to the other participants in the Hague Academy course for 1979, this review is published without the fourth volume.

The second course in this series was *L'extension du statut de combattant à la lumière du protocole I de Genève de 1977,* by Stanisław E. Nahlik (Jagiellonian University, Krakow). He traces the provisions of positive law that specify who is entitled to prisoner-of-war treatment from 1907 (with a brief nod at the Brussels Rules of 1874, but no mention of the 1863 Lieber Code Articles 49–51) to Article 44 of the 1977 Protocol I. After pointing out a number of questions and doubts about Article 44 raised by various participants in the Geneva Conference, he concludes that the new provisions will surely have an important influence even if they were not accepted without reservation by the states that might be concerned in future international armed conflicts.

A more general approach to the evolving law of war was taken by G. I. A. D. Draper (University of Sussex) in his course, *The Implementation and Enforcement of the Geneva Conventions of 1949 and of the Two Additional Protocols of 1978* [*sic*]. In his view, the use of "Protecting Powers" and national education are the major tools the international legal order makes available for enforcing the laws of war, and they do not work well. Turning to more direct means of enforcing the law, Draper points out that reprisals and hostage taking, once common and more or less effective to promote observance of the law, have become either illegal or of marginal importance. Historical experience with trials of war criminals and the "grave breaches" provisions of 1949 and 1977 raise questions of whether tribunals established by the victors or the vanquished can be relied on to serve the ends of justice and provide a deterrent to crime. He also mentions the general reluctance to establish neutral tribunals and the difficulties of achieving extradition under the terms of the Conventions and Protocols. In a most imaginative section he suggests that more attention be paid to the traditional law of compensation for state delicts, to be provided for separately from reparations even after a total victory. Such compensation might be available more easily than reparations, as today peace treaties have gone out of fashion. He is less sanguine about the utility in practice of fact-finding commissions that rely on the cooperation of adversaries. With regard to national liberation movements and armed conflicts not of an international character, Draper finds the problems of enforcement to be overwhelming since the established government against which the struggle is being waged would never accept the kind of supervision necessary to ensure compliance with its obligations; indeed, it is unlikely ever to agree that it had legal obligations in any particular case of this sort. Like Schindler, he seems to consider treaty making the only way to develop the law and to believe that the problem of *jus standi* in cases of alleged breach is insoluble. He thus appears to confuse problems of law creation with problems of enforcement, which are the principal theme of his course.

Two courses focused on natural resources. One by Ian Brownlie (University of London), *Legal Status of Natural Resources in International Law (Some Aspects),* traces the evolution of the concept of permanent sovereignty over natural resources from the enlightened traditional view expressed in UN General Assembly Resolution 1803 (XVII) of December 14, 1962, to recent fundamental documents, such as General Assembly Resolution 3171 (XXVIII) of December 17, 1973, the Declaration on the Establishment of a New Economic

Order of May 1, 1974 in Resolution 3201 (S–VI), and the Charter of Economic Rights and Duties of States in Resolution 3281 (XXIX) of December 12, 1974. He then argues that, read carefully, the rights claimed by capital-importing states are less radical than many Western lawyers have supposed. Examining various high-sounding declarations, international programs, and models for resource sharing, he finds them in general so imprecise and vague that they seem useless as a basis for any actual redistribution of resources. He suggests that some price and resource agreements, such as those establishing buffer stocks, might be more fruitful. On the theoretical side, he finds the increased emphasis on equitable principles too vague to be very helpful, implying as they do a mere delegation of wide discretion to tribunals. On the other hand, joint exploitation under special treaty regimes, like the 1975 Joint Fisheries Zone between Japan and China, the 1920 multilateral Spitzbergen Treaty, and the regime under negotiation in UNCLOS III, he finds effective in assuring a peaceful allocation of scarce resources. He ends by pointing out certain anomalies, including, most interestingly, the apparent conflict between, on the one hand, the rejection by most Northern lawyers of the Calvo Clause as inconsistent with the prerogatives of a potential claimant state, and, on the other hand, their apparent conviction that a concession agreement between a corporation and a foreign state is legally effective to deprive a state of its claimed discretion to exercise its municipal law of property nationalization. Brownlie does not argue the point in detail, but the suggestion calls for consideration of deeper principle by those who so easily find international law to forbid what we do not like, while requiring what we like others to do.

The course by José A. de Yturriaga (Foreign Office of Spain) is a convenient review of *Regional Conventions on the Protection of the Marine Environment.* It goes beyond description of the physical problems in four selected regions (the northeast Atlantic, the Mediterranean Sea, the Baltic Sea, and the Persian Gulf area) to discuss also those conventions that deal with specific pollution problems, such as pollution from land-based sources and pollution from ships (distinguishing between global and regional approaches). It is primarily descriptive. He concludes that the situation is now satisfactory both regionally and globally as far as dumping pollutants is concerned; that implementation of the conventions dealing with land-based pollution is lagging; that failure, so far, to bring into force the 1973 London Convention on the Prevention of Marine Pollution by Dumping of Wastes and Other Matter at Sea impedes control of ship-generated pollution, although regional agreements have filled some of the lacunae; that much remains to be done legally to control the likely spread of pollution from seabed exploration and exploitation and from atmospheric sources other than nuclear testing.

The Legal Status of the Arctic Regions is analyzed by Donat Pharand (University of Ottawa). A concise review of the recent evolution of territorial claims to islands bordering the Arctic Ocean leads him to conclude, somewhat surprisingly in the light of the notorious reluctance of states unequivocally to exercise or to assert formally the powers normally associated with sovereignty in such inhospitable areas, that "territorial sovereignty is now well established in the Arctic" (vol. II, p. 106). Packed with facts and four maps, the course projects a clear picture of current activities and the areas of potential international disagreement. Two points might be mentioned on which some expansion would have been useful. Pharand properly indicates that "self-defense" as normally understood in international law does not justify fully the Arctic Air Defense Identification Zones of Canada and the United States (which extend in places some 380 miles from the nearest American land), particularly as regards civil aircraft. He finds a better rationale in an expanded "protective principle" (p. 110) based on dicta of Vattel and an American "reasonableness" doctrine. But he does not mention what is in fact the principal American rationale for applying the regulations to foreign civil aircraft over the high seas: that obedience to the regulations is a condition of entry into American airspace. To the extent that such a rationale will not suffice, and self-defense is not applicable to the facts of a particular aircraft's approach, it would be shortsighted of the United States to assert a protective principle that could reciprocally be used to restrict American military flights over areas of the high seas off various foreign territories, such as Libya. On the other hand, Pharand's conclusion seems sound that acquiescence over some 30 years in the zones and the increased use of them by other states might by now have made the practice permissible as part of general international law, whatever the initial doubts about their legality.

The other minor area for expansion is in Pharand's discussion of the importance of finding some analogy in well-established law for rationalizing national jurisdiction over some ice floes (pp. 93 *et seq.*). He prefers to treat floating ice by analogy to a "ship," which seems unduly broad; just as under general international law a ship is territory for some purposes only and in some circumstances only, so can ice islands be treated as ships for some purposes and in some circumstances, and as territory or as water for other purposes or circumstances. He is certainly right in regretting the silence of UNCLOS III on this increasingly important legal question.

Of the courses lying on the border between private and public international law, special mention should be made of the unusually clear and stimulating course, *Public Law in the International Arena: Conflict of Laws, International Law, and Some Suggestions for Their Interaction,* given by Andreas Lowenfeld (New York University). While in the main it covers familiar ground in reviewing the expansion of U.S. assertions of legislative jurisdiction from a narrow doctrine based on a misreading of Lord Mansfield to a practice based on remote effects under a vague "protective principle," it puts into simple terms the disquiet scholars have been feeling for several years and raises important questions. Other courses in this borderline area were *International Economic "Soft Law"* by Ignaz Seidl-Hohenveldern (University of Cologne) and *Some Legal Aspects of Industrial Co-operation in East-West Relations* by Jerzy Jakubowski (University of Warsaw).

The *Cours général de droit international privé* for 1979 was given by Professor Edoardo Vitta (University of Turin). Other courses addressing primarily private international law were *Recent Developments of Conflict of Laws Conventions in Latin America* by Gonzalo Parra-Aranguren (University of Caracas); *Choice of Law Problems in International Shipping (Recent Developments)* by Sjur Braekhus

(University of Oslo); and *La Coexistence des droits confessionnels et des droits laïcisés dans les relations privées internationales* by Pierre Gannagé (Saint-Joseph University of Beirut).

One interesting but quite unclassifiable course was a description of the history and current charter of *L'Ordre souverain de Malte* by Béat de Fischer (formerly of the Foreign Office of Switzerland).

ALFRED P. RUBIN
The Fletcher School of Law and Diplomacy

A Modern Introduction to International Law (4th ed.). By Michael Akehurst. Winchester: Allen & Unwin, Inc., 1982. Pp. 304. Index. $28.50, cloth; $12.95, paper.

The fourth edition of Akehurst's *A Modern Introduction to International Law* appears 5 years after its predecessor. Among the major changes are the addition of a new chapter on self-determination, including substantial discussion of the situation in Palestine and in southern Africa; an account of developments in the multilateral law of the sea negotiations (written prior to the April 1982 adoption of the UN Convention); and a treatment of the legal aspects of the seizure of American diplomats in Iran.

Since its first publication in 1970, Dr. Akehurst's book has become one of the most widely used in the genre of the comprehensive, yet compact, introduction to international law. It is designed primarily for use in undergraduate politics and government courses and as an overview for nonspecialists. It continues to earn high marks for its effective presentation of the public and private sides of international law, and of the contextual placement of legal norms in the international political system. The author has also been complimented on his lucid and nontechnical style, his avoidance of bias, and his realistic, but persuasive, argument that international law plays an important role in contemporary world affairs.[1] In most of the chapters, the amount of attention given is appropriate to the topic. The section on states and governments, including recognition, is particularly well done, given the complexity of the issues. The discussion of the problems inherent in interpreting the UN Charter is excellent. Unfortunately, the bibliographic offerings are rather meager.

In this kind of book, simplifications are to be expected; by and large, Akehurst's condensations are valid and indeed useful. He makes his points concisely and in plain language, illustrating but not agonizing over narrowly contentious issues. In the first chapter, entitled "Is International Law Really Law?," he begins immediately to allay the criticisms of the typical student of political science. Admitting that the dominant perception among laymen is that states have little respect for international law, he notes—in language bound to impress skeptics—that it "is not broken more often than any other

[1] See Bruno Simma's review of the first edition of Akehurst's book, at 65 AJIL 643 (1971), and Oliver J. Lissitzyn's of the third edition, at 72 AJIL 956 (1978).

system of law" (p. 2). This should cause second thoughts in the minds of students who tend to impose a much higher standard of achievement on international law than on their national, local, and personal rules schemes.

In another example, rather than laboring over a "perfect" definition of international law, Akehurst neatly solves the problem of how to characterize the subjects of the law in such a definition in this way: "At one time states were the only bodies which had rights and duties under international law, but nowadays international organisations, companies and individuals also sometimes have rights and duties . . . ; however, it is still true to say that international law is *primarily* concerned with states" (p. 1).

In a few instances, brevity is achieved at what is arguably too high a price. In his discussion of the sources of international law, Akehurst sacrifices a certain degree of intellectual rigor in an attempt to clarify the meaning of the troublesome phrase, "general principles of law recognized by civilized nations." He writes:

> [T]here is little agreement about the meaning of the phrase. Some say it means general principles of international law; others say it means general principles of national law. Actually, there is no reason why it should not mean both; the greater the number of meanings which the phrase possesses, the greater the chance of finding something to fill gaps in treaty law and customary law . . . [p. 34].

In addition, his treatment of equity is a bit abrupt: "[I]t is doubtful whether equity forms a source of international law today," and "appeals by international lawyers to considerations of equity [should not] be interpreted to mean that equity is a source of international law" (p. 39). On the other hand, his discussion of customary international law is thorough and excellent, particularly as it addresses the concept of *opinio juris.*

One of the most notable features of this book from the viewpoint of the non-British reader is its frequent mention and sometimes extensive discussion of English law. The focus on English law can in a sense be seen as a bonus for students since indigenous rules can be explained orally and by use of additional reading materials.

In sum, *A Modern Introduction to International Law* constitutes a valuable, though not unflawed, contribution to its genre. While of use primarily in the undergraduate setting, it would not be surprising if it were also popular among law students as a complement to their casebooks. It will therefore be interesting to see whether the forthcoming volume on international law in the West Company's "Nutshell" series, by Thomas Buergenthal and Harold Maier, will displace Akehurst in American law schools.

RICHARD W. NELSON
Washington and Lee University School of Law, Adjunct Professor

International Organization and Integration: Annotated Basic Documents and Descriptive Directory of International Organizations and Arrangements. Vols. I.A and II.A (2d rev. ed.). Edited by P. J. G. Kapteyn, P. H. Kooijmans, R. H. Lauwaars, H. G. Schermers, and M. van Leeuwen Boomkamp. The Hague, Boston, London: Martinus Nijhoff Publishers. Vol. I.A, 1981: pp. lvi + 1322. Index. Dfl.450; $195; vol. II.A, 1982: pp. xxiv + 640. Index. Dfl.235; $99.

The handy 1968 edition of this collection has been, to quote from Professor Louis Sohn's foreword, a "constant travel companion" of participants in international conferences. Alas, the new edition, prepared by a team of Dutch scholars and students, will be considerably less amenable to this function. Although the editors' preface is unclear on this point, the tentative table of contents suggests that in addition to the two hefty volumes currently available, no less than four more will be published, a telling testimony to the proliferation of international organizations and their activities.

The first of the two volumes reviewed here deals with worldwide organizations "deriving from or centered on the United Nations" other than the specialized agencies, which will be dealt with separately. The institutional instruments of the United Nations and of the International Court of Justice (including rules of procedure, staff regulations, arrangements for privileges and immunities, and financial regulations) are followed by an extensive selection of more important resolutions, treaties, and conventions, ranging across the entire spectrum of the activities of the United Nations. The 14 sections in this part deal with the Law Commissions, the major general treaties and resolutions relating to international law, pacific settlement of disputes, peacekeeping, enforcement action, arms control, promotion of economic and social welfare (the "New International Economic Order"), human rights, self-determination, and environmental protection. A descriptive summary introduction under the curious heading of "Directory," is written in standard "officialese" and is "intended in particular for civil servants and journalists." Some of the documents (including the UN Charter itself) are provided with useful annotations and cross-references.

The second volume is devoted entirely to the European Communities. The complete text of the constitutive Treaties establishing the three Communities (the European Coal and Steel Community, EURATOM, and the European Economic Community) with annexed protocols (including the Statute of the Court of Justice and its rules of procedure) are followed by the "Merger Treaty" of 1965 and the complex documents relating to accession to the Communities of Denmark, Ireland, and the United Kingdom in 1973 and of Greece in 1981. The two Treaties amending the original budgetary provisions, however, are not reproduced but are reflected in the constitutive texts. The "Supplementary Treaties" section includes the important Convention on Jurisdiction and the Enforcement of Judgments in Civil and Commercial Matters with the Protocol conferring jurisdiction on the Court of Justice to interpret the Convention. Rather than reproducing the almost identical seven bilateral Free Trade Area Agreements that the Community concluded with the industrialized European countries, members of the European Free Trade Association, the editors present a "composite" or "master" scheme indicating differences in the text of one or another Agreement. The Second Lomé Convention of 1979, which established institutional links between the Community and some 60 African, Pacific, and Caribbean states (to be renegotiated), is set forth in full, and selected miscellaneous materials, such as declarations of the European Parliament, are added. In this volume the introductory summary is somewhat more analytical and operationally oriented and thus more informative than the corresponding section in the first volume. The most helpful feature is the annotations to the three constitutive Treaties containing citations, after the individual articles, to relevant case law and Community legislation and decisions. Although one may question the omission of this or that case or the placement of a reference to a Community act under one Treaty article rather than another, it is this feature more than any other aspect that distinguishes this book from other collections of the same documents.

Both volumes contain tables showing the effective dates of the various instruments and membership of the organizations. Only treaties in force are reported and there is no indication that periodic partial updating is contemplated. The volumes, although inexplicably expensive (considering that the principal texts are available in other official and unofficial collections), will again prove useful to both practitioners and scholars.

ERIC STEIN
Board of Editors

The EEC and Intellectual Property. By Diana Guy and Guy I. F. Leigh. London, Rome, New York: Oceana Publications, Inc., 1981. Pp. xxiv, 375. Index.

This book considers the effect of EEC law on intellectual property, particularly as it affects the traditional exercise of national intellectual property rights. It is not a review of national intellectual property laws.

The authors set as their goal the isolation of the "common thread" running through the judgments of the Court of Justice and the decisions of the Commission. This is found to be the distinction between the "existence" of intellectual property rights, not affected by EEC law, and the "exercise" of such rights, subject to EEC law. The exercise of such rights is particularly subject to the provisions of the EEC Treaty dealing with competition, free movement of goods and, to a lesser extent, free movement of services.

The authors emphasize that one cannot understand the impact of EEC law on intellectual property unless the aim underlying the Treaty is understood, *i.e.*, "the creation of a single community among the ten Member States." While perhaps not readily apparent to Americans accustomed to our federal system of intellectual property protection, in the EEC conflicts are inevitable between the declared aim of the Treaty and the traditional exercise of intellectual property rights. To date, these rights come into existence on a national level and are limited to the national territory. Normally this would mean that the holder of such a right would be able to prevent the importation of products infringing that right from other countries. Within the Common Market, however, the "exercise" of an intellectual property right to block imports of products from other member states could result in a division of the market. Such an exercise of these rights could thereby infringe the Treaty. The major concern of the authors is to show how the Court of Justice and Commission have reacted to this problem.

The great weakness of this and any other book treating a developing area of the law is that it can rapidly become outdated. The authors state the law as it was on December 31, 1980. Since that time the Court of Justice has rendered several major judgments in the area, including, among others, *Merck & Co. v. Stephar BV*;[1] *Dansk Supermarked A/S v. A/S Imerco*;[2] *Musik-Vertrieb membran GmbH and K-tel Int'l v. GEMA*;[3] and *L.C. Nungesser KG and Kurt Eisele v. Commission*[4] (the so-called *Maize* case). Nevertheless, the authors have performed a valuable service in providing a statement of the law up to 1981. Their analysis of the development of the law enhances one's understanding of the more recent judgments of the Court.

THAD W. SIMONS, JR.
Brussels

United Nations Peacekeeping. Documents and Commentary. Vol. IV: Europe 1946–1979. By Rosalyn Higgins. Issued under the auspices of the Royal Institute of International Affairs. New York and Oxford: Oxford University Press, 1981. Pp. xii, 419. Index. $89; £40.

In a review of the first volume in Higgins's broad survey of all UN efforts at peacekeeping, David Wainhouse wrote that "[i]f the [successive] volumes measure up to the first, the author will have performed a valiant and useful service in this important field of UN activity."[1] This reviewer concludes that they do, and she has.

Volume IV examines the two UN peacekeeping operations in Europe: the UN Special Committee on the Balkans (UNSCOB), 1947–1952, succeeded by the Military Observers of the Balkan Sub-Commission, 1952–1954; and the UN Peace-keeping Force in Cyprus (UNFICYP), 1964–1979. The Cyprus force is one of five UN operations currently active (see text below).

The earlier volumes in the series each covered the period 1946–1967. The first volume focused on the Middle East, the second on Asia, and the third on Africa. The geographic breakdowns were employed only for the sake of convenience, and it might be useful to provide a list of each UN peacekeeping venture in chronological order:[2]

[1] Case 187/80, 1981 ECR 2063.
[2] Case 58/80, 1981 ECR 181.
[3] Cases 55 and 57/80, 1981 ECR 147.
[4] Case 258/78, June 8, 1982 (not yet published).

[1] 64 AJIL 985, 985–86 (1970).

[2] The term "peacekeeping" can, of course, be defined in any number of ways. Professor Higgins chose to exclude investigative and fact-finding commissions and diplomatic missions, even though their purpose might be to maintain or restore peace. She decided to include military and paramilitary actions and military observer groups. Some writers would exclude the Korean action from her list.

UNSCOB/Balkan Sub-Commission, 1947–1954 (vol. IV of Higgins)

UN Observers in Indonesia, 1947–1950 (vol. II)

UN Truce Supervision Organization in Palestine (UNTSO), 1949–present (vol. I)

UN Military Observer Group in India and Pakistan (UNMOGIP), 1949–present (vol. II)

UN Enforcement Action in Korea, 1950–1953 (vol. II)

UN Emergency Force (UNEF), 1956–1967 (vol. I)

UN Observer Group in Lebanon (UNOGIL), 1958 (vol. I)

UN Operation in the Congo (ONUC), 1960–1964 (vol. III)

UN Observers and Security Force in West Irian (UNSF), 1962–1963 (vol. II)

UN Yemen Observation Mission (UNYOM), 1963–1964 (vol. I)

UNFICYP, 1964–present (vol. IV)

UN India-Pakistan Observation Mission (UNIPOM), 1965–1966 (vol. II)

Three peacekeeping units organized in the Middle East after 1967 do not appear in the Higgins series:

UN Emergency Force (UNEF II), 1973–1979

UN Disengagement Observer Force (UNDOF), 1974–present

UN Interim Force in Lebanon (UNIFIL), 1978–present

Volume IV uses the same organizational format as each of the earlier volumes. After an introduction, there are chapters on enabling resolutions and voting, functions and mandate, constitutional basis, political control, administrative and military control, composition and size, relations with contributing states, relations with host states, relations with other states involved, finance, and implementation. There is also a checklist of documents and a bibliography for each peacekeeping operation.

The UN peacekeeping experience in the Balkans is of interest above all because it was the first such experience. Boundary disputes arose after the end of the Second World War between Greece on the one hand, and Albania, Bulgaria, and Yugoslavia on the other. Greece also accused those countries of violating its sovereignty by assisting guerrillas within its territory. In December 1946, the UN Security Council established a Commission of Investigation. Further action by the Council, in response to recommendations of the commission and to draft resolutions by several countries, including the United States—which announced the Truman Doctrine in March 1947—was prevented by Soviet veto or, in the case of Soviet resolutions, by majority vote. Finally, in September 1947, the Council removed the dispute from its agenda and asked the Secretary-General to "place all records and documents in the case at the disposal of the General Assembly."[3]

[3] S.C. Res. 555, Sept. 15, 1947.

A month later, the Assembly adopted a United States-sponsored resolution, nearly identical to its vetoed Council draft, which called on Albania, Bulgaria, and Yugoslavia not to aid Greek rebels, and which established the first tentative peacekeeping unit, a Special Committee (UNSCOB) instructed to "observe the compliance by the four governments concerned with the foregoing recommendations" and to "be available to assist [those governments] in the implementation of such recommendations."[4] From early on, the Special Committee made use of military advisers in connection with its observation functions. The Special Committee's interpretation of its mandate, as recorded in its reports, was largely approved by the Assembly, though some delegations, notably that of Australia, voiced reservations. UNSCOB's functions were restated when it was replaced by the Balkan Sub-Commission in 1952.

The formation of UNSCOB foreshadowed the adoption by the General Assembly in 1950 of the "Uniting for Peace" resolution. The Balkan Sub-Commission was a subsidiary body of the Peace Observation Commission established by that resolution. Thus, one of the most important aspects of the Balkans peacekeeping experience was the fact that it illustrated, at a very early stage in the UN's history, the interaction between the Security Council and the General Assembly in the resolution of disputes and the maintenance of peaceful relations among states. The Assembly would act again in the creation of the first UN Emergency Force and of the West Irian Security Force, but the institution of peacekeeping has evolved in such a manner that creating a new force is now all but the exclusive province of the Council.

UNSCOB and the subcommission also provided early examples of the principle of host country consent and of the limits of "enforcement" action. Also of interest are the detailed instructions given to the military observers, which are excerpted in the book under review. In subsequent UN operations, Professor Higgins writes, "either the pressure of time has prevented the formulation of such precise instructions or else they have not been generally published" (p. 37). Greece's borders had quieted and most of the Assembly's objectives in the Balkans had been achieved by 1954. The contribution toward their achievement by the UN peacekeeping units was "real and useful" (p. 66), and the presence of the military observers "helped the external factors to be employed to advantage" (p. 37).

The UN force in Cyprus was created after the United Nations had had more than 15 years of experience in peacekeeping. It is much more complex than the Balkans case and accounts for over three-quarters of Higgins's book.

After the Republic of Cyprus gained independence from Great Britain in 1960, a period of tense cooperation between the Greek and Turkish Cypriot communities ensued. Violence broke out, however, at the end of 1963. British troops, stationed on the island by treaty right, were unable to maintain a cease-fire. The case was brought before the Security Council, initially by Archbishop Makarios and then by Britain, and UNFICYP was created by unanimous vote in March 1964. Fighting continued until August, when the Council's call for a cease-fire was accepted without conditions by the Govern-

[4] G.A. Res. 109 (II), Oct. 21, 1947.

ments of Cyprus and Turkey. UNFICYP immediately consolidated the cease-fire and its own position.

With only a few exceptions, UNFICYP succeeded in keeping the peace, and its mandate was rather routinely renewed. On July 15, 1974, however, a coup by Greek Cypriots in the National Guard removed Makarios from power, though the United Nations continued to recognize him as the lawful President of Cyprus. On July 20, Turkish forces intervened militarily, and by mid-August, Turkey gained control of the north of the island. UNFICYP's original mandate had included a recommendation that it "use its best efforts to prevent a recurrence of fighting and, as necessary, to contribute to the maintenance and restoration of law and order."[5] From its peak level of 7,000 troops, however, the force had been reduced by 1974 to fewer than 3,000. It was not established and was not prepared to deal with a coup and an invasion.

Still, while it was unable to meet all of the challenges of July and August 1974, UNFICYP was effective in providing medical assistance; in making arrangements for the evacuation of foreign nationals, the protection of tourists, and the locating of missing persons; in investigating charges by both sides; and in controlling the Nicosia airport. "Even with the benefit of hindsight," Higgins writes, "it is apparent that UNFICYP did everything that was humanly possible in the circumstances" (p. 371).

Cyprus remains a partitioned island, a Turkish Cypriot state having been declared in the north. The United Nations remains active in the effort to find a permanent political solution to the problem, in part through intercommunal talks under the auspices of the Secretary-General. The UN force continues to observe and maintain the cease-fire, to provide humanitarian relief, and, with the UNFICYP Civilian Police (UNCIVPOL), to maintain physical safety and law and order.[6]

Higgins's stated aim in producing the *United Nations Peacekeeping* series was to go beyond the existing literature—which includes studies of particular operations and broad surveys limited in depth—by thoroughly investigating primary sources. The series uses actual documentary materials to a greater extent than most or all other writings on UN peacekeeping, and the common organizational framework facilitates comparisons among various operations. In that connection, since several UN peacekeeping efforts have received little attention in the literature, it is most important that the author has given "the least known [operations] the same close attention as the best known" (p. ix).

Volume IV has the same technical dependability as the earlier volumes. The series has thus established itself as the compulsory starting point in any future inquiry into UN peacekeeping, be it legal, political, sociological, or even military. Developments are traced and explained chronologically in each functional area. The focus is on the official documents, but these are greatly embellished by connecting commentary that presents a clear picture of the conditions surrounding each documentational step in the process and puts

[5] S.C. Res. 186, Mar. 4, 1964.

[6] *See, e.g.*, the June 1, 1982, report of the Secretary-General on the UN Operation in Cyprus, UN Doc. S/15149.

each into perspective. In essence, the peacekeeping operation is recreated on paper, providing an understanding that probably did not exist in the minds of the principal actors at the time.

However, this is not revisionist history, since Higgins is careful not to impose her own values on the facts as presented by the documents. The furthest she goes in that direction is a disclaimer mentioning her "admiration and respect" for the peacekeepers, both those in the field and those on the 38th floor at headquarters in New York.

This reviewer can do no better than reaffirm the conclusion of Robert Rosenstock in his review of volume III: "Critics, supporters, and students of the United Nations should consult Higgins . . . unless they are prepared to do hundreds of hours of research or risk being dangerously ill-informed. No better synthesis of material is anywhere available . . . ."[7]

RICHARD W. NELSON
Washington and Lee University School of Law, Adjunct Professor

The Expanding Jurisdiction of the United Nations. By M. S. Rajan. Bombay: N. M. Tripathi Private Ltd.; Dobbs Ferry: Oceana Publications, Inc., 1982. Pp. xii, 252. Index. $30.

The changing jurisdiction of the United Nations is topical, but hardly scholarly *terra incognita.* The book under review does not add a great deal in either detail or theory. It consists of eight chapters, commencing with a historical review of the concepts of domestic and international jurisdiction, and then briefly refers to the League of Nations and post-World War II practice. The following six chapters review major incidents and cases brought to the United Nations that concerned internal state administration, non-self-governing territories, economic and social cooperation, human rights, disarmament, and maintenance of peace and security. Those cases include the position of the United Nations in relation to the Franco regime in Spain, the Czechoslovak questions of 1948 and 1968, the Hungarian situation of 1956, and the question of Cyprus. Major cases on non-self-governing territories such as the independence of Indonesia, Morocco, Tunisia, West Irian, Cyprus, Algeria, Oman, and Namibia are essentially reported with insufficient analysis of their political context and their legal significance. The last chapter of the book evaluates the expanding jurisdiction of the United Nations and some of its positive consequences.

There are several problems with Rajan's design, approach, and analysis. The book lacks an independent scholarly perspective with an express statement of criteria employed. Although the author recognizes the ambiguities in the terms "domestic" and "international jurisdiction," he does not offer his own definition. Thus, the description of major UN events, in the first seven chapters, appears aimless and often leaves the reader confused about

[7] 75 AJIL 714, 715 (1981).

its relevance to the title and the purposes of the book. The criteria for characterizing events as falling within domestic jurisdiction are rather superficial, indeed often unstated. No definitions or criteria are developed to explain why certain incidents are within or without domestic jurisdiction. Virtually every case in which the United Nations expanded and exercised its competence is taken to have been within domestic jurisdiction. Nor is there a systematic explanation of why certain cases came to the United Nations or an indication of conditioning factors that influenced their treatment.

MAHNOUSH H. ARSANJANI
United Nations

The Political Role of the United Nations: Advancing the World Community. By John W. Halderman. New York: Praeger Publishers, 1981. Pp. xii, 217. Index. $24.95.

Halderman rests his book on the assumption that much of the failure of the United Nations to maintain peace and security is attributable to the system's structural incapacity to generate consensus rather than to the inherent difficulties of maintaining peace and security in the contemporary world political arena. He attempts to reconstruct the Charter—or as he calls it "the paper instrument"—into an effective constitution. Comparing the Charter to constitutions of democratic societies, he concludes that the success of the Charter will require changes in the identifications and demands of the peoples of the world community.

The function of the United Nations, according to Halderman, is to reduce the intensity of international disputes to manageable proportions. To help bring about a United Nations that will realize this goal, Halderman devotes the subsequent chapters to procedural recommendations for peaceful settlement of disputes and examines some of the past precedents against his approach.

In his view, the UN Charter incorporates sound conceptions but has been misapplied; too much emphasis has been put on enforcement measures or sanctions, as opposed to the peaceful settlement of disputes. Because of this emphasis, the author argues, the United Nations has exceeded or has given the appearance of exceeding its jurisdiction. That has caused distrust of the Organization in the world community. To overcome this distrust, he would separate the peaceful settlement function (largely diplomatic) from enforcement measures. The latter, according to him, should be used only to prevent threats to and breaches of international peace and security, and not to implement decisions of the Security Council or the General Assembly generally, between which he makes no distinction for this purpose. He concludes that the political organs of the United Nations should not go beyond pronouncing themselves on issues through recommendations and should not apply tangible pressure unless the situation constitutes an actual breach of the peace.

Halderman sharply distinguishes recommendations from mandatory measures. In his opinion, neither the General Assembly nor the Security Council, in handling disputes, should act in a formal legal fashion; resolutions of the General Assembly and the Security Council, except those calling for collective measures, are recommendatory. Under this thesis the parties are to acquiesce in the procedure of bringing their dispute to the United Nations and discussing it there, but they will not be "morally or legally" bound to comply with UN resolutions. He believes this strategy would encourage the parties to a dispute to come to the United Nations and discuss their conflict. Knowing that they would not be bound by the decisions, the parties, Halderman believes, would be more likely to reevaluate their positions in the dispute.

In Halderman's thesis, when there are high probabilities that one or all of the parties to the dispute are not going to comply with a UN decision, the decision should not be made, for, he argues, noncompliance with UN decisions would only embarrass the defendant state, inject tension into the atmosphere of subsequent discussions, and discredit the United Nations.

In the author's opinion, "law" in the ordinary sense does not exist in international relations. Hence, the word should be de-emphasized in international dispute handling. The judicial organs of the United Nations, under Halderman's thesis, should be asked to decide disputes only when the parties appear likely to comply with the resulting decision. He considers the decisions on the *Corfu Channel, Namibia,* and *U.S. Diplomats in Tehran* fruitless and institutionally destructive, since one party did not comply with the decision. This, in his opinion, has undermined the Court, added to the hostility, and made the atmosphere unconducive to settlement of those disputes.

Halderman's recommendations stress the role of debate in overcoming resistance. But one can hardly build a political system on that alone. The author himself admits that his thesis rests upon the assumption that the defendant state will accept the right of the Council or Assembly to debate the issue and make recommendations. In the absence of such acceptance, Halderman's thesis will not even begin to work. His approach also relies substantially on the consent of the major powers to withhold their veto right. Further, it appears to assume that every international dispute is isolated from domestic as well as external interaction, and is soluble at the international level. Thus, negotiation by itself will be sufficient to settle it. On the contrary, many international disputes are intimately related to all kinds of internal and international factors. Moreover, Halderman is too sweeping in his depreciation of the value of UN resolutions and political decisions in shaping behavior. Negotiations are extremely useful, but certain maneuvers by the United Nations, including binding resolutions, sanctions, and other forms of collective pressure, may be quite effective in dispute settlement. Another issue ignored in this book is the lawmaking dimension of the UN political and judicial organs, their formulation and maintenance of international norms of conduct—not only for a particular international dispute, but for the longer term and the larger community.

Finally, the time frame for appraisal of success or failure appears unrealistically short in many cases. For example, it is too soon to discuss *Namibia* as an international failure. Although some of the cases examined in the book might have *allegedly* failed to settle particular disputes immediately, they did uphold or formulate certain international norms of behavior that have been stated over and over again in other international dispute settlement procedures as indicators of the community's expectations.

MAHNOUSH H. ARSANJANI
United Nations

Rechtsgleichheit und Selbstbestimmung der Völker in wirtschaftlicher Hinsicht. By Hans Reinhard. (Vol. 74 in the series Beiträge zum ausländischen öffentlichen Recht und Völkerrecht.) Berlin, Heidelberg, and New York: Springer-Verlag, 1980. Pp. xiii, 373. DM 86; $48.20.

The author's intent is to analyze the resolution practice of the United Nations concerning the economic aspects of the principles "equal rights" and "self-determination." To be more specific, the treatise deals primarily with the following General Assembly resolutions: 523 (VI), 626 (VII), 1803 (XVII), 2158 (XXI) (natural resources); 2692 (XXV), 3016 (XXVII), 3171 (XXVIII), 3201 (S–VI), 3202 (S–VI), and 3281 (XXIX).

The introduction (pp. 1–21) gives an outline of the objective of the treatise and serves to interpret the principles of "self-determination" and "equality in substance." It also briefly touches upon preferential treatment, trade in commodities, transfer of technology, and the common heritage principle. The main part starts with an analysis of Article 1 of the two Human Rights Covenants. In his first chapter (pp. 22–32), the author is mainly interested in the relationship among economic self-determination, sovereignty, and human rights. This relationship, however, is primarily dealt with in the light of the legislative history of the provision and not so much from an analytical point of view. Accordingly, the assumption that economic self-determination had to be regarded as a prerequisite to the effective protection of human rights is not jeopardized, though the desire to achieve economic self-determination may result in restricting individual human rights.

Starting with the second chapter, a historical approach becomes more or less dominant. The resolutions are dealt with according to their sequence, which illustrates most clearly that a substantial enrichment of the relevant General Assembly resolutions has taken place over the years. The basis of the analysis again is the legislative history of the relevant resolutions. Chapters B, C, D, and E (pp. 33–95) all deal with the principle of "permanent sovereignty over natural resources" and various related aspects, such as expropriation of foreign property, compensation, multinational enterprises, and international protection of the environment.

The following two chapters (pp. 96–139) are devoted to the principle of "state equality." The author correctly points out that this principle has two aspects, the one aiming at securing state equality in substance, the other at accepting that unequal (less favorable) economic circumstances call for special (preferential) treatment of the respective state or group of states (p. 96). This idea is further elaborated under the topics "prohibition of economic discrimination," "furtherance of economic relations between States having different economic and social systems," "equal participation in the decision making process of international economic organizations," "preferential treatment and GATT," "trade in commodities," "transfer of technology," and "the common heritage principle."

The remaining five chapters deal with what could be called the implementation of the principles of equal rights and self-determination in the economic fields. Chapter H analyzes the deliberations of the International Law Commission with respect to state succession from the viewpoint of the protection of investment; chapter I (pp. 153–92) illustrates the relationship between the exclusive economic zone, as well as the continental shelf regime, and the principle of permanent sovereignty over natural resources. Chapter K (pp. 196–247) addresses the economic rights of peoples under foreign domination. Chapter L (pp. 248–63) questions whether the principles of equal rights and self-determination in economic fields have to be regarded as being part of *jus cogens* and the international *ordre public.* As the author bases himself exclusively on the practice of the United Nations, he does not offer any clear answer as to whether the principle of economic self-determination exists—though it has received widespread acceptance. Because of this approach the treatise does not offer new perceptions concerning the existence, scope, and content of the principle of economic self-determination. However, it contains a careful analysis of the development of this principle within the United Nations and of the expectations attached to it.

C. RÜDIGER WOLFRUM
Institute for International Law, University of Kiel

United States Space Law: National and International Regulation. Binders I and II. Edited by Stephen Gorove. London, Rome, New York: Oceana Publications, Inc., 1982. $85/binder.

In today's society, law and technology are often inseparable companions. In the computer communications field, for example, implementation of transborder data networks is paralleled by the development of national privacy laws. Similarly, in genetic engineering, the patentability of new micro-organisms regulates their rate of development. *United States Space Law* demonstrates clearly that this same pattern exists for space technology.

Since the very beginning of the space age, domestic and international lawmakers have generated a legal framework for the "high frontier." When space technology was embryonic, its attendant legal framework was sparse. Early space law, such as the 1967 Outer Space Treaty, set out the rights and responsibilities of states in very broad terms. Space law was, at that time, the concern largely of foreign ministries, national space agencies, and a select group of international legal scholars.

However, space technology has matured rapidly. Communication satellite launch rates are exceeding one per month. Most of these satellites are built by private firms; hundreds of contracts and millions of persons depend on their continued operation. Earth observation satellite systems, such as the American Landsat and the French Spot, provide remote sensing data from space to public and private entities worldwide. These and many other types of satellites may be launched by the space shuttle or by American and European expendable rockets.

As space technology matures, the scope of the law of activities in outer space becomes far more comprehensive. Today, outer space law is of vital concern to many. With ever more firms moving into the space technology market, and ever more government agencies finding space technology within their domains, knowledge of space law is becoming essential to practicing lawyers and corporate legal departments. Its importance can only grow as space facilities continue to be integrated into the terrestrial economy.

United States Space Law, therefore, is the right work at the right time. What today's high-technology attorney needed was a compendium of outer space law, a single source where such relevant law could be found, studied, and referenced. Oceana Publications has satisfied just this need. Under the expert editorial control of Dr. Stephen Gorove, *United States Space Law* is a cogently organized compilation of significant U.S. law and regulations, including international agreements involving the United States, relevant to utilization of the outer space environment.

In their "preface" to this work, S. Neil Hosenball, NASA's General Counsel, and Richard A. Reeves, a NASA attorney, paint a broad landscape of the dynamic space environment and set forth in succinct fashion the panoply of outer space activities over the past 25 years.

The preparation of a two-volume set such as *United States Space Law* entails challenges in two major categories: selection and organization. With regard to selection, the editor must define the scope of law to include, determine which documents within the defined scope are useful, and decide whether these documents should be reprinted in whole or in part. As to organization, it is necessary to establish both logical structure and useful finding aids.

Gorove's well-deserved reputation as one of America's leading space law scholars provides considerable assurance that the selection challenge is in able hands. Gorove defines the scope of space law to include "domestic and international law arising out of man's activities in relation to the use of outer space." Within this broad scope the volumes include material that ranges from several bilateral agreements between the United States and various countries for the establishment of space vehicle tracking stations to the recent Agreement Governing the Activities of States on the Moon and Other Celestial Bodies.

In determining which space law documents to include, Gorove has emphasized NASA regulations, international treaties, and bilateral agreements. Hence the reader will find, in its entirety, chapter V of Title 14, Code of Federal Regulations, in which NASA publishes its regulations. Also included is the entire National Aeronautics and Space Act of 1958, as amended, and NASA-related portions of over three dozen other acts.

As to international space law, Gorove included 20 multilateral treaties and agreements and a like number of bilateral agreements. The 1963 Nuclear Test Ban Treaty, the 1967 Outer Space Treaty, the Astronaut Rescue and Return Agreement, the Outer Space Liability Convention, and the Convention on the Registration of Objects Launched into Outer Space typify the major outer space treaties included.

Most of the space-related law in these volumes is reprinted in full. The most notable exception is the Convention and Radio Regulations of the International Telecommunication Union (ITU). These documents are heavily edited to emphasize ITU broadcasting-satellite service regulations. However, regulations relating to the ITU's broadcasting-satellite service plan for the Eastern Hemisphere are not included.

In addition to comprehensive coverage of space law, the volumes also include useful ancillary material. For example, in the domestic arena, there are executive branch statements of national space policy, reports on U.S. space programs, and a sample NASA space shuttle launch services contract.

In addition to selection of appropriate material, a compendium of substantive regulation should also be organized logically and provide the user with document-finding aids. *United States Space Law* is organized into national and international categories. Space law and related materials promulgated in the United States are contained in Binder I. International space law, which contains separate multilateral and bilateral sections, is collected in Binder II.

The table of contents is the only finding aid in *United States Space Law.* Unfortunately, the table of contents is only a summary table, and therefore does not list every document the volumes include. One must turn to the sections listed in the summary table of contents to find a listing of the particular contents of each section. There is no topical index or cross-reference system. The inclusion of such topical finding aids would certainly enhance the utility of the volumes.

United States Space Law is in a binder format to facilitate the updating service which the publisher intends to offer. Virtually all materials in the binders are reprints of original documents. Readers familiar with the Space Law Reprints of the U.S. Senate Commerce Committee will recognize much of those useful documents in this collection.

An examination of Gorove's collection certainly leaves one impressed with the breadth of space law today. Indeed, it is hard to believe that any legal discipline could grow so large in so short a time. With increasing numbers of practicing attorneys, government decision makers and academicians in the high-technology field faced with space law questions, the need for a comprehensive collection of relevant law was evident. *United States Space Law* fulfills this need in a useful format.

Furthermore, this is one legal work whose value will certainly increase with time. For space launch capability is increasing from one space shuttle to four or more, and satellites in orbit are increasing in number, growing in size, and diversifying in function. As a result of these trends an ever larger number of companies, government agencies, and scholars will face new space law problems. Answering new space law questions will not be easy, but *United States Space Law* certainly will facilitate the task.

PAUL G. DEMBLING
Of the District of Columbia Bar

A Pole Apart: The Emerging Issue of Antarctica. By Philip W. Quigg. A Twentieth Century Fund Report. New York: New Press (McGraw-Hill Book Company), 1983. Pp. xiv, 299. Index. $19.95.

The current growth of Antarctic fisheries and the future possibilities of commercially exploitable oil and mineral deposits have raised interest in the Antarctic among fishermen, environmentalists, oil men, miners, and officials. The Falklands war has attracted broader public attention to the usually ignored "cold continent." This book is an effort by the Twentieth Century Fund to introduce Antarctic issues to that broader public.

In 218 pages of text, most of which was written before the Falklands war, Quigg discusses the full range of past activity, present controversy, and likely future developments in the Antarctic. Dealing with history, geography, economic potential, environmental constraints, legal controversies, and political concerns in such a short space requires great economy of expression. The chapters dealing with early exploration, scientific activity, and political developments before negotiation of the Antarctic Treaty in 1958–1959 succeed admirably in conveying much information in a short space. The discussion of economic potential lays out the available information and makes a solid argument based on economic and environmental grounds for not acting too quickly, or getting too excited by the immediate prospects of Antarctica. His criticisms of the haphazard nature of U.S. policy making on Antarctic issues have merit, as do the suggestions for improving matters offered almost at the end of the text (p. 216).

Unfortunately, the presentation of the issues most interesting to international lawyers is less successful. Quigg's brief discussion of the juridical weight of the seven Antarctic claims merges abruptly into an examination of the three-way rivalry among Argentina, Britain, and Chile in the Antarctic Peninsula area. This discussion is difficult to follow, particularly since Quigg does not fully explain how the Falklands Islands dispute between Argentina and Britain and the Beagle Channel dispute between Argentina and Chile relate to the Antarctic argument.

Chapter 6, which deals with waning U.S. enthusiasm for applying "common heritage" ideas to Antarctica, the oceans, and outer space would have been much easier to understand if the last paragraph had come first. There (p. 182) Quigg explains it by a theory that policy shifts from global to self-interested as more people, particularly representatives of various interest groups, become involved. Yet there is an equally plausible explanation: recently U.S. policy makers have realized that the notion of "common heritage" tends to be linked to management by a global institution based on the one state, one vote rule which now hands control to others. At a time when many influential Americans view those others, the Group of 77, as unalterably hostile to U.S. interests, waning enthusiasm is to be expected.

Prescriptions for managing Antarctic resources and dealing with the territorial claims also suffer from overly elliptical presentation. Quigg clearly prefers a management scheme that leaves control in the hands of states most active in the Antarctic, but realizes that the Group of 77 is unlikely to accept the Antarctic Treaty Consultative Parties mechanism as it now stands. He proposes some modifications of that mechanism, including earmarking two seats for Third World states serving on a rotating basis. He presents the elements of an argument supporting his contention that the Group of 77 could be persuaded to accept such a scheme, but many readers are likely to remain skeptical that it would settle for such a small share of decision making.

Both dealing with claims and setting up new management institutions present complicated problems that governments have only just begun to address, so it is not surprising that no definitive scheme is offered here. The fragmentary nature of these discussions does mean, however, that Quigg's book is more useful to lawyers for the information and opinions it presents than as a blueprint for Antarctica's future.

M. J. PETERSON
Harvard University

A Joint Venture Agreement for Seabed Mining. By Günther Jaenicke, Erich Schanze, and Wolfgang Hauser. Deventer: Kluwer; Frankfurt am Main: Alfred Metzner Verlag, 1981. Pp. 127. Dfl.38.

The Maritime Dimension. Edited by R. P. Barston and Patricia Birnie. Winchester: Allen & Unwin, Inc., 1980. Pp. 194. Index. $26.95, cloth; $12.50, paper.

U.S. Foreign Policy and the Law of the Sea. By Ann L. Hollick. Princeton: Princeton University Press, 1981. Pp. xii, 496. Index. $32.50, cloth; $15, paper.

Since the Third UN Conference on the Law of the Sea (UNCLOS III) first formally convened in 1974, a spate of legal materials has been published about the perplexing issues, protracted process, and ponderous progress of the negotiations. These three volumes are among the latest additions to the law of the sea literature. Each contains noteworthy insights and new perspectives into the familiar political problems that have served to foment diplomatic frustration over world oceans law for nearly a decade.

The Jaenicke, *et al.* work addresses the legal relationship that would evolve between an International Sea-Bed Authority, its mining arm (the Enterprise), and national consortia investors. As explained by the authors, their chief intent is "to identify [specific legal] problems and to demonstrate that joint ventures between the Enterprise and national companies can be formed in such a way as to pay regard to the special and legitimate interests of both sides and to proffer good prospects for a viable working [relationship]" (p. 5). Drawing upon prior research performed at the Institute for Foreign and International Trade Law in Frankfurt, the authors in effect propose to operationalize legally the parallel exploitation system via a suggested Manganese Nodule Mining Agreement. This proposition consists of some 30 provisional articles, which are organized into three functional sections: "Approval of the Enterprise's Plan of Work"; the "Contract Concerning Fiscal Incentives and Security of Tenure"; and a "Joint Venture Agreement between the Enterprise and the Investor," based on equity participation. Explanatory commentaries are appended to each article in order to clarify the research findings supporting that provision's intent, as well as to link its relevance to other portions of the proposed text and to the 1980 UNCLOS III Draft Convention.[1] Not to be overlooked, the draft proposal covers only the mining (*i.e.*, recovery) phase of the seabed operation and logically assumes that (1) an international seabed mining regime will issue from the current UNCLOS III negotiations; and (2) manganese nodule mining will become not only technically feasible, but also commercially profitable.

The authors' primary contribution, in this reviewer's opinion, is a useful and provocative paradigm—or at least a textual starting point—for negotiating deep seabed mining arrangements between the Enterprise and private investors. Though most assuredly not a panacea, the work achieves its purpose by formulating for serious discussion and policy debate a hypothetical joint venture arrangement that seems economically pragmatic should deep seabed mining efforts become viable large-scale operations in the coming years.

The Maritime Dimension is composed of nine succinct essays that deal cogently with various aspects of the law of the sea. Following an overview historical discussion by Birnie on the pre–1970 evolution of UNCLOS III, Paul Driver and Victor Prescott, respectively, examine the present politics of international fisheries and the potential prospects for deep seabed mining. The essay by Peter Odell analyzes the legal implications generated by offshore hydrocarbon exploitation beyond the limits of national sovereignty in general, and for the North Sea in particular. In subsequent essays, Barston and Birnie aptly assess the problematic dimensions of pollution for the marine environment; Christopher Hayman evaluates the nuances of transoceanic shipping politics; Peter Nailor appraises the contemporary strategic role of naval power; and Barston explains the UNCLOS III negotiating process. The final article by Birnie reviews several recent maritime episodes and persistent problems (*e.g.*, the *Pueblo* (1968) and *Mayaguez* (1975) incidents, the Anglo-Icelandic Cod War (1972), delimitation of the continental shelf, and the future of fisheries commissions) and views them as clearly underscoring the need for an agreed-upon law to manage ocean use. The Barston-Birnie edition provides a terse, albeit wide-ranging, collection of perceptive perspectives on the contemporary law of the sea. As such, it will serve the layman, graduate student, and neophyte scholar well, especially by elucidating the complex, multidimensional quality of the emerging UNCLOS III treaty package.

Of the three volumes, Hollick's study evinces the richest analysis and most incisive scholarship. The work chronicles U.S. oceans policy from 1935 through 1980. In addition, Hollick ventures beneath the surface of historical events to explain in circumspect detail the political, economic, and legal motivations underlying successive policy postures adopted by the U.S. Govern-

[1] Draft Convention on the Law of the Sea (Informal Text), UN Doc. A/CONF.62/WP.10/Rev.3 (1980).

ment. Put squarely, *U.S. Foreign Policy and the Law of the Sea* offers the reader a behind-the-scenes exposure to the drama of how U.S. oceans policy has been formalized during the past 40 years.

The initial third of Hollick's work substantively reviews the political repercussions stemming from the Truman Proclamations in 1945,[2] the resultant claims controversies over international fisheries and the continental shelf that ensued during the next decade, the well-known legal contributions produced at Geneva in 1958, and the less well known, in 1960. Of more contemporary import, the remainder of the study is devoted to scrutinizing U.S. participation in UNCLOS III. Accordingly, the realization during the 1960's that international oceans law merited broad renegotiation, the establishment of the requisite bureaucracy and engagement in the necessary preparatory work during the early 1970's, the launching of the conference in 1974, and, its protracted sessional meetings over the next 7 years—all these facets of the UNCLOS III evolutionary process are appropriately considered and coherently related to the context of U.S. foreign policy initiatives and objectives. Especially intriguing and informative is the author's session-by-session, committee-by-committee, issue-by-issue integrated approach in analytically assaying the ebb and flow of policy formation during the 1970's. Similarly, Hollick effectively investigates decision making within the U.S. Government. The inherent confrontational connection between the executive branch and Congress is explored, with a view to revealing conflicting interagency priorities, diverse interest group pressures, and subsequent congressional responses. As a result, the political process becomes animated and personified, and the reader is shown conclusively that individual personalities loom critical in fashioning and determining policy outcomes, irrespective of the issue.

To sum up, Hollick's study merits praise for its lucid, comprehensive treatment of U.S. oceans policy over the last four decades. The text is amply supported by authoritative documentation, and the attached appendixes and bibliography are welcome. The book should be greatly appreciated as a useful research tool as well, for it furnishes for serious legal scholars a most convenient wellspring of primary source information.

In concluding her volume, Hollick thoughtfully observes that

> [t]he experiences of the past suggest the likely directions of the future, including potential opportunities and problems. While particular events and the timing of emerging problems cannot be precisely pinpointed, general trends can be identified. Based on historical evidence, we can safely assume that, whatever the outcome of UNCLOS III, the evolution of the law of the sea will be an ongoing process. An UNCLOS III treaty might capture the legal picture at one point in time, but any treaty is doomed to be retrospective. Ocean technologies will continue to evolve, generating new uses and new political and economic processes. The law of the sea will have to follow, either through practice and custom or

[2] Policy of the United States with Respect to the Natural Resources of the Subsoil and Sea Bed of the Continental Shelf, Pres. Proc. No. 2667, 3 C.F.R. 67 (1943–1948 Compilation); Policy of the United States with Respect to the Coastal Fisheries in Certain Areas of the High Seas, Pres. Proc. No. 2668, 3 C.F.R. 68 (1943–1948 Compilation).

> future codification conferences or some combination of the two [pp. 381–82].

This reviewer concurs. Like law in general, the law of the sea will remain a dynamic process, in a state of constant flux and readjustment so that it may adapt adequately to meet changing political, economic, and technological conditions in the international milieu. These volumes highlight that realization; more than this, however, they also clearly illustrate the pervasive complexities of world oceans law and point up the paramount need for ongoing scholarly study, critical reflection, and analytical deliberation of pertinent law of the sea issues. The challenge deserves to be met with commitment.

CHRISTOPHER C. JOYNER
The George Washington University

Maritime Law. By Christopher Hill. London, Rome, New York: Oceana Publications, Inc.; London: Pitman Books Limited, 1981. Pp. xxi, 394. Index. $37.50.

The author of this volume serves not only as a member of the staff of a London maritime firm, but also as a lecturer in maritime law and a columnist for two respected shipping journals, a background which enables him to offer to his readers an impressively broad insight into a complex area of international and municipal law. *Maritime Law* was written with a number of audiences in mind: students, practitioners in related areas (*e.g.*, financiers), and nonspecializing lawyers. Its avowed purpose is to provide both an introduction to, and a general text on, the field of British shipping law and practice. To a very large degree it succeeds in adequately presenting the desired range of information to the intended recipients.

The book's contents span almost the entire range of relevant topics, from those most usually expected (such as "Ship mortgages," "Collisions," and "Ownership and registration") to those seldom addressed (for instance, "Seafarers and the ship's Master," "Passengers," and "Harbours and docks"), and touching along the way such important matters as "Towage," "Jurisdiction," "Sale of ship and shipbuilding contracts," "Pilotage," "Oil pollution," "Limitation of liability," and "Salvage." The list is long but not all-inclusive, for the author purposely omitted discussion of the basic categories of marine insurance and carriage of goods by sea, in the hope that existing texts on those topics would be read in conjunction with this book. Other notable gaps relate to the subject of chartering and the growing issues of piracy and maritime fraud. It is perhaps unfortunate that these topics were not included, since each would have benefited from the sort of analysis and summary given the 13 that were presented.

And what is the form of this analysis? Each of the topics is dealt with in a separate chapter in which issues are discussed under a heading that is a question or a summary statement. The style is easygoing and direct, without footnotes, and short case summaries are interspersed to provide anecdotal (yet formal) applications of the rules described. Where appropriate, there are chapter-end appendixes containing the documents noted, and there are excellent case and statutory tables, as well as a complete index.

One finds the book useful in several ways. First, as an introduction to the field it is a document that can be read at a relaxed pace, in sharp contrast to other more "black letter rule" oriented tomes on the same topics. Second, one can, on rereading a given chapter for the express purpose of delving deeply into a narrow subject, discover that there are a great many details and insights—along with appropriate citations—that give the reader a firm foundation in that area. Seldom does one find a single book that can accomplish both tasks with this much success.

There are some weaknesses. Primary among them is the inadequacy of the formats and headings of the topical sections. The information is certainly there, but it is often difficult to locate quickly; too often the reader must simply ignore the section titles. Other problems are less serious, such as overly detailed case summaries, inadequate introductions to certain cases, and excessive treatment of some topics (for example, the Administration of Justice Act, 1956).

The book is very good overall and of great value to its intended users, prompting a hope for subsequent editions with expanded coverage and the elimination of current weaknesses. Also, when the present state of flux in U.S. maritime law has abated, the profession would benefit from a similar volume focused on law and practice on this side of the Atlantic.

PETER A. THOMAS
Washington, D.C.

New Rules for Victims of Armed Conflicts: Commentary on the Two 1977 Protocols Additional to the Geneva Conventions of 1949. By Michael Bothe, Karl Josef Partsch, and Waldemar A. Solf. The Hague, Boston, London: Martinus Nijhoff Publishers, 1982. Pp. xxi, 746. Index. Dfl.340; $145.

In February 1974, a Diplomatic Conference on the Reaffirmation and Development of International Humanitarian Law Applicable in Armed Conflicts convened in Geneva at the invitation of the Swiss Government to draft two Protocols as supplements to the four 1949 Geneva Conventions.[1] The working documents to be used by the conference were two Draft Protocols prepared by the International Committee of the Red Cross (ICRC) with the assistance of a number of preparatory conferences.[2] The task proved more difficult than had originally been expected. As a result, in addition to the 1974 session, lengthy sessions were held in 1975, 1976, and 1977, the two Additional Protocols[3] being completed on June 8, 1977, and the Final Act of the conference signed on June 10, 1977. The formal signing of the Protocols themselves by

[1] The 1949 Geneva Conventions on the protection of war victims, 75 UNTS 31–468; 6 UST 3114–695.

[2] Draft Additional Protocols to the Geneva Conventions of August 12, 1949 (Geneva 1973).

[3] Protocols Additional to the Geneva Conventions of August 12, 1949, 16 ILM 1391–449 (1977).

46 nations took place at Bern on December 12, 1977.[4] *New Rules for Victims of Armed Conflicts,* by Michael Bothe and Karl Josef Partsch, both of the Federal Republic of Germany, and Waldemar A. Solf, of the United States, gives us the background of the evolution of each article of the two Additional Protocols.

The authors necessarily adopted a standard formula for the presentation of each separate article of the two Protocols: (1) the article itself, in full; (2) citation to preexisting law, if any; (3) citations to preconference documentation, if any (although the "Guide to Documentation" states that this "historically begins with the 1973 ICRC draft," there are many citations to pre-1973 documents); (4) citations to the Diplomatic Conference drafting history; (5) citations to any declarations made upon final adoption; (6) citations to any declarations made upon signature of the Protocols; and (7) a personal Commentary by one of the authors, which may be anywhere from one to 25 pages in length, depending upon the complexity of the issues confronting the conference and the dispatch with which those issues were resolved.

It is not a simple matter to review a book such as this one, dealing with many different subjects that frequently have practically no relationship to each other (except that they all fall under the rubric of "humanitarian law of war"), particularly when it is written by three different authors.[5] The reviewer has elected to accomplish the task by selecting three articles from Protocol I each of whose Commentary was written by a different author: Article 1 (Partsch), Article 44 (Solf), and Article 65 (Bothe). It will be found that either the authors were able to merge their personal writing idiosyncracies or that this was accomplished by an anonymous editor, as it is almost impossible to identify the author of a particular Commentary by style and without having recourse to the table of contents (where this information is available).

Article 1 is entitled "General Principles and Scope of Application." Partsch points out (Commentary, pp. 37–52) that the first two paragraphs of the article are general principles while the other two are concerned with the scope of the application of the Protocol; and that while the first three paragraphs were comparatively noncontroversial and were adopted with minimal debate, paragraph 4 was a totally different story, occupying the time of Committee I of the Diplomatic Conference for much of the first (1974) session. (It is also the subject of almost all of the Partsch Commentary.) It is this paragraph which brings within the ambit of the rules applicable in *international* armed conflict those "armed conflicts in which peoples are fighting against colonial domination and alien occupation and against racist regimes in the exercise of their right of self-determination." During the course of the Commentary there are discussions of many of the terms of art used in the quoted provision: "armed conflicts," "peoples," "right of self-determination," "colonial domination,"

[4] As of June 1982 there were 24 parties to Additional Protocol I and 21 to Additional Protocol II. 229 INT'L REV. OF THE RED CROSS 219 (1982).

[5] The "General Introduction and Guide to Documentation" (pp. 1–13) is the joint effort of Professors Bothe and Partsch (its page headings incorrectly identify it as the introduction to Protocol I, written by Professor Bothe alone). The introduction to Protocol II (pp. 604–08) is also a joint product.

"racist regimes," and "alien occupation." The conclusion is reached, and probably with a good deal of merit, that, as Kalshoven has indicated,[6] the net effect of this provision is that it applies to "the peoples of Southern Africa and Palestine." Nevertheless, the drafting and adoption of this provision sharply divided the committee, and there were subsurface indications, which sometimes all but surfaced, that the failure to adopt it would be a signal to the Third World nations that this Diplomatic Conference was to be another instance of an attempt by the developed nations to impose their wills on the underdeveloped and new nations and to maintain the colonial tradition.

It is because of the foregoing that a unique incident concerning this provision deserved, but did not receive, mention in the Commentary. (This was probably because, while it reveals the pressures that were at work, it did not affect the content of the article or its interpretation.) After Article 1 *in toto* had been approved by Committee I (70/21/13) and while the committee's report to the Diplomatic Conference was being considered, India proposed and Committee I adopted a recommendation by which the Diplomatic Conference in Plenary Meeting would be asked not only to follow the normal procedure of taking note of the committee's report, but also to adopt the text of Article 1. This proposal was approved by Committee I[7] and the Plenary Meeting of the Diplomatic Conference complied with it.[8] It was the sole instance during the four sessions of the Diplomatic Conference, which adopted a total of almost 150 separate articles, in which such a procedure was followed by a committee or by the conference. Its obvious purpose was to freeze the conference's position on Article 1(4) and to make extremely difficult, if not impossible, any effective intrasessional campaign to change the content of the paragraph.

The difficulties which Committee I encountered in reaching a decision on Article 1[9] were far exceeded by those which confronted Committee III in the drafting of Article 44, "Combatants and Prisoners of War."[10] Solf opens his Commentary on this article (pp. 243–58) by calling attention to the fact that while Article 1(4) is among the articles of the Protocol that "establish abstract political principles concerning the status of the armed struggles for self determination," the provisions of Article 44 are, in effect, the "concrete application of the principles advanced by these provisions [and] are the conditions under which the combatants of liberation movements enjoy the combatants' privilege" (p. 243, para. 2.1)—in other words, this article implements Article 1(4) by specifying the conditions under which those individuals are to be considered as "privileged combatants," who, when they fall into the hands of their adversary, are entitled to the full protection afforded by the 1949 Geneva Convention Relative to the Treatment of Prisoners of War (Third Conven-

[6] Citing 8 NETH. Y.B. INT'L L. 122 (1977).

[7] Doc. CDDH/I/SR.16, paras. 9–21; 8 OFF. REC. 127–29.

[8] Doc. CDDH/SR.22, paras. 9–21; 5 OFF. REC. 227–29.

[9] The evolution of that article occupies 80 pages of negotiating history in 1 H. LEVIE, PROTECTION OF WAR VICTIMS 1–80 (1979).

[10] The evolution of this article occupies 168 pages of negotiating history in 2 *id.* at 378–545 (1980).

tion).[11] Solf then draws a vivid picture of the several conflicting positions taken by the various delegations during the course of the largely successful attempt to give some practical meaning to Article 4A(2) of the Third Convention, the provisions of which purported to assure prisoner-of-war status to members of resistance groups but which, because they restated the four requirements of Article 1 of the 1907 Hague Regulations,[12] effectively excluded them from such status. This effort was, of course, motivated by the desire to provide privileged combatant status to the so-called freedom fighter, rather than to the members of true "resistance" groups.

Solf traces the day-by-day proposals, arguments, positions, demands, compromises, reports, etc., that were recorded as the debates on this article extended over the second, third, and fourth sessions of the Diplomatic Conference. He then analyzes the contents of the eight paragraphs that now constitute Article 44 of Protocol I. While he does not specifically so state, it would appear that the provisions of paragraph 2 (that violations of the rules of international law applicable in armed conflict do not deprive a combatant of his right to be a prisoner of war) would effectively preclude future claims such as that made by North Vietnam in the late hostilities in that area that every American had been captured *in flagrante delicto* and was, therefore, not entitled to prisoner-of-war status.[13] (It has never been made completely clear what the alleged war crime was, but it was probably that of "making aggressive war," or, even more horrendous, "supporting capitalism"!)

Paragraphs 3 and 4 are the most important, and were the most controversial, provisions of this article. The commentator states that "the obligation of combatants to distinguish themselves from the civilian population was the principal focus of the competing points of view" (p. 251, para. 2.7). He considers that the first sentence of paragraph 3, obligating combatants to distinguish themselves from the civilian population while engaged in an attack or in a military operation preparatory to an attack, is a significant development in the law of armed conflict because the failure to meet that obligation becomes a breach of the rules of international law, rather than being merely a cause for the loss of entitlement to prisoner-of-war status. As a practical matter, it appears that this will mean very little to the individual concerned. Previously he would have been tried as an illegal combatant. Now he will be tried for a violation of the law of war. In either case the maximum punishment is usually death.

[11] 47 AJIL, Supp. 19 (1953).

[12] Regulations Respecting the Laws and Customs of War on Land annexed to the 1907 Hague Convention No. IV, 2 AJIL, Supp. 90 (1908). These requirements are:

1. To be commanded by a person responsible for his subordinates;
2. To have a fixed distinctive emblem recognizable at a distance;
3. To carry arms openly; and
4. To conduct their operations in accordance with the laws and customs of war.

[13] *See* p. 250 n.22.

We are told by Solf that the second sentence of paragraph 3 was a part of the compromise sought in the attempt to protect members of organized resistance movements in occupied territory and members of liberation movements engaged in armed conflict within the scope of Article 1(4), while at the same time not endangering the civilian population (p. 253, paras. 2.7.2 and 2.7.2.1). In these two instances the armed combatant need only distinguish himself "during such time as he is visible to the adversary while he is engaged in a military deployment preceding the launching of an attack" and during the actual military engagement.[14] While a difference between the first and second sentences of paragraph 3 very probably does exist, the distinction between a "military operation preparatory to an attack" (first sentence) and a "military deployment preceding the launching of an attack" (second sentence) appears to be exceedingly fine, even given the additional requirement of visibility.

Paragraph 4 covers the situation that arises when the captured combatant (*i.e.*, a member of an organized resistance group in occupied territory or a member of a liberation movement engaged in an armed conflict within the scope of Article 1(4)) has failed to meet the requirements of the second sentence of paragraph 3, and therefore is not entitled to prisoner-of-war status. Under this paragraph he is nevertheless entitled to "protection equivalent" to that specified by the Third Convention. Solf concludes, however, that this was not intended to prevent his trial, with the appropriate trial safeguards, as an illegal combatant (p. 255, para. 2.8). This appears to be a fully justified interpretation, but there are strong doubts that it would be accepted by a number of Third World countries whose every effort, in the drafting of these provisions, was to protect the "freedom fighter";[15] and they unquestionably intended that protection to cover the freedom fighter like a huge blanket, no matter what he does or fails to do. (Resistance movements in occupied territory were merely a vehicle on which to obtain their objective and were completely incidental, even though in any major conflict their numbers will far exceed that of all the freedom fighters combined.)

Unfortunately, the allocation of articles among the three authors did not require Bothe to write a Commentary on any article that fits into the pattern of Articles 1 and 44. Accordingly, it was necessary to select one on another area that appeared to have sufficient controversial aspects to warrant a fairly substantial Commentary. Article 65 seemed to meet this requirement as much as any of those on which he commented. Moreover, it deals with a subject matter that is new to treaties on the law of war, civil defense;[16] and it is concerned with an aspect of civil defense that is bound to create problems: what actions of civil defense organizations and of their personnel are such as

[14] Both the United Kingdom (p. 721) and the United States (pp. 722–23) made declarations upon signature indicating that to them "deployment" means "any movement towards a place from which an attack is to be launched."

[15] *See, e.g.*, p. 247, para. 2.3(a).

[16] COMMENTARY ON THE 1949 GENEVA CONVENTION RELATIVE TO THE PROTECTION OF CIVILIAN PERSONS IN TIME OF WAR 333–34 (J. Pictet ed. 1958), vol. 4 of the official ICRC Commentary, interprets Article 63(2) of that Convention as relating to civil defense.

to warrant the termination of the protection accorded to them by Article 62 of Protocol I?

Paragraph 1 of Article 65 provides that the protection to which civil defense organizations and their personnel, buildings, shelters, and matériel are entitled "shall not cease unless they commit or are used to commit, outside their proper tasks, acts harmful to the enemy" and even then, only after a warning with a time limit (a type of ultimatum also to be found in Article 13(1) with respect to civilian medical units). Bothe calls attention to the fact that under Article 8(a) and (b) the wounded, sick, and shipwrecked are only protected if they "refrain from any act of hostility"; and that under Article 13(1) the protection of civilian medical units does not cease unless they commit "acts harmful to the enemy." He analogizes these provisions to those of Article 65(1) and states that "it is always what does *not* constitute an act harmful to the enemy that is stated." This is certainly the method adopted in the drafting of Articles 13(2) and 65(2), and it is the implication of Article 28 (concerned with prohibited activities on medical aircraft), another article to which reference is made in the Commentary. It is questionable whether this statement is correct in relation to Article 8(a) and (b).

Once the protection is lost, may it thereafter be regained? Bothe indicates that the answer to this question must be determined by the circumstances. Based on an agreed interpretation, he concludes that while a civil defense organization that performs non-civil-defense functions not harmful to the enemy (and therefore does not perform "exclusively" in the civil defense area as required by Article 61) may regain its entitlement to protection when it returns to civil defense functions, any such organization that commits acts harmful to the enemy may not. With considerable justification he argues that under certain circumstances this result can be unreasonable and he proposes what he terms a "middle solution" under which "[t]he protection should cease as long as there is a reasonable connection with the commission of acts harmful to the enemy" (pp. 412–13, first para. 2.3). There is some question as to the exact meaning of this proposal and also whether, as a practical matter, it could be applied.

The major controversy encountered in the drafting of this article arose with respect to the question of permitting civil defense personnel to carry arms. The problems are obvious: the possession of arms might encourage the commission of acts harmful to the enemy, and armed civil defense personnel might be mistaken for combatants. Bothe considers paragraph 3 of this article, dealing with this question, to be a compromise. The carrying of "light individual weapons" by civil defense personnel is not considered to be an act harmful to the enemy, but where "land fighting is taking place or is likely to take place" the parties should limit these weapons to handguns, *i.e.*, pistols or revolvers. The Commentary includes a quotation from the 1977 Report of Committee II giving the agreed interpretation of a number of the terms used in the paragraph.[17] However, it should be noted that there was no agreement on the specific meaning of the term "light individual weapons." Bothe does

[17] Doc. CDDH/406/Rev.1, para. 58; 13 OFF. REC. 349, 372.

not express an opinion on this compromise solution. This reviewer is forced to concur with the delegations that opposed the carrying of weapons by civil defense personnel. While Article 61(xi) does endow them with the function of "emergency assistance in the restoration and maintenance of order in distressed areas," presumably they will be rendering the emergency assistance to the police (or the military) who will be armed—and if the police are not, it is extremely doubtful that civil defense personnel should be.

It is believed that the foregoing discussion will have indicated that a review of a Commentary written by any one of the three authors will go a long way towards enlightening the reader as to what each article of the two 1977 Additional Protocols says and what it means—or, at least, what the draftsmen probably intended it to mean. There is also little question that anyone interested in recent developments in the law of war should have a copy of this volume readily available for research purposes. However, valuable as this volume should prove to the student of the law of war, it has one objectionable feature (apart from its price). The Swiss Government's 17-volume set entitled *Official Records of the Diplomatic Conference on the Reaffirmation and Development of International Humanitarian Law Applicable in Armed Conflicts* was published in 1979. It is therefore somewhat difficult to understand why the authors elected to use as their sole references the designations that identified the various documents of the conference itself. These original documents are not, of course, generally available, even in the best-equipped libraries. This makes it necessary for the researcher using *New Rules for Victims of Armed Conflicts*, with the *Official Records* as his source for original documents, to waste valuable time locating cited documents in that many-volumed and poorly indexed set. While the authors' "Guide to Documentation" would have the reader believe that this is a comparatively easy chore, the very explanation of how it is done (pp. 12–13) demonstrates the problems involved. The authors could have made life much easier for the researcher by merely adding a cross-reference to the volume and page of the *Official Records* after each citation of a conference document.[18]

If you are interested in the whys and wherefores of recent developments in the law of war, and if you can afford the price, this book should be in your personal library. If you do not wish to make such a large investment for a single volume, be sure to persuade the librarian of the library you use to obtain a copy for its shelves.

HOWARD S. LEVIE

Documents on the Laws of War. Edited by Adam Roberts and Richard Guelff. New York: The Clarendon Press; Oxford University Press, 1982. Pp. xi, 498. Index. $34.50, cloth; $17.95, paper.

In 1973 Dietrich Schindler and Jiří Toman edited *The Laws of Armed Conflicts,* a compilation of 72 conventions, treaties, agreements, reports, resolu-

[18] This was done on a few occasions. *See, e.g.,* p. 250 n.21.

tions, etc., basic to the law of war.[1] In 1981 a revised version of that volume was published with eight new documents, bringing the chronological contents up to June 1977.[2] Now come Roberts and Guelff with *Documents on the Laws of War,* a compilation of 29 such instruments, all but three of which appear in the latest Schindler/Toman volume (a very brief—two pages—extract of the Nuremberg judgment and two documents that postdate the Schindler/Toman 1977 cut-off date, one of which, a creation of the International Committee of the Red Cross, has no real significance). It can readily be seen that, while the price of the volume being reviewed is considerably less than the Schindler/Toman volume, the content is also considerably less.

Each document contains a "prefatory note" that includes some worthwhile historical data concerning the genesis of the particular document and that concludes with some specifics such as date of signing, date of entry into force, authentic language or languages, source, etc.; and each document is followed, where appropriate, by statistical data concerning ratifications, adhesions, and reservations. Much of this, and more, will be found in Schindler/Toman.

In setting forth the criteria followed by the editors in the selection of documents for inclusion, they state that "[e]mphasis is firmly placed on the laws of war which remain applicable today." That is a justifiable criterion: but are they saying that the 1907 Hague Convention No. III Relative to the Opening of Hostilities,[3] which is omitted (by a queer coincidence it is also omitted by Schindler/Toman), is not applicable today, perhaps because war has been "outlawed"? War was "outlawed" by the 1928 Pact of Paris,[4] but France and Great Britain scrupulously followed the requirements of the Convention in 1939. And while they include the 1923 Hague Rules of Aerial Warfare[5] because they "largely corresponded to customary rules and general principles underlying the laws of war on land and at sea," they omit the 1909 Declaration of London on the Laws of Naval Warfare.[6] Does this mean that the Declaration does not, in any part, correspond to "customary rules and general principles underlying the laws of war . . . at sea"? While editors and reviewers will frequently disagree on the selection of documents, and reviewers should not criticize merely because their opinion differs from that of the editors, where the editors have stated with specificity the criterion that governed their document selection, this reviewer believes it justifiable to state that, in his opinion, the editors have not followed their own criterion.

After a careful analysis of the contents of this volume, and cognizant of the contents of the Schindler/Toman volume, this reviewer finds it extremely difficult, if not impossible, to answer the very simple question: why was it considered necessary to publish this book?

HOWARD S. LEVIE

[1] Reviewed at 69 AJIL 927 (1975).
[2] Reviewed at 76 AJIL 209 (1982).
[3] 2 AJIL, Supp. 85 (1908).
[4] 22 AJIL, Supp. 171 (1928).
[5] 32 AJIL, Supp. 12 (1938).
[6] 3 AJIL, Supp. 179 (1909).

The American Road to Nuremberg: The Documentary Record, 1944–1945. By Bradley F. Smith. Stanford: Hoover Institution Press, 1982. Pp. x, 259. Index. $24.95.

This collection of documents is intended to serve as a companion to Professor Smith's historical narrative of the development of the U.S. Government's war crimes policy in the years 1944–1945.[1] Governmental memorandums and drafts are divided chronologically into three "phases," each corresponding to two chapters of Smith's earlier book. A short introduction to each "phase" puts the documents in context. Together the two works provide an interesting comparison of two methods of presenting politico-legal history. The narrative history couches the development of policy in terms of a bureaucratic battle, replete with strategy and confrontation, victories and losses. One faction generally favored an innovative development of international criminal law, particularly a theory of conspiracy that could be used to justify prosecution for acts of questionable international criminality, such as prewar abuse of a state's own nationals. The opposition was more conservative on issues of international law, but was in some cases more willing to dispense with legal niceties. The British, for instance, urged summary execution of top Nazi leaders on political grounds.

The "battle of factions" model may result in a less than dispassionate analysis. For instance, a recommendation by State Department Legal Adviser Green Hackworth to the Secretary of State to "go along" with the views of the War, Navy, and Justice Departments on the issue of whether to try defendants for initiating aggressive war is characterized as "departmental self-abasement" and "total surrender of initiative" (*The Road to Nuremberg*, p. 109). One who is familiar with interdepartmental disagreements in the executive branch might conclude, on the contrary, that a responsible department may, and possibly should, defer to other departments when its perceived interests are small or evenly balanced.

The value of the document collection format is the relative freedom from questionable or opinionated characterizations of historical materials. For example, one War Department memorandum reproduced (p. 97) and set in context (p. 53) in the document collection argues that certain treaties reflect international criminal standards for individuals, although the treaties by their terms only limit actions by the state. Smith, in *The Road to Nuremberg,* calls the argument strained and absurd (pp. 123–24), but the argument stands or falls on its own weight in the document collection. The document format also allows the reader to make his or her own evaluation of the significance of particular proposals or ideas raised. One draft of the executive agreement to be proposed to the Allies, for instance, reserved the right to try defendants for violations of the domestic law "of any of the United Nations" (p. 183). According to Smith, this "highly innovative and dangerous" provision would "have empowered the prosecutors to rummage through the law codes of some

[1] B. SMITH, THE ROAD TO NUREMBERG (1981).

fifty-odd Allied nations in search of offenses that could be charged against the Nazi leaders" (*The Road to Nuremberg,* p. 214). One who is familiar with the international law limitations on the application of domestic criminal proscriptions to nonnationals acting outside the state might conclude on the contrary that the provision merely contemplated, for example, application of Dutch criminal law to Nazi activities in Holland. Indeed, a redraft clearly limited application of domestic law to that of the country in which the violation was committed (p. 206).

The merit of the document collection in affording the freedom to draw one's own conclusions is counterbalanced by an obvious decrease in readability. Moreover, the separate placement of introductory material, documents, and footnotes requires the reader to use two hands and several fingers.

This collection is not intended primarily as a source book for documents that present (as opposed to reflect) legal analysis. It omits, for instance, some memorandums on the effect of the Kellogg-Briand Pact, tantalizingly referred to in the narrative history (pp. 100 and 106). Nevertheless, as a case study in the development of governmental policy affected by international law, it is a positive and highly interesting contribution to the historical literature.

JOHN M. ROGERS
University of Kentucky College of Law

German Private and Commercial Law: An Introduction. By Norbert Horn, Hein Kötz, and Hans G. Leser. Translated by Tony Weir. New York: The Clarendon Press; Oxford University Press, 1982. Pp. xvi, 355. Index. $39, cloth; $24.95, paper.

That American lawyers can have a far-ranging introduction to German law in a single readable volume calls for thanks to the three authors and their translator. The feat does owe something also to the systematic and nonfederal character of German law, since even an expert condenser has not been able to get much beyond an explanation of American procedure and judicial institutions in a one-volume exposition of our law.[1] Still, the selection and condensation involved in this task constitute a major achievement; it ranks the authors in that select band who have opened up for the American audience opportunities to understand the German system, which has rigorously and systematically approached the legal problems of a modern industrial welfare state economy.

The acid test for this volume is comparison with the *Manual of German Law* originally produced by E. J. Cohn and Martin Wolff for the British occupation forces and rewritten in 1968.[2] For the student who would like to acquire a general grasp of the German system and compare its overall structure with our own, one might well recommend the volume under review. Its compact-

[1] A. FARNSWORTH, INTRODUCTION OF THE LEGAL SYSTEM OF THE UNITED STATES (1963).

[2] E. COHN & M. WOLFF, MANUAL OF GERMAN LAW (1950, 1952); E. COHN, MANUAL OF GERMAN LAW (2d ed. 1968).

ness and the fluency of its style make it well adapted to this purpose. It is also 14 busy years more up to date. From a generalist's perspective, its choice of coverage, chiefly contracts, property, and commercial law, makes good sense. A general reader, however, might quarrel with the total omission of criminal law, which is a central feature of a state's legal system even if foreign practitioners seldom become involved with it.[3] The American reader will benefit in addition from the fact that, while the style has a slight leaning toward anglicisms, the substance of the comparisons reflects U.S. practices and institutions—such as the Securities and Exchange Commission—much more than did its predecessor.[4] On the other hand, the practicing lawyer who would like to have at hand a compact and intelligible source to serve as a guide in dealing with German co-counsel about specific problems might still prefer the older book. Its greater bulk does make it possible to cover more topics—perhaps most importantly for a foreigner, the German version of conflicts of law.[5] It also makes possible a greater depth of treatment. For example, an American lawyer involved in a German real estate transaction would come away from the *Manual*'s treatment of the *Grundbuch* or land registry of deeds with a much clearer picture of what it looked like and how it worked than one would from the Horn-Kötz-Leser work.[6]

One addition would have been helpful to this work (and to its predecessor): the inclusion, on a systematic basis, of references to other English-language sources, instead of merely footnotes pointing to almost exclusively German materials.[7] One does have to assume that the typical American reader will have neither access to the materials themselves nor the linguistic capacity to make use of them if he can lay his hands on them. With such an addition the work might really open the doors to systematic exploration of topics through the growing English literature on German law. Still, this is a small complaint in the face of the impressive achievements of this volume.

DETLEV F. VAGTS
Board of Editors

[3] For filling that gap one might start with J. LANGBEIN, COMPARATIVE CRIMINAL PROCEDURE: GERMANY (1977).

[4] The German press, in reviewing translations into German, now usually distinguishes between translations *from* the English and *from* the American. This book was translated into English, not American, but that fact is seldom disturbing, though I was puzzled at "invigilated papers" (p. 36) and "proleptic contractual effect" (p. 108) and had to think a moment about why Boxing Day was an important deadline for the delivery of trees (p. 104).

[5] To fill the gap the reader might wish to have U. DROBNIG, AMERICAN-GERMAN PRIVATE INTERNATIONAL LAW (1972), alongside the volume under review.

[6] *Compare* E. COHN, *supra* note 2, at 190–200 *with* pp. 180–82.

[7] To mention but one source, the World Tax Series volume, H. GUMPEL & C. BOETTCHER, TAXATION IN THE FEDERAL REPUBLIC OF GERMANY (1963), would still usefully supplement the authors' two-page summary of German corporate tax law (pp. 279–81), especially if read in connection with one of the guides produced at regular intervals by the major multinational accounting firms.

Latin American Laws and Institutions. By Albert S. Golbert and Yenny Nun. New York: Praeger Publishers, 1982. Pp. xiv, 573. Index. $39.95.

This is a well-documented and well-organized book of broad scope. A most useful reference work, it contains a wealth of important information and analysis. Each chapter is followed by extensive bibliographic notes. It is explained in the preface that the book has the aim of familiarizing the reader with some of the general legal concepts and institutions of Latin America, and that it does not attempt to cover all the internal or external legal institutions of that region.

The first chapter gives a general background on Latin American sources of law: constitutions, codes, laws, decree-laws, decrees, court decisions, doctrine, customs. In this context the authors briefly examine the Constitutions of Argentina, Bolivia, Brazil, Costa Rica, Mexico, Peru, Uruguay, and Venezuela, and observe: "Today Latin American governments seem in general to be more stable, even those under military rule."

One of the chapters deals with public international law and another contains useful information on the development and codification of private international law, referring to the 13 inter-American conventions and one protocol adopted by the First and the Second Inter-American Specialized Conferences on Private International Law convoked by the Organization of American States (OAS) and held in Panama in 1975, and Montevideo in 1979, respectively. The work accomplished by these two conferences represents an outstanding achievement of the OAS for the progress of law in the Americas.

Other chapters deal with, among other things, trade relations between Latin American and developed countries, Latin American economic integration processes, such as LAFTA and its successor, the Latin American Integration Association (ALADI), the Central American Common Market, and the Andean Pact. The Latin American Economic System and the recent Amazon Pact are briefly analyzed.

The chapter on public international law contains an analysis of the Charter of the OAS and of the Inter-American Treaty of Reciprocal Assistance (TIAR), the so-called Rio Treaty, on which the authors have this comment: "As a practical matter the treaty provided the United States with a defensive tool to be used in the event of a threat to United States security. This pact would have been unnecessary for Latin America alone . . . ." It should be stated in all fairness, however, that the Rio Treaty has been very useful also for small Latin American countries on several occasions, and it can be of special importance in the future not only for small, but also for large, Latin American countries.

A summary of the OAS Charter and activities is also provided, emphasizing the "important principles of international law" established in the OAS Charter, and stressing that "one of the most outstanding features of the inter-American system has been precisely the fact that it has always rested upon the bases of an aggregate of postulates and principles . . . [and] [t]hese have been constantly enunciated and reaffirmed in conference after conference."

If the pertinent information had been available to them, the authors might also have called attention to some of the peculiarities of the OAS, which at present has 30 member countries: the United States and Latin American and Caribbean countries. For example, the United States contributes to the OAS regular budget with a quota of 66 percent. Of the other OAS member countries, the largest contributors, according to the 1982 and 1983 OAS regular budgets, are Brazil (9.36 percent), Argentina (7.47 percent), Mexico (7.02 percent), and Venezuela (3.59 percent). It should be noted that there are 21 OAS member states whose total quota contribution to the OAS regular budget is less than 3 percent. Several reports, recommendations, and resolutions by organs of the OAS have dealt with the need to achieve a better distribution of the contributions of the member states, but no final solution had been adopted as of December 1982.

On the "other side of the coin," there is another peculiarity to be noted and to which a reference was made in a recent Statement of the Association of Retirees of the OAS,[1] indicating that most of the OAS retirees reside in the United States and have to pay income tax on their annuities, which are really a social security benefit. The Statement stresses that the annuities of OAS retirees, paid from the OAS Retirement and Pension Fund, should be tax-exempt, because this Fund "is of an intergovernmental nature, according to the principles and rules established by the OAS Charter, . . . ratified by, and in force in, all member states of the OAS." "If the government of any member state of the OAS imposed or collected taxes on such annuities, these taxes would be received by the Treasury of such a country only," while the "governments of the other member states of the OAS would not receive any portion of those taxes, although they had been imposed and collected on annuities from a Fund to which all the member states of the OAS have contributed over a long period of years and continue contributing" through the OAS regular budget. In addition, according to that Statement, it is obvious that the retired OAS staff members "should pay income tax and other taxes, but only on the income from sources other than the annuity received from the OAS Retirement and Pension Fund, because such an annuity should be tax exempt by reason of its very nature, 'ratione materiae'."

Another OAS peculiarity is the fact that there is no record, as of December 1982, that any Latin American or Caribbean countries, members of the OAS, have taken any official or formal initiative for the adoption of measures either to correct this situation or to provide that the taxes imposed or collected on the annuities of OAS retirees be returned to the OAS Retirement and Pension Fund, which is an intergovernmental fund, and should be treated as such. Not even the countries that contribute with substantial quotas to the OAS regular budget have taken any initiative in this matter. Their contributions, of course, come from the taxpayers of their own countries.

ISIDORO ZANOTTI

General Rapporteur and member of the Council of the Inter-American Bar Association

Former Deputy Director of the OAS Department of Legal Affairs

[1] Statement approved by the Board of Directors of the Association on Jan. 27, 1982, and published in 14 LAW. AM. 99–101 (1982).

Multinational Banks and Underdevelopment. By Maurice A. Odle. New York: Pergamon Press, 1981. Pp. xi, 206. Index. $20.

The author of this book applies a rigorous Marxist analysis to the role of multinational banks in relation to the persistent problem of underdevelopment in the Third World. A basic theme throughout his study is the belief that multinational commercial banking practices in the Third World are elitist, socially inefficient (if not actively counterproductive), and inherently supportive of modern imperialism.

The author begins with a general consideration, in chapter 1, of the role of multinational finance as an instrument of imperialism. In chapter 2, he presents a very useful, if somewhat one-sided, account of the process of penetration of multinational banks in the Third World. Chapters 3 through 5 constitute the core of the author's argument that banking practices have been one of the key factors in underdevelopment. In his view, the banks' attitudes with respect to industrialization projects have been characterized by stultifying conservatism in lending policies. These lending policies have encouraged the development of sectors serving nonbasic needs, and the author concludes, therefore, that these lending policies have resulted in socially inefficient allocation of banks' lending resources.

The author then examines some of the alternative strategies that have emerged to compensate for these inefficiencies. In chapter 6, he considers traditional policies of bank regulation which, in his view, have generally been ineffective in changing bank lending policies in a more development-oriented direction. He reviews some of the newer strategies of intervention in chapter 7 (*e.g.*, more radical regulation, miniaturization and increased competition from indigenous banks, localization and nationalization). These strategies have been decidedly mixed in results and often irregular in their application. In chapter 8 the author considers recent attempts at alternative modes of banking, but these alternatives do not appear to have operated as effective alternatives to the traditional commercial banks. Finally, in chapter 9, he presents an analysis of the increasingly prevalent mode of multinational commercial bank lending, the consortium. The author views this mode as the initiation of a new and even more formidable monopolistic order.

The project that Odle has undertaken is ambitious. Unfortunately, the tone of the book is often accusatory and occasionally shrill. The author's efforts are most satisfactory when he confines himself to a presentation of the cold facts of the case. As a matter of fact, the institutions of multinational commercial banking do not operate as a useful support to development efforts. This fact may simply illustrate the proposition that commercial banking is not an effective instrument for social engineering. Nowhere does the author explain why these commercial enterprises should be instruments of social engineering.

One may commend the author for emphasizing the need for more careful study of the status of multinational commercial banks as a significant subset of multinational enterprises. Nevertheless, the author tends to overlook or trivialize some of the unique features of commercial banking in the course of his analysis. Commercial banking, whether done nationally or multinationally, essentially involves the assessment of credit worthiness and the quantification of risk. Indeed, in extreme cases the failure of a commercial bank to diversify or spread its credit risks would constitute an unsafe and unsound banking practice.[1] This emphasis upon risk analysis, manifested in multinational banking by the prevalence of "country risk" analysis and the rise of consortium lending, is almost axiomatic in commercial banking. Repeatedly throughout his analysis, however, the author explicitly discounts the factor of risk analysis as an explanation of current practices.

For example, in chapter 3 he criticizes banks for the absence of risk taking in their lending decisions. He offers various sociopolitical reasons for this absence, but he does not even mention the possibility that commercial banks, *qua* banks, may be essentially limited by prudent notions of risk analysis and diversification from embarking on "socially efficient" projects. Similarly, it is disingenuous for the author to claim, as he does in chapter 5, that lending for developmental purposes does not involve significant risks that result in higher costs of loans for such purposes.

Nevertheless, the author has at times provided valuable insights into multinational banking and its relationship to current strategies for development. His chapters on new strategies of intervention and on the rise of consortium lending practices are particularly solid contributions to the literature on the regulation of multinational enterprises.

MICHAEL P. MALLOY
New York Law School

Israel Yearbook on Human Rights. Vol. 11. Edited by Yoram Dinstein. Tel Aviv: Faculty of Law, Tel Aviv University, 1981. Pp. 366.

As with its predecessors, the current volume of the *Israel Yearbook on Human Rights* deals with topics of general interest in the field of human rights, as well as some that are of specific Israeli significance.

Of the general articles, two are concerned with problems relating to what the editor calls human rights, human duties, and armed conflict. The editor has written an interesting paper on the laws of war in the air in which he considers the relevance of the customary law of armed conflict, as well as of the 1923 Hague Rules, both in the light of practice and of advances resulting from Protocol I of 1977; the most important sections relate, in this element, to the nature of a lawful attack and the protection of medical aircraft, personnel, and accoutrements. Insofar as nuclear weapons are concerned, he reminds us that conventional bombing may be as devastating as an atomic attack, and that even a "clean" hydrogen bomb will raise problems concerning the scope of destruction (p. 63). The other paper in this section of the *Yearbook* is an analysis by the reviewer of the International Law Commission's draft

[1] For example, for national banks, diversification of credit risk is inherently mandated by statute. *See, e.g.*, 12 U.S.C. §84 (lending limitations).

articles on international criminal law as proposed for inclusion in a convention on state responsibility. He is of the opinion that these articles are more concerned with the political ideologies of the current majority in the United Nations than they are with issues of international criminality, and he takes issue with the suggestion that one can have a criminal code that defines a crime as "an internationally wrongful act which results from the breach by a State of an international obligation so essential for the protection of fundamental interests of the international community that its breach is recognized as a crime by that community as a whole" (pp. 29–33).

Two of the articles under the rubric "Human Rights in a General Context" may be considered as being of Jewish interest. Dr. Lerner looks at the background of the United Nations Declaration against Religious Intolerance and Discrimination, which has now been adopted, while Rabbi Plaut has a short—nonlegal—piece on anti-Semitism in the world today. Of some Jewish interest because of the role that Holocaust survivors played in making the problem real, the essay by Dr. Lador-Lederer concerns what he describes as the "affinity factor" in refugee care, and he calls for a more active and official role for nongovernmental organizations. Within the same rubric is the paper by Dr. Melander on political prisoners. He favors drawing a distinction between political prisoners and political offenders and, after commenting upon the work done by Amnesty International, the International Commission of Jurists, and the International Committee of the Red Cross, spends some time on the International Committee for Migration, which has played a fairly significant role in exchanging imprisonment for exile (p. 81). The two remaining papers in this section deal with specific human rights. Dr. Shapiro-Libai, adviser on the status of women to the Israeli Prime Minister, writes on the concept of sex equality in the context of the UN decade for women and looks at the problem in the light of the Convention on the Elimination of All Forms of Discrimination against Women and of a variety of judicial decisions from different jurisdictions. Perhaps not surprisingly, she is an advocate of affirmative action, recognized by a number of international conventions so long as it is temporary and intended to achieve equality on behalf of a group formerly discriminated against. Finally, in this section, there is the paper by Dr. Ben-Israel who contends that the right to strike is a collective human right on both international and national levels.

Insofar as "Human Rights in a Specific Context" are concerned, only one paper is non-Israeli in emphasis. Dr. Sheleff examines the arbitrariness of the arbitrary rule in death penalty cases in the United States, concluding that the decisions in *Furman* and *Gregg* have created so much confusion and pose such dilemmas that the only proper means of resolving the problems is by complete abolition of the penalty (p. 237). Although the remaining articles in this section are all devoted to problems arising in Israel, Dr. Zaltzman's comments on restrictions on the freedom of expression of state employees in that country are equally relevant in a number of other places. Problems frequently arise in Israel concerning the identity of "the Jew," and Dr. Shava examines the aspect of the question regarding the personal status of Israeli citizens not belonging to a recognized religious community, and whose personal status is governed by civil law in accordance with the Palestine Order-in-Council of 1922. The author is of the opinion that "the personal law of a local citizen is his religious law, whether he belongs to a recognized religious community or one which is not" (p. 244), a proposal that would probably cause more problems than provide solutions in the case of the avowed atheist. Of some affinity to this paper is that by Dr. E. Tabory of Bar Ilan University on religious rights as a social problem, with a call for clear recognition of the right of individuals to exercise their religious freedoms on a collective basis (p. 270). Finally, Dr. M. Tabory of Tel Aviv University, the associate editor of the *Yearbook,* deals with language rights, principally those of the Arab community, especially in the light of proposals that have been made to raise the status of Hebrew by making *it* the state language (p. 304). At present, as became clear during the recent strike of diplomats, both Hebrew and Arabic rank as official languages that the strikers were prepared to use, while they refused to speak in English, since they were working according to rule.

From the point of view of the general reader who, for the main part, is unable to secure access to Israeli materials, the section of the *Yearbook* that may be most useful comprises the last 20 pages or so, in which eight Supreme Court judgments concerning the administered (occupied) territories are summarized and commented upon.

L. C. GREEN
University of Alberta

South African Yearbook of International Law, Volume 6, 1980. Pretoria: The VerLoren van Themaat Centre for International Law, 1981. Pp. xiii, 257. Index. R18,00.

This volume, the sixth in the series, largely continues the format established in earlier volumes. The main section consists of five articles, three of which concern South African legal issues: the South African approach to international adjudication, preindependence agreements between South Africa and the "homelands," and political and legal consequences of the South African plan for a "constellation of States." Two articles consider broader questions: one is on terrorism and the right of self-defense, and the other presents a good summary of developing states' actions to secure changes in the international economic system through international organizations. The section on South African judicial decisions covers the issues of extradition, the "homelands," and immunity of foreign governments. The section on foreign judicial decisions, which makes extensive use of *International Legal Materials,* covers the ICJ hearings in *United States v. Iran,* and four U.S. court cases. The other regular sections that are retained describe UN debates and actions especially relevant to South Africa, present official governmental statements that reflect South Africa's foreign policy, and list treaties signed and ratified by South Africa during the year. The book review section is also continued.

A new element in this volume is an opening comment that attempts to explain and justify a *South African Yearbook of International Law,* partly in response to criticisms of previous volumes. The author argues that law and politics are closely related, that international law is "the most important ingredient of foreign policy," that South Africa has justified all of its external policies (including those of the "homelands") in terms of international law, and that, therefore, international law is of special concern to South Africa and South African interpretations of international law are of special concern to the international community. It would be difficult to argue with the last of these contentions; these interpretations have been at the heart of many private and public international debates. The shortcoming of the *Yearbook,* however, continues to be the absence of any dialogue and any informed criticism of these policies. The question remains as to whether we can still speak of respect for the law or understanding of the international legal process when international legal terminology is used to rationalize and justify some of the most blatant and internationally recognized violations of globally established norms. Nevertheless, the *Yearbook* does continue to provide current information and explanations of South African law and politics and may be a valuable source for political and legal scholars attempting to understand the aberrant behavior of the South African Government.

NATALIE K. HEVENER
University of South Carolina

Foreign Relations of the United States, 1950, Volume IV: Central and Eastern Europe; The Soviet Union. (Dept. of State Pub. 8987.) Washington: U.S. Govt. Printing Office, 1980. Pp. xi, 1548. Index.

This comprehensive compilation of official documentary resources on U.S. diplomatic relations with Central and Eastern Europe during the Cold War consists of two main parts. The first deals with multilateral affairs and the second presents separate sections on bilateral relations with 11 individual countries, arranged alphabetically. The documentation encompasses not only communications to and from the Department of State, circular airgrams, memorandums, reports, and other papers, but also useful editorial notes that explain developments and furnish guidance to related materials published elsewhere. The volume is studded with explanatory and cross-referencing footnotes and contains a handy list of acronyms and symbols and a detailed, 30-page index. Within each section documents are arranged chronologically. Selected and organized by the Office of the Historian, this compendium is one of seven volumes prepared for publication by the Department of State for the year 1950.

The preponderant number of documents emanates from the Department of State—internal communications, reports, and messages flowing between Washington and American diplomatic establishments abroad, other administrative agencies in the national capital, and foreign governments. But they also embrace selected White House papers and other relevant materials pertaining to such agencies as the Commerce, Defense, and Treasury Departments, the Economic Cooperation Administration, the Joint Chiefs of Staff, and the Voice of America, as well as various interdepartmental agencies, a number of multipartite organizations (the Allied High Commission for Germany, the European Coal and Steel Community, the North Atlantic Treaty Organization, and the Organization for European Economic Cooperation), and Western Foreign Ministers subsummit meetings.

Of special interest may be the texts of National Security Council papers dealing with U.S. relations with Austria, the two Germanys, and the Soviet Union and its satellites in Europe; East-West trade; international civil aviation; Soviet threats to U.S. security; the foreign information program and psychological warfare; and other important policy issues. Particularly relevant to those interested in the international legal aspects of American diplomacy are the documents that bear upon human rights commitments, termination of the state of war with Germany, negotiation of an Austrian state treaty, legal status of Berlin and the Saar, severance of diplomatic relations, mistreatment and harassment of U.S. diplomats, arrangements to terminate the wartime lend-lease agreement with the Soviet Union, and the interpretation and application of other treaties and agreements.

The first part (362 pages) focuses on several primary themes: general policies and problems including U.S. efforts to achieve fulfillment by Bulgaria, Hungary, and Romania of their World War II peace treaty stipulations regarding individual rights; civil aviation policy applicable to Eastern Europe; the American attitude toward exile groups and leaders; efforts to strengthen the Voice of America; and the Soviet "Peace Offensive" (related to the outbreak of the Korean War and designed to inhibit the development of the Western alliance). Nearly 200 pages are devoted to synthesizing U.S. trade policy toward Eastern Europe and efforts to achieve an international security export program.

In the second part of the volume (some 1,150 pages on bilateral relations), the segments on Albania, Bulgaria, Czechoslovakia, Finland, Hungary, Poland, and Romania are relatively short (each less than 50 pages). Except for that on Finland, which is devoted largely to the problem of maintaining its independence against Soviet aggrandizement, these sections emphasize efforts to resolve difficulties with emergent postwar governments (especially in the case of Poland); deteriorating diplomatic relations with, and restrictions on U.S. diplomatic and consular agents (Czechoslovakia, Hungary, and Romania); the severance of diplomatic relations (Bulgaria); and attempts to achieve the release of Robert A. Vogeler, an American official of the International Telephone and Telegraph Corporation, arrested in Hungary in November 1949, held incommunicado, and convicted and sentenced in February 1950 to 15 years for alleged espionage and sabotage. The more voluminous section on Yugoslavia (177 pages) contains materials on American policy during the growing conflict between Belgrade and Moscow and the extension of American economic and military assistance.

The documents on Austria (135 pages) concentrate on three principal subjects: negotiation of an Austrian World War II settlement (eventually signed in 1955); interest in the formation of an Austrian defense establishment and arming of the Austrian gendarmerie; and various occupation problems such as efforts by the Allied powers to transfer greater authority to the federal Government in Vienna, the treatment of civil disturbances, and occupation costs.

The most comprehensive bilateral sections concern the Soviet Union (263 pages) and Germany (389 pages). Documents on the USSR embrace such questions as atomic weapons development and control, renewal of the commercial agreement of 1942, trade practices, Soviet treatment of American diplomatic representatives, interference with the U.S. information program, foreign travel restrictions in the Soviet Union, and settlement of World War II lend-lease arrangements.

Several problems affecting Germany as a whole are treated in depth. These encompass the division of Germany and its reunification, termination of the state of war, all-German elections, a Soviet proposal to demilitarize the country, and the status of Berlin. Those that apply specifically to West Germany include the development of the idea of negotiating "contractual arrangements" with the newly created Federal Republic of Germany (to avoid the connotation of a formal treaty or agreement) to supersede the Occupation Statute; West German participation in the Council of Europe, other plans for European integration, and Western security arrangements; and questions relating to West German defense and rearmament. A separate subsection reviews U.S. attitudes regarding the creation of the Democratic Republic of Germany and developments in Communist East Germany.

Given its organization—with approximately 80 percent of the documentation devoted to bilateral relations with individual countries—this compilation is most useful for the study of U.S. policy toward those specific countries. Exceptions that concern American interests in the area as a whole—aside from those addressed in the first portion of the volume—focus upon legal and political settlements for the Axis powers for which peace treaties had not yet been negotiated, the deterioration of diplomatic relations with Eastern European Governments, and retrogression in the treatment of American diplomatic and consular missions and personnel in violation of traditional diplomatic and consular privileges and immunities.

Documents pertaining to additional general functional issues involving Eastern Europe are embodied in other volumes of the *Foreign Relations* series for 1950, especially volumes I (on national security affairs and foreign economic policy),[1] II (on U.S. diplomacy conducted in and through the United Nations),[2] III (on Western Europe),[3] and VII (on the outbreak of war in Korea and its impact on East-West relations in Europe).[4] This is the last of the seven volumes planned for the year 1950. Unfortunately, it has taken 30 years to be published, so that the gap between publication and the year to which this anthology pertains exceeds the shorter schedule preferred by the Department of State and desired by those awaiting its availability.

ELMER PLISCHKE
University of Maryland, Emeritus
Gettysburg College, Adjunct Professor
American Enterprise Institute, Adjunct Scholar

[1] Vol. I was published in 1977.

[2] Vol. II was published in 1976 and reviewed in 71 AJIL 571–72 (1977).

[3] Vol. III was published in 1977 and reviewed in 72 AJIL 691–92 (1978).

[4] Vol. VII was published in 1976 and reviewed in 73 AJIL 160–62 (1979).

Foreign Relations of the United States, 1951, Volume III: European Security and the German Question. Part 1, Dept. of State Pub. 8982. Part 2, Dept. of State Pub. 9113. Washington: U.S. Govt. Printing Office, 1981. Pp. xxxiv, 2065. Index in part 2.

This is a comprehensive compilation of documents on American foreign policy and negotiations that deals with important aspects—largely transitional—in the development of security arrangements for West-Central Europe and relations of the Western occupying powers with the Federal Republic of Germany. It consists of two parts—each constituting a separate volume— the first of which concentrates on European security issues (pp. 1–1316), and the second on the German question (pp. 1317–2029). Both parts contain identical prefaces; tables of contents; helpful lists of abbreviations, symbols, and code names; lists of persons; sources; and lists of photographs. A comprehensive 33-page index is appended to the second part.

The year 1951—the last of the Truman administration—was critical because the Western powers were fearful that the war in Korea might be a prelude to the outbreak of hostilities between East and West in Europe; the North Atlantic Treaty (signed in 1949) was still in the process of being implemented militarily under the command of General Dwight D. Eisenhower; the integration of West Germany into the Western alliance came under serious consideration; and a major modification of relations between the Western occupants and the Federal Republic of Germany was under negotiation. As a consequence, this volume is concerned less with the bipartite relations of the United States than with its multipartite exchanges and negotiations to strengthen NATO and involve West Germany in the defense of Western Europe in exchange for a reduction of Western occupation controls and a commensurate increase in the authority of West Germany over its affairs.

Substantively, the first part deals with such important issues as (1) the institutional and functional development of NATO, the launching of its military command structure, and the admission of Greece and Turkey as its 13th and 14th members (Protocol signed in October, whereas the Protocol for the admission of West Germany was not signed until 3 years later); (2) U.S. financial assistance for the defense of Western Europe; (3) the possibility of convening another session of the Council of Foreign Ministers (CFM), requested by the Soviet Government to consider the matter of fulfilling the clauses of the Potsdam Agreement (1945) regarding the demilitarization of Germany; and (4) a German contribution to West European defense, including plans for the establishment of the European Defense Community (EDC), which would have provided for a West German military commitment without creating a separate German military force (a treaty was eventually signed in May 1952 but was never ratified). Part 1 also presents materials on meetings of the Western Foreign Ministers (of the United States, the United Kingdom, and France) to discuss several of these and other matters, one of which was timed to coincide with their coming to the United States for the San Francisco Conference to sign the Japanese Peace Treaty. Those interested in official documentary resources on this early development of NATO during the height of the Korean War will find this compilation of great value.

Part 2 of this volume deals with two sets of issues. One concentrates on changing relations between the Western occupying powers and the Federal Republic of Germany, and its integration into the Western politico-security system. It presents materials on revising the Occupation Statute for Germany (signed in April 1949) and the Charter of the Allied High Commission (signed in June 1949) by means of "contractual relations" (during negotiations great care was exercised to avoid the expression "contractual agreements") with the Federal Republic, to provide it with greater autonomy and more authority over its political, economic, and foreign affairs; on considering a multipartite security guarantee for West Germany; and on providing for a West German financial contribution to Western defense. The second set of issues includes unification of Germany and all-German elections, Allied rights in Berlin, the economic situation in West Germany, and the attitude of the United States toward developments in the "Soviet Zone of Occupation" (*i.e.*, East Germany—at the time the Western Allies were careful not to dignify it as the Democratic Republic of Germany).

Much of the concern for a viable Federal Republic of Germany as an integral component of the Western security system in Europe—favored by both the United States and West Germany—ran counter to the frequently proclaimed objective of German reunification. Developments during 1951 helped to freeze the division of Germany, and ultimately resulted in the emergence of the two Germanys in the community of nations. This was a crucial transitional period in determining the mutating legal status of Germany in the post-World War II era. At that time it may still have been possible, at least hypothetically, to reunify West and East Germany—but perhaps only if they had been neutralized and divorced from the political orbits of both West and East, which, with hindsight, seems unrealistic in view of the conflict that permeated the relations of the major powers of Europe during the depths of the Cold War. Those interested in a rich reservoir of official resources on developments that pointed in the opposite direction—*i.e.*, toward an emergent, autonomous Federal Republic of Germany integrated into the European Defense Community and eventually in the North Atlantic Treaty Organization—will welcome the detailed documentation contained in this volume.

Aside from the customary mixture of presidential and National Security Council papers, diplomatic telegrams, memorandums, notes, reports on conversations, draft instructions, and similar materials, this compilation contains a substantial quantity of conference documentation, such as lists of conference delegates, minutes of sessions, draft resolutions and agreements, declarations, conference or delegation communiqués, and diplomatic exchanges and commentaries. In addition, its compilers provide the user with useful descriptive, explanatory, and cross-referencing editorial notes.

The conference documents, which constitute a major segment of the volume, pertain to such meetings at the ministerial, diplomatic, and technical levels as (1) the seventh and eighth sessions of the NATO Council (Ottawa in September and Rome in November); (2) a series of meetings between representatives of the Federal Republic of Germany and the Allied Deputy High Commissioners to discuss a German contribution to the defense of Western Europe (January–June); (3) four-power (the United States, the United Kingdom, France, and the Soviet Union) exploratory talks regarding the convening of a session of the Council of Foreign Ministers (Palais Rose, Paris, March–June); (4) conclaves of the Western Big Three Foreign Ministers (the United States, the United Kingdom, and France) in Washington, Paris, and Rome (September and November); (5) sessions of the International Study Group on Germany (the United States, the United Kingdom, and France) which handled the bulk of Allied negotiations on the revisions of the Occupation Statute and the Charter of the Allied High Commission (London, January–May); (6) Western tripartite (the United States, the United Kingdom, and France) and quadripartite (the three Western occupying powers and West Germany) meetings at various levels to discuss the contractual arrangements to modify Allied-West German relations; and (7) the Tripartite Group on Germany (the United States, the United Kingdom, and France) which discussed the West German financial contribution to Western defense and the security controls to remain in effect when the new contractual relations were established (London, October–December). These contractual relations arrangements, when consummated, consisted of a basic agreement on general relations and a series of subsidiary agreements on industrial controls, the status of foreign forces in West Germany, the transfer of specified responsibilities from the occupying powers to West Germany, and West German logistical and financial support.

Those interested in the international law aspects of the issues treated in this compilation will find that it deals with such matters as occupation authority and operations, rights of self-determination and sovereignty, demilitarization and disarmament of a defeated power, status-of-forces arrangements, alliance relations, territorial issues and the unique status of Berlin, and treaty and agreement negotiation, substance, and format.

Each part of this volume is functionally organized, and within each section documents are presented chronologically. It is one of seven planned by the Office of the Historian of the Department of State for the year 1951, three of which have previously been published.[1] Two are about to be published and the final volume is still in process. As usual, this compilation evidences the high standards of coverage, selectivity, structure, style, and treatment that have characterized the *Foreign Relations* series over the years—for which the Department of State is to be commended by both scholars and the public.

ELMER PLISCHKE
University of Maryland, Emeritus
Gettysburg College, Adjunct Professor
American Enterprise Institute, Adjunct Scholar

[1] These volumes have been reviewed in this *Journal* as follows: Vol. I, *National Security Affairs; Foreign Economic Policy* (1979) and Vol. II, *The United Nations; The Western Hemisphere* (1979), reviewed together in 75 AJIL 409–13 (1981); and vol. VI, *Asia and the Pacific,* 2 parts (1977), reviewed in 73 AJIL 536–37 (1979).

Diplomatische Dokumente der Schweiz 1848–1945. Volume 6 (1914–1918). By Jacques Freymond, Isabelle Graf-Junod, and Alison Browning. Bern: Benteli Verlag, 1981. Pp. lxxiv, 902. Indexes.

Diplomatische Dokumente der Schweiz 1848–1945. Volume 7-I (1918–1919). By Antoine Fleury and Gabriel Imboden. Bern: Benteli Verlag, 1979. Pp. lxxviii, 964. Indexes. Sw.F.140.

Diplomatische Dokumente der Schweiz 1848–1945. Volume 9 (1925–1929). Under the direction of Walther Hofer and Beatrix Mesmer, in collaboration with Peter Hurni, Martin Lüdi, and Peter Martig. Bern: Benteli Verlag, 1980. Pp. ci, 966. Index. Sw.F.140.

These three volumes of Swiss diplomatic documents are part of a projected 15-volume series covering the period from 1848 to 1945. The documents are selected and edited through the cooperative work of the history institutes of a group of Swiss universities and the Swiss Federal Archives, under the patronage of the Swiss National Commission for the Publication of Swiss Diplomatic Documents. Volumes are being published in the order in which they are completed.

The goal of the series is not to present a comprehensive and ponderous documentary collection covering all aspects of Swiss international relations, but rather to portray the basic features, themes, and fundamental "givens" that characterize Switzerland's role in international affairs. The documents, kept in the federal archives, include records of Parliament, the Government, and the federal departments. Editorial comment has been kept to a minimum so that the collection can stand on its own as an "original source" useful to scholars and practitioners. In general, the documents are reprinted in their entirety and in the original language.

The organizational presentation of the documents is very well done. The editors focused on intergovernmental relations between Switzerland and selected foreign states as well as on Swiss diplomatic policy in particular substantive areas. These substantive areas will provide readers with a highly useful reference outlining Swiss positions on such diverse questions as neutrality, asylum, banking, recognition of states, revolutionary movements, river navigation, arbitration, human rights, and the League of Nations. A brief table of contents, summarizing the organization of each volume, is followed by an extensive schematic table detailing the number, date, nature (*i.e.*, letter, telegram, report), originator, recipient, and summary contents of each document. Appendixes provide useful information on Swiss governmental organization relevant to foreign affairs.

Volume 6 of the series traces Swiss foreign policy during World War I from the Sarajevo assassination to the armistice on November 11, 1918. Much of the emphasis during this period is on the politics of neutrality and the protection of a small state's independence while a major war rages around it. Although economic issues were frankly very important in Swiss diplomacy, there was also an awareness of humanitarian needs arising from the war. Volume 7 (part I) continues from the armistice up to the signing of the Versailles Peace Treaty on June 28, 1919. Swiss diplomatic interest during this period focused on such issues as the Versailles peace conference, the creation of the League of Nations, Bolshevism and revolutionary movements, economic relations with the Allies, international transportation, and the status of Savoy and Gex.

Volume 9, covering the period 1925–1929, reviews the short period of détente in Europe with the Locarno treaties and Germany's entry into the League of Nations. Swiss diplomacy was involved, both within and outside the League, with the international system for the pacific settlement of disputes. Bilateral relations with various foreign states (*e.g.*, Germany and Russia) also commanded particular attention during these years.

Although there will always be scholarly concern over what might have been "left out" of an edited collection of documents, the collection itself is a welcome addition not only to the published source materials on Switzerland but also to the general literature treating the conduct of international relations. The editors have done excellent work and have provided a valuable service in organizing these materials for interested readers.

FOREST L. GRIEVES
University of Montana

Documentos para la Historia Diplomática de Colombia. Textos. Vol. I: 1820–1830. Vol. II: 1830–1860. By Germán Cavelier. Bogotá: Editorial Kelly. Vol. I, 1976: pp. xxviii, 243; vol. II, 1981: pp. xxxii, 388. Each volume with index.

El Régimen Jurídico de los Tratados Internacionales en Colombia. By Germán Cavelier. Bogotá: Editorial Kelly, 1979. Pp. xi, 604. Bibliography and index.

The first two volumes under review present in a well-organized fashion the texts of several documents of special importance to the diplomatic history of Colombia from 1820 to 1860, and will be of great use to those who are interested in Latin American diplomatic history. The author is an expert on the constitutional and diplomatic history of Colombia, and has written books on these matters. He has occupied high government positions in his own country, such as that of Secretary-General of the Ministry of Foreign Affairs.

These documents also have particular meaning in the context of inter-American relations. For example, volume I contains, among other documents, some treaties of great significance: the bilateral Treaties that Colombia signed with Peru on July 6, 1822, with Chile on October 21, 1822, and with Mexico on October 3, 1823. The objective of these Treaties was to establish a system of union, league, and confederation between Colombia and each of those three countries.

Article 1 of the Treaty between Colombia and Mexico provided for alliance and confederation "forever in peace and war." In Article 2 both countries accepted a perpetual pact of alliance and friendship for their mutual defense, obligating themselves to use their good offices with the governments of the other American countries to enter into a pact of union, league, and perpetual confederation. Article 14 established that a General Assembly of the American countries would meet to consolidate and strengthen their mutual relations. Similar provisions were also contained in the Treaties with Peru and Chile.

These Treaties did not have a long life. They constituted, however, a background of great importance to the preparation of the famous Treaty of Union, League and Perpetual Confederation[1] signed on July 15, 1826, during the Congress of Panama convoked by Simón Bolívar. It was signed by Colombia, Central America, Peru, and Mexico. The Treaty did not come into force, but it held special significance for inter-American relations. It provided, among other things, for the establishment of a General Assembly of the representatives of the parties to the Treaty.[2]

Another document appearing in volume I that is not easy to find in any library is the one with the notes (*apuntes*) of Simón Bolívar written before the Congress of Panama. In his dream of establishing a confederation of the American nations, Bolívar expressed his desire to proclaim in that Congress that no country would be weak in relation to others, that no country would be stronger than others, and that social reforms would be achieved in an environment of peace and freedom.

Volume II also reproduces documents of historical importance. Among others, the following should be mentioned: the Treaty of Confederation signed on February 8, 1848, by Colombia, Peru, Chile, Bolivia, and Ecuador at the First Congress of Lima, held in 1847–1848. Under Article 1 of this Treaty the parties established among themselves a union, league, and confederation to maintain their independence, sovereignty, and the integrity of their respective territories; to this effect they would assist each other with their armed forces and other means of defense. Another step was taken on November 9, 1856, the date on which a Treaty of Confederation was signed by Colombia, Guatemala, El Salvador, Mexico, Peru, Costa Rica, and Venezuela.

These Treaties did not enter into force, but their principles as well as those of the 1826 Treaty were sources or precedents for one adopted many years later, the Inter-American Treaty of Reciprocal Assistance, signed in Rio de Janeiro on September 2, 1947. The so-called Rio Treaty, which created a very well-defined inter-American collective security system, has been ratified by 22 American countries, and has been applied successfully several times. It should be observed that some of the principles and expressions or words contained in the 1826 and 1848 Treaties were also adopted or used in the 1947 Treaty.

The book on the legal regime of international treaties in Colombia is one of the best, or may be the best, by a Latin American scholar on the problem

[1] In almost all translations into English, the title of this Treaty appears as "Treaty of Perpetual Union, League and Confederation." Actually, the title should be "Treaty of Union, League and Perpetual Confederation," because the word "*perpetua,*" in the singular, of the Spanish text refers to "confederation" only. Furthermore, Article 31 of the Treaty uses the phrase "[t]he present Treaty of Union, League and Perpetual Confederation."

[2] It should be noted that the words "General Assembly" were inserted in the OAS Charter as amended in 1967, as the title of the supreme organ of the OAS, which then was called Inter-American Conference.

of incorporating international treaties into national law. It provides excellent guidance to writers of other countries wishing to prepare a book on this subject. The method Cavelier uses is very clear and precise, and he treats the subject in depth. He carefully analyzes the different aspects of the subject, citing texts of documents, doctrine, legislation, events, decisions of the Supreme Court of Justice, and other factors. All the material is presented in an orderly and systematic fashion. His own analysis is of particular importance and interest.

Chronological consideration is given to all the aspects of international treaties, such as appointment of delegates, issuance of credentials, negotiation and approval of treaties, reservations, signature, ratification, exchange of instruments of ratification, entry into force, and denunciation.

The problems raised in Colombia relating to the Cartagena Agreement, which established the so-called Andean Group, and the steps taken, decisions made, and solutions reached concerning these problems, are treated extensively in some of the last chapters of the book. This will be a valuable volume in any law library.

ISIDORO ZANOTTI
General Rapporteur and member of the Council and the Executive Committee of the Inter-American Bar Association
Former Deputy Director of the OAS Department of Legal Affairs

BRIEFER NOTICES

The Law and Practice of International Finance. By Philip Wood. (New York: Clark Boardman Co., Ltd., 1981. Index and table of cases. $75.) This is the second volume in an International Business and Law series. It is a well-done practitioners' guide to the transnational law, mainly private law, of commercial bank lending and international bond issues. The author has attempted, usually with success, to make the work useful to nonspecialists and nonlawyers. Although Wood's orientation concerning legal and banking practice outlooks is basically British, he has been determinedly eclectic on the subject matter of other legal systems deemed relevant to the major objectives of the work.

The international sales transaction, so much in the focus of the activities of the UN Commission on International Trade Policy, is not covered as a specific subdivision of the work. This is a book for lenders, borrowers, bankers, and their counsel, general and local. In areas of notable judicial activity such as legislative jurisdiction, act of state (American version), immunities of states, party autonomy as to choice of law, and forum, the key case law is incorporated into the text, with brief—although on the whole discerning—analysis.

Despite the author's careful efforts, it is likely that nonlawyers and some American lawyers brought up in the introspective (if not ethnocentric) American, "zone of the interior," conflict-of-laws system will not be put entirely at ease by the first three chapters, which concentrate on conflict of laws in a transnational context. However, in defense of the author, it is the reviewer's opinion that he has well synthesized, in hornbook form, the way the creditor-debtor world copes with the diversities of private law legal systems.

International public law and the law in international treaty arrangements, such as the Articles of Agreement of the International Monetary Fund, are brought into the discussion where they fit. The reviewer did not, however, find in the several discussions of espousal of claims for diplomatic protection the classic American disclaimer of official protection for creditor claims, *e.g.*, John Quincy Adams as Secretary of State: "the United States Government is not a collection agency." One is tempted to link this to the almost notorious successes of British creditors, whether the Government be Socialist or Tory, in obtaining energetic diplomatic protection from Her Majesty's Government. The reviewer wishes to add that he welcomes this, because in his opinion the American dichotomy between ownership (shareholder) and creditor claims is increasingly untenable. Today's international private sector creditor is neither an exporter selling on his own account nor a portfolio investor in Bolivian bonds.

Timing has not been altogether fortunate for the coverage of this book, as the double crises of Iranian defaults and the overextension of unsecured commercial and supplier credits to a number of developing countries now in repayment (even of debt service) difficulties have developed into challenges, problems, and lines of action only since the closing date (one assumes) for this book.

COVEY T. OLIVER
Board of Editors

Patent and Trademark Laws of Colombia. By Germán Cavelier. (Bogotá: Editorial Kelly, 1979. Pp. 210. Indexes.) Mr. Cavelier's book is an excellent legal reference. The book begins with an introduction that sets forth the legislative history of the patent and trademark laws of Colombia. The Constitution and pertinent laws that provide the legal authority for patents and trademarks are literally translated in clear and concise language. The book has a fine index of "legal provisions," "international treaties and conventions," and "subjects."

It might have been helpful if Cavelier had discussed administrative and judicial interpretation to date of these laws. Nevertheless, this is definitely a book that any attorney interested in Colombian legal practice should have in his library.

HARRY A. INMAN
Of the District of Columbia Bar

CORRESPONDENCE

Comments on a review by Professor Alfred P. Rubin of *A Collection of Treaties and other Documents affecting the States of Malaysia 1761–1963.* Vols. I and II. Compiled and edited by J. de V. Allen, A. J. Stockwell, and L. R. Wright.

My first inclination is to let a book speak for itself despite adverse criticism. This work, which is some 1,200 pages long and which has been almost 2 decades in the making, certainly has the strength to endure a few hostile sentences from one reviewer. Nevertheless, Professor Alfred P. Rubin has written so intemperate and so injudicious a piece (76 AJIL 218–19 (1982)) that I fear he may have misled his readers. It is to correct the balance that I ask permission to reply.

Let me begin by disposing of three issues raised in the review. First, typing errors: Professor Rubin instances one. Authors are human but computerized typesetting appears to be far more fallible, while photographic reproduction of the original documents (which he seems to be suggesting) would have been unsatisfactory and, in some cases, almost illegible. He next takes us to task for including documents not contained in the *Consolidated Treaty Series* and for omitting others that are. I am not clear about the nature of our transgression here, unless it has been our preparedness to do an editor's job and use our discretion. Third, he charges us with bias because Colonial Office sources are cited more frequently than Foreign Office sources. Of course, Colonial Office documents are generally more relevant to the affairs of the Malay States during the British period. That said, however, a quick count reveals no less than 60 references to Foreign Office files quite apart from the numerous references to the records of the India Office, National Archives of Malaysia, Kedah State Archives, Sarawak Museum, Singapore National Library, etc.

Now I shall deal with Professor Rubin's main objections. His targets are two unexceptional comments upon the positions of Kelantan, Trengganu, and Perak as laid down by the Burney Treaty with Siam in 1826 (*see* the *Collection*, vol. II, p. 307). With reference to Article XII of this treaty we comment that "the position of Kelantan and Trengganu remained ambiguous." Rubin, on the other hand, maintains that Thai sovereignty was conceded in those sultanates. The editors' statement must stand. It is quite clear from what Professor Rubin himself writes that the article in question was open to interpretation. He cites Burney's "interpretation" and he admits that Burney later wavered in his view. There were other interpretations at the time and there have been since.

Governor Fullerton, for example, objected to the article not because it was, as Rubin argues, "intended by its negotiators to affirm Thai sovereignty in Kelantan and Trengganu" but because it might be so construed in some quarters. In fact, as L. A. Mills has shown,[1] Fullerton was disturbed by the phraseology which "was so vague that two entirely opposite meanings could be drawn from it": the British might argue that it precluded Siam from any interference while the Siamese might contend that it gave them "the right of complete subjugation, so long as our [British] trade is not interrupted." Fullerton was not prepared to entertain the second gloss but accepted one which allowed Britain to "protect" the two states "in their independence," and this, said Burney (at least when he faced Fullerton), had always been the objective of the negotiations. In 1860, Colonel Cavanagh, Governor of the Straits Settlements, reporting on the status of the Malay States, wrote: "The districts of Tringanu and Kelantan are . . . protected by the British Government under the Treaty of Bangkok." Cavanagh's report, incidentally, is reproduced in our *Collection* (vol. II, p. 4 *ff.*).

The treaty of 1826 did not, as Professor Rubin would have it, unequivocally concede Thai sovereignty in Kelantan and Trengganu. It is ambivalent on this point. Dr. Mary Turnbull has called the arrangements relating to those sultanates "ambiguous," and Professor Cowan has written that "Burney's

[1] L. A. MILLS, BRITISH MALAYA, 1824–67, at 151 *ff.* (1966).

Treaty with Siam (1826) was a model of diplomatic evasion on the subject" of the position of Kelantan and Trengganu because "it left the question of their status unsettled."[2]

Professor Rubin takes a similarly contrary line with regard to the position of Perak as set out in Article XIV of the Burney Treaty, 1826. Again he relies solely on Burney's testimony when he writes that "Ligor, as a Thai agent, acted correctly in Perak to counter illegal British actions." Again, as in the case of Article XII, we move into the realm of interpretation and to the political uses of the treaty. For, in the opinion of the Governor in Penang, the Chao P'ya of Ligor was permitted by the treaty to interfere peacefully in Perak but his despatch of troops to persuade the Sultan to send the *bunga mas* to Bangkok was a contravention of its terms. This provided the justification for Captain Low's expedition to Perak. Now, as we say on page 370 of volume I, "Low might be thought to have himself infringed the treaty—the Siamese certainly thought so—by advising the Sultan to deprive the pro-Siamese Malays in his court (including the heir apparent) of all powers and to write a letter declaring his wish to be independent of Siam . . . ." Unlike Professor Rubin we have taken into consideration various interpretations of this clause.

Those are his complaints. It is unreasonable of Professor Rubin to condemn the whole work largely on the basis of a difference over a couple of phrases on one page; it is especially unreasonable when it is revealed that his assessments are eccentric and that historical evidence and the judgment of reputable scholars support the editors of this *Collection of Treaties and other Documents.*

A. J. STOCKWELL
Royal Holloway College
University of London

Reply by Professor Alfred P. Rubin:

There seem to be two major issues between myself and the editors of the compilation of treaties and other documents affecting the States of Malaysia. The first concerns the propriety of a reviewer expressing opinions on the reliability of typescript texts[1] and the relationship between the chosen texts and the texts chosen by the editor of another compilation more familiar to readers of this *Journal.* I suppose we must continue to differ on that.

The second goes to the substance of my criticisms of the Colonial Office interpretation of Malaysian history as adopted uncritically in a compilation that purports to be objective. Now, anything written can be made to seem "ambivalent," but in the matters mentioned in my review and in the response, the ambiguities urged by Colonial officials, Cowan, Turnbull, and now by the editors of the compilation, were in fact resolved before and after the events.

[2] C. M. TURNBULL, THE STRAITS SETTLEMENTS, 1826–67, at 256 (1972); and C. D. COWAN, NINETEENTH-CENTURY MALAYA 41 (1961).

[1] The notion that I pored over the volumes and found only one typographical error is amusing and, of course, incorrect.

One example only: Governor Cavenagh [not Cavanagh]'s 1860 Report not only ignored Burney's communications with Thailand and Trengganu cited in the review, but was in fact rejected by the Foreign Office in 1862–1863; the Foreign Office view (which I adopt also) was apparently communicated to the Government of Thailand at that time. It is not mentioned in the compilation.[2]

I did not cite my own books in the review because my expertise was not in question.[3] They deal in some detail with all the questions raised in the review and the response.[4] They were published by the University of Malaya Press and appear in its regular catalog. If the editors of the compilation prefer not to read books reaching conclusions inconsistent with their interpretation of history, they might nonetheless look at the primary documents on which those conclusions are based.

BOOKS RECEIVED*

International Law—General

Bourne, C. B. (ed.). *The Canadian Yearbook of International Law. Volume XIX, 1981.* Vancouver: The University of British Columbia Press, 1982. Pp. 464. Index. $36.

Fawcett, James. *Law and Power in International Relations.* London: Faber and Faber Limited, 1982. Pp. 140. $23.95.

Noel, Jacques. *Le principe de non-intervention: Théorie et pratique dans les relations inter-américaines.* Brussels: Editions de l'Université de Bruxelles; Editions Emile Bruylant, 1981. Pp. iii, 241. BF 580.

Onuf, Nicholas Greenwood (ed.). *Law-Making in the Global Community.* Durham: Carolina Academic Press, 1982. Pp. xv, 214. $29.95.

International Economic Law & Relations

Atimomo, Emiko. *Law and Diplomacy in Commodity Economics: A Study of Techniques, Co-operation and Conflict in International Public Policy Issues.* London: The MacMillan Press Ltd., 1981. Pp. xix, 384. Index. $55. Distributed by Holmes & Meier Publishers, Inc.

Hermann, A. H. *Conflicts of National Laws with International Business Activity: Issues of Extraterritoriality.* London: British-North American Committee, 1982. Pp. xii, 96. £3; $6. Available in the U.S. from the National Planning Association, Washington, D.C.

Lillich, Richard B., and Burns H. Weston (eds.). *International Claims: Contemporary European Practice.* Charlottesville: University Press of Virginia, 1982. Pp. x, 204. Index. $25.

Sandalow, Terrance, and Eric Stein (eds.). *Courts and Free Markets: Perspectives from the United States and Europe.* 2 vols. New York: The Clarendon Press; Oxford University Press, 1982. Pp. 600. $39.50/vol.

[2] *See* PARLIAMENTARY PAPERS 1863 XLIII at 299 for a comprehensive collection of the official documents.

[3] *See* reviews by Alexandrowicz and Emerson in 69 AJIL 459 (1975) and 70 AJIL 398 (1976) respectively.

[4] The negotiation of the Burney Treaty is covered in A. RUBIN, INTERNATIONAL PERSONALITY OF THE MALAY PENINSULA 218–30 (1974), taking the tale to about 1830. The Cavenagh episode is in A. RUBIN, PIRACY, PARAMOUNTCY AND PROTECTORATES 56–70 (1974), covering the period from the end of the first book to about 1909.

* Mention here neither assures nor precludes later review.

Sukijasović, Miodrag. *Multinacionalno Preduzeće: Pravni aspekti.* Belgrade: Institut za Medunarodnu Politiku i Privredu, 1981. Pp. 222. English summary.

Wallace, Cynthia Day. *Legal Control of the Multinational Enterprise: National Regulatory Techniques and the Prospects for International Controls.* The Hague, Boston, London: Martinus Nijhoff Publishers, 1982. Pp. xxii, 387. Index. Dfl.135; $58.50.

World Development Report 1982. Published for The World Bank. New York: Oxford University Press, 1982. Pp. x, 172. $20, cloth; $8, paper.

Law of the Sea & Maritime Law

Anand, R. P. *Origin and Development of the Law of the Sea: History of International Law Revisited.* The Hague, Boston, London: Martinus Nijhoff Publishers, 1983. Pp. xvi, 249. Index. Dfl.115; $49.50.

Laursen, Finn (ed.). *Toward a New International Marine Order.* Proceedings of the NIO Youth Seminar held in Amsterdam, August 1980. The Hague, Boston, London: Martinus Nijhoff Publishers, 1982. Pp. xv, 198. Index. Dfl.100; $39.

Platzöder, Renate (ed.). *Third United Nations Conference on the Law of the Sea: Documents.* Volume 1. New York: Oceana Publications, Inc., 1982. Pp. 537. $100/vol.

Terrorism

Lillich, Richard B. (ed.). *Transnational Terrorism: Conventions and Commentary. A Compilation of Treaties, Agreements and Declarations of Especial Interest to the United States.* Charlottesville: The Michie Company, 1982. Pp. xxi, 281. Index. $25.

Human Rights

Andrews, J. A. (ed.). *Human Rights in Criminal Procedure: A Comparative Study.* The Hague, Boston, London: Martinus Nijhoff Publishers, 1982. Pp. 451. Index. Dfl.195; $85.

Crahan, Margaret E. (ed.). *Human Rights and Basic Needs in the Americas.* Washington: Georgetown University Press, 1982. Pp. xiii, 343. $20, cloth; $8.95, paper.

Franck, Thomas M. *Human Rights in Third World Perspective.* Volume I. London, Rome, New York: Oceana Publications, Inc., 1982. Pp. xxviii, 510. 3 vols. projected. $50/vol.

Hennelly, Alfred, S. J., and John Langan, S. J. (eds.). *Human Rights in the Americas: The Struggle for Consensus.* Washington: Georgetown University Press, 1982. Pp. xiii, 291. $20, cloth; $8.95, paper.

Hevener, Natalie Kaufman. *International Law and the Status of Women.* Boulder: Westview Press, 1983. Pp. xii, 249. Index. $20.

Jakovljević, Boško. *New International Status of Civil Defence as an Instrument for Strengthening the Protection of Human Rights.* Geneva: Henry Dunant Institute; The Hague, Boston, London: Martinus Nijhoff Publishers, 1982. Pp. 142. Index. Dfl.80; $32.50.

Khushalani, Yougindra. *Dignity and Honour of Women as Basic and Fundamental Human Rights.* The Hague, Boston, London: Martinus Nijhoff Publishers, 1982. Pp. 153. Dfl.105; $39.50.

Ramcharan, B. G. (ed.). *International Law and Fact-Finding in the Field of Human Rights.* The Hague, Boston, London: Martinus Nijhoff Publishers, 1982. Pp. x, 259. Index. Dfl.110; $48.

Schwab, Peter, and Adamantia Pollis (eds.). *Toward a Human Rights Framework.* New York: Praeger Publishers, 1982. Pp. ix, 258. Index. $26.95.

van den Berghe, Guido. *Political Rights for European Citizens.* Brookfield: Gower Publishing Co., 1982. Pp. xii, 245. Index. $38.

Environment & Natural Resources

Bush, W. M. *Antarctica and International Law: A Collection of Inter-State and National Documents.* Volume I. London, Rome, New York: Oceana Publications, Inc., 1982. Pp. xxviii, 703. 2 vols. projected. $50/vol.

Grathwohl, Manfred. *World Energy Supply: Resources, Technologies, Perspectives.* Berlin, New York: Walter de Gruyter, 1982. Pp. x, 450. Indexes. DM 120; $54.50.

Zacklin, Ralph, and Lucius Caflisch (eds.), with Gerald Graham and Haritini Dipla. *The Legal Regime of International Rivers and Lakes / Le régime juridique des fleuves et des lacs internationaux.* The Hague, Boston, London: Martinus Nijhoff Publishers, 1981. Pp. xiv, 415. Dfl.170; $69.50.

Air & Space Law

Christol, Carl Q. *The Modern International Law of Outer Space.* New York: Pergamon Press, 1982. Pp. xiii, 932. Index. $85.

Forkosch, Morris D. *Outer Space and Legal Liability.* The Hague, Boston, London: Martinus Nijhoff Publishers, 1982. Pp. xvi, 290. Index. Dfl.100; $43.50.

Kean, Arnold (ed.). *Essays in Air Law.* The Hague, Boston, London: Martinus Nijhoff Publishers, 1982. Pp. xvi, 369. Index. Dfl.170; $74.

Matte, Nicolas Mateesco. *Aerospace Law: Telecommunications Satellites.* Published in conjunction with The Institute and Centre of Air and Space Law, McGill University. Toronto: Butterworths, 1982. Pp. xxi, 354. Index. $95.

International Organizations

Leary, Virginia A. *International Labour Conventions and National Law: The Effectiveness of the Automatic Incorporation of Treaties in National Legal Systems.* The Hague, Boston, London: Martinus Nijhoff Publishers, 1982. Pp. xiv, 191. Indexes. Dfl.120; $52.50.

Murphy, John F. *The United Nations and the Control of International Violence: A Legal and Political Analysis.* Totowa: Allanheld, Osmun & Co., 1982. Pp. xii, 212. Index. $32.50.

European Community Law

Digest of case-law relating to the European Communities. D Series—Judgments of the Court of Justice of the European Communities and selected decisions of courts of Member States on the Convention of 27 September 1968 on Jurisdiction and the Enforcement of Judgments in Civil and Commercial Matters. Luxembourg: Office for Official Publications of the European Communities, 1981. Index. $55.

Korah, Valentine. *Competition Law of Britain and the Common Market* (3d rev. ed.). The Hague, Boston, London: Martinus Nijhoff Publishers, 1982. Pp. xxvii, 352. Index. Dfl.140; $59.

Private International Law

Ferid, Murad, Gerhard Kegel, and Konrad Zweigert. *Gutachten zum internationalen und ausländischen Privatrecht 1979.* Frankfurt am Main: Alfred Metzner Verlag, 1981. Pp. ix, 452. Indexes. DM 244.

Honnold, John O. *Uniform Law for International Sales under the 1980 United Nations Convention.* Deventer: Kluwer, 1982. Pp. 586. Index. Dfl.140; $70, cloth; Dfl.80; $40, paper.

U.S. Law of Foreign Relations

Thomas, Ann Van Wynen, and A. J. Thomas, Jr. *The War-Making Powers of the President: Constitutional and International Law Aspects.* Dallas: SMU Press, 1982. Pp. xiii, 177. Index. $15.

Wolff, Lester L., and David L. Simon (eds.). *Legislative History of the Taiwan Relations Act: An Analytic Compilation with Documents on Subsequent Developments.* New York: The American Association for Chinese Studies, Inc., 1982. Pp. xi, 338. Index. $12.50.

Telecommunications

Codding, George A., Jr., and Anthony M. Rutkowski. *The International Telecommunication Union in a Changing World.* Dedham: Artech House, Inc., 1982. Pp. 414. Index. $38.

Inamura, Kobo. *Satellite Broadcasting: Its pre-history, present and future as a new technology.* Bangkok: Dear Book Co., Ltd., 1981. Pp. 107.

Foreign & Comparative Law

Hopt, Klaus J. (ed.). *European Merger Control: Legal and Economic Analyses on Multinational Enterprises.* Volume I. Berlin and New York: Walter de Gruyter, 1982. Pp. xv, 276. Index. DM 82; $41.

———. *Groups of Companies in European Laws: Legal and Economic Analyses on Multinational Enterprises.* Volume II. Berlin and New York: Walter de Gruyter, 1982. Pp. xv, 352. Index. In English and French. DM 102; $51.

Welch, Jane (ed.). *The Regulation of Banks in the Member States of the EEC* (2d ed.). The Hague, Boston, London: Martinus Nijhoff Publishers; London: Graham & Trotman Ltd., 1981. Pp. viii, 277. Index. Dfl.210; $90.

International Relations & Politics

Mushkat, Mari'on (ed.). *Violence and Peace-Building in the Middle East: Proceedings of a symposium held by the Israeli Institute for the Study of International Affairs.* Munich: K.G. Saur Verlag, 1981. Pp. 192. DM 38.

Papadopoulos, Andrestinos N. *Multilateral Diplomacy within the Commonwealth: A Decade of Expansion.* The Hague, Boston, London: Martinus Nijhoff Publishers, 1982. Pp. ix, 172. Index. Dfl.95; $39.50.

Science & Technology

Bull, Alan T., Geoffrey Holt, and Malcolm D. Lilly. *Biotechnology: International Trends and Perspectives.* Paris: Organisation for Economic Co-Operation and Development, 1982. Pp. 84. Index. $11.

Miscellaneous

Godson, Roy (ed.). *Intelligence Requirements for the 1980's: Clandestine Collection.* Washington: National Strategy Information Center, Inc., 1982. Pp. x, 232. $8.50.

Ingber, Léon (ed.), under the direction of F. De Pauw, P. Foriers, and Ch. Perelman. *Gelijkheid.* Vol. VI. Brussels: Etablissements Emile Bruylant, 1981. Pp. 271. BF 1.268.

INTERNATIONAL LEGAL MATERIALS*

CONTENTS

VOL. XXII, NO. 1 (January 1983)

PAGE

TREATIES AND AGREEMENTS

Switzerland-United States: Memorandum of Understanding to Establish Mutually Acceptable *Means for Improving International Law Enforcement Cooperation in the Field of Insider Trading* 1

Warsaw Convention (Convention for the Unification of Certain Rules Relating to International Carriage by Air): Montreal Protocols 3 and 4 Providing *Higher Liability Limits*

Report of the U.S. Senate Committee on Foreign Relations 13

Excerpt from the Report of the U.S. Delegation to the 1975 Montreal Conference 23

JUDICIAL AND SIMILAR PROCEEDINGS

Inter-American Court of Human Rights:

Advisory Opinion on the *Effect of Reservations on the Entry into Force of the American Convention on Human Rights* 37

Advisory Opinion on the *Definition of Other Treaties Subject to the Interpretation of the Inter-American Court of Human Rights* 51

The Netherlands: District Court at The Hague Judgment in Compagnie Européene des Pétroles S.A. *v.* Sensor Nederland B.V. (*Extraterritoriality of U.S. Export Administration Regulations; Contractual Obligations*) 66

United States:

District Court for the Northern District of Alabama Decision in Jackson *v.* People's Republic of China (*Foreign Sovereign Immunities Act; State Succession; Repayment of Bonds Issued in 1911*) 75

District Court for the Northern District of Illinois Decision in Deere *v.* Lufthansa (*Liability Limits under the Warsaw Convention; Utilization of Last Official U.S. Price of Gold to Determine Limits in U.S. Dollars*) 82

Court of Appeals for the District of Columbia Circuit Order Amending Opinion in the Matter of the Arbitration between Maritime International Nominees Establishment *v.* Guinea (*Foreign Sovereign Immunities Act; ICSID Arbitration; Waiver of Immunity*) 86

Court of Appeals for the Second Circuit Decision in Franklin Mint *v.* Trans World Airlines (*Liability in Limits under the Warsaw Convention; Utilization of Last Official U.S. Price of Gold to Determine Limits in U.S. Dollars; Enforceability of Warsaw Convention in U.S. Courts*) 92

LEGISLATION AND REGULATIONS

Japan: Law on Interim Measures for *Deep Seabed Mining* 102

United Kingdom: *Civil Jurisdiction and Judgments* Act 1982 123

United States: *Foreign Investment in Real Property Tax* Act of 1980, Amendments, and Regulations

Introductory Note 142

Foreign Investment in Real Property Tax Act 144

* ILM subscription, $65; concessionary rate to ASIL members, $30. Address orders to ILM, 2223 Massachusetts Ave., NW, Wash., D.C. 20008. Outside U.S., please add $5.

Amendments to the Internal Revenue Code 149
I.R.S. Regulations concerning the Taxation of Foreign Investment in U.S. Real Property 152

OTHER DOCUMENTS
United Nations Commission on Transnational Corporations:
Information Paper on the *Negotiations to Complete the Code of Conduct on Transnational Corporations* 177
Draft *U.N. Code of Conduct on Transnational Corporations* 192
United States: Department of State Letter with regard to *Act of State Doctrine and Foreign Expropriations* 207

RECENT ACTIONS REGARDING TREATIES
The SDR in Treaty Practice: A Checklist 209
Treaties to which the United States is a Party 214
Treaties to which the United States is not a Party 219

NOTICE OF OTHER RECENT DOCUMENTS (not reproduced) 220

The views expressed in the articles, editorial comments, book reviews and notes, and other contributions which appear in AJIL are those of the individual authors and are not to be taken as representing the views of the Board of Editors or the American Society of International Law.

Manuscripts in triplicate may be sent to the Editors-in-Chief of AJIL, Professors Oscar Schachter and Louis Henkin, Columbia University School of Law, New York, N.Y. 10027. Subscriptions, orders for back numbers, correspondence with reference to AJIL and books for review should be sent to the AMERICAN JOURNAL OF INTERNATIONAL LAW (ISSN 0002-9300), 2223 Massachusetts Avenue, N.W., Washington, D.C. 20008.

AJIL is published in January, April, July, and October and is supplied to all members of the American Society of International Law. The annual subscription to nonmembers of ASIL is $52.00, plus $2.50 for all foreign subscriptions (including ASIL Proceedings). Available back numbers of AJIL will be supplied at $11.00 each. ($21 of membership fee is allotted to AJIL subscription.)

EDITORIAL OFFICE:
BOX 44
COLUMBIA UNIVERSITY SCHOOL OF LAW
NEW YORK, N.Y. 10027

BUSINESS OFFICE:
2223 MASSACHUSETTS AVENUE, N.W.
WASHINGTON, D.C. 20008

The American Society of International Law

2223 Massachusetts Ave., N.W., Washington, D.C. 20008 (202) 265-4313 CABLES "AMINTLAW"

1983 MEMBERSHIP APPLICATION

[ ] REGULAR MEMBERS .... $ 55

[ ] INTERMEDIATE MEMBERS (first 3 years of membership for *those under 30 years of age* at time of application) .... $ 25
Date of Birth ________________

[ ] STUDENT MEMBERS . . . Verification to be completed by a professor or administrative officer of your school: I hereby certify that the applicant is regularly registered in
(school) ________________________________
for academic year __________ Title ________________
Signature ________________________________ $ 15

[ ] SPECIAL CATEGORY (persons *not* resident in a member country of the OECD) .... $ 30

[ ] CONTRIBUTING MEMBERS .... $ 75

[ ] SUPPORTING MEMBERS .... $ 150

[ ] ANNUAL PATRON .... $ 500

[ ] LIFE (one-time dues) $1,000

[ ] PATRON (one-time dues) $5,000

($21 of membership fee is allotted to AJIL subscription)

[ ] Please send me *International Legal Materials* at member rate of $30, plus $5 if outside U.S.

Please enroll me as a member of the American Society of International Law for the calendar year starting January 1, 19____. My check, money order, UNESCO coupon, or payment in a convertible currency is enclosed $____________. I have checked membership category for which I am eligible.

(Please Print)

Name: ....

Address: ....

City: ....

State (or Country): .... Zip: ....

Member, U.S. Bar? .... State: .... Year: ....

Signature: ....

[ ] Check here if you would like to receive a list of Society publications, showing special reduced prices for members.

PLEASE MAKE CHECKS PAYABLE TO *The American Society of International Law*. Contributions above obligatory dues, and all dues if membership is related to your work or profession, are tax deductible in the United States.

NONMEMBER SUBSCRIPTIONS

[ ] *AJIL* incl. ASIL *Proceedings* (add $2.50 if outside U.S.) ..... $ 52

[ ] *International Legal Materials* (add $5.00 if outside U.S.) .... $ 65

American Journal of International Law

ly 1983
ol. 77 No. 3

blished by
nerican Society of International Law

PATRONS OF THE SOCIETY

Honorable ARTHUR H. DEAN
Honorable HERMAN PHLEGER
GENEVIEVE E. TILLAR (deceased)
W. ROBERT MORGAN
BRUNSON MACCHESNEY (deceased)
ALONA E. EVANS (deceased)
JOHN N. HAZARD
Honorable JOHN R. STEVENSON
ARTHUR R. ALBRECHT

In Memoriam

DR. JAMES BROWN SCOTT
HENRY C. MORRIS
ARTHUR K. KUHN
ALEXANDER FREEMAN
STANLEY P. SMITH

PATRONAGE, GIFTS AND BEQUESTS

Upon donation to the Society of $5,000 or more by gift or bequest, any member of the Society or individual eligible for membership may be elected a Patron of the Society. Upon donation of at least $5,000 in the name of a deceased person, such person may be elected a Patron posthumously.

Gifts and bequests may be made in the name of the American Society of International Law, Washington, D.C. Such contributions are deductible from federal returns for income, estate and gift tax purposes. The Society is incorporated by Act of Congress approved September 20, 1950 (64 Stat. 869).

MANLEY O. HUDSON MEDAL

The American Society of International Law bestows from time to time without regard to nationality a gold medal to commemorate the life work of Manley O. Hudson. Such awards are made for preeminent scholarship and achievement in international law and in the promotion of the establishment and maintenance of international relations on the basis of law and justice. Medals have been awarded to Manley O. Hudson (1956), Lord McNair (1959), Philip C. Jessup (1964), Charles De Visscher (1966), Paul Guggenheim (1970), Myres S. McDougal (1976), Eduardo Jiménez de Aréchaga (1978), Richard Reeve Baxter (1981), Oscar Schachter (1981), and Hardy Cross Dillard (1982).

Second-class postage paid at Washington, D.C. and additional mailing office

Postmaster: If undeliverable, send notice on Form 3579 to: American Journal of International Law 2223 Massachusetts Ave., N.W. Washington, D.C. 20008

Printed by Lancaster Press, Lancaster, Pa. 17604

AMERICAN JOURNAL OF INTERNATIONAL LAW

VOL. 77 July 1983 NO. 3

CONTENTS

		PAGE
Towards Relative Normativity in International Law?	*Prosper Weil*	413
Strengthening the Soft International Law of Exchange Arrangements	*Joseph Gold*	443
Freedom of the Air and the Convention on the Law of the Sea	*Kay Hailbronner*	490
Choice of Law under the International Sales Convention: A U.S. Perspective	*Isaak I. Dore*	521
The Law of the Sea Convention and Third States	*Luke T. Lee*	541
Editorial Comments		
On the Degradation of the Constitutional Environment of the United Nations	*Leo Gross*	569
Israel's Air Strike upon the Iraqi Nuclear Reactor	*Anthony D'Amato*	584
Notes and Comments		
On the Inadequate Reach of Humanitarian and Human Rights Law and the Need for a New Instrument	*Theodor Meron*	589
Correspondence		606
The Francis Deák Prize		615
Contemporary Practice of the United States Relating to International Law	*Marian Nash Leich*	616
Judicial Decisions	*Monroe Leigh*	624
Current Developments		
The 1982 Session of the UN Sub-Commission on Prevention of Discrimination and Protection of Minorities	*Jeanette Hantke*	651
Model American Convention on the Prevention and Punishment of Serious Forms of Violence	*Richard B. Lillich*	662
Book Reviews and Notes	*Edited by Leo Gross*	
Pomerance, Michla. *Self-Determination in Law and Practice: The New Doctrine in the United Nations* (Thomas M. Franck)		669
Zartman, I. William, and Maureen R. Berman. *The Practical Negotiator* (Roger Fisher)		670
Catudal, Honoré M. *Kennedy and the Berlin Wall Crisis* (Dean Rusk)		671
Elkind, Jerome B. *Interim Protection: A Functional Approach* (Ted Stein)		673
Mann, F. A. *The Legal Aspect of Money. With special reference to Comparative Private and Public International Law* (4th ed.) (Stephen A. Silard)		676
Atwood, James R., and Kingman Brewster. *Antitrust and American Business Abroad* (2d ed.). 2 vols. (David G. Gill)		679
Jalles, Isabel. *Implications juridico-constitutionnelles de l'adhésion aux Communautés européennes. Le cas du Portugal* (Eberhard H. Röhm)		682
Franck, Thomas M. *Human Rights in Third World Perspective.* Volume I (John N. Hazard)		684
Von Münch, Ingo (ed.). *Festschrift für Hans-Jürgen Schlochauer zum 75. Geburtstag am 28. März 1981* (Günther Handl)		685

Yin, John. *The Soviet Views on the Use of Force in International Law* (John N. Hazard) 687
Dolman, Antony J. *Resources, Regimes, World Order* (Harold K. Jacobson) 688
Anand, Ram Prakash (ed.). *Law of the Sea: Caracas and Beyond. Developments in International Law, 3* (George K. Walker) 689
Chen, Frederick Tse-shyang (ed.). *Proceedings of Conference on Deep Seabed Mining and Freedom of the Seas* (George K. Walker) 689
Vitzthum, Wolfgang Graf (ed.). *Die Plünderung der Meere: Ein gemeinsames Erbe wird zerstückelt* (Uwe Jenisch) 691
Shusterich, Kurt Michael. *Resource Management and the Oceans: The Political Economy of Deep Seabed Mining* (John King Gamble, Jr.) 693
MacDonald, Charles G. *Iran, Saudi Arabia, and the Law of the Sea: Political Interaction and Legal Development in the Persian Gulf* (Roy E. Thoman) 694
Bartell, Joyce J. (ed.). *The Yankee Mariner and Sea Power: America's Challenge of Ocean Space* (Thomas A. Kamm) 695
Rey Caro, Ernesto J. *Estudios de Derecho Internacional* (Domingo E. Acevedo) 697
Lipstein, K. *Principles of the Conflict of Laws, National and International* (Colin Phegan) 699
Courbe, Patrick. *Les objectifs temporels des règles de droit international privé* (Ignaz Seidl-Hohenveldern) 701
Gnesa, Edi. *Die von Israel besetzten Gebiete im Völkerrecht* (Karl Josef Partsch) 703
Newman, Edwin S., and Eugene M. Wypyski (eds.). *United States International Trade Reports.* Binder I (Leo H. Phillips, Jr.) 704
Campbell, Dennis (ed.). *Transnational Legal Practice: A Survey of Selected Countries.* 2 vols. (Michael P. Malloy) 705
Kaye, Harvey, Paul Plaia, Jr., and Michael A. Hertzberg. *International Trade Practice.* 2 vols. (Mark Roy Sandstrom) 707
Postlewaite, Philip F., and Michael P. Collins. *International Individual Taxation* (J. Ross Macdonald) 708
Movchan, A. P. *Prava cheloveka i mezhdunarodnye otnosheniia* (John N. Hazard) 709
Vorotnikov, V. V., and D. A. Lebin (eds.). *Mezhdunarodnye Ekonomicheskije i Nauchno-tekhnicheskije Organizatsii Stran-chlenov SEV. Spravochnik* (Richard Szawlowski) 711
Petrovskij, V. F. (ed.). *Organizatsija Obedinennykh Natsij. Kratkij Spravochnik* (3d ed.) (Richard Szawlowski) 712
Spencer, Robert, John Kirton, and Kim Richard Nossal (eds.). *The International Joint Commission Seventy Years On* (C. Joseph Chacko) 714
Albinski, Henry. *The Australian-American Security Relationship. A Regional and International Perspective* (Ferenc A. Váli) 715
Chiswick, Barry R. (ed.). *The Gateway: U.S. Immigration Issues and Policies* (John W. Williams) 716
Smith, Myron J., Jr. *The Secret Wars: A Guide to Sources in English.* 3 vols. (Allan E. Warnke) 717
Delbrück, Jost, Wilfried Fiedler, and Wilhelm A. Kewenig (eds.). *German Yearbook of International Law. Vol. 22, 1979* (Christina M. Cerna) 718
Bourne, C. B. (ed.). *The Canadian Yearbook of International Law. Volume XIX, 1981* (Forest L. Grieves) 720
Briefer Notices: Amin, 721; Langen, 722; Conforti, 722; Panico, 723; Hakapää, 723; Casad, 724; Sanford, 725; Leu, 726; *List of Treaty Collections,* 726. Correspondence, 727.
Books Received 728

OFFICIAL DOCUMENTS

United Nations General Assembly. Resolution on Principles Governing the Use by States of Artificial Earth Satellites for International Direct Television Broadcasting 733
International Legal Materials. Contents, Vol. XXII, No. 2 (March 1983) 737

The American Society of International Law

The American Society of International Law was organized in 1906 "to foster the study of international law and to promote the establishment and maintenance of international relations on the basis of law and justice."

The Society serves as a meeting place and forum for scholars, teachers, officials, lawyers, and others, from some one hundred countries. In April, it holds a three-day Annual Meeting at which current problems of international law are discussed. The Society also sponsors regional meetings outside of Washington in cooperation with other institutions. Salient questions of international law and relations are considered in depth by panels and study groups organized by the Society's Board of Review and Development. Works of scholarship are often published under the Society's auspices in connection with studies sponsored by the Board, many in the Society's series of *Studies in Transnational Legal Policy.*

The Society periodically issues four publications:

The American Journal of International Law, the leading journal in the field of international law, has been published since 1907. The *Proceedings of the American Society of International Law* carries the papers and discussion of the annual meeting of the Society.

International Legal Materials, a bimonthly, is a unique international collection of texts of current official documents, including legislation, treaties, court decisions, and reports. Subscription rates are $30 a year for members of the Society, $65 for others.

The quarterly *Newsletter* provides members with news of the Society and other organizations in the field.

Society membership is open to all persons of whatever nationality and profession who are interested in its objectives. Dues are: regular, $55; special category, $30 for persons *not* resident in a member country of the Organisation for Economic Co-operation and Development; intermediate, $25; student, $15. Membership application form is printed at the back of each issue of AJIL.

TOWARDS RELATIVE NORMATIVITY IN INTERNATIONAL LAW?

*By Prosper Weil**

1. The purpose of this article is to examine, even at the risk of magnifying them somewhat for clarity, the potential dangers that some recent developments usually studied from other angles—the *jus cogens* theory, the distinction between international crimes and international delicts, the concept of a rule of general international law, the notion of obligation *erga omnes*—bring in their wake for the future of international law as a normative system intended to perform certain functions.

I. Pathology of the International Normative System

2. As an uncontroversial starting point, let us take the statement that "public international law is the aggregate of the legal norms governing international relations."[1] This shows that the concept of international law is defined by both its nature and its functions. Its nature is to be an "*aggregate of the legal norms*" that dictate what its subjects must do (prescriptive norms), must not do (prohibitive norms), or may do (permissive norms) and constitute for them a source of legal rights and obligations. Its functions lie in "*governing international relations.*" International law is therefore at once a "normative order" and a "factor of social organization."[2] These two facets are obviously interdependent. Thus, while the emergence of international law as a "normative order" is due to the need to fulfill certain functions, it will not be capable of actually fulfilling them unless it constitutes a normative order of good quality. In other words, the capacity of the international legal order to attain the objectives it was set up for will largely depend on the quality of its constituent norms. There can therefore be no indifference in regard to anything affecting international legal norms, since without norms of good quality international law would become a defective tool.

The Structural Weaknesses

3. As everyone knows, the international normative system, given the specific structure of the society it is called on to govern, is less elaborate and more rudimentary than domestic legal orders—which, of course, does not mean that it is their inferior or less "legal" than they: it is just different.

* Professor of Law, University of Paris.

This article is a modified and slightly expanded version in English of one published in 86 REV. GÉNÉRALE DROIT INT'L PUBLIC 5 (1982). It appears by kind permission of the editors and publisher of the *Revue Générale.*

[1] 1 P. GUGGENHEIM, TRAITÉ DE DROIT INTERNATIONAL PUBLIC 1 (2d ed. 1967): "le droit international public est l'ensemble des normes juridiques qui règlent les relations internationales."

[2] 1 C. ROUSSEAU, DROIT INTERNATIONAL PUBLIC 25–26 (1971).

Some of its structural weaknesses are too familiar to require lengthy treatment here: not only the inadequacy of its sanction mechanisms, but also the mediocrity of many of its norms. In regard to certain points, international law knows no norm at all, but a lacuna. As for others, the substance of the rule is still too controversial for it effectively to govern the conduct of states. On yet other points, the norm has remained at the stage of abstract general standards on which only the—necessarily slow—development of international law can confer concrete substance and precise meaning.

For some time, however, writers have been apt to point out a further weakness: alongside "hard law," made up of the norms creating precise legal rights and obligations, the normative system of international law comprises, they note, more and more norms whose substance is so vague, so uncompelling, that *A*'s obligation and *B*'s right all but elude the mind. One does not have to look far for examples of this "fragile," "weak," or "soft law," as it is dubbed at times:[3] the 1963 Moscow Treaty banning certain nuclear weapon tests, Article IV of which provides, *inter alia,* that "each Party shall in exercising its national sovereignty have the right to withdraw from the Treaty if it decides that extraordinary events, related to the subject matter of this Treaty, have jeopardized the supreme interests of its country";[4] the numerous treaty provisions whereby the parties undertake merely to consult together, to open negotiations, to settle certain problems by subsequent agreement; and the purely hortatory or exhortatory provisions whereby they undertake to "seek to," "make efforts to," "promote," "avoid," "examine with understanding," "act as swiftly as possible," "take all due steps with a view to," etc. While particularly common in economic matters,[5] these "precarious" norms are similarly encountered in the political field, as witness, apart from the above-quoted Moscow Treaty provision, a recent Advisory Opinion of the International Court of Justice including obligations "to co-operate in good faith" and "to consult together" among the "legal principles and rules" governing the relations between an international organization and a host country.[6] Whether a rule is "hard" or "soft" does not, of course, affect its normative character. A rule of treaty or customary law may be vague, "soft"; but, as the above examples show, it does not thereby cease to be a legal norm. In contrast, however definite the substance of a non-normative provision—certain clauses of the Helsinki Final Act, say, or of the Charter of Economic Rights and Duties of States—that will not turn it into a legal norm.[7] Yet the fact remains that the proliferation of "soft" norms, of what some also call "hortatory" or

[3] *See* Baxter, *International Law in "Her Infinite Variety,"* 29 INT'L & COMP. L.Q. 549 *et seq.* (1980).

[4] 14 UST 1313, TIAS No. 5433, 480 UNTS 43.

[5] Weil, *Le Droit international économique: mythe ou réalité?*, in ASPECTS DU DROIT INTERNATIONAL ÉCONOMIQUE 1 (1972).

[6] Interpretation of the Agreement of 25 March 1951 between the WHO and Egypt, 1980 ICJ REP. 73, 95 (Advisory Opinion of Dec. 20).

[7] The term "soft law" is not used solely to express the vague and therefore, in practice, uncompelling character of a legal norm but is also used at times to convey the sublegal value of some non-normative acts, such as certain resolutions of international organizations, the Helsinki Final Act, and the Stockholm Declaration on the Environment (in addition to Baxter, note 3 *supra,* see the 1973 Hague Academy symposium on THE PROTECTION OF THE ENVIRONMENT AND INTERNATIONAL LAW (1975), esp. the contributions of Goldie, at 513 and 530, and Castañeda, at

"programmatory" law, does not help strengthen the international normative system.

The Conceptual Weaknesses

4. Alongside those structural weaknesses—which a jurist may observe but is powerless to modify—the international normative system also suffers from failings that must rather be ascribed to a certain slackness in intellectual grasp. This time, it is not a question of inherent flaws but of conceptual weaknesses that jurists can strive to remove. One is already familiar and need not be dwelt upon, namely, the lack of rigor too often shown nowadays in handling the distinction between the non-normative and the normative. The other is more recent, and to it we shall devote our attention: it is the conception of variable normativity for which certain theories now in process of elaboration are paving the way.

The Blurring of the Normativity Threshold. 5. The acts accomplished by subjects of international law are so diverse in character that it is no simple matter for a jurist to determine what may be called the normativity threshold: *i.e.*, the line of transition between the nonlegal and the legal, between what does not constitute a norm and what does. At what point does a "nonbinding agreement" turn into an international agreement, a promise into a unilateral act, fact into custom? Of course, this problem of the transition from nonlaw to law occurs in all legal systems, in particular under the guise of the distinction between moral and legal obligation. But the multiplicity of the forms of action secreted by the needs of international intercourse has rendered it more acute in that field than in any other, since in the international order neither prenormative nor normative acts are as clearly differentiated in their effects as in municipal systems. While prenormative acts do not create rights or obligations on which reliance may be placed before an international court of justice or of arbitration, and failure to live up to them does not give rise to international responsibility, they do create expectations and exert on the conduct of states an influence that in certain cases may be greater than that of rules of treaty or customary law. Conversely, the sanction visited upon the breach of a legal obligation is sometimes less real than that imposed for failure to honor a purely moral or political obligation.[8]

---

534 *et seq.;* R.-J. Dupuy, *Droit déclaratoire et droit programmatoire: de la coutume sauvage à la soft law,* in L'ELABORATION DU DROIT INTERNATIONAL PUBLIC 132 (1975), *translated in* DECLARATIONS ON PRINCIPLES: A QUEST FOR UNIVERSAL PEACE 237 (R. J. Akkerman, P. J. van Krieken, & C. O. Pannenborg eds. 1977)). It would seem better to reserve the term "soft law" for rules that are imprecise and not really compelling, since sublegal obligations are neither "soft law" nor "hard law": they are simply not law at all. Two basically different categories are involved here; for while there are, on the one hand, legal norms that are not in practice compelling, because too vague, there are also, on the other hand, provisions that are precise, yet remain at the pre- or subnormative stage. To discuss both of these categories in terms of "soft law" or "hard law" is to foster confusion.

[8] For some recent studies of this problem, see, *inter alia,* Baxter, note 3 *supra;* Schachter, *The Twilight Existence of Non-Binding Agreements,* 71 AJIL 296 (1977); and Bothe, *Legal and Non-Legal Norms: A Meaningful Distinction in International Relations?,* 9 NETH. Y.B. INT'L L. 65 *et seq.* (1980). The question of "the distinction between international texts with a legal bearing and international texts without legal bearing (with the exception of texts emanating from international organizations)" is at present being studied by the Institute of International Law (rapporteur, M. Virally).

If there is one field pervaded by this problem, it is surely that of the resolutions of international organizations. Today, the distinction between decisions, as creative of legal rights and obligations, and recommendations, as not creative of any "legal obligation to comply with them,"[9] has been rejected by some in favor of a more flexible conception: without crossing the normativity threshold, certain resolutions, it is said, nevertheless possess a "certain legal value" that may vary not only from one resolution to another but, within the same resolution, from clause to clause. Henceforth, "there are no tangible, clear, juridical criteria that demarcate with precision the zones of binding force"; there are only "hazy, intermediate, transitional, embryonic, inchoate situations." Even if resolutions do not attain full normative stature, they nevertheless constitute "embryonic norms" of "nascent legal force," or "quasi-legal rules."[10] In other words, there is no longer any straightforward either/or answer to the problem of the normative force of the acts of international organizations; it is all a matter of degree.[11]

6. It is beyond question that we are faced here with a pathological phenomenon of international normativity.

This is so in the first place because the concrete content of this partial or attenuated normativity, said to characterize certain acts, is quite beyond the grasp of intellect. Even recourse to the notion of "soft law"—in a different sense, this time[12]—to summon up the picture of a rule not yet hardened into full normativity, leaves it no less elusive. Some writers have sought to narrow the problem by propounding the notion of "permissive" or "abrogatory" force: without creating any obligation, a resolution is supposed at least to have entitling effects, so that any state acting in conformity with it could not thereby be committing an internationally unlawful act. While powerless to create new norms, the resolution would at least have the power to abrogate existing ones, which would leave states free to cease abiding by them.[13] But this is playing with words, for a permissive norm is a norm like any other norm, and only one norm can abrogate another. Thus, to ascribe permissive or abrogatory force to certain resolutions is tantamount to attributing normative force to them, full and undiluted.

Second, we are faced with a pathological phenomenon because the approach in question is based on a misconception. Nobody would deny that certain

[9] Judge Lauterpacht in South West Africa: Voting Procedure, 1955 ICJ REP. 67, 115 (Advisory Opinion of June 7) (sep. op. Lauterpacht, J.).

[10] These expressions (also to be found, with variants, in the writings of several contemporaries) are borrowed from J. CASTAÑEDA, LEGAL EFFECTS OF UNITED NATIONS RESOLUTIONS 176 (1969); *cf.* his *La Valeur juridique des résolutions des Nations Unies,* 129 RECUEIL DES COURS 205, 320 (1970 I).

[11] *Cf.* award in *Texaco/Calasiatic v. Libya:* UN resolutions "have *varying legal value*"; "while it is now possible to recognize that resolutions of the United Nations have *a certain legal value,* this legal value *differs considerably.*" 17 ILM 28–29, paras. 83 and 86 (1978) (emphasis added).

[12] *See supra* note 7.

[13] R.-J. Dupuy, *supra* note 7, at 146–47. *See also* NGUYEN QUOC DINH, P. DAILLIER, & A. PELLET, DROIT INTERNATIONAL PUBLIC 338 (2d ed. 1980); A. PELLET, LE DROIT DU DÉVELOPPEMENT 63 (1978). Judge Lauterpacht proposed a different analysis: states are under an obligation to examine the resolutions in good faith and, if they decide to ignore them, to give the reasons for their decision. 1955 ICJ REP. at 119.

resolutions serve to prepare, even accelerate, the abrogation of existing norms or the formation of new ones; and it is understandable that states not desiring change in the existing law should oppose the adoption of such resolutions or attach reservations to them, exactly as one might oppose the voting of a resolution or motion by a learned society in the hope of blocking or delaying some development one wished to avert. Resolutions, as the sociological and political expression of trends, intentions, wishes, may well constitute an important *stage* in the process of elaborating international norms; in themselves, however, they do not constitute the formal *source* of new norms. That does not mean, of course, that the jurist should ignore them; but between showing due interest in them and integrating them into the normative system under the cover of a sliding scale of normativity, there is a gap that can be bridged only at the cost of denying the specific nature of the legal phenomenon. Unlike national legislatures, international organizations, though capable of defining the "desired law," do not possess what would be the truly legislative power of themselves transforming it into "established law"; thus, normative force cannot be attributed to resolutions without overriding the distinction between *lex lata* and *lex ferenda.*[14] It is inadmissible within, say, "development law" or "environmental law," to give equal status to conventional or customary rules, on the one hand, and non-normative resolutions, on the other. Neither is there any warrant for considering that, by dint of repetition, non-normative resolutions can be transmuted into positive law through a sort of incantatory effect: the accumulation of nonlaw or prelaw is no more sufficient to create law than is thrice nothing to make something.

Finally, we are faced with a pathological phenomenon because, however much some writers deny the difference between norms and non-norms, states continue clearly to perceive that difference. Otherwise, what explanation could there be for the way they hammer home the fact that they are not legally bound by this or that resolution, declaration, or final act of a conference? When they subscribe to such instruments (or refrain from opposing them), governments neither intend to commit themselves *legally* nor feel they are doing so: "they don't mean it."[15]

7. True, it is not always easy to draw the frontier between the prelegal and the legal. This is a problem that recurs every time law resorts to the technique of the threshold: between the reasonable and the nonreasonable, the equitable and the nonequitable, the essential and the nonessential, the appurtenant and the nonappurtenant.[16] "I know it when I see it": this celebrated formula of a Justice of the United States Supreme Court aptly illustrates this difficulty. It is nonetheless true that the threshold does exist: on one side of the line, there is born a legal obligation that can be relied on before a court or arbitrator, the flouting of which constitutes an internationally unlawful act giving

[14] Virally, *A propos de la lex ferenda,* in MÉLANGES REUTER 519 (1981).

[15] Arangio-Ruiz, *The Normative Role of the General Assembly of the United Nations and the Declaration of Principles of Friendly Relations,* 137 RECUEIL DES COURS 419, 431 (1972 II). *See also* Schwebel, *The Effect of Resolutions of the U.N. General Assembly on Customary International Law,* 73 ASIL PROC. 301, 302 (1979).

[16] *Cf.* de Mérode, World Bank Admin. Trib. Judgment No. 1, para. 43 (1981).

rise to international responsibility; on the other side, there is nothing of the kind.

Variable normativity. 8. And so the international norm is becoming a singularly evasive quarry—or rather one so ubiquitous that it cannot be pinned down. But, as if this hide-and-seek were not frustration enough, recent years have seen a development that attacks the very substance of the norm. All norms are affected, the "hard" no less than the "soft." This time it is no longer a question of determining where the legal norm begins or ends: it is the very nature of the international normative system that is challenged and, by the same token, the functions for which it was created, which are its raison d'être.

9. To appreciate the scale of the problem, it may be useful here briefly to recall, even at the risk of triteness, the content of that "social organization" function alluded to above. The question is, in a word: what is international law *for*?

Long before the modern state arrived on the scene, a *jus inter gentes* had emerged to organize the coexistence and interrelations of heterogeneous national collectivities within what we would nowadays call a pluralistic international community: as Roberto Ago has demonstrated, this phenomenon, whose beginnings are lost in the mists of time, developed markedly throughout the Middle Ages.[17] From the outset, what was eventually to become international law bore the stamp of an end that has never changed: to ensure the coexistence—in peace, if possible; in war, if necessary—and the cooperation of basically disparate entities composing a fundamentally pluralistic society.

Alongside the heterogeneity already existing as between the Romano-Germanic and Byzantine Christendoms and the world of Islam, the collapse in western Europe at the end of the Middle Ages of all higher authority—be it Pope or emperor—resulted in a further heterogeneity as between the new state entities that made their appearance in the Christian world. From there modern international law, with its specifically interstate character, was to take its rise, though without losing the essential features it owed to its remotest prestate origins. The new international society was horizontal like its predecessors, and continued to feature, as they did, a decentralization of political power.

The emergence of legal rules intended to temper this condition of "an-archy," in the proper sense of the term, was stimulated—as it always had been—by a twofold necessity: first, to enable these heterogeneous and equal states to live side by side, and to that end to establish orderly and, as far as possible, peaceful relations among them; second, to cater to the common interests that did not take long to surface over and above the diversity of states. Such have always been the twin roots of international law, and such from the beginning have always been its two essential functions: on the one hand, to reduce anarchy through the elaboration of norms of conduct enabling

[17] Ago, *Pluralism and the Origins of the International Community,* 3 ITAL. Y.B. INT'L L. 3 *et seq.* (1977); and his *The First International Communities in the Mediterranean World,* 53 BRIT. Y.B. INT'L L. 213 *et seq.* (1982). *Cf.* Weil, *Le Judaïsme et le développement du droit international,* 151 RECUEIL DES COURS 253 (1975 III).

orderly relations to be established among sovereign and equal states (as Max Huber put it in a now famous formulation: international law "has the object of assuring the co-existence of different interests which are worthy of legal protection"[18]); on the other hand, to serve the common aims of members of the international community. Coexistence and common aims: this dual function of classic international law—inherited from the *jus inter gentes* of prestate times—was to find expression in the *Lotus* dictum: "International law governs relations between independent States . . . in order to regulate the relations between these co-existing independent communities or with a view to the achievement of common aims."[19]

Despite the profound transformations that international society has undergone, especially since the end of the Second World War, the functions of international law have remained what they have always been since the outset, and there could be no greater error than to contrast "modern" or "present-day" international law with "classic" international law in this respect.

For, more than ever, international society remains at bottom a society of juxtaposition, founded on the "sovereign equality of States," whose "fundamental importance" is emphasized by the 1970 Declaration on Principles of International Law concerning Friendly Relations and Co-operation among States in accordance with the Charter of the United Nations[20]—a revealing expression of "modern" international law if ever there was one. But, while they remain equal, states also remain, more than ever, different from each other, whether in size, political or economic system, ideology, or level of development. Furthermore, the heterogeneity of the components of international society is no longer a mere fact: the right to differ is now proclaimed as one of the attributes inherent in the very notion of sovereignty.[21]

In an international society rendered more diverse than ever by the emergence of a hundred new states, the traditional dual function of international law turns out to be more vital than ever. The 1970 declaration provides telling evidence of this continuity between the functions of "classic" international law and those of "new" international law.[22] Today as yesterday—and the day before—it is the key concepts of "relations" and "coexistence" (now called respectively "friendly" and "peaceful"), on the one hand, and "common aims" (now translated into "cooperation") on the other, that define the functions of international law as an instrument for the regulation of a pluralistic, het-

[18] Island of Palmas (Neth. v. U.S.), 2 R. Int'l Arb. Awards 831, 870 (Perm. Ct. Arb. 1928); *cf.* D. ANZILOTTI, CORSO DE DIRITTO INTERNAZIONALE 39 *et seq.* (4th ed. 1955).

[19] 1927 PCIJ, ser. A, No. 10, at 18.

[20] Annex to UNGA Res. 2625 (XXV) (1970), *reprinted in* 65 AJIL 243 (1971), 9 ILM 1292 (1970).

[21] "Each State has the right freely to choose and develop its political, social, economic and cultural systems." *Ibid.; cf.* Art. 1 of both 1966 Covenants on Human Rights, Annex to UNGA Res. 2200 (XXI) (1966).

[22] "[T]he importance of . . . developing friendly *relations* among nations *irrespective* of their political, economic and social systems or the levels of their development"; "States have the duty to *co-operate* with one another, irrespective of the *differences* in their political, economic and social systems . . ." (emphasis added). The very title of the declaration centers on the concepts of "relations" and "co-operation."

erogeneous society. The *Case concerning United States Diplomatic and Consular Staff in Tehran* enabled the International Court of Justice to highlight and forcefully underline the permanence of this traditional dialectic between difference, on the one hand, and relations and cooperation, on the other: the terms it employed in 1979 and 1980 were a significant echo of the Permanent Court's formulae.[23]

10. If the functions of international law have not changed, the essential features it has acquired over the centuries for the purpose of being able to perform them must be safeguarded in the international law of today.

In the first place, *voluntarism,* as expressed in the celebrated *Lotus* passage: "The rules of law binding upon States . . . emanate from their own free will."[24] This means that states are at once the creators and the addressees of the norms of international law and that there can be no question today, any more than yesterday, of some "international democracy" in which a majority or representative proportion of states is considered to speak in the name of all and thus be entitled to impose its will on other states. Absent voluntarism, international law would no longer be performing its functions.

Furthermore, if the heterogeneity of the components of international society, far from being an obstacle to the formation of international law, is on the contrary its *conditio sine qua non,* it follows that international law will be unable to carry out its function of coordination unless it is *neutral.* This certainly holds true for religious neutrality. As Vattel pointed out so many years ago: "Nations treat with one another as bodies of men and not as Christians or Mohammedans."[25] Closer to our own times, Paul Guggenheim observed that international law is "lay, secularized of necessity; it cannot be otherwise, considering the variety of moral and religious conceptions featured by the different societies making up the international community."[26] But ideological neutrality is also necessary to guarantee the coexistence of heterogeneous entities in a pluralistic society. Both religious and ideological neutrality are inherent in the basic concept of international law.

[23] The rules of diplomacy, the Court held, had proved "essential for the maintenance of peaceful *relations* between States" and were "accepted throughout the world by nations of all creeds, cultures and political complexions." 1980 ICJ REP. 3, 24, 42 (Judgment of May 24) (emphasis added). The institution of diplomacy had proved to be "an instrument essential for effective *cooperation* . . . enabling States, irrespective of their *differing* constitutional and social systems, to achieve mutual understanding"; the obligations thus laid upon states "are of cardinal importance for the maintenance of good *relations* . . . in the interdependent world of today . . . for the security and well-being of the . . . international community . . . , to which it is *more essential than ever* that the rules developed to ensure the *ordered progress of relations* between its members should be . . . respected." 1979 ICJ REP. 7, 19 (Order of Dec. 15); 1980 ICJ REP. at 42, 43 (emphasis added).

[24] 1927 PCIJ, ser. A, No. 10, at 18.

[25] LE DROIT DES GENS, bk. II, ch. XII, §162 (Carnegie ed. 1916, trans. of 1758 ed.), original *quoted in* Marek, *Criminalizing State Responsibility,* 14 REV. BELGE DROIT INT'L 460, 484 (1978–79): "Les peuples traitent ensemble en qualité d'hommes et non en qualité de chrétiens ou de musulmans."

[26] P. GUGGENHEIM, *supra* note 1, at 41: "fatalement un droit sécularisé et laïque; il ne peut en être autrement si l'on tient compte de la variété des conceptions morales et religieuses qui sont celles des différentes sociétés constituant la communauté internationale"; *cf.* his *Les Principes de droit international public,* 80 RECUEIL DES COURS 1, 32–33 (1952 I).

There is, finally, a third feature, which is a corollary of the first two: *positivism.* This term, of course, is not meant to imply that it should be regarded as an essential characteristic of international law that all its norms be "posited" by "formal sources" or result from precise normative facts without ever being the fruit of "spontaneous" formation.[27] No, it is simply intended to emphasize the necessity of envisaging international law as positive law, *i.e.,* as *lex lata.*[28] This means that (as already suggested) the distinction between *lex lata* and *lex ferenda* must be maintained with no abatement of either its scope or its rigor. It also means that, notwithstanding the fact that neither the basis nor the ultimate justification of international law is to be found in the normative system as such, it is still necessary for that system to be perceived as a self-contained, self-sufficient world. Without this positivistic approach, the neutrality so essential to international law *qua* coordinator between equal, but disparate, entities would remain in continual jeopardy.

11. It is these essential features of international law that recent developments have tended to challenge, and have thus threatened to compromise the very functions of the international normative system.

There is now a trend towards the replacement of the monolithically conceived normativity of the past by graduated normativity. While it has always been difficult to locate the threshold beyond which a legal norm existed, at least there used to be no problem once the threshold could be pronounced crossed: the norm created legal rights and obligations; it was binding, its violation sanctioned with international responsibility. There was no distinction on that score to be made between one legal norm and another. But the theory of *jus cogens,* with its distinction between peremptory and merely binding norms, and the theory of international crimes and delicts, with its distinction between norms creating obligations essential for the preservation of fundamental interests and norms creating obligations of a less essential kind, are both leading to the fission of this unity. Normativity is becoming a question of "more or less": some norms are now held to be of greater specific gravity than others, to be more binding than others. Thus, the scale of normativity is reemerging in a new guise, its gradations no longer plotted merely between norms and non-norms, but also among those norms most undeniably situated on the positive side of the normativity threshold. Having taken its rise in the subnormative domain, the scale of normativity has now been projected and protracted into the normative domain itself, so that, henceforth, there are "norms and norms."

[27] *See,* in particular, the criticisms by Ago in *Science juridique et droit international,* 90 RECUEIL DES COURS 851 (1956 II); and *Droit positif et droit international,* 1957 ANNUAIRE FRANÇAIS DROIT INT'L 14.

[28] Though not utterly opposed to use of the term "positive law" (*droit positif*) to cover the whole of the law in force, whether *posé* (*i.e.,* enacted) or *spontané,* Ago would rather it were reserved, in accordance with its etymology, for *jus positivum. Science juridique, supra* note 27, at 60–61. However, the use of "positive law" in the broad sense of *lex lata* seems to have become an accepted commonplace. It is in this sense, for example, that the International Court of Justice, in *North Sea Continental Shelf* (FRG/Den.; FRG/Neth.), referred to the Truman Proclamation as "the starting point of the *positive law* on the subject." 1969 ICJ REP. 3, 32–33, para. 47 (Judgment of Feb. 20) (emphasis added); *cf. id.* at 37, para. 60.

At the same time, normativity is also tending towards dilution. Traditionally, every international norm has had clearly specifiable passive and active subjects: it creates obligations incumbent upon certain subjects of international law, and rights for the benefit of others. The principles governing the relative effect of treaties, the opposability of customary rules, and the capacity to present international claims reflect this individualization of those owing an obligation and those owed a right. But at present both these categories are tending to become indefinite. Where those enjoying rights are concerned, this trend is exemplified by the concept of obligations *erga omnes.* The same development is less perceptible where those with obligations are concerned; however, the profound transformations that for some time now have been affecting the substance of the sources of law, and more particularly the theory of custom and the interrelation of conventional and customary rules, have been gradually fostering the idea that there are certain obligations that are incumbent on every state without distinction. We are nowadays witnessing the appearance, alongside obligations *erga omnes,* of what one is tempted to call obligations *omnium.*

In brief, after international personality, it is now international normativity that is undergoing relativization.

12. Without question, this development is a factor of progress in many respects. By placing the emphasis on "legal conscience," it helps to ensure the primacy of ethics over the aridity of positive law.[29] Without higher moral "values," international law is but a soulless contrivance: that, more or less, is the essential message of these new theories.[30] By thrusting the concept of "international community" into the foreground, they reflect the awareness of increased solidarity and the aspiration to a greater unity overspanning ideological and economic differences; they also impart the frustration of a Third World that has long felt itself powerless and aspires to place its new majority position within international organizations at the service of what it sees as a fight for justice. In view of the multiplication of states and their increasing diversity, this will to transcend the traditional international society made up of juxtaposed egoisms, and to forge an international community animated by the quest for the "common good" and common "values," is all the more precious.[31] One could even see in it an unexpected return to the

[29] Such terms as "legal conscience of states," "awakening of conscience," "universal conscience," "common good of mankind" recur like a leitmotiv on practically every page of the International Law Commission's work on the theories of *jus cogens* and international crimes.

[30] In fact, even before the Second World War, concern to deny states the right to infringe—even by common accord—certain moral rules regarded as superior had led some writers to canvas the concept of peremptory norms or rules of *jus cogens* (for detailed background, see Suy, *The Concept of Jus Cogens in Public International Law,* CARNEGIE ENDOWMENT FOR INTERNATIONAL PEACE, 2 PAPERS & PROC. 17 (1967)). If the idea of rules standing "in a higher category" (A. MCNAIR, THE LAW OF TREATIES 214 (1961)) is thus not entirely new, it used to occupy merely a marginal place in doctrinal writings and, in the minds of its small number of advocates, was intended to be limited to the absolutely unchallenged rules of morality constituting, in Verdross's words, "the *ethical minimum* recognized by all the states of the international community" (*Forbidden Treaties in International Law,* 31 AJIL 571, 574 (1937)). But it is more than a mere difference of degree that separates the modern theory of *jus cogens* from those first faint adumbrations.

[31] On all these trends, see R.-J. Dupuy, *Communauté internationale et disparités de développement,* 165 RECUEIL DES COURS 11 (1979 IV).

historic sources of international law: to "irreducible natural law," no doubt,[32] but also to that fundamental unity of the human race expressed in the 16th century by Vitoria's famous "*Totus orbis, qui aliquo modo est una res publica,*" of which the "international community of States as a whole" is, after all, simply a modernized version.

Accordingly, the potential negative consequences of the relativization of international normativity must at worst be regarded as secondary effects of changes that in themselves are beneficial. Vigilance, however, is imperative, lest too high a price be paid for the progress of international law towards greater moral substance and greater solidarity. At a time when international society needs more than ever a normative order capable of ensuring the peaceful coexistence, and cooperation in diversity, of equal and equally sovereign entities, the waning of voluntarism in favor of the ascendancy of some, neutrality in favor of ideology, positivity in favor of ill-defined values might well destabilize the whole international normative system and turn it into an instrument that can no longer serve its purpose.

II. Normativity Graduated

"Jus cogens" and International Crimes

13. The international normative system has traditionally been characterized by its unity: whatever their formal origins (custom or conventions, for example), whatever their object or importance, all norms are placed on the same plane, their interrelations ungoverned by any hierarchy, their breach giving rise to an international responsibility subject to one uniform regime.

This unity of the normative regime is shattered by the *jus cogens* theory and the distinction between international crimes and international delicts, which introduce what Roberto Ago, as rapporteur of the International Law Commission, called "a 'normative differentiation' between two kinds of rules, and hence, of legal obligations."[33]

To establish the nullity of treaties enshrining norms contrary to others held to be superior, the *jus cogens* theory trends fundamentally towards isolating, within the whole range of international norms, certain norms whose applicability cannot be set aside by particular agreements; *i.e.*, to the "distinction, among the general rules of international law, of the particular category of rules of '*jus cogens*'."[34] In other words, we have a few "peremptory" norms at the summit (elite norms, as it were) of enhanced normativity—"highest ranking" norms,[35] worth a "quality label";[36] then, below them, the great mass

[32] *See* C. De Visscher, *Positivisme et "jus cogens,"* 75 Rev. Générale Droit Int'l Public 5 (1971).

[33] Ago, Fifth report on State responsibility [hereinafter cited as Ago Report], [1976] 2 Y.B. Int'l L. Comm'n, pt. 1, at 3, 32, UN Doc. A/CN.4/SER.A/1976/Add.1 (pt. 1). *Cf.* the Commission's Commentary, Draft articles on State responsibility, in Report of the International Law Commission on the work of its 28th session [hereinafter cited as ILC 1976 Report], *id.*, pt. 2, at 1, 97, 102, UN Doc. A/CN.4/SER.A/1976/Add.1 (pt. 2).

[34] ILC 1976 Report, *supra* note 33, at 102.

[35] C. De Visscher, *supra* note 32, at 9.

[36] P. De Visscher, *Cours général de droit international public,* 136 Recueil des Cours 1, 107 (1972 II).

of merely binding norms, which the International Law Commission eloquently styles "ordinary customary or conventional rules."[37]

In a parallel movement, to establish a differentiation between regimes of international responsibility, the theory of crimes and delicts put forward by the Commission in draft Article 19 of its proposed set of rules on the responsibility of states serves basically to distinguish between, on the one hand, a small number of international obligations so essential to the protection of the international community's fundamental interests that their violation should be sanctioned as an international crime; and, on the other hand, all other international obligations, whose violation would merely constitute an international delict. Here again, international norms are divided into two categories: at the summit, the few that create obligations "the observance of which is of fundamental importance to the international community as a whole"; then, below them, the great mass of norms that create obligations "of lesser and less general importance."[38]

If, as the Commission's work seems to presage, the normative differentiation resulting from these two theories should prove not to be limited to two tiers,[39] we would be witnessing not just a dualization of normativity but a multiplication of intermediate steps, corresponding to different degrees of normative intensity.[40]

14. While this normative differentiation is certainly inspired by unimpeachable moral concerns, it also carries, in both its criterion and its content, some germs of alarming portent for the future of the international normative system.

The Criterion of Differentiation

15. The touchstone of the differentiation is definitely neither formal nor organic.

This is something the International Law Commission has stressed in explaining the distinction between the essential obligations it is a crime to breach and those whose violation is merely a delict: today, as always, "[t]he origin of the international obligation breached by a State does not affect the international responsibility. . . ".[41] And so nothing has changed on this score: the regime of responsibility is established regardless of the origin of the violated norm—convention or custom, lawmaking treaty or contractual treaty, it is all

[37] ILC 1976 Report, *supra* note 33, at 92. [38] *Id.* at 97.

[39] The Commission dismissed the idea "that there is one uniform régime of responsibility for the more serious internationally wrongful acts, on the one hand, and another uniform régime for the remaining wrongful acts, on the other." *Id.* at 117. It is not certain that mere bipolarity is any longer likely to remain a feature of the distinction between norms: thus, one member of the Commission referred to the existence of "more or less important peremptory rules." [1976] 1 Y.B. INT'L L. COMM'N 71, UN Doc. A/CN.4/SER.A/1976.

[40] Hence, in the Commission's work, such expressions as the following: some rules, "already existing, have acquired new vigour and more marked significance" (ILC 1976 Report, *supra* note 33, at 102); "the re-evaluation of rules that had existed since far earlier times" (Ago Report, *supra* note 33, at 53).

[41] Draft articles on State responsibility, ILC 1976 Report, *supra* note 33, Art. 17, at 79, and Commentary, esp. at 80–87.

one. Even the Charter of the United Nations cannot be regarded as giving rise to "essential" norms as such, for the international legal order does not comprise any source specially destined to create so-called constitutional or fundamental principles. The Charter is not a "kind of higher formal source of law"; it is only a treaty, and the norms it enshrines are, from the viewpoint of origin, nothing other than conventional rules.[42]

No more than the distinction between crimes and delicts does the distinction between peremptory norms and ordinary norms derive from any formal or organic considerations. It is acknowledged that peremptory norms may originate in any of the formal sources of international law: conventions, custom, general principles of law—some even say, resolutions of international organizations (which, by some alchemy, would magically transmute non-normative acts into supernormative acts). For the same reasons as for responsibility, the Charter cannot be regarded as an automatic source of superlegality, a "sort of generalized *jus cogens.*"[43]

16. Consequently, the differentiation of norms has to be effected in accordance with an exclusively substantive criterion. "It is not the form of a general rule of international law," wrote the International Law Commission, "but the particular nature of the subject-matter with which it deals that may . . . give it the character of *jus cogens*"; "pre-eminence of [certain] obligations over others is determined by their content, not by the process by which they were created."[44] More precisely, it is recognition of a rule's importance by the international community of states that is the touchstone as between peremptory and ordinary rules, as also between rules whose violation is a crime and those whose violation is a mere delict.

This gives rise to uncertainties and difficulties.

17. The first problem: by what mechanism does a rule graduate from the status of an ordinary norm—which is the general case—to that of a norm of higher grade, which must needs remain the exception?[45]

[42] *Id.* at 86.

[43] H. THIERRY, J. COMBACAU, C. SUR, & C. VALLÉE, DROIT INTERNATIONAL PUBLIC 151 (3d ed. 1981).

[44] Reports of the International Law Commission on the second part of its 17th session and on its 18th session [hereinafter cited as ILC 1966 Reports], [1966] 2 Y.B. INT'L L. COMM'N 169, 248, UN Doc. A/CN.4/SER.A/1966/Add.1; and ILC 1976 Report, *supra* note 33, at 85. Hence, if certain rules in the Charter (not all, as we have seen) belong to the higher grade norms, that is due, not to their inclusion in an instrument supposed formally to be of superior normative status, but to their actual subject matter. Thus, the fact that Article 52 of the Vienna Convention on the Law of Treaties speaks of the threat or use of force "in violation of the principles of the Charter of the United Nations" (and not "in violation of the Charter of the United Nations") derives partly from an intention to make the point that the prohibition of coercion is a rule of general international law whose peremptory character and even normativity are independent of its formal inclusion in the Charter. ILC 1966 Reports, *supra,* at 246–47.

[45] "[T]he majority of the general rules of international law do not have that [peremptory] character." ILC 1966 Reports, *supra* note 44, at 248. "[*J*]*us dispositivum* remains the principle, *jus cogens* the exception. . . . The existence of a peremptory norm of general international law cannot be presumed." Virally, *Réflexions sur le "jus cogens,"* 1966 ANNUAIRE FRANÇAIS DROIT INT'L 5, 25. "The concept of international crime must be restrictive." Ago Report, *supra* note 33, at 90. "[I]t cannot be concluded that an international crime exists unless . . . two conditions are met." ILC 1976 Report, *supra* note 33, at 120.

Central to this norm-mutation process, as we have just seen, is the "international community of states as a whole"; but who or what is this community?

Over the past few years, of course, there have been various telltale signs of a tendency to vague personification of the international community.[46] The international community "accepts and recognizes" the ascent of an ordinary norm to the rank of peremptory norm.[47] It "recognizes" that an international obligation is essential to the protection of its "fundamental interests,"[48] which seems to imply that the community as such possesses such interests. The International Court of Justice considers that a state has obligations to the international community and can enter into commitments towards it;[49] one Member of the Court has even spoken of rules of law that are the "common property of the international community."[50] Perhaps this community may be viewed as identical to the "mankind" whose "common heritage" or "province" is nowadays considered to be the use of outer space, the moon, and the seabed beyond the limits of national jurisdiction.[51] However, for want of adequate organic representation, this community seems impossible to identify separately from its members; but those members—and here the International Law Commission has been quite unequivocal—can only be states, to the exclusion even of international organizations, which the Commission regards as simply "the creation of those States."[52] In brief, the international community means states. But all states, or merely some, and, if so, which? There lies the rub. The answer given by the Commission is well known: a reference to recognition by "the international community as a whole . . . certainly does not mean the requirement of unanimous recognition by all the members of that community, which would give each State an inconceivable right of veto"; what is required is recognition "not only by some particular group of States,

[46] P. REUTER, LA CONVENTION DE VIENNE SUR LE DROIT DES TRAITÉS 21 (1970).

[47] Vienna Convention on the Law of Treaties, Art. 53, UN Doc. A/CONF.39/27 (1969), *reprinted in* 63 AJIL 875 (1969), 8 ILM 679 (1969).

[48] Draft articles on State responsibility, ILC 1976 Report, *supra* note 33, Art. 19, at 75.

[49] *See infra* para. 25.

[50] Judge Lachs in U.S. Diplomatic and Consular Staff in Tehran, 1980 ICJ REP. at 48 (sep. op. Lachs, J.).

[51] Treaty on Principles Governing the Activities of States in the Exploration and Use of Outer Space (1967), 18 UST, TIAS No. 6347, 610 UNTS 205, Art. 1; Agreement Governing the Activities of States on the Moon and other Celestial Bodies, UNGA Res. 34/68, Annex (1979), *reprinted in* 18 ILM 1434 (1979), Arts. 4 and 11; Convention on the Law of the Sea, UN Doc. A/CONF.62/122 and Corrs. 3 and 8 (1982), Art. 136, *reprinted in* 21 ILM 1261 (1982).

[52] Report of the International Law Commission on the work of its 31st session [hereinafter cited as ILC 1979 Report], [1979] 2 Y.B. INT'L L. COMM'N, pt. 2, at 1, 156, UN Doc. A/CN.4/SER.A/1979/Add.1 (pt. 2). Coming 30 years as it did after the hesitance of the *Reparations* Opinion to allow international organizations full international personality, the Commission's reluctance "needlessly" to place "organizations on the same footing as States" (*ibid.*) seems all the more telling in the light of the fact that the Court itself has since made a point of emphatically reiterating the impossibility of regarding an international organization as some sort of "super-State." Interpretation of the Agreement of 25 March 1951 between the WHO and Egypt, 1980 ICJ REP. at 89. *Cf.* de Mérode, World Bank Admin. Trib. Judgment No. 1, para. 28 (1981): "the differences between one organization and another are so obvious that the notion of a common law of international organizations must be subject to numerous and sometimes significant qualifications."

even if it constitutes a majority, but by all the essential components of the international community."[53]

Thus, a rule acquires superior normative density once its preeminence is accepted and recognized by "all the essential components of the international community." But since a state's membership in this club of "essential components" is not made conspicuous by any particular distinguishing marks—be they geographical, ideological, economic, or whatever—what must happen in the end is that a number of states (not necessarily in the majority) will usurp an exclusive right of membership and bar entry to the others, who will find themselves not only blackballed but forced to accept the supernormativity of rules they were perhaps not even prepared to recognize as ordinary norms.

18. And here is a second object of disquiet: if recognition by the international community is to constitute not merely the mechanism whereby an ordinary norm becomes a supernorm but also (as we shall see) the mechanism whereby even ordinary rules of general international law are made, there will be virtually nothing to prevent an irresistible tide of rules of general international law from swelling, one after another, the category of high-grade norms, which in principle was to remain limited and exceptional.[54] There is a danger that the category of ordinary norms will turn out to represent a mere transition stage pending promotion: scarcely is the scale of normativity established than it proves inherently unstable.[55] When one considers the tendency to allow "a certain normative force" to prenormative acts, it even appears that any *sub*norm of general international law might be coaxed upward, in a stealthy rise from nonlaw to superlaw. This process is already becoming difficult to contain.[56] Of course, the risks arising from such indeterminancy would be diminished if, as some had intended, it were left not to the individual states but to the International Court of Justice to appraise the applicability of *jus cogens* in concrete instances.[57] The provisions of Article 66(*a*) of the Vienna Convention on the Law of Treaties provide a glimmer of hope in this respect, but the way they seem to be construed by certain states gives little ground for real optimism.[58]

19. This destined proliferation of supernorms is bound to give rise to a delicate problem where codification conventions are concerned. Everybody knows how difficult, yet at the same time how necessary, it is to distinguish within such a convention between, on the one hand, what is declaratory of

[53] ILC 1976 Report, *supra* note 33, at 119. [54] *Cf. supra* para. 17 and note 45.

[55] The more so in that the concepts of *jus cogens* and international crime are themselves conceived of as essentially evolving. On *jus cogens*, see Vienna Convention, *supra* note 47, Art. 64, and ILC 1966 Reports, *supra* note 44, at 247–49; on international crime, see ILC 1976 Report, *supra* note 33, at 119.

[56] See the example given *infra* note 68.

[57] *See, e.g.*, H. Lauterpacht, *Règles générales du droit de la paix*, 62 RECUEIL DES COURS 95, 308 (1937 IV). Lauterpacht repeated the idea in his 1953 report to the International Law Commission, [1953] 2 Y.B. INT'L L. COMM'N 90, 154 *et seq.*, UN Doc. A/CN.4/SER.A/1953/Add.1. *Cf.* Sir Francis Vallat's statement on behalf of the United Kingdom at the Vienna Conference on the Law of Treaties, OFFICIAL RECORDS OF THE FIRST SESSION 420, para. 25, UN Doc. A/CONF.39/11 (1968).

[58] *See* R.-J. Dupuy, *Les Débats de Vienne sur les procédures du règlement*, 1969 ANNUAIRE FRANÇAIS DROIT INT'L 70, 87–88.

an already formed customary rule or crystallizes a customary rule that had been in process of formation, and, on the other hand, what constitutes a development of the law, *i.e.*, a new norm. It is difficult because the two categories are often closely intermingled; necessary, because, in the first case, provisions are involved expressive of rules opposable to all states, even those not parties to the convention, whereas in the second case only the parties are bound. With normativity split into rules on several tiers, it has now become necessary to distinguish, within each codifying convention, among the purely conventional rules, the ordinary rules of general international law, and the peremptory rules of general international law. This raises, *inter alia,* the problem of derogation through particular agreements from the provisions of such conventions[59] and the problem of reservations. The recent Convention on the Law of the Sea will certainly give rise to difficulties of this kind. One may similarly ask with regard to the provisions on *jus cogens* in Articles 53 and 64 of the Vienna Convention on the Law of Treaties: are they purely conventional rules that are binding solely on states parties to the Convention? are they ordinary rules of customary law, so that states may derogate from them by particular agreements—which would be a denial of the very concept of peremptory norms? or are they *themselves* the expression of norms of *jus cogens,* so that no state is entitled to reject the concept of peremptory norms? The question is not as academic as it might appear.[60]

20. The fundamental instability of normative differentiation explains why the greatest uncertainty prevails when it comes to singling out the norms belonging to the elite in comparison with ordinary norms. This aspect of the problem requires little demonstration here, given the extent to which writers have already dealt with it. In fact, setting aside a core of "innocuous examples, of interest to nobody,"[61] we find ourselves adrift in ever-widening circles of increasing uncertainty:[62] *i.e.*, in an area still featuring, in Roberto Ago's telltale phrase, a "certain unity of views,"[63] encircled by a shadowy margin about whose content opinions differ in the extreme.[64]

[59] Regarding its draft articles on responsibility, the International Law Commission wrote: "In principle, derogations from all the rules in the present draft articles may be made by special agreement, subject to the existence of any rules of *jus cogens.*" ILC 1976 Report, *supra* note 33, at 93. Any reader applying this to the articles one by one will certainly have no easy task of evaluation.

[60] It is precisely because it did not accept the provisions of Articles 53 and 64 that France refused to sign the Vienna Convention on the Law of Treaties. *La Convention de Vienne sur le droit des traités,* LA DOCUMENTATION FRANÇAISE, NOTES ET ÉTUDES DOCUMENTAIRES, No. 3622, at 10 (1969); *cf.* Deleau, *Les Positions françaises à la Conférence de Vienne sur le droit des traités,* 1969 ANNUAIRE FRANÇAIS DROIT INT'L 23. Yet can these provisions nevertheless be opposed to it, either *qua* ordinary norms or *qua* peremptory norms of general international law?

[61] P. REUTER, *supra* note 46, at 20.

[62] This image corresponds to the Commission's own presentation in its 1966 report: "Examples suggested included . . . ; . . . other possible examples." ILC 1966 Reports, *supra* note 44, at 248.

[63] Ago, *Introduction au droit des traités à la lumière de la Convention de Vienne,* 134 RECUEIL DES COURS 297, 324 (1971 III).

[64] For some the norms of higher rank include the rules on countering terrorism and hostage

A particularly sensitive problem is posed by the interrelations of the two normative series: that is to say, on the one hand, peremptory and ordinary norms; on the other, essential and less essential obligations. The International Law Commission has preferred not to tackle this problem head-on but to refer to a certain "parallelism": in certain cases, it has indicated, the two distinctions may diverge, but "normally" they coincide.[65] As an initial approximation, therefore, they will be considered here as virtually synonymous, which is after all normal, since they both spring from a common ethical preoccupation and make recognition by the "international community" a paramount factor.[66]

Content of the Differentiation

21. These uncertainties would not be too serious if it were at least possible to define the precise substantive import of the normative differentiation: in other words, if it were possible to ascertain how the legal regime of international norms varies in accordance with the place of each on the normativity scale.

Whatever their rank, all norms produce legal effects, all are binding, and the breach of any one, no matter which, constitutes an internationally wrongful act. What, then, is the point of distinguishing among them?

The hard-and-fast element of the regime of supernormativity has two sides to it: on one, the limitation placed upon the contractual freedom of states by the introduction of a hierarchy of norms according to subject matter, and the absolute nullity of international treaties containing a clause incompatible with a norm of superior rank; on the other, the applicability of penal sanctions—the content of which remains to be determined—in the event of the breach of any such supernorm.

If the consequences of supernormativity had remained within these bounds, there would be little cause for alarm. It appears, however, that this is not the case, for the assignment of a norm to the upper category, like the actions of

---

taking (Jiménez de Aréchaga, *International Law in the Past Third of a Century,* 159 *id.* at 1, 64 (1978 I)), sovereignty over natural resources (I. BROWNLIE, PRINCIPLES OF PUBLIC INTERNATIONAL LAW 513 (3d ed. 1979)), diplomatic inviolability (Ago, [1976] 1 Y.B. INT'L L. COMM'N 74). On the other hand, while the Commission had mentioned in this connection the principle of self-determination (ILC 1966 Reports, *supra* note 44, at 248), Ago did not refer to it in the lectures cited above (note 63). The Commission has made no secret of the fact that the categories of peremptory norms and essential obligations are both surrounded by uncertainties of many kinds (ILC 1976 Report, *supra* note 33, at 108–09; and 1979 *id.*, *supra* note 52, at 115).

[65] ILC 1976 Report, *supra* note 33, at 119–20. The opinions expressed hereon by the rapporteur (Ago Report, *supra* note 33, at 53; [1976] 1 Y.B. INT'L L. COMM'N 19, 57, 74, 89–90) and various other members of the Commission (*id.* at 67–68, 71) featured certain qualifications.

[66] Thus, I. BROWNLIE, *supra* note 64, at 512, 612; NGUYEN QUOC DINH, P. DAILLIER, & A. PELLET, *supra* note 13, at 690; P.-M. Dupuy, *Observations sur le "crime international de l'Etat,"* 84 REV. GÉNÉRALE DROIT INT'L PUBLIC 449, 461 (1980); and his *Action publique et crime international de l'Etat,* 1979 ANNUAIRE FRANÇAIS DROIT INT'L 539, 551, 553; *cf.* Marek, *supra* note 25, at 468.

the sorcerer's apprentice, seems to provoke a chain reaction that may get out of control.

There is thus, as we shall see, a growing tendency (in no way imposed by Article 53 of the Vienna Convention) to consider that peremptory norms create obligations for all states, and that each state has legal standing to call for those obligations to be fulfilled and to assert the responsibility of any other state that fails to observe them. So this enhanced normativity supposedly generates obligations *erga omnes* and, thereby, an *actio popularis,* which would signify in practice that the nullity prescribed by Article 53 of the Vienna Convention could be invoked by any state. It is with this in mind that the dictum of the *Barcelona Traction* Judgment, which does indeed refer to obligations *erga omnes,* is cited in connection with peremptory norms and norms whose violation constitutes a crime.

Going yet farther, it seems to be assumed that supernorms, once recognized and accepted as such by the "essential components of the international community," will *ipso jure* be opposable to all states, including even those who were against that recognition. At the Vienna Conference on the Law of Treaties, the French delegation had prepared an amendment to the effect that a peremptory norm "shall not be opposable to a State able to prove that it has not expressly accepted it as such," but as it seemed doomed in advance to failure, it was not even tabled.[67] Although a state cannot have invoked against it an ordinary customary rule that it has rejected from the outset, there seems to be no way whatever for it to evade the peremptory character of a norm it has not accepted as such. So what would happen if the "essential components of the international community" saw fit to recognize the supernormativity of a rule that a given state did not even accept as an ordinary norm?[68]

22. One can scarcely overemphasize the uncertainties inflicted on the international normative system by the fragmentation of normativity that the theories of *jus cogens* and international crimes have brought in their wake. A normativity subject to unlimited gradation is one doomed to flabbiness, one that in the end will be reduced to a convenient term of art, covering a great variety of realities difficult to grasp. Like the "variable legal authority" of subnormative acts, the graduated normativity of normative acts is a notion so elusive as to escape comprehension.

III. Normativity Diluted

23. Once the legally binding character of a rule is established, its full definition still requires that the personal subjects of the rights and obligations it creates be determined. Concurrently with the vertical diversification of normativity, however, a trend towards its lateral dilution has appeared, in that the subjects of rights and obligations have been growing ever more indeter-

[67] Deleau, *supra* note 60, at 19.

[68] As, for example, the provisions of General Assembly Resolution 1514 (XV) on decolonization, which the "international community" appears to regard as peremptory rules, whereas France refuses even to see them as ordinary rules of law. *Id.* at 17 and 19.

minate. So much so, that it is growing increasingly difficult to determine not only what a norm consists of, but whom it binds, and in favor of whom.

Obligations Erga Omnes

24. For a state to enjoy a right implies its possession of legal standing to claim performance of the corresponding obligation and, in default, to bring to book the person or persons owing that obligation. In the *Reparations* case, the International Court of Justice stated that "only the party to whom an international obligation is due can bring a claim in respect of its breach."[69] In the *Barcelona Traction* case, the problem was posed in similar terms: "it is the existence or absence of a right, belonging to Belgium and recognized as such by international law, which is decisive for the problem of Belgium's capacity."[70] Thus, not just any state may be regarded as possessing a "legal interest," *i.e.*, a right, in the observance of any international obligation by the state or states on which it is incumbent; in other words, there is no legal obligation whose fulfillment can be demanded by all states, without distinction, as possessors of a corresponding right. While any state has a right to have an international norm adhered to *erga ipsum,* it has no right to the observance *in the absolute* of the whole corpus of international law and the obligations therein enshrined.[71] In sum, no international obligations *erga omnes,* traditionally, exist: it is up to each state to protect its own rights; it is up to none to champion the rights of others. This principle, as has been said, is "characteristic of a general situation of juxtaposition of sovereignties, since it encloses international responsibility within a bilateral relationship opposing the obligation of one state to the personal right of the other."[72]

25. This every-man-for-himself doctrine has not been proof against recent aspirations towards the supremacy of ethical values and oneness of the international community. It is in this setting that one has to view the famous passage from the 1970 *Barcelona Traction* Judgment mentioning that certain obligations exist "towards the international community as a whole." "In view of the importance of the rights involved," the Court declared, "all States can be held to have a legal interest in their protection; they are obligations *erga omnes.*"[73] This dictum the International Law Commission interpreted as meaning that "there are in fact a number, albeit a small one, of international obligations which, by reason of the importance of their subject-matter for the international community as a whole, are—unlike the others—obligations in whose fulfilment all States have a legal interest." It follows, according to the Commission,

> that the responsibility engaged by the breach of these obligations is engaged not only in regard to the State which was the direct victim of the

[69] Reparation for injuries suffered in the service of the United Nations, 1949 ICJ REP. 174, 181–82 (Advisory Opinion of Apr. 11).

[70] Barcelona Traction, Light & Power Co. Ltd., 1970 ICJ REP. 3, 33 (Judgment of Feb. 5).

[71] *See* B. BOLLECKER-STERN, LE PRÉJUDICE DANS LA THÉORIE DE LA RESPONSABILITÉ INTERNATIONALE 50 *et seq.* (1973).

[72] P.-M. Dupuy, *Action publique, supra* note 66, at 543: "caractéristique d'une situation générale de juxtaposition des souverainetés, puisqu'il enferme la responsabilité internationale dans un rapport bilatéral opposant l'obligation de l'un au droit subjectif de l'autre."

[73] 1970 ICJ REP. at 32.

> breach: it is also engaged in regard to all the other members of the international community, so that, in the event of a breach of these obligations, every State must be considered justified in invoking—probably through judicial channels—the responsibility of the State committing the internationally wrongful act.[74]

A few years later, in the *Nuclear Tests* cases, the Court was to analyze certain unilateral statements by French authorities as having been made "*erga omnes.*" Those statements, the Court said, were not "addressed to a particular State" but "to the international community as a whole," and therefore entailed on the part of the French Government an "undertaking to the international community to which [its] words were addressed."[75]

26. The intention behind the *erga omnes* theory, as thus conceived, is to sound the death knell of narrow bilateralism and sanctified egoism for the sake of the universal protection of certain fundamental norms relating, in particular, to human rights. Like the *jus cogens* doctrine and the theory of international crimes, it is inspired by highly respectable ethical considerations. Yet, here too, subjects of doubt and perplexity come crowding in.

This is so, in the first place, because it is no easier, of course, to identify obligations *erga omnes* than peremptory norms or essential obligations. Even if the number of obligations *erga omnes* is in principle to remain small, the examples given by the Court[76] are still mere examples, and we are once more faced with a category capable of an expansion all too likely to get out of hand. One member of the International Law Commission has even referred to "the current rules of the law of the sea" as "obligations *erga omnes*"[77]—which, if words mean anything, can only imply that any State *A* would have a sufficient "legal interest" to take State *B* to task for impeding the innocent passage through *B*'s territorial waters of a vessel flying the flag of State *C*.

But the prime source of perplexity lies in the ambiguity surrounding the precise identity of the *omnes* to whom the obligations are owed. Have the corresponding rights become vested in the "international community as a whole," or in each of its component states *ut singuli*? The first alternative would imply the possession by the international community of some organic representation capable of taking legal action for the protection of its rights, which is certainly not the case. The second would signify that any state, acting separately and on its own behalf, could claim the fulfillment of an obligation *erga omnes* and invoke the international responsibility of any other state committing a breach of it. But then more questions arise. Is it contemplated that there should be some reparation of the classic type? If so, it is hard to see what injury would have been sustained by the applicant or what, apart from a

[74] ILC 1976 Report, *supra* note 33, at 99.

[75] Nuclear Tests (Austl. v. Fr.), 1974 ICJ REP. 253, 269–70 (Judgment of Dec. 20).

[76] "[O]utlawing of acts of aggression, and of genocide, as also . . . principles and rules concerning the basic rights of the human person, including protection from slavery and racial discrimination." 1970 ICJ REP. at 32. Later in the same *Barcelona Traction* Judgment, however, the Court pointed out that "the instruments which embody human rights do not confer on States the capacity to protect the victims of infringements of such rights irrespective of their nationality." *Id.* at 47. This passage is not easy to reconcile with the earlier one.

[77] [1976] 1 Y.B. INT'L L. COMM'N 71.

declaratory judgment, an individual constituent of the *omnes* could claim. Is punishment envisaged? In the absence of any judicial channels organized to that end, that would mean that any state, in the name of higher values as determined by itself, could appoint itself the avenger of the international community. Thus, under the banner of law, chaos and violence would come to reign among states, and international law would turn on and rend itself with the loftiest of intentions.

Obligations Omnium

27. Where those owing international obligations are concerned, we find that the normativity drift, though less blatant than in the case of obligations *erga omnes,* is fraught with even heavier consequences.

According to the familiar classic doctrine expressed in the *Lotus* Judgment, the source and test of a rule's opposability to a given state lie in that state's intention, as "expressed in conventions or by usages generally accepted as expressing principles of law."[78] Where conventional rules are concerned, the formality that presides over the conclusion of treaties and the principle of relative effect have enabled consensualism to be established without ambiguity or restriction: whether a state is committed by a treaty, and as from when, can be precisely ascertained. Matters have never been so clear as regards customary rules: it has always been difficult to determine whether a given state is bound by a rule of that kind and, if so, as from what moment. Nevertheless, thanks to a subtle interplay of tacit intention and nonopposability, acceptance never ceased to be a linchpin of the classic theory of custom. Hence it remained possible for any state unwilling to be bound by a norm, whether of customary or conventional origin, not to be bound by it, and for the states owing this or that international obligation to be as easily identifiable as, conversely, those possessing this or that right.

This situation is changing before our very eyes. Customary rules are now being described as general rules, and general rules are being analyzed as universal rules that are binding on all states without distinction, regardless of individual consent. As for that bastion of voluntarism, the conventional rules, a process is at work of absorbing them into the body of customary rules so as to subject them also to dilution.

The Evolution of the Customary Rule. 28. It was the customary rule, the Achilles' heel of the consensualist outlook, that was most readily to lend itself to the indeterminancy of the subjects of international obligations.

The classic theory of custom depends on a delicate, indeed precarious, equilibrium between two opposite concerns: on the one hand, to permit customary rules to emerge without demanding the individual consent of every state; on the other hand, to permit individual states to escape being bound by any rule they do not recognize as such.

To meet the first of these concerns, the classic theory narrows down the individual participation of each state to each of the two factors it regards as

[78] 1927 PCIJ, ser. A, No. 10, at 18.

indispensable to the formation of a customary rule. The practice that constitutes the corpus of the customary rule is defined as "general," "consistent," "settled," "constant and uniform," "both extensive and virtually uniform"—but never as "unanimous" or "universal." As far back as 1925, Charles De Visscher pointed out that "to rely on a customary rule against a state, it is not always necessary to be able to prove that that state, by its personal actions, contributed to the establishment of the international practice from which the rule derived," and he referred in illustration to customary rules that had come into being on the basis of practices accepted by maritime nations but in whose elaboration the landlocked states had taken no part.[79] Similarly, it is not required that each state, individually and personally, should have had the feeling of "conforming to what amounts to a legal obligation,"[80] which constitutes *opinio juris*, the second traditional condition for the existence of custom.

But while it is possible for a customary rule to coalesce without the *consensus omnium*, the classic theory nevertheless permits a state to escape its application by making known its refusal of it in time: the *Asylum* and *Fisheries* Judgments make this point in categoric terms.[81] It is this opportunity for each individual state to opt out of a customary rule that constitutes the acid test of custom's voluntarist nature.[82]

To put the matter another way: while a customary rule may indeed be formed on the basis of consent that, though general, does not have to be universal, the scope of the normativity attributable to it once formed will likewise be, though general, not necessarily universal. This both facilitates the formation of customary rules and avoids the domination of the minority by the majority.

It is this equilibrium that is threatened today. For the past several years, the degree of generality required of a practice, to enable it to serve as the basis of a customary rule, has been steadily diminished, while, on the contrary, the binding character of such a rule once formed is being conceived of as increasingly general in scope. The result is a danger of imposing more and more customary rules on more and more states, even against their clearly expressed will.

29. The fact of ever-decreasing fastidiousness about the degree of generality demanded of practice is evident from the novel and, in some regards, rather obscure theory of "quasi-universal treaties."

It has never been denied that a provision in a convention, though binding as such only on states parties thereto, could play a role in the formation of a customary rule that would also be binding on third states (provided they had not manifested any objection to it). Even so, it would still be necessary for that provision to have been corroborated by state practice, whether before or after its enactment. In other words, while a provision of treaty law might

[79] De Visscher, *La Codification du droit international*, 6 RECUEIL DES COURS 325, 361–62 (1925 I).

[80] North Sea Continental Shelf, 1969 ICJ REP. at 44.

[81] Colombian-Peruvian asylum, 1950 ICJ REP. 266, 278 (Judgment of Nov. 20); Fisheries (UK v. Nor.), 1951 ICJ REP. 116, 131 (Judgment of Dec. 18).

[82] *Cf.* 1 C. ROUSSEAU, *supra* note 2, at 320; Akehurst, *Custom as a Source of International Law*, 47 BRIT. Y.B. INT'L L. 1, 24 (1974–75); Jiménez de Aréchaga, *supra* note 64, at 30.

find a place in the formation of a customary rule, in which the essential element was the conduct of states, it could never, on its own, be any substitute for that conduct.

Nowadays, there is a tendency to accept that a conventional provision can stand in for the "general" practice, provided the clause in question has been adopted by a sufficient number of states, and in particular by the states whose interests can be regarded as the most nearly affected. In that way a treaty clause can give birth to "instant custom"—or so says the theory of quasi-universal treaties: instruments embodying rules that, simply because they have been accepted *qua* conventional by a large number of states, are supposed to be binding *qua* customary on the others. This is no mere acceleration of the custom-formation process, but a veritable revolution in the theory of custom.

30. To bolster this new view of things, reliance has been placed on that famous passage in the *North Sea Continental Shelf* Judgment where the Court, envisaging the transformation of a conventional rule into a rule of general international law, explains how "it might be that, even without the passage of any considerable period of time, a very widespread and representative participation in the convention might suffice of itself, provided it included that of States whose interests were specially affected."[83] Since the Court indicates elsewhere in the same Judgment that "the passage of only a short period of time is not necessarily, or of itself, a bar to the formation of a new rule of customary international law on the basis of what was originally a purely conventional rule,"[84] nothing more was needed to prompt the conclusion that, in the eyes of the Court, a provision of treaty law adopted by enough sufficiently representative states could undergo instantaneous transmutation into a rule of customary international law. A few months later, in the *Barcelona Traction* case, the Court was explicitly to mention "international instruments of a universal or quasi-universal character."[85]

31. In truth, it is by no means sure that these dicta of the Court bear the construction thus placed upon them.[86] But however frail its jurisprudential underpinning, the theory of quasi-universal treaties has certainly gained ground. According to some, a customary rule prohibiting certain nuclear tests has emerged from the 1963 Moscow Treaty. At least in this case, as in that of the 1958 Continental Shelf Convention, the treaty involved is one already in force. But the apparently all-conquering élan of "instant custom" does not stop there: why, after all, should a treaty not yet in force not also give birth *per se* to new customary rules, thanks to the magic of "instant custom"? Thus, it has been asserted that the Additional Protocol to the Geneva Conventions of August 12, 1949 on the Protection of the Victims of International Armed Conflicts, adopted in 1977 by the Diplomatic Conference on Humanitarian

[83] 1969 ICJ REP. at 42.

[84] *Id.* at 43.

[85] 1970 ICJ REP. at 32.

[86] When the passages quoted from the *North Sea Continental Shelf* Judgment are reinserted in context, it will be seen that the Court by no means discounts the actual conduct of states, to which it in fact attaches, as it has always attached, decisive importance. *Cf.* 1969 ICJ REP. at 41 and 43. As for that quoted from the *Barcelona Traction* Judgment, it refers to the possibility of claiming observance of a rule embodied in a quasi-universal treaty, and not to the possibility of creating, by such a treaty, obligations binding on all states.

Law, has, even before entry into force, established rules which "reflect . . . the universal, or almost universal *opinio juris* on what should henceforth be considered as governing any international armed conflict."[87] Tomorrow we may encounter the application of the same reasoning to this or that provision of the new Convention on the Law of the Sea, even before its entry into force—and a fortiori after. But why stop there? Why should "instant customs" not spring from mere resolutions of international organizations, considering that they are acknowledged to possess a "certain legal value"?

32. There is scarcely any need to emphasize the ambiguities inherent in this theory of quasi-universal treaties. At what point can the participation in a convention be regarded as sufficiently "widespread and representative"? Are only states having ratified or acceded to the convention to be counted, or are all signatories to be included? Are the "states whose interests were specially affected" to be identified by geographic, economic, ideological tests? We have come a long way from the representativity of the maritime states that have created customary norms in the law of the sea, and from the representativity of the founding states of an international organization whose objective international personality, according to the *Reparations* Opinion, becomes opposable to all, thanks to the participation of states "representing the vast majority of the members of the international community."[88]

33. While, under the influence of this development, the generality of practice has been reduced to a minimal requirement, the generality of the normative effects of customary rules has been undergoing the reverse process of constant expansion.

Central to this process is the concept "rule of general international law,"[89] which is both the key to it and the instrument of its advance. This term was not much employed in classic international law, where it denoted a rule applicable except in the event of a particular derogation, more especially of a regional kind: for instance, general—also called universal—international law was contrasted with American international law;[90] and reference was also made to particular historical situations embodying derogations from common or general international law.[91] While continuing sometimes to be taken in that sense,[92] the expression "rule of general international law" is nowadays being increasingly used as a synonym of "customary rule." Thus, in the *North Sea Continental Shelf* Judgment the Court speaks indiscriminately of "customary

[87] Nahlik, *Droit dit "de Genève" et droit dit "de La Haye": unicité ou dualité?*, 1978 ANNUAIRE FRANÇAIS DROIT INT'L 27.

[88] 1949 ICJ REP. at 185.

[89] Manin, *Le Juge international et la règle générale*, 80 REV. GÉNERALE DROIT INT'L PUBLIC 7 (1976).

[90] *Cf.* Judge Alvarez in Asylum, 1950 ICJ REP. at 293–94 (diss. op. Alvarez, J.).

[91] *See, e.g.*, Fisheries Judgment, 1951 ICJ REP. at 30.

[92] In 1976 the International Law Commission was still in certain places contrasting "general" international law to the "particular" international law concluded between two or more states, *e.g.*, its 1976 Report, *supra* note 33, at 92; elsewhere, however, it used the term "general international law" to denote customary, as opposed to conventional, rules, *e.g.*, *id.* at 80–81. Similarly, the expression "peremptory norm of general international law" in Article 53 of the Vienna Convention on the Law of Treaties is mostly construed as referring to rules of universal application, as opposed to rules of regional or bilateral scope. *See, e.g.*, Virally, *supra* note 45, at 15.

international law,"[93] "general international law,"[94] "general or customary international law,"[95] or even (more rarely) "general rule of international law" or "general rule of law."[96] The idea behind this terminological permutation is clear: to establish a contrast between the conventional rule, which only binds states parties to a treaty, and the rule of customary international law, which is more "generally" binding on a less strictly delineated number of states. Above, we have pointed out that a customary rule used not to be opposable to any state that had personally objected to it in appropriate circumstances: generality suffered exceptions. But now the very generality of a rule of customary international law is held to make it binding on all states without distinction. Thus, what used to be *merely* general tends nowadays to be viewed as impervious to individual derogations, as—in a word—universal.

34. This slithering from the customary rule to the general rule, then from the general rule to the universal rule, is strikingly illustrated by that very same Judgment in the *North Sea Continental Shelf* cases, since in it the Court also considered the question whether the equidistance principle of the 1958 Convention, though "not in the nature of a merely conventional obligation" undertaken by the Federal Republic of Germany, might not be opposable to it as "a rule that is part of the *corpus* of general international law," which, "like other rules of general or customary international law, is binding on the Federal Republic automatically and independently of any specific assent, direct or indirect, given by the latter."[97] In fact, the Court gave a negative answer to that question; however, the implication was that the equidistance rule *could* otherwise have been imposed upon the Federal Republic even though it had expressly opposed that rule, and even though it was that very opposition which had lain behind its refusal to ratify the Convention.

35. The opposability of custom was admittedly, hitherto, a presumption, but one that could be overturned by a state in its own particular case. Henceforth, custom is opposable to all, with no possibility of escape. Explicit acceptance of a customary rule has never been required; from now on, even explicit rejection is ineffective. The transition has been made from presumptive acceptance to imposed acceptance.[98] A decreasingly generalized practice—re-

[93] 1969 ICJ REP. at 28, 37, 39, 40, 41, 43, 45.

[94] *Id.* at 24, 28, 41.

[95] *Id.* at 28, 38.

[96] *Id.* at 42. The decision of June 30, 1977 of the court of arbitration in *Delimitation of the Continental Shelf* (France/United Kingdom) (CMND. 7438 (1978), *reprinted in* 18 ILM 397 (1979)) [hereinafter cited as 1977 Decision] also, though less frequently, uses the term "general international law" to indicate customary law (*e.g.*, in para. 62).

[97] 1969 ICJ REP. at 28; *cf.* p. 41. Sometimes the same significance is read into the passage where the Court refers to "general or customary law rules and obligations which, by their very nature, must have equal force for all members of the international community, and cannot therefore be the subject of any right of unilateral exclusion exercisable at will by any one of them in its own favour." *Id.* at 38–39. It is clear, however, that this passage is solely aimed at precluding reservations to provisions that, though conventional as to form, are customary as to substance (*cf. infra* para. 39), and is therefore not concerned with the universally binding character of general rules as such.

[98] *Cf.* Marek, *Le Problème des sources du droit international dans l'arrêt sur le plateau continental de la mer du Nord,* 6 REV. BELGE DROIT INT'L 44, 54 (1970); Manin, *supra* note 89, at 44 *et seq.;* Jiménez de Aréchaga, *supra* note 64, at 28. Admittedly, in the *Barcelona Traction* Judgment, the Court, referring to the evolution of foreign investment protection law, was to observe: "Here as elsewhere, a body of rules could only have developed with the consent of those concerned" (1970

ducible in some cases to a convention signed by the states "specially affected," or even to a resolution by an international organization—may give birth to a norm of customary law, which, under the pretense of its generality, will be universally imposed on all states, including its opponents. This quite upsets the delicate balance on which the classic theory of custom was based, since *opinio juris* is by the same token dissolved in an ill-defined majority consent and more or less reduced to a vague "consensus."[99]

Rarely can so immense an upheaval have taken place under the cloak of a mere terminological mutation.

The Evolution of the Conventional Rule. 36. As one might well expect, the conventional norm has put up greater resistance to this process of increasing indeterminacy of the subjects of international obligations: treaty-conclusion procedures comprise too many tangible signs, and the principle of relative effect is too respectably entrenched, for the distinction between parties and third persons to be easily overcome. Hence, the conventional norm has not been frontally assaulted but cunningly outflanked. The principle remains that an international treaty binds only the states that have become parties to it, and cannot create obligations incumbent upon third states. Yet behind the mask of classicism thus retained there has been a change of substance: in reality, the conventional norm itself may now create obligations incumbent upon all states, including those not parties to the convention in question.

37. What was needed in order to reach this point was, in the first place, to erode the autonomy of the conventional rule vis-à-vis the customary rule. Admittedly, these two categories have never been divided by an insuperable barrier, and it has always been accepted that a treaty could codify or contribute to the formation of a customary norm.[100] But these once exceptional phenomena are now of such frequent occurrence and far-reaching scope as to have become intrinsically altered. Treaty clauses that are declaratory of preexistent customary norms, or crystallize customary norms in process of formation, or attract concordant practice "like iron filings to a magnet":[101] these three variant erasers of the frontier between conventional and customary norms have been too often discussed to require further comment here.

The relationship between the conventional rule and the customary rule goes much farther, however, than the mere "interaction" or "interpenetration" described by writers.[102] The conventional norm—once regarded as the archetypal rule of international law because the purest expression of classic consensualism—is now considered to be a minor variety unable to attain full

---

ICJ REP. at 47); however, Jiménez de Aréchaga sees this, not as the reintroduction of some form of voluntarism into the theory of custom, but as merely a reference "to aggregate consent" (*supra* note 64, at 29).

[99] Stern, *La Coutume au coeur du droit international: quelques réflexions,* in MÉLANGES REUTER, *supra* note 14, at 479. *Cf.* Jiménez de Aréchaga, *supra* note 64, at 29.

[100] As far back as the *S.S. Wimbledon* case, J. Basdevant spoke of a rule possessing "the dual quality of being both a conventional rule and a customary rule." 1923 PCIJ, ser. C, No. 3-I, at 182.

[101] Baxter, *Treaties and Customs,* 129 RECUEIL DES COURS 25, 73 (1970 I).

[102] Marek, *supra* note 98, at 72; Jiménez de Aréchaga, *supra* note 64, at 23, 27.

stature until, ceasing to be "*purely* conventional or contractual," it has "passed into the general *corpus* of international law."[103] The decision of the court of arbitration on the *Delimitation of the Continental Shelf between France and the United Kingdom* bears witness to this tendency towards outright identification of the conventional norm (*in casu,* Article 6 of the Geneva Convention on the Continental Shelf) with the general (understood: customary) norm, since the court regards the former as the "particular expression" of the latter.[104] An even more striking illustration of the premium placed on rules of customary law, held to be of superior quality, was given by the International Court of Justice in the *Case concerning United States Diplomatic and Consular Staff in Tehran,* where it pointed out that the obligations violated by Iran "are not *merely* contractual obligations established by the Vienna Conventions of 1961 and 1963, but *also* obligations under general international law."[105] Time was when no call would have been felt to stray outside the *terra firma* of the conventional norms that bound the parties; here, apparently, the Court did not regard it as sufficient to take that ground but felt it necessary, in order to underscore the normative character of the rules breached by Iran, to point out that those rules had passed into the general corpus of international law—or, in other words, that they were also rules of customary law. And so we find a veritable de-conventionalization of conventional rules taking place on every hand.

38. Once the conventional norm had been absorbed into the customary norm and deprived of its specificity, all that remained to be done, in the second place, was to submit it to that increasing indeterminacy of the subjects of international obligations which we have seen affecting the customary norm. Thus, through the relay of the customary norm—itself qualified as a general rule or rule of general international law—the conventional norm, too, comes to be imposed on all states, including those who never became parties to the convention in question or never even signed it.

39. From this turmoil the law of treaties is emerging profoundly altered. Once hallowed by the prestige of consensualism, now fallen victim to the fascination exerted by the general rule, the conventional norm is being not only devalued against the other sources of law but forced to abandon what hitherto have been the characteristic features of its legal regime. While it is true that the Vienna Convention has confirmed both the classic procedures for the conclusion of treaties and the principle of their relative effect, this confirmation is reduced to an empty shell if a formally conventional provision can be analyzed as being substantively customary, and thus be submitted to the vagaries of a customary rule that, in turn, has become a rule of general international law. In such a situation there is virtually no difference any longer between a state that is a party to the Convention and a state that is not: the norm in question will be applicable to both. Neither will there be any difference between a convention that has entered into force and a convention that has not: did not the International Court of Justice and arbitral tribunals apply

[103] 1969 ICJ REP. at 41.

[104] 1977 Decision, *supra* note 96, para. 70.

[105] 1980 ICJ REP. at 31 (emphasis added); *cf.* pp. 24 and 44; *see also* 1979 ICJ REP. 7, 10, 20 (Order of Dec. 15). In its 1951 Advisory Opinion on *Reservations to the Genocide Convention,* the Court had already made a similar observation. 1951 ICJ REP. 15, 23 (Advisory Opinion of May 28).

provisions of the Vienna Convention on the Law of Treaties many a time before it came into force, and do so in regard to states that had not ratified it, or did not intend to ratify it in future?[106] Whether that Convention is in force or not vis-à-vis a given state is after all, it seems, not so important. Not only that: if it is now possible for a customary rule to spring not merely from an actually adopted convention but even from the "general assent" manifested at an international conference, there no longer remains much difference between "near-agreements" and agreements actually achieved.[107] Many other fundamental aspects of the law of treaties are also being eroded: it is surely out of the question to enter reservations to a treaty provision that has been construed to be a rule of general international law, or to denounce a treaty enshrining such provisions. Besides, what useful purpose would such a denunciation serve, considering that the provisions would continue to be binding on the denouncer as general rules of international law?

In sum, the intention manifested by a state in regard to a given convention is henceforth of little account: whether it signs it or not, becomes party to it or not, enters reservations to such and such a clause or not, it will in any case be bound by any provisions of the convention that are recognized to possess the character of rules of customary or general international law. Thus, while nearly all the distinctions established by the classic law of treaties have finally been more or less blurred, it has at the same time become necessary to differentiate, within each conventional instrument, between those provisions which are subject to the diluted regime of the customary norm and those remaining subject to the strict traditional discipline of classic conventional norms. One shudders to think of the controversies that may lie in wait over the opposability, to states not parties, of certain provisions of the Convention on the Law of the Sea.

IV. Conclusion

40. A system builder by vocation, the jurist cannot dispense with a minimum of conceptual scaffolding. It is impossible, therefore, for him not to feel disturbed by a development that—whatever its merits from other viewpoints—subjects normativity to gradations of strength while at the same time extending its scope *ratione personae* beyond all discernible bounds. Furthermore, the relationships between the various concepts involved raise problems whose solution is far from easy. Do obligations *erga omnes* and obligations *omnium* wholly, or at least partly, overlap, like "peremptory" and "essential" norms? Are the "high-grade" norms precisely those which are also valid *erga omnes* or binding on every state? To succumb to the heady enticements of oversubtlety and loose thinking is to risk launching the normative system of

[106] Legal Consequences for States of the Continued Presence of South Africa in Namibia, 1971 ICJ Rep. 16, 47 (Advisory Opinion of June 21); Fisheries Jurisdiction (UK v. Iceland), Jurisdiction of the Court, 1973 ICJ Rep. 3, 14 (Judgment of Feb. 2); Aegean Sea Continental Shelf (Greece v. Turkey), 1978 ICJ Rep. 3, 39 (Judgment of Dec. 19); Interpretation of the Agreement of 25 March 1951 between the WHO and Egypt, 1980 ICJ Rep. at 92, 95. *Cf.* awards in Beagle Channel, 17 ILM 645 (1978), para. 7, and German External Debts, 19 ILM 1370 (1980), para. 16.

[107] *Cf.* Fisheries Jurisdiction (UK v. Iceland), Merits, 1974 ICJ Rep. 3, 23 (Judgment of July 25).

international law on an inexorable drift towards the relative and the random. It is one thing for the sociologist to note down and allow for the infinite gradations of social phenomena. It is quite another thing for his example to be followed by the man of law, to whom a simplifying rigor is essential.

41. But even that is not the most serious aspect. What is yet more disquieting in this relativization of normativity is that it may eventually disable international law from fulfilling what have always been its proper functions.

The rules of general international law tend no longer to be elaborated, at present, by the states *ut singuli* to which they are addressed, but by the international community of states as a whole. It is also this community which raises certain rules from the rank of "ordinary" to that of "peremptory" or "essential" rules, thus becoming the central agent of both the formation of the rules and their situation on the normativity scale. However, as the international community still remains an imprecise entity, the normative power nominally vested in it is in fact entrusted to a directorate of this community, a de facto oligarchy. There is a danger of the implantation in international society of a legislative power enabling certain states—the most powerful or numerous—to promulgate norms that will be imposed on the others. The fundamental distinction between *lex lata* and *lex ferenda* will be blurred, since the "law desired" by certain states will immediately become the "law established" for all, including the others.

The consequences of such an upheaval are all too obvious. The sovereign equality of states is in danger of becoming an empty catch phrase: for now some states are more equal than others. Those privileged to partake of that legislative power are in a position to make sure that their own hierarchy of values prevails and to arrogate the right of requiring others to observe it. In this way the concepts of "legal conscience" and "international community" may become code words, lending themselves to all kinds of manipulation, under whose cloak certain states may strive to implant an ideological system of law that would be a negation of the inherent pluralism of international society.

42. The shifting of the axis of international law away from states towards the international community would undoubtedly represent a decisive step forward if it corresponded to any real transformation in international relations. If such were the case, there would surely be cause for rejoicing, both on account of the dream-come-true of the unification of the human race, and because of the no less yearned-for victory of the ethical values common to all mankind over the centrifugal forces that had kept nations apart. But, for the time being, it has to be acknowledged that the international community "is an order *in posse* in the minds of men; in the realities of the international scene it is still groping towards existence; it does not represent an actually established order."[108] Regret it as one may, the international scene today is still made up of the juxtaposition of equally sovereign states seeking, irrespective of their differences, to ensure their peaceful coexistence and cooperation. Undeniably,

[108] C. De Visscher, *supra* note 32, at 8: "est un ordre en puissance dans l'esprit des hommes; dans les réalités de la vie internationale elle en est encore à se chercher, elle ne correspond pas à un ordre effectivement établi." On the international community as a "historical" reality and as a "mythical value," see R.-J. DUPUY, LEÇON INAUGURALE (Paris: Collège de France, 1980).

the present trends must command assent insofar as they represent the expression of an *aspiration* towards some more clearly envisioned solidarity, some more assertive legal conscience. But it is impossible to approve them insofar as they are aiming to set up here and now a normative system that the present structures of international society are not ready to accommodate.

By seeking to create today the law of tomorrow's international society, one runs the risk of cutting a key that will not fit the lock it will have to open. By projecting on today's international society the concepts appropriate to a different society, the present trends are indulging in the pleasures of anticipation in ways that, at best, are naively altruistic; at worst, amount to the hijacking of man's "better feelings" for the ends of power or ideology.

43. Adorned with the trappings of modernism, the legal fashions here denounced tend to lull new states—weak and underdeveloped as they often are—into illusions heightened by deceptive rhetoric. Yet, here as elsewhere, it is law with its rigor—not to be confused with rigidity—that comes between the weak and the mighty to protect and deliver. Of course, classic international law has not discharged its functions to perfection—very far from it, since it has failed to prevent wars and has lent itself to being manipulated to the advantage of certain interests of political power. But the reflection that classic international law has been too open to rough handling in the past cannot mitigate the present and future seriousness of any abandonment of its intrinsically positive aspects.

44. Admittedly, all is not yet lost. The theory of international crimes still remains at the teething stage, and, more than a dozen years after the signature of the Vienna Convention on the Law of Treaties, the theory of *jus cogens* has not yet been put to any practical test. Thus, while in the *Case concerning United States Diplomatic and Consular Staff in Tehran* the International Court of Justice stressed the "fundamental character" and "cardinal importance" of the rules governing diplomacy as an institution and pointed to the "universal recognition" they enjoyed, it did not consider it necessary to describe them as rules of *jus cogens* or to define the responsibility of the state that had violated them other than in terms of ordinary responsibility giving rise to a traditional obligation to make reparation. This was a fine opportunity to give concrete shape to the concept of superior norms, but the Court did not take it.[109] As for the obligation *omnium erga omnes,* this likewise has not yet moved on from the stage of the potential to the regime of positive law. There is still some way to go before the dislocation of the normative structure of international law and the perversion of its functions become irreversible facts. There is still time for jurists to react.

[109] Admittedly, it might be possible to place another construction on the silence of the Court. Perhaps it considered that the rules of diplomatic inviolability could validly be set aside or modified by two states in the context of their bilateral relations and that they comprise their own system of sanctions. If so, it would have been for reasons peculiar to the case at hand that the Court regarded it as inappropriate to mention *jus cogens* and international crimes, and not because of any reluctance to accept the actual principle of these theories.

STRENGTHENING THE SOFT INTERNATIONAL LAW OF EXCHANGE ARRANGEMENTS

*By Joseph Gold**

I. The Concept of Soft Economic Law

The concept of "soft law" in international law has been familiar for some years, although its precise meaning is still debated. A distinguished international lawyer, Professor Ignaz Seidl-Hohenveldern, delivered a series of lectures on *International Economic "Soft Law"* at the Hague Academy of International Law in 1979.[1] The concept as applied to economic affairs is of particular interest in relation to the subject matter of this article.

In Seidl-Hohenveldern's discussion, the distinctive characteristic of soft law, at least in relation to economic matters, appears to be the intended vagueness of the obligations that it imposes or the weakness of its commands. This kind of law can be contained in treaties or in other instruments, whether or not adopted under the authority of treaties, that show the softness of their content by such titles as "guidelines" or "declaration of principles." For the purpose of the present article, the essential ingredient of soft law is an expectation that the states accepting these instruments will take their content seriously and will give them some measure of respect.[2] Certain other elements are postulated. First, a common intent is implicit in the soft law as formulated, and it is this common intent, when elucidated, that is to be respected. Second, the legitimacy of the soft law as promulgated is not challenged. Third, soft law is not deprived of its quality as law because failure to observe it is not in itself a breach of obligation. Fourth, conduct that respects soft law cannot be deemed invalid.[3]

It is easy to be too condescending toward soft law, even if firm law would be preferable. Soft law can overcome deadlocks in the relations of states that result from economic or political differences among them when efforts at firmer solutions have been unavailing. A substantial amount of soft law can

* Sir Joseph Gold was formerly the General Counsel and Director of the Legal Department, and is now Senior Consultant, of the International Monetary Fund. It should not be assumed that views of the author expressed in this article are necessarily views of the Fund.

[1] 163 Recueil des Cours 169 (1979 II). *See also* Weil, *Vers une normativité relative en droit international?*, 86 Rev. Générale Droit Int'l Public 5 (1982), translated, modified, and expanded *supra* at p. 413; and Schachter, *Alf Ross Memorial Lecture: The Crisis of Legitimation in the United Nations*, 50 Nordisk Tidsskrift Int'l Ret: Acta Scandinavica Juris Gentium 3 (1981).

[2] One author distinguishes between legal norms and ethical values or political principles and goals, and thinks that the term "soft law" has been applied to the last two of these three categories, with the result that confusion has been created. The term can be, and has been, applied, however, to legal norms that, for various reasons, are not absolute in their firmness. Horn, *Normative Problems of a New International Economic Order*, 16 J. World Trade L. 338, 347–48 (1982).

[3] Baade, *The Legal Effects of Codes of Conduct for Multinational Enterprises*, 22 German Y.B. Int'l L. 11, 39–40 (1979).

be attributed to differences in the economic structures and economic interests of developed, as compared with many developing, countries. Much soft law, therefore, is to be found in the law of universal international organizations, including the decisions of their organs, because the membership of these organizations is so diverse. The soft law of these organizations is the result not of a failure of will or technical skill on their part, but of the deep divisions among members. An organization, to succeed, cannot be too far in advance of the common will of its member states. The influence of states is obvious in the negotiation of constitutive treaties, but that influence exists also when broad powers of administration are vested in organs composed of persons appointed or elected by members of the organization. This control can be considered both a strength and a weakness of international organizations.

The usefulness of soft law as a contribution to the growth of international law is that the application of soft law can produce over time an accretion of firm law. It must be acknowledged, however, that circumstances can force a retreat from firm law, and then soft law may be the only alternative to anarchy. The law relating to exchange arrangements is an example of this development.

What is particularly valuable for the purpose of this article is that a concept of soft law in economic matters can be helpful in understanding the present international monetary system. Seidl-Hohenveldern is aware that soft law governs at least some of the interstate relationships that constitute the international monetary system, but most of the material he cites relates to other international economic relationships. The present article examines in more detail the soft law that applies to exchange arrangements and exchange rates in the international monetary system and some of the consequences of the softness of that law. It is not a purpose of this article to discuss whether or not the present law establishes an international monetary system. Nor is it a purpose to assess the relative merits of the former par value system and present exchange arrangements, except insofar as the law contains safeguards that dispose states to observe their obligations. The topic discussed in this article may be of general interest because it deals with the present balance that has been reached in an important sector of international relations between national sovereignty and international legal regulation. The exchange rate for a country's currency is one of the most important prices in the economy of the country, but at the same time the exchange rate is a relationship with the economies of other countries. The article is concluded with some modest suggestions for strengthening the administration of the present law in the hope that these innovations would strengthen the law itself.

The main legal instrument to be examined is the Articles of Agreement of the International Monetary Fund. It is not the only legal instrument of the system, but the functions of the Fund, the size of its membership, and the volume of its financial resources justify recognition of the Articles as the central instrument of the system. The original Articles were negotiated at the Bretton Woods Conference in July 1944 and took effect on December 27, 1945. The Articles have been modified by two amendments. The First Amendment, which was designed primarily to create the reserve asset called the special drawing right (SDR), became effective on July 28, 1969. The

Second Amendment, which took effect on April 1, 1978, was a fundamental rewriting of the Articles after the breakdown of the par value system.

II. Law of Original Articles

Under the original Articles,[4] an initial par value for each currency was established in agreement with the Fund, which took into account whether the prospective par value could be maintained without undesirable exchange practices and without reliance on an unduly large use of the Fund's resources. Par values were expressed, directly or indirectly, in terms of gold as the common denominator of the system. A member of the Fund could change the par value of its currency after consulting the Fund, and normally only if the Fund concurred in the member's proposed change. In order to concur, the Fund had to be satisfied that a change was "necessary" to "correct" a "fundamental disequilibrium." These quoted words were intended to discourage any tendency to propose changes as responses to transitory conditions or changes that would be inadequate or excessive. The provisions were inspired by the desire to promote the stability of exchange rates, but without imposing rigidity. The Articles did not permit the abandonment of a par value, even if a member wished to float its currency to facilitate transition to a new and sustainable par value. Only an immediate change to a new par value was permissible.

Each member was obliged to ensure that the exchange rates for spot exchange transactions in its territories involving its currency and the currency of another member were not above or below the parity (ratio) between the two currencies by more than the narrow margins specified by the Articles. If any transactions occurred at exchange rates inconsistent with the Articles, the member was accountable to the Fund for a violation whatever the circumstances might be that produced the exchange rates. The Fund could approve multiple currency practices if a member proposed to apply a multiplicity of exchange rates as a temporary strategy for dealing with its balance-of-payments difficulty. A unitary floating exchange rate for a currency was not a multiple currency practice, however, and the Fund had no power to approve and thereby validate it.

The United States was deemed to perform its obligations on exchange rates by voluntarily undertaking to settle international transactions by freely buying and selling gold for dollars, when requested by the monetary authorities of other members, at a price that did not depart from the par value of the dollar by more than the margin prescribed by the Fund for dealing in gold. The United States had negotiated a provision at the Bretton Woods Conference that deemed this practice to be equivalent to performance of the exchange rate obligations imposed on members by the Articles. Members had a choice of measures by which to perform their obligations, provided that the measures they chose were consistent with the Articles. Many members performed their

[4] The First Amendment did not modify the par value system of the original Articles. For detailed examination of the legal aspects of the par value system, see J. Gold, Legal and Institutional Aspects of the International Monetary System: Selected Essays 520–73 (1979) [hereinafter cited as Gold, Selected Essays].

obligations by intervening in the exchange markets by buying and selling dollars, or other currencies convertible into dollars, for their own currencies at exchange rates that were in conformity with the Articles.

The United States was the only member that undertook the free purchase and sale of gold for its own currency as outlined above. The United States came to occupy a central position in the par value system. Other members, when needing to change the par values of their currencies, were motivated, in effect, to establish a new relationship to the U.S. dollar as the central currency of the system. The United States played a passive role by not intervening in the markets on its own behalf to manage exchange rates for the dollar and by creating confidence that the United States would not attempt to devalue its currency. Other members needed this reassurance, not only because of the fear that devaluation of the dollar would have made the United States more competitive, but also because they would have suffered a reduction in the value of the dollars they held in their reserves as the currency with which they intervened in the exchange markets.

It would be disingenuous to claim that there were no fissures in the firm law of the par value system. For example, only a member was authorized to propose a change in the par value of its currency. The Fund could not make a proposal, and could not compel a member to make one, even though the member was in fundamental disequilibrium. That concept was never defined with legal precision. Members were often reluctant for political reasons to announce that they were in fundamental disequilibrium even when, but for that reluctance, they would have been reconciled to a change of par value. The Fund concluded, in interpreting various aspects of the provisions of the Articles on exchange rates, that members were entitled to the benefit of the doubt in the application of the provisions.[5] It is possible that, even when this conclusion was not reached as a matter of interpretation, the Fund was too complaisant in concurring in members' policies on exchange rates, but closer study than has been given to this charge would be required to sustain it. It is undeniable, however, that the number of critics grew who held that the law had contributed to the rigidity of the par value system that the founders had wished to avoid. It was no paradox that stability was not achieved by this rigidity.

Stability was to be achieved by a system in which par values, though changeable, would ensure the maintenance of fixed exchange rates that had been subjected to international scrutiny and had received international endorsement. The most effective safeguard of this system was that the floating of a currency outside the margins around parities was considered the most disturbing breach of the system. Floating was not only serious. It was also obvious to the whole world as a breach. The Fund did not have to exercise judgment or invoke subjective criteria in order to decide that a member, in floating its currency, was in violation of its obligations. The Fund did not have to consider a charge that was controversial and arrive at a judgment that might be politically difficult for that reason. The international shame that followed the obvious breach of the firm obligation to maintain fixed exchange rates on the

[5] *Id.* at 538–39.

basis of parities was the chief practical deterrent to breach. Moreover, a government that considered floating knew that it might have to face castigation by the political opposition in its own country for incurring international odium. Even if a government came to the reluctant conclusion that nothing but the floating of its currency was feasible, the government accepted the burden of proving to the Fund that the rigors of the situation compelled this breach as a temporary expedient. The Fund had a substantial armory of "sanctions" but found it almost completely unnecessary to employ them because of the anxiety of most governments to resume compliance with so fundamental an obligation as the duty to maintain an effective par value endorsed by the Fund.[6]

III. U.S. Action of August 15, 1971

On August 15, 1971, the President announced that the United States would no longer convert foreign official holdings of dollars with gold or other reserve assets, with exceptions that need not be recalled. Furthermore, the United States would not take steps to confine exchange transactions involving dollars within defined margins. The center of the system did not hold.

The U.S. President's announcement meant that the United States had decided to take an action that could not be reconciled with the Articles. What was the breach involved in this action? It may seem strange that the violation was not the withdrawal by the United States of its declared willingness to buy and sell gold freely for dollars with the monetary authorities of other members for the settlement of international transactions, even though the undertaking had become the real foundation of the system. The undertaking was voluntary. The violation was the refusal to take other appropriate measures to confine transactions in U.S. territories involving exchanges of dollars and the currencies of other members within margins that were consistent with the Articles. Another violation was the refusal of the United States to convert official holdings of dollars in accordance with the complex, but limited, obligation of official convertibility under Article VIII, section 4 that all members had to observe once they undertook to perform the obligations of convertibility under Article VIII, sections 2, 3, and 4. If a member gives notice that it will perform these obligations, it cannot shed them at a later date.

Why did the deterrence discussed in section II above fail to prevent the violation of the obligations? The United States is not weaker in its respect for law than other states. The United States was among the first and most insistent in urging, after the breakdown of the par value system, that the Articles should be revised and that members should return to legality. Some other major countries that at first had little or no enthusiasm for engaging in the arduous task of negotiating amendment of the Articles, because a coherent and complete reform was not feasible, had to be persuaded that nevertheless a more modest undertaking would be rewarding.

The United States made known the economic, political, and even the military considerations that had impelled it to decide on the action of August

[6] *Id.* at 148–80.

15, 1971.[7] There is no need to recall these considerations. It is the attitude of the United States to the repudiation of international obligations that is of interest here. Unfortunately, little is known so far of thinking in the U.S. administration on this aspect of the action.

Some information has been provided by a Japanese scholar who has received a number of relevant documents under the U.S. Freedom of Information Act, a statute that he regards with admiration and astonishment.[8] It appears that U.S. Treasury officials began to think as early as January 1971, and probably earlier, of forceful action to devalue the U.S. dollar. The documents disclose that at least one official was concentrating on actions that, though abnormal and dramatic, would be, to the maximum extent, consistent with the Articles. At the heart of the actions that he contemplated was suspension by the United States of the convertibility of foreign official holdings of dollars and closure of the exchange markets in the United States and in certain other countries for a period of 2 weeks beginning 1 week before the Annual Meeting of the Fund's Board of Governors. The United States would initiate within the Fund a uniform proportionate revaluation of all currencies in accordance with the provisions of the Articles as they stood before the Second Amendment.[9] This step would be followed by a devaluation of the U.S. dollar to bring it back to the equivalent of $35 per ounce of fine gold.[10] Other ideas were coupled with these measures as possible reforms of the international monetary system, one of which was phasing out the role of the dollar as a reserve currency without affecting its function as a vehicle currency, but it was recognized that these ideas, in contrast to the action on par values, would have to await amendment of the Articles.

[7] Some of the U.S. criticisms of the way the par value system had worked are set forth in a memorandum the United States submitted to the deputies of the Committee of Twenty in November 1972, entitled The U.S. Proposals for Using Reserves as an Indicator of the Need for Balance-of-Payments Adjustment, ECONOMIC REPORT OF THE PRESIDENT, TRANSMITTED TO THE CONGRESS JANUARY 1973, at 160–74 (1973) [hereinafter cited as ECONOMIC REPORT OF PRESIDENT, 1973]. *See also id.* at 120–31.

[8] Ando, *United States Foreign Economic Strategy as Seen in "Classified" Documents,* The World (Tokyo), Aug. 9, 1981.

[9] Art. IV, sec. 7 (of original Articles and First Amendment). For the original Articles, see 60 Stat. 1401, TIAS No. 1501, 2 UNTS 39. For the First Amendment, see 7 ILM 473 (1968).

[10] An objective of this plan might have been to avoid the need for congressional action because of the delay and publicity that would have been involved in a devaluation of the dollar. It is doubtful, however, that congressional action could have been avoided even though the net effect of the plan would have been no change in the par value of the U.S. dollar in terms of gold. Under section 5 of the U.S. Bretton Woods Agreements Act (Pub. L. No. 79-171, 59 Stat. 512 (1945)), the authorization of Congress was necessary not only for a proposal to change the par value of the dollar but also for U.S. approval of any uniform proportionate change in the par values of all currencies. Article IV, section 7 of the Articles before the Second Amendment required a majority of the total voting power for such a decision under that provision, but in addition the approval was necessary of every member that had 10% or more of the total of quotas. Under that caveat, the approval of the United States and the United Kingdom would have been necessary. The desire to avoid the need for congressional action is an explanation of the character of the action taken on Aug. 15, 1971. *See* K. DAM (who was present at Camp David), THE RULES OF THE GAME: REFORM AND EVOLUTION OF THE INTERNATIONAL MONETARY SYSTEM 188–89 (1982).

It is not known what weight was given to the central proposal described above. A further document, dated May 1971 and written by another U.S. official, is not animated by any obvious wish to work within the Articles in describing a program to achieve a lasting improvement in the balance of payments of the United States, a more equitable sharing of international responsibilities, and reform of the international monetary system. The proposals on monetary and trade matters in this memorandum are close to the measures that were taken on August 15, 1971. A conclusion that can be drawn from these documents is that the kind of action that was taken on that date was not an improvisation at Camp David. A difference of opinion exists among commentators on the question whether the timing of the action was affected by a request of the British authorities on August 12, 1971 that the Federal Reserve draw under swap arrangements in the amount of $750 million. The drawing, which was made on August 13, 1971, had the effect of giving the Bank of England a degree of protection against devaluation of the U.S. dollar by substituting a claim denominated in sterling against the Federal Reserve for dollar holdings redeemed by the Federal Reserve with the sterling it obtained under the swap. It is equally unclear whether the British authorities had contemplated a drawing of the full amount of existing swap arrangements, which amounted to $2 billion, or a request for conversion with gold of the total holdings of dollars by the Bank of England, which exceeded that amount.[11]

The most detailed, as well as the liveliest, account of how U.S. officials arrived at the final decision at Camp David has been provided by William Safire, who was present at the meeting.[12] A feature of the discussion at Camp David, much of which he purports to reproduce verbatim, is that nothing was said about the breach of international obligations, although numerous objections of a political or economic character are reported. Safire does describe what he thinks were the reactions of one participant:

> Even as we kidded around, the men in the room knew that Volcker was undergoing an especially searing experience. He was schooled in the international monetary system, almost bred to defend it; the Breton [*sic*] Woods Agreement was sacrosanct to him; all the men he grew up with and dealt with throughout the world trusted each other in crisis to respect the rules and cling to the few constants like the convertibility of gold. Yet here he was participating in the overthrow of all he held permanent; it was not a happy weekend for him.[13]

[11] K. DAM, *supra* note 10, at 187. He states that "[t]o the top U.S. decisionmakers the British request was the beginning of a run on the U.S. gold bank. The British move led directly to the decision, that weekend at Camp David. . . ." He notes the contest among authors on the facts relating to this incident. *Id.* at 187 n.58. An authoritative account has not yet been published.

[12] BEFORE THE FALL: AN INSIDE VIEW OF THE PRE-WATERGATE WHITE HOUSE 659–86 (1977). Safire quotes a statement by the President that he and John Connally, the Secretary of the Treasury, had agreed on the plan 60 days earlier. *Id.* at 684.

[13] *Id.* at 672–73. For the doubts of Arthur Burns, see p. 673. An article based in part on interviews with "insiders" makes no mention of concern about legal aspects of the action taken on Aug. 15, 1971. Odell, *The U.S. and the emergence of flexible exchange rates: an analysis of foreign policy change,* 33 INT'L ORG. 57 (1979).

The little that is known of the decision taken at Camp David does not dispose of the conclusion that the odium attached to floating was the main deterrent to the breach of obligation under the par value system even if it was not a complete deterrent. If no evidence is available of the discussion of violation of the Articles at Camp David, there is evidence that participants in the decision were impressed with the seriousness of the decision for the international monetary system. It is also safe to assume that at lower levels of the administration there was consideration of the legal character and effects of the decision, although it seems that a high degree of secrecy about the ultimate intentions was maintained even within the administration itself. The decision differs perhaps from earlier decisions by some other members to depart from their obligations under the Articles because the United States appears to have concluded that it had been treated inequitably in the operation of the par value system. Furthermore, the United States seems to have concluded that it could not escape from a predicament that in large part was the result of the policies of other major countries.[14] Certainly, this thesis was the one advanced at a later date when reform was being negotiated.[15] Perhaps also the U.S. administration had concluded that the situation was one that would justify something akin to the defense of *rebus sic stantibus,* although this defense was not put forward in these terms in the Fund or elsewhere. The United States might have found it difficult to reconcile the defense with its resistance to the contention of some members that the U.S. action on the dollar had thrown into desuetude the obligation of members to avoid transactions in gold between themselves at market prices. The tacit assumption by the United States of prolonged or even permanent surplus in its balance of payments on the basis of which the United States had negotiated the original Articles was no longer tenable. The United States had fallen into a condition of persistent deficit and the administration saw no escape that, in its opinion, other members were likely to accept.[16]

IV. Origins of Present Provisions

The provisions of the Second Amendment on exchange arrangements now in operation largely reflect the approach advocated by the United States in the negotiation and drafting of these provisions. The United States argued that the soundness of domestic economic policies should be the primary concern of governments. These policies influence the international position of a country, which in turn affects the exchange rate for its currency. Exchange

[14] Breaking what the United States considered deadlock may help to explain the sense of exhilaration that the decision induced in most participants. W. SAFIRE, *supra* note 12, at 677 ("It was also more fun than any of the men there had ever had in their lifetimes") and 680.

[15] *See* note 7 *supra.*

[16] *See* L. HENKIN, HOW NATIONS BEHAVE: LAW AND FOREIGN POLICY *passim,* and particularly pp. 62, 64–66 (2d ed. 1979). Professor Henkin does not discuss the action of Aug. 15, 1971. No representative of the State Department attended the Camp David meeting, although the Department knew about the meeting. W. SAFIRE, *supra* note 12, at 671. Kenneth W. Dam has advanced some "quasi-legal" points and some points of "considerably broader significance" in support of the U.S. action of Aug. 15, 1971, but they do not rebut the conclusion of illegality. K. DAM, *supra* note 10, at 187–88.

rates should be allowed to change freely to accord with changes in the international position of a country. Floating exchange rates would bring about smooth and prompt adjustments to fundamental economic conditions, keep the balance of payments in equilibrium, and give each country autonomy in conducting domestic monetary policies. It would be unfair to describe this view as benign neglect by each country of the interests of other countries. The position of the United States was that the interests of the international community as a whole are best served by the freedom of each country to pursue sound domestic policies without the constraint of attempting to maintain a particular rate of exchange.

The view of European and other countries was that domestic conditions and the exchange rate react on each other because the exchange rate affects domestic developments. Fluctuations in the exchange rate and uncertainty about it can have detrimental effects on domestic economic activity. These countries held that governments should undertake to maintain as much stability in the exchange rate as they can.

The divergence between the views of the United States and other countries was the result of differences in economic circumstances. The economies of other countries are more dependent than the economy of the United States on international trade, and changes in exchange rates affect their economies more sharply.[17] This difference is one of degree, and it does not mean that international trade is of negligible importance for the United States or that its international trade is not a growing proportion of its total economy. Nevertheless, for the United States it was important that its external position should not interfere with the pursuit of domestic economic policy. U.S. officials thought that floating exchange rates would give them this freedom.

While there was still hope that a system of stable, but adjustable, par values could be restored, although with greater legal flexibility than had been possible under the original Articles, the United States favored firmer law in some respects than had prevailed in the past. The United States saw itself as a country that might have a chronic deficit in its balance of payments unless more pressure was applied to other countries to induce them to modify their policies. Therefore, in its presentation to the Committee of the Fund's Board of Governors on Reform of the International Monetary System and Related Matters (the Committee of Twenty), the United States proposed "objective indicators," defined in terms of reserves, that would put the onus on countries in balance-of-payments surplus (or deficit) to adjust their balances of payments. Adjustment might take the form of changes in the exchange rates for their currencies. This system would be made to work by graduated pressures on the member to which the indicators pointed. The pressures would apply without the necessity for decisions by the Fund. The U.S. representatives argued that public and congressional opinion in the United States, and in other countries as well, would prefer such a mechanistic system to a system that depended on the exercise of discretionary powers by the Fund.[18] The United States was

[17] De Vries, *The Inconstant Dollar,* FOREIGN POL'Y, No. 32, Fall 1978, at 161–83.

[18] ECONOMIC REPORT OF PRESIDENT, 1973, *supra* note 7, at 120–31, 160–74. *See also* INTERNATIONAL MONETARY FUND [IMF], INTERNATIONAL MONETARY REFORM: DOCUMENTS

wrong about the preferences of other members, and it received little support for such firm law.

By the time the drafting of the Second Amendment was undertaken, it had become clear that no par value system of any kind would be acceptable for immediate introduction. The United States had to devise other proposals for the protection of its interests as it saw them. In these circumstances, its proposals moved to the opposite extreme. But now, other members demurred because the U.S. position seemed to advocate law that was too soft and to offer no hope for firmness in the future. Negotiations on the drafting of exchange rate provisions reached a deadlock in the Fund.

The Interim Committee of the Board of Governors on the International Monetary System,[19] which succeeded the Committee of Twenty, requested that the United States and France, as the most dedicated advocates of opposing positions on future rate provisions, collaborate on a proposal that all members could accept. The two countries undertook the task of trying to reach agreement on a solution. They worked in "relative secrecy"[20] until their agreement was made known at the summit conference held at Rambouillet in November 1975. The conference was attended by the heads of state and government of France, the Federal Republic of Germany, Italy, Japan, the United Kingdom, and the United States.[21]

V. Present Article IV

Article IV[22] of the present Articles has been drafted substantially in accordance with the spirit and letter of the agreement reached by the United States and France. Article IV allows each member to choose its exchange arrangements and to determine the external value of its currency under those arrangements. This freedom is made subject to obligations relating to a member's behavior, but these obligations, it will be seen, are soft law and softer than the provisions of the original Articles.

The opening language of Article IV, section 1 sounds like the preamble to a resolution of the General Assembly of the United Nations and is out of harmony with the rest of the language of the Articles:

> Recognizing that the essential purpose of the international monetary system is to provide a framework that facilitates the exchange of goods, services, and capital among countries, and that sustains sound economic growth, and that a principal objective is the continuing development of

---

of Committee of Twenty 26–27, 51–52 (1974) [hereinafter cited as Documents of Committee of Twenty]; and Gold, Selected Essays, *supra* note 4, at 182–216.

[19] IMF, Selected Decisions of the International Monetary Fund and Selected Documents, Ninth Issue 306–09 (1981) [hereinafter cited as Selected Decisions]; Gold, *The Fund's Interim Committee on the International Monetary System*, Fin. & Dev., No. 3, 1979, at 32–35.

[20] *Amendments of the Bretton Woods Agreements Act: Hearing Before the Subcomm. on International Finance of the Senate Comm. on Banking, Housing and Urban Affairs*, 94th Cong., 2d Sess. 13 (1976) [hereinafter cited as *Senate Hearings*].

[21] 4 IMF Surv. 350 (1975).

[22] The text of Article IV is reproduced in Appendix A, p. 487 *infra*.

> the orderly underlying conditions that are necessary for financial and economic stability. . . .

The drafting of this language was an exercise in softening the provision in which it appears. The original version as drafted by U.S. and French officials was as follows: "Recognizing that the essential purpose of the international monetary system is to provide a framework that facilitates the exchange of goods, services, and capital among nations, and that a principal continuing objective is to develop orderly underlying conditions which are a prerequisite for financial stability. . . ."

After a working group, consisting of officials of the two members and the General Counsel of the Fund, was formed, the original language and structure of the provision was transformed for a time to read:

> (a) Each member recognizes that the essential function of the international monetary system is to provide a framework that facilitates the exchange of goods, services, and capital among countries, and that a principal objective of the system at all times should be to develop the orderly underlying conditions that are a prerequisite for financial stability.
>
> (b) In order to contribute to the effective functioning of the international monetary system. . . .

This language was then amended by deleting the introductory language of subparagraph (b) shown above in order to eliminate too firm a relationship between subparagraph (a) and the obligations of members set forth in subparagraph (b) after the introductory language.

Finally, the working group ran subparagraphs (a) and (b) together again, and the language returned to a structure that began with the word "Recognizing." The purpose of restoring this structure is obvious: it was to avoid the impression that recognition of the function of the international monetary system was an independent obligation or the source of independent obligations. The participial clause was intended to do no more than introduce or justify the obligations that follow the clause.[23] "Purpose" was substituted for the more normative "function."[24] The final draft of the working group took the following form: "Recognizing that the essential purpose of the international monetary system is to provide a framework that facilitates the exchange of goods, services, and capital among countries, and that a principal objective is the continuing development of orderly underlying conditions, which are a prerequisite for financial stability. . . ."

This draft was modified by the Executive Board and, as modified, has been incorporated in the Articles. The obligations as stated in Article IV, section 1 after the language that begins with the word "Recognizing" are formulated as follows:

[23] The clause could serve, however, to elucidate the obligations if problems of interpretation arose.

[24] The object was also to create an affinity with the "purposes" of Article I even though they are the purposes of the Fund, while the "purpose" in Article IV is that of the international monetary system.

> [E]ach member undertakes to collaborate with the Fund and other members to assure orderly exchange arrangements and to promote a stable system of exchange rates. In particular, each member shall:
>
> (i) endeavor to direct its economic and financial policies toward the objective of fostering orderly economic growth with reasonable price stability, with due regard to its circumstances;
>
> (ii) seek to promote stability by fostering orderly underlying economic and financial conditions and a monetary system that does not tend to produce erratic disruptions;
>
> (iii) avoid manipulating exchange rates or the international monetary system in order to prevent effective balance of payments adjustment or to gain an unfair competitive advantage over other members; and
>
> (iv) follow exchange policies compatible with the undertakings under this Section.

The original language as proposed by U.S. and French officials was dense and attempted to compensate for the softness of obligations with emphatic language and a multiplicity of verbs:

> [E]ach member pledges to collaborate with the Fund and other members to assure orderly exchange arrangements and to promote a stable system of exchange rates. To this end each member in particular (a) undertakes to direct its economic and financial policies toward the objective of fostering orderly economic growth within the context of relative price stability; (b) accepts without reservation the desirability of stability which results from meeting the criteria of orderly underlying economic and financial conditions and of a monetary system that does not tend to produce erratic disruptions; (c) pledges to disavow practices that serve to manipulate the system in order to gain unfair competitive advantage relative to another member or members and (d) agrees to follow financial and exchange policies compatible with these objectives.

VI. Some Soft Provisions in Present Articles

No attempt will be made to define soft law as a genus of law, but some examples of soft law will be drawn from the present Article IV. The classification and illustrations that follow are not meant to be exhaustive.

(1) *The Fund can make recommendations to its members but without the power to insist that the recommendations are binding.* Under one provision:

> To accord with the development of the international monetary system, the Fund by an eighty-five per cent majority of the total voting power, may make provision for general exchange arrangements without limiting the right of members to have exchange arrangements of their choice consistent with the purposes of the Fund and the obligations under Section 1 of this Article.[25]

The representatives of the United States and France who produced the draft on which the final provisions on exchange arrangements are based had proposed the following text: "The Fund may by an 85 per cent majority of

[25] Art. IV, sec. 2(c).

the total voting power modify as appropriate the general exchange arrangements established under this article."

The general exchange arrangements "established" under Article IV, section 2 in the same draft, and therefore subject to the Fund's power to "modify" them, appeared in the following provision:

> Under the present functioning of the system such arrangements may include maintenance by a member of a value for its currency in terms of the special drawing right or other denominator, other than gold, selected by the member; may include maintenance by a group of members of mechanisms under which each member of such group maintains the value of its currency in relation to other members of such group; and may include other exchange arrangements of a member's choice.

The language that would have created the power to modify exchange arrangements was abandoned when it was pointed out that it could be read to permit amendment of the Articles without observance of the procedure for amendment. The text read in that way would have dispensed with the necessity for approval by legislatures.[26] Moreover, the Fund would have been able to compel members to adopt any general exchange arrangements that it favored.

The provision on the choice of exchange arrangements in the Second Amendment is not substantially different from the draft quoted above:

> Under an international monetary system of the kind prevailing on January 1, 1976, exchange arrangements may include (i) the maintenance by a member of a value for its currency in terms of the special drawing right or another denominator, other than gold, selected by the member, or (ii) cooperative arrangements by which members maintain the value of their currencies in relation to the value of the currency or currencies of other members, or (iii) other exchange arrangements of a member's choice.[27]

The substantive differences appear in the final provision on general exchange arrangements. The Fund's power to "modify" them has disappeared, and it has been made clear that the Fund's power to "make provision for them" is without prejudice to the privilege of members to have exchange arrangements of their own choice.

(2) *The Fund is authorized to adopt "specific principles for the guidance of all members" with respect to their exchange rate policies.*[28] The clue to the softness of this provision is the word "guidance," the implication of which is that a member's neglect of a principle is not automatically a breach of obligation.[29] The principles adopted under this authority can be contrasted, for example, with the Fund's authority under another provision to adopt supplementary general principles for the designation of members to receive SDRs when the Fund is asked by an intending transferor of SDRs to designate a transferee.[30] A des-

[26] GOLD, SELECTED ESSAYS, *supra* note 4, at 319–51.

[27] Art. IV, sec. 2(b).

[28] Art. IV, sec. 3(b).

[29] This statement is subject to the caveat that there will be an automatic breach of obligation if the principle repeats an obligation in Article IV. It will be seen that the Fund's guideline A repeats an obligation.

[30] Art. XIX, sec. 5. For the text of the Second Amendment, see 15 ILM 546 (1976).

ignated member's refusal to accept a transfer in accordance with a supplementary general principle would be an automatic breach of obligation.[31] Although a refusal to follow a recommendation is not in itself a breach of obligation, the Fund could decide that, in the circumstances, the neglect of a specific principle of guidance did amount to a breach of the member's obligations under some provision of the Articles on exchange arrangements.

(3) *The conduct required of a member is expressed not as an obligation to achieve a specified objective but as an obligation to make an effort to achieve an objective.*[32] For example, "each member shall . . . (ii) seek to promote stability by fostering orderly underlying economic and financial conditions and a monetary system that does not tend to produce erratic disruptions."[33] Even an obligation to make an effort may be subject to broad qualification, as is illustrated by the elements italicized in the following provision: "each member shall . . . (i) *endeavor* to *direct* its economic and financial policies toward the objective of fostering orderly economic growth with reasonable price stability, *with due regard to its circumstances.*"[34]

The two obligations in subparagraphs (i) and (ii) are drafted in a style that is in contrast to the other two obligations in the chain of subparagraphs: "(iii) avoid manipulating exchange rates or the international monetary system in order to prevent balance of payments adjustment or to gain an unfair competitive advantage over other members; and (iv) follow exchange policies compatible with the undertakings under this Section." In these provisions, however uncertain their application may be, the verbs ("avoid," "follow") are firm, compared with the verbs in subparagraphs (i) and (ii). The explanation of the softness of subparagraphs (i) and (ii) is that they can have a direct effect on domestic policies. Subparagraphs (iii) and (iv), however, deal directly with exchange policies. It was more difficult to argue in relation to these policies that members' obligations or the Fund's authority should be softened.

(4) *The character of an obligation may make it impossible to recognize by means of objective criteria that a breach of the obligation is occurring.* A judgment of the Fund is always necessary before it can be determined whether or not a member is performing the obligation. The two obligations in subparagraphs (i) and (ii) quoted in (3) above are obvious examples of this category, but even the other two obligations, in subparagraphs (iii) and (iv), and the general obligation of collaboration in the text that precedes the subparagraphs, though not formulated in terms of effort, depend on similar subjective judgments by the Fund before it can be determined that a member is or is not observing its obligations.

[31] Art. XIX, sec. 4; Art. XXIII, sec. 2(a).

[32] A distinction is made sometimes between obligations of result and obligations of conduct. *See, e.g.*, Wyatt, *New Legal Order, or Old,* 7 EUR. L. REV. 147, 152–54 (1982).

[33] Art. IV, sec. 1.

[34] *Ibid.* Richard W. Edwards, Jr., has concluded from public statements of U.S. and French officials and from private inquiries that, in their preparatory work and in later negotiations, the officials did not develop examples of conduct that would be considered violations of subparagraphs (i) and (ii). Edwards, *The Currency Exchange Rate Provisions of the Proposed Amended Articles of Agreement of the International Monetary Fund,* 70 AJIL 722, 737 (1976).

VII. Decisions to Develop Substantive Law

The Fund has authority to develop the present substantive law of exchange arrangements in various ways, even though some of the developments would continue to be soft law. It has been seen already that the Fund can adopt specific principles for the guidance of members' exchange rate policies and can recommend general exchange arrangements. Decisions of either kind would give greater precision to the Fund's function of surveillance, although the legal character of these decisions would not differ from the analysis that has been advanced earlier. The Fund can decide to specify the conduct it expects of members under their obligation to collaborate with it and with other members. The experience of the past shows that decisions of this kind under general obligations of collaboration can have great weight. Even when the decisions are not formulated as obligations, members tend to consider themselves bound to comply with the decisions.[35] In addition to these powers, the Fund can decide to call into existence[36] the par value system that is codified in Schedule C.

The Second Amendment has increased to a remarkable extent the number of decisions for which a special majority is necessary. A special majority is a specified proportion of the total voting power in contrast to the majority of the votes cast, which is the basic majority. The original Articles required special majorities for 9 categories of decisions. The First Amendment increased the number to 21 and the Second Amendment to more than 50, although not all these decisions regulate the conduct of members.[37]

The two special majorities now are 70 percent and 85 percent of the total voting power.[38] The motives for the choice of these two majorities and for their application to categories of decisions were varied and complex, but among the motives was the desire on the part of the United States, the European Community, developing members as a class, and perhaps less visible groupings to have the strength to veto proposed decisions.

The United States is the only single member that can veto proposals to take decisions for which 85 percent of the total voting power is necessary. From time to time, other members have been critical of a power of veto that can be exercised by a single member, and they have negotiated successfully for the requirement of a high majority that would give their group a power to block proposals. The United States has been outspoken in explaining the importance it attaches to the majority of 85 percent for decisions on exchange arrangements:

> These new exchange rate provisions are of critical importance both for the system as a whole and for the United States. They focus on the essential need to achieve underlying stability in economic affairs if exchange stability is to be achieved. They provide a flexible framework for the evolution of exchange arrangements consistent with this broad focus.

[35] Gold, Selected Essays, *supra* note 4, at 34–41, 65, 96, 115, 390–409, 558.

[36] Art. IV, sec. 4.

[37] On the whole subject, see J. Gold, Voting Majorities in the Fund: Effects of Second Amendment of the Articles (IMF Pamphlet Series No. 20, 1977).

[38] *Id.* at 30–33.

> And they help to ensure that the United States is not again forced into the position of maintaining a value for its currency that is out of line with underlying competitive realities and that costs the United States jobs and growth due to loss of exports, increased imports and a shift of production facilities overseas. Under the new provisions, the United States will have a controlling voice in the future adoption of general exchange arrangements for the system as a whole; and will have full freedom in the selection of exchange arrangements to be applied by the United States, regardless of the general arrangements adopted, so long as it meets its general IMF obligations.[39]

A "controlling voice" can prevent, but cannot ensure, the adoption of decisions. The majority of 85 percent of total voting power is necessary for decisions by the Fund to recommend general exchange arrangements and to call into operation the par value system of Schedule C. The other two categories of decision that have been mentioned above can be taken with a majority of the votes cast. These categories are decisions to adopt specific principles for the guidance of members with respect to their exchange rate policies and decisions that make concrete the obligation to collaborate with the Fund and other members to ensure the existence of orderly exchange arrangements and the promotion of a stable system of exchange rates.

The difference between the majorities for decisions to recommend exchange arrangements and to establish specific principles for the guidance of members with respect to their exchange rate policies is striking. The explanation is that the 85 percent majority of total voting power for the former decisions is a survival from the original draft prepared by the American and French officials and quoted in section VI above. That draft may have been inspired by the intention to impose a firmer obligation on members than the eventual obligation.

A special majority was never proposed for the adoption of specific principles, perhaps because "firm surveillance" without principles was not credible, and the need for a special majority could result in the veto of all proposed principles. The use that the Fund could make of the obligation to collaborate was not discussed at any time in the drafting of Article IV.

VIII. U.S. Views of Article IV

The present Article IV is predominantly in accord with the position taken by the United States in the negotiation of the exchange rate provisions of the Second Amendment. U.S. officials and congressional committees[40] have expressed their reactions to Article IV in numerous statements. They have stressed the substitution of the influence of markets on exchange rates for the determination of exchange rates by governments. At the same time, they have explained that governments remain responsible for their international behav-

[39] U.S. National Advisory Council on International Monetary and Financial Policies, Special Report to the President and to the Congress on Amendment of the Articles of Agreement of the International Monetary Fund and on an Increase in Quotas in the International Monetary Fund 23 (1976).

[40] *Senate Hearings, supra* note 20, at 2–5, 19–20.

ior in monetary affairs and that the Fund retains a central position as arbiter or monitor of the international monetary system.

To questions about the effectiveness of the new provisions, spokesmen for the U.S. administration responded that they did not want "supranational government" by an international organization empowered to run the U.S. economy. There should be no substantial limitation on the sovereign right of nations to determine their policies. Nevertheless, these spokesmen drew metaphors from the law to explain the character of the new provisions. Detailed codes of behavior were not included in the Articles because the Articles were a constitution and not a contract. General principles could emerge by a common law approach to individual cases. U.S. officials insisted that the new provisions, although not comparable to the grand design of the original Articles, did constitute an international monetary system. They explained that the critics who rejected this view did so for reasons of nostalgia.[41] "Say not thou, What is the *cause* that the former days were better than these? for thou dost not inquire wisely concerning this."[42]

The metaphors of constitution and common law imply firm rules of law. For the soft law of Article IV to generate firm rules of law, fundamental changes would have to occur in the attitudes that fashioned Article IV. One author, who later became a senior U.S. official with responsibilities in international economic affairs, has explained his opposition to attempts to write (or rewrite) a constitution to govern international monetary matters. His view is more compatible with the rejection of limitations on the exercise of sovereignty than with the vision of a constitution or common law.

> [T]he world economy is very asymmetric in its functioning. For technical reasons, it is both likely and desirable that one or a few currencies will emerge with special status in market transactions. Even when this fact is fully known and acceptable, it cannot always be formally acknowledged and sanctified in treaties, in part for reasons of status touched on earlier in the essay. There thus emerges a discrepancy between what governments say in formal negotiations and what they do, or are willing happily to accept, in day-to-day operations—a discrepancy between their stated

[41] *Id.* at 132–33, 135, 137. *See also To Provide for Amendment of the Bretton Woods Agreements Act: Hearings Before the Subcomm. on International Trade, Investment and Monetary Policy of the House Comm. on Banking, Currency and Housing,* 94th Cong., 2d Sess. 10–12, 37 (1976); *International Monetary Fund Amendments: Hearings Before the Senate Comm. on Foreign Relations,* 94th Cong., 2d Sess. 15–16, 41 (1976); *Briefing on the International Monetary Fund: Hearing Before the Subcomm. on International Trade, Investment and Monetary Policy of the House Comm. on Banking, Currency and Housing,* 94th Cong., 2d Sess. 4 (1976). A similar note is heard within the EMS:

> The institutional framework required for the functioning of the EMS as an exchange arrangement is perfectly adequate for the time being, inclusive of the virtually unlimited credit facilities. Any further institutional steps would amount to transferring certain powers of the participating central banks to a supranational institution, in effect to the nucleus of a European central bank. But essential preconditions for any such shift of powers are lacking, especially in the political field, where the unresolved question of the responsibilities and competence of such an institution and its relations with national and Community bodies is involved.

Karl Otto Poehl, President of the Bundesbank, speech to European Management Forum, Davos (Feb. 3, 1982).

[42] *Ecclesiastes* 7:10.

> preferences and their revealed preferences. In the monetary arena this discrepancy can be observed in attitudes toward the U.S. dollar, both as an intervention currency and as a reserve currency, in attitudes toward the flexibility of exchange rates, and (within Europe) in attitudes toward European monetary unification.
>
> Formal arrangements induce sovereign states to insist on formal symmetry in status, partly to cater to nationalist sentiment at home. Informal arrangements carry no such compulsion. To the extent that asymmetries of treatment are important for efficient functioning, informal arrangements are therefore likely to be superior to formal arrangements that emerge from a negotiating process. In the international monetary sphere, an English-style constitution, built up through a series of acceptable practices, may be both easier to attain and even superior in content to a fully negotiated American-style constitution. Indeed, precisely such informal arrangements seem to mark the current monetary regime of managed flexibility of exchange rates, which few (if any) countries are willing to accept formally but which most (if not all) fully accept in practice.[43]

Skepticism about the usefulness of a negotiated solution in the days when proposed amendments were first put forward did not prevail against the desire for legality, which motivated the United States and some other countries. Even the passage quoted in the preceding paragraph does not abandon legal metaphor. A constitution might evolve, but it should be largely unwritten. A return to legality made a negotiated solution unavoidable, but soft law offered a compromise with skepticism.

A different explanation for the soft law of Article IV can be advanced with some assurance. The Second Amendment was clearly a less comprehensive reform than the one that the Committee of Twenty had sketched in its *Outline of Reform.*[44] At first, the drafters of the Second Amendment assumed that an amendment of the Articles would apply during an interim period only. In the course of this period, a definitive amendment would be negotiated and would become effective after the period ended. Whether the period was predetermined or indefinite, it would be subject to termination by the Fund. These assumptions were abandoned in favor of the negotiation of an amendment that could be permanent because it would permit the evolution of the international monetary system without further amendment. The effect of this change in attitude was to impart a less than peremptory character to the formulation of provisions that would regulate exchange arrangements in the immediate situation. This approach to the provisions was preferred by members whether or not they expected that radical changes would be made in the future. Proposals for evolutionary changes in the regulation of exchange arrangements could be vetoed unless they commanded widespread support among all interests, because of the necessity for high majorities.

[43] Cooper, *Prolegomena to the choice of an international monetary system,* 29 INT'L ORG. 63, 95–96 (1975).

[44] IMF, PROPOSED SECOND AMENDMENT TO THE ARTICLES OF AGREEMENT OF THE INTERNATIONAL MONETARY FUND, A REPORT BY THE EXECUTIVE DIRECTORS TO THE BOARD OF GOVERNORS 1 (1976), *reprinted in* 15 ILM 501 (1976).

IX. Deterrence of Breach under Article IV

The original Articles were a greater deterrent to a breach of obligation because floating was an obvious violation of a fundamental principle of the par value system, while a breach of obligation under the Second Amendment is not recognizable without a decision of the Fund. This difference is not the only distinction that can be made in comparing the deterrent effect of the two versions of the Articles.

Nothing in the present Article IV requires a member to obtain the advance approval of the Fund for the member's choice of its exchange arrangements or for the member's determination of the external value of its currency.[45] The contrast between the par value system and the current Article IV is obvious. Under the par value system, a member was required to reach agreement with the Fund on an initial par value, to consult the Fund before changing a par value, and normally to obtain the Fund's concurrence in a proposed change.

A decision of the Fund that a member is not observing its obligations under the present Article IV would have to be based on policies and practices for which the member had not been required to get the Fund's approval. A requirement of prior approval by an international organization puts greater pressure on members to respect international standards than the possibility that the organization might investigate the consistency with international standards of policies or practices after they have been instituted.

This contrast between what may be called the a priori and the a posteriori approaches has been noted often in comparisons of the procedures of the Fund and the contracting parties to the General Agreement on Tariffs and Trade (GATT). The firmer effect of the a priori approach explains why the Committee of Twenty recommended that members of the Fund should undertake voluntarily not to introduce or intensify trade or other current account measures for balance-of-payments purposes without a finding by the Fund that the balance of payments justified the measures. A member would request such a finding in advance of the introduction or intensification of the measures whenever possible. The Fund's jurisdiction to approve or disapprove restrictions was, and still is, confined to restrictions that are applied directly to payments and transfers for current international transactions. The voluntary pledge would have covered restrictions applied directly to trade and other current account transactions. The pledge never became effective. An undoubted reason for this failure was the firmer character of the a priori principle.[46] This reason explains even more obviously the rejection of a proposal to write into the Second Amendment a provision resembling the pledge. If a member did not request approval under such a provision, or if the member introduced or intensified restrictions notwithstanding the Fund's disapproval of them, the member would be in violation of its obligations under the Articles.

[45] This comment applies only to Article IV, section 1, and not to restrictions, multiple currency practices, or discriminatory currency arrangements under section 2 or section 3 of Article VIII.

[46] Gold, *Recent International Decisions to Prevent Restrictions on Trade and Payments,* 9 J. World Trade L. 63 (1975).

This conduct would not have had the quality of invalidity under the voluntary pledge.

The a priori approach is firmer in operation because it enables an international organization to refuse the required approval of a proposed action without the necessity for a finding that the member is in default. Under the a posteriori system, however, the organization must make such a finding or at least a finding that will be censorious. An international organization is often reluctant to take decisions of this character. Such a decision faces the organization with a dilemma. It must decide what to do next if the member persists in the practice to which the organization has objected or the organization must reconcile itself to a reputation for ineptitude if it does nothing. The Fund has been reluctant in the extreme to adopt censorious decisions.[47] Members might conclude, in the knowledge that such decisions would not be adopted, that they were safe from censure in following practices that were incompatible with the policies of the organization.

X. Some Safeguards against Softness of Article IV

The Second Amendment includes provisions that were intended to be safeguards against the disorders that might develop because of the freedom of members to choose their exchange arrangements and to determine the exchange value of their currencies. These provisions were proposed by the United States in order to get the assurance that it would not be forced again into its former predicament. It had come to analyze that situation as one in which it had been the victim of the freedom that other members had been able to exercise.

The Council

A new organ, the Council, was proposed by the United States in order to give political muscle to the Fund. The Council can be called into existence by a decision of the Board of Governors taken with an 85 percent majority of the total voting power.[48] This organ would occupy a position in the hierarchy of organs below the Board of Governors and above the Executive Board. The Council would be composed on the model of the Executive Board: the number of Councillors would be equal to the number of Executive Directors on the Executive Board and would be appointed by the same constituencies of members that appoint or elect Executive Directors. The Council, composed in this way, would be better fitted to debate and decide issues than the much larger Board of Governors, to which each member appoints a Governor and an Alternate.[49] The Fund would be strengthened because each Councillor would be a Governor, minister in the government of a member, or a person of comparable rank. Persons in these positions, it was assumed, would bring additional strength to the Fund because they would be bolder in their judgments than Executive Directors, but this assumption has been challenged. The

[47] GOLD, SELECTED ESSAYS, *supra* note 4, at 148–216.

[48] Art. XII, sec. 1.

[49] Art. XII, sec. 2(a).

opponents have argued that Governors might be more respectful of their colleagues and more tolerant of each other's policies because of their insight into political difficulties.

The terms of reference of the Council would be to supervise the management and adaptation of the international monetary system, including the continuing operation of the adjustment process and developments in global liquidity; and in this connection the Council would review developments in the transfer of real resources to developing countries. The Council would exercise such powers within these terms of reference as were delegated to it by the Board of Governors. In addition, the Council would consider proposals to amend the Articles.

Originally, it was proposed that the Council would come into existence immediately when the Second Amendment took effect.[50] Developing members disliked the idea of the Council because, as an organ, it would be able to take decisions of the Fund in the exercise of powers.[51] Many of these members feared that, as less powerful countries, they would be subjected to adverse decisions by the Council, while more powerful countries would escape this treatment. Developing members were successful in proposing that the Council should begin to function only when a decision was taken to call it into existence, and that the majority required for that decision should be 85 percent of the total voting power. That majority would assure developing members of a veto if a decision were to be proposed.

The Interim Committee of the Board of Governors on the International Monetary System has been appointed by the Board of Governors to function until the Council is activated. The Committee's terms of reference[52] are similar to those of the Council, but the Committee is not an organ of the Fund. The Committee cannot take decisions or bind members, because it has no authority under the Articles to exercise powers of the Fund. The Committee's authority is confined to recommendations. The organs of the Fund treat these recommendations with respect because of the rank of the persons who compose the Committee, but the conclusion is inescapable that numerous members prefer the Committee to the Council because the Committee cannot take decisions. It is legally possible for an organ, when considering a proposed decision, to modify a recommendation or to propose reconsideration of it by the Committee. There may be no great likelihood that the Executive Board would react to a recommendation in this way, but developing members have preferred not to surrender this legal possibility.

Surveillance

One of the main safeguards against the potential dangers of the soft law on exchange arrangements was intended to be the function that the Fund must perform as an invigilator. Under section 3 of Article IV, the Fund must oversee the international monetary system in order to ensure its effective

[50] GOLD, SELECTED ESSAYS, *supra* note 4, at 238–91.

[51] Schedule D (*see* note 30 *supra*).

[52] SELECTED DECISIONS, *supra* note 19, at 308–09.

operation. In addition, the Fund must oversee the compliance of each member with its obligations under Article IV, section 1. In order to fulfill these functions, the Fund must exercise "firm surveillance" over the exchange rate policies of members, and it must adopt specific principles for the guidance of all members with respect to those policies. The adjective "firm" was retained even though it might suggest uneasiness about the forcefulness of Article IV and even though it might seem to reduce the seriousness of all other functions of the Fund because a similar adjective was not attached to them.

The Fund has adopted detailed decisions on the procedures for surveillance,[53] but repeated appeals are made for firmer surveillance. Almost invariably, these appeals are coupled with warnings about the need for caution. Persuasion, it is said, should be the aim and not prescription. Members have defended the discordance between their appeals and their caveats with explanations that the powers of the Fund are limited.[54]

A consequence of these attitudes is to place major and increasing emphasis on the activities of the Managing Director.[55] His functions in surveillance are indispensable. He exercises influence, not only because of his position and personality, but also because in his approaches to members, however discreet, they understand that he is expressing the views of the Executive Board on exchange rate policies that he has distilled from its debates on general policies and individual consultations. Nevertheless, surveillance, to be firm in its insistence on promoting both the national and the international interest, must involve an adequate role for the Executive Board and a willingness by it to take decisions on the situation of each member. What international lawyers have called the judgment of peers and the mobilization of shame are necessary pressures.[56] Governments can be influenced if they know that the Fund is willing to exercise these pressures. Only an organ composed of persons appointed or elected by members can apply the pressures, because governments assume that these persons are stating the views of other governments. At the present time, the only organ that could find it practicable to take decisions to apply pressures is the Executive Board. The Board of Governors is too large and meets only annually; the Council does not exist; the Interim Committee is not an organ and cannot take decisions.

Even when the debate of the Executive Board is reached as the last stage in consultations under Article IV, the Executive Board completes its debate with "conclusions," in contrast to the "decisions" it takes on other items placed on its agenda.[57] The word "conclusions" was chosen because it sounded less like an assertion of authority than "decisions." Furthermore, the Executive Board does not adopt conclusions that it purports to have formulated itself.

[53] *Id.* at 10–15; IMF, ANNUAL REPORT 1982, at 128–32.

[54] *See* IMF, 1980 SUMMARY PROC. 39–40, 94–97. *See also* IMF, ANNUAL REPORT 1981, at 62.

[55] SELECTED DECISIONS, *supra* note 19, at 14–15; IMF, ANNUAL REPORT 1981, at 62; ANNUAL REPORT 1982, at 130.

[56] GOLD, SELECTED ESSAYS, *supra* note 4, at 151–53. THE EFFECTIVENESS OF INTERNATIONAL DECISIONS (Stephen M. Schwebel ed. 1971).

[57] SELECTED DECISIONS, *supra* note 19, at 14.

It implicitly endorses as the conclusions of its debate the summing up by the Managing Director as Chairman of the Executive Board.

The conclusions in an actual consultation with a member under Article IV were published as a recent example in December 1981, with deletion of the name of the member.[58] The conclusions are reproduced in Appendix B to this article. Nowhere in these conclusions is there a statement of the views of the Executive Board as such. "Many" or "most" Executive Directors are mentioned as holding a particular view. Other references are made to "Executive Directors," followed it is true in one instance by "the Directors," but never is it stated that all Executive Directors, or Executive Directors with a necessary majority of the voting power, have agreed on any one of the conclusions.[59] A member might regard conclusions formulated in this way as a compendium of views on the member's position but not as the collective judgment of an organ of the Fund.[60]

Mr. Jacques de Larosière, the Managing Director of the Fund, has said that consultations have succeeded in dissuading members from resort to abusive practices:

> The question of exchange rates is of central concern for the Fund and its surveillance activities. When a member's exchange rate is at a level which may cause problems, the Fund initiates consultations with that member. While these consultations are discreet, they can be effective. The sanctions available to the Fund are, of course, limited; but the dissuasive effect on a member of an open conflict with the Fund over its exchange rate should not be underestimated. Deliberate manipulation of rates to gain unfair competitive advantage has not become a feature of the system.[61]

The effectiveness of the present law, and of practice under it, does not depend on the Fund's so-called sanctions, which are not limited,[62] because the Fund has rarely invoked them. If obligations cannot be formulated in language that will make breach obvious when it occurs, effectiveness will depend on the explicit expression of censorious judgments by peers whenever censure is justified.[63]

Principles for Guidance of Members

The Fund must adopt "specific principles for the guidance of all members with respect" to their exchange rate policies,[64] but although firm guidance

[58] Brau, *The consultation process of the Fund,* FIN. & DEV., No. 4, 1981, at 13, 16.

[59] It will be apparent also that these conclusions are approbatory.

[60] The Managing Director's views on why the surveillance exercised by the Fund is not stronger are reported in some detail at pp. 21–22 of CHAMBRE NATIONALE DES CONSEILLERS FINANCIERS, L'AJUSTEMENT ÉCONOMIQUE INTERNATIONAL (Paris 1982).

[61] Jacques de Larosière, April 6, 1981, 10 IMF SURV. 104 (1981).

[62] GOLD, SELECTED ESSAYS, *supra* note 4, at 148–81.

[63] The Executive Board, in a decision of April 9, 1982, approved the continuation of surveillance procedures in the light of the Managing Director's summing up of the Executive Board's debate. IMF, ANNUAL REPORT 1982, at 128–32. The summing up is an illuminating account of numerous aspects of surveillance. In the course of it, the Managing Director said: "[I]t is important for members to cooperate by taking seriously into account, in their national process of decision making, the views expressed and conclusions reached by the Board. . . ." *Id.* at 129.

[64] Art. IV, sec. 3(b).

could compensate to some extent for soft law, the forces that produce soft law may be responsible for soft guidance also. A U.S. spokesman has made this tendency apparent in contesting the argument that precise guidelines should have been included in the Second Amendment. The Articles were a constitution and should have the elasticity necessary for adapting practice to changing conditions, but precision was to be avoided in rules of practice as well:

> [M]ore importantly, irrespective of where they might be embodied, I do not agree that the IMF should delineate hard and detailed rules by which each member's performance with respect to exchange policies should be judged. It is in my view neither appropriate nor possible that this important Fund surveillance work through the application of detailed rules and precise formulas. We do not have the capability, the experience or the knowledge, to develop such a set of rules to be applied across a broad spectrum of individual national situations.
>
> It is particularly difficult to apply rigid formulas equitably to economies that differ as profoundly as in the IMF membership where the gross national product of the largest member is 60,000 times as large as that of the smallest member; where some members have no capital markets while others have highly developed and sophisticated markets; where economic structure and elasticities of price and income can vary widely; and where the relative importance of international transactions to domestic economies differs greatly. Rigid rules and formulas simply won't work in such situations.[65]

In some respects, the present guidelines are softer, because they are less detailed and less precise, than the guidelines for the management of floating exchange rates that the Fund adopted on June 13, 1974,[66] before the Second Amendment was drafted. That decision was adopted at a time when exchange arrangements and exchange rates were inconsistent with the Articles, and when the Fund's efforts to minimize disorder were based on the general obligation of members "to collaborate with the Fund to promote exchange stability, to maintain orderly exchange arrangements with other members, and to avoid competitive exchange alterations."[67] The guidelines of 1974 were influenced by the expectation that it would be desirable and possible to establish a system of stable, but adjustable, par values, with legalized floating in some circumstances. The limitation of the 1974 guidelines to currencies that were not pegged in some way was inspired by this expectation.

The Fund, acting under Article IV of the present Articles, has announced three principles for the guidance of all members with respect to their exchange rate policies. These original principles have not been amended or augmented:

> A. A member shall avoid manipulating exchange rates or the international monetary system in order to prevent effective balance of pay-

[65] *Guidelines for Exchange Market Intervention: Hearing Before the Subcomm. on International Economics of the Joint Economic Comm.*, 94th Cong., 2d Sess. 38 (1976) (statement of Edwin H. Yeo, III, Under Secretary for Monetary Affairs, U.S. Dep't of the Treasury).

[66] IMF, SELECTED DECISIONS OF THE INTERNATIONAL MONETARY FUND AND SELECTED DOCUMENTS, EIGHTH ISSUE 21–30 (1976).

[67] Art. IV, sec. 4(a) (of original Articles and First Amendment; *see* note 9 *supra*).

ments adjustment or to gain an unfair competitive advantage over other members.

B. A member should intervene in the exchange market if necessary to counter disorderly conditions which may be characterized inter alia by disruptive short-term movements in the exchange value of its currency.

C. Members should take into account in the intervention policies the interests of other members, including those of the countries in whose currencies they intervene.[68]

In this short list, guideline A is drafted to conform with subparagraph (iii) of Article IV, section 1 and adds nothing to it. Only this guideline contains a peremptory verb ("shall avoid"). Economists have shown that the issues raised by Article IV, section 1 are numerous and complex, so that the absence of agreement should occasion no surprise.[69] The verbs of the other guidelines are hortatory ("should intervene," "should take into account"). The guidelines, whether peremptory or hortatory, are not self-executing. The Fund, which has the ultimate power of interpretation, has not clarified them. Two manifestations of softness become apparent: the concept of guidance is inherently soft, and it can give rise to specific principles that also are soft. It is not surprising that members resist the derivation of firm principles from soft provisions.

Guideline B: Intervention. Of the three guidelines, the practice that is the subject of guideline B has provoked most debate and least agreement. This principle is an echo of the statement in the Rambouillet Declaration that "our monetary authorities will act to counter disorderly market conditions or erratic fluctuations in exchange rates."[70] The language can be traced back at least as far as the joint statement by the Chairman of the U.S. Federal Reserve Board and the Secretary of the U.S. Treasury on July 18, 1973 that the United States would undertake active intervention at whatever times and in whatever amounts that were considered appropriate for maintaining orderly market conditions.[71]

Guideline B is formulated so as to avoid any implication that there is a "right" exchange rate or an obligation to defend a particular exchange rate. The guideline does not mention the "target zones" for exchange rates that were the subject of one of the guidelines of June 13, 1974. The earlier decision noted that medium-term norms or target zones for exchange rates might be advantageous. The decision recognized that in some circumstances a member might wish to consult the Fund about a target zone and its adaptation to changing circumstances. The Fund had a role in defining the target zone. If the Fund considered the target zone to be within the range of reasonable estimates of the medium-term norm for the exchange rate, the member was

[68] SELECTED DECISIONS, *supra* note 19, at 11–12.

[69] Richard N. Cooper, in THE NEW INTERNATIONAL MONETARY SYSTEM 69, 69–71 (Robert A. Mundell & Jacques J. Polak eds. 1977) (and *see generally* pp. 53–108).

[70] 4 IMF SURV. 350 (1975).

[71] DEP'T TREASURY NEWS, No. S253, 1978.

to be free to move toward the target zone even though the other guidelines would not justify measures for this purpose. Moreover, if the exchange rate of a member's currency moved outside what the Fund considered to be the range of reasonable estimates of the medium-term norm to an extent that, in the view of the Fund, was likely to be harmful to other members, the Fund would consult with the member, and, in the light of the consultation, might encourage the member to modify its policies.

The U.S. spokesman who has been quoted above on the subject of guidelines went on to discuss target zones as follows:

> Nor would I agree with those who would call on the Fund to attempt to determine a set of "target" exchange rates toward which each nation's policies should be directed. There are those who believe that a comparison of statistical data on prices or costs in individual countries can reveal appropriate exchange rates. That approach is subject to insurmountable difficulties, both theoretical and practical. While it may indicate that some rates are inappropriate, it cannot be depended on to indicate what rates are proper. It is tantamount to continuous renegotiation of a par value system, based on statistics which are of necessity both partial in coverage and backward-looking in approach. In practice, it may prove to be nothing more than a veiled approach to a return to fixed rates.[72]

Notwithstanding the forcefulness of this statement, some economists continue to be, or have become, attracted to the idea of target zones. These economists seek a stability that is not being achieved by the freedom now exercised by members, but without recommending a par value system.

No authoritative definition exists of the expression "disorderly conditions" in guideline B, or "erratic disruptions" in Article IV, or "erratic fluctuations" in the Rambouillet Declaration. The imprecision of these concepts has enabled the United States to make changes in its policy on exchange rates while purporting always to be making no change because it was adhering to the same policy of readiness to intervene, if necessary, to counter disorderly conditions.

The Carter administration took a series of steps in 1978 that amounted, in effect, to an active policy on the exchange rate for the U.S. dollar.[73] Each step was explained as a move to counteract disorderly conditions in the ex-

[72] *See* note 65 *supra.*

[73] On Jan. 4, 1978, the United States declared that the Treasury's Exchange Stabilization Fund and the swap network would be employed actively in joint intervention with foreign central banks in order to check speculation and reestablish order in the exchange markets. DEP'T TREASURY NEWS, *supra* note 71. The Bundesbank issued a parallel statement. 7 IMF SURV. 1 (1978). On March 13, the monetary authorities of the United States and the Federal Republic of Germany announced that on occasion in the recent past disorder had occurred in the exchange markets, including excessively rapid movements in exchange rates that went beyond what was justified by underlying economic conditions. Both authorities asserted that they would continue to take forceful and cooperative action to counter disorderly conditions in the exchange markets, for which purpose resources were available and would be used. On April 19, 1978, the U.S. Treasury Department announced a series of monthly public auctions of gold, and declared that it planned to study the sale of gold against deutsche mark as a means of obtaining that currency for use in countering disorderly conditions in foreign exchange markets. DEP'T OF THE TREASURY, ANNUAL REPORT OF THE TREASURY ON THE STATE OF THE FINANCES, 1978, at 465.

change markets. The United States took the most dramatic step on November 1, 1978. It announced various measures that it was taking to strengthen the U.S. dollar, including mobilization of the equivalent of U.S. $30 billion in international resources. According to the announcement, recent movements in the exchange rate of the dollar had exceeded any decline related to fundamental factors. The United States, in cooperation with Germany, Japan, and Switzerland, would "intervene in a forceful and coordinated manner in the amounts required to correct the situation."[74]

The Secretary of the U.S. Treasury described the action as "a shift in intervention practices," but one that was aimed at correcting a particular situation. The United States was not "attempting to peg exchange rates or establish targets or push the dollar beyond levels which reflect the fundamental economic and financial realities."[75]

In these and other statements, the U.S. monetary authorities were explaining that there was no change in their policy on the exchange rate for the dollar, but some observers noted that there was at least a greater determination to apply that policy, and that, even if the authorities had no predetermined view of the right exchange rate for the dollar, they might be taking a view on the development of a wrong rate.

After the Reagan administration assumed office, the Treasury announced, in mid-April 1981, that the U.S. authorities had adopted an approach of minimal intervention and that they would intervene only when necessary to counter conditions of disorder in the exchange market.[76] Once again, the same concept of countering disorder was cited, but it was clear that a change in policy had occurred. The Under Secretary of the Treasury for Monetary Affairs, on May 4, 1981, interpreted the policy of the United States of intervening only when necessary to counter conditions of disorder in the market as a return to the pre-1978 concept of intervention.[77] He was skeptical about a more active intervention policy because it would have to rest on the assumption that a few officials were more expert in determining what the exchange rate for the dollar should or should not be than the myriad parties who were dealing in the markets. Furthermore, intervention in the past might have had a destabilizing effect by preventing the dollar from attaining its equilibrium level and by contributing to the steepness of a later decline. U.S. officials have opposed intervention even if official intervention could produce more orderly conditions in exchange markets, because intervention could not change fundamental economic trends. Reports of the Federal Reserve Bank of New York confirm that since the spring of 1981 there has been minimal intervention in the exchange markets on behalf of the U.S. monetary au-

[74] Joint Statement by W. Michael Blumenthal, Secretary of the Treasury, and G. William Miller, Chairman of the Federal Reserve Board, Federal Reserve Press Release, Nov. 1, 1978, *reprinted in* 64 FED. RESERVE BULL., Nov. 1978, at 917.

[75] *The Dollar Rescue Operations and their Domestic Implications: Hearings Before the Subcomm. on International Economics of the Joint Economic Comm.*, 95th Cong., 2d Sess. 13 (1978).

[76] Wall St. J., Sept. 4, 1981, at 6.

[77] *Statement before the Joint Economic Committee,* DEP'T TREASURY NEWS, No. R.158, 1981, at 18.

thorities, although in the quarter ended October 31, 1982, intervention on four occasions amounted to a total of slightly more than $100 million.[78]

The intervention policy of the United States demonstrates that members adopt their own understanding of disorderly conditions and that the concept is sufficiently imprecise to permit sharp changes in policy. One American official has written:

> Disorder, to be sure, is mainly in the eye of the beholder. Rapid rate changes, widening bid and ask spreads, lengthening price gaps from one transaction to the next, a fading away of bids or offers, the degeneration of trading into a one-way market have all been cited as instances of disorder. None need necessarily and inevitably be so regarded.[79]

The refusal of successive U.S. administrations to explain their understanding assures them of flexibility. The Fund's guideline B also avoids a definition, but gives one tentative example of disorderly conditions. They "may" be characterized "inter alia" by disruptive short-term movements in the exchange value of a currency. The example is tautological because of the word "disruptive." A fundamental problem is whether a line can be drawn between the uncertainty that monetary authorities wish to maintain about their intentions in order to make intervention effective and a clarification of guideline B that prevents it from lapsing into inanition.

In some countries a broader view is taken of disorderly conditions than the undefined, but narrow, view taken by the United States, which seems to be confined to conditions provoked by incontrovertible emergencies. The volatility of exchange rates and its consequences are criticized in these other countries.[80] Support is expressed for a more active policy on intervention and for more extensive international understandings on such a policy.[81]

[78] Once again, U.S. officials denied that there was any change of policy, although it was explained that the policy had been misunderstood as one of intervention only at times of "extreme market disorder," while "the actual definition of the guidelines has always been much looser." The United States seemed, however, to be expanding its holdings of foreign currencies. *The U.S. Widens Currency-Trading Role,* N.Y. Times, Dec. 13, 1982, at D1, D10.

[79] Henry C. Wallich (member, Board of Governors of the Federal Reserve System), *Exchange Market Intervention: Issues and Views,* J. Com., Aug. 12 and 13, 1982, at 4A.

[80]

> When the world first moved over to floating exchange rates, firms engaged in international trade seemed to manage surprisingly well with the additional uncertainty. More recently, with the increased volatility of exchange markets, complaints from industry have multiplied. The present degree of volatility inevitably creates great difficulty for firms in planning their sales strategy in foreign markets and complicates investment decisions. It is difficult or impossible for firms to hedge against such uncertainty; and even when they can, it no doubt entails significant expense. Exchange rate volatility must therefore represent a barrier to international trade, with effects not altogether dissimilar to the protectionist barriers which we are accustomed to deplore.

Gordon Richardson, Governor of the Bank of England, at the Annual Banquet of the Overseas Bankers Club, London (Feb. 1, 1982).

[81] Fritz Leutwiler, President of the Swiss National Bank and now President of the Bank for International Settlements, in a speech to the Swiss Forex Club in Zurich on Oct. 24, 1981, did not question the U.S. policy of intervening only in situations of crisis, but he noted that the concept was undefined. It probably had to remain undefined because of the difficulty of foreseeing the character and timing of a critical situation. He urged, however, that the monetary authorities of

One economist, who has written that Article IV, section 2(b) may be described as "codified anarchy," has discussed possible dangers for the United States under the Second Amendment. If all countries other than the United States intervene to manage the exchange rates for their currencies, the effect will be management of the exchange rate for the U.S. dollar whatever the wishes of the United States may be. The situation of the United States would then be the one that ultimately it found objectionable under the par value system.[82] It may be that the U.S. administration does take the view that the U.S. dollar is still the central currency in international monetary arrangements and that it is not the dollar that fluctuates in exchange value but other currencies that fluctuate in relation to the dollar.[83]

Differences of opinion among members of the Fund on whether there should be a more active policy of intervention and what that policy might be

---

the United States, the Federal Republic of Germany, Japan, and Switzerland "should continue in greater depth their talks on the organization of joint intervention. This may seem modest compared with more ambitious plans, but it has the advantage that it is capable of being put into effect." Dr. Leutwiler in a later speech (Feb. 5, 1982) also noted that, although the export element in the U.S. economy is relatively small, the United States should cooperate in preventing the sharpest fluctuations in exchange rates, and that the United States should heed the experience of the European Monetary System in stabilizing exchange rates, notwithstanding the different rates of inflation among members. Intervention by the United States would have an important psychological effect on the markets.

[82] Peter B. Kenen, in THE NEW INTERNATIONAL MONETARY SYSTEM, *supra* note 69, at 202, 208. Professor Kenen adds the following footnote to p. 208:

> The U.S. Government seems to be worried about this problem, and not without justification. The managed float toward which we are drifting contains the seeds of grave international disorder. Large numbers of countries would appear to hold strong views about exchange rates. Many have chosen to peg their currencies; others are intervening actively to prevent or attenuate movements in floating rates. It is not too wrong to say that we have devised a system of gliding parities in which the parities and rates of glide do not have to be announced and are thus hidden from the scrutiny required to guarantee overall consistency. There is, then, the danger that the dollar will become again the *n*th currency in the system—that practice, if not law, will come to resemble in this respect the par value system we have just supplanted. Should this occur, the United States may seek someday to free itself from the constraints imposed by others, by acting as it did in 1971, with convulsive consequences for international financial, economic, and political relationships. Were I to advise the U.S. Treasury, however, I would counsel a response different from the one it appears to have adopted. I would urge the rapid, complete articulation of explicit rules to regulate intervention, rules proscribing any intervention designed to drive exchange rates away from target rates or zones that the IMF, acting on its own initiative, would promulgate from time to time. I leave open a number of complicated questions—whether the IMF should publish the targets and how it should obtain them, to what extent it should rely on its own research, including its own econometric models, and to what extent it should proceed by consultation with the governments concerned. I do believe, however, that we need to move in this direction. Proposals to impose rules for floating that do not include well-defined procedures for setting and altering target rates or zones miss the basic point at issue. The *n*th country problem will not go away. It is sure to arise from the verbiage of Article IV, to plague us when we are most vulnerable to its implications.

See also O. EMMINGER, EXCHANGE RATE POLICY RECONSIDERED 18–20 (Group of Thirty Occasional Papers No. 10, 1982).

[83] There is evidence that this view does prevail to some extent in the domestic law of the United States. *See* Chown, *The Tax Treatment of Foreign Exchange Fluctuations in the United States and the United Kingdom,* 16 GEO. WASH. J. INT'L L. & ECON. 201 (1982).

induce officials who do not regard the present situation as satisfactory to hope that understandings can be negotiated among monetary authorities, and in particular among central banks, outside the Fund.[84] These officials emphasize that understandings, to be useful, cannot be confined to intervention but must extend as broadly as possible to other economic and monetary problems of common interest to the United States and other major countries.

Increasingly strong discontent about the development of exchange rates and the differences of opinion between the United States and other countries on intervention led to a number of understandings at the summit meeting at Versailles on June 4–6, 1982, attended by the heads of government and state of Canada, France, the Federal Republic of Germany, Italy, Japan, the United Kingdom, and the United States. A Joint Statement on Monetary Undertakings was attached to the communiqué issued at the conclusion of the meeting. Paragraph 1 recognizes that greater stability of the world monetary system rests primarily on the convergence of policies designed to achieve common goals. Paragraph 2 announces that the parties attach major importance to the Fund as a monetary institution. The next three paragraphs are formulated as follows:

> 3. We are ready to strengthen our cooperation with the IMF in its work of surveillance; and to develop this on a multilateral basis taking into account particularly the currencies constituting the SDR.
>
> 4. We rule out the use of our exchange rates to gain unfair competitive advantages.
>
> 5. We are ready, if necessary, to use intervention in exchange markets to counter disorderly conditions, as provided for under Article IV of the IMF Articles of Agreement.[85]

Paragraph 4 is drawn from Article IV, section 1(iii) of the Fund's Articles. Paragraph 5 repeats the substance of the Fund's guideline B. Paragraph 3 is an addition to the Fund's preexisting law and practice. In accordance with this paragraph 3, joint discussions are to be held by representatives of the United States, the United Kingdom, Japan, the Federal Republic of Germany, and France, in cooperation with the Fund. The Fund has not announced any decision so far that relates these discussions to new or existing procedures on surveillance.

[84]

> I continue to believe that the way to deal with actual or potential instability of exchange rates is through close co-operation between central banks. The emergence of a multi-currency reserve system over the past decade or so makes such co-operation ever more necessary, especially between the central banks that are responsible for the so-called reserve currencies. Central-bank co-operation has helped us to overcome crises in the past, and we have reason to be confident that it will enable us to deal with any emerging situation. A return to a global system of fixed exchange rates is not on the cards as far as one can see ahead, and effective surveillance of exchange rate policies by the IMF on a worldwide scale is likely to run up against a number of conceptual and practical difficulties, though it may have to play an increasingly greater role over time. Hence the central role of central banks in this area, which after all is an area of special competence for them.

Karl Otto Poehl, President of the Bundesbank, speech to the Conference Board of Europe, London (Oct. 20, 1981).

[85] 11 IMF SURV. 189 (1982).

Another understanding reached at the Versailles meeting, although not recorded in the joint statement, is that experts of the seven countries represented at Versailles would undertake a study, with the help of the Fund's staff, to determine whether intervention had been efficacious in the past.

On December 6, 1982, the Secretary of the U.S. Treasury startled the economic and financial world with an announcement that went beyond the view that stable conditions can be achieved if countries take individual responsibility for pursuing correct policies and reducing inflation. A more collective and more systematic approach to economic problems was necessary, for which purpose a new international conference should be convened in the coming years. In relation to exchange rates, his objective would be greater "viscosity," but he was not advocating a return to fixed exchange rates or a policy of intervention.[86]

Obligation to Collaborate

Article IV, section 1 contains a general obligation of members that is formulated in firm language: "each member undertakes to collaborate with the Fund and other members to assure orderly exchange arrangements and to promote a stable system of exchange rates." This obligation was intended to have a role similar to the obligation that had been set forth in Article IV, section 4(a) before the Second Amendment: "Each member undertakes to collaborate with the Fund to promote exchange stability, to maintain orderly exchange arrangements with other members, and to avoid competitive exchange alterations." That provision had been a reservoir of jurisdiction on which the Fund had drawn in order to exercise authority over exchange rates in the days of the par value system.[87]

Certain features of the new obligation have a special relevance to the subject of the coordination by members of their policies, which is discussed in section XI below. The new obligation dispels any misconception that the four subparagraphs that follow and set forth specific obligations call for policies by each member that are wholly self-regarding. Each member should set its own house in order, but not by policies that create distress in other houses. This concern for others explains why the new obligation requires collaboration with "other members" as well as with the Fund, in contrast to the former general obligation of collaboration, which was formulated as collaboration with the Fund only. Moreover, an objective of collaboration is a stable "system" of exchange rates. The word "system" indicates that the stability to be sought must be worldwide. A similar function is performed by the reference to "the international monetary system" in subparagraph (iii).

The obligation of collaboration can be observed by members without prescriptions by the Fund, but the Fund can give vigor to the obligation by decisions that define how members should behave. The Fund can make clear

[86] N.Y. Times, Dec. 7, 1982, at A1, D8; J. Com., Dec. 7, 1982, at 6A. Later, the Secretary explained that he had in mind some mechanism for more prompt balance-of-payments assistance. N.Y. Times, Dec. 13, 1982, at D1, D11.

[87] GOLD, SELECTED ESSAYS, *supra* note 4, at 390–409.

that it will consider members to be acting in accordance with their obligation if they behave in a particular way. The Fund adopted such decisions under the former Article IV, section 4(a). Decisions of this kind can be taken with a majority of the votes cast. So far, no decisions have been taken under the new obligation.

Consultation

One of the main objectives of the original Articles was that members should make their currencies convertible by giving notice to the Fund of willingness to perform the obligations of convertibility set forth in Article VIII, sections 2, 3, and 4. Members were given the privilege, however, of availing themselves of transitional arrangements under Article XIV, which permitted members to maintain and adapt the restrictions existing when they joined the Fund on payments and transfers for current international transactions without the need for approval by the Fund. If a member decided to avail itself of the transitional arrangements, it was required to consult the Fund annually on the further retention of restrictions that were inconsistent with the obligations of convertibility. The Fund was authorized to encourage a member to withdraw particular restrictions or to abandon them altogether, and if the Fund found that a member persisted in maintaining restrictions without economic justification, the member could be declared ineligible to use the Fund's resources. In practice, the consultations were not limited narrowly to restrictions but covered all aspects of a member's situation that affected its balance of payments, and were completed with decisions of the Executive Board that recorded its views on the member's situation.

Once a member had given notice that its currency was convertible in accordance with Article VIII, the member was no longer required by the Articles to engage in annual consultations.[88] Members were persuaded by the Fund that periodic consultations with it continued to be useful even in these circumstances. A procedure was established for this purpose,[89] but on the understandings that the consultations were voluntary and that they would not be completed with decisions of the Executive Board. The latter understanding illustrates the importance attached by members to possible criticism by their peers in the form of decisions of the Executive Board. Various attempts were made over the years to rescind the understanding and to get agreement on a practice of concluding these consultations with decisions, but the efforts did not succeed. The object of the proposal was to increase the influence of the Fund, for which reason it was not acceptable to members.

When the Second Amendment was being drafted, it seemed unprofitable to resume these efforts in relation to Article VIII. The legal position with respect to consultations under the present Article VIII and Article XIV remains unchanged, but the difference between them has little, if any, practical

[88] A member could be required by the Fund to consult if it was applying measures that required the Fund's approval. SELECTED DECISIONS, *supra* note 19, at 210–11.

[89] *Id.* at 209–11. The justification avoided an authoritarian tone: ". . . the Fund is able to provide technical facilities and advice, and to this end, or as a means of exchanging views on monetary and financial developments. . . ." *Id.* at 210–11.

effect now. The new provisions of Article IV apply to all members. An obligation of consultation without distinction among members was considered a desirable safeguard. Article IV, section 3(b) provides, therefore, that all members must consult with the Fund on their exchange rate policies. The Fund has taken three general decisions so far that regulate these consultations.[90] The first sets forth the principles for the guidance of members' exchange rate policies, the procedures for the Fund's surveillance over these policies, and the circumstances that might be disturbing and might indicate the need for special discussions with a member. The second decision provides for special discussions because of the importance of developments even though they are not disturbing. The third decision clarifies aspects of the earlier decisions and summarizes experience under them.

XI. Some Further Safeguards

Attempts have been made to erect bulwarks against the dangers that present exchange arrangements may create and that the law may not be adequate to prevent. These defenses add to the safeguards discussed in section X above. Some further defenses are considered in this section XI.

European Monetary System

It has become apparent that developments can occur in exchange rates that are not justified by underlying economic conditions. The monetary authorities of a country may conclude that they must counteract these developments. Floating exchange rates may give less independence to determine domestic policies than was expected. Limited *de facto* independence has convinced most members of the European Community that they sacrifice little and gain more by joining the European Monetary System (EMS), which limits their independence *de jure.*[91] The exchange rate and intervention arrangements of the European Monetary System impose obligations on participants in the interest of creating a zone of monetary stability.[92]

Coordination of Policies

The softening of obligations with respect to exchange arrangements has led, not surprisingly, to more emphatic and more repeated exhortations to members to coordinate their policies or to aim at a convergence of them. Sometimes, coordination among all members is urged, and sometimes among participants in the EMS, or the issuers of the expanded number of reserve currencies, or the issuers of the currencies in the basket that determines the exchange value of the SDR, or some other group of countries.

[90] *Id.* at 10–15; IMF, Annual Report 1982, at 128–32.

[91] Kirbyshire, *Floating: A Burden for Trade,* J. Com., Sept. 16, 1981, at 4A.

[92] Committee of Governors of the Central Banks of the Member States of the European Economic Community and the European Monetary Cooperation Fund, Texts concerning the European Monetary System (1979).

A study that has been made of coordination distinguishes among three categories of national economic policies,[93] although these categories are not necessarily exhaustive or always mutually exclusive: (1) policies aimed at a goal that is common for countries, (2) policies that are inherently competitive, and (3) policies that have their main impact within the country applying them. The most obvious example of category (2) for the present purpose is the policy of a change in exchange rate. In contrast to category (1), in which pursuit of common national policies increases the common good, the benefits derived by a country from a change in the exchange rate for its currency are matched by costs borne by other countries. For this reason, international agreements have been made, beginning with the Fund's Articles, to regulate or monitor inappropriate national policies on exchange rates. In the days of the par value system, the world relied on a set of international rules administered by an international organization empowered to take decisions and did not rely on appeals for coordination. The study declares that since 1971,

> the conditions for central decision-making no longer apply for the major currencies. It is truc that the exchange rate policies of all countries, whatever their exchange rate regime, are subject to "firm surveillance" by the Fund; but surveillance of floating rates is inherently difficult. With the disappearance of the rule of the par value system, the avoidance of inappropriate rates for the main currencies has come to rely to a considerable extent on the coordination of exchange rate policies by the main industrial countries. . . .
>
> Fund surveillance of these major currencies constitutes part of the cooperative mechanism about these rates. As a minimum, it can function as a backstop to ensure that these rates do not move outside a reasonable range; with greater exercise of its authority, one could imagine the Fund to garner a much more substantial proportion of the coordination function.[94]

The Fund attempts to garner some proportion of the coordination function by its periodic World Economic Surveys and by the discussion of prospects for coordination in the light of the surveys as the first item on the agenda of meetings of the Fund's Interim Committee. The study referred to concludes that " '[c]oordination' is seen here as a relatively weak form of international influence on national policies. It is a halfway house between, on the one hand, purely national policy formation and, on the other hand, policy-making that is constrained by international rules and surveillance exercised by an international organization."[95]

This conclusion can be accepted if international rules are indeed constraining. If the rules are soft law, they are not at one extremity of the range of possibilities. The rules are then somewhere between the halfway house and the true extremity of firm law. It is difficult to assess the influence of statements by organs or other bodies within the Fund or within other international entities that urge policies on governments. The statements are often formulated in the language of compromise that is typical of committee prose. The statements

[93] J. POLAK, COORDINATION OF NATIONAL ECONOMIC POLICIES (Group of Thirty Occasional Papers No. 7, 1981).

[94] *Id.* at 6, 7.

[95] *Id.* at 3.

may have a sharper focus in the first draft prepared by international civil servants, but the text is then blurred by the ministers or officials who compose the body issuing the statement. The motive for this blurring may be the absence of a true accord[96] or the wish by governments to avoid firm commitments. Even when a clear text does survive in the drafting of a communiqué, an instrument of that character has no binding legal force. Governments are not subject to the reproach that they are neglecting obligations if they give decisive effect to national, rather than international, interests.

The extent to which consultations under Article IV can influence the adjustment of individual balances of payments or the international coordination of policies is affected by the function of these consultations as seen by members. As is discussed in section XII below, the attitude of members to that function is affected by their perception of the degree of uniformity and symmetry achieved by the Fund in the administration of Article IV.

The treatment accepted by the United States is almost always a major influence on the perceptions of members. For example, the policy of consultations with members that had undertaken to perform the obligations of convertibility under Article VIII, which was discussed in section X above, was acceptable to members only when the United States came to the conclusion that it would participate in such consultations. The United States has provided an authoritative exposition of its view of the functions that consultations under Article IV should perform in achieving the international coordination of policies:

> IMF Article IV consultations contribute to international stability in a number of ways. First, such consultations provide information to member governments regarding the national economic policies of other member governments. Such information may be helpful in shaping each member's domestic policies as well as useful in avoiding conflicts because of misunderstandings. Second, Article IV consultations provide a valuable base of information for Fund staff assessments of global economic and exchange-rate developments which in turn provide useful information for national economic authorities. Third, Article IV consultations provide a framework for frank critiques among the representatives of member governments. Fourth, Article IV consultations provide a base from which all nations can develop a better understanding of the economic linkages among nations. And finally, these consultations can help a country to identify and address emerging payments problems at an early stage.[97]

[96] *See* note 60 *supra.*

[97] Economic Report of the President, Transmitted to the Congress February 1982, at 187–88 (1982). *See also* Wash. Post, May 30, 1982, at A16, in discussing the forthcoming summit meeting at Versailles:

> "Perhaps if we can get more guidance [on economic policy] from the IMF—not to make it an international superagency, but it does have a body of knowledge—we could get a greater converging of policy, and there would be less need or cause for intervention," Regan said. Regan said he believed that "the dollar and franc might move together" through such coordination.
>
> It was learned that when British Prime Minister Thatcher heard of the Regan plan, she exploded: "No one is going to tell me how to run economic policy." But Britain and other nations have been assured that there is no such intention. "We wouldn't want to have the IMF order us around, in that sense, either," an administration official said.

The usefulness of consultations as described in this passage cannot be denied, but the functions that are described are considered useful because they provide information and cultivate understanding. No mention is made of the Fund's surveillance of the international monetary system in order to ensure its effective operation or of the compliance of members with their exchange rate obligations. Nor is there any mention of the obligation of members to collaborate with the Fund and with other members to create a stable system of exchange rates. There is no reference, therefore, to the opportunity that consultations can give the Fund to induce members to coordinate their policies.

An observer, who was at one time senior vice president of the Federal Reserve Bank of New York and manager of foreign operations of the Federal Reserve System Open Market Account, has made a pessimistic assessment of the extent to which efforts to develop joint policies have been successful when the policies compete with national preoccupations:

> The institutional framework is still intact. Officials consult regularly at the economic summits, the IMF, the OECD, and the BIS. But their willingness to work together to solve international monetary questions has virtually disappeared. Officials have increasingly used international meetings as platforms to defend or justify their policies at home rather than as opportunities to develop joint strategies to deal with common international and monetary and financial problems. Relations have not deteriorated to blatant policies of beggar-thy-neighbor but the environment has surely become one of every man for himself.[98]

This former official provides a political explanation of the tendency that he has observed. Former governments in a number of industrial countries did not succeed in their economic policies. Electorates then turned to other political parties because they promised new approaches, even if in the past these approaches were considered "offbeat, or even extreme." The successor governments seek as much freedom as possible from international constraints that might hinder the new approaches.

If this analysis is correct, why do governments embarrass themselves by calling for coordination? The declarations are often made by ministers and officials with economic responsibilities. They tend to share a willingness to

[98] Pardee, *International Monetary System Is Adrift*, J. Com., Sept. 15, 1981, at 4A. For his proposals, see *US Urged to Take Initiative*, *id.*, Sept. 16, 1981, at 4A.

See also the following answer by President François Mitterand:

> Q. Is this week's devaluation of the franc symptomatic of a greater disorder within the international monetary system?
>
> A. It is one of the consequences, but not a cause of monetary disorder. There is a currency war, an economic war, and this is one of the most disquieting points for the future of Western relations. Today, it is every man for himself. The U.S., so it says, needs a very high interest rate. That's its business. But it cannot ignore the fact that this measure exacerbates already dangerous movements of capital. Likewise for the fluctuations in the dollar exchange rate. This disorganizes the Western economic system. Since each nation is undergoing a crisis, they all tend toward egotism. Each country first wants to rescue itself, whereas they will only be rescued together.

TIME, Oct. 19, 1981, at 57.

cooperate within the scope of their responsibilities that outruns the political possibilities for harmonized policies. Even when an objective of political integration through economic cooperation has been avowed by a limited group of countries, performance falls short of aspiration.[99]

The dependence of economic aims on political will and the difficulties of developing that will might dispose governments to consider the problem at the highest political level. There has indeed been some disposition to place monetary matters, including exchange arrangements and the coordination of economic policies, on the agenda of summit meetings. The first summit meeting, at Rambouillet, endorsed the solution on exchange arrangements that was incorporated, with no great modification, in the Second Amendment. Later summit meetings have not considered many monetary issues, and have not dealt with them in detail when they were on the agenda, until the meeting at Versailles.[100]

The heads of state and government attending summit meetings have dealt with monetary matters infrequently and sometimes cursorily because these matters are within the responsibilities of the Fund and particularly its Interim Committee. The limited number of states represented at summit meetings provokes resentment among other states, including some whose support for an agreement reached at a meeting is necessary for success. The composition of the Interim Committee according to the model of the Executive Board as established by law protects the Committee against the charge that it is unrepresentative. If the Interim Committee becomes the final arbiter of policy on international monetary matters, the opportunity for promoting political consensus by appeal to the highest political authority attending summit meetings will be unavailable.

XII. Paradox of Present Articles

Since 1971, differential rates of inflation, the shock of increases in the cost of energy, and social and political developments in individual countries have been among the forces that have produced frequent changes in exchange rates. The prospect that conditions such as these would persist was the major reason why members agreed that a par value system could not be restored.[101]

99 *EC Asks Members to Practice Better Economic Cooperation,* J. Com., July 23, 1981, at 23B.

100 The usefulness of these meetings is sometimes challenged.

> The financial commitment [at the Bonn summit] to continue to intervene "to counter disorderly conditions in the exchange market" was interpreted in financial markets as continuation of the status quo and therefore an inability to agree on more concrete guidelines. In particular, it was interpreted as unwillingness on the part of the U.S. to act to stabilize market expectations. It could even be argued that the weak wording of the Bonn summit declaration on this point helped push the U.S. dollar lower in subsequent months.

Atlantic Council Working Group on Political Affairs, Summit Meetings and Collective Leadership in the 1980's, at 25 (1980). This policy paper is a detailed examination of the subject of summit meetings. *See also* Group of Thirty, Annual Report 1982, at 5 (1982); and Owen, *Don't Let This Summit Be the Last,* N.Y. Times, July 19, 1981, at F4.

101

> The Committee [*i.e.,* the Committee of Twenty] recognizes that, in view of present uncertainties related to inflation, the energy situation, and other unsettled conditions, it is not

Not all the consequences of present exchange arrangements were foreseen. The volatility of exchange rates and their tendency to go too far even in the right direction have surprised many economists who favored floating rates in principle and not under the compulsion of economic *force majeure.* The paradox is that the soft law that cannot prevent the undesirable behavior of exchange rates increases the need for firm administration if damage to the purposes of the Fund is to be avoided. But soft law does not predispose members to accept firm administration.

Section X has shown that the Articles provide safeguards against the dangers of soft law. Administration will be firm if these safeguards are applied with vigor. In section XI above, the importance of certain perceptions by members was noted in the discussion of the effectiveness of consultations.

The policies and procedures of the Fund must be acceptable to its members acting through the Executive Directors they appoint or elect or through the ministers or others they appoint to the Interim Committee. Members will not support policies or procedures unless they perceive a net advantage notwithstanding the international constraints they are called on to observe. Uniformity and symmetry in the application of the safeguards would contribute to this perception not simply because of the aesthetic appeal of evenhandedness but also because the surrender of some degree of freedom by each member is a concession of authority to other members. Uniformity is a characteristic of the treatment of the members that are deemed to constitute a class; symmetry is a characteristic of the treatment of classes. Uniform treatment can be said to be the same treatment; symmetrical treatment can be said to be comparable treatment.[102] The treatment of industrialized countries is of particular importance when members decide whether they will accept firm administration. Will the classes of industrialized members and developing members receive symmetrical treatment? Within the class of industrialized members, will the United States and other members receive uniform treatment?[103]

Differences of opinion among members on the character and operation of the present international monetary system may be another impediment to agreement on policies and procedures for administering the system. Some European observers have criticized the Second Amendment as a legalization of disorder and not a reform.[104] They recommend greater official activism,

---

appropriate to attempt to determine the full details of all aspects of the future international monetary system, many of which can better be decided in the light of future developments.

Outline of Reform (June 14, 1974), in DOCUMENTS OF THE COMMITTEE OF TWENTY, *supra* note 18, at 7, *reprinted in* 13 ILM 1004, 1004 (1974).

[102] GOLD, SELECTED ESSAYS, *supra* note 4, at 469–519; Gold, *Symmetry as a Legal Objective of the International Monetary System,* 12 N.Y.U. J. INT'L. L. & POL. 423 (1980).

[103] Other classifications are recognized in the law or practice of the Fund. For example, for some purposes the United States and the issuers of other reserve currencies are perceived to constitute a class. Other perceived classes are: members in deficit and members in surplus in their balances of payments; developed and developing members; among developing countries, oil-exporting and non-oil-exporting countries; members with pegged and unpegged currencies; etc.

[104] *See, e.g., The Prospects for an International Monetary System,* BANK OF ENG., Q. BULL., Sept. 1979, at 280 (The Henry Thornton Lecture, delivered by Gordon Richardson (now Lord Richardson), Governor of the Bank of England, on June 14, 1979 at the City University, London); de Vries, *Jamaica, or the Non-Reform of the International Monetary System,* 54 FOREIGN AFF. 577 (1976); Deniau, *Discipline of Stable Monetary Structure Urged,* J. Com., Dec. 17, 1981, at 4A.

particularly in the management of exchange rates, in order to achieve greater discipline.

American officials have been more sanguine about the existence of an international monetary system and its soundness in concept. They have not favored official activism in the management of exchange rates:

> The United States believes that exchange rates must be allowed to adjust to changing economic and financial conditions. We are not, however, pleased with the degree of exchange rate instability experienced during the past decade. In our judgment, such exchange rate instability reflects unstable economic and financial conditions within countries. The remedy is not a change in institutional arrangements.
>
> Rather, these conditions should be viewed, as recognized in the IMF's surveillance provisions, as evidence of the need for restoration of stable economic and financial conditions.[105]

The statement by the Secretary of the U.S. Treasury of December 6, 1982 manifests concern about the operation of the international monetary system, but not discontent with the concept of present exchange arrangements.

The Managing Director of the Fund has explained that in current conditions it was inevitable that some countries would insist on the advantages of stabilizing exchange rates in the short run while others would emphasize the greater desirability of underlying policies that would produce a stable exchange rate system in the longer run. These different attitudes—to which can be added differences about the role of exchange rates in the adjustment process[106]—have placed limits on the firmness with which surveillance can be conducted:

> Il est donc vrai qu'il y a une situation de fluctuations excessive dans le système international; et il peut paraître que la surveillance exercée par le Fonds Monétaire International, est très modeste, je n'en disconviendrai pas.
>
> Mais pourquoi est-elle modeste, cette action? Je crois quelle est modeste parce que, en fin de compte, les pays membres qui constituent cette collectivité de 145 états sont encore très divisés sur ce que devrait être la gestion harmonisée d'un système international de changes.[107]

XIII. Some Modest Proposals

The international lawyer is predisposed by training to support the transformation of soft law into firm law because he sees that process as the growth of international law. He sees the need for law to avoid collision when the conduct of international relations affects important interests, and he believes that the need can be met more effectively by firm law than by soft law. The economist may consider the process of strengthening the law as undesirable

[105] Donald T. Regan, Secretary of the Treasury and Governor of the Fund for the United States, in International Monetary Fund Board of Governors, Annual Meeting Press Release No. 24, Sept. 30, 1981, at 4.

[106] IMF, Annual Report 1982, at 129.

[107] *See* note 60 *supra*.

if applied to exchange arrangements in present circumstances.[108] He may doubt that firmer rules of law can be formulated, with the present state of knowledge of the economic forces at work, that would be observed in current conditions. Firmer rules of law would be undesirable because they would reduce the choice of policies available to governments. This view may explain why the Fund's guidelines B and C concentrate on intervention and refrain from the mention of other policies or practices that affect exchange rates, and why guideline A is cast in terms of subjective intent rather than objective effect.

Some economists may favor restraint in the establishment of guiding principles because they expect that principles would be directed toward the stability of exchange rates as an end in itself. The promotion of international welfare would be more desirable as the primary objective, and stability should not be sought if it would inhibit welfare.

An assessment of the effectiveness of the present law in achieving the objectives that appear in Article IV, section 1 must recognize the normal disposition of members to act in accordance with the law. No member has announced that it is resiling from the provisions of the Articles on exchange arrangements, and no member has that option. Nor should an assessment neglect the Fund's policies on the use of its resources by members. The policies of a member that directly or indirectly affect its choice of exchange arrangements or the exchange rate for its currency can be influenced by the conditionality the Fund applies under some of its policies when a member in difficulty in its balance of payments seeks to use the Fund's resources under those policies. Conditionality is a portmanteau word that encompasses all the policies that the Fund wishes a member to follow so that it can resolve its problem consistently with the Articles.[109] Conditionality cannot ensure the firm administration of law in relation to all members, however, because numerous members, including major industrialized countries, are not making use, or seeking to make use, of the Fund's resources.

Whatever assessments are made of the present law cannot dispose of the fact that there is widespread dissatisfaction with the conditions that the law has not prevented.[110] At least one achievement of the present law is obvious. The feverish, and often unsuccessful, efforts of the past to defend a par value, and the sense of crisis that was created, no longer disturb the international monetary scene. Miss Prism's instructions to Cecily on the rupee are now unnecessary.[111]

[108] For the view that surveillance would be hampered by more specific guidelines, and that a case-by-case approach under satisfactory procedures will be most effective, see J. ARTUS & A. CROCKETT, FLOATING EXCHANGE RATES AND THE NEED FOR SURVEILLANCE (Essays in International Finance No. 127, Princeton 1978). *But see* Artus, *Toward a more orderly exchange rate system,* FIN. & DEV., No. 1, 1983, at 10–13.

[109] M. GUITIÁN, FUND CONDITIONALITY: EVOLUTION OF PRINCIPLES AND PRACTICES (IMF Pamphlet Series No. 38, 1981); J. GOLD, CONDITIONALITY, particularly at pp. 30–31, 34 (IMF Pamphlet Series No. 31, 1979).

[110] *See, e.g., The Problem of Exchange Rates,* in GROUP OF THIRTY, *supra* note 100, at 27–32; J. ARTUS & A. CROCKETT, *supra* note 108.

[111] ". . . Cecily, you will read your Political Economy in my absence. The chapter on the fall

If agreement were reached on developing the substantive law of exchange arrangements, much room could be found in the present Articles for accommodating development. It is safe to assume that the par value system that is the subject of detailed provisions in the present Articles[112] would not be called into operation. The Fund could act under other provisions, however, to develop substantive rules. It has been seen that the Fund could specify the behavior that it would consider consistent with the obligation of members to collaborate. The Fund could adopt further specific principles for the guidance of all members with respect to their exchange rate policies, and principles could be drafted with greater precision than the three now in existence. The Fund could give greater precision, by interpretation or by decisions on policy, to the four subparagraphs of Article IV, section 1. The Fund could recommend general exchange arrangements to accord with the development of the international monetary system. The first three of these four categories of decisions could be taken with a majority of the votes cast, the fourth with an 85 percent majority of the total voting power.

Opportunities exist for strengthening procedures in combination with the development of substantive rules, but procedures could be strengthened even if new substantive rules are not developed. In primitive societies, it should be recalled, law was secreted in the interstices of procedure. If procedures can be strengthened, the firmer administration of existing rules of law might result in the secretion of new rules. The following developments in procedure are suggested. They have been called modest in the title of this section because they are confined to procedure.

(1) Consultations under Article IV should be completed by the Executive Board with the adoption of avowed decisions instead of "conclusions." The decisions should be formulated as the expression of the collective view of the Executive Board and not as its endorsement of the Chairman's summing up of the views expressed by various Executive Directors. With this change, it would be clearer that the Fund was expressing the judgment of peers.

(2) The basic decision on the procedures for surveillance under Article IV emphasizes extremes of informality and confidentiality.[113] Delay is possible before the Executive Board has an opportunity to examine a member's exchange rate policies. If the Executive Board's eventual response were to be adverse, its criticism would have less impact than if the response had been prompt. The knowledge that the Executive Board might examine exchange rate policies soon after they were introduced might encourage caution on the part of a member that had reason to expect a challenge by its peers. The deterrent effect would be less than is exerted by an a priori approach, but it might be more than is exerted by an a posteriori approach that permits delay.

The solution might be an understanding by the Executive Board that although the detailed procedures of the basic decision on surveillance were to be followed in most instances, the decision did not prevent an Executive Di-

---

of the Rupee you may omit. It is somewhat too sensational. Even these metallic problems have their melodramatic side." Oscar Wilde, *The Importance of Being Earnest.*

[112] Art IV, sec. 4; Schedule C (*see supra* note 30).

[113] SELECTED DECISIONS, *supra* note 19, at 10–14.

rector from invoking Rule C-6 of the Fund's Rules and Regulations if he considered that an unusual situation had arisen: "The agenda for each meeting shall be prepared by the Chairman. The agenda shall include any item requested by an Executive Director."

Whatever understanding might be reached of the circumstances that constituted an unusual situation, uniformity and symmetry would have to be observed. For example, members that pegged their currencies in some way and members that did not would be treated symmetrically. Symmetry implies that the procedure of Rule C-6 would not be confined to members that took action to change a peg, and that the procedure would apply also to the issuers of currencies that were not pegged if changes in exchange rate, whether saltatory or the result of a crawl, were disturbing.

(3) The Council should be called into existence. The decisions of the Council, taken at the level of Ministers of Finance acting as Councillors, would strengthen the Fund. The Council would take decisions, and members that were not acting in accordance with the decisions would have the burden of explaining their failures.

The Council would probably confine its activities to the consideration of general policies. An organ like the Council would be less likely to examine the situation of individual members, although it would not be prevented from doing so in cases of sufficient importance for the international monetary system. The terms of reference of the Council are formulated by the Articles: "The Council shall supervise the management and adaptation of the international monetary system, including the continuing operation of the adjustment process and developments in global liquidity, and in this connection shall review developments in the transfer of real resources to developing countries."[114]

If the Council limited its activities to decisions on general policies, the task of completing consultations under Article IV would continue to be performed by the Executive Board as at present. The role of the Executive Board would be strengthened, however, because it would have the function of calling on members to account for failures to observe the Council's decisions. The undertaking of each member to collaborate with the Fund and other members on orderly exchange arrangements and a stable system of exchange rates[115] would be a powerful instrument in the hands of the Executive Board for influencing members to act in accordance with decisions of the Council on general policies.

(4) In the absence of the Council, the Interim Committee's procedures could be modified. The Committee's terms of reference[116] are substantially similar to those of the Council, although the Committee has no power to take decisions. Supervision of the management and adaptation of the international monetary system could be put on the agenda of the Committee in addition to, or in place of, its consideration of the world economic outlook. The new

[114] Schedule D, para. 2(a) (*see supra* note 30).

[115] Art IV, sec. 1.

[116] SELECTED DECISIONS, *supra* note 19, at 308.

item would be more pointed in recalling that the Committee must concern itself with supervising the evolution of the international monetary system ("adaptation"). The Committee must not concentrate exclusively on the analysis of current economic conditions and short-run prospects. That activity can be subsumed under supervision of the "management" of the system but without exhausting even that concept.

(5) The consultations held among the representatives of the five members whose currencies compose the SDR basket, in which the Fund is to have a role, should be linked in some way to procedures of the Executive Board. Understandings reached among the five members affect the whole community of members. They should have an opportunity, therefore, to comment on those understandings. The most obvious locus of such a discussion would be the Board Room of the Fund.

(6) The documents of the Fund and the "conclusions" reached in consultations under Article IV are confidential and not for public use. Little is known, therefore, of results of the Fund's surveillance. There is, for example, no indication in the *Annual Reports* of the Fund or in its *Annual Reports on Exchange Arrangements and Exchange Restrictions* of the outcome of any action that has been taken under the special procedure for consultations with a member in the interval between periodic Article IV consultations.[117] This procedure could make an effective contribution to surveillance because it is initiated if the Managing Director, "taking into account any views that may have been expressed by other members, considers that a member's exchange rate policies may not be in accord with the exchange rate principles."[118]

The secrecy that envelops surveillance could be pierced in one kind of case without detriment to the confidentiality that members cherish. If a member wished to publish the staff report on a consultation with the member or the "conclusions" reached in the consultation, the Fund should give its consent. A government is likely to request permission to publish only if the document or the "conclusions" are favorable to the government and support its existing or contemplated policies. Nevertheless, it is appropriate for the Fund to give whatever support it can to policies that are consistent with its purposes. Moreover, the member might find it difficult to resist publicity when the reports or "conclusions" in a later consultation are not favorable to the government.

(7) The Monetary Committee of the European Community discusses and recommends actions on monetary matters that affect countries outside the Community as well as within the Community. Actions taken by the Community in these matters must be consistent with the obligations of members of the Community as members of the Fund. Liaison between the Community and the Fund is particularly important now that exchange rate and intervention arrangements and other monetary matters are regulated by an evolving European Monetary System. Furthermore, the experience of the EMS could assist in the evolution of the law relating to exchange arrangements under the Fund's Articles. An official of the Commission of the Community was an observer in meetings of the Committee of Twenty and is an observer in meet-

[117] *Id.* at 12–13, 14.

[118] *Id.* at 14.

ings of the Interim Committee. An official of the Fund should participate in meetings of the Community's Monetary Committee.

There should be no illusion that it would be easy to negotiate acceptance of any of these developments because they relate to procedure. The world has retreated a long way toward the pre-Bretton Woods principle that exchange arrangements and exchange rates are sensitive aspects of sovereignty. There is no evidence yet of willingness to go forward again if any proposal involves, or might involve, a surrender of sovereignty in these matters beyond the modest transfer that has been made at present. Nations are unwilling to take such a step unless they are persuaded that it will result in a net advantage to them. That attitude is reasonable, but unfortunately, nations often conclude that there is advantage only as a last resort after they have reached a condition of crisis.[119]

POSTSCRIPT

Since this article was written, two developments have occurred that are relevant to it. The report of the working group on exchange market intervention commissioned at the Versailles summit became available and was the subject of a statement, issued on April 29, 1983, by the summit finance ministers, central bank governors, and representatives of the European Community. The final paragraph of the statement is as follows:

> Under present circumstances, the role of intervention can only be limited. Intervention can be useful to counter disorderly market conditions and to reduce short-term volatility. Intervention may also on occasion express an attitude toward exchange markets. Intervention will normally be useful only when complementing and supporting other policies. We are agreed on the need for closer consultations on policies and market conditions; and, while retaining our freedom to operate independently, are willing to undertake coordinated intervention in instances where it is agreed that such intervention would be helpful.

The communiqué issued on May 30, 1983 at the Williamsburg summit contains the following paragraphs:

> (2) The consultation process initiated at Versailles will be enhanced to promote convergence of economic performance in our economies and greater stability of exchange rates, on the lines indicated in an annex to this statement. We agree to pursue closer consultations on policies affecting exchange markets and on market conditions. While retaining our freedom to operate independently, we are willing to undertake coordinated intervention in exchange markets in instances where it is agreed that such intervention would be helpful.
>
> (5) We have invited Ministers of Finance, in consultation with the Managing Director of the I.M.F., to define the conditions for improving the international monetary system and to consider the part which might, in due course, be played in this process by a high-level international monetary conference.

[119] *See* M. BRENNER, THE POLITICS OF INTERNATIONAL MONETARY REFORM—THE EXCHANGE CRISIS (1976).

The Annex to the communiqué contains this paragraph: "(3) Exchange Rate Policy. We will improve consultations, policy convergence and international cooperation to help stabilize exchange markets, bearing in mind our conclusions on the Exchange Market Intervention Study."

These statements do not change the law on exchange arrangements or the need to strengthen it as discussed in this article, but the communiqué gives some hope that a strengthening of the law or of practice under it may be undertaken in the future.

Appendix A

Article IV

Obligations Regarding Exchange Arrangements

Section 1. *General obligations of members*

Recognizing that the essential purpose of the international monetary system is to provide a framework that facilitates the exchange of goods, services, and capital among countries, and that sustains sound economic growth, and that a principal objective is the continuing development of the orderly underlying conditions that are necessary for financial and economic stability, each member undertakes to collaborate with the Fund and other members to assure orderly exchange arrangements and to promote a stable system of exchange rates. In particular, each member shall:

(i) endeavor to direct its economic and financial policies toward the objective of fostering orderly economic growth with reasonable price stability, with due regard to its circumstances;

(ii) seek to promote stability by fostering orderly underlying economic and financial conditions and a monetary system that does not tend to produce erratic disruptions;

(iii) avoid manipulating exchange rates or the international monetary system in order to prevent effective balance of payments adjustment or to gain an unfair competitive advantage over other members; and

(iv) follow exchange policies compatible with the undertakings under this Section.

Section 2. *General exchange arrangements*

(*a*) Each member shall notify the Fund, within thirty days after the date of the second amendment of this Agreement, of the exchange arrangements it intends to apply in fulfillment of its obligations under Section 1 of this Article, and shall notify the Fund promptly of any changes in its exchange arrangements.

(*b*) Under an international monetary system of the kind prevailing on January 1, 1976, exchange arrangements may include (i) the maintenance by a member of a value for its currency in terms of the special drawing right or another denominator, other than gold, selected by the member, or (ii) cooperative arrangements by which members maintain the value of their currencies in relation to the value of the currency or currencies of other members, or (iii) other exchange arrangements of a member's choice.

(*c*) To accord with the development of the international monetary system, the Fund, by an eighty-five percent majority of the total voting power, may make provision for general exchange arrangements without limiting the right of members to have exchange arrangements of their choice consistent with the purposes of the Fund and the obligations under Section 1 of this Article.

Section 3. *Surveillance over exchange arrangements*

(*a*) The Fund shall oversee the international monetary system in order to ensure its effective operation, and shall oversee the compliance of each member with its obligations under Section 1 of this Article.

(*b*) In order to fulfill its functions under (*a*) above, the Fund shall exercise firm surveillance over the exchange rate policies of members, and shall adopt specific principles for the guidance of all members with respect to those policies. Each member shall provide the Fund with the information necessary for such surveillance, and, when requested by the Fund, shall consult with it on the member's exchange rate policies. The principles adopted by the Fund shall be consistent with cooperative arrangements by which members maintain the value of their currencies in relation to the value of the currency or currencies of other members, as well as with other exchange arrangements of a member's choice consistent with the purposes of the Fund and Section 1 of this Article. These principles shall respect the domestic social and political policies of members, and in applying these principles the Fund shall pay due regard to the circumstances of members.

Section 4. *Par values*

The Fund may determine, by an eighty-five percent majority of the total voting power, that international economic conditions permit the introduction of a widespread system of exchange arrangements based on stable but adjustable par values. The Fund shall make the determination on the basis of the underlying stability of the world economy, and for this purpose shall take into account price movements and rates of expansion in the economies of members. The determination shall be made in light of the evolution of the international monetary system, with particular reference to sources of liquidity, and, in order to ensure the effective operation of a system of par values, to arrangements under which both members in surplus and members in deficit in their balances of payments take prompt, effective, and symmetrical action to achieve adjustment, as well as to arrangements for intervention and the treatment of imbalances. Upon making such determination, the Fund shall notify members that the provisions of Schedule C apply.

Section 5. *Separate currencies within a member's territories*

(*a*) Action by a member with respect to its currency under this Article shall be deemed to apply to the separate currencies of all territories in respect of which the member has accepted this Agreement under Article XXXI, Section 2(*g*) unless the member declares that its action relates either to the metropolitan currency alone, or only to one or more specified separate currencies, or to the metropolitan currency and one or more specified separate currencies.

(*b*) Action by the Fund under this Article shall be deemed to relate to all currencies of a member referred to in (*a*) above unless the Fund declares otherwise.

Appendix B

An actual conclusion (omitting the name of the member) on a recent Article IV consultation:

Executive Directors have congratulated the . . . authorities on the success of their stabilization efforts, which in the past two years have led to a marked improvement in the balance of payments and to a lowering of the underlying rate of inflation, while allowing a level of economic growth higher than the average for [similarly placed] countries. This remarkable success was seen as largely reflecting the adoption of exchange rate and interest rate policies directed at improving competitiveness and restoring the relative attractiveness of domestic financial assets. The moderation of wage increases and a strong increase in the private savings ratio were seen as important and successful contributing forces.

The Directors were gratified that the stabilization effort has laid the basis for a more sustained rate of growth, and they encouraged the authorities in their efforts to promote a further recovery of investment. Taking into account the recent deterioration in the external current account and in the overall balance of payments, it was important, in the view of Directors, that the exchange rate remain competitive and that interest rates be maintained at levels adequate to attract continued inflows of workers remittances and foreign capital and to mobilize an increasing volume of domestic savings.

Many Directors observed that the situation of public finances, including the unsustainably high public sector deficit as a ratio of GNP, continued to be a cause of concern. They welcomed the efforts currently being made by the authorities to bring about a more equitable distribution of the tax burden, to reduce tax evasion, and to improve productivity in the public enterprise sector. They also stressed the importance of tightening controls over expenditures, especially by the social security system, and the local authorities, and of pursuing appropriate pricing policies, particularly in the public enterprise sector and in the energy field, in order to contain the growth of subsidies. Furthermore they emphasized the importance of increasing the nonmonetary financing of the budget deficit.

Most Executive Directors felt that the authorities' goal of reducing inflation would require a somewhat tighter stance of financial policies. In this respect, concern was expressed about the rapid growth of domestic bank credit in recent months, which was regarded as excessive, and Directors welcomed the authorities' intentions to keep under close scrutiny policies in this area.

Directors expressed satisfaction with the recent measures to liberalize the trade and payments system and the hope that further steps in that direction would be taken.

Finally, Executive Directors expressed their gratification concerning the very positive and fruitful relationship between . . . and the Fund and their confidence that this collaboration will continue to strengthen in view of the medium-term aspects of . . . economic strategy.

FREEDOM OF THE AIR AND THE CONVENTION ON THE LAW OF THE SEA

*By Kay Hailbronner**

I. The Present Legal Regime

Public international air law is based on two principles. The first recognizes each state's full and absolute sovereignty over the air above its territory and territorial waters, including the right to impose its jurisdiction over such airspace. Thus, a state may require any foreign aircraft in its airspace, even if only briefly in transit, to comply with its air transport regulations, for example, those concerning the aircraft and its crew, navigation, and the environment. This right, however, is subject to those international treaty obligations the state has assumed in the interest of safe and efficient air transport. The Convention on International Civil Aviation[1] (hereinafter referred to as the Chicago Convention), generally regarded as the Magna Charta of public international air law, requires each contracting state to "collaborate in securing the highest practicable degree of uniformity in regulations, standards, procedures and organization in relation to aircraft, personnel, airways and auxiliary services in all matters in which such uniformity will facilitate and improve air navigation."[2] To this end, the International Civil Aviation Organization (ICAO) was granted the power to adopt international standards and recommended practices and procedures dealing with matters such as communication systems and air navigation aids, rules of the air and air traffic control practices, as well as registration and identification of aircraft. Contracting states, however, retained the right to depart from such standards or recommended practices, provided they notified the Organization of the differences between their national regulations and those prescribed by an international standard.[3]

The second principle acknowledges the area above the high seas as an aerial highway open to all nations and not subject to the sovereignty of any state. The customary law principle of freedom of overflight,[4] recognized also in Article 2 of the Geneva Convention on the High Seas,[5] is the basis for Article

* Professor of Law, University of Konstanz, Federal Republic of Germany. I would like to acknowledge my appreciation to Wolfgang W. Fritzemeyer of the New York Bar for his assistance in some of the research and in the editing of this article.

[1] *Done* Dec. 7, 1944, 61 Stat. 1180, TIAS No. 1591, 1956 Bundesgesetzblatt [BGB1] II 411, 15 UNTS 295.

[2] *Id.*, Art. 37.

[3] *See* T. Buergenthal, Law-Making in the International Civil Aviation Organization 57 *et seq.* (1969); N. Matte, Traité de droit aérien-aéronautique 195–97 (1964); J. Erler, Rechtsfragen der ICAO 131 *et seq.* (1967).

[4] *See* J. C. Cooper, *Space Above the Seas*, in Explorations in Aerospace Law, Selected Essays by John Cobb Cooper 194 (I. A. Vlasic ed. 1968); Goedhuis, *Sovereignty and Freedom in the Air Space*, 41 Grotius Soc'y Transactions 137 (1956).

[5] 13 UST 2312, TIAS No. 5200, 1972 BGB1.II 1089, 450 UNTS 82.

12 of the Chicago Convention, which states that "over the high seas the rules in force shall be those established under the Convention." Compliance with these rules is therefore obligatory for the contracting states. ICAO's legislative power in this regard is clearly intended to prevent divergences in national regulations that might pose navigational hazards to international air transport. In practice, it has been accepted that it is up to the Council of ICAO to designate certain rules relating to the flight and maneuver of aircraft over the high seas as mandatory, while states may deviate from any other rules not so designated.[6]

Since national air traffic control authorities may extend their services to the airspace above the high seas, it has been considered impractical to change flight regulations whenever an aircraft passes from national airspace to the airspace above the high seas. The Council of ICAO has therefore authorized any contracting state that provides air traffic control services over the high seas to apply the regulations under Annex 1 to its Rules of the Air "in a manner consistent with [those] adopted for airspace under its jurisdiction."[7] Otherwise, each state would have two sets of air traffic service regulations, one applicable to the airspace above its own territory, the other to the airspace over the high seas where it provides air traffic control services. It was also feared that mandatory application of the ICAO standards might deter states from supplying air traffic control services over the high seas.[8]

By developing a uniform aviation code widely accepted by states, the Chicago system has made considerable progress in promoting safe and efficient international air transport. The Chicago Conference, however, did not succeed in establishing a multilateral air transport scheme providing for freedoms of overflight and landing.[9] Therefore, the granting of traffic rights remained essentially within the domain of each state's sovereign powers. Under customary international law, every flight over foreign territory is subject to the consent of the overflown state. Even the right of innocent passage, customarily accorded to ships passing through the territorial sea, has never been extended to foreign aircraft flying over the territorial sea.[10] In addition, there are no general transit rights relating to international airways, analogous to the law

[6] T. BUERGENTHAL, *supra* note 3, at 83.

[7] *See* ICAO Council Doc. 7037 (C 814) at 29–30 (1951); *cf.* Carroz, *International Legislation on Air Navigation over the High Seas,* 26 J. AIR L. & COM. 158, 168–71 (1959).

[8] T. BUERGENTHAL, *supra* note 3, at 83; Carroz, *supra* note 7, at 171; J. ERLER, *supra* note 3, at 144.

[9] According to Article 5, only aircraft not engaged in scheduled international air services shall have the right to make flights into or innocent transit nonstop across a foreign state's territory and to make stops for nontraffic purposes without having to obtain prior permission, and subject to the right of the overflown state to require landing. The attempt to establish a multilateral treaty regime by the International Air Transit Agreement (1956 BGB1.II 442) and the International Air Transport Agreement (for a text, see 2 INTERNATIONAL CIVIL AVIATION CONFERENCE, PROC. 434 (1949)) failed for lack of a sufficient number of ratifications; *cf.* N. MATTE, *supra* note 3, at 241; W. SCHWENK, HANDBUCH DES LUFTVERKEHRSRECHTS 360–61 (1981); Lissitzyn, *Freedom of the Air: Scheduled and Non-Scheduled Air Services,* in THE FREEDOM OF THE AIR 89 (E. McWhinney & M. Bradley eds. 1968); D. JOHNSON, RIGHTS IN AIRSPACE 58 *et seq.* (1965).

[10] La Pradelle, *Les Frontières de l'air,* 86 RECUEIL DES COURS 117, 139 *et seq.* (1954 II); O'Connell, *Innocent Passage of Warships,* in 7 THESAURUS ACROASIUM 405, 446–47 (1977); Moore,

of the sea concept of straits used for international navigation. Instead, a network of bilateral air transport agreements providing for reciprocal traffic rights today forms the pattern of international commercial air transportation.[11]

Under normal circumstances, obtaining permission to pass through foreign airspace will raise no major problems. In extraordinary situations, however, passage rights may be withheld or traffic rights suspended in order to exert political pressure. The freedom of overflight essential to international aviation may be restricted severely as a result of the establishment of prohibited zones, the unreasonable enforcement of national regulations relating to the flight and maneuver of aircraft, or simply the exercise of excessive state control over foreign aircraft in transit. There is sufficient state practice to show that such measures have been taken in the course of conflicts, particularly when the status of a territory was disputed.[12] In those circumstances, the freedom of the airspace above the high seas may provide the only means of maintaining international air services with a third country. Therefore, the regime of the high seas considerably affects commercial aviation interests.

This statement applies a fortiori to state aircraft. State aircraft, defined as aircraft used in military, police, and customs services, are excluded from the scope of the Chicago Convention and are therefore mainly subject to national regulation.[13] With regard to rights of overflight for foreign military aircraft, states are generally reluctant to incur far-reaching obligations. On the whole, freedom of overflight is granted only in particular situations and with the proviso of revocability. Therefore, freedom of the airspace above the high seas is essential to those states whose air forces are poised for flight to any part of the world where their interests are challenged. In a critical situation, military aircraft will need a direct and speedy route to the crisis area. Rerouting or the need to ask for permission to overfly might substantially diminish their efficiency. John Norton Moore underlined the strategic impor-

---

The Regime of Straits and the Third United Nations Conference on the Law of the Sea, 74 AJIL 77, 85 (1980).

[11] W. SCHWENK, *supra* note 9, at 361, has estimated that in 1979 there were approximately 2,924 bilateral air transport agreements in force.

[12] Regarding the dispute between India and Pakistan on the establishment of prohibited zones by Pakistan, which cut off all direct flight routes between the two countries, see N. MATTE, *supra* note 3, at 182–83; J. ERLER, *supra* note 3, at 192. Similar incidents have occurred as a consequence of border disputes between Greece and Turkey, Israel and the Arab states, and Spain and Great Britain.

[13] *See generally* MING-MIN PENG, LE STATUT JURIDIQUE DE L'AÉRONEF MILITAIRE (1957).

Article 3(c) of the Chicago Convention explicitly provides that no state aircraft of a contracting state shall fly over the territory of another state or land thereon without authorization, by special agreement or otherwise, and only in accordance with the terms thereof. ICAO's international aviation code also does not apply to state aircraft. Contracting states only undertake, when they issue regulations covering their state aircraft, to have due regard to the safety of navigation of civil aircraft. In practice, national rules relating to the flight and maneuver of aircraft will normally correspond to ICAO's international standards. With some exceptions for military aircraft, those standards apply as well to state aircraft. For an account of the regulations applicable in the Federal Republic of Germany, see W. SCHWENK, *supra* note 9, at 152–54.

tance of freedom of the airspace over the high seas to the United States when he reported that overflight of land territory during the Yom Kippur War was denied to the United States even by its NATO allies.[14] Similarly, smaller states asked for such permission might refuse it in order to avoid any involvement in a conflict.

The new legal regime of the oceans reflected in the Convention on the Law of the Sea[15] (hereinafter referred to as the Convention) is obviously of paramount importance to the freedom of the air above the oceans. Any extension of sovereign or "quasi-sovereign" jurisdictional powers restricts the freedom of movement of aircraft above the high seas. Thus, the extension of the territorial sea to 12 miles will bring the airspace over the world's most important international straits such as Gibraltar, Hormuz, Bab el Mandeb, Dover, and Malacca under territorial control.[16] Since innocent passage does not embrace any right of overflight, the passage of aircraft will be subject to the coastal state's consent. In addition, recognition of a 200-mile exclusive economic zone might imply authority over movement of aircraft, including restrictions with respect to overflight. Roughly 40 percent of the surface of the world's oceans lies within 200 miles of the shore.[17] If this vast area ever comes to be regarded by coastal states as being wholly or partially subject to their sovereignty relating to flight activities, the traditional concept of the freedom of the air might be drastically curtailed.

In examining some of the air law implications of the Convention, two main issues arise. The first concerns the scope of the right of transit passage for aircraft guaranteed by the Convention in international straits, archipelagic air routes, and exclusive economic zones. The term "transit passage" raises the question of possible restrictions on rights of overflight on the analogy of the traditional concept of innocent passage. Closely related to this issue is the question of "creeping jurisdiction." The Convention has introduced new areas of conflicting rights. International aviation, which is dependent on unambiguous operating rules, may have to face conflicting claims and legal requirements because of the uncertainties in the legal status of those new areas. The most evident uncertainty concerns the application of the ICAO Rules of the Air, which are mandatory in the airspace above the high seas. In addition, jurisdictional claims by coastal states concerning the protection of the environment, weather modification by aircraft, or military activities in the exclusive economic zone may lead to excessive restrictions on foreign aircraft and possible hazards to international aviation.

[14] Moore, *supra* note 10, at 84.

[15] This article was written on the basis of the text of the Convention agreed upon at the 10th session, UN Doc. A/CONF.62/L.78, of Aug. 28, 1981. No changes were made in the relevant provisions in the final text of Oct. 7, 1982, UN Doc. A/CONF.62/122, *reprinted in* 21 ILM 1261 (1982), and opened for signature on Dec. 10, 1982. For the codification process within the United Nations, see Hailbronner & Fritzemeyer, *Das Recht der Vereinten Nationen (2. Teil)—Rechtsquellen, Zuständigkeiten und Arbeitsweise,* 13 JURISTISCHE ARBEITSBLÄTTER 437, 444 *et seq.* (1981).

[16] Richardson, *Power, Mobility and the Law of the Sea,* 58 FOREIGN AFF. 902, 905–06 (1980); Moore, *supra* note 10, at 79.

[17] Vitzthum, *Die Gleichschaltung von Land und Meer,* in DIE PLÜNDERUNG DER MEERE 49, 60 *et seq.* (W. Graf Vitzthum ed. 1981).

The records show that air law implications of the new law of the sea received little attention at the Third Law of the Sea Conference.[18] Interpretation of the Convention therefore has to rely considerably on the general discussion about the legal status of the new areas. Undoubtedly, when the Convention enters into force, new questions may arise that are not foreseen here.

It should be noted that recent announcements by the U.S. Government that it will not ratify the Convention and the reservations expressed by a number of other states[19] do not affect the relevance of our topic. Air law implications of the new law of the sea are mainly related to the legal regimes of territorial waters, international straits, and the exclusive economic zone. If the deep sea mining concept of the Convention should fail, owing to the strong objections of those states capable of engaging in such activities, large parts of the Convention will still have effects on states that have not ratified it. The extension of the territorial sea and the establishment of exclusive economic zones are the result of developments that took place independently of the Convention.[20] This does not necessarily mean that the scope of rights and duties in those areas, as laid down in the Convention, already reflects customary international law. As a part of evolving customary international law, however, those parts of the Convention on which consensus was reached will determine the rights and duties of states in a particular conflict. In this context, it has to be taken into account that many provisions were the result of compromise.[21] The acceptance of "creeping jurisdiction" for the coastal state corresponds, therefore, to enlarged transit rights for aircraft, so that exclusive rights and jurisdiction may be exercised only in accordance with the limitations provided for in the Convention.

II. AIRSPACE ABOVE INTERNATIONAL STRAITS

Article 2 of the Convention reiterates the generally recognized principle of sovereignty over the airspace above the territorial sea. The right of innocent passage through the territorial sea (Article 17 *ff.*) does not include the passage of aircraft. Innocent passage is considered to be prejudicial to the peace, good order, or security of the coastal state if a ship engages in the launching, landing, or taking on board of any aircraft (Article 19(2)(e)). To this extent, the legal

[18] For a summary of the issues raised at the last session, *cf.* UN Press Release SEA/494, Apr. 30, 1982; *see* THIRD UNITED NATIONS CONFERENCE ON THE LAW OF THE SEA, OFFICIAL RECORDS; *see also* THIRD UNITED NATIONS CONFERENCE ON THE LAW OF THE SEA, DOCUMENTS (Werkhefte Nos. 26, 27, and 29 of the Institut für Internationale Angelegenheiten der Universität Hamburg, R. Platzöder ed. 1975, 1976); 1–3 DOKUMENTE DER DRITTEN SEERECHTSKONFERENZ DER VEREINTEN NATIONEN, NEW YORKER SESSIONEN (R. Platzöder ed. 1976).

[19] *Cf.* Frankfurter Allgemeine Zeitung, July 10, 1982, at 5; H. G. KNIGHT, CONSEQUENCES OF NON-AGREEMENTS AT THE THIRD U.N. LAW OF THE SEA CONFERENCE (Studies in Transnational Legal Policy No. 11, 1976).

[20] *Cf.* statement by the Government of the Federal Republic of Germany, in STAND, ENTWICKLUNG UND MÖGLICHE KONSEQUENZEN DER 3. SEERECHTSKONFERENZ DER VEREINTEN NATIONEN, Bundestagsdrucksache No. 9/1171 (June 22, 1981); *see also* Eitel, *Seerechtsreform und Internationale Politik,* 107 ARCHIV ÖFFENTLICHEN RECHTS 100 (1982).

[21] Vitzthum, *supra* note 17, at 67 *et seq.*

regime of the Convention does not differ from the rules of the Geneva Convention on the High Seas.

Article 38, however, stipulates that in straits used for international navigation between one part of the high seas or an exclusive economic zone and another part of the high seas or an exclusive economic zone all aircraft enjoy the right of transit passage, which shall not be impeded. Obviously, the right of transit passage is meant to eliminate possible detrimental consequences to international aviation from the extension of the territorial sea to 12 nautical miles (Article 3). The right of transit passage is defined in Article 38(2) as the "exercise in accordance with this Part of the freedom of navigation and overflight solely for the purpose of continuous and expeditious transit of the strait between one part of the high seas or an exclusive economic zone and another part of the high seas or an exclusive economic zone." The requirement of continuous and expeditious transit, however, "does not preclude passage through the strait for the purpose of entering, leaving or returning from a State bordering the strait, subject to the conditions of entry to that State" (*cf.* the last sentence of Article 38(2)).

The freedom of overflight of international straits conferred by Article 38 raises various questions as to the power of states bordering straits to restrict that freedom and impose obligations on aircraft in transit. Transiting aircraft may considerably affect a littoral state's interests in regulating flight traffic, limiting dangerous or harmful activities such as flight exercises or refueling while in flight, and restricting military activities prejudicial to the defense or security of the coastal state. Spain, which opposed any right of overflight, therefore criticized the 1978 draft proposal for not specifying what activities were to be prohibited to aircraft. Moreover, the proposal did not meet with the Spanish delegation's approval because it did not expressly stipulate the laws and regulations that states bordering straits would be permitted to enact in relation to overflight, and because it did not refer to air corridors, which, on the analogy of the sea lanes provided for in the transit passage regime itself, would have to be established.[22]

Similar criticism was raised by Morocco and Greece. The Moroccan delegation suggested an amendment to Article 39, paragraph 3, providing that aircraft in transit must refrain from activities such as exercises or firing practice, the use of weapons, the taking of photographs, low-altitude and dive-bomber flying, in-flight refueling, and interference with telecommunications.[23] The Moroccan proposal added that aircraft in transit should

> take proper care not to violate the regulations governing air corridors and altitude of flights above the strait as fixed by the State bordering the strait, and to avoid flying over its territory rising above the water, insofar as the air corridor established by the State bordering the strait does not provide for such overflight.

A Greek amendment would have expanded the provision on the coastal state's

[22] Conf. Doc. C.2/Informal Meeting/4 (Apr. 26, 1978); *see also* UN Doc. A/CONF.62/WS/12, at 2 (Oct. 31, 1980).

[23] Conf. Doc. C.2/Informal Meeting/22 (Apr. 28, 1978).

power to regulate transit passage through straits in respect of the "safety of navigation and the regulation of marine traffic" (*cf.* Article 42(1)(a)) by adding the words, "as well as the safety of air traffic and the rules, regulations and procedures of ICAO."[24] Greece suggested another amendment that would have enabled countries bordering straits under their sovereignty to designate predetermined air routes and prescribe traffic procedures for air navigation in straits in the interest of safe and efficient passage.

Neither amendment was approved.[25] Nevertheless, the final text makes clear that transit passage is not guaranteed without limitations. Paragraph 1 of Article 39 provides:

> Ships and aircraft, while exercising the right of transit passage, shall:
>
> (a) proceed without delay through or over the strait;
>
> (b) refrain from any threat or use of force against the sovereignty, territorial integrity or political independence of States bordering the strait, or in any other manner in violation of the principles of international law embodied in the Charter of the United Nations;
>
> (c) refrain from any activities other than those incident to their normal modes of continuous and expeditious transit unless rendered necessary by *force majeure* or by distress;
>
> (d) comply with other relevant provisions of this Part.

The wording of subparagraph (c) may embrace even more duties than those implied by the amendment suggested by Morocco. The concept of transit passage provided for by subparagraph (c) excludes any activity that is not a constituent part of the transit flight. Article 39, however, does not answer the question whether a coastal state may adopt laws and regulations relating to transit passage of aircraft and whether a coastal state has the right to interfere with aircraft in transit not complying with its municipal law or the requirements under Article 39 itself. The Convention confers prescriptive authority on states bordering international straits with respect to the transit passage only of ships. Legislative powers concerning pollution control, navigational safety, customs regulations, etc., apply exclusively to foreign ships exercising the right of transit passage, as Article 42(4) indicates. Article 41, which deals with sea lanes and traffic separation schemes in straits used for international navigation, also does not accord states bordering straits the power to prescribe international air routes and air corridors. The wording of Article 41 clearly covers only the transit passage of ships. Since Articles 38–44 expressly differentiate between ships and aircraft, navigation and overflight, it can hardly be assumed that legislative authority explicitly granted with respect to navigation and ships applies—by analogy or otherwise—to aircraft in transit.

On a first reading, Article 42(5) seems to support a different view. The obligation to bear international responsibility incumbent on the state of registry of an aircraft that is entitled to sovereign immunity rests on the assumption that the aircraft acts "in a manner contrary to such laws and regulations or other provisions of this Part." This assumption, however, does not

[24] UN Doc. A/CONF.62/L.123 (1982).

[25] *See* UN Press Release, *supra* note 18, at 38.

imply that regulations adopted under Article 42 may refer to aircraft in transit. Article 42(4) relates, in the case of ships, to national regulations and laws adopted under that article, as well as to other obligations under the Convention; in the case of aircraft, responsibility is exclusively based on violations of international duties under Article 39.

Nevertheless, it may be argued that the straits regime under the Convention is ambiguous in allowing a coastal state discretion to control aircraft and ships, to discriminate among users, and to interfere with their right of navigation and overflight.[26] After all, the Convention does not explicitly exclude recourse to a coastal state's power to enforce its laws and regulations in the airspace above its territorial sea. Thus, on the analogy of the innocent passage concept, a state bordering straits would be deemed to have those powers which it considers necessary to protect its interests.

Again, regulatory authority relating to transit passage and unilateral enforcement powers have to be treated separately. As far as regulatory competence is concerned, both the wording and the negotiating context argue against the conclusion that the coastal state's legislative authority extends beyond the powers expressly granted by Article 42. This regulatory authority may be exercised only under special conditions and applies mainly to the implementation of international regulations previously adopted and to fishing and loading activities of ships. All amendments to extend this catalog of rights were rejected in order to prevent conflicts from arising out of uncertainties over the legal rights and obligations of ships in transit. As for aircraft in transit, regulatory authority presumably is denied since, unlike the activities of ships in transit, those of aircraft have not been considered potentially prejudicial to the basic interests of states bordering straits.

Any analogy to the powers of a coastal state with respect to the innocent passage of ships through its territorial waters also seems ill-founded because the straits transit regime is evidently covered separately by the provisions of part III of the Convention. Article 45 mentions two exceptional cases in which the regime of innocent passage applies, and Article 36 specifies another exception relevant only to navigation; thus, further reference to the innocent passage regime is excluded. In addition, statements of delegations during the conference cited by Professor Moore[27] demonstrate beyond any doubt that the regime of international straits was adopted in clear contrast to the doctrine of innocent passage, which was generally regarded as an inappropriate approach to the problem of transit through straits.

Article 38(3), which provides that "[a]ny activity which is not an exercise of the right of transit passage through a strait remains subject to the other applicable provisions of this Convention," also does not permit the inference of any regulatory powers to the coastal state. Its purpose is to make clear that activities not covered by the transit passage privilege remain subject to any

[26] Darman, *The Law of the Sea: Rethinking U.S. Interests,* 56 FOREIGN AFF. 373 (1977–78); Reisman, *The Regime of Straits and National Security: An Appraisal of International Lawmaking,* 74 AJIL 48 (1980); *cf. also* Knight, *The 1971 United States Proposal on the Breadth of the Territorial Sea and Passage through Straits,* 51 ORE. L. REV. 759 (1974).

[27] Moore, *supra* note 10, at 93 *et seq.*

other provisions of the Convention dealing with such activities; and it therefore implies that transit passage itself is not subject to other provisions of the Convention, particularly those giving a coastal state regulatory authority with respect to innocent passage in the territorial sea.

The coastal state's lack of regulatory powers over aircraft in transit does not change the legal status of the airspace above international straits. Article 34 states that the regime of passage through straits used for international navigation "shall not in other respects affect the legal status of the waters forming such straits or the exercise by the States bordering the straits of their sovereignty or jurisdiction over such waters and their air space, bed and subsoil." Paragraph 2 of Article 34 indicates that sovereignty may not be used as a claim to supplementary regulatory and enforcement powers over the passage of ships and aircraft. Sovereignty or jurisdiction can only be exercised subject to the provisions in part III of the Convention and to other rules of international law. Restrictions on the freedom of overflight not consistent with the legal regime of transit passage under the Convention are therefore not admissible.[28] However, since the exercise of sovereignty or jurisdiction "in other respects" is not affected by the Convention, aircraft in transit remain subject to a coastal state's general municipal law.

It may not always be easy to draw the line between sovereignty or jurisdiction "in other respects" and the inadmissible regulation of the passage of foreign aircraft. The crucial test will be whether the application of municipal law implies restrictions on the right of overflight granted by the Convention. Municipal law specifications concerning the plane, its crew and passengers, its flight route, noise and emission standards, etc., may not be applied to aircraft in transit, though the crew and passengers remain subject to coastal state jurisdiction in criminal and civil law matters. As noted earlier, Article 39 obliges aircraft to refrain from any activities not incidental to "normal" transit passage. Although this provision cannot be interpreted as giving supplementary regulatory authority to the state bordering the strait, that state is not precluded from making any violation of the international obligations of aircraft in transit a criminal offense.

However, a breach of its duties under the Convention or municipal law by an aircraft in transit does not necessarily give a state bordering straits the right to take unilateral action to prevent passage "prejudicial to the peace, good order or security." The authority of a coastal state under Articles 25 and 30 to take the necessary steps in its territorial sea to prevent noninnocent passage is not applicable, by analogy, to the legal regime of passage through international straits. In contrast to the innocent passage regime, part III does not expressly permit coastal states to interfere with passage under specific circumstances. Rather, it is laid down in Article 44 that "States bordering straits shall not hamper transit passage and shall give appropriate publicity to any danger to navigation or overflight within or over the strait of which they have knowledge. There shall be no suspension of transit passage."

[28] Jaenicke, *Die Dritte Seerechtskonferenz der Vereinten Nationen*, 38 ZEITSCHRIFT FÜR AUSLÄNDISCHES RECHT UND VÖLKERRECHT [ZAÖRV] 438, 471 *et seq.* (1978).

Nevertheless, this provision has been interpreted as not excluding a coastal state's right to secure compliance with an aircraft's duties. A coastal state, as W. Michael Reisman observed, might still be able to characterize passage as "nontransit" and to deny passage unilaterally.[29] In support of this view, it may be argued that anything less than the power to take unilateral enforcement measures might substantially endanger a coastal state's vital interests. In its own sovereign airspace, a state will usually not rely solely on diplomatic and judicial procedures for the solution of a conflict. Therefore, the Convention cannot be presumed as having deprived states bordering straits of their sovereign rights to enforce the law within their own airspace.

Some may read Article 42(5) as implying enforcement powers in case of nonimmune vessels and aircraft, but this interpretation is not logically required. The paragraph may be more reasonably understood as making it clear that sovereign immunity does not relieve the flag state or state of registry from international responsibility in case of a violation. Therefore, no inference can be drawn from that paragraph one way or another about the enforcement powers of a coastal state.

Moore has convincingly demonstrated by a thorough analysis of the wording and the negotiating context that the Convention carefully separates flag state duties from the definition of transit passage rights.[30] In order to avoid repetition, his arguments may be summarized as follows: in contrast to Article 19, which provides that passage "shall be considered to be prejudicial . . . if," Article 39 says, "[s]hips and aircraft, while exercising the right of transit passage, shall." In addition, Moore cites early draft articles and various statements of delegates indicating that transit passage rights should not be linked with vague duties or restrictions that could lead to confrontation.[31] Moreover, other provisions of the Convention clearly distinguish between mere "flag state obligations" of ships in international straits and coastal state authority to take enforcement action. Article 233 gives the right to interfere with the passage of ships only if a foreign ship has committed a violation of its duties under subparagraphs (a) or (b) of Article 42(1), "causing or threatening major damage to the marine environment of the straits."

The distinction made by the Convention between the regime of innocent passage in the territorial sea and the regime of transit passage in international straits would be eliminated if sovereignty could be understood as a superseding right to take unilateral action in order to prevent transit passage. It must be kept in mind that restrictions on the exercise of sovereign powers were conditional on a vast extension of the territorial sea in favor of coastal states. Thus, a coastal state must not deny passage or take any enforcement measures against aircraft in transit that violate their duties under Article 39. Under the Convention, conflicts will usually have to be resolved solely through the normal diplomatic and judicial proceedings.[32]

[29] Reisman, *supra* note 26, at 70.

[30] Moore, *supra* note 10, at 102 *et seq.*

[31] *Id.* at 104.

[32] It is doubtful whether compulsory settlement procedures, provided for in part IV of the Convention, apply to disputes arising out of allegations that a state has abused its right of overflight above international straits. Article 297(1) provides for compulsory jurisdiction:

In exceptional circumstances, the reference to international dispute settlement procedures may be insufficient to protect a coastal state's vital interests. It is doubtful whether resort by a coastal state to its sovereign enforcement powers is also precluded by the regime of transit passage if its security is imminently endangered by an aircraft flying in the airspace above international straits. Even before the regime of transit passage came to be accepted at the Law of the Sea Conference, states laid claim—on the basis of necessity—to air defense identification zones in the airspace above the high seas. However, the legality of establishing large defense zones in which foreign aircraft not complying with certain identification requirements could be intercepted is still doubtful under customary international law (see *infra* pp. 515–19). The Convention cannot be presumed to have barred all recourse to the use of enforcement measures in the airspace above international straits. In case of a "threat or use of force against the sovereignty, territorial integrity or political independence of States bordering the strait" (Article 39(1)(b)), the inherent right of self-defense is not impaired by the Convention.

Beyond the right of self-defense in the case of an armed attack, a coastal state must also be able to protect its vital security interests in its airspace by taking unilateral enforcement action against imminent dangers resulting from activities of an aircraft in transit. Sovereignty over international straits and their airspace implies enforcement rights with respect to a coastal state's vital security interests. This does not amount to abandonment of the concept of guaranteed transit passage. The de-linkage, in the regime of international straits, of rights of transit passage, on the one hand, and duties of transiting ships, on the other hand, is valid in all matters covered by the Convention like pollution control, technical requirements as to the aircraft and its crew, or other activities not incident to the transit passage (Article 39(1)(c)). It applies as well to the general protection of a coastal state's security interests by the establishment of prohibited zones, as demonstrated by Article 52, paragraph 2 in the case of archipelagic sea lanes passage. The protection of a state's vital security interests against imminent dangers requiring immediate reaction, however, is a matter not regulated by the Convention and, therefore, not included in the scope of mere "flag state duties," precluding a state from taking enforcement action in its airspace. The right to deny transit passage, however, must be interpreted very narrowly in order to avoid any undue interference with the freedom of overflight. The danger to vital security interests must be evident, leaving a coastal state no other choice than immediate action if irreparable damage is to be avoided.

(a) when it is alleged that a coastal State has acted in contravention of the provisions of this Convention in regard to the freedoms and rights of navigation, overflight or the laying of submarine cables and pipelines, or in regard to other internationally lawful uses of the sea specified in article 58;

(b) when it is alleged that a State in exercising the aforementioned freedoms, rights or uses has acted in contravention of this Convention or of laws or regulations adopted by the coastal State in conformity with this Convention and other rules of international law not incompatible with this Convention. . . .

Cf. Bernhardt, *Die Streitbeilegung im Rahmen der Neuordnung des Seerechts,* 38 ZAÖRV 971 *et seq.* (1978); Platzöder, *Meerengen, id.* at 710, 730–31.

Article 12 of the Chicago Convention makes compliance with ICAO's Rules of the Air mandatory in the airspace above the high seas. The Convention extends such mandatory compliance to civil aircraft in transit over international straits. Article 39, paragraph 3 says:

> Aircraft in transit passage shall:
>
> (a) observe the Rules of the Air established by the International Civil Aviation Organization as they apply to civil aircraft; state aircraft will normally comply with such safety measures and will at all times operate with due regard for the safety of navigation;
>
> (b) at all times monitor the radio frequency assigned by the competent internationally designated air traffic control authority or the appropriate international distress radio frequency.

Article 39, paragraph 3 therefore ensures uniform application of ICAO's aviation code with respect to civil aircraft, and thus excludes possible divergences between a coastal state's municipal law relating to the flight and maneuver of aircraft and the international Rules of the Air. State aircraft, however, are not strictly obliged to comply with ICAO's Rules of the Air. The Convention does not indicate which criteria should be applied in defining the term "normal." Consequently, subparagraph (a) of Article 39(3) leaves considerable discretion to deviate from the Rules of the Air. Since the legal regime of transit passage precludes use of the littoral state's regulatory authority to fill this gap, state aircraft and, in particular, transiting military aircraft may follow their own rules relating to the flight and maneuver of aircraft. The Spanish delegation raised strong objections to Article 39(3), arguing that state aircraft deemed to be "abnormal" would represent a hazard to air navigation, the populations bordering the straits, and the safety of the states over which they fly.[33] Spain's proposal to delete the word "normally" from the provision, however, received only 21 votes in favor, with 55 against and 60 abstentions.[34] The result of this vote underlines the great importance attached by a large number of states to the unimpeded military and civil use of airways above international straits.

III. Airspace over Archipelagic Sea Lanes

The special geographic situation of archipelagic states, meaning states constituted wholly by one or more groups of islands, "including parts of islands, interconnecting waters and other natural features which are so closely interrelated that such islands, waters and other natural features form an intrinsic geographical, economic and political entity" (Article 46), has led to a slightly different regime of passage for aircraft from the transit passage regime in international straits. Since the sovereignty of an archipelagic state extends to the airspace above the archipelagic waters, basically the same problems arise with respect to the regulatory authority and the enforcement powers of the archipelagic state with regard to aircraft in transit. Vast water areas may be

[33] UN Doc. A/CONF.62/WS/12, *supra* note 22, at 2.
[34] UN Press Release, *supra* note 18, at 38.

subject to the sovereignty of an archipelagic state, which may considerably impair aviation on international routes. The Convention—though recognizing larger security interests of archipelagic states with regard to transiting foreign ships—has established a regime of passage for aircraft very similar to the regime of passage over international straits. Under Article 53, paragraph 2, all aircraft enjoy the right of archipelagic sea lanes passage in air routes. Such passage means "the exercise in accordance with this Convention" of the right of "overflight in the normal mode solely for the purpose of continuous, expeditious and unobstructed transit between one part of the high seas or an exclusive economic zone and another part of the high seas or an exclusive economic zone" (Article 53(3)).

Unlike states bordering international straits under Article 41, however, the archipelagic state may designate special air routes suitable for the continuous and expeditious passage of foreign aircraft over its archipelagic waters and the adjacent territorial sea (*cf.* Article 53(1)). The Convention gives a number of criteria for the establishment of such air routes. They "shall traverse the archipelagic waters and the adjacent territorial sea and shall include all normal passage routes used as routes for international . . . overflight" (Article 53(4)). "[A]ircraft in archipelagic sea lanes passage shall not deviate more than 25 nautical miles to either side" of the axis lines from the entry points of passage routes to the exit points, "provided that such . . . aircraft shall not navigate closer to the coasts than 10 per cent of the distance between the nearest points on islands bordering the sea lane" (Article 53(5)). The archipelagic state may not designate or substitute sea lanes according to its own discretion. Article 53, paragraph 9 obliges the archipelagic state to "refer proposals to the competent international organization with a view to their adoption." The organization may adopt such sea lanes in agreement "with the archipelagic State, after which the archipelagic State may designate, prescribe or substitute them."

Beyond this right, there is no regulatory authority or enforcement power with regard to aircraft in transit. Article 54, by providing for the application "*mutatis mutandis*" of Articles 39, 40, 42, and 44 to archipelagic sea lanes passage, indicates that transit passage of aircraft over archipelagic waters is subject to the same international rules as transit passage of aircraft in international straits.[35] The right of the archipelagic state to suspend innocent passage temporarily in specified areas of its archipelagic waters, if such suspension is essential to the protection of its security, explicitly applies only to transiting ships. Obviously, temporary suspension of passage amounting to the establishment of prohibited zones for military reasons was not considered a necessary precaution with regard to transiting aircraft. Again, the Convention clearly shows its intention to guarantee an unimpeded right of archipelagic sea lanes passage that is not supposed to be subject to claims of unilateral enforcement action. Still, we would suggest that, as in the case of states bordering international straits, the archipelagic state in exceptional circumstances is not precluded from asserting its sovereign right to take immediate action

[35] Moore, *supra* note 10, at 110–11.

against imminent dangers to its security interests resulting from transiting aircraft.

IV. Airspace above the Exclusive Economic Zone

The Legal Nature of the EEZ and the Coastal State's Jurisdiction

The exclusive economic zone (EEZ) is defined by the Convention as "an area beyond and adjacent to the territorial sea, subject to the specific legal régime established in this Part, under which the rights and jurisdictions of the coastal State and the rights and freedoms of other States are governed by the relevant provisions of this Convention" (Article 55). The Convention only very obliquely refers to the legal rights and obligations of states with regard to aircraft in the airspace above the EEZ. In particular, the Convention is silent on the rights of third states vis-à-vis the civil aviation jurisdiction of the coastal state in the airspace above the EEZ and the applicability of ICAO's aviation code, mandatory for aircraft above the high seas. Moreover, the negotiating context provides little guidance. The air law implications of part V belong to the neglected issues of the new law of the sea.[36]

Paragraph 1 of Article 58 provides that in the EEZ all states

> enjoy, subject to the relevant provisions of this Convention, the freedoms referred to in article 87 of navigation and overflight . . . and other internationally lawful uses of the sea related to these freedoms, such as those associated with the operation of ships [and] aircraft . . . , and compatible with the other provisions of this Convention.

Article 87 sets forth the basic principle of the legal regime of the high seas, which declares the high seas open to all states, whether coastal or landlocked. Article 87 incorporates the traditional concept of freedom of the high seas, comprising all activities of aircraft and ships, unless prohibited as harmful, and without discrimination among the users. Overflight, as explicitly mentioned in Article 87(1)(b), is therefore just one example of the lawful uses of the airspace above the high seas. Freedom of the high seas includes, *inter alia,* use of the ocean airspace for military exercises, aerial reconnaissance, and all other activities of civil and military aircraft if due regard is paid to the rights and interests of third states.

It is doubtful, however, whether the reference to Article 87 in Article 58 covers all activities traditionally within the domain of the freedom of the high seas, subject to the provisions of part V. While it is clear that within the EEZ certain sovereign rights of coastal states, as defined in Article 56, preclude unauthorized economic exploration and exploitation by third states, the Convention does not clearly stipulate what legal regime is to apply with regard to activities that are not explicitly covered by Article 56(1)(a). Similarly, it is not altogether clear whether the list of a coastal state's jurisdictional rights with regard to the uses mentioned in Article 56(1)(b) must be regarded as an exhaustive enumeration, precluding any other exercise of jurisdiction in the EEZ.

The solution to the questions raised is linked to the determination of the

[36] *See* Law of the Sea: Neglected Issues, pt. III: Air Space and the Law of the Sea 119–62 (J. K. Gamble ed. 1979).

legal status of the EEZ, one of the most controversial issues at the Law of the Sea Conference. If the EEZ is not part of the high seas, the fundamental principle would seem to be: coastal state jurisdiction with exceptions, to be construed narrowly. If, however, the EEZ remains part of the high seas, freedom of the high seas will prevail and ICAO's aviation code will be applicable. In circumstances not clearly regulated by the Convention, may a coastal state exercise sovereign rights and jurisdiction or does the principle of freedom of the high seas prevail? The answer may be of particular relevance to aviation since in the Convention only the freedom of overflight is mentioned explicitly. A survey of the vast literature on the EEZ does not provide unequivocal answers to the issue.[37] The Group of 77 has succeeded in establishing a "*sui generis*" status of the EEZ based, *inter alia,* on Article 68, under which the provisions of part VII (High Seas) in general do not apply to the EEZ.[38] Although there seems to be no unanimity on the exact legal consequences of this qualification, the *sui generis* concept has mostly been used to "de-link" freedoms granted to third states in the EEZ from the concept of freedom of the high seas. Thus, A. M. Al Mour writes:

> Nevertheless, freedoms enjoyed by other states in the EEZ are in no way equal in their scope to high seas freedoms due to the restrictions imposed on their exercise in accordance with para. (3) of article 58 of the convention. Similarly, other internationally lawful uses of the sea recognized to other states under para. (1) of article 58, are far away from being equal to high seas uses entitled on high seas to all states. In fact, other internationally lawful uses of the sea granted to other states under para. (1) of article 58 are restricted not only by the limitations on their exercise pursuant to para. (3) of this article, but also by the relation which must exist between such uses and other states' freedoms in the EEZ.[39]

On the other hand, it has been observed that the reference to freedom of the high seas in Article 58(1) and to Articles 88–115 in Article 58(2) equals acceptance of the legal regime of the high seas in regard to the EEZ for all practical purposes.[40] One might add that a number of delegations, including that of the United States, have always stressed that the EEZ had to remain a part of the high seas.[41] A look at the negotiating context shows that no agreement could be reached on the legal status of the EEZ.[42] Article 58

[37] *See* Gündling, *Die exklusive Wirtschaftszone,* 38 ZAÖRV 616 (1978); Rojahn, *200 sm-Wirtschaftszone, Meeresfreiheit und Hochseefischerei, Völkerrechtliche Entwicklungslinien,* 19 GERMAN Y.B. INT'L L. 19 *et seq.* (1976); Quéneudec, *La Zone économique,* 79 REV. GÉNÉRALE DROIT INT'L PUBLIC 321 (1975); Rama Puri, *Evolution of the Concept of the Exclusive Economic Zone in UNCLOS III: India's Contribution,* 22 J. INDIAN L. INST. 497 *et seq.* (1980).

[38] *See* Gündling, *supra* note 37, at 653–55, with references to the conference documents at 653 n.105; Jaenicke, *supra* note 28, at 485–91.

[39] Al Mour, *The Legal Status of the Exclusive Economic Zone,* 33 REV. EGYPTIENNE DROIT INT'L 35, 60–61 (1977).

[40] Scerni, *La Zone économique exclusive, son importance, sa nature juridique et les problèmes principaux y relatifs,* in 7 THESAURUS ACROASIUM 157, 183 (1977).

[41] Scerni quotes the head of the U.S. delegation: "It is critical to the United States that the economic zone remains high seas." *Id.* at 182.

[42] For a detailed account, see Jaenicke, *supra* note 28, at 489; *cf. also* Brown, *The Exclusive Economic Zone: Criteria and Machinery for the Resolution of International Conflicts between Different Users of the EEZ,* 4 MAR. POL'Y MGMT. 325 (1977).

represents a compromise, accommodating the *sui generis* approach to objections to that approach.[43] Article 55 supports this view by describing the EEZ as an area subject to the specific legal regime of the Convention.

The lack of agreement about the legal determination of the EEZ is also shown by the "Castañeda formula" in Article 59:

> In cases where this Convention does not attribute rights or jurisdiction to the coastal State or to other States within the exclusive economic zone, and a conflict arises between the interests of the coastal State and any other State or States, the conflict should be resolved on the basis of equity and in the light of all the relevant circumstances, taking into account the respective importance of the interests involved to the parties as well as to the international community as a whole.

Article 59, however, does not resolve the question of exactly what the rights or jurisdictional powers attributed to the coastal state or to other states are, nor does it indicate what legal regime should be applied if a peaceful settlement in accordance with its terms cannot be reached. The reference to equity in Article 59 must be construed as recognition that the legal status of the EEZ is not to be determined according to preconceived terms but on the basis of an evaluation of the respective rights and interests. Thus, the EEZ might be considered as an evolving concept in which the rights and jurisdiction of the coastal state and other states are only partly fixed by the Convention.

This concept, however, does not justify restrictions of the traditional freedom of overflight of the EEZ. Article 59 has to be construed narrowly. The procedure referred to in Article 59 may lead to new jurisdictional rights of the coastal state only insofar as subjects are concerned that are not regulated by the Convention.

One should thus not expect too much of Article 59.[44] In case of a conflict, each side will claim that its rights or jurisdiction, conferred by the Convention or customary international law, is at stake. Therefore, a third state would not be precluded by Article 59 from claiming a right to peaceful military uses of the airspace above the EEZ under Articles 58 and 88. We would suggest that the scope of the rights and jurisdiction of the coastal state in the airspace above the EEZ must be determined according to the "purpose for which the question is asked."[45]

First, those areas will have to be considered in which the Convention gives the coastal state exclusive rights. The concept of "sovereign rights" in Article 56, paragraph 1 implies exclusive economic use of the EEZ by the coastal state. Activities of aircraft of third states relating to "exploring and exploiting, conserving and managing the natural resources, whether living or non-living, of the sea-bed and subsoil and the superjacent waters, and with regard to other activities for the economic exploitation and exploration of the zone,

[43] Oxman, *The Third United Nations Conference on the Law of the Sea: The 1977 New York Session,* 72 AJIL 57, 72 *et seq.* (1978).

[44] *See* Gündling, *supra* note 37, at 655; Quéneudec, *Un Problème en suspens: la nature de la zone économique,* REV. IRANIENNE REL. INTERNATIONALES 39, 40 (1975–76).

[45] Oxman, *supra* note 43, at 74; Heller, *Air Space over Extended Jurisdictional Zones,* in LAW OF THE SEA, *supra* note 36, at 135, 144.

such as the production of energy from the water, currents and winds" (Article 56 (1)(a)), are thus subject to the sovereignty of the coastal state. The use of aircraft to explore and exploit fishery resources, as well as for prospecting in connection with economic exploitation of the EEZ, must be regarded as the coastal state's exclusive right.

On the other hand, the freedoms granted in Article 58 must not be construed too narrowly. The sovereign rights of the coastal state pertain only to the resources of the zone rather than to the zone itself.[46] During the negotiations at the Law of the Sea Conference, it was repeatedly made clear that the freedoms under Article 58 were qualitatively the same as the freedoms of the high seas beyond the EEZ. Thus, the negotiating context supports Bernard Oxman's view "that full freedoms are being preserved, not merely passage rights, and that the application of existing international agreements and regulations regarding navigation, overflight, spacecraft, and submarine cables would be unchanged."[47]

The freedom of overflight and other internationally lawful uses of the sea related to this freedom under Article 58(1) differs from the freedom of overflight of international straits, which are part of the coastal state's territorial sea. Article 58 freedoms include, *inter alia,* use of the airspace above the high seas for military and civil purposes.[48] The exercise of these rights may in a particular case interfere with the coastal state's exclusive economic rights. Flights may threaten the safety of installations for the exploitation of natural resources. Article 58(3) provides:

> States shall have due regard to the rights and duties of the coastal State and shall comply with the laws and regulations adopted by the coastal State in accordance with the provisions of this Convention and other rules of international law in so far as they are not incompatible with this Part.

It should be noted that this provision neither enlarges the regulatory authority of the coastal state under the Convention nor limits the other states' freedoms. Its sole purpose is to make clear that the freedoms under Article 58(1), just like any other right, must not be exercised without taking into account the rights of the coastal state.

Artificial Islands and Installations

According to Article 56(1)(b), the coastal state has jurisdiction "with regard to: (i) the establishment and use of artificial islands, installations and structures; (ii) marine scientific research; (iii) the protection and preservation of the marine environment." Earlier drafts spoke of "exclusive jurisdiction."[49] The text of the Convention avoids such a qualification. Instead, subparagraph (b) of Article 56(1) indicates the scope of these jurisdictional powers by referring

[46] Rama Puri, *supra* note 37, at 509.

[47] Oxman, *supra* note 43, at 69; *see also* Clingan, *Emerging Law of the Sea: The Economic Zone Dilemma,* 14 SAN DIEGO L. REV. 530 (1977).

[48] Jaenicke, *supra* note 28, at 490.

[49] For references, see Gündling, *supra* note 37, at 627.

to the relevant provisions of the Convention and thus clarifies that the coastal state's authority is determined by those provisions.[50] Since the Convention distinguishes between regulatory authority and enforcement powers (*cf.* Articles 60 and 73), the term "jurisdiction" must not be interpreted as a comprehensive power.[51]

Article 60, dealing with artificial islands and installations,[52] may be of particular relevance to aircraft. It is doubtful whether the coastal state's jurisdiction extends to the movements by aircraft above, to, and from those installations. Under Article 60(1) the coastal state has

> the exclusive right to construct and to authorize and regulate the construction, operation and use of:
>
> (a) artificial islands;
> (b) installations and structures for the purposes provided for in article 56 and other economic purposes;
> (c) installations and structures which may interfere with the exercise of the rights of the coastal State in the zone.

While all artificial islands are subject to the coastal state's jurisdiction, installations may be constructed and operated without the coastal state's consent if they are not used for the purposes mentioned in Article 56 or for other economic purposes. Military installations used for aviation purposes are therefore not under the coastal state's exclusive jurisdiction.[53] Proposals to cover *all* installations were rejected since a number of states were prepared to accept the EEZ concept only if military activities within the EEZ, including the movements of aircraft, were not subject to the coastal state's control.[54] Such installations, however, fall under the jurisdiction of the coastal state if they "*may interfere*" with the exercise of its rights in the zone. A proposal by the Federal Republic of Germany to limit the coastal state's authority solely to cases in which installations and structures do interfere with those rights was not accepted.[55]

The wording of Article 60(1)(c) may give rise to conflicts since objective criteria for defining potential interference are not specified.[56] It has to be kept in mind, however, that under the Convention military activities of ships and aircraft are in principle not under the coastal state's control. As an exception to this principle, Article 60(1)(c) must be narrowly construed in order to avoid potential infringement upon other states' rights to use the EEZ for noneconomic purposes.

[50] Jaenicke, *supra* note 28, at 489; *cf.* Gündling, *supra* note 37, at 627.

[51] The term "jurisdiction" is usually understood as granting a special and limited competence over particular events, in contrast to sovereignty, which is understood as a comprehensive and continuous competence. *Cf.* M. McDougal & W. Burke, The Public Order of the Oceans 610 (1962). Not much clarification, however, can be expected from the Convention's terms "exclusive rights," "sovereign rights," "jurisdiction," and "exclusive jurisdiction."

[52] *See generally* Münch, *Les Iles artificielles et les installations en mer,* 38 ZaöRV 933 (1978).

[53] Jaenicke, *supra* note 28, at 487 and 488 n.104.

[54] *Cf.* Gündling, *supra* note 37, at 640.

[55] *See* 3 Dokumente der Dritten Seerechtskonferenz, *supra* note 18, at 719.

[56] *Cf.* Gündling, *supra* note 37, at 640.

Article 60(1) provides for regulatory authority with regard to the construction, operation, and use of such installations and islands. Paragraph 2 adds "exclusive jurisdiction" over those facilities, including "jurisdiction with regard to customs, fiscal, health, safety and immigration laws and regulations." It is questionable whether a coastal state's regulatory authority extends to aircraft movements within the EEZ. The answer, again, depends on the connection in which the question is asked. It is noteworthy that part V lacks a provision corresponding to Article 39(3)(a), which makes ICAO's Rules of the Air mandatory upon aircraft during transit passage in international straits. On the other hand, the coastal state's regulatory authority under Articles 56 and 60 is limited to specific matters and may not easily be extended to the movement of aircraft within the EEZ. Otherwise, control by coastal states over large portions of the airspace above the oceans could be established. The remaining two options, either jurisdiction of the state of registry of the aircraft or attribution of rights and jurisdiction in each particular conflict on the basis of Article 59, hardly seem to be satisfactory. The operation of different legal regimes might endanger air navigation. In the interest of safety, one set of rules would be clearly preferable to a variety of regulations based on each aircraft's nationality.

This problem seems to have escaped the notice of the drafters of the Convention. Paul Heller pointed to the inadequacies of the Informal Composite Negotiating Text by suggesting an amendment that would have given the coastal state jurisdiction over aircraft flying above the EEZ.[57] In support of this proposal, he referred to the recent trend of extending the coastal state's control beyond the original limit of the territorial sea and to the advantage of having a uniform legal regime throughout the coastal state's EEZ.[58]

This solution, despite its advantage of ensuring a uniform set of rules for the territorial sea and the adjacent EEZ, would considerably extend the coastal state's regulatory authority with regard to aircraft flying within or through the EEZ. The coastal state's right to file deviations from international standards with ICAO might lead to restrictions on the freedom of overflight in the guise of regulations concerning the flight and maneuver of aircraft. There are no legal limits, other than procedural requirements under the Chicago Convention, to the exercise by states of their regulatory competence over aviation activities within their airspace.

There is also the danger of inadequate safety standards if the coastal state's regulatory authority were to prevail over ICAO's aviation code. It is therefore suggested that in the airspace above the EEZ, ICAO's Rules of the Air should be mandatory.[59] The basic idea of Article 12 of the Chicago Convention is to provide an international uniform minimum standard of safety, which is not always achieved in national civil aviation. The advantages of such a legal

[57] *See* Heller, *supra* note 45, at 135–53; *cf.* Hailbronner, *Commentary*, in LAW OF THE SEA, *supra* note 36, at 154–58.

[58] Heller, *supra* note 37, at 148.

[59] Where a contracting state accepts the responsibility of providing air traffic services over the high seas, standards and recommended practices may be applied "in a manner consistent with [those] adopted for airspace under its jurisdiction" (*see* text at note 7 *supra*).

regime seem to explain its explicit adoption in the Convention for transit flights through straits and archipelagic waters; but one may hardly deduce from the silence of the Convention an implicit civil aviation jurisdiction with regard to all aircraft movements within the EEZ. Coastal state jurisdiction is expressly limited to specific matters, which ensures that other states' rights may not be unduly hampered by the exercise of wide jurisdictional powers. The concept of residual rights may not be used to support the trend towards "creeping jurisdiction" of the coastal state. According to Article 89, "[n]o State may validly purport to subject any part of the high seas to its sovereignty." If the reference to this provision in Article 58(2) is to have any significance, it can only mean that a coastal state's jurisdiction, as defined by Article 56, cannot be extended to far-reaching control over aircraft movements through or within the airspace above the EEZ.

Unlike the rules relating to the flight and maneuver of aircraft, ICAO's operational standards (*e.g.*, airworthiness, equipment, training of the crew) are not part of the Rules of the Air, which are mandatory in the airspace above the high seas. The state of registry of an aircraft is primarily authorized to enact such regulations and they may deviate from ICAO's standards and recommended practices. Thus, operational aviation rules usually conform to the state of registry's legal order unless a state, exercising its sovereign powers, makes its operational rules—in part or totally—obligatory upon foreign aircraft flying in the airspace above its territory or its territorial sea.[60] In the latter case, territorial sovereignty, comprising regulatory authority and enforcement power with regard to all aviation activities within a state's airspace, overrules the state of registry's operational regulations.

The coastal state's jurisdiction over the EEZ does not extend to the power to prescribe operational rules with regard to foreign aircraft. Operational control of the aircraft flying within the EEZ is not linked to the exercise of the coastal state's sovereign economic rights. Regulatory authority over the operation of foreign aircraft within the EEZ would therefore run counter to the concept of exclusive economic rights and the related jurisdiction of the coastal state over the EEZ. The same legal regime applies to the operational rules for aircraft flying within the EEZ as to those for flights above the high seas.

The situation may be different with regard to aircraft movements to and from installations or artificial islands within the EEZ. Although it may be questioned whether such movements are covered by the "exclusive right to regulate the operation and use of such installations," paragraph 2 of Article 60 indicates that exclusive jurisdiction is meant to be a comprehensive regulatory authority reaching beyond the reference to particular governmental interests (customs, fiscal, health, safety, immigration). Jurisdiction in respect of flights to and from those structures and islands is inseparably interconnected with the coastal state's exclusive rights to construct and use the installations. Landings and takeoffs at airports established within the EEZ inevitably affect

[60] *Cf.* M. McDougal & W. Burke, *supra* note 51, at 1080 *et seq.;* M. McDougal, W. Burke, & I. Vlasic, Law and Public Order in Space 254 *et seq.* (1964); W. Schwenk, *supra* note 9, at 37 *et seq.* and 117.

a coastal state's rights of control over these installations and islands. Prior to the drafting of the Law of the Sea Convention, it was suggested that the coastal state should be granted jurisdiction over activities on such structures when those activities affect its economic or security interests.[61] Since the mere occurrence of landings and takeoffs always affects its interests, it seems reasonable to grant the coastal state exclusive aviation jurisdiction over the structures referred to in Article 60, paragraph 1.[62]

State practice supports this view. National continental shelf regulations usually have extended aviation jurisdiction over such islands, installations, and structures. Landings and takeoffs, as well as the operation of helicopter services to and from those structures, have been subjected to regulations concerning licensing, airport requirements, traffic rules, insurance, and liability.[63] Article 60(2) and Article 80, which refers to artificial islands, installations, and structures on the continental shelf, have codified this practice. Exclusive jurisdiction, however, is vested in the coastal state only with regard to the structures mentioned in Article 60(1). Installations not used for the purposes provided for in Article 56 and other economic purposes are not subject to the coastal state's exclusive jurisdiction.

In addition, the exercise of jurisdiction under Article 60(2) does not justify general restrictions on the freedom of flight over those installations. The right to establish safety zones around those structures is limited to navigation. Aerial safety zones in which freedom of overflight may be suspended or restricted are not mentioned in Article 60. Nevertheless, in order to avoid navigational hazards, the coastal state may require aircraft flying over those facilities to comply with its national traffic regulations relating to such structures. Air traffic control over these installations necessarily implies control of aircraft flying over and around them. In order to avoid conflicts with other states' rights to use the airspace above the EEZ, such installations may not be established—on the analogy of Article 60(7)—where interference with the use of recognized air lanes essential to international aviation may be caused.

Protection and Preservation of the Marine Environment

Under paragraph 1 of Article 56, the coastal state has jurisdiction with regard to the protection and preservation of the marine environment.[64] Part XII of the Convention contains an elaborate set of rules designed primarily to prevent marine pollution from vessels, installations, and land-based sources.

[61] Walker, *Jurisdictional Problems Created by Artificial Islands,* 10 SAN DIEGO L. REV. 662 (1973); Knight, *International Legal Aspects of Deep Draft Harbor Facilities,* 4 J. MAR. L. & COM. 386 *et seq.* (1972–73).

[62] *Cf.* the statement of A. SOONS, ARTIFICIAL ISLANDS AND INSTALLATIONS IN INTERNATIONAL LAW 22 (Occasional Paper No. 22, Law of the Sea Institute, 1974), *quoted in* Heller, *supra* note 45, at 149.

[63] *Cf.* Heller, *supra* note 45, at 150; Lawrence, *Superports, Airports and Other Fixed Installations on the High Seas,* 6 J. MAR. L. & COM. 575, 580 (1975); Schwenk, *Die Anwendung luftrechtlicher Vorschriften bei Flügen von und nach Schiffen und Bohrinseln,* 25 ZEITSCHRIFT FÜR LUFT- UND WELTRAUMRECHT 234 (1976).

[64] *See generally* Kiss, *La Pollution du milieu marin,* 38 ZAÖRV 902 (1978).

The possibility of marine pollution from civil aircraft is mentioned in Article 212.[65] It provides that states shall adopt laws and regulations and take other measures:

> to prevent, reduce and control pollution of the marine environment from or through the atmosphere, applicable to the air space under their sovereignty and to vessels flying their flag or vessels or aircraft of their registry, taking into account internationally agreed rules, standards and recommended practices and procedures and the safety of air navigation.

Furthermore, "States, acting especially through competent international organizations or diplomatic conference, shall endeavour to establish global and regional rules, standards and recommended practices and procedures to prevent, reduce and control such pollution" (Article 212(3)).

Article 212 adds nothing new to the existing pattern of lawmaking under the Chicago Convention and customary international law, with the possible exception that pollution from aircraft is not explicitly mentioned in Article 37 of the Chicago Convention, although standards relating to pollution from the atmosphere may be considered "matters concerned with the safety, regularity and efficiency of air navigation." It is basically up to each state to prescribe pollution standards for its own national aircraft wherever they may be and for all aircraft flying within its own airspace. Enforcement, too, rests with the state of registry of the aircraft or the state exercising its sovereign rights within its airspace. Article 222 obliges those states to enforce such pollution standards and to:

> adopt laws and regulations and take other measures necessary to implement applicable international rules and standards established through competent international organizations or diplomatic conference to prevent, reduce and control pollution of the marine environment from or through the atmosphere, in conformity with all relevant international rules and standards concerning the safety of air navigation.

Articles 212 and 222 exclude coastal state jurisdiction over foreign aircraft that have violated marine pollution and environmental standards as a consequence of their construction or equipment. Under customary international law, however, a state may require foreign aircraft to comply with such standards as a condition to entry into its airspace, provided international treaty obligations are met. The Convention, in providing explicitly for port state authority only in cases of pollution by ships (*cf.* Article 218), does not exclude recourse to a state's sovereign rights in its airspace. However, these sovereign rights would have to be exercised in accordance with the limitations established by the Convention on the state's regulatory authority. Thus, enforcement measures against foreign aircraft and their crews, including prosecution and punishment, may not be based on a violation committed in the airspace above the EEZ or the high seas since the Convention excludes coastal state regulatory

[65] According to Article 236, the provisions of the Convention do not apply to "aircraft owned or operated by a State and used, for the time being, only on government non-commercial service." States, however, shall ensure that such aircraft "act in a manner consistent, so far as is reasonable and practicable, with this Convention" (see, for a critical comment, *id.* at 907).

jurisdiction over those areas. Under international agreements on the protection of the environment, however, states may agree to prosecute such violations wherever they are committed.[66]

It has been asked whether the failure to confer jurisdiction over protection of the marine environment in the EEZ on the coastal state can be considered wise in view of its environmental interests. Professor Carl Christol has remarked that this failure runs "contrary to the establishment of coastal state standards for fisheries running out to 200 miles and to the even more extended authority that a state may exercise with respect to . . . security concerns."[67] It is debatable, however, whether reliance on doubtful claims to control over the high seas for security concerns is an argument in favor of extending coastal state jurisdiction within the EEZ. The exercise of far-reaching environmental authority might impose significant limitations on the freedoms of navigation and overflight. Although the establishment of effective environmental standards for aircraft flying above the EEZ and the high seas would be highly desirable, extension of coastal state jurisdiction would probably not be of much help in achieving this goal. What is generally asked for is the setting of uniform standards by some international machinery rather than a variety of national environmental regulations.

Nevertheless, under certain circumstances a coastal state's environmental interests may be seriously affected by the activities of aircraft above the EEZ.[68] The negative impact of their normal fuel consumption will usually be negligible, but other kinds of fuel and other types of aircraft may pose major concerns.[69] The atmosphere of a coastal state may be seriously endangered by space shuttles passing through the EEZ in the vicinity of its territorial waters, or by the deposit of radioactive materials during weapons tests.[70] In addition, aircraft may influence a coastal state's climate and in so doing create environmental hazards. Weather modification in the airspace above the oceans has recently become a topic of scientific discussion although its practical applicability still seems far off.[71] Finally, the impact of aircraft fuel upon the ozone layer in the atmosphere is currently under study.[72]

The Convention does not dispose of these questions. The use of aircraft in the exploration and exploitation of the natural resources of the waters, including areal surveillance of fishing activities, is covered by Article 56. Part XII deals with the preservation of the marine environment. Environmental

[66] *See* Convention d'Oslo pour la prévention de la pollution marine par les opérations d'immersion effectuées par les navires et aéronefs, Feb. 15, 1972, 1977 BGB1.II 165.

[67] *Cf.* Christol, *Unilateral Claims for the Use of Ocean Airspace,* in LAW OF THE SEA, *supra* note 36, at 130–31.

[68] For a discussion of the claims relating to pollution control, see M. MCDOUGAL & W. BURKE, *supra* note 51, at 848 *et seq.;* M. MCDOUGAL, H. LASSWELL, & I. VLASIC, *supra* note 60, at 308, plead for the application of antipollution regulations in the contiguous zone with respect to aircraft.

[69] Christol, *supra* note 67, at 160.

[70] M. MCDOUGAL & W. BURKE, *supra* note 51, at 852 *et seq.*

[71] Roberts, *The State of the Art in Weather Modification,* in WEATHER MODIFICATION AND THE LAW 1, 20–21 (H. J. Taubenfeld ed. 1968).

[72] Christol, *Aircraft and the International Legal and Institutional Aspects of the Stratospheric Ozone Problem,* 1 ANNALS AIR & SPACE L. 3 (1976).

hazards not specifically related to the marine environment are not dealt with by the Convention. It is not beyond doubt whether, on environmental matters, the Convention can be considered an exhaustive regulation of a coastal state's jurisdiction over the airspace above its EEZ.

Marine Scientific Research

Marine scientific research is the last area in which the coastal state, under Article 56(1)(b) and Articles 245 *et seq.*, is assigned jurisdiction.[73] Marine scientific research, though primarily conducted by ships, may also be engaged in by aircraft in relation to the noneconomic uses of the oceans. While general jurisdiction over research aircraft lies with the state of registry,[74] paragraph 1 of Article 246 gives coastal states the right to regulate, authorize, and conduct marine scientific research in their EEZ's and on their continental shelves. In contrast to Article 245, this right is not "exclusive," but other states may conduct such research only with the consent of the coastal state (Article 246(2)). The somewhat vague obligation to give consent "in normal circumstances" and the exceptions provided for in Article 246(5) leave it basically to the discretion of the coastal state to allow scientific research with respect to the marine environment by foreign aircraft.[75]

V. AIRSPACE ABOVE THE HIGH SEAS AND THE EEZ—ADDITIONAL CLAIMS

Major Claims

The airspace above the high seas is open to aircraft of all states for peaceful purposes (*cf.* Articles 87(1) and 88). The Convention only codifies in this regard the principle recognized by customary international law that no state may validly purport to subject any part of the high seas to its sovereignty. It follows that foreign aircraft in the airspace above the high seas must not be subjected to the control of the adjacent state.[76] Only in very specific circumstances do states have exceptional and limited jurisdictional and enforcement rights with regard to flights of this kind.[77] For example, every state has the right to "seize a pirate . . . aircraft, or . . . aircraft taken by piracy and under the control of pirates, and arrest the persons and seize the property on board" (*cf.* Article 105).[78]

In addition, under customary international law a coastal state may exercise, in a zone contiguous to its territorial sea, such control as is necessary to prevent and punish the infringement of its customs, fiscal, immigration, or sanitary

[73] *See generally* Caflisch & Piccard, *The Legal Regime of Marine Scientific Research and the Third United Nations Conference on the Law of the Sea,* 38 ZAÖRV 848 (1978).

[74] *Id.* at 888.

[75] Gündling, *supra* note 37, at 642–43; Caflisch & Piccard, *supra* note 73, at 873 *et seq.;* Wolfrum, *Der Schutz der Meeresforschung im Völkerrecht,* 19 GERMAN Y.B. INT'L L. 99, 99 (1976).

[76] J. C. COOPER, THE RIGHT TO FLY 126 (1947).

[77] For a general discussion of claims with respect to access to airspace above the high seas, see M. MCDOUGAL & W. BURKE, *supra* note 51, at 782–94.

[78] *Id.* at 806–23.

laws and regulations within its territory or its territorial sea.[79] The concept of the contiguous zone is taken up by the Convention with the modification that it may not extend beyond 24 nautical miles (Article 33). The contiguous zone, now that it is generally situated within the EEZ, is not covered by part VII of the Convention, which relates to the legal status of the high seas. As mentioned earlier, however, the concept of the EEZ did not result in a general extension of the coastal state's jurisdiction with regard to foreign aircraft flying above the EEZ. The jurisdiction of the coastal state in the contiguous zone therefore did not change qualitatively or quantitatively because of the shift to a *sui generis* legal regime for the EEZ. The coastal state may exercise its rights in the contiguous zone with respect to foreign ships and aircraft that violate its laws and regulations. Although the concept of the contiguous zone is generally discussed in the context of the seizure of ships and punishment of their crews, the activities of aircraft in the airspace above areas adjacent to the territorial sea may likewise affect a coastal state's interests (as referred to in Article 33) and give rise to preventive action or prosecution.[80] Since enforcement action against aircraft may result in the loss of human life, interception or shooting as a last resort to enforce compliance with a coastal state's laws is generally not permissible. Such a use of force would be altogether out of proportion to the interests pursued by the coastal state.[81] Even if an order to land is deliberately disregarded, a civil unarmed aircraft that intrudes into foreign airspace may not be fired upon.[82] Similar restrictions apply when enforcement measures are taken against foreign aircraft above the contiguous zone.

The right of hot pursuit is a third matter on which the Convention grants extended coastal state authority along the lines of customary international law.[83] According to paragraph 1 of Article 111, hot pursuit of a foreign ship into the high seas may be undertaken when the competent authorities of the coastal state have good reason to believe that the ship has violated the laws and regulations of that state. Such pursuit must be commenced when the foreign ship or one of its boats is within the internal waters, the archipelagic waters, the territorial sea, or the contiguous zone of the pursuing state, and it may only be continued beyond the territorial sea or the contiguous zone if it has not been interrupted.

It should be noted that paragraph 1 of Article 111 speaks only of the hot pursuit of *ships* by warships or military aircraft (*cf.* Article 111(5) and (6)). Under the Convention, hot pursuit of an aircraft beyond the territorial sea or the contiguous zone is not permissible.

Likewise, the language of Article 109 suggests that unauthorized broad-

[79] *Id.* at 584 *et seq.;* Oda, *The Concept of the Contiguous Zone,* 11 INT'L & COMP. L.Q. 131 (1962).

[80] Martial, *State Control of the Airspace over the Territorial Sea and the Contiguous Zone,* 30 CAN. B. REV. 245 (1952); Head, *ADIZ, International Law and Contiguous Airspace,* 3 ALTA. L. REV. 182 (1964); M. MCDOUGAL, H. LASSWELL, & I. VLASIC, *supra* note 60, at 294 *et seq.* and 308.

[81] *See* K. HAILBRONNER, DER SCHUTZ DER LUFTGRENZEN IM FRIEDEN 87 *et seq.* (1972).

[82] For a comprehensive account of the legal aspects of the treatment of aerial intruders and further references, see *id.* at 41 *et seq.*

[83] *See* N. POULANTZAS, THE RIGHT OF HOT PURSUIT IN INTERNATIONAL LAW (1969).

casting only from ships or installations on the high seas is subject to the jurisdiction of the coastal state where the transmission can be received (Article 109(3) and (4)). Nevertheless, in one of the rare comments on the air law implications of the new law of the sea, it is suggested "that it is not beyond doubt as to whether the provision of Article 109 about unauthorized broadcasting from the high seas applies only to broadcasting from vessels on the high seas, or also to broadcasting from aircraft flying over the high seas."[84] This casual remark raises a question reaching far beyond the problems of unauthorized broadcasting and hot pursuit of aircraft. To what extent does the Convention exhaustively regulate the rights and duties of states in the airspace above the oceans? May a coastal state's jurisdiction be extended to aircraft even though the Convention refers only to ships?

There are several claims to control over the airspace above the high seas or the EEZ, most of them invariably connected with the protection of a coastal state's security or public order, that are not explicitly dealt with in the Convention.[85] It was mentioned earlier that the conflict resolution clause of Article 59 has to be read as recognizing the EEZ as an evolving concept. Rights or jurisdiction of the coastal state or of other states may grow out of the settlement of particular conflicts under Article 59. This interpretation precludes viewing the EEZ as an area in which the rights and obligations of states are exhaustively regulated by the Convention. Particularly with regard to future technological developments that were not foreseen by the drafters of the Convention, rights or jurisdiction may have to be attributed according to Article 59. In addition, there may be specific air law matters that the Convention was not intended to deal with. Like earlier Law of the Sea Conferences, the Third Conference on the Law of the Sea did not purport to settle matters specifically related to the movement of aircraft.[86] On the other hand, freedom of overflight, as an integral part of the legal order of the seas and oceans, is included in the regulatory framework of the Convention. Thus, it is difficult to argue that "certain provisions . . ., although intended to apply to ships, are so drafted that they could either by interpretation or by analogy be considered as capable of application to aircraft also."[87] In case of a particular conflict, claims to the analogous application of other law of the sea provisions have to be examined closely, taking into account the respective interests of the parties concerned.

Air Defense Identification Zones

A major claim to aerial jurisdiction relates to the establishment of air defense identification zones (ADIZ's). According to U.S. regulations,[88] aircraft

[84] Heller, *supra* note 45, at 140.

[85] *See* M. McDougal & W. Burke, *supra* note 51, at 782 *et seq.;* M. McDougal, H. Lasswell, & I. Vlasic, *supra* note 60, at 306 *et seq.*

[86] *See* [1956] 1 Y.B. Int'l L. Comm'n 58, UN Doc. A/CN.4/SER.A/1956.

[87] See a comment by the ICAO on the ILC draft convention, 1 United Nations Conference on the Law of the Sea, Official Records 336, UN Doc. A/CONF.13/31 (1958); *cf.* N. Poulantzas, *supra* note 83, at 302.

[88] Security Control of Air Traffic, 14 C.F.R. pt. 99 (1982); *see* J. Murchison, The Contiguous Air Space Zone in International Law 87–94 (1957).

with the intention of entering U.S. airspace and departing aircraft must provide identification and location reports one hour's flying time before penetrating U.S. airspace. Within ADIZ's, no aircraft may deviate from the flight plan and instructions of the air traffic control authorities. Similar provisions were enacted by the Canadian authorities, with the modification that information is also required from aircraft passing through the Canadian zone even though not flying to Canada.[89] Former French regulations, which applied to the area off the Algerian coast, additionally provided for the right to intercept or fire upon aircraft not complying with such requirements.[90] ADIZ's have usually been justified by analogy to the contiguous zone concept or by the doctrine of necessity.[91] The early identification and control of foreign aircraft has been declared necessary to prevent surprise attacks or infringements upon essential security interests and to ensure the safety of international air traffic.[92]

The security interests of states have also been invoked to establish permanent restricted or prohibited areas adjacent to their coasts. Libya has asserted such aerial zones, extending 100 nautical miles from Tripoli, and U.S. military aircraft have repeatedly been intercepted and fired upon in them.[93] The U.S. Government has strongly protested against such measures and claimed a right of overflight in the zones.

The Convention does not attribute rights or jurisdiction to the coastal state with regard to aerial defense. The coastal state's military security and defense are only casually referred to in Article 39, in connection with the duties of ships and aircraft during transit passage. It is suggested that the Convention was not intended to settle specific problems of restrictions on the freedom of overflight for defense purposes. This does not mean, however, that the Convention has opened the door to claims that have hitherto been regarded as inconsistent with the traditional concept of freedom of overflight. Again, Article 59 must not be considered as carte blanche for claims to jurisdiction in all cases where the Convention does not attribute such rights or jurisdiction. Customary international law has to be taken into account when Article 59 is invoked as a basis for the attribution of rights and jurisdiction.

With regard to prohibited defense areas adjacent to the territorial sea, state practice supports the view that the establishment of permanent restricted aerial zones beyond the airspace above territorial waters would amount to the

[89] Can. Dep't of Transport, Rules for the Security Control of Air Traffic, Notam No. 22/55; *see* J. MURCHISON, *supra* note 88, at 79–86; U. LEANZA, FENOMENI DI ZONA CONTIGUITÀ AEREA NEL DIRITTO INTERNAZIONALE 231–41 (1961).

[90] Zone réglementée No. 230, *reprinted in* Debbasch, *La Zone contiguë en droit aérien,* Ann. I, 24 REV. GÉNÉRALE L'AIR 249, 260 (1961).

[91] J. MURCHISON, *supra* note 88, at 1 *et seq.;* Head, *supra* note 80, at 182 *et seq.;* Hayton, *Jurisdiction of the Littoral State in the "Air Frontier,"* 3 PHIL. INT'L L.J. 369 (1964); Georgiades, *Du nationalisme aérien à l'internationalisme spatial ou le mythe de la souveraineté aérienne,* 16 REV. FRANÇAISE DROIT AÉRIENNE 129 (1962); M. MCDOUGAL, H. LASSWELL, & I. VLASIC, *supra* note 60, at 306 *et seq.; cf.* for a discussion of the arguments referred to in favor of the ADIZ, K. HAILBRONNER, *supra* note 81, at 73 *et seq.*

[92] Christol, *supra* note 67, at 128–30.

[93] 1973 DIGEST OF UNITED STATES PRACTICE IN INTERNATIONAL LAW 302; 1975 *id.* at 451.

exclusive use and control of such areas and would therefore be inconsistent with customary international law.[94] Thus, in protesting against Libya's action, the United States argued that the establishment of such areas is inconsistent with the Chicago Convention and generally recognized principles of international law.[95]

Claims to the temporary exclusive use of certain areas above the high seas may be seen in a different light.[96] Although the legitimacy of weapons testing, involving the temporary closure of large areas of airspace, has been highly controversial,[97] the occasional peaceful military use of the airspace above the high seas must generally be regarded as a legitimate form of enjoyment of the freedom of overflight. Rocket tests have been conducted by the United States and the USSR in the airspace above the high seas.[98] On the other hand, the U.S. hydrogen bomb tests were strongly attacked at the 1958 Conference on the Law of the Sea.[99] As long as restrictions on the freedom of overflight occur as an unavoidable effect of an "*eo ipso*" legitimate enjoyment of the freedom of the high seas, conflicts have to be resolved on the basis of general principles of reasonableness.[100] The establishment of temporary prohibited zones or temporary restrictions on the movements of aircraft in large areas above the high seas may prove to be excessive, harmful to other states, or tantamount to undue interference with international aviation routes.

In contrast to the temporary military use of the airspace over the high seas, the establishment of air defense identification zones on a permanent basis raises the question of the coastal state's *jurisdiction.* While the requirement of identification in itself, without interference with an aircraft's movements, can hardly be considered a restriction on the freedom of overflight, enforcement measures and the imposition of regulations that provide for flight rules and the possible prosecution of the pilot amount to an extension of the coastal state's jurisdiction. The principle enunciated in Article 89 of the Convention, that no state may validly purport to subject any part of the high seas to its sovereignty, is prima facie opposed to any claim of control over foreign aircraft on a permanent basis. Some writers, however, have argued that the only effective self-defense may be interception by defending fighter aircraft or guided missiles, and that must be undertaken before the attackers have ap-

[94] Christol, *supra* note 67, at 129; la Pradelle, *supra* note 10, at 146–47; W. SCHWENK, *supra* note 9, at 116.

[95] 1973 DIGEST, *supra* note 93, at 303.

[96] McDougal & Schlei, *The Hydrogen Bomb Tests in Perspective: Lawful Measures for Security,* 64 YALE L.J. 648 (1955); M. MCDOUGAL, H. LASSWELL, & I. VLASIC, *supra* note 60, at 303; M. MCDOUGAL & W. BURKE, *supra* note 51, at 787.

[97] *See* McDougal & Schlei, *supra* note 96; Margolis, *The Hydrogen Bomb Experiments and International Law,* 64 YALE L.J. 629 (1955); and Gidel, *Explosions nucléaires expérimentales et liberté de la haute mer,* in GRUNDPROBLEME DES INTERNATIONALEN RECHTS, FESTSCHRIFT FÜR JEAN SPIROPOULOS 173 (1957).

[98] M. MCDOUGAL & W. BURKE, *supra* note 51, at 787.

[99] *Ibid.*

[100] For the discussion of the principle of "reasonableness" by the International Law Commission, see [1956] 1 Y.B. INT'L L. COMM'N, *supra* note 86, at 34; M. MCDOUGAL & W. BURKE, *supra* note 51, at 761.

proached. Such a defense would vitally depend on adequate and timely identification.[101] While identification of approaching military aircraft may be required for reasons of security, it is difficult to see how enforcement measures, including interception of foreign aircraft passing through restricted zones and prosecution of their pilots for failure to follow a prescribed route or to file flight plans, can be justified under customary international law. Preventive measures as an exercise of the right of self-defense may only be taken in case of imminent danger if the doctrine of necessity is to be kept within reasonable limits.[102]

In addition, the analogy of air defense identification zones to the concept of maritime contiguous zones has been advanced as a major argument in their favor. This analogy, however, neglects the essential factor that neither the Convention itself nor earlier drafts and codifications recognize special security rights in the contiguous zone. In 1956, the International Law Commission, in explaining its rejection of various proposals to incorporate the concept of security into the contiguous zone scheme, pointed out:

> [T]he extreme vagueness of the term "security" would open the way for abuses and . . . the granting of such rights was not necessary. The enforcement of customs and sanitary regulations will be sufficient in most cases to safeguard the security of the State. In so far as measures of self-defence against an imminent and direct threat to the security of the State are concerned, the Commission refers to the general principles of international law and the Charter of the United Nations.[103]

In spite of heavy criticism, this view prevailed at all the Law of the Sea Conferences.[104] Both the 1958 Geneva Convention on the High Seas and the present Convention clearly allow (and restrict) the exercise of authority for specific purposes, not including security. This concept may be considered "decidedly anachronistic" and "far removed from desirable community policies";[105] it nevertheless reflects the *communis opinio* of states. While it may be true, as McDougal and Burke assert,[106] that claims to the occasional exclusive use of high seas areas have encountered only little objection, claims to extended jurisdiction, including enforcement measures in the airspace above the high seas on a permanent basis, have never been generally accepted, as is shown by the protests of several states against the former French air defense zones off the Algerian coast.[107] It is therefore very doubtful whether claims

[101] J. MURCHISON, *supra* note 88, at 55.

[102] *See* K. HAILBRONNER, *supra* note 81, at 94–97; J. VERPLAETSE, INTERNATIONAL LAW IN VERTICAL SPACE 83 (1960).

[103] Report of the International Law Commission to the General Assembly, 11 UN GAOR Supp. (No. 9) at 39–40, UN Doc. A/3159 (1956), *reprinted in* [1956] 2 Y.B. INT'L L. COMM'N 253, 295, UN Doc. A/CN.4/SER.A/1956/Add.1; *cf.* the report of J. François, UN Doc. A/CN.4/97, at 13–14 (1956), *reprinted in id.* at 1, 5–6.

[104] For an analysis of the discussion, see M. MCDOUGAL & W. BURKE, *supra* note 51, at 604 *et seq.;* K. HAILBRONNER, *supra* note 81, at 88 *et seq.*

[105] M. MCDOUGAL & W. BURKE, *supra* note 51, at 605 and 606.

[106] *Id.* at 594; *see also* M. MCDOUGAL, H. LASSWELL, & I. VLASIC, *supra* note 60, at 310.

[107] For the state practice, see K. HAILBRONNER, *supra* note 81, at 81–87.

to extended jurisdiction for security purposes in the airspace above the high seas have been approved by a considerable number of states.

Hot Pursuit of Aircraft

Finally, the right of hot pursuit, confined by the Convention to the hot pursuit of ships, has been said to embrace the hot pursuit of aircraft as well.[108] Neither state practice nor the opinion of legal writers supports this view,[109] if hot pursuit is understood as the right to intercept foreign aircraft above the high seas. State practice, as reflected in national regulations, usually refers only to the pursuit of ships. While there have been occasional instances of hot pursuit of aircraft in the airspace above the high seas, it is remarkable that such a right has rarely been claimed officially.[110] Usually, the use of force has been justified by invoking the right of self-defense against imminent attack or the sovereign rights of a state within its own airspace.

In addition, the analogy to the law of the sea does not take into account the essential differences between the navigation of ships and the movement of aircraft.[111] Interception of aircraft is likely to endanger the security of the plane and its crew. It is hard to imagine that infringement of a coastal state's regulations could justify the use of force against civil aircraft, but the right to hot pursuit of aircraft could easily have dangerous results and would be open to abuse. The withdrawal of a propósal advanced by Chile during the first Law of the Sea Conference at Geneva, which would have included hot pursuit of one aircraft by another, indicates that a large majority of states have never supported such a right.[112] On the basis of this discussion, the confinement of the concept of hot pursuit to ships in Article 111 of the Convention must be deemed a rejection of extended claims to jurisdiction with regard to foreign aircraft flying in the airspace above the high seas or the EEZ.

Concluding Remarks

The new law of the sea considerably affects the legal regime of the airspace above the oceans. With the extension of sovereign or "quasi-sovereign" powers to coastal states, the traditional rule of the freedom of the air above the high seas no longer appears to guarantee sufficiently the free movement of civil and military aircraft across the oceans. Some of the fears that international aviation may be drastically curtailed have been alleviated by the new concept of transit passage for aircraft in international straits and archipelagic air routes, as well as the right of freedom of navigation in the EEZ. There are questions,

[108] M. McDougal, H. Lasswell, & I. Vlasic, *supra* note 60, at 310; N. Poulantzas, *supra* note 83, at 298 *et seq.*

[109] For a more detailed discussion of this issue, see K. Hailbronner, *supra* note 81, at 100–09.

[110] *Id.* at 101.

[111] *Id.* at 109.

[112] UN Doc. A/CONF.13/5 and Adds. 1–4 (1958), 1 United Nations Conference on the Law of the Sea, Official Records 75, 78–79; 4 *id.* at 90 *et seq.*

however, concerning the exact scope of the right of transit passage, the legal regime of the airspace above the EEZ, and the rights and duties of coastal states concerning transiting aircraft that are yet to be answered.

The Convention does not always provide easy answers to these questions. This is mainly due to the fact that the Convention is to some extent ambivalent. Different parts of the Convention reflect different perceptions of how to reconcile conflicting interests. The determination of the legal status of the EEZ is just one example. A balance between freedom of the air and jurisdictional claims of the coastal states has to be achieved. The approach to finding this balance suggested in this article is based on the assumption that the Convention must be interpreted in favor of the customary law principle of the freedom of the air. The Convention itself has incorporated the traditional concepts of the freedom of the high seas and the airspace above the seas. The attribution of rights and jurisdiction can therefore hardly be understood as an exhaustive new legal framework for the seas and the airspace above the seas but rather as a compromise whereby new rights and powers of states have been acknowledged in areas hitherto regarded as *res communis omnium.* As a result, the extension of territorial sovereignty by coastal states has to be interpreted narrowly. States claiming to have acquired new rights have a burden of proof. They may rely on the Convention only to the extent that it explicitly grants regulatory competence and enforcement power. On the other hand, traditional rights of coastal states to restrict the freedom of aviation in exceptional circumstances are not affected by the Convention.

Consequently, the right of overflight contained in the transit passage regime is not subject to any restrictions by coastal states based on the duties of transiting aircraft referred to in Article 39 of the Convention. It is essential to distinguish clearly between prescriptive regulatory authority and/or enforcement power of the coastal state and duties of transiting aircraft. The Convention neither grants coastal states the power to define "the normal modes of continuous and expeditious transit" nor allows any interference with transiting aircraft. Exceptionally, however, in case of a threat to a coastal state's vital security interests, that state may invoke an inherent right of preventive self-defense recognized under customary international law.

CHOICE OF LAW UNDER THE INTERNATIONAL SALES CONVENTION: A U.S. PERSPECTIVE

*By Isaak I. Dore**

I. Introduction: Genesis of the Convention

The United Nations Convention on Contracts for the International Sale of Goods was adopted on April 10, 1980.[1] The chief reason for its adoption was that the prior Uniform Law on the International Sale of Goods (ULIS)[2] and its supplementary Convention relating to a Uniform Law on the Formation of Contracts for the International Sale of Goods (ULF)[3] had not received widespread support.[4]

Although work began on ULIS in the 1930's, it was not until January 1964, barely 3 months before ULIS was finally negotiated, that the United States became able to participate in the drafting effort, and owing to this short time for preparation, the level of United States participation at the conference was minimal.[5] The United States could not have a number of its serious concerns with ULIS satisfied,[6] the most significant of which was that ULIS was incom-

* Associate Professor of Law, St. Louis University School of Law. The writer gratefully acknowledges the help of Peter Pfund, Assistant Legal Adviser for Private International Law, Department of State, Washington, D.C., for supplying material and information not otherwise available. Special thanks are also due to Professor John Honnold, Goodhart Professor of the Science of Law, University of Cambridge, England, to Darryl Bardusch, and to Dean Jackson for commenting on previous drafts of this article.

[1] The United Nations Convention on Contracts for the International Sale of Goods (hereinafter cited as the Convention) was adopted at a UN Conference of Plenipotentiaries, held in Vienna, Austria, from March 10 to April 11, 1980. For the text, see UN Doc. A/CONF.97/18, Ann. I (1981), *reprinted in* Official Records of the United Nations Conference on Contracts for the International Sale of Goods, UN Doc. A/CONF.97/19, at 178 (1981) [hereinafter cited as Official Records], and 19 ILM 668 (1980).

[2] For the text, see 3 ILM 855 (1964).

[3] For the text, see *id.* at 864.

[4] For a searing critique of ULIS, see Nadelmann, *The Uniform Law on the International Sale of Goods: A Conflict of Laws Imbroglio,* 74 Yale L.J. 449 (1964–65). *See also* Dore & DeFranco, *A Comparison of the Non-Substantive Provisions of the UNCITRAL Convention on the International Sale of Goods and the Uniform Commercial Code,* 23 Harv. Int'l L.J. 49 (1982).

[5] *See* Report of the Delegation of the United States of America to the Diplomatic Conference on the Unification of Law Governing the International Sale of Goods, The Hague, April 2–25, 1964 (submitted to the Secretary of State, Dec. 1, 1964, by Richard D. Kearney, Chairman of the United States Delegation, on file at St. Louis University Law Library). The spirit of the delegation is rather poignantly described in its report as follows: "The United States delegation undoubtedly ran the risk of making itself obnoxious if it proposed at this late stage a large number of changes in the two draft conventions . . . , especially if such instruments were generally acceptable to the other delegations at the conference." *Id.* at 3.

[6] The United States delegation saw four specific weaknesses in ULIS: (1) the Uniform Law was conceived primarily in the light of external trade between nations with a common boundary; (2) insufficient attention had been given to international trade problems involving overseas shipments;

patible with the U.S. Uniform Commercial Code (U.C.C.).[7] Thus, the United States delegation concluded that "it would appear unlikely that the Uniform Act will prove acceptable to America's governmental, commercial, and legal organizations because its many unclear and unworkable provisions do not meet the current needs of commerce and because it varies so markedly in its approach and content from our Uniform Commercial Code."[8]

One of the earliest tasks of the United Nations Commission on International Trade Law (UNCITRAL) was the reexamination of ULIS and ULF with a view to making them more acceptable to all states generally.[9] The United Nations Secretariat was requested by the Commission to invite states to indicate whether they intended to accede to the 1964 Conventions.[10] Not surprisingly, the United States was one of many states that replied that they would not ratify or accede to the Conventions.[11] It further reiterated its earlier objections to ULIS.[12]

It is against this background that the United States favored a fresh codification effort under the auspices of UNCITRAL.[13] This renewed effort led to the adoption of a Draft Convention on Contracts for the International Sale of Goods by the Commission at its 11th session.[14] The Draft Convention was

---

(3) the reciprocal rights and obligations as between seller and buyer, viewed in the light of the practical realities of trade practices, were not well balanced; and (4) the Uniform Law would not be understood by individuals in the commercial field. *Id.* at 6.

[7] The provisions of ULIS were viewed by the U.S. delegation as too abstract and general when compared with the provisions of the U.C.C. Because the ULIS provisions were so general, they could not clearly reflect modern commercial realities and their operation would not be based on "observable and universal commercial events," *e.g.*, with regard to risk of loss, as is the case with the U.C.C. *Id.* at 9–10.

[8] *Id.* at 10.

[9] Report of UNCITRAL on the Work of its First Session, 23 UN GAOR Supp. (No. 16) para. 7, UN Doc. A/7216 (1968).

[10] *Id.* at 19, para. 14.

[11] UN Doc. A/CN.9/11, at 36 (1969).

[12] UN Doc. A/CN.9/11/Add.1, at 34–36 (1969); UN Doc A/CN.9/11/Add.4, at 8 (1969). The observations of the United States and other governments are summarized in UN Doc. A/CN.9/31 (1969), entitled Analysis of Replies and Comments by Governments on the Hague Conventions of 1964: Report of the Secretary-General, *reprinted in* 1 Y.B. COMM'N INT'L TRADE L. 159 (1968–70), UN Doc. A/CN.9/SER.A/1970 [hereinafter cited as 1 YEARBOOK].

[13] At its second session, held in March 1969, UNCITRAL set up a Working Group on the International Sale of Goods to decide which modifications to the 1964 Conventions "might render them capable of wider acceptance by countries of different legal, social and economic systems, or whether it will be necessary to elaborate a new text for the same purpose." Report of UNCITRAL on the Work of its Second Session, 24 UN GAOR Supp. (No. 18) para. 38, UN Doc. A/7618 (1969). The working group was composed of Austria, Brazil, France, Ghana, Hungary, India, Japan, Kenya, Mexico, Tunisia, the USSR, the United Kingdom, and the United States.

[14] The working group held nine sessions. It considered ULIS and ULF at its seventh, eighth, and ninth sessions. The reports of the working group on the work of its first seven sessions are to be found in UN Docs. A/CN.9/35 (1970), A/CN.9/52 (1971), A/CN.9/62 and Adds. 1–2 (1972), A/CN.9/75 (1973), A/CN.9/87 (1974), A/CN.9/100 (1975), and A/CN.9/116 (1976). The reports on the eighth and ninth sessions are in UN Docs. A/CN.9/128 (1977), and A/CN.9/142 (1978). With regard to both ULIS and ULF, the working group recommended that the Commission adopt new texts. These texts were adopted by the Commission at its 10th and 11th sessions. 32 UN GAOR Supp. (No. 17) para. 35, UN Doc. A/32/17 (1977). 33 UN GAOR

adopted, with minor modifications, at a Conference of Plenipotentiaries in April 1980.[15]

That the Convention is an improvement on ULIS has been recognized.[16] Commentators appear to be favorably disposed towards it as a fair compromise among the various legal systems involved in its drafting, and opinion seems to be crystallizing in the United States that the Convention is compatible with American interests.[17]

Supp. (No. 17) para. 28, UN Doc. A/33/17 (1978). At its 11th session the Commission decided to combine the two texts into a single Draft Convention on Contracts for the International Sale of Goods. *Id.*, para. 18.

[15] *See* note 1 *supra*. For a comprehensive analysis of the entire Convention from a substantive as well as a historical point of view, see J. HONNOLD, UNIFORM LAW FOR INTERNATIONAL SALES UNDER THE 1980 UNITED NATIONS CONVENTION (1982).

[16] *See, e.g.*, Report of the United States Delegation to the United Nations Conference on Contracts for the International Sale of Goods (submitted to the Secretary of State by John O. Honnold, Co-Chairman of the Delegation, 1981, on file at St. Louis University Law Library). The report describes the objections of the United States to ULIS and how these objections have been met by the Convention: (1) ULIS was thought to have a "coercive" potential of becoming applicable to transactions of parties of noncontracting states (*see* note 33 *infra*, and J. HONNOLD, *supra* note 15, at 15–16), which has been rectified in the Convention (*see* text accompanying notes 49–57 *infra*); (2) UNCITRAL produced a *single* document on international sales in place of the *two* documents produced by the 1964 Hague Conference (ULIS and ULF), which avoids problems of interpretation; (3) the effect of the course of dealing between the parties in relation to contract formation, considered inadequate under ULIS, has been increased in the 1980 Convention by strengthening the course-of-dealing rules (*cf.* U.C.C. §1-205 (1978)) and by making both course of dealing and trade usage explicitly applicable to formation (Convention, Art. 9); (4) the 1980 Convention eliminated problems of complexity, ambiguity, and nonuniformity that had arisen from the multiple remedial systems and civil law terminology in ULIS and ULF, by providing a single set of remedies for contractual breach (*cf.* U.C.C. §§2-703, 2-711 (1978)) and by thorough advance analysis of the translatability of the Convention's concepts and language; (5) the use in ULIS and ULF of abstract concepts gave rise to interpretational difficulties, whereas the 1980 Convention, in an approach similar to that of the U.C.C., rejects such concepts and is expressed more practically in terms of commercial events that can be uniformly understood (this parallel approach was fostered by "the fact that the U.C.C. is the one important modern formulation of sales law"). Report of the U.S. Delegation, at 11. *See* further pt. II, Honnold, The International Sale of Goods, 27 AM. J. COMP. L. 223 (1979); Lansing & Hauserman, *A Comparison of the Uniform Commercial Code to UNCITRAL's Convention on Contracts for the International Sale of Goods*, 6 N.C. J. INT'L. L. & COM. REG. 63, 64–66 (1980). *See also* Nadelmann, *supra* note 4, at 457 (on what the United States since came to describe as the "coercive" effect of ULIS).

[17] At the annual meeting of the American Bar Association in April 1981, the policy-making House of Delegates adopted a resolution supporting U.S. signature and ratification of the Convention, subject to one reservation discussed below. *See* text accompanying notes 84–87 and 96, *infra*. American Bar Association, Report to the House of Delegates, Resolution recommended by the Section of International Law (1981) (text of resolution and accompanying Background Report [hereinafter cited as ABA Report] on file at St. Louis University Law Library). Apart from noting the compatibility of the Convention with U.S. law (particularly the U.C.C.), the report mentioned four specific benefits to U.S. business interests that would result from U.S. ratification of the Convention: (1) avoidance of difficulties in reaching agreement with foreign buyers and sellers on choice of forum or law; (2) ability of parties, under the Convention, to continue to determine their rights and obligations along the same lines as under the U.C.C. "without fear of foreign 'mandatory' rules"; (3) decrease in costs for legal research on foreign laws because they would be replaced by a single Convention available in an official English text; and (4) reduction of problems

One familiar and crucial standard that American businessmen will use to compare the compatibility of the Convention with U.S. business interests is the Uniform Commercial Code, since one of the major American objections to ULIS was its incompatibility with the U.C.C. The appeal of the Convention to American business entities will therefore in large measure depend on how much it emulates or improves upon the standards of the code, which have already proven to be successful in clarifying and unifying American commercial law.

II. Framework of Comparison

While several approaches may be taken to comparing the Sales Convention with the U.C.C.,[18] this article will be confined strictly to the respective spheres of application of the two codes. Also, it should be recognized that the various competing, and indeed conflicting, legal and political values reflected by the Convention may create future difficulties in its application. The fact that the Convention will have original texts in six languages (each of equal authenticity) may itself generate problems of ambiguity, interpretation, and consistency in application.

Many of these problems, of course, are inherent in any uniform codification effort. Thus, the Uniform Commercial Code of the United States, designed to unify the law among the 50 states and the territories of the United States, was itself a series of compromises. These compromises were aimed at accommodating the different laws of the states as well as their differing commercial interests and practices.[19]

A code seeking to unify the law governing multi-jurisdictional business contracts must, as a necessary first step, define its sphere of application.[20] Failure to do so will jeopardize the goal of uniformity, because several courts may become authorized to hear multi-jurisdictional contracts and different outcomes may be reached by different courts, even within the same country.[21] Thus, the sphere of application of the U.C.C. is defined at the outset in section 1-105. As will be seen below,[22] this section balances the right of the parties to a multi-jurisdictional contract to choose their own law against the basic goal of uniformity, which is promoted by defining the conditions in which the code

---

of proof of foreign law in domestic or foreign courts. *Id.* at 2–3. *See* further Winship, *New Rules for International Sales,* 68 A.B.A.J. 1231 (1982); Ziontz, *A New Uniform Law for International Sale of Goods: Is it Compatible with American Interests?,* 2 Nw. J. Int'l L. & Bus. 129 (1980); Lansing & Hauserman, *supra* note 16, at 80; Dore & DeFranco, *supra* note 4, at 67.

[18] *See, e.g.,* Dore & DeFranco, *supra* note 4, at 49; Lansing & Hauserman, *supra* note 16, at 63.

[19] *See* Mellinkoff, *The Language of the U.C.C.,* 77 Yale L.J. 185 (1967).

[20] *See generally* Nanda, *Forum-Selection and Choice-of-Law Agreements in International Contracts,* in The Law of Transnational Business Transactions (V. Nanda ed. 1981). The foregoing is a fortiori true of international contracts. *See* Delaume, *What is an International Contract? An American and Gallic Dilemma,* 28 Int'l & Comp. L.Q. 258 (1979).

[21] R. Weintraub, Commentary on the Conflict of Laws 90–221, 348–97 (2d ed. 1980).

[22] *See* section III, "Jurisdiction of the U.C.C. and the International Sales Convention," *infra.*

becomes applicable regardless of any specific agreement by the parties as to the applicable law.[23]

The International Sales Convention likewise defines its scope of application in its very first article. It will be seen that when this provision is compared with the corresponding provisions of the U.C.C., the Convention proves itself to be compatible with American interests.[24] Indeed, the United States informed the Secretary-General that it considered the UNCITRAL Draft Convention suitable for submission to the 1980 conference on the ground that it was "more likely to receive widespread acceptance around the world than ha[d] ULIS and ULF,"[25] and in August 1981 the United States signed the Convention.[26]

If the United States ratifies the Convention, the latter will inevitably displace the U.C.C. as governing law with respect to several categories of transactions.[27] This article will therefore examine the scope of the Convention's application to international commercial transactions, focusing specifically on those provisions which allow parties to "opt out" in favor of domestic law. The opting-out provisions are important because they will be seen to provide practical guidelines for American businessmen in deciding whether a specific transaction should be governed by the Convention or the domestic law of the country of one of the contracting parties, which in the case of the United States would be the U.C.C.

III. Jurisdiction of the U.C.C. and the International Sales Convention

Because of a significant overlap in coverage between the Convention and the U.C.C., international commercial transactions involving U.S. parties will continue to generate choice-of-law problems. The rules regarding choice of law will depend on whether the United States has ratified the Convention and whether the individual state of which the foreign businessman is a national has ratified. In the period before United States ratification of the Convention, the U.C.C. will apply as it has in the past. Upon ratification by the United States, both the U.C.C. and the Convention will be potentially applicable to international commercial transactions. If the American party's foreign busi-

[23] Among the underlying purposes and policies explicitly stated by the U.C.C. are those of facilitating commerce through "agreement of the parties" and of making "uniform the law [of commerce] among the various jurisdictions." U.C.C. §1-102(2)(b) and (c) (1978).

[24] *See* text accompanying note 33, *infra*.

[25] Analysis of Comments and Proposals by Governments and International Organizations on the Draft Convention on Contracts for the International Sale of Goods, and on Draft Provisions Concerning Implementation, Reservations and other Final Clauses Prepared by the Secretary-General, UN Doc. A/CONF.97/9, para. 2(b) (1980), *reprinted in* OFFICIAL RECORDS, *supra* note 1, at 71. The comments and proposals are reproduced in UN Doc. A/CONF.97/8 and Adds. 1–7 (1980), cited *ibid.*

[26] Dep't of State Memorandum from Peter H. Pfund, Assistant Legal Adviser for Private International Law, to Members of the Advisory Committee's Study Group on International Sale of Goods, Sept. 24, 1981 (unpub., on file at St. Louis University Law Library).

[27] For further discussion, see section III, *infra*.

ness partner has a place of business in a noncontracting state, the U.C.C. (or the domestic law of the noncontracting state) may apply.[28] If the foreign partner has a place of business in a contracting state, the Convention will apply automatically, unless it is specifically excluded by agreement in accordance with Article 6.[29]

Under each situation, the parties will have some freedom of choice as to the applicable law. Where the U.C.C. applies, the parties under section 1-105(1) may choose the law of either the state of the seller or the state of the buyer (or even a third state), as long as the transaction bears a "reasonable relation" to the state whose law is chosen.[30] Where the Convention applies automatically, such automatic application can be set aside by prior agreement, in favor of the U.C.C. or any other law.[31]

The differences in the potential application of the U.C.C. and the Convention will have important consequences. If the Convention is ratified by a majority of states,[32] it will have *potentially* a much larger scope of application than the U.C.C. Unlike the U.C.C., the Convention does not contain a "reasonable relation" test for determining its applicability to specific transactions. Moreover, in the absence of a choice-of-law clause, the U.C.C. applies only to those transactions which bear an "appropriate relation" to the U.S. state in question. Notwithstanding the wider scope of application of the Convention, the provisions that allow parties to exclude its application when it would otherwise be the governing law evince a strong desire on the part of the drafters to ensure party autonomy in determining the applicable law.

This freedom to "opt out" of the Convention when it would otherwise be applicable shows that the degree of freedom of choice of law hitherto enjoyed by American businessmen under the U.C.C. would not be adversely affected by the Convention. It also answers a fundamental criticism of the United States and many other countries regarding the choice-of-law provisions of ULIS, which were seen as having a "coercive effect."[33]

[28] As will be seen in due course, the Convention applies if the parties have their places of business in different contracting states, or if the rules of private international law lead to the application of the law of a contracting state. *See* the subsection on choice-of-law provisions in the Convention, *infra* p. 529.

[29] Article 6 of the Convention provides: "The parties may exclude the application of this Convention or, subject to article 12, derogate from or vary the effect of any of its provisions."

[30] Section 1-105(1) of the U.C.C. provides in part that "when a transaction bears a reasonable relation to this state and also to another state or nation the parties may agree that the law either of this state or of such other state or nation shall govern their rights and duties."

[31] *See* note 29 *supra* and accompanying text.

[32] Under Article 99(1), the Convention will enter into force 12 months after the date of deposit of the 10th instrument of ratification, acceptance, approval, or accession. As of April 1983, the following states have signed or ratified the Convention. Signatories: Austria, Chile, Czechoslovakia, Denmark, Finland, the Federal Republic of Germany, the German Democratic Republic, Ghana, Hungary, Italy, the Netherlands, Norway, the People's Republic of China, Poland, Singapore, Sweden, the United States, Venezuela, and Yugoslavia. Ratifications: Egypt (accession), France, Lesotho, and Syria (accession).

[33] UN Doc. A/7618, Ann. I, para. 40 (1969). *See also* UN Doc. A/CN.9/31 (1969), *supra* note 12, in 1 YEARBOOK, at 159, 162–64, for a summary of U.S. comments on the scope of application of ULIS. Article I of ULIS, *supra* note 2, provided in part:

SUBSTANTIVE CHOICE-OF-LAW PROVISIONS IN THE U.C.C.

The most important part of the U.C.C. governing choice of law is section 1-105. This section provides, subject to five exceptions,[34] that "when a transaction bears a reasonable relation to this state and also to another state or nation the parties may agree that the law either of this state or of such other state or nation shall govern their rights and duties."[35] The section provides further that "[f]ailing such agreement this Act applies to transactions bearing an appropriate relation to this state."[36] Thus, under section 1-105, for the parties' choice of law to be respected the transaction in question must bear a "reasonable relation" to the state whose law is chosen. These tests are primarily relevant to domestic sales transactions. They may also be relevant to disputes arising from international sales transactions litigated in the United States.

While the word "agree" is not defined in section 1-105 of the U.C.C., section 1-201 on "General Definitions" defines "agreement" as "the bargain of the parties in fact as found in their language or by implication from other circumstances including course of dealing or usage of trade or course of

---

1. The present Law shall apply to contracts of sale of goods entered into by parties whose places of business are in the territories of different States, in each of the following cases:

(a) Where the contract involves the sale of goods which are at the time of the conclusion of the contract in the course of carriage or will be carried from the territory of one State to the territory of another;

(b) Where the acts constituting the offer and the acceptance have been effected in the territories of different States;

(c) Where delivery of the goods is to be made in the territory of a State other than that within whose territory the acts constituting the offer and the acceptance have been effected.

There was widespread dissatisfaction with the above requirements for the applicability of ULIS, and the UNCITRAL Working Group on the International Sale of Goods (*see* notes 13–14 *supra*) concluded that "subparagraphs 1(a), 1(b), and 1(c) of article 1 of ULIS, in many situations left in doubt the question of whether the transaction was governed by the law." Report of UNCITRAL on the Work of its Fourth Session, 26 UN GAOR Supp. (No. 17) para. 58, UN Doc. A/8417 (1971) [hereinafter cited as UNCITRAL, Fourth Report]. Consequently, there was general agreement from a wide geographical mix of states to the present wording of Article 1(1) of the 1980 Convention when it was originally put forward in draft form by a working group of UNCITRAL in 1972 at its third session, UN Doc. A/CN.9/62/Adds. 1–2, Ann. I (1972): *e.g.*, Poland, UN Docs. A/CN.9/SR.72, at 3 (1971), and A/CN.9/SR.74, at 15 (1971); Japan, UN Doc. A/CN.9/SR.72, at 11; Argentina, UN Doc. A/CN.9/SR.74, at 8; Mexico, UN Doc. A/CN.9/SR.74, at 12; Bulgaria, 26 UN GAOR C.6 (1252d mtg.) para. 28, UN Doc. A/C.6/SR.1252 (1971); Norway, UN Doc. A/CN.9/SR.74, at 15; the USSR, *id.* at 13; the United Kingdom, *id.* at 11; the United States, UN Docs. A/CN.9/SR.72, at 9, and A/CN.9/SR.74, at 13; Australia, UN Doc. A/CN.9/SR.74, at 7. *See generally* Report of the Secretary-General: Analysis of Comments by Governments and International Organizations on the draft Convention on the International Sale of Goods as adopted by the Working Group on the International Sale of Goods, ch. 1, Sphere of Application, paras. 1 & 2, UN Doc. A/CN.9/126, pt. B (1977).

[34] The five exceptions are enumerated in U.C.C. §1-105(2) (1978), and cover transactions involving rights of creditors against goods sold, bank deposits and collections, bulk transfers, investment securities, and secured transactions; these transactions are governed by the law of the particular jurisdiction specified by the appropriate U.C.C. section.

[35] *Id.*, §1-105(1). [36] *Ibid.*

performance as provided in this Act."[37] If this definition is used in interpreting "agree" under section 1-105(1), it is clear that the forum may have to look beyond the mere words of the contract to determine whether agreement on choice of law can be implied.[38] It has been suggested that if

> the preponderance of contacts of a transaction are with one jurisdiction, and if the parties were (or should have been) familiar with that jurisdiction's laws, and if nothing is expressly stipulated as to choice of law, the circumstances clearly suggest that the parties implicitly agreed on that law as the applicable law.[39]

This test can in fact be used to avoid the difficulties of implied agreements and to determine which jurisdiction bears an "appropriate relation" to the transaction, as provided in the second part of section 1-105. Under this test, in the absence of an agreement, the jurisdiction with the preponderance of contacts would bear the appropriate relation, and therefore the law of *that* jurisdiction would apply.[40]

For example (simplified for our purposes), if an international contract is made in the United States between a U.S. corporation and a foreign entity and performance is to be in the United States, in the absence of an express choice-of-law clause, the forum would find a "preponderance of contacts of the transaction" with the United States.[41] Such a finding would indicate that

[37] *Id.*, §1-201(3).

[38] *See In re* Bengtson, 3 U.C.C. Rep. Serv. 283 (D. Conn. 1965), in which the district court followed the Official Comment to U.C.C. §1-205, to the effect that

> the meaning of the agreement of the parties is to be determined by the language used by them and by their action, read and interpreted in the light of commercial practices and other surrounding circumstances. This measure and background for interpretation are set by the commercial context, *which may explain and supplement even the language of a formal or final writing.*

Id. at 289 (emphasis added). *See* further Dore & DeFranco, *supra* note 4, at 53. In Amerine Nat'l Corp. v. Denver Feed Co., 493 F.2d 1275, 14 U.C.C. Rep. Serv. 885 (10th Cir. 1974), a contract for the sale of young turkeys was reached in the context of a well-established course of dealing between the parties, and there was no evidence of a sudden change by the seller from its past practice of supplying commercial customers with cross-bred as well as pure-strain turkeys. Thus, the court held that the written contract did not materially depart from the prior course of dealing, and hence the supply of cross-breeds to the buyer was in compliance with the contract, despite buyer's allegation of an oral agreement prior to the formal "Contract of Sale" in which buyer expressed a desire to receive only pure-strain turkeys.

[39] Nordstrom & Ramerman, *The Uniform Commercial Code and the Choice of Law*, 1969 DUKE L.J. 623, 632.

[40] *Ibid.*

[41] The test is not a mechanical one, however, and rather than merely counting contacts, it should weigh their *significance* to the issues before the court. *See generally* Reese, *The Uniform Commercial Code and Its Application in Non-Code States*, 1 U.C.C. Rep. Serv. 802 (1965), for an analysis of the common law conflicts-of-laws tests that are to be used by the forum to determine what law governs the validity of a contract in the absence of an express choice of law by the parties. The controlling law may be, variously: (1) the law of the place where the contract was made; (2) the law of the place of performance; (3) the law intended by the parties to be controlling; or (4) the law of the jurisdiction that has the most "significant contacts" with the transaction. It is useful to note that the "significant contacts" test in (4) is similar to the "preponderance of contacts" test mentioned above, in that both tests can be used to determine the applicable law

the jurisdiction with which there is an "appropriate relation" is the United States, which, in turn, would make *its* law (*i.e.*, the U.C.C.) applicable. The same result would obtain if the United States ratifies the Convention with an Article 95 reservation (discussed below) and the foreign entity's place of business is in a noncontracting state (again, providing there is no express choice-of-law clause in the contract).[42]

When there *is* a choice of law by the parties, the first part of the test in section 1-105 states that the transaction must bear a "reasonable relation" to the state whose law the parties agree to as the governing law.[43] The comment to section 1-105 offers limited guidance for applying this test. It adopts the position laid down in *Seeman v. Philadelphia Warehouse Co.*,[44] which suggests that "ordinarily the law chosen [by the parties] must be that of a jurisdiction where a significant enough portion of the making or performance of the contract is to occur or occurs."[45]

This is not a particularly useful guide; it merely shifts the inquiry to what is "a significant enough portion" of the contract.[46] The reference in the comment to the "making *or* performance of the contract"[47] has been interpreted as implying that the transaction must be examined in terms of its principal components (*viz.*, formation and performance) and that only a *portion* of *either* component need be significant in relation to the jurisdiction whose law is chosen to justify the choice of law.[48]

SUBSTANTIVE CHOICE-OF-LAW PROVISIONS IN THE CONVENTION

Article 1 of the Convention provides in part that the Convention will apply to contracts for the sale of goods between parties whose places of business are in different states when (1) the states are contracting states (Article 1(1)(a)),[49]

---

with reference to the jurisdiction with which there is an appropriate relation. Representative cases illustrating the application of these tests are Neville Chemical Co. v. Union Carbide Corp., 422 F.2d 1205, 7 U.C.C. Rep. Serv. 81 (3d Cir. 1970); and Bache & Co. v. Int'l Controls Corp., 324 F.Supp. 998 (S.D.N.Y. 1971), *supplemented*, 339 F.Supp. 341 (S.D.N.Y. 1972), *aff'd*, 469 F.2d 696, 10 U.C.C. Rep. Serv. 248 (1972). *See also* the Official Comment to U.C.C. §1-105 (1978). The U.C.C. does not distinguish between U.S.-foreign and domestic interstate transactions with respect to application of the "significant contacts" rule.

[42] Article 1(1)(a) of the Convention requires that for the Convention to apply the parties must have their places of business in different states, and the states must be contracting states.

[43] U.C.C. §1-105(1) (1978).

[44] 274 U.S. 403 (1927).

[45] U.C.C. §1-105, Comment 1 (1978).

[46] Each dispute must still be settled on a case-by-case basis, with the added difficulty that the meaning of the key words and phrases such as "agree," "reasonable relation," and "significant enough portion" must be construed contextually.

[47] Emphasis added. The use of words such as "ordinarily," "significant enough," "portion," and "making or performance" merely confirms the elusive nature of the first part of the two-tier test in section 1-105. Because of this difficulty, it would seem reasonable to have *alternative* approaches to the test, *i.e.*, from the point of view of *either* the "making" *or* the "performance" of the contract, instead of a single, rigid, and inflexible approach, and to leave for contextual consideration what "portion" of either the "making" or the "performance" would "ordinarily" be "significant enough."

[48] Nordstrom & Ramerman, *supra* note 39, at 627. On the "reasonable relation" test, see further Dore & DeFranco, *supra* note 4, at 54.

[49] If a party has places of business in more than one state, the relevant place of business for

or (2) the rules of private international law lead to the application of the law of a contracting state (Article 1(1)(b)).[50] In the latter instance, even when the places of business of either or both of the parties are not in contracting states, the Convention becomes applicable if the forum where the case is brought determines that the law of a contracting state will apply, and the forum is itself in a contracting state.[51] A forum in a noncontracting state may apply the Convention[52] or, in certain defined circumstances, the internal law of the contracting state in question.[53] A further application of the principle in Article

---

purposes of Article 1 is to be determined in accordance with Article 10(a) of the Convention. Article 10 provides:

> For the purposes of this Convention:
>
> (a) if a party has more than one place of business, the place of business is that which has the closest relationship to the contract and its performance, having regard to the circumstances known to or contemplated by the parties at any time before or at the conclusion of the contract;
>
> (b) if a party does not have a place of business, reference is to be made to his habitual residence.

[50] *See* further Winship, *supra* note 17, at 1232; J. HONNOLD, *supra* note 15, at 46.

[51] *See* Commentary on the Draft Convention on the International Sale of Goods, UN Doc. A/CN.9/116, Ann. II (1976), *reprinted in* 7 Y.B. COMM'N INT'L TRADE L. 96, 97, col. 1, para. 7 (1976), UN Doc. A/CN.9/SER.A/1976 [hereinafter cited as 1976 Commentary]. Article 1(1)(b) of the Convention has been the subject of a great deal of controversy, and many states have either supported its total deletion from the Convention or have indicated the desire to file a reservation declaring themselves not to be bound by it. *See* text accompanying notes 84–87 and 96, *infra.* Yet when Article 1(1)(b) was put to a vote at the 1980 Conference of Plenipotentiaries that adopted the final text of the Convention, it survived by a very comfortable margin. *See* note 87 *infra.* The controversy, however, antedates the 1980 conference. Proposals were made for its deletion in the early stages of UNCITRAL's attempts to examine methods of making ULIS more acceptable to states. Some of the arguments for deleting an identical provision from a revised draft of ULIS were that:

> (i) The rules of private international law in some States could lead to the application of the law of one State to the obligations of the buyer and of a different law to the obligations of the seller. It would be difficult in such a situation to know whether under paragraph 1(b) all of the provisions of the Convention would be applicable to any dispute between the parties or only those provisions relating to the buyer or the seller, as the case may be.
>
> (ii) Subparagraph 1(b) created the possibility of applying any one of three legal régimes to a contract of sale: the domestic law of the forum, the domestic law of the State of the other party to the contract and the Convention, rather than only two as before.
>
> (iii) If the forum was not in a Contracting State but the rules of private international law of the forum referred the dispute to the substantive law of another State which was a Contracting State, the question would arise whether the forum would feel bound by this subparagraph to apply the Convention rather than the domestic law of the other State.

Report of the Working Group on the International Sale of Goods on the Work of its Sixth Session, UN Doc. A/CN.9/100, para. 17 (1975), *reprinted in* 6 Y.B. COMM'N INT'L TRADE L. 49, 50 (1975), UN Doc. A/CN.9/SER.A/1975. For reasons for the continued resilience of Article 1(1)(b), see notes 54–61 and accompanying text, *infra.* It is not surprising, therefore, that Article 95 of the Convention specifically provides that a signatory state may file a reservation excluding Article 1(1)(b) in relation to itself—a strong palliative to those states opposed to it; *see* text accompanying notes 69 and 84–87, *infra.*

[52] *See* J. HONNOLD, *supra* note 15, at 46.

[53] *See* text accompanying note 91, *infra.*

1(1)(b) is that if two parties from different states designate the law of a contracting state as their governing law, the Convention will apply even though it is not specifically mentioned.[54] The language of the contract may show, however, that the parties intended the domestic law of the contracting state to govern their transaction, in which case the Convention could presumably be displaced in favor of the domestic law.

The provision in Article 1(1) requiring that the places of business of the parties be in different states shows that the Convention is not concerned with the law governing contracts of sale or their formation where the parties have their places of business within the same state.[55] However, experience under ULIS[56] led the drafters of the present Convention to include the criterion in Article 1(1)(a) that the places of business of the parties, in addition to being in different states, must be in contracting states.[57]

Thus, if the parties have places of business in two contracting states, the Convention applies even if the rules of private international law of the forum would ordinarily designate the law of a third contracting state, *e.g.*, the state where the contract was concluded.[58] This result can be obviated only if the litigation takes place in a third noncontracting state (including the state where the contract was concluded), and the rules of private international law of that state would apply the law of the forum, *i.e.*, its own law, or that of a fourth noncontracting state.[59]

However, once the appropriate conditions of Article 1 of the Convention have been met,[60] no specific agreement is needed to make the Convention

---

[54] *See* Commentary on the Draft Convention on Contracts for the International Sale of Goods, Prepared by the Secretariat, UN Doc. A/CONF.97/5 (1980), Commentary on Article 1(1), Basic Criterion, para. 8 [hereinafter cited as 1979 Commentary], *reprinted in* OFFICIAL RECORDS, *supra* note 1, at 14, 15. France and Australia supported Article 1 of the final text at the 1980 Conference of Plenipotentiaries. They asserted that, from the point of view of the ratifying state, because the Convention would govern international sales, its sphere of application should be as wide as possible. Thus, without paragraph 1(b), a court in a contracting state would be obliged to apply domestic legislation regarding internal sales in cases involving parties situated in a noncontracting state, instead of the Convention, which was drafted specifically for international trade, and hence more suitable. In addition, it was pointed out that retaining paragraph 1(b) would give parties in noncontracting states the benefit of a uniform law whenever they dealt with parties from contracting states. At the same time, a contracting state that had a law specially designed for international trade should have the right to apply it in preference to less appropriate legislation. UN Doc. A/CONF.97/C.1/SR.1 (1980), *reprinted in* OFFICIAL RECORDS, *supra* note 1, at 236, 237–38. *See also ibid.*, the Bulgarian view that in the interest of having a truly uniform international sales law, the contracting states should treat the Convention as the *general* law on the international sale of goods and not just as a *special* law on sales between contracting states.

[55] 1979 Commentary, *supra* note 54, at 15, para. 3.

[56] *See* UNCITRAL, Fourth Report, *supra* note 33, para. 58.

[57] The International Chamber of Commerce holds the view that paragraph 1(b), when combined with paragraph 1(a), represents a useful compromise in contrast to the provision in Article 2 of ULIS, *supra* note 2, which excluded the rules of private international law for the purpose of application of the uniform law. UN Doc. A/CONF.97/9 (1980), *supra* note 25, OFFICIAL RECORDS, at 72.

[58] 1979 Commentary, *supra* note 54, at 15, para. 6.

[59] *Ibid.*

[60] *See* text accompanying notes 49–54, *supra*.

applicable to an international sales transaction.[61] Express agreement is required only to *exclude* the Convention (or any part thereof) under Article 6.[62]

In providing for a fairly extensive application of the Convention to international sales transactions, the drafters were prompted by the desire to prevent forum shopping and to avoid reliance on rules of private international law.[63] It was felt that the extensive coverage would more effectively promote uniformity in the law governing the international sale of goods. Despite this underlying policy, there are several notable exceptions to the jurisdiction of the Convention over international sales. It would not apply or its application could be restricted in the following instances: (1) if, under Article 6, the parties specifically exclude or vary its application;[64] (2) if a third noncontracting state takes jurisdiction and decides that its own law or that of another noncontracting state applies;[65] (3) if, under Article 96, a contracting state declares inapplicable, in accordance with Article 12, any provision of the Convention that conflicts with its domestic law;[66] (4) if the goods in question were bought

[61] At the 1980 Conference of Plenipotentiaries, the consensus was that Article 1 was not only a useful compromise, but that it was an improvement over ULIS. The vote in favor of Article 1 of the final text was 42 with none against and 1 abstention. *See* UN Doc. A/CONF.97/SR.6 (1980), *reprinted in* OFFICIAL RECORDS, *supra* note 1, at 199, 200. *See* further the views of Switzerland, the International Chamber of Commerce, Austria, and the United States, UN Doc. A/CONF.97/9 (1980), *supra* note 25, *id.* at 72.

[62] For the text of Article 6, see note 29 *supra.* This basic freedom to "opt out" of the Convention in whole or in part leaves parties from contracting states totally free to select their own law or to agree to only a selective application of the Convention. Articles 1 and 6 of the Convention should satisfy the early objections of the United States to the "coercive effect" of ULIS. *See* text accompanying note 33, *supra.* The exclusion clause of ULIS, Article 3, provided in part that "such exclusion may be express or implied." The drafters of the present Convention decided not to provide for exclusion by implication "lest the special reference to 'implied' exclusion might encourage courts to conclude, on insufficient grounds, that the Convention had been wholly excluded." 1979 Commentary, *supra* note 54, at 17, para. 2, commentary on draft Art. 5 (current Art. 6). The policy of the drafters of the Convention therefore appears to be to ensure as wide an application of the Convention as possible without coercing parties into it. *See also* Dore & DeFranco, *supra* note 4, at 53. It is noteworthy that while Article 6 refers only to the exclusion or modification of the Convention, there is no provision anywhere in the Convention on the question whether the parties can *extend* the applicability of the Convention to transactions that normally fall outside its scope, *e.g.,* where the places of business of the buyer and seller are not "in different states" in accordance with Article 1(1) of the Convention, or where there is a lack of contact with a contracting state, as required by Article 1(1)(a). However, there seems little reason to deny the parties the freedom to apply the Convention *by agreement,* even in such cases. *See* J. HONNOLD, *supra* note 15, at 79–83.

[63] 1979 Commentary, *supra* note 54, at 15, para. 4.

[64] *See* note 62 *supra.*

[65] *See* text at note 59, *supra.*

[66] Article 96 of the Convention provides:

> A Contracting State whose legislation requires contracts of sale to be concluded in or evidenced by writing may at any time make a declaration in accordance with article 12 that any provision of article 11, article 29, or Part II of this Convention, that allows a contract of sale or its modification or termination by agreement or any offer, acceptance, or other indication of intention to be made in any form other than in writing, does not apply where any party has his place of business in that State.

Article 11 provides that a contract of sale need not be in writing, while Article 29(1) permits modification of contracts by "the mere agreement of the parties." *See* J. HONNOLD, *supra* note 15, at 79.

for immediate consumer use;[67] (5) if it is not apparent from the contract that the parties have their places of business in different states;[68] or (6) if, under Article 95, a contracting state files a reservation declaring itself not bound by Article 1(1)(b) of the Convention, which would enable it to apply its domestic law when its jurisdiction results solely from rules of private international law.[69]

As the exceptions under (1) and (2) above have already been discussed,[70] only the remaining four will be examined here.

Article 12 permits a contracting state that has made a declaration under Article 96 to require, contrary to Articles 11, 29, and 14–24, that a sales contract or its modification or termination be in writing. This provision applies if any party has a place of business in that contracting state.[71] Thus, a state such as the USSR, which insists on strict compliance with its legislation in the conclusion of foreign trade contracts, especially with requirements that such

[67] Article 2(a) of the Convention provides: "This Convention does not apply to sales: (a) of goods bought for personal, family or household use, unless the seller, at any time before or at the conclusion of the contract, neither knew nor ought to have known that the goods were bought for any such use." Subparagraphs (b)–(f) of Article 2 further exclude the application of the Convention to sales: by auction, on execution, or otherwise by authority of law; of stocks, shares, investment securities, negotiable instruments, or money; of ships, vessels, hovercraft, or aircraft; and of electricity. For discussion of sales falling in subparagraphs (b)–(f), see J. HONNOLD, *supra* note 15, at 50–56.

[68] Article 1, paragraph 2 of the Convention provides:

> (2) The fact that the parties have their places of business in different States is to be disregarded whenever this fact does not appear either from the contract or from any dealings between, or from information disclosed by, the parties at any time before or at the conclusion of the contract.

For further analysis, see notes 82–83 and text accompanying note 83, *infra.* Paragraph 3 of Article 1 further provides that "[n]either the nationality of the parties nor the civil or commercial character of the parties or of the contract is to be taken into consideration in determining the application of this Convention." Paragraph 3 reinforces the rule that the application of the Convention depends primarily on the parties' having places of business in different contracting states. The relevant place of business is determined each time without reference to nationality of the party. 1979 Commentary, *supra* note 54, at 15, para. 11. Paragraph 3 further excludes from consideration whether the contract is of a civil or commercial character. This is to avoid difficulties that might otherwise arise from the fact that in some legal systems the law relating to sale of goods differs according to whether the parties or the contract are characterized as "civil" or "commercial." *Ibid.*, para. 12. It should be noted, however, that paragraph 3 applies only to the scope-of-application provisions of the Convention. It does not mean that the civil or commercial character of the parties may not be taken into consideration for the purposes of determining such matters as the period of time to be regarded as reasonable for giving notice of lack of conformity of the goods under Article 36(1) of the Convention. *Ibid.*, para. 14.

[69] Article 95 provides: "Any State may declare at the time of the deposit of its instrument of ratification, acceptance, approval or accession that it will not be bound by subparagraph 1(b) of Article 1 of this Convention." The United States, upon signing the Convention in August 1981, declared its intention to file such a reservation. *See* text accompanying notes 84–88 and 96, *infra.*

[70] *See* note 62 and accompanying text, *supra,* for the first exception, and text accompanying note 59, *supra,* for the second exception.

[71] Article 12 of the Convention provides:

> Any provision of article 11, article 29 or Part II of this Convention that allows a contract of sale or its modification or termination by agreement or any offer, acceptance or other indication of intention to be made in any form other than in writing does not apply where any party has his place of business in a Contracting State which has made a declaration under article 96 of this Convention. The parties may not derogate from or vary the effect of this article.

For the text of Article 96, see note 66 *supra.* For the text of Article 11, see note 73 *infra.*

contracts be in writing,[72] could declare void an unwritten contract of sale evidenced by a witness.[73]

Article 12 shows deference to the fact that many states consider it an important element of public policy that contracts or their modification or termination be in writing.[74] Because it is a matter of public policy, the principle of party autonomy is inapplicable to Article 12.[75] The article specifically provides that "the parties may not derogate from or vary the effect of this article."[76]

The fourth category of exceptions to the applicability of the Convention is transactions involving the sale of "goods bought for personal, family or household use."[77] However, if the goods were purchased by an individual for a commercial purpose, the sale would be governed by the Convention.[78]

The rationale for excluding consumer sales from the Convention was to avoid interfering with the various types of domestic consumer protection laws.[79] This seems reasonable since most consumer sales are domestic rather than international in character.[80] However, the exception under Article 2(a) does not apply (that is, the Convention applies) if the seller, at any time prior to or at the conclusion of the contract, did not know and did not have reason to know that the goods were intended for consumer use.[81]

Under Article 1(2) the Convention does not apply if the "fact that the parties have their places of business in different States . . . does not appear either from the contract or from any dealings between . . . [them] at any time before or at the conclusion of the contract."[82] Thus, if a U.S. corporation

[72] Dore, *Plan and Contract in the Domestic and Foreign Trade of the U.S.S.R.*, 8 SYRACUSE J. INT'L L. & COM. 29 (1980). *See also* Osakwe, *Legal and Institutional Barriers to United States-Soviet Trade: Soviet Perspective*, 8 VAND. J. TRANSNAT'L L. 85, 108 (1974); J. HONNOLD, *supra* note 15, at 129–30.

[73] Article 11 provides: "A contract of sale need not be concluded in or evidenced by writing and is not subject to any other requirement as to form. It may be proved by any means, including witnesses." The reason for the inclusion of Article 11 in the Convention was the fact that many contracts for the international sale of goods are concluded by modern means of communication that do not always involve a written contract. 1979 Commentary, *supra* note 54, at 20, para. 2. If a contracting state has a domestic writing requirement that is contravened through an international sales contract, it can, of course, enforce its administrative or penal sanctions against the recalcitrant party, but the contract itself will be enforceable if the state has not filed an Article 12 declaration excluding Article 11. *Ibid.*

[74] *Ibid.*, para. 1.

[75] *Ibid.*, para. 3.

[76] *See* note 71 *supra.*

[77] Art. 2(a), note 67 *supra.*

[78] 1979 Commentary, *supra* note 54, at 16, para. 2. The commentary gives the following examples of sales that would not fall within the Article 2(a) exception and would therefore be governed by the Convention: the purchase of a camera by a professional photographer for use in his business, the purchase of soap or other toiletries by a business for the personal use of the employees, the purchase of a single automobile by a dealer for resale. *Ibid.*

[79] *Ibid.*, para. 3; J. HONNOLD, *supra* note 15, at 50–51.

[80] Thus, "it was felt that the Convention should not apply to the relatively few cases where consumer sales were international transactions, e.g. because the buyer was a tourist with his habitual residence in another country or that the goods were ordered by mail." 1979 Commentary, *supra* note 54, at 16, para. 3 (footnote omitted).

[81] Art. 2(a), *supra* note 67. If the seller knew (or ought to have known) that the goods were being bought for consumer use, the forum would have to decide on an applicable domestic law. *See* 1979 Commentary, *supra* note 54, at 16, para. 4; J. HONNOLD, *supra* note 15, at 51.

[82] Art. 1(2) of the Convention, *supra* note 68.

conducts a transaction in the United States with another entity that at the time appears to have its place of business in the United States, but that in reality is acting as agent for an undisclosed foreign principal, the Convention will not apply even if the United States and the foreign state are both contracting states.[83]

Finally, Article 95 permits a contracting state to file a reservation declaring itself not bound by Article 1(1)(b) of the Convention.[84] The rationale for such a reservation is to prevent the Convention from superceding the domestic law of the contracting state regarding a contract involving a party from a noncontracting state.[85] The United States has already declared its intention to file such a reservation upon ratification.[86] If it does so, a sales contract to which at least one of the parties is from a noncontracting state, and which according to the forum's rules of private international law should be governed by the law of the United States, would be governed by the U.C.C.[87]

[83] Since the basic criterion for the application of the Convention is that the parties have places of business in different states—Art. 1(1) of the Convention, 1979 Commentary, *supra* note 54, at 15, para. 2—if a transaction "appears to be between parties whose places of business are in the same state, [it] is not governed by [the] Convention." 1979 Commentary, at 15, para. 9. Thus, for example, a transaction of sale effected through a broker who did not disclose that he was acting for a foreign principal would not be governed by the Convention. The test, therefore, is an objective one. *See* further J. HONNOLD, *supra* note 15, at 40–42. In an earlier draft, Article 2(a) (Art. 1(2) of the present Convention) excluded transactions where one of the parties "neither knew nor had reason to know" that the place of business of the other party was in a different state. Working Group on the International Sale of Goods, Report on the work of the Second Session, UN Doc. A/CN.9/52 (1971), *reprinted in* 2 Y.B. COMM'N INT'L TRADE L. 50, 52, col. 2 (1971), UN Doc. A/CN.9/SER.A/1971. The working group at its third session felt that this provision was "difficult to apply in view of the subjective element contained in the expression 'neither knew nor had reason to know'." Progress Report of the Working Group on the International Sale of Goods on the Work of its Third Session, UN Doc. A/CN.9/62, Adds. 1–2, Ann. II (1972), *reprinted in* 3 Y.B. COMM'N INT'L TRADE L. 77, 82, 83, cols. 1–2, paras. 9–10 (1973), UN Doc. A/CN.9/SER.A/1972. The working group thereupon substituted the objective criterion in Article 1(2) of a draft of the Convention. *Id.* at 78, col. 1, and 83, para. 10. This draft article is identical to Article 1(2) of the present Convention.

[84] *See* text accompanying note 69, *supra*. For the text of Article 95, see note 69 *supra*. At the 1980 Conference of Plenipotentiaries, Austria urged that reservations to the sphere-of-application provisions of the type permitted under ULIS be disallowed, on the ground that they might endanger the very application of the Convention itself and negate the work of UNCITRAL. UN Doc. A/CONF.97/9 (1980), *supra* note 25, pt. B, Comments and Proposals on Provisions of the Draft Convention, para. 2. On the permissibility of reservations under ULIS, see Nadelmann, *supra* note 4, at 454 *et seq. Cf.* the stand of Argentina in favor of permitting reservations under the present Convention. UN Doc. A/CONF.97/C.1/SR.1, *supra* note 54, OFFICIAL RECORDS, at 237.

[85] The ABA Report, *supra* note 17, makes the following comment on Article 1(1)(b) of the Convention:

> The principal impact of this provision on traders of a Contracting State appears to be that the Convention would be applicable in a greater number of cases but at the expense of the Contracting State's domestic law. The provision also reintroduces the uncertainties of private international law which the . . . [Convention] was designed to avoid.

Id. at 5. For this reason, the report favors a reservation by the United States excluding Article 1(1)(b). *Id.* at 1. *See generally* J. HONNOLD, *supra* note 15, at 47.

[86] *See* note 69 and text accompanying note 26, *supra*.

[87] *See* further text accompanying note 96, *infra*. This preference of a major trading power for a reservation vindicates the stand of the Federal Republic of Germany at the 1980 Conference

The foregoing exceptions could have important ramifications for the Convention. In particular, the ease and frequency with which the exceptions are used by international businessmen or their states could undermine the long-term effectiveness of the Convention (even assuming ratification by a substantial number of countries) by encouraging just the type of forum shopping and reliance on private international law that the Convention is designed to discourage. The international application of the U.C.C. is important in this regard because it is likely to be the source of governing law to which U.S. businessmen will turn if the Convention, for any of the reasons discussed previously, is inapplicable.[88] In light of these issues, the scope of the Convention will be contrasted with that of the U.C.C. in international sales, by examining the potential application of each, both if the Convention is ratified by the United States and if it is not.

THE SCOPE OF THE U.C.C. AND THE CONVENTION COMPARED

The reference in section 1-105(1) of the U.C.C. to "another state or nation" suggests that the drafters intended to cover international transactions involving U.S. business enterprises as well as inter-U.S.-state transactions. However, they do not appear to have anticipated an international code of sales—hence the alternative reference to "the law of another state or nation" rather than to an *international* law of sales.[89]

The applicability of the U.C.C. to international sales involving U.S. parties will depend on: (1) whether the United States ultimately ratifies the Convention (with or without an Article 95 reservation), and (2) whether the nations in which the businesses of the parties to a specific contract are located have ratified the Convention (with or without the reservation). Each variant of these two situations is discussed separately, primarily from a U.S. perspective.

The Situation Prior to U.S. Ratification

Foreign Party from Noncontracting State. Prior to ratification of the Convention by the United States, if a U.S. business entity contracts with a foreign party

---

of Plenipotentiaries. Arguing for the deletion of Article 1(1)(b), Germany submitted that it was highly unusual for an international instrument to bind its signatory states to apply the instrument to nationals of nonsignatory states. It predicted that paragraph 1(b) would cause "serious problems of interpretation and application." UN Doc. A/CONF.97/C.1/SR.1, *supra* note 54, paras. 11–12, OFFICIAL RECORDS, at 236–37. It further predicted that if paragraph 1(b) were not deleted, reservations from contracting states would be likely. *Id.* at 238. Czechoslovakia, the German Democratic Republic, and Sweden also supported the proposal to delete. *Id.* at 237–38. The vote on the proposal to delete paragraph 1(b) was rejected by 25 votes to 7, with 10 abstentions. *Id.* at 238.

[88] *See* text accompanying notes 32–33, 59–62, and 71–87, *supra.*

[89] U.C.C. §1-105(1) (1978). *See* Comment 3 to U.C.C. §1-105, which refers to the code as "in large part a reformulation and restatement of the law merchant and of the understanding of a business community which transcends state *and even national* boundaries" (emphasis added). This statement embodies the drafters' realization of the U.C.C.'s potential for international application. *See also generally* the opinion in Miller v. Wells Fargo Bank Int'l Corp., 18 U.C.C. Rep. Serv. 489 (S.D.N.Y. 1975), in which the court said that the U.C.C. choice-of-law rules may be subject to the limitations that are imposed on the applicability of American domestic law to essentially foreign transactions. This statement implies that the U.C.C. rules would be applicable to a transaction that is not "essentially foreign": *e.g.*, one involving a U.S. enterprise and a foreign party where the "preponderance of contacts" was with the United States.

having a place of business in a *non*contracting state, the parties may choose the U.C.C. to govern their transaction. In the absence of an agreement as to choice of law, the U.C.C. can still apply if the forum's rules of private international law determine that U.S. law will apply.[90] If, however, the rules of private international law of the forum (whether the United States, the foreign state, or even a third noncontracting or contracting state) lead to the application of the law of a contracting state, the forum should apply either the Convention[91] when the contracting state has not filed an Article 95 reservation, or the domestic law of the contracting state when it has filed an Article 95 reservation.

Foreign Party from Contracting State. If (still prior to U.S. ratification) the U.S. business entity's foreign partner is from a *contracting* state that has not filed an Article 95 reservation, and the U.C.C. is designated by the parties as the governing law, then it will apply to a suit brought in the United States, provided the "reasonable relation" test is met. However, if the same parties have not specified a choice of law, the suit is filed in the foreign state, and its rules of private international law lead to the application of its *own* law, the Convention will govern the dispute since the forum state in question is a contracting state.[92] A forum state that *has* filed an Article 95 reservation will apply its *domestic* law, in accordance with the principle that such a reservation narrows the applicability of the Convention to transactions between parties from different *contracting* states.[93] Furthermore, if instead of designating the U.C.C., the parties choose the law of the contracting state that has not filed an Article 95 reservation, the Convention will be applicable to the transaction even though the parties have not specifically mentioned it.[94]

Choice of a Third-State Forum. If the forum state is a *third* noncontracting state and its rules of private international law lead to the application of the law of the United States, the U.C.C. will govern. If the rules designate the law of the state where the foreign entity has its place of business (*i.e.,* the contracting state), the choice of applicable law will depend upon whether the contracting state has filed an Article 95 reservation. Finally, if the forum of the third noncontracting state decides that its rules lead to the application of its *own* law, then the transaction will be governed by its domestic law.

Should the forum state be a third *contracting* state, private international choice-of-law rules would still determine the applicable law. When its rules require the application of U.S. law, the U.C.C. will apply. When its rules require the application of the law of the state where the foreign entity has its place of business, the forum should apply the Convention, provided the state

[90] U.C.C. §1-105(1) (1978). *See* text accompanying notes 35–37, *supra.* It should be noted that section 1-105 states the rule for *U.S.* courts only, and not for foreign courts in noncontracting states. A foreign court may nevertheless apply the U.C.C. if *its* choice-of-law rules so require.

[91] J. HONNOLD, *supra* note 15, at 46.

[92] Art. 1(1)(b) of the Convention. 1979 Commentary, *supra* note 54, at 15, para. 7; J. HONNOLD, *supra* note 15, at 46.

[93] J. HONNOLD, *supra* note 15, at 47.

[94] 1979 Commentary, *supra* note 54, at 15, para. 8. It may nevertheless be possible to infer from the setting and the language of the contract that the parties intended the domestic law of the foreign state to govern their contract and not the Convention. *See* note 54 *supra* and accompanying text.

in question has not reserved against Article 1(1)(b); if it has so reserved, the forum should apply the law that a court of the reserving state would apply, *i.e.*, the domestic law of the reserving state.

When the rules of private international law of the third contracting state require the application of its *own* law, then the forum should apply the Convention, provided the forum state *itself* has not filed an Article 95 reservation. If it has, the court should not apply the Convention in accordance with the principle that a reservation restricts the applicability of the Convention between parties from contracting states only. Since, in the above example, the U.S. party is not from a contracting state, the court in the forum state would apply its domestic law.

The Situation After U.S. Ratification

Foreign Party from Noncontracting State. Although the United States has declared its intention of filing an Article 95 reservation upon ratification of the Convention, let us assume for the moment that it does not. Then, a transaction between a U.S. business and a foreign entity whose place of business is in a noncontracting state could displace the Convention and be governed by the U.C.C. if the parties have so stated. But if the rules of private international law of the forum lead to the application of the law of a contracting state that has not made an Article 95 reservation, the Convention would govern the transaction.[95]

The effect of an Article 95 reservation, so far as the United States is concerned, would be to limit the application of the Convention to those sales contracts in which the places of business of both the buyer and the seller are in different contracting states and the parties have not designated a domestic law as the law of the contract.[96] For example, the United States files the reservation upon ratification, and a U.S. party then concludes a sales contract with a foreign party from a noncontracting state. If a dispute under the contract is litigated in the United States and the rules of private international law lead to the application of U.S. law, then—in view of the reservation—it is the U.C.C. that will apply. The reservation would therefore prevent the Convention from ever applying to transactions in which the foreign entity's place of business is in a noncontracting state and the forum's rules of private international law lead to the application of the law of the noncontracting state or of a contracting state that has filed an Article 95 reservation.

When the forum state is a *third noncontracting* state and its rules of private international law point to the United States, the forum should apply the U.C.C. if the United States has reserved, and the Convention if it has not. When its rules point to the second noncontracting state, the forum should apply the domestic law of that state. Finally, when the rules of the forum require the application of its own law, then its domestic law would govern.

When the forum is a third *contracting* state and its rules point to U.S. law, the forum should apply the Convention if the United States has not reserved,

[95] Art. 1(1)(b) of the Convention. 1979 Commentary, *supra* note 54, at 15, para. 7; J. HONNOLD, *supra* note 15, at 46.

[96] Dep't of State Memorandum, *supra* note 26.

and the U.C.C. if it has. Indication of the noncontracting state would mean that the latter's domestic law should govern. Finally, if the forum's own law is required, the court, as explained in the previous section, would apply its domestic law if the forum state has itself filed an Article 95 reservation, and the Convention if it has not.

Foreign Party from Contracting State. After U.S. ratification, several situations may arise, including: (1) the United States ratifies with an Article 95 reservation, but the foreign party is from a contracting state that has not filed the reservation; (2) the United States ratifies with the above reservation and the foreign party is from a contracting state that has also filed the reservation; and (3) the United States ratifies *without* the reservation and the foreign contracting state has also not filed the reservation.

We have seen that the effect of the Article 95 reservation is to apply the Convention only to sales covered by Article 1(1)(a), transactions between parties whose places of business are in different contracting states. Under (1), (2), and (3) above, in the absence of a specific exclusion of the Convention in accordance with Article 6, the Convention will govern because its basic criterion of applicability will have been met.[97]

Because jurisdictional matters make it more likely that actions will be brought where one of the parties has its principal place of business, parties from two different contracting states will have little worry that the Convention may not govern their transaction. Even if jurisdiction is obtained in another (*i.e.*, a third) contracting state, the Convention directs that it be applied by the forums (courts) of all contracting states. However, a third *noncontracting* state may obtain jurisdiction and determine by the rules of private international law that its own domestic law governs. If its rules require application of the law of either of the other two states, then since the latter two are both contracting states, the forum should apply the Convention.

IV. Conclusion

It has been shown that the applicability of the U.C.C. and/or the Convention to international sales involving U.S. parties will depend on: (1) whether the United States ratifies the Convention; (2) if it does, whether it does so with or without a reservation excluding Article 1(1)(b); and (3) whether the foreign entity's place of business is in a contracting state. Under (3), the applicable law also will depend on whether the foreign contracting state entered a reservation against Article 1(1)(b) upon ratification.

The freedom of a contracting party to exclude Article 1(1)(b) is not the only freedom to narrow the applicability of the Convention. We have seen that under Article 96, a contracting state may declare inapplicable, in accordance with Article 12, any provision of the Convention that conflicts with its domestic law.[98] In addition to these powers of exclusion, the Convention allows the parties themselves to vary or exclude it where it would otherwise be the governing law.[99]

[97] *See* text accompanying notes 49, 57, and 60–62, *supra.*

[98] *See* text accompanying notes 66 and 71–76, *supra.*

[99] *See* text accompanying note 62, *supra.*

We have also seen that while the U.C.C. does contemplate foreign transactions, its drafters do not appear to have anticipated an international code of sales.[100] Furthermore, while the drafters of the Convention clearly intended to prevent "forum shopping," the intention of those who drafted the U.C.C. choice-of-law provisions is less clear.[101] Although it is arguable that the key terms in section 1-105(1), "reasonable relation" and "appropriate relation," could encourage forum shopping,[102] it is also arguable that the terms stipulate a genuine and close connection between the transaction and the law that the forum is to apply to the transaction.[103] The Convention, by contrast, does not contain a "reasonable relation" test, and in the absence of a specific opting out of the Convention, it applies ipso facto and without special agreement if both parties have their places of business in different states and the states are contracting states.[104]

[100] *See* note 89 and accompanying text, *supra.*

[101] The Official Comment to U.C.C. §1-105 is not nearly as explicit on this point as is the commentary to the Convention. *See* 1979 Commentary, *supra* note 54, at 15, para. 4. In order to discern prevention of forum shopping as an intention of the U.C.C. drafters, one must draw inferences from certain language in the comment, which attempts as far as possible to broaden the applicability of the code and highlights the importance of common law policies of giving effect to agreements and of uniformity of result "regardless of where suit is brought." U.C.C. §1-105, Comment 4 (1978). *See also* Reese, *supra* note 41, who makes the point that forum shopping is abhorrent to conflict-of-laws doctrine. The drafters of the U.C.C. may have felt it unnecessary to be explicit as to "forum shopping," on the ground that the common law safeguards endorsed by Comment 4, §1-105, against that phenomenon would be adequate. Note that these safeguards are also incorporated as "Supplementary General Principles of Law" under U.C.C. §1-103 (1978).

[102] Stumberg, *Commercial Paper and the Conflict of Laws,* 6 VAND. L. REV. 489, 503 (1953). It should be noted, however, that the contemplation of the parties as to the governing law and the "significant contacts" test used in the absence of a specific choice of law are factors that are also considered under common law conflict-of-laws theory. The difference is that under traditional conflict-of-laws doctrine, these factors are *alternative* bases for judgment; different jurisdictions may use one or the other or both in deciding the applicable law—whereas under the U.C.C., the parties' right to select the controlling law is *predicated* upon the existence of a "reasonable relation" (probably tested in much the same manner as "significant contacts") between the transaction and the state or nation whose law is sought to be selected. Such "nexus formulation" may thus not even enter into a traditional conflict-of-laws decision, but under the U.C.C. it will be a necessary element regardless of any agreement between the parties.

[103] Cullen, *Conflict of Laws Problems under the Uniform Commercial Code,* 48 KY. L.J. 417, 425 (1960). The detailed version of §1-105 in the original draft of the U.C.C. permitted application of the code to a transaction that "touched" a code state "even in a most casual, or even accidental, way." Cullen concludes that in abandoning the rules permitting minimum contacts, the drafters of the present U.C.C. intended to require "some more substantial contact" with the state in question. This observation relates to the question of what constitutes an "appropriate relation"—*i.e.,* when the parties have not agreed specially as to applicable law—and Cullen considers that such a relation "must be something more than barely reasonable." *Id.* at 422. Where the parties *do* agree as to what law should govern, the law chosen must be that of a jurisdiction bearing a "reasonable relation" to the transaction. Cullen holds that such an agreement must be founded upon a connection between that jurisdiction and "some vital element of the transaction," as expressed in Big Four Mills, Ltd. v. Commercial Credit Co., 307 Ky. 612, 622, 211 S.W.2d 831, 837 (1948). As examples of "vital element" he cites execution (signing), performance, and intent.

[104] *See* text accompanying notes 49, 57, and 60–62, *supra.*

THE LAW OF THE SEA CONVENTION AND THIRD STATES

*By Luke T. Lee**

I. Introduction

The decision of the United States and 22 other countries not to sign the Law of the Sea Convention[1] in Montego Bay, Jamaica, on December 10, 1982,[2] raises the important question of the legal effects of the Convention upon nonsignatories (hereinafter referred to as "third states"). Will the latter be entitled to claim and enjoy treaty provisions beneficial to them, such as those pertaining to military or commercial navigation through international straits, including submerged passage and overflight rights, or will these rights be considered as contractual in nature, exercisable only by states parties? Clearly, the question is of critical importance to the regime of the law of the sea. Since there has been to date no systematic legal analysis of this important question in debates surrounding the Law of the Sea Convention, this essentially legal question has been consigned to general policy pronouncements.[3]

* Director, Office of Planning and Programs, Office of the United States Coordinator for Refugee Affairs. The author was formerly Senior Policy Adviser on the Law of the Sea, Department of State, and a member of the U.S. delegation to the Third United Nations Conference on the Law of the Sea (Drafting Committee). He wishes to record his appreciation to Professors Anthony D'Amato, Leo Gross, Louis Henkin, Oscar Schachter and Louis B. Sohn, as well as Terry Sattler, Esq., for their invaluable comments and suggestions. Responsibility for the views expressed, however, is entirely the author's, and these views have no official standing, in whole or in part.

[1] The United Nations Convention on the Law of the Sea, UN Doc. A/CONF.62/122 (Oct. 7, 1982), *reprinted in* 21 ILM 1261 (1982).

[2] The Convention was signed by 119 delegations when it was opened for signature on Dec. 10, 1982. *See* Closing Statement by the President of Conference on the Law of the Sea, in UN Press Release SEA/MB/14, Dec. 10, 1982. It will remain open for 2 years and will not enter into force until 12 months after being ratified by 60 countries. It is expected that some of the countries that did not sign the treaty in Montego Bay will sign it later, and that some of the countries that signed it may not ratify it. Indeed, on Feb. 7, 1983, the Government of Antigua and Barbuda and the Government of Japan signed the Convention. *See* Addendum to Depositary Notification C.N.297.1982.TREATIES-1 of 17 December 1982, Depositary Notification C.N.7.1983.TREATIES-1 (Feb. 23, 1983).

The text of the treaty was adopted by the Third United Nations Conference on the Law of the Sea in New York on April 30, 1982, by a vote of 130 in favor, 4 against (including the United States), and 17 abstentions. President Reagan announced his decision not to sign the treaty on July 9, 1982. *See* Statement by the President, released by the Department of State on July 9, 1982, 18 Weekly Comp. Pres. Doc. 887 (July 12, 1982).

[3] *See* Ratiner, *The Law of the Sea: A Crossroads for American Foreign Policy,* 60 Foreign Aff. 1006, 1018 (1982) (summary of opposing views).

Contemporary relevant official statements include that of a senior State Department official, who said the administration believed that President Reagan's decision not to sign the Law of the Sea Convention would not affect U.S. ships' access to international waters because the United States is "adequately protected" by existing international law "and we believe we have a sound legal position in terms of assured transit" through some 115 international straits governed by the

This paper explores the bases for the rights of third states under provisions of the Law of the Sea Convention beneficial to them. It explores also the applicability of many provisions in the Convention to states not parties either because such provisions are codifications of antecedent customary law, or because they reflect what has become customary law during and as a result

---

treaty. Washington Post, July 10, 1982, at A5. *See also* N.Y. Times, July 10, 1982, at 5; Christian Science Monitor, July 13, 1982, lead editorial, at 24.

In his testimony before a U.S. Senate body on Sept. 15, 1982, Theodore Kronmiller, Deputy Assistant Secretary of State for Oceans and Fisheries Affairs, stated:

> The exercise by the United States of rights and freedoms under international law can be limited only with our consent. This point holds true with regard both to our right to mine the seabed and to our right to navigate under, on and over the world's oceans, including international straits.

Law of the Sea Negotiations: Hearing Before the Subcomm. on Arms Control, Oceans, International Operations and Environment of the Senate Comm. on Foreign Relations, 97th Cong., 2d Sess. 8 (1982) [hereinafter cited as *Senate Hearing*].

Additionally, James L. Malone, Assistant Secretary of State for Oceans and International Environmental and Scientific Affairs and Chairman, U.S. delegation to the Law of the Sea Conference, stated in his address, "The United States and the Law of the Sea after UNCLOS III," given at the Duke University Symposium on "Law of the Sea–Where Now?," on Oct. 29, 1982 (text to be published in a symposium issue of *Law and Contemporary Problems*):

> Some claim that by rejecting the LOS Convention the U.S. will lose the navigation rights set out in the Convention, rights the United States sought to secure in a comprehensive LOS treaty. If the U.S. does not accept the seabed mining provisions, so goes the argument, the rights set forth in other portions of the Convention are forfeited. This is not so. Particularly with respect to navigation rights, the history of the law of the sea has been predominantly a history of customary rules evolving through state practice. In this area the Convention incorporates existing law, which will continue to apply to all states, not because of the treaty, but because of the customary law underlying the treaty. We are confident that we and our allies have the legal basis to protect our navigational interests outside the Treaty.

Dissenting, Elliot L. Richardson, head of the U.S. delegation to the Law of the Sea Conference from 1977 to 1980, said the United States would not be able to take advantage of the treaty provisions, such as navigational freedom for warships, without signing the treaty: "We can't pick and choose among the rights and responsibilities of the treaty." Christian Science Monitor, July 22, 1982.

Ambassador Tommy Koh, President of the Law of the Sea Conference, likewise stressed that such U.S. interests as military security and resources would not necessarily be protected by customary international law alone if the United States did not become a party to the treaty. The United States would therefore run the risk of having its right to transit passage in straits vital to its global strategic interests, for example, challenged by states parties who considered such matters as governed solely by the Law of the Sea Convention. Straits Times, July 23, 1982. He elaborated further on this point in his closing statement of the conference on Dec. 10, 1982:

> The argument that, except for Part XI, the Convention codifies customary law or reflects existing international practice is factually incorrect and legally insupportable. The régime of transit passage through straits used for international navigation and the régime of archipelagic sea lanes passage are two examples of the many new concepts in the Convention. Even in the case of article 76 on the continental shelf, the article contains new law in that it has expanded the concept of the continental shelf to include the continental slope and the continental rise. This concession to the broad margin States was in return for their agreement for revenue-sharing on the continental shelf beyond 200 miles. It is, therefore, my view that a State which is not a party to this Convention cannot invoke the benefits of article 76.

Meeting of Dec. 10, 1982, UN Doc. A/CONF.62/PV.193, at 23–25 (1983).

of the Conference on the Law of the Sea. It suggests that in some respects, perhaps, the Convention is generating customary law for the future and many provisions therefore may come to apply to nonparty states at some time soon. Excluded from the purview of this paper are third states' roles under the deep seabed mining (part XI), dispute settlement (part XV), and other provisions that are clearly intended to be applicable to "States Parties" only.[4]

II. Presumption against Rights or Duties for Third States

The starting point for analysis is that treaty rights and obligations are legally confined to the contracting parties.[5] The Vienna Convention on the Law of Treaties, reflecting the ancient principle *pacta tertiis nec nocent nec prosunt,* states: "A treaty does not create either obligations or rights for a third State without its consent."[6] The International Court of Justice reaffirmed this principle in the *North Sea Continental Shelf* cases:

> In principle, when a number of States . . . have drawn up a convention specifically providing for a particular method by which the intention to become bound by the régime of the convention is to be manifested—namely by the carrying out of certain prescribed formalities (ratification, accession), it is not lightly to be presumed that a State which has not carried out these formalities, though at all times fully able and entitled to do so, has nevertheless somehow become bound in another way. Indeed if it were a question not of obligation but of rights,—if, that is to say, a State which, though entitled to do so, had not ratified or acceded, attempted to claim rights under the convention, on the basis of a declared willingness to be bound by it, or of conduct evincing acceptance of the conventional régime, it would simply be told that, not having become a party to the convention it could not claim any rights under it until the professed willingness and acceptance had been manifested in the prescribed form.[7]

[4] *See* the table on Rights of Third States to the Law of the Sea Convention, *infra* p. 550.

[5] 1 L. Oppenheim, International Law 925–26 (8th ed. Lauterpacht 1955).

In *Free Zones of Upper Savoy and the District of Gex,* the PCIJ held that "Article 435 of the Treaty of Versailles is not binding upon Switzerland, who is not a party to the Treaty, except to the extent to which that country accepted it." 1932 PCIJ, ser. A/B, No. 46, at 141. *See also* the Upper Silesia Case, 1926 PCIJ, ser. A, No. 7, at 29, in which the Court stated: "A treaty only creates law as between the States which are parties to it; in case of doubt no rights can be deduced from it in favour of third States."

[6] Art. 34, UN Doc. A/CONF.39/27 (1969), *reprinted in* 63 AJIL 875 (1969), 8 ILM 679 (1969). *See* the similar provision in Restatement of the Foreign Relations Law of the United States (Revised) §328(1) (Tent. Draft No. 1, 1980).

[7] North Sea Continental Shelf Cases (Federal Republic of Germany/Denmark; Federal Republic of Germany/Netherlands), 1969 ICJ Rep. 3, 25–26 (Judgment of Feb. 20).

A perhaps overly restrictive and literal view of *pacta tertiis* has been applied in some recent American cases involving the 1958 Geneva Convention on the High Seas. Thus, in United States v. Cadena, 585 F.2d 1252 (5th Cir. 1978), the court of appeals upheld the conviction of the defendant Colombian nationals for conspiracy to import marijuana into the United States despite the fact that defendants were arrested by U.S. Coast Guard personnel who boarded a Canadian-registered vessel some 200 miles off the U.S. coast. The court held, *inter alia,* that provisions of the Convention on the High Seas, 450 UNTS 82, 13 UST 2312, TIAS No. 5200, could not be relied upon by Canada or Colombia, neither of which was a party to the Convention. The court stated, 585 F.2d at 1261: "There is no indication in the treaty, or elsewhere, that it was intended

There are exceptions, however, to the principle *pacta tertiis nec nocent nec prosunt.* These exceptions will be discussed in section III below.

III. Where Rights and Duties Exist for Third States

There are basically two means by which the rights and duties of third states may be affected by a treaty.[8] The first, *stipulation pour autrui,* is an exception to the principle of *pacta tertiis* in that third states may indeed enjoy rights and be encumbered with duties under a treaty in certain circumstances. The other pertains to the interrelationship of treaties and customary international law, which often affects third states' rights and duties. Each of these means will be studied and its relevance to the Law of the Sea Convention examined.

A. *Stipulation pour Autrui*

1. Rights for Third States. Until the conclusion of the Vienna Convention on the Law of Treaties in 1969, publicists could not agree on whether third states could be legally entitled to rights stipulated in their favor in a treaty.[9] The Vienna Convention has effectively settled this issue by providing (Article 36):

---

to confer rights on non-member nations or on vessels of non-member nations, let alone on citizens of non-member nations."

The *Cadena* decision may be criticized for ignoring the fact that the Convention on the High Seas aimed at codifying existing customary international law (*see* text accompanying notes 64–66 *infra*), and hence was binding on all states whether or not parties to it. For the question whether the relevant provisions of the Geneva Convention are "self-executing," in the sense that they have become part of municipal law enforceable by private individuals without separate legislation, see Riesenfeld, *The Doctrine of Self-Executing Treaties and U.S. v. Postal: Win at Any Price?,* 74 AJIL 892 (1980).

For similar decisions involving seizures and arrests in narcotics cases on the high seas, see United States v. Williams, 589 F.2d 210 (5th Cir. 1979), 617 F.2d 1063 (1980); United States v. Postal, 589 F.2d 862 (5th Cir. 1979), *cert. denied,* 444 U.S. 832 (1979); United States v. Conroy, 589 F.2d 1258 (5th Cir. 1979), *cert. denied,* 444 U.S. 831 (1979); United States v. Green, 671 F.2d 46 (1st Cir. 1982). So long as these decisions are not overturned by the U.S. Supreme Court, they retain legal validity, at least in the areas under the jurisdiction of the relevant federal circuit courts.

For an analysis of the *Cadena* and similar cases, see Connolly, *"Smoke on the Water": Coast Guard Authority to Seize Foreign Vessels Beyond the Contiguous Zone,* 13 N.Y.U. J. INT'L L. & POL. 249 (1980).

[8] Although rights and duties are generally regarded as two sides of the same coin, a distinction between third states' rights and duties is found in H. KELSEN, PRINCIPLES OF INTERNATIONAL LAW 345–50 (1952); and in the Vienna Convention on the Law of Treaties, which imposes a more stringent condition for establishing in treaties third states' obligations than it does for rights. In the case of obligations, it requires that third states' acceptance be "in writing" (Art. 35). In the case of rights, however, their "assent shall be presumed so long as the contrary is not indicated, unless the treaty otherwise provides" (Art. 36(1); *see* text accompanying note 10 *infra*).

[9] *See* H. BRIGGS, THE LAW OF NATIONS 870–72 (2d ed. 1952); I. BROWNLIE, PRINCIPLES OF PUBLIC INTERNATIONAL LAW 500–01 (1966).

During World War II, the U.S. Government requisitioned some Finnish ships lying in U.S. ports, settlement for which was still pending when the 1947 Treaty of Peace with Finland came into effect. Under this Treaty, to which the United States was not a party, Finland "waives all claims . . . on behalf of the Finnish Government or Finnish nationals against any of the United Nations whose diplomatic relations with Finland were broken off during the war and which took action in co-operation with the Allied and Associated Powers" (Art. 29). Specifically mentioned

> 1. A right arises for a third State from a provision of a treaty if the parties to the treaty intend the provision to accord that right either to the third State, or to a group of States to which it belongs, or to all States, and the third State assents thereto. Its assent shall be presumed so long as the contrary is not indicated, unless the treaty otherwise provides.
>
> 2. A State exercising a right in accordance with paragraph 1 shall comply with the conditions for its exercise provided for in the treaty or established in conformity with the treaty.[10]

The intent of states parties is thus controlling. Such an intent should not, however, be lightly presumed.[11] While the intent is obvious if the third states are specifically named, it may be inferred from the use of such expressions as "all States" and "every State" in the absence of contrary indications.[12] For, in the words of Judge Jiménez de Aréchaga: "There is, naturally, the possibility of a plurality of beneficiaries, determined in a general way. . . . And treaty stipulations may also benefit 'all nations' or 'all states,' as in the case of provisions referring to transit rights through international waterways: even future states may derive rights from such stipulations."[13]

---

were "claims arising out of actions taken by any of the Allied and Associated Powers with respect to Finnish ships." The position of the Department of State was that no "vested rights" had accrued in the United States as a third-party beneficiary without some positive act of acceptance. *See* 14 M. WHITEMAN, DIGEST OF INTERNATIONAL LAW 337–47 (1970).

As to the question of whether third states can acquire treaty rights only through adhering to an adhesion clause in a treaty, Roxburgh said that, even without such a clause, "third states would, after no very considerable lapse of time, have acquired rights through the development of a customary rule." R. ROXBURGH, INTERNATIONAL CONVENTIONS AND THIRD STATES 66–67 (1917).

[10] It may be noted that the American Law Institute's *Restatement (Second) of the Foreign Relations Law of the United States* (1965) provides (§139(1)): "An international agreement may create a right in favor of a state not a party to it if the agreement manifests the intention of the parties that it shall have this effect." Section 328(3) of Tentative Draft No. 1 (1980) of the revised *Restatement* (note 6 *supra*), however, follows closely the wording of the Vienna Convention on the Law of Treaties.

As for the nature of rights created for third states, such rights may be substantive as well as procedural. The United Nations Charter, for example, confers upon nonmember states a variety of substantive rights under, *inter alia,* Articles 2(4) (freedom from threat or use of force against territorial integrity or political independence by all members) and 2(7) (right to nonintervention in matters essentially within domestic jurisdiction), as well as procedural rights under Articles 32 (participation in discussion of disputes at the Security Council), 35(2) (bringing disputes to the attention of the Security Council or the General Assembly), and 50 (consulting the Security Council on the solution of special economic problems resulting from the implementation of preventive or enforcement measures).

In the case of the Law of the Sea Convention, to the extent that the prospective parties indeed intend to accord rights to third states, such rights are almost exclusively in areas of a substantive nature.

[11] *See* note 7 *supra. See also* the Free Zones case, 1932 PCIJ, ser. A/B, No. 46, at 147–48, in which the Permanent Court of International Justice held that it must be ascertained in each case "whether the States which have stipulated in favour of a third State meant to create an actual right which the latter has accepted."

[12] For contrary indications, see text accompanying notes 18–29 *infra.*

[13] Jiménez de Aréchaga, *Treaty Stipulations in Favor of Third States,* 50 AJIL 338, 356 (1956). *See also* Harvard Draft Convention on the Law of Treaties, with Comment summarizing views of

Less explicit, however, are such terms used in the Law of the Sea Convention as "the coastal States," "the archipelagic States," "land-locked States," and simply "States." Their meanings would hinge upon the context in which they are used.[14] By and large, they may be interpreted to mean "all" or "any" of the coastal states, archipelagic states, landlocked states, or states, respectively, unless a contrary intent can be shown.[15]

The question may be raised as to how a contrary intent can be shown. Article 36(1) of the Vienna Convention provides specifically that third states' rights arise "if the parties to the treaty" so "intend," rather than "if the treaty" so provides or implies. Thus, notwithstanding the use of such expressions as "all States," "any State," and "every State" in the Law of the Sea Convention, the critical question is whether or not states parties indeed intended that third states should enjoy rights under the Convention.

---

authorities and citing cases. 29 *id.*, Supp. 661, 935 (1935); M. WHITEMAN, *supra* note 9, at 334.

The "international waterways" mentioned in Jiménez de Aréchaga's statement refer to the Suez, Panama, and Kiel Canals, whose governing treaties use the expressions "all nations" or "every vessel of commerce or of war, without distinction of flags." *See* Art. I of the 1888 Constantinople Convention, 79 BRIT. & FOREIGN ST. PAPERS 18, 3 AJIL, Supp. 123 (1909); Art. 3 of the 1901 Hay-Pauncefote Treaty between the United States and Great Britain, 32 Stat. 1903, TS No. 401; Art. 18 of the 1903 Hay-Varilla treaty between the United States and Panama, 33 Stat. 2234, TS No. 431; and Art. 380 of the 1919 Treaty of Versailles.

Although Baxter defines "international waterways" as "rivers, canals and straits which are used to a substantial extent by the commercial shipping or warships belonging to states other than the riparian nation or nations" (R. BAXTER, THE LAW OF INTERNATIONAL WATERWAYS 3 (1964)), his analysis of treaties governing passage of ships through international waterways in time of peace (ch. III) is confined to those relating to inter-oceanic canals, *i.e.*, the Suez, Panama, and Kiel Canals. The only treaty he cites (p. 165) as regulating passage through international straits, other than the Geneva Convention on the Territorial Sea and the Contiguous Zone, is the Montreux Convention regarding the Régime of the Straits of 1936, 173 LNTS 213. Under this Convention, passage of all minor warships through the Turkish Straits must be notified through diplomatic channels 8 days in advance of passage, but only the Black Sea powers may send capital ships through the straits after similar notification (Arts. 10 and 11).

Despite the affinity between canals and straits as regards laws regulating freedom of transit in time of peace, their sources are different. In Baxter's words:

> The right of free passage through international straits is a product of state practice hardening into customary international law and thence into treaty. The right of free passage through interoceanic canals is a consequence of the opening of each waterway to usage by the international community. It is the origin of the right in a series of individual grants which distinguishes the law relating to canals from the law of straits [p. 168].

In essence, passage through international straits may be regarded as but one aspect of the freedom of the seas (p. 184), including assimilation to the regime of "innocent passage," whereas canals, absent "express provisions to the contrary," are merely part of the landmasses through which they flow (pp. 184–85). For a discussion of four different approaches to passage through inter-oceanic canals (*i.e.*, "international servitude," the doctrine of third-party beneficiaries, "dispositive right," and "dedication-reliance" theory), see pp. 177–84. For a critique of these approaches, see Lee, *Legal Aspects of Internationalization of Interoceanic Canals*, 33 L. & CONTEMP. PROBS. 158, 162–64 (1968), *reprinted in* THE MIDDLE EAST CRISIS: TEST OF INTERNATIONAL LAW (Halderman ed. 1968).

[14] *See* Article 31(1) of the Vienna Convention on the Law of Treaties, which reads: "A treaty shall be interpreted in good faith in accordance with the ordinary meaning to be given to the terms of the treaty *in their context and in the light of its object and purpose*" (emphasis supplied).

[15] *See supra* note 12.

As stated earlier, such an intent should not be lightly presumed.[16] While the intent of the parties to a treaty can be ascertained generally from the ordinary meaning of the terms used, there are other means of determination, *e.g.*, *travaux préparatoires*, diplomatic correspondence, and voting on pertinent proposals and resolutions. For the purpose of third states' rights under the Law of the Sea Convention, the intent may most appropriately be ascertained from official statements made by representatives of states participating in the Third United Nations Conference on the Law of the Sea, particularly those made during the final part of the 11th session in Montego Bay, Jamaica, on December 6–10, 1982. Such statements fall into two categories: speeches delivered by individual delegations represented in Montego Bay, and declarations made pursuant to Article 310 of the Convention.[17] Both may reflect the intentions of many prospective parties and will be briefly analyzed below.

Although only a few delegations spoke explicitly on the subject of third states' rights in Montego Bay,[18] the speech of Ambassador Arías-Schreiber of Peru[19] was of special significance in view of his representation of the Group of 77, which actually included some 120 states, thereby constituting a great majority of the 167 delegations to the Law of the Sea Conference. In this speech, Ambassador Arías-Schreiber reiterated the "package deal" approach he had outlined on behalf of the group on September 22, 1982, which ruled out any selective application of the Convention and also any third states' rights under it.[20] "[N]o state," he said, "can claim that the new rules and rights established by the Convention apply to that State if it is not a party to the Convention."[21]

In addition to the above-mentioned speeches, 21 declarations were made at the time of the signing of the Convention pursuant to Article 310 of the Convention,[22] and 5 were made upon the signing of the Final Act.[23] More

[16] *See* text accompanying note 7 *supra.*

[17] Article 310 provides:

> Article 309 [Reservations and exceptions] does not preclude a State, when signing, ratifying or acceding to this Convention, from making declarations or statements, however phrased or named, with a view, *inter alia,* to the harmonization of its laws and regulations with the provisions of this Convention, provided that such declarations or statements do not purport to exclude or to modify the legal effect of the provisions of this Convention in their application to that State.

[18] All of these delegations spoke against third states' rights, and none in favor. See the speeches of the delegates from the following countries: Canada (185th mtg. of Dec. 6, 1982, UN Doc. A/CONF.62/PV.185, at 31 (1983)); Cameroon (*id.* at 37); Tanzania (187th mtg. of Dec. 7, 1982, UN Doc. A/CONF.62/PV.187, at 83 (1983)); Byelorussian SSR (189th mtg. of Dec. 8, 1982, UN Doc. A/CONF.62/PV.189, at 46 (1983)); Indonesia (186th mtg. of Dec. 6, 1982, UN Doc. A/CONF.62/PV.186, at 16 (1983)); Iran (191st mtg. of Dec. 9, 1982, UN Doc. A/CONF.62/PV.191, at 32 (1983)); and the USSR (*id.* at 41).

[19] 185th meeting, *supra* note 18, at 63–67.

[20] *See* text accompanying note 112 *infra.*

[21] 185th meeting, *supra* note 18, at 66.

[22] Depositary Notification C.N.297.1982.TREATIES-1, at 3 (Dec. 17, 1982).

[23] *Ibid.*

will undoubtedly be made when states ratify or accede to the Convention.[24] Whatever the legal effect of these interpretative declarations may be,[25] to the extent that they "do not purport to exclude or to modify the legal effect of the provisions of this Convention in their application to" the declarant states, they certainly may manifest an intention of some states as to whether third states enjoy rights under the Convention.

Among the declarations submitted pursuant to Article 310 of the Convention to date, only that of Iran specifically denies third states' rights to certain provisions of the Convention, including those of transit passage through straits.[26] It repeats in essence the Iranian statement made on December 9, 1982.[27]

These statements and declarations are in keeping with a plausible presumption that the Convention was not intended to provide rights for third states. Virtually all states participated in the conference, and the Convention was drafted and negotiated with a view to obtaining adherence by all states. The quest for consensus throughout the conference and the decision not to accept adherence with reservations also suggest a purpose to achieve a universal regime applicable to all states. In this Convention, therefore, it may be argued, the reference to "all States" or "every State" reflects the assumption that all states would be parties to the Convention, not any desire to give rights to states that abstain from adhering. Moreover, many of the provisions codify customary law, and the use of "all States" or "every State" in those provisions may simply reflect that fact, rather than any intention to accord new benefits to third states to which they are not already entitled as a matter of customary law.

The foregoing discussion reveals the professed intention of an overwhelming majority of prospective parties to the Law of the Sea Convention (*i.e.*, all those belonging to the Groups of 77 and of Eastern European States,[28] as well as Canada[29]) to deny third states' rights under the Convention. The question nevertheless remains as to the effect of such an intent upon the interrelationships of other prospective parties to the Convention and third states. One may ask also whether, especially if in the light of developments, the states that have

[24] The declarations of Cuba and the German Democratic Republic, for example, state that they reserve the right specifically to make further declarations in connection with their ratification of the Convention. Depositary Notification C.N.7.1983.TREATIES-1, *supra* note 2, Ann. B, at 5, 7.

[25] *See* McRae, *The Legal Effect of Interpretative Declarations*, 49 BRIT. Y.B. INT'L L. 155, 158–59 (1978); McDorman, *Reservations and the Law of the Sea Treaty*, 13 J. MAR. L. & COM. 481, 509 (1982). The latter makes this observation (*ibid.*):

> The inclusion of Article 310 in a law of the sea treaty will be an invitation for interpretative declarations that declaring States will argue do not modify the legal effects of the treaty and receiving States will argue amount to reservations. The depositary will be unable to say anything definitive, and only third party dispute settlement will be able to make the final determination.

[26] Ann. B, *supra* note 24, at 8.

[27] *Supra* note 18.

[28] *See infra* note 112.

[29] *Supra* note 18.

spoken change their mind, the Convention might yet come to be interpreted to provide rights for third parties.

It may be noted that Article 36(1) of the Vienna Convention on the Law of Treaties does not preclude the possibility of divergent intentions on the part of states parties to accord rights to third states. Accordingly, those prospective parties to the Law of the Sea Convention which have not denied third states' rights or have remained silent may intend that rights be conferred on nonparties and may tacitly agree to that. As far as these parties are concerned, it may thus be assumed that third states are entitled to claim certain rights and benefits under the Convention.

Not only may the terms "all States" and "every State" be used in a context that warrants treating them as *stipulations pour autrui,*[30] but sometimes they may indicate that the rules concerned are customary international law, as are many provisions in the Geneva Conventions on the Law of the Sea.[31] A case in point is the Declaration of Principles of International Law concerning Friendly Relations and Co-operation among States in Accordance with the Charter of the United Nations,[32] in which the word "States" is used interchangeably with "every State," "any State," and "all States" throughout its text. Still another possibility is an expectation that some of the rules will become customary law in the future.

Thus, the terms "all States" and "every State," as used in the Convention on the Law of the Sea, may be held to have any of the following four meanings:

(1) the plain and natural meaning to include all states, whether or not parties to the Convention, as beneficiaries of rights in the Convention;[33]

(2) as synonyms for "states parties" where the intent of the parties is to that effect, as indicated in some statements made in Montego Bay;

(3) as a denotation of customary rules, hence binding upon all states; or

(4) as an intent to generate customary rules.

Care should therefore be taken to ascertain the actual meanings of these terms in the context in which they are used. For example, the terms "all States" and "any State" may mean "States Parties" for Canada and countries that belong to the Groups of 77 and of Eastern European States, but may have their plain and natural meaning for many other states. As applied to straits transit provisions, the terms may indicate preexisting customary rules (*e.g.*, unimpeded surface passage) or new general rules representing progressive development of international law (*e.g.*, submerged passage and overflight rights).

Subject to the foregoing caveats, it may be of interest to review the text of the Convention to determine which among its provisions might be found

[30] *See* text accompanying note 13 *supra.*

[31] *See* text accompanying note 67 *infra.*

[32] UNGA Res. 2625 (XXV) and its Annex (Oct. 24, 1970). For a discussion of the "every State" formula, see G. ARANGIO-RUIZ, THE UN DECLARATION OF FRIENDLY RELATIONS AND THE SYSTEM OF THE SOURCES OF INTERNATIONAL LAW 98, 106, 115–16, 135, and 146 (1979).

[33] *See* text at note 13 *supra.*

TABLE I

RIGHTS OF THIRD STATES TO THE LAW OF THE SEA CONVENTION

Treaty Provisions	States: All States	States: Parties Only
Part		
I. Introduction		X
II. Territorial sea and contiguous zone	X	
III. Straits	X	
IV. Archipelagic states	X	
V. Exclusive economic zone	X	
VI. Continental shelf	X	
VII. High seas	X	
VIII. Islands	X	
IX. Enclosed or semi-enclosed seas	X	
X. Access and transit rights of landlocked states	X	
XI. The Area	X	
Article		
135: Legal status of superjacent waters and airspace	X	
136: Common heritage of mankind	X	
137: Legal status of the Area and its resources	X	
138: General conduct of states relating to the Area	X	
141: Use for peaceful purposes exclusively	X	
142: Rights and interests of coastal states	X	
143(1): Marine scientific research	X	
149: Archaeological and historical objects	X	
All others		X
XII. Marine environment	X	
XIII. Marine scientific research		
Section 6: Dispute settlement and interim measures		X
All others	X	
XIV. Development and transfer of marine technology	X	
XV. Settlement of disputes		X
XVI. General provisions		
Article		
303: Archaeological and historical objects	X	
304: Responsibility and liability for damages	X	
All others		X
XVII. Final provisions		X

to have intended to confer rights only on "States Parties," and which recognize rights for others under one of the three other meanings described above. The accompanying table shows that, among substantive provisions (which exclude dispute settlement (part XV) and the final provisions (part XVIII)), only the deep seabed mining provisions (part XI) pertain clearly to states parties only.

2. *Obligations for Third States.* The Vienna Convention on the Law of Treaties imposes a more stringent condition for establishing third states' obligations in treaties than it does for rights. Article 35 reads: "An obligation arises for a third State from a provision of a treaty if the parties to the treaty intend

the provision to be the means of establishing the obligation and the third State expressly accepts that obligation in writing."

Since third states need not be specifically named but may, in the absence of contrary intentions,[34] be inferred from such expressions as "all States" and "every State,"[35] many provisions of the Law of the Sea Convention may have the effect of imposing obligations on third states if they accept the obligations in writing. Article 3, for example, provides: "Every State has the right to establish the breadth of the territorial sea up to a limit not exceeding 12 nautical miles, measured from baselines determined in accordance with this Convention."

The corresponding duty of every state would thus be to recognize the breadth of the territorial sea established by other states up to 12 miles. The consequences for third states flowing from this duty are many, not the least of which involves straits navigation, to be discussed below.

It will be recalled that the First and Second Geneva Conferences on the Law of the Sea held in 1958 and 1960, respectively, failed to reach agreement on the breadth of the territorial sea. The result of this failure has been to allow all those countries which based their territorial sea on the 3-mile limit to continue their practice of claiming and recognizing such a limit.[36]

Although the number of countries now claiming 12 miles as their territorial seas has increased to 78, as compared to 23 that retain the 3-mile limit,[37] the fact that the latter still include such major maritime powers as the United States, the United Kingdom, the Netherlands, the Federal Republic of Germany, and Australia indicates that the 12-mile limit may not yet have assumed the status of customary law, at least for dissenting states. These states (or at least some of them) not only limit their territorial sea to 3 miles but reject the right of other states to claim a wider territorial sea under which the high seas rights of navigation could be denied. In short, the continued refusal of some states to accept the 12-mile limit as opposable to them would mean that it cannot be regarded as a universal customary norm.

Under the Law of the Sea Convention, the new obligation to recognize an extension of the territorial sea by strait states to the maximum 12-mile limit would effectively exclude 116 straits between 6 and 24 miles wide from submerged passage or overflights by third states that have retained the 3-mile limit. In the words of Ambassador Elliot L. Richardson:

> [T]he legal right to overfly a strait could be gained only with coastal State consent, submarines would be obligated to travel on the surface, and surface vessels would be subject to varying assertions of coastal-State regulatory power. All the world's most important straits would be subject

[34] *See supra* note 12. [35] *See supra* note 13 and accompanying text.

[36] C. J. COLOMBOS, THE INTERNATIONAL LAW OF THE SEA 109 (6th ed. 1967); Dean, *The Second Geneva Conference on the Law of the Sea: The Fight for Freedom of the Sea,* 54 AJIL 751, 788 (1960); Johnson, *Law of the Sea: Developments Since the Geneva Conferences of 1958 and 1960,* 10 INT'L & COMP. L.Q. 587 (1961).

[37] Dep't of State, Office of the Geographer, Summary of Coastal State Claims (mimeo, Nov. 15, 1982, updating LIMITS IN THE SEAS NO. 36: NATIONAL CLAIMS TO MARITIME JURISDICTIONS (4th rev. 1981)).

> to these restrictions; for example: the Strait of Gilbraltar . . . ; the Straits of Malacca and Singapore . . . ; the Strait of Hormuz . . . ; and the Bab el Mandeb Strait. . . . The result could seriously impair the flexibility not only of our conventional forces but of our fleet ballistic missile submarines, which depend on complete mobility in the oceans and unimpeded passage through international straits.[38]

In his statement of March 10, 1983, which accompanied the proclamation of an exclusive economic zone, President Reagan also made the following points:

> First, the United States is prepared to accept and act in accordance with the balance of interests relating to traditional uses of the oceans—such as navigation and overflight. In this respect, the United States will recognize the rights of other states in the waters off their coasts, as reflected in the Convention, so long as the rights and freedoms of the United States and others under international law are recognized by such coastal states.
>
> Second, the United States will exercise and assert its navigation and overflight rights and freedoms on a worldwide basis in a manner that is consistent with the balance of interests reflected in the convention. The United States will not, however, acquiesce in unilateral acts of other states designed to restrict the rights and freedoms of the international community in navigation and overflight and other related high seas uses.[39]

This statement may be regarded as conditional acceptance "in writing" of U.S. obligations to recognize the rights of coastal states, including the 12-mile territorial sea and the exclusive economic zone. If coastal states refuse to accord the United States rights under the Convention,[40] then as far as these states are concerned, the U.S. claims would have to rest on the preexisting customary law high seas freedoms. In that respect, the United States would presumably maintain its rejection of the 12-mile territorial sea of the states refusing to accord the United States its navigation and overflight rights in straits more than 6 miles wide.

To summarize, rights for third states under the *stipulation pour autrui* doctrine are circumscribed by the intent of states parties to the Law of the Sea Convention, should it enter into force. On the basis of the expressed intent of the prospective parties to the Convention at Montego Bay, it may be difficult to apply the doctrine widely. At the same time, any obligations sought to be imposed on third states by the parties to the Convention, including those of recognizing a proclaimed 12-mile territorial sea with the attendant relinquishment of submerged passage and overflight rights through straits of 6- to 24-mile breadth, cannot take effect without the third states' express agreement "in writing."

[38] Richardson, *Power, Mobility and the Law of the Sea,* 58 FOREIGN AFF. 902, 905 (1980). *See also* the statements of Ambassador Koh, President of the Law of the Sea Conference, *supra* note 3, and the Iranian delegation, *supra* note 18.

[39] Statement by the President, March 10, 1983, 19 WEEKLY COMP. PRES. DOC. 383 (March 14, 1983), *reprinted,* together with the proclamation, *infra* at pp. 619–22.

[40] *See* text accompanying notes 18–29 *supra.*

Thus, third states asserting rights under the Convention would have to establish either (1) an agreement (possibly a tacit understanding) with those states parties that accept such rights, or (2) that the rights in question are granted under customary international law. We turn now to the latter question.

B. The Law of the Sea Convention and Customary International Law

Before we examine the relationship between the Law of the Sea Convention and customary international law, a brief discussion of recent developments regarding treaties and customary international law in general is in order.

There has been a trend in recent years to crystallize customary international law into conventional international law.[41] This crystallization invariably involves the dual functions of codification of existing customary international law and the progressive development of international law.[42] Where a treaty rule incorporates existing customary international law, its binding force is attributable not only to the treaty *qua* treaty, but also to the incorporated customary law, which remains binding on all states, whether or not parties to the treaty. Accordingly, a rule of international law may be simultaneously conventional for some states and customary for others.[43] The International Law Commission aptly summed up this relationship between conventional and customary international law some 33 years ago as follows:

> A principle or rule of customary international law may be embodied in a bipartite or multipartite agreement so as to have, within the stated limits, conventional force for the States parties to the agreement so long as the agreement is in force; yet it would continue to be binding as a principle or rule of customary international law for other States.[44]

Recent U.S. practice lends support to such an analysis. Thus, while the United States has not ratified the Vienna Convention on the Law of Treaties, the Department of State, in its Letter of Submittal to the President, stated that "although not yet in force, the Convention is already generally recognized

[41] Lee, *The International Law Commission Re-Examined,* 59 AJIL 545, 545–46 (1965); Baxter, *Treaties and Custom,* 129 RECUEIL DES COURS 25, 101 (1970 I).

[42] Lauterpacht, *Codification and Development of International Law,* 49 AJIL 16, 29 (1955); Lee, *supra* note 41, at 556.

[43] Gamble, *The Treaty/Custom Dichotomy: An Overview,* 16 TEX. INT'L L.J. 305, 312 (1981). *See also* M. SØRENSEN, MANUAL OF PUBLIC INTERNATIONAL LAW 129 (1968); Bos, *The Recognized Manifestations of International Law, A New Theory of "Sources,"* 20 GERMAN Y.B. INT'L L. 9 (1977). Professor Anthony A. D'Amato speaks of a "double source of obligation" in the sense that even if a party should withdraw from a treaty, it would still be bound by the customary international law incorporated therein. *See* A. D'AMATO, THE CONCEPT OF CUSTOM IN INTERNATIONAL LAW 107–08 (1971). *See also* Vierdag, *The Law Governing Treaty Relations between Parties to the Vienna Convention on the Law of Treaties and States not Party to the Convention,* 76 AJIL 779, 786 (1982), in which he uses the term "double regime."

[44] Report of the International Law Commission to the General Assembly, [1950] 2 Y.B. INT'L L. COMM'N 364, 368, UN Doc. A/CN.4/SER.A/1950/Add.1.

This relationship between customary international law and treaties is similar to the relationship between general principles of law—the third source of international law upon which the International Court of Justice may draw—and treaties. Since "general principles" in the law of the sea context are covered under either treaties or customary law, there is no need to deal with them separately in this paper.

as the authoritative guide to current treaty law and practice."[45] Indeed, the United States has on various occasions regarded particular articles of the Convention as codifying existing international law,[46] for example, by citing the Convention in its brief in the *Hostages* case against Iran.[47] American courts have also treated certain provisions of the Convention as authoritative.[48] All of these factors have led the *Restatement of the Foreign Relations Law of the United States (Revised)* to accept the Convention "as presumptively codifying the customary international law governing international agreements, and therefore as foreign relations law of the United States even before the United States adheres to the Convention."[49]

The United States does not stand alone in this regard. The International Court of Justice has taken a similar position. Even before the Vienna Convention on the Law of Treaties entered into force on January 27, 1980,[50] the Court stated in its Advisory Opinion on *Namibia:* "The rules laid down by the Vienna Convention on the Law of Treaties concerning termination of a treaty relationship on account of breach (adopted without a dissenting vote) may in many respects be considered as a codification of existing customary law on the subject."[51]

Inquiry into the relationship between the Law of the Sea Convention and customary international law may be made from two perspectives: incorporation of customary international law into the Convention and the metamorphosis of provisions of the Convention into customary international law.

1. Incorporation of Customary International Law into the Law of the Sea Convention. According to its own terms, the Law of the Sea Convention aims at both the progressive development of international law and its codification.[52] Those provisions of the Convention that codify existing customary international law must be regarded as ipso facto binding upon all states, whether or not parties to the Convention; those that represent the progressive development of international law, on the other hand, unless incorporated in the body of customary international law, will bind only states parties, but not third states. This assumes, of course, that *stipulation pour autrui* does not come into play.

To identify existing customary international law in a treaty text is not always easy but is indispensable. In addition to determining customary law in the

[45] S. Exec. Doc. L., 92d Cong., 1st Sess. 1 (1971).

[46] *See, e.g.*, 1974 Digest of United States Practice in International Law 198, 228, 235.

[47] Memorial of the Government of the United States of America in Case concerning United States Diplomatic and Consular Staff in Tehran (United States of America v. Iran) 42 n.2 (1980). Elsewhere in the same brief, it placed emphasis on those rules which were "firmly embedded in customary international law well before the adoption of the Vienna Convention on Diplomatic Relations" (*id.* at 50–51 n.2).

[48] *See, e.g.*, the *Cadena* case, 585 F.2d 1252 (5th Cir. 1978), in which the court of appeals applied Article 36 to deny rights to citizens of states not parties to the Geneva Convention on the High Seas. The case is discussed in note 7 *supra.*

[49] Restatement (Revised), *supra* note 6, at 72.

[50] United Nations, Multilateral Treaties Deposited with the Secretary-General: Status as at 31 December 1981, UN Doc. ST/LEG/SER.E/1, at 619.

[51] 1971 ICJ Rep. 16, 47 (Advisory Opinion of June 21).

[52] See the penultimate paragraph of the Preamble to the Convention on the Law of the Sea.

usual sources apart from treaties, in general, one would need to look into treaty texts or preambles[53] and judicial decisions,[54] as well as such other sources of varying utility as *travaux préparatoires,*[55] the writing of the most eminent publicists, diplomatic correspondence, the presence or absence of a reservation clause, explicit mention of periodic treaty revisions, application of a treaty only *in futuro,* and consistency or inconsistency with municipal laws of parties and nonparties, as well as with relevant provisions in other treaties, both bilateral and multilateral.[56]

For purposes of illustrating the application of the "incorporation" doctrine, focus will be placed on the straits navigation provisions of the Law of the Sea Convention. Their selection is dictated by the significant interest of the international community in free transit through straits, the uniqueness of straits in international law and practice, and, not least, the military and security role that straits navigation plays in the nuclear world today.

To place straits in their historical perspective: Vattel in the 18th century[57] and other publicists in the 19th century[58] already emphasized the importance of straits transit to international communication and trade. Over the years, several conventions have been concluded for the purpose of regulating transit through specific straits.[59] In the latter part of the 19th century and early in the 20th, the international community undertook the codification of a general

[53] In addition to the Preamble to the Convention on the Law of the Sea cited in the preceding note, see also the Preamble to the Geneva Convention on the High Seas, *supra* note 7.

[54] See, *e.g.*, the *Nottebohm* case ((second phase) (Liechtenstein v. Guatemala), 1955 ICJ REP. 4, 22–23 (Judgment of April 6)), in which the International Court of Justice invoked Articles 1 and 5 of the Hague Convention of 1930 on Certain Questions relating to the Conflict of Nationality Laws (179 LNTS 89) as evidence of the applicable international law, despite the fact that neither Liechtenstein nor Guatemala was a party to the Hague Convention.

[55] This is not intended, of course, to belittle the difficulty of actually applying *travaux préparatoires* to the task of treaty interpretation. As Professor Reisman underscores: "As yet there is no systematic study of the theory and practice of the use of *travaux* in international interpretation." *See* Reisman, *The Regime of Straits and National Security: An Appraisal of International Lawmaking,* 74 AJIL 48, 56 n.20 (1980). *See also* Fitzmaurice, *The Law and Procedure of the International Court of Justice: Treaty Interpretation and Certain Other Treaty Points,* 29 BRIT. Y.B. INT'L L. 1, 6 (1952); A. MCNAIR, THE LAW OF TREATIES 413, 423 (1961); D'Amato, *The Concept of Human Rights in International Law,* 82 COLUM. L. REV. 1110, 1137–38 (1982).

[56] *See* Baxter, *supra* note 41, at 42, 46 *et seq.;* and his *Multilateral Treaties as Evidence of Customary International Law,* 41 BRIT. Y.B. INT'L L. 288, 296, 298 (1965–66).

[57] Vattel distinguished straits that serve as communication links between two portions of the high seas for international navigation from those that have no such function. Passage through straits in the former category may not be refused by straits states, although it may be made conditional upon payment of moderate dues for services such as keeping the straits lighted, marked off, and free from piracy. E. DE VATTEL, LE DROIT DES GENS, bk. 1, ch. 23, §292 (London 1758).

[58] Gérard de Rayneval was one of the first to emphasize the right of passage through straits. G. DE RAYNEVAL, INSTITUTIONS DU DROIT DE LA NATURE ET DES GENS, bk. 2, ch. 9, §7 (Paris 1803). Hautefeuille strongly urged the freedom of navigation in straits, including even those which separate two coasts of the same state. L. HAUTEFEUILLE, DES DROITS ET DES DEVOIRS DES NATIONS NEUTRES EN TEMPS DE GUERRE MARITIME 60 *et seq.* (3d ed. 1868). P. Godey advocated that straits ought to be subject to "un régime tout spécial." P. GODEY, LA MER CÔTIÈRE (Paris 1896). For a brief survey of literature on this subject, see E. BRÜEL, INTERNATIONAL STRAITS 48–69 (1947).

[59] *See* note 63 *infra.*

legal regime for straits,[60] although those efforts eventually proved unsuccessful. In 1949, the International Court of Justice concluded in the *Corfu Channel* case that customary international law recognized special transit rights to pertain in straits used for navigation between two parts of the high seas.[61] All of these developments exerted an influence on the work of the International Law Commission and the 1958 Geneva Convention on the Territorial Sea and the Contiguous Zone.[62]

The question has been posed whether the straits articles in the Law of the Sea Convention reflect customary international law so as to entitle third states also to invoke their provisions.[63] To the extent that the Convention constitutes codification, it relies heavily in relevant areas on the 1958 Geneva Conventions on the Law of the Sea, which in turn, sought in many respects to codify then existing customary law.[64] In this regard, it may be noted that the Preamble to the Geneva Convention on the High Seas reads:

> *The States Parties to this Convention,*
>
> *Desiring* to codify the rules of international law relating to the high seas,
>
> *Recognizing* that the United Nations Conference on the Law of the Sea, held at Geneva from 24 February to 27 April 1958, adopted the following provisions as generally declaratory of established principles of international law,
>
> *Have agreed* as follows. . . .[65]

Accordingly, all of the provisions in the High Seas Convention "must therefore be taken *presumptively* to be declaratory of customary international law."[66]

[60] For a description of efforts made to codify the legal regime for straits, in whole or in part, by the Institute for International Law, the International Law Association, the Inter-parliamentary Union, and the Hague Peace Conference of 1907, see E. BRÜEL, *supra* note 58, at 70–97. *See also* J. MOORE, note 63 *infra*, at 659.

[61] *See* note 90 *infra*.

[62] *See* text accompanying note 68 *infra*.

[63] Apart from the Geneva Convention on the Territorial Sea and the Contiguous Zone, which deals with straits navigation on an inter-regional basis, the following instruments governing navigation through selected straits may be mentioned: the 1936 Montreux Convention regarding the Régime of the Straits (the Bosporus and the Dardanelles) (*see also* note 13 *supra* concerning the Montreux Convention); the 1881 Treaty between Argentina and Chile governing free navigation through the Straits of Magellan, 71 BRIT. & FOREIGN ST. PAPERS 1103; the 1904 Declaration between Great Britain and France relating to free passage of the Straits of Gibraltar, 101 *id.* at 1053, to which Spain adhered in a Declaration with France in the same year, 93 Martens Nouveau Recueil 2d 57; the 1857 Convention between the United States and Denmark to abolish the tolls (referred to as the "Sound Dues") and permit free passage of the Danish Straits, 11 Stat. 719, TS No. 67, *discussed in* 1 J. MOORE, DIGEST OF INTERNATIONAL LAW 660–64 (1906).

See also Cundick, *International Straits: The Right of Access,* 5 GA. J. INT'L & COMP. L. 107, 124–27 (1975).

[64] Jessup, *The United Nations Conference on the Law of the Sea,* 59 COLUM. L. REV. 234, 235 (1959); Fitzmaurice, *Some Results of the Geneva Conference on the Law of the Sea,* 8 INT'L & COMP. L.Q. 73, 74 (1959); Lee, *Jurisdiction over Foreign Merchant Ships in the Territorial Sea: An Analysis of the Geneva Convention on the Law of the Sea,* 55 AJIL 77, 96 (1961).

[65] *Supra* note 7.

[66] Baxter, *Multilateral Treaties, supra* note 56, at 290 (emphasis supplied). For a contrary view, see D'Amato, *supra* note 55, at 1138 (treaties generate custom irrespective of the intent of states parties).

Indeed, where the expressions "all States," "any States," etc., are used, the rules concerned may be regarded as expressing customary international law.[67]

In the Convention on the Territorial Sea and the Contiguous Zone,[68] this would apply to the entire Section III: Right of Innocent Passage (Articles 14–23). Two articles in this Convention bear scrutiny: Article 14(6), which requires submarines, in exercising the right of innocent passage in the territorial sea, "to navigate on the surface and to show their flag"; and Article 16(4), the lone provision dealing with straits explicitly, which merely provides for nonsuspendable innocent passage through straits used for international navigation, without defining the breadth of the straits. Since, under the Geneva Convention, passage through straits is assimilated to passage through the territorial sea (with an additional nonsuspension guarantee), both are subject to the same rule of innocent passage requiring submarines "to navigate on the surface and to show their flag."

The straits navigation provisions of the Law of the Sea Convention,[69] on the other hand, have been interpreted to allow all vessels and aircraft, military as well as civilian, to engage in continuous and expeditious passage through, under, or over international straits overlapped by territorial seas, without prior notification to or authorization from states bordering straits. More specifically, "transit passage" of ships and aircraft through or over straits is governed by part III, and "innocent passage" of submarines and other vessels in the territorial sea by part II. Although submarines in the territorial sea are still required to engage in "surface" navigation and to show their flag,[70] the "transit passage" of ships and aircraft through straits shall be conducted in the "normal mode of continuous and expeditious transit"[71]—which, for modern submarines, may arguably include submerged transit.[72] The word "arguably" is used advisedly in view of not only theoretical disagreements over the existence of an absolute right to submerged passage through straits,[73] but also the fact that some of the straits states have taken the position that neither

[67] Letter on file from Professor Oscar Schachter, dated Jan. 31, 1983.

[68] 516 UNTS 205, 15 UST 1606, TIAS No. 5639.

[69] *See* part III of the Convention. [70] Art. 20.

[71] Art. 39(1)(c).

[72] Moore, *The Regime of Straits and the Third United Nations Conference on the Law of the Sea,* 74 AJIL 77, 89 (1980).

[73] For the view that under the Convention there is an absolute right for submarines to engage in submerged passage through straits, see *id.* at 89, 95–100; Burke, *Submerged Passage through Straits: Interpretations of the Proposed Law of the Sea Treaty Text,* 52 WASH. L. REV. 193, 205 (1977). For the view that such a right is only a conditional one, see Reisman, *supra* note 55, at 71–75.

For the purpose of this paper, it is unnecessary to assess the comparative validity of the absolutist and conditionalist views, since in either case third states' rights, if extant, would be the same as those of states parties. Both views agree that, unlike the "innocent passage" regime under the 1958 Geneva Convention, the Law of the Sea Convention does not exclude submerged passage. Reisman himself acknowledged:

> The point of the present inquiry is not that submerged passage is excluded, but that it is not certain in the text, and, in the absence of express confirmation, is unlikely to defeat coastal competences which are explicit and could be used to require surface passage and, in some circumstances, ban passage and overflight.

Id. at 74–75 n.63.

customary international law nor the Law of the Sea Convention allows the passage of warships and warplanes in general (hence including submarines) through and over straits overlapped by the territorial sea in the absence of prior authorization. The declaration of Yemen made upon the signing of the Law of the Sea Convention at Montego Bay reads:

> 1. The Yemen Arabic Republic adheres to the rules of general international law concerning rights to national sovereignty over coastal territorial waters, even in the case of the waters of a strait linking two seas.
>
> 2. The Yemen Arab Republic adheres to the concept of general international law concerning free passage as applying exclusively to merchant ships and aircraft; nuclear-powered craft, as well as warships and warplanes in general, must obtain the prior agreement of the Yemen Arab Republic before passing through its territorial waters, in accordance with the established norm of general international law relating to national sovereignty.
>
> . . . .
>
> 4. The Yemen Arab Republic declares that its signature of the Convention on the Law of the Sea is subject to the provisions of this declaration and the completion of the constitutional procedures in effect.[74]

Though not mentioning straits specifically, the Iranian declaration would bar warships (hence also submarines) from exercising the right of innocent passage through the territorial sea under both customary international law and the Law of the Sea Convention (citing Articles 19, 21 and 25), unless prior authorization had been obtained.[75]

It may be asked in this connection why the text of the Law of the Sea Convention, after so many years of negotiations and preparation, should still contain such ambiguities as to lend itself to divergent interpretations on some of the key provisions. The answer lies at least in part in a certain reluctance, not only on the part of the major powers, to discuss matters of military import explicitly.[76] The negotiating text, according to Booth, "has adopted the tactic of silence" on military matters, "where the prospects for disagreement are strong, the prospects for legal clarity are weak."[77]

Be that as it may, the distinctions already drawn between the Law of the Sea Convention and the Geneva Convention on the Territorial Sea and the Contiguous Zone, as well as others,[78] make it clear that the straits transit provisions of the former are not based on customary law as reflected in the latter, and that, if the provisions of the latter continue to reflect the current status of customary international law,[79] third states are not entitled to the

[74] Annex B, *supra* note 24, at 14.

[75] *Id.* at 8.

[76] Treves, *Military Installations, Structures, and Devices on the Seabed,* 74 AJIL 808, 811 (1980).

[77] Booth, *The Military Implications of the Changing Law of the Sea,* in LAW OF THE SEA: NEGLECTED ISSUES 328, 340 (J. K. Gamble ed. 1979), *cited in id.* at 811 n.23.

[78] Moore, *supra* note 72, at 90, 95 *et seq.*

[79] For the possibility of the formation of new customary law since the Law of the Sea Conference, see text accompanying notes 99–100 *infra.*

same passage right, be it absolute or conditional,[80] as that accorded to states parties.[81] Indeed, by their willingness at the outset of the negotiations to agree to a universal extension of the territorial sea to 12 miles, provided there was adequate agreement on free transit of straits used for international navigation, the United States and its allies conceded in effect that the straits navigation provisions in the proposed Law of the Sea Convention were not then customary rules of international law.[82]

There remains the question whether the practice of submerged passage is of such a nature as to influence the development of customary international law in any event. This question is answered negatively by W. Michael Reisman:

> By its nature, submerged passage is not the sort of practice that generates customary rights. The notoriety and opportunity for protest by parties thereafter subordinated—requisite components of formation of prescriptive rights—can hardly be fulfilled when the strait state does not or cannot know of the passage or lacks the means of stopping it. And even if such practices were deemed to have generated customary rights in one strait, they could not *eo ipso* be applied to all straits, nor would they be probative of features of surface or aerial passage.[83]

The statement of Professor Reisman raises several interesting questions.

In the first place, there are means for detecting whether submerged passage has occurred.[84] It does not follow necessarily, however, that a strait state must have such means in order to prevent a prescriptive right from accruing. For a developing strait state may well place its priority elsewhere than on acquiring sophisticated listening devices or developing a competent intelligence network in the face of competing demands for scarce resources. That failure to be aware of and to protest submerged passage does not necessarily imply a pre-

[80] *See* note 73 *supra*.

[81] Clearly reflecting this finding is the conclusion of the Report of the Committee on Law of the Sea (July 1982) of the American Branch of the International Law Association (text appended to *Senate Hearing, supra* note 3, at 113, 142):

> The negative observation seems clear that certain important rights sought and claimed by the United States in areas such as freedom of navigation cannot be considered fully secure. But what are the positive contours of the new regime, which may be binding on the United States and others even in the absence of a declared intention to adhere thereto, is a question that will undoubtedly provide stimulus for the fertile imaginations of international lawyers, diplomats and professors for a long time to come.

[82] Stevenson & Oxman, *The Preparations for the Law of the Sea Conference,* 68 AJIL 1, 3 (1974); and *The Third United Nations Conference on the Law of the Sea: The 1974 Caracas Session,* 69 *id.* at 1, 14 (1975).

[83] Reisman, *supra* note 55, at 57.

[84] At the Duke University Symposium on "Law of the Sea—Where Now?," *supra* note 3, Rear Admiral Bruce Harlow stated that "it may be assumed that certain technologically developed strait states have listening arrays and other detective devices that monitor the movement of submerged traffic." Even states without such advanced technology, according to Harlow, "had intelligence and public information from which the existence of the practice could be easily determined." He cited the following as an example: "When a port call notice reveals the presence of a submarine at point A, and call at point B, it requires little shrewdness to conclude that the strait located between points A and B has been utilized for transit."

sumption of consent to submerged passage is cogently explained by MacGibbon:

> Although it is generally conceded that rights can be lost by inaction in the course of time, this is not to assert that failure to protest invariably entails this consequence. There may be circumstances which militate against the inference of acquiescence from failure to protest. Pleas of substance are available, by way of explanation, which, if well-founded, serve to rebut the presumption of consent which might otherwise be raised by a long, unexplained silence. The situations envisaged are those in which the parties have kept the question concerned open—by agreement, by the establishment of a *modus vivendi,* or by the continuance of negotiations; or those in which the inaction and abstention from protest has been that of a party without actual or constructive knowledge of the acts to which the alleged acquiescence relates.[85]

The reference above to "the continuance of negotiations" as one of the excepted situations raises another difficult question: When did the pertinent negotiations begin, in 1958, 1960, or 1974?

On the other hand, it is questionable whether a strait state's inability to stop submerged passage has any influence over the development of customary law based on practice. The inability of states other than the United States and the USSR to stop satellite overflights, for example, has not prevented the development of rules allowing use of the outer space above the atmosphere for such flights.

Finally, it is wrong to suggest that practice deemed to have generated customary rights in one strait "could not *eo ipso* be applied to all straits," unless Reisman had in mind "special customary rights," as opposed to general custom.[86] That general custom can indeed apply to all straits is evident from the historical evolution of the straits regime described above.[87]

The foregoing analysis of the Reisman statement shows the complexity of the issue involved. The many factors combine to make it difficult to provide a clear yes-or-no answer to the creation of prescriptive rights via the practice of submerged passage.

Apart from submerged passage and overflight rights, however, third states may claim the right of "surface" passage of all ships, including warships, through straits under customary law, regardless of the breadth of the straits and without prior notification to or authorization from the coastal states, so

[85] MacGibbon, *The Scope of Acquiescence in International Law,* 31 BRIT. Y.B. INT'L L. 143, 172 (1954). For discussions on a similar subject, see MacGibbon, *Some Observations on the Part of Protest in International Law,* 30 *id.* at 293 (1953); and his *Customary International Law and Acquiescence,* 33 *id.* 115 (1957); O'Connell, *Mid-Ocean Archipelagos in International Law,* 45 *id.* at 1, 60–69 (1971); K. WOLFKE, CUSTOM IN PRESENT INTERNATIONAL LAW 44–45 (1964); [1950] 1 Y.B. INT'L L. COMM'N 4–5, UN Doc. A/CN.4/SER.A/1950.

For the view that "a failure to protest might manifest not acquiescence but a belief that the usage was simply outside the legal realm, belonging to the realm of social courtesy or comity," see A. D'AMATO, *supra* note 43, at 70.

[86] For a lucid discussion on the subject of "special customary rights," see A. D'AMATO, *supra* note 43, ch. 8.

[87] *See* text accompanying notes 57–64 *supra.*

long as the straits are used for international navigation and the passage is "innocent."[87a] According to Brüel, before World War I the law had been established that "the right of passage of *merchant vessels* in international straits was certain, and *warships* were supposed to have the same right—although not with the same degree of certainty."[88] Greater certainty, however, was reflected at the Hague Conference in 1930,[89] and whatever uncertainty that lingered was dispelled when the International Court of Justice held in the *Corfu Channel* case that British warships had the right of innocent passage through Albanian waters:

> It is, in the opinion of the Court, generally recognized and in accordance with international custom that States in time of peace have a right to send their warships through straits used for international navigation between two parts of the high seas without the previous authorization of a coastal State, provided that the passage is *innocent.* Unless otherwise prescribed in an international convention, there is no right for a coastal State to prohibit such passage through straits in time of peace.[90]

2. *Metamorphosis of Provisions of the Law of the Sea Convention into Customary International Law.* Article 38 of the Vienna Convention on the Law of Treaties states: "Nothing in articles 34 to 37 precludes a rule set forth in a treaty from becoming binding upon a third State as a customary rule of international law, recognized as such."[91]

The central issue is how and when a treaty rule acquires the status of customary international law. The *North Sea Continental Shelf* cases[92] show the existence of four precedent conditions:[93]

> (1) The presence of a "fundamentally norm-creating character such as could be regarded as forming the basis of a general rule of law";

[87a] Notwithstanding the Yemeni position described in text accompanying note 74 *supra.*

[88] E. BRÜEL, *supra* note 58, at 202. [89] *Ibid.*

[90] 1949 ICJ REP. 4 (Judgment of April 9).

Compare the Court's decision with a resolution adopted by the Institut de Droit International in Paris in 1894 that contained the following general principle with regard to straits: that straits that serve as a passage from one free sea to another can never be closed. 13 INSTITUT DE DROIT INTERNATIONAL, ANNUAIRE 330–31 (1894–95); 1 J. MOORE, *supra* note 63, at 659.

[91] *Supra* note 6.

[92] 1969 ICJ REP. 3.

The judgment of these cases was characterized by Professor Marek as "un arrêt dont on peut dire sans exagération qu'il est sans précédent dans toute la jurisprudence des deux Cours de La Haye par la richesse de son analyse." Marek, *Le Problème des sources du droit international dans l'arrêt sur le plateau continental de la mer du Nord,* 1970 REV. BELGE DROIT INT'L 44, 45. *See also* Baxter, *supra* note 41, at 33 n.7.

[93] 1969 ICJ REP. at 41–44.

For the use of similar criteria by a national court in reaching the conclusion that a binding international custom could evolve from nonbinding international instruments, including even draft rules or declarations, see the *Shimoda* case, translated into English in the 1964 JAPANESE ANNUAL OF INTERNATIONAL LAW 212–52, *digested in* 58 AJIL 1016 (1964). *See also* Falk, *The Shimoda Case: A Legal Appraisal of the Atomic Attacks upon Hiroshima and Nagasaki,* 59 *id.* at 759 (1965); Lee, The Legal Status of Human Rights Re-Examined, in 1 *Population and Development: Hearings Before the House Select Comm. on Population,* 59th Cong., 2d Sess. 671, 688 (1978).

(2) a "very widespread and representative participation in the convention," including "that of States whose interests were specially affected";

(3) the extensiveness and virtual uniformity of state practice evidencing "a general recognition that a rule of law or legal obligation is involved";[94] and

(4) the passage of some time, short though it may be.[95]

The question may be raised as to whether "new" customary rules on straits transit passage have evolved in the course of the law of the sea negotiations, particularly since "the comprehensive character of, and practically universal participation in, the Conference combine to suggest the inevitable importance

[94] See, however, Professor Bin Cheng's statement on the relationship between repeated state practice and "customary law" regarding outer space: "There need . . . be no usage at all in the sense of repeated practice, provided that the *opinio juris* of the States concerned can be clearly established." Cheng, *United Nations Resolutions on Outer Space: Instant International Customary Law?,* 5 INDIAN J. INT'L L. 23, 36 (1965).

[95] Although the passage of time is necessarily implied in condition (3) above, it is given separate listing here both because the Court dealt with it at length and because of a widespread notion that customary international law is by nature "old" law. Thus, on the time element, the Court had this to say (1969 ICJ REP. at 43):

> [I]t is over ten years since the Convention was signed, but that it is even now less than five since it came into force in June 1964, and that when the present proceedings were brought it was less than three years, while less than one had elapsed at the time when the respective negotiations between the Federal Republic and the other two Parties for a complete delimitation broke down on the question of the application of the equidistance principle. Although the passage of only a short period of time is not necessarily, or of itself, a bar to the formation of a new rule of customary international law on the basis of what was originally a purely conventional rule, an indispensable requirement would be that within the period in question, short though it might be, State practice, including that of States whose interests are specially affected, should have been both extensive and virtually uniform in the sense of the provision involved. . . .

Similarly, in his separate opinion in the *Fisheries Jurisdiction* case between the United Kingdom and Iceland (1974 ICJ REP. 3, 89–90 (Judgment of July 25)), Judge de Castro included a considerable time period as one of four elements necessary for a practice to crystallize into customary international law. *See also* Scott & Carr, *The International Court of Justice and the Treaty/Custom Dichotomy,* 16 TEX. INT'L L.J. 347, 352 (1981).

On the other hand, Sir Gerald Fitzmaurice commented on the time element as follows:

> It is a mistake to think customary law is necessarily "old" law, or that it must take a long time to come into being. It is capable of springing up quite quickly if a sufficiently wide and spontaneous consensus of opinion manifests itself in favour of the view that a given matter is governed by rules that must be considered to be rules of law. Prominent examples of this process in very recent times are to be found, for instance, in the fields of maritime, air and space law, and of war crimes and crimes against peace and humanity. . . .

Fitzmaurice, *The Older Generation of International Lawyers and the Question of Human Rights,* in ESSAYS IN INTERNATIONAL LAW IN HONOUR OF D. ANTONIO DE LUNA 321 note (Madrid 1968).

Tracing the origin of many, if not nearly all, of the rules of customary law to generalizable provisions of treaties, D'Amato concludes that "generalizable provisions in treaties (especially multilateral treaties) ipso facto generate customary rules," though he leaves open the possibility that the passage of "reasonable time" may be required for the development of evidence of custom into binding custom itself. *See* D'Amato, *supra* note 55, at 1146–47.

of its conclusions in shaping the future character of the law, regardless of their present legal status."[96] An affirmative answer would, of course, entitle third states to the same transit rights as states parties, now or at some future time. At bottom is the realization that, although the Law of the Sea Convention has yet to come into force, that fact in itself is immaterial to the question whether the unratified Convention or its earlier drafts have generated customary law. For even if a diplomatic conference fails to adopt a treaty, rules agreed to by that conference may still evolve into customary international law. Thus, in the *Fisheries Jurisdiction* case between the United Kingdom and Iceland, the International Court of Justice, after noting the failure of the 1960 Second Geneva Conference on the Law of the Sea (by one vote) to adopt a text governing both the breadth of the territorial sea and the extent of fishery rights, stated: "after that Conference the law evolved through the *practice* of states on the basis of the *debates and near-agreements* at the Conference. Two concepts have crystallized as customary law in recent years arising out of the general *consensus* revealed at the Conference."[97]

It should be noted that the "new" law of the sea includes new zones of national jurisdiction (the exclusive economic zone, archipelagic waters) and new definitions of existing concepts (continental shelf, the territorial sea, straits transit passage), as well as the totally new concept of the international seabed area as the "common heritage of mankind."[98] However, the "newness" can refer not only to the new rules embodied in the Law of the Sea Convention, but also to the new customary law being formed by recent state practice, which influenced, and was in turn influenced by, the Law of the Sea Conference as a forceful accelerating factor in the development of state practice.[99] The exclusive economic zone may be cited as an example of the latter: notwithstanding the fact that the concept began to receive general sympathy only during the Third United Nations Conference on the Law of the Sea and that the Law of the Sea Convention has not yet entered into force, it is already so widely accepted that the International Court of Justice stated in the *Tunisia-Libya Continental Shelf* case that "the concept of the exclusive economic zone . . . may be regarded as part of modern international law."[100] Can it be said that the straits transit provisions in the Law of the Sea Convention have also acquired the status of customary international law?

If we use the four precedent conditions laid down by the International Court of Justice in the *North Sea Continental Shelf* cases as a yardstick for measuring whether a treaty rule has been transformed into customary international law, it is obvious that the straits transit provisions of the Law of the Sea Convention have met the first, second,[101] and fourth tests. To meet the

[96] Smith, *Innocent Passage as a Rule of Decision: Navigation v. Environmental Protection*, 21 COLUM. J. TRANSNAT'L L. 49, 72 (1982).

[97] 1974 ICJ REP. at 23.

[98] Treves, *supra* note 76, at 812.

[99] *Id.* at 812–13.

[100] Case Concerning the Continental Shelf (Tunisia/Libyan Arab Jamahiriya), 1982 ICJ REP. 18, para. 100.

[101] Although the United States and some 40 other countries, together accounting by one estimation for more than half the global gross domestic product (*see* Meese, *Seabed? No, Bed of Nails,*

third test, however, it would be necessary to show that state practice regarding submerged passage through straits is in fact contrary to the professed intention of many states to deny such a right to third states as manifested by their statements in Montego Bay.[102] The burden of proof rests on those who claim that customary rules on straits transit passage have indeed been changed.[103] It remains to be seen whether or not such a burden can be met.

A variant of the thesis that customary international law may evolve from a widely accepted treaty is one that seeks to explain the universally binding force of a treaty on the basis of its "public law character," especially in the case of the so-called constitutive or semi-legislative treaty. The nature and binding force of such a treaty were explained by Lord McNair as follows:

> When it is remembered that international society has at present no legislature, the treaty is the only instrument available for doing many of the things which an individual State would do by means of its legislature; and the making of rules of law is not the only function of a legislature. It is therefore not surprising that from time to time groups of States should have assumed the responsibility of leadership and used the instrument of a treaty to make certain territorial or other arrangements required, or which they consider to be required, in the interest of this or that particular part of the world. . . . Strictly speaking, a treaty of this kind (which may or may not contain an accession clause) binds at first the parties thereto and no other States. But it is undeniable that after a period of time, to which no fixed duration can be attributed, the mere lapse of time and the acquiescence of other States in the arrangement thus made have the effect of reinforcing the essential juridical element of the treaty and of converting what may at first have been a partly *de facto* situation into a *de jure* one.[104]

The writings of McNair and Brierly[105] on this subject suggest the following ingredients for a "constitutive or semi-legislative" treaty: assumption of re-

---

N.Y. Times, Feb. 21, 1983, at A17), have withheld their signatures from the Convention, the yardstick for the second test—a "very widespread and representative participation in the convention"—should be the number of countries supporting the present text of the straits navigation provisions. Consequently, these provisions have received the near unanimous support of all countries—not only those that have signed the Convention, but also the major nonsignatories such as the United States. *See* statement by Ambassador Thomas A. Clingan, Jr., in Montego Bay, at the 192d meeting of Dec. 9, 1982, UN Doc. A/CONF.62/PV.192, at 2 (1983). *See also* President Reagan's statement on March 10, 1983, *supra* note 39.

[102] *See* text accompanying notes 18–29 *supra*.

[103] *Cf.* Gross, *Passage through the Strait of Tiran and in the Gulf of Aqaba,* in THE MIDDLE EAST CRISIS, *supra* note 13, at 125, 127.

[104] A. MCNAIR, *supra* note 55, at 259. *See also* McNair's separate (concurring) opinion attached to the Advisory Opinion of July 11, 1950 of the ICJ on the international status of South-West Africa, 1950 ICJ REP. 128, 153–55:

> From time to time it happens that a group of great Powers, or a large number of States both great and small, assume a power to create by a multipartite treaty some new international régime or status, which soon acquires a degree of acceptance and durability extending beyond the limits of the actual contracting parties, and giving it an objective existence. This power is used when some public interest is involved. . . .

[105] J. BRIERLY, THE LAW OF NATIONS 326–27 (6th ed. 1963).

sponsibility of leadership by a group of states; using the treaty as an instrument to effect certain territorial or other arrangements required; involvement of regional or global public interests; creation of international situations or entities binding upon all states; acceptance, acquiescence, and durability extending beyond the limits of the actual states parties; and eventual conversion of a universal *de facto* into a *de jure* situation. Among the examples cited were the 1815 treaty signed in Vienna by eight powers establishing the permanent neutralization of Switzerland, to which Switzerland acceded later in the same year;[106] the Aaland Islands Convention of 1856 neutralizing those islands in the Baltic;[107] and the treaty regimes for the Suez, Panama, and Kiel Canals.[108]

In its commentaries on Article 34 of the draft articles on the law of treaties (now Article 38), which concerns the development of treaty rules into binding law through international custom, the International Law Commission cited the Hague Conventions regarding the rules of land warfare, the agreements for the neutralization of Switzerland, and various treaties regarding international rivers and maritime waterways as treaties formulating certain rules or establishing a territorial, fluvial, or maritime regime that thereafter became generally accepted by other states by way of custom. The Commission was careful to point out:

> In none of these cases, however, can it properly be said that the treaty itself has legal effects for third States. They are cases where, without establishing any treaty relation between themselves and the parties to the treaty, other States recognize rules formulated in a treaty as binding customary law. In short, for these States the source of the binding force of the rule is custom, not the treaty. For this reason the Commission did not think that this process should be included in the draft articles as a case of a treaty having legal effects for third States. It did not, therefore, formulate any specific provisions concerning the operation of custom in extending the application of treaty rules beyond the contracting States.[109]

For the same reason, reinforced by that of *stipulation pour autrui,* the Commission refrained from including a provision dealing separately with "treaties creating so-called 'objective régimes', that is, obligations and rights valid *erga omnes.*"[110]

The Commission's reasoning applies equally to the categorization of the Law of the Sea Convention as a treaty creating "objective régimes" with *erga omnes* effect. For, in the final analysis, the source of such effect remains custom, not the treaty.

[106] A. McNair, *supra* note 55, at 260.

[107] J. Brierly, *supra* note 105. The validity of the Aaland Islands Convention was reaffirmed in the declarations of Finland and Sweden in Montego Bay on Dec. 10, 1982, Depositary Notification, *supra* note 22, at 5 and 11, respectively.

[108] A. McNair, *supra* note 55, at 265–68.

[109] Reports of the International Law Commission on the second part of its 17th session and on its 18th session, [1966] 2 Y.B. Int'l L. Comm'n 169, 231, UN Doc. A/CN.4/SER.A/1966/Add.1.

[110] *Ibid. See also* L. Henkin, R. Pugh, O. Schachter, & H. Smit, International Law: Cases and Materials 634 (1980). The Commission cited the 1959 Antarctic Treaty, 12 UST 794, TIAS No. 4780, 402 UNTS 71, as an example of a treaty creating an "objective regime."

To summarize, it is entirely possible for certain norm-creating provisions of the Law of the Sea Convention to evolve into customary international law or to acquire the status of "constitutive or semi-legislative" provisions of a treaty. It is impossible, however, to predict how long this metamorphosis may take or whether it will take place at all. Once the process of evolution or metamorphosis has been completed, the provisions of the Law of the Sea Convention—including those governing submerged passage through straits and overflight rights—will assume the nature of customary rules applicable to all states. This would occur independently of the applicability of *stipulation pour autrui* and without reference to, or the need for determining, what the prior customary rule may have been.

IV. The "Package Deal" Theory

A corollary of *pacta tertiis nec nocent nec prosunt* is the "package deal" theory, regarded as "one procedural innovation of LOS III that perhaps has had the greatest effect upon negotiating techniques."[111] In essence, it means the following:

> In negotiating and adopting the [Law of the Sea] Convention, the Conference had borne in mind that the problems of ocean space were closely interrelated and had to be dealt with as a whole. The "package deal" approach ruled out any selective application of the Convention. According to the understanding reached by the Conference from the outset and in conformity with international law, no State or group of States could lawfully claim rights or invoke the obligations of third States by reference to individual provisions of the Convention unless that State or group of States were themselves parties to the Convention. States which decided to become parties to the Convention would likewise be under no obligation to apply its provisions vis-à-vis States that were not parties. That held true both for the new rules laid down by the Convention for areas under national jurisdiction (inland waters, territorial sea, contiguous zone, exclusive economic zone, continental shelf, archipelagic waters and straits used for international navigation), and for the régime instituted, by virtue of the Convention and the relevant resolutions adopted by the Conference, for the use of the area of the sea-bed beyond the limits of national jurisdiction.[112]

For example, if the straits regime were offered as a quid for the acceptance of the deep seabed regime as a quo, without the quo, there would be no quid.

[111] Eustis, *Procedures and Techniques of Multinational Negotiation: The LOS III Model*, 17 VA. J. INT'L L. 217, 228 (1977).

[112] Statement of Ambassador Arías-Schreiber (Peru), speaking on behalf of the Group of 77 at the 183d plenary meeting of the resumed 11th session on Sept. 22, 1982, as summarized in UN Doc. A/CONF.62/SR.183, at 3–4 (prov. 1982). He added, however, that the Group of 77 had not yet concluded its consideration of this question. Nevertheless, Mr. Kolosovsky (USSR), on behalf of the Group of Eastern European States, expressed full support for the above statement. *Id.* at 4.

The Group of 77 eventually affirmed the above statement. *See* Ambassador Arías-Schreiber's statement at the 185th meeting, note 19 *supra*.

No sign, no benefits! Or, from the strait state's perspective, no sign, no obligations!

At first glance, injection of the "package deal" into the law of the sea negotiations appeared to exacerbate the already difficult task of distinguishing codification of customary international law from the progressive development of international law. For, as Brian Smith observes:

> [M]any provisions may represent neither *lex lata* nor consensus as to *lex ferenda* but only practical accommodations dependent upon an intricate web of interrelated bargains. The degree, therefore, to which a given provision may be defined as evidentiary of the present opinion of States as to existing, emerging, or preferred customary law is difficult to fix.[113]

On deeper analysis, however, proof of customary international law remains the litmus test as to whether third states may enjoy rights stipulated in treaties. For in a real sense, negotiations for any treaty, whether bilateral or multilateral, invariably involve a certain amount of bargaining, compromise, or quid pro quo. The 1958 Geneva Convention on the Territorial Sea and the Contiguous Zone, for example, in addition to codifying existing international law and progressively developing new rules of international law, sought accommodations of divergent national interests in such matters as shipping, fishing, and military security.[114] It entered into force on September 10, 1964, and, as of December 31, 1981, was binding on 46 states.[115] No serious argument has ever been made, however, that states that participated in the negotiations for that Convention but have so far refrained from signing or ratifying it (as well as states that did not participate in its negotiations at all) can be denied the rights or avoid the concomitant duties under customary international law as codified in that Convention. In time, of course, what started out as a "package deal" in negotiations pointing toward a widely accepted multilateral treaty may develop into custom itself.

V. Conclusions

The following conclusions may be drawn about the rights and obligations of third states under the Law of the Sea Convention, looking only at the so-called nonseabed provisions of the Convention.

(1) Although the general rule is that treaty rights or obligations are confined to the contracting parties, there are circumstances under which third states may enjoy rights or incur obligations under or as a result of a treaty.

[113] Smith, *supra* note 96, at 72.

Indeed, the contents of package deals were themselves in a state of flux. For example, in 1973, the United States and its allies were prepared to agree to a universal extension of the territorial sea to 12 miles provided there was adequate agreement on free transit of straits used for international navigation. Stevenson & Oxman, *Preparations, supra* note 82, at 9–10. In 1974, however, "[m]ajor conditions for acceptance of 12 miles as a maximum limit were agreement on unimpeded transit of straits *and acceptance of a 200-mile exclusive economic zone.*" Stevenson & Oxman, *The 1974 Caracas Session, supra* note 82, at 14 (emphasis supplied).

[114] Lee, *supra* note 64, at 96.

[115] Multilateral Treaties, *supra* note 50, at 587.

(2) In principle, third states may benefit from certain provisions of the Law of the Sea Convention on the basis of the principle *stipulation pour autrui.* They need not be specifically named; their rights may be inferred from terms or expressions that manifest the intent to benefit third states. However, the intent of the parties is controlling and intent to confer rights on third parties cannot be lightly presumed. The intent of prospective parties may be reflected in the statements of their delegations or bloc spokesmen, especially at the closing session in Montego Bay, whether or not in the context of Article 310 of the Convention.

(3) Third states may also incur obligations under the Law of the Sea Convention if such obligations were intended by the parties and "expressly" accepted by third states "in writing." The United States position mentioned above may be taken as a conditional acceptance in writing.

(4) Where a preexisting customary rule of international law has been incorporated into the Law of the Sea Convention, all states, whether or not parties to it, continue to be bound thereby. Although it is clear that many such rules have been incorporated, identification of the preexisting customary rules remains a matter of proof, and must be determined in each case.

(5) Third states may also enjoy rights like those provided in the Law of the Sea Convention if its provisions or their substance is transformed into customary international law. It is impossible, however, to predict to what extent this process will occur and how long it may take.

(6) A variant of point (5) above would uphold the universally binding force of those provisions of the Law of the Sea Convention which are endowed with "public law character" as part of a constitutive or semi-legislative treaty. However, as the International Law Commission pointed out, the source of that binding force would remain custom, not the treaty.

(7) Even if the intent of the negotiators of the Law of the Sea Convention was to limit the benefits of all its provisions to the signatories as parties to a so-called package deal, nonparty states may enjoy the same benefits if the particular provision of the Convention reflects preexisting customary international law or has since acquired the status of a customary rule through widespread acceptance as law and confirmation by state practice.

EDITORIAL COMMENTS

On the Degradation of the Constitutional Environment of the United Nations

I.

Manipulating constituent instruments of international organizations in order selectively to punish unpopular member states is not a new phenomenon. Of the states that resorted to war in violation of their obligations under the Covenant of the League of Nations—Japan, Italy, the Soviet Union—only one, the Soviet Union, was expelled from the League when on November 30, 1939 it invaded Finland. On December 14, 1939, the Council, by virtue of Article 16(4) of the Covenant, found "that by its act, the Union of Soviet Socialist Republics has placed itself outside the League of Nations. It follows that the Union of Soviet Socialist Republics is no longer a Member of the League."[1] However, the specific voting rule in Article 16(4) was not complied with on this occasion.[2] While the League insisted "on a strict application of the unanimity requirement; . . . in a period of moral indignation, niceties of procedure are not likely to be observed."[3] But where was moral indignation when Japan attacked China, and Italy attacked Ethiopia, and Germany attacked Poland and thus started World War II? The members of the League and the members of the United Nations now seem to be moved to moral indignation only in selected cases, which deprives indignation of its moral basis. Insofar as the expulsion of the Soviet Union is concerned, a more persuasive explanation has been given by the historian of the League F. P. Walters:

> If no move had been made to submit to the League the issues which had led to war between Germany and Poland, France, and Britain, what result could be expected from its intervention in this new conflict? But the Soviet aggression had loosed a storm of anger from one end of the world to the other. All those States whose policy had been affected by fear and hatred of Communism denounced the perfidy of Stalin in language which none of them used about Hitler.[4]

Thus, the drive to score an ideological victory prevailed over the traditional concern for constitutional propriety. However, coming as it did in the final phase of the League, it could not produce any lasting harm and did not prevent

[1] 20 League of Nations O.J. 506 (1939).

[2] *See* Gross, *Was the Soviet Union Expelled from the League of Nations?*, 39 AJIL 35, 42 (1945). For a contrary view, Nathan Feinberg, *L'Exclusion d'un Membre de la Société des Nations et le principe de l'unanimité,* in Studies in International Law. With Special Reference to the Arab-Israel Conflict 3 (Jerusalem 1979). *See also* Sohn, *Expulsion or Forced Withdrawal from an International Organization,* 77 Harv. L. Rev. 1381, 1387–91 (1964).

[3] Sohn, *supra* note 2, at 1390.

[4] 2 F. Walters, A History of the League of Nations 804–05 (1952).

the forging of the Grand Alliance including the Soviet Union, against Hitler, which was transformed into the United Nations.

In the United Nations strong antagonisms developed in the 1960's as groups of states, many of which only recently had been admitted to membership, set out to impose their views on a dissenting minority of individual states such as Portugal over the colonial question and South Africa over the question of Namibia and apartheid.[5] More recently in the context of the Middle East problem, Israel became the target of intense attempts to isolate, suspend, or expel it. The earlier incidents are of no particular consequence except the patently unconstitutional "suspension" of South Africa from the General Assembly in 1974. Departing from the so-called Hambro formula according to which South Africa was permitted to sit in the Assembly from 1970 to 1973, although the credentials of its representative were rejected, a conniving President of the Assembly, Ambassador A. Bouteflika (Algeria), disregarding precedent and the opinion of the Legal Counsel of the United Nations,[6] gave a ruling interpreting the rejection of credentials as follows:

> On the basis of the consistency with which the General Assembly has regularly refused to accept the credentials of the delegation of South Africa, one may legitimately infer that the General Assembly would in the same way reject the credentials of any other delegation authorized by the Government of the Republic of South Africa to represent it, which is tantamount to saying in explicit terms that the General Assembly refuses to allow the delegation of South Africa to participate in its work.[7]

The representative of the United States, Mr. Scali, challenged the ruling on the ground that it violated Articles 5 and 6 of the Charter, dealing respectively with suspension and expulsion. In the circumstances, the result was predictable: by a vote of 91 to 22 with 19 abstentions, the ruling was upheld.[8]

[5] Sohn, *supra* note 2, at 1409–16; *see* pp. 1412–16 concerning the forced withdrawal of South Africa from the ILO in 1964.

[6] Scope of "credentials" in rule 27 of the rules of procedure of the General Assembly: statement by the Legal Counsel to the President of the General Assembly at his request, UN Doc. A/8160 (Nov. 11, 1970), *reprinted in* 1970 UN JURIDICAL Y.B. 169. The relevant part of the opinion is as follows:

> Should the General Assembly, where there is no question of rival claimants, reject credentials satisfying the requirements of rule 27 for the purpose of excluding a Member State from participation in its meetings, this would have the effect of suspending a Member State from the exercise of the rights and privileges of membership in a manner not foreseen by the Charter. . . . The participation in meetings of the General Assembly is quite clearly one of the important rights and privileges of membership. Suspension of this right through the rejection of credentials would not satisfy the foregoing requirements and would therefore be contrary to the Charter.

Id. at 170–71, para. 6. The Legal Counsel distinguished the case of Hungary from 1956 to 1963 and the case of South Africa in 1970, as in both cases the representation of these members was seated and exercised rights of membership. *Id.* at 170, para 5. He also distinguished the cases of the Congo in 1960, Yemen in 1961, and China. *Ibid.*, para. 4.

[7] UN Doc. A/PV.2281, at 76 (Nov. 12, 1974).

[8] *Id.* at 71–86. The scenario for this meeting of the Assembly might have been written by Professor Sohn. Using an "imaginative" interpretation, he suggested that exclusion of a recalcitrant member might be achieved through a challenge of the credentials on the ground that the

This is not the place to consider further the constitutionality of the exclusion of South Africa from the General Assembly. As the Legal Counsel pointed out, "participation in the meetings of the General Assembly is quite clearly one of the important rights and privileges of membership."[9] It is solidly anchored in Article 9 of the Charter.[10] South Africa was, and continues to be, a member of the United Nations. There is no rival government, and no manipulation of the rules of procedure can prevail over the explicit terms of the Charter without serious degradation of the Organization and the rule of law.[11]

The credentials issue relates to the question whether the delegates are properly authorized—Rule 27 of the Rules of Procedure of the General Assembly—to represent the government, and not to the question whether the government of the member represents the people of the state or a particular ideology. The Charter does not require a representative or democratic form of government as a condition of admission to the United Nations, nor does loss or lack of a representative or democratic character constitute a ground for suspension or expulsion of members.

When the General Assembly on March 2, 1981 resumed its 35th session for the sole purpose of tackling the question of Namibia, a West European, Rüdiger von Wechmar (FRG), was in the chair. As the Government of the Federal Republic had voted against President Bouteflika's ruling in 1974, one

---

government was not a "true" but a totalitarian government or a foreign puppet. This method could be applied even to expel a permanent member of the Security Council, if necessary under the 1950 Uniting for Peace Resolution of the General Assembly. Sohn, *supra* note 2, at 1422–23 & n.202. However, the device to invoke a presidential ruling in order to override the Charter was invented by the United States and applied in the question of Laos. *See* Gross, *The Question of Laos and the Double Veto in the Security Council,* 54 AJIL 118, 127 (1960).

[9] *Supra* note 6.

[10] Article 9 reads: "1. The General Assembly shall consist of all the Members of the United Nations. 2. Each Member shall have not more than five representatives in the General Assembly."

[11] Concerning the legality of the "suspension" of South Africa, see Jhabvala, *The Credentials Approach to Representation Questions in the U.N. General Assembly,* 7 CAL. W. INT'L L.J. 615 (1977); and Ciobanu, *Credentials of Delegations and Representation of Member States at the United Nations,* 25 INT'L & COMP. L.Q. 351 (1976). Jhabvala concluded, at p. 637: "the decision on South Africa was legal." Ciobanu concluded, at p. 380:

> [T]he General Assembly properly exercised its power to inquire into the representation of South Africa in the United Nations, and that its decision of September 30, 1974, to reject the credentials of the delegation appointed by the Government of that State was valid. The same cannot be said of its interpretation of that decision, at the 2281st meeting on November 12 of the same year. . . .

See also McWhinney, *Credentials of State Delegations to the U.N. General Assembly: A New Approach to Effectuation of Self-Determination for Southern Africa,* 3 HASTINGS CONST. L.Q. 19 (1976). Approving the ruling concerning South Africa, McWhinney said:

> In considering the issue of representation, the General Assembly and its Credentials Committee may properly be guided by new international law principles, such as the principle of the self-determination of peoples, developed or extended since the adoption of the Charter, and also, *inter alia,* by relevant World Court opinions, such as the 1971 ruling on the Namibia question.

Id. at 34 (footnotes omitted). It is beyond the scope of this paper to examine the reasoning that led Jhabvala, Ciobanu, and McWhinney to their respective conclusions.

might have expected President von Wechmar to make at least an effort to revive the Hambro formula.[12] However, for reasons that hardly seem convincing, the President chose to play the game according to the rules of the Third World rather than the rules of the General Assembly and the rules of the Charter.[13]

II.

In the cases discussed above, the opponents of unconstitutional proceedings were content to register their reasoned protest but took no further action to stop the degradation of the constitutional foundations of the United Nations. Such verbal protests have been without avail. When Israel became the target of prevailing majorities, the United States manifested its protest in words as well as in deeds.

[12] On that occasion, speaking for his Government, Baron von Wechmar referred to the opinion of the Legal Counsel of Nov. 11, 1970, *supra* note 6, and declared:

> In the opinion of my Government, the credentials of the South African delegation met the requirements of article 27 of the rules of procedure; therefore there were and continue to be no legal grounds for excluding the South African delegation from the General Assembly. . . . We can only hope that this dangerous precedent will remain the only case of its kind, and that the Organization will find its way back to the strict observance of its rules.

UN Doc. A/PV. 2281, at 93–95 (Nov. 12, 1974). As a matter of fact, he not only repeated the dangerous precedent but made it worse by declaring even before the Credentials Committee had made its report on South Africa's credentials: "I shall not recognize requests for participation in this debate until the General Assembly receives a report from the Credentials Committee." UN Doc. A/35/PV.102 (Mar. 2, 1981). The request to which he referred was apparently made by South Africa under Rule 71 of the Assembly's Rules of Procedure: "During the discussion of any matter, a representative may rise to a point of order, and the point of order shall be immediately decided by the President in accordance with the rules of procedure." This incident is summarized in 18 UN MONTHLY CHRON., April 1981, at 7.

[13] The discussion at the 102d plenary meeting is summarized in 18 UN MONTHLY CHRON., April 1981, at 5–8. The President's explanation is on p. 7. Among those who opposed the Assembly action were the Netherlands on behalf of the 10 members of the EEC; Canada; Austria; Turkey; Iceland on behalf of Denmark, Finland, Norway, and Sweden; the United Kingdom; the Federal Republic of Germany; New Zealand; France; Chile; Australia; and the United States. The United States was reported as saying:

> On so fundamental a question as the rights of membership, the passing of time had not given the Assembly a better legal basis for doing in 1981 what it did improperly in 1974. No one has shown that South Africa's credentials failed to meet the requirements of the rules of procedure. To refuse to consider those credentials as required by the rules was to use the guise of credentials to try to accomplish a suspension that lay beyond the powers of the General Assembly.

Id. at 6. In the view of the Federal Republic of Germany, "[i]t was inconsistent with the provisions of the Charter to evaluate the legitimacy and policy of Governments which issued such credentials." *Id.* at 8. France "felt that an organization which did not respect its fundamental laws rendered itself vulnerable." *Ibid.* Chile

> was sorry that it had to stray from the majority of the Latin American countries and its friends from Asia and Africa, but it firmly believed that the sole hope for respect for the small and medium-sized countries was support for the rules of law—and that was the principle which guided Chile in its vote.

Ibid.

Thus, on November 21, 1974, the General Conference of UNESCO rejected an Israeli request to be included in UNESCO's European regional group. As a result, Israel became the only member of UNESCO excluded from its regional group. This action followed an earlier resolution in which the General Conference had condemned Israel for "its persistence in altering the historical features of the City of Jerusalem and by undertaking excavations which constitutes a danger to its monuments." The United States objected to this, saying:

> [T]he essential objective of this resolution is not . . . the preservation or protection of historical sites and monuments. Whatever the claimed intentions of those who sponsored it might be, the resolution in fact imposes a completely unjustified sanction upon a Member State of this Organization for reasons that seem to us to be largely motivated by political considerations.[14]

The Congress on December 30, 1974 voted to withhold the American contribution to the budget of UNESCO.[15] This "counter-sanction" was effective. The General Conference of UNESCO admitted Israel to the European regional group in 1976 and Congress lifted the financial embargo.[16]

A different and stronger sanction was applied by the United States against the International Labour Organisation. It is apparent from the formal notice of intention to withdraw from the ILO given by Secretary of State Henry Kissinger to the Director-General on November 5, 1975 that an accumulation of grievances rather than a single incident motivated it. They were grouped under four heads: (1) the erosion of tripartite representation, which has a long history; (2) selective concern for human rights, which is found to an even greater degree in the United Nations; (3) disregard of due process, of which "[t]he most blatant example was the 1973 [International Labour] Conference's treatment of Israel";[17] and (4) the increasing politicization of the Organisation.[18] The admission of the PLO to participation in the General Conference of the ILO may well have been regarded as a significant illustration

[14] 1974 DIGEST OF UNITED STATES PRACTICE IN INTERNATIONAL LAW 45. For a rebuttal of the alleged danger to monuments, see statement of the American Jewish Congress *quoted in* F. KIRGIS, JR., INTERNATIONAL ORGANIZATIONS IN THEIR LEGAL SETTING 550 (1977). Concerning the exclusion of Israel from the European Group, it was reported that "[a]ccording to one UNESCO official, 'the Arab and Socialist-bloc countries did a full time job' in gathering their support, and non-left-leaning African delegations had voiced resentment about anti-Israeli pressures, 'with much talk of blackmail,' " N.Y. Times, Nov. 22, 1974, §1, at 6, *quoted in* Lang, *UNESCO and Israel,* 16 HARV. INT'L L.J. 676, 681 (1975).

[15] 1974 DIGEST, *supra* note 14, at 47.

[16] 1976 DIGEST OF UNITED STATES PRACTICE IN INTERNATIONAL LAW 49–50. President Ford on Dec. 29, 1976 informed the Congress "that sufficient progress had been made at the recently concluded UNESCO General Conference toward reversing the anti-Israel actions of the 1974 conference to justify a resumption of U.S. funding." *Id.* at 50. It may be noted that the United States National Commission for UNESCO, in a statement approved on Dec. 5, 1974, opposed the withholding of funds for UNESCO. 1974 DIGEST, *supra* note 14, at 46–47.

[17] Alford, *The Prospective Withdrawal of the United States from the International Labor Organization: Rationales and Implications,* 17 HARV. INT'L L.J. 623, 630 (1976).

[18] 1975 DIGEST OF UNITED STATES PRACTICE IN INTERNATIONAL LAW 70–73.

of politicization.[19] However, more or most important may have been the condemnation of Israel by the General Conference in 1974 for "racist" practices in the West Bank in utter disregard of the procedures for which the ILO was justly highly respected.[20]

Pursuant to the notice, President Carter terminated United States membership in the ILO on November 1, 1977, and the reasons for this step, including condemnation of members without due process, were outlined by the Secretary of Labor, F. Ray Marshall.[21] Three years later, on February 18, 1980, after remedial action was taken by the ILO, the United States resumed membership.[22]

In the wake of the destruction of an Iraqi nuclear installation by Israel, the International Atomic Energy Agency suspended Israel from membership in a manner that provides another example of the degradation of the constitution of a specialized agency and its rules of procedure.

The Security Council on June 19, 1981 adopted Resolution 487 (1981) in which, after referring to Article 2(4) of the Charter, it:

> 1. *Strongly condemns* the military attack by Israel in clear violation of the Charter of the United Nations and the norms of international conduct;
>
> 2. *Calls upon* Israel to refrain in the future from any such acts or threats thereof;
>
> 3. *Further considers* that the said attack constitutes a serious threat to the entire IAEA safeguards régime which is the foundation of the non-proliferation Treaty;
>
> 4. *Fully recognizes* the inalienable sovereign right of Iraq, and all other States, especially the developing countries, to establish programmes of technological and nuclear development to develop their economy and industry for peaceful purposes in accordance with their present and future needs and consistent with the internationally accepted objectives of preventing nuclear-weapons proliferation;

[19] F. Kirgis, *supra* note 14, at 207. A particularly ugly incident of politicization of the ILO by the United States occurred in 1970 in connection with the appointment of a Soviet citizen as Assistant Director-General. *See* Schwebel, *The United States Assaults the I.L.O.*, 65 AJIL 136 (1971). On that occasion the U.S. Congress voted to block payment of assessment due to the ILO.

[20] Alford, *supra* note 17, at 630–31. At the same time, the General Conference also discarded standard procedure in condemning Chile for its labor practices.

[21] 1977 Digest of United States Practice in International Law 39–40.

[22] Nash, Contemporary Practice of the United States Relating to International Law, 75 AJIL 363 (1981). In announcing on November 13, 1980 that the United States would rejoin the ILO, President Carter stated:

> Since [the U.S. withdrawal], a majority of the ILO members—governments, workers, and employers—have successfully joined together to return the ILO to its original purposes. Through their efforts, steps have been taken to strengthen the independence of employer and worker delegates, undertake investigations of human rights violations in a number of countries, including the Soviet Union, reinforce the principle of due process, and generally reduce the level of politicization in the ILO.

Ibid.

5. *Calls upon* Israel urgently to place its nuclear facilities under IAEA safeguards;

6. *Considers* that Iraq is entitled to appropriate redress for the destruction it has suffered, responsibility for which has been acknowledged by Israel. . . .[23]

The General Conference of the IAEA at its 25th session adopted a resolution, GC (xxv) Res. 381, on September 26, 1981, in which it decided by a vote of 51 to 8 with 27 abstentions to consider at its next session the suspension of Israel if it failed to comply with the Security Council resolution.[24] The Agency's Statute provides for suspension of a member by a two-thirds majority vote of the General Conference upon the recommendation of the Board of Governors.[25]

The draft resolution for suspension of Israel, submitted at the next session, invoked, *inter alia,* the "persistent violation of the Statute and the purposes and principles of the Charter of the United Nations"[26] and Israel's failure to comply with Security Council Resolution 487 (1981).[27] As the United States representative, Mr. Davis, pointed out, there had been no recommendation from the Board of Governors,[28] and the Israeli "attack did not violate any specific Article of the Statute or any agreement entered into pursuant to the Statute. Nor could a one-time action qualify as 'persistent'."[29] Israel maintained that "[t]here could be no greater damage to the international nonproliferation regime than a politicized IAEA"[30] and that

> [t]o invoke Security Council resolution 487 or any other resolution as grounds for considering the suspension of Israel's rights and privileges of membership was both artificial and illegal. If such political requirements existed, many States represented at the Conference, in particular Iraq, would be in violation of the Statute and therefore subject to suspension.[31]

The United States representative recalled that "[h]is government had consistently opposed proposals to expel or suspend Israel illegally in the past, and continued to do so"; that "[t]he Agency's Statute gave no mandate to attempt to enforce resolutions of the Security Council or other United Nations organizations"; that "[b]ecause the Security Council had not imposed sanctions, suspension by the Agency would run counter to the considered judgment of

[23] UN Doc. S/RES/487 (1981), *reprinted in* 75 AJIL 724–25 (1981).

[24] UN Press Release WS/1043, Oct. 2, 1981, at 6–7.

[25] Article XIX(B) reads:

> A member which has persistently violated the provisions of this Statute or of any agreement entered by it pursuant to this Statute may be suspended from the exercise of the privileges and rights of membership by the General Conference acting by a two-thirds majority of the members present and voting upon recommendation by the Board of Governors.

8 UST 1093, TIAS No. 3873, 276 UNTS 3.

[26] IAEA Doc. GC(XXVI)/OR.245, para. 5 (Oct. 4, 1982) (Tunisia).

[27] *Id.*, para. 19 (Zambia).

[28] *Id.*, para. 12.

[29] *Id.*, para. 9.

[30] *Id.*, para. 28.

[31] *Id.*, para. 27.

the United Nations organ specifically charged with responsibility for the maintenance of international peace and security"; that "after 30 years marked by military action in virtually every region of the globe, no Member State had ever been suspended"; and concluded that "the suspension of Israel from any United Nations body would jeopardize continued United States support for that body and would have grave consequences for its continued participation in it. The illegal suspension of Members would be the dangerous first step toward the unravelling of the whole United Nations system."[32]

In the roll-call vote on the draft resolution to suspend Israel, "[t]here were 43 votes in favour and 27 against, with 16 abstentions. The required two-thirds majority being 47, the draft resolution was rejected."[33]

The reasons for the opposing votes were stated by the United States before, and for the abstentions, by Venezuela after the vote.[34] Since the substantive flaws of the defeated draft resolution could not be excised, its proponents fell back upon the credentials route which has worked so well in the case of South Africa, both in the United Nations and in the International Atomic Energy Agency.[35] At the subsequent meeting, September 24, 1982, the delegate of Iraq recalled that in the Credentials Committee seven delegates had rejected Israel's credentials and six had accepted them. He therefore proposed to amend the operative paragraph of the draft resolution of the committee by adding the words "with the exception of the credentials presented by Israel," on the ground that Iraq "refused to consider Israel to be the legal representative of that region," meaning the Golan Heights, Jerusalem, the West Bank, and the Gaza Strip.[36]

The representative of the United States argued that the rejection of the credentials "would constitute a violation of Article V[37] to the extent that it would be equivalent to suspending the privileges and rights of a Member," and that suspension required a two-thirds majority. He "deplored the attempt to impose policital sanctions on Israel on the occasion of a purely technical question, namely that of determining whether delegations' credentials conformed with the rules laid down" and issued this warning:

> His delegation wished it to be clearly understood that, in the event of de facto suspension of the exercise by Israel of the rights and privileges of membership, which would be illegal, it would withdraw from the current session of the General Conference and that the Government of the United States would reconsider its participation in the Agency's work.[38]

[32] *Id.*, paras. 8, 10, 11, 13, 14.

[33] *Id.*, para. 41. The opposing votes were cast mainly by Western states; the abstentions came from a cross-section of groups other than the socialist and Arab blocs.

[34] *Id.*, para. 42.

[35] *See* IAEA Doc. GC(XXIII) (Dec. 16, 1979).

[36] IAEA Doc. GC(XXVI)/OR.246, para. 16 (Oct. 13, 1982).

[37] The text of Article V(A) reads: "A General Conference consisting of all members shall meet in regular annual session. . . ." Paragraph B reads: "At such sessions, each member shall be represented by one delegate who may be accompanied by alternates and by advisers. . . ." IAEA Statute, *supra* note 25. There is no provision in the Statute for the expulsion of a member.

[38] IAEA Doc. GC(XXVI)/OR.246, *supra* note 36, paras. 17, 18.

The result of the roll-call vote on the amendment proposed by the delegation of Iraq was as follows: "There were 40 votes in favour and 40 against, with 6 abstentions. In accordance with Rule 78 of the Rules of Procedure, the amendment proposed by the delegation of Iraq was not adopted."[39]

What followed was somewhat like the theater of the absurd such as has rarely, if ever, been witnessed at a diplomatic conference. The key roles were played by the President, Mr. Siazon (the Philippines), and Mr. Herron, the Director of the Legal Division of the Agency. As reported, the representative of Madagascar "explained that he had been present at the time of the vote and that he wished his vote to be recorded. His delegation voted 'yes'."[40]

At the request of the President, Mr. Herron

> recalled that a similar situation had occurred at a meeting of the Board the previous year. One Governor had returned to the room *before* the end of the ballot. His advice on that occasion had been that the Governor's vote should be recorded, so as not to deprive a delegation of its sovereign right to vote and in accordance with the principle of international law whereby a defect of form—in that case the late recording of a representative's vote—should not invalidate substance, in other words the vote of the representative in question. In the United Nations Organization, the practice was also based on the desire not to deprive a delegation of its right to vote. The vote of the Malagasy delegation should, therefore, be recorded.[41]

The representative of the United States observed, correctly it is believed, that "the present situation was different because the results of the vote had already been announced," and that "the recording of an additional vote amounted to a reconsideration of the ballot which had already taken place,

[39] *Id.*, para. 25.

[40] *Id.*, para. 26.

[41] *Id.*, para. 27 (emphasis supplied). The legal expert apparently could not distinguish between registering a vote before or after the announcement of the result of the ballot. The delegate of the Netherlands asked the Director of the Legal Division twice "up to what time a delegation could still have its vote recorded after the closure of a ballot," *id.*, paras. 30, 38, only to be told *after* the Iraqi amendment had been adopted that his question "was purely academic." *Id.*, para. 39. Changes in a recorded vote are often requested and noted in the record of the meeting, but no changes in the announced result of the ballot are made. S. BAILEY, THE GENERAL ASSEMBLY OF THE UNITED NATIONS: A STUDY OF PROCEDURE AND PRACTICE 151 (rev. ed. 1964). In connection with the principles of international law regarding defects of form invoked by Mr. Herron, the Judgment (Jurisdiction) of Aug. 30, 1924 in the case of the *Mavrommatis Palestine Concessions* (Greece v. Great Britain) comes to mind. The Permanent Court of International Justice, referring to defects in the Greek Application, declared: "The Court, whose jurisdiction is international, is not bound to attach to matters of form the same degree of importance which they might possess in municipal law." 1924 PCIJ, ser. A, No. 2, at 34. This statement was quoted with approval by the ICJ in the Case Concerning the Northern Cameroons, 1963 ICJ REP. 15, 28 (Judgment of Dec. 2). In his separate opinion in the *Barcelona Traction* case, Judge Wellington Koo put the point more explicitly, saying: "International law, being primarily based upon the general principles of law and justice, is unfettered by technicalities and formalistic considerations which are often given importance in municipal law." Barcelona Traction, Light & Power Co., Ltd. (Preliminary Objections), 1964 ICJ REP. 6, 60–61, para. 32 (Judgment of July 24). However, it is not clear how those statements could relate to voting in the IAEA. *See also* the statement by the United States delegate, *infra* note 48, at 9.

and a decision to hold a fresh ballot required a two-thirds majority."[42] But as the ballot had shown, the advocates of the "*de facto*" suspension did not have the votes to follow the *de jure* road. The President, after noting that "whichever way the decision went, the rights of one State would be affected," decided to affect the right of Israel rather than the "rights" of Madagascar and to follow, without being aware of it, the Bouteflika way by declaring "that the vote of the Malagasy delegation was valid."[43]

The delegate of the United States challenged the President's ruling and by a vote of 37 to 40, with 9 abstentions, "[t]he appeal against the President's ruling was rejected."[44] As a consequence, the result of the first ballot was amended as follows: "In accordance with the President's ruling, the amendment proposed by the delegation of Iraq to the draft resolution . . . was adopted by 41 votes to 40, with 6 abstentions," and thus once again the law was defeated.[45]

The amended resolution was put to the vote and declared adopted by 41 to 39, with 5 abstentions.[46] The British delegate observed that "he was disquieted by the use of procedural means to achieve political ends, by the ruling of the President and by the opinion given by the Director of the Legal Division. . . . In the circumstances, his delegation could not participate further in the General Conference and was obliged to leave."[47] The United States delegate

> declared that he deplored the President's ruling and was appalled by the opinion rendered by the Director of the Legal Division. The credentials of the delegation of Israel should be accepted as they were absolutely in accordance with the established rules. An item such as the examination of delegates' credentials must not be used as a pretext for re-opening a debate which had already been closed by the decision of the General Conference to reject a draft resolution on the suspension of Israel from the exercise of the privileges and rights of membership. The extent to which the Agency has become politicized, as evidenced by the resolution just adopted, was wholly unacceptable to his Government. The Agency had been founded as a technical body to promote the peaceful uses of atomic energy. Instead, it has become a forum for political debates. The persistent abuse of the United Nations system for the pursuit of political vendettas was an exceptionally dangerous course. The politicization of the Agency must cease. In the circumstances, his delegation must withdraw from the General Conference. His Government would reassess its policy regarding United States support for and participation in the IAEA and its activities.[48]

[42] IAEA Doc. GC(XXVI)/OR.246, *supra* note 36, para. 28. *See also* the observation of the British delegate, *id.*, para. 44, and of the French delegate, *id.*, para. 49.

[43] *Id.*, para. 31.

[44] *Id.*, paras. 32, 36.

[45] *Id.*, para. 37.

[46] *Id.*, para. 43. The total vote on the ruling was 86, and 85 on the amended resolution. Mexico abstained on the ruling but voted for the resolution. Ecuador and Venezuela abstained on the ruling but voted against the resolution. Sri Lanka abstained on the ruling and did not participate in the vote on the resolution.

[47] *Id.*, para. 44. The delegate of Italy also declared that he "was obliged to leave the meeting." *Id.*, para. 48.

[48] *Id.*, para. 45. Views critical of the proceedings were also expressed by Japan, Canada, France, Australia, Denmark, Ireland, Greece, and Chile. *Id.*, paras. 46, 47, 49, 50, 51, 53, 54, 55. It may

What effect the action of Great Britain, Italy, and the United States will have on the Agency, the specialized organizations, and the United Nations remains to be seen. The United States has decided to suspend payment of its dues to the Agency,[49] as it did in the case of UNESCO mentioned above. The legality of such financial countermeasures is doubtful despite the Goldberg reservation[50] and the failure of other members to pay their dues for peacekeeping operations.[51] There may be some truth in the old saw to fight fire with fire, but there may be some who will blame the politicization of international institutions on those who oppose it instead of on those who were and are its proponents.[52] In order to break this vicious circle one might consider referring the constitutionality of politicizing proposals or actions to the International Court of Justice, but it is unlikely that the majorities that are responsible for such actions would be willing to vote in favor of a request for an advisory opinion. Still less promising in spite of its apparent attractiveness is the proposal to establish the compulsory jurisdiction of the Court by means of a declaration by the United States pursuant, presumably, to Article 36(2) of the Statute of the Court, that the United States accepts such jurisdiction "in all legal disputes hereafter arising concerning the interpretation or ap-

---

be noted that McWhinney would not have approved of the President's ruling on the case. For "infringements of the Charter or rejections of General Assembly or Security Council resolutions, not directly related to the issue of the representativeness of the delegation seeking accreditation, do not, prima facie, seem to bear upon decisions of the General Assembly and its Credentials Committee in this context." McWhinney, *supra* note 11, at 34.

[49] *See* Miller, *Head of World Arms Agency Sees Peril in U.S. Curbs,* N.Y. Times, Oct. 26, 1982, at A3. The dues amount to $8.5 million, about 26% of the budget. In the same article, Dr. Hans Blix, Director General of the Agency, was reported as saying that a prolonged reassesssment "could cripple" the operations of the Agency. Mr. Gerard C. Smith, a former representative of the United States, stated on his own behalf and on behalf of three other former representatives to the IAEA that they opposed withdrawal from the Agency and refusal (after the current suspension) to pay the assessed contributions. On the other hand, they deplored "the patently illegal action" taken at the General Conference. *Id.* at A29.

[50] *See* Schwebel, *supra* note 19, at 140 n.26. The reservation was made by Ambassador Goldberg on Aug. 16, 1965 in the UN Special Committee on Peacekeeping Operations. He made it

> crystal clear that if any Member can insist on making an exception to the principle of collective financial responsibility with respect to certain activities of the Organization, the United States reserves the same option to make exceptions if, in our view, strong and compelling reasons exist for doing so. There can be no double standard among the Members of the Organization.

UN Doc. A/AC.121/PV.15, at 8–10 (1965), *reprinted in* 60 AJIL 106 (1966).

[51] *See* Nossiter, *U.N. Chief Chides U.S. on Funds,* N.Y. Times, Jan. 4, 1983, at A2. According to Nossiter, the United States owes the UN $612,000 "because Congress has forbidden the use of any funds for the Palestine Liberation Organization and the South-West Africa People's Organization."

[52] For a sample of views, see Maynes, *American Policies in the United Nations,* in U.S. POLICY IN INTERNATIONAL INSTITUTIONS: DEFINING REASONABLE OPTIONS IN AN UNREASONABLE WORLD 403 (S. M. Finger & J. R. Harbert eds. 1978); Ad Hoc Group on United States Policy Toward the United Nations, *A New U.S. Policy Toward the United Nations,* in *id.* at 449; and Klutznick, *American Goals in a Changing United Nations,* in *id.* at 464. *See also* Lyons, Baldwin, & McNemar, *The Politicization Issue in the UN Specialized Agencies,* in THE CHANGING UN: OPTIONS FOR THE UNITED STATES 81 (David A. Kay ed. 1977).

plication of the Charter of the United Nations."[53] One may doubt the need for such a declaration additional to that made by the United States on August 14, 1946.[54] It provides for the compulsory jurisdiction of the Court "in all legal disputes hereafter arising concerning (a) the interpretation of a treaty." It is well established that the Charter is a multilateral treaty and therefore the proposed declaration would do nothing more than clarify, if that were necessary, the range of the term "treaty" in the original declaration. Moreover, the members who are pressing for illegal acts in and out of the United Nations have not accepted and are not likely to accept the compulsory jurisdiction of the Court. Even if the United States could find a willing adversary, and even if the Court would give a judgment, which is doubtful on grounds of standing,[55] its impact on the practice of the United Nations is even more doubtful for the reasons developed by Dr. Ciobanu.

Be that as it may, the reaction of the United States to the illegal proceedings in the IAEA may well have produced a sobering effect[56] on the attempts to expel Israel at the first part of the 37th session of the General Assembly, from September 21 to December 21, 1982.[57] While the session was in progress, Secretary of State George P. Shultz was reported to have "warned that the United States will walk out of any United Nations body that expels Israel, and will halt its contribution to that unit."[58] It may well be that what was afoot was not an attempt at "expulsion," which pursuant to Article 6 would require a prior recommendation of the Security Council, but at a challenge to the credentials of Israel followed by a "Bouteflika" ruling that might deprive Israel, contrary to Article 9 of the Charter, of its right to participate in the work of the General Assembly.[59] Whatever the aim and the strategy may have

[53] Sohn, *Enabling the United States to Contest "Illegal" United Nations Acts,* 69 AJIL 852 (1975); the trial balloon launched by Professor Sohn was promptly deflated by Dan Ciobanu in *Could the Use of the Contentious Procedure of the International Court of Justice Have Any Significant Impact upon the Practice of the United Nations? A Reply to Professor Louis B. Sohn,* 70 AJIL 328 (1976).

[54] 1946–1947 ICJ Y.B. 217–18.

[55] *See* South West Africa Cases, Second Phase, 1966 ICJ REP. 6, 42, para. 73, and 51, para. 99 (Judgment of July 18).

[56] Since the United States walked out from the General Conference of the IAEA, President Reagan signed on Dec. 21, 1982, Pub. L. No. 97-377, which provides in section 159 for suspension of funds to the Agency until its Board of Governors certifies that Israel may fully participate in the Agency. In his address to the General Assembly on Sept. 30, 1982, Secretary of State Shultz referred to the IAEA and said: "As our action last week in Vienna should make clear, we will not accept attempts to politicize—and, therefore, emasculate—such vital institutions." DEP'T STATE BULL., No. 2068, November 1982, at 1, 9.

[57] The writer has been informed that the United States reaction in the IAEA also had a sobering effect on the International Telecommunication Union, whose Plenipotentiary Conference, in October 1982, was faced with similar maneuvers concerning Israel and which were thereupon promptly shelved.

[58] Nossiter, *Iran Challenges Israel's Right to Seat at UN,* N.Y. Times, Oct. 26, 1982, at A15.

[59] It may be recalled that like Secretary Shultz, Resolution 214 (adopted by the U.S. Senate on July 18, 1975) refers to expulsion rather than to illegal suspension via the credentials route. The resolution states that the Senate

> looks with disfavor and concern over persistent attempts by some nations among the so-called nonalined nations of the Third World to expel Israel from membership in the United Nations;

been, the attempt was called off and the upshot was a letter to the President of the General Assembly, Imre Hollai (Hungary), in which 43 members, including the Soviet bloc and a majority of the Arab or Islamic Group, expressed their "reservation on the credentials of the delegation of Israel."[60]

This, however, may not be the end of the unconstitutional drive to "unseat" Israel. For the same group and its allies in the other groups have also been trying another approach, namely, to "de-legitimize" Israel by contending that it has failed to satisfy the conditions of membership laid down in Article 4(1) of the Charter. Aside from the question by dint of what authority the General Assembly may claim the right of "legitimizing" or "de-legitimizing" member states, reference may be made to General Assembly Resolution 37/123A, adopted on December 16, 1982 as part of the by now habitual omnibus resolution on "the situation in the Middle East," as evidence of this approach. After noting in the Preamble "that Israel's record and actions established conclusively that it is not a peace-loving Member State and that it has not carried out its obligations under the Charter of the United Nations," the Assembly, in operative paragraph 12, "[*d*]*etermines once more* that Israel's record and actions confirm that it has persistently violated the principles contained in the Charter and that it has carried out neither its obligations under the Charter nor its commitment under General Assembly resolution 273 (III) of 11 May 1949."[61] In operative paragraph 14, the Assembly "[*r*]*eiterates* its call to all Member States to cease forthwith, individually and collectively, all dealings with Israel in order totally to isolate it in all fields."[62]

The call for isolating Israel is not new. In the wake of the 1973 Yom Kippur War and an OPEC-imposed rise in oil prices, in other words, since the oil

---

> and . . . [t]hat if Israel is expelled from the United Nations the Senate will review all present United States commitments to the Third World nations involved in the expulsion, and will consider seriously the implication of continued membership in the United Nations under such circumstances.

1975 DIGEST OF UNITED STATES PRACTICE IN INTERNATIONAL LAW 65. At the 1975 session of the General Assembly, Libya, Saudi Arabia, and Syria opposed unsuccessfully the acceptance of Israel's credentials. *Id.* at 66; and UN Doc. A/10270 (Sept. 29, 1975).

[60] Nossiter, *supra* note 58. UN Doc. A/37/563 (Oct. 22, 1982); six more members added their signatures, UN Doc. A/37/563/Add.1 (Oct. 25, 1982). For the Israeli response, see UN Doc. A/37/565 (Oct. 25, 1982).

[61] The same text appeared first in GA Res. ES-9/1 of Feb. 5, 1982. By virtue of Resolution 273 (III), the General Assembly, acting upon a recommendation of the Security Council, admitted Israel to membership in the United Nations. In the Preamble, Resolution 273 (III) refers to resolutions of Nov. 29, 1947 and Dec. 11, 1948. The former, numbered 181 (III), provides for the "Future Government of Palestine," and the latter, numbered 194 (III), is entitled "Palestine—Progress Report of the United States Mediator." The reference to these resolutions resulted from a lengthy discussion in the *Ad Hoc* Political Committee in the course of which delegates asked the representative of Israel, Aubrey Eban, to clarify the future policy of Israel concerning refugees, the status of Jerusalem, and other matters. Some delegates may have desired to obtain commitments. However, such efforts turned out to be without result other than the incorporation of references to the resolutions in question. *See* 3 UN GAOR, pt. II, *Ad Hoc* Political Comm. SR, at 179–360 (1949). *See also* Admission of a State to the United Nations, 1948 ICJ REP. 57 (Advisory Opinion of May 28). The Court found that the conditions prescribed in Article 4 of the Charter are of an "exhaustive character." *Id.* at 64.

[62] UN Press Release GA/6787, Jan. 4, 1983, at 56–58.

weapon entered international politics, many states, particularly in Africa, have broken diplomatic relations with Israel. The goal of paragraph 12, however, is nothing else but the exclusion of Israel from the United Nations. Constitutionally, this would require the application of Article 6 of the Charter, specifically a recommendation of the Security Council, which is not likely to be forthcoming. The Soviet and Arab blocs and their allies may have other tactics à la Bouteflika in mind and it will be interesting to see what they will be.

Resolution 37/123A was adopted by a vote of 87 to 23, with 31 abstentions; 16 members were recorded as absent.[63] The long-standing practice of the General Assembly to disregard abstentions in calculating the requisite majorities in Article 18, paragraphs 2 and 3 of the Charter has been based on the Rules of Procedure. Rule 86, entitled "Meaning of the phrase 'members present and voting' in Article 18 of the Charter," reads as follows: "For the purposes of these rules, the phrase 'members present and voting' means members casting an affirmative or negative vote. Members which abstain from voting are considered as not voting." This is not the place to argue that Rule 86 is not an interpretation but a constitutionally doubtful amendment of the Charter. It may have served a useful purpose when the membership was small and it seemed necessary to get on with the business of the Assembly. Nowadays, with a membership of 157 and a large corps of permanent delegations at the headquarters of the United Nations who prepare drafts of resolutions, line up supporters, and actively bargain for votes, there seems no reason why the adoption of resolutions should not be made a little more difficult and more in conformity with Article 18 of the Charter. This could be accomplished by simply eliminating Rule 86 and applying the text of Article 18. The abstaining members certainly participate in the vote and they are recorded accordingly, as are the members that are absent or did not participate in the vote.[64]

[63] *Id.* at 62.

[64] In this context it may be worthwhile to recall the reply by the United States to Resolution 2925 (XXVII) of Nov. 29, 1973, inviting member states to make proposals "for enhancing the effectiveness of the decisions and resolutions adopted by United Nations organs." The United States suggested that

> the General Assembly might consider modifying its rules so that adoption of resolutions would require an appropriate majority of *all* votes cast, counting those who abstain as present and voting. If this change were made, Assembly resolutions would better express the views of a majority of the Assembly, rather than as now on occasion, of a minority whose views prevailed because of a large number of abstentions.

1973 DIGEST OF UNITED STATES PRACTICE IN INTERNATIONAL LAW 52–53 (emphasis in original). At the next session of the Assembly the representative of the United States said on Nov. 29, 1973 that

> recent voting patterns within the United Nations lead us to consider whether or not bloc voting is now too often being used in a manner which raises serious questions for the future effectiveness of this organization. One concern is with the inclination of many U.N. members to support one-sided or simplistic resolutions on complicated or contentious issues, resolutions which do not necessarily represent the weight of world opinion, and which, worse still, have not the slightest chance of being effectively implemented. The United Nations is not an instrument for wish fulfillment. Rather it should be a catalyst for effective action on world problems.

Id. at 54.

A return to the Charter would not prevent the adoption of partisan or ideologically motivated resolutions but would make their adoption more difficult. Resolution 37/123A would not have been adopted by the required two-thirds majority if the abstentions had been included. The total of votes cast was 140 and the required majority would have been 94, that is, 7 votes more than the 87 favorable votes. It may be of interest to recall that the infamous Resolution 3379 (XXX) of November 10, 1975, determining "that Zionism is a form of racism and racial discrimination," would not have been adopted if abstentions had been counted. The vote was 139 and the required majority 93.[65] One need have no illusion about stemming the tide towards majoritarianism in the General Assembly. The reform suggested here would merely put a bridle on it and stimulate the permanent delegations to work a little harder. However, it is well to bear in mind that the two-thirds majority requirement of Article 18(2) can be easily bypassed by the simple majority rule of Article 18(3) combined, if necessary, with a ruling of the President. It would therefore seem that if the United States and other members are serious about preserving the rule of law and preventing a further degradation of the constitutional environment of the United Nations and its agencies such as occurred last year in the IAEA, they will have to vote, regretfully perhaps, more often "with their feet," as the saying goes, and with their purse, and not merely with their voices or hands.

Postscript

After finishing this paper, I was informed that in response to the question "Has any action been taken by the Board of Governors [of the IAEA] to certify Israeli participation in the Agency in conformance with the Kasten/McClure Amendment to the continuing resolution?",[66] the Department of State spokesman stated on February 22, 1983: "I understand . . . that action has been taken which will meet the provision of U.S. law known as the Kasten/McClure Amendment and permit the resumption of U.S. financial contributions."[67] This is further evidence of the effectiveness of the suggested "voting" method.

Moreover, on the same day, at the 600th meeting of the Board of Governors of the IAEA, the Director General, Dr. Blix,

> expressed his gratification that the United States Government, following its reassessment of the Agency's activities, had decided to resume its participation. He recalled that, in a letter of 14 October 1982 sent to all Members of the Board, he had described the factual and legal situation pertaining to Israel's position in the Agency—namely, that Israel remained a fully participating Member of the Agency.[68]

The delegate of India (Mr. Singh) seemed to express some reservation about

[65] *See* Gross, *The United Nations and the United States,* in VÖLKERRECHT UND RECHTSPHILOSOPHIE 403, 406 (P. Fischer, H. F. Köck, & A. Verdross eds. 1980) (footnote omitted).

[66] This amendment refers to the provision in Pub. L. No. 97-377 in note 56 *supra.*

[67] Dep't of State Press Guidance, Feb. 22, 1983, at 1–2.

[68] IAEA Doc. GOV/OR.600, at 3 (March 14, 1983).

the legal aspects of the matter, saying that "the Statute [of the Agency] clearly provided that a measure adopted by the General Conference could not be annulled by the Board of Governors."[69] The delegate of the United States (Mr. Kennedy), "after congratulating the Director General on his statement," referred to the decision of his Government to suspend its participation in the activities of the Agency, and warned that "all Member States would pay a high price if the viability and effectiveness of the Agency were threatened, as they had been, by a tendency to accord increasing importance to political issues extraneous to the Agency's work." Finally, he

> hoped that the organization would put behind it the unfortunate political wrangling of the recent past and return whole-heartedly to the mission conferred upon it by its Statute. The United States was thus prepared to renew its commitment to the Agency within the constraints of the country's laws, but that commitment would depend also on the degree to which other Member States were prepared to respect the principles set forth in the Statute.[70]

LEO GROSS

ISRAEL'S AIR STRIKE UPON THE IRAQI NUCLEAR REACTOR

It is curious that no commentary has appeared in this *Journal* regarding Israel's aerial strike upon the Iraqi nuclear reactor near Baghdad on the morning of June 7, 1981. Perhaps scholarly consensus accords simply with the Security Council resolution of June 19, 1981, which "*strongly condemns* the military attack by Israel in clear violation of the Charter of the United Nations and the norms of international conduct."[1] My limited purpose here is to suggest questions regarding any such simple conclusion, and to invite detailed and considered scholarly analysis of the situation.[2]

The starting point for any legal analysis is Article 2(4) of the Charter.[3] Was Israel's unannounced, premeditated aerial bombardment of the Iraqi reactor a "use of force against the territorial integrity or political independence" of Iraq? On what Professor Julius Stone has called the "extreme" view of 2(4), any unilateral employment of transboundary force not in self-defense against

[69] *Id.* at 11–12.

[70] *Id.* at 12–14.

[1] UNSC Res. 487, 36 UN SCOR (2288th mtg.), UN Doc. S/RES/487 (1981), *reprinted in* 75 AJIL 724 (1981).

[2] *See* Mallison & Mallison, *The Israeli Aerial Attack of June 7, 1981, Upon the Iraqi Nuclear Reactor: Aggression or Self-Defense?*, 15 VAND. J. TRANSNAT'L L. 417 (1982). At the time of the attack, I took the position that the Israeli action was legal under international law, but that Israel owed monetary compensation to Iraq for the actual damage to the nuclear facility and for the four lives that were lost. *The Israeli Air Strike: Hearings Before the Senate Comm. on Foreign Relations,* 97th Cong., 1st Sess. 85–88 (1981).

[3] Article 2(4) provides: "All Members shall refrain in their international relations from the threat or use of force against the territorial integrity or political independence of any state, or in any other manner inconsistent with the Purposes of the United Nations."

an armed attack (Article 51) violates 2(4).[4] But as Stone goes on to argue, this reading—though it commands some support in the *travaux préparatoires*—ignores the terms "territorial integrity" and "political independence."[5]

I suggest that it is open to serious question whether Israel's strike was a use of force against either Iraq's territorial integrity or its political independence. No portion of Iraq's territory was taken away from Iraq by the bombardment. A *use* of the territory—namely, to construct a nuclear reactor—was interfered with, but the territory itself remained integral. Nor was Iraq's political independence compromised. Iraq's *power* was undoubtedly lessened, but in what sense was its governmental authority vis-à-vis other sovereign governments diminished? Of course, if Israel's attack had been preliminary to a military campaign directed against Iraq's territorial integrity or political independence, a purposive interpretation of Article 2(4) would result in a finding of illegality of the initial strike against the nuclear reactor. But there has been no evidence of any Israeli purpose beyond the limited one of destroying the nuclear reactor itself. In this respect, Israel's action was analogous to a limited "humanitarian intervention," such as the Entebbe raid,[6] which can be justified along similar lines as not violative of 2(4).[7]

But there is another component to Article 2(4)—that the use of force must not be "inconsistent with the Purposes of the United Nations." Here a purposive, or teleological, inquiry is explicitly mandated. McDougal and Feliciano, although addressing themselves to self-defense under the Charter, suggest three relevant factors for determining the objectives of the claimant (here, Israel): extension or conservation, degree of consequentiality, and exclusivity or inclusivity.[8] Let us examine briefly the relevant questions under these categorical factors.

As McDougal and Feliciano put it, the question of extension or conservation of values is whether Israel intended to conserve its own values rather than extend them "through acquiring or destroying values held by the opposing participant [Iraq]."[9] In one sense, Israel's action was profoundly conservative: to check possible nuclear proliferation to a regime perceived as unstable or irresponsible. However, having its own nuclear reactor was clearly a value for Iraq. Was Israel's action "therapeutic" in McDougal's view[10]—to remove an enemy's potential for aggression? The difficulty of answering this question leads to McDougal's qualification that a "therapeutic" attack should be "exercisable only by, or under an unambiguous authorization from, the entire community."[11] Yet this qualification is clearly too strong; it swamps

[4] J. Stone, Aggression and World Order 95 (1958).

[5] *Id.* at 97–100. *See, e.g.,* Franck, *Who Killed Article 2(4)?,* 64 AJIL 809 (1970); Henkin, *The Reports of the Death of Article 2(4) Are Greatly Exaggerated,* 65 AJIL 544 (1971).

[6] *See* Boyle, *International Law in Time of Crisis: From the Entebbe Raid to the Hostages Convention,* 75 Nw. L. Rev. 769 (1980).

[7] *See, e.g.,* Lillich, *Humanitarian Intervention: A Reply to Ian Brownlie and a Plea for Constructive Alternatives,* in Law and Civil War in the Modern World 229 (Moore ed. 1974). *Contra,* Brownlie, *Humanitarian Intervention,* in *id.* at 217.

[8] M. McDougal & F. Feliciano, Law and Minimum World Public Order 222 (1961).

[9] *Ibid.*

[10] *Id.* at 223.

[11] *Id.* at 224.

McDougal's own factor for analytical purposes. For it is often politically expedient for the community to condemn a forceful initiative in explicit terms, yet to approve of it in fact by stopping short of reprisals against the initiator. There is a subtle interplay of politics and acquiescence that renders any demand for "unambiguous authorization" unrealistic. The very resolution condemning Israel's aerial strike fell noticeably short of imposing any penalty or sanction against Israel.[12]

With respect to the degree of consequentiality of the values asserted by Israel, there is hardly a more fundamentally important value than the preservation of the lives of the inhabitants of the claimant state. If Iraq were to develop a nuclear weapons capability, the existence of a small state such as Israel would be in jeopardy. In other words, Israel may have been justified in attacking a nuclear reactor in Iraq, where it would not have been justified in attacking a plant that manufactured tanks or conventional artillery, because of the enormous destructive potential of nuclear weapons. Does not any consequentialist perspective require drawing a qualitative line between conventional and nuclear capabilities insofar as an interpretation of Article 2(4) is concerned?

The third factor suggested by McDougal and Feliciano is the exclusivity or inclusivity of Israel's objectives. Professor Thomas Mallison and Ms. Sally Mallison cite the following statement by Prime Minister Begin of Israel in support of their contention that Israel appeared to have acted solely for its own perceived values: "I don't care about the Arab world. I care about our lives."[13] Yet can Begin's statement fairly be read as ruling out any other motivation? Even if it could, is it not possible that a state acting for its own interests could still be carrying out inclusive community interests? If so, what are those interests, and how do they relate to the purposes of the United Nations?

One of the purposes of the United Nations, stated to be a proper concern of the General Assembly, is "disarmament and the regulation of armaments" (Article 11). Armaments are again mentioned in the responsibilities of the Security Council: to "promote the establishment and maintenance of international peace and security with the least diversion for armaments" (Article 26). Apart from the Charter itself, it is clear that the proliferation of nuclear weapons constitutes one of the gravest threats that has ever faced mankind. Given the fact that nuclear weapons cannot be dis-invented, international stability is compromised each time a new government acquires them. The confusion and chaos that would inevitably accompany any aggressive use of nuclear weapons might rapidly escalate into an unintended war of human extinction. Although Israel's unilateral, military, and self-interested aerial at-

[12] *Supra* note 1. The lack of imposition of a sanction, penalty, or reprisal of any kind, whether from the United Nations or any individual nation, tends to support a claim that the act complained of was in fact legal. *See* D'Amato, *The Concept of Human Rights in International Law*, 82 COLUM. L. REV. 1110, 1118–22 (1982); Reisman, *Sanctions and Enforcement*, in THE FUTURE OF THE INTERNATIONAL LEGAL ORDER 273 (Black & Falk eds. 1971).

[13] Mallison & Mallison, *supra* note 2, at 426 (quoting Washington Post, June 9, 1981, at A11, col. 1).

tack on the Iraqi reactor is hardly a peaceful or desirable precedent for the purposes of nonproliferation, it is possible to surmise that the community of nations breathed a little easier after the deed was done. At the time of the attack, Iraq was engaged in a premeditated war of aggression against its neighbor Iran.[14] Is it not arguable that Israel was acting on behalf of inclusive community values in frustrating Iraq's desire for its own nuclear capability?

To be sure, at least two contentions can be made against the claim that Israel was acting on behalf of inclusive interests. First, one might argue that Israel acted simply to preserve its own nuclear hegemony in the Middle East, and thus retain its aggressive posture against its Arab neighbors. However, this argument, even if true, simply restates the position that Israel acted out of self-interest; it does not defeat the claim that such action served to promote inclusive interests.

Second, Iraq is a party to the Non-Proliferation Treaty[15] and has had its nuclear installations inspected on a regular basis by the International Atomic Energy Agency, whereas Israel has refused to place its own nuclear facilities under IAEA safeguards.[16] May we conclude that Iraq's nuclear reactor was in compliance with Iraq's "inalienable right . . . to develop research, production and use of nuclear energy for peaceful purposes," as stated in Article IV of the NPT? The question, of course, is whether IAEA inspection of the facility will continue to be frequent and thorough enough to prevent diversion of fissionable material produced by the reactor to military uses. Clearly, Israel was not convinced. Indeed, is it unreasonable to think that Iraq, or any nation building a nuclear reactor under IAEA safeguards, may at some point bar the inspection team and announce to the world that it has successfully transferred its fissionable material to its weapons program? What is to prevent clandestine transfer at times when the IAEA inspection team is not present or its attention is diverted? Finally, the building of an indigenous nuclear reactor is of inestimable educational value to government scientists who may be sharpening their expertise for the purpose of developing nuclear weaponry. These considerations suggest that the "right" to develop nuclear energy "for peaceful purposes" may be self-defeating, and that Israel's action may be the precursor of a wholesale revaluation of the NPT and the IAEA program. But even if no such revaluation takes place, is it not clear that there is at least a substantial basis for Israel's frontal challenge to the NPT-IAEA system?

I have not dealt with Israel's own purported legal justification for its aerial strike: anticipatory self-defense.[17] How can this be reconciled with Article 51

[14] *See* Falk, *Some Thoughts on the Decline of International Law and Future Prospects*, 9 HOFSTRA L. REV. 399 (1981).

[15] Treaty on the Non-Proliferation of Nuclear Weapons, 21 UST 483, TIAS No. 6839, 729 UNTS 161 (July 1, 1968), *reprinted in* 7 ILM 811 (1968).

[16] Mallison & Mallison, *supra* note 2, at 440–41. The Mallisons argue that by joining the NPT and opening its own nuclear installations to IAEA inspection, Israel would gain leverage over the adequacy of IAEA supervision: "It would have at least been difficult, and probably impossible, for Iraq to refuse additional international inspection had Israel agreed to the same inspection for itself." *Id.* at 428. How can it be "impossible" for a nation to refuse something?

[17] *See id.* at 435–37.

of the Charter, which only allows self-defense "if an armed attack occurs"?[18] There were claims at the time of the Cuban missile crisis of 1962 that the United States quarantine was similarly based upon Article 51,[19] but neither have those claimants in 1962 nor has Israel in 1981 convincingly shown that such a reading of Article 51 would not render it meaningless and in fact open the door to aggression. In particular, we may anticipate that someday tensions between the Soviet Union and the United States may be so high that the only security either nation will have against a war of annihilation will be the clear legal rule prohibiting anticipatory self-defense.[20]

The destructive potential of nuclear weapons is so enormous as to call into question any and all received rules of international law regarding the trans-boundary use of force. Many of the old rationales for these rules no longer apply. At the same time, the shared values underlying the rules apply more emphatically than ever, for the stake is global survival. I have tried to suggest some of the questions that must be asked about as apparently "simple" an incident as the Israeli attack on the nuclear reactor in Iraq. I have also made assertions that, if not convincing, I hope may have heuristic value. I would welcome debate on this question, and analysis in more detail than the sketchy overview given here.

ANTHONY D'AMATO

[18] The argument that there is an inherent right of self-defense apart from the limitation ("if an armed attack occurs") of Article 51 is, according to Professor Henkin, "unfounded, its reasoning is fallacious, its doctrine pernicious." L. HENKIN, HOW NATIONS BEHAVE 141 (2d ed. 1979).

[19] The Mallisons, *supra* note 2 at 423–24, do not convincingly distinguish the Cuban missile crisis from the Israeli aerial strike of 1981. Previously, Professor Mallison had written that the American position in 1962 was justified as self-defense under Article 51. *See* Mallison, *Limited Naval Blockade or Quarantine Interdiction: National or Collective Defense Claims Valid Under International Law*, 31 GEO. WASH. L. REV. 335 (1962). President Kennedy himself carefully refrained from invoking Article 51 in support of the American quarantine, but he did use the language "in support of our own security" in his address of Oct. 22, 1962, 47 DEP'T STATE BULL. 716 (1962), and "to defend the security of the United States" in his Proclamation No. 3504 of Oct. 23, 1962, *id.* at 717, 27 Fed. Reg. 10,401 (1962). *See also* Wright, *The Cuban Quarantine*, 57 AJIL 546, 560 n.53 (1963); MacChesney, *The Quarantine Against Cuba: Legal or Illegal?*, *id.* at 588, 589–90.

[20] *See* Henkin, *The United Nations and Its Supporters: A Self-Examination*, 78 POL. SCI. Q. 504, 532–33 (1963).

NOTES AND COMMENTS

On the Inadequate Reach of Humanitarian and Human Rights Law and the Need for a New Instrument

I. Introduction

Ideally, there should be a continuum of norms that protect human rights in all situations, from international armed conflicts at one end of the spectrum to situations of nonarmed internal conflicts at the other. In every situation, either there should be a convergence of humanitarian and human rights norms,[1] or at least one of these two systems of protection of human rights should clearly apply. The object of this Note is to examine whether there exists an important lacuna in the above model in the area where humanitarian law meshes with human rights law, *i.e.*, in internal conflicts. The renewed interest in humanitarian law caused by the controversy over whether the United States should ratify the two Geneva Protocols Additional to the Geneva Conventions of 1949[2] and the suggestions for a "New International Humanitarian Order"[3] make such an inquiry particularly timely. Only universal human rights instruments will be examined and we shall consider only questions of substance, not of supervision or implementation.[4]

Certain initial general observations may be useful. In the first place, it

[1] *See generally* Meyrowitz, *Le Droit de la guerre et les droits de l'homme,* 88 REV. DROIT PUBLIC & SCIENCE POLITIQUE EN FRANCE & À L'ETRANGER 1059 (1972); Draper, *Humanitarian Law and Human Rights,* 1979 ACTA JURIDICA 193 [hereinafter cited as Draper, *Humanitarian Law*]; Draper, *The Relationship between the Human Rights Regime and the Law of Armed Conflicts,* 1 ISR. Y.B. HUM. RIGHTS 191 (1971) [hereinafter cited as Draper, *Relationship*]; Partsch, *La Protection internationale des droits de l'homme et les Conventions de Genève de la Croix-Rouge,* 26 REV. INT'LE DROIT COMPARÉ 73 (1974); Aldrich, *New Life for the Laws of War,* 75 AJIL 764 (1981); Robertson, *Human Rights as the Basis of International Humanitarian Law,* in PROCEEDINGS OF THE INTERNATIONAL CONFERENCE ON HUMANITARIAN LAW 55 (San Remo 1970); A. CALOGEROPOULOS-STRATIS, DROIT HUMANITAIRE ET DROITS DE L'HOMME: LA PROTECTION DE LA PERSONNE EN PÉRIODE DE CONFLIT ARMÉ (1980); M. BOTHE, K. PARTSCH, & W. SOLF, NEW RULES FOR VICTIMS OF ARMED CONFLICTS (1982). For a list of the principal humanitarian conventions and a discussion of the scope of humanitarian law, see Partsch, *Humanitarian Law and Armed Conflict* [Instalment], 3 ENCYCLOPEDIA OF PUBLIC INTERNATIONAL LAW 215 (R. Bernhardt ed. 1982).

[2] Protocol Additional to the Geneva Conventions of 12 August 1949, and Relating to the Protection of Victims of International Armed Conflicts (Protocol I), *opened for signature* Dec. 12, 1977, 16 ILM 1391 (1977). Protocol Additional to the Geneva Conventions of 12 August 1949, and Relating to the Protection of Victims of Non-International Armed Conflicts (Protocol II), *opened for signature* Dec. 12, 1977, *id.* at 1442.

[3] *See* UN Docs. A/36/245 (1981), A/37/145 (1982), and A/37/746 (1982) on New International Humanitarian Law. *See also* GA Res. 36/136, 36 UN GAOR Supp. (No. 51) at 185, UN Doc. A/36/51 (1981); GA Res. 37/201, UN Doc. A/RES/37/201 (1982).

[4] On the importance of procedures of implementation, see the concurring opinion of Justice Douglas in Joint Anti-Fascist Refugee Comm. v. McGrath, 341 U.S. 123, 179 (1951).

should be observed that humanitarian law has been more systematically codified than ordinary peacetime human rights, a fact that should not be surprising in view of the comparative age of these two systems of law.[5] While humanitarian law has undergone more than a century of fairly intensive codification, human rights instruments are a product of the post-UN Charter era.

Humanitarian law instruments have been accepted far more than human rights instruments as the positive law of the international community. Baxter has observed that "[t]he Hague Regulations of 1907,[6] which have passed into customary international law, and the Geneva Conventions of 1949[7] have achieved almost universal acceptance and are probably binding on a larger number of states than any other treaties save only the constitutional instruments of international organizations."[8] It is remarkable indeed that as of December 31, 1982, there were 152 state parties to each of the four Geneva Conventions.[9] The most parties to any human rights instrument, as of July 1, 1982, were 115 to the International Convention on the Elimination of All Forms of Racial Discrimination.[10] The number of state parties to other instruments was significantly lower: 73 to the International Covenant on Economic, Social and Cultural Rights (Economic Covenant);[11] 70 to the International Covenant on Civil and Political Rights (Political Covenant);[12] 27 to the Optional Protocol to the International Covenant on Civil and Political Rights;[13] 89 to the Convention on Prevention and Punishment of the Crime of Genocide;[14] and 39 to the Convention on the Elimination of All Forms of Discrimination Against Women.[15] In comparing the extent of ratifications of

[5] Baxter, *Some Existing Problems of Humanitarian Law,* in THE CONCEPT OF INTERNATIONAL ARMED CONFLICT: FURTHER OUTLOOK 1 (Proceedings of the International Symposium on Humanitarian Law, Brussels 1974).

[6] Convention Respecting the Laws and Customs of War on Land, with Annex of Regulations, Oct. 18, 1907, 36 Stat. 2277, TS No. 539.

[7] Convention for the Amelioration of the Condition of the Wounded and Sick in Armed Forces in the Field (Geneva Convention No. I), Aug. 12, 1949, 6 UST 3114, TIAS No. 3362, 75 UNTS 31. Convention for the Amelioration of the Condition of the Wounded, Sick and Shipwrecked Members of Armed Forces at Sea (Geneva Convention No. II), Aug. 12, 1949, 6 UST 3217, TIAS No. 3363, 75 UNTS 85. Geneva Convention Relative to the Treatment of Prisoners of War (Geneva Convention No. III), Aug. 12, 1949, 6 UST 3316, TIAS No. 3364, 75 UNTS 135. Convention Relative to the Protection of Civilian Persons in Time of War (Geneva Convention No. IV), Aug. 12, 1949, 6 UST 3516, TIAS No. 3365, 75 UNTS 287.

[8] Baxter, *supra* note 5, at 2.

[9] Information supplied by the International Committee of the Red Cross, January 1983.

[10] 660 UNTS 195; Human Rights International Instruments: Signatures, Ratifications, Accessions, etc. 1 July 1982, UN Doc. ST/HR/4/Rev.4, at 18–19 (1982) [hereinafter cited as Human Rights International Instruments].

[11] GA Res. 2200, 21 UN GAOR Supp. (No. 16) at 49, UN Doc. A/6316 (1966); Human Rights International Instruments, *supra* note 10.

[12] GA Res. 2200, 21 UN GAOR Supp. (No. 16) at 52, UN Doc. A/6316 (1966); Human Rights International Instruments, *supra* note 10.

[13] GA Res. 2200, 21 UN GAOR Supp. (No. 16) at 59, UN Doc. A/6316 (1966); Human Rights International Instruments, *supra* note 10.

[14] 78 UNTS 277; Human Rights International Instruments, *supra* note 10.

[15] GA Res. 34/180, 34 UN GAOR Supp. (No. 46) at 193, UN Doc. A/34/46 (1979); Human Rights International Instruments, *supra* note 10.

human rights and humanitarian instruments, however, account should be taken of the fact that the former instruments apply to day-to-day life, while the latter govern exceptional situations only.

There is a considerable difference between the customary law status of many of the norms contained in the humanitarian law instruments and those in the human rights instruments. It is generally accepted that the Regulations Respecting the Laws and Customs of War on Land annexed to Hague Convention No. IV are now part of the corpus of customary international law.[16] The acceptance of the Hague Regulations as customary law resolves the difficulties posed by Article 2 of the fourth Hague Convention, which states that the provisions contained in the Convention and in the Regulations annexed to it "do not apply except between Contracting Powers, and then only if all the belligerents are parties to the Convention." This *si omnes* or general participation clause can now be regarded as irrelevant.[17]

While the binding nature of the Geneva Conventions of 1949 is generally based on their status as treaties, some of their provisions can be traced to earlier Geneva Conventions and to the Hague Regulations of 1907. Thus, certain provisions of the Conventions of 1949 reflect customary law. This can only be determined *in concreto* with regard to each particular provision. However, the extent to which provisions of the Conventions are declaratory of customary law is of limited significance because of the universal acceptance of these Conventions *qua* binding treaties. Nevertheless, when a government contests the applicability of one of the Conventions, it may be useful for the International Committee of the Red Cross (ICRC) to invoke a certain rule as customary, rather than as a treaty provision.

The status of the 1977 Protocols Additional to the Geneva Conventions of August 12, 1949 is altogether different. By the end of 1982, Protocol I had been ratified by only 27 states and Protocol II by only 23 states.[18] The Protocols have introduced many changes and innovations, some of which are controversial in nature, into humanitarian law. Some scholars view such provisions as not codifying customary law.[19]

While a very important segment of international humanitarian law, *i.e.*, the Hague Regulations of 1907, is customary international law, no major segments of international human rights instruments have similar status. Various provisions of these instruments have attained the status of customary law, but the

[16] *See* text accompanying note 8 *supra*. Judgment of the International Military Tribunal for the Far East of 1948, 15 UNITED NATIONS WAR CRIMES COMMISSION, LAW REPORTS OF TRIALS OF WAR CRIMINALS 13 (1949); Judgment of the International Military Tribunal for the Trial of German Major War Criminals, CMD. 6964, Misc. No. 12, at 64–65 (1946); Baxter, *supra* note 5, at 2; U.S. DEP'T OF THE ARMY, FIELD MANUAL FM 27-10, THE LAW OF LAND WARFARE 6 (1956); 2 U.S. DEP'T OF THE ARMY, PAMPHLET 27-161-2, INTERNATIONAL LAW 249 (1962).

[17] Report of the Secretary-General on Respect for Human Rights in Armed Conflicts, UN Doc. A/7720, at 22 (1969) [hereinafter cited as 1969 Report].

[18] Information supplied by the International Committee of the Red Cross, January 1983.

[19] Thus, the new rules with regard to guerrilla fighters, Article 44, paragraphs 3 and 4, "will become binding upon those States, and those States alone, which ratify the Protocol [I]." Kalshoven, *Reaffirmation and Development of International Humanitarian Law Applicable in Armed Conflicts: The Diplomatic Conference, Geneva, 1974–1977*, 8 NETH. Y.B. INT'L L. 107, 133 (1977).

determination *in concreto* is often difficult. The recent draft of the new *Restatement of the Foreign Relations Law of the United States,* often considered to be a particularly authoritative U.S. source, lists a limited number of human rights, all of which, however, are of central importance, as norms reflecting customary international law:

> A state violates international law if, as a matter of state policy, it practices, encourages or condones
>
> (a) genocide,
> (b) slavery or slave trade,
> (c) the murder or causing the disappearance of individuals,
> (d) torture or other cruel, inhuman or degrading treatment or punishment,
> (e) prolonged arbitrary detention,
> (f) systematic racial discrimination, or
> (g) consistent patterns of gross violations of internationally recognized human rights.[20]

It may also be observed that point (g) opens the door to an expansive interpretation.

II. Growing Convergence: The Jurisprudential Connection

Human rights law and humanitarian law have different historical sources and, originally, different jurisprudential underpinnings. It is not the purpose of this Note to discuss in detail the sources of human rights law.[21] Suffice it to observe that one of the fundamental sources and guiding principles of human rights is the principle of humanity. The ideas that lie behind the law of war and humanitarian law are different in origin.[22] The law of war originates in the tension between military necessity and restraints (whether motivated by humanitarian or other considerations such as economic advantage) on the conduct of belligerents. The weight of these two conflicting factors has changed greatly in the course of history. Originally, military necessity was dominant. The principle of humanitarian restraints, originally in a weak position, is of growing importance, particularly in the elaboration of new instruments, but not necessarily in actual practice. A central concept of the law of war is that of reciprocity, regarded both as a reason behind the norms and as an important factor in their efficacy. Not surprisingly, humanitarian law has focused, historically, on the reciprocal protection of a few strictly limited categories of persons, especially persons "belonging to the enemy."

It goes without saying that the post-UN Charter international human rights instruments have the humanitarian object of recognizing human rights and

[20] Restatement of Foreign Relations Law of the United States (Revised) §702 (Tent. Draft No. 3, 1982). *See generally* D'Amato, *The Concept of Human Rights in International Law,* 82 Colum. L. Rev. 1110 (1982).

[21] For a survey of the philosophical sources and modern theories of human rights, see Shestack, *The Jurisprudence of Human Rights,* in 1 Human Rights in International Law: Legal and Policy Issues 69, 75–98 (T. Meron ed. 1983).

[22] *See generally* Draper, *Humanitarian Law, supra* note 1, at 199–201; M. Veuthey, Guérilla et droit humanitaire 338–47 (1983); G. Best, Humanity in Warfare 157–215 (1980).

extending international protection to them. But it should be pointed out that humanitarian law, while protecting the rights of states and governing their duties, also contains a prominent human rights component, dating back to the 19th century when the law of war had "come to be seen as a law of humanitarian restraints upon the conduct of the belligerents."[23] This humanitarian and humanizing aspect of the law of war finds a significant reflection in the preambular (Martens) clause to Hague Convention No. IV.[24] The post-UN Charter human rights, as reflected in the Universal Declaration of Human Rights (Universal Declaration),[25] had an influence on the humanitarian character of the Geneva Conventions of 1949.[26] The 1977 Additional Protocols also reflect the influence of international human rights, in some instances by taking those rights into consideration,[27] and in others by making explicit reference to them.[28] In matters such as the prohibition of torture and cruel, inhuman, or degrading treatment or punishment, arbitrary arrest and detention, discrimination on grounds of race, sex, language, or religion, and the norm of due process, there exists a very large measure of convergence and parallelism between norms originating in human rights instruments and those originating in instruments on international humanitarian law.[29] There is also growing convergence in the applicability *ratione personae* and *ratione materiae* of these two systems.

The dominance of the humanitarian principle in the most recent elaboration of the laws of armed conflict is apparent, *inter alia,* in Articles 50–56 of Protocol I, which concern the protection of the civilian population in the case of an international armed conflict, and in the provisions of Protocol II, which confer significant human rights on persons living in a country involved in an internal armed conflict. If the former example can be seen as reflecting also the principle of reciprocity, the latter can and should be explained primarily on the basis of the principle of humanity. Indeed, the protection afforded in certain circumstances by humanitarian law to citizens of a particular state vis-à-vis their own government—to be discussed in section III below—did not originate in the principle of reciprocity, but in that of humanity. The idea of humanity has become the common denominator of human rights law

[23] Draper, *Humanitarian Law, supra* note 1, at 201.

[24] This clause reads as follows:

> Until a more complete code of the laws of war has been issued, the High Contracting Parties deem it expedient to declare that, in cases not included in the Regulations adopted by them, the inhabitants and the belligerents remain under the protection and the rule of the principles of the law of nations, as they result from the usages established among civilized peoples, from the laws of humanity, and the dictates of the public conscience.

See generally Strebel, *Martens' Clause* [Instalment], 3 ENCYCLOPEDIA, *supra* note 1, at 252.

[25] GA Res. 217A, UN Doc. A/810, at 71 (1948).

[26] Schindler, *Human Rights and Humanitarian Law,* 31 AM. U.L. REV. 935, 937 (1982).

[27] With regard to the right of self-determination, see Art. 1(4), Protocol I.

[28] *See* Art. 72, Protocol I; Preamble, Protocol II. *See generally* Schindler, *supra* note 26.

[29] For a detailed comparison, see 1969 Report, *supra* note 17; and Report of the Secretary-General on Respect for Human Rights in Armed Conflicts, UN Doc. A/8052 (1970) [hereinafter cited as 1970 Report].

and of humanitarian law. The fact that these two systems of law have different historical and doctrinal origins must not deter us from realizing that a tremendous rapprochement has already taken place between them and that the trends point to an ever greater reliance on the shared idea of humanity.

III. NATIONALITY: APPLICABILITY *RATIONE PERSONAE*

The question of the applicability *ratione personae* of human rights stated in the international human rights instruments and in instruments on international humanitarian law has not been adequately explored in scholarly writings. It is complex and nuanced. This is an area of important convergence, but also of significant differences, in the applicability of the human rights stated in the two types of instruments.

It has been suggested correctly that human rights instruments apply subject to *ratione personae* qualifications that are less restrictive than those provided under some of the Geneva Conventions, which may make applicability dependent on nationality or other status,[30] and incorrectly, that human rights guarantees under the human rights instruments "apply always and everywhere."[31] It is certainly true that the human rights stated in the international human rights instruments apply, in principle, to the relations between the government and the governed and protect the latter against the former regardless of their nationality. But careful consideration shows that this principle is not always followed. To illustrate: Article 2(3) of the Economic Covenant permits developing states, "with due regard to human rights," to determine to what extent they would guarantee to non-nationals the economic rights recognized in that Covenant; and Article 1(2) of the International Convention on the Elimination of All Forms of Racial Discrimination introduces a nationality test in providing that it shall not apply to distinctions, exclusions, restrictions, or preferences made by a state party between citizens and noncitizens.

There may also be limitations of applicability of human rights instruments based on preemption by a different and, on the whole, less generous *lex specialis,* as in the case of prisoners of war.

Another problem arises with regard to the territorial scope of applicability of human rights instruments. Article 2(1) of the Political Covenant provides that each state party undertakes to respect and to ensure to all individuals within its territory and subject to its jurisdiction the rights recognized in the Covenant. Thus, even if a state party does not derogate from the totality of human rights stated in the Political Covenant by invoking Article 4[32] thereof,

[30] 1970 Report, *supra* note 29, at 13. [31] *Id.* at 101.

[32] Article 4 reads as follows:

> 1. In time of public emergency which threatens the life of the nation and the existence of which is officially proclaimed, the States Parties to the present Covenant may take measures derogating from their obligations under the present Covenant to the extent strictly required by the exigencies of the situation, provided that such measures are not inconsistent with their other obligations under international law and do not involve discrimination solely on the ground of race, colour, sex, language, religion or social origin.

the Covenant as interpreted by some scholars would not apply to events occurring outside of the territory of the state concerned.[33] This would be a serious limitation because in armed conflict armies often operate in foreign territory. According to this view, persons in such territory would not be protected by the Covenant. Difficulties may also arise with regard to the applicability of human rights instruments to the population of occupied territories.[34]

It is often taken for granted that human rights stated in the humanitarian law instruments protect only nationals of certain states or persons having a particular status. This is not always accurate.

As regards international armed conflicts, Article 12 of both Geneva Conventions I and II makes it clear that these Conventions apply to certain wounded, sick, or shipwrecked persons without distinction of nationality. A party's own nationals are thus protected persons under these Conventions.[35] This important elimination of the nationality test dates back to the (first Geneva) Convention for the Amelioration of the Conditions of the Wounded in Armies in the Field of August 22, 1864.[36] Article 4 of Geneva Convention III makes it clear, however, that that Convention protects only certain categories of combatants. That the detaining power's nationals are not and cannot be prisoners of war under the Convention is made particularly clear by Articles 87 and 100.

The *ratione personae* position under Protocol I is more complicated. According to Article 1(4), Protocol I applies not only to the situations governed by the 1949 Conventions, but also to certain armed conflicts in which peoples are fighting against colonial or racist regimes and alien occupation. Thus, the provisions of the Protocol may be applicable, subject to Article 1, to certain "wars of liberation" taking place within the territory of a single state between the government and insurgents of the same nationality.[37]

---

2. No derogation from articles 6, 7, 8 (paragraphs 1 and 2), 11, 15, 16 and 18 may be made under this provision.

3. Any State Party to the present Covenant availing itself of the right of derogation shall immediately inform the other States Parties to the present Covenant, through the intermediary of the Secretary-General of the United Nations, of the provisions from which it has derogated and of the reasons by which it was actuated. A further communication shall be made, through the same intermediary, on the date on which it terminates such derogation.

[33] Schindler, *supra* note 26, at 939. For a different interpretation, see Buergenthal, *To Respect and to Ensure: State Obligations and Permissible Derogations,* in THE INTERNATIONAL BILL OF HUMAN RIGHTS 72, 74–77 (L. Henkin ed. 1981).

[34] *See generally* Meron, *Applicability of Multilateral Conventions to Occupied Territories,* 72 AJIL 542 (1978).

[35] *See* Solf, *Human Rights in Armed Conflict: Some Observations on the Relationship of Human Rights Law to the Law of Armed Conflict,* in WORLD IN TRANSITION 41, 44 (H. Han ed. 1979); COMMENTARY ON THE GENEVA CONVENTIONS OF 12 AUGUST 1949: GENEVA CONVENTION FOR THE AMELIORATION OF THE CONDITION OF THE WOUNDED AND SICK IN ARMED FORCES IN THE FIELD 138 (J. Pictet ed. 1952).

[36] Art. 6, 1 Bevans 7, 10; *see* Solf, *supra* note 35, at 43.

[37] *See generally* Aldrich, *supra* note 1, at 770–71; Kalshoven, *supra* note 19, at 122.

It appears that the majority at Geneva in 1977 had intended to grant prisoner-of-war status to combatants in a national liberation war taking place within a single country against a colonial or racist government. Such status could be claimed for citizens of a colonial or racist state in the struggle against their own government,[38] which would thus be regarded as an "adverse Party" in the context of Article 44 of Protocol I.

In accordance with its Article 4, Geneva Convention IV applies only to protected persons, *i.e.,* persons who find themselves, in case of a conflict or occupation, in the hands of a party to the conflict or occupying power of which they are not nationals. Only nationals of a state that is bound by the Convention are protected by it. Nationals of a neutral state who find themselves in the territory of a belligerent state and nationals of a cobelligerent state are not protected persons while their state of nationality has normal diplomatic representation in the state where they are found. Nevertheless, part II of Geneva Convention IV, which concerns the general protection of populations against certain consequences of war, applies, in accordance with Article 13 thereof, without regard to nationality and thus protects nationals from certain acts of their own governments. Article 70 of Geneva Convention IV grants certain rights to nationals of the occupying power vis-à-vis that occupying power.

Article 75 of Protocol I does away with a nationality test. It applies to persons, "[i]n so far as they are affected by a situation referred to in Article 1" of that Protocol, who are in the power of a party to the conflict and who do not benefit from more favorable treatment. Article 75(1) prohibits a wide range of adverse distinctions. Protection is extended to persons in the power of a party of which they are nationals.[39]

An important question is, what is the scope of the phrase "[i]n so far as they are affected by a situation referred to in Article 1"? Although an argument could be made that this language encompasses the entire population of a country involved in a conflict as defined in Article 1, it appears that the object of the Diplomatic Conference that drew up Protocol I was not to revise the entire range of human rights that would otherwise apply between a government and its people. According to this view, which is supported by the

[38] *See generally* Kalshoven, *supra* note 19, at 121–33; Aldrich, *supra* note 1, at 771; Cassese, *A Tentative Appraisal of the Old and the New Humanitarian Law of Armed Conflict,* in THE NEW HUMANITARIAN LAW OF ARMED CONFLICT 461, 469 (A. Cassese ed. 1979). It has been observed that the duty to accord prisoner-of-war status to captured members of the armed forces of an adversary applies to the armed forces of a people

> engaged against a High Contracting Party in an armed struggle for self determination within the meaning of Art. 1(4), *provided,* however, that the struggle qualifies under Art. 1(4) as an international armed conflict, and *provided also* that the authorities of the movement have made the declaration required by Art. 96(3).

M. BOTHE, K. PARTSCH, & W. SOLF, *supra* note 1, at 237–38.

[39] *See* Solf, *supra* note 35, at 44. It has been observed that although the words "national origin" in Article 75 do not refer to nationality but to ethnic group, nationality should be regarded as "an 'other status' or as a status based 'on any similar criteria.' This would mean that the list of banned criteria would not exclude the Parties' own nationals from the enjoyment of the protection provided for by this Article." M. BOTHE, K. PARTSCH, & W. SOLF, *supra* note 1, at 458.

legislative history, the guarantees of Article 75 apply primarily to certain categories of persons especially affected by the conflict, such as collaborators, deserters, and all the nationals of State *A* who serve in the forces of adverse State *B*.[40] It has been observed that this interpretation "respects the jurisdiction of the Parties to the conflict for matters of their internal competence" and suggests that " 'the purpose of the Conference was not to draft a Convention on Human Rights.' "[41]

As regards noninternational armed conflicts, common Article 3 of the four Geneva Conventions protects all persons taking no active part in the hostilities, including even members of armed forces who have laid down their arms and those placed *hors de combat.* Although nationality is not mentioned in Article 3, that article must be read as ensuring humane treatment for all persons involved in internal conflicts regardless of nationality.[42] Nationals of the state party concerned are therefore protected vis-à-vis their own government.[43] This provision is of the greatest importance because Article 3 is often regarded—probably with a measure of exaggeration—as "a 'microcosm' of the remaining humanitarian provisions in each convention."[44]

Protocol II likewise applies to all persons affected by a noninternational armed conflict, including the state's own nationals. This is made clear by Articles 1 and 2. Article 2(1) contains a list of prohibited adverse distinctions, which is identical to that in Article 75(1) of Protocol I.[45] The Protocol, obviously reflecting provisions of the Political Covenant, grants important fundamental guarantees of, *e.g.*, due process and fair trial.[46]

IV. APPLICABILITY *RATIONE MATERIAE*

Dinstein has observed that most human rights are suspended for the duration of hostilities, but that some human rights remain in effect and that "war produces new human rights, which are applicable in war-time in lieu of those suspended."[47] In an interesting discussion of the interplay of human rights in peacetime and wartime, Dinstein has considered several variations. Depending on its content and nature, a peacetime human right may disappear in wartime, be the same in wartime as it is in peacetime, be diminished in wartime, or be expanded in wartime. Wartime human rights may also exist

[40] M. BOTHE, K. PARTSCH, & W. SOLF, *supra* note 1, at 459–60.

[41] *Id.* at 460 (quoting a statement by the Canadian delegation).

[42] COMMENTARY ON THE GENEVA CONVENTIONS OF 12 AUGUST 1949: THE GENEVA CONVENTION RELATIVE TO THE PROTECTION OF CIVILIAN PERSONS IN TIME OF WAR 40 (O. Uhler & H. Coursier eds. 1958).

[43] But it is "possible that certain offences may be regarded as more serious or less serious according to whether they have been committed by citizens of the country concerned or by aliens." *Ibid.*

[44] Draper, *Humanitarian Law, supra* note 1, at 202. Concerning the importance of Article 3, see Robertson, *supra* note 1, at 60–61.

[45] *See* text accompanying note 39 *supra.* For the "fundamental guarantees" provision of Protocol II, see Article 4 thereof.

[46] *See* Art. 6, Protocol II.

[47] Dinstein, *The International Law of Inter-State Wars and Human Rights,* 7 ISR. Y.B. HUM. RIGHTS 139, 148 (1977) [hereinafter cited as Dinstein, *International Law*].

where none exist in peacetime.[48] It is beyond the scope of this Note to enumerate the rights falling into the different categories. This has already been done by Dinstein, Schindler,[49] and others.[50] Instead, we will focus on some problems of the applicability of the human rights stated in the international human rights instruments and in the humanitarian instruments. It may be worthwhile recalling, first, that humanitarian instruments, having been enacted to govern situations of armed strife, are not subject to derogations. Human rights instruments, on the other hand, are generally subject to derogations in various exceptional situations.[51]

The principal difficulty regarding the application of international humanitarian law has been the refusal of states "to apply the conventions in situations where they clearly should be applied. Attempts to justify such refusals are often based on differences between the conflicts presently encountered and those for which the conventions were supposedly adopted."[52] There are, in fact, so many situations in which the applicability of the Geneva Conventions as a whole or of their common Article 3 has been denied[53] that the rule has been rejection of the law, rather than its formal acknowledgment and recognition. Baxter has observed that "[t]he first line of defense against international humanitarian law is to deny that it applies at all."[54] As long as states continue to evade the applicability of humanitarian norms, justifying their evasions by the specific circumstances of particular situations, little solace can be found in the principle that no derogations may be made legally.

International Armed Conflicts

According to common Article 2 of the four Geneva Conventions, the Conventions apply to all cases of declared war or any other armed conflict that may arise between two or more of the contracting parties, even if the state of war is not recognized by one of them. The Conventions apply also to all cases of partial or total occupation of the territory of a contracting party, even if such occupation meets no armed resistance. It has been noted that Article 1(4) of Protocol I expands the above definition of international armed conflicts to include:

> armed conflicts in which peoples are fighting against colonial domination and alien occupation and against racist régimes in the exercise of their right of self-determination, as enshrined in the Charter of the United Nations and the Declaration on Principles of International Law concerning Friendly Relations and Co-operation among States in accordance with the Charter of the United Nations.[55]

[48] *See* Dinstein, *Human Rights in Armed Conflict: International Humanitarian Law,* in 2 HUMAN RIGHTS IN INTERNATIONAL LAW, *supra* note 21, at 345, 350–54 [hereinafter cited as Dinstein, *Human Rights*].

[49] *See* Schindler, *supra* note 26, at 939–40.

[50] *See, e.g.,* 1969 Report, *supra* note 17; and 1970 Report, *supra* note 29, Ann. I.

[51] The question of derogations is discussed in part IV, "Derogations," *infra.*

[52] Aldrich, *Human Rights and Armed Conflict: Conflicting Views,* 67 ASIL PROC. 141, 142 (1973).

[53] *See, e.g., id.* at 143–44; Robertson, *supra* note 1, at 61.

[54] Baxter, *supra* note 5, at 2.

[55] Art. 1(4), Protocol I.

This extension, which has limited parameters,[56] applies only to those parties to the Geneva Conventions that are also parties to Protocol I. The Geneva Conventions and Protocol I state a great number of human rights applicable in international armed conflicts. While not all of the nonderogable rights under the Political Covenant have corresponding rights under the Geneva Conventions, the limited and inadequate catalog of nonderogable rights under the Political Covenant falls short of the totality of human rights recognized by humanitarian instruments.[57]

Noninternational Armed Conflicts[58]

While Protocol II has increased and improved the content of human rights applicable in armed conflicts not of an international character under the provisions of common Article 3, it has raised the threshold of applicability to an exceedingly high level. Article 3, it may be recalled, simply states that in the case of armed conflict not of an international character occurring in the territory of one of the contracting parties, each party to the conflict shall be bound to apply, at a minimum, certain provisions. Article 3 does not define what constitutes a noninternational armed conflict, except by excluding international armed conflicts and by singling out a conflict that takes place in the territory of one contracting party only.

Article 1(1) of Protocol II, concerning the material field of application of the Protocol, purports to develop and supplement common Article 3, "without modifying its existing conditions of application." The article goes on, nevertheless, to state that Protocol II applies to all armed conflicts that are not covered by Article 1 of Protocol I and that

> take place in the territory of a High Contracting Party between its armed forces and dissident armed forces or other organized armed groups which, under responsible command, exercise such control over a part of its territory as to enable them to carry out sustained and concerted military operations and to implement this Protocol.

To avoid any doubts, Article 1(2) adds that those situations of internal disturbances and tensions such as riots, isolated and sporadic acts of violence, and other acts of a similar nature are not armed conflicts. Protocol II is therefore inapplicable to such events. Draper has aptly observed that the material field of application of Protocol II "has been raised to a level of intensity of armed conflict which is virtually commensurate with a classical civil war, but without the need for belligerent recognition."[59] Although the conditions for the applicability of Protocol II are satisfied in a number of

[56] For a discussion and a critique of this delimitation, see Cassese, *supra* note 38, at 467–68. Cassese observes that the extension does not apply to wars of liberation conducted by peoples or minorities except where the regimes against which a struggle is waged are colonial or racist, or in case of foreign occupation.

[57] For a detailed discussion, see 1969 Report, *supra* note 17; and 1970 Report, *supra* note 29.

[58] Internationalized internal armed conflicts will not be considered in this Note. *See generally* Schindler, *International Humanitarian Law and Internationalized Internal Armed Conflicts,* INT'L REV. RED CROSS, No. 230, Sept.–Oct. 1982, at 255.

[59] Draper, *Humanitarian Law, supra* note 1, at 202.

internal conflicts, it is unlikely that many states involved in internal conflicts will be prepared to acknowledge it. Consequently, the prospects for the formal application of the Protocol are poor. Given the frequency and cruelty of noninternational armed conflicts, it is most unfortunate that the threshold of the applicability of Protocol II was raised. It would have been far better if the normative progress made by Protocol II had been accompanied by the lower threshold of applicability under common Article 3, but this was not politically feasible since internal conflicts are viewed by states as the most sensitive ones. Witness the frequent refusal by governments to acknowledge even the applicability of common Article 3. In certain situations, however, the ICRC might be able to persuade some states to refer to the norms contained in Protocol II as agreed standards, without insisting on recognition of the formal applicability of the Protocol.

Derogations

If the observance and implementation of humanitarian law has been plagued by claims of states that the law was inapplicable because of the *sui generis* nature of the circumstances of a particular case, human rights instruments have had their share of difficulties, too. One problem has been the disappointingly low number of states that have ratified some of the principal human rights instruments or acceded to them. Another has been the unfortunate politicization of many United Nations organs involved in the supervision of international human rights.[60] But one of the principal difficulties has turned on the derogation provisions of the Political Covenant, contained in its Article 4. Although the complex question of derogations will not be considered in any detail in the present Note,[61] a few observations on the substantive scope of the "right of derogation" (to distinguish from procedural conditions and safeguards) are necessary.

First, it may be observed that while war or armed conflicts are not explicitly mentioned in Article 4(1) of the Political Covenant, this omission resulted from the consideration that the Covenant should not envisage the possibility of war, even by implication.[62] Nonetheless, it was recognized that war is one of the most "dramatic" public emergencies[63] and might be invoked as a reason for derogations under Article 4. It is not surprising that derogation clauses have proved to be a fertile ground for imaginative justifications by states for the denial of human rights. A recent and important study conducted by Nicole Questiaux[64] groups "deviations" from a "reference model" of nonabusive

[60] *See, e.g.*, Franck & Fairley, *Procedural Due Process in Human Rights Fact-Finding by International Agencies*, 74 AJIL 308 (1980).

[61] *See generally* Buergenthal, *supra* note 33, at 72; Higgins, *Derogations under Human Rights Treaties*, 48 BRIT. Y.B. INT'L L. 281 (1976–77); Hartman, *Derogation from Human Rights Treaties in Public Emergencies*, 22 HARV. INT'L L.J. 1 (1981); Green, *Derogation of Human Rights in Emergency Situations*, 16 CAN. Y.B. INT'L L. 92 (1978).

[62] 1969 Report, *supra* note 17, at 13; and 1970 Report, *supra* note 29, at 90–91.

[63] Buergenthal, *supra* note 33, at 79.

[64] Questiaux, Study of the Implications for Human Rights of Recent Developments Concerning Situations Known as States of Siege or Emergency, UN Doc. E/CN.4/Sub.2/1982/15, at 26–32 (1982).

derogations into several categories, including: (1) states of emergency not notified to other parties to an international instrument; (2) de facto states of emergency, where there is no proclamation or termination of a state of emergency, or where the state of emergency subsists after it has been officially proclaimed and then terminated; (3) permanent states of emergency, where the institution of the state of emergency, with or without proclamation, is perpetuated either as a result of de facto systematic extension or because the constitution has not provided any time limit a priori.

In a number of recent decisions, the Human Rights Committee established under Article 28 of the Political Covenant has refused to accept certain abuses by states of the practice of derogations.[65] Such decisions are important, but given the limited number of states that have accepted the Optional Protocol to that Covenant, their influence is likely to be limited.

How far can states go in derogating, on grounds of public emergency, from international human rights? As regards parties to the Political Covenant, the list of nonderogable rights is clearly stated in Article 4 of that Covenant. But any scrutiny of that list must reveal its inadequacy. For instance, there is no prohibition of arbitrary deportations, even on a massive scale (such measures are prohibited by Article 49 of Geneva Convention IV). On the other hand, the prohibition of imprisonment merely on the ground of inability to fulfill a contractual obligation, stated in Article 11 of the Political Covenant, is not of particular importance in times of emergency.

And what about derogations by states that have not become parties to the Political Covenant? It can hardly be argued that the enumeration contained in Article 4 of that Covenant is to be regarded, *per se,* as binding *erga omnes.* It is significant that the European Convention for the Protection of Human Rights and Fundamental Freedoms[66] and the American Convention on Human Rights[67] contain *different* lists of nonderogable rights. It must also be noted that the enumeration of customary human rights in the draft *Restatement*[68] is different from that given in Article 4. Some of the nonderogable rights under the latter article, such as those stated in Articles 11 and 16 of the Political Covenant, are not even mentioned in the draft *Restatement.* It may thus be argued that the enumeration given in Article 4 is to be considered only as a treaty provision. States that are not parties to the Covenant may not derogate from human rights that are categorical or absolute[69] (their deter-

[65] *See, e.g.,* Views of the Human Rights Committee under article 5(4) of the Optional Protocol concerning Communication No. R.8/34, Report of the Human Rights Committee, 36 UN GAOR Supp. (No. 40) at 130, 132–33, UN Doc. A/36/40 (1981); REV. INT'L COMM'N JURISTS, No. 28, June 1982, at 46–48.

[66] Art. 15, *reprinted in* BASIC DOCUMENTS ON HUMAN RIGHTS 242 (2d ed. I. Brownlie 1981).

[67] Art. 27, *reprinted in id.* at 391, 9 ILM 673 (1970).

[68] *See* text accompanying note 20 *supra.*

[69] Apart from the proposition that states may not derogate from norms that have attained the status of *jus cogens,* Sohn suggests that derogations can only be made to the extent strictly required by the exigencies of the situation, in conformity with a state's obligations under international law, and not in violation of the prohibition of discrimination solely on the ground of race, color, sex, language, religion, or social origin. He also suggests that "some human rights cannot be suspended at all, as several international instruments specify that there can be no derogations" from certain

mination *in concreto* is difficult). Neither can derogations be made that are in conflict with other international obligations of the derogating state or are clearly excessive or arbitrary. This still leaves a large and fertile field for violations of human rights.

V. Concluding Observations

Scholars have assumed that in conflict situations at least, either "human rights" or "humanitarian rights" will apply, not that neither will apply. Draper has thus written that if armed conflict breaks out, the regime of human rights "is there waiting in the background . . . to take over once the conflict abates" and that "a different and exceptional regime, namely that of the law of war, a lower level of the human rights regime but part of it, comes into play as a series of derogations made necessary . . . by the conflict situation."[70] Draper assumes that the regime of the law of war "descends when that of the normal one of human rights lifts in time of armed conflict (international or internal)."[71] Unfortunately, this is not always the case in reality. In many cases of armed conflict, states derogate from peacetime human rights through a number of techniques without recognizing the applicability not only of humanitarian law as a whole, but even of common Article 3. For reasons already explained, the prospects for the application of Protocol II are even worse.

MacBride argues:

> [W]hen a Government wishes to avoid its obligations under the normal provisions of the Law of Human Rights, it will have to take formally the stand that there exists "a public state of emergency threatening the life of the nation": where a Government takes this stand it becomes difficult for it to argue that the Geneva Conventions do not apply either in full or to the limited extent of Article 3.[72]

But difficult or not, states have taken this stand. They have been aided by the fact that humanitarian law and human rights law have not been tightly woven

---

basic human rights. Sohn, *Fundamental Guarantees: Human Rights,* in PROCEEDINGS OF THE SEMINARIO INTERAMERICANO SOBRE SEGURIDAD DEL ESTADO, DERECHOS HUMANOS Y DERECHO HUMANITARIO (Inter-American Institute of Human Rights) (forthcoming). Mme. Questiaux has argued:

> [E]ach State is bound only by the instruments that it has ratified. But the idea of a basic minimum, from which no derogation is possible, is present in a sufficient number of instruments to justify our approaching the matter by reference to a general principle of law recognized in practice by the international community, which could, moreover, regard it as a peremptory norm of international law within the meaning of article 53 of the 1969 Vienna Convention on the Law of Treaties. . . .

Questiaux, *supra* note 64, at 19 (footnote omitted).

See also Hartman, *supra* note 61, at 12 (who suggests that Article 4 does not "codify any customary rule"); Higgins, *supra* note 61, at 282 (who points out that "neither the wording of the various human rights instruments nor the practice thereunder leads to the view that all human rights are *jus cogens*").

[70] Draper, *Relationship, supra* note 1, at 198. [71] *Ibid.*

[72] MacBride, *Human Rights in Armed Conflicts,* 9 REV. DROIT PÉNAL MILITAIRE & DROIT DE LA GUERRE 373, 383 (1970).

into each other. Even states not bent on evading their obligation to observe human rights can plausibly argue that there may arise public emergencies that justify derogations from human rights, but since armed conflict is not involved, do not call common Article 3 into play. The combined effect of derogations from the normally applicable human rights and of the inapplicability of humanitarian law results in denial of elementary protections to denizens of states involved in internal conflicts. The same result occurs when, as unfortunately often happens, states either deny altogether the armed character of internal conflicts or claim that the low level of violence does not reach the threshold required for the applicability of humanitarian instruments. In short, it must be acknowledged that there is a legal uncertainty, or perhaps even a lacuna, in the law.

The complexity of various conflicts and the difficulty involved in determining to which category they belong (*e.g.*, international conflicts, internationalized internal conflicts, internal conflicts of an armed character, civil strife not accompanied by large-scale resort to armed force) and the fact that the applicability of certain norms may depend on the characterization of the conflict make this gap particularly dangerous. It is thus necessary to recognize that an irreducible core of human rights should apply, at a minimum, in this twilight zone.

The need to address the problems arising in that zone has recently been recognized in quite a different area: political risk insurance. The Overseas Private Investment Corporation (OPIC), which in the past has been insuring U.S. investors abroad against certain types of losses caused by war, revolution, and insurrection,[73] now offers protection against "an act of civil strife, terrorism or sabotage," which is defined as a violent act "undertaken by an individual or group with the primary intent of achieving a political objective."[74] This particular coverage will thus be available in a situation of civil strife, *i.e.*, a conflict falling short of revolution or insurrection.

Baxter has argued that the *core* of humanitarian law should be the same for all types of large-scale politically motivated violence.[75] The Universal Declaration might not be well suited to serve such a purpose. Even if no account is taken of its wholesale rejection by some scholars as an instrument applicable

[73] T. MERON, INVESTMENT INSURANCE IN INTERNATIONAL LAW 75 (1976).

[74] Civil Strife Addendum to Section 1.07 of OPIC contract of insurance (No. 12-70 Rev.), supplied by OPIC. *See also* OVERSEAS PRIVATE INVESTMENT CORP. TOPICS, Spring 1983, at 4.

[75] *See* Baxter, *supra* note 5, at 5, 7. For suggestions regarding formulation of core principles of humanitarian law, see M. VEUTHEY, *supra* note 22, at 373–78.

It may be noted that in 1975 the President of the Swiss Red Cross proposed that a declaration be drawn up "setting out in a condensed form the fundamental rules of humanitarian law, and rendering the lofty ideas underlying humanitarian law clearly discernible and easily understandable." INT'L REV. RED CROSS, No. 205, July–August 1978, at 247. A draft of such "fundamental rules of humanitarian law applicable in armed conflicts" was prepared in 1977 at the San Remo Institute of Humanitarian Law by a working group composed of experts from the ICRC, the League of the Red Cross Societies, and National Red Cross Societies. These rules "state in a condensed form the very essence of international humanitarian law applicable in armed conflicts." *Ibid.* The purpose of the text, which consists of seven rules, was to facilitate the dissemination of international humanitarian law. For the rules, see *id.* at 248–49.

in time of war,[76] its Article 29(2) opens the door to limiting the protections extended by the Declaration.[77] It can also be argued that some provisions of the Universal Declaration are not suitable for application in time of conflict.

To view the nonderogable provisions of the Political Covenant as the principal irreducible core of human rights applicable at all times gives rise to several problems. Leaving aside the difficulties concerning the protection of the right to life in time of armed conflict,[78] the unfortunate fact remains that the parties to the Political Covenant comprise only about half of the members of the United Nations. Moreover, there is no consensus that all of the nonderogable rights have already attained the status of categorical rules of customary law and as such, are binding *erga omnes* even in public emergencies. It is also distressing to note that the list of nonderogable rights under the Political Covenant is quite limited and appears to be inadequate to encompass all of the provisions that should be regarded as belonging to an irreducible core of human rights that must be applied at a minimum at all times.

In recent years there has been a proliferation of human rights instruments, not all of them necessary and carefully thought out. It would nevertheless appear that the international community needs a short, simple, and modest instrument to state an irreducible and nonderogable core of human rights that must be applied at a minimum in situations of internal strife and violence (even of low intensity) that are akin to armed conflicts, even though the government concerned contests the armed character of the conflict. The delin-

[76] *See, e.g.*, Meyrowitz, *supra* note 1, at 1081–84.

[77] 1969 Report, *supra* note 17, at 12. Article 29(2) of the Universal Declaration reads as follows:

> In the exercise of his rights and freedoms, everyone shall be subject only to such limitations as are determined by law solely for the purpose of securing due recognition and respect for the rights and freedoms of others and of meeting the just requirements of morality, public order and the general welfare in a democratic society.

[78] As regards the right to life, both the humanitarian instruments and the Political Covenant attempt to regulate the conditions under which capital punishment may be imposed, but neither provides an absolute guaranty of the right to life. In the context of retribution, the right to life is nonderogable under the Political Covenant. As regards humanitarian instruments, provisions relevant to the right to life in international armed conflicts are contained in Articles 100–101 of Geneva Convention III and Articles 68 and 75 of Geneva Convention IV. As regards protection of the right to life in international armed conflicts by Article 6 of the Political Covenant, a UN study suggests that the text of Article 6,

> corroborated by its legislative history, demonstrates that article 6 . . . would not guarantee the right to life as an absolute right without exceptions. . . . [T]o the extent that in present international law "lawful acts of war" are recognized, such lawful acts are deemed not to be prohibited by article 6 . . . if they do not violate internationally recognized laws and customs of war.

1970 Report, *supra* note 29, at 104; *see also id.* at 98–101; 37 UN GAOR Supp. (No. 40) at 93, UN Doc. A/37/40 (1982) (general comments of the Human Rights Committee). Death resulting from "lawful acts of armed conflict" might thus not be considered as arbitrary under Article 6 of the Political Covenant.

As regards protection of the right to life in armed conflicts not of an international character, which is qualified and not absolute, see common Article 3(1)(a) and 3(1)(d) of the four Geneva Conventions. *See also* Dinstein, *The Right to Life, Physical Integrity, and Liberty*, in THE INTERNATIONAL BILL OF RIGHTS, *supra* note 33, at 114, 120.

eation of the situations to which such an instrument would apply is, of course, most difficult. Justified as this may be, it might still be premature to reopen the entire question of derogations in normal (peacelike) emergencies because of the well-known reluctance of states to accept additional restrictions of their sovereignty in this minefield of internal conflicts. Despite a number of encouraging developments suggesting a certain readiness of states to tackle the question of derogations,[79] this might have to be left for later action. The now proposed instrument would therefore attempt to cover situations analogous to those of armed conflict, but not "normal" emergencies. The object of this Note is not to suggest a possible draft of such an instrument, but rather to serve as a catalyst for thought and action, in short to start a process. On the other hand, one may take the view that since states will, in any event, resist additional restrictions on their freedom of action, an attempt should be made from the outset to formulate a statement of nonderogable rights applicable, at a minimum, to all situations.

Some might argue that a solution could be found in better implementation of the existing law, rather than in the adoption of new instruments. But attainment of an effective system to implement the existing law is not probable in the near future. Neither would it help to remedy the weakness inherent in the quantity and quality of the applicable norms.

In working for a new instrument, the international community could build on the principle, already established, that no derogations from humanitarian instruments are permitted. Since all states have agreed to this principle with regard to armed internal conflicts, they should be able to take an additional step and adopt the same principle in an instrument governing human rights in analogous situations. Such an instrument—permitting neither derogations nor limitations—should state rights additional to those few mentioned in the nonderogable provisions of the Political Covenant. The elaboration and adoption of such an instrument, preferably, at least as a first step, in the form of

[79] The Council of Europe has recently adopted the text of Protocol No. 6 to the European Convention, concerning the abolition of the death penalty. Council of Europe Doc. H (83) 3 (1983). Under Articles 1 and 2, the death penalty shall be abolished, except that states may make provision in their laws for the death penalty in respect of acts committed in time of war or of imminent threat of war. "[O]ther public emergency threatening the life of the nation" is thus excluded. And Article 3 provides that "[n]o derogation from the provisions of this Protocol shall be made under Article 15 of the Convention."

A draft resolution proposed in the UN Human Rights Commission by Canada, Peru, and Senegal, which follows upon the Questiaux report, requests that the ECOSOC:

> authorize the Sub-Commission to appoint one of its members to undertake a closer study of the advisability of strengthening and extending the inalienability of the rights enumerated in article 4, paragraph 2 of the International Covenant on Civil and Political Rights, with due consideration being given to national legislations as well as to relevant international and regional conventions and to submit the results of this study to the Commission at its fortieth session.

UN Doc. E/CN.4/1983/L.29 (1983).

Unfortunately, this version was greatly weakened in the revised draft resolution, UN Doc. E/CN.4/1983/L.29/Rev.1 (1983), which was adopted on Feb. 22, 1983 (as Res. 1983/18), UN Doc. E/CN.4/1983/L.10/Add.2, at 6 (1983).

a solemn declaration,[80] which would not require formal accession or ratification by states, should be a priority concern of the international community.

The choice of the competent organ would pose additional problems. Should such a task be undertaken by the ICRC or by the United Nations? We have seen that the fundamental idea of humanity is shared by both human rights and humanitarian law. The subject resides in an area where these two systems meet and mesh. The initiative for action can therefore start from either perspective, but the expertise, the objectivity, and the apolitical character of the ICRC, taken together with the humanitarian law principle of nonderogation, are important arguments in favor of that body.

One day, perhaps, such a declaration could become a basis for Geneva Protocol III, or another international agreement. But even a declaration would strengthen the ICRC, which, without a precise legal mandate and without a clear articulation of international standards, has already been performing the important task of visiting detainees in situations of internal strife.[81] It would be an important addition to the corpus of international human rights.

THEODOR MERON*

CORRESPONDENCE

The *American Journal of International Law* welcomes short communications from its readers. It reserves the right to determine which letters shall be published and to edit any letters printed.

TO THE EDITORS-IN-CHIEF:

March 22, 1983

I am writing you in connection with Mr. John Norton Moore's Editorial Comment, *The Inter-American System Snarls in Falklands War* (76 AJIL 830 (1982)).

Force shall not be used to settle disputes in international relations. No doubt. But oversimplifications are always dangerous.

[80] For the value of declarations, see UN Doc. A/36/245, Annex, at 3 (1981). *See generally* Schachter, *Alf Ross Memorial Lecture: The Crisis of Legitimation in the United Nations,* 50 NORDISK TIDSSKRIFT INT'L RET 3 (1981); and his *The Evolving International Law of Development,* 15 COLUM. J. TRANSNAT'L L. 1, 3–6 (1976).

[81] *E.g.,* in Argentina and Poland. *See* INT'L REV. RED CROSS, No. 230, Sept.–Oct. 1982, at 289, 299, 304. It should be observed that the four Geneva Conventions contain an identical article on the right of "initiative" of the ICRC. *See, e.g.,* Article 10 of Geneva Convention IV, which reads as follows:

> The provisions of the present Convention constitute no obstacle to the humanitarian activities which the International Committee of the Red Cross or any other impartial humanitarian organization may, subject to the consent of the Parties to the conflict concerned, undertake for the protection of civilian persons and for their relief.

* Professor of Law, New York University School of Law.

For example, R. Y. Jennings (in *The Acquisition of Territory in International Law,* at p. 72 (1963)), when considering the case where a state claims legal title to territory actually in the possession of another state, and proceeds to use force in order to *recover* its possession, states:

> If in fact its claim is justified, that is to say *if it does indeed have the legal title to the sovereignty,* then it would seem that this is *not* an employment of force contrary to the provisions of Article 2(4) of the Charter. It cannot be force used against the *territorial integrity* or political independence of another State because the actor State is merely occupying its own territory. The matter is one within its domestic jurisdiction [emphasis added].

The above paragraph serves to illustrate to what extent a violation of the UN Charter might not be as clear-cut as Mr. Moore seems to suggest.

In addition to this, the "use of force" did not start on April 2, 1982. The Argentine Government has argued that the April 2, 1982 reoccupation came "*after*" a British ultimatum threatening the use of force against Argentina unless it evacuated a group of Argentine workmen who had arrived as per the existing agreements at South Georgia Island for the sole purpose of dismantling a whaling station, after having visited the site twice before. In fact, during the second half of March 1982, the British Government sent the H.M.S. *Endurance* (and eventually a second ship) to evict the Argentines. At the least, a nuclear submarine was also sent to the area. The events of April 2 (in which the British suffered no casualties) were, therefore, not action but escalated reaction to a concrete British threat to "use force." The blame should, in view of the foregoing, be distributed in a different manner, and suggesting that resort to force on the part of Argentina was purely unilateral is adding fuel to the fire.

One cannot silence the fact that the Malvinas dispute became a matter of universal concern in the United Nations when in 1946, and in the face of Argentina's opposition based on its territorial claim, the United Kingdom included the islands among the cases under the *decolonization* process. Resolution 1514 (XV) (December 14, 1960) of the UN General Assembly states that "the continued existence of colonialism . . . *militates against the United Nations ideal of universal peace*" and solemnly proclaims "the necessity of bringing to a *speedy and unconditional end colonialism in all its forms and manifestations*" (emphasis added).

Colonialism is not only contrary to the purposes and principles of the UN Charter, but endangers *per se* the world's peace and security. There are UN resolutions which go to the length of stating that colonialism is both an *anachronism* and an *international crime* and thus render legitimate the struggles of peoples, like the Argentine, whose *national unity* and *territorial integrity* have been and are disrupted by alien domination. (See UN General Assembly Resolutions 2105 (XX) (December 20, 1965); 2189 (XXI) (December 13, 1966); 2326 (XXII) (December 16, 1967); 2465 (XXIII) (December 20, 1968); 2548 (XXIV) (December 11, 1969); 2708 (XXV) (December 14, 1970); 2878 (XXVI) (December 20, 1971); 2908 (XXVII) (November 2, 1972); 3163 (XXVIII) (December 14, 1973); 3328 (XXIV) (December 16, 1974); etc.)

A loose reference to "15 active island disputes" and "hundreds of [other] land and sea boundary disputes" (Moore, p. 830) does not overshadow the issue of *colonialism* or the different resolutions enacted by the UN General

Assembly (*i.e.,* 2065 (XX) (December 16, 1965); 3160 (XXVIII) (December 14, 1973); and 31/49 (December 1, 1976)) on this particular case. All of them urged Great Britain and Argentina to find a peaceful solution. Some expressed "grave concern" for the lack of "substantial progress."

The recent General Assembly Resolution 37/9 of November 9, 1982 restated the *incompatibility of the colonial situation on the islands with the UN ideal for peace.* This is the heart of the problem. This is what must be resolved. It furthermore requested (once again) negotiations between both countries on the "sovereign dispute." This time, the United States took a different side, much to the British Conservative Government's regret.

Resolution 502 (April 3, 1982) of the UN Security Council did *not* determine that the Argentine *reoccupation* of the islands was the "act of aggression" (Mr. Moore does). Had it not been a "*colonial dispute*" (evoking Article 7 of the UN Definition of Aggression (GA Res. 3314 of 1974), which excludes the struggle of peoples forcibly deprived of their independence or subject to "*colonial*" or *alien* domination from the meaning of "aggression"), the resolution might have done so under Article 39 of the Charter.

It ordered *both* parties to cease the hostilities. And both appear to have failed to comply. It did determine that there was a "breach of peace," without, curiously enough, stating explicitly which party was responsible for such breach.

One should ask to what extent the spirit, if not the very letter, of the UN Charter is violated when nations holding overseas *colonial* territories taken by force *refuse systematically to negotiate in good faith,* thus violating every single UN General Assembly resolution on the issue, as well as the Charter of the United Nations whose Article 2, paragraph 4 orders its members to settle their international disputes by peaceful means in such a manner that international peace and security, and *justice,* are not endangered (emphasis added).

It might also be worth remembering that Article 51 of the United Nations Charter, which prohibits states from taking justice into their own hands once the Security Council has intervened, was also a victim of the crisis.

Let us now turn to the principle of self-determination in the decolonization process, keeping in mind that, unfortunately, due to the recent events there is, now, one dead soldier (approximately) for each "kelper" (the "kelpers," very recently, have been made full British citizens).

As regards decolonization, Resolution 1514 (XV) of the United Nations General Assembly reaffirmed this principle in its Article 2, but with the specific qualification that it could not be applied to bring about a total or partial disruption of the national unity or territorial integrity of any given country (Article 6). Said caveat cannot be ignored.

Therefore, the principle of "self-determination" is an instrument of decolonization and, evidently, not a vehicle to perpetuate colonial situations that the overwhelming majority of the countries wish and have wished to see terminated.

The principle was aimed at protecting "peoples" (not populations), and this presupposes both geographic separation and ethnic individuality.

The inhabitants of the Malvinas by no yardstick recognized in international law can be characterized as a "people." They can, however, be called a population or a group of inhabitants.

It must be emphasized that Great Britain has had her own experience on this matter, which she obviously tries to dissimulate, but which must be divulged and taken into account. We refer to what happened in another of her colonial enclaves: Gibraltar. The British experience there is, in this connection, very instructive. In 1967, trying to "improve" her position, Great Britain produced a referendum in which the population of Gibraltar exercised its alleged right to "self-determination." The result (as expected) produced 12,138 votes in favor of the permanence of Gibraltar in association with the United Kingdom, and only 44 of all votes cast revealed the wish to be a part of Spain. In the face of the "success" obtained, the British promptly presented the results to the United Nations. There were, notwithstanding, no surprises. The "Committee of 24" (created in 1963 by the General Assembly of the United Nations to implement the decolonization resolution (1514 (XV)), rejected the British claim, stating that the referendum lacked validity because, as in the case of our Malvinas Islands, "imported" population that has replaced a previous one could not give rise to the right of self-determination.

Immediately thereafter, the General Assembly, by Resolution 2353 (XXII) (December 19, 1967), found the referendum contrary to the goals of decolonization and invited the parties to continue negotiations.

The process of decolonization refers not only to the question of people, but also includes cases having to do with territories illegally occupied by colonial powers (irrespective of whether or not there is a local population). The territorial integrity of each country must always be respected. The resolutions of the United Nations General Assembly have expressed, both in the case of Gibraltar (Resolution 2070 (XX) (December 16, 1965)) and in the case of the Malvinas Islands (Resolution 2065 (XX) and Resolution 3160 (XXVIII)) that what must be taken into account is the "interests" of the population, and they have rejected the use of the expression espoused by the British, which referred to the "wishes" of the local population. This, certainly, implies a significant difference.

The interest of the inhabitants of the islands must be taken into account, with all justice and fairness, even though these inhabitants may not amount to a "people," strictly speaking. In doing so, however, one cannot forget the rights of the Argentine people, stripped once and again by force of their legitimate right to the islands.

Some time ago, Martin Luther King said: "For years I have heard the word 'wait.' This wait always meant never. It has been a tranquilizing thalidomide, relieving the emotional stress for a moment only to give birth to an ill-formed infant of frustration." His words seem ironically appropriate in connection with the South Atlantic conflict. (See *What manner of man* by Lerone Bennett, Jr., at p. 141 (2d ed. 1968)).

I would appreciate it if you could publish this letter in full in your Correspondence section. It might help in understanding the Latin American reaction. One-sided approaches, full of bias, do not help to resolve a difficult problem. All matters must be considered. Only then will a lasting peace be gained. Good faith and reason and not the point of a gun shall prevail.

EMILIO J. CÁRDENAS
Professor of Law, University of Buenos Aires

John Norton Moore replies:

Professor Emilio J. Cárdenas of the University of Buenos Aires has advanced a series of arguments seeking to justify the use of force by his Government in the recent attack on the Falkland Islands. The significance of these arguments for the framework of world order makes a response imperative.

In a world drifting dangerously toward anarchy, no principle is more important than that enshrined in Article 1 of the United Nations Charter that international disputes shall be settled by peaceful means and not by armed force. This principle applies not only to clearly recognized *de jure* international boundaries but to *de facto* boundaries of whatever kind, whether they are the subject of territorial disputes between states or are lines within divided nations or cease-fire lines. Failure to recognize *de facto* boundaries would remove normative constraints on use of force from many of the most critical flash points in international life. It would mean that the basic Charter structure regulating coercion is irrelevant to attacks involving divided-nation boundaries as in the Korean War,[1] cease-fire lines as in the Middle East, disputed territories as in the ongoing Iran-Iraq war, disputed borders as between the Soviet Union and China or overlapping Antarctic claims, the many contemporary island disputes, and over two hundred unresolved oceans boundaries.[2]

[1] *See, e.g.*, M. McDOUGAL & F. FELICIANO, LAW AND MINIMUM WORLD PUBLIC ORDER 221–22 (1961).

[2] Cárdenas refers to "[a] loose reference to '15 active island disputes' and 'hundreds of [other] land and sea boundary disputes.' . . ." A partial list, illustrating the extreme potential of boundary and territorial disputes for conflict, may be found in D. DOWNING, AN ATLAS OF TERRITORIAL AND BORDER DISPUTES (1980). A few well-known disputes include:

—overlapping claims on the Antarctic continent and island groups south of 60° latitude—such as the South Shetlands and South Orkneys (including disputes between Great Britain, Argentina and Chile; Argentina refused to accept the referral to the ICJ by Britain in 1955 of the overlapping Antarctic claims of Great Britain and Argentina);

—the Sino-Soviet border;

—the Shikotan and Hobomai Islands (disputed between the Soviet Union and Japan);

—the Danjo Islands and the Takeshima Rocks (disputed between Japan and South Korea);

—the Senkaku/Tiao Yu Tai Islands (disputed between China and Japan);

—the Cambodia-Vietnam border;

—the Paracel Islands (disputed between China and Vietnam);

—the Spratly Islands (disputed between China, Vietnam, Taiwan, and the Philippines);

—the Jammu and Kashmir dispute (between India and Pakistan);

—the Shatt-al-Arab dispute (the subject of an ongoing war between Iran and Iraq);

—the Ogaden region (the subject of a war between Ethiopia and Somalia);

—the Beagle Channel region—including the islands of Picton, Nueva, and Lennox (disputed between Chile and Argentina);

—the El Salvador-Honduras border—including several small islands in the Gulf of Fonseca;

—oceans delimitation concerning the Islands of Saint-Pierre and Miquelon (disputed between France and Canada);

—the maritime boundary between the Soviet Union and Norway;

—the Greece-Turkey Aegean boundary;

The principal reason why the Charter prohibition on the use of force as a means for settling disputes does and must apply in these cases is that any other answer would threaten conflict and destruction out of all proportion to any conceivable advance in "justice" from such wars. Contrary to Cárdenas's view, the United Nations has demonstrated clearly in the Korean War, the Arab-Israeli conflict, and again in the Falklands war that it fully understands the importance of this principle prohibiting the use of force as a means of settling disputes across *de facto* boundaries.

Professor Thomas Franck in a recent editorial arising from the Falklands war in this *Journal,*[3] distinguished for its clear articulation of the importance of the basic Charter principle against use of force for settlement of disputes, quotes Mlle. Edmonde Dever, the Belgian Ambassador to the United Nations, who said during the United Nations Falklands debate:

> If the use of force were to be rewarded, this would encourage any state with territorial ambitions to follow suit. Peace in the world would become even more precarious and many countries, no matter what group they belonged to, would feel threatened. The reaction of many small countries in the world to the Argentine invasion demonstrates, furthermore, that this danger has been understood.[4]

—the continuing division between China and Taiwan (of China?);

—the continuing division of Germany;

—the continuing division of Korea; and

—continuing cease-fire lines and *de facto* boundaries in the Arab-Israeli conflict.

Unfortunately for world order, there is nothing "loose" about the existence of these and many other boundary and territorial disputes and their potential for conflict. In this respect the introduction by David Downing to his atlas of territorial and border disputes is instructive:

> Border disputes provide an all too-convenient platform for the expression of international hostility, and waving the flag and waxing lyrical about the nation's sacred soil are time-honoured methods of silencing internal opposition. . . . But however invidious the role of governments, it cannot be denied that the very existence of ill-drawn borders has played a major role in the fomentation of all this century's major wars.

Id. at 8.

With respect to oceans boundary disputes, Dr. Robert D. Hodgson, the late Geographer of the Department of State, wrote in 1978:

> Over 70 maritime boundaries have been negotiated to date. More than 240 have either not undergone negotiation, are in the process of negotiation, and/or are disputed. Approximately one of five potential maritime limits has been agreed upon, although many of these delimitations, it should be noted, remain incomplete. . . .
>
> Seventy-three maritime boundary disputes have been presently identified. Many of these disputes remain latent and they may not change from the quiescent state until solutions are found. Moreover, over one-third—25 may be so categorized—involve overlapping claims to land territory. Due to this complication, the twenty-five should not be deemed to be maritime boundary disputes in the strictest sense even though the desire to expand control over ocean resources may underlie certain of these disputes. In contrast, others of these derive from prior, in many cases long-standing, disagreements over land boundaries, sovereignty over islands or similar problems.

Hodgson, *International Oceans Boundary Disputes,* OCEANS POL'Y STUDY, No. 4, April 1978, at 37, 38.

[3] Franck, *Dulce et Decorum Est: The Strategic Role of Legal Principles in the Falklands War,* 77 AJIL 109 (1983).

[4] Ambassador Edmonde Dever, UN Doc. S/PV.2363, at 48–50 (1982).

Similarly, Professor Farooq Hassan writes with equal clarity in a recent legal analysis of the Falkland Islands dispute:

> [I]f negotiations fail to solve disputes such as the Falklands crisis, one party's aggression on grounds of self-defense cannot be justified, even if based on historical claims. While the speedy realization of justice in the international arena is difficult to accomplish, allowing the use of force to accomplish that end would, in the process, destroy whatever peaceful options now exist.
>
> . . . [A]rmed solutions of disputes are illegal under contemporary international law as well as under the law of the United Nations.
>
> The Falklands crisis, though widespread armed conflict between the super powers was avoided, illustrates the potential dangers of even limited aggression prior to negotiations. Both the United States and the Soviet Union were involved peripherally on opposite sides and could have become thoroughly enmeshed in the military operations. Regardless of how limited a conflict may appear initially, it may threaten world peace unless the conflict is resolved at the bargaining table. These dangers alone warrant acceptance of an international law prohibiting the use of aggression in territorial disputes.[5]

In sole support of his argument that the Charter prohibition on use of force does not apply to territorial disputes, Professor Cárdenas quotes from the book by Professor Jennings on *The Acquisition of Territory in International Law.* Sadly, he does not give us Jennings's full thoughts on the matter, perhaps understandably since those thoughts seem inconsistent with Cárdenas's assertion of lawful Argentinian action in the Falklands attack. Thus, Jennings adds to the quote cited by Cárdenas:

> But on the other hand all this is only true if the claim to possess title is indeed well founded. And since the establishment of a valid title is, as is easily appreciated from the cases, by no means a simple matter, it is not to be expected that a particular issue of title will usually be so very clear as to justify forcible action by a claimant State on the mere strength of its own case. . . .
>
> . . . [W]here force is alleged to be justified on the ground of an existing legal title, and can on the nature of things only be justified on that ground, there must be a strong presumption against the validity of such an alleged title where the claimant is not willing to have that claim properly determined in a Court of law. And it is submitted that the political organs of the United Nations, if faced with the question whether the use of force was or was not lawful, would be justified in acting on the basis of a presumption that it is unlawful as long as the unwillingness to submit the case to the Court is present. Such a presumption would go some way towards mitigating what is potentially a highly dangerous situation, where a right of recaption may be alleged, yet coupled with the right to maintain a refusal to have the existence of the right challenged in a court of law.[6]

[5] Hassan, *The Sovereignty Dispute over the Falkland Islands,* 23 VA. J. INT'L L. 53, 64–65 (1982).

[6] R. JENNINGS, THE ACQUISITION OF TERRITORY IN INTERNATIONAL LAW 72–73 (1963). Professor Jennings also adds:

> In actual cases the issue is seldom as simple as the case which rests upon strictly legal arguments relative to the existence in law of a present title. Almost invariably the case will

As Cárdenas should know, Great Britain has accepted the compulsory jurisdiction of the International Court of Justice. Argentina, however, not only refuses to submit the Falklands dispute to impartial third-party settlement but has—not incidentally—repudiated a legally binding arbitration by a distinguished arbitral panel that found against it in the Beagle Channel dispute with Chile. Moreover, Jennings's precondition of a "very clear" legal title is by no means met in the Falkland Islands dispute where Argentina relies on a historical claim more than 150 years old and Great Britain relies not only on such a historical claim but also on the last 150 years of effective occupation and a population that overwhelmingly prefers association with Britain.

Most importantly, however, Jennings, writing in the context of a book on territorial acquisition, is simply wrong in implying that any degree of clarity as to legal title overcomes the Charter principle that prohibits the use of force between nations for settlement of disputes. The Charter distinction is between armed attack and defense, not between *de jure* and *de facto* settings. Indeed, the distinction made by Jennings that it might be lawful to use force to take disputed territory, contingent on willingness to submit to third-party dispute settlement, seems more in keeping with the procedural constraints of Articles 12 and 13 of the League Covenant than the substantive constraints on use of force of Articles 1 and 2 of the United Nations Charter. Would Cárdenas accept, pursuant to the Jennings distinction, that Chile has a right militarily to occupy the islands disputed with Argentina in the region of the Beagle Channel? After all, a binding arbitral award by a distinguished arbitral panel would seem "very clear" evidence of title, unlike the Falklands dispute.

Even if Cárdenas were to make his case, reversing 30 years of Charter interpretation and potentially ushering in a new era of global instability, Argentina would still be in clear violation of a binding Security Council resolution (Resolution 502) by failing to withdraw immediately from the Falkland Islands as required by that resolution. And it is notable that General Assembly resolutions on the Falklands call for a "peaceful solution" of the dispute.[7] Moreover, even under his own view, Cárdenas must establish a "very clear" legal title for Argentina, which, as has been noted above, is hardly the case. The only thing clear about title to the Falklands (if title rather than self-determination is the relevant issue) is that title is clearly in dispute.

A second issue raised by Cárdenas also deserves comment. That is the argument that the setting is "colonial," justifying the Argentinian invasion. Strangely, Cárdenas seems not to recognize the paradox presented by his own letter where he states that "in the face of Argentina's opposition based on the territorial claim, the United Kingdom included the islands among the cases under the *decolonization* process." As this quotation suggests, the reality of the Falklands dispute is a territorial dispute between Great Britain and Argentina, complicated by a population that rejects association with Argentina. Great Britain has recognized and indeed led in applying the decolonization process

---

be mixed, including legal arguments to establish a present title, and political arguments, *i.e.* arguments the true tendency of which is that even if the present title is in another it ought to be shifted to the claimant. Now it is perfectly clear that the latter class of argument, be it never so strong and persuasive, cannot, if standing alone, justify in law the use of force to repossess. On the contrary, it is tantamount to an admission that the present legal title is elsewhere; and if that is the position an attempt at self-help must be forbidden by the law.

Id. at 73.

[7] *See* UNGA Res. A/2065 (XX) (1965), and A/3160 (XXVIII) (1973).

to the Falklands. For Britain, however, that means recognizing the self-determination rights of the people of the Falklands. For Argentina it has meant territorial incorporation of the Falklands regardless of the wishes of the people. The issue, then, is not colonization versus decolonization; it is between contending visions of decolonization (if "decolonization" should be the relevant framework for appraisal at all).

In self-determination theory there is sometimes a conflict between the wishes of the people of an entity and the right of a larger population to maintain the territorial integrity of a larger entity. As the recent United Nations action in the decolonization of Belize demonstrates, in settings of ambiguity concerning territorial disputes, self-determination of peoples may prevail over claims to territorial unity.[8] Because the United Nations is well aware of this problem in the Falkland Islands case, it has not taken the position on the merits, crucial to Cárdenas's position, that the process of decolonization of the Falklands should lead to association with Argentina.[9] Rather, the process called for by the United Nations and accepted by Britain could as well lead to respect for the rights of the people of the Falklands to determine their own association and form of governance. In this setting any claim to resort to force to realize the unilateral Argentinian concept of "decolonization" is plain and simple national chauvinism.

Finally, it might be useful to summarize the setting in which Professor Cárdenas seeks to justify his Government's invasion of the Falklands. That setting includes:

—an unprovoked full-scale armed attack by Argentina against a lightly defended Falkland Island garrison in clear violation of Articles 1 and 2 of both the United Nations Charter and the Rio Treaty (the purported pretext of the South Georgia Island whaling station incident, even if not encouraged by Argentina as a pretext, is so minimal as to make a full-scale Argentinian invasion of the Falklands wholly disproportional);

—an attack against an entity that had been at least *de facto* separate from Argentina for over 150 years and whose population overwhelmingly rejects association with Argentina in the setting of a territorial and self-determination dispute that to many reasonable observers provides a stronger case for the British and Falkland Islanders' vision of decolonization and self-determination than for the Argentinian;

—an initiation and continuing acceptance by Great Britain of the United Nations process of decolonization;

—a consistent pattern of refusal by Argentina to accept impartial third-party resolution of the underlying dispute and related Antarctic disputes, and a recent repudiation by Argentina of a binding arbitration finding against it in the Beagle Channel dispute with Chile; and

—a blatant disregard by Argentina of a series of General Assembly resolutions on the Falklands calling for a "peaceful solution" and of a bind-

[8] *See* the excellent note by Maguire, *The Decolonization of Belize: Self-Determination v. Territorial Integrity,* 22 VA. J. INT'L L. 849 (1982).

[9] It might also be noted that the case of Gibraltar, which Professor Cárdenas relies on for support, seems to undercut rather than support his case. For in the Falklands case, unlike that of Gibraltar, the United Nations has not made a determination that the local population should be ignored. Rather, it has expressly called for the need to bear in mind "the interests of the population of the Falkland Islands" in the decolonization process. *See* the resolutions cited in note 7 *supra.*

ing Security Council resolution calling for immediate Argentinian withdrawal from the Falklands.

In this context the effort to justify the use of force by Argentina on the basis of an incomplete Jennings quote is simply grotesque. More importantly, it damages a Charter structure which, however fragile, may be the last hope of mankind. Professor Cárdenas is surely correct, however, that "[o]nesided approaches, full of bias, do not help to resolve a difficult problem."

TO THE EDITORS-IN-CHIEF:

April 11, 1983

Since publication of my article *Recognition of Governments Should Not Be Abolished* in the January issue, a number of scholars, Oliver J. Lissitzyn of Columbia University and Roger S. Clark of Rutgers University being the first, have brought to my attention a change of recognition policy announced by the British Government in mid-1980.

Though the announcement is not entirely clear, it appears to signal adoption of an Estrada Doctrine-like policy of indicating acknowledgment of a new regime's claim to rule by maintaining formal diplomatic relations without making any formal announcement of recognition. The policy and its possible implications for British courts are discussed in an article by Colin Warbrick in volume 30 of the *International and Comparative Law Quarterly* (July 1981), beginning at page 568.

While this information does not affect my argument in any way, it does suggest that the trend toward de-emphasizing recognition of governments is stronger than I indicated.

M. J. PETERSON
Harvard University

THE FRANCIS DEÁK PRIZE

The Board of Editors of the *American Journal of International Law* announces with great pleasure that the Francis Deák Prize for 1983 has been awarded to Ted L. Stein for his *Contempt, Crisis, and the Court: The World Court and the Hostage Rescue Attempt,* which appeared in the July 1982 issue at page 499. As our readers are doubtless aware, the prize is given in honor of the late Francis Deák and recognizes an especially meritorious article in the *Journal* by one of its younger authors.

The Board of Editors congratulates Professor Stein and again expresses its appreciation to Mr. Philip Cohen, President of Oceana Publications, Inc., through whose generosity an award is made to each recipient of the prize.

CONTEMPORARY PRACTICE OF THE UNITED STATES RELATING TO INTERNATIONAL LAW

MARIAN NASH LEICH*

The material in this section is arranged according to the system employed in the annual *Digest of United States Practice in International Law,* published by the Department of State.

JURISDICTION

(U.S. *Digest,* Ch. 6, §3)

Transfer of Offenders and Administration of Foreign Penal Sentences

On March 21, 1983, the American Consul General at Strasbourg, Robert O. Homme, acting on instruction and under a full power signed by Secretary of State George P. Shultz on March 9, 1983, signed the Council of Europe Convention on the Transfer of Sentenced Persons. The Convention, a multilateral treaty providing for the transfer of a foreign prisoner from the country in which he has been sentenced to his home country, was signed at the same time by Austria, Belgium, Denmark, the Federal Republic of Germany, Greece, Luxembourg, the Netherlands, Portugal, Sweden, Switzerland, and Canada.

The Convention is basically similar to existing bilateral treaties between the United States and other countries. It requires triple consent for a transfer to be effected: that of the sentencing state (the state in which the sentence was imposed), of the administering state (the state to which the sentenced person may be, or has been, transferred in order to serve his sentence), and of the sentenced person, or of his legal representative if one of the two states considers it necessary in view of the age or physical or mental condition of the sentenced person. Other conditions for transfer are: (1) that the sentenced person be a national of the administering state; (2) that the judgment (decision or order of a court imposing a sentence) be final; (3) that at the time of the transfer request, the sentenced person still have at least 6 months of the sentence to serve or the sentence be indeterminate; and (4) that the acts or omissions on account of which the sentence was imposed constitute a criminal offense under the law of the administering state or would constitute a criminal offense if committed on its territory. (Article 3, "Conditions for transfer.")

A sentenced person may express interest in being transferred under the Convention to the sentencing state or to the administering state, either of which may request transfer (Article 2, "General principles"). Procedures connected with effecting transfer are set out in Articles 4, "Obligation to furnish information"; 5, "Requests and replies"; 6, "Supporting documents"; and 7, "Consent and its verification."

* Office of the Legal Adviser, Department of State.

Under Article 8, "Effect of transfer for sentencing State," taking of the sentenced person into charge by the administering state's authorities has the effect of suspending enforcement of the sentence in the sentencing state, which may no longer enforce the sentence if the administering state considers enforcement to have been completed. Under Article 9, "Effect of transfer for administering State," the latter must continue enforcement of the sentence immediately or through a court or administrative order, under the conditions set out in Article 10, "Continued enforcement"; or it may convert the sentence through a judicial or administrative procedure into its own decision, and thus substitute for the sanction imposed in the sentencing state a sanction prescribed by its law for the same offense, subject, however, to the conditions set out in Article 11, "Conversion of sentence." Under Article 9, also, if a state cannot under its national law avail itself of one of the alternate procedures specified above to enforce measures imposed in another state party on sentenced persons held not criminally responsible for commission of the offense for reasons of mental condition, and the state is prepared to receive such persons for further treatment, the state may indicate by a declaration addressed to the Secretary General of the Council of Europe the procedures it will follow in such cases.

Articles 10 and 11 read as follows:

Article 10

Continued enforcement

1. In the case of continued enforcement, the administering State shall be bound by the legal nature and duration of the sentence as determined by the sentencing State.

2. If, however, this sentence is by its nature or duration incompatible with the law of the administering State, or its law so requires, that State may, by a court or administrative order, adapt the sanction to the punishment or measure prescribed by its own law for a similar offence. As to its nature, the punishment or measure shall, as far as possible, correspond with that imposed by the sentence to be enforced. It shall not aggravate, by its nature or duration, the sanction imposed in the sentencing State, nor exceed the maximum prescribed by the law of the administering State.

Article 11

Conversion of sentence

1. In the case of conversion of sentence, the procedures provided for by the law of the administering State apply. When converting the sentence, the competent authority:

a. shall be bound by the findings as to the facts insofar as they appear explicitly or implicitly from the judgment imposed in the sentencing State;

b. may not convert a sanction involving deprivation of liberty to a pecuniary sanction;

c. shall deduct the full period of deprivation of liberty served by the sentenced person; and

> *d.* shall not aggravate the penal position of the sentenced person, and shall not be bound by any minimum which the law of the administering State may provide for the offence or offences committed.
>
> 2. If the conversion procedure takes place after the transfer of the sentenced person, the administering State shall keep that person in custody or otherwise ensure his presence in the administering State pending the outcome of that procedure.

Each party may grant pardon, amnesty, or commutation of the sentence in accordance with its constitution or other laws (Article 12), but the sentencing state alone shall have the right to decide upon any application for review of the judgment (Article 13). The administering state must terminate enforcement of the sentence as soon as the sentencing state informs it of any decision or measure as a result of which the sentence ceases to be enforceable (Article 14). The administering state must provide information to the sentencing state concerning enforcement of the sentence: when it considers enforcement to have been completed; if the sentenced person has escaped from custody before enforcement of the sentence has been completed; or if the sentencing state requests a special report (Article 15). Under Article 21, the Convention applies to enforcement of sentences imposed either before or after its entry into force.

Provisions of a general administrative nature are set out in Articles 16, "Transit," and 17, "Language and costs."

Article 18 provides that the Convention shall be open for signature by member states of the Council of Europe and nonmember states that have participated in its elaboration (Canada and the United States). It enters into force upon the first day of the month following expiration of a 3-month period after the date upon which three member states of the Council of Europe have expressed their consent to be bound by the Convention (by instruments of ratification, acceptance, or approval, deposited with the Secretary General of the Council of Europe). Nonmember states may accede to the Convention upon invitation by the Committee of Ministers of the Council of Europe, after consultation with the contracting states, in accordance with the provisions of Article 19.

Article 22 governs the relationship between the Council of Europe Convention on the Transfer of Sentenced Persons and other conventions and agreements, as follows:

> 1. This Convention does not affect the rights and undertakings derived from extradition treaties and other treaties on international co-operation in criminal matters providing for the transfer of detained persons for purposes of confrontation or testimony.
>
> 2. If two or more Parties have already concluded an agreement or treaty on the transfer of sentenced persons or otherwise have established their relations in this matter, or should they in future do so, they shall be entitled to apply that agreement or treaty or to regulate those relations accordingly, in lieu of the present Convention.

3. The present Convention does not affect the right of States Party to the European Convention on the International Validity of Criminal Judgments to conclude bilateral or multilateral agreements with one another on matters dealt with in that Convention in order to supplement its provisions or facilitate the application of the principles embodied in it.

4. If a request for transfer falls within the scope of both the present Convention and the European Convention on the International Validity of Criminal Judgments or another agreement or treaty on the transfer of sentenced persons, the requesting State shall, when making the request, indicate on the basis of which instrument it is made.[1]

Law of the Sea

(U.S. *Digest,* Ch. 7, §1)

United States Oceans Policy

On March 10, 1983, President Reagan announced three decisions bearing upon United States oceans policy, two concerning freedom of navigation and overflight and the third relating to a 200-nautical-mile exclusive economic zone, which the President proclaimed the same day under Proclamation No. 5030.

The President noted that, while the deep seabed mining provisions of the UN Law of the Sea Convention[1] had led to his decision against United States signature (announced on July 9, 1982),[2] the Convention also contained provisions regarding traditional uses of the oceans that generally "confirm existing maritime law and practice and fairly balance the interests of all states." His decisions, the President said, would promote and protect United States oceans interests "in a manner consistent with those fair and balanced results in the Convention and [with] international law." Proclamation of the exclusive economic zone would provide the United States with resource control jurisdiction, including sovereign rights over mineral resources not on the continental shelf, out to 200 nautical miles, but would not change existing U.S. policies concerning the continental shelf, marine mammals, and fisheries.

The President stated, further, that he had elected not to assert United States jurisdiction over marine scientific research within the 200-nautical-mile

[1] Dept. of State Files, L/T. The Department envisages submission of the Convention in the near future to President Reagan for transmittal to the Senate for advice and consent to ratification.

[1] *Done* at Montego Bay, Jamaica, Dec. 10, 1982, UN Doc. A/CONF.62/122 and Corrs. 3 and 8 (1982), *reprinted in* 21 ILM 1261 (1982).

[2] For the announcement, see 18 WEEKLY COMP. PRES. DOC. 887 (July 12, 1982), DEPT. STATE BULL., No. 2065, Aug. 1982, at 71. The Convention had been adopted by the Third UN Conference on the Law of the Sea on April 30, 1982.

See also Law of the Sea and Oceans Policy, id., No. 2067, Oct. 1982, at 48 (statement by Ambassador James L. Malone, the President's Special Representative for the Third UN Conference on the Law of the Sea, before the House Committee on Foreign Affairs, Aug. 12, 1982). The statement reviews the results of the 11th session of the conference and explains why the United States was unable to accept the deep seabed mining provisions of the Convention and voted against its adoption. (The vote for adoption was 130 in favor (France), 4 against, and 17 abstentions (the Federal Republic of Germany, the United Kingdom). Israel, Turkey, and Venezuela also voted against adoption. Some of the 17 states abstaining on the vote subsequently signed the Convention.)

zone, but that the United States would nevertheless recognize the right of other coastal states to exercise a corresponding jurisdiction, if it were exercised "reasonably in a manner consistent with international law." Proclamation of the exclusive economic zone would also enable the United States to take limited additional steps to protect the marine environment. The President added that his policy decisions would not affect application of existing United States law concerning the high seas or existing authorities of any U.S. Government agency.

In conclusion, the President announced that the United States would continue to work with other countries to develop a regime for mining deep seabed minerals beyond national jurisdiction, free of "unnecessary political and economic restraints."[3] He declared that deep seabed mining remained a lawful exercise of the freedom of the high seas open to all nations and that the United States would continue to allow its firms to explore for these resources, and to exploit them when the market permitted.

The major portion of the President's statement follows:

> First, the United States is prepared to accept and act in accordance with the balance of interests relating to traditional uses of the oceans—such as navigation and overflight. In this respect, the United States will recognize the rights of other states in the waters off their coasts, as reflected in the Convention, so long as the rights and freedoms of the United States and others under international law are recognized by such coastal states.
>
> Second, the United States will exercise and assert its navigation and overflight rights and freedoms on a worldwide basis in a manner that is consistent with the balance of interests reflected in the convention. The United States will not, however, acquiesce in unilateral acts of other states designed to restrict the rights and freedoms of the international community in navigation and overflight and other related high seas uses.
>
> Third, I am proclaiming today an Exclusive Economic Zone in which the United States will exercise sovereign rights in living and nonliving resources within 200 nautical miles of its coast. This will provide United States jurisdiction for mineral resources out to 200 nautical miles that are not on the continental shelf. Recently discovered deposits there could be an important future source of strategic minerals.
>
> Within this Zone all nations will continue to enjoy the high seas rights and freedoms that are not resource related, including the freedoms of navigation and overflight. My proclamation does not change existing United States policies concerning the continental shelf, marine mammals, and fisheries, including highly migratory species of tuna which are not subject to United States jurisdiction. The United States will continue efforts to achieve international agreements for the effective management of these species. The proclamation also reinforces this government's policy of promoting the United States fishing industry.

[3] On Sept. 2, 1982, the United States signed an Agreement Concerning Interim Arrangements Relating to Polymetallic Nodules of the Deep Sea Bed with France, the Federal Republic of Germany, and the United Kingdom, which entered into force immediately. TIAS No. 10562, *reprinted in* 21 ILM 950 (1982).

While international law provides for a right of jurisdiction over marine scientific research within such a zone, the proclamation does not assert this right. I have elected not to do so because of the United States interest in encouraging marine scientific research and avoiding any unnecessary burdens. The United States will nevertheless recognize the right of other coastal states to exercise jurisdiction over marine scientific research within 200 nautical miles of their coasts, if that jurisdiction is exercised reasonably in a manner consistent with international law.

The Exclusive Economic Zone established today will also enable the United States to take limited additional steps to protect the marine environment. In this connection, the United States will continue to work through the International Maritime Organization and other appropriate international organizations to develop uniform international measures for the protection of the marine environment while imposing no unreasonable burdens on commercial shipping.

The policy decisions I am announcing today will not affect the application of existing United States law concerning the high seas or existing authorities of any United States Government agency.

In addition to the above policy steps, the United States will continue to work with other countries to develop a regime, free of unnecessary political and economic restraints, for mining deep seabed minerals beyond national jurisdiction. Deep seabed mining remains a lawful exercise of the freedom of the high seas open to all nations. The United States will continue to allow its firms to explore for and, when the market permits, exploit these resources.

The administration looks forward to working with the Congress on legislation to implement these new policies.[4]

Proclamation No. 5030, entitled "Exclusive Economic Zone of the United States of America," reads:

WHEREAS the Government of the United States of America desires to facilitate the wise development and use of the oceans consistent with international law;

WHEREAS international law recognizes that, in a zone beyond its territory and adjacent to its territorial sea, known as the Exclusive Economic Zone, a coastal State may assert certain sovereign rights over natural resources and related jurisdiction; and

WHEREAS the establishment of an Exclusive Economic Zone by the United States will advance the development of ocean resources and promote the protection of the marine environment, while not affecting other lawful uses of the zone, including the freedoms of navigation and overflight, by other States;

NOW, THEREFORE, I, RONALD REAGAN, by the authority vested in me as President by the Constitution and laws of the United States of America, do hereby proclaim the sovereign rights and jurisdiction of the United States of America and confirm also the rights and freedoms of all States within an Exclusive Economic Zone, as described herein.

[4] 19 WEEKLY COMP. PRES. DOC. 383–84 (March 10, 1983).

The Exclusive Economic Zone of the United States is a zone contiguous to the territorial sea, including zones contiguous to the territorial sea of the United States, the Commonwealth of Puerto Rico, the Commonwealth of the Northern Mariana Islands (to the extent consistent with the Covenant and the United Nations Trusteeship Agreement), and United States overseas territories and possessions. The Exclusive Economic Zone extends to a distance 200 nautical miles from the baseline from which the breadth of the territorial sea is measured. In cases where the maritime boundary with a neighboring State remains to be determined, the boundary of the Exclusive Economic Zone shall be determined by the United States and other State concerned in accordance with equitable principles.

Within the Exclusive Economic Zone, the United States has, to the extent permitted by international law, (a) sovereign rights for the purpose of exploring, exploiting, conserving and managing natural resources, both living and non-living, of the seabed and subsoil and the superjacent waters and with regard to other activities for the economic exploitation and exploration of the zone, such as the production of energy from the water, currents and winds; and (b) jurisdiction with regard to the establishment and use of artificial islands, and installations and structures having economic purposes, and the protection and preservation of the marine environment.

This Proclamation does not change existing United States policies concerning the continental shelf, marine mammals and fisheries, including highly migratory species of tuna which are not subject to United States jurisdiction and require international agreements for effective management.

The United States will exercise these sovereign rights and jurisdiction in accordance with the rules of international law.

Without prejudice to the sovereign rights and jurisdiction of the United States, the Exclusive Economic Zone remains an area beyond the territory and territorial sea of the United States in which all States enjoy the high seas freedoms of navigation, overflight, the laying of submarine cables and pipelines, and other internationally lawful uses of the sea.[5]

In conjunction with the President's announcement, the White House released a fact sheet reading in part:

Since President Truman proclaimed U.S. jurisdiction and control over the adjacent continental shelf in 1945, the U.S. has asserted sovereign rights for the purpose of exploration and exploitation of the resources of the continental shelf. Fundamental supplementary legislation, the Outer Continental Shelf Lands Act, was passed by Congress in 1953. The President's proclamation today incorporates existing jurisdiction over the continental shelf.

Since 1976 the United States has exercised management and conservation authority over fisheries resources (with the exception of highly migratory species of tuna) within 200 nautical miles of the coasts, under the Magnuson Fishery Conservation and Management Act. The U.S.

[5] *Id.* at 384–85, 48 Fed. Reg. 10,605–06 (1983).

neither recognizes nor asserts jurisdiction over highly migratory species of tuna. Such species are best managed by international agreements with concerned countries. In addition to confirming the United States sovereign rights over mineral deposits beyond the continental shelf but within 200 nautical miles, the Proclamation bolsters U.S. authority over the living resources of the zone.

. . . .

The concept of the EEZ [exclusive economic zone] is already recognized in international law and the President's proclamation is consistent with existing international law. Over 50 countries have proclaimed some form of EEZ; some of these are consistent with international law and others are not.

The concept of an EEZ was developed further in the recently concluded Law of the Sea negotiations and is reflected in that Convention. The EEZ is a maritime area in which the coastal state may exercise certain limited powers as recognized under international law. The EEZ is not the same as the concept of the territorial sea, and is beyond the territorial jurisdiction of any coastal state.

The President's proclamation confirms that, without prejudice to the rights and jurisdiction of the United States in its EEZ, all nations will continue to enjoy non-resource-related freedoms of the high seas beyond the U.S. territorial sea and within the U.S. EEZ. This means that the freedom of navigation and overflight and other internationally lawful uses of the sea will remain the same within the zone as they are beyond it.

The President has also established clear guidelines for United States oceans policy by stating that the United States is prepared to accept and act in accordance with international law as reflected in the results of the Law of the Sea Convention that relate to traditional uses of the oceans, such as navigation and overflight. The United States is willing to respect the maritime claims of others, including economic zones, that are consistent with international law as reflected in the Convention, if U.S. rights and freedoms in such areas under international law are respected by the coastal state.

The President has not changed the breadth of the United States territorial sea. It remains at 3 nautical miles. The United States will respect only those territorial sea claims of others in excess of 3 nautical miles, to a maximum of 12 nautical miles, which accord to the U.S. its full rights under international law in the territorial sea.

Unimpeded commercial and military navigation and overflight are critical to the national interest of the United States. The United States will continue to act to ensure the retention of the necessary rights and freedoms.[6]

[6] Dept. of State File No. P83 0053-2142.

JUDICIAL DECISIONS

MONROE LEIGH

Act of state doctrine—rejection of "ministerial act" exception—foreign military procurement—act of state defense not applicable where private antitrust defendant involves foreign governments in anticompetitive scheme

WILLIAMS v. CURTISS-WRIGHT CORPORATION. 694 F.2d 300.
U.S. Court of Appeals, 3d Cir., November 29, 1982.

This action involved the applicability of the act of state defense to allegations of federal antitrust and related state law violations. Plaintiff and defendant are competitors in the sale of surplus military aircraft engines and parts to foreign governments. Plaintiff alleged that its potential sales in this market were lost as a result of defendant's anticompetitive activities.[1] Defendant, relying on the act of state doctrine, moved to dismiss plaintiff's suit. The district court denied the motion on the ground that the act of state doctrine does not apply to "ministerial acts" of foreign governments. On interlocutory appeal, the U.S. Court of Appeals for the Third Circuit (per Weis, J.) *held:* that the district court erred in concluding that there was a "ministerial act" exception to the act of state doctrine. The court nevertheless affirmed the lower court's judgment and held that the act of state doctrine was not a barrier to plaintiff's suit because the litigation at issue would not "hinder the conduct of foreign relations by the United States government."[2]

Plaintiff alleged that defendant, in contracting for the sale of surplus engines and parts to certain foreign military establishments, had monopolized the market in violation of section 2 of the Sherman Antitrust Act (15 U.S.C. §2) and had engaged in disparagement, unfair competition, and interference with prospective economic advantage. Defendant's motion to dismiss was based on the contention that plaintiff, in order to prove a causal connection between its lost sales and defendant's activities, would be required to introduce evidence concerning the motivation of the foreign governments in awarding the contracts of sale to defendant. The introduction of such evidence, defendant argued, was barred by the act of state doctrine. The district court, relying on the Third Circuit's decision in *Mannington Mills, Inc. v. Congoleum Corp.*,[3] concluded that there was a ministerial act exception to the act of state doctrine and that evidence submitted by plaintiff raised a triable issue of fact as to whether certain foreign procurement decisions were ministerial or discretionary.

Mannington Mills involved a challenge to the allegedly fraudulent acquisition of patents in foreign countries. In that case, the U.S. Court of Appeals for the Third Circuit, in holding that the act of state doctrine did not bar the

[1] Defendant counterclaimed that plaintiff misappropriated defendant's trade secrets. *See* Williams v. Curtiss-Wright Corp., 681 F.2d 161 (3d Cir. 1982). *See also* Williams v. Curtiss-Wright Corp., 691 F.2d 168 (3d Cir. 1982).

[2] 694 F.2d 300, 304–05.

[3] 595 F.2d 1287 (3d Cir. 1979).

suit, determined that the "granting of patents per se, *in substance ministerial activity,* is not the kind of governmental action contemplated by the act of state doctrine."[4] In the present case, the court held that its earlier statement did not purport to create a new, "ministerial" exception to the doctrine. Rather, the statement "was meant to show that judicial abstention was not necessary in *Mannington Mills* because the routine issuance of patents is 'not the type of sovereign activity that would be of substantial concern to the executive branch in its conduct of international affairs.' "[5]

The court observed that the foundation of the act of state doctrine, which was formerly perceived as residing in the inherent nature of sovereign authority and other principles of international law, has now, in the United States at least, shifted to "the interest in preserving the separation of powers between the branches of government."[6] Accordingly, in considering defendant's motion to dismiss, the court was compelled to determine whether, by exercising jurisdiction, it would intrude on the Executive's conduct of foreign affairs. In this respect, the court observed that plaintiff's complaint did not allege that the foreign governments conspired with defendant in its allegedly illegal conduct. Rather, the complaint treated the foreign governments as "fellow victims." Plaintiff's challenges, the court concluded, were aimed at the anticompetitive effects of defendant's activities, not the validity of the decisions by foreign governments to boycott the plaintiff; and there was nothing in the record to indicate that the foreign policy interests of the United States would in any way be affected, much less hindered, by permitting such a suit to proceed.[7]

In this case, the Third Circuit joins the Fifth and Ninth Circuits[8] in rejecting the dictum in *Hunt v. Mobil Oil Corp.,*[9] which states that a court may never examine the motivation of a foreign government. This dictum has been criticized in the past for immunizing the conduct of private defendants who involve a foreign government in their anticompetitive schemes.[10]

Equally significant is the court's implicit rejection of the argument that the act of state defense dictates different results in suits involving foreign military procurement than it does in suits involving other commercial dealings with foreign governments. In this regard, it may be observed that in passing the Foreign Sovereign Immunities Act (28 U.S.C. §§1602 *et seq.*) Congress evinced an explicit intent to permit suits by foreign sovereigns in situations involving military procurement contracts.[11] Moreover, in a recent case the Ninth Cir-

[4] 694 F.2d at 303 (quoting *id.* at 1294) (emphasis added).

[5] 694 F.2d at 303 (quoting 595 F.2d at 1294).

[6] 694 F.2d at 303 (citing Banco Nacional de Cuba v. Sabbatino, 376 U.S. 398, 423 (1964)).

[7] The court did not rule out the possibility, however, that significant developments could occur as the case proceeded that might require the district court to reconsider the application of the act of state doctrine. 694 F.2d at 305.

[8] *See* Industrial Inv. Dev. Corp. v. Mitsui & Co., 594 F.2d 48, 54–55 (5th Cir. 1979), *cert. denied,* 445 U.S. 903 (1980); Timberlane Lumber Co. v. Bank of America, 549 F.2d 597, 605 (9th Cir. 1976).

[9] 550 F.2d 68, 76 (2d Cir.), *cert. denied,* 434 U.S. 984 (1977).

[10] *See, e.g.,* Industrial Inv. Dev. Corp. v. Mitsui & Co., 594 F.2d at 54–55.

[11] *See* H.R. REP. NO. 1487, 94th Cong., 2d Sess., *reprinted in* 1976 U.S. CODE CONG. & AD. NEWS 6604, 6615.

cuit, relying on *Williams,* also rejected the act of state defense in a suit involving the sale of military equipment to foreign countries.[12]

Finally, as the court in *Williams* recognized, where a suit involves military sales, the foreign government involved may be less willing than otherwise to supply evidence against the defendant with whom it has had dealings. Thus, a plaintiff in such a case may have particular difficulties in sustaining its burden of proof. The court properly concluded, however, that this consideration alone should not thwart the strong interest of the United States in obtaining compliance with its antitrust laws by mandating the dismissal of a suit on act of state grounds.

Export Administration Act—extraterritorial jurisdiction over foreign incorporated subsidiaries of U.S. parent companies upheld in United States court

DRESSER INDUSTRIES, INC. v. BALDRIDGE [*sic*]. 549 F.Supp. 108.
U.S. District Court, District of Columbia, September 13, 1982.

Plaintiffs, Dresser Industries, Inc. and Dresser (France), sued for injunctive relief to prevent defendant, the Secretary of Commerce, from imposing sanctions on Dresser (France) for violations of agency regulations prohibiting certain exports to the Soviet Union. These regulations were promulgated pursuant to the Export Administration Act of 1979 (50 U.S.C. app. §2400 *et seq.* (Supp. IV 1980)), as an exercise of U.S. foreign policy controls in an attempt to apply political pressure on the Soviet Union after martial law was declared in Poland. By *ex parte* proceedings, the Department of Commerce issued a temporary denial order denying Dresser (France) all export privileges;[1] plaintiffs thereupon moved for expedited administrative review. When the Commerce Department failed to act on this request, plaintiffs proceeded to federal district court, seeking a stay of the denial order. The U.S. District Court for the District of Columbia (per Joyce Green, J.) *held:* that in light of the public interest in the enforcement of the regulations at issue, which were viewed by the United States as being essential to the accomplishment of U.S. foreign policy, the prayer for injunctive relief should be denied.

Dresser (France), a wholly owned French subsidiary of Dresser Industries, Inc., had entered into certain contracts to deliver gas pipeline compressors to the Soviet Union. These compressors were manufactured under a license granted by Dresser Industries, Inc., to its French subsidiary. The regulations at issue[2] restricted export or reexport to the Soviet Union of non-U.S.-origin

[12] Northrop Corp. v. McDonnell Douglas, Nos. 80-5165, 81-5172 (9th Cir. Feb. 28, 1983), *rev'g*, Northrop Corp. v. McDonnell Douglas Corp., 498 F.Supp. 1112, 1121 (C.D. Cal. 1980), *summarized in* 75 AJIL 370 (1981). *See also* General Aircraft Corp. v. Air America, 482 F. Supp. 3, 6–7 (D.D.C. 1979).

[1] This order subsequently was amended so as to deny export privileges only with respect to commodities and technology relating to oil and gas exploration, production, transmission, or refinement.

[2] *See* 15 C.F.R. pts. 379, 385, and 399 (1980), *as amended by* 47 Fed. Reg. 141 (Jan. 5, 1982) and 47 Fed. Reg. 27,250 (June 24, 1982). In August 1978, the Commerce Department began controlling oil and gas exploration and production equipment and related technical data destined for the Soviet Union. *See* 43 Fed. Reg. 33,699 (Aug. 1, 1978). The 1982 amendments extended control to transmission and refinement equipment and technical data.

oil and gas equipment and technical data supplied by either (1) foreign firms that were owned or controlled by American companies, or (2) foreign firms that produced such equipment with technical data obtained under a license with persons subject to U.S. jurisdiction. Plaintiffs assailed these regulations and the Commerce Department's sanctions on three grounds, contending: first, that the Export Administration Act did not authorize the assertion of jurisdiction over Dresser (France); second, that the imposition of sanctions violated international law; and third, that the U.S. Government's actions deprived the plaintiffs of property without due process of law. Plaintiffs also argued that the Department's failure to act promptly to grant administrative review had foreclosed their administrative rights to be informed of the alleged violations and to present arguments in opposition to the Department's actions.

Without deciding whether plaintiffs were required to exhaust their administrative remedies, the court applied the traditional criteria for evaluating an application for injunctive relief. Based on the record, the court found that plaintiffs had failed to demonstrate a likelihood of success on the merits. Moreover, in light of the continuing availability of administrative remedies, the court could not find that the plaintiffs would be irreparably harmed if injunctive relief were denied. Turning to the interests of the United States Government and the public, the court determined that injunctive relief could frustrate U.S. foreign policy objectives.[3] Accordingly, plaintiffs' request for injunctive relief was denied. Not long afterwards, the legal controversy created by these export control regulations subsided when the United States reached an accommodation with its European allies and lifted the sanctions imposed on foreign firms.

In the *Dresser* case, it seems apparent that neither of the traditional principles of jurisdiction—territoriality and nationality—justified the extension of U.S. export regulations to Dresser (France). Dresser (France) had no operations within the United States; and although it was owned by a U.S. parent company, it was incorporated in France and therefore, under recognized legal principles, was a national of that country.[4] One could argue that jurisdiction was based on a considerably expanded notion of the "effects doctrine," inasmuch as continued exports to the Soviet Union by Dresser (France) would affect U.S. foreign policy objectives. However, the *Restatement of the Foreign Relations Law,* section 18(b), explicitly states that such effects must be direct and substantial. It is doubtful if the Dresser "effects" met either criterion under the standards heretofore applied. Moreover, such an expansion of the effects doctrine ignores the potentially serious foreign policy implications at-

[3] The court also refused to find that plaintiffs had been denied their due process rights. Commerce Department officials had intimated that a hearing pursuant to 15 C.F.R. §388.19(b)(2) would be held as soon as discovery was completed. This assurance apparently was sufficient to satisfy the minimum due process requirements. 549 F.Supp. 108, 110.

[4] For example, Article XIV (5) of the Convention of Establishment Between the United States of America and France, 11 UST 2398, TIAS No. 4625 (*entered into force* Dec. 21, 1960), states that "companies constituted under the applicable laws and regulations of either High Contracting Party shall be deemed companies thereof."

tendant upon such broad assertions of U.S. jurisdiction,[5] as well as the untenable position in which multinational enterprises are placed where they are subject to concurrent and often inconsistent assertions of regulatory authority by two or more governments.[6]

Foreign Agents Registration Act—standing—no private right of action to enforce registration requirements

COMMITTEE FOR A FREE NAMIBIA v. SOUTH WEST AFRICA PEOPLE'S ORGANIZATION. 554 F.Supp. 722.
U.S. District Court, District of Columbia, December 16, 1982.

The Committee for a Free Namibia, plaintiff in this action, sought an order enjoining defendant, the South West Africa People's Organization, from acting as a foreign agent until such time as defendant complied with the requirements of the Foreign Agents Registration Act of 1938 (22 U.S.C. §§611–621 (1976)).[1] The Act requires all agents of foreign principals who engage in certain activities to file periodic registration statements with the U.S. Department of Justice. Plaintiff alleged that defendant's registration forms contained false statements and omitted material facts concerning its activities. Upon defendant's motion to dismiss, the court (per Parker, J.) *held:* that plaintiff lacked standing to sue, and neither express nor implied authority existed for a private right of action under the Act.[2]

The court first concluded that under Article III of the U.S. Constitution, plaintiff lacked standing to sue because it had failed to demonstrate actual injury to its interests that were traceable to defendant. Plaintiff had alleged that defendant's violations of the Act had directly injured its members by depriving them of information that defendant was required to disclose publicly. The court, however, found this generalized allegation of injury to be indistinguishable from that visited upon the general public. The court also

[5] Consider, for example, U.S. experience in the field of antitrust regulation. In response to the antitrust actions brought against an alleged international uranium cartel, the British Government passed legislation that (1) empowered the British Secretary of State to prevent British compliance with U.S. demands for evidence, (2) limited enforcement of foreign antitrust judgments in Great Britain, and (3) enabled British persons to recover any amount paid in excess of actual damages pursuant to a foreign antitrust judgment. *See* Protection of Trading Interests Act 1980, c. 11, *reprinted in* 21 ILM 834 (1982).

[6] In 1970, John Stevenson, State Department Legal Adviser, noted that the root of many problems caused by extraterritorial application of U.S. laws was the existence of two valid but conflicting claims of jurisdiction. Stevenson, "*Extraterritoriality*" *in Canada-United States Relations,* 63 DEP'T STATE BULL. 425, 430 (1970).

[1] The Committee for a Free Namibia is a voluntary group of U.S. citizens united by a common interest in helping to secure the independence of Namibia, a territory in Africa. In particular, the committee seeks to protect Namibia from external pressure or control exerted by the South West Africa People's Organization. 554 F.Supp. 722, 723.

[2] Defendant also urged the court to dismiss the action for lack of federal question or diversity jurisdiction, lack of personal jurisdiction over defendant, and absence of an actual controversy between the parties. Although an assessment of these claims was unnecessary to dispose of the case, the court noted in passing that plaintiff had failed to allege sufficient facts to establish personal jurisdiction over defendant and had failed to explain adequately the basis for federal question jurisdiction. *Id.* at 723 n.l.

determined that plaintiff had failed to demonstrate a "substantial likelihood" that the relief requested would redress the alleged injury.[3] While such injury was claimed to result from the failure to disclose information, plaintiff had requested an injunction prohibiting defendant from serving as a foreign agent rather than seeking an order compelling proper disclosure.

Even if plaintiff could be accorded standing consistently with Article III, the court continued, it had made only a "superficial showing" that the Act impliedly authorized private enforcement actions. The court listed the four criteria to be considered in determining whether a statute provides an implied right of action[4] and found that plaintiff had failed to satisfy any of the three criteria that were applicable to the present suit. The court reasoned that the Act was intended to provide a centralized reporting system to enable federal officials to monitor the activities of foreign agents for the benefit of the general public rather than any special category of persons. In addition, the legislative history provides no indication that Congress intended to create a private right of action. Finally, a private right of action under the Act would be inconsistent with the legislative scheme, which vests exclusive authority in the federal Government to remedy a broad range of violations, including failure to comply with the registration requirements.

Although the court could have dismissed the case on either of the two grounds discussed above, it addressed briefly defendant's argument that the case presented a political question. In this connection, the court noted that it was not empowered to resolve any dispute involving a "textually demonstrable commitment of an issue to a coordinate political department."[5] The court observed that the Act expressly vests enforcement and administrative responsibility in the executive branch and that plaintiff's claim in this case presented the identical issue that the Act entrusts to the Attorney General to detect and remedy. Accordingly, the court held that the case presented a political question that was beyond its power to decide.

As a matter of statutory and constitutional interpretation, the court in this case correctly concluded that the decision to seek judicial relief for violations of the Foreign Agents Registration Act lies within the sole discretion of the Attorney General.[6] However, although this conclusion is fully consistent with the text and apparent purposes of the Act, it also highlights a limitation on enforcement of the statutory scheme—one which this act shares with other statutes containing criminal provisions. In the event that the Attorney General fails to enforce obligations imposed by the Act, individuals and groups who

[3] *See* Duke Power Co. v. Carolina Envtl. Study Group, 438 U.S. 59, 75 n.20 (1978).

[4] The Supreme Court articulated these four criteria in Cort v. Ash, 422 U.S. 66, 78 (1975): (1) whether plaintiff belongs to the class for whose special benefit the statute was enacted; (2) whether there is any indication of legislative intent to create or deny a private right of action; (3) whether a private right of action is consistent with the underlying purposes of the legislative scheme; and (4) whether the cause of action traditionally falls within the realm of state law.

[5] 554 F.Supp. at 725 (quoting Baker v. Carr, 369 U.S. 186, 217 (1962)).

[6] *See, e.g.*, 22 U.S.C. §618(a) (authorizing the Attorney General to prosecute criminally willful violations of the Act's registration requirements); 22 U.S.C. §618(f) (authorizing the Attorney General to seek injunctive relief to ensure compliance).

may be directly or indirectly affected by a violation are powerless to seek a judicial order enjoining the foreign agent from engaging in activities covered by the Act or compelling the Attorney General to take action.

Jurisdiction over stateless vessels—United States criminal jurisdiction over drug trafficking in international waters

UNITED STATES v. MARINO-GARCIA. 679 F.2d 1373.
U.S. Court of Appeals, 11th Cir., July 9, 1982.

These two consolidated cases present a jurisdictional issue of first impression arising under section 955a(a) of the Marijuana on the High Seas Act of 1980 (21 U.S.C. §955a(a)), the most wide-ranging of a number of recent U.S. statutes designed to combat drug trafficking in international waters. Both cases arose from the U.S. Coast Guard's arrest of vessels on the high seas. In each case, the vessel was carrying substantial amounts of marijuana, the vessel was stateless, and all crewmen involved were foreign nationals. In one case, the trial judge dismissed the criminal indictment on the ground that the Government had failed to establish any nexus between the stateless vessel and the United States. In the companion case, a different trial judge reached the opposite conclusion. On appeal, the U.S. Court of Appeals for the Eleventh Circuit (per Johnson, J.) *held:* that international law permits any nation to subject stateless vessels on the high seas to its jurisdiction and that the exercise of jurisdiction in both cases before the court was therefore proper.

Section 955a(a) proscribes, *inter alia,* possession of a controlled substance by any person on board "a vessel subject to the jurisdiction of the United States on the high seas" with the intent to distribute. The Act's definition of "vessel subject to the jurisdiction of the United States" specifically includes vessels without nationality (21 U.S.C. §955b(d)).

The court began by observing that the statute on its face does not require a nexus between stateless vessels and the United States as a prerequisite to jurisdiction. The court found, however, that the legislative history of section 955a clearly established that the intent of the statute was to extend jurisdiction only to the "maximum . . . permitted under international law."[1] In the court's view, therefore, the critical question was "whether international law imposes any substantive restrictions upon this country's right to extend jurisdiction to all stateless vessels on the high seas."[2]

The court acknowledged that international law generally prohibits countries from asserting jurisdiction over *foreign* vessels on the high seas. While there are recognized exceptions to this rule, all require a nexus of some kind between the foreign vessel and the country asserting jurisdiction.[3] The court

[1] S. REP. No. 855, 96th Cong., 2d Sess. 2 (1980), *quoted in* 679 F.2d 1373, 1379.

[2] 679 F.2d at 1380.

[3] The court identified these exceptions and the international legal principles on which they are based as follows: (1) where a vessel is engaged in illegal conduct intended to have an effect in the nation asserting jurisdiction (the "objective principle"); (2) where a vessel is engaged in activity that threatens the nation's security or governmental functions (the "protective principle"); and (3) where a vessel is engaged in activity that injures the nation's citizens (the "passive principle"). *Id.* at 1380–81.

found, however, that the rule had no applicability to *stateless* vessels on the high seas. In this respect, the court relied primarily on a line of precedent holding that stateless vessels are "international pariahs" with no internationally recognized right to navigate freely on the high seas.[4] Accordingly, the court concluded, all nations have the right to assert jurisdiction over stateless vessels on the high seas. "Such jurisdiction neither violates the law of nations nor results in impermissible interference with another sovereign nation's affairs."[5] The court further concluded that there need not be proof of a nexus between the stateless vessel and the country seeking to effectuate jurisdiction. "Jurisdiction exists *solely* as a consequence of the vessel's status as stateless. Such status makes the vessel subject to action by all nations proscribing certain activities aboard stateless vessels and subjects those persons aboard to prosecution for violating the proscriptions."[6]

While federal courts have previously assumed jurisdiction in cases where a stateless vessel on the high seas had been involved in illegal activity having some connection with the United States, this case is the first federal appellate decision to exercise jurisdiction in the absence of evidence of such connection. Moreover, while the court's holding extended only to stateless vessels, the court in dictum suggested that the proper scope of U.S. jurisdiction over vessels on the high seas might be even broader. A nexus between a vessel and the United States, the court suggested, might well be provided simply by the fact that the vessel was engaged in drug trafficking.[7] Application of this reasoning would suggest that foreign as well as stateless vessels on the high seas, if engaged in drug trafficking, may properly be subjected to United States jurisdiction.

Decisions of Foreign Courts

United Kingdom

Cultural property—territorial theory of sovereignty—seizure as a prerequisite to forfeiture—unenforceability of foreign public laws

Attorney-General of New Zealand v. Ortiz. [1982] 3 W.L.R. 570. Court of Appeal, May 21, 1982.

This case involved a claim for the recovery of cultural property. The property, a rare Maori wood carving, was a national "historic article" under the laws of New Zealand. It was illegally exported from that country in 1973, then purchased by one of the defendants, a private art collector, who later offered it for sale at a London auction house.[1] Upon learning of the offer of

[4] *See, e.g.,* Convention on the High Seas, Art. 6, 13 UST 2312, TIAS No. 5200, 450 UNTS 82; United States v. Monroy, 614 F.2d 61, 64 (5th Cir.), *cert. denied,* 449 U.S. 892 (1980), *summarized in* 74 AJIL 942 (1980).

[5] 679 F.2d at 1383.

[6] *Ibid.* (emphasis in original).

[7] *Id.* at 1378 n.4.

[1] The carving, which had been lost for centuries, was the door of a Maori treasure house. It was found in a swamp in 1972 by a Maori tribesman, who sold it to the third defendant for $6,000.

sale, plaintiff, the New Zealand Government, brought the present action in the United Kingdom seeking an injunction restraining the sale of the article, a declaration that it was the property of the New Zealand Government, and an order for its return. The trial court found in favor of the plaintiff.[2] In a unanimous decision, the Court of Appeal reversed and *held:* first, that since English and New Zealand law required seizure of the article as a prerequisite to forfeiture, the plaintiff was not entitled to possession of the carving; and second, even assuming that the relevant New Zealand statutes provided for automatic forfeiture, that such statutes, as applied outside the territory of New Zealand, would not be enforced by an English court.

In support of its claim for relief in the United Kingdom courts, plaintiff relied on the New Zealand Historic Articles Act 1962, which makes it unlawful for any person to remove a national "historic article" from New Zealand without the Government's express permission and provides that any such article knowingly exported or attempted to be exported in breach thereof "shall be forfeited to Her Majesty."[3] This statute is further implemented by the New Zealand Customs Act 1966, which provides, *inter alia,* that no goods shall be seized except "within two years after the cause of forfeiture has arisen" and that goods "may be seized as forfeited wherever found within the territorial limits of New Zealand."[4]

As framed by the court, the case presented two preliminary issues: (1) whether the Crown "has become the owner and is entitled to possession of the carving" pursuant to the statutes cited above; and (2) whether "in any event the provisions of the said Acts are unenforceable in England as being foreign penal, revenue and/or public laws."[5]

Lord Denning M.R.—in one of his last decisions before retirement—began by observing that although the plaintiff alleged that the statutes in question should be read to call for the "automatic forfeiture" of the carving by virtue of its unlawful export, the law of England is squarely to the contrary. As established by the "great case" of *Lockyer v. Offley* ((1786) 1 T.R. 252), a "forfeiture does not take effect until the goods are seized," at which point the title "relates back to the cause of forfeiture."[6] This principle, Denning found, was likewise mandated by the New Zealand statutes and by international law. If, Denning reasoned, the Historic Articles Act provided for the automatic forfeiture of a historic article illegally exported from New Zealand, then New Zealand could recover such article in any country into which it may have been imported. So interpreted, however, the Act would "infringe the rule of international law which says that no country can legislate so as to affect the rights of property when that property is situated beyond the limits of its

---

The first defendant then purchased it for $65,000 and later offered it for sale to the public through Sotheby's (the second defendant). The estimated value of the carving at the time of auction was £300,000.

[2] 1982 Q.B. 349, [1982] 2 W.L.R. 10.

[3] Historic Articles Act 1962, secs. 5 and 12 (NZ). It was apparently not disputed that the carving at issue was a "historic article" within the meaning of the Act.

[4] Customs Act 1966, secs. 275(4) and 276 (NZ).

[5] [1982] 3 W.L.R. 570, 576.

[6] *Ibid.*

own territory. It is a direct infringement of the territorial theory of sovereignty. . . ."[7]

Addressing the second issue of the case, Denning again relied on the territorial principle of jurisdiction. Assuming that the Historic Articles Act provided for automatic forfeiture on the unlawful export or attempted export of such goods—a provision that could well be expressly legislated by any country attempting to preserve its patrimony—would the law permit the enforcement of such foreign legislation by an English court? Denning answered this question in the negative.[8] It cannot be doubted, Denning observed, that an English court will not entertain a suit brought by a foreign sovereign, directly or indirectly, to enforce the penal or revenue laws of the foreign state.[9] Likewise, Denning reasoned, this rule extends to "other public laws," *i.e.*, laws that are *ejusdem generis* with penal and revenue laws.

> [I]f any country should have legislation prohibiting the export of works of art, and providing for the automatic forfeiture of them to the state should they be exported, then that falls into the category of "public laws" which will not be enforced by the courts of the country to which [such works are] exported, or any other country, because it is an act done in the exercise of sovereign authority which will not be enforced outside its own territory.[10]

Ackner L.J. agreed with Lord Denning's conclusions, but confined his analysis more strictly to statutory interpretation. With respect to the first issue, he agreed that seizure was a prerequisite to forfeiture under the New Zealand statutes; he added, however, that "in view of the time bar [of two years] contained in section 274 of the Customs Act 1966, the Attorney-General falls at the first fence."[11] As for the second issue, Ackner concluded that the New Zealand statutes were penal in nature, since they concerned a public right that the state sought to vindicate through confiscation.

Illicit international trade in cultural property has been the subject of increasing worldwide concern and activity during the past two decades.[12] Recent developments in this area of the law suggest that cases similar to *Ortiz* may well be decided differently in the future.

One major development has been the conclusion of a number of bilateral and multilateral treaties designed to promote international cooperation in controlling the movement of cultural property.[13] The most significant of these

[7] *Id.* at 580 (citing The Apollon, 22 U.S. (9 Wheat.) 362, 370 (1824)).

[8] Denning distinguished, however, between a suit by a foreign state to enforce its laws and a suit between private firms or individuals where foreign laws are at issue. [1982] 3 W.L.R. at 581.

[9] *Cf.* RESTATEMENT (SECOND) OF FOREIGN RELATIONS LAW OF THE UNITED STATES §41, Comment 1 (1965) ("courts in the United States will generally refrain from taking action to give effect to the penal or revenue law of other states, except as provided by international agreement").

[10] [1982] 3 W.L.R. at 585.

[11] *Id.* at 591.

[12] *See generally* Bator, *An Essay on the International Trade in Art,* 34 STAN. L. REV. 275 (1982); L. DUBOFF, THE DESKBOOK OF ART LAW, ch. IV (1977).

[13] *See, e.g.,* Treaty of Cooperation Between the United States of America and the United Mexican States Providing for the Recovery and Return of Stolen Archaeological, Historical and Cultural Properties, July 17, 1970, 22 UST 494, TIAS No. 7088; Pan American Treaty of 1936 on the Protection of Movable Property of Historic Value, 28 OASTS (1962).

is the 1970 UNESCO Convention on the Means of Prohibiting and Preventing the Illicit Import, Export and Transfer of Ownership of Cultural Property (Nov. 14, 1970, 823 UNTS 231, 10 ILM 289 (1971)). While the Secretariat draft of the Convention would have instituted sweeping reforms, prohibiting all parties to the Convention from importing or exporting *any* item of cultural property without authority, the Convention in its final form adopts a much more moderate position. This moderation is reflected in the Convention's three central provisions: Article 7(a) provides that the parties will "take the necessary measures, consistent with national legislation, to prevent museums and similar institutions within their territories from acquiring cultural property . . . which has been illegally exported" from other parties; Article 7(b) contains an undertaking "to prohibit the import of cultural property stolen from a museum or . . . similar institution in another State Party" and, at the request of the other party, to recover and return such property; and Article 9 (the so-called crisis provision) calls for "concerted international effort," including the imposition of import and export controls, in cases where a party's "cultural patrimony is in jeopardy from pillage." Thus, while neither the United Kingdom nor New Zealand was a party to the Convention as of the date of decision in *Ortiz,*[14] it does not appear that the Convention would have dictated a contrary result (short of invocation of the crisis provision) even if they had been parties.

The second major development concerns the judicial application of criminal sanctions in the United States to persons receiving and transporting cultural artifacts deemed to constitute "stolen property." In the leading case of *United States v. McClain* (545 F.2d 988 (5th Cir. 1977)), it was held that persons dealing in foreign cultural property that has been illegally exported from its country of origin may be prosecuted under the National Stolen Property Act (18 U.S.C. §§2314–2315), provided that the country in question has enacted a legislative declaration of national ownership prior to the date of export. In so holding, the court declared that "exportation [in these circumstances] constitutes a sufficient act of conversion to be deemed a theft."[15] Understandably, the holding in *McClain* has become a source of grave concern to the American community of museums, art dealers and private collectors.

[14] Currently, there are approximately 50 parties to the Convention, including the United States. The United States was significantly involved in drafting the Convention, but U.S. implementing legislation was delayed for over a decade. *See* Convention on Cultural Property Implementation Act, 19 U.S.C. §2601 *et seq.* (Supp. V 1981). *See also* 76 AJIL 611 (1982).

[15] 545 F.2d 988, 1003 n.33. The court in *McClain,* however, reversed the lower court's convictions of the defendants on the ground that the foreign country (Mexico) had not unambiguously declared by statute prior to the date of export that it was the owner of all pre-Columbian artifacts located within its territory. *See also* United States v. McClain, 593 F.2d 658 (5th Cir. 1979) (*McClain II*); United States v. Hollinshead, 495 F.2d 1154 (9th Cir. 1974).

Valuation—creditors' rights—date for conversion of currency in context of liquidation proceedings

RE LINES BROS. LTD. [1982] 2 All E.R. 183, [1982] 2 W.L.R. 1010.
Court of Appeal, Civil Division, February 11, 1982.

In this action, liquidators in voluntary dissolution under British corporation law applied for guidance with respect to the valuation of the claim of the respondent, one of the creditors of the liquidating company. The question before the court was whether the debt, which was a contractual obligation denominated and payable in Swiss francs, should be converted into sterling as of the date the liquidation proceedings were commenced in 1971 or, as the respondent contended, at various dates thereafter when partial disbursements were made to all creditors.[1] Because the liquidation period was protracted and because during that period the value of sterling depreciated against the Swiss franc by as much as 40 percent, the issue assumed great commercial importance for the respondent. Unanimously affirming the decision of the lower court, the Civil Division of the Court of Appeal (per Lawton, Brightman and Oliver L.JJ.) *held:* that the sterling equivalent of the debt should be calculated as of the date of the commencement of liquidation.

The respondent argued that this holding was inconsistent with the decision of the House of Lords in *Miliangos v. George Frank (Textiles) Ltd.* ([1975] 3 All E.R. 801, [1976] A.C. 443). In *Miliangos,* the House of Lords had held that a Swiss plaintiff requesting contract damages in a foreign currency could seek a judgment in a British court in that currency. The House recognized, however, that if the judgment were to be enforced in England, a provision would have to be made for converting the foreign currency into sterling. Accordingly, the House addressed the issue of the proper conversion date and determined that while, theoretically, conversion should occur as of the date of payment, theory must yield to the practical necessity of converting the judgment prior to its enforcement. Faced with this practicality, their Lordships agreed (with one dissent) that the conversion date should be the date on which the court authorized enforcement in sterling.

The Court of Appeal distinguished *Miliangos* on the ground that, in *Miliangos,* the plaintiff's claim to a judgment in foreign currency was based on contractual obligations—the plaintiff had bargained to be paid in that currency and only in that currency. Thus, the court reasoned, *Miliangos* reflected a policy of preventing a defendant guilty of breach of contract from benefiting, contrary to his bargain, from a fluctuation in exchange rates. In contrast, the court continued, the creditor's right to recover in a case of liquidation is created and governed by statute; and although the creditor's claim arises out of debt, once the liquidation proceeding has been initiated, his right to recover against the company's remaining assets is dependent upon judicial enforcement among competing liabilities. Thus, the court held, in the context of a liquidation proceeding, a statutory scheme of collective enforcement of lia-

[1] The additional repayment sought by the respondent was available from a substantial residue of the debtor's liquidated estate, which remained available for distribution after the principal amounts of all claims and the expenses of liquidation had been paid.

bilities replaces individual rights to sue on contracts. Applying this reasoning, the court could find no reason to visit the risk of currency fluctuations on one innocent creditor rather than another. The court also held that the decision to choose the date of initiation of the liquidation as the time for evaluating the exchange of currency was based on simplicity and convenience to the liquidators.

THE NETHERLANDS

Export Administration Act—extraterritorial jurisdiction over foreign incorporated subsidiary of U.S. parent company—claim of U.S. jurisdiction rejected in Netherlands court

COMPAGNIE EUROPEENNE DES PETROLES S.A. v. SENSOR NEDERLAND B.V. 22 ILM 66 (1983).
District Court at The Hague, the Netherlands, September 17, 1982.

Plaintiff, a company organized and domiciled in France, brought suit in a Netherlands court against a Netherlands company domiciled in The Hague but owned 100 percent by a U.S.-incorporated parent company to enforce the terms of a contract for the delivery of geophones ultimately destined for the Soviet Union. The contract was concluded in June of 1982. Late in July of 1982, the defendant Dutch corporation notified the plaintiff that it would not be able to meet its delivery obligations because it was bound by the amended United States Export Administration Regulations, which prohibited the export of the goods in question to the plaintiff for delivery to the USSR. The plaintiff asked the Netherlands court to order defendant to deliver the goods under contract by October 18, 1982 or else face penalties accruing thereafter at the rate of 10,000 Netherlands florins per day. Defendant pleaded in defense that it was subject to the jurisdiction of the United States by virtue of the fact that it was owned by a United States parent corporation and hence bound to comply with the United States Export Administration Regulations. Because of threatened sanctions under those regulations, defendant Dutch company contended it was entitled to invoke *force majeure* and to rely on "exonerating circumstances" under section 74 of the Uniform Act governing the International Sale of Goods to avoid the obligations of its contract.

The Netherlands court, after analyzing the factual situation, held as follows:

(1) That the contract was subject to Netherlands law.

(2) That under general principles of international law, a state may not exercise jurisdiction with respect to acts performed outside its borders unless permitted by certain exceptions, such as the nationality principle or the protection principle.

(3) That the case did not fall within the nationality principle because the United States regulatory criterion embodied in the phrase "owned or controlled" by a United States parent corporation was not generally accepted in international law and, moreover, in this case was entirely inappropriate in view of the provisions of Article XXIII of the Treaty of Friendship, Commerce and Navigation between the Kingdom of the Netherlands and the United

States of America,[1] which provides that "[c]ompanies constituted under the applicable laws and regulations within the territories of either Party shall be deemed companies thereof and shall have their juridical status recognized within the territories of the other Party."

(4) That the protection principle exception to territorial jurisdiction is permissible only with respect to protection against the consequences of acts performed outside the territory of the regulating country when such acts "jeopardize the security or creditworthiness of that State" and that such interests do not include the "foreign policy interest that the U.S. measure seeks to protect" in this case.

(5) That the "effects" principle was not available to justify the extraterritorial assertion of United States jurisdiction as an aspect of territorial jurisdiction in this case because the court could not see "how the export to Russia of goods not originating in the United States by a non-American exporter could have any direct and illicit effects within the United States." Therefore, "the jurisdiction rule cannot be brought into compatibility with international law."

Accordingly, the court gave judgment for the plaintiff and assessed costs against the defendant Dutch corporation.

The decision of the Netherlands court in this case illustrates the hostility with which American assertions of extraterritorial jurisdiction have been met in European legal and political circles. Fortunately, the defendant Dutch corporation was ultimately relieved of the pyramiding effect of per diem awards of damages by the accommodation which was worked out diplomatically between the United States and its European allies and which resulted in the revocation of the United States regulations.

INTER-AMERICAN COURT OF HUMAN RIGHTS

Advisory jurisdiction

"OTHER TREATIES" SUBJECT TO THE CONSULTATIVE JURISDICTION OF THE COURT (ART. 64 AMERICAN CONVENTION ON HUMAN RIGHTS) REQUESTED BY PERU. Advisory Opinion No. OC-1/82.*
Inter-American Court of Human Rights, September 24, 1982.

In a decision of first impression, the Inter-American Court of Human Rights declared that its advisory jurisdiction extends to the interpretation of any provision dealing with the protection of human rights set forth in any international treaty applicable in the American states.[1]

[1] *Entered into force* Dec. 5, 1957, 8 UST 2043, TIAS No. 3942.

* Case note prepared by Caroline G. Harris of the Texas Bar, and application pending for the New York Bar.

[1] The Court commenced operations in May 1979. It has rendered one decision under its contentious jurisdiction, Government of Costa Rica (In the Matter of Viviana Gallardo *et al.*), Decision of Nov. 13, 1981, 20 ILM 1424 (1981). It has written two opinions under its advisory jurisdiction; this is the first advisory opinion published by the Court. *See infra* p. 640 for a summary of the second advisory opinion.

The Inter-American Court of Human Rights, a judicial institution created by the Organization of American States (OAS) in the American Convention on Human Rights (American Convention),[2] has both contentious and advisory jurisdiction.[3] Establishing the Court's advisory jurisdiction, Article 64 of the American Convention provides, *inter alia,* that "member states of the Organization may consult the Court regarding the interpretation of this Convention or of other treaties concerning the protection of human rights in the American States."[4] Invoking the Court's advisory jurisdiction, the Government of Peru sought clarification of which treaties other than the American Convention are subject to the Court's advisory purview under Article 64.[5] Peru asked specifically whether the phrase "or of other treaties" refers to treaties adopted only within the framework of the inter-American system, to treaties concluded solely among American states, or to any treaties to which American and non-American states may be parties.[6]

The Court relied on five sources in evaluating the scope of its advisory jurisdiction: the text of Article 64, other provisions of the American Convention (in particular Article 29), the preparatory work of the American Convention, the practice of the Inter-American Commission of Human Rights, and the object and purpose of the Court's advisory jurisdiction within the context of the American Convention. However, the thrust of the opinion centered on the text of Articles 64 and 29, and on the purpose of the Court. The Court emphasized that Article 64 contains no express limitations pertaining to the source of the treaties subject to the Court's advisory jurisdiction. Its only restriction is that the treaties must protect human rights in the American states, a "geographical-political" requirement referring to the states affected by the international obligations, not to the source of the obligations.[7] Since no restrictions were articulated in Article 64, the Court would not presume that any existed.

[2] American Convention on Human Rights [hereinafter cited as American Convention], OASTS No. 6, at 1, OAS OFFICIAL RECORDS, OEA/Ser.K/XVI/1.1, doc. 65, rev. 1, corr. 2 (1970), *reprinted in* 9 ILM 673 (1970), *opened for signature* in San José, Costa Rica, Nov. 22, 1969, *entered into force* July 8, 1978. For the official text, see ORGANIZATION OF AMERICAN STATES, HANDBOOK OF EXISTING RULES PERTAINING TO HUMAN RIGHTS 27, OEA/Ser.L/V/11.50, doc. 6 (English) (1980).

[3] American Convention, Arts. 61–65.

[4] Article 64 provides, in full:

> 1. The member states of the Organization may consult the Court regarding the interpretation of this Convention or of other treaties concerning the protection of human rights in the American states. Within their spheres of competence, the organs listed in Chapter X of the Charter of the Organization of American States, as amended by the Protocol of Buenos Aires, may in like manner consult the Court.
>
> 2. The Court, at the request of a member state of the Organization, may provide that state with opinions regarding the compatibility of any of its domestic laws with the aforesaid international instruments.

[5] Request for an Advisory Opinion Presented by the Government of Peru (1982).

[6] *Id.* at 1–2.

[7] Advisory Opinion No. OC-1/82, at 11 (Inter-Am. Ct. of Hum. Rights, Sept. 24, 1982), *reprinted in* 22 ILM 51, 60 (1983).

Furthermore, the Court would not construe Article 64 in a manner that conflicts with other provisions of the American Convention. Article 29 establishes rules relating to the interpretation of the American Convention.[8] Article 29(b) prohibits the interpretation of any provision of the Convention as "restricting the enjoyment or exercise of any right or freedom recognized . . . by virtue of another convention to which one of the said states is a party." An interpretation of Article 64 that would preclude the Court from considering, categorically, other conventions to which a member state is a party would prevent the Court from complying with Article 29(b). Therefore, the Court could not construe Article 64 restrictively.

The Court augmented its analysis of Articles 64 and 29 with an evaluation of its purpose in the context of the American Convention, a human rights treaty. The Court noted that the purpose of human rights treaties is "to guarantee the enjoyment of individual human beings of those rights and freedoms."[9] In addition, the American Convention is meant to integrate the regional and the universal systems for the protection of human rights. Accordingly, the Court's advisory role is "to assist the American States in fulfilling their international human rights obligations and to assist the different organs of the inter-American system to carry out the functions assigned to them in this field."[10] These purposes are promoted by including within the Court's advisory jurisdiction all treaties that affect human rights in the American states without exclusions based on the source of the treaty or the participation of non-American states in the treaty.

The Court qualified its broad advisory jurisdiction in one respect. It held that "its advisory jurisdiction is permissive in character," empowering the Court to deny a request for an advisory opinion under special circumstances.[11] The Court suggested that special circumstances might exist, for example, where the issue raised concerns either an obligation assumed by a non-American state or the operation of an international organ outside the inter-American system, or where granting the request might weaken the entire system for the protection of human rights established by the American Convention, *e.g.*, where a state's request for an advisory opinion is in reality a device to avoid the Court's contentious jurisdiction.

[8] Article 29 provides, in full:

> No provision of the Convention may be interpreted as:
>
> a. permitting any State Party, group, or person to suppress the enjoyment or exercise of the rights and freedoms recognized in this Convention or to restrict them to a greater extent than is provided for herein;
>
> b. restricting the enjoyment or exercise of any right or freedom recognized by virtue of the laws of any State Party or by virtue of another convention to which one of the said states is a party;
>
> c. precluding other rights or guarantees that are inherent in the human personality or derived from representative democracy as a form of government; or
>
> d. excluding or limiting the effect that the American Declaration of the Rights and Duties of Man and other international acts of the same nature may have.

[9] Slip op. at 8, 22 ILM at 57.

[10] Slip op. at 8, 22 ILM at 57–58.

[11] Slip op. at 9, 22 ILM at 58.

Effect of reservations on entry into force of American Convention on Human Rights

THE EFFECT OF RESERVATIONS ON THE ENTRY INTO FORCE OF THE AMERICAN CONVENTION (ARTS. 74 AND 75). Advisory Opinion No. OC-2/82.*

Inter-American Court of Human Rights, September 24, 1982.

This advisory opinion by the Inter-American Court of Human Rights considers the entry into force of the American Convention on Human Rights (Convention) for states that ratify or adhere to the Convention with reservations. The Court also discusses the scope of its advisory jurisdiction and the standing of the Inter-American Commission on Human Rights (Commission) to request such opinions.

Advisory Opinion No. OC-2/82 was requested by the Commission on June 28, 1982. The Commission asked:

> From what moment is a state deemed to have become a party to the American Convention on Human Rights when it ratifies or adheres to the Convention with one or more reservations: from the date of the deposit of instrument of ratification or adherence or upon the termination of the period specified in Article 20 of the Vienna Convention on the Law of Treaties?[1]

This question arose when the General Secretariat of the Organization of American States (OAS) read Article 75[2] of the Convention as requiring a delay in the Convention's entry into force for states ratifying with reservations until (1) all states parties had accepted or objected to the proposed reservations, or (2) 12 months from the date on which all states parties were notified of the reservations, whichever was earlier, in accordance with Article 20(5) of the Vienna Convention on the Law of Treaties (Vienna Convention). Article 74(2)[3] of the Human Rights Convention provides simply that the Convention enters into force for ratifying states on the date of deposit of the instrument of ratification or adherence.

* Case note prepared by Grant Hanessian of the International Human Rights Law Group, Washington, D.C.

[1] Advisory Opinion No. OC-2/82, at 3 (Inter-Am. Ct. of Hum. Rights, Sept. 24, 1982), *reprinted in* 22 ILM 37, 38 (1983). For the text of the Commission's request, see ANNUAL REPORT OF THE INTER-AMERICAN COURT OF HUMAN RIGHTS 1982, at 28–30, OEA/Ser.1/111.7, doc. 13 (1982). For the U.S. views on the Commission's request, see 77 AJIL 137 (1983).

[2] Article 75 provides: "This Convention shall be subject to reservations only in conformity with the provisions of the Vienna Convention on the Law of Treaties signed on May 23, 1969."

[3] Article 74 provides:

> 1. This Convention shall be open for signature and ratification by or adherence of any member state of the Organization of American States.
>
> 2. Ratification of or adherence to this Convention shall be made by the deposit of an instrument of ratification or adherence with the General Secretariat of the Organization of American States. As soon as eleven states have deposited their instruments of ratification or adherence, the Convention shall enter into force. With respect to any state that ratifies or adheres thereafter, the Convention shall enter into force on the date of the deposit of its instrument of ratification or adherence.
>
> 3. The Secretary General shall inform all member states of the Organization of the entry into force of the Convention.

The Court first determined that it was competent to entertain the request and that the Commission was competent to present it. As to its own competence, the Court had "no doubt whatsoever"; the Court considered that Article 64[4] of the Convention empowered it "to render an authoritative interpretation of all provisions of the Convention, including those relating to its entry into force."[5] As to the Commission's competence to seek the advisory opinion, the Court noted that under Article 64, organs of the OAS may seek advisory opinions on matters "within their spheres of competence." The Court readily found that the Commission was an organ of the OAS, and that, as it was established to promote the observance and protection of human rights, the Commission was competent not only to present this request, but "enjoys, as a practical matter, an absolute right to request advisory opinions within the framework of Article 64(1) of the Convention."[6]

In addressing the substantive question before it, the effect of reservations on the entry into force of the Convention, the Court focused its inquiry on the meaning of the reference to the Vienna Convention in Article 75 of the American Convention. The Court considered relevant Articles 19 and 20 of the Vienna Convention dealing with the formulation of and acceptance and objection to reservations, respectively. The Court first held that as the American Convention says nothing about reservations other than what is provided in Article 75, Article 19(c) of the Vienna Convention applies, permitting "States to ratify or adhere to the Convention with whatever reservations they wish to make, provided only that such reservations are not 'incompatible with the object and purpose' of the Convention."[7]

The Court then considered the various regimes regarding states' acceptance or objection to reservations created under Article 20 of the Vienna Convention. Principal consideration was given to paragraph 4, which establishes that a reserving state's act of ratification or adherence is effective only upon the acceptance of the reservation by at least one other contracting state. This, the Court stated, reflected "the needs of traditional multilateral international agreements which have as their object the reciprocal exchange, for the mutual benefit of the States Parties, of bargained for rights and obligations."[8] But human rights treaties, and specifically the American Convention, were found by the Court to be of a different character. Their object and purpose was not the reciprocal exchange of rights and obligations between states but

> the protection of the basic rights of individual human beings, irrespective of their nationality, both against the State of their nationality and all other contracting States. . . . [T]he States [Parties] can be deemed to submit themselves to a legal order within which they, for the common good, assume various obligations, not in relation to other States, but towards all individuals within their jurisdiction.[9]

[4] For the text of Article 64, see *supra* p. 638 n.4.

[5] Slip op. at 5, 22 ILM at 40.

[6] Slip op. at 6, 22 ILM at 41.

[7] Slip op. at 9, 22 ILM at 44.

[8] Slip op. at 12, 22 ILM at 46.

[9] Slip op. at 12, 22 ILM at 47. The Court noted similar descriptions of the purposes of the European Convention by the European Commission on Human Rights, Austria v. Italy, Application No. 7881/60, 4 EUR. Y.B. HUM. RIGHTS 116, 140 (1960); and of the Convention on the

The Court further observed that the American Convention, unlike other human rights treaties, confers on private parties the right to file a petition with the Commission against any state party to the Convention. By contrast, communications by states parties may only be received where both the petitioning state and the state complained against have accepted the Commission's jurisdiction over such complaints. Thus, the Court reasoned, "the Convention must be seen for what in reality it is: a multilateral legal instrument or framework enabling States to make binding unilateral commitments not to violate the human rights of individuals within their jurisdiction";[10] "it would be manifestly unreasonable" to consider that the reference in Article 75 to the Vienna Convention requires application of Article 20(4). "[N]o useful purpose," the Court held, would be served by delaying the effect of a state's act of ratification or adherence until a state party formally accepts the reserving state as a party.[11]

Instead, the Court found that Article 75 of the Convention refers to Article 20(1) of the Vienna Convention and thus authorizes all reservations compatible with its object and purpose. Consequently, such reservations do not require the acceptance of any state party. The Court noted that Article 20(1), allowing "a reservation expressly authorized by a treaty," does not mandate that the authorized reservation be "specified" by a treaty, in contrast to Article 19(b), which refers to "specified reservations."

States parties desiring to object to reservations as incompatible with the object and purpose of the Convention are free, the Court stated, to make use of the "adjudicatory and advisory machinery established by the Convention,"[12] but have no interest in delaying the entry into force of the Convention or in delaying the protection of individuals within the boundaries of the reserving state. The Court concluded that "the Convention enters into force for a State which ratifies or adheres to it with or without a reservation on the date of the deposit of its instrument of ratification or adherence."[13]

Decisions of the Iran-United States Claims Tribunal*

Jurisdiction—corporate nationality

FLEXI-VAN LEASING INC. v. THE ISLAMIC REPUBLIC OF IRAN. Claim No. 36, Order of December 15, 1982.
GENERAL MOTORS CORPORATION v. THE ISLAMIC REPUBLIC OF IRAN. Claim No. 94, Order of January 18, 1983.
Iran-United States Claims Tribunal, The Hague.

Prevention and Punishment of the Crime of Genocide by the International Court of Justice in its Advisory Opinion on Reservations to the Convention on the Prevention and Punishment of the Crime of Genocide, 1951 ICJ REP. 15.

[10] Slip op. at 14, 22 ILM at 48.

[11] Slip op. at 14, 22 ILM at 49.

[12] Slip op. at 15, 22 ILM at 49.

[13] Slip op. at 16, 22 ILM at 50.

* From time to time, the *Journal* will report decisions of interest of the Iran-United States Claims Tribunal.

These cases involved a challenge by the respondent, the Islamic Republic of Iran, to the jurisdiction of the Iran-United States Claims Tribunal over claims filed by two publicly held U.S. corporations, Flexi-Van Leasing, Inc. and General Motors Corporation. Article II(1) of the Claims Settlement Agreement between Iran and the United States empowers the Tribunal to hear, *inter alia,* certain claims of U.S. "nationals" against Iran; and Article VII(1)(b) of the Agreement defines the term "national" of the United States to include

> a corporation or other legal entity which is organized under the laws of . . . the United States or any of its states or territories, the District of Columbia or the Commonwealth of Puerto Rico, if, collectively, natural persons who are citizens of such country hold, directly or indirectly, an interest in such corporation or entity equivalent to fifty per cent or more of its capital stock.

Article VII(2) of the Agreement defines "claims of nationals" of the United States as claims owned continuously by U.S. nationals from the date on which the claim arose to January 19, 1981, the date on which the Agreement entered into force. The respondent alleged that the claimants had failed to present evidence to satisfy either of these Article VII requirements. In response to this jurisdictional challenge, Chamber One of the Tribunal, in two decisions rendered by Judge Lagergren, set forth the types of evidence that generally must be presented by publicly held corporations in order to prove U.S. nationality and continuous ownership of claims. In addition, the Chamber af-

---

The Tribunal was established in 1981 pursuant to a Claims Settlement Agreement between the Islamic Republic of Iran and the United States. The Claims Settlement Agreement is part of the Algiers Accords which led to the release of 52 Americans held hostage in Iran from Nov. 4, 1979 to Jan. 19, 1981. The Accords consist of two Declarations issued by the Government of the Democratic and Popular Republic of Algeria on Jan. 19, 1981, together with a number of technical implementing agreements. The first Declaration, generally known as the General Declaration, provided for the release of the hostages in return for a number of actions and undertakings by the United States, including the transfer of Iranian assets frozen in the United States. The second Declaration, generally known as the Claims Settlement Agreement, established a new international arbitral body, the Iran-United States Claims Tribunal. Article II(1) of the Claims Settlement Agreement gives the Tribunal jurisdiction, *inter alia,* over "claims of nationals of the United States against Iran and claims of nationals of Iran against the United States, and any related counterclaims, . . . aris[ing] out of debts, contracts . . . , expropriations or other measures affecting property rights"; and Article II(2) of the Agreement gives the Tribunal jurisdiction over "official claims of the United States and Iran against each other arising out of contractual arrangements between them for the purchase and sale of goods and services."

Article III of the Claims Settlement Agreement provides that the Tribunal shall consist of nine members (three appointed by the United States, three by Iran, and three third-country arbitrators chosen by the six party-appointed arbitrators) or such larger multiple of three as the two Governments may agree. Claims may be decided by the full Tribunal or by a panel of three members of the Tribunal as the Tribunal President shall determine. Presidential Order No. 1 of Oct. 19, 1981 (as amended by Presidential Order No. 8 of March 24, 1982) created three Chambers to hear claims arising under Article II(1) and (2) of the Agreement. The administrative decisions and presidential orders do not specify that the decisions of one Chamber are binding on the others. However, Article IV of the Agreement provides that all decisions and awards shall be final and binding and that any award that the Tribunal may render against either Government shall be enforceable against that Government in the courts of any nation in accordance with its laws.

forded the claimants in the present cases additional time to produce such evidence.[1]

The Chamber first described the general principles that should be followed for purposes of establishing corporate nationality. The respondent had contended that in order to satisfy the requirements of Article VII, a U.S. claimant that was publicly held must produce lists of the names and addresses of all its shareholders and detailed evidence of the U.S. nationality of over 50 percent of its shareholders with respect to both the date on which the claim arose and January 19, 1981. The Chamber held, however, that it is "neither possible nor necessary" for claimants to provide such voluminous submissions and that any such requirements would impose "excessive burdens on the parties and the Tribunal."[2] Relying on standards set by prior international arbitral tribunals,[3] the Chamber concluded that it could require whatever evidence of corporate nationality it deemed to be sufficient under the circumstances of each case and that it was free to draw reasonable inferences from such evidence.

As to the particular evidence required, the Chamber held that there must be evidence to support each claimant's two jurisdictional allegations: first, that the claimant was, during the relevant time period, a corporation organized under the laws of the United States; and second, that during the same period, 50 percent or more of the capital stock of the claimant was held, directly or indirectly, by natural persons who were citizens of the United States.

With respect to the first requirement, the Chamber held that a corporation could meet this burden by producing a certificate by a government official of the U.S. state of incorporation stating the date on which the claimant was incorporated and that the claimant continues to exist. The Chamber concluded that if such certificate shows that the claimant was organized before the claim arose, if the date of the certificate is after January 19, 1981, and if no convincing rebuttal evidence is produced, "the Chamber will draw the reasonable inference that the corporation was continuously in existence from the date the claim arose until at least January 19, 1981."

With respect to the second requirement, the Chamber determined that in most cases a corporate claimant must submit two additional documents in order to make a prima facie showing that at least 50 percent of its voting stock was owned continuously by U.S. nationals during the relevant time period: (1) copies of those pages of the corporation's proxy statements issued by the corporation in connection with its Annual Meetings closest in time to the date

[1] Judge Mahmoud Kashani, the Iranian-appointed member of Chamber One, filed a dissent to the order in *Flexi-Van*.

[2] The Chamber also pointed out that the list of a U.S. corporation's stockholders is not a matter of public record. Furthermore, it noted that during the period from the date on which Flexi-Van's claim arose to January 19, 1981, Flexi-Van had approximately 6 million shares of common stock outstanding, owned at various relevant times by approximately 4,300 to 5,500 stockholders. Similarly, during the relevant period, General Motors Corp. had outstanding more than 300 million shares of common stock, owned by approximately 1.5 million stockholders.

[3] *See, e.g.*, William Parker (U.S.A.) v. United Mexican States, 4 R. Int'l Arb. Awards 39 (1926); George Pinson (France) v. United Mexican States, 5 R. Int'l Arb. Awards 327 (1928).

on which the claim arose and to January 19, 1981, showing the number of shares of each class of capital stock entitled to vote at the meetings and information with respect to any beneficial owners of 5 percent or more of the corporation's voting stock, with a sworn statement by a corporate official that such proxy statements are true and complete copies; and (2) a notarized affidavit by a corporate officer stating the percentage of voting stock held by stockholders of record with addresses in the United States as shown on the stockholders list used in connection with the corporation's Annual Meeting closest in time to January 19, 1981.[4]

Specifically, the Chamber held that these documents would be required in cases where the proxy statements showed that principal holders of voting stock (those owning 5 percent or more) held less than 40 percent of the total voting stock entitled to vote at the annual meeting.[5] However, in cases where the total number of voting shares owned by all holders of 5 percent or more of such stock was greater than 40 percent, the Chamber held that it may require the claimant to submit further evidence concerning the nationality of a sufficient number of those principal holders to enable the Chamber to make a reasonable determination of nationality on a case-by-case basis.

In arriving at this conclusion the Chamber made a number of findings of particular interest. First, the Chamber took judicial notice of official United States Government statistics demonstrating that in the vast majority of cases the percentage of foreign ownership of the stock of U.S. corporations has been less than 10 percent. Second, the Chamber observed that stock ownership of publicly traded U.S. corporations is in constant flux and that therefore a corporate claimant was justified in measuring its stock ownership on a periodic rather than a daily basis. The Tribunal concluded that the most practical and appropriate dates of measurement were the dates of Annual Meetings of stockholders closest in time to the date on which the claim arose and to January 19, 1981. Third, the Chamber found that information in corporate proxy statements filed with the U.S. Securities and Exchange Commission comprises an "appropriate source of reliable evidence" with respect to the nationality of stockholders.

Finally, the Chamber addressed the issue of establishing the corporate nationality of a subsidiary corporation. In this connection, the Chamber held that the parent must meet the requirements set forth above and also provide two additional documents to show that the subsidiary was a U.S. national and that 50 percent or more of the subsidiary was owned by natural persons who were citizens of the United States. First, the subsidiary must submit a certificate

[4] The first requirement was set forth by Chamber One in the *Flexi-Van* order; the second was added in the *General Motors* order. *Cf.* The Management of Alcan Aluminium Ltd. v. Ircable Corp., AWD 41-91-3 (May 3, 1983) (Chamber 3), in which Chamber Three held that while it may draw reasonable inferences based upon probabilities, a showing by the claimant that, at the relevant times, between 52 and 53% of its shareholders had reported U.S. addresses did *not* provide an adequate basis for the inference that U.S. nationals held 50% or more of the claimant's shares.

[5] The Chamber noted that this requirement was reasonable because even if as much as 40% of all the voting stock is owned by non-U.S. nationals, the remaining shares held by non-nationals could not, in accordance with U.S. Government statistics, reasonably be expected to exceed 10%.

by a government official of the U.S. state of incorporation showing the date of incorporation and whether the subsidiary existed after January 19, 1981. Second, the parent must provide a certificate by a firm of independent certified public accountants stating that the parent's financial statements for the relevant period accurately reflect the parent's ownership of the claimant subsidiary.

The basic standards of proof set forth in these orders have been accepted by the other Chambers of the Tribunal.[6]

Jurisdiction—dual nationality

ESPHAHANIAN v. BANK TEJARAT. AWD 31-157-2.
Iran-United States Claims Tribunal, The Hague, March 29, 1983.

Claimant, Nasser Esphahanian, a naturalized U.S. citizen, filed a claim against respondent, Bank Tejarat, an Iranian banking entity, in the Iran-United States Claims Tribunal, alleging wrongful dishonor of a check. Under Article II(1) of the Claims Settlement Agreement between Iran and the United States, the Tribunal has jurisdiction to hear, *inter alia,* certain claims of U.S. "nationals" against Iran. The respondent sought dismissal of the present claim, contending that the Tribunal had no jurisdiction because the claimant was an Iranian national. The respondent argued that the claimant's Iranian nationality was never renounced in accordance with Iranian municipal law and that Iran does not recognize dual nationality. The respondent further argued that, in any case, the theory of absolute nonresponsibility of a state for claims of its own citizens against the state prohibited the Tribunal from exercising jurisdiction. In response, the claimant argued that the Tribunal had jurisdiction over dual nationals by virtue of Article VII(1) of the Claims Settlement Agreement, which defines a "national" as a "citizen" of either Iran or the United States without restriction regarding dual nationals. In a decision authored by Judge Bellet, Chamber Two of the Tribunal rejected both the claimant's and the respondent's arguments and held that the proper test for determining the Tribunal's jurisdiction over dual nationals was that of the claimant's "dominant and effective nationality." Applying this test, the Chamber held that it had jurisdiction to hear the claim, and it awarded damages to the claimant.

In ascertaining the proper test of nationality to be applied to claimants before the Tribunal, the Chamber first made a threshold determination concerning the applicable source of law. The Chamber held that in the absence of a specific provision in the Claims Settlement Agreement on the issue of dual nationals, the Chamber must determine the meaning of the text through

[6] *See, e.g.,* Rexnord Inc. v. The Islamic Republic of Iran, AWD 21-132-3 (Jan. 10, 1983) (Chamber 3). It has been reported that both Chambers Two and Three have told claimants at prehearing conferences that the documents required by the *Flexi-Van* and *General Motors* orders would be acceptable as proof of corporate nationality.

application of the rules of the Vienna Convention on the Law of Treaties.[1] In this respect, the Chamber observed that paragraph 3(c) of Article 31 of the Vienna Convention directs the Chamber to take into account "any relevant rules of international law applicable in the relations between the parties."

Turning to applicable international legal precedents, the Chamber began by analyzing the 1930 Hague Convention on Certain Questions relating to the Conflict of Nationality Laws (the Hague Convention).[2] The Chamber observed that the Hague Convention provides in Article 4 that "[a] State may not afford diplomatic protection to one of its nationals against a State whose nationality such person also possesses." The Chamber distinguished this rule from a case, "such as the present one, where a dual national, by himself, brings before an international tribunal his own claim against one of the States whose nationality he possesses." In applying international law, the Chamber determined that its position was similar to that of a court of a third state faced with the claim of a dual national against one of the states of his nationality. Again relying on the Hague Convention,[3] the Chamber held that in such a case it should determine its jurisdiction by adopting the test of the claimant's dominant and effective nationality.

The Chamber supported this conclusion by reference to international arbitral precedents,[4] recent legal literature, and the structure of the Algiers Accords themselves. With respect to the Accords, the Chamber made three observations in support of its holding. First, the Chamber found that the Agreement creating the Tribunal was not a typical exercise of diplomatic protection in which a state, seeking some form of international redress for its nationals, creates a tribunal to which it, not its nationals, is a party. Rather, under the Accords, the Governments are not parties to the arbitration of claims of their nationals; the nationals themselves present their own claims.[5] Second, the two Governments were not before the Tribunal solely in their capacities as sovereign states because, under the Accords, each Government

[1] Both Iran and the United States have acknowledged before the Tribunal that international agreements between them, including the Claims Settlement Agreement, are to be interpreted in accordance with the rules embodied in the Vienna Convention on the Law of Treaties of May 23, 1969, *reprinted in* 63 AJIL 875 (1969), 8 ILM 679 (1969). *See* Memorials filed before the Tribunal on Nov. 23, 1981 in case A/1 by Iran (p. 22) and by the United States (p. 11).

[2] 179 LNTS 89.

[3] Article 5 of the Hague Convention, *supra* note 2, states that "within a third State, a person having more than one nationality shall be treated as if he had only one" and that third states "may, in [their] territory, recognize exclusively amongst the nationalities possessed by such individual, either the nationality of the country in which he mainly and principally resides, or the nationality of the State to which, according to the circumstances, he appears to be more attached in fact" (quoted by Chamber Two).

[4] Judge Bellet relied particularly on the Nottebohm Case (Liechtenstein v. Guat.), 1955 ICJ Rep. 4; and the Mergé Case (U.S. v. Italy), 14 R. Int'l Arb. Awards 236 (1955).

[5] Article III(3) of the Claims Settlement Agreement states that "[c]laims of nationals of the United States and Iran . . . shall be presented to the Tribunal either by claimants themselves, or, in the case of claims of less than $250,000, by the Government of such national." In the latter case, Chamber Two noted, the Governments act only as counsel.

guaranteed the debts of juridical persons not part of the Government itself.[6] Thus, the Governments assumed responsibility for private as well as public law duties. Third, the Tribunal was "substituted for the national courts of both countries with a flexibility not found in either." Moreover, since there is no *lex fori* binding on the Tribunal,[7] the two Governments "knew or should have known that, when dealing with dual nationals, the Tribunal would have no choice but to give effect to the 'real and effective nationality [of the claimant] . . . based on the stronger factual ties between the person concerned and one of the States whose nationality is involved.' "[8]

Applying this test to the claimant, the Chamber held that the following were important factors in determining the claimant's dominant and effective nationality: the claimant's place of residence, voting record, property ownership, place of schooling, payment of taxes, family ties, military service and investments. In addition, the Chamber closely examined the claim itself to determine whether it arose from benefits not otherwise available to a foreign national in Iran. In this respect, the Chamber determined that all of the actions relevant to the claim could have been lawfully taken by a non-Iranian. The Chamber therefore concluded that the claimant was a U.S. national within the meaning of the Claims Settlement Agreement and that the Tribunal had jurisdiction to decide his claim.

Judge Shafie Shafeiei, the Iranian member of Chamber Two, refused to sign the majority opinion, stating that it was "tainted with improper motives" and could not be legally justified. The Government of Iran also strongly protested the decision, requesting that the issue of jurisdiction over claims by dual nationals be decided by the Full Tribunal as an interpretive dispute under Article VI(4) of the Claims Settlement Agreement.[9] The Tribunal has agreed to the Iranian request and has scheduled a hearing for October 6, 1983 to consider this issue.

[6] Article VII(3) and (4) of the Claims Settlement Agreement includes within the definition of Iran and the United States "any agency, instrumentality, or entity controlled" by either of the two Governments.

[7] Article V of the Claims Settlement Agreement states: "The Tribunal shall decide all cases on the basis of respect for law, applying such choice of law rules and principles of commercial and international law as the Tribunal determines to be applicable. . . ."

[8] Quoting the Nottebohm Case, 1955 ICJ REP. at 22. To this conclusion, the Chamber added "an important caveat": it reserved the right to deny jurisdiction to dual nationals on equitable grounds in cases of fraudulent use of nationality.

[9] Article VI(4) of the Claims Settlement Agreement gives the Tribunal jurisdiction over "[a]ny question concerning the interpretation or application" of the Agreement "upon the request of either Iran or the United States." Under Presidential Order No. 1 of Oct. 19, 1981, only the Full Tribunal has jurisdiction to hear cases arising under this paragraph. Under Article IV(1) of the Claims Settlement Agreement, all decisions and awards of the Tribunal are final and binding. Thus, the hearing scheduled for Oct. 6, 1983 before the Full Tribunal will not affect the award in *Esphahanian*, the value of which the claimant received in May 1983.

Jurisdiction—interpretation of "other measures affecting property rights"

GRIMM v. THE GOVERNMENT OF THE ISLAMIC REPUBLIC OF IRAN. AWD 25-71-1.
Iran-United States Claims Tribunal, The Hague, February 11, 1983.

Claimant, the widow of the Managing Director and General Manager of the Oil Service Company of Iran, filed a claim in the Iran-United States Claims Tribunal against respondent, the Government of the Islamic Republic of Iran, for loss of support and punitive damages relating to the assassination of her husband in Iran in 1978. The claimant based her claim on an alleged breach by the respondent of its responsibility under international law to exercise due diligence in affording protection to her husband, an alien in Iran. The claimant asserted that the respondent's failure to protect her husband gave rise to a claim that fell within the jurisdiction of the Tribunal. Article II(1) of the Agreement provides, *inter alia,* that the Tribunal is empowered to hear claims arising out of "debts, contracts . . . , expropriations or other measures affecting property rights." In a decision authored by Judge Lagergren, Chamber One of the Tribunal held that the claim did not fall within the meaning of the phrase "other measures affecting property rights" and dismissed the claim for lack of jurisdiction.

The Chamber based its holding on three grounds. First, the Chamber reasoned that a failure to protect the claimant's husband could affect only the life and safety of Mr. Grimm, not the rights of the claimant. The Chamber held that compensation for mental anguish, grief and suffering could not be a property right affected by the alleged failure to provide adequate protection since the right to such compensation, if any, arose out of the assassination. Since this right did not exist prior to the assassination, it could not be affected by the failure to protect.

Second, applying the principle of *ejusdem generis,* the Chamber concluded that the phrase "other measures affecting property rights" should be construed as "generically similar to 'expropriations' " and that the "alleged failure to provide protection is in no way similar to expropriations." In this respect, the Chamber observed that in connection with another claim before the Tribunal,[1] the United States Government had argued that claims for the tortious destruction of property were not intended by the parties to come within the Tribunal's jurisdiction.

Third, the Chamber relied on the fact that the Claims Settlement Agreement does not contain an explicit grant of jurisdiction for damages suffered by surviving dependents. The Chamber observed that it is generally recognized that a provision which establishes the scope of the jurisdiction of an arbitral tribunal should be given a restrictive interpretation. Referring to the language of the United States-Mexican General and Special Claims Conventions of 1923 and the Berlin Treaty of Peace of 1921, the Chamber noted that each of these agreements expressly addressed damages suffered by persons

[1] Haji-Bagherpour v. The United States of America, AWD 23-428-2 (Jan. 26, 1983) (Chamber Two).

as distinct from damage to property. Accordingly, the Chamber concluded that "[i]f the Governments [of the United States and Iran] had intended to bring damages to surviving dependents within the ambit of the Tribunal's jurisdiction, it can be assumed that they would have done so by incorporating express language to that effect."

Judge Holtzmann, the American-appointed arbitrator in Chamber One, forcefully dissented, arguing that the ordinary meaning of "property rights" under international law includes a surviving dependent's right to financial support and that the respondent's failure to protect the life of the claimant's husband resulted in a property loss to the claimant that was "squarely within the jurisdiction of this Tribunal." The dissent emphasized that the claim was not for failure to provide protection to the claimant's husband or for injury to him. Rather, the claimant alleged damages suffered when her husband's financial support was taken away from her. According to the dissent, such support has long been recognized as a property right by international arbitral tribunals and legal commentators. Thus, the absence of any language in the Agreement explicitly granting jurisdiction to the Tribunal over damages suffered by surviving dependents was irrelevant.

The dissent also contested the majority's conclusion that "other measures affecting property rights" is simply a category of "expropriations." Such an interpretation, Holtzmann argued, was not supported by the language of Article II(1) of the Claims Settlement Agreement, particularly in light of the broad reading that "expropriation" has otherwise received by the Tribunal.[2] In the view of the dissent, the phrase " 'other measures affecting property rights' . . . simply adds a further category, leaving the Tribunal open to find liability arising out of any measures which result in diminution of the value of property."[3]

[2] *See* Harza Engineering Co. v. The Islamic Republic of Iran, AWD 19-98-2 (Dec. 30, 1982) (Chamber Two) ("the phrase 'expropriations or other measures affecting property rights' has broad meaning under international law").

[3] The dissent also noted that the majority's interpretation of "other measures" was not supported by the U.S. pleadings in *Haji-Bagherpour, supra* note 1, since that case "arose in a different context and the Award of Chamber Two was made without 'addressing the issue at hand' in this case."

CURRENT DEVELOPMENTS

The 1982 Session of the UN Sub-Commission on Prevention of Discrimination and Protection of Minorities

The United Nations Sub-Commission on Prevention of Discrimination and Protection of Minorities held its 35th annual meeting in Geneva from August 16 to September 10, 1982, and considered a broad range of human rights issues as diverse as allegations of human rights violations, establishment of legal norms, and promotion of research. The Sub-Commission, consisting of 26 "experts" elected on the basis of equitable geographic distribution, is accountable to the governmental Commission on Human Rights, which in turn is subsidiary to the Economic and Social Council (ECOSOC). Assisting this hierarchy is the UN Centre for Human Rights, formerly known as the UN Division of Human Rights.

In recent years, controversy has arisen over the increasingly independent stance adopted by the Sub-Commission in much of its work.[1] However, the Sub-Commission's broad reading of its originally narrow jurisdiction (as reflected in its title) has not been directly challenged by its parent bodies and has been widely supported by nongovernmental organizations (NGO's).

At its 35th session,[2] the Sub-Commission proved itself eager to attain tangible, substantive results in certain areas, *e.g.*, detention, though it was less successful in others. An ever-present tension between members' political views and independent expertise continued to haunt the Sub-Commission, but there were constructive developments such as the increasing effectiveness of working groups and the Sub-Commission's growing awareness of the important relationships among studies, standards, and implementation of human rights.

Violations of Human Rights

ECOSOC's Resolution 1503 (XLVIII) empowers the Sub-Commission to examine and bring to the attention of the Commission communications "which appear to reveal a consistent pattern of gross and reliably attested violations of human rights and fundamental freedoms."[3] Communications are received

[1] In 1981 some members of the Commission strongly criticized the Sub-Commission for the expanded role the latter sought at its 33d session in 1980. *See* Gardeniers, *The U.N. Sub-Commission on Prevention of Discrimination and Protection of Minorities: Recent Developments,* 4 HUMAN RIGHTS Q. 353 (1982). For analyses of the Sub-Commission's 1980 and 1981 sessions, see *id.;* Hannum, *Human Rights and the United Nations: Progress at the 1980 Session of the U.N. Sub-Commission on Prevention of Discrimination and Protection of Minorities,* 3 HUMAN RIGHTS Q. 1 (1981); and the Current Developments Notes by Hannum, and Gardeniers, Hannum, & Kruger in 75 AJIL 172 (1981), and 76 AJIL 404 (1982), respectively.

[2] The report of the Sub-Commission is UN Doc. E/CN.4/Sub.2/1983/4 (1983), also listed as UN Doc. E/CN.4/Sub.2/1982/43 (1982) [hereinafter cited as 1982 Report].

[3] ESC Res. 1503 (XLVIII), 48 UN ESCOR Supp. (No. 1A) at 8, UN Doc. E/4832/Add.1 (1970).

from individuals, NGO's, governments, and other sources and are handled in closed session by the Working Group on Communications. Owing to the confidentiality of the "1503 procedure," no public announcements are made of the actions, if any, taken by the working group; however, it seems safe to assume that the working group considered and forwarded to the Commission communications concerning Afghanistan, Argentina, East Germany, Haiti, Indonesia, Iran, Paraguay, Uruguay, and Turkey. Iran was publicly discussed at the 1983 session of the Commission,[4] while East Germany was reportedly dropped from consideration. At this session of the Sub-Commission, it was quite clear from unofficial comments by working group members that the number of communications brought before the working group under the "1503" label has increased dramatically and that appropriate changes must be made to accommodate this growing workload. To this end, a Sub-Commission draft resolution—ultimately deferred—suggested that the number of working group members be increased from five to eight or that the group meet twice yearly, requested that votes under the communications item be taken by secret ballot, and decided "that Government employees would be placed in an impossible position if they were required to vote on questions involving their own countries."[5]

Under ECOSOC Resolution 1235 (XLII), the Sub-Commission may "examine information relevant to gross violations of human rights and fundamental freedoms."[6] In this connection, the Sub-Commission approved the transmission (via the Secretary-General and the Chairman of the Commission on Human Rights) of a condemnatory telegram to the Government of Israel, which expressed grave concern at the "vast human suffering resulting from the invasion of Lebanon and the blockade and massive bombardment of Beirut" and called for "the full co-operation of Israel, and all other States and parties concerned" in humanitarian efforts.[7] As has proved to be the case in the recent past, this session's debate on Israel resulted in a number of recommendations and findings, including condemnation of the Israeli occupation of Lebanon, demand for Israeli withdrawal from all occupied Palestinian territories, and support for Palestinian self-determination, sovereignty, and independence.[8]

Though public debate did touch upon alleged human rights violations in the Soviet Union, Cyprus, and North and South Korea,[9] no resolutions were

[4] Iran was the subject of Commission Res. 1983/34. *See* UN Doc. E/CN.4/1983/L.10/Add.3, at 23 (1983).

[5] UN Doc. E/CN.4/Sub.2/1982/L.6 (1982), with amendments in UN Doc. E/CN.4/Sub.2/1982/L.31 (1982).

[6] ESC Res. 1235 (XLII), 42 UN ESCOR Supp. (No. 1) at 17, UN Doc. E/4393 (1967).

[7] For the text, see Sub-Comm'n Dec. 1982/2, 1982 Report at 110.

[8] *See* Res. 1982/18, *id.* at 91–92.

[9] For a summary of debate on Item 7 (violation of human rights and fundamental freedoms), including discussion of these and other countries, see UN Press Releases HR/1237–38, Aug. 17, 1982; 1247, Aug. 24, 1982; 1248–49, Aug. 25, 1982; 1250–51, Aug. 26, 1982; UN Docs. E/CN.4/Sub.2/1982/SR.2–3, 13–17, 33–35 (1982). For a list of all countries referred to in Item 7 debate, see UN Doc. E/CN.4/Sub.2/1982/CRP.1/Add.7, para. 6 (1982).

passed on these countries, and a resolution concerning Poland was deferred.[10] The Sub-Commission did adopt a resolution addressing violations in Afghanistan.[11]

Complaints of human rights violations ranging from disappearances to torture to genocide were leveled against various Latin American countries, including Mexico, Nicaragua, Honduras, Paraguay, Argentina, and Uruguay;[12] but only Guatemala, Chile, and El Salvador were the subjects of resolutions.[13]

Two resolutions of universal scope also were adopted under this agenda item. The first requests that ECOSOC permit the Sub-Commission to appoint a special rapporteur to revise and update the Study on Genocide;[14] the second seeks extension of the mandate of the Working Group on Enforced or Involuntary Disappearances, and designation of the subject as of "highest priority" for the Sub-Commission's 36th session.[15]

As in 1981, a Sub-Commission resolution was passed supporting East Timor's demands for self-determination.[16] In addition, assaults against the cultural and religious rights of Kurds in Turkey and Iraq and Baha'is in Iran were again noted, and allegations of aggression and other wrongful acts by Vietnam against Democratic Kampuchea were revived. As in the past, the 1982 Sub-Commission adopted resolutions concerning both Iran[17] and Kampuchea.[18] The latter country was also the subject of an oral report by Asbjørn Eide, expert from Norway. An unsuccessful effort to direct a telegram to the Government of Haiti, in order to facilitate the presence of observers at an upcoming trial with political overtones in that country, also was made.[19]

Several other countries, most of them African, were mentioned but were not the subject of extensive debate or resolutions: Albania, Benin, Cuba, Ethiopia, Madagascar, Malawi, Uganda, and Zaire. South Africa, of course, was the exception to this tendency to pass over African nations. The delivery

[10] *See* UN Doc. E/CN.4/Sub.2/1982/L.9 (1982). The resolution would have the Sub-Commission receive information next year on the results of the Secretary-General's study of the situation in Poland.

[11] *See* Res. 1982/21, 1982 Report at 94–95. The resolution welcomes future information on "the use of illegal weapons in Afghanistan" and recommends that the Commission "give special attention and high priority to the situation in Afghanistan at its thirty-ninth session."

[12] *See supra* note 9.

[13] *See* Res. 1982/17, 19, and 26, respectively, 1982 Report at 90–91, 93, and 100–01, respectively.

[14] *See* Res. 1982/2, *id.* at 72, with accompanying text, Sub-Commission Draft Res. I, *id.* at 1, adopted without change by the Commission at its 1983 session. *See* Human Rights Comm'n Res. 1983/24, UN Doc. E/CN.4/1983/L.10/Add.2, at 16 (1983).

[15] *See* Res. 1982/5, 1982 Report at 74–75. The mandate of the working group was continued for another year by the Commission at its 1983 session. *See* Human Rights Comm'n Res. 1983/20, UN Doc. E/CN.4/1983/L.10/Add.2, at 9 (1983).

[16] *See* Res. 1982/20, 1982 Report at 93–94, with accompanying text, Sub-Commission Draft Res. VII, *id.* at 6.

[17] *See* Res. 1982/25, *id.* at 99, which expresses approval of efforts to have the Secretary-General establish direct contact with Iran and determines that the human rights situation in Iran deserves continuing scrutiny.

[18] *See* Res. 1982/22, *id.* at 96.

[19] *See* UN Press Release HR/1248, Aug. 25, 1982.

of speeches condemning apartheid coincided with the Sub-Commission's expression of condolences to the family of the late Ruth First, a slain white who fought against apartheid.[20] The two superpowers emerged relatively unscathed from the general public debate; the United States was scrutinized primarily on the treatment of migrant farmworkers,[21] and also on indigenous people's rights, and the USSR survived the passage of a resolution on Afghanistan and the deferment of one on Poland.

In addition to these country-specific allegations, this year reference was made to alleged violations of the rights of refugees in general, Romany people (often called "gypsies"), certain UN staff members, disabled persons worldwide, and prisoners in Manchuria subject to medical experimentation by the Japanese during World War II.[22] As a result of intensive NGO lobbying, the Sub-Commission adopted a resolution to gather information from many sources on ways to promote the human rights of disabled persons, and to examine how government spending cuts affect programs for such persons, in order to help them assert their rights.[23] The issue of disabled persons' rights is one that seems to be largely independent of the ideological, economic, racial, sexual, or other such prejudices that often surround human rights questions.

The Sub-Commission also had before it a note by the Secretariat on the 1963 Study of Discrimination in Respect of the Right of Everyone to Leave Any Country, Including His Own, and to Return to His Country. The Sub-Commission subsequently adopted a resolution requesting C. Mubanga-Chipoya to report "current trends" in this area, in particular to address employment discrimination, problems of the "brain drain" from developing countries, and the restriction on the right to leave permissible under Article 12(5) of the Covenant on Civil and Political Rights.[24]

To attempt to depoliticize debates between government observers[25] reminiscent of the political atmosphere of the Commission and other UN bodies, the Sub-Commission adopted a statement expressing the view that "in order to avoid inter-State recriminations which are detrimental to [the Sub-Commission's] work as an expert body, observers for States should in future . . . not implicate other States in a deliberately abusive manner."[26]

The Sub-Commission also adopted a resolution aimed at obtaining au-

[20] For the text of the telegram of condolence, see Sub-Comm'n Dec. 1982/6, 1982 Report at 111.

[21] The Minority Rights Group presented a paper on this topic. *See* UN Doc. E/CN.4/Sub.2/1982/21, para. 19 (1982).

[22] A draft decision on this last subject submitted by Messrs. Whitaker and Carey, UN Doc. E/CN.4/Sub.2/1982/L.13 (1982), was rejected by the Sub-Commission.

[23] *See* Res. 1982/1, 1982 Report at 71–72.

[24] *See* Res. 1982/23, *id.* at 97.

[25] Tension also arose between observers and experts, as was the case between Mrs. de Sousa, alternate from Panama, and the Government observer from Uruguay. *See* UN Press Release HR/1249, Aug. 25, 1982, where the observer responded strongly to a statement made by the expert found in UN Press Release HR/1247, Aug. 24, 1982, and accused the expert of being "deceived"; UN Doc. E/CN.4/Sub.2/1982/SR.15, para. 10 (1982). These documents do not, however, adequately reflect the high degree of negative feeling (indeed bitterness) that the observer's comments conveyed.

[26] Sub-Comm'n Dec. 1982/12, 1982 Report at 112.

thorization from ECOSOC for on-site visits by "one or more members of the Sub-Commission, following a decision by the Commission on Human Rights . . . , with the approval of the government concerned," to "any country as regards which the Commission has received reliably attested allegations of a gross and consistent pattern of violations of human rights and fundamental freedoms."[27] The Commission, however, once again decided to postpone consideration of this issue.[28]

Slavery

Issues falling under the label of slavery and slavery-like practices were dealt with both in the presessional Working Group on Slavery and in a special rapporteur's update of the Sub-Commission's 1966 Report on Slavery. The working group's report[29] included a recommendation that written allegations by NGO's against states should be brought to the attention of the states concerned for their observations and comments, and that these states should be invited to participate in discussions during the following session of the working group. The proposals in the report for studies on the sale of children, street children, and female circumcision indicate the working group's willingness to stretch its definition of "slavery."

Benjamin Whitaker's updating of the 1966 Report on Slavery[30] explores the range of contemporary manifestations of slavery and slavery-like practices, including such infrequently publicized subjects as involuntary abortion, genital mutilation, dowry killings, and exploitation of hard-drug addicts. The report also canvasses action in the field taken at the national and international levels and offers a series of conclusions and recommendations, only a few of which can be mentioned here. For example, the report recommends that increased pressure be put upon states to sign or ratify relevant conventions and that the United Nations and its agencies "actively offer Member States such co-ordinated legal, technical, administrative, educative, financial and other practical assistance and co-operation as is desirable to eliminate conditions conducive to slavery and slavery-like situations."[31] In addition, the United Nations Development Programme should help rehabilitate slaves and suggest ways that development programs could be adapted to help fight slavery.

Other recommendations call for a better diagnosis of the causes or roots of slavery; the updating and expanding of the existing list of slavery experts and more involvement of these experts and also NGO's in the work of the United Nations; the provision of legal aid to slavery victims; more regular reporting and publication of all slavery cases globally; expert participation in country visits and improved information gathering; and the establishment of

[27] Res. 1982/14, *id.* at 84, with accompanying text, Sub-Commission Draft Res. VI, *id.* at 5.

[28] *See* Human Rights Comm'n Dec. 1983/105, UN Doc. E/CN.4/1983/L.10/Add.6, at 2 (1983).

[29] UN Docs. E/CN.4/Sub.2/1982/21 and Corr. 1 (1982).

[30] The updated report is contained in UN Docs. E/CN.4/Sub.2/1982/20 and Add.1 (1982). The 1966 report, prepared by Mr. Awad, is UN Pub. Sales No. 67.XIV.2 (1967).

[31] UN Doc. E/CN.4/Sub.2/1982/20/Add.1 (1982), Recommendation (ii)(a).

working groups to protect women and children (and/or that the Slavery Working Group be expanded to better cover these areas).[32]

The Sub-Commission passed two resolutions, one calling for the transmission of the updated report to the Commission,[33] the other generally—but not exactly—following the recommendations in the report.[34] The latter resolution also requests that Mr. Mudawi and Mrs. Warzazi prepare the report on female sexual mutilation. The Slavery Working Group undoubtedly will have an eventful future; until now, its work has led both to the authorization of an observation trip by Messrs. Bossuyt and Mudawi to Mauritania[35] and to an announcement by the Dominican Republic that it will participate in the working group's meetings at the next session.[36]

Indigenous Populations

The major question was how the presessional Working Group on Indigenous Populations[37] would interpret its mandate at its first session, for its initial work would greatly influence its future capabilities and ultimate impact. Its mandate, as set forth in the ECOSOC resolution authorizing the establishment of the working group, is twofold:

> (1) to "review developments pertaining to the promotion and protection of the human rights and fundamental freedoms of indigenous populations, including information . . . from Governments, specialized agencies, regional intergovernmental organizations and non-governmental organizations in consultative status, particularly those of indigenous peoples, to analyse such materials, and to submit its conclusions to the Sub-Commission"; and
>
> (2) to "give special attention to the evolution of standards concerning the rights of indigenous populations."[38]

In its deliberations on procedural issues, the group rejected—for the time being—the idea of distributing some form of detailed questionnaire and considered instead the desirability of focusing attention on several specific areas of concern regarding discrimination against indigenous populations (*e.g.*, the right to life, natural resources, religion, and self-determination) and gathering information on these subjects. The group unanimously supported extending its sources of information beyond those mentioned by ECOSOC, to experts and recognized authorities in the field, though with the important caveat that its "consent" is required and that submissions must not be irrelevant, abusive,

[32] *Id.*, Recommendation (xxi).

[33] Res. 1982/9, 1982 Report at 77–78, with accompanying text, Sub-Commission Draft Res. III, *id.* at 3. The Commission at its 1983 session adopted Sub-Commission Draft Res. III without a vote. *See* Human Rights Comm'n Res. 1983/25, UN Doc. E/CN.4/1983/L.10/Add.2, at 17 (1983).

[34] Res. 1982/15, 1982 Report at 85–88.

[35] *See* Sub-Comm'n Dec. 1982/7, *id.* at 111.

[36] *See* UN Doc. E/CN.4/Sub.2/1982/21, at 4 n.4 (1982). This year the conditions of migrant labor in that country were criticized before the working group.

[37] The report of the working group is contained in UN Doc. E/CN.4/Sub.2/1982/33 (1982).

[38] *See* ESC Res. 34 of May 7, 1982, as found in UN Doc. E/CN.4/Sub.2/1982/33, at 3 (1982).

or voluminous.[39] The working group thus has opened its forum to the very voices most likely to have been victims of the discrimination under scrutiny.[40]

The working group appears to have steered a middle course between two very different problems: on the one hand, many government observers asserted that the indigenous populations forum should not duplicate that of the "1503" Working Group on Communications by becoming a judicial or quasi-judicial "chamber of complaints";[41] on the other hand, some NGO's stressed that indigenous populations need specialized access to the United Nations. The working group decided that it would not receive complaints as such but would like to receive information—especially from indigenous persons—on alleged violations of human rights to help enable it to assess the adequacy of the existing national and international protection of indigenous peoples and to carry out its other mandated activities.

Beyond the complex questions of procedure and definition, the working group considered the evolution of substantive standards in the field of human rights for indigenous populations. It was noted that while existing standards, *e.g.*, those expressed in national, regional, and international instruments, might theoretically provide adequate protection for indigenous populations, in practice such standards have not been effective, perhaps because indigenous peoples are not specifically mentioned in most of those instruments. The group heard examples of several types of alleged violations involving the rights to life, physical integrity, and security (including alleged genocide or ethnocide in Guatemala, El Salvador, and Bangladesh);[42] the right to self-determination and the development of indigenous culture, traditions, language, and way of life; the right to freedom of religion and traditional religious practices (mentioning the case of the Black Hills in the United States);[43] the right to land and to natural resources (referring to Canada, the United States, Australia, Peru, Bolivia, Panama, Bangladesh, and the Philippines);[44] civil and political rights; and the right to education.

In its conclusions, the working group emphasized—literally—that it "*did not want, at this first and explorative session, to adopt firm recommendations to the Sub-Commission.*"[45] However, it took note of principles of openness and accessibility (particularly to representatives of indigenous populations) and suggestions for improving such accessibility by allocating funds for bringing such representatives to Geneva or by holding the group's meetings in regions containing indigenous people. Despite its unwillingness to act as a quasi-judicial body, the group agreed that "developments" could be examined so as to "elucidate whether existing or emerging standards are adhered to."[46] It concluded that there was a particular need to examine the application of existing standards on genocide and that the group should "discuss the possibility of

[39] Working group report, *supra* note 37, para. 84.

[40] The group did note, though, that documents submitted by NGO's or others without consultative status would not be distributed as UN documents, *id.*, para 23(ii), and that their statements would be viewed only as representing individual opinions, not that of any group.

[41] *Id.*, para. 24.

[42] *See id.*, paras. 77–81.

[43] *See id.*, paras. 86–88.

[44] *See id.*, paras. 89–99.

[45] *Id.*, para. 110.

[46] *Id.*, para. 114.

drafting one or more declarations . . . [and at] some time in the future it might also contemplate drafting a convention" on substantive standards.[47]

The Sub-Commission passed a resolution requesting the continuation of the special rapporteur's Study of the Problem of Discrimination against Indigenous Populations (the Cobo Study)[48] and another commending the group's work, generally endorsing its conclusions, and requesting that the Commission and ECOSOC establish a fund to help representatives of indigenous populations participate in the working group's meetings in Geneva.[49]

Detention

In contrast with its inactivity last year, this year's sessional Working Group on Detention presented a detailed list of recommendations to the full Sub-Commission.[50] The Sub-Commission passed a resolution on the basis of these recommendations that deals with several aspects of detention, *e.g.*, arrest, incommunicado detention, and trial, and suggests rather specific guidelines to be established in these problem areas. For example, incommunicado detention "should be discouraged and should be forbidden for periods exceeding 24 hours from the moment of arrest," every detainee "should be publicly announced," and anyone arrested or detained "should be entitled to be visited by members of his family and a lawyer of his choice, preferably within 24 hours after arrest and regularly thereafter."[51]

The Sub-Commission showed its concern that there be independent checks in the detention process by recommending, for example, that detention and interrogation spots be unexpectedly and independently inspected. Other recommendations center on limitation of *in camera* trials and military jurisdiction. In addition, "every detainee should be examined, preferably by a doctor of his own choice, within 48 hours after arrest and regularly thereafter," provision should be made "allowing a person sentenced to death proper time or opportunity for appeal," and extrajudicial executions should be prevented.[52]

The Sub-Commission further proposed a special study on how to implement international habeas corpus and anticipatory bail, sought an increase in the number of working group meetings for next year, and decided that next year the group "should give special attention to hearing and receiving information . . . [on] torture or cruel, inhuman or degrading treatment or punishment," with such work to be continued on an annual basis.[53]

The Sub-Commission hopes to receive (via the Secretary-General) "reliably attested information" from many sources concerning arrest and detention on vague or no grounds, duration of pretrial detention, "procedural guarantees

[47] *Id.*, para 126.

[48] Res. 1982/29, 1982 Report at 103–04.

[49] Res. 1982/31, *id.* at 105–06. At its 1983 session, the Commission supported establishing a fund for such a purpose, though contributions from member states are to be voluntary. Human Rights Comm'n Res. 1983/23, UN Doc. E/CN.4/1983/L.10/Add.2, at 14–15 (1983).

[50] The recommendations of the working group are found in its report, UN Doc. E/CN.4/Sub.2/1982/34, at 6, 7 (1982).

[51] *See* Res. 1982/10, 1982 Report at 78–81.

[52] *Ibid.*

[53] *Ibid.*

for preventive (administrative) detention, especially under states of emergency," existing incommunicado detention (when is it tolerated and how is it regulated?), extraterritorial abduction, and "suicides" in detention under "suspicious circumstances."[54] The Sub-Commission also asked the Secretary-General to provide a survey of maximum detention periods under existing national laws and decisions of international organs of investigation and settlement.

This year Special Rapporteur Nicole Questiaux presented her report on the effect of states of siege or emergency upon human rights.[55] Many emergency regimes, she finds, become permanent and institutionalized and result in the breakdown of normal institutions and of the rule of law. Mme. Questiaux's recommendations are of two sorts: the first are aimed at better developing the role of specialist international surveillance organs, and the second are geared towards strengthening the substantive guarantees found in international law, *e.g.*, by extending the list of rights of absolute inalienability.

Mental Health

The Sub-Commission reviewed a report on mental ill-health written by Special Rapporteur Erica-Irene Daes.[56] The report consists of a "concise review of the topic of mental illness and the protection of persons who are mentally ill or suffering from mental disorder," along with "draft guidelines, principles and guarantees" for the protection of persons detained on those grounds.[57] Mrs. Daes's report will undoubtedly be useful to many human rights organizations currently seeking to end psychiatric detention of human rights activists, particularly in the Soviet Union.

Research and Studies

Perhaps the most well-received report presented to the Sub-Commission at its 35th session was that of Raúl Ferrero, special rapporteur for a study on the New International Economic Order (NIEO) and the Promotion of Human Rights.[58] Discussion in the Sub-Commission focused on the indivisibility and interdependence—or linkage—of human rights and an NIEO. Although emphasis was placed upon the global character of the problem of development, the justness of the NIEO, the role of disarmament in promoting development, and the influence of colonialism on the present international economic order, it was also stressed that underdevelopment does not justify violations of human rights.

On a related topic, the Sub-Commission requested authorization to entrust Mr. Eide with preparation of a study on the right to adequate food as a human right, with special attention to "the normative content of the right to food

[54] *Ibid.*
[55] UN Doc. E/CN.4/Sub.2/1982/15 (1982).
[56] UN Doc. E/CN.4/Sub.2/1982/16 (1982).
[57] *Ibid.*
[58] This year Mr. Ferrero only presented part I, UN Docs. E/CN.4/Sub.2/1982/19/Rev.1 and Add.1 (1982).

and its significance in relation to the establishment of the new international economic order."[59] Other requests received included an updated list of banks, transnational corporations, and other organizations providing "assistance" to South Africa;[60] a preliminary report on conscientious objection to military service;[61] a "concrete programme of action" drafted by Abdelwahab Boudiba to address the problems of child labor outlined in his 1981 report on that subject;[62] and Justice Chowdhury's final report on discrimination in the administration of criminal justice.[63]

Discussion of the agenda item, "The effects of gross violations of human rights on international peace and security," seemed to bring together both actual allegations and general studies of human rights violations and point to one conclusion: gross violations *do* threaten international peace and security. Sub-Commission experts noted that apartheid, genocide, racism, and denial of self-determination are among the many gross violations that threaten world stability (as can be seen particularly from experience in the Middle East and southern Africa). One expert suggested that total disarmament should be seen as a collective human right.

The Sub-Commission deferred action on a resolution expressing the hope that states would release "all persons detained for their views who have not used or advocated violence, so that . . . [v]iolations of human rights will not afford a pretext to other States for using force to end such violation."[64] However, another resolution requested that the Security Council consider how most effectively to handle violations that threaten international peace; that the International Law Commission take the issue into account "when elaborating the draft code of offences against the peace and security of mankind"; and that the Sub-Commission consider "preparing principles and, in particular, establishing criteria to govern [relevant] situations."[65]

The Sub-Commission did forward to the Commission concrete proposals concerning possible terms of reference for the mandate of a High Commissioner for Human Rights. The proposed mandate would allow the High Commissioner, *inter alia,* to "initiate direct contacts with Governments, whenever such action appears necessary or desirable, to safeguard or assist in restoring respect for human rights," with particular attention to be given to "urgent situations" and "mass and flagrant violations."[66] The Sub-Commission proposed that the High Commissioner be nominated by the Secretary-General and elected by the General Assembly, and that he receive a 5-year mandate.[67]

[59] Res. 1982/7, 1982 Report at 76–77, with accompanying text, Sub-Commission Draft Res. II, *id.* at 2.

[60] UN Doc. E/CN.4/Sub.2/1982/10 (1982).

[61] UN Doc. E/CN.4/Sub.2/1982/24 (1982).

[62] *See* Note by the Special Rapporteur, UN Doc. E/CN.4/Sub.2/1982/29 (1982).

[63] UN Doc. E/CN.4/Sub.2/1982/7 (1982).

[64] UN Doc. E/CN.4/Sub.2/1982/L.22 (1982).

[65] Res. 1982/11, 1982 Report at 82, with accompanying text, Sub-Commission Draft Res. IV, *id.* at 3–4.

[66] Res. 1982/27, *id.* at 101–02.

[67] *Ibid.*

At the 39th session of the Commission, there was considerable debate on the proposed mandate of a High Commission for Human Rights, with several member states, led by Argentina, consid-

Organizational Matters

After closed meetings on Item 3, "Review of the status and activities of the Sub-Commission and its relationship with the Commission on Human Rights and other United Nations bodies," a public summary of the major issues under this item was presented.[68] (This review will be discussed further below.) In addition, the Sub-Commission deferred a resolution that sought to increase the size of the working group on communications established under the "1503" procedure or have it meet twice yearly; to have it vote on communications by secret ballot; and to require members who are government employees to abstain from voting on questions involving their own countries.[69] Deferment of these recommendations—all clearly aimed at increasing the effectiveness of the communications complaint procedure—highlights the politicization still evident in the Sub-Commission.

The Sub-Commission also failed to adopt two draft resolutions: one recognized, *inter alia,* the need for "an autonomous body . . . composed of independent experts which would report directly to" and be elected by ECOSOC;[70] the other provided "that one alternate to every member, from the same country, may be elected simultaneously . . . and that a member may be replaced by an alternate only when the alternate has been elected in this way."[71]

Observations

To view this session in its proper context, the Sub-Commission must be understood as one link in a long chain stretching over the years and weaving throughout the UN system. Thus, the 35th session cannot be fully evaluated until its initiatives are considered by the Commission on Human Rights and ECOSOC. When the cycle of hierarchical reporting is eventually completed, the Sub-Commission, in turn, will respond at its 36th session in 1983.

Review of the status and activities of the Sub-Commission as a distinct agenda item was a step forward in the quest to clarify and/or change substantive and procedural rules governing the Sub-Commission's competence. The discussion addressed questions about alternates, scope of work, and organizational independence that continually arose during debate on other agenda items. As the Sub-Commission assumes an increasingly active role, its

---

ering that the Sub-Commission had not provided the "first study" on possible terms of reference for a High Commissioner, envisioned in the Commission's Resolution 1982/22. The Commission ultimately decided to invite the Sub-Commission to "re-submit their proposals to the Commission," taking into account Resolution 1982/22 of the Commission and debate at its 39th session. The Commission decided to continue consideration of the question at its next session. Human Rights Comm'n Res. 1983/49, UN Doc. E/CN.4/1983/L.10/Add.7, at 2 (1983).

[68] UN Docs. E/CN.4/Sub.2/1982/CRP.1/Add.4 (1982), and E/CN.4/Sub.2/1982/SR.5/Add.1 (1982).

[69] *See supra* note 5.

[70] UN Doc. E/CN.4/Sub.2/1982/L.1 (1982).

[71] UN Doc. E/CN.4/Sub.2/1982/L.3 (1982). At its 39th session, the Commission did recommend to ECOSOC that states be required also to nominate alternates when nominating candidates for membership of the Sub-Commission, and that "no other person may serve as an alternate for a member, except that expert elected with him." *See* Human Rights Comm'n Res. 1983/21, UN Doc. E/CN.4/1983/L.10/Add.2, at 11 (1983).

procedural and substantive limitations may be questioned more intensely by its parent bodies as well as by its own members. For the time being, however, the Sub-Commission has its work set rather comfortably within the bounds of its own competence and political limitations. Its increasing concentration on issues of slavery, detention, and indigenous rights should improve continuity and balance some of its more erratic decision making.

The increased use of working groups and special rapporteurs is to be welcomed. Although government observers at times attempted to turn the Sub-Commission into a forum for political rhetoric, in the narrower confines of the working groups their comments were more relevant and helpful. In addition to the smaller likelihood of disruption of their work, the working groups and special rapporteurs, by focusing on relatively narrow topics, can achieve greater concentration and analysis than the full Sub-Commission. NGO participation is also much more effective in the less formal atmosphere of working groups, where an NGO is likely to be seen more as a helpful resource than as an antagonist. Work by these smaller entities will become even more effective if the Sub-Commission is authorized to obtain better information through on-site fact-finding, with the consent of the government concerned.

The successes and failures of the Sub-Commission's 35th session must ultimately be the responsibility of the members themselves, for their attitudes and ideas are instrumental in setting the tone of the session and in delineating the breadth and depth of the Sub-Commission's work. Despite the overtly political stances of some members, as a group the present Sub-Commission (half of which was elected for the first time in 1981) seems to be rapidly acquiring the needed expertise and experience to match the commitment to human rights that most of its members bring to Geneva.

JEANETTE HANTKE*

MODEL AMERICAN CONVENTION ON THE PREVENTION AND PUNISHMENT OF SERIOUS FORMS OF VIOLENCE

This Model Convention for the Americas, the product of a 5-year effort by the American Bar Association's Standing Committee on World Order under Law,[1] initially was inspired by the successful conclusion of the European Convention on the Suppression of Terrorism in 1977.[2] Like its predecessor,

* This Note was prepared for the International Human Rights Law Group of Washington, D.C., by the author, who represented the Procedural Aspects of International Law Institute/International Human Rights Law Group at the 1982 session of the Sub-Commission. The author wishes to thank Hurst Hannum and Grant Hanessian for their help in preparing this report.

[1] In preparing this Model Convention, the Standing Committee received financial support from the American Bar Association and the Law Enforcement Assistance Administration through Department of State Contract No. 1724-920087. The research for and first drafts of the Model Convention were the work of Professor Bert B. Lockwood, Jr., Director of the Urban Morgan Institute of Human Rights, University of Cincinnati College of Law, who served as consultant to the committee. *See also* note 5 *infra* and accompanying text.

[2] European Convention on the Suppression of Terrorism, *signed* Jan. 27, 1977, *entered into force* Aug. 4, 1978 (CMD. 7031), *reprinted in* R. LILLICH, TRANSNATIONAL TERRORISM: CONVENTIONS AND COMMENTARY 120 (1982), 15 ILM 1272 (1976).

it takes a regional approach to combating transnational terrorism, but it also includes—in Articles 7 and 9–11—a unique system, potentially involving the Inter-American Court of Human Rights, that seeks to guarantee that individual rights will not be abused in the name of fighting terrorism. An earlier version of the Model Convention[3] was approved in principle by the House of Delegates of the American Bar Association at its mid-winter meeting in 1982,[4] and, after a joint American Society of International Law/American Bar Association conference reviewed this version later last year, the Standing Committee requested a small group of its members to revise the instrument into its present form.[5]

It should be noted at the outset that the draft Convention does not adopt a comprehensive definition of terrorism for the Americas. Instead, like its European counterpart, it incorporates by reference in Article 1 the definitions of specific terrorist offenses found in existing international instruments, recognizing that such definitions represent the consensus of a deliberative process that considered the views of states that are potential parties to the Model Convention. The draft Convention, however, carries this "piecemeal approach"[6] two steps further: first, it includes offenses within the scope of two human rights treaties—the Genocide Convention[7] and the Inter-American Judicial Committee's Draft Convention Defining Torture as an International Crime;[8] and, second, in one instance it breaks new ground by creating a crime of "nuclear sabotage."

Much of the balance of the draft Convention is standard terrorist convention boilerplate. States under Article 2 are required to incorporate Article 1 offenses into their domestic law, while Articles 3 and 8 establish the "extradite or prosecute" obligation common in such conventions. Article 7, however, intended to prevent abuses under antiterrorist laws, is a useful innovation in that it assures alleged terrorists who are apprehended all the relevant legal guarantees found in the American Declaration of the Rights and Duties of Man[9] and in the American Convention on Human Rights.[10] Moreover, Ar-

[3] ABA Standing Committee on World Order under Law, Model American Convention on the Prevention and Punishment of Certain Serious Forms of Violence Jeopardizing Fundamental Rights and Freedoms (ABA Div. Pub. Serv. Activities, July 1980).

[4] ABA, SUMMARY OF ACTION OF THE HOUSE OF DELEGATES, 1982 MIDYEAR MEETING 5 (Chicago 1982).

[5] This group consisted of Donald K. Duvall, Richard B. Lillich, and Harry A. Inman, current Chairman of the Standing Committee.

[6] On the advantages of the "piecemeal approach" to legislating against transnational terrorism, see Procedural Aspects of International Law Institute [PAIL], Future International Efforts to Ensure the Prosecution and Punishment of Acts of International Terrorism: The Use of Treaties 3–11 (Dec. 1976).

[7] Convention on the Prevention and Punishment of the Crime of Genocide, *opened for signature* Dec. 9, 1948, *entered into force* Jan. 12, 1951, 78 UNTS 277, *reprinted in* R. LILLICH, INTERNATIONAL HUMAN RIGHTS INSTRUMENTS 130.1 (1983).

[8] Draft Convention Defining Torture as an International Crime, approved by the Inter-American Juridical Committee, Feb. 6, 1980, 19 ILM 618 (1980).

[9] American Declaration of the Rights and Duties of Man, *signed* May 2, 1948, OAS OFFICIAL RECORDS, OEA/Ser.L./V/II.23, doc. 21, rev. 6 (English 1979), *reprinted in* R. LILLICH, *supra* note 7, at 430.1.

[10] American Convention on Human Rights, *signed* Nov. 22, 1969, *entered into force* July 18,

ticles 9–11 are truly creative provisions that seek to encourage extradition in proper cases and discourage it in improper ones (Articles 5–6) by authorizing the Inter-American Court of Human Rights, at the request of either state involved in the extradition process, to render an advisory opinion as to whether extradition in a given case would violate the provisions of the draft Convention.

While the Model Convention is not the perfect legal solution to transnational terrorism—for instance, it finesses the thorny "political offense exception"[11] rather than meeting it head on—it is a useful, up-to-date, and occasionally innovative regional approach to combating transnational terrorism that warrants the serious attention of all states. Steps already are underway that, it is hoped, ultimately will lead to its adoption and widespread ratification within the Western Hemisphere.

Model American Convention on the Prevention and Punishment of Serious Forms of Violence*

Recognizing the universally accepted principle that every human being has the right to life, liberty, and the security of his person,

Aware that acts of terror against innocent persons continue to violate this principle and occur throughout the Western hemisphere,

Wishing to take effective measures to ensure that perpetrators of such acts do not escape prosecution and punishment,

The Member States of the Organization of American States Have Agreed upon the Following Articles:

Article 1

The following offenses shall come within the scope of this Convention:

a. an offense within the scope of the Convention for the Suppression of Unlawful Seizure of Aircraft, signed at The Hague on 16 December 1970;

b. an offense within the scope of the Convention for the Suppression of Unlawful Acts Against the Safety of Civil Aviation, signed at Montreal on 23 September 1971;

c. an offense within the scope of the Convention to Prevent and Punish the Acts of Terrorism Taking the Form of Crimes Against Persons and Related Extortion That Are of International Significance, signed at Washington on 2 February 1971;

1978, OASTS No. 36, at 1, OAS Official Records, OEA/Ser.L/V/II.23, doc. 21, rev. 6 (English 1979), *reprinted in* R. Lillich, *supra* note 7, at 190.1.

[11] *See* PAIL, The Political Offense Exception to Extradition and Transnational Terrorists: Old Doctrine Reformulated and New Norms Created (June 1977), *reprinted in* Carbonneau, *id.*, 1 ASILS Int'l L.J. 1 (1977). *See also* C. van den Wijngaert, The Political Offence Exception to Extradition: The Delicate Problem of Balancing the Right of the Individual and the Public International Order (1980).

* Reprinted with permission of the American Bar Association.

d. an offense within the scope of the Convention on the Prevention and Punishment of Crimes Against Internationally Protected Persons Including Diplomatic Agents, signed at New York on 14 December 1973;

e. an offense within the scope of Article 11(e) of the Universal Postal Convention, signed at Tokyo on 14 November 1969;

f. an offense within the scope of the Genocide Convention, adopted by the General Assembly of the United Nations on 9 December 1948;

g. an offense within the scope of Articles 13–16 of the Convention on the High Seas, signed at Geneva on 29 April 1958;

h. an offense within the scope of the Convention on the Physical Protection of Nuclear Material, signed at Vienna and New York on 3 March 1980;

i. the crime of "nuclear sabotage," which shall mean a willful act of violence against a nuclear facility in reckless disregard of the possible deleterious consequences or endangerment to life and property in the neighboring communities. Any person or persons committing, participating in, directly inciting, or encouraging the commission of an act of nuclear sabotage shall be held accountable, irrespective of the motive involved;

j. an offense within the scope of the Draft Convention Defining Torture as an International Crime, approved by the Inter-American Juridical Committee on 6 February 1980;

k. an offense within the scope of the International Convention against the Taking of Hostages, signed at New York on 4 December 1979.

Article 2

Each Contracting State shall incorporate the offenses included in Article 1 into its domestic law, make the offenses punishable by severe penalties, and establish jurisdiction to prosecute such offenses.

Article 3

1. Each of the offenses included in Article 1 shall be deemed to be included as extraditable offenses in any extradition treaty existing between Contracting States. Furthermore, Contracting States undertake to include such offenses as extraditable offenses in every extradition treaty to be concluded between them.

2. If a Contracting State that makes extradition conditional upon the existence of a treaty receives a request for extradition from another Contracting State with which it has no extradition treaty, it shall consider this Convention as the legal basis for extradition in respect of offenses included in Article 1. Extradition shall be subject to the procedural conditions provided for by the law of the requested State.

3. Contracting States that do not make extradition conditional upon the existence of a treaty shall recognize the offenses included in Article

1 as extraditable offenses between themselves subject to the procedural conditions provided for by the law of the requested State.

4. The offenses included in Article 1 shall be treated, for the purpose of extradition between Contracting States, as if they had been committed not only in the place in which they occurred but also in the territories of the Contracting States.

5. This Convention does not exclude any criminal jurisdiction exercised in accordance with domestic law.

Article 4

1. Contracting States shall afford one another the greatest measure of assistance in connection with criminal proceedings brought respecting offenses included in Article 1. The law of the requested State concerning mutual assistance in criminal matters shall apply in all cases.

2. The provisions of paragraph 1 of this article shall not affect obligations under any other treaty, bilateral or multilateral, which governs, in whole or in part, mutual assistance in criminal matters.

Article 5

Under this Convention Contracting States shall not extradite a person alleged to have committed an offense included in Article 1 if the requested State has substantial grounds for believing that the request for extradition has been made for the purpose of prosecuting or punishing a person on account of his race, religion, nationality, membership in a particular social group or political opinion, or that that person's position may be prejudiced for any of these reasons.

Article 6

Nothing in this Convention shall be interpreted as imposing an obligation to extradite if the requested State has substantial grounds for believing that the request for extradition for an offense included in Article 1 has been made for the purpose of obstructing or preventing the prosecution or punishment of a person alleged to have committed an offense included in Article 1.

Article 7

Any person, who is in the custody of a Contracting State and who is suspected of committing an offense included in Article 1, is entitled to all the relevant legal guarantees set forth in the American Declaration of the Rights and Duties of Man and in the American Convention on Human Rights.

Article 8

A Contracting State in whose territory a person suspected to have committed an offense included in Article 1 is found shall, if it does not extradite that person, submit the case, without exception whatsoever and without undue delay, to its competent authorities for the purpose of prosecution. Those authorities shall make their decision in the same manner as in the case of any offense of a serious nature under the law of that State.

Article 9

Upon receipt of a request for extradition for an offense included in Article 1, a Contracting State may refer the matter to the Inter-American Court of Human Rights pursuant to Article 64 of the American Convention on Human Rights for an advisory opinion as to whether granting the request for extradition would violate the provisions of this Convention. In like manner, a Contracting Party, which has made a request for extradition for an offense included in Article 1, may refer the matter to the Inter-American Court for an advisory opinion.

Article 10

Extradition shall not be granted for an offense included in Article 1 while a request for an Advisory Opinion from the Inter-American Court of Human Rights pursuant to Article 9 of this Convention is pending.

Article 11

The Contracting States urge the Inter-American Court of Human Rights to adopt procedures to ensure the expeditious handling of requests for advisory opinions pursuant to the provisions of this Convention.

Article 12

The provisions of all treaties and arrangements existing between Contracting States are modified to the extent that they are incompatible with this Convention.

Article 13

This Convention shall remain open for signature by the Member States of the Organization of American States.

Article 14

This Convention shall be ratified by the signatory States in accordance with their respective constitutional procedures.

Article 15

The original instrument of this Convention, the English, French, Portuguese, and Spanish texts of which are equally authentic, shall be deposited in the General Secretariat of the Organization of American States, which shall send certified copies to the signatory Governments for purposes of ratification and to the several secretariats of the United Nations for registration and publication, in accordance with the provisions of Article 102 of the United Nations Charter. The instruments of ratification shall be deposited in the General Secretariat of the Organization of American States, which shall notify the signatory Governments of such deposit.

Article 16

This Convention shall enter into force among the States that ratify it when they deposit their respective instruments of ratification.

Article 17

Contracting States may make reservations to this Convention at the time of signature, ratification, approval or accession, provided that any such reservation is not incompatible with the aims and purposes of the Convention.

Reservations may not be entered with respect to Article 7.

Article 18

This Convention shall remain in force indefinitely, but any of the Contracting States may denounce it. The denunciation shall be transmitted to the General Secretariat of the Organization of American States, which shall notify the other Contracting States thereof. One year following the denunciation, the Convention shall cease to be in force for the denouncing State, but shall continue to be in force for the other Contracting States.

Article 19

The original instrument of this Convention, the English, French, Portuguese and Spanish texts of which are equally authentic, shall be deposited with the General Secretariat of the Organization of American States, which shall send a certified copy to the General Secretariat of the United Nations for registration and publication, in accordance with the provisions of Article 102 of the United Nations Charter. The General Secretariat of the Organization of American States shall notify the member states of the Organization and the states that have acceded to the Convention of signatures, deposits of instruments of ratification, accessions or denunciations, as well as of reservations, if any.

RICHARD B. LILLICH*

* University of Virginia Law School.

BOOK REVIEWS AND NOTES

EDITED BY LEO GROSS

Self-Determination in Law and Practice: The New Doctrine in the United Nations. By Michla Pomerance. The Hague, Boston, London: Martinus Nijhoff Publishers, 1982. Pp. xi, 154. Index. Dfl.90; $39.50.

This is a concise, comprehensive bill of particulars charging that the "New United Nations Law of Self-Determination" is a ghastly perversion of the Wilsonian dream. It is not only destabilizing, an invitation to violence and racism, but also antidemocratic—as practiced by the majority of states in the international system and registered in General Assembly votes.

Those readers who follow the writings and utterances of Ambassador Jeane Kirkpatrick cannot but have noticed that the United Nations operates on the basis of a double standard. It will come as no great surprise that Michla Pomerance has amply documented the existence of a double standard or, rather, many double standards in the area of self-determination.

However, even the well-informed reader may not have noticed the finer points of United Nations double-dealing. Thus, the Assembly has insisted that Fijian voting on the eve of independence involve participation by all adults, including the nonindigenous Indian majority. On the other hand, the Assembly has warned Britain that preindependence voting in Bermuda must protect against the influence of (white) expatriates. Similarly, the United Nations sponsors self-determination through revolutionary violence by preferred "freedom fighters," while condemning the use of force by the inhabitants of Mayotte to sever an unwanted link with the Comoros. And while the United Nations insists that the 5,000 inhabitants of St. Helena be offered the independence option, it does not wish the same option offered to the inhabitants of Gibraltar.

These evidences of the "double standard" lead different observers to different conclusions. Pomerance draws the lawyer's conclusion that the self-determination standard of the United Nations is not law but naked advantage seeking by partisan participants in the system. That, too, will not come as a surprise to most observers, let alone participants. What the book does not do is to go a step beyond this debunking of the East River Bag Lady to a consideration of appropriate strategies for transforming this (evidently) unsatisfactory institutional decline. Should the West take more initiatives—for example, to attempt to expand the jurisdiction of the General Assembly's Special Committee on Decolonization to include all non-self-governing territories, including states that do not regularly schedule free and open elections? Or should it try to get the International Court, in an advisory opinion, to define "non-self-governing" in relation to states that are independent but ruled without popular consent? If such efforts were to be rejected by the UN majority, should the West be building a record for leaving it? Who would join in? What would be put in its place?

The author makes a good argument for despair about the United Nations in one relatively small area of its activity. A similar case can be made in respect of almost everything else, from disarmament to women's rights. But what conclusion are we to draw from these counsels? What lies beyond despair?

THOMAS M. FRANCK
Board of Editors

The Practical Negotiator. By I. William Zartman and Maureen R. Berman. New Haven and London: Yale University Press, 1982. Pp. xiii, 250. Index. $20.

Zartman and Berman's book is a valuable contribution to the expanding literature on negotiation. The authors have produced a work that both proposes prescriptive formulations and offers, by virtue of its methodology, useful insights into some major past international negotiations and some key negotiators.

While the book relies to a large degree on existing literature (there is a good review of the principal findings by other authors), its primary innovation is the use of data gathered from interviews with and questionnaires addressed to senior diplomats, UN ambassadors, and other high-ranking negotiators from a number of different nations. Americans on the list include Averell Harriman, Charles Yost, and Gerald Ford.

The systematic use of the views and reactions of international practitioners makes for interesting reading and reveals some surprising results. For example, Zartman and Berman find that the influence of culture on the negotiation process may not be as significant as it is often thought to be. Nearly 50 percent of the respondents did not see culture as a dominant factor in negotiations. Furthermore, a high number classified the negotiating styles of cultures not their own in the very same way as their culture was classified by others. The authors wisely refrain from drawing any major conclusions from this, but they do suggest that, among other things, there might be an emerging "international diplomatic culture" that works to cancel or at least diminish the impact of national cultural differences on negotiations.

Conceptually, Zartman and Berman present a phasic view of negotiation. They see negotiation as involving three distinct stages: a stage of deciding whether to negotiate, a stage of developing a general formula about the negotiation, and a stage of negotiating details. Some confusion is present as to which aspects of the approach are meant to be descriptive and which prescriptive. In either instance, various limits to the applicability of the approach, as developed, become evident. This is something of which the authors seem aware when they acknowledge that negotiation is neither a sequential nor a finite process. They correctly observe that "moves can go in all directions, including backtracking," and to their credit urge creativity in the interpretation of their proposals.

One notable merit of the Zartman and Berman approach is that it draws attention to the different challenges that the negotiation process may present as it advances—or fails to advance—from initial talks to the signing of an agreement. This might be particularly important in the case of long-term negotiations, such as the SALT and START talks. The identification of prenegotiation as a phase in itself is also noteworthy and should encourage further inquiry among those who suspect that this part of negotiating makes special demands of the negotiator.

As a whole, *The Practical Negotiator* contains an intelligent series of observations and suggestions. A good number of the latter are put axiomatically without much guidance ("trust is enhanced when there is an early return on the agreement"), so that practitioners may not find immediate utility in them. For scholars and researchers, however, some of the propositions advanced are enlightening and others, though perhaps ultimately refutable, are challenging. Zartman and Berman suggest, for example, that in certain cases "concessions may be misinterpreted, cooperativeness may be mistaken for weakness, and innovativeness may engender suspicion."

In the end, most of the limits to the authors' inquiry might be reflective, not of any major flaw in their scholarship, but of the current early stage of negotiation research and theory. Certainly, more efforts of the type made here are needed for us to come to understand better the international negotiating process.

ROGER FISHER
Board of Editors

Kennedy and the Berlin Wall Crisis. By Honoré M. Catudal. Berlin: Berlin Verlag, 1980. Pp. 358. Index. DM 36.

Professor Honoré Catudal has given us a lively, readable, and largely accurate account of the events surrounding the building of the Berlin Wall in August 1961—at least as seen and experienced by the Americans who were directly involved. After a first chapter that deals with Washington's reaction to the closing of East to West traffic through Berlin, the author returns to the opening weeks of 1961 and deals briefly with other matters affecting Berlin, such as Khrushchev's initiative on Berlin in February, reflected in communications with Chancellor Adenauer; the debacle of the Bay of Pigs; and President Kennedy's visit to Europe in May and June, especially the summit meeting in Vienna between Kennedy and Khrushchev. Of particular importance was the "ultimatum" on Berlin presented by Khrushchev to Kennedy at that Vienna meeting.

Professor Catudal winds up telling a story, freeing himself from the several models constructed by academics about decision-making theory. He must have discovered quite early in his study of this affair that real people dealing with real problems in a real world simply do not squeeze themselves into intellectual models formulated by professors. He used freely a considerable number of interviews he had with American officials who were involved with the Berlin Wall. These included both civilian and military participants; the interviews were reinforced by an examination of many documents, the more important of which are included as appendixes.

This book illustrates some of the problems faced by historians in handling personal interviews. Each person necessarily sees the world through his own eyes and from his own vantage point. If the 16 members of EXCOM were to write out their individual accounts of the Cuban missile crisis, the historian would find 16 rather different stories, which could not be fully reconciled into a single consistent account. When interviews are held some years after the event, the historian must make allowances for faulty memory, personal biases, and that ever-present danger in the preparation of memoranda of conversations—the afterthoughts that cause some to record what they later wished they had said. The Germans call these *Treppengedanken,* the thoughts one has on the steps on the way out.

There are similar problems for the historian in dealing with documents, especially in situations where all the relevant documentation is not yet available. Even full documentation is not definitive because the documents are surrounded by many discussions among the principal participants that are not in the record at all. The real meaning of a document and the role it played in particular decisions are sometimes elusive.

Catudal succeeds in capturing most of the key elements in the Berlin Wall crisis. He properly points out that it was predictable and predicted that East Germany and the Soviet Union would be forced to stop the "hemorrhage" of East Germans moving to the West in rapidly increasing numbers, but exactly how and when was not precisely known.

From the point of view of the West, the key to the entire Berlin Wall crisis appears in the author's first chapter in the form of a remark attributed to Foy Kohler, namely, that the prevention of the flow of people from East to West was not a *casus belli* for the West. Everything else about the Wall followed upon that central point. Winston Churchill's "Iron Curtain" already extended from the Baltic to the Black Sea; closing the hole in Berlin did not change the underlying strategic or political relationship. A probe by force against the initial barbed wire barriers could not, even if locally unopposed, prevent erection of a barrier 50 or a 100 yards further inside East Berlin. The East Germans and Russians had long since established complete control over East Berlin and East Germany, reducing the notion of Four Power responsibility over all of Berlin to the thinnest facade. Those who believed that the East Germans and Russians would simply back down upon a slight show of Western force were not prepared to face up to second, third, and fourth steps if the back-down did not occur. In any event, no NATO Government (including the Federal Republic of Germany) favored the use of armed force to break through the barbed wire or the Wall.

The Berlin Wall was built in the midst of a genuinely serious crisis arising from Khrushchev's pressure against the presence of the three Western powers in West Berlin and free access to that city. Here was a genuine *casus belli* for the West and no one underestimated the dangers connected with Khrushchev's June 1961 ultimatum. The Wall was a shameful demonstration of the measures necessary to keep East Germans from abandoning ship, but it was not critical to the safety and freedom of the people of West Berlin. Catudal does not, in this short book, go into much detail on the larger issues. Lord Home, the British Foreign Secretary, and this reviewer decided to talk about Berlin with the Russians—and talk and talk and talk. We did not see any possibility of reaching fresh agreements on Berlin because the positions of East and West were so far apart. But we talked, interminably and repetitively. A reporter once asked this reviewer at the time what my hopes were with regard to Berlin and I replied, "I would like to pass this problem along to my successor." Years later, the two Germanys recognized each other, both joined the United Nations, and a new Four Power Agreement on Berlin was concluded during the Nixon administration.

In the present book the author deals with the psychological and political anxieties spurred by the Wall in West Berlin and, to a lesser extent, in the Federal Republic. The people of West Berlin were naturally dismayed by the sealing off of East Berlin, but the Wall also stirred deep anxiety about their own safety. Attempts were made to provide assurance to the West Berliners by the presence of General Lucius Clay, a visit by Vice President Lyndon Johnson, and, somewhat later, the dramatic visit of President John F. Kennedy to West Berlin. It should be noted, however, that maintaining the confidence of people living in an obviously exposed position in West Berlin is not all that simple.

At one point, Catudal attempts to divide the actors working on the Wall problem between "hard-liners" and "soft-liners." Such attempts are not very useful; the attitudes of the actors moved across the spectrum of attitudes with almost imperceptible variations; no clear dividing line between white and black can be accurately drawn. For example, this reviewer agreed completely with President Kennedy that the Berlin Wall was not a *casus belli* but that the safety of and access to West Berlin clearly was; did those views make me "hard-line" or "soft-line"?

In his conclusion, the author offers a rather intriguing sentence: "Contrary to what many researchers in this field (i.e. decision making theory) often assume, this case study suggests that rationality (however construed) may indeed play a crucial role in how decisions are reached and actions undertaken in the area of foreign policy." If there are researchers who doubt the role of rationality in decisions, they should examine the thousands of cables that go out of the Department of State on every working day and reflect upon the fact that we have put behind us more than 37 years since a nuclear weapon has been fired in anger.

DEAN RUSK
The University of Georgia School of Law

Interim Protection: A Functional Approach. By Jerome B. Elkind. The Hague, Boston, London: Martinus Nijhoff Publishers, 1981. Pp. xxiv, 287. Index. Dfl.140; $59.

Professor Elkind of the University of Auckland has written the first book-length treatment of the subject of interim measures of protection since Edward

Dumbauld's *Interim Measures of Protection in International Controversies*, published in 1932.[1] Elkind's book fills an important gap in the literature and should be welcomed by academics, students, and practitioners alike who have lamented the absence of a convenient reference work on this subject.

The book is divided into four main parts. In part I, Elkind outlines what he terms a "functional approach" to the identification of "general principles of law" within the meaning of Article 38(1)(c) of the ICJ Statute. He makes clear that a principal objective of the book as a whole is to demonstrate the utility of this approach by illustrating its application to several of the major legal problems arising in connection with interim measures of protection. Part II reviews the evolution of Article 41 of the Statute and the related Rules of Court, and also includes a summary description of each of the cases in which indication of interim measures has been requested. This portion of the book usefully pulls together the rather scattered references to interim measures in the *travaux préparatoires* of the Statute and various versions of the Rules. One wishes, nonetheless, that Elkind had tried to impose more structure on the material, rather than contenting himself with a narrative recitation of the comments made by the jurists involved in the drafting process. The third portion of the work explores some of the principal legal issues arising in connection with interim measures orders, *e.g.*, whether they have binding force, whether they may be made on something less than a final determination of jurisdiction on the merits, and whether they are appropriate for the sole purpose of preventing aggravation of the dispute. Part IV is a summary of the principal conclusions reached earlier.

Comparative analysis has bulked large in discussions of "general principles of law" under Article 38(1)(c). As Elkind points out, however, the rationale for such analysis is rarely made explicit (pp. 4–6, 10–12). On what theory are principles found in municipal legal systems properly treated as sources for principles applicable on the international plane? Elkind provides his own answer to this question:

> The methodology proposed is to compare the *interests* protected by international law with those protected by various municipal systems of law. If we see, in a number of municipal systems, interests protected which are similar to those protected by international law, we may examine those interests in order to deduce the principles which most effectively protect them.
>
> We can go one step further. A study of the operation of such principles in those municipal systems which contain them may reveal to us the rules which are essential to their effective operation given the interests which are to be protected [p. 18, emphasis added].

This is an interesting and creative approach. As one who has combed the codes of various legal systems without any very clear idea of the reasons for doing so, but with a clear sense of obligation to undertake such a survey, I appreciate Elkind's effort to provide an explicit theory. The theory itself is not without difficulties, which Elkind fails to dispel. Most importantly, Elkind

[1] Reviewed in 27 AJIL 192–93 (1933).

fails to provide us with any very clear idea of what he means by "interests," the basic units of analysis in his framework. Nor does he provide us with sufficient guidance in identifying parallel or analogous interests on the municipal and international planes. The problem is illustrated by his suggestion that the interests protected by the concept of private property are analogous to those protected by the concept of sovereignty (p. 18). There may be analogies between these concepts; both have roles in distinguishing the *meum* from the *teum,* as well as the individual from the communal. Still, the concept of private property is rooted in notions of desert, allocative efficiency, and minimum entitlement; in contrast, the concept of sovereignty remains first and foremost an attribution of decision-making competence.

It is much easier to agree with Elkind that interim measures orders on the international level serve functions akin to those served by provisional remedies in municipal legal systems (p. 30). He correctly asserts that the two functions of such remedies are to prevent frustration of the judicial process and to discourage resort to violence (pp. 30–31).

Elkind's attempts to apply his overall approach to the resolution of particular issues meet with varying success. His discussion of the question of jurisdiction to indicate interim measures is a fine, thoughtful one, and makes good use of the comparative analysis presented. Elkind finds the jurisdictional base for the indication of such measures in Article 35 of the Court's Statute, together with Article 93 of the UN Charter (pp. 176–77). He supports this view with a demonstration that jurisdiction *ratione personae,* which can be presumed in most cases before municipal tribunals, is a sufficient jurisdictional predicate for provisional remedies (p. 177). It follows, he argues, that the authority to indicate interim measures does not and cannot depend upon a certainty or a very high probability of jurisdiction on the merits. He suggests, indeed, that the authority exists even in a case where a very weak title of jurisdiction on the merits has been adduced (p. 192). Although the first of these conclusions seems sound, the latter neither conforms to existing law[2] nor closely corresponds to the municipal rules that Elkind surveys (pp. 186–91). His survey seems to show that there is a rather close division between municipal systems where a prima facie showing (or a showing of probable success) is required and those in which no such showing is necessary (p. 192). In this circumstance, Elkind is forced to choose the "better rule"; his methodology has no further light to shed on why municipal systems protecting the same interest do so in relevantly different ways.

The same resort to teleology unaided by Elkind's comparative law method recurs elsewhere in the work, notably on the question whether interim measures orders are binding. The argument seems to be that such orders must be binding because they otherwise would be pointless (pp. 162–63). That may be true; it may even be the limit of wisdom on the question. But as a demonstration of the utility of Elkind's overall approach, it is disappointing.

[2] The Court seems to have settled on the view that a prima facie showing of jurisdiction on the merits is required. *See* Case Concerning U.S. Diplomatic and Consular Staff in Tehran, 1979 ICJ REP. 3, 13; Nuclear Tests Case, 1973 ICJ REP. 99, 101; Fisheries Jurisdiction Case, 1972 ICJ REP. 12, 15–16.

Perhaps the best portion of the book concerns the circumstances in which an indication of interim measures is appropriate (pp. 209–30). Elkind's discussion is fresh and insightful, and contains a particularly valuable analysis of the *Aegean Sea Continental Shelf* case (pp. 211–19). Here, moreover, the comparative material is used to very good effect.

The Court's experience with interim measures orders has not been a happy one. As Elkind notes, every such order issued by the present Court has been disregarded. Yet despite this dismal record, states still find it useful to seek and obtain such orders. The respondent who flouts an order of the Court transforms a bilateral conflict of interests into a confrontation between one law-abiding and one willful contestant. The political benefits of placing one's adversary in that posture of defiance are instinctively understood and sought after by political leaders. The prospect, then, is for practice under Article 41 of the Statute to continue to bulk large in the work of the Court. Elkind's work, notwithstanding the reservations already expressed, is thus a significant contribution to an important subject that has been too long without a comprehensive scholarly treatment.

TED STEIN
University of Washington School of Law

The Legal Aspect of Money. With special reference to Comparative Private and Public International Law (4th ed.). By F. A. Mann. New York: The Clarendon Press; Oxford University Press, 1982. Pp. lvi, 602. Index. $69.

The first edition of this book was published 45 years ago, in 1938, as an important and novel contribution in English. It was intended to be the first work "to treat the legal aspects of money in a systematic and comprehensive manner," and its preface noted the absence of any English or American work dealing with the subject on such a broad basis.

The work of Mann is well known in the monetary field, and in a sense the current, fourth, edition is the summing up of this work. The question that it raises for a reviewer is how to approach the achievement that it represents in a balanced way, by recognizing its qualities, such as the once pioneering intellectual scope and imagination, the painstaking labors reflected by the extensive historical research filling its numerous footnotes, and the rigor of the author's logic in many areas, while at the same time appraising objectively, as the reviewer must, its current value.

The core of the book is built around the principle of "nominalism," and much of it is devoted to an explanation of the implications and ramifications of this principle in the law. For the author, the principle is also an article of faith. This principle

> means that a monetary obligation involves the payment of so many chattels, being legal tender at the time of payment, as, if added together according to the nominal value indicated thereon, produce a sum equal to the amount of the debt. In other words, the obligation to pay £ 10 is discharged if the creditor receives what at the time of performance

> are £ 10, regardless of both their intrinsic and functional value. It follows that a monetary obligation has no other "value" than that which it expresses [p. 84].

The nominalist principle rests on two foundations: the state theory of money, on which the author's concept of legal tender is based ("only those chattels are money to which such character has been attributed by law, i.e. by or with the authority of the State," p. 13), and the freedom of contract. Legislative and judicial acceptance of this principle would mean that the nominal (that is, face) value of legal tender money would be axiomatic, and this would provide a clear, consistent, and hence predictable basis for contracting parties to make their own arrangements, such as protective clauses if they so desire, to deal with possible changes in the economic value of money (or foreign exchange) as it may affect their relationship. Legislative interference with such freedom of contract, particularly in a retroactive way, or by courts assuming the role of the legislature in abridging protective clauses out of some misguided sense of public policy, and thereby frustrating the will of the parties, is strongly condemned (p. 175).

Nominalism as a legal principle leads to interest in protective clauses. Historically, given the evolution of monetary systems both at the national and at the international levels, "the law of protective clauses has largely developed within the framework of the gold clause" (p. 138). With the obsolescence of gold clauses, due to the demonetization of gold internationally which has resulted in fluctuating market prices for gold, the available techniques from which parties may choose to take account of changes in the economic value of money for their contracts are index clauses, foreign exchange clauses, and unit of account clauses.

Most of the current value of the book is in the explanation of the relevant concepts and the tracing of this evolution in the law of money, first and foremost in English law, but with a comparative approach based primarily on German, but also on French and U.S. sources. Much of this material is of historical interest now, because of revolutionary changes in the national and international law of money in the last decade that have transformed vast areas of legal analysis into legal history. The principal changes that have had this effect for the material covered extensively in the book are the undesirability of gold clauses; fluctuating exchange rates leading to the abandonment of the centuries-old breach-day rule by the House of Lords in *Miliangos v. George Frank (Textiles) Ltd.* ([1975] 3 All E.R. 801) in favor of judgments in appropriate cases in foreign currency or its national currency equivalent at the time of execution of judgment; and the lifting of exchange controls in the United Kingdom.

By contrast, the material dealing with the private international law of exchange control (pp. 401–33) continues to be a useful research tool, particularly on account of the historical wealth of research collected in the footnotes.

This brings the reader to the less valuable parts of the book. The perspective of nominalism, with its sharp focus on the unit of account function of money, seems to have created a basic problem for the author. The problem seems traceable to two factors: first, the limited perspective, which was perhaps understandable as self-restraint at the outset in order to keep the subject within manageable limits; and second, developments in the international monetary system that had changed the subject so pervasively that the restraint became a severe handicap to understanding.

The limited perspective is seen in a strongly defended and often repeated distinction between what the author wished to cover, which he calls "legal," and what he did not, which he calls "economic." Thus, the view is taken that in answering questions pertaining to the nature or meaning of money, "economic theory is unlikely to assist the lawyer to any appreciable extent" (p. 5). Accordingly, "such problems as monetary policy, the management and supply, the quantity and soundness of money are no concern of the lawyer" (*ibid.*). As "modern economic literature rarely deals with . . . any question material to the lawyer" (*id.*, n.12), "money is not the same as credit" (p. 6), "nor does the fact that bank money largely functions as money prove that in law it necessarily and invariably is money" (*ibid.*), it must follow that "it does not fall within the scope of a discussion of the legal problems of money to describe in detail the numerous matters which are included in the organization of a monetary system" (p. 29). Excluded from the discussion are, then, the role and activities of central banks, monetary policy, monetary reserve assets (pp. 29–30), Eurocurrency (p. 62), and so on, all of which are topics that have interesting and complex legal aspects. This should not be a problem in itself, in that every author is entitled to his own definition of the subject he wishes to explore, but problems start when misunderstandings and erroneous opinions begin to appear and gather force in parts of the work where the author attempts, all the same, to describe topics with which he is not fully familiar. Thus, the world according to Mann has little room or use for the International Monetary Fund, which he regards as "primarily a credit institution or a bank in that it retained the function to provide or procure international credit or 'liquidity' for the benefit of member States" (p. 34), while "the Fund's powers and tasks as a monetary institution, on the other hand, are hardly more than nominal in character and effect, however wordily and grandiosely they may have been expressed in the amended Article IV" (pp. 34–35). These judgments follow from the author's concept of legal tender, which seems to reject implicitly the theory that "money" can be created by international agreement short of a full-fledged monetary union.

From the author's perspective, a distinguishing feature of the Fund's operations and transactions is not what they seek to, or do, accomplish, but that they "give rise to many difficulties of interpretation" (p. 507), and the system of Special Drawing Rights is dismissed as "a facility defined in terms of even greater obscurity" (*ibid.*). The obscurity evidently becomes the basis for such easily avoidable mistakes as saying that the rules of reconstitution which, by the way, were abrogated in 1981, "probably involve the repayment of the currency received" (p. 509). But then, the "obscure" SDR, understood in one place as a combination of national currency values rather than as a standard of international value (p. 531), becomes the laconically stated basis for solving the problem of the unforeseen absence of an official price of gold in the application of gold clauses "when it became the practice to adopt the SDR as an international unit of account" (pp. 155–56). The inconsistency is derived clearly from the author's guiding principle: "the reasons which rendered it necessary and appropriate to exclude the law of banking and credits from the scope of this book require and justify the conclusion that the admittedly peculiar type of credit which the SDR represents should in the present context [patterns of monetary organization] not be discussed in detail" (p. 509).

The IMF and the SDR are not alone in being so summarily dismissed from what the author understands as the public international law of money (part IV of the book). He finds the texts concerning the European Monetary System "very confusing," and "as usual in these cases, the terminology cannot easily be understood by a lawyer" (p. 504, n.79). An effort to understand is viewed as not only useless, but as carrying grave risks, because no less an authority than Sir Winston Churchill is invoked against dissent: "There is no sphere of human thought in which it is easier for a man to show superficial cleverness and the appearances of superior wisdom than in discussing questions of currency and exchange" (*ibid.*). The warning applies, apparently, to all matters treated in the book, because it is chosen as the leading quotation in the preface to the third edition, and is recalled in the fourth. The history and practices relating to the European Currency Unit (ECU) are viewed, accordingly, as "extraordinarily confusing and complex; the details are devoid of general interest, but were described in contributions of great specificity" (p. 506).

The reader may wonder at this point if such a limited understanding of the subject, which seems to develop inexorably from the exclusion of the economic background and context, is in fact the revenge of economics, which Mann has sought to banish, so emphatically and categorically, from the law of money.

This shortcoming, with its consequences for several parts of the book, should not blind us, however, to the historical value of this work in presenting and clarifying the evolution of the nominalist principle in the law, for which it earned a place of prominence among the seminal works on national monetary law.

STEPHEN A. SILARD*
International Monetary Fund

Antitrust and American Business Abroad (2d ed.). 2 vols. By James R. Atwood and Kingman Brewster. Colorado Springs: Shepard's/McGraw-Hill, 1981. Pp. lxiv, 770. Index. $120.†

The publication of a second edition of Kingman Brewster's treatise on the application of the U.S. antitrust laws in foreign commerce has been long awaited. The two volumes, which are primarily the work of Atwood, build

* Mr. Silard is writing in a personal capacity. The views expressed do not necessarily reflect those of the International Monetary Fund.

† The reviewer was Associate Director of the project assisting Mr. Brewster on the first edition.

on the Brewster base and follow the format of the original 1958 book, but, although many Brewster ideas and concepts from the first edition have survived the birth of the second (notably the seminal conflict-of-laws approach), Brewster rightly notes that the second edition "is more forthrightly prescriptive than the prior book was about the ends and means of antitrust policy." As Brewster states in his preface, such changed emphasis is highly desirable in view of the marked changes in the political and economic contexts in which antitrust law operates.

This edition follows the original structure of the first edition, dealing first with basic jurisdictional and substantive concepts and then examining the law's impact on specific areas relating to exports, imports, licenses, and the ownership of foreign enterprises. The second volume considers the impact of international and foreign antitrust law and the administration of U.S. antitrust law, including the dimensions of both discovery and remedies. The final section of the work evaluates the law's impact on American business abroad, suggests a process for improvement of the law's application and, finally, reaches conclusions and recommendations for action.

The book is thus directed to both the practitioner and the policy maker. Its message to the latter is more profound and important. Atwood speaks for the growing consensus among those interested and informed concerning the international application of the U.S. antitrust laws when he identifies the need for their improvement.

> In our judgment, United States antitrust law should reflect better than it does, both in its substance and its administration, the international nature of America's foreign commerce. When foreign rather than domestic commerce is at issue, a wide range of American policy interests comes into play, and strict adherence to the policy of competition alone, however laudable in the domestic context, is simply too rigid to serve the United States' economic and political objectives in today's world [vol. 2, p. 311].

He notes a number of compelling arguments: the goal of minimizing unnecessary friction with friendly foreign interests, the need for a mechanism to achieve the "clearly lawful and orderly overriding of antitrust by other high priority national policies," the growth of international competitive norms and laws and, finally, the possibly unfavorable effect upon U.S. business of the foreign application of these laws.

Like Brewster, Atwood surveys the jurisdictional issue and opts for the conflict of laws/comity approach as the best among various alternatives to minimize jurisdictional disagreement. He finds that the best jurisdictional rule is that of *Timberlane:*[1] "whether, in the face of conflicting government interests, the contacts and interests of the United States are sufficient in the particular circumstances to support the exercise of extraterritorial jurisdiction."

[1] Timberlane Lumber Co. v. Bank of America, 549 F.2d 597 (9th Cir. 1976). Judge Choy expressly notes his reliance upon the jurisdictional "rule of reason" proposed by Brewster's first edition. The proposed revision of the Restatement, Foreign Relations Law, urges a similar approach in proposed section 403, although, in the reviewer's opinion, the proposal is imperfectly repeated in proposed section 415.

Atwood concedes that so generalized a rule will be difficult to administer and fraught with uncertainty either in general or in particular cases, and he is aware of the issue of judicial competence. Many would question whether federal district judges and the adversarial trial process will more often than not reach sound judgment in this delicate balancing process; others will ask whether the courts of one nation should retain the sole responsibility to conduct the balancing process. In the final analysis, however, no better approach has yet been suggested.

Since the publication of Atwood's second edition, Congress has passed the Export Trading Company and Foreign Trade Antitrust Improvements Act of 1982. Title IV of the combined Acts enacts several of Atwood's policy recommendations. The statute codifies the policy statement of the 1977 Antitrust Division's *Guide for International Operations* that foreign conduct and transactions are reached by U.S. antitrust laws only if they produce a direct, substantial, and reasonably foreseeable anticompetitive effect upon U.S. commerce. Similarly, Atwood's suggestion that foreign consumers need not be protected by the U.S. antitrust laws has been largely enacted into law, in Title IV's provision that only those involved in U.S. export business may complain of restraints on U.S. exports.

Atwood is profoundly right in his observation that the private antitrust suit is and continues to be the loose cannon on the deck. "Because private suits are not subject to such interdepartmental procedures or Presidential surveillance, and because private plaintiffs are not constrained by the discipline of public accountability, they have raised particularly serious comity and foreign policy problems from time to time" (vol. 2, p. 340). The author would not eliminate all private suits in the foreign commerce area, but he would limit the availability of the treble damage remedy. It is heartening to note that he finds that even under present law a plaintiff is not entitled to automatic treble damages in foreign commerce litigation (vol. 2, p. 341, n.65). He urges that, beyond this, legislation is desirable to create a presumption in such litigation that only single damages would be available to the private plaintiff, unless that plaintiff can demonstrate that foreign conduct is not central to the complaint, not undertaken by foreign nationals, and unlawful where it occurred. Finally, he urges an active amicus role by the Justice Department in consultation with State.

The scholarship and wisdom of the treatise are profoundly impressive. There are a few areas where the authors make prescriptions that seem inconsistent with their prior analysis. For example, the suggestion that the act of state doctrine should not be a defense in antitrust litigation (vol. 2, p. 353) seems to ignore the treatise's previous analysis of this doctrine (vol. 1, pp. 235–74), as well as Judge Choy's decision in *International Association of Machinists v. OPEC* (649 F.2d 1354 (9th Cir. 1981), *cert. denied,* 102 S.Ct. 1036 (1982)). The argument that the availability of comity, sovereign immunity, and *Noerr-Pennington* makes the defense unnecessary can just as easily be turned on its head; the existence of other alternatives demonstrates the continuing utility and relevance of the doctrine. But these are truly minor caveats.

Atwood and Brewster is and will continue to be one of the most authoritative works on international antitrust to be published.

DAVID G. GILL
Of the New York Bar

Implications juridico-constitutionnelles de l'adhésion aux Communautés européennes. Le cas du Portugal. By Isabel Jalles. Brussels: Etablissements Emile Bruylant, 1981. Pp. 309. F.1.378.

That the unification of Europe is not a matter of tariffs or politics only becomes clear after reading this book.

Portugal's proposed accession to the European Communities again brings to light that compatibility—or the lack thereof—between national laws and Community laws as a condition for the accession constitutes an area of great concern in the negotiating process.

In analyzing the conflicts between national laws and Community laws, Jalles focuses on juridical-constitutional questions.

In 1964 Advocate-General Maurice Lagrange reached the conclusion that a member country, if faced with the issue of compatibility of its constitution with one of its laws derived from the EC Treaty, had only two choices: to modify the constitution or to denounce the Treaty. It is with the first choice in mind that the author makes her demand for a revision of Portugal's Constitution, a proposal that would apply to any other country wishing to become a member of the European Communities. This proposition is not so much based upon the internal political considerations that introduced into Portugal's Constitution in 1976 the concepts of "national independence," "democracy," and "socialism," but, rather, upon technical conflicts in substantive law itself.

However, the political environment in which the Constitution of 1976 functions must be borne in mind in order to appreciate the author's proposals that Portugal: (1) establish a system for implementing international treaties and for its accession to supranational organizations; (2) provide for the possibility of a transfer of sovereign powers to a supranational organization; and (3) render the whole Constitution "homogeneous" with the Constitutions of the other Western European countries.

Portugal formally applied for accession to the European Communities in 1977, shortly after Greece and Spain had indicated their interest in joining. This was the first time that the Communities had entertained applications from southern European countries.

While the accession of the United Kingdom, Ireland, and Denmark, during the early seventies, was generally a smooth process, political obstacles remain to the accession of the countries of southern Europe. This is, in part, because some member states want to stay clear of competition from these countries, especially in the area of agricultural products, and, in part, because of the latter's different historic experience during the Second World War from that of the founding members. If these and other countries join, regulations for agricultural and other products will probably change. The "opening to the South" has been slowed down, so far, by objections largely from France. In any event, such an accession will tend to increase the present trend towards a confederacy rather than a union, a development which has been led by France for some time.

The Constitutions of the present member states contain, to varying degrees, provisions that permit the delegation of sovereign national powers to a supranational organization. The purest form of this concept is contained in the Constitution of the Federal Republic of Germany, the Basic Law of Bonn of 1949. The authors of the West German Constitution were, in a way, fortunate because they truly found a new beginning at the end of World War II. Having lost so much in that war, Germany was most receptive to the ideal of a united Europe, and the West German Constitution bears witness to this. It provides, in Article 25, that the commonly accepted rules of international law not only form an integral part of German law, but also—and this distinguishes the German Constitution from others—that international law "shall have priority over national law and shall directly create rights and obligations for all residents of the Federal Republic of Germany."

In contrast, under the present Portuguese Constitution, it is conceivable that a judge would find that law derived from an international convention to which Portugal is a party is "unconstitutional" because the Portuguese Constitution fails to provide for a mechanism for the integration of international law.

If Portugal became a member of the European Communities, this would create an insurmountable conflict because the EC Treaty not only constitutes an international convention but, in addition, creates a supranational body of organizations. The terms "autonomy" and "supranationality" in the EC Treaty, according to the European Court in *COSTA/ENEL*, mean that an

> independent body of law, integrated in the legal system of its member states since the entering into force of the Treaty, is superimposed on their jurisdictions by the E.C. Treaty.
>
> . . . by instituting a Community of unlimited duration, acting through its own agencies, with an independent legal status, being internationally represented and with real powers based upon a limitation of jurisdiction and delegation of privileges of the member states, they themselves have limited their sovereign powers and have created a legal corporation.

In its *Racke* decision, the European Court in 1979 confirmed the lawmaking powers of the European Communities whereby EC laws shall take effect in each member country directly upon publication in the *Official Journal of the European Communities.*

Even among the six founding members this has led to problems because Germany and Italy have constitutional high courts that have exclusive jurisdiction to review the constitutionality of all domestic law, which—at least so far as Italy is concerned—includes law that is derived from international treaties.

On the other hand, France and the Benelux countries (like Anglo-Saxon countries) have rejected such an absolute right of control, under the principle of separation of powers and the supremacy of parliament.

The European Court, most recently in *Variola* and in *Simmenthal,* has taken the position that Article 189 of the EC Treaty requires compliance of member states with Community laws. The Treaty lacks provisions for resolving a conflict between the Court of Justice of the European Communities and a constitutional court of a member country, over the constitutionality of a national law based on Community law. Perhaps, as the author suggests, the creation of a court of conflicts will become necessary in the future.

In developing her concept for a revision of the Portuguese Constitution, the author provides a most interesting and thorough discussion of the constitutional experience of each of the present member countries with EC laws. This part of the book will be worthwhile for practitioner and scholar alike. It contains numerous citations of national and EC case law. The extensive bibliography and table of cases, listed by country, make this book a useful tool for anyone interested in the unification of Europe in general and the constitutional issues related thereto in particular, work that has been the basis for this book. The American reader will appreciate the good fortune of the United States, where the accession of a state was much simpler because the state (being new) was willing to model its laws after those of existing states, whereas in Europe the accession of new countries, with their already existing and often sophisticated constitutions reflecting their respective histories of two thousand years, required a complex process of legal harmonization.

In the case of Portugal, it seems clear that, as a condition to accession, its Constitution has to be amended before it can sign the Protocol of Accession and join the European Communities. When this will take place is still unclear. The original time schedule has long been exceeded. The next target date is January 1984.

EBERHARD H. RÖHM
Of the New York Bar

Human Rights in Third World Perspective. Volume I. By Thomas M. Franck. London, Rome, New York: Oceana Publications, Inc., 1982. Pp. xxviii, 510. 3 vols. projected. $50/vol.

Franck has brought to the casebook his profound knowledge of public law in anglophonic Asia and Africa. In a set of volumes cast in the form of the familiar North American teaching tool, he has set out hard-to-find constitutions, judicial opinions, and his own incomparable "Notes" with the suggestion that the materials can be helpful to students in preparing for legislative and judicial roles in their homelands. The "Notes" are the fascination for the Western reader, for they explain the wordiness of Third World constitutions. To Franck, draftsmen have distrusted their expatriate judges who often remain on the bench after independence, and they are unwilling to give them for development the terse phrases of the first ten amendments of the U.S. Constitution. They prefer to spell out the rules. One has the sense that the mass of grievances of the colonial period have swelled up in the hearts of the draftsmen who are determined to protect citizens from abuse of bureaucratic power and who believe that constitutional phraseology can prevent such abuse.

The Westerner will also sense that judges in the developing world, and especially in India, live under a tradition that calls for little restraint in wordiness. Franck gives his readers the remarkable debate over whether a constitutional bill of rights may be amended under the constitution's provisions for amendment or whether a new constitutional convention is required to redraft the social compact in consideration of changed political grounds. Natural lawyers and positivists have debated the topic for decades as legal philosophers. In the developing world judges depart from the terse phrases of British judges to adopt arguments normally reserved in the West for philosophers in academic halls.

Franck poses the question whether human rights are to be looked upon by newly liberated statesmen as imported from their former metropoles or as indigenous to their precolonial history. He inclines to the latter position, and calls upon the well-known anthropological studies of African tribal procedures to prove his point. Generally, Franck argues that citizens' interests are to be fostered most effectively by respect for legal procedures rather than by revision of substantive law. Without saying so specifically, he implies that a focus on the ownership and use of property, now so common among the socialists of the Third World, will be inadequate to satisfy citizens if procedure is subordinated to substantive results. He calls upon Third Worlders to remain faithful to what he sees as their birthright, even while attempting to foster the material well-being of their traditional community-oriented societies by enacting and implementing socialist-oriented substantive law.

JOHN N. HAZARD
Board of Editors

Festschrift für Hans-Jürgen Schlochauer zum 75. Geburtstag am 28. März 1981. Edited by Ingo von Münch. Berlin, New York: Walter de Gruyter, 1981. Pp. xv, 1023. DM 370; $185.

A collection of essays that lacks a specific substantive unifying theme, as this one does, is not only always difficult to review but frequently makes for less than rewarding reading. Since papers committed to such a *Festschrift* will generally get less publicity and consequently have less impact than publications in better indexed and circulating legal periodicals, *Festschrift* pieces often evince the characteristics of an author's uninspired discharge of a social obligation vis-à-vis the colleague to be honored. On balance, the present volume, I am happy to report, does not suffer from this rather common malaise.

Wedged in between an introductory essay by the editor and a list of the honoree's publications are 49 papers. With the exception of three contributions written in English, all are in German. The topics they cover are wide-ranging, extending from German public law to international law and the law of the European Communities. Thematically diverse as these papers may be, in the aggregate they amount to an impressive overview of some of the major contemporary transnational legal problems. The result, in other words, is a volume that presents quite a treasure box, the contents of which, alas, can only briefly and very selectively be hinted at in this review.

By far the largest number of essays addresses human rights issues. Simma contributes an important paper on the international enforceability of treaty-stipulated human rights provisions. He argues persuasively that irrespective of whether the human rights treaty provides for a specific international complaints procedure, a violation of its provisions ultimately entitles the complaining state to take any other action that would be a legitimate response under general international law to the violation of the obligation concerned. On this issue, Bindschedler, in an essay on the protection of human rights and nonintervention, comes out—wrongly, I believe—on the other side. Tomuschat presents an exacting analysis of the principles of equality and non-discrimination under the International Covenant on Civil and Political Rights, in which he calls our attention to the fact that the Covenant lacks a comprehensive nondiscrimination clause. Other papers on the protection of individuals include those by Delbrück (the conventional prohibition of discrimination against women), Schröder (the transnational reach of German constitutional rights), Schwarze (legal remedies of individuals against directly effective EEC regulations), and Uibopuu (extraterritorial effects of the recognition of refugee status).

Several papers focus on the lawmaking process. Scheuner and Frowein review elements of lawmaking in the jurisprudence of the European Court of Human Rights and the European Commission of Human Rights, respectively. Bothe, in an essay on "soft law" in the European Communities, makes some interesting general remarks. He correctly criticizes the concept as misleading and emphasizes the political context as determining expectations of compliance. Unfortunately, at least in this essay, he does not develop further the jurisprudential underpinnings of his approach; nor does he acknowledge the direct relevance to this subject of the work of McDougal, Lasswell, and Reisman.

Among the contributions dealing with the law of armed conflicts, Kimmich's paper on the influence of international humanitarian law on the nuclear weapons question is especially noteworthy: here is yet another voice suggesting the international illegality of the use of not only strategic but also possibly tactical nuclear weapons.

Mosler provides an expert guide to the problems raised by nonparticipation of a party in the proceedings before the ICJ. Kewenig assesses the concept of the common heritage of mankind as a key vehicle for promoting fundamental changes in North-South relations. There are three papers on international organizational questions, by Seidl-Hohenveldern, Steiger, and Suy. An equal number of contributions (by Magiera, Rengeling, and Zweiger) brings into focus the need for a "democratization" of the institutions of the EEC by strengthening the powers of the European Parliament.

Finally, Blumenwitz offers a useful review of the persistent controversy over the notion of "*Inland*" (domestic territory) in West German law and thus a commentary on the continued political commitment, 10 years after normalization of inter-German relations, to the preservation of a legal fiction that symbolizes the ideal of eventual German reunification.

GÜNTHER HANDL
Wayne State University Law School

The Soviet Views on the Use of Force in International Law. By John Yin. Hong Kong: Asian Research Service, 1980. Pp. 189. Index.

Soviet attitudes on the use of force prove that for the USSR international law is perceived to be an effective instrument of Soviet policy. That is the message of Dr. John Yin. Educated in Chungking before the Communist era and subsequently in the United States, Yin has assiduously examined great numbers of Soviet texts in comparison with traditionalist Western writings to produce an encyclopedic-style monograph where every sentence is footnoted. Clearly, he has had access to an unexpectedly complete library of Soviet materials.

His study of a narrow, but critical, topic is nearly exhaustive, although there are gaps. For example, in his discussion of aggression he unaccountably omits comment on the Soviet positions taken in the formulation of Resolution 3314 (XXIX) of the General Assembly defining aggression. Generally, however, he is thorough in coverage of the literature, though his prose is replete with malapropisms and orientalisms.

Some conclusions deserve note in a review. He argues that it is Soviet policy to maintain the power of the Security Council (where it has the veto) and to restrain the Secretary-General. This is because it fears that the Secretary-General's role has expanded over the years (p. 75). Hence, the effort to install a "troika" in the office, giving the Second World a veto. Also, he is to be denied command of armed forces. These forces are seen by Soviet authors as never to be more than the forces of the contributing states. Thus, Trygve Lie's proposal that he be given a small force was opposed lest it become the nucleus of an army, and even headquarters police have been opposed with the argument that host nations should protect UN installations. The UN forces in Korea are seen always as "a unified command under the United States." Yin finds this position correct, since President Truman first dubbed them "a unified command under the U.S." (p. 79).

Yin demonstrates his annoyance with Soviet positions when he adds cutting characterizations following his exposition of texts. Thus, he asks, after paralleling Soviet criticism of Nazi shootings of surrendering Soviet troops with

Soviet statements that capitulation is a serious crime, "We may wonder why not let the Germans shoot the capitulationists, because they would certainly face the firing squad after returning to their own country?" (p. 60). Again, in considering the Soviet analysis of tsarist incursions into Siberia as benefiting tremendously the minorities of the East by joining them in a progressive cultural and economic union with the more advanced Russian people, he asks, "May we not say that because Hitler's conquest of Eastern Europe has the salutary though unintended outcome of turning it into a soviet satellite, his war has progressive character?" (p. 113). And again, in treating Soviet views on "just" and "unjust" wars, he concludes, "In other words, the entry of the Soviet Union into a war puts automatically a lofty imprint on it, and her leaving the war makes it unjust" (p. 127).

The author lists all Soviet vetoes in the Security Council to mid-1979 (122 out of 165), and he appends a good bibliography, which can be a useful source for scholars seeking access to Soviet materials. Authors of general texts wishing to insert Soviet views on the topics they are treating will also find the volume helpful.

JOHN N. HAZARD
Board of Editors

Resources, Regimes, World Order. By Antony J. Dolman. Published in cooperation with the Foundation Reshaping the International Order (RIO). New York: Pergamon Press, 1981. Pp. xiv, 413. Indexes. $37.50, cloth; $10.95, paper.

The announced purpose of this book by Dolman, a Senior Fellow at the Foundation Reshaping the International Order (RIO), is to "identify possible ways in which planning and management capabilities at the world level could be strengthened" (p. 3). Although the goal of enhanced planning and management capabilities is never explicitly articulated, implicitly it would clearly be to accelerate the development of developing countries so as to reduce economic inequalities among states.

The book begins with a comprehensive review of the several analyses of the global economy that were published in the late 1970's. The conclusion of the review is that neoclassical, radical, and Marxist analyses are inadequate as explanations for the state of the world economy and as prescriptions for making it better; new analytical paradigms are needed. Then there is a summary of the program to achieve a "New International Economic Order" (NIEO) and an analysis of the obstacles to the realization of this program.

The remaining four chapters of the book are devoted to an exposition of Dolman's own strategy for improving the global economic order. This strategy, which draws heavily on the work of RIO, involves strengthening international institutions, progressively broadening application of the concept of the common heritage of mankind, developing systems of international taxation, and establishing international control over the development and utilization of technology, especially technology that has both harmful and beneficial uses.

That none of Dolman's suggestions is completely novel is both a strength and a weakness of his strategy. All of the steps that he would like states to take have historical antecedents; thus, they are plausible. Several of the suggestions, however, have been in the political arena for some time, but states—or at least the most powerful among them—have not chosen to implement them. Dolman offers no persuasive explanation as to why states might respond more positively at this juncture. Indeed, his telling analysis of the obstacles to the realization of the NIEO program could be used to demonstrate the infeasibility of his own strategy. To the extent that precedents for his suggestions have been implemented and that the world economy is not any better than it is, according to Dolman's own bleak appraisal, one wonders why doing more of the same would make it better.

The book is marked by a strong anticapitalist bias. There are many statements such as the following: "Western civilization gave birth to capitalism and capitalism spawned barbarism" (p. 80). Capitalism and its market mechanism have widely recognized flaws, yet they also have important strengths. Dolman's treatment of capitalism is ideological and rhetorical, not analytical.

One could dismiss the book by dubbing it the ultimate 1970's-style prescription for global reform, hardly a guide for action in the 1980's. Yet one cannot escape the feeling that whenever states choose to strengthen international institutions, and given the pace of technological development it is unlikely that this choice can be postponed indefinitely, Dolmans's book will be a useful source, providing a broad review of the possible steps that could be taken.

HAROLD K. JACOBSON
Board of Editors

Law of the Sea: Caracas and Beyond. Developments in International Law, 3. Edited by Ram Prakash Anand. New Delhi: Radiant Publishers; The Hague: Martinus Nijhoff Publishers, 1980. Pp. viii, 399. Index. Dfl.110; $58.

Proceedings of Conference on Deep Seabed Mining and Freedom of the Seas. Edited by Frederick Tse-shyang Chen. Bridgeport: University of Bridgeport School of Law; Westport: United Nations Association of Connecticut, 1981. Pp. viii, 84. $3.50.

These books, the product of symposia, will be useful in filling gaps in the secondary literature on law of the sea issues.

Caracas and Beyond publishes papers presented at the December 1976 seminar held in the International Legal Studies Division of the School of International Studies, Jawaharlal Nehru University in New Delhi. The papers were updated through 1977, and a 20-page postscript carries the UNCLOS III story through 1979. The United Nations Association of Connecticut began its 3-year celebration of the 400th anniversary of the birthday of Hugo Grotius in 1980 with a conference on deep seabed mining and freedom of the seas, cosponsored by the Grotius Society of International Law of the University of Bridgeport Law School. The result was the *Proceedings.*

Caracas and Beyond is entirely the product of Indian legal scholars, diplomats, scientists, and international lawyers. The law- and economics-based chapters often reflect India's views and therefore developing nations' insights on the evolving law of the sea. The editor's introduction, in its survey of the topics that follow, brings to mind Lord Wilberforce's remark at the 1982 annual dinner meeting of the American Society of International Law, that an international lawyer "must be a bit of all things" today. Professor Anand's paper, *Winds of Change in the Law of the Sea,* is followed by Law Minister H. R. Gokhale's analysis of developments through 1976. Chapters by V. S. Mani, O. P. Sharma, Anand, M. K. Nawaz, S. P. Sharma, Saroj Mohan, and V. C. Govindaraj are trend studies of principal issues at UNCLOS III: islands and archipelagoes, international straits navigation, the continental shelf, exclusive economic zones (EEZ's), fisheries jurisdiction, and the problems of geographically disadvantaged states, *i.e.,* landlocked or shelf-locked nations or those with narrow continental shelves or short coastlines. V. K. S. Varadhan and P. Sreenivasa Rao have essays on the most troublesome aspects of UNCLOS III, seabed resources and the structure and powers of the International Sea-Bed Authority. J. N. Saxena explores compulsory jurisdiction alternatives for the Authority, and S. Rama Rao traces trends in dispute settlement mechanisms proposed during UNCLOS III. Scattered through the book are interdisciplinary chapters on other perspectives of ocean management: mineral resources of the continental margin, by V. Asthana; legal aspects of marine science research, by Rahmatullah Khan; a scientist's view of marine research, by R. R. Subramaniam; and a survey of marine pollution and international law, by Tarsem Lal Gill.

The *Proceedings* of the Connecticut symposium are a useful follow-up to *Caracas and Beyond.* By April 1981, when the conference was held, the final version of the Convention had appeared.[1] The United States, under the Reagan administration, had announced, on March 2, 1981, its decision for a policy review of the Convention. Shabtai Rosenne, Ambassador-at-Large and Chairman of the Israel delegation to UNCLOS III, opened his conference remarks by expressing the "anger and bitterness" of UNCLOS delegates over the U.S. decision. The remainder of his remarks gives the background to UNCLOS, with particular emphasis on seabed issues, and concludes with the assertion that Grotius would have approved the UNCLOS III diplomatic process. John Norton Moore, former U.S. Ambassador to UNCLOS III, postulates three models of LOS negotiations, and advocates a "balanced" or pragmatic model of supporting a treaty that preserves navigational freedoms and access to deep seabed minerals over the Carter administration's view that the present treaty was the best obtainable under the circumstances, or the ideological/skeptical model that postulates no need for a treaty at all.

Mario Carías, Honduras' Permanent Representative to the United Nations and head of its UNCLOS III delegation, sketches the draft provisions relating

[1] UN Doc. A/CONF.62/WP.10/Rev.3 (1980), *reprinted in* 19 ILM 1129 (1980).

to seabed mining, and concludes that a convention on the subject is necessary. Ralph J. Gillis, an international lawyer previously with the Marine Resources Section of the U.S. Justice Department, states the reasons for seabed miners' opposition to the Convention. Professor Chen applies a policy science analysis to the problem, concluding that "the acquisition of an adequate conception of the common interest stands as a propitious beginning" for considering the UNCLOS III treaty terms for seabed mining. Myres McDougal comments that embarking on UNCLOS III was a mistake and that the real issue is the power, not the wealth, process, and that the challenge is to make law that has "some semblance of democracy and some semblance of responsibility."

Procedural and substantive events have occurred since the Connecticut conference. On January 19, 1982, President Reagan reaffirmed the U.S. commitment to the multilateral treaty process. On April 30, the Convention was adopted by 130 to 4, with 17 abstentions, the United States voting no. On July 9, the President announced that the United States would not sign the treaty. And on March 10, 1983, the President proclaimed a 200-mile EEZ, U.S. recognition of other states' rights to navigation and overflight on a reciprocal basis, and the U.S. determination to "exercise and assert its navigation rights . . . consistent with the balance of interests reflected in the Convention." The Preparatory Commission, authorized by resolution of the conference, has begun drafting rules for the Sea-Bed Authority.

Despite these developments—and there will be more as the treaty proceeds through the ratification process elsewhere—the books reviewed remain a useful contribution to pre-Convention trends and thinking for those who follow the law of the sea, whose issues, as Anand so aptly puts it, have "become as fluid as its waters."

GEORGE K. WALKER
Wake Forest University

Die Plünderung der Meere: Ein gemeinsames Erbe wird zerstückelt. Edited by Wolfgang Graf Vitzthum. Frankfurt am Main: Fischer Taschenbuch Verlag, 1981. Pp. 327. DM 7,80.

This paperback, available at a very moderate price, was initiated by Vereinigung Deutscher Wissenschaftler (VDW), an interdisciplinary group of German scientists. The editor, Professor Vitzthum, belongs to the rare species of German law of the sea experts. The other authors are outstanding lawyers, economists, historians, and political and natural scientists.

Under the provocative title *The Plundering of the Oceans: A common heritage is fragmentized,* four main chapters with 14 different contributions, each followed by a short bibliography, cover all aspects of the new ocean regime.

The preface by E. Pestel and the first chapter are devoted to philosophical and historical aspects of man and the sea. This "typical German" approach is one of the rare efforts of profound criticism of the new law of the sea. The generous enrichment of coastal states in terms of ocean space and resources is clearly a radical change from Grotius's philosophy of *mare liberum.* In fact, the new Convention will be an ironic 400th birthday present for the great Dutch lawyer, born in Delft on April 10, 1583. In his preface, Pestel advocates, as a possible means of achieving rational use and peace in the oceans, the establishment of 10–15 large regional economic zones in order to accommodate the rivalry of some 160 states.

The philosophical contribution by K.-M. Meyer-Abich tries to answer the question whether man will live better with the industrial revolution of the oceans than without it. The question of man's proper place in nature has been asked time and again in history. Meyer-Abich hopes that this great challenge may produce better understanding among nations and between man and nature.

Golo Mann, the brother of Elisabeth Mann Borgese, gives an extremely witty analysis of *The Germans and the Sea,* describing the maritime history of this nation of "terrestrial animals." The old antinomy of land and sea is taken up by W. Vitzthum who comes to the conclusion that, in view of industrial and military progress, the oceans become *res occupata* as the land has always been. This "terranization" or nationalization of the coastal third of the world's oceans benefits but a few lucky states with lengthy coastlines. A side effect of this development is that many of the least developed Fourth World countries are cut off irrevocably from marine resources by virtue of their geographical situation. The International Sea-Bed Authority, as custodian of the common heritage of mankind, paralyzed by its own bureaucracy, is allocated what is left after the great "rip-off." Vitzthum rightly complains about the manifest lack of any grand design in the new law of the sea, which can best be described as "balkanization" of the seas. It is this part of the book that best fits its provocative title, whereas the following chapters examine in detail different aspects of the new law.

In the second chapter, the essays on militarization of the seas (J. Herbig), the risks and opportunities for world shipping (H.-J. Stöcker), aquaculture (E. Mann Borgese), marine pollution (H. Thiel), ecological consequences of deep seabed mining (J. Schneider), and modern problems of marine scientific research (G. Hempel, the director of the German Polar Institute) are each substantial contributions covering the relevant technical, legal, economic, and political implications, as well as specific German interests.

The interdisciplinary approach is maintained in the third chapter, on law and politics of the industrialization of the seas. Here the emphasis is on the economic realities of seabed mining (H.-G. Stalp) which may be completely frustrated by the new seabed regime. The old and permanent conflict of liberal market economy versus protectionist planned economy is discussed in detail, as well as national interim legislation and its interfaces with the international regime. An incidental remark about the problem of transfer of technology, which was solved in a reasonable way in a German-Arabian joint venture in the Red Sea, deserves more elaboration than the author provides, since the joint venture would be an example of how to overcome the deadlock in the deep seabed mining conflict between signatories and nonsignatories of the new Convention. R. Wolfrum's subject is the renationalization of fisheries, the dark future of existing international fishery organizations, and the impact of the exclusive economic zone. M.-I. Kehden, one of the fathers of the chapter on Marine Environment of the UN Convention on the Law of the Sea, gives a detailed picture of old and new remedies against pollution from vessels. The new rules of enforcement against ships under foreign flags by means of a graduated system of intervention and control, as well as the new safeguards in favor of unimpeded shipping, are the highlights of this contribution.

The fourth chapter consists of R. Dolzer's analysis of *Germany and the Law of the Sea Conference* and H.-P. Ipsen's *European Community and the Sea,* two articles that are necessary to understand the economic and political situation of the Federal Republic of Germany during the law of the sea debates.

The book was originally designed to encourage a broad discussion on the pros and cons of the UN Law of the Sea Conference. It is at the same time an excellent source of materials for all those who are interested in the philosophical background, in specific German law of the sea problems, or in neglected issues like the EEC and the law of the sea.

UWE JENISCH
Kiel

Resource Management and the Oceans: The Political Economy of Deep Seabed Mining. By Kurt Michael Shusterich. Boulder: Westview Press, 1982. Pp. xx, 344. Index. $22.50.

This is a thoroughly worthwhile book that embarks on a difficult task. According to Shusterich:

> This book analyzes the various domestic and international issues that have been raised about the management of the global commons. It provides an analysis and history of the major issues and developments of the United States and international laws on marine policy and resource management. The book does so by focusing on the case of deep seabed mining, while pointing to the broader range of political implications involved that may influence exploitation for other resource commons [p. xvii].

This is a tall order, but one that the author handles well.

There are seven main sections to the book plus 16 appendixes: (1) "Ocean Mining: A Complex Policy Issue"; (2) "United States Government: Political and Institutional Responses"; (3) "Mining the Deep Seabed: A Complex and Innovative Industry"; (4) "UNCLOS III, The Group of '77, and the *New International Economic Order*"; (5) "Complex Interdependence and the Political Process of Ocean Politics"; (6) "Precedents for Other Global Commons"; and (7) "The Current Status of U.S. Ocean Mining Policy." All seven sections are good, in that they provide solid, accurate description and analysis. The section on the NIEO seems to stray somewhat from the book's main focus, but the impact of NIEO aspirations on the new law of the sea cannot be ignored. Section 6, in endeavoring to draw parallels between mining of the deep seabed and other commons, is very interesting and stimulating. The author sees parallels with other types of global commons including "the high seas, international airspace, the electromagnetic spectrum, outer space, geostationary orbits, and Antarctica" (p. 161). One could take issue with the specifics of certain comparisons, *e.g.*, with the moon (p. 164). Nevertheless, the attempt to find parallels with and to generalize from the seabed experience is important. However, it must be acknowledged that the uncertain status of the seabed regime (both legally and operationally) makes such speculation as risky as it is important.

The most unusual thing about the book is the appendixes. In sharp contrast to most monographs, they are excellent, providing one of the best, most concise statements available about the history and development of deep seabed mining. Everything is here, from a physical description of nodules (Appendix 1) and diagrams of ocean mining systems (Appendix 5) to a table of state involvement in deep seabed mining consortia (Appendix 16). The appendixes are the best part of the book!

The potential audience for a book like this is reasonably clear. Those who have been *immersed* in studying the law of the sea for the last decade will find little new, but will still like the appendixes. Those with less familiarity with the law of the sea will find the book to be one of the best treatments of the legal and political issues surrounding the deep seabed regime. One last point: as with many recent books, a highly inaccurate title has been selected. This is too bad because the book is quite capable of standing alone with an appropriate title.

JOHN KING GAMBLE, JR.
The Behrend College
The Pennsylvania State University

Iran, Saudi Arabia, and the Law of the Sea: Political Interaction and Legal Development in the Persian Gulf. By Charles G. MacDonald. Westport: Greenwood Press, 1980. Pp. xv, 226. Index. $28.50.

The author, a professor of international relations at Florida International University, has produced an excellent study that is of value to specialists in international law and Middle Eastern affairs, as well as those with more general interests. The focus of the book is the Persian Gulf.

In Chapter 1, "The Persian Gulf Context," the author discusses his selection of "phase analysis" as his main theoretical tool to examine the process of interaction in the Gulf region. This method of analysis "breaks the process of interaction into the participants, the situations encountered, the objectives or goals of the participants, the base values or capabilities of the participants, and the strategies chosen by the participants to accomplish their goals in the given situations with their given capabilities" (p. 29).

The second chapter provides a general survey of what is at stake in the development of the law of the sea in the Persian Gulf. Examples abound concerning the importance of the Gulf. Oil tankers pass through the Strait of Hormuz at the rate of one every 15 minutes. As of 1973, about 70 percent of the world's proven offshore recoverable oil reserves were located in the Gulf. Also, commercial fishing appears to have a bright future. Estimates place the annual potential as high as 600,000 tons, whereas the current annual catch in the Gulf has been only about 75,000 tons.

In this reviewer's opinion, chapter 4, "Claims to Authority Over Offshore Resources," is the most outstanding part of the book. Excellent maps accompany the author's analysis of the various agreements. The first delimitation of submarine boundaries between two Persian Gulf states was set forth in the Saudi Arabia-Bahrain agreement of 1958. It provided for the establishment of a central boundary line to delimit the submarine areas of the two states, but also delimited a hexagonal area to be under Saudi jurisdiction, with revenue generated from oil resources in the area to be shared equally by Saudi Arabia and Bahrain.

MacDonald notes that Saudi Arabia and Iran have played significant roles in the development of the law of the sea through innovative approaches to the continental shelf concept and their provisions for the delimitation of offshore resource boundaries. He observes that the Saudis' emphasis on the concept of contiguity in the context of the Persian Gulf (*i.e.,* its lack of a continental shelf) led the International Law Commission to extend the concept of the continental shelf to apply to the Persian Gulf. Furthermore, the author points out that the use of "equitable principles" by Iran and Saudi Arabia in the delimitation of offshore resource boundaries set a major precedent by emphasizing the importance of context. "[T]he practice of Iran and Saudi Arabia was exonerated by (and probably contributed to) the findings of the International Court of Justice in the North Sea continental shelf cases . . ." (p. 152).

Scenarios for the future are explored in chapter 6, "Claims in Transition." In reviewing developments at the Third UN Conference on the Law of the Sea, the author notes the broad community acceptance of a 200-mile exclusive economic zone. If applied by the littoral states, this principle would enclose the Persian Gulf for resource jurisdiction. The author feels that the Gulf states will move toward the establishment of a special regional regime. Should this happen, the Persian Gulf could lose its status as part of the high seas. In effect, the Gulf would become a closed sea. "Such an action might be tied to questions concerning the status of the Persian Gulf as a zone of peace and security, especially with expressed desire of the gulf states to avoid a superpower presence" (p. 193).

ROY E. THOMAN
West Texas State University

The Yankee Mariner and Sea Power: America's Challenge of Ocean Space. Edited by Joyce J. Bartell. Los Angeles: University of Southern California Press, 1982. Pp. 299. $20. Distributed by Transaction Books.

This book represents a collection of papers from a conference sponsored by the Center for Study of the American Experience at the University of

Southern California. The conference took place in March 1981 and assembled 15 recognized experts in the fields of naval history and strategy; international law and politics; marine transport and port authority; ocean engineering, mining, and petroleum extraction; and fishing and oceanography. As the book jacket announces, "these sea specialists examine the diversity of America's uses of the earth's oceans, trace the ongoing evaluation of seagoing America, and assess United States sea power today and the nation's future in ocean space."

A synthesis of the sometimes diverse views of the authors is contained in the opening chapter by pioneering oceanographer Athelstan Spilhaus, Distinguished Scholar in Residence at the Center during 1980–1981 and originator of the National Sea Grant program. Spilhaus defines American sea power as a three-legged stool, with a Navy leg, a sea resources leg, and a marine transport leg. He summarizes the historical development, current sea uses, and projections for the future from the disciplines reported at the conference and notes that the authors find the United States faltering in its momentum toward mastery of the sea environment. He joins the conference chairman, Don Walsh, in his assessment that a long-term commitment to a concerted U.S. national ocean policy framework must be forthcoming. Their central thesis is an eloquent argument for more U.S. Government attention to the ocean frontier from both a policy and a budget perspective.

Of interest to the international lawyer and political scientist is the examination by Arvid Pardo of the development of the law of the sea, the U.S. attitude toward which he characterizes as being pragmatic rather than principled. It should be noted that the conference took place prior to the U.S. decision to refuse to sign the UN Convention on the Law of the Sea, while 117 other nations did so on December 10, 1982.[1] Pardo criticizes the United States for acting cavalierly in this regard, especially in view of the Truman Proclamations of 1945, which he blames for opening a Pandora's box of other national claims to the offshore resources beyond traditional boundaries. He also argues interestingly for an "Ocean Space West Point" in conjunction with a needed national ocean policy for the United States.

Ann L. Hollick also addresses the political issues leading to conclusion of the Convention, but in a more positive vein, and she appears to have been prescient in predicting that the United States would not sign in view of the problems it had with the deep seabed mining authority provisions.

John E. Flipse tacitly represents the thinking of the deep seabed mining consortiums in his chapter on ocean mining, a treatise on current and projected technology. Other ocean engineering capabilities are lucidly set forth by Rechnitzer's article on ocean research, and by the fascinating discussion of offshore oil production technology by L. Donald Maus, which describes current capabilities to drill at incredible depths down to 4,900 feet.

Perhaps an unintended illustration of the difficulty of gaining consensus for a national ocean policy is the conflict of opinion among the experts themselves. This is strikingly demonstrated by two articles on the naval defense issue: one

[1] San Francisco Chronicle, Dec. 11, 1982, at 7. *See* text, 21 ILM 1261 (1982); signatures, *id.* at 1477.

by Brookings Institute author, Michael MccGwire, and the other by Richard Ackley, retired submarine commander and former U.S. Naval Attaché to Moscow. While MccGwire states that worldwide naval supremacy is no longer useful and international cooperation is the way of the future, Ackley's in-depth and scholarly thesis argues persuasively for a resurgence of naval power by rebuilding to a 600-ship Navy to meet the global commitments it is presently assigned.

Brand and Brockel describe the state of U.S. marine transport and port capacity, while naval historians Symonds and Hattendorf trace the 17th- to 20th-century sinusoidal pattern of America's commitment to support maritime endeavors, with nods to Mahan and Clausewitz. Finally, to the delight of those of artistic persuasion, John Craven waxes lyrical in a satisfying contemplation of music, art, poetry, and literature inspired by the ocean and its littoral in his *Images of the Sea*.

Bartell's editing brings a cohesiveness to what otherwise could be an uneven collection in a conference of this magnitude and complexity. An excellent reference for those interested in maritime matters, these articles, some of which were rewritten by their authors following the conference, contain a creditable overview of U.S. sea power today. The book is recommended as a current statement on affairs of the sea.

THOMAS A. KAMM
Golden Gate University

Estudios de Derecho Internacional. By Ernesto J. Rey Caro. Córdoba: Universidad Nacional de Córdoba, 1982. Pp. 250.

This book contains six essays written by Professor Rey Caro (Universidad Nacional de Córdoba) between 1977 and 1981. Two essays are devoted to topics on the law of the sea and one focuses on the subject of human rights. Another essay is devoted to the peaceful settlement of disputes within the Organization of American States, while the remaining two are on the international law of the environment.

The first essay, *Argentina and current aspects of the law of the sea,* does not concern itself with international law *per se.* It is essentially an analysis of the legislation enacted by Argentina since 1869 with regard to its territorial sea and, since 1944, with regard to its continental shelf. The essay also discusses Argentina's claim to jurisdiction over the so-called epicontinental sea, which is described in a decree issued by the Government of Argentina in 1946 as "the waters covering the submarine platform," *i.e.,* the shelf's superjacent waters. The discussion of the evolution of the concepts of "patrimonial sea" and economic zone, in the introduction to this essay, is brief and unsatisfactory. For instance, the author states that "it is in the so-called 'Declaration of Santo Domingo' of June 1972 that several states of the American Hemisphere publicly asserted their sovereign rights over the patrimonial sea," but he provides no further reference in connection with that statement. There is no mention of the Specialized Conference of the Caribbean Countries on Problems of the

Sea, which adopted that declaration by a majority of the 15 participating states. One would also have expected to find in a study of this kind at least a brief reference to the manner in which certain unilateral claims of jurisdiction over the adjacent seas, such as those advanced by Argentina, have influenced the development of the concept of the exclusive economic zone (EEZ). Moreover, there seems to have been no perception that, by the time this essay was written (September 1977), the concept of "patrimonial sea" had already been embodied in the EEZ concept and incorporated by the Third UN Conference on the Law of the Sea, as part V, in the Informal Single Negotiating Text, which formed the basis for the 1982 UN Convention on the Law of the Sea.

The essay entitled *Territorial Sea and Continental Shelf: Jurisdiction of the Nation and of its Provinces* is a well-documented study on the coastal jurisdiction of the federal Government of Argentina, over the territorial sea and the continental shelf, vis-à-vis the jurisdiction of the constituent provinces. It provides an interesting comparative analysis of similar federal-state coastal jurisdictions in the United States, Mexico, and Brazil.

The most extensive study concerns the subject of human rights. Under the title *Human rights thirty years after the Universal Declaration,* the author discusses several important multilateral instruments and mechanisms for the protection of human rights. These include the UN Charter, the Universal Declaration adopted by the UN General Assembly in 1948, the European Convention, and inter-American instruments on the subject of human rights. Unfortunately, the discussion is conceptual rather than functional in focus, with little or no consideration of state practice. There is no doubt that this essay constitutes a valuable contribution to the study of an issue of great importance, particularly in Latin America. Yet, it is most astonishing that in a study stressing the theoretical rather than the practical aspects of the problem, the author concludes, without qualifications, that: "Despite the many denunciations of human rights violations, which continue to stir public opinion in the countries and in the competent bodies of the international organizations, the record for the last 30 years shows a favorable balance, both within the UN system and within the regional systems" (p. 172). No background discussion or relevant material is furnished anywhere in the study to substantiate a generalization of this kind. It seems odd, in any case, to indulge in a statement of this nature when so many reliable and authoritative reports, prepared both by national and international organizations, have shown that certain "regimes," so contemptuous of the fundamental rights of their citizens, have, among other violations, eliminated or "made to disappear" thousands of men and women never found guilty of any crime.[1]

In his essay on *Peaceful Settlement of Disputes within the Organization of American States* the author covers so many issues in relatively few pages that, inevitably, he cannot avoid indulging in generalizations. Much of the work consists of a discussion of topics that have been sufficiently discussed in other writings. On

[1] The *Sunday Times* of London reported on Nov. 7, 1982 (p. 19) that approximately 90,000 people have "disappeared" during the last decade in Latin America alone.

a different level, the reader should be warned of certain omissions such as on page 231 where five states (Brazil, Chile, Colombia, Paraguay, and Peru) that are parties to the American Treaty on Pacific Settlement are not mentioned as such. On the other hand, El Salvador, a country that denounced that Treaty in November 1973, is listed as one of the current parties to the Treaty.

Finally, the two essays on the international law of the environment differ on two counts: the depth of analysis and the amount of space devoted to the topics. *International Law of the Environment* is a well-written and well-documented work. Specialists in the subject will certainly find this article to be a welcome addition to the existing literature in the field. On the other hand, the essay on the *International Legal Protection of the Work Environment,* which primarily highlights the work of the International Labour Organisation and the existing international legislation with regard to the protection of the work environment, is too sketchy to be very useful.

As sometimes happens with collections of this kind, the essays, even though written by the same author, are of uneven quality. However, despite the observations voiced above, Rey Caro has made a valuable contribution to the study of issues of great importance in contemporary international law.

DOMINGO E. ACEVEDO
Queens' College
University of Cambridge

Principles of the Conflict of Laws, National and International. By K. Lipstein. The Hague, Boston, London: Martinus Nijhoff Publishers, 1981. Pp. xii, 144. Index. Dfl.75; $33.

As the preface to this book states, it is a reproduction, with slight changes, of a course of lectures given by the author at the Hague Academy of International Law in 1972.[1] The only changes of substance are (1) the addition of a series of questions raised by recent writings on the effect of domestic public policy on the application of private international law rules embodied in public international law, and (2) some rewriting of the section on spatially conditioned or self-limiting rules.

The book is divided into four parts: I, "The nature and function of Private International Law"; II, "The relationship between Public and Private International Law"; III, "The structure and interpretation of rules of Private International Law"; and IV, "Conclusions." Part I is a survey of the principal theories of conflict of laws from Roman times to the "new doctrines" of Ehrenzweig, Currie, and Cavers. Lipstein is one of that select band of his generation who fled continental Europe already schooled in the civil law and grafted onto their earlier experience long and distinguished careers in an Anglo-Saxon legal environment. The full breadth and depth of Lipstein's scholarship is evident in this concise, but illuminating, account, which is made the more interesting by parallels he draws between the ideas of earlier con-

[1] 135 RECUEIL DES COURS 104–229 (1972 I).

tinental theorists and the modern American writers (*e.g.*, the Statutists and Currie; Wächter and Ehrenzweig). Part III contains an elaboration of the fundamental characteristics of choice-of-law rules under such headings as structure; characterization; spatially conditioned internal rules; transposition substitution and adaptation; renvoi; preliminary question; and conflict of laws in time. The discussion of the preliminary, or incidental, question is particularly thorough and brings much clarity to a question frequently clouded in obscurity. The expanded treatment given to spatially conditioned rules, a subject on which Lipstein has written elsewhere[2] but which is too often neglected in expositions on the choice-of-law process, especially in the United States, is to be welcomed.

One conspicuous difference between the lectures and the book which is based on them is in the title. *The General Principles of Private International Law* has become *Principles of the Conflict of Laws, National and International.* The significance of this change may be twofold. By emphasizing the national as against the international, the title draws attention to the problem of adapting modern American theories, developed almost entirely to solve conflict of laws between the states of one nation, to the task of solving genuinely international conflicts arising between nation-states. This difference between the national and international character of conflict-of-laws rules is discussed in part I, section 19, "The International Use of the New Doctrines." But a second reason for highlighting the national vs. international distinction is to draw attention to the question whether conflict-of-laws rules as applied in the international context are in their nature and origin national or international. This question is touched upon in part I and faced squarely in part II where the author considers the somewhat diverse topics of the general influence of public on private international law, choice of law in international tribunals, and the application in domestic tribunals of international law rules on expropriation. There are an increasing number of instances in which consideration has had to be given in domestic tribunals to the relevance of international law standards, many of which[3] Lipstein dismisses as concerned only with self-limiting rules that do not raise the question of the application of foreign law and are not therefore proper private international law problems. But this is not easy to reconcile with the attention given later (in part III) to spatially conditioned rules (another name for self-limiting rules). There are an increasing number of problems in the broad context of private international law to which public international law standards may be relevant, such as the validity of service of process abroad;[4] jurisdiction and choice-of-law questions raised by the revision of the rules of sovereign immunity;[5] the power to reverse foreign judgments

[2] *E.g.*, *Conflict of Laws 1921–1971, The Way Ahead,* [1972 B] CAMBRIDGE L.J., at 67, 72–77; *Inherent Limitations in Statutes and the Conflict of Laws,* 26 INT'L & COMP. L.Q. 884 (1977).

[3] In criminal law, labor law, tax law, bankruptcy law, antitrust legislation, procedure and jurisdiction and exchange control legislation.

[4] Federal Trade Commission v. Compagnie de Saint-Gobain-Pont-à-Mousson, 636 F.2d 1300 (D.C. Cir. 1980); Note, 16 TEX. INT'L L.J. 565 (1981).

[5] Dellapenna, *Suing Foreign Governments and Their Corporations,* pts. 1–9, 85 COM. L.J., at 167 (1980); 86 *id.* at 346, 438, 486 (1981); 87 *id.* at 8, 129, 244, 303, 375 (1982).

under "clawback" statutes.[6] Examples can also be found of private international law concepts finding their way into public international law rules.[7] This interplay requires constant reconsideration of the relationship between public and private international law and might profitably have been the subject of a more expanded part II of the book.

To the extent that more might have been added within the existing framework of part II without any damage to the cohesion of what was already there, its publication with only minor alteration, almost 10 years after the Hague lectures were delivered, is an opportunity lost. But to say this is not to overlook the value of the book. The lectures were the distillation of many years of scholarly activity. They were and still are a most important contribution to international law in its widest sense. If the book has made these lectures more accessible, it has served a very useful purpose.

COLIN PHEGAN
University of Sydney

Les objectifs temporels des règles de droit international privé. By Patrick Courbe, with a preface by Jacques Foyer. Paris: Presses Universitaires de France, 1981. Pp. 505. Index. F.200.

The author attacks the "classical" thesis, which resolves intertemporal conflicts arising mainly out of changes in the connecting factors (*conflit mobile*) or from changes in the *lex causae,* by reference to the rules on intertemporal conflicts figuring in the foreign law that applies under the conflict-of-law rules of the forum. It is regrettable that the author could not include in his research the work done by the Institut de Droit International in this field, following a report by Graveson on the problem of choice of time in private international law.[1] However, the author shows himself well acquainted with earlier writings by the participants in this effort. The resolution on this topic adopted by the Institute in 1981 approves to a very large extent the views that the author, on the basis of these earlier publications, has held to be the dominant "classical" rules.

Yet, according to the author, these rules lead to unsatisfactory results in many cases, which can be remedied only by recourse to *ordre public* arguments. In long and thorough discussions of terminology as well as of problems of legal philosophy raised by conflicts of law in time and space, the author criticizes these "classical" rules for not giving due weight to the fact that in such a situation a judge of a foreign forum, and not a judge from the country concerned, is asked to apply this country's rules on intertemporal conflicts of law. Due account should be paid to the foreign element thus involved. The

[6] Danaher, *Anti-Antitrust Law: The Clawback and Other Features of the United Kingdom Protection of Trading Interests Act, 1980,* 12 LAW & POL'Y INT'L BUS. 947 (1980); Note, 81 COLUM. L. REV. 1097 (1981).

[7] AMERICAN LAW INSTITUTE, RESTATEMENT OF THE FOREIGN RELATIONS LAW OF THE UNITED STATES (REVISED), Tent. Draft No. 2 (1981), §402.

[1] 58 INSTITUT DE DROIT INTERNATIONAL, ANNUAIRE, pt. I, at 1 (1979).

author rightly rejects the view advanced by Szaszy, that in such a case the judge of the forum should apply the forum's rules on intertemporal conflicts. However, the author likewise rejects the view that, in such a case, a forum judge should apply the intertemporal rules of the *lex causae* as would a judge of the country concerned. According to Courbe, such conflicts should be resolved by a thorough analysis of the rules established by the forum state for the solution of conflicts of laws in space. Usually such a conflict rule will determine only which foreign law shall be applicable in a certain case. Only in rare instances will such a rule establish also that the foreign law concerned should be applied as it was at the time of a certain event, *e.g.*, at the death of the *de cuius.*

According to the author, conflict rules that do not contain such explicit references may be interpreted in such a way that they will offer guidance also in respect of intertemporal conflicts. Such interpretation will have to fall back on the underlying motives that induced the state concerned to establish these rules. These motives will be applicable as well to conflicts of law in time as to conflicts of law in space. As the solutions found in the conflict-of-law rules of the several states give due weight to the foreign element involved in such situations, these rules, in general, will conform in a better manner with international interests than would any reference to intertemporal rules established by a state for domestic use.

The author proceeds to show the practicability of this method of solving intertemporal conflicts. He refers mainly to cases decided by French courts, replacing in part, and reinterpreting in part, dicta of these courts so as to render the results reached compatible with his theories.

Where changes in a foreign law on nationality affect the status of a person as a French national, *e.g.*, retroactive annulment of the validity of a marriage of a foreign woman to a Frenchman, this foreign law should be applied as it was at the time of the marriage. Otherwise, the intertemporal rules of the *lex causae* would apply.

Where the forum law requires proof of reciprocity as a condition for granting certain procedural rights, the foreign law should be taken into consideration as it was at the time when the suit was brought and not as it was at the time of the events forming the subject matter of the law suit.

As for the form of legal acts, the presumed will of the parties should be preferred to the social interests underlying a change in the *lex causae.* Courbe wants to solve such conflicts by deciding always in favor of the validity of the acts concerned.

As far as the substantive content of international contracts is concerned, any choice of law indicated by the parties should be interpreted as freezing this law as it was at the time of the conclusion of the contract, unless the contract violates *jus cogens* of the forum state or possibly also a new *jus cogens* rule of the *lex causae.* However, application of such a rule of the *lex causae* may run counter to the *ordre public* of the forum.

In cases where the judge of the forum has to determine the law applicable to the contents of an international contract, he would apply this foreign law, including its rules on intertemporal conflict.

Marriage contracts, according to the implied will of the parties, should be interpreted as referring to the applicable foreign law frozen as it was at the time of the marriage. According to the presumed will of the *de cuius,* a foreign law held applicable for the succession to movables likewise should be frozen at the time of the death of the *de cuius.*

If the tendency to introduce the U.S. notion of the "proper law of torts" into the law of European states grows in strength, intertemporal conflicts concerning the application of foreign laws of tort should likewise be solved by recourse to the law thus held applicable in the version having the closest connection with the tort concerned.

The author has amassed a vast amount of legal and philosophical arguments in support of his unconventional views. These arguments fit well, one into the other. Yet the author has not fully convinced me as far as the practicability of his solution is concerned. Does not the "classical" solution revised and corrected, where necessary, by recourse to *ordre public* arguments lead to similar solutions by methods easier to understand?

IGNAZ SEIDL-HOHENVELDERN
Vienna

Die von Israel besetzten Gebiete im Völkerrecht. By Edi Gnesa. Zürich: Schulthess Polygraphischer Verlag, 1981. Pp. xxvi, 223. Sw.F.42.

The administration of the territories occupied by Israel has already been treated by many writers, not always *sine ira et studio.* The present author wants to be impartial and objective and he attains this goal with great skill, while evaluating impressive documentation from official and unofficial sources. One can totally agree with his conclusions concerning the measures taken in the legal, educational, and sanitary fields, and also with his investigations into the protection of the individual against torture, the administrative internment of civilians, deportation and collective punishments by the destruction of houses, and the Israeli policy of settlements in Arab territories. His method of applying rules of international law without any compromise, but with criticism, is convincing.

It may seem doubtful whether it is possible to do justice to the very complex history of the origins of the situation with his rather positivistic approach. Thus, he treats the acts of occupation or annexation before explaining to whom the occupied territories belonged according to law. If they should have been under Israeli sovereignty in 1948, there could be no question of an occupation in 1967.

The author is of the opinion that the population of the former mandate, insofar as it did not come under the jurisdiction of the newly founded State of Israel in 1948, continued to be the sovereign of the West Bank, East Jerusalem, and the Gaza Strip. Egypt and Jordan only acted as trustees for the population, which did not definitely abandon its sovereignty in favor of these states. Even if one accepts this thesis, it should be made clear: (1) who belongs to the population of these territories (only those who resided there before the mandate ended and continued to reside there, or also the refugees who left the State of Israel in order to settle there or in neighboring countries?); (2) whether and how this population entrusted Egypt and Jordan with provisionally administering the territories on their behalf; (3) on what basis an occupant can be regarded as a trustee if he does not behave as such, but claims (as Jordan did) to be the sovereign. These questions have not been answered sufficiently.

According to the author, both East Jerusalem and the West Bank are being occupied illegally by Israel. The West Bank should be restored to its sovereign, a future Arab state. A revival of the partition of the city would, however, be unrealistic and meet with difficulties. In this case, the author himself is aware of the legal impasse. He recommends negotiations.

The pros and cons expressed in the discussions are carefully analyzed. The participants are sometimes identified as pro-Israeli or pro-Arab. I am not sure whether he has not done an injustice to some of them. Even some Israeli writers have voiced strong criticism of their Government.

The study includes the events and also the literature up to the end of 1980.

KARL JOSEF PARTSCH
Bonn / Ingelheim

United States International Trade Reports. Binder I. Edited by Edwin S. Newman and Eugene M. Wypyski. London, Rome, New York: Oceana Publications, Inc., 1981. $100/binder.

International trade has increasingly become central to the economic wellbeing of this nation. In 1981, American exports reached the level of approximately $234 billion. In the same year, the developing countries, now representing the fastest growing markets in the world, accounted for $95 billion (41 percent) of total U.S. exports. Approximately one-third of all U.S. exports were made to U.S. affiliates and subsidiaries abroad. This helps them gain a foothold in foreign markets for further exports. The continued growth of the U.S. economy is now largely dependent on how effectively this country can compete for these markets.

The problem of imports into the United States has also taken on greater significance in recessionary times. Increasingly, there have been protectionist cries for import relief to protect ailing industries against foreign competition. This situation is exacerbated by what many observers believe is an overvalued dollar. Inevitably, this has led to increased trade litigation.

Recognizing the increased importance of modern trade litigation and its complexities, Congress enacted the Customs Court Act of 1980. This Act redesignated the U.S. Customs Court as the U.S. Court of International Trade and created a system for the judicial review of civil actions arising out of import transactions and federal statutes affecting international trade.

This book undertakes to make readily available the decisions of the Court of International Trade and of the appellate court, the Court of Customs and

Patent Appeals, from November 1, 1980. In this initial volume, decisions through March 1981 have been included.

The binder includes the reprint of an excellent article by the Chief Judge of the Court of International Trade, the Honorable Edward D. Re. The article is a comprehensive exposition of the historical antecedents of the Court, its composition, and its jurisdiction. The binder also includes the text of the Customs Court Act of 1980, the Rules of the Court of International Trade, and the text of Title X of the Trade Agreements Act of 1979 setting forth review procedures applicable to countervailing duty and antidumping duty matters. The publishers plan soon to include Customs Service decisions relating to international trade as well as rulings of the International Trade Commission.

The editors have enhanced the utility of the work by providing a systematic set of cross-references. This series of binders, as updated, should serve as a valuable resource tool for practitioners and students of trade litigation.

LEO H. PHILLIPS, JR.
Overseas Private Investment Corporation

Transnational Legal Practice: A Survey of Selected Countries. 2 vols. Edited by Dennis Campbell. Deventer: Kluwer Law and Taxation Publishers, 1982. Pp. xii, 387. Index. Dfl.180; $90.

This book appears under the aegis of the Center for International Legal Studies, Salzburg, Austria, of which the editor is Director. Recognizing the ever-quickening process of the "transnationalization" of business activity, the editor has brought together a collection of short essays on the rules and restrictions in this setting with respect to the practice of law in a variety of countries.[1]

Just as business has for some time now been conducted without regard to specific national boundaries, so also the legal community that advises transnational business clients has found itself dealing with legal questions that are in some degree transnational. When the legal adviser follows the client into this new environment, questions necessarily arise concerning the competence of counsel to continue the advisory function in the new legal setting. This book is intended to provide the transnational practitioner with basic data concerning the limitations on the practice of law in various jurisdictions. To the extent that there are specific local rules governing the activities of this sort of practitioner or of individuals specializing in foreign law, these provisions are particularly noted.

[1] The countries covered are Australia, Austria, Belgium, Brazil, Denmark, England and Wales, Finland, France, the Federal Republic of Germany, Ghana, Greece, Hungary, Ireland, Israel, Italy, Japan, Kenya, Kuwait, Malaysia, the Netherlands, the Netherlands Antilles, Norway, Panama, the Philippines, Poland, Scotland, Spain, Sweden, Switzerland, and the United States. In addition, an essay on the impact of principles governing the European Communities on member state rules is also included.

The coverage of this work is necessarily selective, but the jurisdictions are treated in a useful and clear manner. For practitioners who are already knowledgeable about a given jurisdiction, there will be no surprises or revelations. For the practitioner who is following a client into a new legal environment, the information contained in these essays will undoubtedly be an invaluable first stop on the road to familiarity. For comparativists, this work is also likely to be a useful reference tool. Not all of the essays provide the language of the governing provisions, in text or appendix, and this may limit the utility of the work to that of an initial reference point only.

It is obvious that transnational legal practice is not an entirely new invention, but the degree to which practitioners are likely to find themselves in transnational situations has certainly been increasing apace. Furthermore, host jurisdictions are increasingly becoming aware of the need for regulation of transnational legal practice and for understanding its nature. Consequently, a survey of this sort is certainly timely, and it will undoubtedly continue to be of interest.

While the essays are not lengthy, each provides a fairly solid introduction to rules of practice. Each addresses the general requirements for the practice of law, and, wherever pertinent under local rules, the essays identify and discuss such issues as (1) restrictions on the practice of law by noncitizens; (2) registration requirements for practitioners licensed in other jurisdictions who wish to establish a practice or otherwise conduct business in the jurisdiction; (3) the present extent of activity of foreign practitioners within the jurisdiction, and the nature of activities permitted to such practitioners; (4) the nature and extent of permissible cooperation and collaboration between foreign practitioners and local counsel; (5) practical information concerning the way one can contact appropriate local counsel; and (6) in some cases, identification of any expected future developments of interest to the foreign practitioner.[2]

While the essays are selective and practical for the most part, the introductory essay by the editor and Jack J. Coe, Jr., will be of more general academic interest to many readers. This well-footnoted article summarizes the historical emergence of transnational practice and the legal issues raised by this practice, with some attention to comparative analysis of developments in U.S. practice (*e.g., In re Griffiths*[3]) and EC practice (*e.g., Reyners v. Belgian State*[4]). The article also surveys the responses of groups interested in the continuing development of the contours of transnational practice, including the transnational bar itself and legal educators.

Because this work deals with an area of practical importance to legal practitioners, its usefulness to each reader will be determined by his own practical needs. On the whole, the project undertaken by the editor and his able contributors is a notable and worthwhile addition to the literature.

MICHAEL P. MALLOY
New York Law School

[2] The closing date for the essays was February 1981.

[3] 413 U.S. 717 (1973).

[4] Case 2/74, 1974 ECR 631.

International Trade Practice. 2 vols. By Harvey Kaye, Paul Plaia, Jr., and Michael A. Hertzberg. Colorado Springs: Shepard's/McGraw-Hill, 1981. Index. $150 for 2 vols.

This two-volume practice-oriented work is the Shepard's/McGraw-Hill International Practice series's contribution to the expanding international trade law library. The volume seeks to provide a working guide to an area of the law that has been gaining importance among practitioners in light of the increasing significance of international trade to the U.S. economy. Coauthored by three highly qualified and experienced attorneys, and reasonably priced, this work represents a solid treatment of the major substantive areas of current trade practice.

The two loose-leaf binders are divided into six parts and will be updated periodically by supplements. Part I provides a basic introduction to the various government agencies that administer the international trade laws of the United States, including the International Trade Commission, the Office of the U.S. Trade Representative, the International Trade Administration of the Department of Commerce, and the U.S. Customs Service. Part II is a study of section 337 of the Tariff Act of 1930. Its comprehensive treatment of imports involving unfair trade practices benefits from the authors' own particular experience and expertise in this area. Parts III and IV are devoted to the antidumping and countervailing duty laws, as modified by the Trade Agreement Act of 1979. Part V details sections 201 and 406 of the Trade Act of 1974 and thus describes respectively the U.S. laws providing import relief from fairly traded imports and from imports from Communist countries causing market disruption.

The volumes also contain appendixes that should be helpful to the practitioner. The appendix material includes the Revenue Act of 1916, the Tariff Act of 1930 as amended through the Trade Agreements Act of 1979, relevant regulations of the International Trade Commission and the International Trade Administration, certain articles of the General Agreement on Tariffs and Trade, and the Agreement on Interpretation and Application of Articles VI, XVI, and XXIII of the GATT (Subsidies Code), as well as other selected documents.

In general, the work represents a concise, yet thorough and well-footnoted, analysis of the major laws affecting the import side of U.S. international trade. The usefulness of the volumes will depend, of course, upon the quality and frequency of the promised supplements. Full-time trade practitioners may have need of more intensive trade reporting services such as the *U.S. Import Weekly* of the Bureau of National Affairs, Inc. However, at less than one-third the price of the latter, Kaye, Plaia, and Hertzberg's international trade practice publication represents an attractive resource for those requiring knowledge of the major U.S. laws and programs affecting an area of law that is becoming important to an ever-growing number of lawyers in this country.

Mark Roy Sandstrom
Of the District of Columbia Bar

International Individual Taxation. By Philip F. Postlewaite and Michael P. Collins. Colorado Springs: Shepard's/McGraw-Hill, 1982. Pp. xxv, 507. Index.

In the preface to *International Individual Taxation,* the authors set forth the following laudable goals: to provide the novice with a comprehensible explanation of international individual taxation and "to afford the experienced user the most complete and thorough resource material in the field." In addition, they hope to emphasize tax planning techniques. The authors largely accomplish their first goal, fail in their second, and are only partially successful in their third.

The book, divided into four parts, begins by describing in part 1 the concepts of "residence," "source of income," "engaged in trade or business," and "effectively connected income." Part 2 describes the taxation of Americans abroad, of former citizens, and of possessions operations, and the foreign tax credit. Part 3 discusses tax treaties. The last part is concerned with the taxation of partnerships.

The following comments are merely illustrative of some of the book's problems. The book begins with a treatment of the concept of "residency." Drawn largely from regulations and rulings, this section is far too general to be useful to a practitioner. While it more or less adequately sets forth certain rules that may be culled from these limited sources, it largely ignores the voluminous case law. Moreover, although it sets forth the rules for certain categories of individuals (*e.g.,* students, seamen, nonresident commuters, etc.), it merely states that, aside from these rules, one must look to the facts and circumstances. Yet either for planning purposes or in an attempt to determine one's chances in litigation, this is not terribly useful information. One must know, for example, how the courts have interpreted the type of visa status possessed by the individual, or the weight they have attached to contacts (economic, social, or familial) in the United States, as contrasted with those in the individual's country of origin. There are a number of articles that have outlined these considerations. Regrettably, only one such article is cited in a footnote (p. 7, n.18), and there is no meaningful discussion in the book itself describing these factors and their possible interactions.

The next section of the book discusses the concepts of "engaged in trade or business" and of "effectively connected income," concepts that govern the regime of U.S. taxation applied to a nonresident alien or foreign corporation on types of income from sources either in the United States or abroad. Certain subsections are so short as to lack value (*e.g.,* to what extent will trading in stocks or securities by a dealer or nondealer lead to trade or business status?) or meaningful discussion; for example, there is considerable authority concerning when ownership of real property by a nonresident or foreign corporation will result in U.S. trade or business status. This authority is never analyzed by the authors, with the exception of one footnote (p. 57, n.180). Moreover, several possible situations are simply not treated. There is authority, for example, that an individual or corporation purchasing goods in the United States for sale abroad will not be considered to be engaged in a

U.S. trade or business. Surely, such an issue deserves mention. The "effectively connected" concept (notoriously complex) is treated far too cursorily, and it would have been helpful at least to cite the several excellent articles written on the subject in the aftermath of the Foreign Investors Tax Act of 1966, which adopted the concept. The discussion of the Foreign Investment in Real Property Tax Act of 1980 (FIRPTA), which concludes part 1, is treated in approximately seven pages. There is no analysis of the almost infinite number of problems created by this legislation. Moreover, the first supplement to *International Individual Taxation* indicates that one can expect little or no additional commentary to the original text; the supplement appears primarily to consist of a list of relevant cases, rulings, and articles. Thus, one will have to turn elsewhere to achieve a satisfactory understanding of FIRPTA, or other rapidly changing areas of the tax law.

Space considerations preclude many further examples. To mention but two additional problems that clearly are of major concern to internationally oriented practitioners, no real help is given regarding planning around the *Aiken Industries* case, which concerned the possibility of treaty shopping, and the book's treatment of foreign entity classification leaves one inadequately prepared for the difficulties facing a practitioner in determining whether exotic foreign entities, such as a Liechtenstein *Anstalt,* are associations taxable as corporations, partnerships, or trusts.

Thus, for the practitioner the bottom line is that the text (302 pages) is too short to set forth adequately the extremely complex rules governing this area of the tax law, to evaluate them, and to suggest tax planning strategies. Because of that complexity, much of the text is given over to recapitulation of the applicable regulations. There is some information concerning tax planning possibilities, though it often lacks sufficient specificity. In summary, *Individual International Taxation* may be characterized as an acceptable introduction to this area of the tax law; however, for the practitioner it remains a somewhat simplified, uncritical excursion through a body of law that may now be so complicated as to defy in any one book satisfactory achievement of the goals set by the authors.

J. ROSS MACDONALD
Of the New York Bar

Prava cheloveka i mezhdunarodnye otnosheniia (Human Rights and International Relations). By A. P. Movchan. Moscow: Izdatel'stvo "Nauka," 1982. Pp. 144. 50 kopecks; $1.90.

The Soviet jurist sitting on the Committee established by the Human Rights Covenants provides his thoughts on the problems to be expected in protecting human rights and on the role of the Committee. Although replete with denunciation of Western powers and especially of the United States for talking loudly but refusing to act effectively by ratifying the Covenants and by adopting the Equal Rights Amendment to its Constitution, the monograph is more than an indictment. It provides clues as to what to expect from the Committee so long as the United States remains aloof.

Movchan takes credit for having guided the Committee toward adoption of what he calls a "Gentlemen's agreement" rejecting as evidence information gained from radio, television, and the press, as well as that published by non-governmental organizations such as Amnesty International and the International Commission of Jurists. In his view, this has created in the Committee "a business-like atmosphere in reviewing the reports of signatory states." Further, he claims for the socialist members credit for another "Gentlemen's agreement" that the Committee must strive to take all decisions by consensus (pp. 5–6). He rejects fears that the Committee will be thwarted by vetoes, for he accepts the Legal Adviser's view that abstentions and partial disagreements do not prevent arriving at consensus. Readers with knowledge of Committee practice may doubt the far-reaching effect of the "Gentlemen's agreements" to which the author refers.

Attention is given to the impact of Article 2(7) of the UN Charter upon protection of human rights. Movchan sees that international practice has already provided a reconciliation. This is found in the rejection of complaints filed by individuals and in the recommendation by organs of the United Nations that states protect their citizens by their own municipal legislation, notably against discrimination on grounds of race, sex, language, or religion. It is to be found also in UN preparation of international conventions requiring states to enact protective legislation and in the establishment of a special international mechanism to verify the performance by states of treaty obligations (p. 25).

The sore point, as Movchan sees it, lies in the attempt to introduce individual cases into discussion. President Carter is excoriated for his worldwide human rights campaign, which Movchan sees as causing hostility and lack of confidence among states and as undermining the Helsinki Act (p. 17). The author has only praise for the Act as recognition that states have the right to choose their own political, social, economic, and cultural systems. He believes that U.S. efforts to arouse public opinion over treatment of citizens by signatories clearly conflict with this obligation (p. 22). He quotes Eastern and Western authorities in support of the traditional Soviet position that individuals are not subjects of international law.

Movchan denies that human rights of individuals can be subsumed under the situations likely to endanger international peace and security, for he finds nothing in the record to suggest that this interpretation was contemplated at San Francisco. To his mind, the only situations that meet the test of the Charter are those defined by General Assembly resolutions: genocide, apartheid, colonialism, foreign occupation and rule, aggression, threat to national sovereignty and territorial integrity, refusal to recognize the right of self-determination, and the right to permanent sovereignty over resources (pp. 32–33).

Further proof of his position on complaints of individuals is adduced from the prohibition on the Committee's hearing such complaints unless signatories sign the supplementary Protocol, and even on its hearing complaints brought by signatories against cosigners who have not recognized the Committee's competence to hear such complaints (p. 29).

As to freedom of information, Movchan says that the Soviet delegate to the drafting committee preparing the Covenants warned against unbridled use of this freedom. Movchan insists that limitations on this freedom exist, as evidenced by provisions in all legal systems protecting state security. He believes that limitations must exist internationally against warmongering and propaganda for fascist regimes. He opposes distribution across national frontiers of information by radio and the press when the purpose is to attack governments or the structure of society (p. 103).

The monograph suggests that loss of enthusiasm for the Covenants in the United States since President Carter's defeat is creating a propaganda advantage for those seeking to reduce the prestige of the United States in much of the world. One hopes that fact will again be understood by policy makers in the United States and that they will come to accept the arguments of members of this Society for ratification of the Covenants. Harm is being done to the United States in world public opinion, and Movchan's monograph, as it is distributed in translation, indicates how much harm can be expected. Further, membership on the Committee after ratification might provide a counterweight to present positions.

JOHN N. HAZARD
Board of Editors

Mezhdunarodnye Ekonomicheskije i Nauchno-tekhnicheskije Organizatsii Stran-chlenov SEV. Spravochnik (The International Economic and Scientific-Technical Organizations of the Member Countries of COMECON. Reference book). Edited by V. V. Vorotnikov and D. A. Lebin. Moscow: "Mezhdunarodnye Otnoshenija," 1980. Pp. 252.

The Council for Mutual Economic Assistance (COMECON), which was created in 1949 as Stalin's retort to the Marshall Plan and the Organization for European Economic Cooperation (now the OECD), became really active during the second half of the fifties. A great wave of developments, both regarding the Organization's activities and the creation of numerous "specialized agencies," took place in the sixties, and even more in the seventies.

At present, apart from COMECON itself, there are 35 multilateral international organizations of the "family," plus 15 bilateral ones, too many even to have their names mentioned in a review of this size. After Cuba joined in 1972 and Vietnam in 1978, COMECON's membership was 10 (Albania, nonactive since the early sixties, is not even mentioned). Yugoslavia is a sort of associate member. There exist cooperation agreements between COMECON and Finland, Iraq, and Mexico. Several African and Asian countries attend the yearly sessions of the Council of COMECON. And in 1980, the Foreign Minister of Mozambique declared that there was a good possibility of his country's joining COMECON (*cf. Trybuna Ludu,* Warsaw, December 1, 1980).

This book tries, in its introduction (p. 3), to convey a somewhat exaggerated picture of the strength of the COMECON group, qualifying it as "not only the most dynamic and progressive, but also the strongest economic force in the world." It may be that the rate of industrial growth—starting from a much lower point of departure—was generally always higher than in the West. But what of the rest? The authors try to make an impression by citing the total population of the group, which, in the late seventies, was indicated as 434 million. But obviously, this is not what really counts.

The book then covers COMECON and the 50 minor multilateral and bilateral organizations of the group. The information given is not always totally satisfying. Thus, *e.g.*, while it mentions (p. 32) that COMECON's original 1959 Charter was amended in 1962, 1974, and 1979, there is no mention of the amendments, in 1974 and 1977, of the 1963 Agreement on Multilateral Settlements in Transferable Roubles and the Establishment of the International Bank for Economic Cooperation (referred to on p. 157). On page 40 the reader fails to see any figure on the total staff of COMECON's Secretariat, but this "omission" is typical of all relevant Soviet and East European literature (in 1977 this reviewer was told at the headquarters of COMECON in Moscow that it was over 2,000—and it is probably still growing).

On the whole, the book is a useful source of pertinent information. In spite of a dramatic decrease in economic growth rates since the mid-seventies (and even the previously unheard-of phenomenon of "negative industrial growth" in the case of Hungary in 1980 and Poland in 1981 and 1982), as well as other serious troubles, especially with and around Poland, the "COMECON family" is still viable. Literature on it, therefore, deserves attention in the West.

RICHARD SZAWLOWSKI
Vancouver, B.C.

Organizatsija Obedinennykh Natsij. Kratkij Spravochnik (United Nations Organization. Short reference book) (3d ed.). Edited by V. F. Petrovskij. Moscow: "Mezhdunarodnye Otnoshenija," 1980. Pp. 143.

Soviet literature on international organizations in general, and the United Nations in particular, is fairly voluminous. Concerning Western regional organizations, the tenor is mostly critical, if not bluntly militant, especially where "aggressive" NATO is concerned.

Regarding the organizations of the UN "family," to most of which the USSR belongs, the tone is much more moderate. In a book of the *spravochnik* type, most parts offer correct information free of ideological and political admixtures. One exception, of course, must be the introduction.

Here the introduction maintains, without mentioning the former League of Nations at all (evidently because of the expulsion of the Soviet Union from it in December 1939), that the United Nations is "basically" the first attempt of this kind in history (p. 3). Almost all attention is concentrated on its political activities; activities in the economic and social fields are only mentioned by name in one paragraph of 12 lines (p. 7). Certain important achievements, *e.g.*, in the human rights field, are not mentioned at all.

Regarding the USSR and the United Nations, the reader is informed that Lenin had already envisaged the possibility and usefulness of an international center for the support of international peace, with the participation of both socialist and capitalist countries. Further, one reads that "in principle" all large-scale initiatives and proposals aimed at the reduction of the danger of war and the improvement of international relations have been presented to the United Nations by the Soviet Union and other socialist countries (p. 4). Such things as, *e.g.*, the Uniting for Peace resolution are "forgotten" and, consequently, the genesis of the Emergency Special Sessions of the General Assembly is not explained (p. 15). In a situation where the USSR increasingly supports the convocation of Emergency Special Sessions, there is evidently no place for earlier condemnations of that resolution.[1]

As an illustration of relevant Soviet achievements, the case of Resolution 34/103 of the General Assembly on the Inadmissibility of the Policy of Hegemonism in International Relations is given. It "limits the incorrect use of the term 'hegemonism,' the attempts to present the policy of our country in a false light" (p. 5). This resolution, one reads, has "concrete addressees": China, Israel, South Africa, and the "American imperialists."

On the whole, one reads that

> [t]he Soviet Union assesses the future prospects of the UN with optimism. It bases itself on the fact that the role and proportional political weight of the socialist and other peace-loving countries are constantly increasing, and that the policy of peace which these countries pursue in the UN corresponds, in the final analysis, with the interests of all states-members of the UN [p. 8].

In the detailed part, information on the United Nations and its six main organs, its committees, commissions, and other bodies, is given, followed by brief notes on the specialized agencies and the IAEA. Soviet participation— or nonparticipation— in the latter organizations is indicated, though it is not explained why, *e.g.*, the USSR joined the ICAO only in 1970 and has not, so far, joined FAO. Also left unexplained is why in some organizations only the USSR is a member, but not Soviet Byelorussia and the Soviet Ukraine. Regarding the IBRD, the IMF, the IDA, and the IFC, it is stated that the USSR is not a member "because they are used by the bourgeois states in the interests of monopolistic capital, and for interference in the sphere of international economic relations" (p. 117). The weak point of such a radical diagnosis is that readers may ask why, then, under such circumstances, Romania joined the Fund and the World Bank in 1972, and Hungary the Fund in 1982.

For the Soviet reader generally, though, this booklet seems to be not a bad source of basic information on the UN system.

RICHARD SZAWLOWSKI
Vancouver, B.C.

[1] *Cf., e.g.*, the attacks in G. MOROZOV, ORGANIZATSIJA OBEDINENNYKH NATSIJ 219–20, 227–29 (1962); or M. JANOVSKIJ, GENERAL'NAJA ASSAMBLEJA OON 47–60 (1971).

The International Joint Commission Seventy Years On. Edited by Robert Spencer, John Kirton, and Kim Richard Nossal. Toronto: The Centre for International Studies, University of Toronto, 1981. Pp. xiv, 158. Index. $10.

The International Joint Commission (IJC), established by the Boundary Waters Treaty of 1909 between the United States and Great Britain (on behalf of Canada), was to celebrate in 1981 its 70th anniversary of service to the two countries. In preparation for this event, the Centre for International Studies (Toronto) invited to a conference "sixty experts" from the United States and Canada, along with the Chairmen and members of the IJC, as well as certain officials from the foreign offices of the two countries. The volume under review is "the product of that conference."

Out of their deliberations, seven important papers emerged that succinctly cover the history, the organization, and the work of the IJC from its foundation up to 1979, as well as the various handicaps the IJC encounters in the fulfillment of its fundamental objectives under the Treaty. As Professor Maxwell Cohen (McGill University), then Chairman of the Canadian Section of the IJC, remarked, "an unreserved unanimity exists about the usefulness of the Commission since its beginnings, and similarly, there is no less unanimity about the need for its services in the future," a view generally endorsed by the other contributors. Several, however, have pinpointed the hindrances that the Commission faces in the speedy and effective discharge of its duties. For example, the IJC "has no independent power of inquiry. Only Washington and Ottawa can initiate an investigation." So, too, the IJC has no police or executive power to enforce its decisions under Article III of the Treaty, or its recommendations under other articles. There has been, moreover, a tendency on the part of the two Governments to remove difficult boundary problems from the hands of the IJC and vest them in diplomats—as happened in the case of the Columbia River Project of 1956. To get over this type of problem, a proposal was made in 1970 to convert the IJC into a "supra-national" agency, but this the two Governments have not so far endorsed. Professor Don Munton, Director of Research, Canadian Institute of International Affairs, refers to several other proposals to make the IJC more effective as an instrument of international cooperation, but these are still only proposals.

Besides the seven authoritative essays, the book has an equally valuable preface and an introduction, a helpful glossary of terms, a list of the 107 applications so far processed by the Commission, a select bibliography, a helpful index, and a copy of the 1909 Treaty. This small volume furnishes the latest information on the commendable and effective work of the IJC in settling disputes between contiguous sovereign states, a subject worthy of study by all interested in the peaceful methods of settling problems of international relations, especially between the United States and Canada.

C. JOSEPH CHACKO
Widener University, Emeritus

The Australian-American Security Relationship. A Regional and International Perspective. By Henry Albinski. New York: St. Martin's Press, 1982. Pp. 257. Index.

The Japanese threat of invasion during World War II completely reversed Australia's perceptions on foreign policy. It then became evident that the British motherland was no longer able to provide protection to its offspring. It was the American military campaign in the Pacific that saved Australia; henceforth this island-continent was to depend for its safety on the assistance of the United States. Formal acknowledgment of this new situation was given in 1952 by the tripartite defense treaty between the United States, Australia, and New Zealand, known as the ANZUS Treaty. Under the terms of this Treaty the United States committed itself to defend Australia (and New Zealand) in the event of external aggression, and these two states pledged to support the United States should the latter become involved in a defensive war.

The work under review is thus well justified in speaking of a special Australian-American security relationship. In fact, the book's title is an understatement because the author extends his analysis over Australia's entire foreign and security problems. Albinski assesses these problems, together with the respective American positions and attitudes, in the broad spectrum of practically all the world. Chapters are devoted to such geographic areas as the greater Asian Pacific region, Southeast Asia (with proper emphasis on the ASEAN community), the Indian Ocean and its hinterland (which includes the African countries limitrophe to this ocean), and the South Pacific region. Naturally, the direct contacts between Australia and the United States are given particular attention.

From the perspective of international law, the Australian interpretation of a passage of the ANZUS Treaty deserves special mention. The Treaty refers to assistance to be provided by the signatories in the event of "armed attack on the metropolitan territory of any of the Parties, or on the island territories under its jurisdiction, *in the Pacific,* or on its armed forces, public vessels or aircraft, *in the Pacific*" (italics supplied). This wording is of significant interest to Australia, which is surrounded by both the Pacific and the Indian Oceans. When the Treaty was concluded in 1952, the British Navy ruled supreme over the Indian Ocean. But by the early 1970's, Britain had withdrawn from east of Suez, and America had become involved in the protection of navigation routes in the Indian Ocean as well as in the Pacific. Australia, invoking the "spirit" of the commitment, wishes to interpret the ANZUS Treaty extensively (instead of narrowly or literally) so as to include obligations on all parties in the event of an aggression that might also occur in the Indian Ocean against territorial dependencies, public ships, or aircraft of the parties.

The text is accompanied by impressive documentation. It is a solid and unimpeachably objective piece of scholarship.

FERENC A. VÁLI
University of Massachusetts at Amherst

The Gateway: U.S. Immigration Issues and Policies. Edited by Barry R. Chiswick. Washington and London: American Enterprise Institute for Public Policy Research, 1982. Pp. 476. $22.95, cloth; $12.95, paper.

Last year two major pieces of legislation affecting the way America approaches its immigration situation were introduced in the Congress (S. 1765 and H.R. 4832, the Omnibus Immigration and Control Act, and S. 2222 and H.R. 5872, the Immigration Reform and Control Act of 1982, both in the 97th Congress, 1st session). Both bills would make substantial changes in a number of areas of U.S. immigration law, including implementation of summary exclusion proceedings, ability to declare "immigration emergencies" with the right of interdiction on the high seas, and institution of sanctions against employers. There is an excellent chance that these bills will be reintroduced in the second session of this Congress.

The proposed legislation is just one of many responses America is generating to its devastating immigration problems. This extensive and scholarly study by the American Enterprise Institute is another response. It is a collection of 11 essays, and responsive commentary, generated at an April 1980 conference, cosponsored by AEI and the University of Illinois College of Business Administration. As the essays indicate, the conference was concerned with "the scarcity of substantive research on which to base public policy" (p. 1). The essays are organized to reflect the four sessions of the conference: the supply of and demand for immigrants; the progress of immigrants; the economic impact of immigrants; and alternative immigration policies.

Skimming the essays and commentary, the reader will quickly realize that the focus of the work is economic and social, not legal or practical. In fact, two-thirds of the participants were economists. This is not to diminish the usefulness of the volume. It begins to alleviate the paucity of economic analysis of our immigration situation, especially the essays by Jeffrey Williamson, Barry Chiswick, and Julian Simon on aspects of the economic impact of immigrants. These and the other essays should be of interest to scholars and researchers who are delving into the background of the problems.

However, the book is of less use to the lawyer, legislator, or public policy maker who is battling on the "front lines." Several of the essays, including David Reimer's survey of American immigration policies and practices and Larry Morgan and Bruce Gardner's proposal for a U.S. guest-worker program are easily accessible to the noneconomist. In fact, Reimer's essay should probably be required reading for our legislators. However, the analytical approach to the majority of the material in this book will discourage most noneconomists. This is unfortunate because the authors have taken a significant step toward establishing a factual basis for the creation of effective immigration policies. I was disappointed, given the title and the cosponsors, that *The Gateway* proved so difficult for the layman to get through.

JOHN W. WILLIAMS

The Secret Wars: A Guide to Sources in English. Vol. I: Intelligence, Propaganda and Psychological Warfare, Resistance Movements, and Secret Operations, 1939–1945. By Myron J. Smith, Jr. Santa Barbara: ABC-Clio, Inc., 1980. Pp. lxii, 250. Indexes. $42.50.

The Secret Wars: A Guide to Sources in English. Vol. II: Intelligence, Propaganda and Psychological Warfare, Covert Operations, 1945–1980. By Myron J. Smith, Jr. Santa Barbara: ABC-Clio, Inc., 1981. Pp. lxxxii, 389. Index. $67.50.

The Secret Wars: A Guide to Sources in English. Vol. III: International Terrorism, 1968–1980. By Myron J. Smith, Jr. Santa Barbara: ABC-Clio, Inc., 1980. Pp. xxxvi, 237. Index. $37.50.

The persistent use of covert operational techniques and organized nonmilitary violence to achieve political objectives challenges any optimism for the establishment of a comprehensive international legal system. Yet it is a serious mistake for all in the international legal community to hold the belief that organized political violence is beyond the scope of public international law. It is becoming essential to have a comprehensive understanding of the nature of organized political violence in order to anticipate its impact upon public international law.

A contribution to the understanding of modern intelligence, covert political activity, and organized terrorism is *The Secret Wars.* Myron J. Smith, Jr., has compiled several bibliographies on military affairs, but here he focuses primarily on the development of modern intelligence and its operations.

Modern international terrorism has evolved from subversive techniques employed during World War II and from the developing course of East-West relations. In this sense, a continuity exists among the three volumes, despite the apparently different subjects. Each volume contains a lengthy chronology of events, an extensive list of reference materials, magazines, and journals, and a bibliographic list of personalities concerned with each topic.

The first volume was the most difficult bibliography to assemble since so much has been published on the course of World War II. However, this volume is intended to list publications concerned with the effects of intelligence gathering and its operations. For example, only military campaigns directly affected by intelligence operations are included. In addition, the role of resistance movements, special forces, and paramilitary units all have an exclusive list of publications according to region. Together with the sources concerned with "land, sea and air" intelligence and operations, an inclusive list of entries on the historical origins of modern intelligence provides the basis for the second volume.

Similar areas of interest appear in the volume covering the postwar era. There are more entries on propaganda and psychological warfare, listed according to country. The primary emphasis is on "intelligence, espionage and covert operations," which are listed according to country or region. Considerable attention is given to entries on national intelligence agencies, especially the American intelligence community including the Central Intelligence

Agency. Of additional interest, alleged conspiracies as well as established or proven covert operations are included.

The most interesting volume is the third, which includes the following areas, some quite delimited in scope: terrorist tactics, armaments, and international law and terrorism, each with specialized subheadings. Also included are terrorist group activities, arranged according to region and country. The list of entries pertaining to international law includes criminal jurisdiction, and international organizations and conventions relating to terrorism. Another section includes international law and aerial hijacking. The list of entries of this set appears complete to date of publication.

ALLAN E. WARNKE
The University of British Columbia

German Yearbook of International Law. Vol. 22, 1979. Edited by Jost Delbrück, Wilfried Fiedler, and Wilhelm A. Kewenig. Berlin: Duncker & Humblot, 1980. Pp. 581. DM 168.

Since 1976 the editors of the *Yearbook* have used an English title and most of the contributions have been written in English. Many of those written in German and French have English summaries and, as a result, the *Yearbook* reaches a larger audience since it has overcome the traditional language barrier. This volume contains 18 articles on the theory and practice of international law, six reports on the activities of international organizations, and approximately 66 pages of book reviews. Considerations of space do not permit a review of all this material.

The lead article by Hans Baade is an interesting analysis of how voluntary, not legally enforceable codes, guidelines, and other declarations concerning the conduct of multinational enterprises are slowly transformed into customary international law despite the reluctance of international organizations to adopt legally binding instruments in the first place.

A number of articles concern issues related to the Law of the Sea Convention. Carl August Fleischer of the Norwegian delegation to the UN Law of the Sea Conference discusses problems that have arisen as a result of the extended 200-mile economic zone in the waters north of the territories of Norway and the Soviet Union. Choon-Ho Park presents a hypothetical analysis of the problems of maritime jurisdiction in the China seas arising from the 200-mile zone boundaries between China and its adjacent and opposite states. Jorge A. Vargas, in his excellent historical article, *The Legal Nature of the Patrimonial Sea,* traces the evolution of the juridical features of the Latin American concept of the "patrimonial sea," first used by Gabriel Valdés in 1970 (then Chilean Minister of Foreign Affairs in the Government of Eduardo Frei). Edmundo Vargas Carreño, who first defined the concept, gave it the meaning it has today: that marine resources off the coast of any state should be utilized by such a state for the benefit of its inhabitants and for the promotion of its socioeconomic development. The patrimonial sea concept was transformed into the "exclusive economic zone" (EEZ) concept at the Third

UN Law of the Sea Conference, and is the single most important contribution made by Latin America to the new international law of the sea.

The United States and Unilateral Action: Changing Patterns of Fisheries Conservation and Management by Thomas A. Clingan, Jr., reads easily after this discussion of the evolution of the EEZ concept, since it deals with the U.S. Fishery Conservation and Management Act of 1976, by which the United States unilaterally declared a 200-mile fishery conservation zone off its coasts and granted to itself exclusive fishing rights within that zone. Although the United States has not become a party to the Law of the Sea Convention, this 1976 Act followed the trend of the Law of the Sea Conference, and the author informs us that the level of foreign fishing in the U.S. zone has been significantly reduced.

Geoffrey Yarema, in *The Impact of Cargo Preference Legislation on the International Obligations of the United States,* discusses the impact of a state's unilateral action of giving preferential treatment to its own vessels, which consequently discriminates against vessels of other countries. He convincingly argues that whereas a state may reserve its coastal trade to nationals under international law, no corresponding right to reserve foreign trade is recognized.

Michael Bogdan's unusual article on *The International Legal Status of Governing Political Parties in One-Party States* argues that since the majority of states are "more or less totalitarian," this fact affects the traditional liberal concepts of international law. Disagreeing with Hersch Lauterpacht, the author submits that a government should be held responsible not only for acts of state organs but even for acts of political parties if they are as closely identified with the government as the Soviet Communist Party, the Fascist Party in Italy, or the Kuomintang in China.

The fine article by Yves Sandoz of the International Committee of the Red Cross (ICRC), *Le Droit d'initiative du Comité international de la Croix-Rouge,* describes how the ICRC, acting as a humanitarian body, at first exercised a very limited function, which only slowly expanded due to the ICRC's seizing the initiative. It did so by proposing to states that it be permitted to undertake certain actions to relieve suffering caused by armed conflict. These actions were subsequently ratified by statutes and the 1929 and 1949 Geneva Conventions. Much institutional human rights work owes its evolution to the actors' having seized such an initiative and it is an important point that is well made in this article.

The *Reports* section covers the work of the following international organizations: the International Court of Justice (1977 and 1978), the International Law Commission (1978), the Council of Europe (1978), the Organization of American States (1977 and 1978), and the Nordic Council (1978). The reports on the Council of Europe and the Organization of American States present excellent information on the human rights work of these organizations.

CHRISTINA M. CERNA
Of the District of Columbia Bar

The Canadian Yearbook of International Law. Volume XIX, 1981. Edited by C. B. Bourne. Vancouver: The University of British Columbia Press, 1982. Pp. 464. Index. $36.

The present volume of the *Yearbook* includes four very interesting and timely articles that address important international issues: the conflict in Cyprus, Third World debts, protection of diplomats, and Canadian-U.S. dispute resolution.

The conflict in Cyprus, sometimes overlooked as a current international problem because it no longer appears regularly in newspaper headlines, continues to be unresolved, perhaps because the 1974 Turkish military intervention seems to have "stabilized" the intercommunal situation on the island. The author of the first article, R. St. J. Macdonald, examines the international legal dimensions of the conflict, which transcend the specific dispute on Cyprus. The legal questions concern the legality of Turkey's intervention as well as its continued military presence, questions of sovereignty and recognition, rules of occupation, protection of human rights, and the effectiveness of the UN system of peace and security. While the conflict in Cyprus will only be solved through diplomatic negotiation, the author believes that renewed discussion and clarification of the complex legal issues may well facilitate and advance such negotiation.

France Morrissette reviews in substantial detail the debt problem of the developing countries—a problem that some observers feel has reached crisis proportions and that could threaten the stability of the world's financial structure. A primary conclusion of Morrissette's study is that the developing countries do not bear sole responsibility for their debt problem; rather, various international actors must share the blame. The author offers an evaluation of public and private loan activities, particularly during the 1960's and 1970's, as well as a discussion of the often anarchic character of loan-rescheduling mechanisms, which generally serve the interests of the lenders more than those of the developing countries. Various methods of rescheduling loans are proposed, along with a new institutional mechanism for implementing the author's proposals.

The third article, by L. C. Green, examines trends in the law concerning diplomats. Clearly, the notion of diplomatic privileges and immunities is one of the more established principles of international law. A review of case law, international agreements, and actual state practice, however, reveals a readiness to place national political goals before diplomatic niceties. The Iranian actions toward the American Embassy in Tehran, and the courageous Canadian stance regarding diplomatic protection, represented just one episode in the modern political turmoil surrounding the diplomatic function. Perhaps diplomacy would be best served, the author feels, if nations concentrated more on the selection and training of their diplomats as well as on consciously trying to live up to the standards embodied in the many conventions to which they have agreed.

Using a joint 1979 Canadian/American Bar Association report as a point of departure, the final article, by Erik B. Wang, treats the adjudication of

Canadian-U.S. disputes. Wang's study is important, not only because it offers an enlightening review of the history of dispute settlement between the two countries, but also because it clarifies and explains the current legal mechanisms and political atmosphere regarding dispute settlement that exist between Canada and the United States. Wang tabulates past disputes and how they were resolved. He notes the difficulties in determining who "won" or "lost," and suggests that the Canadian perception of being a "chronic loser" is misplaced. The decision to resort to adjudication is political and often painful, but Canada and the United States must decide what kind of a relationship they want. Modern disputes over such matters as maritime boundaries, fisheries, and acid rain will test that relationship.

The *Yearbook* also includes the usual rich coverage of notes and commentary, Canadian practice in international law, and book reviews.

FOREST L. GRIEVES
University of Montana

BRIEFER NOTICES

International and Legal Problems of the Gulf. By Sayed Hassan Amin. (Wisbech: Middle East and North African Studies Press Ltd., 1981. Pp. 235. Indexes. £16.50; $41.25.) The gulf with which this volume is concerned is, of course, the Persian (or Arabian) Gulf, which has its full share of international and legal problems—among them the controversy over its proper name, to which a chapter is devoted. Those addressed by the author, a jurist of Iranian origin now settled in the United Kingdom, are strictly maritime, and the approach is legal rather than political. They include the legal status of the Gulf itself and of the Strait of Hormuz, the problems of fishery regulation, and the control of marine pollution. But the bulk of the book is given over to a history and discussion of the water and shelf boundaries in the Gulf, both settled and unsettled. Also treated under this heading are various island disputes, as well as the Iran-Iraq war, which is traced in large part to the conflict between the two states over their water boundary in the Shatt al-Arab.

The book contains little material not already available elsewhere. The author's conclusions and suggested solutions are in general orthodox and unsurprising, though his emphasis on the need for increased regional cooperation on common problems is welcome. It is regrettable that the style is somewhat disjointed and repetitive, the documentation is uneven, and some slips and errors impair the reliability of the text. The study as a whole is more superficial, and hence less valuable, than other recent works on the Gulf, such as those by Ramazani[1] and MacDonald.[2] But the author is to be commended for his generally evenhanded treatment of opposing views in an area where partisan approaches have often seemed too prevalent.

RICHARD YOUNG
Board of Editors

[1] R. K. RAMAZANI, THE PERSIAN GULF AND THE STRAIT OF HORMUZ (1979). Reviewed by this reviewer in 74 AJIL 467–68 (1980).

[2] C. MACDONALD, IRAN, SAUDI ARABIA, AND THE LAW OF THE SEA (1980). Reviewed in this issue, at p. 694.

Transnationales Recht. By Eugen Langen. (Heidelberg: Verlagsgesellschaft Recht und Wirtschaft mbH, 1981. (Schriftenreihe Recht der internationalen Wirtschaft, vol. 20.) Pp. 241. Indexes. DM 110.) This book is the last publication of a distinguished (now deceased) scholar-practitioner. He advances the thesis, supported by some other modern writers and occasional arbitral decisions, of the existence of a "stateless" transnational private law governing international contracts in the absence of contractual or legislative provisions prescribing the applicability of a national legal order. Although the author argues that national courts in litigations arising out of international transactions also may derive their rules of decision from such transnational law, the main field of application of this denationalized law is found in international arbitrations. Langen buttresses his conception by elaborate references to the mandates of "the nature of things" and "reason." In addition, he relies on many ideas garnered from the natural sciences. As the author notes, his thesis is still fighting for general recognition, but has found a number of followers in practice as well as in scholarly writings.[1] Provisions on applicable law contained in modern rules of arbitration, adopted by various international arbitration institutions, tend towards the goals set by the author.

STEFAN A. RIESENFELD
Board of Editors

Lezioni di Diritto Internazionale (2d ed.). By Benedetto Conforti. (Naples: Editoriale Scientifica, 1982. Pp. xi, 289. Index. L.18.000.) This is the second edition of Professor Conforti's *Notes from Lectures on International Law,* published in 1977, now titled *Lectures on International Law,* in which he has brought the volume up to date with practice of recent years. More attention has been given to international economic relations and additional detail has been included on the law of treaties, the functions of international organizations, and especially human rights.

The work is divided into four chapters preceded by an introduction that defines international law and explains the creation, validation, and contemporary enforcement of norms and how the state is a subject of international law, as well as a creator and protector of rights for individuals through contemporary practice. The first two chapters deal with norms, while the last two chapters are more novel in that they analyze the application of international norms to the internal organs of a state, and then the means, by international agencies and courts, of verifying the application of such norms within a state.

The assessment of the application of international norms naturally deals more with Italian illustrations, of particular interest to foreign readers because Italy is one of the few states with a written Constitution that specifies, "the Italian legal system conforms to the norms of international law generally recognized."

Although a large part of the book, designed as lectures for students in jurisprudence, will not seem unusual to specialists in international law, Conforti must be complimented for a logical and lucid style, for the substantial international bibliographies preceding every section to be discussed, and for providing insight on how international law is taught by a leading Italian scholar of both international law and the United Nations.

GERARD J. MANGONE
University of Delaware

[1] *See* Croff, *The Applicable Law in an International Arbitration: Is It Still a Conflict of Laws Problem?,* 16 INT'L LAW. 613 (1982).

La Politica Commerciale Convenzionale della CEE nel sistema commerciale internazionale. By Giuseppe Panico. (Milan: Dott. A Giuffrè Editore, 1979. Pp. vii, 372.) The book provides an analysis, mainly from a legal point of view, of the role of the European Economic Community and its rapidly spreading network of trade and economic cooperation agreements (of varying scope and content) with other nations within the framework of world trade relations. This framework, as the author emphasizes, has itself shifted from a universal system of free and nondiscriminatory trade, as established in the original articles of GATT, to a matrix of arrangements favoring nonreciprocal concessions for developing nations, as reflected in the reformed GATT. The work is divided into three main parts, each of which, though not bearing a distinct title, is subdivided into two or three chapters with special captions.

The first part focuses on the compatibility of the multifaceted economic relations between the EEC and groups of developing nations with the provisions of the original and revised GATT. The second part is devoted to the powers of the European Communities, as a matter of Community and international law, to enter into bilateral and multilateral agreements with other nations relating to trade and economic development. Finally, the third part discusses three special problems: (1) the legal forms of the participation of the EEC in GATT and UNCTAD and the commodity agreements sponsored by them; (2) the legal aspects of the preferential arrangements between the EEC and regional groups, in particular the Lomé Convention with the ACP countries, the coordinated incipient free trade area agreements with the EFTA members, the harmonized arrangements with the Mediterranean Arab nations, the special agreements with the members of ASEAN, and the economic cooperation agreement with Canada; and (3) the commercial agreements of the EEC with the state trading countries of Eastern Europe and the People's Republic of China.

The book aims at comprehensiveness and a unified perspective on the varied international economic policies of the EEC. The text is followed by a geographically arranged list of the existing trade and economic agreements between the EEC and third countries, including a brief characterization of each item. The book is not easy, but it is worthwhile reading.

STEFAN A. RIESENFELD
Board of Editors

Marine Pollution in International Law. Material Obligations and Jurisdiction, with Special Reference to the Third United Nations Conference on the Law of the Sea. By Kari Hakapää. (Helsinki: Suomalainen Tiedeakatemia, 1981. Pp. 341. Indexes.) Pollution of the marine environment could prove an ideal subject for a cameo study to anyone wishing to discover the delights and frustrations of international law. Beginning with the initiative of the United States on oil pollution in 1926 and up to the 1982 Law of the Sea Convention, the law is contained mainly in treaty form but, where agreement has failed or ratifications proved tardy, it is also found in the classical precepts of customary law. The subject also exemplifies the interdisciplinary nature of modern international law: the norms of the marine scientist, the conflicting claims of developed and developing nations, the economics of the confrontation of maritime powers and coastal states.

In this short work, originally presented as a dissertation in the University of Helsinki, the author provides us with an extraordinarily interesting introduction to the study of marine pollution. Introduction, because it is soon obvious that detailed study of this many faceted branch of the law requires perseverance. The author chooses to examine two areas: first, the material obligations of states with regard to pollution of the sea, that is to say, the rules and standards on such matters as discharges, ship design and construction, manning and equipment, and designation of sea lanes and schemes for traffic separation; and, second, jurisdictional rules, the competence of states to establish and enforce environmental regulations. He leaves untouched discussion of rules on such matters as environmental monitoring and assessment, contingency plans, and mutual assistance, and he avoids the large and complex area of liability. By isolating material obligations and jurisdiction and examining each of these in relation to the various areas and zones of the sea and seabed, the author has highlighted the major legal problems to be faced in creating international marine pollution norms and, in this way, has produced a concise and readable survey of the present law. As a conclusion, if not always a climax, to each area of study he has considered the contribution of UNCLOS III and the Law of the Sea Convention. It is enlightening for the student to see a summary of the Convention's provisions in this field in the context of a review of the whole branch of law.

By selecting for study the problems of material obligation and jurisdiction with regard to marine pollution, the author has shown clearly and concisely how the international lawyer works, how he tackles his subject, and how he must be aware always of the competing interests of modern life.

RALPH BEDDARD
The University, Southampton

Civil Judgment Recognition and the Integration of Multiple-State Associations: Central America, the United States of America, and the European Economic Community. By Robert C. Casad. (Lawrence: The Regents Press of Kansas, 1982. Pp. xiii, 258. Index. $25.) Professor Casad focuses his attention on the judicial institutions of the six countries of Central America. He explores the role played by the system of mutual recognition and enforcement of civil judgments among states in a multiple-state association and the process by which those states become integrated into a larger political-economic entity. The author describes and analyzes the existing national systems as well as the judgment recognition provisions of the Bustamante Code (the multilateral Convention signed by all of them). Of particular interest is the clarification that Casad brings to the problems of terminology and legal concepts of Latin American legal systems that often mislead those coming from an Anglo-American legal background. Casad also compares the Central American system to the system existing in the United States (the full faith and credit clause) and in the European Economic Community. The book also includes an examination of the proposed inter-American judgment recognition convention which is intended to replace the Bustamante Code. Casad finds that its ratification would not lead to a significant improvement over the current regime. He believes that any convention designed to be acceptable to all the nations of the Western Hemisphere could hardly be expected to prescribe the kind of certain, ready recognition of judgments that he advocates for the countries of Central America. Any such regime tailored to the conditions of Central America should be reinforced by a Central American court.

The book is a fascinating study in the comparison of economic integration and recognition of judgments. The book's special value to practitioners is in its discussion of the process of enforcing foreign judgments in Central America.

THAD W. SIMONS, JR.
Brussels

U.S. Foreign Policy and Multilateral Development Banks. By Jonathan E. Sanford. (Boulder: Westview Press, 1982. Pp. xiv, 279. Index. $22.) It can be exciting for the practicing lawyer as well as the political science teacher to discover an "all-you-need-to-know-about" book. Sanford's short, though detailed and documented, volume is one such book. The reader is immediately impressed with both Sanford's thoroughness and his logical organization. It lives up to its cover description as "the first major description and analysis of the overall goals and processes that govern U.S. participation in multilateral development banks."

Sanford is a senior political analyst with the Congressional Research Service of the Library of Congress. Just prior to and during publication of the book, he was on temporary leave to serve as a majority (Democratic) staff consultant with the House Committee on Banking, Finance and Urban Affairs. Although containing the words "urban affairs" in its title, this is the House committee concerned with U.S. participation in the multilateral development banks, including the International Finance Corporation, the International Development Association, and the regional development banks (Inter-American, Asian, and African).

The book is divided into seven chapters: an introductory overview of the banks and U.S. foreign policy; a summary of American goals and policy involving banks; a history of U.S. policy; three detailed studies of the banks—from the perspective of the executive branch, from the perspective of Congress, and through the tumultuous interplay of executive-legislative relations; and an analysis of the effect of U.S. policy in achieving its goals. The book includes a lengthy collection of footnotes and a thorough bibliography and index.

Reflecting Sanford's own experience, the book heavily emphasizes American policy from the point of view and activities of the legislative branch. The result is that he downplays events and policy activities focused in the executive branch. However, this study breaks new ground in that too few books study American policies, especially U.S. foreign policy, from the congressional perspective. In fact, I am considering using Sanford's book as one of the textbooks in my undergraduate political science course on executive-legislative relations.

Sanford, in his final chapter, "Influence and Effectiveness: Ends and Means for Foreign Policy," distinguishes between "the concepts 'influence' and 'control' as regards U.S. participation in multilateral banks" (p. 181). Based on many of the goals examined in his second chapter, Sanford concludes that "the United States has a good deal of influence in the banks," but it "does not control the banks" (p. 181). American attempts to exert effective control over the banks have exacerbated the growing politicization of these institutions. Sanford closes his evaluation with several warnings. In particular, he warns that the United States "runs the risk of damaging its effectiveness and injuring the multilateral banks if it tries to make the MDB program its primary vehicle and main forum for promoting action" on issues such as human rights, nuclear proliferation, and foreign investments (p. 233). Furthermore, American attempts to manipulate the banks will only cause other nations to attempt the same.

JOHN W. WILLIAMS

Introducción al derecho internacional penal. By Hans-Joachim Leu. (Caracas: Ministerio de Relaciones Exteriores, 1982. Pp. 174. Index.) This book is divided into six chapters. Chapter 1 is devoted to a lengthy and not particularly helpful discussion of the general principles of international law. In chapter 2, which comprises nearly half of the book, the author summarizes the arguments in the debate on establishing international criminal law as a separate field of law. This chapter contains an excellent review of the activity of the United Nations, starting with its early concerns with genocide and ending with its more recent attempts to deal with international terrorism, torture, and apartheid. Chapters 3 and 4 describe some international aspects of Venezuela's criminal law. In chapter 5 there is a brief summary of the arguments concerning the possibility of creating an international criminal court. Chapter 6 is a documents supplement containing the United Nations Draft Code of Offences against the Peace and Security of Mankind, as well as another draft of this same Code prepared by the Foundation for the Establishment of an International Criminal Court.

Written in a style accessible to students in the first years of their legal education, this book does not, however, deal with important topics in international criminal law such as judicial assistance, recognition of foreign criminal judgments, abduction, extradition, and asylum. This lack stems from the author's exclusive concern with the substance of international criminal law, which causes him to neglect the importance that questions of procedure have in this area of law.

This book is the first in a series published by the Institute of International Affairs of Venezuela's Ministry of Foreign Affairs. We hope that future titles in this series will match the high standard of scholarship found in this book.

J. FAUNDEZ
University of Warwick

List of Treaty Collections. United Nations, Office of Legal Affairs, Codification Division. (A Symposia Press reprint, 1981. Pp. xv, 174. Index. $40. Distributed by Wm. W. Gaunt & Sons, Inc.) This reprint edition was originally published in 1956, following Resolution 686 (VII), adopted by the General Assembly on December 5, 1952, which authorized the Secretary-General to undertake the publication of a list of treaty collections. The compilation contains collections published from 1726 up to the date of the first publication of this book, altogether more than seven hundred titles. The *List* is divided into three parts. Part I contains the general collections (*e.g.*, Martens, *Recueil de traités;* British and Foreign State Papers; Hudson, *International Legislation; Treaty Series* of the League of Nations and the United Nations), but includes also indexes, bibliographies, and handbooks generally relating to treaties. The second part is devoted to collections by subject matter; the subjects are presented in alphabetical order, ranging from clearing agreements to recognition of foreign judgments. Part III contains collections of 70 states, *i.e.*, nearly all states existing in 1956. Here, too, collections by subject matter of treaties concluded by a given country are taken into consideration where not already included in part II.

Owing to the nature of a reprint edition, neither the collected treaties of states that have emerged since 1956 nor more recent collections of then already existing states could have been taken into account. One should try to fill this gap. The book reviewed here shows this gap very clearly since, for the period covered, it is itself a most valuable source of information. It has been out of print for too long a time.

ECKART KLEIN
University of Mainz

CORRESPONDENCE

TO THE EDITORS-IN-CHIEF:

May I ask space for a brief comment on Mr. Kirgis, Jr.'s review of my book *Israel and Palestine* (The Johns Hopkins University Press, 1981) in 76 AJIL 875–76 (1982).

Your reviewer flatly asserts that the argument of my first four chapters is that "the Palestinian Arabs have no right of self-determination, or other valid territorial claim . . . because the post-World War I arrangements recognized a Jewish national home in all of Palestine."

This assertion is not correct. The basic thesis of the opening chapter on "the time frame" of Jewish and Arab self-determination rights is that the liberation or self-determination principle was already applied, after World War I, to both Jewish and Arab national aspirations, and resulted in about a dozen Arab sovereignties over an area hundreds of times greater and richer than the tiny allocation to Israel (pp. 9–26).

The argument, then, is that any *ex post facto* separate claims of Palestinian Arabs as part of the Arab nation should be targeted "not on Israel alone, but on the Arab States and Israel in common and in some due proportion to the benefits they respectively received in the overall allocation" after World War I.

Mr. Kirgis, Jr. claims to have "shorn" my argument of "its rhetoric."

Readers of your *Journal* may already have suspected that his account may also (or rather!) have shorn my argument of its argument—and not merely on the above matter. I confirm and regret that that is indeed the case.

JULIUS STONE
Hastings College of the Law
University of California

Reply by Professor Frederic L. Kirgis, Jr.:

Professor Stone's selective quotation from my review makes it sound as though I attributed to him a rejection of any legitimate Arab territorial claim anywhere in post-World War I Palestine. He did not make such an extreme assertion, nor did I attribute it to him. Had Professor Stone quoted the full passage from the review, it would have been clear that I intended to attribute to him only the argument that Palestinian Arabs have no current right of self-determination or other territorial claim in the area of Palestine west of the Jordan River.

BOOKS RECEIVED*

International Law—General

Buirette-Maurau, Patricia. *La Participation du Tiers-Monde à l'élaboration du droit international: Essai de qualification.* Paris: Librairie Générale de Droit et de Jurisprudence, 1983. Pp. xvi, 242. F.140.

Cheng, Bin (ed.). *International Law: Teaching and Practice.* London: Stevens & Sons, 1982. Pp. xxix, 287. Index. $54. Distributed by Carswell Legal Publications.

Ferencz, Benjamin B. *Enforcing International Law—A Way to World Peace: A Documentary History and Analysis.* 2 vols. London, Rome, New York: Oceana Publications, Inc., 1983. Pp. xix, 890. Index. $45/vol.

Green, N. A. Maryan. *International Law: Law of Peace* (2d ed.). Plymouth: Macdonald and Evans, 1982. Pp. xxxiv, 254. Index. £12.50; $26.50. Distributed by Sheridan House Inc.

Jennings, R. Y., and Ian Brownlie (eds.). *The British Year Book of International Law, 1981.* Vol. 52. Oxford: The Clarendon Press; Oxford University Press, 1982. Pp. viii, 550. Index. £40; $99.

Merrills, J. G. *Anatomy of International Law: A Study of the Role of International Law in the Contemporary World* (2d ed.). London: Sweet & Maxwell, 1981. Pp. xv, 146. Index. $21.75.

Netherlands Yearbook of International Law. Vol. XIII, 1982. T.M.C. Asser Institute, The Hague. The Hague: Martinus Nijhoff Publishers, 1982. Pp. 511. Index. Dfl.110; $44.

Remiro Brotons, Antonio. *Derecho internacional público. I. Principios fundamentales.* Madrid: Editorial Tecnos, 1982. Pp. 341.

van Holk, L. E., and C. G. Roelofsen (eds.). *Grotius Reader.* The Hague: T.M.C. Asser Instituut, 1983. Pp. xi, 244. Dfl.17.50.

International Economic Law & Relations

Díaz-Alejandro, Carlos F., and Gerald K. Helleiner. *Handmaiden in Distress: World Trade in the 1980s.* Ottawa: North-South Institute; Washington: Overseas Development Council; London: Overseas Development Institute, 1982. Pp. xvi, 30.

Effros, Robert C. (ed.). *Emerging Financial Centers: Legal and Institutional Framework.* Washington: International Monetary Fund, 1982. Pp. xvi, 1150. $35.

Erler, Georg. *Studien zum internationalen Wirtschaftsrecht und Atomenergierecht.* Cologne: Carl Heymanns Verlag, 1982. Pp. 337. Index.

Hodgson, John S., and Mark G. Herander. *International Economic Relations.* Englewood Cliffs: Prentice-Hall, Inc., 1983. Pp. xvi, 441. Index. $24.95.

Mádl, Ferenc. *The Law of International Transactions.* Budapest: Akadémiai Kiadó, 1982. Pp. 205. $19.50.

McGovern, Edmond. *International Trade Regulation: GATT, the United States and the European Community.* Exeter: Globefield Press, 1982. Pp. xxxv, 457. Index. £20; $40.

Prissert, Pierre, and Alain Piquemal. *Stratégie et économie des échanges internationaux.* Paris: La Revue Banque, 1982. Pp. 295. F.89.

Rosenthal, Douglas E., and William M. Knighton. *National Laws and International Commerce: The Problem of Extraterritoriality.* Published under the auspices of The Royal Institute of International Affairs. London, Boston, and Henley: Routledge & Kegan Paul, 1982. Pp. xi, 96. £3.95; $10.

Yusuf, Abdulqawi. *Legal Aspects of Trade Preferences for Developing States: A study in the influence of development needs on the evolution of international law.* The Hague, Boston, London: Martinus Nijhoff Publishers, 1982. Pp. xx, 185. Index. Dfl.100; $43.50.

* Mention here neither assures nor precludes later review.

Law of the Sea & Maritime Law

Alexandersson, Gunnar. *The Baltic Straits.* The Hague, Boston, London: Martinus Nijhoff Publishers, 1982. Pp. xi, 132. Index. Dfl.75; $32.50.

Bassett, Frank E., and Richard A. Smith. *Farwell's Rules of the Nautical Road* (6th ed.). Annapolis: Naval Institute Press, 1982. Pp. xviii, 551. Indexes.

Ellen, Eric, and Donald Campbell. *International Maritime Fraud.* London: Sweet & Maxwell, 1981. Pp. viii, 174. Index. £8; $19. Distributed by Carswell Legal Publications.

Jónsson, Hannes. *Friends in Conflict: The Anglo-Icelandic Cod Wars and the Law of the Sea.* London: C. Hurst & Company; Hamden: Archon Books, 1982. Pp. xi, 240. Index.

Karatzas, Theodoros B., and Nigel P. Ready. *The Greek Code of Private Maritime Law.* The Hague, Boston, London: Martinus Nijhoff Publishers, 1982. Pp. viii, 98. Index. Dfl.75; $32.50.

Lapidoth-Eschelbacher, Ruth. *The Red Sea and the Gulf of Aden.* The Hague, Boston, London: Martinus Nijhoff Publishers, 1982. Pp. xiv, 265. Index. Dfl.150; $65.

McDorman, Ted L., Kenneth P. Beauchamp, and Douglas M. Johnston. *Maritime Boundary Delimitation: An Annotated Bibliography.* Lexington and Toronto: D. C. Heath and Company, 1983. Pp. xiii, 207. Indexes.

O'Connell, D. P. Edited by I. A. Shearer. *The International Law of the Sea.* Volume I. New York: The Clarendon Press; Oxford University Press, 1982. Pp. xxxiii, 634. Indexes. $74.

Pazarci, Hüseyin. *La Delimitation du Plateau Continental et les Iles.* Ankara: The University of Ankara, 1982. Pp. ix, 343. 300 TL.

Pueyo Losa, Jorge. *El Archipiélago Oceánico: Regulación jurídico-marítima internacional.* Madrid: International Law Association (Sección Española), 1981. Pp. 346.

Use of Force & Law of War

Rousseau, Charles. *Le Droit des conflits armés.* Paris: Editions A. Pedone, 1983. Pp. viii, 629. Index. F.320.

Terrorism

Adeniran, Tunde, and Yonah Alexander (eds.). *International Violence.* New York: Praeger Publishers, 1983. Pp. xvi, 265. Index. $29.95.

Miller, Abraham H. (ed.). *Terrorism: The Media and the Law.* Dobbs Ferry: Transnational Publishers, Inc., 1982. Pp. xi, 221. Index. $25.

Wardlaw, Grant. *Political Terrorism: Theory, Tactics and Counter-Measures.* New York: Cambridge University Press, 1983. Pp. 218. Index. $29.50, cloth; $9.95, paper.

Human Rights

Buergenthal, Thomas, Robert Norris, and Dinah Shelton. *Protecting Human Rights in the Americas: Selected Problems.* Kehl, Strasbourg, Arlington: N. P. Engel, Publishers, 1982. Pp. xvii, 337. $19.

Degan, Vladimir-Duro. *Medunarodno Pravo i Medunarodna Sigurnost: Pravni domašaj helsinškog Završnog akta.* Sarajevo: "Svjetlost," Oour Izdavačka Djelatnost, 1982. Pp. 161. Index.

Dinstein, Yoram (ed.). *Israel Yearbook on Human Rights. Volume 12.* Tel Aviv: Faculty of Law, Tel Aviv University, 1982. Pp. 333.

Flanz, Gisbert H. *Comparative Women's Rights and Political Participation in Europe.* Dobbs Ferry: Transnational Publishers, Inc., 1983. Pp. xix, 520. Index. $45.

Foriers, Paul, Léon Ingber, and Paul-F. Smets. *Droit Naturel.* (Vol. B/11 in the series Introduction bibliographique à l'histoire du droit et à l'ethnologie juridique.) Brussels: Editions de l'Université de Bruxelles, 1982. Pp. 130.

Hertzberg, Sandra, and Carmela Zammuto. *The Protection of Human Rights in the Criminal Process under International Instruments and National Constitutions.* Toulouse: Editions Erès, 1981. Pp. 208.

Kälin, Walter. *Das Prinzip des Non-Refoulement.* Bern and Frankfurt am Main: Peter Lang, 1982. Pp. xxviii, 365. Sw.F.68.90.

Kitz, Heinz-Eberhard. *Die Notstandsklausel des Art.15 der Europäischen Menschenrechtskonvention.* Berlin: Duncker & Humblot, 1982. Pp. 105. DM 44.

Robertson, A. H. *Human Rights in the World: An Introduction to the Study of the International Protection of Human Rights* (2d ed.). New York: St. Martin's Press, 1982. Pp. viii, 243. Index. $25.

Vasak, Karel (ed.). *The International Dimensions of Human Rights.* 2 vols. Revised and edited for the English edition by Philip Alston. Westport: Greenwood Press; Paris: UNESCO, 1982. Pp. xxiv, 755. Indexes. $55.

International Criminal Law

Conot, Robert E. *Justice at Nuremberg.* New York: Harper & Row, Publishers, 1983. Pp. xiii, 593. $22.50.

Lael, Richard L. *The Yamashita Precedent: War Crimes and Command Responsibility.* Wilmington: Scholarly Resources Inc., 1982. Pp. xii, 165. Index. $19.95.

Environment & Natural Resources

Bush, W. M. *Antarctica and International Law: A Collection of Inter-State and National Documents.* Volume II. London, Rome, New York: Oceana Publications, Inc., 1982. Pp. xii, 589. 3 vols. projected. $50/vol.

Craven, John P. *The Management of Pacific Marine Resources: Present Problems and Future Trends.* Published in cooperation with The Hubert H. Humphrey Institute of Public Affairs. Boulder: Westview Press, 1982. Pp. xix, 105. Index. $12.95.

Nanda, Ved P. (ed.). *World Climate Change: The Role of International Law and Institutions.* Boulder: Westview Press, 1983. Pp. x, 264. Index. $20.

Air & Space Law

Bhatt, S. *Aviation, Environment and World Order.* Atlantic Highlands: Humanities Press, 1980. Pp. 181. Index.

Górbiel, Andrzej. *Outer Space in International Law.* Łódź: Uniwersytet Łódzki, 1981. Pp. 175. Zł.109.

Steinberg, Gerald M. *Satellite Reconnaissance: The Role of Informal Bargaining.* New York: Praeger Publishers, 1983. Pp. viii, 200. Index. $27.95.

International Organizations

Ameri, Houshang. *Politics and Process in the Specialized Agencies of the United Nations.* Brookfield: Gower Publishing Co., 1982. Pp. xiii, 284. Index. $46.

Bowett, D. W. *The Law of International Institutions* (4th ed.). Published under the auspices of The London Institute of World Affairs. London: Stevens & Sons, 1982. Pp. xv, 431. Index. $44.75, cloth; £12.50; $29.50, paper. Distributed by Carswell Legal Publications.

Di Blase, Antonietta. *Nazioni Unite e istituti specializzati: La rilevanza giuridica del coordinamento.* Naples: Jovene Editore, 1982. Pp. 439. Indexes. L. 20,000.

Kapteyn, P. J. G., P. H. Kooijmans, R. H. Lauwaars, H. G. Schermers, and M. van Leeuwen Boomkamp (eds.). *International Organization and Integration: Annotated Basic Documents and Descriptive Directory of International Organizations and Arrangements.* Vol.I.B (2d rev. ed.). The Hague, Boston, London: Martinus Nijhoff Publishers, 1982. Pp. xxxvi + 760. Index. Dfl.240; $99.

Kranz, Jerzy. *Głosowanie wazone w organizacjach miedzynarodowych.* Warsaw: Ossolineum, 1982. Pp. 191. Index.

European Community Law

Braxator, Kamil. *Die Zwischenstaatlichkeitsklausel in den Wettbewerbsvorschriften des EWG-Vertrages und des Freihandelsabkommens Schweiz-EWG.* Bern and Frankfurt am Main: Peter Lang, 1982. Pp. 266. Sw.F.49.

Gijlstra, D. J., H. G. Schermers, E. L. M. Völker, and J. A. Winter (eds.). *Leading Cases on the Law of the European Communities* (4th ed.). Deventer: Kluwer Law and Taxation Publishers, 1982. Pp. xxi, 599. Dfl.70; $28.

Gijlstra, D. J., and E. L. M. Völker (eds.). *Materials on the Law of the European Communities* (1st ed.). Deventer: Kluwer Law and Taxation Publishers, 1983. Pp. xxi, 530. Dfl.75; $31.

Kerse, C. S. *EEC Antitrust Procedure. Supplement 1982.* London: European Law Centre Ltd., 1982. Pp. ix, 41. £7.

Private International Law

Actes et documents de la Quatorzième session (1980). Book I—Miscellaneous matters. Book II—Consumer sales. Edited by the Permanent Bureau of the Hague Conference on private international law. The Hague, 1982. Book I: pp. 298; book II: pp. 201. G.135.

Actes et documents de la Quatorzième session (1980). Book III—Child abduction. Edited by the Permanent Bureau of the Hague Conference on private international law. The Hague, 1982. Pp. 481.

U.S. Foreign Relations: Law & Policy

Brown, Peter G., and Henry Shue (eds.). *The Border That Joins: Mexican Migrants and U.S. Responsibility.* Totowa: Rowman and Littlefield, 1983. Pp. x, 254. Index. $26.50, cloth; $17.95, paper.

Keynes, Edward. *Undeclared War: Twilight Zone of Constitutional Power.* University Park and London: The Pennsylvania State University Press, 1982. Pp. ix, 236. Index. $17.95.

Kirkpatrick, Jeane J. *The Reagan Phenomenon—and Other Speeches on Foreign Policy.* Washington and London: American Enterprise Institute for Public Policy Research, 1983. Pp. xv, 230. Index. $14.95.

Foreign Relations of the United States, 1951, Volume V: The Near East and Africa. (Dept. of State Pub. 9114.) Washington: U.S. Govt. Printing Office, 1982. Pp. xxxv, 1497. Index.

Foreign Relations of the United States, 1951, Volume VII: Korea and China. Part 1, Dept. of State Pub. 9270. Part 2, Dept. of State Pub. 9271. Washington: U.S. Govt. Printing Office, 1983. Pp. xii, 2091. Index in part 2.

Foreign Relations of the United States, 1952–1954, Volume XIII: Indochina. Part 1, Dept. of State Pub. 9210. Part 2, Dept. of State Pub. 9211. Washington: U.S. Govt. Printing Office, 1982. Pp. xxvii, 2497. Index in part 2.

Conflicts & Disputes

Israel in Lebanon: The Report of the International Commission. Seán MacBride, Chairman. London: Ithaca Press, 1983. Pp. xxii, 282. £4.50.

Nedjatigil, Zaim M. *The Cyprus Conflict—A Lawyer's View* (2d ed.). Mersin: A-Z Publications, 1982. Pp. xii, 248. Index. £6.

Srivastava, M. P. *The Korean Conflict: Search for Unification.* New Delhi: Prentice-Hall of India Private Limited, 1982. Pp. v, 120. Rs.29.

Arms Control & Disarmament

Carroll, Berenice A., Clinton F. Fink, and Jane E. Mohraz. *Peace and War: A Guide to Bibliographies.* Santa Barbara and Oxford: ABC-Clio, Inc., 1983. Pp. xxiii, 580. Indexes. $42.50.

No Substitute for Peace. A Report by the Centre for Conflict Studies, University of New Brunswick, Canada, 1982. Pp. 72. $2.

Däubler, Wolfgang. *Stationierung und Grundgesetz: Was sagen Völkerrecht und Verifassungsrecht zu neuen Massenvernichtungswaffen (ABC-Waffen) in der Bundesrepublik?* Reinbek bei Hamburg: Rowohlt Taschenbuch Verlag GmbH, 1982. Pp. 221. Index. DM 8.80.

Foreign & Comparative Law & Politics

China—Trade and Investment Bibliography of English Language Publications. Melbourne: Australian Law Council Foundation, 1982. Pp. 162. A$25.

Bernhardt, Rudolf, and Ulrich Beyerlin (eds.). *Deutsche Landesreferate zum Öffentlichen Recht und Völkerrecht.* (XI. Internationaler Kongress für Rechtsvergleichung, Caracas 1982.) Heidelberg: C. F. Müller Juristischer Verlag, 1982. Pp. xii, 283. DM 118.

Decker, David R., and Ignacio Duran. *The Political, Economic, and Labor Climate in Colombia.* Philadelphia: Industrial Research Unit, The Wharton School, University of Pennsylvania, 1982. Pp. xi, 129. Index. $18.

Feldbrugge, F. J. M., and William B. Simons (eds.). *Perspectives on Soviet Law for the 1980s.* The Hague, Boston, London: Martinus Nijhoff Publishers, 1982. Pp. xvii, 266. Index. Dfl.75; $32.50.

Lerrick, A., and Q. J. Mian. *Saudi Business and Labor Law: Its Interpretation and Application.* London: Graham & Trotman, 1982. Pp. xx, 289. Index. £71.50; $154.

Maggs, Peter B., Gordon B. Smith, and George Ginsburgs (eds.). *Law and Economic Development in the Soviet Union.* Boulder: Westview Press, 1982. Pp. xi, 293. Index. $21.50.

Mak, W., and H. Molijn. *Introduction to Trade Mark Law in the Benelux.* Deventer: Kluwer, 1982. Pp. 139. Index. Dfl.67.50; $27.

Seidl-Hohenveldern, Ignaz. *Die Überleitung von Herrschaftsverhältnissen am Beispiel Österreichs.* Vienna and New York: Springer-Verlag, 1982. Pp. ix, 186. DM 98; $39.20.

Tornaritis, Criton G. *The Evolution of the Law Relating to Land in Cyprus.* Nicosia, 1982. Pp. 35.

International Relations & Politics

Arlinghaus, Bruce E. (ed.). *Arms for Africa: Military Assistance and Foreign Policy in the Developing World.* Lexington and Toronto: D. C. Heath and Company, 1983. Pp. xiv, 233. $26.95.

Dawisha, Adeed, and Karen Dawisha (eds.). *The Soviet Union in the Middle East: Policies and Perspectives.* Published for the Royal Institute of International Affairs. New York: Holmes & Meier Publishers, 1982. Pp. 172. Index. $17.50, cloth; $9.50, paper.

Holloway, David. *The Soviet Union and the Arms Race.* New Haven and London: Yale University Press, 1983. Pp. x, 211. Index. $14.95; £7.95.

Keeton, George W., and Georg Schwarzenberger (eds.). *The Year Book of World Affairs 1983.* Published under the auspices of The London Institute of World Affairs. London: Stevens & Sons, 1983. Pp. vi, 312. Index.

Matheson, Neil. *The 'Rules of the Game' of Superpower Military Intervention in the Third World 1975–1980.* Washington: University Press of America, 1982. Pp. viii, 159. $21.25, cloth; $9.75, paper.

Vasquez, John A. *The Power of Power Politics: A Critique.* New Brunswick: Rutgers University Press, 1983. Pp. xiv, 303. Indexes. $27.50.

Miscellaneous

Bar-Niv, Zvi H. (ed.). *International Labour Law Reports, Volume 3.* Alphen aan den Rijn and Rockville: Sijthoff & Noordhoff, 1980. Pp. xix, 399. Dfl.200; $87.50.

Clarke, Malcolm A. *International Carriage of Goods by Road: CMR.* London: Stevens and Sons, 1982. Pp. xxvi, 212. Index. Distributed by Carswell Legal Publications.

Kolvenbach, Walter. *Cooperation between Management and Labor: A survey of co-determination mechanisms in European corporations.* Deventer: Kluwer Law and Taxation Publishers, 1982. Pp. 89. Dfl.65; $26.

OFFICIAL DOCUMENTS

Resolution Adopted by the General Assembly*

37/92. *Principles Governing the Use by States of Artificial Earth Satellites for International Direct Television Broadcasting*

The General Assembly,

Recalling its resolution 2916 (XXVII) of 9 November 1972, in which it stressed the necessity of elaborating principles governing the use by States of artificial earth satellites for international direct television broadcasting, and mindful of the importance of concluding an international agreement or agreements,

Recalling further its resolutions 3182 (XXVIII) of 18 December 1973, 3234 (XXIX) of 12 November 1974, 3388 (XXX) of 18 November 1975, 31/8 of 8 November 1976, 32/196 of 20 December 1977, 33/16 of 10 November 1978, 34/66 of 5 December 1979 and 35/14 of 3 November 1980, and its resolution 36/35 of 18 November 1981 in which it decided to consider at its thirty-seventh session the adoption of a draft set of principles governing the use by States of artificial earth satellites for international direct television broadcasting,

Noting with appreciation the efforts made in the Committee on the Peaceful Uses of Outer Space and its Legal Sub-Committee to comply with the directives issued in the above-mentioned resolutions,

Considering that several experiments of direct broadcasting by satellite have been carried out and that a number of direct broadcasting satellite systems are operational in some countries and may be commercialized in the very near future,

Taking into consideration that the operation of international direct broadcasting satellites will have significant international political, economic, social and cultural implications,

Believing that the establishment of principles for international direct television broadcasting will contribute to the strengthening of international co-operation in this field and further the purposes and principles of the Charter of the United Nations,

Adopts the Principles Governing the Use by States of Artificial Earth Satellites for International Direct Television Broadcasting set forth in the annex to the present resolution.

100th plenary meeting
10 December 1982

* UN Doc. A/RES/37/92 (Feb. 4, 1983), adopted by the General Assembly on the report of the Special Political Committee, UN Doc. A/37/646 (1982).

ANNEX

Principles Governing the Use by States of Artificial Earth Satellites for International Direct Television Broadcasting

A. *Purposes and objectives*

1. Activities in the field of international direct television broadcasting by satellite should be carried out in a manner compatible with the sovereign rights of States, including the principle of non-intervention, as well as with the right of everyone to seek, receive and impart information and ideas as enshrined in the relevant United Nations instruments.

2. Such activities should promote the free dissemination and mutual exchange of information and knowledge in cultural and scientific fields, assist in educational, social and economic development, particularly in the developing countries, enhance the qualities of life of all peoples and provide recreation with due respect to the political and cultural integrity of States.

3. These activities should accordingly be carried out in a manner compatible with the development of mutual understanding and the strengthening of friendly relations and co-operation among all States and peoples in the interest of maintaining international peace and security.

B. *Applicability of international law*

4. Activities in the field of international direct television broadcasting by satellite should be conducted in accordance with international law, including the Charter of the United Nations, the Treaty on Principles Governing the Activities of States in the Exploration and Use of Outer Space, including the Moon and Other Celestial Bodies, of 27 January 1967, the relevant provisions of the International Telecommunication Convention and its Radio Regulations and of international instruments relating to friendly relations and co-operation among States and to human rights.

C. *Rights and benefits*

5. Every State has an equal right to conduct activities in the field of international direct television broadcasting by satellite and to authorize such activities by persons and entities under its jurisdiction. All States and peoples are entitled to and should enjoy the benefits from such activities. Access to the technology in this field should be available to all States without discrimination on terms mutually agreed by all concerned.

D. *International co-operation*

6. Activities in the field of international direct television broadcasting by satellite should be based upon and encourage international co-operation. Such co-operation should be the subject of appropriate arrangements. Special consideration should be given to the needs of the developing countries in the use of international direct television broadcasting by satellite for the purpose of accelerating their national development.

E. *Peaceful settlement of disputes*

7. Any international dispute that may arise from activities covered by these principles should be settled through established procedures for the peaceful

settlement of disputes agreed upon by the parties to the dispute in accordance with the provisions of the Charter of the United Nations.

F. *State responsibility*

8. States should bear international responsibility for activities in the field of international direct television broadcasting by satellite carried out by them or under their jurisdiction and for the conformity of any such activities with the principles set forth in this document.

9. When international direct television broadcasting by satellite is carried out by an international intergovernmental organization, the responsibility referred to in paragraph 8 above should be borne both by that organization and by the States participating in it.

G. *Duty and right to consult*

10. Any broadcasting or receiving State within an international direct television broadcasting satellite service established between them requested to do so by any other broadcasting or receiving State within the same service should promptly enter into consultations with the requesting State regarding its activities in the field of international direct television broadcasting by satellite, without prejudice to other consultations which these States may undertake with any other State on that subject.

H. *Copyright and neighbouring rights*

11. Without prejudice to the relevant provisions of international law, States should co-operate on a bilateral and multilateral basis for protection of copyright and neighbouring rights by means of appropriate agreements between the interested States or the competent legal entities acting under their jurisdiction. In such co-operation they should give special consideration to the interests of developing countries in the use of direct television broadcasting for the purpose of accelerating their national development.

I. *Notification to the United Nations*

12. In order to promote international co-operation in the peaceful exploration and use of outer space, States conducting or authorizing activities in the field of international direct television broadcasting by satellite should inform the Secretary-General of the United Nations, to the greatest extent possible, of the nature of such activities. On receiving this information, the Secretary-General should disseminate it immediately and effectively to the relevant specialized agencies, as well as to the public and the international scientific community.

J. *Consultations and agreements between States*

13. A State which intends to establish or authorize the establishment of an international direct television broadcasting satellite service shall without delay notify the proposed receiving State or States of such intention and shall promptly enter into consultation with any of those States which so requests.

14. An international direct television broadcasting satellite service shall only be established after the conditions set forth in paragraph 13 above have

been met and on the basis of agreements and/or arrangements in conformity with the relevant instruments of the International Telecommunication Union and in accordance with these principles.

15. With respect to the unavoidable overspill of the radiation of the satellite signal, the relevant instruments of the International Telecommunication Union shall be exclusively applicable.

INTERNATIONAL LEGAL MATERIALS*

CONTENTS

VOL. XXII, No. 2 (March 1983)

PAGE

TREATIES AND AGREEMENTS

Conference of Plenipotentiaries on the *Protection and Development of the Marine Environment of the Wider Caribbean Region:*

Final Act 221

Convention for the Protection and Development of the Marine Environment of the Wider Caribbean Region 227

Protocol concerning Co-operation in Combating Oil Spills in the Wider Caribbean Region 240

Diplomatic Conference for the Adoption of the UNIDROIT Draft Convention on *Agency in the International Sale of Goods:*

Final Act 246

Convention on Agency in the International Sale of Goods 249

Gambia-Senegal: Agreement and Protocols concerning the *Establishment of a Senegambian Confederation*

Agreement 260

Protocol on the *Institutions* 266

Protocol on the *Financial Regulations* 276

Protocol on *Co-ordination of Policy in the Field of External Relations* 283

International Law Association: Draft Convention on *State Immunity* 287

Organization of American States: Inter-American Draft Convention on *Jurisdictional Immunity of States* 292

United Nations Conference on *Succession of States in Respect of State Property, Archives and Debts:*

Final Act 298

Vienna Convention on Succession of States in Respect of State Property, Archives and Debts 306

LEGISLATION AND REGULATIONS

China: *Economic Contract* Law 330

United States:

Clayton Act Amendment Modifying *Amount of Damages Payable to Foreign States which Sue for Antitrust Violations* 348

Department of Commerce, International Trade Administration, Regulations Implementing the *Export Administration Act*

Revision of *Export Controls Affecting the USSR and Poland* 349

Revision of *Enforcement Provisions* 353

Department of Justice, Immigration and Naturalization Service, *Asylum Procedures under the Refugee Act of 1980* 362

Export Trading Company Act of 1982 363

JUDICIAL AND SIMILAR PROCEEDINGS

European Court of Human Rights: Judgment in the Case of Foti and Others (*Unreasonable Delay in Italian Court Proceedings*) 380

* ILM subscription, $65; concessionary rate to ASIL members, $30. Address orders to ILM, 2223 Massachusetts Ave., NW, Wash., D.C. 20008. Outside U.S., please add $5.

United States:
Court of Appeals for the District of Columbia
Decision in Persinger *v.* Iran (*Foreign Sovereign Immunities Act; Presidential Authority to Extinguish Claims of US Hostages*) 404
United States Petition for Hearing Persinger *v.* Iran (*Court's Construction of Foreign Sovereign Immunities Act*) 419
Court of Appeals for the Eleventh Circuit Decision in Harris Corporation *v.* National Iranian Radio and Television (*Foreign Sovereign Immunities Act; Preliminary Injunction to Prevent Payment on Standby Letter of Credit*) 434

OTHER DOCUMENTS
General Agreement on Tariffs and Trade: Ministerial Declaration on the *World Trading System* 445
United Nations General Assembly Resolutions:
On Principles Governing the *Use by States of Artificial Earth Satellites for Direct Television Broadcasting* 451
On a *World Charter for Nature* 455
United States: Proclamation on an *Exclusive Economic Zone* 461

RECENT ACTIONS REGARDING TREATIES TO WHICH THE UNITED STATES IS A PARTY 466
RECENT ACTIONS REGARDING TREATIES TO WHICH THE UNITED STATES IS NOT A PARTY 471
NOTICE OF OTHER RECENT DOCUMENTS (not reprinted) 472

Manuscripts in triplicate may be sent to the Editors-in-Chief of AJIL, Professors Oscar Schachter and Louis Henkin, Columbia University School of Law, New York, N.Y. 10027. Subscriptions, orders for back numbers, correspondence with reference to AJIL and books for review should be sent to the AMERICAN JOURNAL OF INTERNATIONAL LAW (ISSN 0002-9300), 2223 Massachusetts Avenue, N.W., Washington, D.C. 20008.

AJIL is published in January, April, July, and October and is supplied to all members of the American Society of International Law. The annual subscription to nonmembers of ASIL is $52.00, plus $2.50 for all foreign subscriptions (including ASIL Proceedings). Available back numbers of AJIL will be supplied at $11.00 each. ($21 of membership fee is allotted to AJIL subscription.)

EDITORIAL OFFICE:
BOX 44
COLUMBIA UNIVERSITY SCHOOL OF LAW
NEW YORK, N.Y. 10027

BUSINESS OFFICE:
2223 MASSACHUSETTS AVENUE, N.W.
WASHINGTON, D.C. 20008

American Journal of International Law

ctober 1983
ol. 77 No. 4

blished by
nerican Society of International Law

PATRONS OF THE SOCIETY

Honorable ARTHUR H. DEAN

Honorable HERMAN PHLEGER

GENEVIEVE E. TILLAR (deceased)

W. ROBERT MORGAN

BRUNSON MACCHESNEY (deceased)

ALONA E. EVANS (deceased)

JOHN N. HAZARD

Honorable JOHN R. STEVENSON

ARTHUR R. ALBRECHT

ALWYN V. FREEMAN (deceased)

In Memoriam

DR. JAMES BROWN SCOTT

HENRY C. MORRIS

ARTHUR K. KUHN

ALEXANDER FREEMAN

STANLEY P. SMITH

PATRONAGE, GIFTS AND BEQUESTS

Upon donation to the Society of $5,000 or more by gift or bequest, any member of the Society or individual eligible for membership may be elected a Patron of the Society. Upon donation of at least $5,000 in the name of a deceased person, such person may be elected a Patron posthumously.

Gifts and bequests may be made in the name of the American Society of International Law, Washington, D.C. Such contributions are deductible from federal returns for income, estate and gift tax purposes. The Society is incorporated by Act of Congress approved September 20, 1950 (64 Stat. 869).

MANLEY O. HUDSON MEDAL

The American Society of International Law bestows from time to time without regard to nationality a gold medal to commemorate the life work of Manley O. Hudson. Such awards are made for preeminent scholarship and achievement in international law and in the promotion of the establishment and maintenance of international relations on the basis of law and justice. Medals have been awarded to Manley O. Hudson (1956), Lord McNair (1959), Philip C. Jessup (1964), Charles De Visscher (1966), Paul Guggenheim (1970), Myres S. McDougal (1976), Eduardo Jiménez de Aréchaga (1978), Richard Reeve Baxter (1981), Oscar Schachter (1981), and Hardy Cross Dillard (1982).

Second-class postage paid at Washington, D.C. and additional mailing office

Postmaster: If undeliverable, send notice on Form 3579 to: American Journal of International Law 2223 Massachusetts Ave., N.W. Washington, D.C. 20008

Printed by Lancaster Press, Lancaster, Pa. 17604

AMERICAN JOURNAL OF INTERNATIONAL LAW

VOL. 77 October 1983 NO. 4

CONTENTS

PAGE

Fisheries under the United Nations Convention on the Law of the Sea *Shigeru Oda* 739

The Extraterritorial Application of the German Antitrust Laws *David J. Gerber* 756

ICSID Arbitration and the Courts *Georges R. Delaume* 784

The General Admission of Aliens under International Law *James A. R. Nafziger* 804

Editorial Comment

Human Dignity as a Normative Concept *Oscar Schachter* 848

Notes and Comments

The Teaching of International Human Rights Law in U.S. Law Schools *Richard B. Lillich* 855

Soviet Theory of International Law for the Seventies *Kazimierz Grzybowski* 862

Correspondence 872

Contemporary Practice of the United States Relating to International Law *Marian Nash Leich* 875

Judicial Decisions *Monroe Leigh* 878

Current Developments

Discovery of Documentary and Other Evidence in a Foreign Country *Robert B. von Mehren* 896

The African Charter on Human and Peoples' Rights *U. O. Umozurike* 902

The Iran-United States Claims Tribunal *Marian Nash Leich* 913

Book Reviews and Notes *Edited by Leo Gross*

Moskowitz, Moses. *The Roots and Reaches of United Nations Actions and Decisions* (Inis L. Claude, Jr.) 915

Conot, Robert E. *Justice at Nuremberg* (Benjamin B. Ferencz) 917

Dinstein, Yoram (ed.). *Models of Autonomy* (Allan Gerson) 918

Parry, Clive (ed.). *The Consolidated Treaty Series, 1648–1919.* 231 vols. + index vol. (Robert A. Friedlander) 922

Zuijdwijk, Ton J. M. *Petitioning the United Nations: A Study in Human Rights* (John Carey) 924

Hevener, Natalie Kaufman. *International Law and the Status of Women* (Rita E. Hauser) 926

Khushalani, Yougindra. *Dignity and Honour of Women as Basic and Fundamental Human Rights* (Rita E. Hauser) 926

Gold, Joseph. *The Fund Agreement in the Courts: Volume II. Further Jurisprudence Involving the Articles of Agreement of the International Monetary Fund* (Robert Litan) 927

Galenson, Walter. *The International Labor Organization: An American View* (Virginia A. Leary) 929

Kruglak, Gregory T. *The Politics of United States Decision-Making in United Nations Specialized Agencies: The Case of the International Labor Organization* (Virginia A. Leary) 929

Bowett, D. W. *The Law of International Institutions* (4th ed.) (Richard W. Nelson) 933
Sybesma-Knol, R. G. *The Status of Observers in the United Nations* (Lawrence S. Finkelstein) 935
Kusumowidagdo, Judo Umarto. *Consultation Clauses as Means of Providing for Treaty Obedience: A Study in the Law of Treaties* (Maria Frankowska) 936
Christol, Carl Q. *The Modern International Law of Outer Space* (Martin Menter) 937
Charney, Jonathan I. (ed.). *The New Nationalism and the Use of Common Spaces: Issues in Marine Pollution and the Exploitation of Antarctica* (Susanne Tongue) 940
Johnston, Douglas M. (ed.). *The Environmental Law of the Sea* (Susanne Tongue) 941
Schwarz-Liebermann von Wahlendorf, H. A. *The Forms of Action at International Law* (Jerome Elkind) 942
Duffar, Jean. *Contribution à l'étude des privilèges et immunités des organisations internationales* (Philippe Cahier) 943
Hague Conference on Private International Law. *Actes et documents de la Quatorzième session (1980). Books I and II* (Kurt H. Nadelmann) 944
Newton, William H., III. *International Estate Planning* (Nancy K. Mintz) 947
Schoenblum, Jeffrey A. *Multistate and Multinational Estate Planning.* Vols. I and II (Nicholas R. Doman) 948
Welch, Jane (ed.). *The Regulation of Banks in the Member States of the EEC* (2d ed.) (Joseph Gold) 950
Korah, Valentine. *Competition Law of Britain and the Common Market* (3d rev. ed.) (A. V. Lowe) 952
Van den Berghe, Guido. *Political Rights for European Citizens* (Ralph Beddard) 953
Degenhardt, Henry W. *Treaties and Alliances of the World* (3d ed.) (William S. Kenney) 955
Chatterjee, S. K. *Legal Aspects of International Drug Control* (Frank W. Swacker) 956
Bull, Alan T., Geoffrey Holt, and Malcolm D. Lilly. *Biotechnology: International Trends and Perspectives* (Frederic A. Eustis, III) 957
Laszlo, Ervin, and Donald Keys (eds.). *Disarmament: The Human Factor* (Guy Du Bose) 959
Ebinger, Charles K. (proj. dir.). *The Critical Link: Energy and National Security in the 1980s* (Francis A. Boyle) 961
Péteri, Zoltán, and Vanda Lamm (eds.). *General Reports to the 10th International Congress of Comparative Law* (Detlev F. Vagts) 962
Streinz, Rudolf. *Meinungs- und Informationsfreiheit zwischen Ost und West* (Henn-Jüri Uibopuu) 963
Galenskaia, L. N. *Pravovoe polozhenie inostrantsev v SSSR* (John N. Hazard) 964
Sumner, Colin (ed.). *Crime, Justice and Underdevelopment* (Ved P. Nanda) 965
Atimomo, Emiko. *Law and Diplomacy in Commodity Economics* (Michael G. Schechter) 968
Sukijasović, Miodrag. *Multinacionalno Preduzeće: Pravni Aspekti* (Zvonko R. Rode) 969
Pooley, James. *Trade Secrets: How to Protect Your Ideas and Assets* (Lawrence R. Caruso and Linda A. Caruso) 970
Soviet Year-Book of International Law 1981 (John N. Hazard) 971
Annuaire Français de Droit International. Vol. XXVI, 1980 (Andrew Drzemczewski) 973
Chiu, Hungdah (ed.). *Chinese Yearbook of International Law and Affairs.* Vol. 1 (1981) (Shao-chuan Leng) 975
Netherlands Yearbook of International Law. Vol. XIII, 1982 (Edward Dumbauld) 976
Zhou Gengsheng. *Guoji Fa.* 2 vols. (Hungdah Chiu) 977
Wang Tieya and Wei Min (eds.). *Guoji Fa* (Hungdah Chiu) 977
Wang Tieya and Tian Ruxuan (comps.). *Guoji Fa Ziliao Xuanpian* (Hungdah Chiu) 977
Briefer Notices: Ingber (ed.), 980; Alexander and Myers (eds.), 980; Dunn, 981; Ginsburgs and Slusser, 982. Correspondence, 982.
Books Received 986
International Legal Materials. Contents, Vol XXII, No. 3 (May 1983) and No. 4 (July 1983) 990
Table of Cases 993
Index 996

The American Society of International Law

The American Society of International Law was organized in 1906 "to foster the study of international law and to promote the establishment and maintenance of international relations on the basis of law and justice."

The Society serves as a meeting place and forum for scholars, teachers, officials, lawyers, and others, from some one hundred countries. In April, it holds a three-day Annual Meeting at which current problems of international law are discussed. The Society also sponsors regional meetings outside of Washington in cooperation with other institutions. Salient questions of international law and relations are considered in depth by panels and study groups organized by the Society's Board of Review and Development. Works of scholarship are often published under the Society's auspices in connection with studies sponsored by the Board, many in the Society's series of *Studies in Transnational Legal Policy*.

The Society periodically issues four publications:

The American Journal of International Law, the leading journal in the field of international law, has been published since 1907. The *Proceedings of the American Society of International Law* carries the papers and discussion of the annual meeting of the Society.

International Legal Materials, a bimonthly, is a unique international collection of texts of current official documents, including legislation, treaties, court decisions, and reports. Subscription rates are $30 a year for members of the Society, $65 for others.

The quarterly *Newsletter* provides members with news of the Society and other organizations in the field.

Society membership is open to all persons of whatever nationality and profession who are interested in its objectives. Dues are: regular, $55; special category, $30 for persons *not* resident in a member country of the Organisation for Economic Co-operation and Development; intermediate, $25; student, $15. Membership application form is printed at the back of each issue of AJIL.

FISHERIES UNDER THE UNITED NATIONS CONVENTION ON THE LAW OF THE SEA

*By Shigeru Oda**

Introduction—Some Preliminary Observations

Fisheries under the Traditional Dualism

Under the traditional rules of international law, the sea was divided into the high seas and the territorial seas and in each case different rules and regulations obtained.[1] As for the exploitation of fishery resources, the coastal state possessed unquestioned rights to regulate any such exploitation within its territorial sea and to apply its domestic legislation fully to any person engaged in such activities. Similarly, the coastal state was free to prohibit fishing by foreigners in its territorial sea and thus to monopolize those fishery resources. On the high seas, however, no state was allowed, at least in principle, to impose its jurisdiction upon any foreign vessel, since fishing on the high seas fell under the general regime of the high seas. The existence of these two disparate regimes, namely, exploitation under the full control of the coastal state and exploitation free from interference by any country, was a fundamental presumption underlying the exploitation of fishery resources.

As the breadth of the territorial sea inherently coincided with the coastal state's monopoly of fishery resources, it was of great importance to determine just how far the territorial sea should extend from the coast. Any expansion of the territorial sea would imply encroachment on the fishing rights that other states might otherwise have enjoyed in an area previously regarded as part of the high seas. Hence, policies concerning territorial seas have been affected by the balance of the dependency of each nation's fishery interests on its own offshore zone on the one hand, and on the offshore zones of other nations on the other. At the United Nations Conference on the Law of the Sea (hereinafter referred to as UNCLOS) held at Geneva in 1958, some developed nations were strongly opposed to the expansion of the territorial seas from 3 miles to a much wider extent. For the United States, the navigation of vessels, particularly warships, in the offshore waters of other coastal nations was a sensitive issue. The United States was even ready to forsake fishery interests if free navigation of warships in the offshore waters of other coastal states could be guaranteed. Thus, the U.S. delegation suggested trading the wider (12-mile) fishery zone

* Member, International Court of Justice.

[1] No particular reference is made here to any other publication, as this subsection merely confirms the author's long held view, expressed in such works as INTERNATIONAL CONTROL OF SEA RESOURCES (1963); *International Law of the Resources of the Sea,* 127 RECUEIL DES COURS 353 (1969 II) (reprinted ed. with Supp. 1979); THE LAW OF THE SEA IN OUR TIME, I: NEW DEVELOPMENTS 1966–1975 (1977).

for a narrower (6-mile) territorial sea.[2] This proposed package deal did not bear fruit, however, at either UNCLOS I (1958) or UNCLOS II (1960).

In the past, it was generally recognized that some control over exploitation of the resources of the vast oceans was needed if their optimum utilization was to be assured, and no nation ever contested the necessity for conserving high seas fisheries. Indeed, conservation was a basic concept of fishery science. Yet it was a basic principle of international law that all states were free to fish on the high seas unless otherwise bound by specific international agreements. Prior to UNCLOS I, several conservation treaties were concluded that provided for the effective regulation of fishing on the high seas. The idea of equal access to fisheries and equal limitations on fishing was fundamental to the conservation program provided for in each convention. In this field, as in many others, the underlying rationale of free competition has been one of the basic values endorsed in the modern period. Furthermore, enforcement of the provisions of these conventions, or of any measures subsequently adopted by international commissions set up pursuant to them, fell within the responsibility of each contracting party with respect to the fishing vessels flying its flag. This obligation derived from the freedom of the high seas, the dominant general principle whereby any vessel on the high seas enjoyed immunity, in time of peace, from the control and authority of any power other than its flag state.

The Convention on Fishing and Conservation of the Living Resources of the High Seas (hereinafter referred to as the High Seas Fisheries Convention) adopted at UNCLOS I, in which the concept of conservation was enshrined, retained the basic characteristics of traditional high seas fisheries rules. It set forth a new concept of special interests of the coastal state, which is to be construed so as to entitle the coastal state, even when its nationals are not fishing off its coast (beyond its national jurisdiction), to participate with other fishing states in prescribing any conservation measure applicable to offshore fisheries (Article 6, paragraphs 1 and 2). Yet it did not disturb the established rule of freedom of the high seas, under which fishing vessels need observe only the law of their own flag state. Although the coastal state is also empowered to adopt unilateral measures in certain circumstances (Article 7, paragraph 1), the expression "adopt unilateral measures" should not be construed as enabling the coastal state to extend its control directly over nationals of other states. Rather, in certain circumstances, fishing states are obliged to apply the measures unilaterally adopted by the coastal state to their own nationals.

The New Concept of Fishery Regulations

More than two decades have passed since UNCLOS I and UNCLOS II. It took nearly one decade, or 15 years if the work of the Sea-bed Committee

[2] Canada and United States of America, UN Doc. A/CONF.19/L.11 (1960), SECOND UNITED NATIONS CONFERENCE ON THE LAW OF THE SEA, OFFICIAL RECORDS, SUMMARY RECORDS OF PLENARY MEETINGS AND OF MEETINGS OF THE COMMITTEE OF THE WHOLE [hereinafter cited as UNCLOS II, OFF. REC.], UN Doc. A/CONF.19/8, at 173.

is taken into account, for the global negotiations conducted at UNCLOS III to result in the United Nations Convention on the Law of the Sea, signed at Montego Bay, Jamaica, on December 10, 1982. It introduces various new regimes with respect to fisheries.

The 1982 Convention has 21 articles providing for the new concept of the 200-mile exclusive economic zone (hereinafter referred to as EEZ) (part V, Articles 55–75). In fact, for offshore fisheries in particular, this concept has made meaningless the traditional dualism of the territorial seas and the high seas. The EEZ is a *sui generis* regime, and the argument as to whether it still remains a part of the high seas seems to be purely academic. In the 200-mile EEZ the coastal state has "sovereign rights for the purpose of exploring and exploiting, conserving and managing the natural resources," including fishing (Article 56, paragraph 1), while other states may continue to enjoy the freedoms of navigation and overflight and others that they could have enjoyed on or above the high seas (Article 58, paragraph 1).

On the other hand, the basic idea of freedom of fishing is still retained for the high seas, with some modifications. While the 1958 Convention provides for rules to be applicable to the high seas beyond the territorial seas, the right to fish under the 1982 Convention shall apply to the areas beyond the EEZ, which extends to 200 miles from the coast. Secondly, while freedom of fishing has undoubtedly been considered as one of the basic freedoms of the high seas for many centuries, fishing on the high seas today is placed under some restrictions. Although suggestions were often made at UNCLOS III to drop fishing from the list of the freedoms of the high seas, the 1982 Convention mentions, as one of six such freedoms, "freedom of fishing, subject to the conditions" concerning conservation and management of the living resources of the high seas (Article 87, paragraph 1(e)), and it devotes five articles to high seas fisheries (Articles 116–120).

Brief mention should also be made of the general framework of dispute settlement under the 1982 Convention. While at UNCLOS I an optional protocol for the settlement of disputes was prepared in parallel with the four Geneva Conventions, the 1982 Convention provides a comprehensive system for the settlement of disputes, 21 articles of part XV being devoted to this subject (Articles 279–299). As a basic principle, the states parties are required to settle any dispute concerning the interpretation or application of the Convention by peaceful means in accordance with the United Nations Charter (Article 279). If a dispute arises, they must proceed expeditiously to exchange views regarding settlement of the dispute by negotiation or other peaceful means (Article 283). While the states parties have the right to agree to settle disputes by any peaceful means of their own choice (Article 280), they are bound to refer disputes to a general, regional, or bilateral arrangement if they have accepted this special procedure in advance (Article 282). In addition, a suggestion is made in the Convention for conciliation proceedings (Article 284). The Conciliation Commission, constituted on an ad hoc basis and in principle consisting of five members to be chosen from a list of conciliators drawn up and maintained by the United Nations Secretary-General, shall hear the parties, examine their claims and objections, and make proposals to the parties with a view to reaching an amicable settlement (Annex V). Where no settlement has been made on the interpretation and application of the Convention by recourse to any of these procedures, the dispute may be referred to the International Court of Justice or a tribunal by unilateral request of any of the parties (Article 286).

Four tribunals—the International Tribunal for the Law of the Sea, the International Court of Justice, an arbitral tribunal, and a special arbitral tribunal—are mentioned, and the states parties, when signing or ratifying the Convention or at any time thereafter, shall be free to choose by means of a written declaration one or more of these four institutions for the settlement of disputes (Article 287). Apart from the International Court of Justice, which does not require any specification, detailed provisions for the International Tribunal for the Law of the Sea, an arbitral tribunal, and a special arbitral tribunal are laid down in Annexes VI, VII, and VIII, respectively. If the parties to a dispute have accepted the same procedure among these four means, a dispute may be subjected only to that procedure. If not, the dispute may be submitted only to an arbitral tribunal (Article 287, paragraphs 4 and 5). A state party to the Convention that is a party to disputes not covered by a declaration in force is deemed to have accepted arbitration (Article 287, paragraph 3). All four tribunals are expected to apply the Convention and other rules of international law not incompatible with the Convention (Article 293, paragraph 1). But if the parties to a dispute so agree, the tribunal may make the decision *ex aequo et bono* (Article 293, paragraph 2). Any dispute between states parties may be submitted to these institutions only after local remedies have been exhausted, as required by international law (Article 295).

Purpose of this Paper

This paper simply reflects the impressions gained by the author after reading the provisions relating to marine fisheries in the 1982 Convention. The author cannot conceal his apprehension that some difficulties will be encountered in applying the fisheries regime introduced by this Convention, and that the new machinery for dispute settlement that it introduces may not only come up against practical difficulties but even fail to function properly in the resolution of fishery disputes.

I. Fishery Regulations Applicable in the EEZ

Restrictions on Regulations

In prescribing the rules and regulations applicable to fisheries in the EEZ, the coastal state will be placed under certain obligations regarding the conservation and optimum utilization of fishery resources (Articles 61 and 62).

Determination of the Allowable Catch. The reference to conservation of the living resources differentiates the EEZ from the territorial sea and the concept of a fishery zone that had become institutionalized in the 1960's. This new idea was not current when some earlier drafts on the EEZ were proposed. For instance, there was no such suggestion in the Kenyan proposal[3] of 1972 and the proposal of three Caribbean states[4] in 1973, both of which were presented in the United Nations Sea-bed Committee. The obligation of the coastal state regarding conservation first appeared in proposals made by six Eastern European nations[5] and the United States[6] in 1974 at UNCLOS III. In fact, some developed nations, including the United States, that had previously been skeptical about or even hostile to the 200-mile zone proposal, fell back on the notion of imposing conservation of fishery resources on the coastal state once they realized that the general trend towards the EEZ could no longer be ignored.

The idea of determination of the allowable catch of living resources in the EEZ appeared in the six Eastern European nations' proposal of 1974, which provided that, except for highly migratory species, the annual allowable catch should be determined for each species of fish or other living marine resources.[7] The first draft prepared by UNCLOS III in 1975 (Informal Single Negotiating Text)[8] dropped the specification "for each species"; at the same time, more complex provisions were included so that the provisions as retained in the 1982 Convention read: "The coastal State shall determine the allowable catch of the living resources in its exclusive economic zone" and "shall ensure through proper conservation and management measures that the maintenance of the living resources in the exclusive economic zone is not endangered by over-exploitation" (Article 61, paragraphs 1 and 2). The conservation measures may limit not only the annual allowable catch, but also the species that may be caught, fishing seasons, fishing areas, and even fishing gear (Article 62, paragraph 4(b) and (c)). It can be argued that it is not appropriate for the coastal state always to be required to determine the allowable catch of the living resources in the EEZ and that it is extremely difficult to perform this obligation properly.

Optimum Utilization of Fishery Resources. Another new concept, promotion of the optimum utilization of fishery resources, is introduced in the 200-mile EEZ, as differentiated from the territorial sea. The 1982 United Nations Convention suggests that while the "coastal State shall determine its capacity to harvest the living resources of the exclusive economic zone," "it shall, through agreements or other arrangements and pursuant to the terms, con-

[3] Kenya, Draft articles on exclusive economic zone concept, UN Doc. A/AC.138/SC.II/L.10 (1972), 27 UN GAOR Supp. (No. 21) at 180, UN Doc. A/8721 (1972).

[4] Colombia, Mexico, and Venezuela, Draft articles of treaty—Territorial sea, UN Doc. A/AC.138/SC.II/L.21 (1973), 28 UN GAOR Supp. (No. 21, Vol. III) at 19, UN Doc. A/9021 (1973).

[5] Bulgaria, Byelorussian SSR, German Democratic Republic, Poland, Ukrainian SSR, and USSR, Draft articles on the economic zone, Arts. 11–14, UN Doc. A/CONF.62/C.2/L.38 (1974), 3 THIRD UNITED NATIONS CONFERENCE ON THE LAW OF THE SEA, OFFICIAL RECORDS [hereinafter cited as UNCLOS III, OFF. REC.] 214, 215.

[6] United States of America, Draft articles for a chapter on the economic zone and the continental shelf, Art. 12, UN Doc. A/CONF.62/C.2/L.47 (1974), 3 UNCLOS III, OFF. REC. at 222, 223.

[7] Draft articles, note 5 *supra,* Art. 12.

[8] UN Doc. A/CONF.62/WP.8/pt.II, Art. 50, paras. 1 and 2 (1975), 4 UNCLOS III, OFF. REC. at 160.

ditions, laws and regulations [to be established by it], give other States access to the surplus of the allowable catch," when it "does not have the capacity to harvest the entire allowable catch" (Article 62, paragraph 2). In the proposal regarding a 12-mile fishery zone, which was rejected at UNCLOS II because it failed to gain the required two-thirds majority (though there were 54 votes in favor, with 28 against and 5 abstentions),[9] it was stated that traditional foreign fishing should be guaranteed, but that it was still to be phased out sooner or later unless guaranteed by concessions granted at the discretion of the coastal state. However, under the 200-mile EEZ, foreign fishing will be categorically guaranteed for the surplus of the allowable catch when the coastal state cannot itself "harvest the entire allowable catch."

It is important to note that the coastal state's capacity to harvest living resources may not always be meant to depend solely on the capital and technology of its national economy. Each coastal state is free to introduce foreign capital and to obtain technical assistance from foreign nations, and it is also free to allow any foreign nations or foreign enterprises it chooses to engage in fishing activities through concessionary agreements and to secure the maximum of the total allowable catch for itself, even though it might not wish to use this catch for the consumption of its own nationals.

Was it the intention of these provisions that the expression "does *not have the capacity* to harvest" might mean "does *not care* to harvest"? After all, fishing not only is carried out for the livelihood of fishing villages on the coast, or for the supply of animal protein for the nationals of the coastal state, but also is a part of the national industry—serving both home and foreign markets—and must be looked at as well from the angle of the labor or social policy of the coastal state. Thus, how can one say with any assurance that even the "least developed" coastal state does not have the capacity, or does not care, to harvest its entire allowable catch? If this interpretation is correct, any least developed country may be considered always to have the *capacity* to harvest the total allowable catch.

Access of Other States to the Surplus. As suggested before, other states are given access to the surplus of the allowable catch only through agreements or other arrangements. Conclusion of these agreements or other arrangements may be extremely difficult. The 1982 Convention suggests that, in giving access to other states, the coastal state should take all relevant factors into account, of which the following are specified concretely:

> the significance of the living resources of the area to the economy of the coastal State concerned and its other national interests, the provisions of articles 69 and 70 [relating to landlocked states and geographically disadvantaged states], the requirements of developing States in the subregion or region in harvesting part of the surplus and the need to minimize economic dislocation in States whose nationals have habitually fished in the zone or which have made substantial efforts in research and identification of stocks [Article 62, paragraph 3].

[9] UNCLOS II, OFF. REC., note 2 *supra*, at 30.

It is not clear how the significance of the living resources of the area to the economy of the coastal state and its other national interests will be relevant to the allocation of the surplus among other states. In addition, the criteria for allocating the surplus to other states will be extremely difficult to determine. After all, how can the coastal state take these relevant factors into account, and with what "other State," and what "agreements or other arrangements" is the coastal state going to have? It is surely hard to imagine that a coastal state that "does not have the capacity to harvest the entire allowable catch" will be ready and able to engage in so complex an exercise.

Surplus for Landlocked and Geographically Disadvantaged States. Access to the surplus is particularly guaranteed to landlocked states and geographically disadvantaged states, the more so if they are developing nations (Articles 69 and 70). Apart from some technical difficulties in drawing the line between developed nations and developing nations, application of this provision will be somewhat difficult if there are two or more coastal states in the same subregion or region. The landlocked states or the geographically disadvantaged states would have to find out in whose EEZ they would have the right to fish and, if they participated in exploiting the EEZ of two or more states, what percentage they would share. Furthermore, the guarantee of "the right to participate on an equitable basis" (Article 69, paragraph 1; Article 70, paragraph 1) does not seem to ensure a share of the catch equal to that allocated to other states. The application of equity will be especially problematic in view of the various factors to be taken into account whenever more than two handicapped nations participate in exploiting the EEZ of more than two coastal states.

While the terms and modalities of such participation shall be established by the state concerned, it will not be easy to decide which country "the State concerned" will be, even by considering the relevant economic and geographical circumstances of all the states concerned. Let us take one landlocked state as an example. For Switzerland, the adjoining coastal states may be West Germany, France, and Italy, but it would be most impracticable for West Germany, situated on the North Sea, Italy on the Mediterranean Sea, and France on the Atlantic and Mediterranean to negotiate with Switzerland on a regional level about its participation in exploiting living resources. In addition, the requirement that other states may only participate through agreements is considered to mean that the exercise of such a right by a landlocked state might depend on the consent of the adjoining state concerned.

One may well be surprised to find a provision in the 1982 Convention that restricts transfer of the rights of landlocked or geographically disadvantaged states to third states or their nationals for the purpose of participating in the exploitation of an appropriate part of the surplus "by lease or licence, by establishing joint ventures or in any other manner which has the effect of such transfer" (Article 72, paragraph 1). Was it not originally intended, as reflected in the proposals of the 22 landlocked and geographically disadvantaged states[10]

[10] Afghanistan, Austria, Belgium, Bhutan, Bolivia, Botswana, Finland, Iraq, Laos, Lesotho, Luxembourg, Mali, Nepal, the Netherlands, Paraguay, Singapore, Swaziland, Sweden, Switzer-

at UNCLOS III in 1974, that participation of these states in the exploitation of living resources might be permissible, *inter alia,* in the form of joint collaboration ventures? If the rights of these states are limited by Article 72, the raison d'être of those provisions conferring special status on these states will be very doubtful, considering that they may legitimately wish to participate in fishing for the sake not only of supplying animal protein to their own populations, but also of increasing national employment opportunities or even of developing marine fishing as an integral part of their national industry.

Fishery Regulations Unamenable to Dispute Settlement

As previously suggested, it would be extremely difficult to implement the whole scheme requiring the coastal state to determine the allowable catch for the purpose of conservation and its capacity to harvest the fishery resources, and to give access to the surplus of the allowable catch to other states, in view of the fact that the ideas themselves are not always well defined in the Convention. However ideal they may appear, the coastal state's obligations in the EEZ in respect of conservation and optimum utilization of fishery resources will surely result in great difficulties when put into practice, and disputes are bound to occur if other states protest the failure of the coastal state to conserve living resources, its arbitrary refusal to determine the allowable catch or its harvesting capacity, or its refusal to allocate EEZ resources among the states concerned.

Such disputes may be settled, if not by negotiation, then by recourse to any procedure agreed upon by the parties concerned or by their submission to the conciliation procedure (Article 297, paragraph 3(b)). However, it should be noted that the Conciliation Commission cannot substitute its discretion for that of the coastal state (Article 297, paragraph 3(c)) and, at any rate, the report drawn up by the Commission cannot be binding (Annex V, Article 7 (2)). In addition, the lack of any substantive law (as evidenced in the ambiguity of the concept of surplus of allowable catch and the lack of criteria for granting other states access to the surplus) will greatly hinder the settlement of disputes of this nature. Yet under the 1982 United Nations Convention, such disputes are exempted from compulsory settlement by the four different categories of tribunal (Article 297, paragraph 1). The coastal state is not obliged to submit to compulsory settlement

> any dispute relating to its sovereign rights with respect to the living resources in the exclusive economic zone or their exercise, including its discretionary powers for determining the allowable catch, its harvesting capacity, the allocation of surpluses to other States and the terms and conditions established in its conservation and management laws and regulations [Article 297, paragraph 3(a)].

---

land, Uganda, Upper Volta, Zambia, Draft articles on participation of land-locked and other geographically disadvantaged States in the exploration and exploitation of the living and non-living resources in the area beyond the territorial sea, particularly Art. 4, UN Doc. A/CONF.62/C.2/L.39 (1974), 3 UNCLOS III, Off. Rec. at 216.

II. Exercise of Fisheries Jurisdiction in the EEZ

Violations of Regulations in the Zone

Arrest of Offenders. Although, as stated above, there are some limitations on the coastal state's power to prescribe the contents of fishery regulations, the authority of the coastal state to enforce those regulations in the EEZ is in nature equivalent to that in the territorial sea. The coastal state will have jurisdiction over all such activities, whether carried out by its own nationals or by foreigners, and will apply its legislation governing these activities to any and all nationals. Any person charged with a violation of these laws and regulations may well be seized by the police of the coastal state.

Disputes may arise when coastal authorities arrest a vessel for alleged violation of a coastal state's regulations enacted in conformity with the Convention. The captain of the arrested vessel may allege that while the vessel was fishing in compliance with the coastal regulations, their enforcement was not properly carried out. Yet such appeals will have to be primarily disposed of before the judicial authorities of the coastal state, and not only as a result of the application of the rule of local remedies. For in the Convention it is precisely those disputes concerning law enforcement activities in regard to the exercise of sovereign rights or jurisdiction in the EEZ which a state may exclude from compulsory procedures (Article 298, paragraph 1(b)). Thus, an incident arising out of enforcement of the coastal state's fishery regulations, such as the boarding, inspection, and arrest of foreign vessels, may not be unilaterally submitted by the flag state of the arrested vessel to any procedure of compulsory settlement, unless it is claimed that such measures were taken outside the EEZ.

Punishment of Offenders. Any person charged with violating the fishery regulations of the coastal state may be punished, if found guilty, by the courts of that state. Yet there is a restriction on the type of punishment in the 1982 Convention. In its judicial proceedings against the arrested vessel and crew, the coastal state is obliged to impose a financial penalty only (Article 73, paragraph 3). However, since there is no international standard for such financial penalties, it seems that the degree of these penalties would fall exclusively within the domestic jurisdiction of each coastal state, unless otherwise provided for in international law.

On this point, furthermore, an ambiguity of interpretation remains as to whether the restriction to a financial penalty should apply only to those foreign vessels allowed by the coastal state to fish the surplus of the allowable catch under Articles 62, 69, or 70 or, more broadly, to vessels that might not have been authorized at all to fish in the EEZ. While no positive indication seems to have been given in either the provision or the drafting process of UNCLOS III, it seems likely that in practice the first interpretation will be followed.

Prompt Release of Detained Vessels

It is characteristic of the 1982 Convention that the coastal state is obliged, upon the posting of reasonable bond or other security, promptly to release a vessel and crew that it has arrested for the alleged violation of coastal fishery regulations (Article 73, paragraph 2). This concept was introduced because it was feared that unreasonably prolonged detention of fishing vessels might cause an enormous amount of damage to the fishing industry; but it will certainly cause some difficult problems in practice.

Obligation of Prompt Release. Firstly, whatever the reason may be for the supposed violation of the coastal state's regulations by foreign fishing vessels, the prolonged detention of these vessels will itself constitute a violation of the Convention by the coastal state; thus, the coastal state would be responsible for noncompliance with the Convention. The Convention suggests a particular mechanism that is of interest in the legal sense. Where the flag state of the detained vessel alleges that the coastal state has failed, neglected, or refused to comply with the provision for the prompt release of the vessel and its crew, upon the posting of a reasonable bond or other financial security, "the question of release from detention may be submitted to any court or tribunal agreed upon" by the two states in question (Article 292, paragraph 1).

But which court or tribunal should be the one agreed upon by the states concerned? Theoretically, it is possible to consider a domestic court of the coastal state. However, since the competence for the release of the arrested vessels may in most cases fall to the court of first instance of the coastal state, it would be extremely inappropriate to bring the case before another domestic judicial body of that state. In addition, it would be quite impracticable to institute any new tribunal within such a short period as 10 days from the time of detention, which is the time suggested for reaching such an agreement between the states concerned.

If such an agreement is not reached within 10 days of the commencement of detention, the question of release may be brought before any of the four courts or tribunals accepted by the detaining state under Article 287 or, if the parties do not otherwise agree, before the International Tribunal for the Law of the Sea (Article 292, paragraph 1). As stated in Article 292, paragraph 3, "[t]he court or tribunal . . . shall deal only with the question of release, without prejudice to the merits of any case before the appropriate domestic forum against the vessel, its owner or its crew"; these four courts or tribunals are not expected to pronounce on the merits of whether the arrest of a foreign vessel for its alleged violation of the coastal regulations would be justified under international law or not, or whether the coastal regulations are consonant with the requirements of the Convention or not. On the contrary, they are simply expected to order the prompt release of the vessels that have been arrested.

As in the case of financial punishment, the author finds it likely that the obligation of prompt release will in practice be applied only to those vessels which have been authorized by the coastal state to fish the surplus of the resources.

Reasonable Bond or Other Security. If an arrested vessel has been detained by the coastal authorities and not promptly released, this could either constitute an actual violation of the Convention by the coastal state, however justifiable the actual arrest might have been, or be justified by it only on the grounds that the bond or other financial security it has deemed reasonable and demanded has not been deposited by the arrested vessel. In turn, such a failure to post bond could be defended on the ground that the required amount is not in fact reasonable. This leads us to suggest that the court or tribunal may only be expected to pronounce on whether the bond or other financial security demanded by the coastal state is reasonable or not.

Yet the arrested vessel is to be promptly released on the understanding that the captain or owner will be tried before a judicial court of the coastal state in due course. In fact, however, the appearance of the captain or owner of the arrested vessel at the judicial proceedings of the coastal state that has arrested the vessel is highly unlikely. In addition, no hint is given in the United Nations Convention of what is "reasonable bond or other security." It must be pointed out that the reasonableness of a bond or other security can never be proved from an objective point of view. Thus, the amount of the bond or other security might in practice be fixed by each coastal state at an amount equivalent to the fine that might be imposed by its courts at a later stage. In other words, any fine constituting final punishment will in practice be "preempted" in the shape of a bond or other security for arrested vessels, which are to be promptly released, while any return for the purpose of a court appearance will be improbable.

Indeed, no rules exist in international law that suggest a universal standard for fines to be imposed for violations of coastal regulations by foreign vessels, so that it would be extremely difficult for any court or tribunal to carry out the suggestion in the 1982 Convention that it determine the reasonableness of the bond or other financial security to be deposited. It is often said that the International Tribunal for the Law of the Sea will play an important role in the matter—this is one reason among others advanced to justify establishing that institution—but one must reluctantly conclude that this is likely to prove a vain hope. The establishment of international standards through case law is after all a slow and uncertain process dependent on the good will of states. Thus, although a coastal state faithful to the 1982 United Nations Convention is expected promptly to release an arrested vessel or its crew, the dispute that may arise over the amount of bond or other security will certainly give rise to some difficult problems in connection with the functioning of the court or tribunal set up for the settlement of disputes.

III. High Seas Fisheries: Exercise of State Jurisdiction

The Principle of Nonexercise of State Jurisdiction

The measures to be taken for high seas fisheries must be agreed upon by the states concerned. The fishery regulations of any state can only apply to, and be enforced upon, a fishing vessel flying the flag of that state on the high seas, and the authority of a state cannot be exercised upon a vessel flying the flag of another nation. Because this basic scheme does not change under the United Nations Convention on the Law of the Sea, there will be hardly any disputes on the exercise of the competence or jurisdiction of any particular state as far as high seas fisheries are concerned. The mere attempt at exercising such competence will be tantamount to a clear violation of the basic principle of the freedom of the high seas. Even so, some provisions in the 1982 Convention appear to leave room for misunderstanding in this connection.

Some Ambiguities in Certain Provisions of the 1982 Convention

Both the 1958 Geneva Convention and the 1982 United Nations Convention equally provide for "the right [of all States] for their nationals to engage in fishing on the high seas" (Article 1(1) and Article 116, respectively), but the right to fish under the 1958 Convention, which was "subject . . . to the interests and the rights of coastal States as provided for in this Convention," is now redrafted in the 1982 Convention so as to be subject to "the rights and duties as well as the interests of coastal States provided for, *inter alia,* in article 63, paragraph 2, and articles 64 to 67" (Article 116(b)). Of course, concurrently with the establishment of the EEZ, the high seas have shrunk from their 1958 extent and will moreover offer fewer species—now consisting almost wholly of highly migratory varieties—for fishermen to harvest.

But, apart from that, the use of the expression "*inter alia*" could lead us to ask whether there are any rights and duties or interests of coastal states recognized in the 1982 Convention, other than those which are spelled out in the provisions mentioned above. It must be noted that the 1982 Convention is different in principle from the 1958 Convention, which, without putting forward the concept of the EEZ, provided that the coastal state was entitled to have some special or preferential rights in its coastal areas. Under the 1982 Convention, the coastal state is not granted, apart from the case of some species specifically mentioned in Articles 63–67, any competence or rights in fisheries beyond the EEZ. If this is the case, it is submitted that the expression "*inter alia*" surely gives rise to some doubts as to what lies behind this provision and its inspiration.

Furthermore, a sentence reading, "All States have the right for their nationals to engage in fishing on the high seas subject to . . . *duties* . . . of coastal States provided for, *inter alia,* in article 63, paragraph 2, and articles 64 to 67" (Article 116(b)) (emphasis of "duties" added), is bound to raise difficulties of interpretation. In the 1958 Convention there was no reference to the duty of the coastal state except for the general obligation in respect of conservation imposed equally on all states (Article 1, paragraph 2). On the other hand, the 1982 Convention, which in Article 63, paragraph 2 and Articles 64, 66, and 67 deals also with some species that migrate between the EEZ and the high seas, contains certain other requirements imposed on the coastal state as such. Yet these requirements are not such as to restrict "the right . . . to engage in fishing on the high seas" to the coastal state alone, but, with some exceptions in the case of anadromous stocks, amount to a total prohibition of high seas fishing by *all states* for anadromous and catadromous species (Article 66, paragraph 3(a) and Article 67, paragraph 2). The 1982

Convention speaks also of the duties of states concerned to come to agreement on conservation measures (Article 63, paragraph 2; Article 64) and in the exceptional cases involving anadromous stocks, on enforcement of regulations (Article 66, paragraph 3(d)). The Convention does not seem to contain any provision to contradict the principle that a vessel on the high seas is subject solely to the authority of its flag state. Hence, it is difficult to imagine the intended effect of the proviso that the right to fish is subject to "duties" of the coastal state. Indeed, the insertion of the word "duties" tends to obscure the nature and limits of the EEZ concept.

IV. High Seas Fisheries: Cooperation of States

Ambiguous Concept of Cooperation

A basic idea still inherent in the 1982 Convention is that any fishery regulations on the high seas may only be enacted by agreements among the states concerned. Yet some incomplete provisions in the Convention seem to be drawn from a somewhat ambiguous concept of the cooperation of states.

Management of Living Resources. The Convention suggests "co-operation of States in the conservation and management of living resources" of the high seas (Article 118). The reference to the "management" of living resources needs some explanation. The United States proposal on high seas fisheries[11] of 1974, which initiated this provision, mentioned cooperation of states not in the "management" but in the "exploitation" of living resources. The substitution of "management" in a preliminary text of 1975 (Informal Single Negotiating Text[12]) at UNCLOS III seems very important, and appears to be due to the fact that the optimum utilization of living resources is specifically mentioned in connection with the regime of the EEZ. However, the content of management is not defined concretely in connection with high seas fisheries in the Convention.

The duty of cooperation in this provision thus seems rather abstract, and there is no provision describing how it can be performed in a concrete way. Furthermore, in the second sentence of this article, which reads, "States . . . shall enter into negotiations with a view to taking the measures necessary for the conservation of the living resources concerned," the concept of management is ignored, and the subregional fisheries organizations in the third sentence exist only for the purpose of conservation. The drafting of this article seems very imprecise.

Determination of the Allowable Catch. The following provision is found: "In determining the allowable catch and establishing other conservation measures for the living resources in the high seas, States shall . . ." (Article 119, paragraph 1). The words "determining the allowable catch" appear rather strange because the concept of the allowable catch for high seas fisheries appears for

[11] United States of America, Draft article for inclusion in a chapter on the high seas—living resources, UN Doc. A/CONF.62/C.2/L.80 (1974), 3 UNCLOS III, Off. Rec. at 239.

[12] Note 8 *supra,* Art. 105.

the first time only in this provision. Mention should have been made that determination of the allowable catch is to be one of the conservation measures for high seas fisheries. In the United States proposal of 1974, on which this provision was based, it was provided that "States, acting individually and through regional and international fisheries organizations, have the duty to apply . . . conservation measures," and as one of the conservation measures mentioned there was a reference to the establishment of the allowable catch.[13] This reference is no longer found in the 1982 Convention. Considering the drafting process, this provision thus seems to be incomplete.

Nondiscrimination against Fishermen of Other States. The provision that "States concerned shall ensure that conservation measures and their implementation do not discriminate in form or in fact against the fishermen of any State" (Article 119, paragraph 3), which also originated in the United States proposal[14] of 1974, is not at all clear. A similar provision had appeared in Article 7, paragraph 2(*c*) of the 1958 Convention, in relation to the possibility that unilateral measures might in exceptional cases be taken by a coastal state outside its territorial sea (*cf. id.*, paragraph 1). The present Convention, however, is quite different, for, having made provision for the EEZ, it does not contemplate any situation in which a coastal state would take *unilateral* measures affecting foreign vessels on the high seas beyond its 200-mile EEZ. Where vessels of two or more states are engaged in fishing in the vast expanses of the high seas, the new Convention provides that conservation measures should be taken only by agreement among the states concerned, while only the flag state will be entitled to enforce conservation measures on a vessel. Thus, it is very difficult to see how a situation could arise in which the adoption or implementation of conservation measures could be so selective as to discriminate in form or fact against the fishermen of any state. One may therefore regard Article 119, paragraph 3 as technically superfluous; as an admonition *ex abundanti cautela,* however, it may be found, especially by minor exploiting states, to serve some useful purpose.

Conservation and Management of Marine Mammals. There is a further provision in the section on conservation and management of the living resources of the high seas that may be found difficult to interpret properly, namely, Article 120, which provides: "Article 65 also applies to the conservation and management of marine mammals in the high seas." Article 65 is a provision partly relating to the right of a coastal state or the competence of an international organization "to prohibit, limit or regulate the exploitation of marine mammals more strictly than provided for" in part V on the EEZ, which originated in the EEZ proposal of the United States[15] of 1974. There, however, the provision began with the words "notwithstanding the provisions of this chapter [EEZ] with respect to full utilization of living resources." It may be possible to suggest separate treatment for marine mammals and other living resources in the EEZ. Yet even Article 65, which lacks both the original words

[13] Note 11 *supra,* para. 2.

[14] *Id.,* para. 2(d).

[15] Note 6 *supra,* Art. 20.

suggested by the United States and any further provision defining the right of a coastal state or the competence of an international organization to that effect, seems to be equivocal. At any rate, Article 65, the provision relating to marine mammals in the EEZ, will acquire meaning only when optimum utilization of these resources is to be ensured. However appropriate this may be as regards the EEZ, no duty of states for optimum utilization of high seas resources, or marine mammals of the high seas, is suggested in the 1982 Convention. Thus, the provision seems in context to be devoid of any sense.

Conservation of Highly Migratory Species. Mention should be made of the duty of states under the new Convention to cooperate with a view to conservation and optimum utilization of certain highly migratory species. Article 64 concerning these species may probably be better understood by looking at its drafting process. The Informal Single Negotiating Text of 1975, in which the existing text of Article 64 originated, first defined the rights of the coastal state over these species in its EEZ and then suggested the cooperation of that state with other states if those species were found beyond the EEZ.[16] If the present text is to be interpreted along these lines in spite of the equivocal drafting, this provision would have found a more appropriate place not in the section on the EEZ but rather under part VII on the high seas, in connection with cooperation on high seas fisheries.

Disputes Concerning Cooperation on High Seas Fisheries

If there is any difference of opinion among nations on high seas fisheries, this will simply be due to failure in cooperation on joint conservation measures. The 1958 Convention suggested a specific conciliation body, called a "Special Commission," in case negotiations broke down. This machinery was never used, apparently because the states concerned were able to come to successful agreement by negotiation, taking into account not only scientific data (in terms of resource conservation) but also various political or diplomatic factors, or because they simply did not have sufficient overlapping interests to provide an incentive to agreement or compromise. The actual situation is not different from the time of the 1958 Convention. Under the 1982 United Nations Convention it is simply the general provisions concerning the settlement of disputes that shall apply to such a dispute on high seas fisheries. Who is to determine whether and when negotiations for the conservation of fishery resources have failed? One may doubt whether there will be an incentive for any state to resort to dispute settlement in order to reach an agreement on joint measures for high seas fisheries, in view of the fact that, unless otherwise agreed by states concerned, the state will continue to be free to fish on the high seas without restriction.

One must always bear in mind that fishing is carried out by fishermen not only for their own consumption, but also for financial profit or for the social or political interest of the state, and conservation of the limited amount of

[16] Note 8 *supra,* Art. 53, paras. 1 and 2.

renewable resources, a subject of fishery science, will not in itself yield any guiding principles to solve the thorny political and social problems inherent in these facts. That being so, it will inevitably be the power of diplomatic negotiation of each nation, not any legal principle, that will be determinant in settling the difference of views among nations with regard to the allocation of fishery resources. Unlike fisheries disputes in the EEZ, disputes concerning high seas fisheries, it is true, are not exempted from compulsory settlement under the 1982 Convention. Yet, while the persistent difference of views among nations will make a mutually satisfactory solution difficult, their dispute will hardly be of so predominantly legal a character as to be suitable for submission to any judicial body. Once conservation has been ensured, the regulation of competition for the high seas catch is surely, under the present regime, a political, not a legal, concern.

In fact, the 1958 High Seas Fisheries Convention providing for the obligation to negotiate among the states concerned was virtually ignored in practice for the past 20 years, and there have been few instances of international agreements or national legislation referring to it. The basic problems facing us in respect of high seas fisheries concern the search for universally agreed principles according to which a limited amount of these resources should be allocated among nations, all of whom will undoubtedly clamor for greater shares.[17] Just as the 1958 Convention did not provide any solution to the problems of allocation of fishery resources among states, thus failing to be implemented in any concrete case, so the 1982 Convention—even allowing that, with its accent on the EEZ, it puts high seas fisheries in a rather different context—has likewise overlooked the importance of these basic problems of allocation by simply suggesting cooperation among nations for the conservation of these resources. The institution for the settlement of disputes, if requested to tender its views on conservation of high seas fisheries, will inevitably be faced with the difficult issues surrounding the philosophy of fishery resource allocation.

V. CONCLUSION

In concluding this article, the author is aware that he may be blamed for not supplying a solution to the problems in question, having simply raised some somewhat controversial issues.

The concept of the EEZ was introduced in concrete form in early 1973 at the Asian-African Legal Consultative Committee,[18] and, after some debate at the Sea-bed Committee in 1973 and at UNCLOS III in 1974, it became in

[17] In this part the author is also suggesting his long-standing view expressed in his previous works, as referred to in note 1 *supra*, and, in addition, *Sharing of Ocean Resources—Unresolved Issues in the Law of the Sea*, in THE MANAGEMENT OF HUMANITY'S RESOURCES: THE LAW OF THE SEA 49 (Hague Academy of International Law/UN University Workshop, 1981).

[18] Revised Draft Articles on the Exclusive Economic Zone (submitted by Kenya as Member of the AALCC), ASIAN-AFRICAN LEGAL CONSULTATIVE COMMITTEE, REPORT OF THE 14TH SESSION (New Delhi, Jan. 10–18, 1973), at 61.

1975 a firm policy of the Informal Single Negotiating Text of UNCLOS III. While the basic idea prevailed and was established very rapidly, no concrete provisions concerning this concept received any extensive examination or debate at UNCLOS III. In addition, since the institution of the EEZ was conceded as an essential right of the coastal state, the predominant thinking was that any dispute between states regarding it should not be amenable to compulsory settlement. Despite the fact that the concept has now been widely accepted as a permanent institution of international law, the relevant provisions seem bound to invite many difficulties of interpretation once any concrete problems arise. Hence, however cut and dried they may seem, the type of regime that will be developed by future practice remains to be seen.

The provisions of the 1982 Convention concerning the rights to high seas fisheries, the obligations of states regarding the conservation of fishery resources, and the cooperation among states for their management and conservation in that area are derived from the provisions of the 1958 High Seas Fisheries Convention. The new institution of the EEZ, however, proceeded from quite different doctrinal bases, and it seems all too likely that it will have repercussions on high seas fishery policies that will lead to some confusion. In addition, no attention was paid to the question why the 1958 High Seas Fisheries Convention seemed unable to function properly, or why that Convention was not applied in practice—either internationally or nationally—over the past two decades. The 1982 Convention does not even hint at the question of the allocation of high seas fishery resources (a subject wholly unresolved in 1958). Meanwhile, with regard to seabed mineral resources, a new international regime of the deep ocean floor has been emerging from the discussions of UNCLOS III for international control of these resources based upon the basic concept of the common heritage of mankind. Who can say that the same trend will not be followed in regard to ocean fishing? Surely, discussions similar to those now taking place on seabed mineral resources will eventually be held on the new concept of the common heritage of mankind as applicable to ocean fishing.

THE EXTRATERRITORIAL APPLICATION OF THE GERMAN ANTITRUST LAWS

*By David J. Gerber**

The extraterritorial reach of national economic regulation, particularly of antitrust laws, is one of the most controversial topics in the international legal community, largely because that community has failed to develop jurisdictional principles that both accommodate the regulatory needs of regulating states and are discriminating enough to avoid impinging on the legitimate interests of other states. As a result, international conflicts related to the assertion of jurisdiction have greatly increased in both frequency and intensity.[1]

Assertions of extraterritorial jurisdiction by the United States have been the focal point of the controversy. Until the 1970's, the United States was the only country with both well-developed and strictly enforced antitrust laws and a legal regime permitting broad application of those laws to foreign conduct. Consequently, it was the only country with significant experience in applying antitrust provisions to conduct occurring outside its territorial boundaries.

Outside the United States, the extraterritoriality issue has been seen largely in a defensive context—namely, how to respond to excessive jurisdictional claims by the United States. These problems have reached critical dimensions. While American courts and commentators flail about in search of principles to use in grappling with jurisdictional issues,[2] major allies have ceased trying to cooperate with the United States to avoid excessive conflicts of jurisdiction and have turned to so-called blocking legislation to attempt to protect their nationals and enterprises from the reach of United States antitrust laws.[3]

The extraordinary difficulties that American law has encountered in this area may be ascribed to two major causes: (1) an inability to define more clearly and concretize the "effects" principle, which is the basis for extending American jurisdiction over foreign conduct; and (2) a failure adequately to take into account the sovereign interests of other states.

Recent West German law developments illuminate the dimensions of these two problems and provide guideposts toward useful solutions. In recent years,

* Associate Professor, IIT/Chicago-Kent College of Law.

[1] *See, e.g.*, Samie, *The Extraterritorial Enforcement of United States Antitrust Laws: The British Reaction*, 16 INT'L LAW. 313 (1982).

[2] *See, e.g.*, Timberlane v. Bank of America, 549 F.2d 597 (9th Cir. 1976); Mannington Mills, Inc. v. Congoleum Corp., 595 F.2d 1287 (3d Cir. 1979); and Dominicus Americana Bohio v. Gulf & Western Indus. Inc., 473 F.Supp. 680 (S.D.N.Y. 1979).

[3] *See, e.g.*, Lowe, *Blocking Extraterritorial Jurisdiction: The British Protection of Trading Interests Act*, 75 AJIL 257 (1981); Toms, *The French Response to the Extraterritorial Application of United States Antitrust Laws*, 15 INT'L LAW. 585 (1981); Herzog, *The 1980 French Law on Documents and Information*, 75 AJIL 382 (1981).

German antitrust provisions have become stricter in many respects than their United States counterparts, and, especially in regard to international mergers, they are enforced at least as vigorously as are U.S. laws. Moreover, the extraterritorial reach of German antitrust law is, at least arguably, longer than that of U.S. antitrust law. Germany's experience is thus highly relevant to the American dilemma, especially because German law has taken important steps to alleviate the two above-mentioned causes of the American difficulties. Specifically, Germany has placed conceptual limits on the "effects" principle and used public international law to devise means of taking into account the interests of countries affected by extraterritoriality.

This article therefore has two main purposes: to describe the extraterritoriality issue in the German context,[4] and to relate the German experience with extraterritoriality to the pressing need to find international law solutions to an issue laden with the potential for ever-increasing international conflict.[5]

I. The Context: German Antitrust Law

In order to understand the extraterritorial application of German antitrust law, it is important to be aware of several basic characteristics of the German antitrust law system.[6]

German antitrust law operates within the framework of the civil law tradition. The principles of law are generally to be found in the codelike structure of the Law against Restraints on Competition (the GWB) rather than in court decisions.[7] This statutory orientation of German antitrust law contrasts sharply with the lack of systematic structure in United States antitrust law. Moreover, it corresponds with a far greater role for the legislative branch in German antitrust law than is the case in the United States.

The basic principles on which the GWB is based, however, derive from American experience. As the first true antitrust statute in German history, the GWB became law in 1957 after years of careful study of U.S. antitrust law by German scholars. German antitrust law thus has a much shorter history

[4] Not to be forgotten here are the needs of practitioners who are, or should be, aware of the practical importance of understanding the reach of German antitrust law. Any company that participates in an acquisition or joint venture involving either a German company *or* a company that is doing business in the German market may find itself affected by German antitrust rules.

[5] The issue of the extraterritorial application of German antitrust law is both substantively and procedurally separate and distinct from the application of the antitrust law of the European Community. The provisions of the Treaty of Rome, however, have been interpreted to require that the actions of national cartel authorities may "not jeopardize the uniform application throughout the Common Market of the Community cartel rule." Wilhelm v. Bundeskartellamt, 1969 ECR 1, [1969–1970 Transfer Binder] COMMON MKT. REP. (CCH) ¶8056, at 7867. *See also* B. HAWK, UNITED STATES, COMMON MARKET AND INTERNATIONAL ANTITRUST 476 (1979).

[6] For a detailed description of German antitrust law in English, see K. STOCKMANN & V. STRAUCH, FEDERAL REPUBLIC OF GERMANY, 5 WORLD LAW OF COMPETITION (J. Kalinowski ed. 1981). For a leading German textbook, see F. RITTNER, WIRTSCHAFTSRECHT (1979).

[7] Gesetz gegen Wettbewerbsbeschränkungen, 1957 Bundesgesetzblatt [BGBl] I 1081 (July 27) [hereinafter cited as GWB]. For a useful German-English presentation of the text of the statute as well as a short commentary, see A. RIESENKAMPFF & J. GRES, LAW AGAINST RESTRAINTS OF COMPETITION (1977, Supp. 1980).

than does American antitrust law, with the result that little, if any, of it is "cast in stone."

The administration of the antitrust laws in Germany—and thus the constellation of forces affecting the development of the law—is also significantly different from the American system. One major difference is the fact that there are relatively few private antitrust suits under the German system, although the statute permits such suits under certain circumstances.[8] This has particular importance for the extraterritoriality issue because it means that in most types of cases, including merger cases, the problems created by private suits, which have helped to confound American efforts in this area,[9] play little or no role.

German antitrust law is enforced primarily by a government agency, the Bundeskartellamt (Federal Cartel Office or FCO), which can issue orders prohibiting violations of the statute and setting fines for such violations. The decisions of the FCO have a distinctly judicial character. Its actions must be approved by organs within it that are charged with judicial impartiality. As a result, the decisions of the FCO are often accorded interpretive weight similar to that of judicial decisions.

The decisions of the FCO are appealable to the regular courts. Since the FCO is located in Berlin, appeals are made to the Federal Appeals Court for Berlin, the Kammergericht (KG). By virtue of this arrangement, the KG has taken on special importance in the antitrust area. In reviewing the decisions of the FCO, the KG and the Supreme Court for Civil Matters (Bundesgerichtshof or BGH) both view their roles as that of interpreters of the will of the legislature. They generally do not consider their roles as including the search for "lawmaking" solutions.[10]

II. The Structure of the Extraterritoriality Issue

The American attorney who attempts to understand the extraterritoriality issue in its German setting is immediately faced with a conceptual structure that can be misleading. Consequently, it is necessary to delve briefly into some of the differences in the structure of the extraterritoriality issue in the two legal systems.

In the United States the antitrust laws may be applied to conduct occurring outside the country whenever the court has *power* over the parties (jurisdiction in personam) as well as authority to adjudicate the subject matter. These two concepts of jurisdiction are seen as unrelated. The extent of personal jurisdiction is a domestic issue, measured primarily according to due process prin-

[8] Private suits are permitted in cases where there has been a violation of a provision that is intended to provide so-called individual protection (*Individualschutz*)—*i.e.*, protection of individual competitors rather than protection of the institution of competition itself. *See* GWB §35.

[9] Many of the recent American cases involving extraterritorial application of the antitrust laws have been private suits. *See Panel Discussion on Antitrust and International Trade*, 49 ANTITRUST L.J. 1217, 1221 (1980), and cases cited.

[10] *See generally* Rittner, *Das Ermessen der Kartellbehörde*, in FESTSCHRIFT FÜR HEINZ KAUFMANN 307 (1972).

ciples. It is not related to the question whether there may be international law limits on the right of American courts to apply American antitrust law extraterritorially, an issue usually treated within the context of subject matter jurisdiction.[11]

The role of public international law in the application of the American antitrust laws is vague and uncertain. In *United States v. Aluminum Co. of America* (*Alcoa*),[12] Judge Learned Hand stated:

> [W]e are not to read general words, such as those in this [Sherman] Act, without regard to the limitations customarily observed by nations upon the exercise of their powers. . . . We should not impute to Congress an intent to punish all whom its courts can catch, for conduct which has no consequences within the United States. . . . [W]e shall assume that the Act does not cover agreements, even though intended to affect imports or exports, unless its performance is shown actually to have had some effect upon them.[13]

Since Congress could not be presumed to have violated norms of international law, and since international law requires domestic effects as a basis for prescriptive jurisdiction over foreign conduct, the effects principle was incorporated in American law. The role of international law is thus indirect and framed in the context of congressional intent.

What, then, of situations where the effects principle provides a jurisdictional base, but the application of U.S. antitrust laws to foreign conduct could lead to conflicts with other nations? The answer in American law relies on the concept of comity.[14] American courts take the position that where the United States has a basis for the exercise of jurisdiction, it has a right to exercise that jurisdiction, and there is no further legal issue. Nevertheless, a court may decide, as a matter of comity, to refrain from exercising that right in cases of potential conflict.[15]

Under German law the conceptual structure of the extraterritoriality issue is fundamentally different.[16] The analysis centers on two main questions. First, does the relevant choice-of-law rule mandate the application of German law? And second, would the application of German law violate public international law?

In the antitrust context the relevant choice-of-law provision is section 98(2) of the GWB, which provides that the GWB is to be applied wherever a restraint of competition has domestic effects.[17] Thus, the effects principle is explicitly anchored in the GWB.

[11] *See generally* Ongman, *Be No Longer a Chaos: Constructing a Normative Theory of the Sherman Act's Extraterritorial Scope,* 71 NW. U.L. REV. 733, 735 (1977).

[12] 148 F.2d 416 (2d Cir. 1945).

[13] *Id.* at 444.

[14] *See generally* Yntema, *The Comity Doctrine,* 65 MICH. L. REV. 9 (1966).

[15] *See* Maier, *Extraterritorial Jurisdiction at a Crossroads: An Intersection between Public and Private International Law,* 76 AJIL 280 (1982).

[16] For a comparison, see I. SCHWARTZ, DEUTSCHES INTERNATIONALES KARTELLRECHT 154–57 (1962).

[17] For text, see text accompanying note 22 *infra.*

If the restraint of competition has the required effects, the next question is whether international law prohibits the application of the GWB to the particular circumstances of the case. This issue must be taken much more seriously by German courts than by their American counterparts, for the German Constitution mandates that general international law binds the legislature and the courts.[18] For years the requirements of international law were considered to have been met by virtue of the fact that the effects principle was an approved basis of jurisdiction under international law. This answer is no longer sufficient, however, and German law now requires that additional international law requirements be met that are designed to avoid conflicts with the sovereignty of foreign states.

Where the conflict-of-laws rule mandates the application of the GWB, and international law does not prohibit the exercise of jurisdiction, a German court will apply German antitrust law, provided that the court is "internationally competent" (*zuständig*).[19] The concept of international competence performs a function similar to that of the concept of personal jurisdiction in American law. It is not to be confused with the issue of the GWB's extraterritorial reach. It refers to the requirement that the court have a sufficient relationship to the facts of a given case to adjudicate the issues.[20] This is determined solely by reference to domestic law, which focuses on factors such as whether the defendant has sufficient contacts with the state to be subjected to its judicial power.[21]

III. THE "EFFECTS" CONCEPT CODIFIED AND PURIFIED

The focal point of the extraterritoriality issue in German antitrust law is easily located. The effects principle is codified in section 98(2) of the GWB: "This statute applies to all restraints of competition which have an effect within the territorial scope of the statute, even when they are caused outside of the territorial scope of the statute." The extraterritorial reach of the German antitrust laws centers on the construction and application of this provision.

The legislative history of section 98(2) is not extensive, but it leaves little doubt as to what the legislature intended.[22] According to the report of the committee of the federal legislature (Bundestag) that proposed the GWB, "The committee intends to achieve with the very general and broad version of the last half-sentence [of section 98(2)] that all restraints of competition that have domestic effects fall within the statute, regardless of where and by

[18] *See* GRUNDGESETZ art. 25 (W. Ger.).

[19] *See generally* G. KEGEL, INTERNATIONALES PRIVATRECHT, ch. 22 (4th ed. 1977); and J. SCHRÖDER, INTERNATIONALE ZUSTÄNDIGKEIT (1971).

[20] *See generally* A. HELDRICH, INTERNATIONALE ZUSTÄNDIGKEIT UND ANWENDBARES RECHT (1969).

[21] The court must also have "jurisdiction" (*Gerichtsbarkeit*). In the German view, however, jurisdiction is an accessory of sovereignty and exists generally, except as limited by public international law. Thus, it should not be confused with American concepts of jurisdiction. *See generally* I. SCHWARTZ, *supra* note 16, at 138.

[22] The legislative history is reviewed in *id.* at 17–21.

whom such restraints were agreed upon or caused."[23] All "restraints of competition that have domestic effects" were thus intended to fall within the statute.

The only limitations on the scope of extraterritoriality mentioned by the committee were (1) practical limitations relating to the international competence of German courts to adjudicate some foreign-related cases, and (2) the limitations of international law. The committee stated:

> The possibilities for the cartel officials to take action against such restraints will obviously depend on whether the participants in such agreements are represented within the area of application of this statute by statutory representatives, attorneys in fact, or agents and whether the participant enterprises are, according to the principles of international law, subject to the jurisdiction of the Federal Republic and whether German law is applicable to the agreements.[24]

The committee, however, does not appear to have expressed any specific ideas about what the limitations deriving from international law might involve.

The scope of section 98(2) is intended to be extremely broad. It fails, in fact, to limit the "effects" concept in any way, and it thus can be said to contain a "pure" effects principle, completely shorn of limiting concepts. Moreover, section 98(2) appears to be the only codification of a "pure" effects doctrine.[25]

The German effects principle is therefore broader than the American effects principle on which it was based.[26] Even in *Alcoa* the court required that the domestic effects had to be *intended* in order to establish a basis of jurisdiction.

The purity of the GWB's effects principle may, in part, be explained by the timing of its codification. Section 98(2) was part of the GWB when it was enacted in 1957. Since there had never before been a true antitrust statute in Germany, German legislators had had little experience with the problems of extraterritorial jurisdiction. Their main source of guidance in this context was the United States, but at that time American experience was also misleading. Following the precedent of the *Alcoa* case, the United States had been expanding the jurisdictional ambit of the antitrust laws for more than a decade, but the broad assertion of extraterritorial jurisdiction by the United States had not yet led to the widespread and intense resistance from affected countries that has developed in recent years.[27] This was most likely due to the

[23] BUNDESTAGSDRUCKSACHE NO. 3644, at 40 (June 28, 1957) [this quotation and all others of German sources were translated by the author].

[24] *Ibid.*

[25] Bunte, *Völkerrechtliche Fragen bei Auslandszusammenschlüssen,* 1981 WIRTSCHAFT UND WETTBEWERB [WuW] 605, 606.

[26] Huber, *Auswirkungstheorie und extraterritoriale Rechtsanwendung im internationalen Kartellrecht,* 10 ZEITSCHRIFT FÜR UNTERNEHMENS UND GESELLSCHAFTSRECHT 509, 511 (1981).

[27] To be sure, significant international conflicts related to the extraterritorial application of antitrust laws had begun to occur earlier in the postwar period. *See* J. ATWOOD & K. BREWSTER, ANTITRUST AND AMERICAN BUSINESS ABROAD §4.13 (1981).

dominant position of the United States in the post-World War II period, which made many foreign states reluctant to confront it openly on this issue. In these circumstances, the U.S. experience gave misleading signals to the German legislators.

In addition, in its initial form the GWB was a relatively mild statute that contained few provisions likely to cause conflicts in the international arena. Moreover, the newly formed and inexperienced FCO was expected to try to avoid controversy and to be restrictive in its attempts to enforce the GWB in international cases. Thus, the broad effects principle must have seemed innocuous to its framers, and it is only with the tightening of the GWB's substantive provisions and the change in the climate of international legal relations that the conflicts inherent in the exclusive use of this principle have become apparent.

IV. Peaceful Development: Nonmerger Cases

The development of the extraterritoriality issue in German antitrust law has gone through two distinct phases: a relatively peaceful stage of incremental development and relative confidence in the adequacy of the solutions being proffered, and the stormy, controversial period of intense uncertainty in which it finds itself at present. This dichotomy has corresponded largely to the types of cases in which extraterritorial application has been asserted. During the initial phase of development, the FCO was concerned with extraterritoriality in the nonmerger context, looking primarily at international licensing agreements, vertical restraints, and international cartels. The second phase has centered on the problems of applying the statute's merger control provisions to international mergers and acquisitions. Although our specific focus in this article is on the merger context, developments during the preceding period set the stage for that drama.

The Issue Framed

During the initial decade and a half of the life of the GWB, extraterritoriality was, at best, a secondary issue. The newly created FCO was careful to avoid asserting itself in areas that were likely to lead to international conflicts and/or excessive controversy about its enforcement activities.[28] In several international cases in which the exercise of jurisdiction might have been expected to lead to international conflict, the FCO sidestepped the potential problems by naming as defendants only the domestic participants in the allegedly anticompetitive arrangements. In 1971, for example, the FCO determined that the GWB should apply to an international shipping conference with members in many countries, but it named only the domestic participants as defendants.[29] The FCO's position during this period was that the GWB

[28] *See generally* Markert, *Die Anwendung des GWB auf internationale Wettbewerbsbeschränkungen,* in Zehn Jahre Bundeskartellamt 205 (1968).

[29] FCO, Sept. 10, 1971, WuW/E BKartA 1361 (Fernost-Schiffahrtskonferenzen).

could be applied to foreign conduct wherever such conduct had substantial anticompetitive domestic effects, but it generally avoided testing this position in court.

There were international cases, however, in which the FCO did attempt to apply the GWB against foreign defendants with limited contacts in Germany. It found on several occasions, for example, that section 98(2) empowered it to review the validity of international licenses where they involved either domestic licensors and foreign licensees or foreign licensors and domestic licensees.[30] Yet even where the FCO did extend the application of the GWB to foreign conduct, it seldom engaged in significant analysis of the transnational reach of the statute.

The FCO's success in avoiding confrontation with regard to the extraterritorial scope of the GWB is attested to by the fact that during this period the issue of extraterritoriality seldom played a role in cases appealed to the regular courts, and the first major Supreme Court case dealing directly with the construction of section 98(2) was not decided until 1973.

The lack of elaboration of this issue by the FCO and the courts did not mean, however, that there were no developments in the area. The developments were largely provided, as is often the case in German law, by legal scholarship. Two seminal studies—by Rehbinder and Schwartz[31]—in the 1960's arrived at similar conclusions with regard to several basic questions regarding the application of section 98(2).

The most important of these conclusions was that the effects principle enunciated in section 98(2) was unequivocally in accord with the requirements of public international law. Rehbinder and Schwartz concluded not only that the effects principle was clearly justified under international law, but that it was perhaps the only reasonable basis for a conflict-of-laws principle in international antitrust law. This proposition was quickly accepted by the legal community, and it has become a cornerstone of all subsequent discussions of the issue.

These conclusions, however, led to a trap. Having established that the effects principle satisfied the jurisdictional requirements of international law, German law assumed, as had American law, that this was the end of the issue. The special postwar circumstances, the relatively low level of international business interdependence, and the relative weakness of the GWB allowed extraterritoriality to appear to be a one-dimensional issue. These elements obscured the fact that by so limiting the role of international law, German law was prevented from considering the interests of other states. More than a decade would pass before the nature of the trap thus created would become apparent and this one-dimensional approach to extraterritoriality would lead to serious controversy.

[30] *See* U. Immenga & E. Mestmäcker, Kommentar zum GWB 1904–09 (1982).

[31] E. Rehbinder, Extraterritoriale Wirkungen des deutschen Kartellrechts (1965); and I. Schwartz, *supra* note 16.

Limiting the Effects Principle

In the interim, however, the sculpting of the effects principle was the central focus of the extraterritoriality issue. There was full agreement in the legal community that section 98(2) could not mean what it seemed to mean. It could not be construed to mean that any violation of any part of the GWB that had any kind of effect in Germany would be subject to the GWB. This interpretation would involve an extraordinarily broad application of the GWB that would be both unworkable and a constant embarrassment. The issue was how to go about limiting the effects principle.

The basic approach developed by German scholarship in the 1960's was to tie the effects principle directly to the protective purposes of the GWB, in general, and to the protective purposes of the specific provision of the GWB whose violation was at issue, in particular.[32] The "general protective purpose" of the statute is to protect free *domestic* competition. It requires, therefore, that the GWB be applied only where there is harm to the *domestic* competitive system.

More important is the requirement that domestic effects include only those which violate the specific protective purpose of the statutory provision being applied. Whenever a statutory provision is alleged to have been violated, the court must analyze the "sphere of protection" established by that provision. For an effect to be cognizable for purposes of section 98(2), it must interfere with that protected sphere. Only when the violation of a provision "injures" or "invades" the protected sphere of that provision are its effects relevant. The acceptance and development of this principle by the BGH was a key element in its first major decision dealing specifically with section 98(2).

The long awaited occasion for Supreme Court guidance concerning the application of section 98(2) finally came in 1973 in the *Oil Field Pipes* decision.[33] Ironically, it was not a case of extending extraterritorial jurisdiction at all. Rather than extending jurisdiction on the basis of effects, it limited the reach of the GWB. The central issue in the case was whether section 98(2) should apply to prevent application of the GWB to an agreement that was made in Germany, but that related solely to the export of goods from Germany and thus arguably had no "domestic effects."

The case involved an agreement among leading European—including German—and Japanese producers of oil field pipes to establish a cartel arrangement affecting markets outside of Germany. Section 6 of the GWB permits participation in such cartels by German companies, provided they are limited to regulating competition in markets outside of Germany. In order to qualify for this exemption from the antitrust laws, however, such agreements, including revisions thereof, must be reported to the FCO. Failure to report such an arrangement is punishable by fine.

The participants here failed to report a major revision of their cartel arrangement to the FCO, and the FCO fined the German participants for vi-

[32] *See, e.g.*, I. SCHWARTZ, *supra* note 16, at 32.

[33] BGH, July 12, 1973, WuW/E BGH 1276 (Ölfeldrohre) [hereinafter cited as Ölfeldrohre].

olation of the statute. The appeals court reversed the FCO's decision, and the BGH confirmed. The court held that the arrangement had no "domestic effects," and therefore that the GWB was not applicable to it.[34] According to the court, "Section 98(2) of the GWB, as the determinative conflict-of-laws rule, contains not only an extension but also a limitation on the area of application of the GWB to certain foreign-related facts."[35]

The decision's importance lies less in its specific holding, however, than in its enunciation of the general principles of construction to be used in applying section 98(2), in particular its treatment of the concept of "domestic effects." The court affirmed and established the "protected sphere" limitation that had been developed by Rehbinder and others during the previous decade. The key language in the decision dealt with this issue.

> In light of the variety of conceivable effects of foreign restraints on competition on the domestic market, a limitation and concretization of the concept of domestic effects is required in order to prevent the unlimited expansion of the international application of the substantive rules. . . . As §98(2) is not a substantive law rule, but rather a conflict-of-laws principle, . . . clarity concerning . . . which foreign-related effects fall within the GWB can only be achieved by construing §98(2) in relation to the general protective purpose of the statute as a whole and the protective purpose of the relevant substantive rules. Thus, the consequences of foreign-related restraints on competition can be viewed as "domestic effects" only when they constitute a domestic violation of the area of protection of the particular substantive rule.[36]

This decision helped set the stage for the second phase of development of the issue of extraterritoriality in German antitrust law.

V. The Breaking Point: Mergers and Acquisitions

The principles that were developed during the initial phase of development of the extraterritoriality issue had appeared to many to be adequate. The "effects" concept had been accepted as being in conformity with international law, and it had been sufficiently concretized to allow it to be applied in a reasonable and effective manner.

By the end of the decade, however, this picture had begun to change. As merger cases became the focus of international application of the GWB, confidence in the adequacy of the existing scheme was shaken. The principles developed for defining and concretizing the effects test of section 98(2) no longer seemed satisfactory, for it became clear that they did not provide a means of avoiding the potential for international conflict inherent in extraterritorial assertions of jurisdiction.

[34] The decision was overturned in the 1980 revisions of the GWB, by which the GWB was expressly made applicable to export cartels. *See* Viertes Gesetz zur Änderung des Gesetzes gegen Wettbewerbsbeschränkungen, 1980 BGBl.I 458 (April 26). *See also* Grauel, *Zur Novellierung des §98 Abs.2 GWB betr. Exportkartelle,* 1981 WuW 763.

[35] Ölfeldrohre, *supra* note 33, at 1277.

[36] *Id.* at 1278–79.

The German Merger Control Provisions

In 1973 the GWB was amended to include premerger notification requirements and to authorize the FCO to prohibit certain mergers,[37] and the potential problems of applying the GWB to foreign mergers quickly became the key issue in the area of extraterritoriality. They have remained so since, and with the 1980 amendments to the GWB,[38] which further tightened the merger control provisions, they have become one of the most controversial subjects in German law.[39]

Three separate sections of the GWB relate to mergers, and each has a distinct function. One section establishes reporting requirements; another provides premerger notification rules; and the third contains the rules that authorize the FCO to take action to prevent mergers.

The reporting provisions are contained in section 23, which has been part of the GWB since its inception. They are designed to provide information on the basis of which the FCO can monitor merger activity. When a merger meets certain market share or size criteria,[40] the acquisition and certain basic details about it must be reported to the FCO "without delay" after consummation of the transaction. The scope of coverage is very broad, applying to virtually all significant acquisitions.

A much more limited category of acquisitions is subject to the premerger notification requirements of section 24a of the GWB. Acquisitions meeting these requirements must be reported to the FCO *before* they are consummated, and they may not be consummated until a fixed period of time has elapsed without a negative response from the FCO.[41] In essence, the criteria here are that the merger be anticompetitive and likely to violate the substantive merger control provisions. The premerger notification provisions were added to the GWB in 1973.

A third type of merger control provision was also added to the GWB in 1973—namely, the substantive merger control provisions. Section 24 gives the FCO authority to prohibit mergers "[w]here it is to be expected as a result of the merger that a market-dominating position will be created or strengthened . . . unless the participants can demonstrate that as a result of the merger improvements in competitive conditions will occur that outweigh the disadvantages of the market domination." Although the FCO is thus directed to prohibit a merger that will result in creating "a market-dominating posi-

[37] Zweites Gesetz zur Änderung des Gesetzes gegen Wettbewerbsbeschränkungen, 1973 BGBl. I 917 (Aug. 3).

[38] *See supra* note 34.

[39] *See, e.g., Extraterritoriale Rechtsanwendung unter Berücksichtigung der Entwicklung im U.S. Antitrustrecht,* 1982 WuW 22.

[40] For text, see *infra* note 54.

[41] In order to alleviate unnecessary hardship in premerger notification cases where it is obvious that the requirements of §24 will not be met, the Minister of Economics on May 30, 1980, ordered the FCO to respond to notification in such cases "without delay." Bundesanzeiger No. 103 (June 7, 1980), *reprinted in* 1980 WuW 591.

tion,"[42] it is given the discretion to refrain from prohibiting such a merger if it is shown that these negative results will be outweighed by improvements in competitive conditions.[43]

The Effects Principle in the Merger Context

Development of the Legal Concepts. In 1975 the FCO took an important step regarding the application of the effects principle to international mergers.[44] Recognizing the potential for confusion and controversy in applying the new merger provisions in an international context, the FCO in that year issued guidelines intended to clarify the extraterritorial scope of the merger provisions.[45] These guidelines established several aspects of what has come to be the accepted analysis of extraterritoriality in merger cases, and they continue to reflect the FCO's policy in the area.

The starting point of the guidelines is the basic principle enunciated in *Oil Field Pipes* that the protective purpose of each of the individual substantive provisions must determine the scope of its international application. The critical analytical development provided by the guidelines pertained, however, to what this meant in the merger context, in particular to the question of what constituted the "restraint of competition" required by section 98(2). According to the guidelines:

> The purpose of §23 *et seq.* of the GWB is to deal with concentration, for it can harm competition. The concept "restraint of competition" in §98(2) is the summary designation for all restraints of competition subject to the substantive provisions of the GWB. In regard to §23 *et seq.* of the GWB, the restraint of competition within the meaning of §98(2) is the merger as such. Whether the intensity of domestic competition is actually diminished is not relevant.

By defining the "restraint of competition" for purposes of section 98(2) as the merger itself, the FCO was forging an important link in the present chain of analysis,[46] for this obviates the need to ask about actual effects in merger cases and thus greatly reduces the scope of inquiry.[47]

[42] The concept of market domination is defined in detail in §22 of the GWB.

[43] A losing party may also request "special permission" from the Minister of Economics, who may allow a merger where "the restraint of competition is outweighed by macroeconomic advantages of the merger or the merger is justified by a transcending public interest." GWB §24(3).

[44] Since the statute specifically refers to the effects principle as the relevant conflict-of-laws concept, the nationality principle is not considered a sufficient basis of jurisdiction. U. IMMENGA & E. MESTMÄCKER, *supra* note 30, at 1878.

[45] FCO, TÄTIGKEITSBERICHT (Annual Report) 45 (1975). For text, see also W. KLEINMANN & R. BECHTOLD, KOMMENTAR ZUR FUSIONSKONTROLLE 467 (1977). For a discussion of merger control in Germany and an English translation of the guidelines, see Markert, *Merger Control in Western Europe,* in COMPETITION IN INTERNATIONAL BUSINESS 293 and 332 (O. Schachter & R. Hellawell eds. 1981).

[46] Critics of the guidelines have attacked this assumption, arguing that the merger should not itself be considered a restraint of competition. *See generally* Huber, *supra* note 26.

[47] If, for purposes of applying §98(2) to the reporting requirement of §23, a "restraint of

Having declared that the merger was itself the restraint of competition for purposes of section 98(2), the FCO then took the position that the place where the merger was realized would determine whether it had the required domestic effects. According to the FCO's scheme, mergers "realized" within the country automatically created domestic effects, whereas mergers realized outside the country created domestic effects only under certain circumstances. "Realized within the country" includes, for example, the acquisition of the assets or shares of a domestic corporation as well as the creation of a domestic joint venture corporation. The acquisition outside of Germany of a foreign corporation with a domestic subsidiary is deemed—with respect to the subsidiary—to be realized within the country.

Other mergers realized outside the country are deemed to have domestic effects if "through the merger the structural requirements for domestic competition are effected and at least one domestic enterprise (including subsidiaries and other related enterprises) is involved." This category includes, for example, acquisitions of foreign enterprises by German companies.

According to the FCO, some mergers realized outside the country have domestic effects by virtue of the activity of the involved foreign corporations on the domestic market; in other such cases domestic effects will be found only where additional factors are present. For example, domestic effects exist where, prior to the merger, both the acquiring and acquired enterprises were active within the country, either directly or through subsidiaries or agents. Domestic effects *may* exist where only one of the participating companies was active, but in such cases other direct domestic economic effects must be found. The examples given include situations where, in the event the merger is consummated, the foreign participant (generally, the target company) is "likely" to supply the domestic market or to transfer significant technology to the domestic enterprise.

The guidelines have been an important aid in clarifying the position of the FCO, at least in regard to section 23, and the FCO continues to attach weight to them.[48] Moreover, they have established several basic propositions regarding the application of section 98(2) to merger cases. They have, however, been sharply criticized for vagueness and oversimplification.[49]

Some of the issues raised by the guidelines were dealt with in the BGH's *Organic Pigments* decision,[50] which was the first major Supreme Court case involving the application of section 98(2) in the merger area. The central issue was whether the GWB's reporting provisions were applicable to the acquisition in the United States of a division of a U.S. corporation that had been doing

---

competition" required proof of actual anticompetitive effects, far fewer mergers would be required to be reported, and the task of the FCO would be far more difficult.

[48] For a statement of the present position of the FCO, see Niederleithinger, *Zur Problematik einer Praeventivkontrolle von Auslandszusammenschlüssen,* 1981 WuW 469.

[49] *See, e.g.,* Harms, *Zusammenschlusskontrolle,* in GEMEINSCHAFTSKOMMENTAR 60 (4th ed. 1981).

[50] BGH, May 29, 1979, WuW/E BGH 1613 (Organische Pigmente) [hereinafter cited as Organische Pigmente].

business in Germany by another U.S. corporation that was the subsidiary of a German corporation.

The defendant company took the position that the reporting provisions could not extend to the transaction. It argued that the reporting requirements were merely procedural rules designed to improve the ability of the FCO to enforce substantive provisions. Since they were not substantive provisions (*Sachnormen*), they could have no "protected sphere." Therefore, since a provision of the GWB could be applied only where its protected sphere had been violated, section 23 could not be applied to such a transaction.

The BGH refused to accept this logic and held that the reporting requirements were substantive provisions within the meaning of the *Oil Field Pipes* decision. In the opinion of the court, the merger control provisions of the GWB represented a differentiated approach to merger control, with each of the three sets of provisions serving a specific purpose in that scheme. In the court's view, "This differentiated regulatory scheme resulted from the fact that the legislature did not view mergers as necessarily inimical to competition and therefore created a graduated statutory scheme designed to limit the interference of the state to necessary levels."[51] The reporting provisions were thus considered an independent and substantive component of this structure. As substantive provisions, their extraterritorial application was to be measured directly, in terms of whether or not the "effects" of the transaction invaded the "protected sphere" of the provisions.

Since the size criteria of section 23 had been met by the participants in the merger, albeit with the inclusion of foreign sales data, the question was whether this was sufficient to require the merger to be reported. Apparently concerned, however, about the possibility of "unlimited expansion" of the extraterritorial application of the provision, the BGH answered in the negative. It imposed a further modification on the statutory scheme by asking whether the merger, in addition, had a "direct effect" on the German market. Presupposing—without discussing the issue—that the acquisition was itself the restraint of competition whose effects were to be measured, the court stated that "the issue of whether the acquisition of the organic pigments division of ACC created relevant domestic effects depends entirely on whether the acquisition had a direct effect on the competitive conditions in the domestic market."[52] In the following paragraph it also required that the effect be "substantial."

The court found such direct and substantial effects on the basis of two factors. First, the merger eliminated actual competition because the acquired enterprise ceased to be a domestic competitor. Second, the acquiring corporation's German subsidiary increased its sales as a result of the merger and gained access to the know-how of the acquired company. The court, however, did not provide further guidance for the use of the "direct" and "substantial" tests in other cases.

[51] *Id.* at 1614.

[52] *Id.* at 1615.

The court's failure to follow its own prescribed line of analysis confused the extraterritoriality issue. It introduced independent limiting principles of "directness" and "substantiality," but it failed to indicate how these limiting principles were to be applied and how they related, if at all, to the issue of the provision's protected sphere.[53]

Application of the Effects Principle to Specific Merger Provisions. In analyzing whether a merger must be reported or notified to the FCO, the substantive merger prevention provisions of section 24—*i.e.*, the issue of whether the merger involves the "creation or strengthening of a market-dominating position"—are irrelevant. As required by the *Organic Pigments* decision, each of the three merger control provisions is treated separately.

The criteria for the reporting and premerger notification provisions are of two kinds: a market share test in section 23 and absolute size tests in sections 23 and 24a.[54] The market share test of section 23 presents little difficulty in the international context, for it refers solely to shares of the domestic market. In general, reporting is required on the basis of market share only where the participants have a combined domestic market share of at least 20 percent, regardless of whether the merger takes place within the Federal Republic. Here the effects principle is satisfied by the fact that a merger involving this level of domestic involvement necessarily affects the protected sphere of section 23.

The absolute size criteria of sections 23 and 24a present more complex issues. Where the parties to a merger meet these standards with respect to the domestic market, the respective reporting and notification obligations obviously arise. Unresolved, however, is whether foreign sales and foreign employees may be counted in determining if the size criteria have been met. The case law suggests that these criteria need not in all cases be fulfilled domestically, but may be met, at least in part, by the inclusion of foreign data. The theory is that the "absolute size criteria are an indication of the competitive parameters of the enterprise,"[55] and therefore sales that occur outside

[53] *See generally* U. IMMENGA & E. MESTMÄCKER, *supra* note 30, at 1887–94 and 1911–15.

[54] The text reads, in relevant part, as follows:

> [§23] (1) The merger of enterprises shall immediately be reported to the Federal Cartel Office, if
>
> 1. the merger results in or increases a market share of at least 20% within the entire territory in which this Law applies or within a major portion thereof, or if one of the participating enterprises has a market share of at least 20% in another market, or
>
> 2. the participating enterprises combined had at any point during the fiscal year preceding the merger at least 10,000 employees during such period or combined sales of at least 500 million DM.
>
> [§24] Notification of a proposed merger shall be given to the Federal Cartel Office if at least two of the participating enterprises had sales of DM 1 billion or more during the preceding fiscal year. . . .

[55] U. IMMENGA & E. MESTMÄCKER, *supra* note 30, at 1912.

the domestic market, for example, must be considered in measuring the domestic effects of the merger.[56]

Because the inclusion of foreign data in applying the absolute size criteria could greatly broaden the extraterritorial application of the provision, the BGH's "direct and substantial" requirement must also be met in such cases. Only if such a merger has a "direct and substantial" effect on domestic competition are the requirements of section 98(2) considered to be fulfilled.

The interaction of these rules can best be understood by reviewing the basic categories of relevant situations. When a domestic enterprise is acquired, reporting, or, as the case may be, premerger notification, is required whenever either the market share criteria are met domestically or the absolute size criteria are met on a worldwide basis. The theory is that the acquisition of a domestic enterprise necessarily entails the required effect on domestic competition, and the market share and size criteria simply measure the intensity of that effect.

In the case of foreign mergers, the situation is unchanged with respect to the market share criterion of section 23. Since, however, the absolute size criteria may be met either domestically or outside the country, the "direct and substantial" test must be applied—*i.e.*, the merger must not only meet the stated criteria, but it must also have a direct and substantial effect on competitive conditions on the domestic market.

There have been too few cases to clarify the issue of when effects are "direct and substantial," but a distinction is generally drawn between situations involving at least one domestic participant and those which are totally foreign. When one of the participants is a domestic enterprise, domestic effects result if, for example, both parties to the merger are actual or potential competitors on the domestic market or if the acquisition results in growth in the "competitive resources" of the domestic enterprise.[57]

In the case of a foreign merger in which there are no domestic participants, the required effect on domestic competition will normally be found only when one of the participants has substantial sales in the domestic market prior to the merger.[58] It is not clear, however, whether this condition must necessarily be fulfilled in order to find such effect.

As for the substantive merger control provisions, section 24 authorizes the FCO to prohibit a merger that is expected to result in the creation or strengthening of a domestic market-dominating position, provided the resulting improvements in competitive conditions do not outweigh the anticompetitive consequences. Since the creation or strengthening of a dominant position on the domestic market is defined by the statute as a serious domestic effect, the only issue that remains is when, in fact, a *foreign* merger may create or strengthen such a position.

[56] Allowing only domestic size data to be used in applying these tests would significantly restrict the scope of those provisions, but critics of the FCO argue that this would more fully reflect the GWB's "protective purpose" guidelines. *See, e.g.*, Harms, *supra* note 49, at 59–61.

[57] U. IMMENGA & E. MESTMÄCKER, *supra* note 30, at 1912.

[58] *Id.* at 1914.

The determination of this issue generally centers on a series of presumptions relating primarily to market share and size. A discussion of the elaborate system of statutory presumptions would go beyond the scope of this article, but the applicable principles are generally the same as those outlined above for the reporting and premerger notification provisions—*i.e.*, market share presumptions relate solely to the domestic market, while presumptions based on size relate to the enterprise as a whole, regardless of where, for example, sales occur.

By tying the jurisdictional concept of domestic effects to the protective purposes of the statutory provisions being applied, German law has substantially sharpened its "effects" analysis. It has developed a definable and manageable framework for continuing refinement of the protective purposes of particular provisions and the types of foreign conduct that can interfere with them. Additional refinement is necessary, however, especially in regard to the role and content of the "direct and substantial" requirement.

The Limits of Sovereignty

While merger cases have provided the context for further development of the effects principle, they also have confronted German antitrust law with a new aspect of the extraterritoriality issue—namely, the problem of external jurisdictional restraints. The reason is that extraterritorial application of the GWB threatens to collide with the sovereign interests of other states. Refining and developing the limits of the effects theory serves to reduce the likelihood of such conflicts, but the effects concept can itself neither take them into account nor respond to them.

Owing in large part to the restrained enforcement policies of the FCO during the first decade and a half of the GWB's existence, the potential for external conflict was seldom directly encountered in the nonmerger cases. Recent cases, however, have shifted the focus from reliance on the effects principle to filter out inappropriate exercises of jurisdictional positions to recognition and clarification of principles of jurisdictional restraint.

Prior to the *Organic Pigments* decision in 1979, there had been little consideration of the issue of external restraints in German law.[59] The extraterritoriality problem was viewed essentially as a matter of properly defining the effects principle. Even in *Organic Pigments* the BGH refused to take the issue seriously.[60] Attempting to convince the court that section 23 should not apply to a foreign merger, the defendant corporation had there argued that the principles of international law prohibited the application of a nation's *public law*—*e.g.*, regulatory laws—to foreign transactions. The judges were unimpressed. The court stated:

[59] *But see* K. MEESSEN, VÖLKERRECHTLICHE GRUNDSÄTZE DES INTERNATIONALEN KARTELLRECHTS (1975), discussed *infra* note 65.

[60] *See* Kersten, *Zur Anwendbarkeit des GWB auf ausländische Unternehmenszusammenschlüsse mit Inlandswirkungen,* 1979 WuW 721.

> The appellant cannot . . . claim that according to international law all states are obligated to mutual accommodation and therefore in principle may not apply their public law [*öffentliches Recht*] to fact situations which have arisen in foreign countries. The appellant thus fails to appreciate the importance of the conflict-of-laws principle of §98(2) GWB, which does not focus on the foreign conduct but on the effects that occur within the country.[61]

In effect, the court's position was that the relevance of international law to the extraterritoriality issue was limited to the question whether the effects principle was or was not sanctioned by it.[62]

The *Organic Pigments* case did not, however, as it could not, put an end to the external restraints issue. Awareness of the potential for international conflict inherent in the application of section 98(2) to foreign mergers quickly led to increasing concern in the legal community.[63] This development was primarily due to three factors. The first involved the internal legal situation in Germany. The merger control provisions that had been introduced in 1974 had given the FCO the authority to attack international mergers, an authority the FCO had now shown it was quite willing to use. Moreover, the FCO's authority in this area was further strengthened in 1980. Second, several of Germany's neighbors (including France and Britain) had introduced, or were considering, blocking legislation to thwart the extraterritorial application of foreign (particularly United States) antitrust laws within their respective borders.[64] Finally, the extraordinary international expansion of German investment, especially in the United States, vastly increased the potential for international application of merger control provisions and concomitantly increased the sensitivity of Germany's international corporations to their exposure in this area.

Consequently, when in late 1980 the KG handed down its *Bayer/Firestone* opinions, the situation looked much different from its appearance a year and a half earlier in *Organic Pigments.*[65] The *Bayer/Firestone* case represented the first major test of the FCO's authority to prohibit a foreign merger, and with it the external restraints issue reached center stage.

[61] Organische Pigmente, *supra* note 50, at 1615.

[62] The fact that there was a domestic enterprise involved in the merger put the court in the position of having little incentive to look toward international ramifications. Its basic position was that "there is no legal basis to remove the reporting obligation of the domestic enterprise merely because the interests of the [acquiring foreign enterprise], which it indirectly controls, are affected." *Ibid.*

[63] *See, e.g.,* Autenrieth, *Die Anzeigepflicht beim Zusammenschluss ausländischer Unternehmen,* 1980 RECHT DER INTERNATIONALEN WIRTSCHAFT 820.

[64] *See supra* note 3.

[65] The intellectual background for this change in position was the excellent study by Professor Karl Matthias Meessen published in 1975. Meessen confirmed that the effects principle remained a valid basis for jurisdiction under international law, and he made several important suggestions with regard to its application. He also discussed the external restraints issue and laid the foundation for subsequent case law developments with regard to it. *See* K. MEESSEN, *supra* note 59, and text accompanying note 72 *infra.*

In May 1980, Bayer France, a wholly owned French subsidiary of a Canadian holding company owned by Bayer AG, a German corporation, reported to the FCO in accordance with applicable reporting requirements that it intended to purchase a division of Firestone France S.A., located in France. Firestone France was a French subsidiary of Firestone, Inc., a U.S. corporation. The contract required as a condition of the acquisition that necessary governmental approvals be obtained, and the French Government had approved the plan. The FCO held, however, that the acquisition violated the GWB and ordered that it not proceed.

Curiously, the FCO's decision failed to discuss the external restraints issue, in spite of the fact that it had been a focus of discussion about the case, and the KG held that this omission was in itself a sufficient basis for dismissing the case and allowing the merger.[66] According to the court:

> [I]n the case of an acquisition which is to take place directly between two or even three foreign enterprises and which, as the FCO admits, has its center of gravity [*Schwergewicht*] outside the country, the [FCO] must deal with the issue whether §98(2) is applicable and whether as a result of the recognizable effects outside the country there are international law barriers to the proposed prohibition that are based on factors other than internal factors.[67]

Less than 2 years earlier, the BGH in *Organic Pigments* had held that the existence of "effects" was all that international law required. In *Bayer / Firestone* the KG explicitly required that the FCO take into account external restraints imposed by international law.

The court was given the opportunity to carry its thinking further, for the defendant corporation also sought an order allowing the transaction to be carried out immediately.[68] The court granted the order not only on the basis of procedural mistakes made by the FCO during the case and the lack of consideration of the external restraints issue, but also on the basis of "serious doubt" about whether the FCO's prohibition was susceptible of legal justification:

> These [doubts] result from the fact that . . . the center of gravity of the acquisition plan—which was prohibited *in its entirety*—is outside the country, while within the country, in contrast, a relatively unimportant additional restraint of competition would result from the strengthening of a market-dominating position of Bayer. The competent French legal office approves of the acquisition and the competent French authorities welcome it on the basis of economic and sociopolitical considerations. In this situation, prohibition of the acquisition with respect to the involved foreign enterprises [presents] a conflict between the conflicts-of-law rule of §98(2) of the GWB . . . and generally recognized principles of international law, namely, the principles of (1) reasonable forum contacts

[66] KG, Nov. 26, 1980, WuW/E OLG 2411 (Synthetischer Kautschuk I, 1980).

[67] *Id.* at 2417.

[68] KG, Nov. 26, 1980, WuW/E OLG 2419 (Synthetischer Kautschuk II, 1980).

> in international administrative law and (2) the principle of nonintervention.[69]

The court thus framed the entire issue much differently than it had been framed in *Organic Pigments.* The effects principle, the application of which had previously been seen as satisfying the requirements of international law, was no longer sufficient to satisfy those requirements.

The KG admitted that under section 98(2) the merger created a domestic effect, for there was a strengthening of a domestic market-dominating position. It held nevertheless that the prohibition violated international law principles of external restraint—namely, the principles of nonintervention and reasonable forum contacts:

> Since the prohibition . . . relates to the entire acquisition and thus, due to the contractual conditions requiring the approval of all responsible government bodies, prevents consummation of the transaction even by the foreign enterprises, which are primarily involved here, it constitutes a violation of the above-named and generally recognized rules of international law. . . . In a special case such as this one, in which the acquisition takes place only between foreign enterprises, the assets sold are located outside the country and [their foreign] production is only to a very limited extent available to the participants domestically, the prohibition cannot be allowed to have legal force.[70]

The court thus held that the application of international law prevented the FCO from taking the proposed action.[71]

The court did not elaborate the basis for its claim that these international law principles restrained its jurisdictional reach. It referred instead to the leading work by Professor K. M. Meessen, *Völkerrechtliche Grundsätze des internationalen Kartellrechts* (1975), in which these points were developed.[72] Meessen concluded that restraint principles were applicable in jurisdictional cases. He argued, in particular, that the principle of nonintervention had become an accepted principle of international law, and that it should therefore be applicable to jurisdictional issues, provided only that it could be concretized and given substance. He then suggested as a basis for this concretization process the tests that were implicitly adopted by the court in *Bayer / Firestone* and more fully developed by the FCO in the case that was to follow.

The FCO wasted no time in finding another case in which to press its position. Having been chastised for failure to take into account the issue of external restraints in the *Bayer / Firestone* case, it was careful to present a carefully reasoned argument to support its prohibition of a proposed acquisition in *Rothmans / Philip Morris.*[73]

[69] *Id.* at 2420. [70] *Id.* at 2420–21.

[71] The case has been widely discussed in the legal literature. *See, e.g.,* Ebenroth & Autenrieth, *Die Fusionkontrolle beim Zusammenshcluss ausländischer Unternehmen unter indirekter Beteiligung eines inländischen Unternehmens,* DER BETRIEBS-BERATER, Jan. 10, 1981, at 16.

[72] *See* K. MEESSEN, *supra* note 59, ch. 5.

[73] FCO, Feb. 24, 1982, WuW/E BKartA 1943 (Morris/Rothmans) [hereinafter cited as Morris/Rothmans].

In a highly publicized opinion,[74] the FCO prohibited a merger outside of Germany between two non-German corporations. The case involved the purchase by Philip Morris, Inc., an American corporation (Philip Morris), of 50 percent of the shares of the Rothmans Tobacco Company, a British corporation (Rothmans), from a South African holding company called the Rembrandt Group, Ltd. (Rembrandt). Rothmans, in turn, controlled the Martin Brinkmann AG, a German corporation that was a major competitor of Philip Morris in Germany (Brinkmann). The remaining 50 percent of the Rothmans shares continued to be held by Rembrandt, and the sale constituted part of an arrangement by which Rembrandt and Philip Morris would exercise joint and equal influence over Brinkmann through Rothmans. Rothmans became, in effect, a joint venture corporation of Rembrandt and Philip Morris, the purpose of which was to provide joint distribution, research, and production efforts between the former competitors. In contrast to the *Bayer / Firestone* case, the acquisition here had already been carried out. Moreover, although the plan of acquisition entailed transactions other than the purchase of Brinkmann, the FCO sought to act against it only insofar as it affected the German economy—namely, by prohibiting the acquisition of Brinkmann.[75]

The FCO ordered that the acquisition be prohibited with respect to Brinkmann on the grounds that it would lead to the strengthening of a market-dominating position on the part of the leading German cigarette makers, *i.e.*, a tightening of the oligopoly that controlled the cigarette market. The acquisition would have resulted in the merger of Philip Morris's German subsidiary with Brinkmann, and thus a merger of the third largest seller (Brinkmann, 16.9 percent) with the holder of the fourth largest market share (Philip Morris, 14.3 percent).

The most controversial issue, however, was the jurisdictional basis of the decision. Building on the principles enunciated by the KG in *Bayer / Firestone,* the FCO specifically addressed itself to the external restraints imposed by international law, carefully responding to the objections expressed by the court in that case. It articulated a clear standard on which to base its extraterritorial reach:

> The authority for [this decision] is based on the effects principle, which is recognized by international law and which establishes the jurisdiction of a state to regulate matters that have a *direct* effect within its borders. Limitations on this authority can only result from the principle of non-

[74] *See, e.g.*, N.Y. Times, March 5, 1982, at D4.

[75] The FCO officially informed the Governments of the United States, the United Kingdom, and South Africa that it was considering taking action against the merger and gave them an opportunity to be heard. The United States did not respond to this opportunity. The Government of the United Kingdom held consultations with the FCO, and, on the basis of certain assurances from the FCO, it declared that it had no objection to the issuance of a prohibition order. The South African Government objected to the proceedings. It argued that the actions of the FCO would violate the international law principle of nonintervention because they would violate the rights of South African nationals to dispose of their foreign assets.

intervention in the internal affairs of other states as well as the international law prohibition on abuse [of jurisdiction].[76]

Thus, the FCO explicitly based its authority on the "effects principle, which is recognized by international law," and then stated that the only limits on this authority were also provided by international law, the principles of nonintervention and abuse of jurisdiction.

These two principles are designed to incorporate and, perhaps, encapsulate the kinds of limitations referred to in the KG's *Bayer/Firestone* decision.[77] In formulating its version of these international law principles, the FCO had to deal with the stated concerns of the KG about external restraint without becoming too vague and without unduly limiting the reach of the GWB.

By applying the nonintervention principle of international law to the extraterritoriality issue, the FCO entered essentially new territory. This use of the nonintervention principle represented a new development in international law, but it also meant that there existed little guidance as to how the nonintervention principle should be adapted to its new role.

According to the FCO, the nonintervention principle prevented the exercise of prescriptive jurisdiction over a foreign merger where the interests of the regulating state in the exercise of such jurisdiction were significantly outweighed by governmental interests of a foreign state in the completion of the merger.

The nonintervention principle thus referred only to "governmental interest[s]," which the FCO described as fundamental state interests such as "politico-economic interest[s]." It did not apply to the interests of foreign individuals or corporations "because they are not subjects of international law."[78]

This important limitation on the scope of the nonintervention principle was a major issue, for the Republic of South Africa had argued against the FCO's proposed actions on the ground that the property interests of its citizens would be affected, which thus violated its own interests. It argued that its interests were governmental interests because it was obligated "to protect the property interests of South African nationals and enterprises." According to the FCO, however, such interests were not governmental interests for these purposes because they did not constitute an "original, state interest" of South Africa.[79] It thus distinguished between primary interests of states, such as regulatory interests, and derivative interests, which arise from the protection of private interests.

[76] Morris/Rothmans, *supra* note 73, at 1953.

[77] The external restraints concepts in the FCO's test were similar to those used by the KG in *Bayer/Firestone.* Both the FCO and the KG utilized the nonintervention principle, but the FCO utilized the international law abuse of jurisdiction principle in place of the reasonable forum contacts principle mentioned in *Bayer/Firestone.* This change represented a clear improvement because the abuse of jurisdiction principle is directly related to the external restraints issue, whereas the reasonable forum contacts concept is not.

In addition, the FCO significantly developed the content of the respective principles. The KG had only mentioned them in *Bayer/Firestone.*

[78] Morris/Rothmans, *supra* note 73, at 1953. [79] *Id.* at 1954.

The FCO's nonintervention principle required that the respective governmental interests be weighed according to a defined standard. According to the FCO, "Only when the interests of the foreign state in the execution of the merger significantly outweigh the German interest in preventing it can there be a violation of the nonintervention principle."[80] A significant preponderance of governmental interests on the part of the foreign state was thus required to establish a violation of the principle.

The second principle of international law that the FCO applied was the prohibition against abuse of jurisdiction, and here again the FCO found its proposed actions to be unobjectionable. It described the principle as follows: "The international law prohibition against abuse presupposes a crass disproportionateness between the domestic regulatory interests and the disadvantages that the affected foreign enterprises or the corresponding states suffer through the issuance of the sovereign act."[81] This principle had appeared previously in international law doctrine,[82] but it had apparently not been used in this context.

For purposes of this test, the FCO took into account both private and governmental interests and defined the types of interests to be included. It required that the *regulatory interests* of the state exercising jurisdiction be weighed against the harm that would be suffered either by the foreign enterprises involved *or* by foreign governments.

Which types of private harm are to be considered is not specified, but the FCO's treatment of several arguments advanced during the proceedings sheds light on its views in this regard. Injury to the property rights of South African shareholders of Rembrandt was not relevant to this balancing of interests, the FCO ruled, because the South Africans had, in effect, accepted the risk that the activities of a major multinational enterprise would "bring it into conflict with the national legal system of a state in whose markets it was active."[83] Similarly, the fact that the FCO's intervention would require the merger to be partially dissolved did not inflict relevant harm on the South African shareholders, who had argued that a partial dissolution would substantially reduce the value to them of the acquisition.

The standard to be applied in determining whether there was such abuse was one of "crass disproportionateness." A jurisdictional abuse would be found only where the specified disadvantages were crassly disproportionate to the interests of the regulating state. The FCO concluded that such disproportionateness could not be established in the instant case. According to the FCO, "The merger leads . . . to a substantial narrowing of the oligopoly dominating an economically very significant domestic market and therefore to a serious deterioration of the competitive structures."[84] Therefore, reasoned the FCO, there could be no disproportionateness.

The external restraints principles employed by the FCO are directly related

[80] *Id.* at 1953–54.

[81] *Id.* at 1954.

[82] *See* K. MEESSEN, *supra* note 59, at 203.

[83] Morris/Rothmans, *supra* note 73, at 1955.

[84] *Id.* at 1954.

to the avoidance of international conflict, for they provide a defined and structured balancing mechanism by which foreign interests can be taken into account. The tests represent novel usages of international law principles, and, although they require further refinement,[85] they expand the potential role of international law in this context.[86]

VI. Concluding Perspectives

Taking their cue from American experience, the drafters of the GWB started in 1957 with what appeared to be a simple and reasonable proposition—*i.e.,* that foreign anticompetitive conduct that had domestic "effects" should be subject to German antitrust law. After all, jurisdiction based on such effects had been held to be justified under international law. The German GWB did not even limit the effects principle; *any* effects within Germany appeared to justify extraterritorial application of the statute. As in the United States, the effects principle appeared to have almost magical powers: its mere existence seemed to solve the problem of extraterritoriality.

It soon became clear, however, that the effects principle would have to be modified, for construing it as broadly as it was written exceeded the limits of what was generally acceptable within the international community. Domestic effects resulting from foreign anticompetitive conduct could reasonably provide a basis for extraterritorial application of the law only under certain conditions.

At this point, German law took a portentous step. It sought to reduce the extraterritorial scope of the GWB by simply modifying the effects principle. It provided that only effects of a certain *level and intensity* would constitute a basis of jurisdiction. It asked, "What kinds of limitations must be put on the effects concept so that it will not reach too broadly?" But in order to answer that question it looked primarily to its *own* interests and applied modifying principles such as "direct" and "substantial" that referred to those interests.

The weakness of this approach is fundamental. Modifying the effects principle represents a one-dimensional solution to a two-dimensional problem. Conflicts between states are the core of the extraterritoriality issue. Modifying the effects principle reduces the *likelihood* of conflicts by reducing the number of situations in which effects can justify the exercise of jurisdiction, but it does not relate directly to the goal of conflict reduction, because it contains no means of accommodating the interests of other states. Its sole reference point is the regulating state.

This basic deficiency of an exclusively effects-based approach to extraterritoriality has become apparent in both Germany and the United States during

[85] *See, e.g.,* Meessen, *Zusammenschlusskontrolle in auslandsbezogenen Sachverhalten,* 143 Zeitschrift für das gesamte Handelsrecht 273, 282 (1979).

[86] Defendants have appealed, but officials of the European Community are reported to be considering taking action in the case, in which event the German courts would presumably not have the opportunity to review the FCO's decision. *See supra* note 5.

the last decade, and both countries have taken steps to remedy it. In some respects, these steps have been similar; in others, there have been significant differences.

German law has adopted a two-dimensional test that is designed to take into account foreign as well as domestic interests and also to minimize external conflict. The test has two components. The first is a carefully defined "effects" principle that allows effects to provide a basis for extraterritorial jurisdiction only when they are substantial and directly injurious to the purposes sought to be achieved by the specific provisions being applied. The second component relates directly to the issue of whether the state has overstepped its bounds and encroached on the sphere of sovereignty of another state, either by interfering with the governmental interests of that state or by abusing the jurisdictional authority that international law has conferred upon it.

United States law has also responded to this challenge, principally through the introduction of a so-called jurisdictional rule of reason.[87] This "rule" requires that in deciding whether to exercise jurisdiction in accordance with the notion of comity, a court is to "balance" the interests of the states involved and refrain from exercising jurisdiction where the interests of the foreign state "outweigh" the interests of the United States.

A comparison of German and American law regarding three central aspects of the extraterritoriality issue suggests similarities in approach that may reflect an emerging consensus in the international community and that highlight the potential value of the German experience to the further development of the legal principles in this area. These aspects are: the functioning of the effects principle, the use of interest-balancing concepts, and the role of international law.

In both the United States and Germany, "effects" has been the central concept in defining the extraterritorial reach of the antitrust laws, but there are significant differences between the two countries with regard to its content and function. In the United States, the concept has been little developed, and there is even uncertainty about which "effects" the concept refers to.[88] It is generally considered to refer, however, to effects on U.S. commerce—*i.e.*, to general economic effects caused by the anticompetitive conduct.[89] Using general economic effects as its reference point, American law has been able to make the test more precise only by introducing modifying concepts such as "direct" and "substantial," which refer to the level and intensity of such effects. Such modifying principles can yield only the vaguest of guidelines for court action, and, partially as a result of that fact, American law has had little success in forging the effects principle into a useful and discriminating legal principle.

[87] *See* cases cited *supra* note 2.

[88] *But see* National Bank of Canada v. Interbank Card Ass'n, 666 F.2d 6 (2d Cir. 1981), which represents an effort to sharpen the analytical structure of American law by requiring that the relevant effects also be anticompetitive.

[89] *E.g.*, Timberlane v. Bank of America, 549 F.2d 597 (9th Cir. 1976).

In Germany, on the other hand, the effects concept has been gradually concretized and defined by relating it to the procompetitive purposes of the statutory provisions being applied. The effects of foreign anticompetitive conduct serve as a basis for jurisdiction only where they interfere with the protective purposes of the specific statutory provision that defines such conduct as anticompetitive. This allows the legal process to define incrementally the specific elements that will constitute a basis for international jurisdiction—namely, the protective purposes of the respective statutory provisions and the kinds of effects that interfere with them.

Recognizing the need for flexibility in dealing with potential conflict situations, both legal systems have introduced balancing-of-interests concepts. Both states have recognized that world order demands that the effects principle be complemented by the use of legal mechanisms reflecting the interests of all states involved in the exercise of international regulatory jurisdiction.

The respective balancing tests, however, have significantly different characteristics. In the United States the balancing of interests does not, strictly speaking, take place within the domain of law.[90] It is performed within the context of "comity" and is thus essentially a discretionary political issue.[91] It is generally seen as informing a judge's answer to the question, "Having the right to apply our law to this situation, do we wish to abstain?"[92]

Corresponding to its nonlegal context is the fact that the balancing-of-interests test has not acquired a conceptual structure. The kinds of interests to be weighed are given little definition, and there are no standards to guide the weighing process. The court is merely instructed to look at a long list of factors,[93] attach relative weights to each, and weigh them against each other. How this is to be done is left to the discretion of the court. As a result, there is no basis for consistency in decision making, and there appears to be no way to arrive at even a modicum of predictability in judicial behavior.

The balancing concepts developed by German law are significantly more structured. First, both the nonintervention principle and the abuse of jurisdiction principle are applied in a *legal* rather than a political context. They require that a judge interpret and apply a principle of law. Conclusions reached on the basis of such application are legal conclusions, and each case is related to every other case by that fact.

In addition, the interests to be weighed are defined. In applying the nonintervention principle, for example, the regulating state's "governmental in-

[90] Tentative Draft No. 2 of the *Restatement of Foreign Relations Law* (*Revised*), *infra* note 97, seeks to place balancing issues in a legal rather than a political and discretionary context. The draft is summarized in 75 AJIL 987 (1981).

[91] *See* Maier, *supra* note 15, at 281.

[92] The opinions in *Timberlane* and in other cases following it have been obscure on the issue of how the balancing test relates to the issue of subject matter jurisdiction. The analysis appears to be, however, that the effects test controls the right to exercise jurisdiction and the balancing test relates to whether we *should* exercise that jurisdiction.

[93] A recent list of factors is contained in Mannington Mills v. Congoleum Corp., 595 F.2d 1287 (3d Cir. 1979).

terests" are weighed against the "governmental interests" of other states that may be affected. Such interests are the only interests to be weighed. The abuse principle involves weighing the governmental interests of the regulating state, on the one hand, against the governmental interests of foreign states and the private interests of the merger participants, on the other hand.

Furthermore, each test has a standard of measurement. When the nonintervention principle is applied, governmental interests of the regulating state will suffice to justify the exercise of jurisdiction, unless the governmental interests of the foreign state *significantly outweigh* them. The exercise of jurisdiction will violate the abuse principle only if injuries to foreign interests are "crassly disproportionate" to the interests of the regulating state.

Both German and United States law recognize that international law places certain limits on the right of a state to exercise prescriptive jurisdiction over conduct outside its borders. Moreover, until recently, both systems considered that the requirements of international law were satisfied by use of the effects principle. The exercise of international jurisdiction based on a modicum of domestic effects was not considered capable of violating international law.

This remains the basic U.S. position concerning international law; it has not fundamentally changed. Introduction of the concept of a jurisdictional rule of reason reflects awareness of the importance of developing principles of conflict avoidance. The critical factor, however, is that this approach does not look to international law for guidance. It is conceived as a domestic United States solution based on United States law models. It is perhaps in part for this reason that its introduction seems not to have convinced other states that their interests will be adequately taken into consideration by its application.

In Germany, on the other hand, the courts and the FCO have responded to these changing conditions by altering their position with respect to international law.[94] They have moved from a one-dimensional effects-centered approach to a two-dimensional approach that includes both an effects test and an external restraints test. They have adapted external restraints concepts of international law and applied them to an area in which they previously had not been used. In doing so, they have substantially expanded the role of international law in the extraterritoriality context. In the German scheme, that role is no longer limited to sanctioning the effects principle as a basis for jurisdiction; it now includes the development and application of conflict-avoidance principles.

These external restraints concepts will undoubtedly require further refinement and clarification, but they seem well suited to the purposes for which they are being utilized. The principle of nonintervention is an established component of the international law system, whose purpose is to establish restraints on state action in violation of foreign sovereignty.[95] It is for the same

[94] *See generally* Meng, *Neuere Entwicklungen im Streit um die Jurisdiktionshoheit der Staaten im Bereich der Wettbewerbsbeschränkungen,* 41 ZEITSCHRIFT FÜR AUSLÄNDISCHES ÖFFENTLICHES RECHT UND VÖLKERRECHT 469 (1981).

[95] K. MEESSEN, *supra* note 59, at 203.

purpose that German law has adapted this principle for use in the extraterritoriality context. The concept of abuse of jurisdiction is an extension of the international law principle of reasonableness.[96] In the extraterritoriality context, it performs the important function of complementing the nonintervention principle by taking into account private as well as governmental harm.

Most important, perhaps, is the fact that German law has placed international law at the center of its effort to resolve the extraterritoriality problem. The experience of both countries in this area has been plagued by the generally deficient state of international law, which is, in turn, attributable to the fact that states have been reluctant to look to international law rules and processes for the resolution and avoidance of international jurisdictional conflicts. Consequently, guidance in the form of experience shared by other countries has been minimal, and the clarification and development of principles of external restraint has been thwarted.

In each of these areas, both German and American law have responded to international conflicts and the increasing potential for such conflicts. They have incorporated into their respective legal approaches to the issue of extraterritoriality mechanisms limiting the scope of the effects principle and taking into account foreign interests. This process is critical to the avoidance of international conflict based on the exercise of international jurisdiction, and can only be characterized as a major international law development.

The particular importance of German law in this process derives from the fact that German law has proceeded further than United States law in sharpening its analytical tools. American law has taken refuge in relatively vague notions such as "comity" and "jurisdictional rule of reason," and, as a result, it has yet to develop the conceptual and analytical strength necessary to accomplish its conflict-avoidance purposes effectively.[97]

A related and perhaps even more important fact is that German law has sought, and found, conceptual guidance and structure in the processes of public international law.[98] This is of critical importance, because a comparison of United States and German developments suggests that achieving a workable international jurisdictional framework may require greater reliance on public international law as a source of conflict-avoidance principles.

[96] *Id.* at 205.

[97] The draft *Restatement of Foreign Relations Law* (1981) seeks to meet this need by concluding that "reasonableness" is a principle of international law and by specifying the various considerations and the relevant circumstances that need to be weighed in determining whether an exercise of jurisdiction is unreasonable as a matter of law. *See* RESTATEMENT OF THE FOREIGN RELATIONS LAW OF THE UNITED STATES (REVISED) §403, Comment and Reporters' Notes (Tent. Draft No. 2, 1981).

[98] This is to suggest neither that the German approach here outlined has been fully accepted in Germany nor that it is without weaknesses. *See, e.g.,* Harms, *supra* note 49.

Indeed, in regard to the specific issue of premerger notification, American law has achieved a more effective solution to the problems raised. Not coincidentally, however, this is an area in which American law relies not on case law principles, but on recent statutory developments. *See* 15 U.S.C. §18A (1981).

ICSID ARBITRATION AND THE COURTS

*By Georges R. Delaume**

The Convention on the Settlement of Investment Disputes Between States and Nationals of Other States (the Convention)[1] provides for a truly international arbitration machinery,[2] operating under the auspices of the International Centre for Settlement of Investment Disputes (ICSID).

Within the framework of the Convention and of the Regulations and Rules adopted for its implementation, ICSID arbitration constitutes a self-contained machinery functioning in total independence from domestic legal systems. The autonomous character of ICSID arbitration is clearly stated in Article 44 of the Convention, according to which:

> Any arbitration proceeding shall be conducted in accordance with the provisions of this Section and, except as the parties otherwise agree, in accordance with the Arbitration Rules in effect on the date on which the parties consented to arbitration. If any question of procedure arises which is not covered by this Section or the Arbitration Rules or any rules agreed by the parties, the Tribunal shall decide the question;

and in Article 26 of the Convention, which provides: "Consent of the parties to arbitration under this Convention shall, unless otherwise stated, be deemed consent to such arbitration to the exclusion of any other remedy."[3]

By submitting to ICSID arbitration, the parties therefore have the assurance that they may take full advantage of procedural rules[4] specifically adapted to their needs and, equally important, that the administration of these rules will

* Senior Legal Adviser, International Bank for Reconstruction and Development. The views expressed in this paper are those of the author and do not necessarily represent those of the IBRD or of ICSID.

[1] 17 UST 1270, TIAS No. 6090, 575 UNTS 159.

[2] The Convention also provides for conciliation of investment disputes. The first request for conciliation was registered by the ICSID Secretariat on Oct. 5, 1982. However, because this article exclusively concerns issues arising in the context of ICSID arbitration, no more will be said about ICSID conciliation facilities.

[3] Pursuant to the second sentence of Article 26, the rule formulated in that provision is subject to one exception: as a condition of its consent to ICSID arbitration, a contracting state may require the exhaustion of local administrative or judicial remedies.

So far, this exception has had little practical significance. None of the ICSID clauses known to the secretariat requires exhaustion of local remedies. Nor do investment laws referring to ICSID as a means of settling investment disputes and the overwhelming majority of bilateral investment protection treaties, with the exception of those concluded by Romania. The Romanian treaties all provide that consent to ICSID arbitration is limited to issues of compensation following preliminary adjudication by the Romanian courts. G. DELAUME, TRANSNATIONAL CONTRACTS, para. 15.18 (1982 updating).

[4] The parties enjoy the same freedom of choice in the selection of the substantive rules applicable to their relationship. *See* Art. 42 of the Convention. For concrete illustrations, see G. DELAUME, note 3 *supra*, para. 15.24.

be exempt from the scrutiny or control of domestic courts in states that are parties to the Convention (contracting states).

In the context of the Convention, domestic courts must abstain from taking any action that might interfere with the autonomous and exclusive character of ICSID arbitration. In other words, if a court in a contracting state becomes aware that a claim before it may call for adjudication under ICSID, the court ought to stay the proceedings pending proper determination of the issue by ICSID. So long as such determination is not made and the possibility exists that the claim may fall within the jurisdiction of ICSID, the court must refrain from further consideration of the matter and refer the parties to ICSID to seek a ruling on the subject. It is only in the event of an adverse decision by ICSID (which may result from a refusal by the Secretary-General to register a request for arbitration or from a decision of an ICSID arbitral tribunal holding that the issue involved does not fall within its "competence"[5]) that the court in question could resume hearing the case, assuming, of course, that it would have an independent basis for entertaining jurisdiction over the parties and the subject matter of the dispute.

This "rule of abstention," which is essential to the proper implementation of the Convention,[6] finds its sanction in Article 64 of the Convention, according to which: "Any dispute between Contracting States concerning the interpretation or application of this Convention which is not settled by negotiation shall be referred to the International Court of Justice by application of any party to such dispute, unless the States concerned agree to another method of settlement."

Since this rule of abstention is directly relevant to the "interpretation" or "application" of the Convention, failure by a domestic court to comply with the rule might expose its own state to the type of international claim that is referred to in Article 64.

Under the Convention, the sole role assigned to domestic courts relates to the recognition and enforcement of ICSID awards. As discussed below,[7] that role is one of judicial assistance intended to promote the effectiveness of such awards.

Recently, courts in the United States and in France have been given the opportunity to consider these basic features of the Convention. In the United States, *Maritime International Nominees Establishment v. The Republic of Guinea (MINE v. Guinea)*[8] touches upon issues concerning the rule of abstention, but

[5] *See* notes 21 to 23 *infra* and accompanying text.

[6] The rule of abstention was clearly advocated in the Brief for the United States as Intervenor and Suggestion of Interest in *MINE v. Guinea* (*see* note 8 *infra* for references): "To prevent United States courts from improperly asserting jurisdiction over ICSID cases, and to accord the necessary deference to ICSID's jurisdictional autonomy, the United States submits that a rule of abstention should be followed in U.S. courts." Brief No. 81-1073, at 48–49 (Oct. 1981).

This argument is consistent with that made by the United States in regard to claims that might fall within the jurisdiction of the Iran-United States Claims Tribunal. *See* Statement of Interest of the United States, Crocker Nat'l Bank v. The Government of Iran, No. 79 Civ. 6493 (S.D.N.Y., Statement filed Feb. 26, 1981), *reprinted in* 20 ILM 363, 374 (1981).

[7] *See* part II of this paper.

[8] 693 F.2d 1094 (D.C. Cir. 1982), *reprinted in* 21 ILM 1355 (1982), *as amended,* 22 ILM 86

falls short of considering all its implications. In contrast, the French decision in *Benvenuti & Bonfant Co. v. The Government of the People's Republic of Congo (B&B v. Congo)*[9] neatly implements the provisions of the Convention concerning the recognition and enforcement of ICSID awards.

Because these decisions are the only ones that have so far been rendered in the context of the Convention, they deserve particular attention and careful analysis.

I. *MINE v. GUINEA* AND THE RULE OF ABSTENTION

In 1971, MINE, a Liechtenstein corporation, and the Republic of Guinea entered into a contract providing for the creation under the laws of Guinea of a joint venture, known as SOTRAMAR, whose purpose was to provide shipping services to transport bauxite mined in Guinea to foreign markets.

The contract provided for the settlement of disputes first by conciliation and, if conciliation failed, by arbitration by a panel of three arbitrators appointed by the "President"[10] of ICSID. The site of arbitration was not specified. This dispute settlement clause may have been intended as an ICSID conciliation/arbitration clause.[11] However, technically it could not be treated as such. All that it accomplished, as do similar clauses,[12] was to designate ICSID as an appointing authority; it did not constitute consent to ICSID conciliation/arbitration under the Convention. The parties must have subsequently become aware of the shortcomings of this clause. In 1975 they agreed upon a new stipulation that provided expressly for the submission of disputes to ICSID.[13]

(1983). For the decision of the district court, see 505 F.Supp. 141 (D.D.C. 1981), *reprinted in* 20 ILM 669 (1981).

[9] S.A.R.L. Benvenutti [*sic*] & Bonfant v. Gouvernement de la république du Congo (Cour d'appel Paris, June 26, 1981), 20 ILM 878 (1981) (in English translation), and 108 J. DROIT INT'L 843 (1981) (original French).

[10] The reference should have been to the "Chairman" of the Administrative Council of ICSID.

[11] *See* the amended decision of the court of appeals, 22 ILM at 88–89, nn.11 & 12 and accompanying text.

[12] A typical illustration is found in the provisions consistently stipulated in guarantee agreements between Brazil and foreign lenders relating to loans made to Brazilian public entities. Brazil is not yet a member of ICSID and there is therefore no possibility of bringing potential disputes between the lenders and Brazil within the scope of the Convention. However, the parties have found a way to place such disputes under the aegis of ICSID: they provide for ad hoc arbitration and stipulate that if one arbitrator is not appointed within certain time limits, the appointment will be made by the Secretary-General of ICSID at the request of the most diligent party.

Other stipulations requesting that the Secretary-General of ICSID act as appointing authority are submitted from time to time to ICSID.

[13] The consent clause read as follows:

> SUBMISSION OF DISPUTE TO THE INTERNATIONAL CENTER FOR THE SETTLEMENT OF INVESTMENT DISPUTES
>
> The Government of the Republic of Guinea (hereinafter called "the Host State") and Maritime International Nominees Establishment (hereinafter called "the Investor") hereby agree to submit to the International Center for the Settlement of Investment Disputes (hereinafter called "the Center") in order to settle by arbitration by virtue of the Convention for the Settlement of Investment Disputes between States and Nationals of other States the

What happened next is not clear. By Guinea's account, MINE agreed to file the consent and a formal arbitration request with ICSID. MINE took no such step and, some 3 years later, filed a petition in the United States District Court for the District of Columbia to compel arbitration under section 4 of the Federal Arbitration Act (FAA),[14] asserting jurisdiction under both the Foreign Sovereign Immunities Act (FSIA)[15] and the FAA.

MINE served process upon Guinea by mailing copies of the relevant documents via registered mail to the Ministry of Foreign Affairs in Conakry, Guinea. MINE also sent the same documents by certified mail to the Embassy of Guinea in Washington, D.C. Guinea did not respond.

In June 1978, the district court heard argument on MINE's petition. Guinea made no appearance and the court entered an order granting MINE's petition and ordering arbitration before the American Arbitration Association (AAA).

In September 1978, MINE filed a demand for arbitration before the AAA, and served notice of the demand by the same method it had followed earlier. Arbitration hearings took place in 1979–1980. Guinea did not appear or file any response and in June 1980, the arbitrators rendered an *ex parte* award against Guinea in excess of $25 million.

In August 1980, MINE returned to the district court, filing a motion to confirm the award and enter judgment thereon under section 9 of the FAA. Once again MINE served process upon Guinea by the method followed earlier.

On December 9, 1980, Guinea entered the proceedings for the first time and filed a motion to dismiss for lack of jurisdiction. Guinea argued that neither the FAA, the Rules of the AAA, nor the FSIA provided the court with subject matter jurisdiction and that the court's earlier order to compel AAA arbitration rested on an incorrect premise because ICSID arbitration was available.

On January 12, 1981, the court confirmed the award and entered judgment. According to the court:

> (1) by agreeing to arbitration under the auspices of ICSID, Guinea had implicitly agreed to submit to arbitration in the United States, since ICSID headquarters are located in Washington, D.C.;
>
> (2) consent to arbitration in the United States constituted a waiver of Guinea's immunity from suit under section 1605(a)(1) of the FSIA;
>
> (3) numerous meetings in Connecticut and the District of Columbia relating to the contract showed that Guinea had conducted substantial

---

following disputes: All disputes existing between the "A" and "B" shareholders of SOTRAMAR deriving from the Convention of August 19, 1971 between the Host State and the Investor. The parties hereby precise [*sic*] that the investor is Swiss. Any Court of arbitration constituted on the occasion of a dispute submitted to the Center by virtue of the present agreement shall be composed of one arbitrator nominated by each party and one arbitrator nominated by the President of the Board of Directors of the Center who will assume the [chair]manship of the Court.

[14] 9 U.S.C. §4 (1976).

[15] 28 U.S.C. §§1330, 1602–1611 (1976).

commercial activities in the United States, within the meaning of section 1605(a)(2) of the FSIA, sufficient to give jurisdiction to the court; and

(4) since the court had jurisdiction over Guinea, the order compelling arbitration was proper and the court had authority to confirm the award.[16]

This decision was more than questionable. In the first place, it ignored the fact that under section 1604 of the FSIA, the provisions of the Act apply only "subject to existing international agreements to which the United States is a party." The Convention is clearly one of these agreements. Consequently, the court should have acknowledged the exclusive character of ICSID arbitration under Article 26 of the Convention and on that ground alone stayed the proceedings.

Aside from this fundamental consideration, the court's assumption that ICSID arbitration necessarily takes place in the United States was incorrect. To be sure, Article 62 of the Convention provides that in the absence of agreement between the parties, ICSID proceedings take place at the seat of the Centre, *i.e.*, in Washington, D.C. However, pursuant to Article 63, the parties may agree that the proceedings will take place in another location, *i.e.*, at the seat of arbitration institutions with which ICSID has made appropriate arrangements. Such arrangements have been concluded with the Permanent Court of Arbitration at The Hague, and with the Asian-African Legal Consultative Committee and the Regional Centre for Commercial Arbitration (in Kuala Lumpur), and the Regional Centre for Commercial Arbitration (in Cairo). In addition, the parties are free to choose another situs of arbitration, subject only to the approval of the arbitral tribunal after consultation with the Secretary-General of ICSID. In fact, the majority of ICSID proceedings have been held outside the United States.[17]

Under the circumstances, to assimilate an ICSID clause to an ordinary agreement providing for arbitration in the United States,[18] and to derive from

[16] 505 F.Supp. 141 (D.D.C. 1981), 20 ILM 669 (1981). *See* Shifman, *Maritime International Nominees Establishment v. Republic of Guinea: Effect on U.S. Jurisdiction of an Agreement by a Foreign Sovereign to Arbitrate before the International Centre for Settlement of Investment Disputes,* 16 GEO. WASH. J. INT'L L. & ECON. 451 (1982).

[17] In practice, ICSID proceedings have taken place in the following locations:

Proceedings No.	First Meeting of the Tribunal	Hearings
(1)	The Hague	Paris
(2)	Geneva	Geneva and Lausanne
(3)	Washington, D.C.	Washington, D.C.
(4)	Washington, D.C.	Washington, D.C.
(5)	Washington, D.C.	Washington, D.C.
(6)	No meeting	None
(7)	Paris	Paris
(8)	Paris	Paris
(9)	The Hague	The Hague
(10)	Washington, D.C.	Paris
(11)	New York City	Paris

[18] Pursuant to §1605(a)(1) of the FSIA, a state is not immune when it has waived its immunity

this a basis for the jurisdiction of U.S. courts under the FSIA, was simply an untenable position.

Guinea appealed. It claimed, *inter alia,* that the district court had erred in ruling that Guinea was not immune under the FSIA and that consent to ICSID arbitration deprived the district court of jurisdiction. The Court of Appeals for the District of Columbia Circuit reversed the district court's decision, but only on the ground that Guinea was entitled to immunity from suit. The court considered that neither the negotiations surrounding the SOTRAMAR contract nor the circumstances of its breach offered sufficient contacts with the United States to deny Guinea immunity under section 1605(a)(2) of the FSIA.

Turning to the waiver of immunity allegedly found in the consent to ICSID arbitration, the court of appeals held that such consent was not a waiver of immunity within the meaning of section 1605(a)(1) because:

> MINE has insisted, and is estopped from denying, that United States courts were powerless to compel an ICSID arbitration under this particular arbitration agreement. . . . Given that this point is now established for purposes of this litigation, we have no trouble holding that this particular ICSID agreement was not an agreement "to arbitrate in another country" that waives sovereign immunity under the FSIA. A key reason why pre-FSIA cases found that an agreement to arbitrate in the United States waived immunity from suit was that such agreement could only be effective if deemed to contemplate a role for United States courts in compelling arbitration that stalled along the way. . . . As this particular ICSID agreement concededly did not foresee such a role for United States courts, we hold that it did not waive Guinea's sovereign immunity even though the agreed-to arbitration would probably take place on United States soil;[19]

and that, in any case, the transaction did not bear sufficient contacts with the United States to found jurisdiction under section 1605(a)(2) of the FSIA.[20]

The Rationale of the Decision

As appears from the above-quoted language of the judgment of the court of appeals, the court based its decision on the consideration that U.S. courts

---

"either explicitly or by implication." The legislative history mentions as an example of implicit waiver the case "where a foreign state has agreed to arbitration in another country." H. REP. NO. 1487, 94th Cong., 2d Sess. 18 (1976).

There has been some divergence of opinion on the question whether by referring to "another country," the authors of the FSIA had in mind the United States or considered that so long as the situs of arbitration was outside the territory of the state involved, submission to arbitration constituted an implicit waiver of immunity. *See* Ipitrade Int'l S.A. v. Federal Republic of Nigeria, 465 F.Supp 824 (D.D.C. 1978); Verlinden B.V. v. Central Bank of Nigeria, 488 F.Supp 1284 (S.D.N.Y. 1980), *aff'd,* 647 F.2d 320 (2d Cir. 1981), *rev'd and remanded,* 103 S.Ct. 1962 (1983); Libyan American Oil Co. v. Socialist People's Libyan Arab Jamahirya, 482 F.Supp. 1175 (D.D.C. 1980), and the U.S. amicus curiae brief *reproduced in* 20 ILM 161 (1981).

[19] 693 F.2d at 1102–03 (footnote omitted).

[20] *Id.* at 1103. Since this article is limited to that part of the decision concerning ICSID, it will

could not "compel an ICSID arbitration," and therefore that consent to ICSID did not waive Guinea's immunity under the FSIA. These two points deserve further elaboration.

The consideration that domestic (and not only U.S.) courts cannot "compel" ICSID arbitration is correct in the sense that any other solution would directly interfere with the prerogatives of the Secretary-General of ICSID and of ICSID arbitral tribunals.

Under Article 36(3) of the Convention, the Secretary-General is given the right to refuse to register a request for arbitration if he finds, on the basis of the information supplied by the requesting party, that the dispute is "manifestly outside the jurisdiction" of ICSID. This "screening power" must be exercised with great care. As there is no appeal from the Secretary-General's decision, a refusal to register a request would be a definite bar to the use of ICSID facilities.[21]

Registration of a request by the Secretary-General is only one step in a two-stage process. It has no bearing upon the ultimate power of an ICSID arbitral tribunal to rule on its own "competence" (Article 41(1) of the Convention). Among other decisions,[22] that of the tribunal in the *Holiday Inns* case[23] illustrates this remark. The claimants, a Swiss and a U.S. company, filed claims against the Government of Morocco both in their own names and on behalf of certain subsidiaries incorporated in Morocco. The tribunal held that it had jurisdiction and could hear the principal claimants, but that the subsidiaries were not entitled to participate in the proceedings. As discussed later,[24] this type of issue is not excluded from being raised in the context of the dispute between MINE and Guinea, should it be submitted to ICSID.

Under the circumstances, it is apparent that no domestic court can "compel" ICSID arbitration. However, this does not mean that a domestic court can remain indifferent to the alleged existence of an ICSID arbitration agreement. As stated earlier, the proper course of action for the court in such circumstances is to stay the proceedings and to refer the parties to ICSID. This is an issue that the court in *MINE v. Guinea* deliberately refused to

---

not discuss the jurisdictional aspects of the case under §1605(a)(2) of the FSIA. See in this respect G. DELAUME, note 3 *supra*, para. 11.10.

[21] So far, the Secretary-General has never refused to register a request for ICSID arbitration. However, before agreeing to register a request, the Secretary-General has on occasion sought supplementary information to make sure that, prima facie, the conditions set forth in the Convention were satisfied.

[22] Alcoa Minerals of Jamaica, Inc./Kaiser Bauxite Co./Reynolds Jamaica Mines Ltd. and Reynolds Metals Co. v. Government of Jamaica, Decision of July 5–6, 1975, as summarized in Schmidt, *Arbitration under the Auspices of the International Centre for Settlement of Investment Disputes (ICSID): Implications of the Decision on Jurisdiction in Alcoa Minerals of Jamaica Inc. v. Government of Jamaica,* 17 HARV. INT'L L.J. 90, 96 *et seq.* (1976); Société Ltd. Benvenuti & Bonfant srl v. Government of the People's Republic of the Congo, Decision of Jan. 17–19, 1978, summarized in ICSID, FIFTEENTH ANNUAL REPORT 1980/1981, at 41.

[23] Holiday Inns/Occidental Petroleum v. Government of Morocco, Decision of the arbitral tribunal of July 1, 1973, as summarized by Lalive, *The First "World Bank" Arbitration (Holiday Inns v. Morocco)—Some Legal Problems,* 51 BRIT. Y.B. INT'L L. 123, 137 *et seq.* (1980).

[24] *See* notes 37 to 39 *infra* and accompanying text.

consider, which is somewhat surprising because the court was perfectly aware of the exclusive remedy rule set forth in Article 26 of the Convention and of the "self-executing" character of ICSID "processes."[25] The court also noted that the State Department had urged the court "to find that agreements to arbitrate with ICSID do not contemplate the involvement of domestic courts, at least not before a final ICSID decision is to be enforced."[26]

Disregarding these considerations, the court concluded that it did not have to reach these precise questions because, as stated above, MINE was estopped from denying that U.S. courts were powerless to compel ICSID arbitration and that under the circumstances consent to ICSID arbitration could not be considered as a waiver of immunity within the meaning of the FSIA.

In the final analysis, therefore, this decision, like that of the district court, is based on considerations found in the domestic law of the forum, *i.e.*, the FSIA. It should have been based instead on grounds consistent with the purposes of the Convention and the international character of ICSID arbitration. The court should have taken into account certain basic features of the Convention, which are characteristic of the ICSID machinery and are of direct relevance to issues of immunity.

One of the major purposes of the Convention is to maintain a careful balance between the interests of investors and those of contracting states.

The Convention gives investors direct access to an international forum and assures them that the refusal or abstention of the state party to a dispute to participate in the proceedings cannot prevent the institution, conduct, and conclusion of the proceedings, and the recognition and enforcement of an ICSID award. For the purposes of the Convention, therefore, consent to ICSID arbitration constitutes an irrevocable waiver of immunity from suit by the state involved. Thus bound, that state is barred from raising any plea of immunity that would frustrate the proceedings or the recognition of the resulting award. Within the framework of the Convention, immunity from suit is eradicated at the outset.

In exchange, the Convention protects contracting states from other forms of foreign or international litigation. Because consent to ICSID arbitration is just as binding upon the investor as it is on the state party to the dispute, that state is assured that the investor cannot bring action in a non-ICSID forum, whether in the investor's own state or somewhere else. In other words, both parties must respect the exclusive character of ICSID remedies. Furthermore, the Convention expressly provides that when an investor and a contracting state have agreed to submit investment disputes to ICSID arbitration, the state whose national is party to the agreement may not espouse the case of its national, give that national diplomatic protection, or bring an international claim in respect of the dispute.[27]

[25] 693 F.2d at 1102.

[26] *Ibid.*

[27] Art. 27 of the Convention. The effect of this provision is limited to the period starting from the date of consent to the rendition of an award. If, after an award is rendered, the contracting state party to the dispute refuses to comply with the award, the right of diplomatic protection will revive. *See* note 61 *infra* and accompanying text.

Under the circumstances, it is clear that the Convention, and not the FSIA, supplied the correct answer to the problem that confronted the court of appeals. *MINE v. Guinea* must therefore be regarded as a missed opportunity to give the decision its proper legal setting.

The Rule of Abstention Illustrated

Investment disputes often raise delicate questions of law and fact that require careful determination by either the Secretary-General or ICSID tribunals or both. Examples borrowed from ICSID's experience, as well as certain issues involved in *Mine v. Guinea,* that might arise if that case is one day submitted to ICSID illustrate the nature of the problem and the implications of the rule of abstention.

Consent to ICSID Arbitration. In *MINE v. Guinea,* MINE alleged that the 1975 agreement providing for ICSID arbitration was deficient in certain respects and, in particular, because it had not been signed by Guinea. According to MINE, these defects made it impossible for MINE to submit the dispute to ICSID.[28]

On the basis of the affidavits and evidence presented by MINE, the district court found that MINE "could not have proceeded under the contract"[29] or, in other words, that ICSID arbitration was not available. This finding was regrettable. Not only did it substitute the court's judgment for that of ICSID, but it showed an ignorance of the fact that consent to ICSID may be a matter significantly more complex than the court was led to assume.

Article 25(1) of the Convention merely states that consent must be "in writing"; it does not specify the type of instrument in which consent may be expressed.

In most cases, consent takes the form of an ICSID arbitration clause in an investment agreement. However, consent does not have to be recorded in a single instrument and can be expressed in an exchange of letters or other documents. Consent may also result from a unilateral offer by one of the parties subsequently accepted by the other party. Examples are found in domestic investment laws intended to promote investments and in investment protection treaties concluded by contracting states.[30] In such cases, the state involved may agree in advance to submit investment disputes to ICSID arbitration and "consent" becomes binding when the investor indicates that it also agrees to this method of settlement. The investor's acceptance of the offer may be recorded either at the time of the investment or subsequently,

[28] *See* Shifman, note 16 *supra,* at 454–55.

[29] 505 F.Supp. at 142 n.2. *See also* the amended opinion of the court of appeals, 22 ILM at 88, according to which: "Because exhibits filed by MINE itself in connection with its motion to confirm demand this very conclusion, we cannot say that the District Court's factual finding was clearly erroneous" (footnote omitted).

[30] G. DELAUME, note 3 *supra,* paras. 15.07–15.08. *See also* Broches, *Bilateral Investment Protection Treaties and Arbitration of Investment Disputes,* in THE ART OF ARBITRATION—LIBER AMICORUM PIETERS SANDERS 63 (1982); Mann, *British Treaties for the Promotion and Protection of Investments,* 52 BRIT. Y.B. INT'L L. 241 (1982).

including, at the limit, when the investor submits a request for arbitration to ICSID.

In view of these various alternatives, ascertaining that consent exists is a task that must be discharged with great care. Additional difficulties are not excluded. This point is nicely illustrated by *Alcoa Minerals of Jamaica Inc. / Kaiser Bauxite Co. / Reynolds Jamaica Mines Ltd. and Reynolds Metals Co. v. The Government of Jamaica.*[31] The original agreements between each of the plaintiffs and Jamaica provided, *inter alia,* for the "stabilization" of certain taxes and for ICSID arbitration. Some years later, Jamaica notified ICSID that it intended to exclude from its consent disputes arising out of "an investment relating to mineral and other resources."[32] This notification was intended to be both prospective and retrospective in effect. One month after the notification, Jamaica decided to increase significantly the amount of taxes payable by the plaintiffs. The plaintiffs instituted arbitration proceedings, and it was held that since the initial consent of Jamaica was unconditional and unqualified, no retrospective effect could be given to the notification.[33] Following these decisions, the disputes were amicably settled.

Although these proceedings took place exclusively in an ICSID context, it is not difficult to imagine that one party might try to have some of the issues involved adjudicated in a non-ICSID forum, contrary to its consent to ICSID arbitration.[34] In such a case, the forum in question should observe the rule of abstention, for the reasons stated earlier.

The Nationality of the Investor. Only disputes between a contracting state (or under certain conditions, one of its subdivisions or agencies[35]) and a "national" of another contracting state may be submitted to ICSID arbitration. Geared to the promotion of investments, the Convention excludes from its scope disputes between international persons, including contracting states, and disputes between private law persons. Subject to an important qualification, which is discussed below, the Convention also excludes disputes between a contracting state and one of its nationals.

Under Article 25(2) of the Convention, the term "national" applies to both physical and juridical persons. So far, the nationality of physical persons has raised no difficulty. However, the determination of the nationality of a juridical person is directly relevant to a further examination of *MINE v. Guinea.*

It is generally agreed that for the purposes of the Convention, the nation-

[31] The procedural history of these cases is recorded in ICSID, *supra* note 22, at 34–39. *See also* Schmidt, note 22 *supra.*

[32] Regarding the right of a contracting state to notify ICSID of the classes of disputes that it would or would not submit to ICSID, see notes 43 to 45 *infra* and accompanying text.

[33] Schmidt, note 22 *supra,* at 103.

[34] *Compare* in the case of a non-ICSID arbitration the facts involved in Revere Copper & Brass Inc. v. Overseas Private Inv. Corp. (OPIC), 17 ILM 1321 (1978).

[35] Under Article 25(1) of the Convention, each contracting state is free to designate to ICSID the particular public entities that it considers eligible to become parties to ICSID proceedings. Such a designation is not enough, however, to authorize a subdivision or agency to consent to ICSID arbitration. Under Article 25(3) of the Convention, such consent also requires the approval of the contracting state involved unless that state notifies ICSID that its approval is not required. Doc. ICSID/8/Rev.9 (Dec. 31, 1981) refers to the designations that have been made.

ality of a juridical person is determined on the basis of its place of incorporation or seat (*siège social*). Consequently, a corporation or other juridical person incorporated in Contracting State *A* and investing in Contracting State *B* is eligible to be a party to ICSID arbitration. A corporation incorporated in State *B* would not be so eligible, because of lack of diversity.[36]

This situation would change, however, if State *B* agreed to treat the corporation as a national of another contracting state because it was under the "foreign control" of nationals of that state.[37] This exception to the general rule is intended to account for the situation, which is not rare, in which a host government insists that foreign investors channel their investment through a locally incorporated company. The exception permits investors to comply with such a requirement while preserving their right to submit investment disputes to ICSID.

During the proceedings in *MINE v. Guinea,* MINE raised a novel question, which is not dealt with in the appeals court's decision but deserves mention because of its possible implications for the future. MINE is a Liechtenstein company. Liechtenstein is not a contracting state. Therefore, the basic condition set forth in the Convention would have been lacking, were it not for the fact that in the 1975 agreement the parties agreed to treat MINE as a "Swiss" national, Switzerland being a contracting state.

MINE argued that this characterization of itself as "Swiss" was invalid because it exceeded the scope of Article 25(2)(b) of the Convention.[38] According to MINE, the scope of that provision should be limited to situations in which the company involved is incorporated in the host contracting state. If a company were incorporated in a third state, neither the company nor the host state would have the power to agree upon the nationality of that company, even if it was controlled by nationals of another state. Guinea challenged the validity of this argument on the ground that, consent being the paramount feature of the ICSID Convention, the parties to an ICSID clause were free to determine the nationality of the investor as they deemed appropriate in the light of the surrounding circumstances.

The question is a difficult one. To be sure, most of the discussions relating to the successive drafts of what became Article 25(2)(b) focused primarily on the case of companies incorporated in the host state, yet under foreign control, and on the possible definition of what should be understood by "foreign control." Nevertheless, the *travaux préparatoires* of the Convention show that the discussions covered a much broader range and that the general feeling was that since consent is the cornerstone of the Convention, each contracting state, at the time it agreed to ICSID conciliation/arbitration should be free to determine to its own satisfaction whether it was willing to treat a particular company as the "national" of another contracting state, regardless of the place of incorporation of that company.[39]

[36] *See* the *Holiday Inns* case mentioned in the text at note 23 *supra.*

[37] Art. 25(2)(b) of the Convention.

[38] Brief for Appellee and Addenda thereto, at 57, 61–66 (D.C. Cir. filed May 22, 1981).

[39] 2 ICSID, LEGISLATIVE HISTORY OF THE CONVENTION ON THE SETTLEMENT OF IN-

Whether this issue will be submitted to ICSID in the context of possible proceedings is unknown at this time. All that can be said is that the complexity of the issue and its significance for the "interpretation" and "application" of the Convention place the final determination clearly beyond the cognizance of domestic courts.

The Notion of Investment. Neither the *Legislative History of the Convention* nor Article 25(1) supplies a precise definition of "investment," even though that term is of fundamental importance to the implementation of the Convention.

The Convention was drafted at a time when most investments took the form of concessions, joint ventures, or loans made by private financial institutions to foreign public entities and, to a certain extent, of arrangements concerning industrial property rights. Since then, new forms of association between states and foreign investors have appeared, such as profit sharing, service and management contracts, contracts for the sale and erection of industrial plants, turn-key contracts, international leasing arrangements, and agreements for the transfer of know-how and of technology.

In the context of contemporary thinking and practices, an economic concept of investment is progressively being substituted for the traditional notion of investment in capital. The progressive reception of that concept can only give new meaning to the Convention and widen its scope. In effect, ICSID arbitration clauses known to the secretariat refer to a variety of transactions corresponding to the modern notion of investment.[40] This is a fact that bodes well for the future of the Convention and is testimony to its adaptability to a new investment climate.

However, and particularly in regard to transactions characterized by the supply of services rather than by capital contributions, it must be acknowledged that the nature of the transaction is not always apparent at the outset. Marginal cases falling between investments proper and commercial ventures are not rare and may fit in either category depending upon the more or less complex features of individual transactions.

For these reasons, the ICSID Secretariat has, over the years, consistently reminded the parties to ICSID clauses of the importance of, first, stating in the instrument recording their consent that the particular transaction between them constitutes an investment for the purposes of the Convention, and second, of supplementing such a statement with a description of the salient features of the transaction, such as those concerning its nature, size, and duration.[41]

At the same time, the secretariat has been careful to recall that

> the definition agreed upon by the parties does not deprive: (i) the Secretary-General of his right to refuse to register a request for ICSID

VESTMENT DISPUTES BETWEEN STATES AND NATIONALS OF OTHER STATES 260, 359, 447–50, 851–52 (1970).

[40] These clauses are found in arrangements concerning the industrial or agricultural development of a particular state or the development of its touristic or port facilities, as well as in turnkey contracts and contracts for the transfer of technology, especially in matters of electronics and air transportation.

[41] *See* ICSID Model Clauses, Doc. ICSID/5/Rev.1, sec. 2 (1981).

> Conciliation/Arbitration if he finds, on the basis of the information contained in the request, that the dispute is manifestly outside the jurisdiction of ICSID (e.g., because it is a "commercial" rather than an "investment" dispute); or (ii) the Conciliation Commission/Arbitral Tribunal from ruling that the dispute in question is or is not within its own competence.[42]

This admonition is directly addressed to the parties. As a reminder of the prerogatives of the Secretary-General and of ICSID tribunals, it should be equally relevant in the event of possible litigation in the courts of contracting states. So much the more when it is recalled that, pursuant to Article 25(4) of the Convention, any contracting state may notify ICSID of the class or classes of disputes that it may be willing or not to submit to ICSID arbitration.

To date, only four contracting states have used this option. Three states have notified ICSID that they intended to exclude investment disputes relating to "oil and pertaining to acts of sovereignty" (Saudi Arabia[43]), or to "the mineral and other natural resources" of the contracting state (Guyana and Jamaica[44]). Papua New Guinea has specified that "it will only consider submitting those disputes to the Centre which are fundamental to the investment itself."[45]

Admittedly, the language of these declarations is broad and may require interpretation. Because of the obvious need to secure uniformity of interpretation, the matter, if it should be raised, would fall exclusively within the jurisdiction of ICSID.

II. *B&B v. Congo*: Recognition and Enforcement of ICSID Awards

On April 16, 1973, an Agreement was executed by the Government of the People's Republic of Congo and the Italian company Benvenuti & Bonfant to create a semi-public company for the manufacture of plastic bottles. This Agreement included, under Article 12, the following arbitration clause:

> Any dispute between the parties arising out of the performance of this Agreement that could not be amicably settled shall be submitted to arbitration within the framework of the Convention on the Settlement of Investment Disputes between States and Nationals of Other States, of March 18, 1965, prepared by the I.B.R.D. The proceedings shall be conducted in the French language. The parties hereby agree to abide by the arbitral award and undertake to comply with its terms, and to waive any right to any appeal or other power [*sic*] of such award. The costs of arbitration shall be borne equally by the parties.

Following the creation of the PLASCO company, that company and the SODISCA company entered into a contract, dated April 21, 1973, for the delivery on a turn-key basis of a plant to manufacture thermo-plastic bottles and a plant to bottle mineral water. Disputes arose, however, between the parties to the April 16, 1973 Agreement.

[42] *Ibid.*

[43] Doc. ICSID/8/Rev.9, *supra* note 35 (this document is being revised and updated).

[44] *Ibid.* [45] *Ibid.*

On December 15, 1977, Benvenuti & Bonfant addressed a request for arbitration, dated December 12, 1977, to the International Centre for Settlement of Investment Disputes.[46] The arbitral tribunal rendered its award on August 8, 1980.[47]

In subsequent proceedings, B&B petitioned the court of first instance in Paris, France (*Tribunal de Grande Instance*) to give recognition to the award. On December 23, 1980, the President of the tribunal granted the petition, subject, however, to the following reservation: "We rule that no measure of execution, or even a conservatory measure, can be taken pursuant to said award, on any assets located in France without prior authorization" (as translated from the French). B&B objected to the reservation, but by order dated January 13, 1981,[48] the President of the tribunal refused to amend or delete that part of his earlier order that had been challenged. B&B appealed. However, before the appellate decision is considered on its own merits, an interim remark is needed to place both that decision and the order of the President of the lower court in proper perspective.

The French courts do not, as yet, subscribe to the monolithic doctrine of immunity that increasingly prevails in a number of countries.[49] Having accepted the restrictive doctrine of immunity in regard to immunity from suit, the French courts are still hesitant to apply the same doctrine to immunity from execution. All that can be said at this time is that a new trend of thinking is in progress and that if the claimant were to succeed in establishing the commercial use or intended use of a foreign state's property, a plea of immunity from execution might fail.[50] So far, however, the burden of proof imposed upon the claimant has proved overwhelming and incapable of making a real dent in the immunity rule.

Thus, in the most recent case on the subject,[51] creditors of the Iranian Government and Iranian entities had attached funds owed to Iran by the French Government. The court acknowledged that

> [t]he appellee corporations are correct in contending that immunity from execution is not absolute and that it may be disregarded in exceptional circumstances when the property attached is intended by the foreign State's decision for the pursuit of a purely commercial transaction carried on by it or by an entity created by it for the purpose . . . [as translated].

[46] The procedural history of this case is summarized in ICSID, *supra* note 22, at 40–42.

[47] The text of the award in English translation appears in 21 ILM 740 (1982), with a correction in *id.* at 1478.

[48] Benvenuti & Bonfant S.A.R.L. v. Gouvernement de la République du Congo (Trib. gr. inst. Paris, Jan, 13, 1981), 108 J. DROIT INT'L 365 (1981).

[49] *See* G. DELAUME, note 3 *supra*, paras. 12.02–12.04.

[50] Englander v. Statni Banka Ceskoslovenska (Cass. ch. lre, Feb. 11, 1969), 96 J. DROIT INT'L 923 (1969); Clerget v. Représentation commerciale de la République démocratique du Viet-Nam (Cass. ch. lre, Nov. 2, 1971), 99 *id.* at 267 (1972); Caisse algérienne d'assurance vieillesse des non-salariés v. Caisse nationale des barreaux français (Cass. ch. lre, Dec. 7, 1977), 67 REV. CRITIQUE DROIT INT'L PRIVÉ 532 (1978). *See also* G. DELAUME, note 3 *supra*, para. 12.03.

[51] République islamique d'Iran, OIAEFI and OEAI v. Société EURODIF and SOFIDIF (Cour d'appel Paris, Apr. 21, 1982), 1982 REV. ARBITRAGE 204, 110 J. DROIT INT'L 145 (1983). *See also* Bourel, *Arbitrage international et immunités des Etats étrangers,* 1982 REV. ARBITRAGE 119.

Nevertheless, the court vacated the attachment because it was not established that the funds involved were earmarked for commercial purposes and they should therefore be considered as part of the general assets of Iran, and, as such, be immune from measures of execution. The court also held that the fact that the parties had agreed to submit to arbitration under the rules of the International Chamber of Commerce and to give effect to the resulting award did not constitute a waiver of immunity from execution by Iran.

An attempt to introduce more fairness into the implementation of the emerging immunity rule was made in only one case and by the same lower court that subsequently issued the order relating to the *B&B v. Congo* award. Thus, a summary of that earlier decision may be of assistance in understanding the probable rationale of the *B&B* order. The decision took place in the context of the *LIAMCO v. Libya* litigation, which concerned the recognition and enforcement of the *LIAMCO* award[52] in a number of countries, including France.[53] After obtaining recognition of the award in France, LIAMCO proceeded to attach assets of Libya held in French banks. Libya sought to have the attachments vacated, and the French Public Attorney intervened in the proceedings to claim that under the "absolute" doctrine of immunity no measure of execution could obtain against Libya's assets. The court did not agree with this abstract formulation of the doctrine of immunity and considered that the doctrine should be applied in the light of the circumstances of each case. However, the court vacated the attachments on the ground that the evidence before it made it impossible to ascertain whether the assets involved were intended to be used for sovereign or for commercial activities. Unwilling, nevertheless, to let this issue die, the court took the unprecedented step of appointing a committee of three independent persons to determine the precise use of the assets in question.[54] What the outcome of this unusual procedure would have been will forever remain unknown since a settlement ended the litigation.

Still, it is clear that in issuing the *B&B* order, the President of the court was influenced by the *LIAMCO* decision. In words that echo those used in *LIAMCO*, the President said:

> Since it is not immediately possible to segregate the funds or property intended to be used for a sovereign or a public activity and those relating to a simple economic or commercial activity subject to private law, it has not appeared appropriate to us, in the absence of prior investigation, to allow a situation to occur that might interfere with the sovereignty of a foreign State by means of measures of compulsion exclusive of any notion of comity and international independence [as translated].

The major difference between *B&B* and *LIAMCO* is that in *B&B* the President of the court did not wait until the award had been recognized to address

[52] Libyan American Oil Co. (LIAMCO) v. Government of the Libyan Arab Republic, 20 ILM 1 (1981), 62 ILR 140 (1982).

[53] Proceedings took place also in the United States, Sweden, and Switzerland. *See* G. DELAUME, note 3 *supra*, para. 12.03.

[54] Procureur de la République v. Société LIAMCO (Trib. gr. inst. Paris, March 5, 1979), 106 J. DROIT INT'L 857 (1979).

the issue of sovereign immunity and sought to deal with both issues in a single decision. In so doing, the President reached the paradoxical result of granting recognition to the award, while at the same time depriving the award of any practical significance.

On appeal, the Court of Appeal disagreed with the President's reasoning.[55] In general terms, which should be borne in mind in non-ICSID situations, the court held that an order granting recognition to a foreign award is not in itself an act of execution, and that the President had exceeded his authority by dealing at that stage of the proceedings with matters of immunity from execution.

More specifically, the court held that the reservation concerning measures of execution made in the President's order should be deleted since it was directly contrary to the provisions of the ICSID Convention. The court recalled that Article 54(1) of the Convention provides that each contracting state shall recognize an ICSID award and enforce the pecuniary obligations imposed by that award as if it were a final judgment of a court in the recognizing state.

The court also noted that the procedure for the recognition and enforcement of ICSID awards is made as simple as possible, and that under Article 54(2) of the Convention, any party to an ICSID award may obtain recognition and enforcement by furnishing a certified copy of the award to the competent court or authority designated for the purpose by each contracting state.[56] The court said:

> [T]hese provisions offer a simplified procedure for recognition and enforcement (*exequatur simplifié*) and restrict the function of the court designated for the purposes of the Convention by each Contracting State to ascertaining the authenticity of the award certified by the Secretary-General of the International Centre for Settlement of Investment Disputes. . . .
>
> . . . [T]he lower judge, requested pursuant to Article 54 of the Convention of Washington, could not, therefore, without exceeding his authority, deal with the second step, that of execution, to which relates the question of the immunity from execution of foreign States.[57]

Practical Significance of the Decision

The decision of the Court of Appeal of Paris deserves approval. By segregating the issue of recognition and enforcement of an ICSID award from subsequent measures of execution, it is in complete accord with the provisions of the Convention. This is the time to recall that Article 55 of the Convention acknowledges that the procedure for recognition set forth in Article 54 shall in no way "be construed as derogating from the law in force in any Contracting State relating to immunity of that State or of any foreign State from execution."

[55] For references, see note 9 *supra*.

[56] The ICSID Secretariat keeps a current list of the judicial and other authorities designated by contracting states.

[57] 20 ILM at 881.

As a matter of great practical significance, the combination of these two provisions means that (1) as soon as an ICSID award is recognized, it becomes a valid title on whose basis measures of execution can be taken, provided, however, that (2) where such measures are directed at state property (as opposed to the property of an investor), execution is possible under the law of the contracting state in which execution is sought.

Immunity from Execution in the Context of the Convention

The Narrowing Hurdle of Immunity from Execution. Because Article 55 of the Convention surrenders measures of execution to domestic rules of immunity, it is possible that, as in the case of other arbitral awards, those rendered within the framework of the Convention will be subject to different treatment in contracting states.

This solution is to be regretted. However, it could not be avoided in view of the opinions expressed during the drafting stages of the Convention by governmental representatives and the lack of consensus on the meaning and scope of immunity from execution, considered both in its domestic and in its international implications. Insofar as domestic rules of immunity are concerned, they are substantially the same today as at the time the Convention was drafted. In many cases, execution against the public assets of a state is not permissible. The situation may be different in regard to assets owned by other public entities, particularly those engaged in commercial activities, although in this case also domestic rules continue to exhibit variations.

In contrast, since the Convention entered into force in 1966, the rules applicable to immunity from execution considered in an international environment have undergone significant changes. Today, the restrictive doctrine of immunity has made marked progress in a number of countries, and especially in those where most of the world's leading financial centers are located and assets of foreign states are likely to be found.[58] Although the restrictive doctrine of immunity is not uniformly applied, it can only contribute to giving a new practical significance to ICSID awards. The investor in whose favor such an award is rendered is now in a position, with increasing chances of success, to engage in "forum shopping" in order to take advantage of new immunity rules in existence or in the making.

Furthermore, the parties have the opportunity, at the time they consent to submit disputes to ICSID arbitration, to provide expressly that the contracting state involved waives immunity from execution in connection with enforcement of an ICSID award. A typical illustration is found in an agreement relating to a joint venture for the exploitation of diamond deposits in Sierra Leone, according to which: "The State and DIMINCO hereby expressly waive the right to avail themselves of any privilege or immunity of jurisdiction in respect of any arbitration pursuant to this Agreement or the execution or enforcement of any award or judgment as a result thereof."[59]

[58] Such as the United States, the United Kingdom, Canada, and Western European countries. *See* G. DELAUME, note 3 *supra*, ch. XII.

[59] Diminco Agreement (1970), Ratification Act, 1970, approving an Agreement between the

Other examples are found in loan contracts between financial institutions and contracting states, such as the following:

> The parties hereto expressly waive hereby the right to avail themselves of any privilege or immunity of jurisdiction in respect of any arbitration pursuant to this Agreement or the execution or enforcement of any award or judgment as a result thereof.
>
> The Republic hereby agrees that, should any Bank or any holder of any Note bring any judicial proceeding in relation to any matter arising under this Agreement or any of the Notes, including without limitation any arbitration proceeding and any action to enforce any arbitral award, no immunity from such judicial proceeding, from attachment of the Republic's property or from execution of judgment shall be claimed by or on behalf of the Republic or with respect to its properties, any such immunity being hereby waived by the Republic.

These provisions accord with the consistent practice of lenders regarding waivers of immunity in loan agreements with foreign governments.[60]

Sanctions for Noncompliance with an ICSID Award. If an investor fails to comply with an ICSID award, the contracting state party to the dispute will find in Article 54 of the Convention effective means of enforcing the award against the investor and its property. As already mentioned, the great advantage of the Convention over other international conventions regarding the enforcement of foreign arbitral awards is that not even public policy can be raised as a defense against the binding character of ICSID awards. Against an investor, and subject to the recognizing court or authority, an ICSID award is a title that is immediately executory.

The situation may be otherwise if the noncomplying party is the contracting state party to the dispute, since a plea of immunity from execution might effectively bar measures of execution against that state and its assets. This possibility cannot be ignored. However, the fact that under the Convention contracting states do not surrender their right to immunity from execution in no way relieves these states from their treaty commitments. Thus, it is clear that if a contracting state party to a dispute pleaded immunity, either in its own courts or in those of another contracting state, in order to frustrate the enforcement of an ICSID award, that state would violate its obligation to comply with the award. Moreover, the state involved would be exposed to various sanctions, which are expressly provided for in the Convention.

In the first place, failure to comply would restore the right of the contracting state whose national is the award creditor to give diplomatic protection to its national and to bring an international claim on its behalf. Under Article 27(1) of the Convention, diplomatic protection is suspended during the period beginning with the date of consent to ICSID arbitration and ending with compliance with the terms of an ICSID award. It may also terminate with the

---

Government of Sierra Leone and Sierra Leone Selection Trust Limited, CI SIERRA LEONE GAZETTE, No. 89, Supp., Schedule E, para. 2 (Dec. 17, 1970).

[60] G. DELAUME, note 3 *supra*, para. 12.05.

dismissal of the investor's claim by the arbitral tribunal. However, Article 27(1) provides expressly that diplomatic protection may be exercised again if the contracting state party to the dispute fails "to abide by and comply with the award rendered in such dispute."[61]

In the second place, since noncompliance would affect the "application" of the Convention, the contracting state whose national is involved would have the right to use the remedy provided for in Article 64 of the Convention, namely, to submit the question to the International Court of Justice.[62]

CONCLUSION

Two judgments can hardly be considered an established "jurisprudence." However, if the rule of abstention is complied with, as it should be, case law will probably be limited to issues relating to the recognition and enforcement of ICSID awards. Even then, cases cannot be expected to be abundant. In the first place, it is a fact that out of 16 disputes that have been submitted to ICSID, six of which are pending,[63] seven have been the object of settlement or dis-

[61] Certain bilateral investment treaties parallel Article 27(1) of the Convention by providing for the suspension of diplomatic protection unless the dispute is held not to fall within the scope of the ICSID Convention or one of the contracting parties does not comply with an ICSID award. Two examples follow.

(1) The United Kingdom and Bangladesh, Treaty of June 19, 1980, CMND. 8013, Art. 8(2):

> Neither Contracting Party shall pursue through diplomatic channels any dispute referred to the Centre unless
>
> (a) The Secretary General of the Centre, or a conciliation commission or an arbitral tribunal constituted by it, decides that the dispute is not within the jurisdiction of the Centre, or
>
> (b) the other Contracting Party should fail to abide by or to comply with any award rendered by an arbitral tribunal.

(2) The Belgo/Luxembourg Economic Union and Singapore Treaty of Nov. 17, 1978, Moniteur (Belgium), March 10, 1981, at 2722, Art. 9(4):

> Aucune des Parties Contractantes ne poursuivra la solution d'un différend par la voie diplomatique, lorsque celui-ci se trouve soumis au Centre, à moins que:
>
> (a) le Secrétaire Général du Centre estime que le différend dépasse manifestement la compétence du Centre conformément à l'Article 36(3) de la Convention ou que le Tribunal d'arbitrage constitué selon l'Accord décide que le différend n'est pas de la compétence du Centre;
>
> (b) l'autre Partie Contractante omette de respecter ou de se soumettre aux termes de la décision du tribunal d'arbitrage.

[62] *See* text at note 6 *supra.*

[63] (1) Amco Asia Corp., Pan American Development Ltd. and P.T. Amco Indonesia v. Government of Indonesia; (2) Klöckner Industrie-Anlagen GmbH, Klöckner Belge, S.A. and Klöckner Handelsmaatschappij B.V. v. United Republic of Cameroun and Société Camerounaise des Engrais (SOCAME) S.A.; (3) Société Ouest Africaine des Betons Industriels (SOABI) v. Government of Sénégal; (4) Swiss Aluminium Ltd. (ALUSUISSE) and Icelandic Aluminium Co. Ltd. (ISAL) v. Government of Iceland; (5) The Liberian Eastern Timber Corp. (LETCO) v. Government of The Republic of Liberia; Tesoro Petroleum Corp. v. Government of Trinidad and Tobago.

continuance,[64] and only three have ended in an award.[65] Of these three awards, only the one relating to *B&B v. Congo* has been the object of recognition proceedings. In no case have measures of execution been sought. The inference, therefore, is that the awards have been complied with in accordance with the provisions of Article 53(1) of the Convention or that the parties have ultimately reached an amicable settlement.

These encouraging results speak for themselves and for the effectiveness of the ICSID machinery.[66] In the light of these considerations, the theoretically troublesome issue of sovereign immunity from execution seems to lose a great deal of its practical significance.

[64] Holiday Inns/Occidental Petroleum v. Government of Morocco; Alcoa Minerals of Jamaica, Inc./Kaiser Bauxite Co./Reynolds Jamaica Mines Ltd. and Reynolds Metals Co. v. Government of Jamaica (three separate cases); Guadalupe Gas Products Corp. v. Federal Military Government of Nigeria; SEDITEX Engineering Beratungsgesellschaft für die Textilindustrie m.b.H. v. Government of the Democratic Republic of Madagascar.

[65] Adriano Gardella Spa. v. Government of Ivory Coast (unpub.); AGIP s.p.a. v. Government of the People's Republic of the Congo, 64 RIVISTA DIRITTO INTERNAZIONALE 863 (1981) (original French), 21 ILM 726 (1982) (English translation); Ltd. Benvenuti & Bonfant srl. v. Government of the People's Republic of the Congo, note 47 *supra*.

[66] Another encouraging factor concerns ICSID membership. Until recently, ICSID membership was unevenly distributed. It included only limited Arab participation and no participation at all from Latin American countries. The situation has dramatically changed.

Aside from Egypt, Morocco, Sudan, and Tunisia, who were among the first countries to ratify the Convention, Kuwait, Saudi Arabia, and the United Arab Emirates became contracting states in 1979, 1980, and 1981, respectively. This phenomenon is significant; it shows that these countries, which are great importers of technology and investments, are themselves engaged in huge investments abroad with regard to which ICSID may be, and should increasingly become, particularly attractive.

Even more spectacular is the fact that Paraguay ratified the Convention on Jan. 7, 1982, and that the Convention has been signed by Costa Rica and El Salvador. The adhesion of these Latin American countries to ICSID is an event of historical importance. It shows an awareness of the changes that have recently taken place in the investment climate. It is well known that the financing of economic development projects from public, national or international, sources is becoming increasingly difficult. Under the circumstances, countries seeking outside financial assistance for the development of their economy must seek new ways of attracting foreign private capital. ICSID membership is one of the ways that this can be accomplished because it gives both investors and the host state means for settling possible investment disputes under the auspices of a specialized international organization whose impartiality is assured.

THE GENERAL ADMISSION OF ALIENS UNDER INTERNATIONAL LAW

*By James A. R. Nafziger**

I. INTRODUCTION

One often reads or hears that a state has a right to exclude all aliens from its territory unless a treaty obligation requires admission.[1] Frequently, that proposition prefaces discussion of such issues as immigration quotas, expulsion and deportation of aliens,[2] justiciability and procedural due process in litigation involving immigration questions, and the duty of states to protect aliens. Sometimes the proposition is colored by such words as "of course," "no longer open to serious question," or "unquestionably"—clues, at least, that some questions and doubts may be in order.

The claimed right of exclusion is usually considered an attribute of sovereignty and territoriality and is defended as an inherent power necessary for the self-preservation of the state. In other words, if a sovereign "could not exclude aliens it would be to that extent subject to the control of another power."[3] Consequently, for reasons of state, sovereign decisions concerning the general admission of aliens are said to be immune from legal appraisal even if particular decisions distort the more or less natural flow of human dispersion. That is the conventional wisdom. In reality, however, the lofty aim of preserving the state may be a less cogent explanation of exclusionary legislation than nativism and more specific fears that aliens will displace local workers, contribute to social tensions, or impose an economic burden on the state.

This article challenges the exclusionary proposition on several grounds. It points out that juristic writing relied on to support the proposition requires legitimate reasons for exclusion in individual cases, such as necessity or self-preservation. States have customarily admitted aliens and have at times considered themselves bound to justify exclusion on grounds of public safety,

* Professor of Law, Willamette University College of Law. The author wishes to thank Oscar Schachter and Anthony A. D'Amato for their helpful comments and suggestions.

[1] A common formulation of the proposition first appeared in Nishimura Ekiu v. United States, 142 U.S. 651, 659 (1892), quoted in text at note 115 *infra*.

[2]

> "[E]xclusion" means preventing someone from entering the United States who is actually outside of the United States or is treated as being so. "Expulsion" means forcing someone out of the United States who is actually within the United States or is treated as being so. "Deportation" means the moving of someone away from the United States, after his exclusion or expulsion.

Kwong Hai Chew v. Colding, 344 U.S. 590, 596 n.4 (1953). Although the issues of alien exclusion, expulsion, and deportation are interrelated and governed by similar principles, the present study will examine only the issue of alien exclusion.

[3] Chae Chan Ping v. United States (The Chinese Exclusion Case), 130 U.S. 581, 604 (1889).

security, public welfare, or threat to essential institutions. Although some courts may have characterized the practice of admission as a voluntary waiver of the right to exclude or a self-imposed limit on the exercise of the right, it is reasonable to regard the practice and the accompanying justification as recognition of a qualified duty to admit some aliens in some circumstances. Moreover, commonly cited judicial opinions and related authority, at least in English-language sources, are unconvincing; they often misinterpret other authority, contradict contemporaneous statements of *opinio juris,* and rest on questionable, often racist presumptions. The international significance of migration and the interdependence of states lend support to the argument that the general admission of aliens should not be regarded as an untrammeled discretionary power within the exclusive domestic jurisdiction of states. Therefore, although a state has no duty to admit all aliens who might seek to enter its territory, the present article argues for a qualified duty to admit aliens when they pose no danger to the public safety, security, general welfare, or essential institutions of a recipient state. Admittedly, this formulation is so broad as to permit expansive discretion by states, but affirming it may encourage states, in their mutual interest, to develop more precise rules, principles, and procedures to govern the general admission of aliens.

Since most states in practice do admit *some* aliens, any existence in theory of a sovereign right to exclude all of them might seem immaterial.[4] That is, if states in practice do not exercise whatever right they may have to exclude all aliens, the proposition might seem inconsequential. Nevertheless, the proposition warrants scrutiny, for it influences both municipal and international decision making. The widespread presumption that there is an absolute right of exclusion affects the degree to which, and the circumstances under which, states do admit aliens. For example, immigration laws might be more generous if it were not for the widely held premise of municipal authorities that the admission of each and every alien is a privilege. Also, the state practice of admitting some aliens has not succeeded in dispelling widespread uncertainty about standards of international solidarity, mutual aid or cooperation, and burden sharing. Individual and community expectations are unstable. Seemingly endless crises of migration in the modern world beg for a clear articulation of authentic rules, principles, and procedures of international law to govern the general admission of aliens. Unfortunately, the proposition that a state may exclude all aliens inhibits such legal development by concealing state practice and interdependence, international legal constraints, and the actual policy choices presented to municipal decision makers.[5] Finally, the

[4] Numerous publicists have noted this discrepancy between theory and reality, *e.g.,* E. BORCHARD, THE DIPLOMATIC PROTECTION OF CITIZENS ABROAD OR THE LAW OF INTERNATIONAL CLAIMS 46 (1915); C. FENWICK, INTERNATIONAL LAW 319 (4th ed. 1965); A. HERSHEY, THE ESSENTIALS OF INTERNATIONAL PUBLIC LAW AND ORGANIZATION 369 n.52 (1939); Oda, *The Individual in International Law,* in M. SØRENSEN, MANUAL OF PUBLIC INTERNATIONAL LAW 469, 481 (1968); J. STARKE, AN INTRODUCTION TO INTERNATIONAL LAW 345 (1972).

[5] Hucker, *Migration and Resettlement under International Law,* in THE INTERNATIONAL LAW AND POLICY OF HUMAN WELFARE 327 (R. Macdonald, D. Johnston, & G. Morris eds. 1978). Also, "[l]es questions d'immigration ne sont pas du tout laissées à la compétence arbitraire d'un

proposition has inhibited comprehensive global deliberations among states concerning the admission of aliens other than those belonging to such special classes as refugees and stateless persons. Thus, the state practice of admitting aliens, or at least some of them, does not mean that the proposition is insignificant.

This article has several boundaries of its own. First, for analytic purposes, it examines only the clearest, most common, most comprehensive formulation of the proposition, that is, that a state has a right to exclude all aliens. There are, however, numerous variations that generally qualify or restrict the proposition.[6] For example, some versions limit its scope to individuals and well-defined classes or categories of aliens;[7] other, rather ambiguous versions speak of a sovereign right (or power) to "(freely) regulate," "set limitations on," "restrict," "control," or "exercise discretion over" immigration.[8] Second, this article will focus on more or less permanent migration rather than on the admission of such transient classes of aliens as diplomats, temporary workers, visitors, or students.[9] Third, the article will devote only passing attention to such specially protected classes of aliens as refugees and stateless persons. These classes may be *sui generis* or their existence, in the aggregate, may indeed contradict the general claim of a sovereign right to exclude all aliens. Finally, although this article focuses on the most commonly cited justifications for the proposition, such as the principle of sovereignty, other legal reasons are sometimes given. For example, it has been suggested that the fact that scarcely any states freely admit aliens supports their right to exclude all aliens.[10] It has also been argued, as a peculiar variation of the territorial principle, that sovereign power to control national borders prevents the moral

---

Etat seul, car le droit international limite sa compétence en la matière, en vue du bien commun de l'humanité." A. VERDROSS, LES RÈGLES INTERNATIONALES CONCERNANT LE TRAITEMENT DES ÉTRANGERS 25 (1932).

[6] G. GOODWIN-GILL, INTERNATIONAL LAW AND THE MOVEMENT OF PERSONS BETWEEN STATES 20, 94–96, 196–97 (1978).

[7] *E.g.,* 1 M. SIBERT, TRAITÉ DE DROIT INTERNATIONAL PUBLIC 575 (1951).

[8] *E.g.,* 1 L. CAVARÉ, LE DROIT INTERNATIONAL PUBLIC POSITIF 275 (2d ed. 1961); Lung-chu Chen, Remarks, 67 ASIL PROC. 127, 130–31 (1973); 5 J. VERZIJL, INTERNATIONAL LAW IN HISTORICAL PERSPECTIVE 417 (1972); Wildes, *The United States Immigration Service v. John Lennon: The Cultural Lag,* 40 BROOKLYN L. REV. 279, 281 (1973), *reprinted in* 1 IMMIGRATION & NATIONALITY L. REV. 407, 409 (1976–77); Hucker, *supra* note 5, at 327; G. GOODWIN-GILL, *supra* note 6, at 196–97; RESTATEMENT OF FOREIGN RELATIONS LAW OF THE UNITED STATES (REVISED) §722, Reporters' Note 1, at 247 (Tent. Draft No. 3, 1982).

[9] *See generally* L. CAVARÉ, *supra* note 8. The distinction between permanent and temporary jurisdiction is material to an appraisal of national laws. For example, a state may allow the entry of large numbers of temporary guest workers without the same level of commitment to permanent hospitality that another state provides by accepting fewer immigrants who, however, have a greater likelihood of being eligible for permanent residence or citizenship. Kindleberger, *Mass Migration, Then and Now,* 43 FOREIGN AFF. 647, 656–57 (1965). Also, the focus of this article will be on the admission of natural, rather than juristic persons such as corporations. For a discussion of the problems of applying analogies drawn from natural to juristic persons, see W. LEVI, CONTEMPORARY INTERNATIONAL LAW: A CONCISE INTRODUCTION 176 (1979).

[10] *E.g.,* J. STARKE, *supra* note 4; Oda, *supra* note 4.

obligation to accept some immigration from becoming a broader, legal obligation.[11]

II. Historical Analysis

Modern Origins of the Proposition

The proposition that a state has the right to exclude all aliens is of recent origin. Several insights emerge from sampling the writings of influential publicists of various nationalities who have recited the absolutist version of the proposition.[12] Many of these writers, citing no authority, apparently regard the proposition as self-evident. The sovereign's right to exclude aliens is simply a maxim. When authority is cited, by far the most frequent is Anglo-American case law from the period 1889–1893, followed in order by highly selective snippets from the writings of Emmerich de Vattel, excerpts in digests of international law from 19th-century United States diplomatic correspondence, and black-letter pronouncements apparently rendered *ex cathedra* by earlier publicists.[13] The validity and significance of this authority will be examined later.

[11] Nickel, *Human Rights and the Rights of Aliens,* in THE BORDER THAT JOINS 31, 42 (P. Brown & H. Shue eds. 1983); *Labor Mobility: The Global Bracero Problem,* 73 ASIL PROC. 119, 130 (1979).

[12] Aybay, *The Right to Leave and the Right to Return: The International Aspect of Freedom of Movement,* 1 COMP. L. Y.B. 121, 122 (1978); J. BRIERLY, THE LAW OF NATIONS 276 (6th ed. 1963); C. DE VISSCHER, THÉORIES ET RÉALITÉS EN DROIT INTERNATIONAL PUBLIC 228 (3d ed. 1960); 1 C. HYDE, INTERNATIONAL LAW CHIEFLY AS INTERPRETED AND APPLIED BY THE UNITED STATES 216, 217 (2d ed. 1951); Hyndman, *Asylum and Non-Refoulement—Are These Obligations Owed to Refugees Under International Law?,* 57 PHIL. L.J. 43, 68 (1982); Johnson, *Refugees, Departees and Illegal Migrants,* 9 SYDNEY L. REV. 11, 24 (1980); H. KELSEN, PRINCIPLES OF INTERNATIONAL LAW 372–73 (2d ed. 1966); W. LEVI, *supra* note 9; H. MOSLER, THE INTERNATIONAL SOCIETY AS A LEGAL COMMUNITY 55–56 (1980); Oda, *supra* note 4; 1 L. OPPENHEIM, INTERNATIONAL LAW 675–76 (8th ed. Lauterpacht 1955); S. SINHA, NEW NATIONS AND THE LAW OF NATIONS 97 (1967); J. STARKE, *supra* note 4; G. VON GLAHN, LAW AMONG NATIONS: AN INTRODUCTION TO PUBLIC INTERNATIONAL LAW 214 (3d ed. 1976); A. VON OVERBECK, NIEDERLASSUNGSFREIHEIT UND AUSWEISUNGSRECHT (1907); P. WEIS, NATIONALITY AND STATELESSNESS IN INTERNATIONAL LAW 45 (1956); S. WILLIAMS & A. DE MESTRAL, AN INTRODUCTION TO INTERNATIONAL LAW CHIEFLY AS INTERPRETED AND APPLIED IN CANADA 105 (1979); 1 W. WILLOUGHBY, THE CONSTITUTIONAL LAW OF THE UNITED STATES 251 (1910). Three criteria determined the selection of authority in this sampling: apparent influence on jurists, political scientists, and public decision makers; historical balance; and nationality balance. The latter proved to be particularly problematic because of the preponderance of the proposition among British and American writers. Nonetheless, some ten nationalities are represented among the above publicists. An examination of 20th-century digests of international law published by the U.S. Government offers one additional insight: the trend has been from an elaborate discussion of the proposition in 4 J. MOORE, A DIGEST OF INTERNATIONAL LAW 67, 151 *et seq.* (1906), to a shorter, somewhat ambiguous restatement of the proposition in 3 G. HACKWORTH, DIGEST OF INTERNATIONAL LAW 692–94, 717 (1942), to an even shorter, somewhat cryptic recital of case law in 8 M. WHITEMAN, DIGEST OF INTERNATIONAL LAW 573–75, 581 (1967). Among these digests the trend toward abstraction of the proposition under study parallels a trend, chronologically, among the publicists in the above sampling.

[13] These publicists are sometimes misinterpreted. Edwin M. Borchard, *e.g.*, sometimes cited as authority for the proposition under study, is ambiguous. He is careful to summarize contending

For now, it is only a slight exaggeration to note that authority today for the proposition absolving the sovereign of any legal duty to admit aliens is derived "almost exclusively"[14] from turn-of-the-century common law precedent, even in writings from some countries outside the common law tradition. The proposition arose just as the American and other frontiers of new settlement disappeared and at the peak of emigration from Europe and the Orient to the United States and the British Empire. Because these historical circumstances developed during the heyday of Austinian and Holmesian positivism, with its peculiar limitation of law to sovereign commands, the nativistic pronouncements of courts became engraved in stone.

In contrast, a number of continental and Latin American jurists have tended to assert the principles of interdependence and freedom of movement, to reject the exclusionary proposition, or to qualify its applicability in terms of *ordre public.*[15] In particular, the principle of interdependence challenges the proposition even though states have seldom expressly accepted that the principle obligates them to admit aliens.[16]

"Ancient" Principles of International Law

Despite the apparently modern origin of the proposition as a legal matter,[17] a 1972 opinion of the United States Supreme Court referred to "ancient principles of the international law of states"[18] to uphold the power of the United States Government to exclude all aliens if it so wanted. Although that opinion did not further identify the ancient principles, its observation probably accords with conventional wisdom. To show that the observation is nevertheless misleading, this article will delve into the history of restrictions on mi-

---

positions and to limit the exclusionary position to "[c]ourts in the United States and Great Britain." E. BORCHARD, *supra* note 4, at 45. He then refers to an "ultimate power" to exclude aliens which, however, "would violate the spirit of international law and endanger [a state's] membership in the international community" (*id.* at 46). He states that the "grounds of exclusion are fixed by the public interests of each state" with respect to "dangerous or undesirable" aliens (*id.*) and recognizes that an "arbitrary or unjust exclusion" would give rise to a political, though not a legal, pecuniary claim (*id.* at 48). While noting the contending principles of interdependence and sovereign exclusivity, and while referring to "the recognized inherent power of a state to exclude foreigners," Borchard concludes as follows:

> At the present day the *right* of admission and sojourn on the part of unobjectionable aliens is almost universally *recognized.* Qualifications of the *right,* which are to be found in the possibilities of exclusion, expulsion and the fixing of conditions of sojourn by the state, must in practice be based upon reasonable grounds.

Id. at 37 (emphasis added).

[14] M. KONVITZ, THE ALIEN AND THE ASIATIC IN AMERICAN LAW 18 n.53 (1946).

[15] *E.g.,* 1 P. FAUCHILLE, TRAITÉ DE DROIT INTERNATIONAL PUBLIC 894–95 (8th ed. 1926); P. FIORE, INTERNATIONAL LAW CODIFIED AND ITS LEGAL SANCTION 42 (E. Borchard trans. 1918) (1890); M. SIBERT, *supra* note 7, at 571; Irizarry y Puente, *Exclusion and Expulsion of Aliens in Latin America,* 36 AJIL 252, 254–56, 270 (1942): A. VERDROSS, *supra* note 5, at 25.

[16] R. PLENDER, INTERNATIONAL MIGRATION LAW 39 (1972) (an excellent commentary on these issues).

[17] Hucker, *supra* note 5, at 338.

[18] Kleindienst v. Mandel, 408 U.S. 753, 765 (1972).

gration. Certainly, any historical summary, even confined to the West, is hazardous. One is reminded of an antiquarian's acknowledgment that "[t]he charm of guessing ancient motives from the records of ancient deeds fascinated me—there is much in the pursuit to a gambler. . . ."[19] Fortunately, the gambler's risk of grossly distorting the history of restrictions on migration is minimized by a fairly obvious pattern of free movement.

Before the late 19th century, there was little, in principle, to support the absolute exclusion of aliens. Closed cities, or other territory to which no aliens are admitted, have been rare, at least in the West. Biblical injunctions, which influenced the articulation of international law by 17th- and 18th-century publicists, favored free transboundary movement.[20] To be sure, the early Greeks sharply distinguished "citizens" from "barbarians," and later distinguished among citizens, naturalized aliens, public guests, domiciled aliens, nondomiciled aliens, and strangers.[21] Nevertheless, the early antagonism of the Greek city-states toward foreigners matured, with occasional ripples of xenophobia, into hospitality toward them, especially in Athens and the Hellenistic Empire.[22] For example, the *Funeral Oration* of Pericles included a criticism of the alien exclusion acts of the Lacedaemonians of Sparta.[23] Plato, and to a limited extent Aristotle, himself an alien, favored the qualified admission of aliens under express conditions.[24] The Romans were even less exclusive than the Greeks. Roman cosmopolitanism, imperial policy, aspira-

[19] D. HOGARTH, ACCIDENTS OF AN ANTIQUARY'S LIFE 2 (1910).

[20] The most widely quoted, today at least, is from *Leviticus* 19:33–34: "And if a stranger sojourn with thee in your land, ye shall not vex him. But the stranger that dwelleth with you shall be unto you as one born among you, and thou shalt love him as thyself; for ye were strangers in the land of Egypt. . . ." Contemporary doctrine of the Roman Catholic Church has conditioned limitations by states on the influx of immigrants upon "real and genuine reasons of the common good" and never "to the detriment of other people." A. ZIMMERMAN, PIUS XII AND INTERNATIONAL MIGRATION: A REPORT OF THE COMMITTEE ON SOCIAL QUESTIONS OF THE CATHOLIC ASSOCIATION FOR INTERNATIONAL PEACE 3–4 (1959); *accord*, POPE PAUL VI, NEW NORMS FOR THE CARE OF MIGRANTS 9 (1969).

[21] J. JONES, THE LAW AND LEGAL THEORY OF THE GREEKS 49 (1956); 1 C. PHILLIPSON, THE INTERNATIONAL LAW AND CUSTOM OF ANCIENT GREECE AND ROME 145 (1911).

[22] J. JONES, *supra* note 21; C. PHILLIPSON, *supra* note 21, at 32–3, 125, 128.

[23] THUCYDIDES, THE PELOPONNESIAN WARS 49, 67 (Washington Square Press ed. 1963).

[24] THE LAWS OF PLATO (J. M. Dent & Son, Ltd. ed. 1960). For example, in book VIII, Plato wrote as follows:

> Any foreigner who pleases may become a resident in the country on certain express conditions. It shall be understood that we offer a home to any alien who desires to take up his abode with us and is able to do so; but he must have a craft, and his residence must not be prolonged more than twenty years from the date of his registration.

Id. at 239. In book XII, Plato prefaced a discussion of rules restricting the admission of aliens by summarizing contending arguments, including the following:

> [T]o refuse all admission to the foreigner and permit the native no opportunity of foreign travel is, for one thing, not always possible, and, for another, may earn a State a reputation for barbarism and inhumanity with the rest of the world; its citizens will be thought to be adopting the ill-sounding policy of "exclusion of aliens" and developing a repulsive and intractable character; but reputation, for good or ill, with the outer world ought never to be under-valued.

tions of universal dominion, and fiscal needs contributed to a liberal policy of naturalization so long as assimilation was from within the vast empire.[25] The openness of the Romans to foreigners, reinforced by the Stoic tradition and early church doctrine, shaped medieval universalism. There was ample freedom of movement for eligible classes of travelers even though feudal serfs were not free to leave their estates, safe-conduct passes were at times necessary, and medieval cities strictly controlled immigration.[26] Despite the Prince's prerogatives as *custos regni*, the imperatives of trade fairs, leagues, and more diffused economic intercourse protected free movement and choice of residence, at least in times of peace.[27] A provision of the Magna Charta, repealed only in 1969, protected the freedom of merchants to travel "in accordance with ancient and lawful customs."[28] Later, mercantilism encouraged immigration on the theory that wealth was related partly to the number of productive workers a sovereign could muster.[29]

The Classic Publicists

The Westphalian system of nation-states complicated the free movement of persons by confirming more rigid territorial boundaries. Significantly, however, the classic publicists, faced with a new tension between traditional freedom of movement and the emerging concept of the sovereign state, denied the state an absolute right to exclude aliens. "Of things which belong to Men in Common," according to Hugo Grotius, were, among others: the right to temporary sojourn, a permanent residence for refugees "expelled from their homes," the right of foreigners to be free of discrimination on the basis of nationality, the right of foreigners to possess deserted and unproductive soil, and the right of foreigners to the necessities of life, such as food, clothing, and medicines.[30] Although Grotius said little more about admitting aliens, he quoted Strabo, who had concluded that it was "characteristic of barbarians to drive away strangers," and Saint Ambrose, who wrote that "those who keep foreigners out of their

---

Id. at 343–44. On Plato's hostile attitude toward barbarians remaining outside the Greek city-states, see Arnopoulos, *Platonic Ideas on International Affairs,* 2 HELLENIC REV. INT'L REL. 33, 40–41 (1981).

Compared with Plato, Aristotle had rather little to say about migration or the rights of aliens. In the context of his theory of citizenship, he seems to have viewed aliens not as strangers but as a class of acceptable residents with less status than citizens. E. BARKER, THE POLITICAL THOUGHT OF PLATO AND ARISTOTLE 294–301 (Dover ed. 1959). Aristotle seems to have recognized limited treaty rights of aliens. THE POLITICS OF ARISTOTLE 93 (Oxford ed. 1958).

[25] C. PHILLIPSON, *supra* note 21, at 213, 256. In Cicero's words, "[t]o debar foreigners from enjoying the advantages of the city is altogether contrary to the laws of humanity." M. CICERO, DE OFFICIIS, bk. III, ch. xi, at 47 (Loeb Classical Library ed. 1923).

[26] M. CRANSTON, WHAT ARE HUMAN RIGHTS? 33, 36 (1973).

[27] *See, e.g.,* H. HENRIQUES, THE LAW OF ALIENS AND NATURALIZATION 9–10 (1906).

[28] For a useful bibliographical note, with authoritative citations, see R. PLENDER, note 16 *supra,* at 40 n.12.

[29] M. CRANSTON, *supra* note 26, at 36.

[30] 2 H. GROTIUS, DE JURE BELLI AC PACIS, bk. II, ch. II, at 186–205 (Carnegie Endowment trans. 1925).

city are by no means worthy of approval."[31] Perhaps most important was the Grotian provision for a right of foreign refuge, so long as those "expelled from their homes [no causes stipulated] submit themselves to the established government and observe any regulations . . . necessary in order to avoid strifes."[32]

Francisco de Vitoria, applying the Roman *jus gentium,* logical inferences from history, and the imperative of noblesse oblige, sought to confirm the right of Spaniards to travel and sojourn freely in Indian-held lands of the New World, "provided they do no harm to the natives."[33] He argued that a freedom to migrate freely, having been established "from the beginning of the world" and operating at that time in Europe, ought therefore to be respected everywhere. To deny admission to foreigners might even constitute an act of war.[34] Christian Wolff later sharpened the statements of Grotius, Vitoria, and other publicists into a principle of free movement, subject to several stipulated exceptions within the discretion of states.[35] In the growth of an international law of migration, Wolff was instrumental in taking account of political realities by according limited regulatory powers to the sovereign to protect morals, religion, public safety, and public welfare, while maintaining the principle of free migration.

Samuel Pufendorf similarly denied to the sovereign a right to exclude aliens, so long as they had lawful reasons, including economic ones, for seeking admission into states. In one of the first explicit, more or less modern statements of sovereign powers over the admission of aliens, Pufendorf wrote somewhat vaguely as follows: "Every state may reach a decision according to its own usage on the admission of foreigners who [do not come to it out of necessity or deserving of sympathy]. Only no one can question the barbarity of showing an indiscriminate hostility to those who come on a peaceful mission."[36]

Vattel's synthesis of natural law and positivism, with an emphasis on the latter, strongly influenced the development of modern migration law.[37] Unfortunately, though Vattel was sympathetic to the plight of migrants, his writing has been misinterpreted as supporting the proposition under study. Because of his influence, we should carefully consider what he actually wrote.

Regarding admission of aliens, Vattel's book, *Le Droit des gens,*[38] although it

[31] *Id.* at 202. [32] *Id.* at 201–02.

[33] F. DE VICTORIA, DE INDIS ET DE IURE BELLI RELECTIONES 151 (E. Nys ed. 1917).

[34] *Ibid.*

[35] According to Wolff, a state could refuse entry to a foreigner where

> there is fear lest the morals of the subjects may be corrupted, or lest prejudice may be aroused against religion, or even lest criminals be admitted because of whom injury threatens the State, and other things which are detrimental to public welfare. . . . [Moreover,] since nations are free, the decision in these matters must be left to the nations themselves and that decision must be respected.

C. WOLFF, JUS GENTIUM SCIENTIFICA PERTRAETATUM §§148–149 (Clarendon ed. 1934).

[36] 2 S. PUFENDORF, DE JURE NATURAE GENTIUM, bk. VIII, at 365 (Oxford ed. 1934) (as indicated by brackets, the present author has corrected a faulty, misleading translation from the Latin in this edition; *see id.,* vol. 1, at 248).

[37] G. GOODWIN-GILL, *supra* note 6, at 95.

[38] E. DE VATTEL, THE LAW OF NATIONS (J. Chitty ed. 1839). On the interrelationship between

is often ambiguous, adopted and refined many of the principles of Grotius and Pufendorf. Significantly, however, Vattel distinguished the internal law of nations, rooted in natural law, from the external law, rooted in what today one might call positivism. Internal law establishes sovereign duties as a matter of conscience and principle, whereas external law establishes sovereign rights as a matter of will.[39] Because of this quasi-Kantian distinction, where no effort is made to reconcile the two concepts, *Le Droit des gens* "could be cited on both sides in almost every controversy."[40] That criticism is particularly accurate in explaining the selective adaptation from Vattel that helped shape the modern rationale for a right of states to exclude all aliens. Two statements, which refer only (and rather narrowly) to the applicable external law rooted in *raison d'état,* have been repeatedly extracted from Vattel's far broader discussion of migration in *Le Droit des gens.* These statements are, first, that

> [t]he sovereign may forbid the entrance of his territory either to foreigners in general, or in particular cases, or to certain persons, or for certain particular purposes, according as he may think it advantageous to the state: There is nothing in all this that does not flow from the rights of domain and sovereignty: every one is obliged to pay respect to the prohibition; and whoever dares to violate it, incurs the penalty decreed to render it effectual.[41]

Second, "the lord of the territory may, whenever he thinks proper, forbid its being entered."[42]

Vattel's rationale under the internal law of nature for these sovereign prerogatives is as follows:

> By an evident consequence from what has been said, a nation ought carefully to avoid, as much as is possible, whatever might cause its destruction, or that of the state, which is the same thing.
>
> A nation or state has a right to every thing that can help to ward off imminent danger, and to keep at a distance whatever is capable of causing it ruin; and that from the very same reasons that establish its right to the things necessary to its preservation.[43]

This statement is qualified, however, by a cross-reference to two later sections that create certain exceptions to the external law and establish the sovereign's duties under the internal law, more or less *erga omnes,* to allow free passage

---

the ideas of Grotius and those of Vattel, see P. REMEC, THE POSITION OF THE INDIVIDUAL IN INTERNATIONAL LAW ACCORDING TO GROTIUS AND VATTEL (1960).

[39] For a discussion of this distinction, see P. REMEC, *supra* note 38, at 197. For an example of the distinction in Vattel's discussion of the rights of foreigners, see E. DE VATTEL, *supra* note 38, bk. II, §135, at 183–84.

[40] Parry, *The Function of Law in the International Community,* in M. SØRENSEN, *supra* note 4, at 1, 25.

[41] E. DE VATTEL, *supra* note 38, bk. II, §94, at 169–70.

[42] *Id.* §100, at 171–72. Grotius argued for a right of passage in the absence of a genuine threat to the sovereign. H. GROTIUS, *supra* note 30, at 198.

[43] E. DE VATTEL, *supra* note 38, bk. I, §§19–20, at 6.

through and residence in its territory.[44] The exceptions to the right to exclude aliens include such Grotian principles as the right of procuring provisions by force, the qualified right of making use of the things that belong to others, the right of passage, and for those exiled or banished from their own country, the right of dwelling in a foreign country.[45] All of these are premised on the notion of a primitive state of communion[46] and the Grotian right of necessity. For example, Vattel elaborated the right of procuring provisions by force, as follows:

> The earth was designed to feed its inhabitants; and he who is in want of every thing is not obliged to starve, because all property is vested in others. . . . Extreme necessity revives the primitive communion, the abolition of which ought to deprive no person of the necessaries of life. . . . *The same right belongs to individuals, when a foreign nations [sic] refuses them a just assistance.*[47]

Vattel's commentary on the right of "fugitives or exiles" is particularly illuminating as an exception to sovereign prerogatives under his concept of positive external law.[48]

[44] *Id.*, bk. II, §§131–139, at 182–85.

[45] Respectively, *id.* §§120, 121, 123, and 125, at 178–80.

[46]

> In the primitive state of communion, men had, without distinction, a right to the use of every thing, as far as was necessary to the discharge of their natural obligations. And, as nothing could deprive them of this right, the introduction of domain and property could not take place without leaving to every man the necessary use of things,—that is to say, the use absolutely required for the fulfillment of this natural obligation. . . . This right is a necessary remnant of the primitive state of communion.

Id. §117, at 177.

[47] *Id.* §120, at 178 (emphasis added).

[48]

> For, on the other hand, every nation has a right to refuse admitting a foreigner into her territory, *when he cannot enter it without exposing the nation to evident danger, or doing her a manifest injury.* What she owes to herself, the care of her own safety, gives her this right; and, in virtue of her natural liberty, it belongs to the nation to judge, whether her circumstances will or will not justify the admission of that foreigner. . . . He cannot, then, settle by a full right, and as he pleases, in the place he has chosen, but must ask permission of the chief of the place; and, if it is refused, it is his duty to submit.
>
> *However . . . no nation can, without good reasons, refuse even a perpetual residence to a man driven from his country.* But, if particular and substantial reasons prevent her from affording him an asylum, this man has no longer any right to demand it.

Id., bk. I, §§230–231, at 107–08 (emphasis added).

By "exiles" Vattel referred to both involuntary departures pursuant to superior order and voluntary departures "to escape some punishment, or to *avoid some calamity.*" *Id.* §228, at 107 (emphasis added). Vattel concluded this discussion by indicating the circumstances under which a state may exclude "fugitives or exiles," as follows:

> Thus, a nation, whose lands are scarcely sufficient to supply the wants of the citizens, is not obliged to receive into its territories a company of fugitives or exiles. Thus, it ought even absolutely to reject them, if they are infected with a contagious disease. Thus, also, it has a right to send them elsewhere, if it has just cause to fear that they will corrupt the manners of the citizens, that they will create religious disturbances, or occasion any other disorder, contrary to the public safety. In a word, it has a right, and is even obliged, to follow, in this respect, the suggestions of prudence. But this prudence should be free from unnecessary

According to Vattel, the state is also restrained by the requirements of internal law. The sovereign must thus allow free passage through, and residence in, its territory.[49] Vattel gave a few examples of the liberty of residence, denied the sovereign a right to discriminate unreasonably against aliens on the basis of nationality, and admonished states to be courteous to aliens.[50]

It is essential to understand, as leading judicial opinions and scholarly writings often have not, that Vattel thought sovereignty was subject to internal law, however loosely it might operate in terms of conscience and duties of humanity. Indeed, despite his frequent ambiguities, Vattel made this point explicit when he referred to the internal law of free passage and residence as "the line of conduct which a nation is, by her duty to other nations, *bound to observe* in the exercise of her rights."[51] Failure to satisfy this duty is an abuse of an external right, which for Vattel was a breach of law.

Vattel thus took sovereign duties as well as rights seriously. Even if the sovereign theoretically has the right, or "inherent power" in modern terminology, to exclude aliens absolutely, he cannot do so in some instances because of his qualified duty to admit some foreigners. Interpretations of Vattel's commentary on foreign migration have, however, consistently ignored both the subtleties on the duty side[52] and his qualifications of the sovereign "right" to exclude foreigners.[53] The explanation for this distortion or selective reading of Vattel lies, perhaps, in the later ascendancy of positivism, especially during the formative period of immigration law at the end of the last century. Concepts such as "conscience," "duties of humanity," and the like, vital to Vattel, were

---

> suspicion and jealousy; it should not be carried so far as to refuse a retreat to the unfortunate, for slight reasons, or on groundless and frivolous fears. The means of tempering it will be, never to lose sight of that charity and commiseration which are due to the unhappy. We must not suppress these feelings even for those who have fallen into misfortune through their own fault. For, we ought to hate the crime, but love the man, since all mankind ought to love each other.

Id. §231, at 107–08.

49

> In explaining the effects of domain we have said above . . . that the owner of the territory may forbid the entrance into it, or permit it on such conditions as he thinks proper. We were then treating of his external right,—that right which foreigners are bound to respect. But now that we are considering the matter in another view, and as it relates to his duties and to his internal right, we may venture to assert that he cannot, without particular and important reasons, refuse permission, either to pass through or reside in the country, to foreigners who desire it for lawful purposes. For, their passage or their residence being in this case an innocent advantage, the law of nature does not give him a right to refuse it: and, though other nations and other men in general are obliged to submit to his judgment . . . he does not the less offend against his duty, if he refuses without sufficient reason:—he then acts without any true right; he only abuses his external right.

Id., bk. II, §135, at 183–84.

50 *Id.* §§135, 136, 137, 138, at 184–85.

51 *Id.* §130, at 182 (emphasis added); *see* P. REMEC, *supra* note 38, at 197.

52 *E.g.*, M. AKEHURST, A MODERN INTRODUCTION TO INTERNATIONAL LAW 21 (3d ed. 1977).

53 An exception is the opinion in the landmark alien expulsion case, Fong Yue Ting v. United States, 149 U.S. 698 (1893).

passé to the positivists. Perhaps the interrelationship between external and internal law has been ignored because modern positivism views internal law as no more than nonbinding, moral obligation. Whatever the cause, misinterpretations of *Le Droit des gens* have had a profound influence on the case law, to be discussed later,[54] that is cited to support contemporary claims of the state's right to exclude absolutely.

Sir William Blackstone, though less influential in this sphere than elsewhere, nevertheless wrote about it in a strikingly modern vein. Although he is somewhat cryptic, skirting the edges of the issue of a sovereign's legal duty, Blackstone seems to have identified the modern tension between sovereign rights theory and actual practice. Consider the following passage:

> [B]y the law of nations no member of one society has a right to intrude into another . . . *those being ever excepted who are driven on the coast of necessity, or by any cause that deserves pity or compassion.* Great tenderness is shown by our laws . . . with regard . . . to the admission of strangers who come spontaneously: for so long as their nation continues at peace with ours, and they themselves behave peaceably, they are under the King's protection. . . .[55]

The Era of Immigration Laws

The tenderness of the law, as observed by Blackstone, soon turned to toughness under England's first immigration statute, Lord Grenville's Alien Act of 1793.[56] Responding to the threat of refugees from the French Revolution and Jacobin infiltrators, this Act regulated the landing of aliens and provided for their registration, subsequent residence, and punishment for noncompliance with the statute. For nearly a century after the French Revolution, however, freedom of movement was encouraged in the West by an expanding economy, an unusual compatibility of demographic interests between source and destination countries, Manifest Destiny in the Western Hemisphere, and the predominance of liberal thought conducive to the free circulation of human beings and capital.[57]

A mid-19th-century opinion of a United States court encapsulated the liberal, even laissez faire, spirit of the era: "The policy of our nation has always been to bestow the right of citizenship freely, and with a liberality unknown to the old world. I hold this to be our sound and wise policy still. . . ."[58] On the eve of a more restrictive period of U.S. policy, a leading publicist, though apparently a poor forecaster, expressed the contemporary generosity as follows: "It deserves to be remarked, however, that non-intercourse and restriction are fast disappearing from the commercial arrangements of the world,

[54] *See* text at notes 98–133 *infra.*

[55] 1 W. BLACKSTONE, COMMENTARIES ON THE LAWS OF ENGLAND 259 (1783) (emphasis added).

[56] 33 Geo. 3, ch. 4 (1793). For a discussion of this measure and its aftermath, see H. HENRIQUES, *supra* note 27, at 11–13.

[57] C. DE VISSCHER, *supra* note 12, at 228.

[58] Lynch v. Clarke, 1 Sand. Ch. 583, 661 (N.Y. 1844).

and that jealousy of foreigners is vanishing from the minds of all the more civilized nations, in the East as well as in the West."[59]

Yet, by the end of the 19th century, many geographical frontiers in the Western world had been reached. Mounting economic and political tensions contributed to municipal regulations and restrictions characterized by nationalism and protectionism.[60] For the first time, governments began systematically to deny admission to certain classes of aliens. The First World War and the Great Depression intensified nation-state cleavages and precipitated the enactment of more comprehensive restrictions. Nevertheless, it is important to keep in mind that these restrictions applied to specific *classes* of aliens. The new laws did not support the proposition of comprehensive exclusion. Of the specific classes, the most significant was Oriental labor. Toward the end of the 19th century, Oriental migration into the United States, Australia, New Zealand, and Canada led to the enactment of discriminatory exclusion laws in all four countries. Nativism in the common law countries was particularly instrumental, if not definitive, in conditioning the landmark judicial decisions that upheld exclusionary laws.[61]

III. A Critique of Theoretical Justifications

The proposition that a state may exclude all aliens often appears as a maxim. No justification is given. When it is provided, the most common philosophical justification is the sovereign's inherent powers to govern all activity in and entering its territory. A related concept is that of an autonomous, communal self-determination to choose all other members of a national polity. Because the right to exclude is so often justified simply as a sort of given attribute of a sovereign's inherent powers, a brief critique of this concept is appropriate. The following analysis not only sheds doubt on the validity of the concept, but reveals that the concept itself is qualified.

"Inherent Power(s)"

Municipal courts often ignore international law by according "inherent powers" to the sovereign state. The modern rationale for these powers is found in Vattel's concept of self-preservation by which a state may take all just measures that do not offend the law of nature.[62] A state is therefore

[59] T. Woolsey, Introduction to the Study of International Law 89 (1879).

[60] C. de Visscher, *supra* note 12, at 228–29.

[61] R. Plender, *supra* note 16, at 48–52. On the laws of New Zealand, see Williams, *New Zealand Immigration Policies and the Law—A Perspective*, 4 Otago L. Rev. 185, 190–91 (1978). A prominent Canadian scholar has made an interesting observation on early developments in his country, as follows: "Canadian immigration thinking has been an exercise in sustaining an uneasy balance among a variety of forces, all tugging in different directions. Some appeared at an early date—for example, Quebec's early resistance to immigration in contrast to general encouragement from the English-speaking provinces." J.-G. Castel, International Law Chiefly as Interpreted and Applied in Canada 472 (1976).

[62] E. de Vattel, *supra* note 38, vol. 1, §§19–20, at 6. *See also* Gordon, *The Immigration Process and National Security*, 24 Temp. L.Q. 302, 319 (1950–51).

entitled to perform its "highest duty," which, in the words of *The Chinese Exclusion Case,* is

> [t]o preserve its independence, and give security against foreign aggression and encroachment . . . , and to attain these ends nearly all other considerations are to be subordinated. It matters not in what form such aggression and encroachment come, whether from the foreign nation acting in its national character or from vast hordes of its people crowding in upon us.[63]

This "highest duty" of the sovereign implies a right of self-preservation. The question remains, however: what measures are reasonable and necessary to preserve the state? That question is usually ignored. Instead, the mere right of self-preservation, together with the sovereign's plenary authority and jurisdiction within its territory,[64] is said to be sufficient to justify the sovereign's "inherent right" or "power"[65] to exclude aliens. In the absence, however, of something like "vast hordes of [aliens] crowding in upon"[66] a state, self-preservation would not seem to be at issue, for an act of self-preservation must be limited to what is strictly imposed by an emergency. If the self-preservation of the state is not at issue, the concept of inherent powers, in an international sense,[67] is dubious. Moreover, in today's world, at least, the concept is vacuous. Even if the sovereign is regarded as some sort of Leviathan, the acknowledg-

[63] 130 U.S. at 606.

[64] In U.S. jurisprudence, Chief Justice Marshall wrote a classic formulation of this concept of territorial jurisdiction, as follows:

> The jurisdiction of the nation within its own territory is necessarily exclusive and absolute. It is susceptible of no limitation not imposed by itself. Any restriction upon it, deriving validity from an external source, would imply a diminution of its sovereignty to the extent of the restriction, and an investment of that sovereignty to the same extent in that power which could impose such restriction.

Schooner Exchange v. M'Faddon, 11 U.S. (7 Cranch) 116, 136 (1812). Historical circumstances on troubled seas help explain the vigor of the above language. Note, however, the following dicta qualifying the territorialist presumption:

> The world being composed of distinct sovereignties, possessing equal rights and equal independence, whose mutual benefit is promoted by intercourse with each other, and by an interchange of those good offices which humanity dictates and its wants require, *all sovereigns have consented to a relaxation in practice, in cases under certain peculiar circumstances, of that absolute and complete jurisdiction within their respective territories which sovereignty confers.*
>
> *This consent may, in some instances, be tested by common usage, and by common opinion, growing out of that usage.*

Ibid. (emphasis added).

[65] On a functional definition of "power," see R. DAHL, MODERN POLITICAL ANALYSIS 50, 51 n.8 (1963) (quoting others).

[66] 130 U.S. at 606.

[67] In the U.S. constitutional context, where decision makers sometimes use the terms "powers," "rights," and "authority" interchangeably, the concept of inherent powers is rooted in the transferral of power from the British Crown and in early constitutional history. Also, the concept of inherent powers is often, and confusingly, used interchangeably with the constitutional concept of "implied powers," which are conferred by judicial inference to give effect to governmental powers expressed in the Constitution. The basis for the constitutional doctrine of implied powers, as expressed in United States v. Curtiss-Wright Export Corp., 299 U.S. 304 (1936), is highly

ment of a sovereign's "inherent power" cannot help determine whether a particular exercise of sovereign power, such as the exclusion of aliens, is legitimate or simply a function of brute force.[68] Whether used to describe either a categorical right or an expectation of obedience,[69] the concept of a sovereign's inherent powers makes little sense as a basis for excluding all aliens, absent a threat to a sovereign's self-preservation, necessity, or a conferral by global constitutive processes of other powers for whose effectuation the exclusion of aliens is appropriate.

"Sovereignty"

Modern theories of "sovereignty" are often identified with, or derived from, the positivism of John Austin; however, one can trace the modern concept at least as far back as the 16th-century writer, Jean Bodin. He proposed, quite simply, a "puissance souveraine, absolue et perpetuelle d'une République," consisting of authority to make municipal law.[70] Later, Hobbes's personalization of the sovereign, James I's theocratization of the sovereign person, Hegel's idealization of the sovereign state, and legal positivism, all contributed to the concept of a sovereign's inherent powers. Just as important was a new dimension to the meaning of sovereignty. Although for several centuries theories of sovereignty sought simply to analyze and justify the vertical structure of the state, they later took on a second meaning to define the horizontal relationship of one state to another.[71] Sovereignty as against other states seems to have been a product of the concept that a personal sovereign serves to represent that state in all community forums.[72] In assuming this new dimension, the concept of sovereignty became ambiguous in its relationship to the law of nations and served to confuse international legal theory.[73] Two versions of this confusion are the voluntarist and auto-limiting theories, ac-

---

questionable. Note, *Constitutional Limits on the Power to Exclude Aliens,* 82 COLUM. L. REV. 957 (1982); Note, *Constitutional Limitations on the Naturalization Power,* 80 YALE L.J. 769 (1971).

[68] On the functions of centralized power, see H. LASSWELL, POLITICS: WHO GETS WHAT, WHEN, HOW (Meridian ed. 1958).

[69] On the concept of obedience, see, *e.g.*, H. SIMON & C. BARNARD, ADMINISTRATIVE BEHAVIOR 126 (The Free Press 2d ed. 1965).

[70] *See* J. ALLEN, A HISTORY OF POLITICAL THOUGHT IN THE SIXTEENTH CENTURY 412–13 (Methuen ed. 1960).

[71] M. AKEHURST, *supra* note 52, at 22.

[72] GREAT JURISTS OF THE WORLD 497 (Macdonell & Manson eds. 1914) (in a discussion of Vattel's concept of sovereignty).

[73] As one writer reminds us:

> The notion that the validity of international law raises some peculiar problem arises from the confusion which the doctrine of sovereignty has introduced into international legal theory. Even when we do not believe in the absoluteness of state sovereignty we have allowed ourselves to be persuaded that the fact of their sovereignty makes it necessary to look for some specific quality, not to be found in other kinds of law, in the law to which states are subject.

J. BRIERLY, *supra* note 12, at 54. In other words:

> The concept of sovereignty was misleading even when it was first announced in the 16th century in support of the divine right of kings. Pursued in the late 20th century, it seems

cording to which states are only bound by rules they have imposed upon themselves. An extreme version of the confusion is the positivistic notion that international law is only positive morality.

Nevertheless, sovereignty among states, though "very deeply rooted" in "national sentiment and in the psychology of people,"[74] is limited. Today, the concept has "become an institution, an international social function of a psychological character, which has to be exercised in accordance with a new international law."[75] Thus, sovereignty "cannot be either the basis or the source of the law of nations."[76] Rather, the term refers simply to the institutionalized independence of states, subject to international law.[77] Beyond that, the concept, as applied to issues of migration, is undefined and undefinable.[78]

The political theory of a sovereign's inherent powers to exclude aliens is therefore questionable as valid legal theory. Even if it was once valid, the theory is questionable today.[79] Indeed, one prominent writer turned the key words around to refer to "inherent limitations of the sovereign power over reception of aliens."[80]

Domestic Jurisdiction

Whatever its merits, the theory of a sovereign's inherent power to exclude aliens has been significantly recast today in terms of the reserved domain of domestic jurisdiction.[81] Indeed, concern for sovereign control over immigra-

---

> likely to lead to vertical concepts where horizontal thinking is required; to rigid rules that bear no relation to reality. . . .

Lowenfeld, *Sovereignty, Jurisdiction, and Reasonableness: A Reply to A. V. Lowe,* 75 AJIL 629, 629 (1981).

[74] The Corfu Channel Case, 1949 ICJ REP. 1, 43 (individual opinion by Judge Alvarez).

[75] *Ibid.*

[76] H. LAUTERPACHT, THE FUNCTION OF LAW IN THE INTERNATIONAL COMMUNITY 96 (1933). Similarly, H. L. A. Hart denied the validity of the

> *a priori* argument which attempts to deduce the general character of international law from an absolute sovereignty, which is assumed, without reference to international law, to belong to states.
>
> It is worth observing that an uncritical use of the idea of sovereignty has spread similar confusion in the theory both of municipal and international law, and demands in both a similar corrective. . . . [The question for international law is] what is the maximum area of autonomy which the rules allow to states?

H. HART, THE CONCEPT OF LAW 218 (1961). *But see* the writings of some contemporary political scientists who emphasize sovereignty and the nation-state as the basic structural feature of the present international system, *e.g.*, Aron, *The Anarchical Order of Power,* in CONDITIONS OF WORLD ORDER (S. Hoffmann ed. 1968); K. WALTZ, MAN, THE STATE AND WAR (1959).

[77] Customs Regime between Germany and Austria, 1931 PCIJ, ser. A/B, No. 41, at 57 (individual opinion by Judge Anzilotti).

[78] C. GORDON & H. ROSENFELD, IMMIGRATION LAW AND PROCEDURE 2–16 (1978).

[79] M. AKEHURST, *supra* note 52, at 22.

[80] 2 D. O'CONNELL, INTERNATIONAL LAW 696 (1970).

[81] "Nothing contained in the present Charter shall authorize the United Nations to intervene

tion was instrumental in crystallizing the newly formulated concept of "domestic jurisdiction" under Article 15(8) of the Treaty of Versailles.[82] Given the then prevailing anxieties about immigration, it is remarkable that the Council of the League of Nations, not individual claimant states, was given the role to apply international law in defining the newly formulated concept of domestic jurisdiction.

The concept of domestic jurisdiction is dynamic. Although restrictions on states cannot be presumed, we shall see that there are legal limitations on state discretion to exclude aliens. Even leaving these limitations aside, state discretion must be viewed dynamically in a historical context of international relations. That is,

> [t]he question whether a certain matter is or is not solely within the jurisdiction of a State is an essentially relative question; it depends upon the development of international relations. Thus, in the present state of international law, questions of nationality are, in the opinion of the Court, in principle within this reserved domain.[83]

International law therefore requires municipal institutions to appraise decisions and practices within the reserved domain of domestic jurisdiction in order to determine whether they should remain immune from transnational supervision, given "the development of international relations."[84] The Court did not intend that domestic jurisdiction should be self-defined, more or less expediently, by the laws, policies, and diplomatic practices of a particular state at a particular time.[85] States cannot simply do as they please without regard to the exigencies of world order. For example, in the *Nottebohm Case*, the International Court of Justice eliminated an extravagant determination of

---

in matters which are essentially within the domestic jurisdiction of any state or shall require the Members to submit such matters to settlement under the present Charter. . . ." UN CHARTER art. 2(7).

82

> If the dispute between the parties is claimed by one of them, and is found by the Council, to arise out of a matter which by international law is solely within the domestic jurisdiction of that party, the Council shall so report, and shall make no recommendation as to its settlement.

Treaty of Peace between the Allied and Associated Powers and Germany, June 28, 1919, 1919 FOREIGN RELATIONS OF THE UNITED STATES, THE PARIS PEACE CONFERENCE, Vol. 13, at 55, 88, 2 Bevans 43, 53.

83 Tunis-Morocco Nationality Decrees, 1923 PCIJ, ser. B, No. 4, at 24 (Advisory Opinion of Feb. 7).

84 C. JENKS, THE COMMON LAW OF MANKIND 283–85 (1958). For an early, rather idealistic assertion that immigration is not solely within the domestic jurisdiction of states and that the moral right to immigrate might "in time" become a legal right, see Manisty, *The Right of Immigration,* 12 GROTIUS SOC'Y TRANSACTIONS 1–3 (1927).

85 *But see* the following dictum, as a principle of municipal constitutional law, in Harisiades v. Shaughnessy, 342 U.S. 580, 588–89 (1952): "any policy toward aliens is vitally and intricately interwoven with contemporaneous policies in regard to the conduct of foreign relations, the war power, and the maintenance of a republican form of government." *Accord,* Carlson v. Landon, 342 U.S. 524, 534–35 (1952).

nationality, as a basis for diplomatic protection, from the reserved domain of states.[86]

It is uncertain to what extent, "in the present state" of conventional law, questions of alien admission or exclusion fall *solely* within the reserved domain of domestic jurisdiction. On one hand, international agreements sometimes place questions of immigration within that reserved domain. For example, Article 12 of the International Covenant on Civil and Political Rights, in establishing freedom of movement for "everyone lawfully within the territory of a State," apparently allows each signatory to interpret the word "lawfully" for itself.[87] The Constitution of the Intergovernmental Committee for Migration[88] acknowledges that control of immigration is vested within the domestic jurisdiction of states, and defers to municipal law. On the other hand, the drafters of other agreements have refused to endorse an absolute faculty of exclusion within the discretion of states.[89]

More importantly, from a global perspective, one may persuasively maintain that the issue of alien exclusion should not be essentially one of domestic jurisdiction. Migration by its nature is international and has international consequences, as does immigration law, particularly in creating tensions between states.[90] States themselves describe immigration problems as international and understand that such problems may require international solutions. Moreover, judicial opinions and legal scholars have referred to limits on sovereign discretion, as will be shown.

As the world heats up, a Brownian movement of persons and populations challenges the global order. Conflagration begets migration. Carried to the extreme, an unfettered sovereign discretion to exclude aliens may inhibit the

[86]

> According to the practice of States, to arbitral and judicial decisions and to the opinions of writers, nationality is a legal bond having as its basis a social fact of attachment, a genuine connection of existence, interests and sentiments, together with the existence of reciprocal rights and duties. It may be said to constitute the juridical expression of the fact that the individual upon whom it is conferred, either directly by the law or as the result of an act of the authorities, is in fact more closely connected with the population of the State conferring nationality than with that of any other State.

Nottebohm Case (Second Phase) (Liechtenstein v. Guat.), 1955 ICJ REP. 4, 23 (Judgment of Apr. 6).

[87] International Covenant on Civil and Political Rights, GA Res. 2200 (XXI), 21 UN GAOR Supp. (No. 16) at 52, UN Doc. A/6316 (1966), *entered into force* Mar. 23, 1976. Article 6 of the International Covenant on Economic, Social and Cultural Rights, GA Res. 2200 (XXI), 21 UN GAOR Supp. (No. 16) at 49, UN Doc. A/6316 (1966), *entered into force* Jan. 3, 1976, "recognize[s] the right to work, which includes the right of everyone to the opportunity to gain his living by work which he freely chooses or accepts." *Id.* at 50. It is doubtful, however, that this right contemplates that immigration laws will be liberalized to effect its provisions.

[88] Constitution of the Intergovernmental Comm. for European Migration, *opened for signature* Oct. 19, 1953, 6 UST 603, TIAS No. 3197, 207 UNTS 189 (renamed to exclude the word "European").

[89] D. O'CONNELL, *supra* note 80, at 696 (with particular reference to the convention drafted by the Conference on Treatment of Foreigners and the Convention between the American Republics regarding the Status of Aliens in their Respective Territories).

[90] One writer speaks of "l'influence dangereuse des pratiques restrictives de l'immigration sur les tensions internationales." C. DE VISSCHER, *supra* note 12, at 228; *see also* pp. 230–31.

normal process of human migration and thereby strain the global order,[91] whose preservation and progressive development might be said to constitute the highest duty of international law.

Another justification for exclusive domestic jurisdiction, as applied to immigration decisions, is that members of a national polity should be allowed to choose all new members, as a matter of communal self-determination.

> Affluent and free countries are, like élite universities, besieged by applicants. They have to decide on their own size and character. More precisely, as citizens of such a country, we have to decide: Whom should we admit? Ought we to have open admission? Can we choose among applicants? What are the appropriate criteria for distributing membership?[92]

The important point, however, is that even though national polities must generally answer these questions for themselves, they must take account of constraints. Thus, the right to exclude, as a matter of self-determination or a "particular community's understanding of self," is said to be subject to the principle of mutual aid, which may indicate a modification of admission policies.[93]

For these reasons, it is highly questionable whether the general admission of aliens either is or ought to be left wholly to the domestic jurisdiction or unlimited self-determination of states. Theory nevertheless dies hard. In practice, no matter how dormant the concept of a sovereign's inherent powers to exclude any or all aliens, or the corollary that exclusion is a matter lying solely within domestic jurisdiction, they remain engraved in the Anglo-American municipal decisions and derivative writings that have shaped the proposition under study. Because of the international flavor of alien exclusion cases, municipal courts seem prone to reify, or at least to orient their analysis toward, the concept of a sovereign's inherent powers within the nation-state system. Although historically and analytically the concept may be doubtful in its application to alien admissions, it looms large in judicial and legislative discussions concerning the general admission of aliens. It has a life of its own. Moreover, mindless acceptance of the concept of a state's exclusive jurisdiction inhibits the growth of international cooperation and lawmaking in response to intrinsically international, and important, issues of migration.

[91] *E.g.:*

> If the power to exclude is beyond review and redress, it might be assumed that entry may be authorized on whatever conditions the state may choose to impose, including a general condition that an alien enters at his peril. This in turn might suggest that any action by the state affecting an alien after he is admitted may be regarded as an unreviewable exercise of power. If law and the behavior of men and states conformed to so abstract and extreme a logic, foreignness would imply absence of legal protection, and there would be little possibility of a meaningful international legal order.

M. KATZ & K. BREWSTER, THE LAW OF INTERNATIONAL TRANSACTIONS AND RELATIONS 8 (1960).

[92] M. WALZER, SPHERES OF JUSTICE 32 (1983).

[93] *Id.* at 51.

The Curtiss-Wright *Doctrine*

In the United States, judicial support for the theory of a sovereign's inherent right or powers of international scope is especially misleading. The opinions that will be examined in the next section typically turn on a sovereign's inherent powers, not within a global context as a means of openly and candidly avoiding international law, but rather within a federal context as a means of resolving constitutional issues. The rationale for many of the municipal decisions seems to be a reworking of the *Curtiss-Wright* doctrine.[94] Accordingly, the "lot of aliens" is "peculiarly a subject for international diplomacy,"[95] not in the absence of an international legal duty, but because of constitutional requirements involving an allocation of powers within a government.

Moreover, *Curtiss-Wright* itself established a litmus test of international law. Despite its extravagant language about sovereign powers, the *Curtiss-Wright* doctrine is rooted in a concept of sovereignty that recognizes a state's membership in the family of nations. Citing an alien expulsion case, among others, the Court determined that certain powers inhere in the sovereign because they are "inseparable from the conception of nationality [warranted by] the law of nations."[96] The Court, quoting from an earlier opinion, concluded that national governments are vested with "all the powers of government *necessary* to maintain an effective control of international relations."[97] Thus, *Curtiss-Wright* seems to have established a limited, not an absolute, standard for testing what laws are within a sovereign's unfettered "inherent" powers.

IV. The Alien Exclusion Cases: Questionable Authority

The highly selective statements already examined from Vattel's *Le Droit des gens*,[98] together with socioeconomic circumstances and legal positivism of the late 19th century, conditioned the classic United States and British judicial decisions to uphold a limited exclusion of aliens. These decisions have been cited as authority throughout the world. In giving formal respectability to the trend of limited exclusion in state practice, decisions of the highest Anglo-American courts between 1889 and 1893, in the historical context of increased immigration pressures from the Orient, were thus definitive, if not dispositive.[99] Recognition of this historical context is critical to a full appraisal of the exclusionary proposition's validity today. Against this background the following section will show that both the authority and especially later restatements of that authority are highly questionable.

[94] The federal Government has inherent powers over external affairs. More specifically, the right and power of the United States in the field of international relations "are equal to the right and power of the other members of the international family." Thus, for example, the federal Government may expel undesirable aliens so long as expulsion is justified by "the law of nations." 299 U.S. at 318.

[95] Harisiades v. Shaughnessy, 342 U.S. at 591.

[96] 299 U.S. at 318.

[97] *Ibid.* (emphasis added).

[98] *See* text at notes 37–54 *supra*.

[99] M. Konvitz, *supra* note 14, at 18.

United States Supreme Court Opinions

Under the Constitution, the U.S. Supreme Court established in 1933 that the power of Congress to prescribe the terms and conditions upon which aliens may enter or remain in the United States is "no longer open to serious question."[100] However, critical questions remain. As a preliminary constitutional consideration, to what extent must the plenary power of Congress bear a reasonable relationship to such interests as public health, safety, morals, general welfare, fiscal integrity, and national security?[101] To what extent do statements about the authority of the political branches of government properly define sovereign power internationally? That is, to what extent, if any, was the Supreme Court speaking of the constitutional powers of the political branches as an international, rather than a strictly federal, consideration? To what extent, to the contrary, does international law limit sovereign prerogatives? Are the Court's exclusionary principles still valid even though they were premised on the Court's acceptance of nativism, racial prejudice, and ideological repugnance?

The pertinent case law is firmly rooted in reasons of state, that is, in the state's "highest duty" of self-preservation. It is therefore instructive to ask what circumstances were perceived as a threat to the country's survival when the Court gave its opinions. The answer is simple. Of the three landmark cases decided during the period 1889–1893, two upheld legislation designed to exclude or expel what were explicitly feared to be nonassimilable yellow hordes,[102] and the third[103] upheld the exclusion of a Japanese, ostensibly on the basis of her indigency.

In *The Chinese Exclusion Case,* the Court first established that congressional authority to exclude aliens was plenary, was derived from the inherent power of the sovereign, and could abrogate valid treaties.[104] Because that landmark decision has been repeatedly, if not ritually, invoked, it merits careful consideration. The case involved a Chinese laborer who had lived in the United

[100] United States *ex rel.* Volpe v. Smith, 289 U.S. 422, 425 (1933).

[101]

> The proper constitutional test for restrictions on entry is the two-level test applied to legislation generally. Where the restriction does not involve a suspect classification or impinge on fundamental rights, a restriction on entry would have to bear a reasonable relationship to a legitimate government interest. Present immigration law contains various exclusion provisions which would need to meet the test of a reasonable relationship to a legitimate state interest. We may consider these as falling under the broad interests of public health and safety, public morals, fiscal integrity, and national security, though these categories overlap to a degree.

Note, *Immigrants, Aliens, and the Constitution,* 49 NOTRE DAME LAW. 1075, 1082 (1974). Related issues of municipal constitutional law lie beyond the scope of this study.

[102] The Chinese Exclusion Case, 130 U.S. 581 (1889); Fong Yue Ting v. United States, 149 U.S. 698 (1893). *See* Hesse, *The Constitutional Status of the Lawfully Admitted Permanent Resident Alien: The Pre-1917 Cases,* 68 YALE L.J. 1587, 1588 (1959).

[103] Nishimura Ekiu v. United States, 142 U.S. 651 (1892).

[104] 130 U.S. 581, *passim* (1889). The power of Congress to regulate immigration had been found in the Commerce Clause. The Head Money Cases, 112 U.S. 580 (1884).

States for 12 years but was denied reentry after a visit to China. The denial was based on a recently enacted federal statute that precluded the admission of Chinese nationals. A unanimous Court upheld the constitutionality of that statute. The petitioner's exclusion was thereby upheld even though he had obtained a certificate of reentry prior to his departure from the United States, even though the underlying statute had been passed during his return voyage from China, and even though the statute violated the express terms of treaties between the United States and China.

The Court held that the statute applied to the petitioner despite his particular circumstances, and that under the Supremacy Clause of the Constitution, an Act of Congress could abrogate treaty privileges such as those in a U.S.-Chinese agreement that would have entitled the petitioner to reenter the United States. The "later in time" principle apparently applied, although it is somewhat difficult to reconcile the decision to exclude this petitioner with the long heeded doctrine of *Murray v. Charming Betsy* under which statutes are to be construed so as to comply with international law.[105]

It is usually overlooked that the Court in *The Chinese Exclusion Case* did not leave congressional power unbridled. Congress "can exclude aliens," but its power was said to be restricted by "the Constitution itself and considerations of public policy and justice which control, more or less, the conduct of all civilized nations."[106] Although the Court did not specify the requirements of justice, it inferred a public policy of excluding Chinese laborers that was "essential to the peace of the community on the Pacific Coast, and possibly to the preservation of our civilization there."[107] Indeed, "[i]t seemed impossible for [Chinese subjects] to assimilate with our people or to make any change in their habits or modes of living."[108] Thus, if the presence and incapacity of aliens to assimilate were considered by Congress "to be dangerous to [the country's] peace and security,"[109] even a peaceful treaty relationship between the United States and China was immaterial.

The Court quoted diplomatic correspondence taken from Wharton's *International Law Digest* to support the power of the federal Government "to exclude foreigners from the country whenever, in its judgment, the public interests require such exclusion."[110] Actually, the cited correspondence expressed only a qualified power to exclude. These qualifications included a foreign presence sufficient to be deemed a source of danger or dangerous to the peace of the state and otherwise expressed "policy or other grounds."[111] As examples, the Court specifically noted that paupers, criminals, and persons afflicted with incurable diseases were excludable.[112] By extension, the presence of Chinese laborers was deemed to be dangerous to the peace of the

[105] 6 U.S. (2 Cranch) 64, 117–18 (1804), where Chief Justice Marshall wrote that "an Act of Congress ought never to be construed to violate the law of nations if any other possible construction remains."

[106] 130 U.S. at 604.

[107] *Id.* at 594.

[108] *Id.* at 595. In the Lawyer's Edition of the opinion, the word "seemed" appears as "seems." 32 L. Ed. 1068, 1072.

[109] 130 U.S. at 606.

[110] *Ibid.*

[111] *Id.* at 607–08.

[112] *Id.* at 608.

country. Under those circumstances, Congress had determined that the interests of the country required racial exclusion.

In quick succession after *The Chinese Exclusion Case,* the Supreme Court delivered two further opinions, *Nishimura Ekiu v. United States* and *Fong Yue Ting v. United States,* which largely completed the elaboration of judicial doctrine, not only for the United States but for much of the modern world. In *Ekiu* the Court upheld a provision of the Immigration Act of 1891[113] that prohibited the admission of a "person likely to become a public charge."[114] *Ekiu* is significant principally because of the debut there of the most common version of the proposition under study, as follows:

> It is an accepted maxim of international law, that every sovereign nation has the power, as inherent in sovereignty, and essential to self-preservation, to forbid the entrance of foreigners within its dominions, or to admit them only in such cases and upon such conditions as it may see fit to prescribe. Vattel, lib. 2, §§94, 100; 1 Phillimore (3d ed.) c. 10, §220.[115]

The cited authority is questionable. Sir Robert Phillimore had formulated "a received maxim of International Law, that the Government of a State may prohibit the entrance of strangers into the country."[116] It is unclear whether Phillimore was referring to "strangers" individually, collectively, or both. Moreover, the only authority he cited for the "received maxim" was limited British practice, which, as he was careful to note, occurred only temporarily and "during periods of revolutionary disturbances."[117] As a matter of state practice, Phillimore also noted the policy of "wise States," including Rome, to "open wide the door for the reception and naturalization of foreigners."[118]

In citing Vattel's statements about sovereign rights under the external law, the Court ignored pertinent exceptions as well as those sovereign duties to aliens under internal law which have been previously examined.[119] The opinion in *Ekiu* is therefore tendentious, and its talismanic dictum ill-founded.

In *Fong Yue Ting,* the Court extended its doctrine from instances of exclusion to those of expulsion. In doing so, the Court cited *The Chinese Exclusion Case* and two of the latter's excerpts from Wharton. Of particular interest is the Court's citation to the authority of four publicists, again including Phillimore and Vattel in support of the right of exclusion. The Phillimore citation is the same as that in *Ekiu,* but that of Vattel, which is different, significantly qualified sovereign rights under the law of nations. The Court once again ignored not only the exceptions in Vattel's restatement of external law but also his articulation of a binding internal law. More importantly, the Court relied on the following passage from Vattel:

[113] 26 Stat. 1084 (1891).

[114] 142 U.S. at 662.

[115] *Id.* at 659.

[116] 1 R. PHILLIMORE, INTERNATIONAL LAW 320 (3d ed. 1879).

[117] *Ibid.*

[118] *Id.* at 446.

[119] *See* text at notes 44–53.

> Every nation has the right to refuse to admit a foreigner into the country, *when he cannot enter without putting the nation in evident danger, or doing it a manifest injury.* What she owes to herself, the care of her own safety, gives her *this right;* and in virtue of her natural liberty, it belongs to the nation to judge, whether her circumstances will or will not justify the admission of that foreigner. . . .[120]

This passage is significant, for Vattel clearly qualified the right of a state to restrict the admission of aliens. He did not, therefore, endorse the proposition under study. Thus, in concluding that states had a right to exclude aliens absolutely, the Court relied on authority that limited that right.

Subsequent jurisprudence, though ample, is generally addressed to procedural or constitutional matters. Most of the remaining opinions of the U.S. Supreme Court that allude to exclusionary doctrine, often rather cryptically, are fundamentally concerned with questions of federal power, justiciability, or procedural due process.[121] Also, at least one of the opinions seems to turn partly on the since discarded distinction between rights and privileges[122] to receive governmental benefits.

Kleindienst v. Mandel,[123] a case decided in 1972, while concerned primarily with congressional powers and justiciability of political questions, is the Court's latest significant elaboration of exclusion doctrine.[124] The Court's discussion of federal powers and justiciability relied upon the most extreme statements from earlier opinions on the plenary powers of Congress. These statements seem to presume, a fortiori and erroneously, that the Court had acknowledged no checks at all upon congressional authority to exclude aliens.

The Court disposed of the international legal question by citing *The Chinese Exclusion Case* and *Fong Yue Ting* to evidence "ancient principles of the international law of nation-states"[125] as support for the power to exclude aliens. Again, the Court confused international and constitutional legal issues by passing quickly over the former. The Court has had a habit of leaping over the international legal hurdle into the issue of justiciability or of incorrectly applying *The Chinese Exclusion Case* and *Fong Yue Ting* by failing to inquire into the existence of a genuine danger to the nation's peace and security. One of

[120] E. DE VATTEL, *supra* note 38, bk. I, §230, at 107, *quoted with minor rewording in* 149 U.S. at 707 (emphasis added).

[121] *See, e.g.,* Lem Moon Sing v. United States, 158 U.S. 538, 543 (1895); Fok Yung Yo v. United States, 185 U.S. 296, 302 (1902); United States *ex rel.* Turner v. Williams, 194 U.S. 279, 294 (1904); Keller v. United States, 213 U.S. 138, 143–44 (1909); Mahler v. Eby, 264 U.S. 32, 40 (1924); United States *ex rel.* Knauff v. Shaughnessy, 338 U.S. 537, 542 (1950); Harisiades v. Shaughnessy, 342 U.S. at 587–88; Shaughnessy v. United States *ex rel.* Mezei, 345 U.S. 206, 210 (1953); Galvan v. Press, 347 U.S. 522, 531 (1954).

[122] United States *ex rel.* Knauff v. Shaughnessy, 338 U.S. at 542, 544. Graham v. Richardson, 403 U.S. 365, 374 (1971), a case involving access by aliens to state welfare benefits, is one of several Court opinions that have explicitly rejected the materiality of the distinction between a "right" and a "privilege."

[123] 408 U.S. 753 (1972).

[124] *See also* Plyler v. Doe, 457 U.S. 202, 225 (1982); Landon v. Plasencia, 103 S.Ct. 321, 329 (1982).

[125] 408 U.S. at 765.

two vigorous dissents to *Kleindienst v. Mandel* correctly cited *The Chinese Exclusion Case* on this point, and both it and the other dissent, which refers to "the majority's baroque approach," questioned whether the Court should rely today upon precedent that had upheld racial and ideological tests for the admission of aliens.[126]

In sum, even a strict constitutional constructionist[127] could find little compulsion in the case law for the proposition that a state may exclude all aliens absolutely. Three of the four leading opinions are nearly a hundred years old, three applied exclusion doctrines principally to uphold racial or ideological tests acceptable then but questionable today, and one misapplied cited authority. Moreover, three of the four opinions predated comprehensive immigration laws, and therefore may have gone as far as they did in lieu of broad statutory rules. Most importantly, the definitive opinions in *The Chinese Exclusion Case* and *Fong Yue Ting* qualified the excludability of aliens by citing international legal authority to the effect that a state can exclude aliens *only when they present a danger to the peace and security of the country.* Subsequent opinions that failed to acknowledge this limitation on sovereign power mostly addressed other issues such as the allocation of powers among branches of the federal Government. Reaffirmations of the exclusive power of the political branches of government to make rules for the admission of aliens have been "legion."[128] Other opinions relied upon a semantic distinction, since discarded, between a right and a privilege, or, as in *Kleindienst v. Mandel,* simply failed to cite precedent contextually, completely, and correctly.

British Opinions

The classic British opinion is *Musgrove v. Chun Teeong Toy.*[129] Decided by the Privy Council in 1891 on facts remarkably similar to those in *The Chinese Exclusion Case,* that decision upheld a provision of the Chinese Act of 1881 (Victoria, Australia), as follows:

> No authority exists for the proposition that an alien has [a legal right to enter British territory]. Circumstances may occur in which the refusal

[126] *Id.* at 770 (Douglas, J., dissenting) and 781 (Marshall, J., dissenting), respectively. *See also* Harisiades v. Shaughnessy, 342 U.S. at 598 (Douglas, J., dissenting); and Galvan v. Press, 347 U.S. at 534 (Douglas, J., dissenting).

[127] In *The Chinese Exclusion Case* the Court formulated a mechanistic role for the judiciary, as follows:

> When once it is established that Congress possesses the power to pass an act, our province ends with its construction, and its application to cases as they are persented for determination. . . . We do not mean to intimate that the moral aspects of legislative acts may not be proper subjects of consideration. Undoubtedly they may be, at proper times and places, before the public, in the halls of Congress, and in all the modes by which the public mind can be influenced. Public opinion thus enlightened, brought to bear upon legislation, will do more than all other causes to prevent abuses; but the province of the courts is to pass upon the validity of laws, not to make them, and when their validity is established, to declare their meaning and apply their provisions. All else lies beyond their domain.

130 U.S. at 603.

[128] Kleindienst v. Mandel, 408 U.S. at 765–66.

[129] 1891 A.C. 272.

> to permit an alien to land might be such an interference with international comity as would properly give rise to diplomatic remonstrance from the country of which he was a native, but it is quite another thing to assert that an alien excluded from any part of Her Majesty's dominions by the executive government there, can maintain an action in a British Court . . . involving delicate and difficult constitutional questions affecting the respective rights of the Crown and Parliament, and the relations of this country to her self-governing colonies. . . .[130]

Thus, *Musgrove,* like the U.S. opinions, addressed issues of an alien's standing to sue and justiciability of subject matter, in view of "delicate and difficult constitutional questions." On its face, *Musgrove* seems more absolutist and protective of sovereign prerogatives than the U.S. opinions. Under *Musgrove,* a state's right to exclude may apparently be challenged only extrajudicially, that is, by diplomatic remonstrance as an interference with international law. An alien has no standing to raise a claim in court.[131] Under the formative case law of the United States, however, an exclusionary measure could presumably be challenged for lack of a danger to peace and security of the country. A recent British opinion confirms that "[*a*]*t common law* no alien has any right to enter this country except by leave of the Crown; and the Crown can refuse leave without giving any reason."[132]

Whatever the differences, the British and U.S. opinions are similar in largely ignoring or glossing over the international legal dimension. Why? As a British expert has poignantly observed, the answer may be that counsel for petitioners in both of the formative cases, *Ekiu* (U.S.) and *Musgrove* (UK), failed to develop the principle of free movement on behalf of their clients; nor did they direct the court's attention to a line of writing and state practice obligating the state to admit aliens.[133] In failing their clients, lawyers in *Ekiu* and *Musgrove* failed posterity.

V. Customary International Law

Despite its questionable provenance in political theory, history, and judicial precedent, has the exclusionary proposition ripened into custom? If not, has international custom established the obverse proposition, that a state has at

[130] *Id.* at 282–83. There was reliance on *Musgrove* 17 years later. 2 BURGE'S COMMENTARIES ON COLONIAL AND FOREIGN LAWS 140 (Renton & Phillimore eds. 1908).

[131] G. GOODWIN-GILL, *supra* note 6, at 23.

[132] R. v. Governor of Pentonville Prison, *ex parte* Azam, [1973] 2 All E.R. 741, 747 (emphasis added); *see also* Schmidt v. Secretary of State for Home Affairs, [1969] 1 All E.R. 904, 907, where Lord Denning wrote as follows: "I have always held the view that in common law no alien has any right to enter this country except by leave of the Crown: and the Crown can refuse leave without giving any reason."

[133]

> In neither case was there prolonged discussion about the principle of free movement. Thus, Sir W. Phillimore, Q.C. and J. W. McCarthy, for Chun Teeong Toy, conceded that "every state may by international law exclude aliens", [1891] A.C. 272, 276. In *Nishimura Ekiu v. U.S.*, Mr. Lyman I. Mowry, for the appellant, merely referred to international law to support his assertion that the powers conferred by the Act were of such an extraordinary nature that it was the evident intention of Congress that a record of the proceedings should be kept: 142 U.S. 651, 658.

R. PLENDER, *supra* note 16, at 51 n.80.

least a qualified duty to admit aliens? In an effort to answer these questions, this section will explore the following sources and evidences of customary international law: scholarly commentary, draft regulations, particularly those adopted by the Institute of International Law in 1892, state practice, and regional practice.[134] This analysis of custom first reviews its quantitative or material elements and then the qualitative or psychological element of *opinio juris*. International lawyers generally regard *opinio juris* as a requirement for the establishment of custom although some argue that, like the corpus of general practice itself, the animus of *opinio juris* is only a test to controvert "prima facie evidence that [the general practice of states] is accepted as law."[135]

Material Elements

Scholarly Commentary and Draft Regulations. It is important to begin with a survey of scholarly writings. Though inconclusive, they clarify the contending interpretations of customary law, help evaluate the relative persuasiveness of each interpretation, and articulate *opinio juris*.

Modern publicists seem to concur on two points: that a state may exclude aliens under some circumstances at least, and that it must meet its treaty obligations to admit aliens. Otherwise, the publicists disagree. There are at least ten categories: publicists who (1) accept the proposition a priori or categorically in a legal sense and without qualification (states may do as they please);[136] (2) accept the proposition in only a theoretical sense or in principle;[137] (3) accept the proposition but would render diplomatically or legally responsible any state that denies admission to an alien in an arbitrary or unjust manner;[138] (4) seem to accept the proposition but only as it relates, somewhat ambiguously, to individual applicants and well-defined classes;[139] (5) accept

[134] Another, somewhat different version of this section will appear as *International Law Bearing on the Entry of Aliens Regardless of Refugee Status*, XIII THESAURUS ACROASIUM (1983).

[135] North Sea Continental Shelf Cases (W. Ger./Den.; W. Ger./Neth.), 1969 ICJ REP. 3, 231 (Judgment of Feb. 20) (Lachs, J., dissenting). This article relies on Professor Anthony D'Amato's concept of *opinio juris*, which requires authoritative articulation of a rule, in advance of or concurrent with a state practice. A. D'AMATO, THE CONCEPT OF CUSTOM IN INTERNATIONAL LAW 74 *et seq.* (1971).

[136] *E.g.*, J. BRIERLY, C. DE VISSCHER, C. HYDE, H. KELSEN, W. LEVI, Oda, L. OPPENHEIM, S. SINHA, and G. VON GLAHN, *supra* note 12.

[137] *E.g.*, C. FENWICK, *supra* note 4; A. JEANCOURT-GALIGNANI, L'IMMIGRATION EN DROIT INTERNATIONAL 97 (1908).

[138] E. BORCHARD, *supra* note 4, at 48; C. BOUVÉ, A TREATISE ON THE LAWS GOVERNING THE EXCLUSION AND EXPULSION OF ALIENS IN THE UNITED STATES 14, 15 (1912); L. EVANS, LEADING CASES ON INTERNATIONAL LAW 135 (2d ed. 1922); E. STOWELL, INTERNATIONAL LAW: A RESTATEMENT OF PRINCIPLES 193 (1931); W. HALL, A TREATISE ON INTERNATIONAL LAW 223 (4th ed. 1895); D. O'CONNELL, *supra* note 80, at 695–96; W. WILLOUGHBY, *supra* note 12, at 251.

[139] Pradier-Fodéré, Remarks, 12 INST. DROIT INT'L ANNUAIRE 192 (1892–94); M. SIBERT, *supra* note 7, at 575. A related statement is that "there is no general right for a foreign national to enter a country." Jagerskiold, *The Freedom of Movement*, in THE INTERNATIONAL BILL OF RIGHTS 166, 174 (L. Henkin ed. 1981).

the proposition, but only to protect the public safety, health, morals, or general welfare of a recipient state, or to serve its most vital public interests (or who reject the proposition except to protect those values);[140] (6) accept the proposition except when applied arbitrarily or discriminatorily on the basis of race or geographical origin;[141] (7) accept the proposition except when applied in a racially discriminatory manner or in violation of the principle of *non-refoulement* of refugees;[142] (8) reject the proposition but recognize broad sovereign authority, limited by international law, to exclude some aliens;[143] (9) reject the proposition but allow states to exclude aliens upon the submission of "definite reasons" to "the foreign government covered," presumably at the immigration source;[144] and (10) reject the proposition flatly, on the principle that a state cannot prevent foreigners from entering its territory.[145] Historically, Anglo-American writers have tended to favor the proposition under the principle of absolute sovereignty, whereas European continental and Latin American writers have favored freer movement under the principle of inter-

[140] E. BORCHARD, *supra* note 4, at 46; P. FAUCHILLE, *supra* note 15, at 894–95; Fiore, Remarks, 12 INST. DROIT INT'L ANNUAIRE 193 (1892–94); 1 J. KENT, COMMENTARIES ON AMERICAN LAW §35 n.(a) (O. W. Holmes, Jr., ed. 1884); Irizarry y Puente, *supra* note 15, at 254–56, 270. "Any government [may exclude aliens] when entry would be likely to endanger the public health, welfare and safety or threaten national security." STAFF REPORT OF THE [U.S.] SELECT COMMISSION ON IMMIGRATION AND REFUGEE POLICY, U.S. IMMIGRATION POLICY AND THE NATIONAL INTEREST, SUPPLEMENT TO THE FINAL REPORT AND RECOMMENDATIONS OF THE COMMISSION 762 (1981) (emphasis added). *Cf.* this statement with more ambiguous "undesirability" criterion. *Id.* at 723.

As the Swiss jurist, Johann K. Bluntschli, wrote in a classic formulation of this viewpoint:

> Aucun état n'a le droit d'interdire d'une façon absolue aux étrangers l'entrée de son territoire, et de fermer le pays au commerce général.
>
> . . . .
>
> Chaque état a le droit d'interdire l'entrée de son territoire à certains étrangers pour motifs politiques ou judiciaires.
>
> 1. *L'exclusion de certains étrangers doit être motivée par l'ordre, la sûreté ou le bien publics,* sinon elle serait en contradiction avec le principe de la liberté des relations internationales. . . .
>
> . . . .
>
> *Lorsqu'un gouvernement interdit sans motif l'entrée du territoire à un étranger* dûment légitimé, ou l'expulse sans cause et avec des formes blessantes, l'état dont cet étranger est citoyen a le droit de réclamer contre cette violation du droit international, et de demander au besoin satisfaction.

J. BLUNTSCHLI, LE DROIT INTERNATIONAL CODIFIÉ 228–29 (5th Guillaumin ed. 1895) (emphasis added).

[141] The practice of certain newly independent states supports the proposition only when exclusion is nondiscriminatory and "necessary" to implement a state's "national or public interest." ASIAN-AFRICAN LEGAL CONSULTATIVE COMMITTEE, REPORT OF THE FOURTH SESSION 56, 59–60, *discussed in* S. SINHA, *supra* note 12, at 97.

[142] G. GOODWIN-GILL, *supra* note 6, at 196.

[143] L. CAVARÉ, *supra* note 9, at 275; D. O'CONNELL, *supra* note 80, at 695–96; Hucker, *supra* note 5, at 327; M. SIBERT, *supra* note 7, at 571; E. STOWELL, *supra* note 138, at 193; A. VERDROSS, *supra* note 5, at 25.

[144] A. HEFFTER, DAS EUROPÄISCHE VÖLKERRECHT DER GEGENWART AUF DEN BISHERIGEN GRUNDLAGEN §33 (5th ed. 1867); T. WOOLSEY, *supra* note 59, at 88–89.

[145] P. FIORE, *supra* note 15, at 42.

dependence.[146] In practice, this geographical distinction has become somewhat less significant.

Numerous writers who have commented that a state may deny entry to all aliens either fail to indicate authority, or rely on questionable authority or interpretations of that authority. Of those writers who would limit or reject the proposition, the most numerous and persuasive seem to fall in the fifth and eighth categories. Logically, the fifth category simply articulates a specific class or classes of excludable aliens within the ambit of the eighth category. Semantically, it makes little difference whether we begin by accepting the proposition, subject to a major qualification, or by rejecting the proposition, subject to the exclusion of some aliens. Either way, a consensus of persuasive publicists confirms the teachings of the classic publicists and early case law, namely, that a state may exclude some, but not all, aliens. The best evidence of a more specific rule, though tentative, is as follows: a state may exclude aliens if, individually or collectively, they pose serious danger to its public safety, security, general welfare, or essential institutions.

Ironically, the formative period of restrictionist policy at the end of the 19th century occurred just as the Institute of International Law was formulating a liberal proposal for a state's duty to admit aliens. The Institute's adoption in 1892 of the proposed International Regulations on the Admission and Expulsion of Aliens,[147] although less significant today,[148] nevertheless refutes later claims that the international legal community acquiesced in the exclusionary proposition when it was formulated. The regulations distinguished clearly between the legal right of a state to admit or not to admit aliens as "a logical and necessary consequence"[149] of its sovereignty and independence, and the obligations of "humanity and justice." Thus, the Institute called upon a state, in exercising that legal right, to have due regard, as a matter of humanity and justice, to the right and liberty of foreigners wishing to enter that state's territory, to the extent compatible with its security.[150] Three of the provisions are particularly noteworthy today:

> ARTICLE 6. Free entrance of aliens to the territory of a civilized State, may not be generally and permanently forbidden except in the public interest and for very serious reasons, for example, because of fundamental differences in customs or civilization, or because of a dangerous organization or gathering of aliens who come in great numbers.
>
> ARTICLE 7. The protection of national labor is not, in itself, a sufficient reason for non-admission.

[146] R. PLENDER, *supra* note 16, at 38 & n.15.

[147] 12 INST. DROIT INT'L ANNUAIRE 218 *et seq.* (1892–94). For minutes of the proceedings convened to draft the regulations, see *id.* at 184–218 [hereinafter referred to as Procès-verbal des séances]. For an English translation of the regulations, see RESOLUTIONS OF THE INSTITUTE OF INTERNATIONAL LAW 104 *et seq.* (J. Scott ed. 1916). For a summary of the background and earlier draft of the regulations, see *id.* at 88–90.

[148] R. PLENDER, *supra* note 16, at 53.

[149] Preamble, RESOLUTIONS, *supra* note 147, at 104.

[150] *Ibid.*

ARTICLE 12. Entrance to a country may be forbidden to any alien individual in a condition of vagabondage or beggary, or suffering from a malady liable to endanger the public health, or strongly suspected of serious offenses committed abroad against the life or health of human beings or against public property or faith, as well as to aliens who have been convicted of the said offenses.[151]

A proposed amendment would have permitted states to exclude individuals on the basis of "race, customs, or civilization."[152] The Eighth Commission of the Institute, which drafted the regulations, decided against those bases for exclusion, however, and in favor of a more limited sovereign role consistent with prevailing theory and reality. Thus, the Institute affirmed the existing law on exclusion and proposed a set of stable principles for the future.

General Custom: State Practice. Although no state appears to accept a theory of unlimited free movement, the general practice of states has long favored the qualified admission of aliens despite periodic currents of xenophobia.[153] That practice continues today. For example, although a survey during the world depression revealed that "the doors which once opened are now but slightly ajar,"[154] immigration laws enacted in troubled economic circumstances, now as before, keep the door somewhere between ajar and open.[155] Sometimes states have consented in bilateral and regional agreements to accept limited obligations of general admission.[156] Aside from these treaty obligations, most modern states have continuously admitted aliens under municipal law and have acquiesced in the admission of their own nationals by other states. In sum, the duration, repetition, continuity, and generality of this state practice, which constitute the material elements of custom, help refute the proposition that a state may exclude all aliens. Thus, the issue is not whether the material elements of state practice ratify the absolutist proposition (they clearly do not), but whether, in the development of international relations, states have a minimum or qualified duty to admit *some* aliens under normal circumstances. Let us examine the evidence.

Municipal laws vary in their hospitality to aliens applying for admission. Generally, the laws accommodate specific categories of aliens besides affirming a state's duty to readmit its own nationals. A limited range of eligible nonimmigrants and immigrants includes applicants who have acquired a right of residence; diplomats and consuls; representatives of and to international organizations; members of armed forces assigned for local duty under international agreements; victims of *force majeure;* and traders, investors, and others

[151] *Id.* at 105–06. *Cf.* STAFF REPORT ON IMMIGRATION, *supra* note 140.

[152] Procès-verbal des séances, *supra* note 147, at 192.

[153] E. BORCHARD, *supra* note 4, at 46; Oda, *supra* note 4, at 481.

[154] Fields, *Closing Immigration throughout the World,* 26 AJIL 671 (1932). On current nativism in Western Europe, see Yerkey, *W. Europe immigrants live in no man's land,* Christian Sci. Monitor, March 30, 1982, at 1, col. 4.

[155] *E.g.,* Australia (Australian News, Oct. 29, 1981); Belgium (COUNCIL OF EUROPE INFORMATION BULL., No. 10, Nov. 1981, at 31, 35, 47).

[156] G. GOODWIN-GILL, *supra* note 6, at 160–61, 197; J. STARKE, *supra* note 4, at 345.

whose migration is protected by treaty.[157] Although eligible persons within these categories are primarily transient, municipal laws disclose a state practice, often extending beyond treaty obligations, of admitting three important categories of aliens as immigrants for indefinite stays: refugees, dependents of resident aliens or citizens, and applicants from nearby or otherwise closely affiliated countries. Conversely, municipal laws often qualify statutory obligations to admit aliens, for reasons of national or public security, health, indigence, criminality, or labor displacement.[158] Ethnic and racial discrimination against alien applicants, though dubious under contemporary international law, nevertheless continues to exist.[159] Even so, the most important, if obvious, point remains: municipal laws, as evidence of state practice, generally reveal a willingness to admit well-defined classes of aliens for more or less permanent residence. Because interpretations of United States and British practices have strongly influenced other states, a summary of trends in the laws of those two countries is instructive.

Of four categories of immigration policy—unrestricted immigration, qualitative restrictions, quantitative restrictions, and prohibitions of all immigration—the trend in U.S. history has been from the first to a combination of the second and third categories.[160]

[157] R. PLENDER, *supra* note 16, at 71–88, 94–126; G. GOODWIN-GILL, *supra* note 6, at 136–37. On laws affirming a state's duty to readmit its own nationals, see Hucker, *supra* note 5, at 329; P. WEIS, *supra* note 12, at 50.

[158] For a list of national immigration laws, see R. PLENDER, *supra* note 16, at 298–323. For an extensive sampling of these laws, see INDIVIDUAL RIGHTS AND THE STATE IN FOREIGN AFFAIRS (E. Lauterpacht & J. Collier eds. 1977), as follows: Austria, at 38–39; Belgium, at 61–63; Cameroon, at 83; Canada, at 105–06; Chile, at 147–49; COMECON, at 438–42; Denmark, at 199–200; Egypt, at 223–26; the Federal Republic of Germany, at 253; France, at 282–84; Israel, at 321–29; Italy, at 375; Mexico, at 399–400; Poland, at 438–39; Sri Lanka, at 471–72; Switzerland, at 510–11; Thailand, at 568–71; Uganda, at 590–91; the United Kingdom, at 616–17; the United States, at 657–60. *Accord*, with regard to the "new nations of Asia and Africa in the 1960's," S. SINHA, *supra* note 12, at 97–98. Generally, African states have relatively generous immigration laws, especially toward refugees. Anderson, *America in Africa, 1981*, 60 FOREIGN AFF. 658, 679 (1982). Occasional mass expulsions are an exception.

[159] For example, the influential immigration laws of the United States, Canada, and the United Kingdom all included discriminatory provisions in the past. Whereas those of the United Kingdom protect the concept of patriality to distinguish some British citizens from others, those of the United States and Canada seek to replicate existing demographic patterns, to ensure assimilability of aliens, and to encourage the highly skilled to enter, typically from the more highly developed industrial countries. G. GOODWIN-GILL, *supra* note 6, at 92–93.

[160]

> [T]he United States, since 1921, has followed the second and third courses by imposing both qualitative and quantitative restrictions on aliens seeking to enter the United States as immigrants. This period was preceded by some forty-five years of qualitative restrictions and this period, in turn, by more than one hundred years of immigration unrestricted by federal legislation.

F. AUERBACH, IMMIGRATION LAWS OF THE UNITED STATES 4 (E. Harper ed. 1975). *See generally id.* at 4–48; E. ABBOTT, HISTORICAL ASPECTS OF THE IMMIGRATION PROBLEM (1926); E. ABBOTT, IMMIGRATION—SELECT DOCUMENTS AND CASE RECORDS (1924); R. DIVINE, AMERICAN IMMIGRATION POLICY, 1924–1952 (1957); R. GARIS, IMMIGRATION RESTRICTION (1927); E. HUTCHINSON, LEGISLATIVE HISTORY OF AMERICAN IMMIGRATION POLICY 1798–1965 (1981); D. TAFT & R. ROBBINS, INTERNATIONAL MIGRATIONS (1955); Higham, *American Immigration Policy in Historical Perspective*, 21 L. & CONTEMP. PROBS. 213 (1956).

Colonial hospitality to immigration[161] contributed to "a cosmopolitan community from the very beginning."[162] After the Revolution, leading founders of the Republic, with the salient exception of Thomas Jefferson, appear to have favored fairly open immigration.[163] The views of James Madison are representative.[164] A laissez faire policy of unrestricted admissions prevailed for nearly a hundred years, with the exception of the notorious Alien and Sedition Acts of 1798.[165] The concept of Manifest Destiny and the sheer fact of a vast territory available for settlement and development favored immigration throughout the 19th century. State and federal governments encouraged immigration and the Supreme Court forbade the states from levying landing taxes, on the grounds that they interfered with congressional prerogatives under the Commerce Clause of the Constitution.[166] The opinion in *Lynch v. Clarke,* which was discussed earlier in this study,[167] is characteristic of the period. The first qualitative restrictions to exclude several narrowly defined classes of aliens led to the comprehensive quantitative restrictions of quota systems enacted in 1921 and 1924.[168] These laws followed the trend in the West, after the outbreak of World War I, of erecting limited national barriers.

161

> I have referred somewhat at large to the usages and legislation of the colonies, to show that so far from limiting, or abridging in any mode, the common law rule of claiming allegiance and conferring rights as subjects; the whole scope and tendency of their legislation and their acts, were to obtain for their infant communities, all the population, and all the citizens that could be brought within their territory. They invited in all nations to multiply the people, which laboriously employed are the true riches of any country.

Lynch v. Clarke, 1 Sand. Ch. 583, 650 (N.Y. 1844).

162 E. PROPER, COLONIAL IMMIGRATION LAWS 88 (1900).

163 *Id.* at 90–91.

164

> [Mr. Madison] wished to maintain the character of liberality which had been professed in all the Constitutions & publications of America. He wished to invite foreigners of merit & republican principles among us. America was indebted to emigration for her settlement & Prosperity. That part of America which had encouraged them most had advanced most rapidly in population, agriculture & the arts. There was a possible danger he admitted that men with foreign predilections might obtain appointments but it was by no means probable that it would happen in any dangerous degree.

J. MADISON, JOURNAL OF THE FEDERAL CONVENTION 507 (E. Scott ed. 1840).

165 1 Stat. 570 *et. seq.* (1798). The Alien Act authorized the President to deport any alien whom he deemed to be dangerous to the nation. After its expiration in 1800, there was no restrictive federal legislation until 1875. On immigration history in the period immediately after the Alien Act of 1798, see *Immigration Following the Peace of 1815,* 10 NILES' WEEKLY REG., June 27, 1816, at 412, *reprinted in* E. ABBOTT, HISTORICAL ASPECTS, *supra* note 160.

166 *See* Note, *supra* note 101, at 1076.

167 1 Sand. Ch. 583. *See* text at note 58.

168

> The first act of Congress restricting immigration, passed in 1875, excluded prostitutes and convicts. Later statutes excluded idiots, lunatics, and those likely to become public charges. In 1882, Congress passed the first act excluding Chinese immigration, and since that time has been active in legislating restrictions on immigration. It has barred immigration on grounds of political opinions; and, under the quota system, first adopted in 1921, fostered an explicitly racial and eugenic scheme of immigration aimed at encouraging immigration from northern and western Europe rather than southern and eastern Europe and Asia, while at the same time placing a fixed limit on yearly immigration. Racial quotas were not dropped until 1965 by an act which replaced exclusion on racial grounds with a preference system.

Since the enactment of the comprehensive Immigration and Nationality Act of 1952, as amended,[169] the trend in the statutory law has been toward abandoning racial restrictions and relying upon nondiscriminatory quotas and qualitative criteria that favor economic potential and family reunification. Current practice discourages the admission of unskilled and semiskilled laborers by applying regulatory presumptions against them.[170] Otherwise, current laws, though perhaps bearing a "striking resemblance to King Minos's labyrinth in ancient Crete,"[171] are rather generous in their deference to the imperatives of human migration.

Arguably, judicial opinions, which were discussed earlier in depth, provide some basis, though shaky, for identifying United States practice with the proposition that the sovereign may exclude all aliens. Nevertheless, very few opinions have unambiguously accorded plenary discretion to the sovereign as a matter of international law. Of the opinions, the earliest and most often cited either explicitly qualified sovereign discretion or cited authority to that effect. Although the racist underpinnings of the formative opinions are repugnant today, the courts were careful to uphold exclusionary measures on the basis that the aliens seemed to pose a manifest danger to the peace and security of the country.

The most important British legislation, beginning with the anti-Jacobin measures of 1793, includes several 20th-century statutes.[172] The British immigration system is premised on selective controls over certain classes of aliens, some deference to aliens from within the British Commonwealth, and broad executive discretion. As an important example, British subjects from countries other than the United Kingdom enjoy a limited right, not shared by other aliens, to be heard upon the state's refusal of entry. Elsewhere, among the older members of the British Commonwealth such as Canada,[173] Australia,[174] and New Zealand,[175] policies and laws in the past have generally tended to encourage immigration from the traditional source countries, other European

---

Note, *supra* note 101, at 1076; *see also* Adams, *A Dubious Host,* WILSON Q., New Year's 1983, at 100.

[169] 8 U.S.C. §§1101–1503 (1976).

[170] 8 U.S.C. §1182(a)(14) (1976) provides that an employer must hire U.S. nationals unless none are "able, willing, qualified . . . and available." On the difficulties and inequities of overcoming this presumption, see Singhal, *Labor Certification Under Revised Regulations,* 51 S. CAL. L. REV. 823 (1978); Note, *Alien Labor Certification,* 60 MINN. L. REV. 1034 (1976).

[171] J. WASSERMAN, IMMIGRATION LAW AND PRACTICE (3d ed. 1979); *accord,* Gim, *Immigration Law Deficiencies and the Need for Reform,* in ASIAN IMMIGRANTS AND THEIR STATUS IN THE UNITED STATES 1 (H. Chiu ed. 1979): "Our immigration laws are unfair, anachronistic, even primitive in their severity."

[172] For a summary, see INDIVIDUAL RIGHTS, *supra* note 158, at 616.

[173] "Lacking a larger design, Canadian immigration history can be read as a series of pragmatic reactions to relatively short-term interests and pressures, influenced by the emergence of the concept of Canada's 'absorptive capacity' for immigrants at any given time." J.-G. CASTEL, *supra* note 61, at 472; *see also* collection of Canadian judicial opinions, in CANADA AND THE LAW OF NATIONS 269–83 (M. MacKenzie & L. Laing, eds. 1938); Hucker, *Immigration, Natural Justice and the Bill of Rights,* 13 OSGOODE HALL L.J. 649, 650–55 (1975).

[174] *See* Johnson, *supra* note 12, at 26 *et seq.;* and note 155 *supra.*

[175] *See* Williams, *supra* note 61, at 188 *et seq.*

countries, and to a lesser extent, from other countries of the British Commonwealth. Although the United Kingdom is less hospitable to alien entries from other Commonwealth countries than it once was, some members of the Commonwealth have kept a fairly open door to each other. For example, the Caribbean Community explicitly encourages mutual cooperation concerning free mobility of persons, as evidenced by the Petit St. Vincent Initiative Agreement.[176]

Special Custom: Three Examples of Regional Practice. What, more generally, is the regional practice? Regional arrangements, which offer a relatively effective means for accommodating the flow of human migration,[177] help confirm the state practice of admitting well-defined classes of aliens.

Among a majority of countries within the Western Hemisphere, exclusionary measures are contemplated by Article 1 of the Convention between the American Republics regarding the Status of Aliens in their Respective Territories: "States have the right to establish by means of laws the conditions under which foreigners may enter and reside in their territory."[178] Whatever gloss may have been placed on this provision, it is doubtful that the word "conditions" should be stretched to justify an absolute exclusion of aliens. Under a good faith interpretation, the plain meaning of the term "conditions" would seem to refer rather narrowly to the technical process of admitting aliens. Such an interpretation would give greatest effect to the cooperative objectives of the Convention. The Calvo Doctrine, favored by most of the signatories of the Convention, would not lead to a different interpretation, for its insistence upon national treatment of aliens would not purport to address the issue of which aliens are eligible for entry in the first place. Thus, Article 1 of the Convention would simply confirm the right of states parties to adopt their own technical procedures for processing aliens into their territories.

Under the Treaty of Rome, members of the European Communities must abolish "any discrimination based on nationality between workers of the Member States as regards employment, remuneration and other conditions of work and employment."[179] In Article 48(3), workers are ensured free movement within the Common Market nations and enjoy the rights:

[176] Turack, *Freedom of Movement in the Caribbean Community,* 11 DEN. J. INT'L L. & POL. 37, 49 (1982).

[177] *E.g.:*

> There appears little likelihood of the emergence of a system of world order which would curtail in any fundamental way the exclusive competence of states to decide who will be admitted or allowed to remain in their territory. On the basis of past trends, any surrender of authority is likely to be gradual and primarily confined to regional groupings, of which the E.E.C. is the obvious example, in which the members share compatible political systems, a reasonable equivalence in economic development, and a largely homogeneous ethnic and racial composition.

Hucker, *supra* note 5, at 340.

[178] 46 Stat. 2753, TS No. 815, 132 LNTS 301, *signed* Feb. 20, 1928.

[179] Treaty Establishing the European Economic Community, Art. 48(2), *done* Mar. 25, 1957, 298 UNTS 3. Article 3(c) provides that the Community shall include within its activities "the abolition, as between Member States, of obstacles to freedom of movement for persons."

(a) to accept offers of employment actually made;
(b) to move about freely for this purpose within the territory of Member States;
(c) to stay in any Member State in order to carry on an employment in conformity with the legislative and administrative provisions governing the employment of the workers of that State; and
(d) to live . . . in the territory of a Member State after having been employed there.

Article 49 of the Rome Treaty prescribes procedures for implementing the free movement of workers, Article 50 requires that "Member States shall, within the framework of a joint programme, encourage the exchange of young workers," and Article 51 provides for the adoption of "such measures in the field of social security as are necessary to provide freedom of movement for workers. . . ."

The European Court of Justice has supported intraregional migration and significantly limited sovereign discretion over the admission of aliens by ruling that restrictions of free movement for reasons of *ordre public,* security, or public health are exceptional and hence subject to strict interpretation.[180] Within a larger community of states, the European Commission of Human Rights has assured procedural due process to applicants who are denied admission into member countries.[181] These developments, though treaty-based, disclose significant special custom.

The third and last example, the Final Act of the Conference on Security and Cooperation in Europe ("Helsinki Accords"),[182] establishes an important qualified right of migration. Generally, the Accords confirm an obligation to admit aliens for purposes of family unification, especially to accommodate workers, and marriage.[183] The Accords also confirm that municipal legal restrictions on the obligation to help reunite families and prospective marriage

[180] Turack, *Freedom of Transnational Movement: The Helsinki Accord and Beyond,* 11 VAND. J. TRANSNAT'L L. 585, 603–04 (1978).

[181] *Re* Application No. 434/58 (X v. Gov't of Swed.), 28 ILR 242 (Eur. Comm'n on Human Rights 1959). The Commission's dictum on the obligations of members is illuminating:

> Under general international law a State has the right, in virtue of its sovereignty, to control the entry and exit of foreigners into and out of its territory. It is true that a right or freedom to enter the territory of States, Members of the Council of Europe, is not, as such, included among the rights and freedoms guaranteed in Section I of the Convention. However, a State which signs and ratifies the European Convention on Human Rights and Fundamental Freedoms must be understood as agreeing to restrict the free exercise of . . . its right to control the entry and exit of foreigners, to the extent and within the limits of the obligations which it has accepted under that Convention.

Id. at 250–51.

[182] Conference on Security and Cooperation in Europe: Final Act, *reprinted in* 14 ILM 1292 (1975) [hereinafter cited as Accords]. For bibliographies of literature pertaining to the Accords, see U.S. DEP'T OF STATE NEWSLETTER, Oct. 1980, at 60; Granier, *Human Rights and the Helsinki Conference on Security and Cooperation in Europe: An Annotated Bibliography of United States Government Documents,* 13 VAND. J. TRANSNAT'L L. 529 (1980). Although arguably not legally binding in themselves, the Accords provide a comprehensive, morally compelling expression of norms that, by influencing state behavior, may constitute *lex ferenda.*

[183] *See* Nafziger, *The Right of Migration under the Helsinki Accords,* 1980 S. ILL. L.J. 395.

partners are subject to scrutiny under the human rights provisions of the United Nations Charter.[184]

Special Classes of Aliens: Refugees and Stateless Persons. Stateless persons and refugees are entitled to the same minimum rights and protections as other aliens. Treaty law, when applicable, provides additional protection.[185] The law of refugees, for example, relies on such distinctive concepts as asylum and *non-refoulement.* There is, however, no international legislation requiring states to grant asylum, parole, or other means of documented entry to refugees.[186] The United Nations Declaration on Territorial Asylum, adopted by the General Assembly in 1967, says only that asylum is "a peaceful and humanitarian act and that, as such, it cannot be regarded as unfriendly by any other State."[187] Similarly, the principle of *non-refoulement,* though widely followed, may not yet be binding as custom on all states although regional custom has adopted the principle. Aside from custom, the principle of *non-refoulement* is expressed in the Declaration on Territorial Asylum; in the 1951 Convention Relating to the Status of Refugees;[188] by incorporation, in the 1967 Protocol to the latter agreement;[189] and in other agreements, such as the American Convention on Human Rights.[190]

A majority of the UN membership is party to the 1951 Convention and 1967 Protocol, which establish minimum standards for the treatment of refugees once they are declared to be entitled to that status by recipient states.[191] Since these agreements are usually not regarded as self-implementing, the regime established under them relies heavily on municipal legislation.[192] For

[184] Accords, *supra* note 182, at 1314.

[185] Stateless persons are protected primarily by two international agreements. *See* Convention relating to the Status of Stateless Persons, Final Act of the United Nations Conference on the Status of Stateless Persons, *done* Sept. 28, 1954, 360 UNTS 117; Convention on the Reduction of Statelessness, *done* Aug. 30, 1961, UN Doc. A/CONF.9/15 (1961). A summary of the law of refugees follows in the text.

[186] Report of the United Nations High Commissioner for Refugees, 34 UN GAOR Supp. (No. 12) at 4, UN Doc. A/34/12 (1979). On the international law of refugees, see A. GRAHL-MADSEN, TERRITORIAL ASYLUM (1980); A. GRAHL-MADSEN, THE STATUS OF REFUGEES IN INTERNATIONAL LAW (2 vols. 1966, 1972). Article 14 of the Universal Declaration of Human Rights provides, as follows, for an individual right to seek asylum, but does not provide specifically for a duty upon a state to grant it: "(1) Everyone has the right to seek and to enjoy in other countries asylum from persecution. (2) This right may not be invoked in the case of prosecutions genuinely arising from non-political crimes or from acts contrary to the purposes and principles of the United Nations."

[187] Preamble, UNGA Res. 2312 (XXII), 22 UN GAOR Supp. (No. 16) at 81, UN Doc. A/6716 (1967), *reprinted in* 62 AJIL 822 (1968).

[188] Art. 33, Convention relating to the Status of Refugees, *done* July 28, 1951, 189 UNTS 137 (does not require states to grant entry, but guarantees numerous basic rights to lawfully admitted political refugees displaced before 1951). *See also* OAU Convention Governing the Specific Aspects of Refugee Problems in Africa, *done* Sept. 10, 1969, *reprinted in* 8 ILM 1288 (1969).

[189] Protocol relating to the Status of Refugees, *done* Jan. 31, 1967, 19 UST 6223, TIAS No. 6577, 606 UNTS 267 (supplements 1951 Convention for persons displaced after 1951).

[190] Art. 22, para. 8, American Convention on Human Rights, *entered into force* July 18, 1978, ORGANIZATION OF AMERICAN STATES, HANDBOOK OF EXISTING RULES PERTAINING TO HUMAN RIGHTS 27, OEA/Ser.L/V/11.50, doc. 6 (1980).

[191] Report of the UN High Commissioner, *supra* note 186, at 13.

[192] *Ibid.*

present purposes, the most significant point is that the global practice of admitting special classes of aliens under treaty and municipal law sheds further doubt, though inconclusive, on the validity of the exclusionary proposition.

Opinio Juris

As we have seen, special customary law imposes duties on states to admit aliens in certain regions and classes. In the aggregate, special custom also suggests the likelihood of a more general custom of admitting some aliens under some circumstances. To establish a general custom, however, it must be shown that states generally admit those aliens from a sense of obligation or at least in order to be consistent with existing rules (*opinio juris*). One could argue that any of several factors satisfies this "psychological" element of custom: for example, the acquiescence of states in the admission of their nationals by other states; the reiteration in treaties of the pervasive practice of admitting aliens; or a more vaguely defined consensus of expectations supporting the practice of generally admitting aliens. Even more persuasively, there is evidence to confirm *opinio juris* on the basis of existing or contemporaneous articulations of a qualified duty to admit aliens.

Although municipal immigration statutes themselves do not articulate *opinio juris*, one can turn to judicial interpretations of them. Judicial authority, however, is split. While some courts, in both civil and common law countries, have endorsed an "absolute right to exclude,"[193] others have endorsed a "qualified duty to admit" rule.[194] Recently, the New Zealand Supreme Court called the absolutist proposition "xenophobic" in view of both the contrary custom of alien admissions under the New Zealand Immigrant Act and the observation that "the Royal prerogative to keep foreigners at bay has been superseded by the modern transportation and the mass population movements of the 20th century."[195] The global trend, however, is uncertain.

Although this brief survey of case law is inconclusive, there is important evidence of *opinio juris* in and surrounding the formative case law of the United States. It will be recalled that dicta in those opinions, which cited international authority, justified immigration restrictions on the basis not simply of a sov-

[193] *E.g.*, Vaaro v. R., [1933] 1 D.L.R. 359, 362 (Canada); Salebhoy v. The Controller of Immigration, 36 ILR 348 (Burma Chief Ct. 1963); Expulsion of Foreign National Case, 32 ILR 255 (Admin. Ct. App. North Rhine-Westphalia 1961); Residence of Alien Trader Case, 21 ILR 209 (Admin. Ct. App. Münster 1954) (the court indicated, however, that "a State is not allowed to shut itself off from general international intercourse," *id.* at 210); Lin Jung-A'ai v. Japan, 26 ILR 479 (Japan S. Ct. 1957); and McLean v. Setoyama, *reported in* 23 JAPAN. ANN. INT'L L. 176, 180 (1980) (Japan S. Ct. 1978).

[194] *E.g.*, Marcon, 1952 Recueil des arrêts du Conseil d'état 525 (France) (administrative discretion in the admission of aliens must be based on the interests of public security); Chandra v. Minister of Immigration, [1978] 2 N.Z.L.R. 559, 568. The Latin American practice seems generally to have required such grounds for exclusion as a threat to the political stability, defense, public order, or social tranquility of the state, although discretion to make those determinations is vested in the state. Irizarry y Puente, *supra* note 15, at 254–56.

[195] [1978] 2 N.Z.L.R. at 568.

ereign's inherent powers, but of a danger at that time to the peace and security of the country. Even more tellingly, the Government officially concurred that restrictive measures were acceptable because they responded to the perception of a serious threat to the state. Contemporary statements of Secretary of State Foster and Presidents Harrison, Cleveland, and Roosevelt reveal that the Government thought that it had to show that the new immigration restrictions could be reconciled with the principle of open admission and to clarify how the restriction of certain classes bore a relation to the self-preservation of the state or the protection of its people from clearly defined threats.[196] Although, arguably, these statements may not disclose the necessary psychological element in current state practice, they do indicate it in the earlier state practice upon which the proposition, in its modern form, was based.

Scholarly commentary and draft regulations, as discussed above, have further articulated a qualified duty to admit aliens, and states have had reason to know of these articulations.[197] Therefore, the practice of states has conformed with either a qualified duty to admit some aliens under some circumstances or a highly qualified version of the exclusionary proposition, that aliens may be excluded only if they objectively pose a serious danger, individually or collectively, to the state, its people, or essential institutions.

VI. General Principles and Salient Values

Universal prescriptions protect the right of migrants to return to their own countries,[198] but not explicitly the right to enter another country. Universal principles, however, disclose some basis for inferring a qualified duty to admit aliens. Under the UN Charter, members have pledged themselves to take "joint and separate action in co-operation with" the United Nations to help achieve fundamental human rights and socioeconomic development.[199] The

[196] J. Moore, *supra* note 12, at 153–60. Nishimura Ekiu v. United States, 142 U.S. at 659, quoted in text at note 115 *supra*, stands out as an exception among pronouncements cited in Moore's *Digest*.

[197] On the "reason to know," see A. D'Amato, *supra* note 135, at 86–87. Elsewhere, Professor D'Amato specifically questions whether the long-standing receptivity of states to tourists has been "articulated to be a matter of international *law*," but he does not discuss whether state practice of admitting aliens on a more permanent basis, the subject of this study, satisfies the requirements of *opinio juris*. *Id.* at 77–78.

[198] Article 13 of the Universal Declaration of Human Rights, UNGA Res. 217 (III) (A), UN Doc. A/810, at 71 (1948), provides as follows: "1. Everyone has the right to freedom of movement and residence within the borders of each State. 2. Everyone has the right to leave any country, including his own, and to return to his country." Articles 15, 23, and 25 of the Declaration establish basic rights to change one's nationality, to work freely under favorable conditions, and to secure an adequate standard of living. Application of these provisions does not specifically require more liberal national immigration laws. The provisions serve, nevertheless, as a reminder that the global community is increasingly animated by a unifying concept of universal equal opportunity and by a growing awareness of the social waste and economic disequilibrium inherent in nation-state centrism. *See also* Higgins, *The Right in International Law of an Individual to Enter, Stay in and Leave a Country*, 49 Int'l Aff. 341, 344–50 (1973).

[199] UN Charter arts. 55 and 56; *see also* text at notes 87–88 *supra*.

contours of that requirement, while unclear, support at least two inferences. First, the prescription in the Universal Declaration of Human Rights of "the right to leave" would seem to require states, taken together, to respect the right by not totally barring entry. Second, as a matter of helping achieve socioeconomic development, it is arguable that states should consider the role of migration in helping redistribute global resources by facilitating the access of people to those resources.

Several opinions of the World Court are relevant in this connection. As noted earlier, dicta in the *Tunis-Morocco Nationality Decrees* case would require states, in defining nationality, to take account of changing international relations.[200] Later, in its Advisory Opinion on the *Treatment of Polish Nationals and Other Persons of Polish Origin or Speech in the Danzig Territory*,[201] the Permanent Court of International Justice confirmed treaty rights of Polish nationals to free and secure access to Danzig. The Court refused in that case to express any opinion on the question whether a state can exclude all foreigners from its territory.[202] It is unclear whether the Court's refusal meant that it did not accept the absolutist position or that it did not need to reach that issue. Only later, in a controversial dissent to the main opinion in the *Nottebohm Case*, did a judge, without citing authority, refer to the "unfettered right" of states to refuse admission to aliens.[203] Today the issue might fall within the framework of the dictum in the *Barcelona Traction* case, in which the Court articulated obligations of states *erga omnes*, including those derived "from the principles and rules concerning the basic rights of the human person."[204]

Within other international frameworks, states have committed themselves to cooperate in the admission of aliens under normal circumstances. For example, the World Population Plan of Action[205] developed new norms to facilitate human migration. This document, the culmination of the 1974 World Population Conference in Bucharest, recommends, *inter alia*, that governments facilitate migration and thereby help reunite families. The document further urges countries affected by significant numbers of migrant workers to conduct bilateral or multilateral consultations with a view to harmonizing policies that influence these movements, and to conclude pertinent bilateral or multilateral agreements. The more developed countries are encouraged to cooperate bilaterally or regionally in creating favorable employment opportunities at the national level in countries concerned with the outflow of

[200] 1923 PCIJ, ser. B, No. 4, at 24.

[201] 1932 PCIJ, ser. A/B, No. 44, at 4 (Advisory Opinion of Feb. 4).

[202] *Id.* at 41.

[203] 1955 ICJ REP. at 46.

[204] Case Concerning the Barcelona Traction, Light & Power Co., Ltd. (New Application) (Belg. v. Spain), 1970 ICJ REP. 4, 32 (Judgment of Feb. 5).

[205] UN Doc. E/CONF.60/WG/L.55/Add.3 (1974), *reprinted in* 71 DEP'T STATE BULL. 440 (1974). Although the World Population Plan of Action is not legally binding in the classical sense of an international agreement, it has much the same juridical weight as, for example, the Helsinki Accords. The plan was adopted without a vote by the conference, and on Dec. 17, 1974, the General Assembly adopted Res. 3344 (XXIX), by a vote of 131–0–1, on the World Population Plan of Action.

migrant workers. By endorsing the plan, each conference participant has assumed an international obligation to assist in the rational processes of human migration.

The Brandt Commission on North-South Issues focused attention on human migration as a component of global development and on the critical need for developed countries to liberalize their immigration laws and policies to facilitate migration.[206] Scholarly commentary concurs. For example, a leading scholar recently observed that, short of massive programs for resettling unemployed workers and refugees, "it remains the duty of each country to open its own borders as widely as possible, without looking for excuses or waiting for others to act."[207] Specifically, "there is a moral duty of host states not simply to get rid of the foreign work force when a recession hits, nor to apply retroactive measures in order to thin its ranks."[208] The parochial fear of job displacement by aliens, dating back at least to the Middle Ages,[209] ought not to govern the formulation of rational migration policy.

The realities of global development have encouraged consideration of the fledgling ideal that "any person should be able to enter any country he might choose."[210] To some commentators, the right of emigration under international law implies a duty to allow entry into another country.[211] One can also discern new recognition by some states of a right to family unity.[212] Short of truly free movement, global order may be well served by further elaboration of the rights to leave, stay, and return, toward freer movement of migrants into those communities with which they have "actual and significant ties."[213]

Aside from these newly articulated ideas, the sources of a qualified duty of states to admit aliens include several established principles that underlie much of the positive law of human rights. These principles are freedom of movement,

[206] INDEPENDENT COMMISSION ON INTERNATIONAL DEVELOPMENT ISSUES, NORTH-SOUTH, A PROGRAMME FOR SURVIVAL 108–13 (W. Brandt ed. 1980).

[207] S. HOFFMANN, DUTIES BEYOND BORDERS 224–25 (1981).

[208] *Id.* at 225.

[209] M. CRANSTON, *supra* note 26, at 36.

[210] Aybay, *supra* note 12, at 125.

[211] Note, *e.g.*, the following:

> Moreover the right to leave a country cannot be fully exercised unless there is a right of entry into another country. If there is an obligation upon a state to let everyone leave it, there must be a corresponding obligation on other states to let people enter it without discrimination. Barriers imposed by states on entry, such as quota systems or racial and religious requirements, must be lifted.

Hussein A. Hassouna, Remarks, 67 ASIL PROC. 135, 136 (1973). *Accord,* M. SIBERT, *supra* note 7, at 575; David Yeres, U.S. Dep't of Justice, Remarks, ASIL Annual Meeting (Apr. 26, 1979); J. GREGORY, HUMAN MIGRATION AND THE FUTURE 50 (1928). *But see* M. WALZER, *supra* note 92, at 40, 42 *et seq.* Professor Walzer finds immigration and emigration to be "morally asymmetrical."

[212] G. GOODWIN-GILL, *supra* note 6, at 197; Helsinki Accords, *supra* note 182, at 1314.

[213] 67 ASIL PROC., *supra* note 211, *passim. See also* Higgins, *supra* note 198; J. Inglés, Study of Discrimination in respect of the Right of Everyone to Leave Any Country, Including His Own, and to Return to His Own Country, UN Doc. E/CN.4/Sub.2/220/Rev.1 (1963); Lung-chu Chen, *supra* note 8, at 127.

perhaps "the first and most fundamental of man's liberties";[214] good faith; mutual aid; humanity and hospitality; comity; and mutual intercourse.[215] Also, a duty of states to admit at least some aliens manifests several specific values of global order:[216] the encouragement of peace by easing demographic pressures,[217] the enrichment of national cultures,[218] the redistribution of economic resources,[219] and the pursuit of such humanitarian objectives as satisfaction of

[214] M. CRANSTON, *supra* note 26, at 31.

[215] *See* Virally, *Review Essay: Good Faith in Public International Law,* 77 AJIL 130 (1983) (on the principle of good faith); M. WALZER, *supra* note 92, at 33 (on the principle of mutual aid); T. WOOLSEY, *supra* note 59, at 23–24 (on the other principles). A distinguished U.S. scholar, Livermore, long ago observed in a different but not inapposite context, as follows:

> The people of an independent nation may, if they please, surround their territory with an impassable wall, and totally exclude all intercourse with other nations. But if a desire to promote their own interest induces them to cultivate an intercourse with other people, they must necessarily adopt such principles, as a sense of common utility and of justice will inspire. . . .

S. LIVERMORE, DISSERTATIONS ON THE QUESTIONS WHICH ARISE FROM THE CONTRARIETY OF THE POSITIVE LAWS OF DIFFERENT STATES AND NATIONS 27–28 (1828).

[216] Freedom of migration, generally speaking, "continues to be important for promoting mutual understanding and cooperation among peoples. To that extent, this right serves as an instrument of peace and reduces world tension." Jagerskiold, *supra* note 139, at 166 (*but see* n.139). Social scientific research has given greater resonance to the value of freer migration by contradicting popular fears of a country's low absorptive capacity, of the moral danger posed by an influx of immigrants, of a serious displacement of indigenous labor, and so on. *See, e.g.,* Reubens, *Immigration Problems, Limited-Visa Programs, and Other Options,* in THE BORDER THAT JOINS, *supra* note 11, at 187, 194–203; Segal, *The Half-Open Door,* WILSON Q., New Year's 1983, at 116, 127; Bustamante, *Undocumented Migration from Mexico: Research Report,* 11 INT'L MIGRATION REV. 149 (1977); W. CORNELIUS, BUILDING THE CACTUS CURTAIN: MEXICAN IMMIGRATION AND U.S. RESPONSES, FROM WILSON TO CARTER (1981); W. CORNELIUS, MEXICAN MIGRATION TO THE UNITED STATES: CAUSES, CONSEQUENCES, AND U.S. RESPONSES (Center for International Studies, Massachusetts Institute of Technology, Monograph Series of the Migration and Development Study Group, 1978); W. CORNELIUS, ILLEGAL MIGRATION TO THE U.S.: RECENT RESEARCH FINDINGS, POLICY IMPLICATIONS AND RESEARCH PRIORITIES (1977); C. Davidson, Characteristics of Deportable Aliens Located in the Center of the United States (unpub. paper presented at the Annual Meeting of the Population Association of America, Washington, D.C., March 1981); D. NORTH & M. HOUSTOUN, THE CHARACTERISTICS AND ROLE OF ILLEGAL ALIENS IN THE U.S. LABOR MARKET: AN EXPLORATORY STUDY (1976). On a few of the salient migration issues in need of social scientific research, see W. GOULD & M. BARKUN, INTERNATIONAL LAW AND THE SOCIAL SCIENCES 279–80 (1970).

[217] C. DE VISSCHER, *supra* note 12, at 231; Bellot, Remarks, in *Problems of Peace and War,* 12 GROTIUS SOC'Y TRANSACTIONS 5 (1927).

[218] Nafziger, *A Policy Framework for Regulating the Flow of Undocumented Aliens into the United States,* 56 OR. L. REV. 63, 79 (1977).

[219]

> [R]esponsible nations might deliberately strive for a relatively quick assimilation of the underprivileged as against the high cost of maintaining present restrictions. What seems radical in terms of past policies may come to seem more like common sense in a world situation fewer alternatives. A policy of gradualism extending intermigration privileges between select nations would be one type of beginning. If some nations were to begin opening their boundaries, it would probably put others at a political disadvantage so that they could not stand

family reunification and the basic human needs of migrants.[220] Access to a better life in foreign territory may be fundamental to the achievement of human dignity by enabling individuals in some instances to have the essential alternative of participating in the social processes of another state.[221]

VII. CONCLUSION

The proposition that states have an absolute right to deny territorial access to all aliens has unusual resilience and resonance, but little historical or jurisprudential foundation. From Vattel forward, even those publicists who have acknowledged a sovereign power or capacity to exclude all aliens have also insisted upon the rightful exercise of that power,[222] "tempered by the facts of modern civilization."[223] For example, racial, geographical, and other forms of discrimination have long been regarded even by exclusionists as "tokens of arrogance"[224] that defy both explanation and community expectations. Because the roots of the exclusionary proposition lie in questionable interpretations of scholarly writings and political theory and in judicial opinions that condoned racial discrimination, the proposition itself is questionable. Moreover, an analysis of decisions reveals important, though largely forgotten, limitations on the authority of a state to exclude aliens.

Because state practice refutes the proposition that states have an unfettered right to exclude all aliens, some might question the need to reexamine it. The answer is simple: abstract as it is, the proposition appears to be instrumental in shaping exclusionary provisions of municipal law and policy and in forestalling the emergence of human migration as a comprehensive topic on the international legal agenda. Consequently, global discussions have only begun on one of the most serious issues of our era, the general admission of aliens.

It is essential that migration issues be unshackled from the dubious proposition that a state may exclude all aliens. Instead, there is a firm basis for articulating a qualified duty of states to admit aliens.[225] What needs to be done next is to make that duty more concrete and specific. States might therefore begin to negotiate and formulate agreements to govern the general admission of aliens. In particular, the world community might consider the preparation

---

still. A new geopolitics could begin on that basis, one with sufficient latitude for political realism.

Nett, *The Civil Right We Are Not Ready For: The Right of Free Movement of People on the Face of the Earth,* 84 ETHICS 212, 227 (1971).

[220] Nafziger, *supra* note 218, at 86–87.

[221] *See* M. MCDOUGAL & W. REISMAN, INTERNATIONAL LAW IN CONTEMPORARY PERSPECTIVE 925 (1981).

[222] *Supra* note 138. *See also* Boffolo Case (Italy v. Venez.), 10 R. Int'l Arb. Awards 528 (1903), which addressed an issue of expulsion by Venezuela of an Italian national.

[223] W. HALL, A TREATISE ON INTERNATIONAL LAW 211 (6th ed. 1909).

[224] C. HYDE, *supra* note 12, at 218.

[225] "Considering the universal restrictions placed on immigration in this century, and the almost total exclusion of aliens by some countries, it is surprising to discover that there is a widespread

of a comprehensive multilateral convention to govern the admission of aliens. Even the mere exercise of negotiating and drafting a convention on the general admission of aliens might be worthwhile.[226]

Where should the global community begin in attempting to articulate a more precise statement of the qualified duty to admit aliens? A careful reading of the very authority upon which the discredited proposition relies suggests one point of departure: that a state may legitimately exclude aliens only if, individually or collectively, they pose serious danger to its public safety, security, general welfare, or essential institutions.[227] That formulation is so broad as to permit expansive discretion by states. Therefore, to be workable, it must be refined. Although it is as yet difficult to formulate a more precise norm of general application and plausibility, this study has identified some common circumstances of controlled entry. More extensive study of the state practice may help define a workable, qualified duty of states to admit aliens.

Above all, the global community should seek, by the operation of law, to facilitate natural processes of human migration as a means of accommodating basic human needs and human dignity. To be sure, the initiation of global deliberations may not be easy. Periodic waves of xenophobia and the persistent narcissism of states may inhibit efforts. States may be timid about establishing acceptable international procedures and institutions to enforce compliance with an acceptable formulation of the qualified duty of admission. In the words of the International Law Commission, "it is one thing to define a rule and the content of the obligation it imposes and another to determine whether that obligation has been violated and what should be the consequences of the violation."[228] Also, states may be reluctant to discuss thorny substantive issues such as the traditional discrimination against specific classes of aliens, the relative absorptive capacities of states,[229] the status of economic migrants as refugees, international solidarity and burden sharing—in sum, all the issues arising out of the ageless quest of individuals for a better life elsewhere.

Once the general admission of aliens becomes a topic for comprehensive discussions on the international agenda, the global community should be prepared to address issues that are only now becoming apparent in the context of economic development.[230] For example, should states be expected to keep relatively open doors in times of inflation, limited resources, and recession? Does the brain drain, that is, the departure of skilled or enterprising migrants,

---

consensus of opinion, particularly on the Continent, favouring a general duty in international law to receive aliens." D. O'CONNELL, *supra* note 80, at 695.

[226] Thomas, *Undocumented Aliens: Some International Aspects,* 73 ASIL PROC. 131, 136 (1979).

[227] *See, e.g.,* notes 48, 49, 111, 120, and 140 *supra.*

[228] [1970] 2 Y.B. INT'L L. COMM'N 178, UN DOC. A/CN.4/SER.A/1970/Add.1.

[229] Ironically, developing countries least able to absorb immigrants often bear the greatest burdens of admitting aliens. Carlin, *Significant Refugee Crises Since World War II and the Response of the International Community,* 1982 MICH. Y.B. INT'L LEGAL STUD. 3, 12–21; Anderson, *supra* note 158, at 679.

[230] *See* Schechter, *The Views of "Charterists" and "Skeptics" on Human Rights in the World Legal Order,* 9 HOFSTRA L. REV. 357, 388–89 (1981).

improperly hurt source countries by denying them benefits justified by the cost of raising and educating those migrants? Or, does emigration help source countries, on balance, by reducing population and birth rates and by generating cash remittances in foreign exchange? Do developed countries owe developing countries some kind of duty both to accept migrants and to dispense financial aid? In determining state obligations, what weight should be given to the absorptive capacities of states, ethnic heterogeneity that is already divisive within a state, massive unemployment, or underemployment? The questions seem endless.

Troublesome issues abound, to be sure, but they would at least be manageable within a comprehensive international framework. As a first step, it is imperative, once and for all, to acknowledge the invalidity of the proposition that a state has a right to exclude all aliens. This article has argued, instead, that a state has a qualified duty to admit some aliens under more or less normal circumstances. Recognition that the general admission of aliens is subject to international legal constraints should encourage states, in their mutual interest, to begin to formulate specific obligations of general admission. At present, the clearest formulation, which would need to be refined, is that a state has a qualified duty to admit aliens when they pose no serious danger to its public safety, security, general welfare, or essential institutions.

EDITORIAL COMMENT

Human Dignity as a Normative Concept

The "dignity of the human person" and "human dignity" are phrases that have come to be used as an expression of a basic value accepted in a broad sense by all peoples.

Human dignity appears in the Preamble of the Charter of the United Nations as an ideal that "we the peoples of the United Nations" are "determined" to achieve. The words are part of the second paragraph of the Preamble, which reads in full as follows: "to reaffirm faith in fundamental human rights, in the dignity and worth of the human person, in the equal rights of men and women and of nations large and small."

The term dignity is also included in Article 1 of the Universal Declaration of Human Rights: "All human beings are born free and equal in dignity and rights. They are endowed with reason and conscience and should act towards one another in a spirit of brotherhood."

In some subsequent instruments, we find the expression "respect for the inherent dignity of the human person." For example, the International Covenant on Civil and Political Rights provides in Article 10 that "[a]ll persons deprived of their liberty shall be treated with humanity and with respect for the inherent dignity of the human person." A similar provision is found in the American Convention on Human Rights (Article 5).

The International Covenant on Economic, Social and Cultural Rights states in Article 13 that "education shall be directed to the full development of the human personality and the sense of its dignity."

The Helsinki Accords in Principle VII affirm that the participating states will promote the effective exercise of human rights and freedoms, "all of which derive from the inherent dignity of the human person."

References to human dignity are to be found in various resolutions and declarations of international bodies.[1] National constitutions and proclamations, especially those recently adopted, include the ideal or goal of human dignity in their references to human rights.[2] Political leaders, jurists and philosophers have increasingly alluded to the dignity of the human person as a

[1] *See, e.g.*, the ILO Declaration of Philadelphia (May 10, 1944) affirming the right of all persons to pursue their well-being and development "in conditions of freedom and dignity"; the UN Standard Minimum Rules for the Treatment of Prisoners (1955) (Rule 60); the UN Declaration on the Elimination of Discrimination against Women (1967); the UN Declaration on the Use of Scientific and Technological Progress in the Interests of Peace and for the Benefit of Mankind (1975). The latter declaration notes that scientific and technological achievements can be used to the detriment of human dignity.

[2] Article 1 of the German Federal Constitution states: "Human dignity is inviolable. It is the duty of all governmental power to respect and protect it." There is a considerable legal literature in German on this article. For a recent commentary by the President of the German Constitutional Court, see Benda, *Die Menschenwürde*, in HANDBUCH DES VERFASSUNGSRECHTS DER BUNDESREPUBLIK DEUTSCHLAND 107 (1983).

basic ideal so generally recognized as to require no independent support. It has acquired a resonance that leads it to be invoked widely as a legal and moral ground for protest against degrading and abusive treatment. No other ideal seems so clearly accepted as a universal social good.

II. The Meaning of the "Inherent Dignity of the Human Person"

We do not find an explicit definition of the expression "dignity of the human person" in international instruments or (as far as I know) in national law. Its intrinsic meaning has been left to intuitive understanding, conditioned in large measure by cultural factors. When it has been invoked in concrete situations, it has been generally assumed that a violation of human dignity can be recognized even if the abstract term cannot be defined.[3] "I know it when I see it even if I cannot tell you what it is."

In some situations an abstract definition is not needed; but it is not entirely satisfying to accept the idea that human dignity cannot be defined or analyzed in general terms. Without a reasonably clear general idea of its meaning, we cannot easily reject a specious use of the concept, nor can we without understanding its meaning draw specific implications for relevant conduct.

An analysis of dignity may begin with its etymological root, the Latin "dignitas" translated as worth (in French, "valeur"). One lexical meaning of dignity is "intrinsic worth." Thus, when the UN Charter refers to the "dignity and worth" of the human person, it uses two synonyms for the same concept. The other instruments speak of "inherent dignity," an expression that is close to "intrinsic worth."

What is meant by "respect" for "intrinsic worth" or "inherent dignity" of a person? "Respect" has several nuanced meanings: "esteem," "deference," "a proper regard for," "recognition of." These terms have both a subjective aspect (how one feels or thinks about another) and an objective aspect (how one treats another). Both are relevant to our question, but it seems more useful to focus on the latter aspect for purposes of practical measures.

One general answer to our question is suggested by the Kantian injunction to treat every human being as an end, not as a means. Respect for the intrinsic worth of every person should mean that individuals are not to be perceived or treated merely as instruments or objects of the will of others. This proposition will probably be generally acceptable as an ideal. There may be more question about its implications. I shall suggest such implications as corollaries of the general proposition.

The first is that a high priority should be accorded in political, social and legal arrangements to individual choices in such matters as beliefs, way of life, attitudes and the conduct of public affairs. Note that this is stated as a "high

[3] Several judicial decisions have applied the concept of dignity without attempting to define the concept in general terms. *See, e.g.*, the decision of the European Court of Human Rights in Lawless v. Ireland (Merits), 1 EHRR 15, 39 (Judgment of July 1, 1961) (individual op. Maridakis, J.). The courts of West Germany have also handed down several interesting decisions applying the constitutional provision on human dignity. *See* Benda, *supra* note 2.

priority," not an absolute rule. We may give it more specific content by applying it to political and psychological situations. In the political context, respect for the dignity and worth of all persons, and for their individual choices, leads, broadly speaking, to a strong emphasis on the will and consent of the governed. It means that the coercive rule of one or the few over the many is incompatible with a due respect for the dignity of the person. It also means that governments are not to use coercion to impose beliefs and attitudes on those subject to their rule or to extend their authority into areas of human life that are essentially personal and familial. The question of the proper boundaries between the public and the private, and between the sphere governed by the "general will" and that left to the individual remains to be answered in particular cases. But the idea that such boundaries need to be drawn and that an appropriate priority should be accorded to individual choices is not without significance. It clearly runs counter to many existing political ideologies and practices.

The conception of respect for dignity suggested above can also be given more specific meaning by applying it to actions of psychological significance. Indeed, nothing is so clearly violative of the dignity of persons as treatment that demeans or humiliates them. This includes not only attacks on personal beliefs and ways of life but also attacks on the groups and communities with which individuals are affiliated. Official statements that vilify groups or hold them up to ridicule and contempt are an especially dangerous form of psychological aggression resulting in a lack of respect by others for such groups and, perhaps even more insidious, destroying or reducing the sense of self-respect that is so important to the integrity of every human. We can also point to the widespread practice of using psychogenic drugs or other forms of psychological coercion to impose conformity and ideological obedience. These should clearly be seen as violations of the inherent dignity of the person. Put in positive terms, respect for the intrinsic worth of a person requires a recognition that the person is entitled to have his or her beliefs, attitudes, ideas and feelings. The use of coercion, physical or psychological, to change personal beliefs is as striking an affront to the dignity of the person as physical abuse or mental torture.

Our emphasis on respect for individuals and their choices also implies proper regard for the responsibility of individuals. The idea that people are generally responsible for their conduct is a recognition of their distinct identity and their capacity to make choices. Exceptions may have to be made for those incapable of such choices (minors or the insane) or in some cases for those under severe necessity. But the general recognition of individual responsibility, whether expressed in matters of criminal justice or civic duties, is an aspect of the respect that each person merits as a person. It is also worth noting as a counterpart that restraint is called for in imputing responsibility to individuals for acts of others such as groups of which they are members. In general, collective responsibility is a denigration of the dignity of the individual, a denial of a person's capacity to choose and act on his or her responsibility.

We do not by this last comment mean to separate individuals sharply from the collectivities of which they are a part. Indeed, we believe that the idea of human dignity involves a complex notion of the individual. It includes recognition of a distinct personal identity, reflecting individual autonomy and responsibility. It also embraces a recognition that the individual self is a part of larger collectivities and that they, too, must be considered in the meaning of the inherent dignity of the person. We can readily see the practical import of this conception of personality by considering political orders that, on the one hand, arbitrarily override individual choice and, on the other, seek to dissolve group ties. There is also a "procedural" implication in that it indicates that every individual and each significant group should be recognized as having the capacity to assert claims to protect their essential dignity.

We are led more deeply into the analysis of human dignity when we consider its relation to the material needs of human beings and to the ideal of distributive justice. Few will dispute that a person in abject condition, deprived of adequate means of subsistence, or denied the opportunity to work, suffers a profound affront to his sense of dignity and intrinsic worth.[4] Economic and social arrangements cannot therefore be excluded from a consideration of the demands of dignity. At the least, it requires recognition of a minimal concept of distributive justice that would require satisfaction of the essential needs of everyone.

Some would probably go beyond this and contend that substantial equality is a necessary condition of respect for the intrinsic worth of the human person. "Each person is as good as every other" may be inferred as a plausible maxim. In particular, relations of dominance and subordination would be viewed as antithetical to the basic ideal. If this is so, great discrepancies in wealth and power need to be eliminated to avoid such relations. However, the counterargument can be made that such egalitarian objectives cannot be realized without excessive curtailment of individual liberty and the use of coercion. This familiar confrontation of conflicting political philosophies need not be pursued here, but it is worth noting that demands for the respect of human dignity will almost surely lead into the continuing debate between advocates of equality and advocates of freedom.

These observations on the meaning of respect for the inherent dignity of the human being suggest the far-reaching implications of an ideal that has not yet been given substantial specific content. At the same time, our analysis indicates that a determinate core of meaning may be elucidated that is in keeping with widely accepted (though not universally accepted) values. This core of meaning has not been formulated as an explicit definition. To do so would result in another highly abstract formula. What is important is the extent to which the analysis leads to more concrete acceptable norms of con-

[4] Benda considers that the German constitutional provision on human dignity imposes a constitutional duty on the state to protect individuals against material want (*materieller Not*). *See* Benda, *supra* note 2, at 113, 115. The right to public assistance has been linked to Article 1 of the Constitution by the Supreme Administrative Court, No. 55, 1 BVerwGE 159 (1954). There is an old judgment of the Constitutional Court stating that Article 1 standing alone did not impose a duty of protection against material want (No. 22, 1 BVerfGE 97, 104 (1951)), but this opinion does not represent the views held generally today. I am indebted to Professor Stefan Riesenfeld for information on the German constitutional law concerning this point.

duct. I have sought to indicate this in my comments. As a further step in this direction, I shall next suggest some examples of conduct and ideas antithetical to or incompatible with respect for the inherent dignity of the human person.

II. Conduct and Ideas Antithetical or Incompatible with Respect for Inherent Dignity

The following list embraces two categories: one relates to conduct and ideas that directly offend or denigrate the worth and dignity of individuals; the second, to conduct and ideas that are implicitly incompatible with the basic ideas of the inherent dignity and worth of human persons. The line between the two categories is not a sharp one, but the distinction is helpful to the task of identifying relevant factors and to considering how to respond to incompatible acts and attitudes. The examples given are not limited to official acts and statements. Affronts to dignity may come from nonofficial sources. They should not be excluded for that reason, although a different position might be taken if the question were whether such affronts should be grounds for legal action.

(1) Statements that demean and humiliate individuals or groups because of their origins, status or beliefs.

(2) Vilification or derision of beliefs that people hold in reverence. Teaching that particular races, ethnic groups or religions hold "ridiculous" or dangerous views, or otherwise belittling cherished beliefs.

(3) Denial of the capacity of a person to assert claims to basic rights.

(4) Punishment of detained persons by psychological or physical means that are meant to humiliate or ridicule their beliefs, origins or way of life.

(5) Dissemination of negative stereotypes of groups (ethnic, religious, social) and implications that members of such groups are inferior.

(6) Psychiatric treatment that involves coercive means to change beliefs or choices that are lawful.

(7) Restrictions on opportunities and means to maintain family life as, for example, by denying access to family members or requiring members of families to inform authorities of the acts or beliefs of others.

(8) Denial of educational or employment opportunities to persons on ground of their membership in groups or their beliefs.

(9) Restrictions on equal participation in political processes because of beliefs, status or origin.

(10) Degrading living conditions and deprivation of basic needs.

(11) Abuse and insolence by officials, especially to persons suffering from infirmities or social opprobrium.

(12) Medical treatment or hospital care insensitive to individual choice or the requirements of human personality.

III. Human Dignity and Human Rights

The relation of human dignity to human rights is of particular interest to our thesis.

The Helsinki Final Act declares in Principle VII that all human rights and fundamental freedoms "derive from the inherent dignity of the human person." This statement should be understood in a philosophical rather than historical sense. As history, it would probably be more correct to say the opposite: namely, that the idea of dignity reflects sociohistorical conceptions of basic rights and freedoms, not that it generated them. However, as a philosophical statement, the proposition that rights derive from the inherent dignity of the person is significant. It clearly implies that rights are not derived from the state or any other external authority.

One may ask whether a philosophical statement of this broad character has any practical consequence. The answer lies in the degree to which general ideas influence perceptions and attitudes affecting conduct. The general idea that human rights are derived from the dignity of the person is neither truistic nor neutral. It has two corollaries that challenge conceptions prevalent in some societies and ideologies. The first corollary is the idea that basic rights are not given by authority and therefore may not be taken away; the second is that they are rights of the person, every person. It is not unrealistic to assume that ideas of this kind will have a role in challenging existing attitudes. When they are found in official declarations, they become part of the instruments of change, sometimes loudly proclaimed, at other times almost imperceptibly affecting ideas of legitimacy.

There is a further implication to be drawn from the recognition of human dignity as a "source" of human rights. Drawing upon the conception of human dignity and the intrinsic worth of every person, we can extend and strengthen human rights by formulating new rights or construing existing rights to apply to new situations. The analysis of human dignity given earlier is suggestive of such possibilities. As an example, one might suggest that aliens now commonly deprived of rights to take part in civic and political life should as a matter of respect for their worth be given such rights. Other examples might perhaps be inferred from the recognition that vilification and demeaning of group beliefs and aspirations are affronts to dignity and that official behavior involving such vilification or demeaning should be considered as a violation of the rights of the person.

This latter example raises another general question: namely, whether violations of dignity should as a rule be dealt with through legal action and the assertion of rights. I would suggest the contrary. Respect for human dignity may be realized in other ways than by asserting claims of right. In many cases, the application of a "rights approach" to affronts to dignity would raise questions involving existing basic rights such as free speech. In other cases, respect for dignity may be more appropriately and effectively attained through social processes such as education, material benefits, political leadership and the like. Various situations involving apparent violations of dignity may be alleviated by a code of conduct or of good manners such as those followed in some parliamentary bodies or educational institutions. Simply making people aware of language and acts that would be considered disrespectful of the worth of others could have a beneficial effect. Steps may be taken to foster better understanding by those in power and in the information media of the sensitivities of persons and groups to slurs and belittling comment. Informal channels for dealing with alleged affronts to dignity might be more suitable and effective than litigation in many cases. In such areas of public administration as social welfare, health care and prison administration, there is ample room for the elimination of actions that impinge on the self-respect of those in need of aid.

These observations indicate that the central idea of human dignity has a wide range of applications outside of the sphere of human rights. It is therefore of some importance to treat it as a distinct subject and to consider ways that respect for dignity can be fostered through public and private agencies.

OSCAR SCHACHTER

NOTES AND COMMENTS

The Teaching of International Human Rights Law in U.S. Law Schools

The teaching of international human rights law in U.S. law schools has come a long way in the past two decades. Twenty years ago a survey conducted by the American Society of International Law made no mention of the subject.[1] In 1965, the late Egon Schwelb, "Mr. Human Rights," in what he himself characterized as a "novel departure,"[2] offered a seminar on "The International Protection of Human Rights" at Yale. During the next half-dozen years, similar offerings were made available at California (Berkeley), Harvard, Virginia, and several other institutions. By 1971, when a panel at the annual meeting of the Society considered "The Teaching of International Aspects of Human Rights,"[3] at least 13 law schools offered either a course or a seminar in international human rights law.[4]

With the publication of two course books during the 1970's,[5] plus the public interest in human rights sparked by the Carter administration, the number of such offerings by U.S. law schools increased steadily, albeit far less spectacularly than most international human rights lawyers had hoped. Indeed, the major conclusion of a two-day conference in 1979 on "Teaching International Human Rights Law in Law Schools and Universities," organized by the International Human Rights Law Group of the Procedural Aspects of International Law Institute (PAIL) under a grant from the National Endowment for the Humanities, was that far too few schools had a separate international human rights law offering. Since the narrative report of the conference never has had wide circulation[6] and since, in the opinion of this writer, its conclusions remain as valid today as they were 4 years ago, they are set out below and then reviewed in

[1] Teaching of International Law and Related Courses in American Law Schools (ASIL Occasional Paper, 1964).

[2] International Legal Studies: A Survey of Teaching in American Law Schools 1963–1964, at 92 (ASIL, R. Edwards, Jr., ed. 1965).

[3] Panel, *The Teaching of International Aspects of Human Rights,* 65 ASIL Proc. 240 (1971).

[4]

> Those professors currently teaching a course in human rights are Sohn at Harvard, Bilder at Wisconsin and Michigan, Carey at N.Y.U., Newman at Berkeley, Nanda at Denver, Henkin at Columbia, Marroney [*sic*] at Syracuse, Van Dyke at Iowa, Lillich at Virginia, Del Russo at Howard and Georgetown, and McDougal at Yale.

Panel, *supra* note 3, at 255 (remarks of Bert B. Lockwood, Jr., reporting on a 1971 survey of international human rights law courses conducted by the University of Virginia School of Law).

[5] L. Sohn & T. Buergenthal, International Protection of Human Rights: Cases and Materials (1973); and R. Lillich & F. Newman, International Human Rights: Problems of Law and Policy (1979). *See* notes 12–13 and 22 *infra* and accompanying text.

[6] Teaching International Human Rights Law in Law Schools and Universities (PAIL Institute, Oct. 1980). Copies of the report may be obtained for cost by writing Hurst Hannum, Esq., Executive Director, Procedural Aspects of International Law Institute, Room 1027, 1346 Connecticut Ave., N.W., Washington, D.C. 20036.

light of a recent PAIL survey on the teaching of international human rights law in U.S. law schools.

(1) *Relatively few law schools offered a course or seminar on international human rights law.* At the conference, it was reported that in 1979 only 15 law schools offered a course or seminar on the subject. A follow-up PAIL survey in early 1980 revealed that 20 institutions intended to offer a course or seminar during the 1980–1981 academic year.[7] Nevertheless, this figure still represented only 11.9 percent of the 168 schools then listed by the Association of American Law Schools (AALS). Among the law schools that did not offer international human rights law at the time were such nationally ranked institutions as California (Berkeley), Chicago, Cornell, Michigan, Texas, UCLA, and Yale.[8] Thus, despite considerable progress, the subject had yet to become an accepted elective in the normal law school curriculum.

(2) *Lack of student demand and interested instructors were the principal reasons for the relatively few international human rights law offerings.* Many conference participants observed (even 4 years ago) that student interest in the subject was not what one might expect. Law students were worried about passing their bar examinations and getting good jobs; international human rights law did not appear to be helpful in either regard. Peer group pressure and the mistaken belief that international human rights law was not "law" also militated against such offerings.

Another reason frequently mentioned for the relatively few offerings was the lack of interested instructors. Nine of the 21 persons then teaching international human rights law actually attended the conference; in addition to these 21, only a handful of academics occasionally taught the subject. This lack of law faculty interest was underscored by the 1980 PAIL survey: 4 of 9 law schools reporting that they did not have an offering or intend to have one in the future cited as a reason lack of faculty interest (UCLA being one such school), while 4 of the 13 schools stating that they did not have an offering but intended to have one in the near future indicated either that they had no interested faculty member in residence or that, if they did, he or she did not offer such a course or seminar on a regular basis (Cornell and Yale being among such law schools). Clearly, the lack of interested full-time instructors on law school faculties was

[7] They were American, Arizona State, Catholic, Cincinnati, Dayton, Denver, Harvard, Howard, Iowa, Minnesota, NYU, Ohio Northern, Pace, Rutgers (Camden), Santa Clara, Stanford, SUNY (Buffalo), Temple, Virginia, and Wisconsin. All but Catholic, Howard, and Wisconsin still have such an offering in their regular curricula. *See* notes 16–18 *infra.*

A contemporaneous survey by the American Bar Association, perhaps reflecting "the wish is the parent of the thought" principle, listed 47 law schools "offering or planning to offer one or more courses primarily concerned with international human rights." ABA Subcommittee on Human Rights Education, The ABA National Survey on Human Rights Teaching, App. (Dec. 1979). Included in the list were all the institutions mentioned in the 1980 PAIL survey—except for Howard, NYU, and Stanford—plus 32 other law schools. Well over half of the latter never offered such a course or seminar and, as the recent PAIL survey discovered, have no present intention of doing so.

[8] California (Berkeley) and Michigan now have such an offering, as does Texas during its summer session. *See* notes 16–18 *infra.* Cornell and Yale have offered a course or seminar upon occasion, but Chicago and UCLA remain delinquent. *See* text at note 24 *infra.*

a serious obstacle to increasing the number of international human rights law offerings.

(3) *International human rights law should be taught as a separate course or seminar at every law school.* It should come as no surprise that there was unanimous agreement among the conference participants on this point, with most of the discussion focusing on the content of such an offering and who should be allowed to take it.

A consensus emerged that the offering, while stressing civil and political rights, should consider economic, social, and cultural rights as well. Moreover, it should strike a balance between introducing the students to the substantive law of international human rights and familiarizing them with international and domestic procedures for enforcing this law. A clinical component, field work, or internship should be offered whenever possible, as this would teach needed skills and show students that international human rights law has a practical application.

With respect to who should be allowed to enroll in a basic international human rights law course or seminar, there was general agreement that it should be open to both law school students and university graduate students, and perhaps undergraduates as well. Several participants made the point that an interdisciplinary student body was to be encouraged since it would benefit all concerned. Moreover, the offering should be structured in such a way that a course in public international law need not be a prerequisite, although such a course, as well as courses in administrative, constitutional, and criminal law, naturally would be most helpful.[9]

(4) *International human rights law should be taught in other international law courses.* Conference participants suggested that in law schools not offering a course or seminar in international human rights law, the instructor in public international law carve out a major section for it either in the basic course, a course in international organizations if one was offered, or both. Recent international law course books have made it easier to accomplish this objective by devoting much more space to international human rights law than their predecessors.[10] Even when a law school offers international human rights as a separate entity, it should continue to be taught in the basic international course, since the latter will remain for some time the only one that most law students will take.

(5) *International human rights law should be infused into as many noninternational law courses as possible.* As an alternative to a course or seminar on international human rights law, or (preferably) in addition to one, conference participants agreed that there should be an international human rights law

[9] On the question of prerequisites, the conference discussion tracked that of the ASIL panel in 1971. *See* Panel, *supra* note 3, at 257–58.

[10] *See, e.g.*, L. Henkin, R. Pugh, O. Schachter, & H. Smit, International Law 804–28 (1980); J. Sweeney, C. Oliver, & N. Leech, The International Legal System 573–650 (2d ed. 1981); and B. Weston, R. Falk, & A. D'Amato, International Law and World Order 466–595 (1980). So, too, does the most recent international organizations course book. *See* F. Kirgis, Jr., International Organizations in Their Legal Setting 744–919 (1977).

component or at least dimension to such established law school courses as constitutional law, civil rights/liberties, criminal law, administrative law, and labor law. While there was general consensus in favor of this approach on the theoretical level, several participants thought it difficult to implement practically. Ideally, everyone agreed, international human rights norms should be integrated into all courses, but that was a major undertaking that would take years to accomplish.[11]

(6) *International human rights teaching materials should be revised and new materials published.* Reviewing existing law school course books, the participants agreed that the Sohn and Buergenthal work was too long, included too much historical material, and was not sufficiently process-oriented.[12] On the other hand, the action-oriented approach of Lillich and Newman, while appealing to students, led to skimpy coverage of substantive international human rights law.[13] Conference participants recommended that in their next editions both books include much more material on the two UN Covenants[14] and on the role of specialized agencies and nongovernmental organizations. It also was suggested that a good handbook was needed to supplement both books, as well as for general purposes. The need for collections of basic documents and selected readings also was stressed.

The present writer believes the above six conclusions are as valid now as they were in 1980. Data obtained from a short questionnaire sent to all 170 AALS or ABA-accredited U.S. law schools in August 1982, followed up by numerous telephone calls during June 1983, confirm this belief.[15] The most recent PAIL survey specifically substantiates the two major points (1 and 2) made above.

In the first place, there has been a continued steady increase in the number of law schools offering a separate course or seminar in international human rights law—from 13 in 1971, to 20 in 1980, to 46 at present. Of these 46 schools, 4 (or 3 percent of the 146 schools reporting) offer both a course and a seminar;[16] 17 (or 12 percent) offer a course;[17] and 25 (or 17 percent) offer

[11] For the first steps in that direction, see text accompanying note 34 *infra.*

[12] The 1980 PAIL survey revealed that this course book was being used at two law schools. Teaching International Human Rights Law in Law Schools and Universities, *supra* note 6, App. C. For its present adoptions, see text accompanying note 22 *infra.*

[13] The 1980 PAIL survey revealed that this course book was being used at 14 law schools. *Ibid.* For its present adoptions, see text accompanying note 22 *infra.*

[14] International Covenant on Civil and Political Rights, *adopted* Dec. 16, 1966, *entered into force* Mar. 23, 1976, GA Res. 2200 (XXI), 21 UN GAOR Supp. (No. 16) at 52, UN Doc. A/6316 (1966), *reprinted in* R. LILLICH, INTERNATIONAL HUMAN RIGHTS INSTRUMENTS 170.1 (1983); International Covenant on Economic, Social and Cultural Rights, *adopted* Dec. 16, 1966, *entered into force* Jan. 3, 1976, GA Res. 2200 (XXI), 21 UN GAOR Supp. (No. 16) at 49, UN Doc. A/6316 (1966), *reprinted in* R. LILLICH, *supra,* at 180.1.

[15] The data that follow are based upon questionnaires returned by or information orally supplied by 146 of the 170 accredited U.S. law schools, or 86%. Apologies are made in advance for the errors inherent in such a survey.

[16] American, Columbia, New York Law School, and Virginia.

[17] Antioch, Boston University, California (Berkeley), Capital, Connecticut, Dayton, Franklin Pierce, Georgetown, Iowa, Notre Dame, Ohio Northern, Rutgers (Camden), Rutgers (Newark), Southwestern, Stanford, SUNY (Buffalo), and Texas.

only a seminar.[18] Thus, 32 percent of the law schools recently surveyed offer either a course or a seminar, or both.[19] Moreover, 9 additional schools (or 6 percent of the schools surveyed) indicated that they intended to schedule such an offering in the future.[20] Hence, as many as 55 law schools (or 38 percent of those surveyed[21]) may soon be teaching international human rights law.[22]

This increasing acceptance of international human rights law in law school curricula is encouraging, but for two obvious reasons it still rates only about one and a half cheers. First, 62 percent or more of the U.S. law schools surveyed[23] still do not teach the subject, including such perennial "top ten" institutions as Chicago, Pennsylvania, and Yale, and such other leading schools as Cornell, Duke, Illinois, Indiana, Tulane, UCLA, USC, and Washington.[24] Second, even at those 46 institutions teaching the subject, support for it is very thin: seminars predominate over courses by a three to two margin, and many offerings are scheduled only every other year,[25] during summer sessions,[26] or even as part of overseas summer programs.[27] While hard figures are unavailable, it seems likely that no more than 750 U.S. law students are taking an international human rights law offering each academic year.

Second, as in 1979–1980, the lack of student demand and interested instructors appears to be the major roadblock to increasing the teaching of international human rights law in U.S. law schools. At least a dozen law schools—including some surprising ones[28]—reported that there was no perceived demand from students for such an offering. Nearly half again as many

[18] Albany, Arizona State, Bridgeport, Cincinnati, Cleveland State, Denver, Florida, George Mason, George Washington, Harvard, JAG School (Army), Loyola (Los Angeles), Michigan, Minnesota, NYU, Northern Illinois, Northwestern, Nova, Pace, Pittsburgh, Santa Clara, Southern Illinois, Stetson, Temple, and West Virginia.

[19] Of the 24 accredited law schools not reporting, however, it would not be unreasonable to assume that relatively few had an international human rights law offering. Thus, the percentage of *all* U.S. law schools having such an offering is probably closer to 26% than to 32%.

[20] Akron, Boston College, Catholic (Puerto Rico), Campbell, Detroit College, Richmond, Texas Southern, Utah, and Wayne State. Three of these schools reported a similar intention to the ABA in 1979 but never followed through (*see* note 7 *supra*), which makes one somewhat skeptical about whether they will now.

[21] This percentage probably should be adjusted downward for the reason suggested in note 19 *supra*.

[22] At the 46 law schools currently teaching the subject, five instructors report using Sohn and Buergenthal as teaching materials and 26 have adopted Lillich and Newman. *Compare* text accompanying notes 12–13 *supra*. Thirteen instructors use their own materials, generally for seminars, while no information is available on the materials used in the other offerings.

A two-volume text edited by Theodor Meron, *Human Rights in International Law: Legal and Policy Issues*, is appearing late in 1983 and will also be available for teaching the subject.

[23] The percentage of all U.S. law schools not teaching the subject probably is somewhat higher for the reason suggested in note 19 *supra*.

[24] In 1979, Yale and five of the eight schools in the latter category reported to the ABA that they were offering or intended to offer an international human rights law course. *See* note 7 *supra*. Now none of these schools contemplates such an offering, certainly a disappointing slippage of expectations.

[25] *E.g.*, Ohio Northern.

[26] *E.g.*, Texas.

[27] *E.g.*, Notre Dame.

[28] *E.g.*, Duke.

law schools—once more including some surprising ones[29]—indicated that no faculty member was interested in teaching the subject. Other law schools advised that funding priorities prevented them from offering a course or seminar on such a specialized subject.[30] The hoped-for economic recovery, of course, may generate both the financial resources and ultimately the increased student interest needed to support and justify new international human rights law offerings. Moreover, the fact that more students are taking such offerings right now will provide law schools with a pool of potential interested instructors in the future. Nevertheless, without being unduly pessimistic, it would be optimistic to expect that more than 50–60 schools, roughly one-third of accredited U.S. law schools, will teach international human rights law on a regular basis during the balance of this decade.

If this prognosis is correct, then international human rights lawyers in academia, in addition to solidifying their offerings in the curricula of their law schools and building up the number of students enrolled in them, should concentrate their pedagogical efforts in two other areas, both stressed by the participants in PAIL's 1979 conference, namely, making sure that international human rights law is adequately covered in the basic international law course[31] and that it also is infused into as many noninternational law courses as possible (points 4 and 5 made above). The first objective already seems to have been achieved, at least in large measure.[32] The second objective will take much more time and effort to realize,[33] although PAIL already has a pilot project on "The Linkages between International Human Rights and U.S. Constitutional Law" in train[34] and hopes to receive funding soon for a similar project in the field of criminal law and procedure. In sum, while a lot has been accomplished since Dr. Schwelb's "novel departure" 20 years ago, and the prospects for further achievements in the teaching of international human rights law in U.S. law schools look more than passing fair, much remains to be done.

Appendix

List of Law Schools Currently Teaching International Human Rights Law (June 1983)

SCHOOL	INSTRUCTOR	FORM OFFERED
Albany	Gordon	Seminar
American	Buergenthal	Course & seminar
Antioch	Kerry Baca & Tonme	Course

[29] *E.g.*, USC.

[30] *E.g.*, Colorado.

[31] And, of course, encouraging more students to take such a course.

[32] *See* text at note 10 *supra.*

[33] *See* text at note 11 *supra.*

[34] This project, supported by grants from the Dana Fund, the Exxon Education Fund, the Ford Foundation, and the Blaustein Institute, seeks—through exposing constitutional law professors to international human rights law and preparing supplementary materials for their use in teaching the basic constitutional law course—to infuse or integrate international human rights norms into one key area of the law school curriculum. Further information about the project may be obtained by writing PAIL, whose address is given in note 6 *supra.*

SCHOOL	INSTRUCTOR	FORM OFFERED
Arizona State	Kader	Seminar
Boston University	Partan	Course
Bridgeport	Arens	Seminar
California (Berkeley)	Newman	Course
Capital	Turack	Course
Cincinnati	Lockwood	Seminar
Cleveland State	Picker	Seminar
Columbia	Henkin & Schachter	Course & seminar
Connecticut	Ioffe	Course
Dayton	Sultan	Course
Denver	Cox & Nanda	Seminar
Florida	Nagan	Seminar
Franklin Pierce	Saunders	Course
George Mason	Ebiasah	Seminar
Georgetown	Drinen	Course
George Washington	Mallison	Seminar
Harvard	Ferguson	Seminar
Iowa	Weston	Course
JAG School (Army)	Dowell & Gravelle	Seminar
Loyola (Los Angeles)	Garbesi	Seminar
Michigan	Stein	Seminar
Minnesota	Weissbrodt	Seminar
New York Law School	McDougal & Chen	Course & seminar
New York University	Meron	Seminar
Northern Illinois	Stern	Seminar
Northwestern	Nathanson	Seminar
Notre Dame	Fawcett	Course
Nova	Feinrider	Seminar
Ohio Northern	Friedlander	Course
Pace	Sinha	Seminar
Pittsburgh	Gerety (on leave 1983–84)	Seminar
Rutgers (Newark)	Paul	Course
Rutgers (Camden)	Clark	Course
Santa Clara	Shelton	Seminar
Southern Illinois	Dore	Seminar
Southwestern	Hoffman	Course
Stanford	Barton	Course
Stetson	Del Russo	Seminar
SUNY (Buffalo)	Leary	Course
Temple	Richardson	Seminar
Texas	Kramer (Summer 1983)	Course
Virginia	Martin & Young-Anawaty	Course & seminar
West Virginia	Friedberg	Seminar

RICHARD B. LILLICH*

* Howard W. Smith Professor of Law, University of Virginia School of Law, and President, Procedural Aspects of International Law Institute.

SOVIET THEORY OF INTERNATIONAL LAW FOR THE SEVENTIES

I. THE NEW APPROACH

Ever since the purge of the ranks of Soviet publicists in the thirties, their function has been to serve Soviet external policies.[1] It is there that one must look for the rationale of modifications in their views as to the role of international law in the current period. While the central doctrine of peaceful coexistence is still in place as the basic Soviet concept of modern international law, the seventies witnessed a new approach by Soviet publicists to the study of Western writings on international law. This new approach had important consequences as regards their doctrines and theoretical formulations.[2]

The new tone, clearly detectable in Soviet writings, reflects the conviction that to develop and grow, the Soviet Union must abandon its position of economic isolation. The world economy is no longer seen as consisting of two separate economic orders: the socialist and the capitalist.

> The West has achieved a high level of technical development in key industrial areas. It is therefore essential that socialist countries establish close cooperation with the West to move forward. The progress of each country is inseparable from participation in the world-wide exchange of material and spiritual values. Specialization is unavoidable.[3]

As Soviet economic interests called for a new approach, the policy of détente was energetically pursued, which led to the Helsinki Declaration of 1975 and a veritable deluge of pacts and treaties aiming at normalizing relations with the West.

On the scientific front, the new policy was outlined by Professor Tunkin, upon whose shoulders the mantle of authority, once worn by Vishinski, now rested. The transition was accomplished in two stages. Tunkin's book, *The Theory of International Law,* which clearly established the idea that there is a single world science of international law, was published in 1970.[4] Then in 1972, at the meeting of the Soviet Association of International Law, he harshly criticized his Soviet colleagues for an uncritical and undiscerning rejection of

[1] *See* K. GRZYBOWSKI, SOVIET PUBLIC INTERNATIONAL LAW 4–9 (1970); E. MCWHINNEY, THE INTERNATIONAL LAW OF DÉTENTE 12–13 (1978).

[2] Frenzke, *Zur Entwicklung des Sowjetischen Völkerrechtslehre,* 25 OSTEUROPA RECHT 272 (1979). *But see* Butler, *Some Reflections on the Periodization of Soviet Approaches to International Law,* in CONTEMPORARY SOVIET LAW: ESSAYS IN HONOR OF JOHN HAZARD 213, 213–14 (1974).

[3] EKONOMICHESKIE SVIAZI VOSTOK-ZAPAD 12–13, 35 *ff.* (N. P. Shmelev ed. 1976). Grzybowski, *Comecon,* in R. STARR, EAST-WEST BUSINESS TRANSACTIONS 125 (1974).

Even before the public call to cooperate economically with the West, a number of socialist countries joined GATT. It seems certain that they provided a trade channel to the Soviet Union, which remained outside GATT's formal membership. *See* Dobroczynski's article in POLITYKA, No. 38, Nov. 6, 1982.

[4] G. I. TUNKIN, TEORIA MEZHDUNARODNOGO PRAVA (1970).

Western writings on political grounds only.[5] His exposé stressed three points: the unity of the international community (in spite of the two camps theory), the unity of international law as governing the international community at large, and the unity of legal science on international relations.[6]

In a very few years Soviet publicists have produced a number of studies that have developed Tunkin's basic views and at the same time have upheld two singular features of the Soviet understanding of contemporary reality: first, that the Soviet Union and its allies represent the most important force in international relations, and second, that Soviet scholars are better equipped than others (owing to the Marxist-Leninist understanding of history) to analyze international relations and the development of international law.[7]

The overall effect of Tunkin's admonitions was a willingness to utilize methodology as developed in the West, including modern techniques of research and organization, to achieve a systematic presentation of the doctrines and institutions of international law. Professor Levin, who developed Tunkin's views, insisted that at the present stage, stress should be laid on the study of law and international relations in the world context. These relations constitute the environment in which the dialectical process towards higher forms of social organization takes place.[8] He further charged Soviet writers with failing to distinguish between international law, a system of rules, and the science of international law, which treats topics outside the law in force. It is the scientists who organize legal rules in a systematic order according to a theoretical concept.[9]

Modernization of the research method was the subject of a major work by Baskin and Feldman. While the materialist interpretation of history is still seen as the only sure guide to the study of law, research techniques developed in the West may be profitably used to supplement and illustrate the process of change and evolution with greater precision and accuracy. Thus, for instance, statistical methods can be used to explain changes in the structure of the international community, by tracing the development and functions of international organizations. The same applies to systemic studies, model building, cybernetics and game theory, opinion polls and opinion soundings—though traditional juridical research, analysis of texts, historical interpretations, and comparative methods are not to be abandoned.[10]

Baskin and Feldman further insist that the study of international law cannot be confined to the current period. Its norms and institutions in force today have a long history extending even to precapitalist times. National sovereignty,

[5] K. GRZYBOWSKI, *supra* note 1, at 10 *ff.*, on Vishinski's role in the 1938 conference of Soviet legal scholars.

[6] Tunkin, *Zadatchi, nauki mezhdunarodnogo prava v svete reshenii XXIV sjezda KPSS*, SOVETSKOE GOSUDARSTVO I PRAVO, No. 7, 1972, at 34.

[7] G. I. TUNKIN, *supra* note 4, at 156, 232; J. J. BASKIN & D. I. FELDMAN, MEZHDUNARODNOE PRAVO PROBLEMY METODOLOGII 19 *ff.* (1971); D. B. LEVIN, AKTUALNYE, PROBLEMY TEORII MEZHDUNARODNOGO PRAVA (1974).

[8] D. B. LEVIN, *supra* note 7, at 114, 127 *ff.*

[9] *Id.* at 78–94.

[10] J. J. BASKIN & D. I. FELDMAN, *supra* note 7, at 47 *ff.*, 62.

national liberation, and self-determination were recognized as postulates of law by the Peace of Westphalia (1648), although only now have they been given proper dimensions. Only the universalist perspective will permit proper understanding of the institutions of current international law.[11]

Levin's criticism of Soviet writings on international law was further developed in two important articles on the organization of teaching tools used at Soviet universities. The 1977 volume of the *Soviet Yearbook of International Law* carried an important article on the methods of legal research,[12] while in 1981 a Moscow University publication contained an article on the programming of textbooks for teaching international law.[13]

II. The International Community Today

Soviet publicists see the present international community as consisting of states with full rights under international law, nations striving for national independence and self-determination, and general and regional international organizations (the United Nations and its agencies), which participate in the development of international law. In studying the international community, attention must be paid to Soviet social organizations which, though lacking independent status under international law, nevertheless participate in international relations and take an active part in the progressive development of international law.

The current Soviet description of the international community has abandoned the theory of three camps. Soviet publicists have returned to the original description of the world by Lenin, in which the socialist state (now the socialist system) is confronted only by the capitalist system.[14] No mention is made of the tripartite division introduced by Khrushchev, who classified the developing countries, former colonies of the fallen empires, as a separate grouping (called Peace Zone).[15]

Soviet publicists of today are faced with the fact that the new members of the international community have adopted different attitudes to socialism in the Soviet form. The publicists have singled out those among them who have a positive attitude towards the Soviet Union. They are referred to as socialist-oriented states. These states enjoy a privileged position vis-à-vis the Soviet Union and other socialist states.[16] Under current international law, which has established the duty of material assistance to the newly emergent states, the Soviet Union and other socialist states have a legal obligation to assist only

[11] *Id.* at 51–53.

[12] Feldman, *O sisteme mezhdunarodnogo prava,* 1977 SOVETSKII YEZHEGODNIK MEZHDUNARODNOGO PRAVA 91–116.

[13] Talalayav, *Programmirovannye uchebniki i uchebnyi process, na primere uchebnika mezhdunarodnogo prava,* VESTNIK MOSKOVSKOGO UNIVERSITETA (Seria Pravo, Jan. 1981). The first textbook departing from the traditional organization of Soviet manuals was G. V. IGNATENKO & D. D. OSTAPENKO, MEZHDUNARODNOE PRAVO (1978). *Cf.* Frenzke, *supra* note 2, at 290–91.

[14] LENIN, 33 SOCHINENIIA 123 (5th ed. 1956).

[15] Pravda, Feb. 15, 1956.

[16] G. B. STARUSHENKO, MIROVOI REVOLUTSIONNYJ PROTSESS I SOVREMENNOE MEZHDUNARODNOE PRAVO 22, 247, 285 (1978).

the socialist-oriented states.[17] The difference between socialist states and states of socialist orientation consists in the presence of several variables: power monopoly in the hands of the Communist parties, organization of public and economic institutions according to the Soviet model, and the acceptance of the leadership of the working class by other toilers, in the first place the working peasantry.[18]

Two factors are seen as shaping international relations in the current period. First, the international community consists of states on an uneven level of economic development.[19] Second, "The character of international relations is—as it must be—determined by the social structure of the states that play a dominant role in the international arena."[20] One of these states is the Soviet Union, victorious in World War II, which established the socialist system and is supported by the working class of the entire world. The Soviet Union assumed the role once played by revolutionary France at the end of the 18th century.[21]

Soviet scholars study the international community as a social environment in constant flux. Its evolution is reflected in the new international law, a law of peaceful coexistence, which is "a specific form of class struggle between socialism and capitalism" controlled by "the immutable laws of societal development in the contemporary stage, which cannot be changed or repealed by people." While peaceful coexistence is a law of normal relations between states, it does not apply to relations between colonial powers and colonial peoples.[22] The key problem in the new international community is the emergence of new nations.

Although international law prohibits the export of revolution, socialist states have the right to afford moral and political assistance to nations struggling for independence. They also have the right to give weapons to new states when they are requested by a new socialist government, or when a colonial power militarily assists antiliberation forces.[23]

The right of self-determination belongs not only to entire nations, but also to parts of nations that form nonsocialist states. This explains the splitting of Germany and Korea. The right of self-determination does not belong to a province or an ethnic group that is already a part of a socialist country. Therefore, Namibia is entitled to self-determination, while Eritrea, which is a part of socialist Ethiopia, cannot claim that right. While splitting national entities in order to establish a socialist country is legal, it is illegal to organize plebiscites and referendums to protect the right of a minority to remain with a colonial power.[24]

[17] *Id.* at 183–89.

[18] *Id.* at 248.

[19] MARKSISTKO-LENINSKAIA TEORIA GOSUDARSTVA I PRAVA, OSNOVNYE INSTITUTI I PONIATIA 230 (1970).

[20] D. B. LEVIN, *supra* note 7, at 104, 114–27.

[21] G. I. TUNKIN, *supra* note 4, at 104–14.

[22] *Id.* at 38–39.

[23] D. B. LEVIN, *supra* note 7, at 127.

[24] G. B. STARUSHENKO, *supra* note 16, at 100–01, 249 *ff.* G. V. IGNATIENKO, MEZHDUNARODNOE PRAVO I OBSHCHESTVENNYJ PROTSESS 110–12 (1972).

The legality of wars of liberation is also reflected in the treatment of those who take part in the armed struggle. Foreigners hired to fight on the side of progressive forces are volunteers and enjoy the protection of the laws of war. Those hired by colonial powers or reactionary forces opposing self-determination are mercenaries and criminals. Thus, restrictions on intervention in the internal affairs of other countries must be dialectically interpreted. Under the influence of the forces of progress, the United Nations has adopted a number of resolutions that created a legal right to assist the struggling nations, although formally such assistance amounts to intervention in internal affairs.[25]

The same dialectical interpretation applies to the protection of human rights. Intervention in the internal affairs of capitalist states in order to promote the self-determination of colonial peoples is legal. At the same time, similar intervention into the internal affairs of socialist states is prohibited by international law.[26]

International organizations, whether general or regional, have a special role in the progressive development of international law. In addition to the law-making activities specified in their charters, or involving treaties with states or other international organizations, they play an extremely important role in developing the principles of international law. Those principles, either by means of resolutions adopted by the socialist and capitalist states or through the practice of states, then become a part of customary international law. Resolutions such as those on decolonization, national control of natural resources, modification of the principle of nonintervention in favor of the self-determination of nations, and elimination of racism and national discrimination are the achievements of the United Nations General Assembly.[27]

Not all international regional organizations are progressive. Their character and role in the international community and ability to develop international law depend upon their political color. The Organization of African Unity and the group of nonaligned nations, for example, are able to contribute to the development of general international law. Others, such as the Arab League, are reactionary, and therefore unable to promote the progressive development of law governing international relations.[28]

Soviet social organizations active in the international arena have an important place in the movement to reform international law. Their role is to influence public opinion abroad and to support Soviet policies. Soviet social organizations, according to the terminology of Soviet publicists, serve as transmission belts to the population of foreign countries, very much in the same manner as they transmit the propaganda generated at the highest level of authority to the populace in the Soviet Union itself. In this sense they are an extension of the Soviet Government abroad.

The active role of Soviet social organizations has a well-established tradition. In the initial period of the Soviet state, when foreign powers were withholding recognition of the revolutionary Government, the Russian Red Cross, and the

[25] G. B. STARUSHENKO, *supra* note 16, at 13–14, 289–304.

[26] *Id.* at 94, 200.

[27] *Id.* at 27 *ff.*

[28] *Id.* at 75, 132, 174–78.

Tsentrosoiuz, allegedly a national association of the Russian cooperatives, acted as diplomatic agencies or state trading organizations.

At present, three types of Soviet organizations pursue the goals of Soviet foreign policy. First are the friendship societies, such as Association U.S.S.R.-France and the Institute of Soviet-American relations, which seek to establish a common front with their counterparts in other countries. In the next group are various professional organizations, trade unions, the Soviet component of the Parliamentary Union, the Union of Architects, workers in the movie industry, the Red Cross, the national United Nations organizations, the International Organization of Democratic Lawyers, the World Organization of Democratic Youth, etc., which use their members in international professional and cultural organizations to propagandize Soviet policies.

Last come organizations with a specific political program such as the World Council for Peace, the Association of Fighters for Peace, and World Peace Congresses, which make propaganda aimed at winning the acceptance of the Soviet policy line by public opinion abroad. Their actions lead to the adoption of declarations, political demands directed at foreign governments, and proposals of agreements between the Soviet Union and other countries. Special emphasis is placed on propaganda for disarmament and the abolition of atomic weapons.[29]

III. Principles and Sources of International Law

Already in his early work (1956), Professor Tunkin defined international law as a "totality of norms, developed on the basis of agreements between the states." This simple and straightforward definition had the great advantage of being true to fact. Its weakness lay in the difficulty of fitting it into the basis-superstructure model, a must for a Soviet jurist. General international law, as Tunkin saw it at that time, was one and the same for all international relations, independent of the class character of the members of the international community. As such, Tunkin's view met with considerable opposition among more orthodox Soviet scholars, among them Korovin himself.

The doctrine of one general international law was put to test by the events in Hungary and Poland in 1956. It was necessary to find a doctrine that would justify Soviet armed intervention in Hungary and the political pressures in Poland. Tunkin had to recant and retreat from his position. International law was split into two systems, one in force in nearly the entire international community, the other within the socialist system. Although their norms and institutions were nearly identical and applied with equal authority to the relations of socialist states in the general international community, socialist international law was vitally affected by the doctrine of socialist internationalism. Socialist international law protected not only the national sovereignty of the socialist states, but also the interests of the entire socialist camp and the achievements of the working class. It authorized armed intervention vis-à-vis other

[29] V. V. Kravchenko, Obshchestvennye organisatii SSSR na mezhdunarodnoi arene (1969).

members of the socialist system in situations threatening its cohesion, and it acknowledged the leading role of the Communist Party of the Soviet Union.[30]

The invention of socialist international law posed a dilemma, however, when the unity of the world economy was proclaimed. Prior to 1970, Soviet scholars were satisfied with the doctrine that although norms of public international law sounded almost identical for socialist and capitalist states alike, they served states with different social orders and different social classes: the entire population, or the working class, in socialist countries, and the bourgeoisie or other exploiting classes in the other system. Once the economic unity of the world was proclaimed, this solution would not do. The difficulty was finally resolved by the construct that international law is a creation in the superstructure of the economic relations between the members of the entire community of states. These are not primary economic relations, but secondary, once removed from the internal economic order. International economic relations are neither socialist nor capitalist, and consequently, general international law is also neutral as regards class character. As such, it can be developed and adhered to by the states of the two systems.

This concession, which removes the basis-superstructure model from international relations, goes even deeper. Tunkin's concession to common sense admits that internal legislation, which may be a source of rules and institutions of international law and of international obligations, may also be an expression of genuine agreement. Here, obviously, the secondary theory fails. Thus, it may be concluded that regarding international relations, the basis-superstructure model has for all practical purposes been abandoned.[31]

The next doctrinal problem that required adjustment is the issue of historical determinism. Capitalist states, in their agreements to reform or lay down the principles of international law, could not be understood as accepting and upholding the Marxist understanding of history.

According to Tunkin, international law created by agreement is not a direct consequence of the immutable laws of societal development. It is true that the legal ideas of the 1917 October Revolution were incorporated into contemporary international law. However, international law as such is not socialist, and is independent of the laws of societal development. It is an autonomous legal system wholly controlled by agreement. Indeed, the present condition of the international community corresponds with the laws of societal development, and therefore Western writers who foresee its development into a superstate are wrong.[32] It is important to understand that the principle of peaceful coexistence applies to interstate relations only. Otherwise, laws of societal development are laws of armed revolutionary struggle. The concept of a warless world (Falk, Mendlovitz, Schwarzenberger, Jessup) is therefore

[30] G. I. TUNKIN, OSNOVY SOVREMENNOGO MEZHDUNARODNOGO PRAVA 158 (1956); *cf.* also G. I. TUNKIN, *supra* note 4, at 237, 431 *ff.;* D. B. LEVIN, *supra* note 7, at 2, 15, 25–26; K. GRZYBOWSKI, *supra* note 1, at 20–21.

[31] G. I. TUNKIN, *supra* note 4, at 236–37, 309; G. V. IGNATIENKO, *supra* note 24, at 8 *ff.;* D. B. LEVIN, *supra* note 7, at 25–26.

[32] G. I. TUNKIN, *supra* note 4, at 21 *ff.*, 45 *ff.*, 156 *ff.* and *passim.*

based on a misguided understanding of history.[33] The cardinal function of international law is the internationalization of the revolutionary struggle.[34]

Current international law consists of principles that prescribe the conduct of states and governments. They include prohibition of aggression, peaceful settlement of disputes, self-determination of peoples, peaceful coexistence, disarmament, respect for human rights, and prohibition of war propaganda. The role of the great powers is crucial to the formulation of principles of international law. A rule not accepted by the great powers, even one of the great powers, has no real significance.[35]

According to Tunkin, treaty and custom are two basic forms in which consensus of states may be expressed. In reaching international agreement, resolutions of the UN General Assembly are given a special place. Should the states of the two opposed systems accept a UN resolution, and should this resolution correspond to the provisions of the Charter, it may then reach the level of formal agreement between states. This acceptance will give it the status of an international treaty.

In addition to treaty and custom, Tunkin's theory of sources lists subsidiary processes of norm formation, which though leading to an agreement or customary norm of international law, constitute an intermediate stage. They include the decisions of the International Court and arbitral tribunals, teachings of publicists, internal legislation, decisions of national courts, and activities of social organizations. They must be accepted by both systems, frequently quoted in interstate diplomatic practice, or affirmed in international treaties concluded by a limited number of countries. They then may become a part of general international law, accepted by the international community. An example of such a treaty is the Treaty of Paris of 1928, which prohibited wars of aggression.[36]

IV. Three Systems of International Law

The creation of a separate legal system for socialist international relations was followed logically by the concept of a capitalist international law, in addition to the general international law in force between all states of the world. Formally, the capitalist system is identical with general international law. However, as it regulates relations characterized by contradictions, it is dialectically inferior. Capitalist states profess to respect the principles of national sovereignty and noninterference, when in fact they demonstrate a constant tendency to violate the rights of weaker states.

[33] G. V. Ignatienko, *supra* note 24, at 122–23.

[34] *Id.* at 129–30.

[35] All Soviet writers of the epoch accept the consensual theory of general international law. However, only Tunkin developed the theory of consensus in full. *See* G. I. Tunkin, *supra* note 4, at 49, 270; I. M. Minasian, Pravovye osnovy Leninskoi diplomatii 61–148 (1970); N. A. Ushakov, Sovetskoe gosudarstvo i provgressyvnoe razvitie mezhdunarodnogo prava (1977); G. B. Starushenko, *supra* note 16, pt. I, at 46–54. *See* USSR Const. art. 28 (1977).

[36] D. B. Levin, *supra* note 7, at 112 *ff.*, 167–68, 177; G. B. Starushenko, *supra* note 16, at 143; G. I. Tunkin, *supra* note 4, at 431, 440.

The qualitative superiority of the socialist system of international law results from the absence of contradictions and the presence of harmony in socialist relations. Socialist internationalism, which became the legal principle of the socialist system, guarantees not only the national sovereignty of socialist states, but also socialist construction and progress towards communism. Speaking in Poland after the invasion of Czechoslovakia in 1968, Brezhnev affirmed that the Soviet Union stands for strict respect for the sovereignty of socialist states and noninterference in their internal affairs.[37]

While Brezhnev's doctrine may be dialectically true, its direct consequence is the serious limitation of the national independence of weaker socialist countries vis-à-vis the Soviet Union, especially that of states bordering the Soviet Union, or where the Soviet Union maintains its garrisons. One may presume that the doctrine of socialist sovereignty applies to Afghanistan, but that the Soviet Union respects the integrity of the People's Republic of China in spite of its sins against socialist internationalism.[38]

The regime established by the Soviet Union in Eastern Europe may be usefully compared to the powers and influence exercised in Europe by the Holy Alliance in the first half of the 19th century. It was based on a specific concept of legitimism combined with the right to intervene in the affairs of any European country in defense of its principles.[39]

V. Soviet Theories and the Science of International Law

In addition to those Western writers who attacked the doctrine of national sovereignty and promoted the idea of a warless world under world government, Soviet publicists have also reviewed, sometimes very critically, other jurisprudential tendencies. Three of them merit singular attention.

Soviet scholars now assert that capitalist jurisprudence is dominated by the monistic school of the supremacy of international law (Kelsen, Scelle, Verdross). According to the monistic school, national legal systems derive their authority from international law. This position is not only scientifically wrong, but also reactionary in the Soviet view. It is an open attack on the institution of the national sovereignty of nations. It supports the political aim of imperialistic circles in their effort to establish supranational organizations, which would justify their intervention into the internal affairs of small and middle-sized countries.

[37] G. I. Tunkin, *supra* note 4, at 431–40. According to Article 30 of the 1977 USSR Constitution, the USSR—as a component part of the world socialist system, of the socialist alliance—strengthens the friendship and cooperation, and comradely mutual aid with the socialist countries on the basis of the principle of socialist internationalism, and actively participates in economic integration and socialist division of labor.

[38] G. B. Starushenko, *supra* note 16, at 232.

[39] Charles Martens, in the preface to his *Causes célèbres du droit des gens* (1827), acknowledged that at the time of the supremacy of the Holy Alliance, the right of armed intervention was one of the principles of international law. At the time of his writing, it had already been applied twice, against Piedmont and the Kingdom of Naples. The basis of that right was the Treaty of Paris of Nov. 20, 1815.

Monistic theory was adopted in a number of national constitutions (the French, West German, Italian, Dutch, and Danish).[40] These provisions have nominal significance only. When governmental interests of an imperialist state come into conflict with rules of international law, imperialist lawyers rely rather on the rules of municipal law. Thus, the monistic view is not only untrue in theory, but also in practice.

Soviet publicists find some merit in the views of moderate monists (Verdross, Rousseau), who acknowledge the possibility of conflicts between international law and municipal legal systems. Moderate monists advocate solving such conflicts by recourse to international tribunals for the settlement of disputes, first of all, to the International Court.[41]

The dualistic school, which is on the decline in the Western world, is more to the liking of Soviet publicists. The views of Triepel, Anzilotti, Hyde, Dahm, and Scheuner are closer to reality. Although formalistic in nature, and not concerned with relations between municipal and international legal systems, the dualistic school, and the mutual influence of these systems upon each other, describes actual practice in international relations.[42]

Yet an understanding of the relationship between the two legal systems—the municipal and the international—is essential to understanding current international relations. By and large, Soviet scholars share the views of Tunkin, who suggested that "a proper solution of the conflicts between internal and international law may be found only by explaining real links between them, in the process of formulating provisions of international law on one hand, and in the process of applying the provisions of international law on the other." Soviet legal science stands on the proposition of strict national sovereignty, and follows a dualistic theory; at the same time, it recognizes close connections between these two systems, and the desirability, even necessity, of maximal coordination.[43]

The sources of the errors of Western scholars—even those who express views acceptable to Soviet publicists—lie in their formalistic approach to the study of international law. They are unable to comprehend the close connections between its development and progress and the role of social and revolutionary forces in the present international community in general, and the role of the Soviet Union in particular.[44]

The sharpest criticism is reserved for the school of McDougal and his followers, specifically for their studies of international relations from the nonlegal position and their failure to distinguish between policy and a legal rule. They are charged with overemphasizing the role of power in international relations and for continuing the traditions of deniers of international law (Spinoza, Puchta, Austin, Lasson).[45]

[40] D. B. LEVIN, *supra* note 7, at 205–06; J. J. BASKIN & D. I. FELDMAN, *supra* note 7, at 24–31.

[41] D. B. LEVIN, *supra* note 7, at 209.

[42] *Ibid.*

[43] *See ibid.;* G. I. TUNKIN, *supra* note 4, at 233.

[44] D. B. LEVIN, *supra* note 7, at 209.

[45] J. J. BASKIN & D. I. FELDMAN, *supra* note 7, at 52–60; G. I. TUNKIN, *supra* note 4, at 297–302; D. B. LEVIN, *supra* note 7, at 22.

The attack of Soviet publicists on McDougal and his followers is somewhat surprising. Certainly, McDougal does not deny the role and function of international law in the international community. His approach to the study of international law (and municipal law as well) includes the element of policy in the form of unilateral claims as they contribute to norm formation. The norm formation process, as described by McDougal, has to include the element of power. The interplay of unilateral policy claims, and their acceptance by the international community, is essential to the development of "World Public Order," as he calls the system of rules governing international relations.

Compared with McDougal's approach, Soviet theories also lay emphasis on power and policy. But while McDougal avoids dividing the process of norm formation into two categories of social phenomena, Soviet scholars combine in their theories two incompatible elements: norm formation, a voluntaristic process, with the immutable laws of societal development. Intellectually speaking, is this warranted? Is it explained by historical facts? These questions go beyond the scope of the present study. It must be noted, however, that Soviet theories lead to some unexpected results. Socialist internationalism, which is a rule of positive law within the socialist system, is enforced by force, while socialist international law prohibits the use of force. In consequence, sovereign equality has a different meaning within the socialist system than in relation to the capitalist states.[46]

KAZIMIERZ GRZYBOWSKI*

CORRESPONDENCE

TO THE EDITORS-IN-CHIEF:

June 8, 1983

In his article, *The Tunisia-Libya Continental Shelf Case: Geographic Justice or Judicial Compromise?* (77 AJIL 219 (1983)), Mark B. Feldman presents an authoritative view of the Judgment of the International Court of Justice concerning the continental shelf delimitation between those two countries. Among the various opinions given in this article, the following may be considered among the more important from the point of view of consequences for future cases.

(1) Feldman states that the Court's Judgment is a step forward towards the formulation of integrated principles to be applied both to the continental shelf and to the economic zone. He concludes that the legal analysis of the Court appears well suited to the delimitation of the exclusive economic zone (pp. 220 and 238).

The Convention on the Law of the Sea consolidates the rules and criteria for the delimitation of the economic zone and the continental shelf. Though the Court did not deal with the delimitation of the economic zone, its legal thinking could well accommodate delimitation problems concerning both the economic zone and the continental shelf; and by dropping the physical features of the shelf as criteria for delimitation and refusing to accept any kind of

[46] *See* Pechota, *The Contemporary Marxist Theory of International Law,* 75 ASIL PROC. 149 (1981).

* Duke University School of Law.

natural seabed boundary, the Court opened the door, even before the Convention enters into force, to the consolidated treatment of both areas regarding delimitation.

It would be an anomaly for the economic zone of one state to be superimposed on the continental shelf of another state, but state claims favoring that odd situation have to be noted. In areas up to 200 miles, that anomaly may now be eliminated as the consequence of the interaction of logic, expediency, and judicious interpretation of the new conventional rules. Beyond 200 miles, the continental margin may underlie the high seas.

(2) Feldman states that "[b]y this time, it is beyond dispute that 'equitable principles' form the foundation of the law of maritime boundary delimitation" (p. 228). However, the Judgment "does not identify any equitable principles as such" (p. 229).

As a matter of fact, the Judgment does not specify any equitable principles as a concrete legal basis for the determination of the delimitation line. There are many references in the Judgment to equitable principles, but they are not spelled out. In the *North Sea Continental Shelf* cases, it was unnecessary to specify the equitable principles. The Court did not apply them but advised the parties to take them into account in order to achieve a negotiated and agreed delimitation. In the *Libya-Tunisia* case, the Court itself determined the dividing line of the continental shelf by applying equitable principles. As Feldman states, the general rule that the delimitation "is to be effected in accordance with equitable principles, and taking account of all relevant circumstances," is "too general in itself to provide much guidance for future cases" (p. 238).

It may be expected that in future cases the Court will wish to specify the equitable principles it applies to the delimitation of the continental shelf and the economic zone. Otherwise, as several scholars and the dissenting members of the Court in the *Libya-Tunisia* case fear, the Court may increasingly make decisions *ex aequo et bono* in this undefined area of general rules of law. The subtitle of Feldman's article is meaningful: *Geographic Justice or Political Compromise?*

REYNALDO GALINDO POHL

TO THE EDITORS-IN-CHIEF:

July 12, 1983

Ebere Osieke's article, *The Legal Validity of Ultra Vires Decisions of International Organizations* (77 AJIL 239 (1983)), discusses the interesting and troublesome question of the right of member states to reject decisions of international organizations when they regard the decisions as *ultra vires.* He concludes that there is no consensus recognizing such a right, and that it therefore cannot be regarded as a generally accepted principle of international law or of the law and practice of international organizations.

Osieke's article is a most valuable contribution. I agree that there is no broad right of rejection or of auto-interpretation exercisable by member states whenever they think an organization's act is *ultra vires.* I think, though, that there may be a right of rejection or of auto-interpretation in narrowly defined circumstances.

As Osieke has noted, the problem arises primarily when an organization makes a decision that purports to bind the member states. The decision is not properly subject to rejection or auto-interpretation by member states, even if it is made by a political organ and is not reviewable by any other body within the organization, when it (1) is made by an organ that clearly has authority to make a determination regarding matters of the kind in question; (2) may plausibly be said to be taken for a recognized purpose of the organization; *and* (3) is not contrary to a manifest restriction or prohibition in the organization's constituent instrument or established practice.

If condition (1) is not met, that is, if the organ does not have clear authority to make determinations in the field in question, the *Expenses* case seems to say that the determination may nevertheless bind members if it purports to do so. Some passages in the *Namibia* Advisory Opinion might be read to say the same thing. But the Court's reasoning on this point in the *Expenses* case seemed to confuse the internal and external effects of the *ultra vires* doctrine. Moreover, the subsequent failure of the organization effectively to challenge the French and Soviet rejection of the decisions in question suggests that there may be a right of rejection or auto-interpretation when the acting organ does not have clear authority to make a determination in the field in question.

Rarely is there a failure to meet condition (2) or (3). The instances in which such a failure has most arguably occurred are those involving South Africa's suspension or expulsion from specialized agencies of the United Nations. When the World Meteorological Organization suspends, or the Universal Postal Union expels, South Africa for reasons having nothing to do with meteorology or postal communications, it would seem to violate condition (2). Quite arguably, the WMO also violated condition (3), since it has an express provision in its constituent instrument on suspension of members, and its attempt to fit South Africa's suspension into that provision was far-fetched indeed. It is possible that the UPU violated condition (3) as well, since it has no provision in its constituent instrument for expulsion, and long-standing practice in the specialized agencies seemed to preclude expulsion without such a provision.

Members concerned about the lawfulness of international organizations' acts have not acquiesced in the suspension or expulsion of South Africa when condition (2) or (3) has not been met. One can certainly argue from their nonacquiescence, and from the negative inferences that may be drawn from language in the *Expenses* case, that there is a right of rejection or auto-interpretation when either of these conditions is not met.

Let me say finally that recognition of a right of rejection or auto-interpretation in the cases involving South Africa, mentioned above, implies nothing about approval of the South African practices that provoked the WMO and UPU majorities to do what they did. The point has to do strictly with the effect of *ultra vires* acts of organizations on their member states.

FREDERIC L. KIRGIS, JR.
Washington and Lee University School of Law

CONTEMPORARY PRACTICE OF THE UNITED STATES RELATING TO INTERNATIONAL LAW

MARIAN NASH LEICH*

The material in this section is arranged according to the system employed in the annual *Digest of United States Practice in International Law,* published by the Department of State.

ALIENS

(U.S. *Digest,* Ch. 3, §3)

Deportation—Request for Cuban Acceptance of Mariel Returnees

In a note handed to the Chief of the Cuban Interests Section of the Czechoslovak Embassy at Washington on May 25, 1983, the Department of State requested that the Government of Cuba take back certain Cuban nationals who had come to the United States in 1980 during the Mariel boatlift and who are ineligible on substantive grounds to remain in the United States. Attached to the note was a list of the names of 789 Cubans held in federal detention facilities for these reasons.

The Department set out the problem presented by the ineligible, or deportable, Cuban nationals, as well as the current United States policy regarding visa applications from Cubans, in a press release issued the same day, that read in part:

> During . . . [the] period [of the Mariel boatlift], some 125,000 Cubans entered the United States without authorization. The vast majority were law-abiding, were allowed to join relatives and friends, and soon found homes and employment. A few thousand were detained by the Immigration and Naturalization Service because of serious criminal conduct in Cuba. Many of these remain in detention. Additionally, others have been convicted of crimes in this country and have served or are currently serving sentences in state or local prisons. Finally, some are ineligible to remain in the United States for other substantive reasons. The Cuban government has refused to take back any of these persons.
>
> Under Section 243(g) of the Immigration and Nationality Act, the Department is required to discontinue the issuance of immigrant visas in any country upon notification by the Attorney General that said country, upon request, denies or unduly delays acceptance of the return of its nationals found ineligible to remain in the United States under U.S. immigration law. The Attorney General has so notified the Secretary of State.
>
> Coincident with the Mariel boatlift, the U.S. Interests Section in Havana was obliged to discontinue the issuance of visas because hundreds

* Office of the Legal Adviser, Department of State.

of Cuban applicants, seeking escape from Cuban police action outside the building, took refuge in its premises.[1] The Section later resumed the issuance of nonimmigrant visas and of immigrant visas to immediate relatives (spouses, minor children and parents) of U.S. citizens, and to certain U.S. permanent residents who had been in Cuba for protracted stays, but it continued not to issue immigrant visas to other applicants.

With the concurrence of the Attorney General, and pursuant to regulatory authority, the U.S. Interests Section in Havana will continue its current policy of issuing immigrant visas in the above categories.

We will also continue issuing nonimmigrant visas in Havana, as well as immigrant visas in all categories to Cuban applicants in third countries. Once all the Cuban nationals who came with the Mariel boatlift who are ineligible to remain in the United States for substantive reasons have been returned to Cuba, the way will be clear for the U.S. Interests Section in Havana to resume issuance of immigrant visas in all categories to Cuban applicants.

Finally, we wish to make it very clear that members of the Cuban community who came with the Mariel boatlift and who maintain "Cuban-Haitian entrant" status will not be affected by this initiative. Neither will members of the Cuban-American community who came before Mariel.[2]

On July 7, 1983, Judge Marvin H. Shoob of the U.S. District Court for the Northern District of Georgia ruled illegal the continued incarceration without hearings of (Mariel) Cubans who had been determined not releasable under the Attorney General's Status Review Plan or who were incarcerated because their paroles into the United States by the Attorney General under section 212(d)(5) of the Immigration and Nationality Act (8 U.S.C. §1182(d)(5)) had been revoked.[3]

Judge Shoob held that the Attorney General had statutory authority to detain excludable aliens for an indefinite period, if immediate exclusion was impracticable. After an initial period, however, during which detention might reasonably be imposed as an aid to effecting an alien's exclusion, he considered that the Constitution required further detention to be justified upon the basis of a procedurally adequate finding that the detainee, if released, "is likely to abscond, to pose a risk to the national security, or to pose a significant threat to persons or property within the United States."

The court found that the Attorney General's Status Review Plan, which it described in its order, did not afford detainees procedurally adequate hearings. New detention hearings must be provided for each detainee, the court said, that embodied the procedural guarantees detailed in full in its order.

[1] *See* 75 AJIL 144–45 (1981).

[2] Dept. of State Press Release No. 192, May 25, 1983.

[3] The ruling was issued in Fernandez-Roque v. Smith, Civ. A. Nos. C81-1084A, C81-938A, and C81-1350A (N.D. Ga. July 7, 1983), three consolidated cases, two being class actions, that involved petitions for writ of habeas corpus. *See also* Fernandez-Roque v. Smith, 91 F.R.D. 117, *modified,* 91 F.R.D. 239 (1981); Fernandez-Roque v. Smith, 557 F.Supp. 690 (1982); and Soroa-Gonzales v. Civiletti, 515 F.Supp. 1049 (1981).

Aircraft Crimes

(U.S. *Digest,* Ch. 8, §3)

Hijackings to Cuba

Following hijackings of Capitol Air flights from San Juan, Puerto Rico, to Miami, Florida, on May 1 and May 12, the Department of State, in a note to the Cuban Interests Section of the Embassy of Czechoslovakia, dated May 18, 1983, again urged the Government of Cuba to alter its current policy of not providing information on the fate of persons who succeeded in hijacking commercial aircraft to Cuba.

The note reiterated representations about a series of hijackings, that the Department had made in two earlier notes within an 11-month period: (1) that they had been conducted in conditions of extreme danger to the lives of the passengers and the crew and in some instances serious injuries had resulted; and (2) that Cuba could discourage hijackers from using it as a haven by returning them to the appropriate jurisdiction for trial (and, if found guilty, punishment), or by trying them in Cuba and giving public notice of this fact. Failure to publicize the punishments hijackers received, the Department maintained, encouraged further commission of the international crime of hijacking.

The Department noted the "fortuitous" fact that the two Capitol Air hijackings had not resulted in loss of life or serious injury and stressed that every hijacking involved the risk of a major aviation disaster causing death or serious injury to passengers, crew, and, potentially, ground personnel or bystanders. All nations, including Cuba, the Department said, had a common interest in discouraging this practice.

In its note of May 18, the Department of State requested that the persons involved in the two Capitol Air hijackings be returned or, as a minimum, that they be identified and prosecuted under Cuban law and, if found guilty, that they be sentenced commensurately with the gravity of their offenses. The Department requested, further, that, in the interest of deterring similar criminal acts in the future, whatever convictions were obtained be made public.[1]

[1] Dept. of State File No. P83 0064-0926. On June 15, 1983, the Cuban Government responded to the request for information with a list of names and sentences extending back over a period of more than 3 years, to April 1980.

On Feb. 15, 1973, the United States and the Republic of Cuba had signed notes incorporating a Memorandum of Understanding on Hijacking of Aircraft and Vessels and Other Offenses (TIAS No. 7579, 24 UST 737, *entered into force* Feb. 15, 1973), under which each party was obliged to return hijackers of aircraft or vessels to the party of their registry, or to prosecute them in the territory reached. On Oct. 15, 1976, Cuba formally denounced the Memorandum of Understanding, pursuant to the 6-months clause of the agreement, to take effect on Apr. 15, 1977. Cuba had not returned any hijackers pursuant to the 1973 agreement while it was in effect, but it returned two hijackers in September 1980.

JUDICIAL DECISIONS

MONROE LEIGH

Constitutional law—Fourth Amendment—exclusionary rule inapplicable despite violation of international law

UNITED STATES v. HENSEL. 699 F.2d 18.
U.S. Court of Appeals, 1st Cir., January 25, 1983.

Defendants Hensel, and others, were convicted by jury trial in federal district court of conspiracy to import and distribute marijuana in the United States. On appeal, defendant Hensel claimed, *inter alia,* that certain evidence obtained by the U.S. Coast Guard during a high-seas search of a Honduran vessel piloted by defendant should have been excluded because it was obtained in violation of international law. The U.S. Court of Appeals for the First Circuit (per Breyer, J.) affirmed the conviction and *held:* that even if the high-seas search violated international law, the Fourth Amendment to the Constitution does not require that the evidence thus obtained be excluded.

Defendant was the pilot of a Honduran shrimp boat that was located 65 miles off the coast of Nova Scotia when Canadian Coast Guard authorities, with the assistance of the U.S. Coast Guard, stopped the boat, boarded it, conducted a search, and confiscated 18 tons of marijuana. Hensel asserted that whether or not probable cause existed to search the Honduran boat, the search was conducted without the permission of the Honduran Government and thus violated international law. Therefore, the search was unreasonable and required application of the exclusionary rule.

The court of appeals agreed that the Coast Guard's statutory mandate to conduct searches on the high seas did not authorize searches in violation of international law.[1] "The rule is well established . . . that 'an act of congress ought never to be construed to violate the law of nations, if any other possible construction remains. . . .' "[2] Moreover, despite dictum in *United States v. Williams*[3] that American authorities can conduct high-seas searches without flag state permission, the court observed:

> [I]nternational law does not allow one nation to search on the high seas vessels belonging to another except in very special circumstances. As a fundamental rule, the proposition "that a merchant ship flying the flag

[1] The relevant statutory language provides as follows:

> The Coast Guard may make . . . searches, seizures, and arrests upon the high seas . . . for the prevention, detection, and suppression of violations of laws of the United States. For such purposes . . . [Coast Guard] officers may . . . go on board of any vessel subject to the jurisdiction, or to the operation of any law, of the United States . . . and search the vessel. . . .

14 U.S.C. §89(a) (1976).

[2] 699 F.2d 18, 27 (quoting Murray v. The Charming Betsy, 6 U.S. (2 Cranch) 64, 118 (1804)).

[3] 617 F.2d 1063, 1076 (5th Cir. 1980).

> of a recognized State is immune from all interference on the high seas by the ships of any other than her own State" is widely accepted.[4]

The court observed that only a few exceptions specified in the Convention on the High Seas[5] would permit active interference with a foreign merchant vessel. An attempt to apply these exceptions, however, would have required either factual determinations not made by the district court or "a difficult exploration of the murky waters of international law."[6] Therefore, the court assumed, *arguendo,* that the U.S. Coast Guard had violated both statutory and international law and proceeded to discuss whether suppression was appropriate.

Citing two prior Supreme Court decisions,[7] the court stated that the absence of statutory authority for a search did not automatically require application of the exclusionary rule. Since the search was supported by probable cause, it did not violate Hensel's Fourth Amendment rights. Moreover, in *United States v. Ramsey,*[8] the Supreme Court had indicated that the exclusionary rule should be applied only if the individual seeking its application falls within the zone of interests protected by the violated statute.

> In this case, the statute and regulation arguably violated (insofar as they incorporate principles of international law) were designed not to protect the privacy rights of ship captains, but rather to protect the rights of foreign sovereigns. In such a situation, . . . "[T]here is no basis for concluding that violation of these international principles must or should be remedied by application of the exclusionary rule . . . unless Fourth Amendment interests are violated."[9]

The court observed that a "related way to reach the same conclusion" was to say that defendant lacked "standing" to invoke the exclusionary rule for any violation of international law that invaded the rights of the Honduran Government. "The rule of international law in the case at bar is a rule designed to secure peace among nations, not to protect the privacy of individuals. . . . In brief, international law protects Honduras, not [the defendant]. And Honduras, as far as this record reveals, does not care."[10]

Unlike the Fifth Circuit in *United States v. Williams,* the First Circuit has taken a cautious view of what constitutes a permissible search on the high seas absent

[4] 699 F.2d at 27 (quoting C. COLOMBOS, THE INTERNATIONAL LAW OF THE SEA 311 (6th ed. 1967)).

[5] 13 UST 2312, TIAS No. 5200 (*entered into force* September 30, 1962). The Convention allows the search of another state's flag ship on the high seas if the searching authority (1) suspects that the foreign ship is engaged in piracy or slave trade, or that the ship is in fact a domestic vessel, (2) is engaged in hot pursuit, (3) has obtained the permission of the flag state, or (4) believes the foreign ship threatens the security of its own nation. *Id.*, Arts. 14–23.

[6] 699 F.2d at 29.

[7] United States v. Caceres, 440 U.S. 741 (1979); United States v. Giordano, 416 U.S. 505 (1974).

[8] 431 U.S. 606 (1977).

[9] 699 F.2d at 30 (quoting United States v. Cadena, 585 F.2d 1252, 1261 (5th Cir. 1978)).

[10] 699 F.2d at 30. The court also rejected the arguments of Hensel and his codefendants regarding hearsay, sufficiency of the evidence and procedural defects at trial. *See id.* at 30–41.

the flag state's permission. Whereas the Fifth Circuit apparently would permit such a high-seas search if it were supported by reasonable suspicion of criminal activity, the First Circuit would limit such searches to certain internationally defined instances—*e.g.*, piracy and slave trade. However, the First Circuit's opinion engrafts the "zone of interests" standing requirement, articulated by the Supreme Court in *Association of Data Processing Services Organizations, Inc. v. Camp,*[11] onto the application of the exclusionary rule. A similar rationale was adopted by the U.S. Court of Military Appeals in *United States. v. Whiting,*[12] wherein the court held that the victim of a search, allegedly conducted in violation of the NATO Status of Forces Agreement,[13] could not invoke the exclusionary rule since the treaty did not confer rights on individuals. Whether the same type of "zone of interests" rationale is applicable where the victim of the illegal search is seeking compensatory relief is unclear.

Although not discussed by the court, it should also be noted that the recently concluded United Nations Convention on the Law of the Sea[14] permits a warship[15] to board a foreign ship only if there is a reasonable ground for suspecting that the foreign ship is engaged in piracy, slave trade, unauthorized broadcasting, is not flying a flag or is suspected of being of the same nationality as the warship.[16] Furthermore, the Convention grants a right of "hot pursuit" if a coastal state has good reason to believe the foreign ship has violated the laws of that state.[17] However, the pursuit must begin when the foreign ship is "within the internal waters, the archipelagic waters, the territorial sea or the contiguous zone of the pursuing State, and may only be continued outside the territorial sea or the contiguous zone if the pursuit has not been interrupted."[18] As of July 1, 1983, 127 nations—but not the United States—have signed the Convention. It will come into force when 60 nations have deposited ratifications. As of this date, 6 ratifications have been deposited.

Foreign Sovereign Immunities Act—immunity of a foreign state from prejudgment attachment—explicit waiver of immunity

S & S MACHINERY CO. v. MASINEXPORTIMPORT. 706 F.2d 411.
U.S. Court of Appeals, 2d Cir., April 26, 1983.

Plaintiff, S & S Machinery Co., a U.S. corporation, sued to recover damages resulting from the delivery of allegedly defective goods by defendant, Masinexportimport, a Romanian foreign trading company. Pursuant to a purchase agreement between the parties, plaintiff had made payment by irrevocable letters

[11] 397 U.S. 150 (1970).

[12] 12 M.J. 253 (1982), *summarized in* 76 AJIL 624 (1982).

[13] 4 UST 1792, TIAS No. 2846 (*entered into force* Aug. 23, 1953).

[14] UN Doc. A/CONF.62/122 (Oct. 7, 1982) (*opened for signature* Dec. 10, 1982), *reprinted in* 21 ILM 1261 (1982).

[15] "Warship" is defined as a ship "belonging to the armed forces of a State bearing the external marks distinguishing such ships of its nationality, under the command of an officer duly commissioned by the government of the State . . . and manned by a crew which is under regular armed forces discipline." *Id.*, Art. 29.

[16] *Id.*, Art. 110.

[17] *Id.*, Art. 111.

[18] *Ibid.*

of credit issued to codefendant, the Romanian Bank for Foreign Trade, as defendant's collection agent. Concurrently with the commencement of its action, plaintiff sought and was granted prejudgment attachment of assets held by defendants in the United States and moved for an injunction against the negotiation of drafts or other negotiable paper pursuant to the letters of credit. After removal of the action from state court, the U.S. District Court for the Southern District of New York vacated the attachment of assets and dissolved an injunction against negotiation of the letters of credit. The U.S. Court of Appeals for the Second Circuit (per Timbers, J.) affirmed and *held:* (1) that defendants were agencies or instrumentalities of Romania within the meaning of section 1603(b) of the Foreign Sovereign Immunities Act (28 U.S.C. §§1330, 1602–1611 (1976)) (FSIA), (2) that defendants had not explicitly waived immunity from prejudgment attachment in accordance with section 1610(d)(1) of the Act, and (3) that the district court had correctly refused to grant, by injunction, relief which it was prohibited from providing by attachment.

Section 1603 of the FSIA provides that for most purposes of the Act a "foreign state" includes an "agency or instrumentality" of the foreign state. As a threshold determination, the court concluded that the defendants qualified as agencies or instrumentalities of Romania, observing that the legislative history of the Act specifically identified state trading corporations and central banks as the kinds of entities intended to be included within the meaning of these terms.[1]

Turning to the central issue of the case, the court considered whether defendants were entitled to the protection of section 1609 of the Act, which provides that, subject to certain enumerated exceptions, "property in the United States of a foreign state shall be immune from attachment arrest and execution." One exception to this rule is contained in section 1610(d)(1) of the Act, which provides, *inter alia,* that the property of a foreign state used for commercial activity in the United States shall not be immune from attachment prior to the entry of judgment if the foreign state has "explicitly waived its immunity" from such attachment. Plaintiff claimed that an explicit waiver of immunity could be found in the "Business Facilitation" clause of the subsisting United States-Romania trade agreement, which states that:

> Nationals, firms, companies, and economic organizations of either Party shall be afforded access to all courts and, when applicable, to administrative bodies as plaintiffs or defendants, or otherwise, in accordance with the laws in force in the territory of such other Party. *They shall not claim or enjoy immunities from suit or execution of judgment or other liability in the territory of the other Party* with respect to commercial or financial transactions, except as may be provided in other bilateral agreements.[2]

The court of appeals disagreed, holding that "waivers of immunity from suit or from execution of judgment have no bearing upon the question of immunity

[1] *See* H.R. Rep. No. 1487, 94th Cong., 2d Sess. 15–16, *reprinted in* 1976 U.S. Code Cong. & Ad. News 6604, 6614.

[2] Agreement on Trade Relations between the United States and the Romanian Government, April 2, 1975, Art. IV, para. 2, 26 UST 2305, 2308–09, TIAS No. 8159 (emphasis added).

from prejudgment attachment."[3] The court observed that the only language in the treaty that might be construed as a waiver of immunity from such attachment was the phrase "other liability in the territory of the other Party." However, relying upon dictum in its previous decision in *Libra Bank Ltd. v. Banco Nacional de Costa Rica,*[4] the court held that the phrase "other liability" does not explicitly waive immunity from prejudgment attachment. It is by no means clear, the court reasoned, that prejudgment attachments are liabilities; rather, the better view is that such attachments are provisional remedies authorized to assure that prevailing parties will have meaningful recoveries. Thus, the court held that the phrase "other liability" does not unequivocally express the will of the parties to waive immunity from prejudgment attachment. In reaching this conclusion, the court reiterated its holding in *Libra Bank* that section 1610(d)(1) does not require the verbatim recitation of the words "prejudgment attachment"; it does, however, require that the asserted waiver "demonstrate unambiguously" the foreign sovereign's intention.[5]

Finally, the court ruled that once the lower court had correctly determined that defendants were protected from prejudgment attachment, it properly refused to sanction any other means to effect the same result, since the FSIA would become meaningless if courts could eviscerate its protections merely by denominating their restraints as injunctions rather than attachments.

The instant case does little to clarify the meaning of the term explicit waiver of prejudgment attachment. Although it is well established that the words "prejudgment attachment" need not appear in a document in order to meet the requirement of section 1610(d)(1), the Second Circuit has again[6] declined to be more explicit in its own reasoning. Such narrow case-by-case interpretations of section 1610(d)(1) do little to guide potential litigants into sound contracts or to reduce the need for judicial involvement in commercial affairs.

Political question doctrine—act of state doctrine—role of the United States in foreign military sales—application of U.S. antitrust laws to military sales

NORTHROP CORPORATION v. MCDONNELL DOUGLAS CORPORATION. 705 F.2d 1030.
U.S. Court of Appeals, 9th Cir., February 28, 1983, as amended May 9, 1983.

This case involved the applicability of the political question and act of state doctrines in an action alleging federal antitrust and related violations. Plaintiff,

[3] 706 F.2d 411, 417.

[4] 676 F.2d 47 (2d Cir. 1982), *summarized in* 76 AJIL 851 (1982).

[5] 706 F.2d at 416. In this respect, the court contrasted its present conclusion with that in *Libra Bank,* where it had construed the waiver of "any right or immunity for legal proceedings including suit judgment and execution" to constitute an explicit waiver of immunity from prejudgment attachment within the meaning of §1610(d)(1). The court also contrasted the explicit waiver requirement of §1610(d)(1) with the requirement of §1610(a) of the Act, which provides that a foreign state's immunity from attachment as an aid in the *execution* of a judgment can be waived implicitly as well as explicitly.

[6] *See* Libra Bank Ltd. v. Banco Nacional de Costa Rica, 676 F.2d 47 (2d Cir. 1982).

Northrop Corporation, and defendant, McDonnell Douglas Corporation, are competing manufacturers of military aircraft for sale to the United States and foreign governments. In 1974, at the request of the United States Government, the parties entered into teaming arrangements under which they agreed to cooperate in the development and production of military aircraft. Under this agreement, plaintiff was limited to marketing aircraft suitable for land-based operation, and defendant was limited to marketing carrier-based aircraft. Plaintiff's suit alleged that defendant's marketing of land-based aircraft to foreign countries violated the agreement and that it had lost potential sales as a result of such anticompetitive activities. The district court granted defendant's motions for dismissal and summary judgment.[1] The U.S. Court of Appeals for the Ninth Circuit (per Boochever, J.) reversed and *held, inter alia,* that neither the political question doctrine nor the act of state doctrine was a barrier to plaintiff's suit, and it remanded the case for further proceedings on the merits.[2]

In support of its argument that the political question doctrine barred the suit, defendant invoked three of the six determinative factors listed in the leading case of *Baker v. Carr.*[3] The court concluded, however, that, regardless of which of these factors were considered, the political question doctrine was not a bar to plaintiff's suit because the challenged activity was neither authorized nor directed by the United States; thus, there could be no conflict between the political branches and the judiciary with respect to the issues raised by plaintiff. Rather, plaintiff's claims presented "legal issues, involving private commercial activity which the judiciary is uniquely equipped to resolve."[4]

Defendant also argued that plaintiff's suit was barred by the act of state doctrine, which precludes U.S. courts from sitting in judgment on the acts of a foreign state.[5] Defendant contended that plaintiff's claim would require the court to review the procurement decisions of foreign sovereigns in order to decide whether defendant's conduct was causally connected to plaintiff's loss of foreign sales. Plaintiff conceded that military procurement decisions by foreign sovereigns are acts of state. It argued, however, and the court of appeals agreed, that the resolution of its claims would not necessitate direct judicial inquiry into such decisions. As determined by the court, plaintiff could adequately establish

[1] 498 F.Supp. 1112 (C.D. Cal. 1980), *summarized in* 75 AJIL 370 (1981).

[2] The court also reversed the lower court's dismissal of the defendant's counterclaim, which the lower court described as the "mirror image" of the plaintiff's complaint. 705 F.2d 1030, 1036, 1058–59.

[3] 369 U.S. 186 (1962). Defendant contended that the following three factors identified plaintiff's claim as involving a political question, thereby warranting dismissal: (1) the impossibility of deciding the case without expressing lack of respect for the coordinate branches of government; (2) the unusual need for adherence to a political decision already made; and (3) the potentiality for embarrassment to the executive branch from multifarious pronouncements by various governmental departments. 705 F.2d at 1046–47.

[4] 705 F.2d at 1047.

[5] The court noted that "[t]he act of state doctrine is essentially the foreign counterpart to the political question doctrine. Both doctrines require courts to defer to the executive or legislative branches of government when those branches are better equipped to handle a politically sensitive issue." *Id.* at 1046.

the *fact* that it had suffered damages by proving the increased costs associated with duplicating technology that defendant was contractually obligated to furnish to plaintiff. The court left open, however, the question whether plaintiff could ultimately establish the *amount* of its damages without implicating foreign procurement decisions, reserving this issue for determination on remand.[6] Finally, the court determined that even if plaintiff's harm from future misconduct could be measured solely by reference to lost sales, there was no reason to extend the act of state doctrine to future decisions by foreign governments. Thus, the court held that plaintiff would be entitled to an injunction barring defendant from selling its aircraft to foreign countries provided that the district court found a likelihood that defendant's actions would cost the plaintiff *some* amount of future sales—a finding that "would not create the foreign policy tensions that the act of state doctrine was designed to avoid."[7]

The court also rejected four additional arguments raised by defendant. First, defendant contended that 22 U.S.C. §2356 (1976) provided the exclusive statutory remedy for an action involving foreign military sales.[8] In rejecting this argument, the court pointed out that section 2356 by its terms applies only where proprietary information involving military equipment is disclosed. Section 2356 thus could not provide the exclusive remedy for all cases involving foreign military sales. Moreover, because plaintiff's suit did not seek relief based on unauthorized disclosures, section 2356 was inapplicable.

Second, defendant argued that the United States was a necessary party to the suit, whose joinder was required. The court concluded, however, that the United States was not a necessary party because (1) complete relief could be fashioned without joining the United States, and (2) the United States would not be prejudiced by a ruling in favor of plaintiff. With respect to the latter point, the court observed that defendant was not obligated to supply any aircraft to the United States; thus, enjoining defendant would not affect U.S. procurement policy any more than would a refusal by defendant to manufacture the aircraft for its own commercial reasons.

Third, defendant contended that it was entitled to summary judgment because the teaming arrangement upon which plaintiff based all of its claims was a *per se* antitrust violation. However, the court declined to apply *per se* treatment to the teaming arrangement on the ground that the agreement did not prohibit the parties from competing for sales of their respective versions

[6] *Cf.* Williams v. Curtiss-Wright, 694 F.2d 300, 304 (3d Cir. 1982), *summarized in* 77 AJIL 624 (1983).

[7] 705 F.2d at 1048.

[8] 22 U.S.C. §2356 provides in pertinent part:

> (a) Whenever, in connection with the furnishing of assistance under this chapter—
>
> . . .
>
> (2) information, which is (A) protected by law, . . . is disclosed by the United States Government or any of its officers, employees, or agents in violation of such restrictions,
>
> the exclusive remedy of the owner . . . is to sue the United States Government for reasonable and entire compensation for such practice or disclosure in the district court . . . or in the Court of Claims. . . .

of the jointly developed aircraft. Moreover, given the nature of the military weapons industry, the agreement was likely to have procompetitive effects. Thus, a rule-of-reason analysis was required, and the contested facts in the record precluded summary judgment on the issue of whether the agreement was in fact reasonable.

Finally, defendant argued that transactions involving commercial military sales were immune from the antitrust laws because of the pervasive regulation governing the industry. The court rejected this argument, reasoning that the statutes and regulations governing commercial military sales themselves evinced an intent not to modify or eclipse application of the antitrust laws.[9] In this connection the court also observed that the inadequacy or nonexistence of agency structures to remedy anticompetitive behavior in the military aircraft industry militated against the granting of such immunity.

This case represents the most comprehensive rejection to date of the notion that manufacturers or sellers of military weapons are subject to legal standards different from those applicable to manufacturers or sellers of other commercial products.[10] As the court's opinion ably demonstrates, a dispute such as the one involving Northrop and McDonnell Douglas can be resolved by the courts without posing a threat to U.S. policy and without requiring U.S. courts to sit in judgment on acts of foreign countries.

Sovereign immunity—alien as plaintiff under Foreign Sovereign Immunities Act—"arising under" clause of Article III of the U.S. Constitution

VERLINDEN B.V. v. CENTRAL BANK OF NIGERIA. 103 S.Ct. 1962.
U.S. Supreme Court, May 23, 1983.

This suit between an alien plaintiff and a foreign sovereign defendant provided the U.S. Supreme Court with its first opportunity to examine in depth the jurisdictional aspects of the Foreign Sovereign Immunities Act of 1976 (28 U.S.C. §§1330, 1602–1611 (1976)) (FSIA). Plaintiff Verlinden B.V., a Dutch corporation, brought suit under the FSIA in federal district court against the Central Bank of Nigeria, an agency of the Nigerian Government. The complaint sought damages for an anticipatory breach of an irrevocable letter of credit established in Verlinden's favor with the Morgan Guaranty Bank in New York. Judge Weinfeld in the Southern District of New York held that the Act contemplates suits by an alien plaintiff against a foreign sovereign, but dismissed the instant action because the controversy did not have sufficient contacts with the United States to meet any of the standards of the FSIA for assertion of jurisdiction over the defendant.[1]

[9] 705 F.2d at 1057 (citing 10 U.S.C. §§2301 *et seq.*, 22 U.S.C. §§2751 *et seq.*, 22 C.F.R. §§121.01 *et seq.*, 32 C.F.R. §§1–100 *et seq.*).

[10] *Cf. Williams, supra* note 6 (rejecting act of state defense in antitrust suit between competing manufacturers of military weapons).

[1] 488 F.Supp. 1284 (S.D.N.Y. 1980).

The Court of Appeals for the Second Circuit affirmed on a different ground.[2] It held that, insofar as the Act authorized suits by alien plaintiffs against foreign sovereigns, it exceeded the scope of Article III of the U.S. Constitution. In its view, neither the diversity clause nor the "arising under" clause of Article III was broad enough to support jurisdiction over actions by foreign plaintiffs against foreign sovereigns. In particular, it held that because sovereign immunity was a defense to be raised affirmatively by the defendant, the case did not "arise under" the FSIA.

In a unanimous decision, the U.S. Supreme Court reversed and *held:* that the FSIA authorizes suits brought by alien plaintiffs against foreign sovereigns and that Congress possessed sufficient power under Article III of the Constitution to vest the federal courts with jurisdiction over such suits. In brief, the Court reasoned that such suits "arise under" federal law within the meaning of Article III because in every suit brought under the FSIA the district court is required to apply the substantive rules of immunity provided by the Act.[3]

Chief Justice Burger's opinion for the Court began by examining the origin and structure of the FSIA. The Court pointed out that after the U.S. Government adopted the restrictive theory of sovereign immunity in 1952, "foreign nations often placed diplomatic pressure on the State Department," and, on occasion, "political considerations led to suggestions of immunity in cases where immunity would not have been available under the restrictive theory."[4] In addition, in cases in which the State Department did not participate, courts were left to make determinations of immunity by reference to prior State Department decisions. This split of authority between the executive and judicial branches had led to governing standards that were "neither clear nor uniformly applied."[5]

The Court noted that the FSIA was enacted in order to free the Government from these case-by-case diplomatic pressures, to clarify the governing standards and to assure litigants that decisions would be made on purely legal grounds under fair procedures. Thus, the FSIA contains a "comprehensive set of legal standards governing claims of immunity"[6] in all civil actions. "For the most part," the Court observed, "the Act codifies, as a matter of federal law, the restrictive theory of sovereign immunity."[7] Accordingly, a foreign state is generally immune from the jurisdiction of U.S. courts unless the case falls within one of the exceptions specified in the Act.

The Supreme Court agreed with the courts below that the Act by its terms authorizes a foreign plaintiff to bring suit against a foreign sovereign in federal

[2] 647 F.2d 320 (2d Cir. 1981) (per Kaufman, C.J.), *summarized in* 75 AJIL 965 (1981).

[3] The defendant Central Bank of Nigeria refused to argue before the U.S. Supreme Court. However, the Supreme Court appointed the attorney for an amicus curiae, the Republic of Guinea, to argue in support of the decision below. The Republic of Guinea has been involved in litigation raising similar issues. *See* Maritime Int'l Nominees Establishment v. Republic of Guinea, 693 F.2d 1094 (D.C. Cir. 1982), *summarized in* 77 AJIL 318 (1983).

[4] 103 S.Ct. 1962, 1968.

[5] *Ibid.*

[6] *Ibid.*

[7] *Ibid.*

court, observing that the language of 28 U.S.C. §1330(a), vesting the federal district courts[8] with jurisdiction over "any non-jury civil action against a foreign state . . . with respect to which the foreign state is not entitled to immunity," contains no indication of any limitation based on the citizenship of the plaintiff. The Court also concluded that "considered as a whole, the legislative history reveals an intent not to limit jurisdiction under the Act to actions brought by American citizens."[9] In this respect, the Court acknowledged the concern expressed at congressional hearings that U.S. courts might be turned into small "international courts of claims" if alien plaintiffs could bring suit under the Act; it pointed out, however, that "Congress protected against this danger not by restricting the class of potential plaintiffs, but rather by enacting substantive provisions requiring some form of substantial contact with the United States."[10]

Turning to the "core question" of whether Congress had exceeded its Article III powers in authorizing suits by foreign plaintiffs, the Court reasoned that an action against a foreign sovereign "arises under" federal law because such a lawsuit "necessarily raises questions of substantive federal law at the very outset."[11] In every such action, the court must apply the standards for immunity under the FSIA, since subject matter jurisdiction depends on the existence of one of the specified exceptions. The Court rejected the reasoning of the court below—that the federal question must appear on the face of a well-pleaded complaint—on the ground that the "well-pleaded complaint" rule was developed in cases construing the "arising under" language of a statute (28 U.S.C. §1331) rather than a constitutional provision.[12]

The Court also rejected the appeals court's view that the FSIA was simply a jurisdictional statute. While acknowledging that some prior cases had stated that a federal case could not "arise under" a purely jurisdictional statute,[13] the Court found that the FSIA involved an exercise of Congress's Article I

[8] The FSIA contemplates that its standards will be applied in both federal and state courts. *Id.* at 1969. However, in view of the political sensitivity of such cases and the importance of developing a uniform body of law, the Act guarantees to foreign states the right to remove any action to federal court (28 U.S.C. §1441(d)) and specifically provides that any claim against a foreign sovereign may be brought in federal court at the outset (28 U.S.C. §1330(a)). *Ibid.*

[9] *Ibid.*

[10] *Id.* at 1970. The Court noted that the Act also contains an exception for cases in which sovereign immunity had been waived, 28 U.S.C. §1605(a)(1), but the Court characterized this provision as "an exception to the normal pattern of the Act, which generally requires some form of contact with the United States." *Id.* at 1959 n.15. The Court reserved the question whether, by waiving its immunity, a foreign state could consent to suit based on activities wholly unrelated to the United States. In addition, the Court noted that the traditional doctrine of *forum non conveniens* did not appear to have been affected by the Act.

[11] *Id.* at 1971. The Court acknowledged that the relevant House report (H.R. REP. NO. 1487, 94th Cong., 2d Sess. 17 (1976)) states that sovereign immunity must be pleaded as an affirmative defense, but reasoned that, because subject matter jurisdiction turns on the existence of an exception to foreign sovereign immunity, the district court must determine that immunity is unavailable regardless of whether the foreign state enters an appearance. 103 S.Ct. at 1971 n.20. *See* Ipitrade Int'l v. Federal Republic of Nigeria, 465 F.Supp. 824 (D.D.C. 1978).

[12] 103 S.Ct. at 1971–72 (citing Louisville & Nashville R. Co. v. Mottley, 211 U.S. 149 (1908); Gully v. First Nat'l Bank, 299 U.S. 109 (1936)).

[13] 103 S.Ct. at 1972–73 (citing Mossman v. Higginson, 4 U.S. (4 Dall.) 12 (1800); The Propeller Genesee Chief v. Fitzhugh, 53 U.S. (12 How.) 443, 451–53 (1852)).

powers and that it set forth a comprehensive set of rules governing immunity. Because the FSIA "codifies the standards governing foreign sovereign immunity as an aspect of substantive federal law,"[14] every action against a foreign sovereign "necessarily involves application of a body of substantive federal law, and accordingly 'arises under' federal law, within the meaning of Article III."[15]

Finally, the Court held that the instant action could proceed only if one of the statutory exceptions from immunity were satisfied. Although the district court had held that the action did not fall within any of these exceptions, the court of appeals had not reached this issue. Accordingly, the Court remanded the case to the court of appeals for a determination as to whether jurisdiction existed under one of the exceptions set forth in the Act.[16]

From the perspective of U.S. constitutional law, reversal of the court of appeals decision was important in order to establish that Congress's power to grant jurisdiction to the federal courts was not limited by the narrow interpretation accorded to the "arising under" language of 28 U.S.C. §1331. However, in holding that an alien plaintiff is entitled to invoke the Act, the Supreme Court did not find that Congress had intended to encourage such suits. Rather, the Court identified several means through which suits by alien plaintiffs can be limited to those having substantial contact with the United States, including careful application of the exceptions to immunity set forth in the Act and invocation of the doctrine of *forum non conveniens.* Assuming that the Act is applied in this way, the *Verlinden* decision may prove of primary benefit to foreign subsidiaries of U.S. corporations, which may be better able than other alien plaintiffs to meet the minimum jurisdictional contacts requirements of the federal courts.

Sovereign immunity—offset of value of nationalized property against commercial debt—burden of proving taking in violation of international law

ALBERTI v. EMPRESA NICARAGUENSE DE LA CARNE. 705 F.2d 250. U.S. Court of Appeals, 7th Cir., April 18, 1983.

In this action for wrongful conversion and request for a declaratory judgment, plaintiffs sought to offset the value of expropriated property against a commercial debt. Plaintiffs had previously owned 35 percent of a Nicaraguan corporation engaged in beef slaughtering and packaging. In 1979, the Government of Nicaragua nationalized the business and began operating it as Empresa Nicaraguense de la Carne (ENCAR). Plaintiffs were not compensated

[14] 103 S.Ct. at 1973.

[15] *Ibid.*

[16] In this regard, the Court noted that the court of appeals had upheld jurisdiction in several related cases in which it found a "direct effect" on the United States from Nigeria's commercial activity. *See, e.g.,* Texas Trading & Milling Corp. v. Federal Republic of Nigeria, 647 F.2d 300, 310–13 (2d Cir. 1981), *cert. denied,* 454 U.S. 1148 (1982), *summarized in* 75 AJIL 968 (1981). However, the Court stressed that these cases involved claims by *American* suppliers operating within the *United States.* 103 S.Ct. at 1974.

for their expropriated stock, valued at over one million dollars. Thereafter, plaintiff Alberti International ordered beef from defendant ENCAR, which was delivered to plaintiff in Florida. Plaintiff did not pay the amount owed for the beef, approximately $740,000.

Plaintiffs filed an action in Illinois state court seeking recovery for wrongful conversion of plaintiffs' interest in the meat-slaughtering business and seeking a declaratory judgment approving plaintiffs' right to offset the value of their stock against the value of the beef purchased. The action was removed to federal district court where defendants moved to dismiss on grounds of improper service of process, lack of subject matter jurisdiction, lack of personal jurisdiction, and the act of state doctrine. The lower court granted the motion on all grounds without opinion. The U.S. Court of Appeals for the Seventh Circuit (per Pell, J.) affirmed and *held:* that under the Foreign Sovereign Immunities Act (28 U.S.C. §§1330, 1602–1611 (1976)) (FSIA), defendants were immune from suit and that the district court consequently lacked subject matter and personal jurisdiction.

Plaintiffs argued that defendants were subject to suit under section 1605(a)(2) of the FSIA, which provides an exception to sovereign immunity in cases where an action is "based upon a commercial activity carried on in the United States by the foreign state." The court disagreed, finding that there was no controversy regarding plaintiffs' commercial debt; rather, the dispute was based on the "quintessential Government act" of nationalization. Accordingly, the court declined to permit the transformation of a governmental dispute into a commercial one through the "simple expedient of attempting to offset an unrelated commercial debt."[1]

The court also rejected plaintiffs' reliance on section 1607(c) of the Act, which removes immunity with respect to counterclaims when a foreign state brings suit in U.S. courts. The court ruled that this section expressly requires that the foreign state initiate the action and that a preemptive declaratory judgment action cannot serve as a counterclaim.[2]

Finally, the court considered plaintiffs' argument that the suit should proceed on the basis of section 1605(a)(3) of the Act, which provides that a foreign state is not immune if "rights in property taken in violation of international law are in issue," and the property is owned or operated by an agency or instrumentality of the foreign state which is engaged in commercial activity in the United States. The court observed that there are "differences of opinion between the various nations and commentators" regarding the form, timing and calculation of compensation for nationalization; the "generally accepted formulation is that the expropriating nation must provide 'prompt, adequate and effective' compensation."[3] The court acknowledged that "there is little agreement on the meaning of these terms,"[4] and proceeded to consider whether international law requires

[1] 705 F.2d 250, 254.

[2] The court noted, however, that plaintiffs were free to file a counterclaim and raise the §1607(c) argument in a pending lawsuit in Florida, which had been brought by defendant ENCAR to recover on the commercial debt. *Ibid.*

[3] *Id.* at 255.

[4] *Ibid.*

actual payment prior to or immediately upon nationalization. Looking to the legislative history of the FSIA, as well as various commentators, the court concluded that the expropriating nation must only afford property owners a means of obtaining payment within a reasonable time after nationalization.

The parties disputed whether Nicaragua had established such procedures, but the court found it unnecessary to answer this question. Rather, drawing on the legislative history of the FSIA, the court held that defendant had to establish a prima facie case of immunity, by proving: (1) that it is a "foreign state" as defined by the FSIA, and (2) that plaintiff's claim relates to a "public act."[5] If the defendant demonstrates these elements, the court reasoned, the burden of going forward shifts to the plaintiff to rebut the presumption of immunity, which it may do by offering evidence that one of the statutory exceptions to immunity (*i.e.*, one of the exceptions found at sections 1605–1607 of the Act) applies.

The court noted that the term "public act" is circularly defined in the legislative history as "an act not within the exceptions in sections 1605–1607."[6] Reasoning that it would be nearly impossible and, in any case, wasteful for a defendant to prove the inapplicability of each such exception, the court ruled that defendants need only demonstrate that the suit related to a governmental act of the foreign state. The court held that, in the present case, the undisputed fact that a nationalization was involved was sufficient to show the requisite governmental act; defendants did not have to make the more particularized showing that the act was not in violation of international law. Therefore, the burden had shifted to plaintiffs, who "could easily indicate which [statutory] exception is applicable and produce minimal support as to its applicability" by affidavit or otherwise.[7] Because plaintiffs had presented no evidence that a statutory exception was applicable, the court found that they had failed to rebut defendants' prima facie showing of immunity. Accordingly, the court concluded that the district court lacked subject matter and personal jurisdiction over defendants.[8]

This is the first appellate decision that addresses in detail the practical issues of proving the applicability of the immunity exceptions of the FSIA.[9] The Act, as the court noted, appears to contemplate that a defendant prove a negative, *i.e.*, that the exceptions to sovereign immunity do not apply. As the court points out, however, plaintiff's identification of its claimed exceptions

[5] *Id.* at 256 (quoting H.R. REP. NO. 1487, 94th Cong., 2d Sess. 17, *reprinted in* 1976 U.S. CODE CONG. & AD. NEWS 6604, 6616 [hereinafter cited as House Report]).

[6] 705 F.2d at 256.

[7] *Ibid.*

[8] The court of appeals also vacated for lack of jurisdiction the district court's decision that the act of state doctrine precluded recovery. In addition, the court expressly affirmed the lower court's holding that service of process by mail upon the Nicaraguan Ambassador to the United States in Washington, D.C. was defective under §1608 of the FSIA.

[9] *Cf.* Arango v. Guzman Travel Advisors Corp., 621 F.2d 1371, 1378 (5th Cir. 1980), in which the U.S. Court of Appeals for the Fifth Circuit noted, without close discussion, the foreign state's burden of proving the "non-applicability of specified exceptions." Lower courts have imposed the burden of producing evidence on the foreign state. *See, e.g.*, Matter of Sedco, Inc., 543 F.Supp.

minimizes unnecessary uncertainty and avoids wasting time. Significantly, the court took the additional step of requiring the plaintiffs to make a specific evidentiary showing that an exception applies, thereby protecting the foreign state from the costs of meeting meritless claims. The effect of this protective measure is to place both the responsibility for producing evidence and the risk of nonproduction upon the plaintiff. It should be observed that while the FSIA plan, as explained in the legislative history, may have posed some practical difficulties, the court's solution departs from the FSIA's allocation of the burden of proof to the foreign state invoking immunity.[10] At least in this case, where there was no dispute regarding the fact of nationalization, the court effectively eliminated the foreign state's burden by requiring only a general statement by defendant to prove a prima facie case of immunity.

Decisions of the Iran-United States Claims Tribunal

Expropriation—standard of compensation

ITT Industries, Inc. v. The Islamic Republic of Iran. AWD 47-156-2 (concurring opinion of George H. Aldrich).
Iran-United States Claims Tribunal, The Hague, May 26, 1983.

Claimant, ITT Industries, Inc., a U.S. corporation, filed a claim against respondent, the Islamic Republic of Iran, in the Iran-United States Claims Tribunal,[1] alleging that respondent had expropriated its 25 percent equity interest in an Iranian corporation, IKD Iran. Claimant alleged that such expropriation occurred when respondent, pursuant to Iranian law, assumed control of the company by appointing all members of the Board of Directors, thereby ousting the directors elected by the shareholders, including the one director selected by claimant.[2] Following a hearing before Chamber Two of the Tribunal, but prior to the issuance of the Chamber's award, the parties agreed to settle the claim and filed a Joint Request for an Arbitral Award on Agreed Terms, which was accepted by the Chamber.[3] George H. Aldrich, the American member

---

561 (S.D. Tex. 1982); De Sanchez v. Banco Central de Nicaragua, 515 F.Supp. 900 (E.D. La. 1981); Jet Line Services, Inc. v. M/V Marsa El Hariga, 462 F.Supp. 1165 (D.Md. 1978).

[10] *See* House Report, *supra* note 5, at 6616.

[1] For background information on the Iran-United States Claims Tribunal, see 77 AJIL 642 (1983).

[2] Respondent's action was taken pursuant to the Legal Bill Concerning the Appointment of Provisional Director or Directors for Supervising Production, Industrial, Commercial, Agricultural and Service Units Whether in Public or Private Sector of June 14, 1979 and the Protection and Development of Iranian Industries Act of July 7, 1979. Article 2 of the Bill provides that, upon appointment of directors, "the earlier directors and persons in charge will be stripped of their competence" and "[s]hareholders are not allowed in any way to appoint directors in their stead."

[3] Pursuant to Article 34(1) of the Tribunal's Rules of Procedure, if, before an award is made, the parties agree on a settlement of the dispute, they may request that the Tribunal accept the settlement and record it in the form of an arbitral award on agreed terms. In Case No. A/1, Aug. 3, 1982, the Tribunal held that Article 34 allows the Tribunal to approve a settlement after making such examination concerning its jurisdiction as it deems necessary. It also held that while

of Chamber Two, filed a concurring opinion to the award,[4] in which he concluded, first, that the assumption of control of IKD Iran's Board of Directors by Government appointees constituted an expropriation of claimant's property and, second, that the taking warranted prompt, adequate and effective compensation, which he valued at 75 percent of the par value of claimant's quantum of ownership of the company's stock.

In determining that an expropriation had occurred, Aldrich observed that property may be taken under international law through interference by a state in the use or enjoyment of that property, "even where legal title to the property is not affected." Relying on a variety of international legal authorities, he declared that while the assumption of control over property by a government does not automatically justify a conclusion that the property has been taken by the government, "such a conclusion is warranted whenever events demonstrate that the owner was deprived of fundamental rights of ownership and it appears that this deprivation is not merely ephemeral."

Turning to the relevant facts at issue, Aldrich found that over 2 years after respondent's assumption of control, claimant had received no profits of the company, no opportunity to participate in its management and no information on its financial affairs. Moreover, claimant had been given no reason to believe that it would soon, if ever, be offered restoration of its property rights. Thus, while Aldrich did not question respondent's right to appoint directors for the company pursuant to Iranian laws, he concluded that by doing so, respondent had rendered claimant's rights of ownership "so meaningless as to be the equivalent of an expropriation of those rights."[5]

With respect to the appropriate measure of compensation, claimant urged adopting the standard contained in the Treaty of Amity between Iran and the United States,[6] while respondent contended that even if the Treaty was still in force (which it questioned), it was inapplicable in this case because the claim at issue was owned indirectly through a Swedish subsidiary. Aldrich determined, however, that the treaty issue need not be decided because "the applicable rules of international law are not significantly different" whether the Treaty of Amity is applied or not.[7] In either case, "a taking of property

---

the Tribunal will not review the reasonableness of the settlement, it can refuse to record a settlement if it does not appear to be appropriate in view of the framework provided by the Algiers Accords.

[4] Aldrich stated that his rationale for issuing the opinion, despite the settlement of the claim, was his belief that the settlement should not "deprive the parties or the public of these views on important questions of international law," particularly since "the settlement may well have been inspired, at least in part, by the Respondent's desire to prevent these views from appearing in the Award."

[5] Citing Barcelona Traction, Light & Power Co., Ltd. (Belgium v. Spain), 1970 ICJ REP. 3, 36 (Judgment of Feb. 5).

[6] Treaty of Amity, Economic Relations and Consular Rights between the United States and Iran, Aug. 15, 1955, 8 UST 899, TIAS No. 3853.

[7] Aldrich noted, however, that the International Court of Justice held that the Treaty was still in force in 1980. *See* Case Concerning United States Diplomatic and Consular Staff in Tehran (U.S. v. Iran), 1980 ICJ REP. 3, 28 (Judgment of May 24).

must be accompanied by the prompt payment of just compensation which is effective and adequate to compensate fully for the value of the property taken." Turning to the measure of compensation in the instant case, Aldrich found that "[i]n the absence of a market to determine market value, the Tribunal must endeavor to find the value of the company as a 'going concern' at the time of taking."[8] This value, he reasoned, is arrived at less by appeal to "theoretical constructs" than by analysis of the particular circumstances of the case.

In this connection, Aldrich rejected valuations asserted by both the respondent and the claimant, concluding that "the relevant date for the determination of value is the date of the taking." That Iran might experience revolution was "a risk assumed by investors in Iran, as in any country," Aldrich reasoned, and "any reduction in value of investments as a result of revolution cannot be ignored by the Tribunal." Thus, the Islamic Revolution was not a "wrong" for which claimant was entitled to compensation under international law; and in computing compensation, the Tribunal's task was to ascertain the real value at the moment of taking, "excluding only any decline in value resulting from the threat of taking or other acts attributable to the Government itself."

As for the assigning of a currency figure to compensate claimant for the expropriated value of its investment, Aldrich observed that the Tribunal would generally have to decide whether to appoint an expert or to make its own best estimate of the evidence presented by the parties. As neither party in the present case had requested the appointment of an expert, Aldrich offered his own best estimate of the value of the property at issue, concluding that the real value of claimant's shares in IKD Iran had declined to approximately 75 percent of their par value.[9]

Force majeure—impossibility and frustration of contract—affirmative counterclaims

GOULD MARKETING, INC. v. MINISTRY OF NATIONAL DEFENSE OF IRAN. ITL 24-49-2.
Iran-United States Claims Tribunal, The Hague, July 27, 1983.

A claim for contract damages was filed by claimant, Gould Marketing, Inc., against respondent, the Iranian Ministry of National Defense, in the Iran-United States Claims Tribunal. The contract at issue required claimant to provide respondent with military radios and related services, including a field service representative on site in Iran, from 1976 to 1986. As a result of civil disturbances in Iran, claimant withdrew its field service representative in December 1978 but continued to provide factory repair services in the United States through August 1979. In June 1979, respondent failed to make a scheduled contract

[8] Citing Chorzów Factory case, 1928 PCIJ, ser. A, No. 17, at 47 (compensation defined as "the value of the undertaking at the moment of dispossession, plus interest to the date of payment").

[9] Aldrich estimated compensation on this basis in terms of Iranian rials; he did not, however, convert the amount into a dollar figure, provide a conversion rate, or discuss the time at which the exchange of currencies should be computed. Likewise, he did not address the issue of interest, though he alluded to it by quoting earlier in his opinion from the *Chorzów Factory* case. *See supra* note 8.

payment of over a million dollars. In its claim before the Tribunal, claimant sought damages for goods delivered and services rendered through 1979 and also for all future scheduled payments due from respondent for the term of the contract. Respondent disputed certain elements of claimant's alleged performance and contended that claimant had breached the contract by withdrawing its field service representative from Iran. In addition, respondent counterclaimed for approximately ten times the amount of the claim. In an interlocutory award,[1] Chamber Two *held*: that *force majeure* conditions prevailing in Iran during 1978–1979 justified nonperformance by both parties. The Chamber also determined, however, that a final award could not be rendered until additional arguments were heard "on the general question of what consequences should result from the discharge of the contract through frustration or impossibility."[2]

Before reaching the merits of the case, the Chamber considered two jurisdictional questions. The first was whether the Tribunal had jurisdiction over that portion of the claim seeking payments due under the contract subsequent to January 19, 1981. Article II(1) of the Claims Settlement Agreement, which establishes the scope of the Tribunal's jurisdiction with respect to claims by nationals of one country against the Government of the other,[3] confers jurisdiction for claims "outstanding" as of January 19, 1981, the date of the Agreement. Claimant contended that if it were unable to claim for payments due under the contract after January 19, 1981, it would be left without recourse against respondent with respect to such payments. Citing its award in *Kimberly-Clark Corp. v. Bank Markazi,*[4] Chamber Two rejected this argument, noting that while the Claims Settlement Agreement "deprives this Tribunal of jurisdiction over claims not outstanding on 19 January 1981, it does not purport to affect the jurisdiction of any other tribunals." Accordingly, the Chamber dismissed that portion of the claim relating to payments due after January 19, 1981.

The second preliminary issue was whether the Tribunal had jurisdiction over respondent's counterclaim to the extent it exceeded the amount of the claim. Claimant argued that since the Tribunal lacked jurisdiction over claims instituted by Iran against United States nationals,[5] it had no power to issue an affirmative award against claimant. In a precedential ruling, Chamber Two rejected claimant's argument, holding that "[s]o long as a counterclaim falls within the requirements of Article II(1), . . . the counterclaim is within our jurisdiction

[1] Article 32(1) of the Tribunal's Rules of Procedure authorizes the Tribunal to make "interim, interlocutory, or partial awards," in addition to final awards.

[2] Mr. Shafie Shafeiei, the Iranian member of Chamber Two, did not sign the award. In a statement appended to the award, Messrs. Bellet and Aldrich noted his absence. This statement recounts that Shafeiei had been notified of the Chamber's intention to devote the month of July to "final deliberations in this and the other pending cases, in view of the 1 August effective date of Chairman Bellet's resignation from the Tribunal." Noting that Shafeiei had absented himself, leaving no address or telephone number where he could be reached, Bellet and Aldrich stated that "an arbitral tribunal cannot permit its work to be frustrated" and issued the award without Shafeiei's signature.

[3] For background information on the Claims Settlement Agreement, see 77 AJIL 642 (1983).

[4] AWD 46-57-2 (May 25, 1983) (Chamber 2).

[5] *See* Case Concerning Jurisdiction of the Tribunal with Respect to Claims by the Islamic Republic of Iran against Nationals of the United States of America, No. A/2 (Dec. 21, 1981) (Full Tribunal).

even if it exceeds the amount of the claim." The Chamber concluded that since respondent's counterclaim arose directly out of the contract that constituted the subject matter of the claim, the counterclaim was within the Tribunal's jurisdiction.

Turning to the merits, the Chamber noted that claimant and respondent each denied the existence of *force majeure* conditions excusing the other's performance. Nevertheless, the Chamber determined that by December 1978 "classic *force majeure* conditions" existed in Iran's major cities. These conditions were defined by the Chamber as "social and economic forces *beyond the power of the state to control* through the exercise of due diligence."[6] As such, injuries caused by the operation of such forces are

> not attributable to the state for purposes of its responding for damages. Similarly, as between private parties, one party cannot claim against the other for injuries suffered as a result of delays in or cessation of performance during the time *force majeure* conditions prevail, unless the existence of these conditions is attributable to the fault of the respondent party.

The Chamber found that claimant had failed to prove that the *force majeure* conditions existing in Iran in 1978–1979 were attributable to acts for which the Government of Iran was responsible. Accordingly, just as these conditions excused claimant from maintaining its field service representative in Iran, "it also follows that the Ministry's failure to pay the June 1979 milestone [payment] must be similarly excused."[7] The Chamber also observed that a suspension of the parties' performance obligations "could not continue indefinitely," and found that by mid-1979 neither party could realistically hope for resumption of the other's performance. Accordingly, the Chamber concluded that the continued existence of *force majeure* conditions had, by mid-1979, "ripened into a termination of the . . . contract," since by that time "[p]erformance had become essentially impossible."

Having reached this conclusion, the Chamber determined that it could not issue a final award without considering additional questions concerning the consequences of the discharge of the contract through frustration or impossibility. These questions, on which the Chamber requested additional argument, included, *inter alia:* (1) Should the parties be left in the situation in which they found themselves after frustration of the contract, or should the Tribunal conduct an accounting to determine whether the claimant has been paid more or less than its performance would justify? (2) If an accounting were made, should experts be appointed by the Tribunal? (3) On what bases should such an accounting be made? and (4) How should such an accounting take into consideration the subsequent prohibition by the United States of exports to Iran of military equipment and services covered by the contract?[8]

[6] Emphasis added.

[7] In this respect, the Chamber observed in passing that the Islamic Republic was "to some extent in control of the direction of the revolution" during the months February through June 1979; it concluded, however, that claimant had failed to establish that such *force majeure* conditions had been transformed during those months into conditions sufficiently attributable to Iran to make its nonpayment in June 1979 a breach of contract.

[8] Chamber Two has scheduled oral argument on these questions for Oct. 29, 1983.

CURRENT DEVELOPMENTS

Discovery of Documentary and Other Evidence in a Foreign Country

There are substantial differences between attitudes in the United States and those in foreign jurisdictions towards litigation in general and pretrial discovery in particular. Thus, in the United States, there is a breadth of pretrial discovery that cannot be found in any other legal system. Moreover, factual investigation in the United States is largely controlled and conducted by the attorneys for the litigants rather than by the judiciary which, in many other legal systems, is responsible for such investigations in a litigated matter.

Thus, any American effort to discover evidence in a foreign country before trial meets at the outset attitudes and practices that are different from and often hostile to American attitudes and practices. These differences have an impact upon discovery abroad, as will appear later. Before considering this impact, however, it is helpful to present an overview of the devices through which the American practitioner may seek to secure evidence abroad.

Devices Available in the U.S. System for Discovery of Evidence Abroad

At the outset, it should be emphasized that the discovery devices most often used in U.S. litigation to secure evidence abroad are the rules of procedure of the court in question. Parties to the litigation use the applicable rules to force each other to give discovery of the scope and depth usual in American litigation. This approach has led to significant foreign responses—particularly blocking statutes. The sanctions for failure to comply with discovery demands appropriate under the court rules are sanctions imposed by the trial court; they may, in some instances, include the entry of judgment for the party that has been denied discovery.

Where, however, discovery from third parties not subject to the jurisdiction of the trial court is sought, the local discovery rules are generally not applicable and recourse must be had to international agreements. On the whole, however, such agreements play a role vastly less important than the court rules.

Multilateral Conventions. In 1964, before the United States was a party to any multilateral discovery convention, the Federal Rules of Civil Procedure were amended to provide foreign litigants, without any requirement of reciprocity, with wide federal assistance in obtaining evidence in the United States for use either here or abroad:[1]

> The amendments named the Department of State as a conduit for the receipt and transmission of letters of request. They authorized the use in the federal courts of evidence taken abroad in civil law countries, even if its form did not comply with the conventional formalities of our normal

[1] Rule 28(b); 28 U.S.C. §§1781 and 1782 were also amended.

rules of evidence. No country in the world has a more open and enlightened policy.[2]

A few years after these amendments, in October 1968, the Hague Convention on the Taking of Evidence Abroad in Civil or Commercial Matters was negotiated.[3] The Convention rests on the fundamental concept that it sought to find a method of gathering evidence "tolerable to the authorities of the State where it is taken and, at the same time, utilizable in the forum where the action will be tried."[4] The Convention entered into force for the United States on October 7, 1972.[5]

The Convention provides for three different methods of securing evidence abroad: (1) letters of request, (2) the use of consular agents, and (3) the use of commissioners. Since the purpose of this paper is not to examine the details of these mechanisms as such, they will not be discussed further here.

Although the Hague Convention has been available to litigants in American courts for more than a decade, there are relatively few significant judicial decisions dealing with the Convention. However, some issues of importance regarding its relation to local rules of civil procedure have been touched upon and are worthy of consideration.

First, it should be noted that Article 27 of the Convention provides that internal laws granting assistance to foreign courts upon terms more favorable than those contained in the Convention are preserved. Therefore, foreign litigants, whether or not of contracting parties, may avail themselves of more liberal federal and state provisions for obtaining evidence and are not restricted to the Convention.

What, however, is the position of an American litigant seeking evidence abroad? Should he be required to have prior resort to the Convention before using local discovery procedures? This question was considered by the Court of Appeals, First District, of California in *Volkswagenwerk A.G. v. Superior Court.*[6] In that case, Volkswagenwerk (VW) was properly joined as a defendant in a California action for bodily injuries and loss of consortium. Over its objection, the trial court had entered a discovery order pursuant to the local rules that would have required VW to permit inspection of its plant and documentary records, and to give other discovery, in Wolfsburg, West Germany. VW sought review of the trial court's order arguing, *inter alia,* that the discovery order encroached impermissibly upon the judicial sovereignty of West Germany. The court of appeals reversed the trial court. It looked at the federal cases and summarized their results as follows:

[2] Amram, *The Proposed Convention on the Taking of Evidence Abroad,* 55 A.B.A.J. 651 (1969).

[3] 23 UST 2555, TIAS No. 7444.

[4] *See* Report of the U.S. Delegation on the Convention, 8 ILM 804, 806 (1969).

[5] This is the only multilateral convention on this subject to which the United States is a party. It should be noted, however, that the United States has participated in the negotiation of the Inter-American Convention on Letters Rogatory, 14 ILM 328 (1975). This Convention and its Additional Protocol of 1980 were signed by the United States, but neither has yet been ratified. On the Protocol, see Trooboff, Current Developments Note, 73 AJIL 704 (1979).

[6] 123 Cal. App. 3d 840, 176 Cal. Rptr. 874 (App. 1982).

> Federal cases which have dealt with procedures tantamount to international discovery have generally recognized that what is required is a case-by-case process of balancing the interests of the respective sovereignties to reach an appropriate "accommodation of the principles of the law of the forum with the concepts of due process and international comity." (Cf., e.g., *In re Westinghouse Elec. Corp. Uranium, etc.* (10th Cir. 1977) 563 F.2d 992, 996–999; *Arthur Andersen & Co. v. Finesilver* (10th Cir. 1976) 546 F.2d 338, 341–342.) The same federal cases also generally affirm in the first instance the jurisdictional power of federal courts to order a party *to give discovery* in another country, and generally apply the "balancing approach" only when the responding party has failed to give full discovery and seeks to avoid *sanctions* by asserting the conflict of sovereign demands upon it. (*Ibid.;* cf. also *Societe Internationale v. Rogers* (1958) 357 U.S. 197, 211–212. . . .)[7]

After noting that it agreed with the approach of the federal cases, the court of appeals suggested that the "balancing approach" should be used initially rather than only after compliance with the discovery order has been refused. It concluded that "the trial court, in the exercise of judicial restraint based on international comity, should have declined to proceed other than under the Hague Convention at this stage."[8]

This is an interesting approach which, in terms of international comity and the spirit underlying the Hague Convention, has much to recommend it. The impact of this decision on the relation between local court rules and the Hague Convention has not yet fully emerged; the court's recommendation in the *Volkswagenwerk* case could be a significant departure.

The Californian courts did not, however, take into account an aspect of the Hague Convention that may checkmate the approach suggested in *Volkswagenwerk.* Article 23 of the Convention provides that a contracting state may declare in connection with its adherence to the Convention that it will not execute letters of request issued for the purpose of obtaining pretrial discovery of documents as known in common law countries. With the exception of the United States, all contracting states, including West Germany, have made such declarations. In *Volkswagenwerk* the plaintiff was seeking pretrial discovery of documents located in West Germany. In view of West Germany's reservation under Article 23 of the Convention, therefore, a German court could have refused to execute a letter of request.

A second issue of significance is whether Articles 11 and 21 of the Convention, which permit a person to refuse to give evidence if it is prohibited by the law of the state of execution, have an effect upon discovery sought without the aid of the Convention. In *Compagnie Francaise d'Assurance v. Phillips Petroleum Co.,*[9] an American defendant sought an order pursuant to Rule 37(a) of the Federal Rules to compel a French plaintiff to produce documents located in France. The production of such documents was precluded by French

[7] 176 Cal. Rptr. at 884.

[8] *Id.* at 885. *Accord,* Pierburg GmbH & Co. KG v. Superior Court of Los Angeles County, 137 Cal. App. 3d 240, 186 Cal. Rptr. 876 (App. 1982).

[9] No. 81 Civ. 4463 (S.D.N.Y. Jan. 24, 1983).

law. The plaintiff argued that the court had "to decline to order the requested discovery" because of Articles 11 and 21 of the Convention.

Although both the United States and France had signed the Convention, the court rejected the argument because "nothing in the legislative history of the Hague Convention nor in the Congressional proceedings at the time of its adoption, suggests that Congress intended to replace, restrict, modify or repeal the Federal Rules."[10] The approach of the *Volkswagenwerk* case, of course, postpones consideration of this issue by its conclusion that international comity requires initial resort to the Convention.

A third question of interest is the effect of the Convention upon the application of the doctrine of *forum non conveniens.* At least one court has held that the existence of the Convention is not sufficient to tip the scales in favor of the United States court as a convenient forum. The United States Court of Appeals for the District of Columbia, in *Pain, et al. v. United Technologies Corp.,*[11] held that the trial court had correctly dismissed a consolidated wrongful death action brought by American, French, Norwegian, British and Canadian plaintiffs against the designer and manufacturer of a helicopter that crashed into the North Sea while en route from Bergen, Norway to an offshore drilling platform. The court, although recognizing that the Convention provides a compulsory system to obtain evidence abroad, emphasized that the numerous exceptions that can be raised by the requested state render that system "far from perfect," and it also noted the "exceedingly high" cost of obtaining evidence abroad. It concluded that the action should be dismissed upon the agreement of the defendant to waive the statute of limitations and concede liability with respect to any suit brought in a foreign country.

A federal district court used the Convention differently in *Hodson v. A. H. Robins Co., Inc., et al.*[12] In that case, English citizens sought to recover for injuries allegedly caused by an intrauterine contraceptive device manufactured by A. H. Robins Company, Inc. (Robins) in Virginia and inserted and removed by British physicians in the United Kingdom. Robins argued that plaintiffs' medical records and other evidence on the issues of causation and the extent of the plaintiffs' damages were located in England, beyond the subpoena power of the court. The court looked, in part, to the Hague Convention in denying Robins's motion:

> Furthermore, some of the necessary evidence located in the United Kingdom can be obtained through the channels of international judicial assistance available under the Hague Convention on the Taking of Evidence Abroad, to which the United States and the United Kingdom are signatories. The Convention provides for the use of a letter of request or letter rogatory to obtain evidence where the compulsory powers of a foreign court are needed. Of course, this system is less than perfect and will not completely replicate the access to evidence which would exist if all relevant material were located in this country, but does provide the parties to a trial here reasonable procedures by which to obtain evidence

[10] *Id.*, slip op. at 11.
[11] 637 F.2d 775 (D.C. Cir. 1980).
[12] 528 F.Supp. 809 (E.D. Va. 1981).

present in a foreign forum. Deficiencies would likewise exist if the situation were reversed, and the trials held in England.[13]

Bilateral Agreements. The United States has concluded a number of bilateral treaties for mutual assistance in the administration of justice involving investigation into certain specific matters, as, for example, the improper payments allegedly made overseas by the Boeing Company,[14] the Lockheed Aircraft Corporation,[15] and others.[16]

These agreements apply exclusively to investigations conducted by agencies with law enforcement responsibilities, in connection with criminal, civil or administrative proceedings to which such agencies are a party.[17] The obligation of the requested state to provide assistance to the requesting state is phrased in general terms—"the parties shall use their best efforts"—and includes supplying "information, such as statements, depositions, documents, business records, correspondence or other materials . . . concerning alleged illicit acts."[18] These agreements also usually provide that the parties shall use their best efforts to "assist in the expeditious execution of letters rogatory."[19] It should be noted that judicial assistance under these agreements is granted only if the actions to be taken by the requested state are not in violation of its domestic law.[20]

Finally, the Agreement between the United States and the Federal Republic of Germany, effected by Exchange of Notes, dated February 11, 1955, and January 13 and October 8, 1956, on Taking of Evidence (taking of testimony of German nationals by U.S. consular officers stationed in Germany) should be mentioned.[21] The Agreement, as confirmed in the Exchanges of Notes dated

[13] *Id.* at 820 (footnotes omitted).

[14] *See* the Agreements concluded with Canada, 28 UST 2463, TIAS No. 8567; Venezuela, 28 UST 5219, TIAS No. 8623; the Sudan, 28 UST 7482, TIAS No. 8723; Pakistan, 28 UST 7488, TIAS No. 8724; India, 28 UST 7497, TIAS No. 8726; and Nepal, 30 UST 2495, TIAS No. 9347.

[15] *See* the Agreements concluded with Japan, 27 UST 946, TIAS No. 8233; Nigeria, 27 UST 1054, TIAS No. 8243; Colombia, 27 UST 1059, TIAS No. 8244; the Netherlands, 27 UST 1064, TIAS No. 8245; Spain, 27 UST 3409, TIAS No. 8370; Turkey, 27 UST 3419, TIAS No. 8371; Australia, 27 UST 3424, TIAS No. 8372; the Federal Republic of Germany, 27 UST 3429, TIAS No. 8373; Italy, 27 UST 3437, TIAS No. 8374; Iran, 28 UST 5205, TIAS No. 8621; Belgium, 27 UST 1966, TIAS No. 8292; and Greece, 27 UST 2006, TIAS No. 8300.

[16] In connection with the General Tire & Rubber Co. and the Firestone Tire & Rubber Co. investigations, see the Agreement concluded with Mexico, 28 UST 2083, TIAS No. 8533; in connection with the Gulfstream American Corp. investigation, see the Agreement concluded with Togo, 30 UST 3477, TIAS No. 9401; in connection with the Jamaica Nutrition Holding Ltd. investigation, see the Agreement concluded with Jamaica, 30 UST 3868, TIAS No. 9430; in connection with the Westinghouse Electric Corp. investigation, see the Agreement concluded with Egypt, 30 UST 3996, TIAS No. 9441; and in connection with the McDonnell Douglas Corp. investigation, see the Agreement concluded with the Netherlands, 30 UST 2500, TIAS No. 9348.

[17] *See, e.g.,* Arts. 3 and 5 of the Agreements with Japan, note 15 *supra,* and Canada, note 14 *supra.*

[18] *See, e.g.,* Art. 2 of the Agreements with Japan and Canada.

[19] *See, e.g.,* Art. 7 of the Agreement with Japan and Art. 8 of the Agreement with Canada.

[20] *See, e.g.,* Art. 9 of the Agreement with Japan and Art. 10 of the Agreement with Canada.

[21] *See* TIAS No. 9938.

October 17, 1979, and February 1, 1980, is still considered in force even though the Hague Convention on the Taking of Evidence Abroad is now in force between the two countries.

Conclusion

The opinion of Lord Denning in *Smith Kline & French Laboratories Ltd. v. Block*[22] begins with this rather baroque metaphor: "As a moth is drawn to the light, so is a litigant drawn to the United States." Moths may sometimes be consumed by the light to which they are drawn and there is at least one hazard (particularly applicable to corporations and other business entities) that litigants face when they go to the United States. This hazard is created by the necessary submission of the foreign party to the American court's rules with respect to discovery. If the defendant seeks discovery of the plaintiff and the court enters an order compelling discovery, the plaintiff may be faced with the dilemma that to give discovery will offend the blocking statutes of its own state.

In *Societe Internationale v. Rogers*,[23] the U.S. Supreme Court held that, where a Swiss plaintiff did not comply with a discovery order on the ground that to do so would violate Swiss penal law, the complaint should not be dismissed because plaintiff had made a good faith effort to comply with the order.

After the *Rogers* case, the United States Court of Appeals for the Second Circuit, in a series of cases beginning with *First National City Bank v. Commissioner*,[24] held that a plaintiff should not be required to produce documents if to do so would violate the law of the state of the document's situs. The Second Circuit reaffirmed this position in a number of later decisions.[25]

Beginning in the mid-1970's, however, a contrary position was taken in other circuits. For example, in *United States v. Vetco*,[26] the Ninth Circuit, holding that the interests of the United States should prevail, affirmed an order of the district court requiring a defendant to produce documents located in Switzerland despite possible criminal liability under Swiss law.[27]

Thus, under some circumstances, the blocking statutes that other countries have enacted to curb American discovery may inhibit the efforts of parties to American litigation to prosecute or defend an action. There is no easy solution to this problem. It cannot be dealt with in terms of the Hague Convention because that Convention does not require the requested state to supply evidence where to do so would violate its domestic law.[28]

[22] Court of Appeal, May 13, 1982.

[23] 357 U.S. 197 (1958).

[24] 271 F.2d 616 (2d Cir. 1959).

[25] *See also* Ings v. Ferguson, 282 F.2d 149 (2d Cir. 1960); *In re* Chase Manhattan Bank, 297 F.2d 611 (2d Cir. 1962); United States v. First Nat'l City Bank, 396 F.2d 897 (2d Cir. 1968); and Trade Dev. Bank v. Continental Ins. Co., 469 F.2d 35 (2d Cir. 1972).

[26] 644 F.2d 1326 (9th Cir. 1981).

[27] *See also* Arthur Andersen & Co. v. Finesilver, 546 F.2d 338 (10th Cir. 1976); *In re* Uranium Antitrust Litigation, 480 F.Supp. 1138 (N.D. Ill. 1979); and Commission v. Banca della Svizzera Italiana, 92 F.R.D. 111 (S.D.N.Y. 1981).

[28] *See* Arts. 11 and 21 of the Convention, *supra* note 3.

One must reluctantly conclude that, from the United States point of view, the Hague Convention appears to have contributed little to the solution of the problem of discovery of documentary and other evidence in a foreign country. Although this conclusion is not surprising in view of the substantial differences between the U.S. attitude and the attitudes of other signatories to the Convention towards discovery, it does illustrate the limitations that domestic factors place upon the effectiveness of international agreements and the difficulty of establishing procedures to harmonize legal systems with conflicting views on the conduct of litigation.

ROBERT B. VON MEHREN*

THE AFRICAN CHARTER ON HUMAN AND PEOPLES' RIGHTS

During the 1970's human rights appeared to enjoy low esteem in Africa. The basic documents in inter-African relations were the UN and the OAU Charters. In its Preamble, as well as four substantive articles,[1] the UN Charter refers to respect for human rights as a basis for international relations. The principles of human rights were further elaborated in the Universal Declaration of Human Rights of 1948 whose principles, in the view of some writers, have become part of customary international law.[2] This Declaration was in turn elaborated on in the International Covenant on Economic, Social and Cultural Rights of 1966.

In its Preamble and purposes, the OAU Charter reaffirms the principles of the UN Charter and the Universal Declaration of Human Rights. It also refers to the right of self-determination, the eradication of colonialism, and the welfare and well-being of African people. The Organization of African Unity was concerned about the persistence of colonialism in the former Portuguese colonies of Mozambique and Angola and the unilateral declaration of independence by Southern Rhodesia under a racist minority regime. It gave material, moral, and diplomatic support to the liberation movements of those territories. It is committed to the achievement of human rights and self-determination by the people of South Africa and Namibia.

The OAU maintained an indifferent attitude to the suppression of human rights in a number of independent African states by unduly emphasizing the principle of noninterference in the internal affairs of member states at the expense of certain other principles, particularly the customary law principle of respect for human rights. President Sékou Touré's prohibitory assertion that

* Of the Board of Editors. This paper is based on remarks made by the author at a conference held May 11–12, 1983 in London, sponsored by the International Law Association, on the subject "Extra-territorial Application of Laws and Responses Thereto." The author wishes to acknowledge the very helpful assistance of Carlo Croff, a member of the Italian Bar.

[1] UN CHARTER arts. 1, 13, 55, and 76.

[2] Waldock, *Human Rights in Contemporary International Law and the Significance of the European Convention,* 14 INT'L & COMP. L.Q., Supp. No. 11, at 1, 15 (1965); Bilder, *The Status of International Human Rights Law: An Overview,* in 1 INTERNATIONAL HUMAN RIGHTS IN LAW AND PRACTICE 8 (rev. ed. J. Tuttle 1978).

the OAU was not "a tribunal which could sit in judgement on any member state's internal affairs"[3] was typical of the inhibition the members imposed on themselves, not so much to protect their legitimate states' rights as to fend off international concern for gross abuses of human rights in some African states.

For instance, the massacres of thousands of Hutu in Burundi in 1972 and 1973 were neither discussed nor condemned by the OAU, which regarded them as matters of internal affairs.[4] The notorious regimes of Idi Amin of Uganda (1971–1979), Marcias Nguema of Equatorial Guinea (1969–1979), and Jean-Bedel Bokassa of the Central African Republic (1966–1979) escaped the criticism of the OAU and most of its members, Tanzania, Zambia, and Mozambique being the exceptions. In fact, the correct interpretation of the OAU Charter, coupled with the international obligations of African states *qua* members of the United Nations and of the international community generally, reveals that respect for human rights had become an obligatory norm of international law binding on all of them.[5] Tanzania's invasion of Uganda, far from being condemned, could be justified as humanitarian intervention to protect the human rights of Ugandans against a ruthless and obstreperous regime. Some of the consequences have been undesirable, but the way has been opened for a change and a better government.[6]

As far back as 1961, African jurists meeting in Lagos under the auspices of the International Commission of Jurists suggested an African Human Rights Charter under which would be created a court to which individuals or groups could have recourse.[7] A similar call was made in Dakar by jurists from French-speaking African states in 1967.[8] The African Bar Association later proposed a commission of human rights to operate along the same lines as Amnesty International in London and the International Commission of Jurists in Geneva.

In 1967 Nigeria proposed at the 23d session of the Commission on Human Rights that the United Nations establish regional commissions where none existed. An 11-member ad hoc study group thought that such commissions should

[3] AFRICAN RESEARCH BULL. (Political, Social and Cultural Series) 5329B (1979).

[4] For earlier conflicts between Hutu and Tutsi in Burundi and Rwanda, see B. ANDEMICAEL, PEACEFUL SETTLEMENT AMONG AFRICAN STATES: ROLES OF THE UNITED NATIONS AND THE ORGANIZATION OF AFRICAN UNITY 17–20 (UNITAR 1972).

[5] Umozurike, *The Domestic Jurisdiction Clause in the O.A.U. Charter,* AFRICAN AFF. (London), No. 311, April 1979, at 197; Okongwu, *The O.A.U. Charter and the Principles of Domestic Jurisdiction in Intra-African Affairs,* 13 INDIAN J. INT'L L. 589 (1973); Akinyemi, *The Organization of African Unity and the Concept of Non-Interference in Internal Affairs of Member-States,* 46 BRIT. Y.B. INT'L L. 393 (1972–73); J.-F. Lalive, *The Protection of Human Rights within the Framework of Existing Regional Organizations,* in HUMAN RIGHTS IN NATIONAL AND INTERNATIONAL LAW 330 (A. H. Robertson ed. 1968); Markovic, *Implementation of Human Rights and the Domestic Jurisdiction of States,* in INTERNATIONAL PROTECTION OF HUMAN RIGHTS 47 (A. Eide & A. Shou eds. 1968); Welch, *The O.A.U. and Human Rights: Towards a New Definition,* J. MOD. AFR. STUD., Sept. 1981.

[6] Wani, *Humanitarian Intervention and the Tanzania-Uganda War,* HORN AFR., No. 2; Umozurike, *Tanzania's Intervention in Uganda,* 20 ARCHIV VÖLKERRECHTS 301 (1982).

[7] INTERNATIONAL COMMISSION OF JURISTS [hereinafter cited as INT'L COMM'N JURISTS], AN AFRICAN CHARTER ON THE RULE OF LAW (1961).

[8] BULL. INT'L COMM'N JURISTS, No. 29, March 1967, at 1.

be set up by the members of the region themselves and not imposed from outside.[9] The Commission then invited the UN Secretary-General to organize seminars in those regions where no human rights commissions existed with a view to discussing the need for them.

At the commemoration of the 20th anniversary of the Universal Declaration of Human Rights held in Tehran in 1968, Nigeria renewed its campaign for the establishment of regional commissions.[10] The next year, the participants in the UN seminar in Cairo, attended by 19 African states, requested, *inter alia,* that the UN Secretary-General communicate its report to the OAU Secretary and membership with the recommendation that a regional commission be set up and that OAU members give full support to it. The OAU summit held in Monrovia in July 1979 resolved that the Secretary-General should set the process in motion for a commission on human rights, and a UN seminar in Monrovia attended by 30 African states later in the same year produced a draft for the OAU Working Committee that was established.[11] In three meetings, held once in Dakar in 1979 and twice in Banjul in 1980 and 1981, the last attended by OAU ministers, the final draft was produced; it was adopted unanimously by the OAU heads of state at the summit conference in Nairobi in June 1981.

Developments on the international scene favored the idea of an African Charter on Human Rights. Chief among these was the emphasis that President Carter placed on human rights in the international relations of the United States. The Helsinki Final Act of 1975, signed by the United States, Canada, and 33 European countries, emphasized respect for human rights. Watch committees were subsequently set up to monitor observance and this kept the issue alive in international politics. The suffering of millions of people in Southeast Asia in the 1970's, with its phenomenon of the "boat people," stirred the conscience of mankind. Though unsuccessful, an attempt was made to include human rights in the renewed EEC–A-C-P pact, the Lomé II Convention.[12] The stage was thus set both internally and externally for the debut of the African Charter on Human and Peoples' Rights.[13]

Political and Civil Rights

The Charter guarantees, without qualifications, the following traditional political and civil rights: the rights to equality, a fair hearing, and personal

[9] UN Doc. E/CN.4/966, paras. 41–44 (1968).

[10] The current President of the World Court, Judge T. O. Elias, was closely connected with the preparation of the background papers for the three conferences in 1961, 1967, and 1968 in his capacity as Attorney-General and Minister for Justice in Nigeria.

[11] UN Seminar on the Establishment of Regional Commissions on Human Rights with Special Reference to Africa, Monrovia, 10–21 September 1979, UN Doc. ST/HR/SER.A/4 (1979). *See* COMMISSION TO STUDY THE ORGANIZATION OF PEACE, 29TH REPORT, REGIONAL PROTECTION AND PROMOTION OF HUMAN RIGHTS IN AFRICA (1980) [hereinafter cited as COMMISSION REPORT].

[12] Young-Anawaty, *Human Rights and the ACP-EEC Lomé II Convention,* 13 N.Y.U. J. INT'L L. & POL. 63 (1980).

[13] The text approved by the OAU Ministerial Conference in the Gambia, January 1981, is *reprinted in* 21 ILM 59 (1982), and 27 INT'L COMM'N JURISTS REV. 76 (1981). *See* further Eze, *Prospects for International Protection of Human Rights in Africa,* AFR. REV., No. 1, 1974, at 79, 83.

dignity. The components of fair hearing are elaborated in Article 7: namely, the rights to defense, to counsel of one's choice, to appeal, to trial within a reasonable time by an impartial court or tribunal, and to the presumption of innocence. Other rights are qualified. Thus, the right to life, liberty, freedom of conscience, freedom of expression, freedom of association, assembly, and movement may be limited or derogated from by law. There is no derogation clause as such, nor is it stated that such laws must be "strictly required by the exigencies of the situation," as in the European Convention[14] and some national constitutions.[15] Article 13 guarantees the right to participate in government either directly or through freely chosen representatives and protects access to public property and services on the basis of nondiscrimination. The independence of the judiciary is also protected.

The Charter recognizes the rights of groups including the family, children, the aged, and the infirm who are entitled to special protection and support. The right of peoples to self-determination is recognized and is elaborated in the right to existence, equality, and nondomination. Peoples shall freely determine their future and "have the right to the assistance of the States Parties to the present Charter in their liberation struggle against foreign domination."[16]

The mass expulsion of non-nationals is prohibited. Mass expulsion is defined under this clause as that directed against national, racial, ethnic, or religious groups. The mass expulsion of *illegal* aliens by an order of the Nigerian Government in 1983 will not fall under the prohibition. An alien is expected to travel with the necessary papers and obtain the necessary visas or permits. The ECOWAS (Economic Community of West African States) free travel accord allows nationals of member states to visit for 3 months without a visa. Any stay in excess of that period goes through the normal channels. The Secretary-General of ECOWAS confirmed that Nigeria had not committed a breach of the treaty of association,[17] but the large-scale suffering of the refugees could have been avoided by earlier remedial actions and a later deadline for the departing aliens.[18]

Economic, Social and Cultural Rights

The Charter protects the right to property but provides that it may be "encroached upon in the interest of public need or the general interest of the

[14] Convention on Human Rights and Fundamental Freedoms (European Convention on Human Rights), 213 UNTS 221, Art. 15(1).

[15] *E.g.*, §41 of the Nigerian Constitution.

[16] Afr. Charter, Art. 20.

[17] "Dr. Quatara [Executive Secretary of ECOWAS] explained that the quit order did not in any way conflict with any provision of ECOWAS protocol of free movement of persons within the community." Nigerian Chronicle, Jan. 29, 1983, at 16. Dating back to the sub-Saharan droughts of a few years ago, the Nigerian Government allowed aliens without papers from neighboring states to flood the country. The unsettled situation in Ghana encouraged over a million Ghanaians to take advantage of the liberal immigration policy. The strain on the employment market and social services, and the increasingly high crime rate, at last forced the Government to reassess its national interests.

[18] *See also* Eze, *ECOWAS and Freedom of Movement: What Prospects for Nigeria?*, NIG. F., March 1981, at 22.

community and in accordance with the provisions of appropriate laws."[19] There is no mention of compensation, whether "prompt, effective and adequate"[20] in the traditional Western sense or "appropriate"[21] or reasonable in the UN sense. The Charter also guarantees the right to work "under equitable and satisfactory conditions"[22] and to equal pay for equal work. If this obliges governments to provide jobs, it is likely to be honored more in breach than in observance owing to sheer incapacity or circumstances beyond the control of African states, which have few industries and a limited wage system. The bulk of the people are peasants living off the land for mere subsistence. The ability to create jobs is further restricted by the unequal international trading system, which places the Third World at a disadvantage.

The right to enjoy the best attainable state of physical and mental health is also guaranteed, as is the right to education and to participation in cultural life. These rather onerous provisions serve to remind the member states to extend the benefits of their resources to the generality of their citizenry rather than to a minority, as now seems to be the case in many states.

Other rights of peoples recognized in the Charter include the right to pursue their economic and social development. States parties to the Charter may freely dispose of their national wealth and resources with a view to strengthening African unity and solidarity.

The Right to Development

The Charter recognizes the right to development as belonging to all peoples and encompassing economic, social, and cultural aspects.[23] Because states have a duty to ensure the exercise of the right to development,[24] it may be said that all peoples have a right to a general satisfactory environment favorable to their development. They also have a right to national and international peace and security under the Charter.

The right to development, if it is indeed a right in international law, is new. It was first enunciated by the President of the Senegal Supreme Court, Keba M'baye, in an address to the Institute of International Law of Human Rights in Strasbourg in 1972. He suggested that all rights are intertwined with the right of existence, with a progressively higher standard of living, and therefore with development. He referred to Articles 55–56 of the UN Charter and 22–27 of the Universal Declaration of Human Rights, and to statutes of the specialized agencies in which international cooperation and solidarity are important.[25] In 1978, as President of the International Commission of Jurists, he further adumbrated on the right at the Dakar Conference on the Devel-

[19] Afr. Charter, Art. 14.

[20] Note of Aug. 3, 1938, *reproduced in* U.S. DEP'T OF STATE, COMPENSATION FOR AMERICAN-OWNED LANDS EXPROPRIATED IN MEXICO (Inter-American Series No. 16, 1939).

[21] UNGA Res. 1803 (XVII) (Dec. 14, 1962).

[22] Afr. Charter, Art. 15.

[23] *Id.*, Art. 22(1).

[24] *Id.*, para. 2.

[25] M'baye, *Le Droit de développement comme un droit de l'homme,* 5 REV. DROITS DE L'HOMME 523, 526 (1982).

opment of the Law of Human Rights. At the request of the Commission of Human Rights, the UN Secretary-General made a study in which he concluded that a large number of principles based on the UN Charter and human rights texts and declarations confirm the existence of the right in law.[26] This conclusion was later confirmed by the General Assembly.[27]

The right to development appears to cover all of self-determination[28] and much more than that. In itself, it appears not to have attained the definitive status of a rule of law despite its powerful advocates. Its inclusion in the African Charter will be as effective as the Charter itself. The negative duty not to impede the development of states may go down well; the positive duty to aid such development, in the absence of specific accords, is a higher level of commitment that still rests on nonlegal considerations.

Duties

The Charter breaks new ground by including individual duties in an international instrument.[29] Hitherto, rights were usually enumerated that, by implication, imposed duties on states. The Charter, on the other hand, recognizes the duty of the individual to the family, society, the state, and the international African community. Duties to the family include respect, care of parents, and preservation of the family's harmonious development; duties to the state include preserving and strengthening social and national solidarity, contributing to national defense, and paying taxes.

Who will be answerable for a large-scale breach of individual duties—the states or individuals? The states' responsibilities for these duties imply a minimum obligation to inculcate the underlying principles and ideals in their subjects.[30]

The Commission on Human Rights

The Charter sets up an 11-member Commission, which includes not more than one national of the same state. Members are normally elected for a 6-year period. Their emoluments and allowances are paid out of the OAU regular budget. The Charter states that they shall be individuals with the highest reputation and relevant competence, especially in the field of law. The Commission shall lay down its rules of procedure and elect its chairman and

[26] UN Doc. E/CN.4/1334, para. 305 (1979). *See also* DEVELOPMENT, HUMAN RIGHTS AND THE RULE OF LAW: REPORT OF THE CONFERENCE HELD IN THE HAGUE, especially Mestdagh, *The Right to Development,* at 143–74 (1981).

[27] UNGA Res. 34/46 (Nov. 23, 1979).

[28] U. UMOZURIKE, SELF-DETERMINATION IN INTERNATIONAL LAW (1972).

[29] Afr. Charter, Art. 29.

[30] *Id.,* Art. 25:

> States parties to the present Charter shall have the duty to promote and ensure through teaching, education and publication, the respect of the rights and freedoms contained in the present Charter and to see to it that these freedoms and rights as well as corresponding obligations and duties are understood.

vice-chairman for a 2-year period. All the members, including the elected officers, are eligible for reelection. The OAU Secretary-General shall appoint the Commission's secretary and supporting staff.

The main duty of the Commission is to promote and protect human rights through documentation, studies, seminars, symposiums, and conferences to disseminate information; to encourage other human rights institutions; "and should the case arise, give its views or make recommendations to Governments."[31] It shall formulate principles and rules for the solution of human rights problems, interpret the Charter "at the request of a State Party, an institution of the OAU or an African organization recognized by the OAU,"[32] and perform other functions given to it by the Assembly.

Communications from States. A state that believes that another state has violated the Charter shall communicate the alleged breach to the violator in writing and send copies to the Secretary-General and to the chairman of the Commission. If the matter is not satisfactorily resolved within 3 months, either state may submit the matter to the Commission. The accusing party may also submit the matter directly to the Commission, which, before dealing with the matter, must ensure that local remedies have been exhausted, unless the matter would be unduly prolonged.

The states concerned may submit written or oral representations to the Commission. Having received these and other materials and "having tried all appropriate means to reach an amicable solution based on the respect of Human and Peoples' Rights," the Commission is directed to send a report and its recommendations to the state concerned and to the OAU Assembly.[33] In any event, it is required to send an annual report on its activities to each Ordinary Session of the Assembly.

Communications from Nonstate Entities. The Commission may receive communications from nongovernmental organizations and individuals. To ensure that the process is not abused, the Charter provides, *inter alia,* that such communications must not be couched in language insulting to a state or its institutions or to the OAU, and must not be based exclusively on information from the mass media. Whether the Commission considers such a complaint shall be decided by a simple majority of its members.

If a communication reveals a special case of a series of serious or massive violations of human and peoples' rights, the Commission shall draw the Assembly's attention to it. The Assembly may then request an in-depth study of the situation by the Commission and a report of its findings and recommendations. The Commission shall refer a case of emergency to the Chairman of the Assembly who may ask for an in-depth study. The Commission is expected to work in secrecy "until such time as the Assembly . . . shall decide otherwise."[34] Reports on the activities of the Commission considered by the Assembly or factual reports whose publication the Assembly directs are exceptions to this confidentiality provision.

[31] Afr. Charter, Art. 45(1)(a).

[32] *Id.*, para. 3.

[33] *Id.*, Art. 52.

[34] *Id.*, Art. 59(1).

Distinctive Features of the African Charter

The African Charter on Human and Peoples' Rights was preceded by the European Convention on Human Rights in 1950 and the American Convention on Human Rights in 1969. While similar to them in some ways, it has distinct features that reflect the special character of the African legal systems.

One such feature is the absence of a court. Despite some calls for provision of an African court of human rights,[35] the drafters of the African Charter concluded that the formal adversarial procedures common to Western legal systems were inappropriate. African customs and traditions emphasize conciliation rather than judicial settlement of disputes.[36]

While the structures of the African, American, and European Commissions are similar, they function differently. For example, individuals and groups have a qualified right to petition the African Commission similar to the unqualified right to petition the American Commission.[37] The European Commission, on the other hand, receives individual and group petitions only if the state against which the complaint is made has declared its recognition of the Commission's competence to receive them.[38] As stated earlier, states parties to the African Charter may petition the Commission orally or in writing. The European Convention provides that any state party may refer complaints about another state party to the Commission.[39] The American Convention gives states parties the option to declare recognition of the Commission's competence to receive complaints from other states parties; the complainant must also have recognized the Commission's competence to receive state complaints.[40]

Whereas the Courts under the American and European Conventions can review cases brought first before the Commissions, there is no such "second avenue" of redress under the African Charter. The Organization of African Unity cannot give redress under the Charter. It can only request that the Commission undertake studies and make reports, findings, and recommendations to it; order publication of Commission reports; and consider the activities reports of the Commission.[41] Nowhere is the Assembly entitled to make recommendations unless such power may be implied from the OAU Charter generally.

A third distinctive feature of the African Charter is the absence of a derogation clause. Article 15 of the European Convention and Article 27 of the American Convention specify that rights may be derogated from in times of war or public emergency that threatens the life[42] of the nation. They also specify those rights which are nonderogable. As was discussed above, certain rights under the African

[35] *See, e.g.,* Esiemokhai, *Towards Adequate Defence of Human Rights in Africa,* 13 VERFASSUNG & RECHT IN ÜBERSEE 151, 156–57 (1980).

[36] COMMISSION REPORT, *supra* note 11, at 30–31.

[37] Afr. Charter, Art. 56; American Convention on Human Rights, Art. 44, 9 ILM 673 (1970).

[38] European Convention, Art. 25(1).

[39] *Id.,* Art. 24.

[40] American Convention, Art. 45.

[41] Afr. Charter, Arts. 58 and 59.

[42] The American Convention allows derogations "[i]n time of war, public danger, or other emergency that threatens the independence or security of a State Party."

Charter are qualified and others are stated in absolute terms; there is no single clause, however, that clearly defines the nonderogable rights or, more importantly, that describes the circumstances under which qualified rights may be limited. In its *Report on Regional Protection and Promotion of Human Rights in Africa,* the Commission to Study the Organization of Peace noted, "The question is not whether any such suspensions are permissible, but when and to what extent."[43] Declarations of emergency for military, political, or even economic reasons are thus discretionary—tempered, unless stated otherwise, only by states' duty "to promote and ensure through teaching, education and publication, the respect of the rights and freedoms contained in the present Charter."[44]

The right to participate in government, included in the African Charter[45] and the American Convention,[46] is absent from the European Convention. All three documents provide for the right of workers to organize themselves, though under the African Charter, this right is only implicit in the right to free association.[47]

The African Charter includes civil and political as well as specific economic and social rights. The American Convention, while integrating political and social rights, provides separately for the progressive development of economic, social, and cultural rights referred to in the amended OAS Charter.[48] Economic and social rights are promoted in the European system under the European Social Charter.

Unlike the European and American Conventions, drafted much earlier in time, the African Charter emphasizes the right to development. While exposition of this emerging right is beyond the scope of this study, it should be noted that its inclusion reflects developing states' desire to catch up economically with the developed states.[49]

Finally, the Charter reaffirms faith in general international law on human and peoples' rights based on UN and African instruments. As a subsidiary means of determining the principles of law, it refers to

> other general or special international conventions, laying down rules expressly recognized by member States of the Organization of African Unity, African practices consistent with international norms on human and peoples' rights, customs generally accepted as law, general principles of law recognized by African States as well as legal precedents and doctrine.[50]

[43] COMMISSION REPORT, *supra* note 11, at 31.

[44] Afr. Charter, Art. 25. [45] *Id.*, Art. 15(1).

[46] American Convention, Art. 23.

[47] Afr. Charter, Art. 10; American Convention, Art. 16(1); European Convention, Art. 11(2).

[48] American Convention, Art. 26. *See* Alston, *Development and the Rule of Law: Prevention versus Cure as a Human Rights Strategy,* in DEVELOPMENT, HUMAN RIGHTS, *supra* note 26, at 31, 46–53.

[49] *See* Alston, *supra* note 48, at 98–107.

[50] Afr. Charter, Art. 61. *Contrast* Statute of the International Court of Justice, which, in Article 38, directs the Court to apply: (a) international conventions; (b) international custom; (c) general principles of law recognized by civilized nations; and (d) as subsidiary means and subject to Article 59, "judicial decisions and the teachings of the most highly qualified publicists of the various nations."

The Charter thus subscribes to the consent theory on the binding effect of international law, denying validity to those norms the parties either have not consented to or played no part in formulating. This is a conservative and commonsensical approach in a world of unequal political, economic, and military powers and of disparate interests but requiring accepted norms for mutually beneficial relations.

Assessment and Conclusions

The African Charter on Human and Peoples' Rights has combined an impressive array of individual rights and duties, group rights, and state rights and duties. Some of these, like the right to development and the right to national and international peace and security, appear to be new additions to the list of internationally recognized rights. The possession of a right usually implies a duty for others to conform to a pattern of behavior. Even if it is accepted that there is a negative duty not to contravene these rights, a positive duty to support them, desirable as it may be, appears as yet to be futuristic, a *lex ferenda* rather than a *lex lata.* Whether these new rights have matured into principles of international law is still a matter of controversy.

An enumeration of rights and duties may not achieve the intended ends, but it serves to give them publicity and entrench them in the minds of men. Enforcement may be a different matter and at the international level may be precarious. On examination of the reporting system and in light of the recent problems of the continent, it seems likely that the Commission will be more concerned with civil and political rights; should it venture into economic and social ones, it would find too many problems in too many countries to cope with. How it copes with its responsibilities when the Charter comes into force will be keenly watched.[51]

The concept of duties stressed in the Charter is quite likely to be abused by a few regimes on the continent, if the recent past can be any guide to future developments. Such governments will emphasize the duties of individuals to their states but will play down their rights and legitimate expectations. There have been a few governments that were not persuaded that the welfare of the governed was their main business. In such situations, the dichotomy between the governors and the governed was acute. It is wholesome, however, to emphasize duties along with rights in order to maintain a proper balance.

If the most notorious abuses of human rights in Uganda, the Central African Republic, and Equatorial Guinea took place after the Charter came into force, would there have been any difference in the course of events? Bearing in mind the slow process of the Commission, the communications, the inquiries, the recommendations, and the in-depth studies (all in confidence until publication is authorized), it is extremely doubtful that the number of lives lost would have been reduced by a significant degree. Nevertheless, it is certain that the

[51] Under Article 63, the Charter will come into force 3 months after the Secretary-General of the OAU receives instruments of ratification or adherence by a simple majority of the OAU member states. At present, 26 will constitute such a majority, not counting the Saharawi Arab Democratic Republic.

limits of the domestic jurisdiction doctrine would have been more openly discussed, to the greater discomfiture of the tyrants.

African states have been very slow in ratifying the Charter with its minimally enforceable responsibilities.[52] How long will it take a majority of African states to ratify the Charter and enable it to take effect? Bello, for example, forecasts with uncanny pessimism that a continental arrangement like the Charter will be "illusory and unworkable," "an exercise in sheer futility."[53] He prefers an arrangement that would embrace like-minded states, starting with Kenya, the Ivory Coast, Nigeria, Senegal, Tanzania, and Zambia. The possible alternatives are a weak compromise arrangement for all African states such as at present, or a higher level of effectiveness in an agreement with like-minded states. It may be that a pan-African arrangement will enhance the credibility of the OAU and be helped by it.[54]

Article 60 directs the Commission to draw inspiration from the UN and OAU Charters, from the Universal Declaration of Human Rights, and from other human rights instruments. It may be that the Commission, in keeping with this provision, will develop beyond the narrow confines set by the present African Governments.

Human rights have grown beyond the exclusive concern of individual states. The UN Charter set in motion in clear terms the process for their internationalization. Further steps were taken in the Universal Declaration of Human Rights, the Covenants on Human Rights, and other instruments. The OAU Charter made references to them; yet it was still possible for some regimes to insist that they were matters of exclusive domestic jurisdiction. The Charter on Human and Peoples' Rights has cleared any doubts that may persist as to the international status of human rights, and African states cannot contract out of customary international law, which undoubtedly includes respect for human rights. It follows that whether or not the Charter is ratified, the essential human rights principles in it are binding.

The adoption of the Charter should therefore be regarded as a milestone in the development of human rights on the continent, its imperfections notwithstanding. Little drops of palm wine fill the calabash up the tree. It is now left for concerned individuals, groups, and institutions to carry on the struggle for the rehabilitation of the human personality after the degradations of the slave trade and colonialism.[55]

U. O. UMOZURIKE*

[52] As of October 1983, the Charter had been ratified by Congo, the Gambia, Guinea, Liberia, Mali, Nigeria, Rwanda, Senegal, Togo, and Tunisia.

[53] Bello, *Human Rights: The Rule of Law in Africa,* 30 INT'L & COMP. L.Q. 628, 634, 636 (1981).

[54] The Working Group on the Encouragement of Universal Acceptance of Human Rights was set up in 1979 by the Sub-Commission on Prevention of Discrimination and Protection of Minorities to consider, *inter alia,* what assistance the United Nations could give to encourage the ratification of human rights treaties. *See* further Weissbrodt, *A New United Nations Mechanism for Encouraging the Ratification of Human Rights Treaties,* 76 AJIL 418 (1982).

[55] *See* further U. UMOZURIKE, INTERNATIONAL LAW AND COLONIALISM IN AFRICA (Nigeria 1979).

* Professor of Law, University of Calabar, Nigeria.

THE IRAN-UNITED STATES CLAIMS TRIBUNAL

In a notice issued by David P. Stewart, Administrator for Iranian Claims, under date of June 24, 1983, the Department of State informed claimants before the Iran-United States Claims Tribunal at The Hague of recent developments at the Tribunal with specific regard to settlement of claims. The notice read in part:

> On two recent occasions, the Tribunal had refused to certify as Tribunal awards settlements submitted by U.S. claimants and Iran. In one case the amount of the proposed settlement significantly exceeded the amount of the claim. In the other, the settlement was in the full amount of the claim plus interest, but the settlement required that, after the settlement had been paid from the Security Account at the N.V. Settlement Bank of Netherlands, more than half of the amount of the settlement would be paid to Iran for taxes allegedly owed. The U.S. claimant had previously denied that any such taxes were owed. The United States—and, to the best of the Department of State's knowledge, all U.S. claimants—has consistently denied that Iranian counterclaims for taxes are within the Tribunal's jurisdiction.
>
> Both proposed settlements were rejected because the parties were unable to demonstrate that the settlements did not include matters other than settlement of claims within the Tribunal's jurisdiction. The Tribunal has no authority to certify as awards payable from the Security Account settlements that do not, in whole or in part, represent claims within its jurisdiction. (*See* the Tribunal's Decision of May 14, 1982, in Case No. A/1.) Such settlements, moreover, may improperly deplete the Security Account and thereby diminish the security provided by the account for other claims of U.S. nationals.
>
> Under these circumstances, the Department of State cautions U.S. claimants that any proposed settlements in excess of the amounts claimed or otherwise appearing to encompass matters not properly before the Tribunal will be closely scrutinized by the Tribunal and may be rejected. Consultation with department officials in Washington or The Hague before submission of such settlements may be helpful in avoiding Tribunal rejection.
>
> The Department further notes that, as a United States Government agency, it is obligated to call to the attention of the Internal Revenue Service any matters that may present questions concerning the administration of the internal revenue laws of the United States. This may include settlements that purport to include the payment of Iranian taxes.[1]

Responding to a request from Senator Barry Goldwater for information regarding a constituent's claim against Iran, Powell A. Moore, Assistant Secretary of State for Legislative and Intergovernmental Affairs, wrote to Senator Goldwater on July 28, 1983:

> Since the Department's last correspondence with claimants concerning developments at the Tribunal, some progress has been made with regard

[1] 48 Fed. Reg. 30,817–18 (1983). The notice supplemented information published in Public Notice 819, Aug. 20, 1982, 47 *id.* at 37,993 (1982), and prior notices.

to the preparation of the small claims (under $250,000) for arbitration. Although the Department does not at this time know which of the small claims the Tribunal will select to arbitrate first, the Tribunal has now adopted a method of categorizing the claims according to common types of losses. It is anticipated that the Tribunal may select "test cases" from each of these categories sometime during this fall so that it can proceed to establish pleading schedules for the first of these "test cases." By holding "test case" hearings and issuing precedent decisions binding on the remaining claims within particular categories, the Tribunal could avoid the time-consuming necessity of holding individual hearings for each of the 2,800 small claims. Further, the Tribunal has recently approved the recruitment of additional personnel to work exclusively on the small claims. It is hoped that these additional staff members will be hired by the Tribunal in the next few months to begin the extensive task of reviewing the small claims. Once precedent "test case" decisions have been rendered, the small claims personnel also will begin to evaluate the supporting evidence for the remaining claims for purposes of recommending individual decisions on them to the Tribunal.

It should be emphasized that all of these measures taken by the Tribunal with regard to the small claims occurred after long periods of debate and over strong objections from the representatives of the Islamic Republic of Iran, who have continuously maintained that the small claims should be considered by the Tribunal only on a case-by-case basis.

The Department of State shares the claimants' frustration over the length of time necessary to arbitrate the claims against Iran. In addition to the nearly 2,800 small claims, however, there are nearly a thousand claims of other United States nationals before the Tribunal, as well as certain claims of the United States and Iran against one another. The Department is working with the Tribunal to expedite the arbitration of these claims. Given the sheer number and complexity of the claims pending before the Tribunal, however, it is only reasonable to expect that arbitration of all the claims will take at least several years.

It is also possible that the 2,800 claims of less than $250,000 each may at some time be settled by a lump-sum agreement between the United States and Iran, in which case they would be withdrawn from the Tribunal and referred to the U.S. Foreign Claims Settlement Commission in Washington, D.C. for adjudication. Legislation authorizing the Commission to adjudicate these claims was recently reintroduced in Congress. In the event of a lump-sum settlement, claimants would still have the obligation of proving their claims, although proceedings before the Commission would likely be much quicker than at the Tribunal. It is, however, unlikely that even in the event of such a settlement, many of the small claimants could expect to receive payment on Commission awards before 1985.[2]

MARIAN NASH LEICH*

[2] Dept. of State File No. P83 0099-0867.

* Office of the Legal Adviser, Department of State.

BOOK REVIEWS AND NOTES

EDITED BY LEO GROSS

The Roots and Reaches of United Nations Actions and Decisions. By Moses Moskowitz. Alphen aan den Rijn: Sijthoff & Noordhoff, 1980. Pp. x, 210. Index. Dfl.66; $28.50.

Publications that make a predominantly negative appraisal of the United Nations fall into two categories: the literature of opposition, and the literature of disillusion. Those whose work falls into the former category tend to regard international organization in general, and in principle, as a foolish and futile enterprise and perhaps even a nefarious and dangerous one. Authors of the second variety are sometime supporters of and optimists about international organization, persons who have been impressed by the potentialities of the United Nations but disappointed and discouraged—perhaps even alarmed and outraged—by its deviation from their hopes and expectations. Writers of the first sort say "I told you so." Writers of the second sort say "It is hard to believe." Both have harsh things to say about the United Nations.

The literature of disillusion may be further divided, into that complaining of the ineffectiveness of the United Nations and that deploring its misuse. The former expresses regret about the good deeds that the Organization is unable to perform, and the latter is concerned about the misdeeds that must be attributed to it.

For obvious reasons, opponents of the United Nations had the critical field to themselves in its earliest days, but disillusion was not long in emerging. Evidence of the weakness of the United Nations stirred friends of the Organization to examine the causes and possible cures of its frailty. Its continued failure to develop as a decisive force in the international arena has left them so dispirited that they have largely lapsed into silence; there is not much point in writing about an ineffectiveness that has come to be taken for granted. Hence, the more recent literature of disillusion is predominantly of the sort that deplores the effectiveness of the United Nations in doing things that ought not to be done. Moskowitz's book clearly falls into this subcategory.

The line of criticism pursued by Moskowitz emphasizes themes that have become familiar. He discusses the bulldozing tactics of the anticolonial movement: its riding roughshod over restraints laid down in the Charter, its capture of the doctrine of national self-determination for itself alone, and its distortion of the antiaggression doctrine to extract from it a license for violence in the anticolonial cause. He devotes chapters to the Organization's preoccupation with the chastisement of South Africa and of Chile, noting in particular how the theme of human rights has been exploited as cover for ideological campaigns. He gives extended attention to the anti-Israeli bias that pervades the handling of Middle Eastern issues in the United Nations. This litany does not allow room for striking originality, but the author manages to make his treatment of the subject more valuable and more convincing than most. He writes more in sorrow than in anger, avoiding shrillness but giving eloquent expression to the indignation inspired by the partisanship of the Organization, its contempt for its own constitutional limitations, its use of double standards, its willingness to disregard and distort the facts that ought to undergird its judgments, and other sins against moral and intellectual integrity.

In considerable measure, Moskowitz sees the evils of the United Nations as good things gone bad. He recognizes, for instance, that the rejection of a strict construction of the Charter was essential to the survival and healthy development of the early United Nations; however, the demand for flexibility has given way to an abandonment of restraint. He acknowledges the nobility of international concern for human rights; yet, the United Nations has proved unable either to manage the internal affairs of its member states or to prevent the cynical manipulation of the ideal of human rights—and it was the vain ambition to do the former that led to exposure to the latter.

The author evokes contemplation of the disappointed hopes that have been attached to the development of international organization in the 20th century. The world needs, and international agencies ought to be able to promote and provide, such things as impartial mediation, thorough investigation and honest presentation of the facts about disputed situations, mobilization of pressure upon disputants to be moderate and reasonable, and effective representation of international interests. All too often, the products of international organization have been the approximate opposites of these.

Why? What can we do about it? It is easier to answer the first question than the second. The bright hopes rested upon the expectations that states would be substantially transformed by their involvement in international organizations and that the organizations would become significant members of the system in their own right—prominent and beneficent nonstate actors, uniquely useful because of their peculiar nature. Disillusion follows from the discovery that the United Nations consists of states that persist in behaving like states; the alchemy of multilateralism has neither converted national sinners into internationally minded saints nor created a great "Something Other" to preside over the multistate system with Olympian impartiality. The indictment of the United Nations is essentially that states have not been reformed or displaced by the Organization.

What can be done about it? Moskowitz examines various schemes for institutional and procedural reform, designed to curb the excesses of the Organization and press it to observe some reasonable standard of due process. Quite properly, he declines to attach great importance to such schemes. In the end, he comes to the view, as do I, that the political rehabilitation of the United Nations is dependent upon a change in the spirit of those who use it and form its character. Participants in its processes must have the decency not to abuse the Organization and the courage not to permit its abuse. The United Nations has no magic formula for producing such qualities as moderation, fairness, intellectual honesty, and moral integrity—or for surviving as a useful political force without them.

INIS L. CLAUDE, JR.
University of Virginia

Justice at Nuremberg. By Robert E. Conot. New York: Harper and Row, Publishers, 1983. Pp. xiii, 593. Index. $22.50.

The trial of German war criminals by the International Military Tribunal at Nuremberg was undoubtedly one of the most sensational trials in history. Its record filled dozens of volumes and countless studies commented on the legal ramifications of the effort by victorious powers to bring Nazi criminals to justice. Robert Conot has sought to capture the drama of the proceedings in an imaginative narrative. His focus moves chronologically from the trial concept to the organization of the court, imprisonment of the accused, preparations for prosecution and defense, and the deliberations by American, British, French, and Soviet judges whose verdicts meant death or imprisonment for the convicted. The account is embellished with fanciful descriptions and bits of titillating gossip that would detract from the seriousness of the subject were the book intended for legal scholars. But for the public with no recollection of the Hitler era or its aftermath, *Justice at Nuremberg* offers a highly readable and reasonably accurate outline of what the international trial was all about.

The author describes documentary and confirmed proof of unimaginable barbarities, including the "Final Solution of the Jewish Question," the program of working civilians to death,[1] the murder of millions of prisoners-of-war, inhuman medical experiments, and perversions of justice. The undeniable truth is contrasted with the feigned ignorance and "know-nothing" attitude of defendants like Field Marshal Hermann Goering (who cheated the hangman by suicide), Foreign Minister Ribbentrop, the "venomous vulgarian" Julius Streicher, and others directly involved in mass murder. The madness of defendant Rudolf Hess (the only Nazi war criminal still incarcerated) and the questionable sincerity of the confessions by Hitler's Armaments Minister Albert Speer are described, as well as the acquittals of several of the accused, including finance wizard Hjalmar Schacht. In a section on "The Krupp Fiasco," Conot tries to lay to rest the persistent myth that industrialist Alfried Krupp was an innocent lamb who was later forced to stand trial only because his senile father had to be dropped as a defendant.

Lawyers may be particularly interested in the difficulties encountered in trying to sustain the conspiracy theory on which the prosecution based much of its case. The cross-examination of Goering by U.S. Prosecutor Robert Jackson, as compared with the questioning by Britain's Maxwell Fyfe, makes interesting reading. Unfortunately, the book deals only cursorily with the 12 subsequent

[1] *See* 75 AJIL 702 (1981).

proceedings at Nuremberg, under the direction of Jackson's Associate Trial Counsel General Telford Taylor, in which the historical record was augmented and the principles of international justice were further developed. Perceptively, the author draws attention to Judge Francis Biddle's report to President Truman in which the American judge noted that the significance of the Nuremberg trial would depend upon action by the United States in drafting a code of international criminal law.[2] This exhilarating chronicle correctly concludes: "The world . . . can ignore the lessons of Nuremberg only at its peril" (p. 522).

BENJAMIN B. FERENCZ
Of the New York Bar

Models of Autonomy. Edited by Yoram Dinstein. Tel Aviv: Faculty of Law, Tel Aviv University; New Brunswick and London: Transaction Books, 1981. Pp. x, 319. Index. $39.95.

In January 1980, the Egyptian-Israeli negotiations over autonomy for the West Bank and Gaza were faring badly. Believing that "it could make a contribution to the success of the negotiations," the Tel Aviv University Faculty of Law convened a small international conference of lawyers, historians, and political scientists to analyze various "models" of autonomy and to examine the framework for autonomy set forth in the Camp David Accords. "It was hoped," according to Yoram Dinstein, the editor of the collected papers presented at that conference, "that among those models certain elements which could be helpful to the negotiations might perhaps be gleaned."

Alas, these hopes were never realized. The Egyptian-Israeli talks over Palestinian autonomy ground to a halt in March 1982. Egypt has since referred to the need for "confidence-building measures," by Israel—meaning cessation of Israeli settlements and modification of other practices in the West Bank and Gaza—to get the talks back on track. As of this writing, June 1983, they have yet to be reconvened.

The Egyptian-Israeli inability to find a common ground was not, however, due to any lack of model formulas, or lack of imagination or resourcefulness by either side. It was the absence of the will to compromise over ultimate objectives, coupled, at least ostensibly, with Egypt's increasing discomfiture over Israeli occupation and other practices, that brought the talks to a halt. The Egyptians, increasingly intent on having autonomy pave the way for Palestinian self-determination, sought to interpret the many ambiguous terms of the Camp David Accords in this light. Egypt's Minister of State for Foreign Affairs, Dr. Boutros Ghali, has often been quoted as characterizing Palestinian autonomy as a belated instance of decolonization whereby an occupied people, after a transition period, would progress towards self-determination and the exercise of sovereignty. By contrast, the Israelis wanted the agreed-upon structure for autonomy during the 5-year interim period prescribed by the Accords to serve not merely as an interim measure but as a model for permanent relations. Accordingly, unlike their Egyptian counterparts, they sought to interpret such

[2] *See* 75 AJIL 674 (1981).

crucial terms in the Accords as "full autonomy to the inhabitants," "administrative council," and "withdrawal" of military government in ways designed to frustrate Palestinian self-determination, or the option of independence, at the end of the transition period.

This must have been apparent to Dinstein. His concluding essay reveals no great enthusiasm for any of the models of autonomy canvassed during the conference as aids to the Egyptian-Israeli negotiations, and his introduction makes clear that his aim in reproducing these papers is more restricted than the one that inspired the conference organizers. He hoped it would "serve as a useful tool to scholars and laymen puzzled by the increasingly important issue of autonomy, and interested in examining it more closely."

Dinstein succeeds in achieving his stated purpose. The volume demonstrates that autonomy is a flexible concept that has been and can be used to advantage in a great many different contexts where power sharing is the only means to resolve an otherwise insoluble conflict. The volume also focuses on some of the intriguing legal questions presented by the Camp David autonomy process, although the editor himself appears to be less sanguine about that framework than the other contributors.

The book has four parts: an introduction to the theory and practice of autonomy, case studies of autonomy, a discussion of legal aspects of autonomy with special reference given to the autonomy negotiations between Israel and Egypt, and the editor's own views on autonomy.

In the first part Louis Sohn and Rudolf Bernhardt, in separate essays, distinguish between autonomy and other political arrangements. Sohn traces the evolution of the concepts of autonomy and self-government in the UN Charter and early practice of the United Nations. He concludes that autonomy, unlike self-determination and independence, allows for "direct control over areas of special concern to [the autonomous region], while allowing the larger entity, which retains certain powers over that area, to exercise those powers which are in the common interests of both entities." Bernhardt then discusses federalism and points out that, unlike autonomy, federalism entails cooperation in such matters of central importance as defense and foreign policy.

The case studies begin with several illuminating essays about autonomy in Europe: Greenland, South Tyrol, the Basque region, the Balkan states, and the Sudeten. Only Christoph Shreuer, writing on South Tyrol, makes a serious effort to relate the case under discussion to the Palestinian autonomy negotiations. He notes several factors that made that problem less intractable than the case of the West Bank and Gaza: the far lower level of hostility in South Tyrol-Italy relations; the existence of a system of autonomous regions in Italy, of which South Tyrol was but a special part; the operation of an organized and responsible political leadership by the South Tyrolese; and the fact that the South Tyrolese never sought self-determination in their own state.

Next, Puerto Rico and the 13 American colonies are discussed. Natan Lerner fails to make clear that, notwithstanding UN resolutions to the contrary, Puerto Rico has repeatedly exercised its right to self-determination in plebiscites and that the population freely voted for association with the United States.

Robert Friedlander's thesis that autonomy is only useful transitionally is not persuasive and is refuted by some of the other papers, including the preceding essay on Puerto Rico.

The section on Africa begins with a learned discussion by Haim Shaked of the 1972 agreement that ended the conflict in the Southern Sudan and established a framework of autonomy for that region. Shaked cautions against easy analogies to the Palestinian case: most significant is the fact that, unlike Israel in its relation to its Arab neighbors,

> [t]he African majority (to which the Southern Sudanese African minority belongs both ethnically and culturally), which resides in States bordering on the Sudan on two sides, never disputed, let alone objected to, the right of the non-African predominantly Arab North, to maintain an independent sovereign state which contains the South as an integral, legitimate part of its territory.

Also in this part are two essays on the breakdown of the autonomy arrangements that prevailed in Eritrea from 1952 to 1962. Haggai Erlich argues that "by raising unrealistic expectations, by granting a constitution and establishing institutions that had no practical chance of existing, the arrangement did contribute, and most significantly, to the creation of bitter frustration among the Eritreans" and ultimately to the breakdown of autonomy in the region. Theodor Meron and Anna Pappas place the blame on the Ethiopians and on the United Nations and argue that "even with greater and clearer safeguards to Eritrean autonomy, Ethiopia would have sooner or later moved to annex Eritrea" and that "if Eritrean autonomy were to be given any chance of survival, adequate international guarantees should have been provided."

From the standpoint of the international lawyer, the essays in the concluding part are of the most immediate interest. They address the concept of autonomy in international law and, in particular, as embodied in the Camp David Accords. Unfortunately, they are uneven in quality. The most comprehensive in scope and depth of analysis is the essay on the concept of autonomy in international law by Hurst Hannum and Richard Lillich. Drawing upon their recent two-volume study, *The Theory and Practice of Governmental Autonomy*, prepared under contract to the Department of State, the authors offer a number of generalizations based on their analysis of 22 cases of nonsovereign entities and federal states. In the great majority of autonomous entities, the local executive's role in foreign affairs is usually minimal; residual powers of a locally elected legislative body are generally reserved for the principal or sovereign state; most autonomous judicial systems enjoy fairly complete independence; the extent of local police powers and control over natural resources varies greatly; and, while the issue of control over land is one of the most divisive and complex in Middle East negotiations, it is not an issue that has often been addressed in other autonomy negotiations. Hannum and Lillich end by noting that there "may be the beginning of a trend away from independence and full statehood as the only answer to the problems perceived by ethnic communities within existing states or by non-self-governing territories which have yet to emerge fully on the international stage." Autonomy, they thus stress, "remains a useful, if imprecise, concept within which flexible and unique political structures may be developed to respond to that complexity."

This brings us, finally, to the issue of Egyptian-Israeli negotiations and the Camp David framework for autonomy. Mayer Gabay, Director-General of Israel's Ministry of Justice, contends that ambiguity, though "often referred to as the flaw of the Camp David Accords may eventually be seen as their great achievement." Because "there were apparently irreconcilable differences with respect to the details of the solution, the challenge for the lawyers was to find legal formulae which could provide the framework now called the Camp David Accords, yet not to exclude certain differing views of the parties." It was hoped, Gabay explains, "that the passage of time, the appearance of all the parties to the issues and the clarification of political options would finally lead to a detailed acceptable solution."

Itamar Rabinovich and Amos Shapira, in the next two essays, essentially share Gabay's view about the necessity of ambiguity for the success of the Camp David conference. Rabinovich, expanding upon Gabay's theme that Camp David was grounded, not unreasonably, in the hope that intervening political developments would improve the chances of success for autonomy, analyzes the factors that led to the disappointment of those hopes: Jordan's refusal to join the negotiations, the increase in PLO influence in the West Bank and elsewhere, the hardening of Arab and Jewish attitudes towards the West Bank, and the Begin Government's decision to oppose the option of first establishing autonomy in Gaza.

Dinstein does not, however, share many of his colleagues' assumptions about the Camp David autonomy process. He refers, in his concluding essay, to the negotiators' efforts as simply "this tendency to obfuscate issues." And he suggests that Egyptian-Israeli positions were inherently irreconcilable: "When two parties are negotiating a certain move, thinking that it will produce mutually contradictory results, one of them (at least) is bound to be grievously disappointed."

Moreover, Dinstein proceeds to assess the legal validity of the claim to sovereignty over the West Bank that the Begin Government said it would assert, or at least reserved the right to assert. "As far as the West Bank is concerned," he writes, "the sovereign State is the kingdom of Jordan. Jordanian sovereignty over the region is derived from the exercise of the right of self-determination by the inhabitants [referring to the Jericho Conference of 1948 and the general elections held in 1950]." Israel's current legal status in the West Bank is deemed to be clearly that of a belligerent-occupant. Although this may indeed be the view of most legal scholars, the matter is hardly free of controversy and it is therefore surprising that Dinstein chose not to note other views relevant to these questions.

Finally, it is to be noted that all four pieces on the Camp David process raise a wide range of important issues that are, unfortunately, not fully addressed. This is especially true of the contributions by Shapira and Dinstein. Shapira, in his essay *Reflections on the Autonomy: The Camp David Accords and the Obligation to Negotiate in Good Faith,* observes that "the Camp David Accords did not resolve, nor did they purport to resolve," the issue of autonomy but aimed rather "to set out a process of negotiations for resolution of the Palestinian problem while preserving Israel's vital interests." What is required now, Shapira contends, citing Articles 26 and 31 of the Vienna Convention on the Law of Treaties, is that the autonomy negotiations be conducted on the basis of "good faith." (Good faith negotiations are also referred to in the March 20, 1979 letter accompanying the signing of the Israel–Egypt Peace Treaty.) But what does "good faith" mean in this context? To what extent does customary international law relative to such matters as self-determination govern the interpretation of the Camp David Accords? Have the parties met their obligations to negotiate in good faith? And what are the consequences of a breach of this requirement? These are all questions that come to mind upon reading Shapira's thought-provoking piece, but which are ultimately left for the reader to ponder.

Similarly, Dinstein's essay, which ends on the following rather wistful note—"One can only express the hope that autonomy, designed to boost the prospects of peace in the Middle East, will not become its bane"—cries out for more explanation. Does Dinstein suggest that the concept of autonomy, designed to serve as a conduit to discussions over the final status of the territories, has outlived its usefulness? Does he maintain that the "creative ambiguity" of the Accords merely defers, and makes more difficult, resolution of the hard questions? The reader is left hoping that Dinstein and his colleagues might in future writings expand more fully on these ideas.

Regardless of any particular shortcomings of the papers, this volume is a significant contribution to greater understanding of the matrix of historical, legal, and political forces that can affect success or failure in negotiations for autonomy. It makes clear that in several important respects negotiating autonomy for the West Bank is a more difficult task than that presented in other instances. Nevertheless, in this reviewer's judgment, autonomy for the West Bank and Gaza, pursuant to the framework established by the Camp David Accords, will more and more be seen by the parties to the conflict as the only way out of their current dilemma. To say no to autonomy is to preserve the status quo. To say yes is to create a framework for movement that could lead to a variety of different outcomes, including a form of autonomy as an ultimate solution. In this climate, intelligent discussions of autonomy, like those provided in this volume, deserve the attention of all concerned with conflict resolution.

ALLAN GERSON

The Consolidated Treaty Series, 1648–1919. 231 vols. + index vol. Edited by Clive Parry. Dobbs Ferry: Oceana Publications, Inc., 1969–1981. $10,000/set.

One of the more remarkable editorial enterprises of recent decades has been Clive Parry's *Consolidated Treaty Series,* completed just before his untimely death in 1982. Parry intended his massive compilation, comprising 226 basic volumes with five supplements and a single index-guide (so far uncompleted), to replace the older, hard-to-obtain, and incomplete 19th-century *Recueil des principaux traités,* first edited by George Frédéric de Martens. The importance of the latter work is indicated by the inclusion in Parry's first volume of Martens's famous discourse on treaty collections, originally published in 1802. Nevertheless, Parry's contribution is demonstrably unique, and it provides an indispensable reference source to be used in connection with the later *League of Nations* and *United Nations Treaty Series.*

Reproductions of the treaty texts are presented in five different languages: Latin, German, French, Spanish, and English. (The Latin texts are sometimes accompanied by a translated version.) English texts of treaties and conventions are provided wherever possible or practicable. Each document is introduced by the author, but whereas the early volumes contain many one-page introductions, the middle volumes limit the introductory material to short paragraphs, and the last 46 volumes, plus the five supplements, give only a one-line description along with a list of printed sources where the treaty or convention may be found. There is a table of contents in each volume which includes the date of the treaty or convention, a descriptive title, the language or languages in which it appears, and the relevant page numbers. A table of abbreviations is provided for locating the sources cited in the final 46 volumes and five supplements.

The *Consolidated Treaty Series* begins with the year 1648–1649, commonly accepted as the genesis of classical international law, and the entire first volume is limited to those treaties and conventions relating to the so-called Peace of Westphalia. Appropriately, the last two regular volumes on the year 1919 are concerned primarily (but not exclusively) with the peace treaties and agreements relating to the end of the First World War. Other subjects for that seminal year include: extradition, postal matters, commerce, diplomatic bags, immigrants, and air navigation. The five supplementary or appendix volumes deal solely with treaties and agreements concluded by the Netherlands East India Company during the 17th and 18th centuries, covering more than five hundred documents governing Dutch commercial activity in India, the Near East, and East Asia. The treaty texts presented are in the Dutch language. Although the reader is provided with an occasional English translation, this practice is only infrequent and therefore not much use to scholars who lack proficiency in Dutch.

Unfortunately, Parry was able to complete only one index volume, covering the years 1648–1809,[1] before his death. With the exception of approximately 50 treaties, this index includes the documents contained in the first 59 volumes. Each entry provides the date of the instrument, the title or descriptive heading, reference to the particular volume and page where it can be located, and information as to other textual sources. There is also a 25-page list of general treaty collections and chronologies and their dates of publication.

The *Series* was truly an immense undertaking and provides a fitting mon-

[1] This volume is the result of a joint endeavor by Parry and Professor Paul Irwin.

ument to Professor Parry's excellent reputation as a scholar, editor, and teacher. It is indispensable for the historian, invaluable for the legal academic, and instructive for the student. This is a collection in the grand tradition, and everyone with an interest in international law should be aware of its existence.

ROBERT A. FRIEDLANDER
Ohio Northern University

Petitioning the United Nations: A Study in Human Rights. By Ton J. M. Zuijdwijk. Hampshire: Gower Publishing Co., Ltd.; New York: St. Martin's Press, 1982. Pp. xv, 397. Index. $35.

The first fifth (75 pages) of this potentially important book narrates the evolution over three decades of the UN's petition-reviewing jurisdiction in the field of human rights. Starting with the Human Rights Commission's voluntary denial, at its first session in 1947, of "power to take any action in regard to any complaints concerning human rights," Zuijdwijk sketches the subsequent efforts of governments, nongovernmental organizations, and individuals to give teeth to the UN Charter's human rights provisions. When the author went to press in mid-1979 (p. xiv), he was able correctly to conclude that "a wide spectrum of countries has come under investigation within the framework of [ECOSOC] resolution 1503" (p. 39). This he attributes to "skilful manipulation of the anti-colonialism and anti-*apartheid* movements" (p. 375).

Zuijdwijk's initial promise to trace Resolution 1503's "legislative history" (p. 1) is not fulfilled as well as it might have been, and should be in an early second edition. He has examined the written record in detail but largely ignored available human sources. The recollections of individuals would greatly enhance the book's usefulness. An example is the Commission's 1947 self-denial mentioned above, which is recited without a word of explanation for such bizarre behavior. Since the contributor of the preface, John P. Humphrey, figured prominently in these events as Commission Secretary and his writings are frequently cited, it is curious that his elucidation is omitted. Moreover, the book contains occasional revelations, such as the fact that in 1963, while head of the UN Human Rights Division, Humphrey wrote a speech for a private citizen; thus, at this late date there could hardly be any objection to naming those who set back, until 1967, the first exercise of UN authority to question mistreatment of citizens by governments (other than the South African Government and those in charge of non-self-governing territories).

Humphrey could well be given direct credit for the 1967 initiative, since, as a member of the Sub-Commission on Prevention of Discrimination and Protection of Minorities, it was he who first introduced there a resolution that the situations in Greece under "the Colonels" and in Haiti be referred to the Human Rights Commission (p. 21). At the same time, the author might have noted that the resolution as adopted, with an appendix documenting the conclusions, set a precedent for systematically drawing on both confidential and public sources under ECOSOC Resolution 1235. The Sub-Commission's authority to examine alleged violations of human rights now rests in Resolution 1235 and the later 1503, also inspired by Humphrey.

The Sub-Commission's existence is not explained by Zuijdwijk, nor is any light shed on its near demise in 1952, referred to only in a footnote (p. 57, n.62). In view of the "important function" he describes the Sub-Commission as playing (p. 16), more information about that body's nongovernmental "expert" makeup, so different from that of other UN organs, would have given the reader a clearer perception of possible reasons for the events discussed. Likewise, the Commission's struggles could be better understood in the context of other problems its governmental members were confronting at various stages.

The author could have achieved a more complete exegesis and certainly a more interesting narrative by explaining the weight of a single comma: no mention appears of the struggle between those, on the one hand, who favored a jurisdictional formula encompassing "the violation of human rights and fundamental freedoms, including policies of racial discrimination and segregation and of *apartheid* in all countries," and those, on the other hand, who prevailed in adding a comma before "in all countries."[1]

One paragraph and one footnote each (pp. 35–36; pp. 68–69, nn.204–05) are scarcely adequate to take notice of the UNESCO and ILO procedures for dealing with complaints in their spheres, particularly in contrast with the whole chapters on other human rights procedures and the tribute later paid to those of the ILO as "important and . . . effective" (p. 120).

Zuijdwijk's second section discusses five legal questions concerning the human rights authority taken to itself by the United Nations without benefit of treaty. The author's manifest bias in support of this authority robs his treatment of any appearance of objectivity, and he does not attempt in each case to deal with opposing arguments. The impressiveness of the book is not enhanced by footnote statements such as: "The time has come . . . to admit that the U.N. is in the process of changing the basic structure of international law" (p. 112, n.95).

Zuijdwijk's chapter on proposals for a UN High Commissioner for Human Rights shows how dangerous predictions can be even if pessimistic. His 1979 conclusion that "[i]t seems safe to assume that the High Commissioner proposal is now dead" (p. 129) was proven wrong within 2 years by a renewed initiative in the Sub-Commission, pursued favorably by a majority of the Commission in 1983.[2] More serious than being wrong about the future is to examine the past superficially. The author's reliance on Humphrey, a Canadian, for "what the Americans had in mind" (p. 119) in 1963, meaning what U.S. State Department policy consisted of, cannot be called resort to primary sources. Similarly, it is not worthy of the subject or the author for him to state, without reference to any source, that "the U.S. State Department had lost interest in the [High Commissioner] plan following the assassination of President Kennedy" (p. 120).

[1] The issue is skirted at pp. 15, 17.

[2] Comm'n on Human Rights Resolution 1983/49, adopted by a vote of 24 in favor, 11 against, 7 abstentions, according to the Commission's report, UN Doc. E/1983/13. The Sub-Commission in September 1983 gave its further support by a vote of 16 in favor, 3 against, 3 abstentions, UN Doc. E/CN.4/Sub.2/1983/L.14 as amended.

The chapter on Trusteeship Council procedures for dealing with petitions contrasts them with those of other UN organs. The author notes the usefulness of participation by the administering power in the discussions (p. 147), recalling his earlier stress on the legitimizing value of drawing accused governments into Resolution 1503 dialogues.

While this Council's method, unlike the 1503 procedure, gets high marks for dealing with individual cases, it is that of the Human Rights Committee, a treaty-created body under the Covenant on Civil and Political Rights, that rates being called "the best procedure within the U.N. system for the examination of petitions" (p. 361), and "the only attempt within the U.N. system to deal with cases from individuals in a quasi-judicial procedure and to render an opinion on the merits of the case" (p. 363).

Tightening-up is needed regarding Zuijdwijk's notion of a "law of the United Nations" (p. 238) as to human rights, also called "U.N. human rights law" (pp. 315, 380), a corpus of rules binding on states without their explicit consent. He should also find out from Humphrey and others, and explain to his readers, why the 1963 South Vietnam investigating team rushed home the day after a new regime invited it to stay (p. 237). Also to be explained is why the report found no facts but only restated the evidence (p. 239).

A strong case is made for the usefulness of hearing witnesses testify (p. 349) and for rules of procedure adopted in advance (p. 330), but there is no discussion of the possible usefulness of cross-examination.[3] The final conclusion, that a new body should replace the Sub-Commission, is given only a portion of the book's last paragraph and should be either supported or dropped.

JOHN CAREY*
Of the New York Bar

International Law and the Status of Women. By Natalie Kaufman Hevener. Boulder: Westview Press, 1983. Pp. xii, 249. Index. $20.

Dignity and Honour of Women as Basic and Fundamental Human Rights. By Yougindra Khushalani. The Hague, Boston, London: Martinus Nijhoff Publishers, 1982. Pp. 153. Dfl.105; $39.50.

These two slender volumes would complement the library of any student of human rights since they deal with the status of women under international law.

Hevener's book is essentially for reference. It makes available in one place those international legal documents that treat women as a separate, identifiable group. Hevener breaks down these instruments into three categories. The protective conventions, which came earliest, seek to shield women in their employment conditions, such as by prohibiting night work, employment in mines, and certain types of plantation labor. The second category of convention is

[3] The possibility of cross-examination is referred to implicitly or explicitly at pp. 306, 332, 333, and 337.

* The reviewer was a member of the Sub-Commission on Prevention of Discrimination and Protection of Minorities at its 1983 session.

corrective in nature, intended to ameliorate a distinct social problem or restriction. This type of convention covers matters such as loss of nationality at time of marriage, restrictions on prostitution, sale of women for forced labor, slavery and similar practices, child labor, and other personal abuses.

The third category, which is the most recent, is intended to prevent discrimination on the basis of sex in a wide variety of fields, with normative sex-neutral provisions as the underlying rationale. Hevener makes clear that nondiscrimination conventions, nevertheless, may also contain corrective or protective elements. The Maternity Protection Convention, which calls for nondiscrimination in employment, contains special arrangements for pregnant workers and mothers. A woman's job is secured during pregnancy and the early child-rearing period.

Hevener also summarizes recent nontreaty action, such as the Declaration and World Plan of Action for Women adopted at Mexico City in 1975 to open International Women's Year.

The compilation of the texts and compendia of nations that have ratified the various conventions makes this a most worthwhile reference book.

Khushalani's book concerns a most arresting subject in international law: the protection of the dignity and honor of women in times of conflict, including protection against rape on a mass scale, such as occurred in Bangladesh in 1971. The author reviews the basic laws governing the conduct of war, particularly the Hague Conventions of 1899 and 1907, and the Geneva Conventions of 1949. She traces the development of the concept of "crimes against humanity" and "war crimes." It is the author's conclusion that mass rape violates the laws of war and constitutes as well a "crime against humanity."

The author is firm in her belief that persons committing or participating in the crime of mass rape, in violation of normative standards of international law, are war criminals and, thus, liable to punishment by every state. Indeed, she stresses the international obligation to punish such war criminals, whether the war in question be deemed just or unjust by any standard, but she laments that it has rarely, if ever, been the case in fact.

The author more than makes her case. Whether this type of war crime, committed against innocent women, will ever arrest the attention of states, alas, remains to be seen.

RITA E. HAUSER
Of the New York and District of Columbia Bars

The Fund Agreement in the Courts: Volume II. Further Jurisprudence Involving the Articles of Agreement of the International Monetary Fund. By Joseph Gold. Washington: International Monetary Fund, 1982. Pp. xii, 499. Indexes. $17.50.

This is the second volume of a work, whose first volume appeared in 1962,[1] by the distinguished former Director of the Legal Department of the International Monetary Fund.

[1] The earlier volume was *The Fund Agreement in the Courts, Volume I* (1962), reviewed in 57 AJIL 961–63 (1963).

As the title suggests, this is not a book likely to interest a general legal audience. However, for those lawyers with specialties in international commercial law, the volume brings together in one place a series of articles—some that have previously been published and some that have not—by an eminent legal scholar on a wide variety of topics related to the Articles of Agreement of the IMF that have surprising relevance to private litigation.

As the author explains in the introduction, at one time it was thought that because the Articles were a treaty applicable to nation-states they had little relevance for private parties. In addition, the economic character of the Articles contributed to a widespread neglect of their legal impact.

That attitude began to change after the Fund signaled its serious commitment to the Articles by adopting an authoritative decision on June 10, 1949 on legal aspects of Article VIII, section 2(b), which declares that certain contracts offensive to the exchange control regulations of a member country of the Fund other than the forum country shall be treated as unenforceable by the forum. The judicial opinions in various countries that have applied and interpreted this article, which has spawned more litigation and controversy than any other provision of the IMF Articles, are discussed in several of the chapters of this second volume. Chapter 2, in particular, is devoted entirely to a series of U.S. cases involving this provision in which American courts have been called upon to adjudicate insurance policy claims that grew out of the Cuban nationalizations in 1959. Insurance companies in these cases invoked Article VIII, section 2(b) to support their contention that they were bound by Cuban regulations to pay on those policies only in Cuba, and not to policyholders in the United States who had since emigrated from Cuba. This argument was accepted in an influential decision by the Florida Supreme Court in *Confederation Life Association v. Ugalde* (164 So.2d 1, *cert. denied,* 379 U.S. 915 (1964)), which held that because Cuban currency was involved in such insurance claims the IMF Articles required recognition of the Cuban exchange control laws permitting payment only in Cuba.

The rest of the book covers a wide range of other topics related to the IMF Articles, including questions involving the combined effects of the GATT and the Articles on exchange control, the many judicial decisions on units of accounts defined in terms of gold, and other legal issues involving exchange rates.

The most interesting of these other topics, at least to this reader, is the discussion in chapter 12 of the relationship between the IMF Articles and the freeze on Iranian assets imposed by President Carter in November 1979. Much of this chapter provides commentary on the arguments of legal scholars and judges in various countries as to whether the U.S. freeze ran afoul of certain provisions of the Articles.

While there is little question that the author has rendered an erudite treatment of all of these issues, it would have been useful if he had expanded his introduction (beyond the eight short pages that are found at the front) to tie together the different themes that appear in the individual chapters. Because he did not, the reader is left to search in different places of the volume for explanations of key provisions of the Articles. Moreover, in many instances, the reader is given little background to the treatment of often quite technical subjects.

These organizational criticisms notwithstanding, Gold's second volume on the treatment of the IMF Articles by the courts in various countries should stand as an authoritative reference work for international specialists for years to come.

ROBERT LITAN
Of the District of Columbia Bar

The International Labor Organization: An American View. By Walter Galenson. Madison: The University of Wisconsin Press, 1981. Pp. xi, 351. Index. $21.50, cloth; $7.75, paper.

The Politics of United States Decision-Making in United Nations Specialized Agencies: The Case of the International Labor Organization. By Gregory T. Kruglak. Washington: University Press of America, 1980. Pp. ix, 290. $21.25.

Why did the United States withdraw from the International Labour Organisation in 1977—the first, and thus far, only U.S. withdrawal from a UN agency? And why did it return in 1980? The two recent studies reviewed here document the long-standing ambivalence of the U.S. commitment to the ILO and suggest factors leading to the unusual action of withdrawal. They also suggest that the U.S. Government as well as U.S. employers and worker organizations should reevaluate the significance of the ILO for the United States and take a more active and positive role within the ILO in the future.

There is much support for the view that the United States withdrew from the ILO because of George Meany's deep-seated anticommunism which found the membership of the USSR an abomination in an organization in which the AFL-CIO participated. The United States rejoined the ILO, according to this explanation, shortly after George Meany was no longer on the scene. That the influence of Meany in the U.S. decision was significant—perhaps decisive—is evident. But the "Meany as sole cause" explanation is superficial. Since the United States joined the ILO in 1934 there has been, on the one hand, a persistent conviction in U.S. circles that ILO activities, including the setting of labor standards, are irrelevant to the U.S. scene and, on the other hand, a fear that ILO labor standards might have an effect on U.S. domestic labor standards. These contradictory views have resulted in either a belief in the irrelevancy of the ILO or hostility towards it. Thus, neither U.S. labor leaders nor employers have evidenced great enthusiasm for the ILO. As a result, the Government has placed a low priority on ILO affairs which ultimately led to the withdrawal from the Organisation.

In 1975, the Ford administration, in a letter from Secretary of State Kissinger, gave the required 2-year notice of intent to withdraw from the ILO. The Kissinger letter cited erosion of tripartite representation, a double standard on human rights, lack of due process, and increasing politicization within the

ILO as reasons for the contemplated withdrawal. In 1977, President Carter announced the U.S. withdrawal.

The U.S. withdrawal from the ILO and its subsequent reentry in 1980 were major events in the history of U.S. relations with the United Nations and its specialized agencies. Despite widespread dissatisfaction with other UN agencies, in particular UNESCO, the United States has not in other cases taken the radical step of withdrawal. The decision by President Carter to leave the ILO was also an anomalous one by an administration committed to the promotion of human rights, since the ILO, despite the Kissinger criticism, has been a pioneer and a leader in the development of effective human rights supervisory systems.

The Kruglak book is a study of decision making within the three U.S. constituencies concerned with ILO matters: the Government, the AFL-CIO, and the Chamber of Commerce. The author uses the U.S. refusal to pay its assessed dues to the ILO in 1970, in violation of international law, as the focal point for a case study of the politics of U.S. decision making. He points out that, although the 1970 decision was precipitated by the appointment of a Soviet national as Assistant Deputy-General of the ILO, the underlying issues involved in the 1970 crises remained unresolved and were directly related to the later decision to withdraw.

The ILO is the only UN agency in which nongovernmental organizations—employer and worker organizations—are given full and direct participation. In theory, such organizations are to be independent of their governments, but since the founding of the ILO in 1919 many, perhaps most, have not been. The desire for universality of membership has pragmatically been given precedence within the ILO over the principle of independent employer and worker representation. Only relatively few countries in the world have truly independent employer and worker organizations. Kruglak cites this conflict between the principle of universality and the principle of independent industrial organization representation (to which most other ILO member states have become reconciled) as a continuing problem in U.S.-ILO relations and the source of the antagonism of George Meany towards the ILO—an antagonism that greatly influenced the U.S. decision to withdraw. Valuable information is provided by Kruglak on conflicting goals and lack of coordination among the Departments of State, Labor, and Commerce in U.S. attitudes towards the ILO. Of concern to international lawyers is the failure of Congress to take into account the international legal responsibilities of the United States in its decision to withhold legally assessed dues to the ILO in 1970. In considering the lack of enthusiasm towards the ILO by the U.S. Government and labor and employer organizations, Kruglak concludes that

> the low level of priority accorded to the ILO by the government unit became self-fulfilling and self-sustaining. Given the manpower and resources allocated by the executive branch, it would have been physically impossible for those responsible to develop a viable, long range outlook, or for that matter, even to participate effectively on a day-to-day basis. Delegations were sent to ILO meetings understaffed and ill-prepared to develop and defend positions of interest to the United States government;

> and consequently, criticism was voiced that the arena was being lost to the Communist and Third World States [pp. 7–8].

Kruglak analyzes decision making during the 1970 controversy in terms of various paradigms. He utilizes current political and social theories of "Analytic, Organizational, Bureaucratic, and Social Psychological Inputs" concerning decision making, only to conclude that his study "had produced data which would suggest that the decision-making process in this instance has been influenced by a wide range of variables exceeding the parameters of traditional decision-making paradigms" (p. 4). In other words, the paradigms have shed little light on this particular case study.

The research undertaken by Kruglak on U.S.-ILO affairs is extensive and useful. His conclusions, however, are tentative and hesitant and do little to explain U.S. relations to other international organizations. The author's effort to fit the facts of this case study into paradigms of decision making was obfuscating and distracting to this reviewer. The interest of the Kruglak study lies not in theories concerning decision making but in the author's extensive documentation of U.S.-ILO relations. Readers not enamored of theoretical frameworks of decision making may profitably skip part of the book to ferret out this worthwhile documentation.

Professor Galenson's book is specifically focused on the U.S. withdrawal from the ILO. His study attempts to (1) explain why the United States withdrew from the ILO, and (2) explore and evaluate the two main functions of the ILO: the setting of international labor standards and the administration of technical assistance to less-developed countries. The discussion of the first purpose takes up five chapters. The treatment of the second occupies two chapters. A final chapter concerns the future role of the United States in the ILO.

This is a curious work. The two sections of the book dealing with the explanation for the withdrawal and the evaluation of the main functions of the ILO are so dissimilar in tone and interpretation of events that one is led to conclude that the author is schizophrenic towards the ILO. In chapters analyzing the reasons for the U.S. withdrawal, Galenson provides an apologia for the U.S. position enunciated in the original Kissinger letter of intent to withdraw: alleged lack of due process and a double standard in the ILO work on human rights, erosion of tripartism, and increasing politicization in the ILO. His analysis here adds little to the reasons mentioned in the Kissinger letter, appears tendentious at times, and displays slight comprehension or sympathetic understanding of the reasons why our Western allies, observing the same events within the ILO, chose to remain ardent supporters of the Organisation and to oppose U.S. withdrawal. Galenson refers repeatedly in these chapters to the lack of support for the U.S. position on various matters within the ILO from our own Western allies. His reiteration of the solitary position of the United States leads one to think of the proud mother observing her son on parade: "Everyone is out of step but my Bill!" His view of the ILO in these chapters is essentially negative. That view is considerably mitigated in his later chapters.

The two chapters on technical assistance and the setting of international labor standards are comprehensive, informative, and thoughtful. They evidence a sophisticated understanding of both the deficiencies and successes of ILO action coupled with an understanding of the complexity of work in these areas. Galenson rightly observes that the ILO devotes most of its energies to these two endeavors, but "they scarcely figured in the U.S. decision to withdraw. In fact, very little is known about them in the United States" (p. 22). In earlier chapters the author criticizes the alleged lack of due process and a double standard in the human rights work of the ILO. In the chapter on standard setting he observes, however, that the machinery set up by the ILO to supervise its human rights conventions is "generally regarded as superior to that of any other international organization" (p. 232). He praises the impartiality of the ILO Committee of Experts, which has not bowed to political pressures, and he points out that the committee has cited deficiencies of socialist bloc countries in implementing ILO conventions. His general conclusion concerning ILO action in these two chapters appears positive.

As mentioned earlier, the erosion of tripartism is frequently mentioned as a persistent U.S. complaint concerning the ILO. The author, however, observes that this complaint alone would probably not have resulted in a U.S. withdrawal. A large number of union representatives at ILO conferences are not independent of governmental control and this has been true since the early days of the ILO. The ILO Constitution does not require that such representatives be independent of governmental control. Yet, the attainment of independent trade unions in member states remains an ILO objective, as the recent outstanding efforts of the ILO with regard to Poland make evident. The U.S. return to the ILO is a welcome acceptance of the importance of universality in the Organisation, coupled with a recognition that there is value in supporting an international organization whose aim is so fully compatible with American ideals despite difficulties in attaining those ideals.

Galenson cites anti-Israeli resolutions at the annual ILO Conference and the admission of the PLO to observer status at the Conference as among the most decisive issues in the final U.S. decision to withdraw. Israel itself, however, has shown no inclination to withdraw from the ILO and an Israeli worker presently sits as a deputy member of the ILO Governing Body.

Much of Galenson's negative comments relating to the ILO concern political actions (such as controversial resolutions) at the 3-week annual ILO Conference. His positive comments relate to the regular on-going work of the ILO. His final chapter contains some thoughtful remarks concerning future participation in the ILO. Particularly noteworthy are his suggestions that the United States should ratify key ILO conventions relating to human rights. The U.S. record on ratification—seven conventions among more than 150—has been a source of embarrassment to the United States and remains a disgrace. The author concludes by urging the United States to take a more active role in the Organisation in the future.

While the two books under review provide interesting information on U.S. participation in the ILO, and on ILO activities in general, they lack the sophisticated analyses of the International Labour Organisation contained in other writings, for example, by Robert Cox and John P. Windmuller. The reader is left finally with the perplexing question of why U.S. participation in the ILO has been so inadequate since in terms of U.S. interest, the ILO, as Galenson notes, "remains potentially the most important of all the specialized international agencies" (p. 276).

VIRGINIA A. LEARY
State University of New York at Buffalo

The Law of International Institutions (4th ed.). By D. W. Bowett. Published under the auspices of The London Institute of World Affairs. London: Stevens & Sons, 1982. Pp. xv, 431. Index, bibliography. $44.75, cloth; £12.50, $29.50, paper. Distributed by Carswell Legal Publications.

Professor Bowett's book is, in most respects, excellent as a concise introductory text for use by students of law or international relations, or by anyone with a general interest in the activities of international organizations. This new edition is therefore welcome.

The book is divided into four parts, and includes a historical introduction. Parts I–III are essentially descriptive, treating in turn global, regional, and judicial institutions. Part IV, which is more analytic, addresses certain institutional problems common to all international organizations.

In a treatment of the functions and powers of the principal organs of the United Nations, Bowett discusses Charter provisions and UN practice with useful references to specific cases and resolutions. He gives special attention to the powers and responsibilities of the Security Council and General Assembly in peace and security matters.

Under the heading "Organizations of limited competence," the author summarizes, very briefly, the functions of the UN specialized agencies and GATT. Appearing for the first time in this edition are the World Intellectual Property Organization, the International Fund for Agricultural Development, and the UN Industrial Development Organization. This is followed by a comparative survey of provisions on institutional structure and a discussion of the "legislative" or "law-making" sanctioning and enforcement procedures of the specialized agencies. Part I concludes with a few paragraphs—new to the fourth edition—on the Organization of Petroleum Exporting Countries.

In Part II, on regional institutions, the following changes in the new edition are of particular interest. In the discussion of the Organisation for Economic Co-operation and Development, there is mention of the autonomous International Energy Agency, set up in 1974. A paragraph in the third edition (p. 178) stating that, with the expansion of membership in the EEC, the "demise" of the European Free Trade Association seemed "only a matter of time," has been excised. In the section on the European Communities, there is mention of the 1979 accession of Greece to membership, of the first direct parliamentary elections in 1979, of the Lomé Conventions of 1975 and 1979, of the European Council of heads of state or government, formalized in 1974, and of the Court of Auditors, set up in 1975.

In the section on Latin American organizations, a reference to the establishment in 1979 of the Inter-American Court of Human Rights has been added. There are also descriptions of the Latin American Economic System, established in 1975; the Andean Pact organization, a 1969 outgrowth of the Latin American Free Trade Association (LAFTA); the 1978 Treaty for Amazonian Cooperation; the Latin American Integration Association, established in 1980 to replace LAFTA; and the Caribbean Community, which replaced the Caribbean Free Trade Area in 1974.

Sections on the Central Treaty Organization and the South-East Asia Treaty Organization appearing in earlier editions have been deleted in their entirety; the dissolution of the latter in 1977 is mentioned in passing, but that of the former, in 1979, is nowhere to be found. A discussion of the Association of South East Asian Nations has been added. The 1975 treaty giving an institutional framework to the West African Economic Community is mentioned, and the evolving structure of the Economic Community of East Africa is discussed.

In Part III, on judicial institutions (including administrative tribunals), the only changes of note in the fourth edition are an expanded discussion of interlocutory proceedings in the International Court of Justice, and a treatment of the International Centre for Settlement of Investment Disputes (whose constituent instrument entered into force in 1966).

Part IV, on common institutional problems, is essentially unchanged save for some updating. It comprises two chapters: international personality, and the impact of international organizations on the doctrine of sovereign equality of states. The former includes treaty-making powers, privileges and immunities, the responsibility of international organizations for their acts, the law governing their activities (choice of law and jurisdictional questions), and the dissolution of organizations and problems of succession. In the final chapter, Bowett examines "how far, by a constant process of development and experiment," the theoretical consequences of the doctrine of sovereign equality (*e.g.*, unanimity in decision making) "have been evaded by different techniques" (p. 383). Thus he discusses such topics as observer status, "associate" membership, suspension, withdrawal, and expulsion, as well as reservations to constituent instruments and nonratification of amendments. The book ends, rather abruptly, with a discussion of some of the budgetary issues faced by international organizations.

The author has—understandably, given the objective of conciseness—been selective in updating the book. Most of the additions to the fourth edition are brief and other alterations are relatively few and minor. Unfortunately, the revision process has fallen short in the correction of errors, many of which persist from one edition to the next. This, and the fact that in a number of instances facts and figures are not updated, makes the book a dubious buy, particularly at its current price. The following errors are a representative sampling:[1] references on pages 2 and 3 to the Congress, and the Conference, of Berlin of 1871—presumably the intended reference is to the Congress of 1878—appear in all four editions. On page 166, there is a reference to the 1948

[1] Several errors noted in a review of the first edition by Professor Leo Gross, 59 AJIL 419 (1965), remain uncorrected.

"Treaty" of Bogotá, and on page 216 to the "Pack" (*sic*) of Bogotá, while on page 219 the author makes clear that in each of those instances he is really referring to the Charter of Bogotá. These references remain unchanged from the first edition. A reference on page 211 to the "ESCC Community," which in the context is both redundant and wrong, appeared first in the second edition and remains undetected. A reference on page 216 to "the present decade" remains unchanged since the second edition was published 13 years ago. A correct reference on page 223 to the General Secretariat of the Organization of American States, formerly the Pan-American Union, is followed in subsequent paragraphs by references to the former title. A list on page 385 of the specialized agencies of which "the Republic of Vietnam is a Member" persists despite the change of government in 1975.

Except for doubts about the thoroughness of the revision process, this book is to be recommended within the bounds of its objective as a basic introduction for use mainly by undergraduate students.

RICHARD W. NELSON
Catholic University of America, Visiting Lecturer in Law

The Status of Observers in the United Nations. By R. G. Sybesma-Knol. Brussels: Vrije Universiteit Brussel, 1981. Pp. xi, 484. Index.

The title of this work is misleading. Its main focus, to be sure, is on observers in the United Nations. Its coverage of that subject is extensive and includes nonmember states, nonmembers of particular organs, regional international organizations, other international organizations, liberation movements, and other nonstate actors including nongovernmental organizations. The topics covered include only briefly and in passing specialized agencies or other bodies in the UN system, either as participants in the United Nations itself or as venues for participation by other actors. The work goes beyond its title, however, in two respects. It deals with all forms of external participation in the United Nations and in the League of Nations before it, not just those involving formal "observer" status. Thus, there are excursions into such diverse subjects as the continued participation of various countries in the ILO and in the economic and social activities of the League after they had withdrawn from League membership, and the treatment of Liechtenstein's application to become a party to the Statute of the International Court of Justice. Second, the author felt compelled to detail not only the arrangements involving nonmember participation in the United Nations but, often, the historical background of the origins and development of the agencies concerned. The reader is thus exposed to sketchy and not always entirely accurate historical synopses about the OAS, the Arab League, the PLO, and the Council of Europe, among many others. By contrast, the chapter on NGO's is brief and mainly rehearses well-known information about the system stemming from Article 71 of the Charter under which NGO's relate to the United Nations. On this subject, readers would be better served by the recent work by Chiang Pei-heng.[1] Not only does Chiang offer a fuller treatment of UN relations with NGO's, but her study also captures the tension resulting from the predominantly Western pluralist origins of the NGO's and what Chiang describes as "functionalist, statist and bureaucratic tendencies in the UN."

The conclusion that emerges from the analysis is that the network of non-member relations with the United Nations is dense, variegated, and of uneven significance. The untidiness of all but the NGO system of relations inspires the author, somewhat hesitantly, to advocate consideration of a more orderly regulation of the system. The reasons, however, do not extend beyond a fastidious distaste for untidiness and hardly support the idea that the results would justify the effort and the attendant real costs of trying to introduce a more orderly scheme.

The main virtue of this book is its author's conscientious success in compiling in one place an exceptionally full set of information about the relations between the United Nations and the broad panoply of external participants.

LAWRENCE S. FINKELSTEIN
Northern Illinois University

Consultation Clauses as Means of Providing for Treaty Obedience: A Study in the Law of Treaties. By Judo Umarto Kusumowidagdo. Stockholm: Almqvist & Wiksell International, 1981. Pp. 321. Kr.345; $63.50. Distributed by Transnational Publishers, Inc.

Consultation clauses, known since the Congress of Vienna, have proliferated in the last 40 years. Although some detailed analyses of certain clauses exist, a broader study of the subject has been lacking. The book under review is a response to that need. The author undertook the endeavor convinced that consultation clauses have a significant role to play in an increasingly interdependent world.

He focuses on such clauses embodied in "treaties of common interests," a category which, without adequate justification, he limits to treaties dealing with economic rather than political matters. In the main part of the book (pp. 107–286), Kusumowidagdo describes the use of consultation clauses in several treaty arrangements, *inter alia,* those regulating apportionment of rights (*e.g.,* bilateral air transport agreements, treaties regulating the use of common resources, and double taxation agreements), and those establishing international economic organizations, both regional (*e.g.,* the EEC) and global (*e.g.,* GATT and the IMF), or borrowing agreements (concluded within the IBRD, the IDA, and between states). However, NATO, the Warsaw Pact, the OAS, and SALT I are omitted.

The author contends that consultation clauses mitigate the arbitrary exercise of rights of the parties to treaties and help to ensure their proper observance. He offers specific proposals for refining these clauses, although he admits that no "model clauses" need be designed (pp. 302–03).

[1] NON-GOVERNMENTAL ORGANIZATIONS AT THE UNITED NATIONS: IDENTITY, ROLE, AND FUNCTION (1981).

Another important point is Kusumowidagdo's contention that under customary international law states have a duty to consult with each other prior to action in matters of common interest and concern. Somewhat surprisingly, no mention is made in this context of Article 3 of the Charter of Economic Rights and Duties of States (1974), which imposes such a duty in cases of exploitation of natural resources shared by two or more countries.

The book is enigmatic in both conceptualization and form. The problems of fact, legal reasoning, and last, but not least, expression loom large. The following quotation concluding the inquiry into the municipal law of several states typifies the difficulties a reader of this ambitious study may encounter:

> By using the preceding process of *reductio ad absurdum,* that is a juridical formulation by comparative law to discover what is general among legal principles and to establish the universality of a precept and its place in the corpus of international law, as an ancillary discipline to international law, we conclude that the concept of an obligation of each party to consult other parties within a group prior to action affecting common interest or common concern in which everyone of them recognizes the existence of this common interest or common concern is a general principle of law which is bound to become a universal legal principle [pp. 71–72].

Uncritical editing and inattention to detail serve to compound the other problems with this work.

MARIA FRANKOWSKA
Treaty Research Center
University of Washington

The Modern International Law of Outer Space. By Carl Q. Christol. New York: Pergamon Press, 1982. Pp. xiii, 932. Index. $85.

The author's expertise in the emerging field of space law is reflected in this prodigious book, to which Christol brings a wealth of experience as a professor of political science and international law. The chapter titles reveal the breadth of subjects covered—from treaties already in effect to legal issues yet unresolved. Repeated emphasis is placed on the need to have an understanding of the applicable science and technology in formulating governing legal principles. The extension of the rule of law to outer space by the formulation of substantive legal principles, standards, and rules, as part of a tailored legal regime, is presented as mandatory if order is to prevail in the exploration, use, and exploitation of resources of the space environment. It may be noted that the initial 1967 Outer Space Treaty provides that "States Parties to the Treaty shall carry on activities in the exploration and use of outer space . . . in accordance with international law, including the Charter of the United Nations."[1] The author's background, knowledge, and experience in international law instill confidence in his views on the law governing space activities.

[1] Treaty on Principles Governing the Activities of States in the Exploration and Use of Outer Space, Including the Moon and Other Celestial Bodies, Jan. 27, 1967, 18 UST 2410, TIAS No. 6347, 610 UNTS 205 (effective Oct. 10, 1967).

This book provides a wealth of reliable source material for the beginning reader in space law, as well as for the more knowledgeable reader. Many of its chapters are concerned with subjects considered at sessions of the UN Committee on the Peaceful Uses of Outer Space (COPUOS) and its two subcommittees (Legal Sub-committee and Scientific and Technical Sub-committee). The author describes the position of states in succeeding sessions on issues considered. Delegates to sessions of COPUOS or its subcommittees should find this description helpful in acquainting them with, or refreshing their recollection of, past consideration of issues.

The "consensus" principle used in decision making by COPUOS and its subcommittees is portrayed: a proposed provision in the drafting of a treaty or other position paper undergoes revision until objection is no longer raised. The value of this procedure is that it makes the final document more readily acceptable to the UN General Assembly and to later signature and ratification by states. It has resulted in the drafting of five treaties within COPUOS, four of which are currently in effect;[2] the fifth will become effective 30 days after the filing of but one further instrument of ratification.[3]

Christol examines such subjects studied and discussed by COPUOS and its subcommittees as international direct television broadcasting by satellite; remote sensing from space of Earth resources; definition or delineation of outer space; use of nuclear power sources in space-vehicle propulsion; space transportation systems, *e.g.*, the U.S. Space Shuttle; and the positioning of geostationary orbital (GEO) satellites,[4] including the equatorial states' claim of sovereignty over the portion of the orbit above them, and the concern of the World Administrative Radio Conferences (WARC's), past and planned, with allocation of GEO positions and portions of the radio spectrum for satellite communication.

The initial 1967 Outer Space Treaty looked to international cooperation in space exploration and use for the benefit of all mankind. This desire is further reflected in the subsequent space law treaties and in other formulations of the COPUOS Legal Sub-committee. However, the author notes that ideological and cultural differences influence states in their consideration of new scientific and technological development. In the debates on remote sensing, the principal issues noted are lawful earth sensing from free outer space versus

[2] The 1967 Principles Treaty, *ibid.;* Agreement on the Rescue of Astronauts, the Return of Astronauts and the Return of Objects Launched into Outer Space, Apr. 22, 1968, 19 UST 7570, TIAS No. 6599, 672 UNTS 119 (effective Dec. 3, 1968); Convention on International Liability for Damage Caused by Space Objects, Mar. 29, 1972, 24 UST 2389, TIAS No. 7762, 26 UN GAOR Supp. (No. 29) at 25, UN Doc. A/8429 (1972) (effective Oct. 9, 1973); Convention on Registration of Objects Launched into Outer Space, Jan. 14, 1975, 28 UST 695, TIAS No. 8480, 29 UN GAOR Supp. (No. 31) at 16, UN Doc. A/9631 (1975) (effective Sept. 15, 1976). The texts of these treaties and the status of their ratifications are set forth in the appendixes of the book.

[3] Agreement Governing the Activities of States on the Moon and Other Celestial Bodies, 34 UN GAOR Supp. (No. 20) at 33, UN Doc. A/34/20 (1979); and Annex to UNGA Res. 34/68, Dec. 14, 1979. The treaty, thus far, has been signed by 11 states (not including the United States or the USSR) and has been ratified by Chile, the Philippines, the Netherlands, and Uruguay.

[4] Twenty-two thousand three hundred miles above the Earth's equator; at this altitude the satellite's speed in orbit is synchronous with the rotation of the Earth and thus the satellite maintains a consistent, although not fixed, hovering position over the same area of the Earth.

the claim of infringement of sovereignty (*i.e.*, to the entitlement of a state to privacy of its natural resources, and to barring transmission of its sensed data without its consent). In direct telecommunications broadcasting from satellites, the issue concerned the contended right of all persons to receive a free flow of information without regard to borders versus the contention of infringement of sovereignty (*i.e.*, of a state's right to determine whether to admit broadcasting signals beamed to it). Since the publication of this book, the UN General Assembly has adopted a resolution stating "governing principles" for direct television broadcasting that purports to establish such service following agreement with the receiving state.[5] However, as the resolution is not binding international law, the discussion by the author on this issue remains relevant.

On the subject of space transportation system (STS) operations, the author discusses the extension of civil and criminal law of the launching state, vesting of authority in the commander of the spacecraft, the legal status of the vehicle, and the advisability of formulating "uniform international standards" for the operation and activities of space objects, and particularly for a private sector launch of a space object from foreign soil.

The consideration given to other subjects provides the reader with detailed information and guidance on unresolved problems such as those raised by the "Moon Treaty" on an international undertaking to establish an international regime to govern exploitation of the natural resources of the moon when exploitation "is about to become feasible," and those raised by the claims of developing states to "special consideration" in the "equitable sharing . . . in the benefits derived from these resources" under the "common heritage of mankind" principle.[6]

Each chapter of the book is self-contained: for each subject considered, the author provides historical, scientific, and technical background, the legal issues involved and appropriate quotations from authoritative sources, a detailed summary and conclusions, and an impressive bibliography. While self-containment of chapters necessarily produces some repetition, the comprehensive tailored treatment of a subject in a given chapter should prove a timesaver to the researcher concerned only with that subject. The researcher will be further aided by an excellent subject index.

The author asserts that space law is a modern body of law that will continue to evolve and expand; that when measured by any standard, it has achieved enormous maturity in an exceedingly brief time; and that international lawyers would be hard pressed to identify other areas of international law where so many achievements have resulted in so short a time.

With the Space Shuttle now operational, and with the rapidly growing interest of the private sector in future commercial space endeavors, this informative book is timely and should prove helpful to persons interested in the issues involved in this new, but rapidly expanding, field of law.

MARTIN MENTER
Washington, D.C.

[5] UNGA Res. 37/92, Dec. 10, 1982, *reprinted in* 77 AJIL 733 (1983).

[6] *See* Art. 11, 1979 Moon Treaty, *supra* note 3.

The New Nationalism and the Use of Common Spaces: Issues in Marine Pollution and the Exploitation of Antarctica. Edited by Jonathan I. Charney. Published under the auspices of The American Society of International Law. Totowa, N.J.: Allanheld, Osmun & Co., 1982. Pp. ix, 343. Index. $39.50.

There is, of course, nothing new about nationalism. The historical sections of this book about ocean pollution and Antarctica highlight the continuing power of nationalism on these areas, which are traditionally thought to be exemplary of international cooperation. To the extent that there are international regimes for the oceans and Antarctica, they are the result of past trade-offs between competing claims that derived from national interests. The "new nationalism" of the title refers to the more recent claims to benefits derived from exploiting these areas, which are seen as the common heritage of mankind. Such claims reinforce and entrench existing national demands, and the resultant polarization in the global community diminishes the prospect of development of realistic management schemes for the world's resources.

However, some headway has been made in the area of marine pollution, which is dealt with in part 1 of this book. In her chapter on the prevention of pollution from vessels, Jan Schneider concludes that there has been some impressive development towards a viable international regime, although more remains to be done. Attempts at international cooperation to control pollution from land-based sources have not been so successful. Professor Whipple's useful summary of pollutants and their sources, supported by scientific and technical data and an overview of national programs of various countries, suggests that the problem may be quite serious and difficult to solve. Judith Kildow's interesting analysis of the political and economic dimensions of the issue confirms this conclusion, as does the account of the legal aspects by Robert McManus.

The establishment of an international regime for the development of resources in Antarctica is a somewhat similar story told in the second, and larger, part of the book. Dr. Zumberge and Professor Pontecorvo, who are the authors of two chapters on potential mineral resources, exhaustively examine the availability of resources, possible environmental problems of their extraction, and the economics of exploitation. Professor Bilder analyzes the legal and political situation in the area and explores realistic future strategies for a mineral resource regime. He concludes that despite the difficulties posed, agreement will probably be reached on practical measures to deal with immediate problems and ultimately longer term solutions. The final chapter, in which James Barnes discusses the emerging Convention on the Conservation of Antarctic Marine Living Resources exemplifies the difficulties of formulating a universally agreed strategy that have been adverted to in the previous chapters. The conclusion is that while mineral resources are unlikely to be exploitable in the foreseeable future, a regime for their exploitation is likely to be established.

Despite their obvious frustration with national claims that hinder solutions to the important issues addressed, the authors patiently explore past efforts at regulation, the realities of the present regimes, and possibilities for the future without being alarmist or unduly pessimistic. Although most of them have served with U.S. advisory committees and agencies on the subject, they do not demonstrate bias and realistically explain and take into account the attitudes of developing countries and their impact on the international regulation of resources. The main message is that absence of scientific and technical data is a serious concern. In the case of the oceans, the fear is that without proof of the danger to the environment, there is unlikely to be significant further cooperation to abate pollution. The lack of data on Antarctica's minerals and the environmental impact of their exploitation is seen as a potential hindrance to the formulation of a responsive legal regime. However, this collection with its concise and well-argued analysis and detailed documentation of those sources that are available goes some way towards alerting us to the need for renewed efforts at mobilizing awareness and action on these issues.

SUSANNE TONGUE
The Fletcher School of Law and Diplomacy

The Environmental Law of the Sea. Edited by Douglas M. Johnston. Gland, Switzerland: International Union for Conservation of Nature and Natural Resources, 1981. Pp. 419.

In the excitement over the seabed mining provisions of the recent Law of the Sea Convention, other important aspects of the new regime for the oceans are frequently overlooked. This publication focuses our attention on one of them, marine conservation.

The book is the product of a 2-year study by the Commission on Environmental Policy, Law and Administration of the International Union for Conservation of Nature and Natural Resources. Although it was written before adoption of the new Convention, the authors relied on the environmental provisions of the 1980 Draft Convention which were not significantly altered in the final treaty. The result is a welcome and expert analysis of the effect of the provisions in the Convention that relate to the environment.

The first chapter describes the historical development of the environmental law of the sea, recalling the advances made in a relatively short time and the role played by environmental awareness in helping to bring about the convening of UNCLOS III. The second, and largest, chapter traces the development of controls for the conservation and management of living resources, concluding with an analysis of the most recent treaties. It provides for lay persons a very lucid account of the complex subject of fisheries. The third chapter on prevention and control of marine pollution includes analysis of various sources of pollution: from vessels (the main focus of the UNCLOS III provisions), ocean dumping, land-based operations, seabed activities, and finally, seabed mining, which is perceived as a potential environmental threat. These three chapters provide a historical overview of marine conservation in the context of the impact of the new Convention on previous arrangements. A supplementary theme of the book is the importance of regional arrangements in implementing environmental protection measures, and in the chapter devoted exclusively to this subject, there are useful charts of current and evolving regional agreements for conservation of marine species and marine pollution prevention control, as well as for protection and conservation of the marine environment. Finally, and most importantly, the study culminates in a series of sound conclusions and recommendations for future action. Since the new Convention does not provide a comprehensive approach to environmental considerations but does extend national responsibility for marine conservation, the authors conclude that the future of the oceans depends primarily on states and international organizations assuming the responsibility for implementation and development of protection and preservation measures for the marine environment. The authors suggest a world ocean conservation strategy and global and regional coordination of activities. In addition to timely ideas as to how the new provisions can be elaborated and implemented, they put forward concrete proposals for the future roles of various organizations, together with methods that could be employed to coordinate their programs.

Because the study is composed of essays by various experts, there tends to be duplication of information, particularly with regard to historical details. Since there is no index, even after a thorough examination of the detailed table of contents, one cannot be sure that everything on a particular subject has been uncovered. This is unfortunate since the book purports to be, and inevitably will be used as, a comprehensive source book. However, if information is sought on one subject—*e.g.*, fisheries, ocean dumping—it is possible to find a complete and sufficient account in one place. Furthermore, the extensive footnotes at the end of each essay provide a variety of sources for further investigation. The editors have done a good job in pulling the strands of each essay together in the concluding chapter. The overall impression is that all the contributors are realistically appreciative of the effectiveness of international law in resolving conflicts between conservation and development, and somewhat optimistic about controlling abuse of our oceans.

SUSANNE TONGUE
The Fletcher School of Law and Diplomacy

The Forms of Action at International Law. By H. A. Schwarz-Liebermann von Wahlendorf. Published by author. Pp. iii, 55.

This idiosyncratic little book is hardly a book at all. It is an essay and is about the length of a moderate-sized law review article. It has no index and is apparently written for a very limited audience. There is not a single footnote or other citation to authority. One is either familiar with the references in the text or one is not.

The style is turgid. To understand it one must wade through a welter of qualifying phrases, subordinate clauses, and parenthetical statements.

The essay is a philosophical exegesis apparently inspired by Frederick William Maitland's essay *The Forms of Action at Common Law.*[1] If it is to be understood at all, it must be in terms of its subtitle, "The Spirit of English Law and International Law." The author, professor of comparative law and legal philosophy

[1] F. W. MAITLAND, THE FORMS OF ACTION AT COMMON LAW (1936). The essay first appeared in MAITLAND, EQUITY (1906).

at the University of Lyon, believes that the development of forms of action in English law (and *actiones* in Roman law) constitutes a unique contribution to the understanding of law from which the international community, "struggling with essentially comparable problems," might be able to draw some lessons. This contribution lies in the facility with which English law and Roman law have succeeded in "implicitly formulating issues of cardinal importance for the development of society by finding corresponding formulae relevant in terms of law" (p. 2). The international legal order can be helped to "reach its full strength and vigour" only by pondering what is at issue. English law does this by formulating the law on the basis of pleadings which define the issues (pp. 16–17). The methodology of English law is thus useful in the study of international law.

The essay considers the procedures and techniques by which the issues might be formulated and goes on to look at a number of specific issues arising from "the essential prerequisites of the growth of civilized life," which the author says are few in number and linked to the task of ensuring the peace (p. 14).

The point deserves to be made without detracting from the possible contributions of other systems of law. It is, however, a pity that it is not made more lucidly or developed more systematically.

JEROME ELKIND
The University of Auckland

Contribution à l'étude des privilèges et immunités des organisations internationales. By Jean Duffar. Paris: Librairie Générale de Droit et de Jurisprudence, 1982. Pp. 391. Index. F.280.

The privileges and immunities of international organizations have been examined in a large number of articles, but usually only from certain restricted angles. Comprehensive studies are rather rare and relatively old. To cite but one example, *International Immunities* by the late Wilfred Jenks was published in 1961.

Duffar's work will therefore be welcomed by all those who have to deal in one way or another with the law of international organizations. It is based on a careful survey of a great number of treaties, municipal and international cases, and the practice of organizations; the author also adduces unpublished material. Considerable attention is devoted to the privileges and immunities of the European Communities, whose operation is not well known. Had the author limited his endeavor primarily to description, his work would still be quite valuable; but he goes beyond that level by placing his study in a theoretical framework.

The rationale of the privileges and immunities of international organizations is generally identified with the freedom they require in order to discharge their functions. Starting from this idea, the author goes on to develop its implications. According to him, "the privileges and immunities of international organizations answer the need for security and independence particularly necessary to public institutions." Because they also pursue the public interest, public services in municipal law enjoy a similar privileged status. Duffar holds that the privileged status of municipal public services and of international organizations differs only in degree, not in kind. It is thus not surprising that both types of entities, municipal and international, are constantly compared.

This fundamental stance explains the rather peculiar structure of the work. The first part focuses on the right of autonomy, both institutional and jurisdictional. The second part deals with the right of privacy, which consists essentially in the inviolability of the premises and the freedom of communications. The third part discusses patrimonial rights, *i.e.*, protection of goods, as well as fiscal and customs privileges.

Duffar's argument is admittedly ingenious; but is it entirely satisfactory? In the first place, a general caveat has to be entered. The comparison between municipal public services and international organizations holds good only for states such as France (to which the author constantly refers) that have developed an elaborate administrative law; but this is not equally true of all countries. Moreover, if this comparison is convincing as far as patrimonial rights of these entities and their power over their agents are concerned, it is much less to the point if one considers their jurisdictional immunity and the inviolability of their premises. To be sure, certain governmental buildings (parliament, military buildings, etc.) are subject to a special regime in matters of search, but this inviolability is always relative, whereas the inviolability of international organizations is absolute. The author himself draws an analogy between international organizations and diplomatic missions; but the extensive privileges enjoyed by such missions flow from the fact that they represent foreign governments, just as the privileges accorded to international organizations, insofar as they differ from those accorded to municipal public services, are based upon the organization's international status. What is argued to be a difference only in degree of privilege is thus clearly the product of a fundamental difference in nature between the privileged entities.

Lawyers tend to study international organizations from a descriptive point of view. Without neglecting this approach, Duffar's work, whatever objections it may raise, also contains many valuable observations on the theory of international organizations. His book will prove most useful.

PHILIPPE CAHIER
Geneva

Conférence de La Haye de droit international privé. Actes et documents de la Quatorzième session (1980). Book I—*Matières diverses;* Book II—*Ventes aux consommateurs.* The Hague, 1982. Book I: pp. 298; book II: pp. 201. G.135.

At the 14th, 1980, session of the Hague Conference on Private International Law, two new Conventions were produced, one on Child Abduction (the materials are in vol. II (1983)), and the other on International Access to Justice, dealing with Legal Aid, Security for Costs, and Arrest and Detention in Civil Matters (to be in vol. III). Furthermore, a Convention on the Law Applicable to Certain Consumer Sales received tentative approval, its fate to be decided in light of the results of work begun on revision of the Hague Convention of 1955 on the Law Applicable to International Sales of Goods. The Conference agreed that the Sales Convention does not prevent states parties to it from applying special rules on the law applicable to consumer sales (bk. I, p. 62). The material on consumer sales is in the second book of the volume under review.

Important decisions affecting the future of the Hague Conference are reported in book I. The postwar Conference of 1951 had delegates from nations that had participated in the prewar, 1928, Conference. This included two states from the East, Czechoslovakia and Yugoslavia. At the 1951 meeting, the Conference gave itself a Charter, making it an intergovernmental agency, with a Permanent Bureau and regular sessions to be held. Functions of an executive committee were given to the Netherlands Standing Committee on Private International Law. This included preparation of the sessions and the final word on what could be on the agenda. Since then the number of participating states has grown steadily. Today it is 29 or 30.[1] From outside Europe there are the United States (1964), Canada, Australia, Argentina, Venezuela, Egypt, and Israel.

Frictions developed when the European Economic Community embarked upon work in private international law, the aim being a Convention on the Law Governing Contracts, its rules to apply generally (not merely regionally). Led by the U.S. delegation, non-EEC delegations suggested that the Hague Conference undertake such work on the broad Conference level. By a narrow vote in 1972, the Community blocked Conference work on the subject. Later attempts to gain approval had no better result.[2] The last one was made at the 1980 Conference session, and the pages on the discussion in the volume under review (bk. I, pp. 232–35) make for good reading. From the U.S. side, a statement was read into the record on what the objective of the Hague Conference was thought to be (Prof. Willis Reese, bk. I, p. 239).

Finding itself caught in the middle, the Netherlands Government Standing Committee let it be known that decisions would be in close consultation with the Conference Commission on Policies, to meet regularly between sessions (bk. I, pp. 185–86). Those at the session saw no need for a change in the Charter.

The composition of the Conference raised another problem. In 1980, under the auspices of the United Nations, an International Convention, prepared by UNCITRAL, was concluded at Vienna on Contracts Governing the International Sale of Goods.[3] Depending upon ratifications, the substantive law

[1] *See* Droz, *The Hague Conference on Private International Law 25 Years after the Founding of its Permanent Bureau: Achievements and Prospects,* 168 RECUEIL DES COURS 23 (1980 III).

[2] *See* Nadelmann, *Clouds over International Efforts to Unify Rules of Conflict-of-Laws,* L. & CONTEMP. PROBS., No. 2, 1977, at 54, 64.

[3] Vienna Convention of Apr. 11, 1980 on Contracts Governing the International Sale of Goods, 19 ILM 268 (1980).

on international sales may become uniform. The rules of private international law would still have to be resorted to, even if all nations ratified the Vienna Convention, which is not likely. The Convention itself refers to the rules of private international law, first, for identification of its international range of application, and second, to fill gaps left by the Convention.[4] The question of unification of the rules of private international law, consequently, presents itself. Among the Hague Conventions in force, there is the Convention of June 15, 1955, on the Law Governing International Sales of Goods.[5] Its rules have become general domestic law in eight states parties to the Convention, Belgium, Denmark, Finland, France, Italy, Norway, Sweden, and Switzerland (1972).

The choice existed between work by UNCITRAL and an endeavor by the Hague Conference to rewrite the 1955 Convention to make it more widely acceptable. Agreement was reached for the Hague Conference to go ahead with the work, with states not members of the Conference but having participated in the UNCITRAL work on unification of the substantive law to be invited to participate (bk. I, p. 63). Work on this enlarged basis has already started. A similar problem will be faced when it is decided to rewrite the Geneva Conflicts Conventions of 1930 and 1931 on Bills of Exchange and Checks, respectively, which were produced under the auspices of the League of Nations.

However, work on an enlarged basis already took place at the 1980 session. Under the Vienna Convention on the Law of Treaties, parties to a convention must be invited to participate in revision work. The agenda of the Hague Conference included rewriting a part of the Hague Convention of 1954 on International Civil Procedure. Parties to that Convention who were not members of the Hague Conference were invited and took part in the work. Among others, the USSR was represented (vol. III).

The decision to broaden participation was unanimous, but concern was expressed from several sides about the general opening of the Conference, which would unavoidably affect the quality of the work (bk. I, pp. 216–21). The old routine will be continued for regular work on coming projects. Efforts are currently being focused on the validity and recognition of trusts, the question of the law applicable to arbitration clauses and, possibly, elaboration of a convention on the law applicable to decedents' estates (bk. I, p. 64).

At the session, the question of the method to be used for Conference work was brought up. In 1960, the U.S. Observer Delegation had pointed to possible advantages in using uniform legislation in addition to international conventions. To secure U.S. accession, a concession was made on paper. While use of international conventions would remain the principal form, use of the

[4] Arts. I(1)(b) and VII(1) of the Convention. *See* J. HONNOLD, UNIFORM LAW FOR INTERNATIONAL SALES UNDER THE 1980 UNITED NATIONS CONVENTION 64, 96 (1982).

[5] 510 UNTS 147, 1 AM. J. COMP. L. 275 (1952) (trans.) (the Convention was prepared in 1951). For present status, see 2 ASSER INSTITUUT, LES NOUVELLES CONVENTIONS DE LA HAYE 189 (2d ed. 1980). A comment by Rabel on the 1931 draft is in 3 E. RABEL, CONFLICT OF LAWS: A COMPARATIVE STUDY, ch. 37 (1950, 2d ed. Bernstein 1964). The draft remained practically unchanged.

method of uniform legislation should not be excluded. Three Hague Conventions have been ratified by the United States, all in the field of international judicial assistance.

Choice-of-law conventions, so far, have not been ratified. The enactment of legislation may be found safer. In the discussion, reference was made to the low number of ratifications. The question was asked whether the Permanent Bureau had ever tried to identify effects of Hague Conference work achieved indirectly, that is, not by ratification. A promise to look into it was made (bk. I, p. 239).

Noting that other international bodies, including UNCITRAL, have increasingly been issuing "Recommendations," the Permanent Bureau determined that using recommendations might be advantageous (bk. I, p. 222). A resolution was adopted saying that, "while maintaining as its principal purpose the preparation of international conventions, the Conference may nevertheless use other procedures of less binding effect, such as recommendations or model laws, where, having regard to the circumstances, such procedures appear to be particularly appropriate" (bk. I, p. 63). Indeed, at the session two recommendations were adopted, one involving use of forms in the matter of the Convention on the Civil Aspects of International Child Abduction and the other regarding information to accompany requests for service of documents abroad (bk. I, pp. 65, 67).

Due, notably, to work in the conflict-of-laws field by regional organizations, such as the EEC, the Council of Europe, and the Organization of American States, the travails of the Hague Conference are not over. Complaints also come from the Third World which claims that its interests are not sufficiently represented. The work on international sales will provide an opportunity to look further into the questions. The services of an agency with the experience accumulated at The Hague should not be lost.

As for the technical aspects of volume I, an excellent bibliography of some 50 pages on literature covering the postwar Hague Conference work is at the end of the first book (pp. 249–94). If it appeared in a separate volume, the existence of the bibliography might become better known. A table giving the status of ratifications of the Conventions could be added.

KURT H. NADELMANN
Harvard Law School

International Estate Planning. By William H. Newton, III. Colorado Springs: Shepard's McGraw-Hill, 1981. Index. $75.

Multijurisdictional estate planning has become more prevalent in recent years. An increasing number of estate-planning clients have both U.S. and foreign contacts. These include U.S. citizens residing abroad, U.S. citizens with foreign investments, non-U.S. persons with investments in the United States, and non-U.S. persons with foreign assets who become U.S. persons. The goal of the

U.S. estate planner is to avoid, on behalf of his client, a proliferation of estate administration proceedings in numerous jurisdictions and to minimize overall tax liability to the extent possible.

The scope of Newton's treatise is ambitious. It covers 11 broad subjects: the planning and jurisdictional aspects of international estates; conflicts of law; U.S. taxation of citizens, residents, and domiciliaries of the United States who have contacts with foreign jurisdictions; U.S. taxation of nonresidents and nondomiciliaries of the United States, including a section on FIRPTA; tax treaties; trusts, including the taxation of trusts, trust grantors, and trust beneficiaries; the generation-skipping transfer tax; partnerships and the taxation of partners; corporations, including domestic and foreign personal holding companies, controlled foreign corporations, foreign investment companies, and DISC's; international transfers of foreign situs property; and probate and administration. In addition, the book includes a supplement (updating it to January 1982), several appendixes (the Convention produced by the 1972 Hague Conference on Private International Law concerning the international administration of estates; schedules of U.S. income and transfer tax treaties; and schedules of U.S. taxation or exemption, as the case may be, of the U.S. source personal service income and nonpersonal service income of foreigners), tables cross-referencing cited authorities to the text, and an index.

Newton's work is comprehensive in stating the rules relevant to developing international estate plans, but it lacks analysis and substantive discussion. It covers numerous topics, but without depth. It fails to provide the "insight into supplemental theories and approaches to international estate planning" that the author promises in the preface.

The text is essentially a summary of its extensive footnotes. It does not attempt to synthesize conflicting authority, nor does it propose possible solutions or approaches. Despite these deficiencies, the treatise presents a well-documented overview of the rules pertinent to the planning of international estates. It should be valuable to a nonspecialist in need of a primer summarizing existing authority.

NANCY K. MINTZ
Of the District of Columbia Bar

Multistate and Multinational Estate Planning. Vols. I and II. By Jeffrey A. Schoenblum. Boston and Toronto: Little, Brown and Company, 1982. Vol. I: pp. xxxvii, 809; vol. II: pp. xxxvii, 721. Index. $125 for 2-vol. set.

This is not another book on a subject amply explored by other books. It is a major treatise in an area in which articles on some phases of the subject abound but general, all-encompassing up-to-date treatises are missing, particularly in the English language. This book is primarily, but not exclusively, destined for the American reader. It is a useful and thorough encyclopedia of multistate and multinational estate problems.

An international lawyer would have preferred to see a book on the strictly international aspects of the multijurisdictional dimensions of estate planning. But Schoenblum, professor of law at Vanderbilt University, wanted to corral under his multijurisdictional umbrella multistate aspects of the subject as well. Aside from a few isolated exceptions, the multistate coverage is limited to the United States.

It is the book's point of departure that the geographic mobility of business, government, and society resulted in a rapid expansion of multijurisdictional estate situations, and that multijurisdictional contacts affect virtually every estate. The author finds the same conflicts and choice-of-law principles in multistate contexts. Furthermore, he sees the basic difference between single jurisdictional planning and administration, on the one hand, and multijurisdictional planning and administration, on the other hand.

Professor Schoenblum goes so far as to suggest that, on the basis of recent developments, the neglect of multijurisdictional aspects of estate planning may be considered a serious breach of professional responsibility, if not the basis of a cause of action for malpractice. His judicial precedents showing the finding and enforcement of liability on the part of estate-planning lawyers are from courts in the United States, principally from California. No precedents are cited by the author for finding professional liability or malpractice on the part of the estate-planning lawyer in connection with faulty multinational estate planning.

One of the most noteworthy chapters is on "Trusts in Multinational Estate Planning." The treatment of this subject in 170 pages is the most thorough and the best organized this reviewer has encountered anywhere. The reader will be interested in the discussion of the common law trust in civil law courts. The author has well-selected material from various civil law countries, not assembled in any other single place. Another very interesting section of this chapter of the book deals with the adoption and use of trusts in a number of civil law jurisdictions. The Trust Code of Louisiana enacted in 1964 is discussed, along with the role of the trust in Puerto Rico, Panama, Quebec, Mexico, Liechtenstein, and Israel. The brief summaries of the trust law provisions of such "off-shore" jurisdictions as the Bahamas, Bermuda, Barbados, the British Virgin Islands, Grenada, the Cayman Islands, and St. Vincent are of interest to the multinational estate planner.

Liechtenstein and Switzerland have developed their own trust substitutes. The status of the Liechtenstein *Stiftung* (foundation) and that of the *Anstalt* (establishment) have been the subject of litigation in English and American courts. Nonresident aliens of the United States are increasingly resorting to the use of Liechtenstein *Anstalt*s in their estate and tax planning. Through the use of the *Anstalt* the nonresident alien has a legal device with which to avoid liability for U.S. federal estate taxes with respect to securities and other intangible property located in the United States. The clear and concise analysis by Schoenblum of these Liechtenstein devices as trust substitutes is of particular interest to the multinational estate planner. There are, as the author elaborates, vast differences between civil and common law jurisdictions in the matter of wills and estates.

The 1961 Hague Convention on the Conflict of Laws Relating to the Form of Testamentary Dispositions does not provide or specify any particular form of will. Nor does it deal with the capacity of the testator or of witnesses. Instead, it offers a set of choice-of-law options under which a will is considered valid. Schoenblum raises a number of questions in suggesting that the Hague Convention did not resolve all questions for the determination of the validity of the wills. It must be conceded that in an intensely mobile world the Hague Convention contributes to the safeguarding of the testamentary freedom of the citizens and residents of the ratifying countries.

The International Institute for the Unification of Private Law was the driving force behind the Washington Convention of 1973. This conference produced and offered for signature a Convention Providing a Uniform Law on the Form of an International Will and a Recommendation concerning the Safekeeping and Registration of Wills. Schoenblum is even more critical of some of the provisions of the Washington Convention. He points out the considerable difficulties of an international convention on the subject of wills for a country that has a federal system. The authors of the Washington Convention showed deference to the constitutional system of the United States, but according to Schoenblum, the federal Government would still be intruding in an area of law historically reserved for the states. He argues against the United States ratifying this Convention because the ratification would represent encroachment on state law. We can join the author in his prognosis that in the foreseeable future the United States will not ratify the Hague and the Washington Conventions. In view of the wide differences in law among the various jurisdictions in the field of validity and construction of wills, and their legal effect, the historical choice-of-law approach will continue to prevail and apply.

NICHOLAS R. DOMAN
Of the New York and District of Columbia Bars

The Regulation of Banks in the Member States of the EEC (2d ed.). Edited by Jane Welch. The Hague, Boston, London: Martinus Nijhoff Publishers; London: Graham & Trotman Ltd., 1981. Pp. viii, 277. Index. Dfl.210; $90.

It has become increasingly clear that the activities of commercial banks have as great an impact on national and international economic well-being as the activities of national and international monetary authorities. At the present time, the focus of interest everywhere is on the international effects of the conduct of banking. The tendency (in the sixties) to regard the banks as the knights of the internationalization of capital markets and (in the seventies) of the recycling process that followed the oil crisis has been replaced (in the eighties) by the tendency to regard the banks as the knaves of the crisis of indebtedness. The reactions to the change in attitude have been that tighter official regulation by national authorities and a more intensive cooperation among these authorities are necessary if disaster is to be avoided. These reactions are producing adaptations in the law and practice of national and international authorities and conjoint initiatives by the banks themselves.

The times could not be more propitious for the publication of the second, and greatly revised, edition of this book, first published in 1978. The European Community is a major economic and financial area and its banking facilities have worldwide importance. This book summarizes the regulations imposed by each of the 10 members of the EC on both the national and international banking business that is subject to its jurisdiction. For the EC, there is a further problem: the coordination of banking legislation as an aspect of the integration of the area. For this reason, a new chapter has been included in the present edition. Chapter 11 summarizes the provisions of EC law under the same headings that are used in the chapters dealing with national regulations. Two directives of the Council of Ministers, adopted in 1973 and 1977, have affected the content of the banking legislation of members of the EC, but the complete body of law that applies to banking includes other pronouncements of EC entities, provisions of the Treaty of Rome, some of which do not refer expressly to banking, and decisions of the European Court of Justice. A number of these decisions have direct effect in member states.

The EC Commissioner for Financial Institutions notes, in the foreword, that the movement toward uniformity is still in its early stages. The banking edifice, he writes, is a delicately balanced structure, and it would be wrong to make precipitate changes. One can imagine how much greater must be the difficulty of reaching agreement among a broader and more disparate assemblage of countries.

The regulations of EC members are the subject matter of the first 10 chapters. The same format appears in each chapter, so that the regulatory requirements of members can be compared with ease. The format consists of 18 headings. Some examples will illustrate the range of the survey: the institutions covered, basic legislation, the supervisory system, restrictions on domestic or foreign branching, restrictions on the kinds of business conducted, solvency and liquidity ratios, controls on foreign exchange business, monetary and credit controls, deposit insurance, and subsidiaries and branches of foreign banks.

The last heading in each chapter is a list of so-called background sources. These lists are helpful bibliographies on the subject of the chapters. Throughout the material under other headings, references occur to the specific legal provisions that are being summarized. The information is set forth in clear English and occupies fewer than three hundred pages. Both virtues are probably the result of courageous paraphrase by the editor. It must be added that supervisory authorities, a professional association, and other experts have assisted in the preparation of the volume.

The book is to be welcomed as a valuable work of reference. Only its price will give the purchaser a *frisson.*

JOSEPH GOLD
International Monetary Fund

Competition Law of Britain and the Common Market (3d rev. ed.). By Valentine Korah. The Hague, Boston, London: Martinus Nijhoff Publishers, 1982. Pp. xxvii, 352. Index. Dfl.140; $59.

There is a dearth of monographs offering a comprehensive introductory survey of the competition laws—both those emanating from the British Parliament and those emanating from the European Communities—applicable in the United Kingdom. Korah enjoys a dominant position in the market for such books and the result is that there is little pressure on her to be as efficient as possible in meeting consumer demand. Consequently, while the third edition of her book is the best treatment of the subject available in monograph form, it is not as good as it could be.

The book begins with a short introduction to some of the economic issues central to competition law and then considers in turn the regulation of monopolies, mergers, anticompetitive practices, restrictive practices, and resale price maintenance under the municipal law of Britain. Most of the remaining third of the text is directed to the Common Market rules concerning restrictive practices, abuses of dominant position, and the exercise of intellectual property rights. Two particularly helpful chapters at the end consider various kinds of commercial arrangements under both national and Community law, and offer comments on the differences in the approaches adopted by the regulatory bodies whose work is discussed in the book. The text is followed by an appendix, which consists of excerpts from the more important legal instruments to which the book refers.

Korah's aim was "to stimulate and help understanding rather than to produce a comprehensive treatise." To this end, her account of the law is interspersed with comments, ranging from criticisms of the economic policies adopted by authorities responsible for enforcing competition law to purely practical advice to businessmen on dealing with those authorities. While the information on practical aspects of competition policy is interesting, and many of her criticisms are stimulating, they sometimes obscure the central argument of a book whose style is already demanding upon the concentration of the reader. The book is probably most useful to those who already understand the elements of the subject. Those seeking a basic introduction may prefer the more systematic, if less stimulating, approach of other works. Introductions to Common Market competition law abound: Korah herself has written *An Introductory Guide to EEC Competition Law and Practice,* which provides a concise account of the subject. Readers seeking an introduction to British competition laws may well find more useful than the work under review Korah's estimable commentary on the British law, which will be published in D. J. Gijlstra's *Competition Law in Western Europe and the USA.* Although that commentary is more detailed, the material is presented in a clearer fashion (and with far fewer misprints) than is the survey in this monograph. But for those who want a single-volume introduction to both sets of laws, there is no real alternative to this book.

At present, the book seeks not only to provide a survey of the institutions and principles of competition law, but also to offer practical advice and academic stimulation. The book might achieve a more satisfying, unified approach if it were to focus more clearly on one of these aims, any of which Korah could undoubtedly achieve. A little competition in the field might encourage such a development.

A. V. LOWE
University of Manchester

Political Rights for European Citizens. By Guido van den Berghe. Brookfield, Vt.: Gower Publishing Co., 1982. Pp. xii, 245. Index. $38.

In June 1979, elections were held, in the nine countries that made up the European Communities, for seats in the European Parliament. Prior to this time, representatives of the member states had been chosen by state legislatures from among their own parliamentarians. Only a minimum of provisions were laid down at Community level for these first elections; other electoral procedures were to be governed in each member state by its own national provisions, pending the eventual entry into force of a uniform system. This meant that many important and, as regards European unification, crucial matters were left to national decision-making bodies. In this short study, van den Berghe examines the rights of individuals in member states to stand and vote in the 1979 elections, especially in light of the fact that ultimately there will be uniform electoral procedures.

The title immediately reveals the basic problems that the study sets out to investigate. What are "European citizens" and can they have political rights outside the area of jurisdiction of their state of nationality? Consideration of these questions requires the reader, at the start, to contemplate the nature of the European Communities.

The author, a research fellow at the European University Institute at Florence, points out that private persons, whether natural or legal, are considered subjects of Community law. This is not to say that individuals, nationals of the member states of the Community, are European citizens, which, in legal terms, could only come about following the establishment of a political union of the member states. Similar terms such as "Community citizen" or "Market citizen" are also used by writers, and it is argued by some that these too are inappropriate while the Community lacks civil and political jurisdiction over the nationals of member states. Nevertheless, in their own specific fields, the three European Communities do grant rights to individuals; since 1975 the European Parliament has been calling for the Community to draw up a catalog of fundamental rights and, in addition, each of the member states of the Community is a contracting party to the European Convention on Human Rights. Faced with such evidence, it seems foolish to maintain for too long the legal technicalities that might deny individuals within the Community political rights by dint of their "European citizenship."

The Treaties establishing the European Communities contain identical provisions concerning the formation of the European Parliamentary Assembly. Each (EEC Article 138(3), ECSC Article 21(3), and EAEC Article 108(3)) requires the Assembly to propose ways of electing its members by "direct universal suffrage" and entrusts the Council with recommending the adoption of such provisions by member states "in accordance with their respective constitutional requirements." It is at this point that it becomes apparent that nationals of member states are not identically treated with regard to their political rights and duties, and herein lie many of the difficulties that the Assembly and national legislatures faced in trying to bring about direct elections. The majority of European Community states have some form of proportional representation, but some have a simple relative majority system. Some states make voting a legal requirement and others require voters to be living in their territory on election day or on a qualifying date.

Ideally, the right to stand and vote in an election for an institution of the Community should be allocated equally to all persons normally resident within the area covered by the Community. This, however, is too much to expect from states still staggering from the implications of Community membership in some cases, and reluctant to make an irretrievable surrender of sovereignty in others.

The Council and Assembly of the European Community soon discovered that immediate attempts to establish a European norm for direct elections were doomed to failure and proceeded instead towards direct elections governed by the individual states' laws, subject only to intergovernmental agreements on such matters as double voting, non-national suffrage, and participation while absent from country of nationality (absentee voting). Only after the first elections would attempts at uniform procedure be introduced.

Van den Berghe, in the major chapter of the book, considers each of the member states in turn and examines the legislative proposals and debates leading up to the elections of June 1979. This illuminating chapter reveals much about both the workings and discussions of the various legislatures and their level of "European-mindedness," as well as that of the executives of the states concerned. The next chapter, which tries to examine the participation in the elections of citizens of the member states resident abroad, is somewhat of a disappointment because of the uneven level of information available. Van den Berghe then gives brief, but useful, consideration to principles with regard to voting and standing of citizens resident abroad that might be incorporated into a future uniform procedure, and also in procedures for municipal elections. Finally, he considers, somewhat sketchily, the right to vote under the United Nations Covenant on Civil and Political Rights and in the jurisprudence of the European Commission of Human Rights.

Generally, the book examines a fascinating aspect of the building of the European edifice. One of the greatest problems that faces researchers of all kinds is the mode and form of publication of results. Direct elections to one of the institutions of the European Community happened in 1979, apparently despite the lack of enthusiasm of the member states. Evidently, it was felt that once direct elections were established, it would prove simpler to unify them and build them into a pragmatic exercise of European unification. The need for direct elections and the political and legal difficulties involved in their institution are richly documented in an interesting and readable fashion in this work. Since procedures to create a uniform electoral system are still to be decided upon and implemented, however, the present reviewer is left with reservations as to whether publication of a book on this topic at this stage was worthwhile, particularly since much of the treatment is necessarily uneven.

RALPH BEDDARD
The University, Southampton

Treaties and Alliances of the World (3d ed.). Compiled and written by Henry W. Degenhardt. Detroit: Gale Research Co., 1981. Pp. ix, 409. Index. $70.

This book attempts to furnish a guide through the maze that has resulted from the proliferation of bilateral and multilateral treaties, international alliances, and agreements. It contains a compilation of the major treaties and the principal international alliances, organizations, and associations through the end of 1980. In some instances, the full text of the treaty is set forth but, for most of the treaties, only the operative articles and salient points are included. Some treaties are merely referred to by title and date. The author furnishes concise background information on most of the treaties and in many instances reports on subsequent developments. The detailed descriptions of the organization and operations of the international councils, organizations, and associations reflect the scholarly quality of the author's research. A series of maps indicate at a glance the countries that are members of 14 major international organizations. Diagrams of the organization of the West European Union and of the structure of the North Atlantic Treaty Organization supplement the description of those organizations. Tables of the independent countries in Africa and of the independent states of the Americas show membership in various regional organizations.

The author does not express opinions on the legal effect of the facts reported. For example, the fact that the U.S. Senate, in ratifying the Panama Canal Neutrality Treaty, approved a number of amendments and reservations introduced by opponents to the Treaty is reported, but Degenhardt does not indicate or express an opinion on the legal effect of such amendments and reservations.

The material is organized into two major categories, *viz.*, subject matter and regions of the world.

There are some deficiencies. The major one is the failure to furnish citations of sources where the documents may be found. In some instances, amendments to the treaties are not indicated. The index would be more helpful if it had included additional specific topics. However, this deficiency is lessened by the clarity of the organization of the contents.

This book is of particular value as a handbook for journalists, college students, and attorneys in general practice. However, even an expert in international law will find it useful.

WILLIAM S. KENNEY
Of the District of Columbia Bar

Legal Aspects of International Drug Control. By S. K. Chatterjee. The Hague, Boston, London: Martinus Nijhoff Publishers, 1981. Pp. xxiv, 587. Index. Dfl.285; $124.

Dr. S. K. Chatterjee's book deserves the highest acclaim from those interested in the substance and nuances of international drug control. His work reflects diligent scholarship, understanding, and thoughtful evaluations of the multiplicity of international efforts to gain a degree of effective drug control. His approach is very practical. In most cases his appraisals of the legal aspects of drug regulatory steps are fully justified by the historical experiences that he records with clear insight as to their impact on the events, actors, and circumstances involved. The book includes, in addition to numerous cited references, a selective bibliography of books, articles, and technical reports of the World Health Organization, as well as documents and protocols.

After tracing the origins of drug abuse, the author notes that despite their short life span, the early suppression attempts of the League of Nations paved the way for such success as has been subsequently realized in this area of international law, both by treaty and customary law. When the author takes the reader through the UN machinery, the technical assistance programs, and the separate agreements and protocols, his analysis of the conflict between sociological objectives and the political and economic realities takes on added value.

A U.S. report entitled "White Paper on Drug Abuse," submitted to President Ford on September 29, 1975 by the Domestic Council Drug Abuse Task Force, observed:

> International treaties complement U.S. efforts to control drug abuse and have formalized the drug concerns of other nations. The Single Convention on Narcotic Drugs of 1961 is the best treaty now in force for controlling narcotic substances. The international machinery established by the Single Convention has a mixed record. It has worked well in limiting legal production of narcotic drugs to amounts needed for medical and scientific use. It has been less successful in getting countries to fulfill their treaty commitments to root out illegal production and trafficking.

Nonetheless, it is acknowledged that helicopter spraying, if widely used, is the surest and most economical means of eradicating illegal crops. However, only a few countries use it. The National Narcotics Intelligence Consumers Committee has adopted the UN view that the willingness of governments to control illicit narcotics crops depends upon their being able to provide producers with viable alternative sources of income. For less-developed countries with shaky governments, however, crop control brings difficult political choices. The more pressure brought to bear upon such countries by the fully developed countries, the more the developing countries will demand from them by way of economic and technical assistance. It is hoped that when their economies are doing well, they will share in the burden of effective control.

Chatterjee believes that both the greed represented by the drug trade and states' assertion of their sovereignty must be tempered in the service of reducing the world misery supported by the use of illicit drugs, while preserving their legal cultivation. While he does not recommend a specific new legal order, his examination and chronicle of the present situation provide a framework and focus that should inspire international lawyers and others to build improvements for a healthier society. The book as a text should be required reading for all who assume responsibility for the major considerations involved in international drug control.

FRANK W. SWACKER
Of the Virginia Bar

Biotechnology: International Trends and Perspectives. By Alan T. Bull, Geoffrey Holt, and Malcolm D. Lilly. Paris: Organisation for Economic Co-Operation and Development, 1982. Pp. 84. Index. $11.

This is a report on the status of biotechnology and represents an early step by the Committee for Scientific and Technological Policy of the Organisation for Economic Co-operation and Development in evaluating biotechnology. The report analyzes the state of biotechnology and assesses what OECD member governments should do to foster its beneficial development.

The report begins by creating a broad definition of biotechnology intended to facilitate analysis and comparison. The authors of the report have tried to pick a broadly inclusive definition that is at the same time clearly delimited. They define biotechnology as "the application of scientific and engineering principles to the processing of materials by biological agents to provide goods and services" (p. 21). This definition is sufficiently broad to include many conventional techniques often neglected in discussions of biotechnology (*e.g.,* sewage treatment and grape sugar fermentation). It thus avoids the parochial view of biotechnology as consisting only of the new and exciting aspects of biotechnology such as "genetic engineering."[1] Such a broad definition is useful and probably more accurate than those focusing on the newer technologies in that it emphasizes recombinant DNA technologies as merely the newest manifestation of a centuries-old industry. Too many commentators have failed to realize that recombinant DNA technologies are an evolutionary tool that expands (albeit substantially) a preexisting technology. Man has created modified organisms for many years, although not with the degree of control and direction now possible.

After setting out the definition quoted above, the authors analyze the central issue of the report: the most important areas for OECD member governments to address to encourage biotechnology development. The authors describe a number of areas in which governmental support is crucial. For example, more funding is needed in areas such as research in plant microbiology, host systems other than *E. coli,* and fermentation technology, as well as in the area of increased training in the basic sciences. Much of this needed research could be carried out at academic institutions funded by private and public sources. While there is little discussion in the report of government funding problems, the writers

[1] The phrase "genetic engineering" is itself colloquial terminology. In many instances the phrase "recombinant DNA technologies" would more precisely describe the relevant technologies.

do describe the tension in industry/university relationships generated by private funding. The authors argue that it is not now possible "to reach agreement on which [mechanism for university/industry collaboration in biotechnology] is best" (p. 60), but imply that a single solution is possible. Unfortunately, the attempt to specify a single resolution to such a complex problem seems naive. There are many approaches now being tested by experience and it seems likely that different mechanisms will best suit different situations. Any attempt to fit many different relationships into a single form is at best fraught with difficulty.

The report also highlights several other areas that have received even less attention than those mentioned above, but that deserve new consideration, particularly in the international arena. For example, there is a very significant need for increased culture and plant stock collections. These collections can provide the basic source material for later genetic modification of existing organisms. The loss of these resources may be irrecoverable. There is also a significant need for greater attention to the analysis of the effects of biotechnology on the development of world trade and economics, as well as on the world ecosystem. Biotechnology is, and has been, a major force in world economics. If recombinant DNA technologies prove as useful a tool as they now appear to be, we can expect substantial changes in biotechnology and its effect on world economics. If governments desire control of the impact of such technologies, they must *now* try to understand their effects.

In highlighting the issues described above, the book provides a useful introduction to the problems and issues of modern biotechnology from the governmental point of view. However, the report underestimates the speed of accomplishment in biotechnology and the present state of development in the industry. The report proceeds from the premise that biotechnology is still in its early infancy and suggests that now is the time for biotechnology "to leave the stage where [it] was the subject of an uncontrolled publicity cult" (p. 9). In so arguing, the report overreacts to the excessively rosy predictions once made for the pace of new biotechnology achievement. The authors argue that commercial development will be much slower than anticipated. Experience in the industry has been just the reverse. Many developments, including *commercial* developments in the health care field, have been more, not less, rapid than anticipated. A review of the report's "market predictions for implementation in production of genetic engineering procedures" demonstrates many areas in which industry has already proven such estimates to be unduly pessimistic (see Appendix IV). For example, alpha (leukocyte) interferon is already being produced in commercial quantities and is in phase III testing in humans, though the report argues that genetic production will not be implemented until 1987. A similar prediction for genetically produced insulin reaching the market in 1987 fails to realize that such insulin is now being sold commercially in the United States. Modern biotechnology is moving very rapidly in the health sciences. Whether it will progress as rapidly in other industries remains to be seen. The danger to governments in assuming that this technology will develop more quickly than it, in fact, does is less than that of underestimating its rate of development, as the authors do.

In sum, this book provides a useful starting point for governmental analysis of priorities in encouraging biotechnology and in assessing its impacts. It is not intended to be, and is not, a comprehensive source book. However, if the OECD desires to produce useful guides for its members, it and its advisers must realize that the rate of development in parts of modern biotechnology is so rapid that quicker response is necessary. Otherwise, governments will be reacting rather than planning. While the nature of science is such that it does not await governmental direction, its development may nonetheless be modified by proper incentives. Whether the OECD governments should or could create the necessary incentives are very different and difficult issues—ones assumed without sufficient discussion by the authors of this report.

FREDERIC A. EUSTIS, III
Of the New York Bar

Disarmament: The Human Factor. (Proceedings of a Colloquium on the Societal Context for Disarmament, sponsored by UNITAR and Planetary Citizens, held at the United Nations, New York, 1978.) Edited by Ervin Laszlo and Donald Keys. New York: Pergamon Press Inc., 1981. Pp. x, 164. Index. $12.50.

This work is a collection of essays and group discussions that were first presented as papers at a symposium on disarmament at UN headquarters in late 1978. The central premise is that disarmament is not solely a political or economic issue, but rather an issue involving human values and how the individual perceives the correlation between security and military spending. All of the distinguished participants were speaking as world citizens and were not openly identified by the state or organization that they represented. The material is organized into four parts, starting with "Introductory Survey: The Neglected Human Factors of Disarmament," and continuing with "Global Community Values" (part II), "Threat Perception and Psycho-social Factors" (part III), and last, "Alternative Mechanisms for Guaranteeing Peace and Security" (part IV). The essays in each part focus on a slightly different perspective of disarmament and the human factors that could prevent its realization.

The practical value of this work is not in its reiteration that a serious world problem exists, but rather in the authors' assessment of solutions for arms curtailment. Most of the authors do not limit themselves to discussing disarmament as merely an abstract ideal, or a goal divorced from current global realities. Admittedly, there has been an increased public awareness and outcry over the arms race in the 5 years since these papers were first delivered. However, even though the human element is no longer one of the most neglected issues in the arms race (as repeatedly mentioned in the book), this does not detract from the work's relevancy. Because there has been no downslide in the arms race or lessening of world tension since 1978, these papers may be even more welcome today.

Although this book contains a rich collection of ideas, its merit will ultimately depend on its insight on the causes of the arms problem and the validity of the various solutions proposed by the authors. One of the more realistic solutions is the Unilateral Initiatives Approach discussed in part I by William Epstein. Epstein suggests that the arms race has accelerated because of unilateral moves taken by individual states. In his judgment, a reversal can take place by unilateral moves, modest at first, in the opposite direction. Of course, no state would take action that would make it vulnerable. However, each step would put pressure on and serve as an offer to the other side to make a reciprocal move. One of Epstein's main points is that such an approach would curtail the arms race much faster than bilateral negotiations (which could take years).

Since the current national security system is based on armaments, it is arguable that statesmen possess a psychological block against total disarmament. A fortiori, it can be argued that disarmament will not occur until there is a collective shift in how the individual perceives security. Robert Muller takes this position in part III when he argues that disarmament cannot happen under the present value system (this proposition is advanced by several of the other writers). It is interesting to note, however, that Bryant Wedge believes that a shift regarding security is already taking place in the military's concept of its role. This issue of consciousness raising as a condition precedent to halting the arms race resulted in a lively debate in chapter II. One who took an opposing view is David Singer who believes that the arms buildup, in and of itself, perpetuates the type of value system that will always see a need for arms. He concludes that it is pointless to wait for a consciousness change to end the arms race because the values will not change in the states involved in an arms buildup. Singer's solution is to start disarming immediately. While it is self-evident that this approach will erase the current fear of a nuclear holocaust, disarmament alone will not eradicate the seemingly inherent human propensity for violence and arms as a means to achieve security. The reason is that even if it is taken as axiomatic that arms perpetuate our current value system, they do not cause it. It is laudable then, that the book views the arms problem as two-sided. There exists, on the one hand, the immediate danger, and on the other, the need to find suitable alternatives to our present form of security in order to ensure permanent peace.

An innovative, but not entirely novel, alternative is proposed by Bryant Wedge in his chapter, *Reducing Hurt Feeling and Fear as a Prerequisite for Arms Reduction.* Wedge advocates setting up full-scale educational peace academies that would focus on training peacemakers equipped to act as national and international mediators in contentious disputes. To make this a workable prospect, he states that these cadres must be clothed with sufficient authority and respect to generate obedience. His point is that mediation could be used to bring the parties concerned to the point of formal diplomatic negotiation before any armed conflict. It is doubtful, however, that in today's world such a method would be any more effective than the efforts currently being taken by such organizations as the United Nations. Basically, it amounts to a bilateral agreement to cooperate, without which no method of mediation or negotiation can work.

Donald Keys discusses two psychological attitudes that, up until now, have been a hindrance in international arms control negotiations. He makes the empirical observation that nations have a recurrent tendency both to dehumanize the enemy and to conduct negotiations from a position of force (which the other side adopts as a defense). However, he does not mean to imply that states should negotiate and conciliate on the presumption that the other side should be categorically and naively trusted. Underestimating the motives of the opponent can spell disaster. Keys states that the optimum negotiating standard should be fair and dependable, and supported by a sincere desire for peace.

Since these essays were originally presented as short talks, none of the material forms a systematic blueprint for action. However, their purpose is to serve as a starting point in both increasing the reader's awareness that definite and plausible substitutes to arms exist and exploring why our world is arms oriented to begin with. The lucid and revealing treatment of this subject makes this collection both necessary and highly recommended.

GUY DU BOSE
Of the California Bar

The Critical Link: Energy and National Security in the 1980s. Charles K. Ebinger, Project Director, The Center for Strategic and International Studies. Cambridge: Ballinger Publishing Co., 1982. Pp. xxx, 260. Index. $29.75.

Some of the policy recommendations contained in this detailed study of the world energy problem by Georgetown University's Center are of interest to international lawyers concerned with American national security policies. The authors criticize the Reagan administration's "strategic consensus" approach to Middle East foreign policy decision making, arguing that the immediate threat to Persian Gulf stability is not Soviet intervention but a continuation of the Arab-Israeli dispute. The security of the Persian Gulf oil lifeline to Europe and Japan cannot be divorced from the attainment of an overall peace settlement between Israel and its Arab neighbors. The interventionary U.S. Rapid Deployment Force (RDF) could not succeed at its appointed tasks of seizing and operating Persian Gulf oil fields in the event of another cutoff by local governments, or of protecting petroleum installations from destruction by indigenous or externally supported saboteurs. Consequently, providing military assistance to African and Middle Eastern countries (*e.g.*, Somalia, Kenya, Oman) in return for RDF access rights or facilities is a policy of doubtful utility that can only undermine the domestic legitimacy of host governments and enmesh the United States on the wrong side of regional disputes. The authors recommend against establishing RDF facilities in Turkey, and recognize that an extension of NATO's area of operations to include the Gulf would not be acceptable to its membership.

If the Soviet Union invades northern Iran, however, the authors recommend that the United States seize the Iranian port of Chahbahar on the Indian Ocean. No rationale is offered for America mimicking a Soviet violation of international law. As the authors point out, to the extent Gulf oil can be transported via pipelines terminating on the Red Sea, the strategic importance of controlling the Straits of Hormuz diminishes. This curious advice highlights the major intellectual defect of the authors' overall policy prescriptions for resolving the security dilemma presented by Gulf oil production: they wholeheartedly embrace the Carter doctrine, while their arguments repudiate the feasibility of its essential ingredients. Far better for the United States to disavow the Carter doctrine, the Reagan corollary, and the RDF, and concentrate instead upon building up regional self-defense arrangements such as the Gulf Cooperation Council, in which the United States would play no formal role except within the context of the right of collective self-defense recognized by Article 51 of the UN Charter.

FRANCIS A. BOYLE
University of Illinois

General Reports to the 10th International Congress of Comparative Law. Edited by Zoltán Péteri and Vanda Lamm. Budapest: Akadémiai Kiadó, 1981. Pp. 1048. $75.

One might think it natural for this *Journal* to relegate the reviewing of this book to its sister, the *American Journal of Comparative Law.*[1] That would, however, do an injustice to the amount of material of interest to international lawyers that is contained in this large volume of reports delivered to the Tenth Congress of the International Academy of Comparative Law. The volume contains, in addition to introductory formalities, 48 general reports which are in turn based upon as many as 21 national reports (not published in the volume).[2] Of these, two are addressed quite explicitly to the relationship between international and comparative law—one by Hanna Bokor-Szegö (p. 659) and the other by William Butler (p. 673).[3] They remind us that the "general principles of law recognized by civilized nations," referred to in Article 38 of the Statute of the International Court of Justice, cannot be developed as a source of international law without careful comparative analysis. Even a customary rule of the law of nations depends on the identification of evidences of national assent to the asserted rule that will generally be found imbedded in a matrix of domestic rules. Increasingly, both international and comparative lawyers find themselves concerned with multilateral conventions that make uniform operative rules for private parties; generating acceptable treaty rules depends upon thorough knowledge of the separate national practices that are to be harmonized and, later, the interpretation of those rules must be sensitive to national practices.

Several articles, expressly or by inference, bear upon those interactions. For example, the article by Sundberg (p. 605) on the chartering of aircraft combines analysis of national rules on the question with that of issues of the applicability and meaning of several multilateral conventions. The articles by Pereznieto

[1] For a previous review of the *Reports to the 5th Congress,* see 55 AJIL 1033 (1961).

[2] A major service in locating many of these national reports as published elsewhere is rendered by Szladits, *A Bibliography of Reports of the International Congresses of Comparative Law, 1932–1974,* 25 AM. J. COMP. L. 684 (1977), updated in 30 *id.* 709 (1982).

[3] Another work growing out of that project is *International Law in Comparative Perspective* (W. Butler ed. 1979).

Castro (Mexico) (p. 311) and Meznerics (Hungary) (p. 331) on guarantees for foreign investors deal with a topic long thought to be within the province of international lawyers; one can conjecture that the authors' ability to detach themselves from strictly nationalistic views of the problem has much to do with the degree to which they were able to absorb a comparativist perspective on the situation. Gray's study of products liability (p. 191) focuses on proposals for unification and harmonization of the topic emanating from the Council of Europe and the Council of the European Community. Simmonds's study (p. 677) of the "New International Economic Order" relies only in a most general sense upon comparative work and would seem to be quite comfortably within the field where international lawyers work.

Plainly, these articles should be accessible to those who think of themselves as international rather than comparative lawyers and one can only regret the relative inaccessibility of this trove of scholarship.

DETLEV F. VAGTS
Board of Editors

Meinungs- und Informationsfreiheit zwischen Ost und West: Möglichkeiten und Grenzen intersystemarer völkerrechtlicher Garantien in einem systemkonstituierenden Bereich. By Rudolf Streinz. Ebelsbach: Verlag Rolf Gremer, 1981. Pp. xxii, 290. Indexes. DM 89.

The book under review discusses the feasibility of an international system for the protection of a basic human right, the right to hold opinions and to freedom of expression, including the freedom to seek, receive, and impart information (Article 19 of the International Covenant on Civil and Political Rights of the United Nations), as well as its possible limits. The author's major preoccupation is to what extent such a right may exist in the contemporary heterogeneous world in which the North-South disagreement has become almost as prominent as the traditional East-West conflict. States belonging to virtually all categories have committed themselves—at least verbally—to guarantee this right under different international instruments. Still, there exists no universally recognized concept of the right in question; some states interpret it mainly in accordance with their political perceptions or in conformity with the alleged needs of their society, and they jealously protect their sovereignty against noxious interference from outside.

The author starts with a description of international instruments—treaties and others—pertaining to the freedom of opinion and expression and then turns to an analytic discussion of the divergent concepts of this right under different constitutional systems. His examples are, *pars pro toto,* the United States and the USSR as major world powers, and the Federal Republic of Germany and the German Democratic Republic as secondary powers. Here, he contrasts the Western-democratic approach to human rights with its socialist counterpart. Derived from municipal law and judicial practice, the conflicting approaches are then examined in the next section within the framework of international law, with special regard to the implementation of international instruments for the protection of human rights. His last chapter is devoted to universal and intersystem protection of the right to opinion and expression, its possibility and limits.

The main value of this well-documented book lies in the very scholarly analysis of the difference between human rights approaches in the East and West. The desire of states of different social and political systems to maintain their status quo and to broaden their influence in the international arena is correctly regarded as the main impediment to an effective international system of protecting the individual's right to opinion and expression. The reviewer can fully agree with the author's final remarks, that only an understanding of the limits of the right in question permits its full exploration, and that the international community should strive for the implementation, improvement, and enforcement of existing instruments rather than for the elaboration of new ones.

HENN-JÜRI UIBOPUU
University of Salzburg Law School

Pravovoe polozhenie inostrantsev v SSSR (The Legal Status of Foreigners in the USSR). By L. N. Galenskaia. Moscow: "Mezhdunarodnye Otnosheniia," 1982. Pp. 159. 65 kopecks; $2.50.

The enactment on June 24, 1981 of a comprehensive Law on the Legal Status of Foreigners in the USSR has stimulated publication of a handbook treating not only the principles of the Law, but the obligations assumed by the USSR in treaties and the substantive municipal law to be applied under the rule of "national treatment" adopted by the new Law. The result is a booklet of such importance to foreigners that it should be translated into many languages and made available at frontier kiosks.

For international lawyers the study has theoretical interest as well as practical value. Because national treatment has been made the rule, the author has to enumerate exceptions. She does so by adopting what seems to have become popular among the cited Eastern European authors, namely, a distinction between "rights" and "freedoms." Under this distinction, foreigners enjoy the "freedoms" guaranteed in the Constitution to Soviet citizens (speech, press, assembly, conscience, etc.), but they do not enjoy the "rights," *i.e.*, active and passive electoral rights, participation in state administration, membership in certain social organizations, and practice of certain professions.

Of course, she finds it necessary to indicate that the freedoms are limited for both citizens and foreigners: no one may claim a right to harm the Soviet state or its citizens through exercise of a freedom. Further, she thinks the distinction between rights and freedoms would be clearer if they were denominated "political rights" and "democratic freedoms." For the foreign reader unaccustomed to the Europeans' struggles over the choice of satisfactory terminology, the chapter on theory may seem pedantic, but to cognoscenti it is not without interest.

The practical value of the booklet is enhanced by references to Soviet practice. The most prominent cases of expulsions of foreign offenders are chronicled with their offense. It is indicated that expulsion is preferred over imprisonment for foreigners convicted of crime, and we learn that in 1976 alone more than 50 foreigners were expelled.

Evidently, the foreigners who most concern policy makers are not Western businessmen or tourists but Eastern Europeans who reside permanently within the USSR but do not acquire citizenship. Under the Citizenship Law of 1978, marriage confers no citizenship rights, so there are mixed marriages. This raises questions of the status of children and the rights of a foreign spouse. Even temporary visitors may create problems in conflict of laws as a result of torts or contractual relationships. Income tax applies to the earnings of foreigners unless there exists a double tax treaty providing otherwise.

As for the law of asylum, practice has divided refugees into two groups: those who are permitted to remain permanently, and those who must move on as soon as possible. None are returned to a homeland where their life would be endangered. All may enter without visas and remain until their status is settled.

There is no discussion of the remedies available to foreigners under general international law. The assumption is that municipal law provides adequate procedures, and these are augmented in many cases by treaties, such as consular conventions permitting those in prison to meet with consuls and to receive letters and packages, privileges not accorded Soviet citizens. Also, the provisions of the UN Covenants may help citizens of contracting states, as the USSR is a party. Finally, there may be diplomatic negotiation, which Soviet policy has always favored; presumably, the Soviet side will not accept resolution of disputes by outsiders unless a treaty so provides, as there has always been a reluctance to be put into a situation that cannot be controlled. If the volume is to be translated, it would be helpful if these established positions could be stated specifically so that those who do not know them could be made aware of them.

JOHN N. HAZARD
Board of Editors

Crime, Justice and Underdevelopment. Edited by Colin Sumner. London: Heinemann Educational Books Ltd., 1982. Pp. xvi, 345. Indexes. $55.

The editor, Colin Sumner, who teaches criminology at Cambridge University, reproaches Western criminological theory for remaining "virtually silent on crime in the underdeveloped countries" (p. i). He is also critical of scholars in development studies and legal scholars as well for neglecting the "role of crime and criminal law in social development" (pp. 3–4).

Sumner explains that this book, another in the Cambridge Studies in Criminology series, is

> an attempt to get beyond the dominant view that the "crime problem" in the third world primarily means urban, working-class juvenile delinquency accelerating rapidly due to the pressure of "modernisation", and that the "justice problem" there is the inability of "native" officials and politicians to grasp the rules and procedures that constitute the rule of law [p. xi].

The focus of the book is thus, in Sumner's words, on understanding "the connections between the process of imperialism and underdevelopment and the whole range of law violations and legal institutions current in post-colonial societies. In short, it is about *capitalism* and the forms of crime and justice it begets" (pp. 11–12).

The orthodox criminological analysis of crime in the Third World, as a phenomenon caused by failure of regulation in those societies to keep pace with abrupt social change, is soundly criticized by Sumner in his opening essay. He examines in detail Clinard and Abbott's work, *Crime in Developing Countries* (1973), as an illustration of the orthodox criminology which equates "development" with "modernisation" and focuses narrowly on urban, working-class crime in the Third World, ignoring official corruption, rural crime, crime by businessmen, and crimes of state and the multinationals. He is critical of their recommendations for crime prevention, especially of their proposal that "some funds earmarked for economic development and welfare should be devoted to crime control, in the form of manpower, buildings and transport for the police, prisons and courts" (p. 18). Why, he asks, are they not concerned with the upper-class criminology, the relation of the police to the causes of the growth of crime, or with political biases in legislation and law enforcement? He faults them for producing a criminology for developing countries which is "logically inconsistent, theoretically weak, and empirically problematic" (p. 21), and which, he asserts, "could only serve as an ideological agency for the class-controlled procedures of the capitalist state" (*ibid.*).

Arguing in favor of the use of an internationalist, historical, and comparative perspective in understanding the nature of crime in the developing countries, Sumner traces crime in the postcolonial states to their "unjust past" and to the effects of the international capitalist system on the national economies. He criticizes orthodox criminology since it "fails to recognize the reality of underdevelopment and could only produce policies which would sustain the classes, inside and outside the third world, benefiting from the imperialistic connections" (p. 26). It also neglects the role of criminal law in colonialism, for the "penetration of capitalism into the weaker areas of the globe, now the third world, involved the use, non-use and abuse of the criminal law. . . . Without this state power, nothing would have been possible, for it helped create and sustain the labour force needed for capital" (p. 35). He contends that "[c]riminological work based on 'modernisation' theory is ahistorical, astructural, and pro-state; it can not therefore produce knowledge of the historical, structural and cultural specificity of particular forms of criminal practice and criminal law" (p. 36).

Case studies in the book are on labor and land policies in Tanganyika under the British rule, by Issa Shivji and C. Louise Sweet (pp. 40–89); the creation of a body of "customary" law by the colonialists in Senegal, by Frances G. Snyder (pp. 90–121); prostitution among the urban poor of early Nairobi, Kenya, by Janet M. Bujra (pp. 122–42) and robbery among the urban poor of modern Cali, Colombia, by Chris Birkbeck (pp. 162–91); origins and impact of the new village court systems in Papua New Guinea, by Abdul Paliwala and Peter Fitzpatrick (pp. 192–247); and crime and the criminal justice system in Cuba, by James Brady (pp. 248–300). The contributors, all academicians, corroborate Sumner's thesis that criminal law and the criminal justice system were used and abused by colonial powers in the creation of a new class structure and in shoring up colonial interests.

Brady, who teaches sociology at the University of Massachusetts, has written extensively on Cuban society and the criminal justice system in Cuba. His essay, *The Revolution Comes of Age: Justice and Social Change in Contemporary Cuba,* is set in a social and historical context. Cuba, he observes, is not following the Soviet model in government, justice, or party building. The primary concern of an attorney in today's Cuba "is not necessarily to 'win' the case, but to promote the revolution" (p. 289). He identifies Cuba's most serious crime problems as those related to domestic conflict, juvenile delinquency, black market speculation, and violations of labor discipline. Cuba's success in reducing its prison population is attributed in part to its reliance on informal sanctions, fines or short-term detentions in handling common criminals. He applauds Cuba's efforts toward ensuring women's equality. While acknowledging that Cuba in 1959 showed "many features not unlike those in many advanced capitalist countries" (p. 297), Brady concludes that for the Third World, the Cuban lesson is that "socialism offers the best hopes of achieving economic independence and reducing crime and social inequality, and political corruption" (p. 299).

The studies are well researched and documented. However, the book abounds in Marxist jargon. Also, it is arguable that the radical perspective offered in the book, to wit, that colonialism and capitalism are responsible for the growth of serious crime in Third World countries, suffers from a similar weakness to that which the book's contributors find in orthodox criminology. It is selective, makes broad generalizations, and builds a case on some untested assumptions and hypotheses. To illustrate, Cuba is said to have had "remarkable success" in reducing violent crime because of the socialist revolution there. Thus, socialism is offered as a model for other Third World countries as their best hope of reducing crime and social inequality. However, many socialist states have been unable to find satisfactory solutions to these questions. The real value of the book lies in the serious questions the contributors and Sumner raise about crime and underdevelopment—questions that should not be ignored.

VED P. NANDA
University of Denver College of Law

Law and Diplomacy in Commodity Economics: A Study of Techniques, Co-operation and Conflict in International Public Policy Issues. By Emiko Atimomo. London: The Macmillan Press Ltd., 1981. Pp. xix, 384. Index. $55. Distributed by Holmes & Meier Publishers, Inc.

Ever since the inauguration of UNCTAD's Integrated Programme for Commodities in 1976, interest in international commodity agreements has greatly increased, as has the intensity of the negotiating process itself. Thus, an additional work in this field is certainly welcome.

Atimomo's book is divided into two parts: "General Characteristics of International Economic Law and Diplomacy" and "Conflict and Co-operation in Commodity Diplomacy." The former is of greater interest to the student of international law; it is also a more significant contribution to the relatively slim literature on international commodity agreements.

In that part, Atimomo seeks to provide a legal analysis of commodity agreements and procedures of ratification and acceptance, as well as legal processes. Throughout, he tries to elucidate the concept of international economic law, taken to be a more flexible law needed to accommodate to an era of economic interdependence in which the interests of producers and consumers are not always coincident. He exemplifies this concept by pointing to the seemingly binding nature of provisional acceptance of such commodity accords as the International Coffee Agreement of 1968.

More generally, he tries to identify the commonalities and differences between and among recent commodity agreements. The focus is on tin and coffee, but he uses numerous other examples. The decision to carefully and laboriously work through two particularly important accords has its merits, but these are diminished somewhat when one recognizes the atypicality of some of the provisions of these agreements as well as the fact that a full understanding of even these two accords would require that one work through sections not discussed here at all. Moreover, there are clear limitations to going carefully through commodity agreements that are constantly being altered. Still, this section does provide the reader with some unique materials, crucial to anyone contemplating international commodity negotiations. These insights are magnified in those too infrequent instances where the author provides his own personal observations as to how an accord might have been improved or why a particular provision was accepted.

The second part of the book suffers both from being outdated—most of the discussion is current only through 1976—and the author's failure to exploit sufficiently secondary source materials. The use of primary documents, however, is exemplary: meticulous and extensive. Most of the discussion of commodity accords in this part of the book is much too cryptic to be of any value. Moreover, the failure to differentiate sufficiently among members of the Group of 77, much less discuss extensively the tensions therein, is a defect which can only be remedied by reading this section in tandem with Robert Rothstein's more narrowly focused, but much more analytically powerful book, *Global Bargaining.*[1]

[1] R. ROTHSTEIN, GLOBAL BARGAINING: UNCTAD AND THE QUEST FOR A NEW INTERNATIONAL ECONOMIC ORDER (1979).

Reference to Rothstein might also have chastened Atimomo's enthusiasm for UNCTAD as a negotiating forum. Somewhat ironically, Atimomo is much more impressive in noting the nuanced differences among the developed countries' positions as they relate to commodity conflict and cooperation than he is in drawing distinctions among developing countries' interests and views.

On the other hand, this part does offer a unique and extensive discussion of ECOWAS (Economic Community of West African States) and CEAO (Communauté économique de l'Afrique de l'Ouest), although their particular relevance to the subject at hand is a little less obvious.

In spite of these drawbacks—especially in part 2—Atimomo does achieve his expressed goal: "to show the interdependence between law and diplomacy in the area of international economic transactions, be it of a common market type or a relationship between consumers and producers of raw materials." In the process of doing this, he has certainly evidenced that "law and diplomacy in this area are still in evolution, although certain characteristic features have started to emerge as distinct from traditional law and diplomacy" (p. 329).

MICHAEL G. SCHECHTER
James Madison College
Michigan State University

Multinacionalno Preduzeće: Pravni Aspekti. By Miodrag Sukijasović. Belgrade: Institut za Medjunarodnu Politiku i Privredu, 1981. Pp. 222, with English summary.

The author, a prolific Yugoslav writer and a scholar in the field of international trade relations, published this study on the legal aspects of multinational enterprises from a standpoint which appears to be between the positions taken by the representatives of industrial powers and the spokesmen for undeveloped and socialist countries. He first outlines the history of multinational enterprises from the early companies in medieval Europe up to modern times, with more than 10,000 multinational enterprises in existence.[1] The author describes the deep differences in the opinions of the industrial countries and those of the undeveloped or not yet fully developed states of Asia, Africa, and Central and South America. He seems to consider that the viewpoint of the socialist countries is sometimes closer to the position taken by Western industrialized states, even though the socialist states almost always support the undeveloped countries in any controversy with the Western world.

The author, who prefers the use of the term "multinational enterprises" rather than "multinational corporations" or "transnational enterprises," describes in some detail the studies of, and attention given to, the numerous legal problems arising out of the spreading of multinational enterprises. He refers to the projects undertaken by the European Economic Commission, the Organisation for Economic Co-operation and Development (whose members are

[1] Report of the UN Centre on Transnational Corporations, UN Doc. E/C.10/38 (1978).

the industrialized nations), the work of the so-called Andean Group (of South America), and the substantial research done by numerous agencies of the United Nations.

The author is especially familiar with the projects of the United Nations Commission on Transnational Corporations, the Economic and Social Council of the United Nations, and the UN Industrial Development Organization, as well as with the results of the UN Conference on Trade and Development.

The main legal issues concerning these commissions and organizations are the conflicts arising out of the controversy between host governments and the multinational enterprises, and also between the host governments and the governments of parent companies. The host governments assert that the affiliates quite often exercise an undue economic and political influence in their countries, hurting their interests and creating problems and conflicts. They accuse the parent companies of considering the status of their affiliate companies to be somewhat extraterritorial, and it often happens that they ignore or circumvent the law and practices of the host countries, especially in fiscal, currency, personnel, and other matters.

The author's conclusion is that the controversies could be lessened by the establishment of an international treaty, whereby the governments of the investor nations and of the host countries would agree that the multinational enterprises be internationally registered (presumably at the United Nations), and then both parent companies and affiliates would be treated as an international trade association. It is, of course, doubtful whether the industrial countries would accept such a solution.

ZVONKO R. RODE
Of the District of Columbia Bar

Trade Secrets: How to Protect Your Ideas and Assets. By James Pooley. Berkeley: Osborne/McGraw-Hill, 1982. Pp. 145. Index. $19.95.

This slender volume is not aimed at lawyers regularly engaged in trade secret work. It is for employers and their employees whose companies utilize trade secrets in their domestic and international business.

Mr. Pooley did not set out to write a scholarly tome. But, what he did set out to do, he did very well. A central theme underlying the book is that ideas, intellectual property, technology, or "proprietary information," are assets. Any sensible businessman should make reasonable efforts to protect an internationally valuable asset.

In this era of dramatic attempts at domestic and international industrial and commercial espionage, *Trade Secrets* explains in simple language how a businessman can recognize his trade secrets and how they differ from, but interrelate with, his patents and copyrights. The author also advises the reader on how to protect trade secrets, how to be alert to antitrust implications, how to avoid litigation, and, if necessary, how to litigate. At every stage the emphasis is on the practical and on helping the businessman to know when to call his lawyer.

Mr. Pooley gives the following advice: "Most secrets are lost through employee inadvertence. . . . Employee education in the trade secret area, like safety, must be continuous and not simply the focus of a single meeting or campaign prompted by an unpleasant experience" (pp. 57–58). Then, he goes on to suggest practical ways this can be done.

Trade Secrets is summarized:

> The idea that intellectual property is a real but often overlooked business asset is the central theme of this book. To that premise, I add the undisputed assumption that the protagonists in trade secret disputes would do better by staying out of these legal battles. Finally, to avoid the apparently unavoidable fight you must prepare to win it. The employer's process is simply stated: first, identify your proprietary information; second, create a continuing system for classifying and protecting it; and third, act swiftly and decisively when its integrity is threatened. For employees who want to capitalize on their own ideas the process is: first, clarify what is yours and what isn't; second, carefully plan your new activity to minimize the perceived threat to your employer; and finally, execute your plans in a professional, deliberate fashion.
>
> Whatever your perspective, remember everything you do is in preparation for a possible lawsuit. No matter how good your intentions are, appearances control the outcome [p. 122].

Trade Secrets makes the most of its many opportunities to caution businessmen to secure legal advice at the optimum time. One example is:

> Above all, if any serious possibility of litigation exists, consult a qualified lawyer at the earliest possible time. Relatively little preparation can pay off enormously if a lawsuit later develops, or even by avoiding a lawsuit that otherwise would have been filed. And remember, securing legal consulting services to avoid litigation costs a fraction of the legal fees required to defend a lawsuit [p. 113].

Indeed, it seems that one useful purpose of *Trade Secrets* would be for lawyers, especially in-house corporate counsel, to invite the attention of appropriate client personnel to this book.

Lawrence R. Caruso
Linda A. Caruso
Of the District of Columbia Bar

Soviet Year-Book of International Law 1981. Moscow: Publishing House "Nauka," 1982. Pp. 408. 4 rubles, 80 kopecks; $10.75.

Three themes stand out in the 1981 Soviet *Year-Book:* (1) force and the threat of force are unacceptable instruments of the international policy of states; (2) multilateral treaties create a combination of treaty and customary norms some of which bind nonsignatories; and (3) international law must be expanded to cover new areas, notably the protection of the environment and outer space.

In addition, Gregory I. Tunkin once again takes up his pen in a leading article to argue that there can be only one unitary general international law, which is binding on all because it has been coordinated by the wills of states of various social and economic systems. Tunkin has long opposed those, even within the socialist camp, who have argued that two systems of international law exist, one capitalist and one socialist.

To implement the first theme, N. N. Ulyanova rehearses Soviet attempts to persuade others to conclude a "World Treaty on the Nonuse of Force." She finds unconvincing Western arguments against the Soviet draft, denying that such a treaty would be redundant in view of existing Charter obligations and that it would create two legal regimes if all UN members did not sign it. She believes that such a treaty would revive the topic in the public's eyes and would concretize the Charter's general statement of the rule. She adds that a further advantage would be to earmark states that refuse to sign the treaty as likely violators of the Charter's provisions. The Soviets have frequently had this argument on their lips, for they see in returning to the Charter not only a chance to refresh discussion but also to extend it to add principles thought advantageous to Soviet diplomacy.

On the second theme, J. A. Grigelenis argues that with regard to the sanctity of frontiers, the Final Act of Helsinki was based on *jus cogens* and, hence, has binding force. He thinks its principles applicable not only in Europe but, he hopes, in Asia, Africa, and Latin America; presumably, he has his eyes on the Soviet frontier with China, which continues to be a bone of contention in Sino-Soviet relations. M. A. Korobova develops the theme further. Although making no claim that rules created by a multilateral treaty are binding automatically on nonsignatories, she argues that one application of a treaty rule in diplomatic or treaty practice by a nonsignatory will serve as evidence that the multilateral rule has been extended to that nonsignatory. Although she adheres to the long-standing rule of Soviet diplomacy that no state can be bound without its consent, she finds that a nonsignatory is subject to a moral obligation to observe rules of peace and security established in multilateral treaties.

On the third theme, A. S. Timoshenko argues that although environmental law has not yet become an independent branch of international law, there is a trend in that direction. He argues for a universal codifying convention that would comprehensively regulate aspects now appearing only in nonbinding expressions of intent. R. V. Dekanosov then discusses the "common heritage of mankind" as a principle concerned with the preservation and rational use of international resources. L. B. Imnadze follows on the same theme, but adds, in reflection of Soviet interests, that common heritage must not be applied to restrict freedom of the high seas as regards navigation. Common heritage is a means of preventing monopolization of the resources of the sea by a single state.

American critics of their own Foreign Sovereign Immunities Act will find interesting S. I. Ivanov's criticism of it. He adheres rigidly to the Soviet position that no state can be subjected against its will to the jurisdiction of another, even in commercial matters. He finds that U.S. judges are "not hurrying to go over totally to the unconditional automatic denial of sovereign immunity with regard to so-called commercial activity of states" (p. 244). His proposal is that the matter of sovereign immunity be codified through the usual procedures of the International Law Commission rather than by legislation such as that of the United States and of the United Kingdom.

As usual, the *Year-Book* contains a bibliography not only of Soviet writing, but of Eastern European socialist authors. Once again the German Democratic Republic's authors are the most prolific, with the Czechs a close second. Polish and Romanian literature is unaccountably missing, perhaps because the local editors failed to meet a deadline. Also missing is the usual summary of discussion at the annual meeting of the Soviet Association of International Law, although Tunkin's leading article is marked as having been presented at the 1982 meeting.

English summaries of leading articles improve with each year's book, not only in the quality of the language but also in the breadth of coverage. Maybe it is time to include among them the "scientific reports," which are often as interesting as the articles themselves.

JOHN N. HAZARD
Board of Editors

Annuaire Français de Droit International. Vol. XXVI, 1980. Paris: Editions du Centre National de la Recherche Scientifique, 1981. Pp. 1316.

It is not difficult to stress yet again the importance of this *Annuaire:* it has provided, over the years, a balanced and authoritative account of international law as perceived, by and large, through the eyes of lawyers and academics in the French-speaking world. This edition is no exception, and it is only sad to reflect upon the lack of a publication of similar stature elsewhere.

The *Annuaire* continues to produce substantial and original work of enduring interest; and perhaps more importantly, provides a thorough and comprehensive survey of virtually all major developments for the year 1980. Whether as a reference work on French practice on the international plane or as a bibliographical guide to publications in the field of international law, it is an extremely rich mine of information for the researcher; certainly a sine qua non for any serious francophone international lawyer.

Space permits reference to only a few articles of particular interest to the reviewer. The article by C. Cadoux, *The Birth of a Nation: Zimbabwe,* merits attention, in that it may be recalled that the struggle for independence included, for the first time in the history of the United Nations, the use of sanctions in accordance with chapter VII of the UN Charter. In this context the author found it somewhat regrettable that both the United States and the United Kingdom preempted the formal revocation of sanctions by the Security Council; one must tend to agree that such unilateral action appeared to many as insensitive, to say the least. This being said, one can concur with the author's conclusion that as of December 21, 1979, the United Nations "a donc fermé définitivement le dossier de la Question de la Rhodésie du Sud," but a rider may be added: that this might not necessarily be true in respect of "le dossier de la Zimbabwe."

P.-H. Imbert provides an incisive critique of the French attitude in accepting human rights treaty obligations in his article *France and Human Rights Treaties.* The author is very critical of the delay in France's adherence to the UN Covenant on Civil and Political Rights, and even more so in respect of the way in which this was done. He rightly admonishes the "portée limitée" of the French commitment, in particular, in light of the nonacceptance of the Covenant's facultative provisions, namely, interstate applications under Article 41 and the right of individual petition provided for in the Optional Protocol. One can only wonder what Imbert would write were he to analyze the U.S. Government's attitude to the same instrument.

What is the status of a former head of state? Take the examples of Napoleon I, King Constantine of Greece, Edward VIII, Haile Selassie, and the Shah of Iran. And what have been the legal repercussions of Taiwan's removal from the United Nations and other international forums? These fascinating and yet complex issues are discussed by E. Decaux and A. Manin, respectively. In the case of Taiwan (approximately half of whose exports are absorbed by U.S. and Japanese markets) the question is posed: how long will 18 million inhabitants continue to vegetate on the margins of legality? The destiny of China is—so Chinese mythology tells us—in the hands of three bearded gods. Although the gods of happiness (Foo) and prosperity (Loo) have kept a watchful eye over Taiwan, will the same be true in respect of Sho, the god of longevity?

The wealth of information contained in this volume is truly vast. The well-documented Camp David Agreement, the *LIAMCO* arbitration and the ICJ *Hostages* case are discussed. So, too, is the less-publicized ICJ Advisory Opinion on the *Interpretation of the Agreement between the WHO and Egypt* of December 1980, and the arbitral decision of May 16, 1980 concerning the external debts of the Federal Republic of Germany (all of which, incidentally, are reproduced in *International Legal Materials*), as well as the case law of the UN and ILO Administrative Tribunals and decisions of a variety of European regional instances.

A few useful articles and commentaries on the law of the sea deserve mention: one by T. Treves relating to the peaceful use of the seas (as now provided in Article 301 of the UN Law of the Sea Convention), and another by B. Oxman which analyzes the significance of the U.S. Deep Seabed Hard Mineral Resources Act of 1980. This Act, as well as similar legislation in the United Kingdom, the Federal Republic of Germany, and France, has been the cause of much (perhaps justified?) criticism.[1] Now that such "interim" legislation also exists in the USSR,[2] Japan, and Italy, it may be an opportune time to reflect upon the reported intention of UNCLOS III President T. B. Koh to ask the General Assembly of the United Nations to request an advisory opinion from the ICJ

[1] *See, e.g.,* the article by Brown, *The Impact of Unilateral Legislation on the Future Legal Regime of Deep-Sea Mining,* 20 ARCHIV DES VÖLKERRECHTS 145–82 (1982).

[2] Actually, in the USSR, it was an edict enacted by the Presidium of the Supreme Soviet on April 17, 1982. *See* Izvestiia, Apr. 18, 1982, at 1–2, 21 ILM 551–53 (1982).

on this subject.[3] Interestingly, in the wider context of this subject, note can be taken of a decision of the Cour d'appel de Rennes of March 26, 1979 (commented upon on pp. 822–27). In this case the French law of July 16, 1976, creating an exclusive economic zone of 188 nautical miles around the Republic's coastline, was accepted as a reflection of customary international law superseding those parts of the 1958 Geneva treaty regime which might be inconsistent with it. Might this, and similar domestic court decisions, be of some relevance to the United States, especially in light of the recent and somewhat controversial declaration of March 10, 1983, in which President Reagan proclaimed the existence of an exclusive economic zone around the coastline of the United States?

Does there exist, in the English-speaking world, a yearbook of comparable stature?

ANDREW DRZEMCZEWSKI
The Polytechnic of North London

Chinese Yearbook of International Law and Affairs. Vol. 1 (1981). Edited by Hungdah Chiu. Published by the Occasional Papers/Reprints Series in Contemporary Asian Studies, Inc. for the Chinese Society of International Law—Chinese (Taiwan) Branch of International Law Association, Baltimore, 1982. Pp. 294. Index. $7.

This publication is intended to provide a forum for scholarly discussion on international legal aspects that touch the Republic of China (ROC) on Taiwan. It is divided into 10 major areas, including articles, current legal developments in such areas as trade, investment, and human rights in the ROC, reviews of books published in Taiwan, and lists of official or unofficial agreements concluded by the ROC or its semi-official organs. This volume generally covers the period from January 1, 1979 to December 31, 1980, although there are some later references as well.

In view of Taiwan's delicate international status, its close relations with the United States, and the continuing role it plays in U.S.-People's Republic of China relations, one should find the five articles in this volume useful and interesting: *The International Law of Recognition and Multi-system Nations—With Special Reference to the Chinese (Mainland-Taiwan) Case* (Hungdah Chiu), *Taiwan's International Status* (Ralph N. Clough), *The Taiwan Issue in Peking's Foreign Relations in the 1970s: A Systematic Review* (Lyushun Shen), *Foreign Investment in the Troubled Waters of the East China Sea* (Ying-jeou Ma), and *Legal Development in U.S.-ROC Trade from January 1, 1979 through June 1, 1981* (David Simon).

SHAO-CHUAN LENG
University of Virginia

[3] *See* Financial Times, May 1, 1982.

Netherlands Yearbook of International Law. Vol. XIII, 1982. T. M. C. Asser Institute, The Hague. The Hague: Martinus Nijhoff Publishers, 1982. Pp. 511. Index. Dfl.110; $44.

As in preceding years, this useful publication contains leading articles, together with a synopsis of Dutch state practice, treaties, domestic legislation with international impact, judicial decisions, and scholarly literature for the period covered. The articles are particularly interesting. Legal problems arising out of underwater salvage of sunken treasure ships, of the Russian submarine investigated by Howard Hughes's *Glomar Explorer,* and of other historic artifacts from the ocean bottom are discussed by Professor Lucius Caflisch of the Graduate Institute of International Studies, Geneva. The scope of individual judges' dissenting or concurring opinions in the World Court is probed by Farrokh Jhabvala of Florida International University, Miami. Territory in international law is the subject of the article by M. N. Shaw of the University of Essex. Dr. Peter J. van Krieken treats the topic of repatriation of refugees. Ko Swan Sik, of the *Yearbook* board of editors, reviews legal aspects of the proposed export by a Dutch company of two submarines and a nuclear power plant to the Taiwan Navy. Whether unauthorized broadcasting from a purportedly Panamanian ship outside Dutch territorial waters justified seizure of the transmitting equipment on board is explored by Professor H. Meijers of Amsterdam and R. C. R. Siekmann of the Asser Institute (publisher of the *Yearbook*).

This edition of the *Yearbook* covers a very active year. The account of state practice occupies almost one hundred pages. The concise catalog of treaties requires 31 pages, and the treatment of municipal legislation takes up 15 pages, while 94 pages are devoted to court cases. The volume of litigation on civil and human rights has increased to such an extent that beginning with this volume of the *Yearbook* complete coverage will not be attempted, but only cases "interesting from the viewpoint of general international law" will be mentioned (p. 360). Cases involving admission of aliens and grant of residence and work permits continue to be numerous. In one reported case two children of a Moroccan father who are now living with his polygamous wife in Morocco were refused permission to reside in the Netherlands. It was held that this was not a violation of his "right to respect for his private and family life" guaranteed by Article 8 of the European Convention on Human Rights (p. 350). The same result was reached with respect to members of a nomadic Gypsy tribe who claimed that their group constituted a single extensive family (p. 357). However, that article in conjunction with Article 14 (which provides that enjoyment of the rights set forth in the Convention "shall be secured without discrimination on any ground such as sex . . . social origin . . . birth or other status") required Dutch courts to treat a bastard's mother's sister as one of his "blood-relations" for purposes of guardianship of the minor child, contrary to the actual intent of the national legislator (p. 364). But Article 4 (forbidding "slavery or servitude" and "forced or compulsory labor") was held not to prevent the club for which a professional football player was under contract to play from exacting a substantial transfer fee from the club to which he wished to be traded, a sum that the latter club was not willing to pay (pp. 414–15).

EDWARD DUMBAULD
U.S. Senior District Judge

Guoji Fa (International Law). 2 vols. By Zhou Gengsheng. Beijing: Shangwu yinshuguan (Commercial Press), 1981. Pp. iv, 815. PRC $2.45; $1.65.

Guoji Fa (International Law). Edited by Wang Tieya and Wei Min. Beijing: Falu chubanshe (Law Publisher), 1981. Pp. x, 568. PRC $2.20; $1.45.

Guoji Fa Ziliao Xuanpian (Selected Materials on International Law). Compiled by Wang Tieya and Tian Ruxuan. Beijing: Falu chubanshe, 1982. Pp. vi, 1081. PRC $3.95; $2.70.

Thirty-two years after the establishment of the People's Republic of China (PRC), the mainland Chinese have finally published two treatises and one source book on international law. This reflects the post-Mao Chinese leadership's policy to end China's self-imposed isolation in the world community. During the last stage of Mao's rule—the so-called Great Proletarian Cultural Revolution Period (1966–1976)—no scholarly writing on international law was published.[1] As a matter of fact, it was not until March 30, 1979, almost two and a half years after the death of Mao, that the first article on international law was published in the official *Renmin ribao* (People's Daily) urging the strengthening of the study of international law in the PRC. The authors of that article, Wang Tieya and Wei Min, are responsible for compiling the treatise and Wang for the source book on international law under review here.

The manuscript of the treatise by Zhou Gengsheng was completed in 1964 but was not published, except in very limited numbers with internal circulation only, until 1976. The author died in 1971. The present edition for public circulation was published in October 1981. Because the publication date is 17 years after the manuscript was completed, a substantial part of the book is out of date and some terms or statements are not even consistent with the PRC's current policy. For instance, in several places, the author refers to the United States as "American imperialism" (pp. 128, 486, 687), a term the PRC now refrains from using in publications available to the public. On the other hand, it is not clear whether the author, in 1964, sensed the deterioration in Sino-Soviet relations; he still exaggerated the Soviet contribution to certain principles of international law in a few references. For instance, he wrote that the Soviet Union was the first major power to adhere to the 1928 Paris Treaty for the Renunciation of War (p. 200). He failed to mention that the Treaty was proposed by the United States and France and that it was these two countries who invited

[1] For a summary of the study of international law in the PRC before 1965, see Hungdah Chiu, *Communist China's Attitude Toward International Law,* 60 AJIL 263–66 (1966).

all others, including the Soviet Union, to adhere to the Treaty. In some places, the author apparently relied on Soviet doctrines to identify some rules of international law. Thus, on the question of the subjects of international law, the author insists that only states are proper subjects and denies that international organizations are at least limited subjects of international law. This appears to reflect the Soviet view as expressed in a 1957 textbook edited by F. I. Kozhevnikov,[2] which was translated into Chinese in 1959 (p. 89 of the Chinese version).

The organization of the book is primarily based on Oppenheim's treatise on international law, edited by H. Lauterpacht (vol. I, 8th ed. 1955 and vol. II, 7th ed. 1952), though Zhou's treatise covers only the law of peace. Reliance on Oppenheim poses some problems, because by the time the author completed the manuscript, Lauterpacht's Oppenheim was 9 years old and did not totally reflect some important subsequent developments in international law. For instance, in volume 1 of Lauterpacht's Oppenheim, the question of the continental shelf was discussed in part II, "The Objects of the Law of Nations"; chapter II, "The Open Sea"; section X, "The Subsoil beneath the Bed of the Open Sea" (pp. 629–35). The author follows this pattern of considering the continental shelf as part of the regime of the high seas by discussing this problem in chapter 8, "High Seas," section 2, "The Principle of Freedom of the High Seas" (pp. 482–86), though he does refer to the 1958 Geneva Convention on the Continental Shelf.

After an introduction, the following topics are discussed: the subjects of international law, states, the recognition and succession of states, residents (individuals), territory, high seas, diplomatic relations, treaties, international organizations, and peaceful settlement of international disputes. Each chapter is very well written and is annotated with references to works of all major American and European writers, including occasional references to Soviet and Japanese writers. The most frequently consulted writer is, of course, Oppenheim, and the most frequently cited journal is the *American Journal of International Law*. Ironically, there are no Chinese writers' views cited in the book. The explanation may be that at the time the author completed the manuscript, almost all Chinese international lawyers had been purged in the 1957 Anti-rightist Campaign or in the 1959 Anti-rightist Opportunism Campaign and it was simply too risky to cite their work in the manuscript. The only PRC writer cited is Wang Tieya, for his compilation of Chinese treaties before 1949[3] (p. 644) and not for his scholarly writing. Whenever appropriate, the author also refers to the PRC's practice of international law in each chapter. However, almost all of the PRC practices he discusses are taken from *Zhonghua Renmin Gangheguo Duiwai Guanxi Wenjian Ji* (Collection of External Relations Documents of the People's Republic of China) and other publicly available sources and thus reveal no new information.

The international law book edited by Wang and Wei is a textbook for use in universities or colleges—the first one on international law ever published in the PRC. It is a collected work; in addition to the two editors who also participated

[2] MEZHDUNARODNOE PRAVO. The English translation was published in 1961.

[3] *See* Chiu, *supra* note 1, at 266.

in writing some chapters, there are 18 authors. The book is characterized as a "tentative" edition and the editors' note invites criticism and suggestions for preparation of future editions. The introduction examines the concept of international law, its history, sources, and codification, as well as its relationship to municipal law. The body of the text covers fundamental principles of international law, subjects, territory, law of the sea, airspace and outer space, residents (individuals), diplomatic and consular relations, treaties, international organizations, international economic law, settlement of international disputes, and the law of war (including a section on neutrality). Unlike Zhou's treatise, this book does not have extensive notes to explain its sources, though in some chapters it does have a few explanatory notes. The contents of the book are fairly up-to-date and it addresses almost all areas covered in some recent Western textbooks on international law. In some places, it also presents some Chinese practices of international law, such as the introduction of international law to China (pp. 15–19), Chinese nationality law (pp. 247–50), and aliens' legal status in the PRC (pp. 258–60). Generally speaking, it is a fairly well-written introduction for Chinese college students who wish to learn about international law, though a few improvements could be made. The book contains no glossary of Chinese international law terms and their English equivalents; thus a student, after studying this book, would still have difficulty in reading English literature on international law for further research or understanding. This is especially important in the PRC where few international law books and articles in Chinese exist. Moreover, a list of major treatises on international law and an index would greatly facilitate the reading of this book.

The source book compiled by Wang and Tian is a comprehensive collection of all major treaties and declarations or resolutions adopted primarily by the General Assembly of the United Nations. In total, it contains 88 documents adopted between 1919 and 1979. Some documents do not have Chinese texts, so the compilers have translated them into Chinese. All documents are within the scope of what is usually referred to as the law of peace. The law of war documents and those international law documents relating to China are excluded. Even with such omissions, the book is still over one thousand pages.

The way the documents are grouped into chapters causes some confusion, because it is done neither chronologically nor according to subject matter. Yet a closer inspection reveals that documents of a similar character do follow one another in a sequence which is obscured by the chapter divisions, but seems to be the following: fundamental principles of international law (documents 1–10), subjects of international law (documents 11–19), residents (individuals) (documents 20–43), law of the sea (documents 44–46), territory (document 47), airspace and outer space (documents 48–60), diplomatic and consular relations (documents 61–67), international economic law (documents 68–71), international organizations (documents 72–84), and settlement of international disputes (documents 85–88). In a future edition, these documents should be arranged under different chapters for the convenience of readers. Despite this minor problem, this collection should be useful to Chinese students and practitioners if they want to learn more about modern international law beyond the textbook level.

In view of the post-Mao PRC's interest in expanding its contacts with the outside world, it is only natural for the PRC to strengthen the study of international law in China. The publication of the three books reviewed here is an indication of that trend. We can expect PRC writers to contribute more to the literature of international law in the future.

HUNGDAH CHIU
University of Maryland School of Law

BRIEFER NOTICES

Gelijkheid. Vol. VI. Edited by Léon Ingber, under the direction of F. De Pauw, P. Foriers, and Ch. Perelman. (Brussels: Etablissements Emile Bruylant, 1981. Pp. 271. BF 1.268.) Equality is a concept relevant to international law with respect to protection of minorities (as in the peace treaties of World War I) and protection of human rights under the European Convention of 1950 and the International Covenants of 1976. The material in the sixth volume of *Equality* (unlike some of the earlier volumes in the series) is highly theoretical and interdisciplinary. There is more emphasis on philosophy than on specific counsel for practitioners. The volume, a publication of the Center for Philosophy of Law of the Free University of Brussels, is dedicated to the memory of Professor René Dekkers, one of the Center's long-time supporters. His brief article on equality and inequality in Chinese thought opens the volume. According to Confucius, human virtue is found in harmony with nature, and nature manifests inequality in many forms. Léon Ingber, adjunct-director of the Center, then discusses law and equality. K. Dassen treats equality theory and case law. The remaining articles launch into nonlegal areas. Jozef van Billingen compares the philosophy of John Rawles and J. Haberman; M. Lambrechts analyzes that of Michel Foucault. L. Apostel and W. Callebaut apply the methods of economics, "systems theory" and "quality of life research" based on "social indicators." This area of research is said to have been initiated by President Lyndon Johnson and developed during the past 15 years (pp. 107–08). Hugo de Schampfeleire contributes a historical study of the idea of equality from antiquity to the *ancien régime.* Readers who have the time and inclination to pursue abstruse ratiocination of the type elaborated in these studies will find this volume interesting.

EDWARD DUMBAULD
U.S. Senior District Judge

Terrorism in Europe. Edited by Yonah Alexander and Kenneth Myers. (New York: St. Martin's Press, 1982. Pp. 216. Index. $25.) This collection of articles on European terrorism varies in quality from the purely propagandistic to the scholarly. Into the former category falls the introduction by the coeditors, who argue without any substantiation that most manifestations of antistate violence throughout Western Europe are orchestrated by Moscow as part of a conscious program to destabilize the NATO alliance. In contrast, Dennis Pluchinsky's detailed catalog of European terrorist attacks successfully explains most of the violence without any reference to a Soviet-inspired conspiracy, thus implicitly repudiating the introduction's thesis. A perceptive article by Marie Fleming traces the intellectual origins of modern European terrorism back to 19th-century anarchists, not Marxists. Yosef Nedava seems to advance the extraordinary proposition that in the absence of an international criminal court, an individual might be entitled to take the enforcement of international law into his own hands by assassinating those alleged to be guilty of the crime of genocide against his people. An excellent article by Juliet Lodge and David Freestone examines the history of political opposition by the members of the European Economic Community to the adoption of a common legal policy for the purpose of suppressing terrorism, an opposition which was finally overcome to some extent by the novel device of their 1979 Dublin Agreement to apply the general terms of the Council of Europe's Convention on the Suppression of Terrorism to the EEC. And Matthew Lippman presents a thumbnail sketch of the anti-terrorist acts which the British Government has promulgated for application to Northern Ireland in abrogation of the traditional due process protections afforded to individuals in Great Britain. Case studies on Italy's Red Brigades, Spain's ETA, and German terrorism complete this uneven volume.

FRANCIS A. BOYLE
University of Illinois

Controlling the Bomb: Nuclear Proliferation in the 1980s. By Lewis A. Dunn. (New Haven and London: Yale University Press, 1982. Pp. xii, 209. Index. $21, cloth; $6.95, paper.) This book begins with a superficial presentation of the historical progression of nuclear weapons proliferation since 1945. After glancing over India's decision to explode a "peaceful" nuclear device and ignoring the origins of Israel's nuclear weapons capability, it proceeds to catalog the most recent developments in proliferation-related occurrences and policies on a country-by-country basis. The author's arguments as to why nuclear weapons proliferation is a dangerous phenomenon verge on the platitudinous (except to those in the Reagan administration who do not perceive the danger). Some of his concluding policy recommendations can be read to provide justification for the Reagan administration's dismantling of President Carter's strict antiproliferation regime and its replacement by the promiscuous philosophy of America becoming a "reliable supplier" of nuclear knowledge, training, technology, materials, and expertise—in other words, a reliable proliferator.

The author cleverly manipulates nonproliferation arguments to criticize progressive developments in the field of nuclear arms control: proposals for a U.S. no-first-use pledge, for a comprehensive test ban treaty, and for large reductions in U.S. strategic nuclear forces; and the lack of European popular support for deployment of NATO's new theater nuclear weapons. Certainly, the greatest preventive to further nuclear proliferation would be a massive reduction in both U.S. and Soviet nuclear weapons inventories. Yet the author does not even address the fundamental question of whether any nonproliferation regime can ultimately succeed unless and until the two superpowers take seriously their obligations under Article 6 of the Non-Proliferation Treaty.

Dunn wrote this book while a senior professional staff member of the conservative Hudson Institute, then joined the Reagan administration as Special Assistant for Nuclear Affairs in the State Department. The book is worth reading for the insight it may provide into what the Reagan administration's otherwise nebulous proliferation policies are or could become. In whatever forum, however, the persuasiveness of Dunn's set of policy prescriptions is sharply undercut by his failure to construct the historical foundation and political analysis necessary to support them.

FRANCIS A. BOYLE
University of Illinois

A Calendar of Soviet Treaties 1958–1973. By George Ginsburgs and Robert M. Slusser. (Alphen aan den Rijn and Rockville: Sijthoff & Noordhoff, 1981. Pp. xx, 908. Index. Dfl.300; $150.) Drs. Ginsburgs and Slusser continue in this volume the use of techniques found successful in their earlier *Calendar* of 1959 to discover hard-to-find foreign relations documentation of the USSR. They examine not only standard treaty series of the USSR, the United Nations, and treaty partners, but also journals, newspapers, and even memoirs. The result is a compendium of information going far beyond treaties to cover communiqués, statements, memorandums, and even news reports. All entries include dates of ratification by the USSR and coming into force. Without question, the use of this method makes the *Calendar* unique.

The key chronological listings are supplemented by a country index that facilitates research on Soviet foreign relations with the country concerned. Thus, the reader can trace limited concern with Rwanda or Guyana, or widely developed concern for relations with France or Czechoslovakia. Research librarians will find the *Calendar* invaluable, of course, but even the browser who looks beyond the endless columns of type can glean general impressions of the trend of politics, for the USSR has become one of the principal molders of international law. Although custom has for decades been accepted by Soviet diplomats as a source of law, there is still preference for the creation of law through agreement. This method permits control as custom does not. Even the columns on multilateral treaties are given political significance by the inclusion of notations on Soviet reservations. It becomes evident that the USSR rejects third-party interpretation if its bargaining power is sufficient to permit it to do so.

JOHN N. HAZARD
Board of Editors

CORRESPONDENCE

TO THE EDITORS-IN-CHIEF:

Authors should normally take in silence any criticism from reviewers. But Howard Levie, in his review (77 AJIL 383 (1983)) of the book we edited, *Documents on the Laws of War* (Oxford University Press, 1982), relies heavily on one argument which is both central to the character of the whole book and based on a faulty reading of it. We thus feel bound to reply.

Levie accepts the principle of selection of documents which was set out in the book: "Emphasis is firmly placed on the laws of war which remain applicable today." But he questions whether we have followed our own criterion. Two matters are cited:

(1) In pointing out that we omitted the text of the 1907 Hague Convention III Relative to the Opening of Hostilities, he asks, rhetorically, whether the editors are therefore saying that this agreement "is not applicable today"? How-

ever, in the introduction, under the heading "Principles of Selection in this Volume," we state that this Convention was omitted because it relates more to *ius ad bellum* than to *ius in bello.* This is again indicated on page 43.

(2) He says:

> And while they include the 1923 Hague Rules of Aerial Warfare because they "largely corresponded to customary rules and general principles underlying the laws of war on land and at sea," they omit the 1909 Declaration of London on the Laws of Naval Warfare. Does this mean that the Declaration does not, in any part, correspond to "customary rules and general principles underlying the laws of war . . . at sea"?

The vital word "because" in the above sentence is misleading. As is amply clear from pages 17 and 121–23 of our book, our main reason for including the 1923 Hague Rules was that they clarify an aspect of the laws of war which is not covered by any international agreement in force. On the same criterion, the text of the 1909 London Declaration (which is twice mentioned in the book) was deliberately omitted.

In short, if we are to be charged with not following our own criteria of selection, we would prefer to be criticized on the ground of our actual reasoning, as stated in the book, and not on the basis of what our criteria are presumed, incorrectly, to have been.

On the issue of whether our book is necessary at all in view of Schindler and Toman's excellent and much larger collection on the laws of war, every other reviewer of our book has reached a conclusion different from that of Dr. Levie. Moreover, Dr. Jiří Toman, whose generous encouragement and advice is mentioned in our book, has all along seen the point of a book of documents which, by focusing on the currently applicable laws, could be less heavy and expensive than his own volume, and more up-to-date: a view which he has emphatically reiterated since publication of our work. But this is a matter on which opinions may differ, and it is not for us to quarrel with Dr. Levie's view: only with the particular argument about our selection of documents which he makes in his review.

ADAM ROBERTS
St. Antony's College, Oxford

RICHARD GUELFF
Coudert Frères, Paris

Howard S. Levie replies:

I have never believed that any reviewer should be called upon to vindicate his personal reactions to and criticisms of the book reviewed; and now that I have had an adverse criticism contained in a review challenged by the editors of such a book I see no reason to change that position. Perhaps my feelings about the book reviewed were influenced by the fact that I have grave reservations as to the propriety of taking a collection of documents on a highly specialized and somewhat esoteric subject successfully put together by other editors, sifting its contents, and then producing it as a "new" volume—particularly when this procedure is subsequently justified by the scholarly reasoning that such a volume would be "less heavy and expensive."

I would add one point: the examples I gave in my review and which the editors now attempt to justify were exactly that—examples only. Others could have been given.

TO THE EDITORS-IN-CHIEF:

I am a little surprised at the review of my book *The Expanding Jurisdiction of the United Nations* by Dr. Mahnoush H. Arsanjani in the April 1983 issue of the *Journal* (77 AJIL 365 (1983)). From the brief review, it seems either the reviewer has not read the book as carefully as an author is, in fairness, entitled to expect from a learned reviewer or that she intended to dispose of the review of the book in a hurry.

The reviewer observes that there are some "problems" about the "design, approach, and analysis." I suggest that these "problems" arise primarily because the reviewer has failed to take note of the fact that the present volume is essentially complementary to the author's earlier volume *United Nations and Domestic Jurisdiction* (2d ed. 1961). This fact has been evidenced in the preface, as well as repeatedly throughout the present volume. The "independent scholarly perspective with an express statement of criteria employed" (the lack of which in the present volume she complains of) is fully laid out in that volume (which had been commended by, among others, Hersch Lauterpacht, Leland Goodrich, Oliver Lissitzyn, and C. G. Fenwick).

The reviewer remarks that I do not offer my own "definition" of the terms "domestic" and "international jurisdiction." Surely, when neither the body of international law nor the law of international organizations cares to expressly define these terms, what is (and who is) she complaining against? So far as I am concerned, I have stated categorically (p. 232) that a definition of these terms is "an utterly pointless exercise"; that "any definition is undesirable, impracticable and useless"; and that "the scope of jurisdiction cannot, and should not, be defined in the abstract—whether generally or enumeratively."

The reviewer remarks that the analysis of the cases that have come before UN organs "appears aimless and often leaves the reader confused about its relevance to the title and the purposes of the book" and that there is "insufficient analysis of their political context and their legal significance." Apparently, the reviewer has either not read through these case studies carefully or understood the focus of the analyses. If the reviewer had cared to look up my 1961 volume, she would have noticed that I had analyzed the cases (during the first 10 years of the functioning of the United Nations) as thoroughly as she possibly expects me to have done in the present volume. The reasons why I did so in the earlier volume and not in the present one are explained largely by the different foci of the two studies and "the radical change in the outlook of members," as I stated in the preface to the present volume. It is rather extraordinary for the reviewer to complain that the analysis of the cases "appears aimless." It so appears to the reviewer because she has failed to note that in the analysis of the cases, I am severely concerned with only one, limited, aspect of the question, namely, the issue of jurisdiction of UN organs. I have naturally highlighted only those aspects of the cases which, in my opinion, are relevant to this limited point—with only such additional facts of the cases as are absolutely necessary and relevant to make that point clear. If a reader (or a reviewer) desires more background to the cases, he ought to look up the *Year Book of the United Nations* or UN documents.

And, finally, the reviewer complains that "[t]he criteria for characterizing events as falling within domestic jurisdiction are rather superficial, indeed often unstated. No definitions or criteria are developed to explain why certain incidents are within or without domestic jurisdiction." It is this comment, more than any others, that makes me feel that the reviewer has either not read the book carefully or is unfairly cavalier in her comments. For, in a large concluding chapter, this is precisely what I have done. Under each of the seven categories of questions, I have sought to analyze the likely criteria applied by UN organs for the determination of their jurisdiction with respect to them *and* added my own criticism and comment. This is in addition to the explanations I have given in the chapters on case studies. I have certainly given (pp. 175–95) (contrary to the reviewer's remark) "a systematic explanation of why certain cases came to the United Nations or an indication of conditioning factors that influenced their treatment." Furthermore, in the concluding section (pp. 195–236) I have sought to go beyond the cases that came up before the UN organs (until 1975) and taken a look at the factors and contingencies that are likely to affect (positively and negatively) the exercise of jurisdiction by UN organs in the future.

I hope the learned reviewer would care to look up the book again and "review" her own review in the interests of fairness to the author and the standing of the *Journal.*

M. S. RAJAN
School of International Studies
Jawaharlal Nehru University

Mahnoush H. Arsanjani replies:

Dr. Rajan's innuendo against me that his book was not read or not read carefully requires no comment. His cavil that my review gave insufficient attention to his book on domestic jurisdiction, first published in 1958 and revised in 1961, which, he tells us, won some favorable reviews then, is irrelevant. That was a book conceived a quarter of a century ago and on a different subject. While an author may wish to have his work reviewed and rereviewed through the decades, that was not the function of this reviewer. The author's insistence that the reader wishing to understand his 1982 book must also read his 1961 (and presumably his 1958) work is also unfounded. Nothing in the preface or the chapters of the 1982 book indicates such an interrelationship or such a demand by the author of his readers. Quite the contrary. The preface states that the focus of inquiry of these books is different: "I wish to emphasize that the focus of the present volume is different from that of the earlier volume." The author continues: "when I reverted to the subject recently [*i.e.,* some 20 years later] I found that the earlier approach was no longer appropriate." It is at least astonishing to be chastened now for not having rereviewed a work the author himself has declared archaic.

The author's testimony that he purposely chose *not* to define terms constantly used in his book can in no way change the criticism. Whether his nonfeasance was intentional or not, the scholarly reader is entitled, if not obliged, to understand what the author means by the terms he is using. Indeed, what does he mean by jurisdiction itself: to make law, to apply law? Though the author is not required to make meaningful all the technical terms he describes, he can be expected to make clear what he is talking about. In the last chapter, he does at last try to propose a criterion for characterizing events as falling within or outside domestic jurisdiction. I appraised this effort as superficial. The punch line of this chapter is "whether or not a question is a matter of international concern/interest depends upon the collective judgement of the most representative organ of the international community" (p. 171). Is this criterion anything but general? Is it consequential? On its own terms, what is the most representative organ of the international community? The General Assembly? The Security Council? The Economic and Social Council? The International Court of Justice? How does one assess when this collective judgment has taken place? Through resolutions? Decisions? Through the actual behavior of the member states outside the United Nations? How does one deal with inconsistencies between the voting of member states in the United Nations and their behavior outside the United Nations? What are the elements that affect such a judgment? Alas, these central questions are neither raised nor answered.

As for the author's efforts to appraise cases, I judged them inadequate. Upon a rereading, I find no reason to change my opinion.

BOOKS RECEIVED*

International Law—General

Bernhardt, Rudolf (ed.). *Encyclopedia of Public International Law. Instalment 3: Use of Force. War and Neutrality. Peace Treaties (A–M).* Pp. xv, 299. *Instalment 4: Use of Force. War and Neutrality. Peace Treaties (N–Z).* Pp. xv, 377. Published under the auspices of the Max Planck Institute for Comparative Public Law and International Law. Amsterdam: North-Holland Publishing Company, 1982.

Bleckmann, Albert. *Grundprobleme und Methoden des Völkerrechts.* Freiburg and Munich: Verlag Karl Alber, 1982. Pp. 348. DM 48.

Duculescu, Victor. *Continuitate si discontinuitate in dreptul international* (Continuity and Discontinuity in International Law). Bucharest: Editura Academiei, 1982. Pp. 176.

Gutiérrez Girardot, Rafael, Helmut Ridder, Manohar Lal Sarin, and Theo Schiller (eds.). *New Directions in International Law: Essays in Honour of Wolfgang Abendroth—Festschrift zu seinem 75. Geburtstag.* Frankfurt/Main and New York: Campus Verlag, 1982. Pp. 592. DM 178.

Van Bogaert, E. R. C. *Volkenrecht.* Antwerp: Kluwer Rechtswetenschappen, 1982. Pp. xxi, 648. Index.

International Economic Law & Relations

Le droit des relations économiques internationales: Etudes offertes à Berthold Goldman. Paris: Librairies Techniques, 1982. Pp. xvi, 427. F.288.

Fernández Tomás, Antonio. *El Control de las Empresas Multinacionales.* Madrid: Editorial Tecnos, 1983. Pp. 311.

Vers une érosion du droit des brevets d'invention? Nairobi 1981. Colloque de l'IRPI sur la révision de la Convention de Paris (Paris, 9 février 1982). Paris: Librairies Techniques, 1982. Pp. 100. F.80.

Sanders, Pieter (ed.). *Yearbook Commercial Arbitration.* Volume VIII–1983. Published under the auspices of the International Council for Commercial Arbitration. Deventer: Kluwer, 1983. Pp. xiv, 468. Dfl.82.50; $33.

Welt, Leo G. B. *Countertrade: Business Practices for Today's World Market.* New York: American Management Associations, 1982. Pp. 72. $10.

Jurisdiction & Immunities

Lowe, A. V. *Extraterritorial Jurisdiction: An Annotated Collection of Legal Materials.* Cambridge: Grotius Publications Limited, 1983. Pp. xxiii, 273. Index. £25; $45.

Stevenson, John R., Jeffrey F. Browne, and Lori Fisler Damrosch. *United States Law of Sovereign Immunity relating to international financial transactions.* London: Euromoney Publications Ltd., 1983. Pp. 158. $145.

* Mention here neither assures nor precludes later review.

State Responsibility

Przetacznik, Franciszek. *Protection of Officials of Foreign States according to International Law.* The Hague, Boston, London: Martinus Nijhoff Publishers, 1983. Pp. xix, 390. Indexes. Dfl.160; $65.50.

Law of the Sea & Maritime Law

Conforti, Benedetto (ed.). *La Zona economica esclusiva.* Milan: Dott. A. Giuffrè Editore, 1983. Pp. vi, 209. L. 12.000.

Jayaraman, K. *Legal Regime of Islands.* New Delhi: Marwah Publications, 1982. Pp. x, 169. Index. Rs.45; $9.

Jiménez Piernas, Carlos Bartolomé. *El Proceso de formación del derecho internacional de los archipiélagos.* 2 vols. Madrid: Universidad Complutense de Madrid, 1982. Pp. l, 1217.

Morales Paúl, Isidro. *La Delimitación de Areas Marinas y Sub-Marinas al Norte de Venezuela.* Caracas: Academia de Ciencias Políticas y Sociales, 1983. Pp. 315. Index. Bs.100.

Post, Alexandra Merle. *Deepsea Mining and the Law of the Sea.* The Hague, Boston, Lancaster: Martinus Nijhoff Publishers, 1983. Pp. xxiii, 358. Dfl.160; $69.50.

Rao, P. Chandrasekhara. *The New Law of Maritime Zones.* New Delhi: Milind Publications Private Limited, 1983. Pp. xx, 423. Indexes. Rs.200.

Treves, Tullio (ed.). *Lo Sfruttamento dei fondi marini internazionali.* Milan: Dott. A. Giuffrè Editore, 1982. Pp. xii, 195. L. 12.000.

Conflicts & Disputes

Bailey, Sydney D. *How Wars End: The United Nations and the Termination of Armed Conflict, 1946–1964.* Volumes I and II. New York: The Clarendon Press; Oxford University Press, 1982. Vol. I: pp. xxi, 404. Index. $89. Vol. II: pp. xxxii, 715. Index. $98.

Perl, Raphael. *The Falkland Islands Dispute in International Law and Politics: A Documentary Sourcebook.* London, Rome, New York: Oceana Publications, Inc., 1983. Pp. xiii, 722. $45.

Rousseau, Charles. *Droit International Public. Tome V: Les rapports conflictuels.* Paris: Editions Sirey, 1983. Pp. xvi, 504. Index. F.240.

Sauvignon, Edouard. *Les Etats-Unis et la Seconde Guerre d'Indochine: Analyse des arguments américains.* Grenoble: Editions CEDSI, 1982. Pp. 49. F.30.

Use of Force & Law of War

Veuthey, Michel. *Guérilla et Droit Humanitaire* (2d ed.). Geneva: Le Comité international de la Croix-Rouge, 1983. Pp. xl, 451. Index. $5, paper.

Dispute Settlement

Kirgis, Frederic L., Jr. *Prior Consultation in International Law: A Study of State Practice.* Charlottesville: University Press of Virginia, 1983. Pp. ix, 389. Index. $35.

Terrorism

Dimitrijević, Vojin. *Terorizam.* Belgrade: Radnička Štampa, 1982. Pp. 272. Index.

Friedlander, Robert A. *Terrorism: Documents of International and Local Control. Volume III: From the Terror Decade of the 1970's to the Dangerous Decade of the 1980's.* London, Rome, New York: Oceana Publications, Inc., 1981. Pp. xiv, 614. $40.

——. *Terror-Violence: Aspects of Social Control.* London, Rome, New York: Oceana Publications, Inc., 1983. Pp. xxix, 299. Index. $35.

Human Rights

Bernhardt, Rudolf, Wilhelm Karl Geck, Günther Jaenicke, and Helmut Steinberger (eds.). *Völkerrecht als Rechtsordnung—internationale Gerichtsbarkeit—Menschenrechte: Festschrift für Hermann Mosler.* Berlin, Heidelberg, New York: Springer-Verlag, 1983. Pp. xiv, 1057. DM 298; $123.10.

Drzemczewski, Andrew Z. *European Human Rights Convention in Domestic Law: A Comparative Study.* New York: The Clarendon Press; Oxford University Press, 1983. Pp. xiv, 372. Indexes. $63.

Forsythe, David P. *Human Rights and World Politics.* Lincoln and London: University of Nebraska Press, 1983. Pp. xiv, 309. Index. $25.95, cloth; $8.50, paper.

States of Emergency: Their Impact on Human Rights. A study prepared by the International Commission of Jurists. Geneva, 1983. Pp. iii, 477. Sw.F.40; $19.50.

Lillich, Richard B. (ed.). *International Human Rights Instruments. A Compilation of Treaties, Agreements and Declarations of Especial Interest to the United States.* Buffalo: William S. Hein & Co., 1983. $50.

Maier, Irene (ed.). *Protection of Human Rights in Europe: Limits and Effects.* Proceedings of the Fifth International Colloquy about the European Convention on Human Rights. Heidelberg: C.F. Müller Juristischer Verlag, 1982. Pp. xviii, 378. Index. DM 168; $70.

Sieghart, Paul. *The International Law of Human Rights.* New York: The Clarendon Press; Oxford University Press, 1983. Pp. xxiv, 569. Index. $89.

Tornaritis, Criton G. *The Operation of the European Convention for the Protection of Human Rights in the Republic of Cyprus.* Nicosia, 1983. Pp. 21.

Environment & Natural Resources

Wetstone, Gregory S., and Armin Rosencranz. *Acid Rain in Europe and North America: National Responses to an International Problem.* A Study for the German Marshall Fund of the United States. Washington: Environmental Law Institute, 1983. Pp. xvi, 244.

Air & Space Law

Ballarino, Tito. *Diritto aeronautico.* Milan: Giuffrè Editore, 1983. Pp. xii, 308. Index. L. 16.000.

Diederiks-Verschoor, I. H. Ph. *An Introduction to Air Law.* Deventer: Kluwer Law and Taxation Publishers, 1983. Pp. xxii, 185. Index. Dfl.90.

International Organizations

Feld, Werner J., and Robert S. Jordan, with Leon Hurwitz. *International Organizations: A Comparative Approach.* New York: Praeger Publishers, 1983. Pp. xxii, 332. Index. $33.95, cloth; $13.95, paper.

Jordan, Robert S. (ed.). *Dag Hammarskjöld Revisited: The UN Secretary-General as a Force in World Politics.* Published under the auspices of the University of South Carolina. Durham: Carolina Academic Press, 1983. Pp. xvi, 197. Index. $16.50.

Rucz, Claude. *Le Conseil Economique et Social de l'O.N.U. et la Coopération pour le Développement.* Published under the auspices of the Centre d'Etudes et de Recherches Internationales et Communautaires de l'Université d'Aix-Marseille III. Paris: Economica, 1983. Pp. xii, 501. Index. F.125.

Seara Vázquez, Modesto. *Tratado general de la organización internacional* (2d ed.). Mexico: Fondo de Cultura Económica, 1982. Pp. 1103. Indexes.

European Community Law

Furmston, M. P., R. Kerridge, and B. E. Sufrin (eds.). *The Effect on English Domestic Law of Membership of the European Communities and of Ratification of the European Convention on Human Rights.* The Hague, Boston, London: Martinus Nijhoff Publishers, 1983. Pp. viii, 428. Dfl.103; $56.50.

Völker, E. L. M. (ed.). *Protectionism and the European Community.* Deventer: Kluwer Law and Taxation Publishers, 1983. Pp. xii, 199. Dfl.70.

Foreign & Comparative Law & Politics

Brown, W. J. *"O" Level Law* (2d ed.). London: Sweet & Maxwell, 1982. Pp. xiv, 227. Index. Distributed by Carswell Legal Publications.

Butler, W. E. *The Mongolian Legal System: Contemporary Legislation and Documentation.* The Hague, Boston, London: Martinus Nijhoff Publishers, 1982. Pp. xxiii, 995. Dfl.450; $195.

——, (ed.). *The Legal System of the Chinese Soviet Republic, 1931–1934.* Dobbs Ferry: Transnational Publishers, Inc., 1983. Pp. 212. Index. $35.

Butler, W. E., and A. J. Nathanson (comps./eds.). *Mongolian-English-Russian Dictionary of Legal Terms and Concepts.* The Hague, Boston, London: Martinus Nijhoff Publishers, 1983. Pp. xxvii, 718. Dfl.300; $130.

Buzzard, John Huxley, Richard May, and M. N. Howard. *Phipson on Evidence* (13th ed.). London: Sweet & Maxwell, 1982. Pp. ccvi, 1166. $142.50. Distributed by Carswell Legal Publications.

Cassese, Antonio (ed.). *Control of Foreign Policy in Western Democracies: A Comparative Study of Parliamentary Foreign Affairs Committees. Volume I: Parliamentary Foreign Affairs Committees—The National*

Setting. Pp. 381. *Volume III: The Impact of Foreign Affairs Committees on Foreign Policy.* Pp. 142. Padua: CEDAM, 1982. Copublished with Oceana Publications, Inc. $60/set.

Cavelier, Germán. *La Prioridad en el derecho marcario.* Bogotá, 1982. Pp. 42.

De Bauw, François, and Bernard Dewit. *China Trade Law: Code of the Foreign Trade Law of the People's Republic of China.* Brussels: Etablissements Emile Bruylant; Deventer: Kluwer, 1982. Pp. 572. Indexes. BF 2.300; Dfl.169; $68.

Hamblin, C., and F. B. Wright. *Introduction to Commercial Law* (2d ed.). London: Sweet and Maxwell, 1982. Pp. xxiii, 302. Index. Distributed by Carswell Legal Publications.

Hołyst, Brunon. *Comparative Criminology.* Lexington and Toronto: D.C. Heath and Company, 1979. Pp. xiii, 409. Indexes. $35.95.

Landynski, Jacob W. *Fundamental Rights and Public Policy in the New Supreme Court.* Jerusalem: The Magnes Press, The Hebrew University, 1982. Pp. 51. $3.

Livadas, Christopher. *The Winding-Up of Insolvent Companies in England and France.* Deventer: Kluwer Law and Taxation Publishers, 1983. Pp. xxxvi, 384. Dfl.175; $70.

Punch, Maurice (ed.). *Control in the Police Organization.* Cambridge and London: The MIT Press, 1983. Pp. xvi, 346. Index. $30.

Thornhill, A. R., and R. Venables (eds.). *Tax Planning with Precedents* (9th ed.). London: Sweet & Maxwell, 1982. Pp. xxix, 420. Index. $66. Distributed by Carswell Legal Publications.

Todd, Stephen. *Limitation Periods in Personal Injury Claims.* London: Sweet & Maxwell, 1982. Pp. xxii, 131. Index. Distributed by Carswell Legal Publications.

Tornaritis, Criton G. *The Legal Links between Cyprus and the Balkans especially Macedonia during the Byzantine Era.* Nicosia, 1982. Pp. 24.

Walton, Anthony, and Mary Vitoria. *Russell on the Law of Arbitration* (20th ed.). London: Stevens & Sons, 1982. Pp. lviii, 602. Index. $96.75. Distributed by Carswell Legal Publications.

Lord Wedderburn of Charlton, Roy Lewis, and Jon Clark (eds.). *Labour Law and Industrial Relations: Building on Kahn-Freund.* New York: The Clarendon Press; Oxford University Press, 1983. Pp. vii, 250. Index. $37.50.

Weiler, Joseph H. H. *Control of Foreign Policy in Western Democracies: A Comparative Study of Parliamentary Foreign Affairs Committees. Volume II: The Transnational Setting: The European Parliament and its Foreign Affairs Committees.* Padua: CEDAM, 1982. Copublished with Oceana Publications, Inc. Pp. 161.

International Relations

Cumings, Bruce (ed.). *Child of Conflict: The Korean-American Relationship, 1943–1953.* Seattle and London: University of Washington Press, 1983. Pp. xiv, 335. Index. $22.50.

Lang, Winfried. *Der internationale Regionalismus: Integration und Desintegration von Staatenbeziehungen in weltweiter Verflechtung.* Vienna and New York: Springer-Verlag, 1982. Pp. xiii, 217. Index. DM 98; $43.60.

Medina Ortega, Manuel. *Teoría y formación de la sociedad internacional.* Madrid: Editorial Tecnos, 1983. Pp. 624.

Miscellaneous

Bator, Paul M. *The International Trade in Art.* Chicago and London: The University of Chicago Press, 1983. Pp. vii, 108. $16, cloth; $6.95, paper.

Bourrinet, Jacques, and Maurice Flory. *L'Ordre Alimentaire Mondial.* Published under the auspices of the Centre d'Etudes et de Recherches Internationales et Communautaires de l'Université d'Aix-Marseille III. Paris: Economica, 1982. Pp. 332. F.85.

Ingber, Léon. *L'Egalité.* Volume VIII. Published under the auspices of the Centre de Philosophie du Droit de l'Université Libre de Bruxelles. Brussels: Etablissements E. Bruylant, 1982. Pp. 628. BF 2.491.

Sepúlveda, César. *La Frontera Norte de México. Historia, conflictos, 1762–1982* (2d ed.). Mexico: Editorial Porrúa, S.A., 1983. Pp. 222.

Shyam, Manjula R. *Metals from the Seabed: Prospects for Mining Polymetallic Nodules by India.* New Delhi: Oxford & IBH Publishing Co., 1982. Pp. xvi, 165. Rs.72.

Sivard, Ruth Leger. *World Military and Social Expenditures, 1982.* Leesburg: World Priorities, 1982. Pp. 44. $4.

Vedder, Christoph Wilhelm. *Die auswärtige Gewalt des Europa der Neun.* Göttingen: Verlag Otto Schwartz & Co., 1980. Pp. xxi, 297. Index. DM 68.

INTERNATIONAL LEGAL MATERIALS*

CONTENTS

VOL. XXII, NO. 3 (May 1983)

PAGE

REPORTS

Israel: Final Report of the Commission of Inquiry into the *Events at the Refugee Camps in Beirut* 473

TREATIES AND AGREEMENTS

Asian-African Legal Consultative Committee *Agreements Promoting Arbitration*

Introductory Note 521

Asian-African Legal Consultative Committee-Regional Centre for Commercial Arbitration (Kuala Lumpur)-International Centre for Settlement of Investment Disputes: Agreement regarding General Arrangements between the Regional Centre and ICSID 522

Asian-African Legal Consultative Committee-Regional Centre for Commercial Arbitration (Cairo)-International Centre for Settlement of Investment Disputes: Agreement regarding General Arrangements between the Regional Center and ICSID 524

Asian-African Legal Consultative Committee-Regional Centre for Commercial Arbitration (Kuala Lumpur)-Tokyo Maritime Arbitration Commission: Co-operation Arrangement for the Administration of International Maritime Arbitrations 526

Council of Europe:

Convention on the *Transfer of Sentenced Persons* 530

Protocol to the Convention for the Protection of Human Rights and Fundamental Freedoms concerning the *Abolition of the Death Penalty* 538

France-United States: Convention on the *Transfer of Sentenced Persons* 542

Governmental Conference for the Adoption of the European Agreement concerning the *Provision of Medical Care to Persons during Temporary Residence*

Final Act 550

European Agreement concerning the Provision of Medical Care to Persons during Temporary Residence 553

Institute of International Finance, Inc.: Articles of Incorporation to Form an *Organization of Lending Institutions* 569

SEDCO, Inc.-United States: Agreement concerning *Settlement of Claims Arising from the 1979 Oil Well Blowout and Oil Spill in the Gulf of Mexico* 580

JUDICIAL AND SIMILAR PROCEEDINGS

Iran-United States Claims Tribunal: Decision with regard to Issues Arising in Connection with the Establishment and Operation of the Security Account *(Standard Applied in Recording a Settlement as an Award on Agreed Terms; Interest Earned on the Security Account; Payment of Bank Fees Associated with the Security Account; Indemnification of Depositary of the Security Account)* 591

United States:

District Court for the District of Columbia Decision in Asociacion de Reclamantes *v.* the United Mexican States *(Act of State Doctrine; Claims Settlement)* 625

* ILM subscription, $65; concessionary rate to ASIL members, $30. Address orders to ILM, 2223 Massachusetts Ave., NW, Wash., D.C. 20008. Outside U.S., please add $5.

Supreme Court Decision in Verlinden *v.* Central Bank of Nigeria *(Foreign Sovereign Immunities Act; Recourse of Foreign Nationals to U.S. Courts)* 647

LEGISLATION AND REGULATIONS
Israel: *Commissions of Inquiry* Law and Amendments 658
Romania: Decree on the *Obligations of Persons Emigrating to Repay Debts and Expenses for Education* 667

OTHER DOCUMENTS
Council of Europe:
Committee of Ministers Recommendation concerning the *Protection of Users of Computerised Legal Information Services* 669
Committee of Ministers Recommendation on *Measures to be Taken in Cases of Kidnapping followed by a Ransom Demand* 675
Parliamentary Assembly Recommendation on *Extradition of Criminals* 681
United Nations: General Assembly Resolution on *Protection against Products Harmful to Health and the Environment* 683
United States: Presidential Message to Congress on *Trade with Hungary, the People's Republic of China, and Romania* 685

RECENT ACTIONS REGARDING TREATIES TO WHICH THE UNITED STATES IS A PARTY 686
RECENT ACTIONS REGARDING TREATIES TO WHICH THE UNITED STATES IS NOT A PARTY 691
NOTICE OF OTHER RECENT DOCUMENTS (not reprinted) 692

VOL. XXII, NO. 4 (July 1983)

TREATIES AND AGREEMENTS
Canada-United States: Agreement concerning the *Test and Evaluation of United States Defense Systems in Canada* 693
Contracting Parties of the Convention on *Wetlands of International Importance* Especially as Waterfowl Habitat: Protocol to Amend the Convention 698
Denmark-Finland-German Democratic Republic-Federal Republic of Germany-Poland-Sweden-Union of Soviet Socialist Republics: Protocol Amending *Convention on Fishing and Conservation of Living Resources in the Baltic Sea and the Belts to Provide for EEC Membership* 704
Israel-Lebanon: Agreement on *Withdrawal of Troops from Lebanon* 708
Sweden-United States: Supplementary Convention on *Extradition* 736

JUDICIAL AND SIMILAR PROCEEDINGS
Federal Republic of Germany: District Court of Kiel Judgment concerning *United States Grand Jury Subpoenas for Bank Records in the Krupp Case* 740
International Chamber of Commerce Court of Arbitration: Award in the *Arbitration between S.P.P. (Middle East) Limited, Southern Pacific Properties Limited and the Arab Republic of Egypt, the Egyptian General Company for Tourism and Hotels* 752
Switzerland: Swiss Supreme Court Opinion concerning *Judicial Assistance in the Santa Fe Case* 785
United States:
Court of Appeals for the District of Columbia Circuit Decision in Collins *v.* Weinberger (*NATO Status of Forces Agreement; Treaty Interpretation*) 799
Court of Appeals for the First Circuit Decision in Wald *v.* Regan (*Treasury Regulations Preventing Travel to Cuba; Trading with the Enemy Act*) 805

Court of Appeals for the Second Circuit Decision in Associated Container Transportation (Australia) *v.* United States (*Investigatory Powers under the Antitrust Act; Act of State Doctrine*) 824
Court of Appeals for the Seventh Circuit Decision in Alberti *v.* Empresa Nicaraguense De La Carne (*Foreign Sovereign Immunities Act; Service of Process; Nationalizations; Counterclaims*) 835
Supreme Court: Decision in First National City Bank *v.* Banco Para El Comercio Exterior De Cuba (*Foreign Sovereign Immunities Act; Nationalizations; Counterclaims*) 840
Supreme Court: Decision in Container Corporation of America *v.* Franchise Tax Board (*California's Unitary Business Principle Applied to Foreign Subsidiaries for Corporate Franchise Tax Assessment*) 855

LEGISLATION AND REGULATIONS
United States:
Department of Commerce, International Trade Administration, Interpretations of *Antiboycott Regulations* 879
Department of the Treasury, Internal Revenue Service, Regulations concerning the *Taxation of Foreign Investment in U.S. Real Property* 883

OTHER DOCUMENTS
Canada-France-Federal Republic of Germany-Italy-Japan-United Kingdom-United States:
Williamsburg Declaration on *Economic Recovery* 885
Williamsburg Joint Statement on *Security Issues* 894
Committee on Banking Regulations and Supervisory Practices: Revised Basle Concordat on *Principles for the Supervision of Banks' Foreign Establishments* 900
Organisation for Economic Co-operation and Development:
Council Decision concerning the *Minimum Pre-marketing Set of Data in the Assessment of Chemicals* 909
Council Communique Outlining *Strategy for a Sustained Recovery* 914
International Energy Agency Governing Board Communique concerning *Energy Requirements and Security* 918
United States: Comptroller of the Currency and Federal Reserve Board Revisions to the *Minimum Capital Guidelines* 930

RECENT ACTIONS REGARDING TREATIES TO WHICH THE UNITED STATES IS A PARTY 938
RECENT ACTIONS REGARDING TREATIES TO WHICH THE UNITED STATES IS NOT A PARTY 943
NOTICE OF OTHER RECENT DOCUMENTS (not reprinted) 944

Manuscripts in triplicate may be sent to the Editors-in-Chief of AJIL, Professors Oscar Schachter and Louis Henkin, Columbia University School of Law, New York, N.Y. 10027. Subscriptions, orders for back numbers, correspondence with reference to AJIL and books for review should be sent to the AMERICAN JOURNAL OF INTERNATIONAL LAW (ISSN 0002-9300), 2223 Massachusetts Avenue, N.W., Washington, D.C. 20008.

AJIL is published in January, April, July, and October and is supplied to all members of the American Society of International Law. The annual subscription to nonmembers of ASIL is $52.00, plus $2.50 for all foreign subscriptions (including ASIL Proceedings). Available back numbers of AJIL will be supplied at $11.00 each. ($21 of membership fee is allotted to AJIL subscription.)

EDITORIAL OFFICE:
BOX 44
COLUMBIA UNIVERSITY SCHOOL OF LAW
NEW YORK, N.Y. 10027

BUSINESS OFFICE:
2223 MASSACHUSETTS AVENUE, N.W.
WASHINGTON, D.C. 20008

Table of Cases

(*Italicized* page numbers indicate where decisions are excerpted or cases discussed at length. Abbreviations: arb., arbitration; IACHR, Inter-American Court of Human Rights; ICJ, International Court of Justice; PCIJ, Permanent Court of International Justice.)

Afroyim v. Rusk, 300–1
Agreement of 25 March 1951 between the WHO and Egypt (ICJ), *253,* 414
Alberti v. Empresa Nicaraguense de la Carne, *888–91*
Alcoa case. *See* United States v. Aluminum Co. of America
Alcoa Minerals of Jamaica Inc./Kaiser Bauxite Co./Reynolds Jamaica Mines Ltd. and Reynolds Metals Co. v. Government of Jamaica (arb.), 793
Alfred Dunhill of London, Inc. v. Cuba, 142
Anglo-French Continental Shelf arbitration. *See* United Kingdom-France Continental Shelf
Arthur Andersen & Co. v. Finesilver, 898
Association of Data Processing Services Organizations, Inc. v. Camp, 880
Asylum case (ICJ), 434
Attorney-General of New Zealand v. Ortiz, *631–4*
Baker v. Carr, 883
Banco Nacional de Cuba v. First National City Bank, 145
Banco Nacional de Cuba v. Sabbatino, 142, *145, 146*
Barcelona Traction (ICJ), 430, 431, 435, 842
Bayer/Firestone (Synthetischer Kautschuk) case, *773–5,* 776, 777
Benvenuti & Bonfant Co. v. Government of the People's Republic of Congo, 786, *796–9,* 803
Bergesen v. Joseph Muller Corp., *308–10*
Briggs & Stratton Corp. v. Baldrige, *310–2*
Cabell v. Chavez-Salido, 165
Callas v. United States, 159
Case against Buscetta, *164*
Certain Expenses of the United Nations (ICJ), *241–2, 246, 249, 253, 254,* 874
China National Technical Import Corp. v. United States, *315–7*
[The] Chinese Exclusion Case, *817, 824–6,* 827–8
Committee for a Free Namibia v. South West Africa People's Organization, *628–30*
Compagnie Europeenne des Petroles S.A. v. Sensor Nederland B.V., *636–7*
Compagnie Francaise d'Assurance v. Phillips Petroleum Co., 898–9
I Congreso del Partido, 158
Corfu Channel case (ICJ), 91, *93–4,* 556, *561*
Costello v. United States, 299
Dames & Moore v. Regan, 165, 313, *314–5*
Dresser Industries, Inc. v. Baldridge, *626–8*
[The] Effect of Reservations on the Entry into Force of the American Convention (Arts. 74 and 75) (IACHR), *137–41, 640–2*
Egle v. Egle, *167–8*
[Nishimura] Ekiu v. United States, *826,* 829
Esphahanian v. Bank Tejarat (arb.), *646–8*
Estate of Silme G. Domingo v. Ferdinand E. Marcos, *305–7*
Ethiopian Spice Extraction Share Co. v. Kalamazoo Spice Extraction Co., 144
Ex parte Republic of Peru, 306, 307
Fernandez-Roque v. Smith, *876*
First National City Bank v. Commissioner, 901
Fisheries case (UK v. Norway) (ICJ), 284, 434
Fisheries Jurisdiction case (UK v. Iceland) (ICJ), *26, 563*
Flexi-Van Leasing Inc. v. The Islamic Republic of Iran (arb.), *642–6*
Fong Yue Ting v. United States, *826–7,* 828
Franklin Mint Corp. v. Trans World Airlines, Inc., *320–2*
General Motors Corp. v. The Islamic Republic of Iran (arb.) *642–6*
Genocide Convention Case (ICJ), 140
Gould Marketing, Inc. v. Ministry of National Defense of Iran (arb.), *893–5*
Grimm v. The Government of the Islamic Republic of Iran (arb.), *649–50*
Haig v. Agee, 165
Hodson v. A. H. Robins Co., Inc., *899–900*
Holiday Inns/Occidental Petroleum v. Government of Morocco (arb.), 790
Hostages case. *See* US Diplomatic and Consular Staff in Tehran
Hunt v. Mobil Oil Corp., 625
Immigration and Naturalization Service v. Wang, 165
In re Aircrash in Bali, Indonesia on April 22, 1974, *153–5*
In re Citizenship of X, *160–1*
In re Prejudgment Garnishment against National Iranian Oil Co., *159–60*

In re Rekhou, *161–2*
In re Westinghouse Electric Corp. Uranium Antitrust Litigation, 898
Interhandel Case (ICJ), 340
International Association of Machinists and Aerospace Workers v. Organization of Petroleum Exporting Countries, 165
ITT Industries, Inc. v. The Islamic Republic of Iran (arb.), *891–3*
Jurisdiction of the ICAO Council (ICJ), *246*
Kalamazoo Spice Extraction Co. v. The Provisional Military Government of Socialist Ethiopia, *142–3, 144–6*
Kennedy v. Mendoza-Martinez, 301
Kilroy v. Prince of Wales, 306
Kimberly-Clark Corp. v. Bank Markazi (arb.), 894
Kleindienst v. Mandel, *827–8*
Legal Status of Eastern Greenland (PCIJ), 267–8
LIAMCO arbitration. *See* Libyan American Oil Co.
LIAMCO v. Libya. *See* Procureur de la République v. Société LIAMCO
Libra Bank Ltd. v. Banco Nacional de Costa Rica, 882
Libyan American Oil Co. v. Government of the Libyan Arab Republic (arb.), 798
Lockyer v. Offley, 632
Lotus case (PCIJ), 419, 420, 433
Lynch v. Clarke, 835
Mannington Mills, Inc. v. Congoleum Corp., 624–5
Marine Steel Ltd. v. Government of the Marshall Islands, *158–9*
Maritime International Nominees Establishment v. Republic of Guinea, *318–20, 785–95*
Maritime Safety Committee of IMCO (ICJ), 244
Matter of Sedco, Inc., *149–51*
Matter of the Republic of the Philippines, 160
McCulloch v. Maryland, 276
Miliangos v. George Frank (Textiles) Ltd., *635*
Murray v. The Charming Betsy, 825
Musgrove v. Chun Teeong Toy, *828–9*
Namibia case (ICJ), *241*, 554, 874
Northrop Corp. v. McDonnell Douglas Corp., *882–5*
North Sea Continental Shelf cases (ICJ), *26*, 219, 220, *224–8*, 230, 231, 235, 236, 238, 434, *435, 436–7, 543, 561–2*, 563, 873
Nottebohm Case (ICJ), 820–1, 842
Nuclear Tests cases (ICJ), 130, 132, *268–9*, 271, 278, 432
Oil Field Pipes (Ölfeldrohre) case, *764–5*, 767, 769
Organic Pigments (Organische Pigmente) case, *768–70, 772–3*, 774, 775
"Other Treaties" Subject to the Consultative Jurisdiction of the Court (Art. 64 American Convention on Human Rights) Requested by Peru (IACHR), *637–9*
Pain v. United Technologies Corp., 899
Perez v. The Bahamas, 165
Persinger v. Islamic Republic of Iran, *312–5*
Pfizer v. Government of India, 304
[The] Philippine Admiral, 158
Piper Aircraft Co. v. Reyno; Hartzell Propeller, Inc. v. Reyno, 165
Plyler v. Doe, *151–3*
Procureur de la République v. Société LIAMCO, *798–9*
Psinakis v. Marcos, 306
Re Lines Bros. Ltd., *635–6*
Reparation for injuries suffered in the service of the United Nations (ICJ), 431, 436
Republic of Mexico v. Hoffman, 306
République islamique d'Iran, OIAEFI and OEAI v. Société EURODIF and SOFIDIF, *797–8*
Rex v. Cia. Pervana de Vapores, S.A., 165
Rothmans/Philip Morris (Morris/Rothmans) case, *775–9*
Russell Jackson v. The People's Republic of China, *146–8*
San Antonio School District v. Rodriguez, 152
San Diego Gas & Electric Co. v. San Diego, 155
S & S Machinery Co. v. Masinexportimport, *880–2*
Schneider v. Rusk, 300–1
Seeman v. Philadelphia Warehouse Co., 529
Shoji America, Inc. v. Avagliano, 165
Smith Kline & French Laboratories Ltd. v. Block, 901
Societe Internationale v. Rogers, 898, 901
Spacil v. Crowe, *306–7*
S.p.a. Imprese Marittime Frassinetti e S.p.a. Italiana Lavori Marittimi e Terrestri c. Repubblica Araba di Libia, *163–4*
Speiss v. C. Itoh & Co. (America), 165
Syndicat Unique des Vignerons de l'Aude, *163*
Texas Trading & Milling Corp. v. Federal Republic of Nigeria, 165
Timberlane Lumber Co. v. Bank of America, 136, 137
Tinoco Case (arb.), 35
Treatment of Polish Nationals and Other Persons of Polish Origin or Speech in the Danzig Territory (PCIJ), 842
Tunisia-Libyan Arab Jamahiriya Case concerning the Continental Shelf (ICJ), *219–38*, 563, *872–3*

Tunis-Morocco Nationality Decrees (PCIJ), 820, 842
United City Merchants (Investments) Ltd. v. Royal Bank of Canada, *155–7*, 165
United Kingdom-France Continental Shelf (arb.), 228, 232, 237, 439
United States v. Aluminum Co. of America, *759*, 761
United States v. Brown, 134
United States v. Curtiss-Wright Export Corp., *823*
United States v. Hensel, *878–80*
United States v. Lee, 307
United States v. Marino-Garcia, *630–1*
United States v. McClain, 634
United States v. McRary, 165
United States v. Ramsey, 879
United States v. Robinson, 300
United States v. Vetco, 901
United States v. Whiting, *134*, 880
United States v. Williams, 878, 879–80
US Diplomatic and Consular Staff in Tehran (ICJ), *295–6*, 420, 426, 439, 442, 554
Vance v. Terrazas, 301–2
Verlinden B.V. v. Central Bank of Nigeria, 165, 320, *885–8*
Volkswagenwerk A.G. v. Superior Court, *897–8*, 899
Washington Public Power Supply System v. Western Nuclear, Inc., *136–7*
Williams v. Curtiss-Wright Corp., *624–6*
Youngstown Sheet & Tube Co. v. Sawyer, 314

INDEX

(The following abbreviations refer to sections of the *Journal: BN,* Briefer Notices; *BR,* Book Reviews and Notes; *CD,* Current Developments; *Corr.,* Correspondence; *CP,* Contemporary Practice of the US Relating to International Law; *Ed.,* Editorial Comments; *JD,* Judicial Decisions; *LA,* Leading Article; *NC,* Notes and Comments; *OD,* Official Documents. Other abbreviations include: EEC, European Economic Community; EEZ, Exclusive Economic Zone; FRG, Federal Republic of Germany; GATT, General Agreement on Tariffs and Trade; IAEA, International Atomic Energy Commission; ICJ, International Court of Justice; ICSID, International Centre for Settlement of Investment Disputes; ILC, International Law Commission; IMF, International Monetary Fund; MTN, Multilateral Trade Negotiations; OAU, Organization of African Unity; PRC, People's Republic of China; SWAPO, South West Africa People's Organization; UK, United Kingdom; UNCLOS III, Third United Nations Conference on the Law of the Sea; UNGA, United Nations General Assembly; UNSC, United Nations Security Council; US, United States.)

Aaland Islands Convention (1856), 565

Acevedo, Domingo E. *BR* of Rey Caro, 697

Act of state doctrine, 331, 889: and adjudication of expropriation cases, *CP,* 141–3; *JD,* 144–6; *JD,* 163–4; and antitrust suits involving foreign governments' military procurement, *JD,* 624–6; *JD,* 882–5

Afghanistan, 111, 123, 124, 652, 653, 654, 870

African Bar Association, 903

(The) African Charter on Human and Peoples' Rights, *CD,* 902: right to development under, 906–7, 910, 911

African countries, 582: Charter on Human and Peoples' Rights, *CD,* 902; and Falklands War, 117

Ago, Roberto, 233, 331, 332, 418: on international legal norms, 423, 428

Aircraft, Convention for the Suppression of Unlawful Seizure of (1970), 664

Akehurst, Michael. A Modern Introduction to International Law (4th ed.), *BR,* 357

Albania, 47, 93–4, 561, 653

Albinski, Henry. The Australian-American Security Relationship. A Regional and International Perspective, *BR,* 715

Aldrich, George H., 891–3

Alexander, Yonah, & Kenneth Myers (eds.). Terrorism in Europe, *BN,* 980

Algeria, 42, 516, 518: effect of lack of reciprocity on Evian Accords with France, *JD,* 161–2

Algiers Accords: authority of US President to extinguish claims under, *JD,* 312–5; settlement of "small" US claims under, 166, 167. *See also* Claims Settlement Agreement

Aliens, 853: federal jurisdiction in cases involving, *CP,* 135; general admission of under international law, *LA,* 804; illegal, entitlement to education under US Constitution, *JD,* 151–3; under African Human Rights Charter, 905; US request for Cuban acceptance of illegal Mariel immigrants, *CP,* 875–6. *See also* State responsibility

Aliens, Convention between the American Republics regarding the Status of (1928), admission under, 837

Allott, Philip. Power Sharing in the Law of the Sea, *LA,* 1

Al Mour, A. M., on legal status of EEZ, 504

(An) Alternative to the Law of the Sea Convention, *Ed.,* 281

Ambrose, 810

Amelioration of the Conditions of the Wounded in Armies in the Field, Convention for the (1864), 595

American Arbitration Association, 309, 318, 319, 787

American Bar Association (ABA), 858: Model American Convention on terrorism, *CD,* 662: text, 664; proposal on requests by national courts for ICJ advisory opinions, 126–9

American Convention on Human Rights, 601, 663, 666, 839, 848: advisory jurisdiction under, *JD,* 637–9; 640–1; and African Human Rights Charter, 909–10; reservations to and entry into force: Inter-American Court on, *JD,* 640–2; US State Department views, *CP,* 137–41
American Declaration of the Rights and Duties of Man, 663, 666
American Law Institute, and federal jurisdiction based on alienage, 135–6. *See also* Restatement of Foreign Relations Law of the United States (Revised); Restatement (Second) of Foreign Relations Law of the United States
American Society of International Law, on teaching of human rights law, 855
Amin, Idi, 903
Amin, Sayed Hassan. International and Legal Problems of the Gulf, *BN,* 721
Amnesty International, 903
Anand, Ram Prakash (ed.). Law of the Sea: Caracas and Beyond. Developments in International Law, 3, *BR,* 689
Angola, 902
Annuaire Français de Droit International. Vol. XXVI, 1980, *BR,* 973
Antigua and Barbuda, and Falklands War, 119
Antitrust: extraterritorial application of FRG law, *LA,* 756; notes from foreign governments to US courts, *CP,* 136–7; recovery of damages by foreign states, *CP,* 303–5; suits involving foreign governments' military procurement and act of state defense, *JD,* 624–6; *JD,* 882–5
Arab League, 866
Arab states, 6, 84, 94, 581, 582, 586: boycott of Israel and US law, *JD,* 310–2
Arbitration, 158, 292, 613, 614: agreement not contemplating role for US courts and immunity, *JD,* 318–20; enforcement, *JD,* 308–10; by ICSID, and the courts, *LA,* 784. *See also* Dispute settlement; Iran-United States Claims Tribunal
Archipelagic sea lanes. *See* Law of the sea
Argentina, 652, 653: position on Falklands war, 607. *See also* Falkland Islands
Argios Dimitrios incident, 101–2
Arsanjani, Mahnoush H. *BR* of Halderman, 366; *BR* of Rajan, 365: response to *Corr.* on, 985
Arías-Schreiber, Alfonso, on third states' rights under LOS Convention, 547
Aristotle, 809
Armed conflicts: international, applicability of law on, 589, 595, 596–7, 598–9, 602, 603; non-international, applicability of law on, 595–6, 597, 599–600, 602, 603, 605. *See also* Geneva Conventions for the protection of war victims; Hague Conventions on laws of war
Artificial islands, 622: establishment of states on, *JD,* 160–1; and transit of aircraft, 506–10
Asian-African Legal Consultative Committee, 754, 788
Association of American Law Schools (AALS), 856, 858
Association of Southeast Asian Nations (ASEAN), 45
Asylum, 27, 839
Atimomo, Emiko. Law and Diplomacy in Commodity Economics: A Study of Techniques, Co-operation and Conflict in International Public Policy Issues, *BR,* 968
Atwood, James R., & Kingman Brewster. Antitrust and American Business Abroad (2d ed.). Vols. 1–2, *BR,* 679
Auburn, F. M. Antarctic Law and Politics, *BR,* 180
Austin, John, 808, 818, 871
Australia, 59, 551, 657: and admission of aliens, 816, 828–9, 836–7
Austria, 616: and recognition of governments, 43
Aviation: air defense identification zones, 500, 515–9; Freedom of the Air and the Convention on the Law of the Sea, *LA,* 490; US representations to Cuba re hijackings, *CP,* 877. *See also* Aviation, Convention for the Suppression of Unlawful Acts against the Safety of Civil; International Civil Aviation, Convention on; Warsaw Convention
Aviation, Convention for the Suppression of Unlawful Acts against the Safety of Civil (1971), 664

Bab el Mandeb, 91, 105, 493, 552
Balance of power, 287
Bangladesh, 657

Barston, R. P., & Patricia Birnie (eds.). The Maritime Dimension, *BR,* 373
Bartell, Joyce J. (ed.). The Yankee Mariner and Sea Power: America's Challenge of Ocean Space, *BR,* 695
Baskin, J. J., on study of international law, 863–4
Baxter, R. R.: on humanitarian law, 590, 598, 603; on recognition of governments, 31
Bays. *See* Geneva Convention on the Territorial Sea and the Contiguous Zone; Law of the sea: UN Convention
Beddard, Ralph. *BN* of Hakapää, 723; *BR* of van den Berghe, 953
Bedjaoui, Mohammed, 324: on majority decisions of international organizations, 251
Begin, Menachem, 586
Belgium, 616: on recognition of governments, 42–3; UN Ambassador on Falklands war, 110–1, 611
Belize, and Falklands war, 117, 297, 614
Bellet, Pierre, 646
Berlin Treaty of Peace (1921), 649–50
Berman, Maureen R., & I. William Zartman. The Practical Negotiator, *BR,* 670
Birnie, Patricia, & R. P. Barston (eds.). The Maritime Dimension, *BR,* 373
Blackstone, William, on admission of aliens, 815
Blix, Hans, on Israeli participation in IAEA, 583
Blocking statutes, 756, 773, 896: and US courts, 901
Boczek, Boleslaw A. *BR* of Kneifel (2 works) and of Weber, 196
Bodin, Jean, 818
Boisson, Philippe. La Sécurité en Mer, *BR,* 182
Bokassa, Jean-Bedel, 903
Bolivia, 657
Book Reviews and Notes, 169, 345, 669, 915
Boomkamp, M. van Leeuwen, P. J. G. Kapteyn, P. H. Kooijmans, R. H. Lauwaars, & H. G. Schermers (eds.). International Organization and Integration: Annotated Basic Documents and Descriptive Directory of International Organizations and Arrangements. Vols. I.A and II.A (2d rev. ed.), *BR,* 359
Borgese, Elisabeth Mann. *BR* of Boisson, 182
Botelho, Bruce M. *BN* of Rumpf, 208
Bothe, Michael, Karl Josef Partsch, & Waldemar A. Solf. New Rules for Victims of Armed Conflicts: Commentary on the Two 1977 Protocols Additional to the Geneva Conventions of 1949, *BR,* 377
Bouchez, L. J., on regime of bays, 86–7
Bourne, C. B. (ed.). The Canadian Yearbook of International Law. Vol. XIX, 1981, *BR,* 720
Bouteflika, A., ruling on South African credentials to UNGA, 570, 571–2, 578, 580, 582
Bowett, D. W. The Law of International Institutions (4th ed.), *BR,* 933
Boyle, Francis A. *BN* of Alexander & Myers, 980; *BN* of Dunn, 981; *BR* of Ebinger, 961
Brandt Commission (Independent Commission on International Development Issues), 843
Brazil, 45: on Falklands war, 115, 116; and GATT Tokyo Round, 61, 63, 66
Bretton Woods Agreement, 155, 157, 449. *See also* International Monetary Fund
Bretton Woods Conference, 444, 445
Brewster, Kingman, & James R. Atwood. Antitrust and American Business Abroad (2d ed.). Vols. 1–2, *BR,* 679
Brezhnev, Leonid, 870
Brierly, J., 564–5
Broadening the Advisory Jurisdiction of the International Court of Justice, *Ed.,* 124
Browning, Alison, Jacques Freymond, & Isabelle Graf-Junod. Diplomatische Dokumente der Schweiz 1848–1945. Vol. 6 (1914–1918), *BR,* 400
Brown-John, C. Lloyd. *Corr.* on Falklands war, 297
Brüel, E., 561
Buergenthal, Thomas. *See* Sohn/Buergenthal
Bulajić, Milan. Međunarodno pravo ekonomskog razvoja: Pravni aspekti novog međunarodnog ekonomskog poretka, *BR,* 193

Bull, Alan T., Geoffrey Holt, & Malcolm D. Lilly. Biotechnology: International Trends and Perspectives, *BR*, 957
Burke, W. T., 518
Burundi, 903
Byrne, Edward M. Military Law (3d ed.), *BR*, 198

Cahier, Philippe. *BR* of Duffar, 943
Calvo Clause, 286
Calvo Doctrine, 286, 837
Cambodia (Kampuchea), 111, 123, 653: recognition of, 38, 45
Campbell, Dennis (ed.). Transnational Legal Practice: A Survey of Selected Countries. Vols. 1–2, *BR*, 705
Camp David Framework (1978), 97, 99–100, 102, 103, 104
Canada, 155, 616, 618, 657, 774, 878, 899, 904: and admission of aliens, 816, 836-7; and air defense identification zones, 516; and GATT Tokyo Round, 59, 68; Quebec and Falklands, 297; and third states' rights under LOS Convention, 548, 549
(The) Canadian Yearbook of International Law. Vol. XIX, 1981, *BR*, 720
Canenbley, Cornelis (ed.). Enforcing Antitrust against Foreign Enterprises, *BR*, 189
Cárdenas, Emilio J. *Corr.* on *Ed.* by Moore, 606
Carey, John. *BR* of Zuijdwijk, 924
Caribbean Community, 837
Carnahan, Burrus M. *Corr.* on constitutional and treaty rights of US military personnel abroad, 134
Carter, Jimmy, 312, 574, 855, 904: exchange rate policy, 468–9; and SALT I Treaty, 267, 272
Caruso, Lawrence R., & Linda A. Caruso. *BR* of Pooley, 970
Caruso, Linda A., & Lawrence R. Caruso. *BR* of Pooley, 970
Casad, Robert C. Civil Judgment Recognition and the Integration of Multiple-State Associations: Central America, the United States of America, and the European Economic Community, *BN*, 724
"Castañeda formula," regarding EEZ, 505
Catudal, Honoré M. Kennedy and the Berlin Wall Crisis, *BR*, 671
Cavelier, Germán. Documentos para la Historia Diplomática de Colombia. Textos. Vol. I: 1820–1830. Vol. II: 1830–1860, *BR*, 401; Patent and Trademark Laws of Colombia, *BN*, 404; El Régimen Jurídico de los Tratados Internacionales en Colombia, *BR*, 401
Center for Study of the American Experience. Rights and Responsibilities. International, Social, and Individual Dimensions, *BR*, 201
Central African Republic, 903, 911
Central America, recognition policy based on democratic legitimism, 38
Central American Court of Justice, on passage through Gulf of Fonseca, 87
Cerna, Christina M. *BR* of German Yearbook of International Law, 718
Chacko, C. Joseph. *BR* of Spencer, Kirton, & Nossal, 714
Chafee, John, and amending Foreign Corrupt Practices Act, 340–4
Chamberlain, Neville, 110
Charney, Jonathan I. (ed.). The New Nationalism and the Use of Common Spaces: Issues in Marine Pollution and the Exploitation of Antarctica, *BR*, 940
Chatterjee, S. K. Legal Aspects of International Drug Control, *BR*, 956
Chen, Frederick Tse-shyang (ed.). Proceedings of Conference on Deep Seabed Mining and Freedom of the Seas, *BR*, 689
Chicago Convention. *See* International Civil Aviation, Convention on
Chile, 116, 519, 613, 653
China, Imperial: declarations by diplomats as binding agreements, 267; and 1911 railway bonds, 146–7; US and UK exclusion of nationals, 824–9
China, People's Republic of (PRC), 111, 118, 251, 610, 870: Belgian recognition of, 43; liability for 1911 railway bonds, *JD*, 146–8; nonrecognition of generally, 38; reciprocal access of US nationals to courts, *JD*, 315–7; US nonrecognition of, 34–5

China, Republic of (pre-1949), 39, 569: and 1911 railway bonds, 147
China, Republic of (Taiwan), 34, 46: and 1911 railway bonds, 147, 148
China Council for the Promotion of International Trade (CCPIT), on reciprocal access of US nationals to PRC courts, 316–7
Chiswick, Barry R. (ed.). The Gateway: U.S. Immigration Issues and Policies, *BR*, 716
Chiu, Hungdah. *BR* of Zhou, of Wang & Wei, and of Wang & Tian, 977; Chinese Yearbook of International Law and Affairs. Vol. 1 (1981), *BR*, 975
Choice of law: in FRG antitrust, 759; under UN Convention on Contracts for the International Sale of Goods, *LA*, 521
Choice of Law under the International Sales Convention: A U.S. Perspective, *LA*, 521
Christol, Carl, 512: The Modern International Law of Outer Space, *BR*, 937
Claims. *See* Claims Settlement Agreement; ICSID Arbitration and the Courts; Iran-United States Claims Tribunal; State responsibility
Claims Settlement Agreement (Iran-US): claims of dual nationals under, *JD*, 646–8; claims of publicly held corporations under, *JD*, 642–6; counterclaims under, 894–5; "other measures affecting property rights" under, *JD*, 649–50; "outstanding" claims under, 894. *See also* Algiers Accords; Iran-United States Claims Tribunal
Clark, Roger S. *BR* of Tay in collaboration with Connelly & Wilkins, 349
Claude, Inis L., Jr. *BR* of Moskowitz, 915
Cleveland, Grover, 841
Collins, Michael P., & Philip F. Postlewaite. International Individual Taxation, *BR*, 708
Colombia, 304: on Falklands war, 115, 116, 119
Comity, 798, 828–9, 844: and US extraterritorial jurisdiction, 137, 759, 780, 781, 783, 898, 899
Commission to Study the Organization of Peace, 910
Common heritage of mankind, 16, 426, 563: deep seabed minerals as, 282–3, 284–5, 755
Compensation, under African Human Rights Charter, 906. *See also* Expropriation
Conciliation: and African Human Rights Charter, 909; under LOS Convention, 21, 741–2, 746. *See also* Dispute settlement
Conforti, Benedetto. Lezioni di Diritto Internazionale (2d ed.), *BN*, 722
Congo, People's Republic of, 796
Connelly, Graeme. *See* Tay, Alice Erh-Soon
Conot, Robert E. Justice at Nuremberg, *BR*, 917
Consensus: and evolution of customary law, 563; in GATT Tokyo Round and UNCLOS III, 75, 77, 78; as legislative process at UNCLOS III, 5–8, 25; and political decisions of international organizations, 252
Contemporary Practice of the United States Relating to International Law, 135, 298, 616, 875
Continental shelf. *See* Law of the sea
Contracts: Choice of Law under the International Sales Convention: A U.S. Perspective, *LA*, 521; *force majeure* and nonperformance, *JD*, 893–5. *See also* International Sale of Goods, Convention relating to a Uniform Law on the Formation of Contracts for the
Costa Rica, and recognition of governments, 38
Council of Europe, Convention on the Transfer of Sentenced Persons (1983), *CP*, 616–9
Courbe, Patrick. Les objectifs temporels des règles de droit international privé, *BR*, 701
Cuba, 653: US diplomatic relations with, 46; US 1962 quarantine and self-defense, 588; US representations re hijackings, *CP*, 877; US request for acceptance of ineligible Mariel immigrants, *CP*, 875–6
Cultural property, territorial sovereignty over, *JD*, 631–4
Cultural Property, Convention on the Means of Prohibiting and Preventing the Illicit Import, Export and Transfer of Ownership of (1970), 634
Current Attempts to Revise International Law—A Comparative Analysis, *NC*, 286
Current Developments, 166, 323, 651, 896
Cyprus, 652–3
Czechoslovakia, 110, 870, 875, 877

Dam, Kenneth W. The Rules of the Game: Reform and Evolution in the International Monetary System, *BR*, 185

D'Amato, Anthony. An Alternative to the Law of the Sea Convention, *Ed.*, 281; Israel's Air Strike upon the Iraqi Nuclear Reactor, *Ed.*, 584
———, Burns H. Weston, & Richard A. Falk. International Law and World Order: A Problem-Oriented Coursebook, *BR*, 350
Danish Straits, 96
Dashwood, Alan, & Derrick Wyatt. The Substantive Law of the EEC, *BR*, 188
Davis, Kenneth C., 300
Declaration of the Government of the Democratic and Popular Republic of Algeria Concerning the Settlement of Claims. *See* Claims Settlement Agreement
Deep seabed. *See* Law of the sea
Degenhardt, Henry W. Treaties and Alliances of the World (3d ed.), *BR*, 955
de Larosière, Jacques: on IMF consultations on exchange rates, 465; on surveillance by IMF, 481
Delaume, Georges R. ICSID Arbitration and the Courts, *LA*, 784
Delbrück, Jost, Wilfried Fiedler, & Wilhelm A. Kewenig (eds.). German Yearbook of International Law. Vol. 22, 1979, *BR*, 718
Dembling, Paul G. *BR* of Gorove, 369
Denmark, 268, 616, 871
Denning, Lord, 901: on territorial sovereignty over cultural property, 632–3
Developing countries, 127, 444, 457, 480, 484, 574, 594, 654, 847, 910: and GATT Tokyo Round, 53, 54, 56–7, 58–60, 63–4, 65, 66, 70, 71–3, 74, 76–9, 81; and proposal for IMF Council, 463; and revising international law, 294–5; under LOS Convention, 18, 744, 745
Dever, Edmonde, on Falklands war, 110–1, 611
De Visscher, Charles, 434
Dillard, Hardy Cross, 246
Dinstein, Yoram, on human rights in wartime, 597–8
——— (ed.). Israel Yearbook on Human Rights. Vol. 11, *BR*, 391; Models of Autonomy, *BR*, 918
Diplomatic Agents, Convention on the Prevention and Punishment of Crimes against Internationally Protected Persons Including (1973), 665
Diplomatic conferences. *See* International conferences
Diplomatic courier and bag, ILC progress on, 324, 336–7, 338
Diplomatic missions, notes from to US courts, *CP*, 136–7
Diplomatic privileges and immunities, of Philippine and Polish consular offices in US, *CP*, 302–3
Diplomatic protection of nationals abroad, 286, 290–1, 647, 821: and ICSID arbitration, 791, 801–2
Diplomatic relations, 41: in lieu of recognition, 47–9; recognition of governments in absence of, 44–6; with unrecognized governments, 34–5, 46. *See also* Recognition
Discovery of Documentary and Other Evidence in a Foreign Country, *CD*, 896
Discrimination Against Women, Convention on the Elimination of All Forms of, 590
Dispute settlement, 116, 869: and Falklands, 610–3, 614; under ILC draft articles, 325, 327–8; under LOS Convention, 11, 18, 19, 21–2, 25, 247–8, 256, 327, 499–500, 515, 543, 550, 741–2, 746, 747–9, 753–4, 755; under Tokyo Round agreements and the GATT, 79–80, 82. *See also* Arbitration; Conciliation; International Court of Justice; Iran-United States Claims Tribunal
Documents, discovery in a foreign country, *CD*, 896. *See also* Blocking statutes; Evidence
Dolman, Antony J. Resources, Regimes, World Order, *BR*, 688
Doman, Nicholas R. *BR* of Schoenblum, 948
Dominican Republic, 656
Dore, Isaak I. Choice of Law under the International Sales Convention: A U.S. Perspective, *LA*, 521
Dover Straits, 493
Drago Doctrine, 286
Draper, G. I. A. D., on applicable law in armed conflicts, 599, 602
Dreyfus, Simone. Droit des relations internationales, *BN*, 209
Drzemczewski, Andrew. *BR* of Annuaire Français de Droit International. Vol. XXVI, 1980, 973
Du Bose, Guy. *BR* of Laszlo & Keys, 959

Duchy of Sealand, requirements for creation of state, *JD,* 160–1
Duffar, Jean. Contribution à l'étude des privilèges et immunités des organisations internationales, *BR,* 943
Dulce et Decorum Est: The Strategic Role of Legal Principles in the Falklands War, *Ed.,* 109
Dumbauld, Edward. *BN* of Fischer with Wälde, 211; *BN* of Ingber, 980; *BR* of Netherlands Yearbook of International Law. Vol. XIII, 1982, 976
Dunn, Lewis A. Controlling the Bomb: Nuclear Proliferation in the 1980s, *BN,* 981

East European states, 6, 250, 870: proposal re fishery conservation, 743; and third states' rights under LOS Convention, 548, 549. *See also* Soviet bloc
East Timor, 653
Ebinger, Charles K. (proj. dir.). The Critical Link: Energy and National Security in the 1980s, *BR,* 961
Economic Community of West African States, 905
Edwards, R. Randle, on reciprocal access of US nationals to PRC courts, 316–7
"effects" doctrine: in FRG antitrust, 757, 759–62, 763–5, 767–77, 779–81, 782, 783; in US practice, 756, 759, 761, 779–81, 782, 783
Egypt, 253: access to Gulf of Aqaba under Peace Treaty with Israel, *LA,* 84
ElBaradei, Mohamed, response to *LA* by, *LA,* 84
Elkind, Jerome B. *BR* of Schwarz-Liebermann von Wahlendorf, 942; Interim Protection: A Functional Approach, *BR,* 673
El Salvador, 87, 653, 657: and recognition of governments, 38
Environment. *See* International liability for lawful acts; Law of the sea: Fisheries, Marine environment
Epps, Valerie. *BR* of Van den Wijngaert, 175
Equatorial Guinea, 903, 911
Equitable principles, 622: in delimiting continental shelf, 6, 20, 22–3, 219, 222, 224–5, 226, 228–34, 236, 238, 873
Essequibo, 297
Estrada Doctrine, on recognition of governments, 41–2, 615
Ethiopia, 34, 569, 653, 865: compensation for expropriation under treaty with US, *CP,* 141–3; *JD,* 144–6
European Commission of Human Rights, 838
European Convention on Human Rights, 601: and African Human Rights Charter, 905, 909–10
European Convention on the International Validity of Criminal Judgments, 619
European Convention on the Suppression of Terrorism (1977), 662
European Court of Human Rights, 909
European Court of Justice, 838: advisory jurisdiction, 126, 128; applicability of Council regulations in EEC states' courts, *JD,* 163
European Economic Community, 6, 837, 904: and exchange rates, 457, 475, 485–6; and GATT Tokyo Round, 55–6, 58, 59, 64–5, 68, 70, 71, 75; and ILC draft articles, 325–6. *See also* European Court of Justice; Treaty of Rome
European Monetary System (EMS), 475, 485
"European" origin of international law, and efforts at revision, 289–91
European Social Charter, 910
Eustis, Frederic A., III. *BR* of Bull, Holt, & Lilly, 957
Evensen, Jens, 324
Evidence: of corporate nationality and continuous ownership of claims, 643–6; *Corr.* on admissibility in international adjudication, 295; discovery of documentary and other in a foreign country, *CD,* 896; and exceptions to Foreign Sovereign Immunities Act, 890–1; exclusionary rule and international law, *JD,* 878–80; in loss of nationality cases, 302. *See also* Blocking statutes
Exclusive economic zone (EEZ). *See* Law of the sea
Expropriation, 27, 649, 650: by Libya, whether cognizable in Italian courts, *JD,* 163–4; by Nicaragua, and sovereign immunity, *JD,* 888–91; standard of compensation, *JD,* 891–3; and treaty provision for compensation, *CP,* 141–3; *JD,* 144–6

Extradition, 27: and Convention on transfer of offenders, 618; under Model American Convention on terrorism, 663–4, 665–7
(The) Extraterritorial Application of the German Antitrust Laws, *LA*, 756

Falk, Richard A., 290–1, 868
———, Burns H. Weston, & Anthony A. D'Amato. International Law and World Order: A Problem-Oriented Coursebook, *BR*, 350
Falkland Islands, war between Argentina and UK over: *Corr.* on legal issues, 297; *Ed.* on legal principles and, 109
Faundez, J. *BN* of Leu, 726
Feldman, D. I., on study of international law, 863–4
Feldman, Mark B. The Tunisia-Libya Continental Shelf Case: Geographic Justice or Judicial Compromise?, *LA*, 219; *Corr.* on, 872
Feliciano, F., on determining objectives of state claiming self-defense, 585–6
Ferencz, Benjamin B. *BR* of Conot, 917
Fiedler, Wilfried, Jost Delbrück, & Wilhelm A. Kewenig (eds.). German Yearbook of International Law. Vol. 22, 1979, *BR*, 718
Finger, Seymour Maxwell, & Joseph R. Harbert (eds.). U.S. Policy in International Institutions: Defining Reasonable Options in an Unreasonable World, *BN*, 207
Finkelstein, Lawrence S. *BR* of Sybesma-Knol, 935
Finland, 569: and recognition of governments, 43
Fischer, Peter (ed.), with Thomas W. Wälde. A Collection of International Concessions and Related Instruments, *BN*, 211
Fisher, Roger. *BR* of Zartman & Berman, 670
Fisheries under the United Nations Convention on the Law of the Sea, *LA*, 739
Fishing, fisheries. *See* Law of the sea
Fitzmaurice, Gerald, on competence of political organs to determine validity of their acts, 241
Fleury, Antoine, & Gabriel Imboden. Diplomatische Dokumente der Schweiz 1848–1945. Vol. 7-I (1918–1919), *BR*, 400
Flint, David. *BN* of Dreyfus, 209
Force, use of, 872: and expulsion from League of Nations, 569–70; and Falklands war, *Ed.*, 109; 607, 610–5; Latin American efforts to prevent, 286–7, 294; UN Charter Art. 2(4) and Israeli raid on Iraq, 584–6
Foreign property, revision of international law on state responsibility, *NC*, 286
Foreign Relations of the United States: 1950, Vol. IV: Central and Eastern Europe; The Soviet Union, *BR*, 394; 1951, Vol. III: European Security and the German Question, *BR*, 397
Foster, John W., 841
France, 130, 430, 569, 636, 745, 773, 774, 865, 871, 874, 899: and air defense identification zones, 516, 518; amendment of IMF Articles, 452–5, 458; effect of decrees reenacting EEC Council regulations, *JD*, 163; and exchange rates generally, 472; extraterritorial jurisdiction over US subsidiary incorporated in, *JD*, 626–8; and Falklands war, 113, 118; fisheries practice and Tunisia-Libya case, 223, 224, 233, 235; and production of documents abroad, 898–9; recognition and enforcement of ICSID award, 785–6, 796–9, 803; on recognition of governments, 42–3, 45; supremacy of treaty over prior statute, *JD*, 161–2; unilateral declarations as binding agreements, 268, 432
Franck, Thomas M. *BR* of Lachs, 169; *BR* of Pomerance, 669; Dulce et Decorum Est: The Strategic Role of Legal Principles in the Falklands War, *Ed.*, 109; 611; Human Rights in Third World Perspective. Vol. I, *BR*, 684
Frankowska, Maria. *BR* of Kusumowidagdo, 936
Freedman, Eric E., *Corr.* on *LA* by, 295
Freedom of the Air and the Convention on the Law of the Sea, *LA*, 490
Freeman, Alwyn, *Ed.* on, 285
Freymond, Jacques, Isabelle Graf-Junod, & Alison Browning. Diplomatische Dokumente der Schweiz 1848–1945. Vol. 6 (1914–1918), *BR*, 400
Friedlander, Robert A. *BR* of Parry, 922

Galenskaia, L. N. Pravovoe polozhenie inostrantsev v SSSR, *BR,* 964
Galenson, Walter. The International Labor Organization: An American View, *BR,* 929
Galindo Pohl, Reynaldo. *Corr.* on *LA* by Feldman, 872
Galloway, L. Thomas, 44
Gamble, John King, Jr. *BR* of Shusterich, 693
García-Amador, F. V. Current Attempts to Revise International Law—A Comparative Analysis, *NC,* 286
(The) GATT and Multilateral Treaty Making: The Tokyo Round, *LA,* 51
General Agreement on Tariffs and Trade (GATT), 461: early tariff negotiations, 52–3, 66–7; Kennedy Round, 53, 54, 57, 67, 68, 73, 74, 75; Tokyo Round, *LA,* 51: the groups, 62–6, 68–9, 70, 75; informal consultations, 69–71, 75–6, 82, 83; relation of MTN agreements to the GATT, 79–80, 81–2; request-and-offer technique, 66–8, 69, 74–5, 76, 82–3. *See also* Tokyo Declaration
(The) General Admission of Aliens under International Law, *LA,* 804
Geneva Convention on Fishing and Conservation of the Living Resources of the High Seas (1958), 752, 755: dispute settlement under, 753, 754; freedom to fish under, 740, 741, 750
Geneva Convention on the Continental Shelf (1958), 17, 19, 26, 228, 236, 435, 437, 439
Geneva Convention on the High Seas (1958), 15, 87, 518, 665, 879: as codifying customary international law, 556–7; freedom of overflight under, 490–1, 495
Geneva Convention on the Territorial Sea and the Contiguous Zone (1958), 20, 101: inland seas (bays) under, 85–6, 87–8; on straits passage, 556, 557, 558–9; straits passage provision and Gulf of Aqaba, 84, 91–4; and third states, 557, 558–9, 567
Geneva Conventions for the protection of war victims (1949): applicability, 594, 595–7, 598–600, 601, 602–3; and human rights law, 590, 591, 593, 602–3
Geneva Conventions for the protection of war victims, Additional Protocols to (1977), 589, 593: legal effect, 591; Protocol I, 591, 593: applicability, 595–7, 598–9; and "instant custom," 435–6; Protocol II, 591, 593: applicability, 597, 599–600, 602
Geneva Conventions on the Law of the Sea (1958), 549, 556: relation to 1982 LOS Convention, 12–20, 22
Genocide, Convention on Prevention and Punishment of the Crime of, 590, 663, 665
Gerber, David J. The Extraterritorial Application of the German Antitrust Laws, *LA,* 756
German Yearbook of International Law. Vol. 22, 1979, *BR,* 718
Germany (pre-1945), 569
Germany, Democratic Republic of, 652
Germany, Federal Republic of (FRG), 230, 281, 304, 437, 507, 551, 616, 745, 871: agreement with US on testimony of nationals, 900–1; and exchange rates, 452, 469, 472; and expulsion of South Africa from UNGA, 571–2; extraterritorial application of antitrust laws, *LA,* 756; immunity of foreign state-owned commercial entity, *JD,* 159–60; nationality of citizen of state on man-made island, *JD,* 160–1; and pretrial discovery of documents, 897–8; and recognition of governments, 43
Gerson, Allan. *BR* of Dinstein, 918
Gibraltar, 91, 493, 552: compared to Falklands, 118, 121–2, 297, 609
Gidel, Gilbert, on passage through straits, 92
Gill, David G. *BR* of Atwood & Brewster, 679
Ginsburgs, George, & Robert M. Slusser. A Calendar of Soviet Treaties 1958–1973, *BN,* 982
Glennon, Michael J. The Senate Role in Treaty Ratification, *LA,* 257
Gnesa, Edi. Die von Israel besetzten Gebiete im Völkerrecht, *BR,* 703
Golbert, Albert S., & Yenny Nun. Latin American Laws and Institutions, *BR,* 388
Gold, Joseph. *BR* of Welch, 950; The Fund Agreement in the Courts: Vol. II. Further Jurisprudence Involving the Articles of Agreement of the International Monetary Fund, *BR,* 927; Strengthening the Soft International Law of Exchange Arrangements, *LA,* 443
Goldklang, Jack M. House Approves Proposal Permitting ICJ to Advise Domestic Courts, *CD,* 338
Good Faith in Public International Law, *NC,* 130
Gordon, Edward. *BR* of Singh, 177
Gorove, Stephen (ed.). United States Space Law: National and International Regulation. Binders I and II, *BR,* 369

Graf-Junod, Isabelle, Jacques Freymond, & Alison Browning. Diplomatische Dokumente der Schweiz 1848–1945. Vol. 6 (1914–1918), *BR*, 400

Greece, 93–4, 616: ancient, and admission of aliens, 809; and transit passage of aircraft, 495–6

Green, L. C. *BR* of Israel Yearbook on Human Rights. Vol. 11, 391

Grieves, Forest L. *BR* of The Canadian Yearbook of International Law. Vol. XIX, 1981, 720; *BR* of Diplomatische Dokumente der Schweiz 1848–1945. Vols. 6, 7-I, & 9, 400

Griffin, Joseph P. *BR* of Kerse, 191

Griffin, Ronald C. *BR* of Canenbley, 189

Gros, André, 296: on ICJ Tunisia-Libya decision, 224, 235, 237; on states' right to reject decisions of international organizations, 253

Gross, Leo, 92: Book Reviews and Notes, 169, 345, 669, 915; on majoritarianism in UNSC, 250; on states' right of auto-interpretation, 254; On the Degradation of the Constitutional Environment of the United Nations, *Ed.*, 569

Grosse-Jütte, Annemarie, & Rudiger Jütte (eds.). The Future of International Organization, *BR*, 172

Grotius, Hugo, on admission of aliens, 810–1, 812, 813

Group of 77, 6, 115, 250: on legal status of EEZ, 504; on third states' rights under LOS Convention, 547, 548, 549. *See also* Developing countries; New International Economic Order; Nonaligned countries; Third World

Grzybowski, Kazimierz. *BR* of Polish Yearbook of International Law, Vol. X, 1979–1980, 205; Soviet Theory of International Law for the Seventies, *NC*, 862

Guatemala, 653, 657: and Falklands war, 117; and recognition of governments, 38

Guelff, Richard, & Adam Roberts (eds.). Documents on the Laws of War, *BR*, 383: *Corr.* on, 982

Guggenheim, Paul, 420

Guinea, Republic of, immunity under arbitral agreement not contemplating role for US courts, *JD*, 318–20; 786–94

Gulf of Aqaba, regime under Egyptian-Israeli Peace Treaty, *LA*, 84

Gulf of Fonseca, passage through, 87

Guy, Diana, & Guy I. F. Leigh. The EEC and Intellectual Property, *BR*, 360

Guyana, 796: and Falklands war, 117, 118

Hague Academy. *See* Recueil des Cours de l'Académie de droit international de La Haye

Hague Codification Conference (1930), 287, 561

Hague Conference on Private International Law. Actes et documents de la Quatorzième session (1980). Books I & II, *BR*, 944

Hague Convention on Certain Questions relating to the Conflict of Nationality Laws (1930), on claims by dual nationals, 647

Hague Convention on the Taking of Evidence Abroad in Civil or Commercial Matters, US practice under, 897–900, 901–2

Hague Conventions on laws of war (1907), 565: 4th Convention, 593: Regulations under as customary law, 590, 591

Hailbronner, Kay. Freedom of the Air and the Convention on the Law of the Sea, *LA*, 490

Haiti, 652, 653

Hakapää, Kari. Marine Pollution in International Law. Material Obligations and Jurisdiction, with Special Reference to the Third United Nations Conference on the Law of the Sea, *BN*, 723

Halderman, John W. The Political Role of the United Nations: Advancing the World Community, *BR*, 366

Hand, Learned, on effects principle, 759

Handl, Günther. *BR* of von Münch, 685

Hantke, Jeanette. The 1982 Session of the UN Sub-Commission on Prevention of Discrimination and Protection of Minorities, *CD*, 651

Harbert, Joseph R., & Seymour Maxwell Finger (eds.). U.S. Policy in International Institutions: Defining Reasonable Options in an Unreasonable World, *BN*, 207

Harrison, William Henry, 841

Hassan, Farooq, on Falklands dispute, 612

Hauser, Rita E. *BR* of Hevener and of Khushalani, 926

Hauser, Wolfgang, Günther Jaenicke, & Erich Schanze. A Joint Venture Agreement for Seabed Mining, *BR,* 373
Havana Charter, basis for early GATT negotiations, 52
Hazard, John N. *BN* of Ginsburgs & Slusser, 982; *BR* of Franck, 684; *BR* of Galenskaia, 964; *BR* of Movchan, 709; *BR* of Mukherjee & Mukherjee, 171; *BR* of Soviet Year-Book of International Law, 1980, 203; *BR* of Soviet Year-Book of International Law, 1981, 971; *BR* of Yin, 687
Hegel, G. W. F., 2, 818
Heller, Paul, 508
Helsinki Final Act (Helsinki Accords), 414, 862, 904: and admission of aliens, 838–9; on human dignity, 848, 853; legal effect, 270
Henkin, Louis (ed.). The International Bill of Rights: The Covenant on Civil and Political Rights, *BR,* 347
Herron, L. W., on IAEA voting procedure, 577
Hertzberg, Michael A., Harvey Kaye, & Paul Plaia, Jr. International Trade Practice. Vols. 1–2, *BR,* 707
Hevener, Natalie K. *BR* of South African Yearbook of International Law, Vol. 6, 1980, 393; International Law and the Status of Women, *BR,* 926
Hickenlooper Amendment, applicability of, 145–6
Higgins, Rosalyn. United Nations Peacekeeping. Documents and Commentary. Vol. IV: Europe 1946–1979, *BR,* 361
High seas. *See* Law of the sea
Hill, Christopher. Maritime Law, *BR,* 376
Hingorani, R. C. Prisoners of War (2d ed.), *BN,* 211
Historic title: and Falklands war, 118–9; in Tunisia-Libya case, 223–4, 235, 237
Hobbes, Thomas, 818
Hofer, Walther, & Beatrix Mesmer, in collaboration with Peter Hurni, Martin Lüdi, & Peter Martig. Diplomatische Dokumente der Schweiz 1848–1945. Vol. 9 (1925–1929), *BR,* 400
Hohfeld, Wesley, 9
Hollick, Ann L. U.S. Foreign Policy and the Law of the Sea, *BR,* 373
Holmes, Oliver Wendell, 808
Holt, Geoffrey, Alan T. Bull, & Malcolm D. Lilly. Biotechnology: International Trends and Perspectives, *BR,* 957
Holtzmann, H., 650
Honduras, 87, 653: and recognition of governments, 38; US search of vessel on high seas, *JD,* 878–80
Hormuz, Strait of, 493, 552
Horn, Norbert, Hein Kötz, & Hans G. Leser. German Private and Commercial Law: An Introduction, *BR,* 386
Hostages, International Convention against the Taking of (1979), 665
House Approves Proposal Permitting ICJ to Advise Domestic Courts, *CD,* 338
Huber, Max, 419
Human dignity, 904–5: and admission of aliens, 845, 846; as a normative concept, *Ed.,* 848
Human Dignity as a Normative Concept, *Ed.,* 848
Humanitarian law. *See* War, law of
Human rights, 432, 573, 843–4, 866, 869: advisory jurisdiction under American Convention, *JD,* 637–9; 640–1; The African Charter on Human and Peoples' Rights, *CD,* 902; and human dignity, 848, 853–4; of individuals under American Convention, 641–2; law and humanitarian law, on the inadequate reach of, *NC,* 589; law, teaching in US law schools, *NC,* 855; and Model American Convention on terrorism, *CD,* 662. *See also* (The) 1982 Session of the UN Sub-Commission on Prevention of Discrimination and Protection of Minorities
Hume, David, 1
Hungary, 581, 867

ICSID Arbitration and the Courts, *LA,* 784
Imboden, Gabriel, & Antoine Fleury. Diplomatische Dokumente der Schweiz 1848–1945. Vol. 7-I (1918–1919), *BR,* 400

India, 111, 246, 304, 583–4: and Falklands war, 122; seizure of Goa, 120, 123
Indonesia, 652: accession of West New Guinea and East Timor, 120, 121, 123, 124
Ingber, Léon (ed.). Gelijkheid. Vol. VI, *BN*, 980
Inman, Harry A. *BN* of Cavelier, 404
Institute of International Law (Institut de Droit International), 1892 proposal on admission of aliens, 830, 832–3
Inter-American Commission on Human Rights, 137, 638, 642: standing to request advisory opinions, 640–1
Inter-American Court of Human Rights, 909: advisory jurisdiction, *JD*, 637–9; 640–1; and Model American Convention on terrorism, 663, 664, 667; reservations and entry into force of Convention: opinion on, *JD*, 640–2; request for views of governments on, *CP*, 137–41
Intergovernmental Committee for Migration, 821
Inter-governmental Maritime Consultative Organization (IMCO), 621: confirmation of acts of improperly constituted committee, 244
Intergovernmental organizations, and recognition of governments, 33, 34, 36, 44, 48. *See also* International organizations
Interim Commission for the International Trade Organization (ICITO), 76
Internal conflicts, need for applicable instrument, 589, 599–600, 603–6
International Atomic Energy Agency (IAEA): safeguards and Israeli 1981 raid on Iraq, 587; suspension of Israel, 574–80, 583–4
International Bank for Reconstruction and Development (IBRD, World Bank), 796
International Centre for Settlement of Investment Disputes (ICSID): agreement to arbitration by and immunity, 318–9, 786–92; arbitration by, and the courts, *LA*, 784
International Chamber of Commerce, 798
International Civil Aviation, Convention on (Chicago Convention, 1941), 245: rules and standards applicable to territorial and high seas, 490–2, 501, 508, 511, 517
International Civil Aviation Organization (ICAO), 243, 490, 496: legal validity of challenged decisions, 245, 246; Rules of the Air and high seas, 491, 493, 501, 503, 504, 509; Rules of the Air and international straits, 501, 508
International Commission of Jurists, 903, 906
International Committee of the Red Cross (ICRC), 591, 600, 606
International conferences, 511, 563: and recognition of governments, 33, 34, 36
International Convention on the Elimination of All Forms of Racial Discrimination, 590, 594
International Court of Justice, 243, 244, 292, 324, 327, 332, 414, 420, 426, 427, 442, 613, 742, 785, 802, 820–1, 869, 871: and admission of aliens, 842; and binding force of unilateral declarations, 268, 269; broadening advisory jurisdiction of: *Ed.*, 124; 256; US House approval of proposal on, *CD*, 338; compulsory jurisdiction re UN Charter interpretation, 579–80; on conventional rules and custom, 435, 436–7, 439, 554, 563; *Corr.* on admission of evidence by, 295; on delimitation of continental shelf, 19, 22, 23, 25–6: Tunisia-Libya decision, *LA*, 219: *Corr.* on, 872; on good faith, 130, 131, 132; implied distinction between freedom and power, 26; on international straits passage, 91, 93–4, 556, 561; on legal validity of acts of UN organs, 241–2, 246, 249, 253, 254, 256, 874; on obligations *erga omnes*, 431–2; possible views on seabed mining by nonsignatories to LOS Convention, 282–5; on practice, consensus and custom, 563; on treaties and third states, 543; on Western Sahara, 120
International Court of Justice, Statute of, 21, 22, 124, 125, 220, 229, 579
International Covenant on Civil and Political Rights, 590, 597, 605, 654, 821, 848, 858, 912: applicability, 594–5, 599, 604; derogations under, 600–2
International Covenant on Civil and Political Rights, Optional Protocol, 590, 601
International Covenant on Economic, Social and Cultural Rights, 590, 594, 848, 858, 902, 912
International Labour Organisation (ILO), 251: and Israel, 573–4; legal effect of acts under challenged declaration, 244–5
International Law Commission, 7, 57, 74, 556, 660, 846: on codification vs. progressive development, 275, 553; on *jus cogens* and international crimes, 423–7, 429; on obligations *erga omnes*, 431–2; on security rights in contiguous zone, 518; 34th session of, *CD*, 323; on treaties and custom, 565, 568
International Legal Materials (Contents), 216, 411, 737, 990

International liability for lawful acts, ILC progress on defining, 324, 333–6, 338

International Monetary Fund (IMF), 321: "soft" law in Articles of Agreement, *LA*, 443: consultation under Art. IV, 465, 475, 477–8, 483, 484, 485, 488–9; deterrence of breach under Art. IV, 461–2; intervention under Art. IV, 467–73, 482, 486–7; par value system, 445–52, 457, 458, 461, 466, 471, 473, 476, 479, 482, 483; UK Court on unenforceable exchange contracts, *JD*, 155–7

International organizations, 51, 511, 752–3, 833, 857: competence to determine legality of their decisions, 241–3; degradation of constitutional environment of, *Ed.*, 569; ILC draft articles on treaties between states and, etc., 324, 325–8; legal validity of *ultra vires* decisions of, *LA*, 239; *Corr.* on, 873; normative status of resolutions, 416–8, 425, 438; requests to ICJ for advisory opinions, 125, 126; right of member states to challenge decisions, 240–1; "soft" law of, 444, 461; in Soviet theory, 864, 866

International Sale of Goods, Convention on Contracts for the (1980), choice of law under, *LA*, 521: exceptions to jurisdiction, 525, 526, 531, 532–6, 539: Art. 95 reservations, 529, 533, 535, 536, 537–9

International Sale of Goods, Convention relating to a Uniform Law on the Formation of Contracts for the (1964), 521, 522

International Sale of Goods, Uniform Law on the (ULIS, 1964), 531, 636: US views on, 521–4, 526

International trade: Arab boycott of Israel and US antiboycott laws, *JD*, 310–2; currency conversion date in liquidation proceedings, *JD*, 635–6; proposed amendment of US Foreign Corrupt Practices Act, *CD*, 340; Strengthening the Soft International Law of Exchange Arrangements, *LA*, 443; treaty-making process at Tokyo Round, *LA*, 51; UK judicial enforcement of IMF Agreement, *JD*, 155–7. *See also* Antitrust; Choice of Law under the International Sales Convention; United States: Export Administration Act

Investment disputes. *See* International Centre for Settlement of Investment Disputes; Settlement of Investment Disputes Between States and Nationals of Other States, Convention on the

Iran, 111, 123, 439, 587, 610, 652, 653, 797–8: *Corr.* on evidence in *Hostages* case, 295; former hostage's claims, *JD*, 312–5; French policy on recognizing, 43; immunity of state-owned commercial entity in FRG, *JD*, 159–60; on innocent passage of warships, 558; on third states' rights under LOS Convention, 548. *See also* Iran-United States Claims Tribunal

Iran-United States Claims Tribunal: concurring opinion on expropriation and standard of compensation, *JD*, 891–3; on *force majeure* and nonperformance of contracts, *JD*, 893–5; handling of "small" claims, 913–4; jurisdiction for damages to surviving dependents, *JD*, 649–50; jurisdiction over dual nationals, *JD*, 646–8; jurisdiction over publicly held corporations, *JD*, 642–6; proposed legislation on costs of, 166–7; on settlements not within its jurisdiction, 913

(The) Iran-United States Claims Tribunal, *CD*, 913

Iraq, 111, 123, 610, 653: 1981 Israeli raid and IAEA, 574–8; *Ed.* on 1981 Israeli raid, 584

Ireland, Republic of: and Falklands war, 116, 118; and recognition of governments, 43

Israel, 111, 250, 611: access to Gulf of Aqaba under Peace Treaty with Egypt, *LA*, 84; Arab boycott and US law, *JD*, 310–2; attempts to suspend or expel from international organizations, 570–84; 1981 raid against Iraq, 574–8: *Ed.* on, 584; UN Sub-Commission on invasion of Lebanon, 652

Israel's Air Strike upon the Iraqi Nuclear Reactor, *Ed.*, 584

Israel Yearbook on Human Rights. Vol. 11, *BR*, 391

Italy, 161, 569, 579, 745, 796, 871: admissibility of evidence taken abroad, *JD*, 164; cognizability of Libyan expropriation, *JD*, 163–4; and exchange rates, 452, 472; fisheries practice and Tunisia-Libya case, 223, 224, 233, 235; and recognition of governments, 43; jurisdiction over felonies by citizens abroad, *JD*, 164

Ivory Coast, 912: and recognition of governments, 43

Jackson, John H., on MTN agreements, 80–1

Jacobson, Harold K. *BR* of Dolman, 688

Jaenicke, Günther, Erich Schanze, & Wolfgang Hauser. A Joint Venture Agreement for Seabed Mining, *BR*, 373

Jalles, Isabel. Implications juridico-constitutionnelles de l'adhésion aux Communautés européennes. Le cas du Portugal, *BR*, 682

Jamaica, 796: ICSID arbitration on mineral agreements, 793
Japan, 118, 569, 654, 764: and exchange rates, 452, 469, 472; and GATT Tokyo Round, 55–6, 58, 59, 68
Jay, John, on binding nature of treaties, 257
Jefferson, Thomas, 835
Jenisch, Uwe. *BR* of Vitzthum, 691
Jennings, R. Y.: on broadening advisory jurisdiction of ICJ, 256; and use of force in territorial disputes, 607, 612, 613, 615
Jessup, Philip C., 868: on revising international law, 288–9, 290, 292
Jiménez de Aréchaga, Eduardo, 226–7: on natural prolongation of continental shelf, 227; on treaties and third states, 545
Johnston, Douglas M. (ed.). The Environmental Law of the Sea, *BR*, 941
Jordan, and regime for Gulf of Aqaba, 85, 90, 94, 102
Joyner, Christopher C. *BR* of Auburn, 180; *BR* of Jaenicke, Schanze, & Hauser, of Barston & Birnie, and of Hollick, 373
Judicial assistance: recognition and enforcement of ICSID awards by domestic courts, 785–6, 791, 796–800, 802; US bilateral treaties on, 900–1
Judicial Decisions, 144, 308, 624, 878
Jurisdiction: advisory, broadening ICJ's: *Ed.*, 124; 256, 579; US House approval of proposal on, *CD*, 338; advisory, under American Convention on Human Rights, *JD*, 637–9; 640–1; of coastal state over foreign aircraft, 498–501, 503–20; compulsory, of ICJ to interpret UN Charter, 579–80; Convention on transfer of offenders, *CP*, 616–9; to determine reciprocity in treaty application, *JD*, 161–2; domestic, and admission of aliens, 819–22; extraterritorial, notes from foreign governments to US courts, *CP*, 136–7; extraterritorial, over foreign incorporated subsidiaries of US companies, *JD*, 626–8; *JD*, 636–7; extraterritorial, under FRG antitrust laws, *LA*, 756; over felonies by citizens abroad, *JD*, 164; fisheries, under LOS Convention, *LA*, 739; over foreign entity under Texas long-arm statute, *JD*, 149–51; lack of, and administrative relief in nationality cases, *CP*, 298–302; over stateless vessels on high seas, *JD*, 630–1; territorial, over US embassies abroad, 314; of US courts and Panama Canal Treaty, *CD*, 167. *See also* Antitrust; Choice of Law under the International Sales Convention; Iran-United States Claims Tribunal; (The) Legal Validity of Ultra Vires Decisions of International Organizations; United States: Foreign Sovereign Immunities Act
Jütte, Rudiger, & Annemarie Grosse-Jütte (eds.). The Future of International Organization, *BR*, 172

Kamm, Thomas A. *BR* of Bartell, 695
Kampuchea. *See* Cambodia
Kant, Immanuel, 2, 812, 849
Kapteyn, P. J. G., P. H. Kooijmans, R. H. Lauwaars, H. G. Schermers, & M. van Leeuwen Boomkamp (eds.). International Organization and Integration: Annotated Basic Documents and Descriptive Directory of International Organizations and Arrangements. Vols. I.A & II.A (2d rev. ed.), *BR*, 359
Kasten/McClure Amendment, on Israeli participation in IAEA, 583
Katō, Ichirō, Nobuo Kumamoto, & William H. Matthews (eds.). Environmental Law and Policy in the Pacific Basin Area, *BN*, 210
Kaye, Harvey, Paul Plaia, Jr., & Michael A. Hertzberg. International Trade Practice. Vols. 1–2, *BR*, 707
Kelsen, Hans, 133
Kenney, William S. *BR* of Degenhardt, 955
Kenya, 743, 912: and Falklands war, 117; and recognition of governments, 43
Kerse, C. S. EEC Antitrust Procedure, *BR*, 191
Kewenig, Wilhelm A., Jost Delbrück, & Wilfried Fiedler (eds.). German Yearbook of International Law. Vol. 22, 1979, *BR*, 718
Keys, Donald, & Ervin Laszlo (eds.). Disarmament: The Human Factor, *BR*, 959
Khrushchev, Nikita S., 864
Khushalani, Yougindra. Dignity and Honour of Women as Basic and Fundamental Human Rights, *BR*, 926

King, Martin Luther, Jr., 609
Kirgis, Frederic L., Jr. *BN* of Hingorani, 211; *Corr.* on *LA* by Osieke, 873; response to *Corr.* on *BR* by, 727
Kirkpatrick, Jeane, and Falklands war, 111, 112, 113
Kirton, John, Robert Spencer, & Kim Richard Nossal (eds.). The International Joint Commission Seventy Years On, *BR,* 714
Klein, Eckart. *BN* of List of Treaty Collections, 726
Kneifel, J. L. Fluggesellschaften und Luftverkehrssysteme der sozialistischen Staaten UdSSR, Polen, CSSR, Ungarn, Bulgarien, Rumänien, Kuba, Jugoslawien und der VR China, *BR,* 196; Staatliches und internationales Luftverkehrsrecht der sozialistischen Staaten UdSSR, DDR, Polen, CSSR, Ungarn, Bulgarien, Rumänien, Kuba, Jugoslawien und der VR China, *BR,* 196
Kooijmans, P. H., P. J. G. Kapteyn, R. H. Lauwaars, H. G. Schermers, & M. van Leeuwen Boomkamp (eds.). International Organization and Integration: Annotated Basic Documents and Descriptive Directory of International Organizations and Arrangements. Vols. I.A & II.A (2d rev. ed.), *BR,* 359
Korah, Valentine. Competition Law of Britain and the Common Market (3d rev. ed.), *BR,* 952
Korea, Democratic People's Republic of (North), 652–3
Korea, Republic of (South), 113–4, 652–3
Kötz, Hein, Norbert Horn, & Hans G. Leser. German Private and Commercial Law: An Introduction, *BR,* 386
Kruglak, Gregory T. The Politics of United States Decision-Making in United Nations Specialized Agencies: The Case of the International Labor Organization, *BR,* 929
Kumamoto, Nobuo, Ichirō Katō, & William H. Matthews (eds.). Environmental Law and Policy in the Pacific Basin Area, *BN,* 210
Kusumowidagdo, Judo Umarto. Consultation Clauses as Means of Providing for Treaty Obedience: A Study in the Law of Treaties, *BR,* 936

Lachs, Manfred. The Teacher in International Law, *BR,* 169
Lagergren, Gunnar, 643, 649
Lamm, Vanda, & Zoltán Péteri (eds.). General Reports to the 10th International Congress of Comparative Law, *BR,* 962
Landlocked and geographically disadvantaged states, and fisheries provisions of LOS Convention, 744, 745–6
Langen, Eugen. Transnationales Recht, *BN,* 722
Laos, 114
Lapidoth, Ruth. The Strait of Tiran, the Gulf of Aqaba, and the 1979 Treaty of Peace between Egypt and Israel, *LA,* 84
Laszlo, Ervin, & Donald Keys (eds.). Disarmament: The Human Factor, *BR,* 959
Latin America: on admission of aliens, 808, 831–2; efforts to revise international law, 286–7, 288, 294–5
Lauwaars, R. H., P. J. G. Kapteyn, P. H. Kooijmans, H. G. Schermers, & M. van Leeuwen Boomkamp (eds.). International Organization and Integration: Annotated Basic Documents and Descriptive Directory of International Organizations and Arrangements. Vol. I.A & II.A (2d rev. ed.), *BR,* 359
Law against Restraints on Competition (GWB) (West Germany): external jurisdictional restraints on, 760, 772–9, 780, 781–3; merger control under, 757, 762, 765–79; and US antitrust law, 757–60, 761–2, 763, 779–83. *See also* "effects" doctrine
Law of the sea
  Archipelagic waters, 566: transit passage of aircraft, 493, 500, 501–3, 519
  Continental shelf: aviation jurisdiction over structures on, 510; Commission on the Limits of, 17–8; outer edge, 17–8; under LOS Convention, 13, 14, 16, 566; US position on, 620, 622
  Continental shelf, delimitation, 12, 19–24: equidistance method, 219, 222–3, 227–8, 235–6, 237–8, 437; natural prolongation, 219, 222–8, 232, 238; perpendicular line, 224, 228, 231–2, 233–4, 236–7; proportionality, 220, 231, 232–3, 236, 238
  Deep seabed, 13: mining under LOS Convention and the US, 281–5, 619, 620, 621; regime of LOS Convention, 12, 16–7, 494, 543, 550, 566, 619, 755 (*see also* International Sea-Bed Authority)

Exclusive economic zone, 563: delimitation, 20–4, 220, 236, 238, 872–3; fisheries regime, 741, 742–9, 751, 752–3, 754–5; transit of aircraft, 493–4, 503–16, 519–20; under LOS Convention generally, 12, 13, 14–6, 17, 281, 566; US proclamation of, 552; *CP*, 619–23
Fisheries, 506, 512: conservation and management under LOS Convention, 741, 742–6, 747, 748, 750–4, 755; ICJ on jurisdiction, 26; and Tunisia-Libya ICJ decision, 223–4, 230, 233, 234–5, 237, 238; US position on, 619, 620, 622–3, 739–40, 743
High seas, 12, 13, 14–6: admissibility of evidence illegally obtained on, *JD*, 878–80; authority of Coast Guard over vessels on, *JD*, 630–1; fisheries regime, 739, 740–1, 749–54, 755; transit of aircraft, 490–3, 503–4, 509, 511–2, 513–20, 552, 620, 623, 741; US position on, 620, 621, 622, 623
International Sea-Bed Authority, 16, 18–9, 25: review powers of Disputes Chamber re acts of, 247–8, 256
Marine environment, 12, 281: and transit of aircraft, 505–6, 510–3; US position on, 620, 621, 622
Marine scientific research, 12, 17: and transit of aircraft, 513; US position on, 619–20, 621
Territorial sea, 18, 432, 621–2, 623: aircraft in contiguous zone, 514, 518; breadth of and third states, 551–2, 559; delimitation, 19–24; fisheries policy before LOS Convention, 739–40, 741, 742, 743, 752; and Gulf of Aqaba, 84–5, 88–91, 99–103; and inland seas (bays), 85–8, 91; passage through straits generally, 91–4, 555–6; regime under LOS Convention, 12, 13–4, 15, 880; Strait of Tiran, 94–7, 99–103; transit passage of aircraft, 491–501, 502, 506, 516, 519–20, 541, 549, 560; transit passage through international straits, 12, 95–6, 97, 101, 107–8, 281, 541, 548, 549, 551–2, 556–61, 562–4, 566–7
UN Convention, 229, 436, 440, 872–3, 880: an alternative to, *Ed.*, 281; classification of persons, sea areas, and relations, 8–11, 13, 28–30, 563; codification vs. development, 428, 542–3, 548, 549, 567; fisheries under, *LA*, 739; freedom of the air and, *LA*, 490; power sharing under, *LA*, 1; regime of bays, 86, 88, 91, 106; rights under as shared powers, 27; straits passage, 84–5, 95–7, 99, 102, 106; and third states, *LA*, 541: provisions incorporating or developing customary law, 554–66, 568 (*see also* Deep seabed, Territorial sea)
See also Dispute settlement
(The) Law of the Sea Convention and Third States, *LA*, 541
Lauterpacht, Elihu, on legal validity of majority decisions of international organizations, 250–1
League of Nations, 613, 820: and binding force of unilateral declarations, 267; expulsion of USSR, 569–70; and revision of international law, 287, 288. *See also* Permanent Court of International Justice
Leary, Virginia A. *BR* of Galenson and of Kruglak, 929
Least developed countries, 744: and GATT Tokyo Round, 57, 59, 72
Lebanon, 111, 652
Lebin, D. A., & V. V. Vorotnikov (eds.). Mezhdunarodnye Ekonomicheskije i Nauchno-tekhnicheskije Organizatsii Stran-chlenov SEV. Spravochnik, *BR*, 711
Lee, Luke T. *BR* of Lillich, 202; The Law of the Sea Convention and Third States, *LA*, 541
(The) Legal Validity of Ultra Vires Decisions of International Organizations, *LA*, 239; *Corr.* on, 873
Leich, Marian Nash. Contemporary Practice of the United States Relating to International Law, 135, 298, 616, 875; The Iran-United States Claims Tribunal, *CD*, 913; The Panama Canal Treaty and Jurisdiction of U.S. Courts, *CD*, 167; The Proposed Iran Claims Act of the United States, *CD*, 166
Leigh, Guy I. F., & Diana Guy. The EEC and Intellectual Property, *BR*, 360
Leigh, Monroe, 142: Judicial Decisions, 144, 308, 624, 878
Leng, Shao-Chuan. *BR* of Chiu, 975
Lenin, 863, 864
Leser, Hans G., Norbert Horn, & Hein Kötz. German Private and Commercial Law: An Introduction, *BR*, 386
Leu, Hans-Joachim. Introducción al derecho internacional penal, *BN*, 726
Levie, Howard S. *BR* of Bothe, Partsch, & Solf, 377; *BR* of Roberts & Guelff, 383: response to *Corr.* on, 983
Levin, D. B., on international law theory, 863, 864
Libya, 43: and air defense identification zones, 516, 517; cognizability of expropriation by in

Italy, *JD*, 163–4; ICJ delimitation of continental shelf with Tunisia, *LA*, 219; *Corr.* on, 872; recognition and enforcement of oil arbitration awards, 798
Liechtenstein, 318, 786, 794
Lillich, Richard B., 292: Model American Convention on the Prevention and Punishment of Serious Forms of Violence, *CD*, 662; The Teaching of International Human Rights Law in U.S. Law Schools, *NC*, 855
——— (ed.). The Family in International Law: Some Emerging Problems, *BR*, 202; International Aspects of Criminal Law: Enforcing United States Law in the World Community, *BR*, 173
Lillich/Newman, human rights course book, 858
Lilly, Malcolm D., Alan T. Bull, & Geoffrey D. Lilly. Biotechnology: International Trends and Perspectives, *BR*, 957
Lipstein, K. Principles of the Conflict of Laws, National and International, *BR*, 699
List of Treaty Collections, *BN*, 726
Litan, Robert E. *BR* of Dam, 185; *BR* of Gold, 927
Locke, John, 24, 25
Lomé II Convention, 904
Lowe, A. V. *BR* of Korah, 952
Luxembourg, 251, 616

MacBride, Sean, on derogations under human rights law, 602
MacDonald, Charles G. Iran, Saudi Arabia, and the Law of the Sea: Political Interaction and Legal Development in the Persian Gulf, *BR*, 694
Macdonald, J. Ross. *BR* of Postlewaite & Collins, 708
MacGibbon, I. C., on failure to protest and acquiescence, 560
Madison, James, 835
Maggs, Peter B. *BR* of Bulajić, 193
Mahiou, Ahmed, 324
Malacca, Strait of, 493, 552
Malagasy Republic (Madagascar), 653: vote re Israeli credentials to IAEA, 577–8
Malloy, Michael P. *BR* of Campbell, 705; *BR* of Odle, 390
Malvinas, Islas. *See* Falkland Islands
Maneli, Mieczyslaw. Juridical Positivism and Human Rights, *BR*, 199
Mangone, Gerard J. *BN* of Conforti, 722
Mann, F. A. The Legal Aspect of Money. With special reference to Comparative Private and Public International Law (4th ed.), *BR*, 676
Marcos, Ferdinand E. and Imelda, 305–6
Marcoux, Laurent, Jr. *BR* of Rights and Responsibilities. International, Social, and Individual Dimensions, 201
Marshall Islands, applicability of sovereign immunity to, *JD*, 158–9
Marx, Karl, 2, 24, 25, 863, 868
Matthews, William H., Ichirō Katō, & Nobuo Kumamoto (eds.). Environmental Law and Policy in the Pacific Basin Area, *BN*, 210
M'Baye, Keba, 906
M'Bow, Amadou-Mahtar, on majority decisions of international organizations, 251
McCaffrey, Stephen C. The Thirty-fourth Session of the International Law Commission, *CD*, 323
McDougal, Myres S., 518: on determining objectives of state claiming self-defense, 585–6; Soviet view of works, 871–2
McNair, A., on semi-legislative treaties, 564–5
McRae, D. M., & J. C. Thomas. The GATT and Multilateral Treaty Making: The Tokyo Round, *LA*, 51
Meagher, Robert F. *BR* of Olson, 186
Meessen, K. M., on jurisdictional restraint in antitrust cases, 775
Menter, Martin. *BR* of Christol, 937
Meron, Theodor. On the Inadequate Reach of Humanitarian and Human Rights Law and the Need for a New Instrument, *NC*, 589
Mesmer, Beatrix, & Walther Hofer, in collaboration with Peter Hurni, Martin Lüdi, & Peter Martig. Diplomatische Dokumente der Schweiz 1848–1945. Vol. 9 (1925–1929), *BR*, 400

Mexico, 653: on Falklands war, 114–5, 116; immunity of governmental agency re oil spill, *JD*, 149–51; and recognition of governments, 38, 39, 41–2, 45

Mintz, Nancy K. *BR* of Newton, 947

Model American Convention on the Prevention and Punishment of Serious Forms of Violence, *CD*, 662: text, 664

Moore, John Norton, 96, 492–3: *Corr.* on *Ed.* by, 297; 606; response to *Corr.*, 610; on straits passage, 497, 499

Morelli, Gaetano, on states' right to reject decisions of international organizations, 254

Morocco, 39, 790: and transit passage of aircraft, 495, 496; and Western Sahara, 120–1, 123, 124

Morrisson, Clovis C., Jr. The Dynamics of Development in the European Human Rights Convention System, *BR*, 345

Moskowitz, Moses. The Roots and Reaches of United Nations Actions and Decisions, *BR*, 915

Movchan, A. P. Prava cheloveka i mezhdunarodnye otnosheniia, *BR*, 709

Mozambique, 902, 903

Mukherjee, Indrani, & Sakti Mukherjee. Major Issues in International Law, *BR*, 171

Mukherjee, Sakti, & Indrani Mukherjee. Major Issues in International Law, *BR*, 171

Multinational corporations. *See* Transnational corporations

Myers, Kenneth, & Yonah Alexander (eds.). Terrorism in Europe, *BN*, 980

Nadelmann, Kurt H. *BR* of Hague Conference on Private International Law, 944

Nafziger, James A. R. *BR* of Weston, Falk, & D'Amato, 350; The General Admission of Aliens under International Law, *LA*, 804

Namibia, 570, 571, 865, 902: suit in US court re activities of SWAPO, *JD*, 628–30

Nanda, Ved P. *BR* of Sumner, 965

Nationality: and applicability of humanitarian and human rights law, 594–7; exception to territorial jurisdiction, 636–7; of juridical persons and ICSID arbitration, 793–5; loss of, appeals procedures and administrative relief, *CP*, 298–302; loss of through creation of state on man-made island, *JD*, 160–1; under Algiers Accords, *JD*, 642–6; *JD*, 646–8. *See also* Diplomatic protection

Nationalization. *See* Expropriation

National liberation, 905: Soviet view of wars of, 866

Natural resources, 866: offshore, and Tunisia-Libya ICJ decision, 220, 230, 232, 233–4, 235, 237. *See also* Law of the sea: Fisheries, Marine environment

Negotiations. *See* General Agreement on Tariffs and Trade

Nelson, Richard W. *BR* of Akehurst, 357; *BR* of Bowett, 933; *BR* of Higgins, 361

Netherlands, 120, 551, 616, 871: Antilles, and Falklands war, 119; extraterritorial jurisdiction over US subsidiary incorporated in, *JD*, 636–7

Netherlands Yearbook of International Law. Vol. XIII, 1982, *BR*, 976

New International Economic Order, 4, 66, 78–9, 251: and human rights, 659–60; and ILC international liability articles, 335; and revision of international law of state responsibility, *NC*, 286

New International Humanitarian Order, 589

Newly industrialized countries, and GATT Tokyo Round, 58, 59

Newman, Edwin S., & Eugene M. Wypyski (eds.). United States International Trade Reports. Binder I, *BR*, 704

Newman, F. *See* Lillich/Newman

Newton, William H., III. International Estate Planning, *BR*, 947

New Zealand, 59, 268: and admission of aliens, 816, 836–7, 840; Court on applicability of sovereign immunity to Marshall Islands, *JD*, 158–9; unenforceability of cultural property laws in UK courts, *JD*, 631–4

Nguema, Marcias, 903

Nicaragua, 87, 653: litigation over nationalized property, *JD*, 888–91; and recognition of governments, 38

Nigeria, 885, 912: proposal for human rights commissions, 903–4

(The) 1982 Session of the UN Sub-Commission on Prevention of Discrimination and Protection of Minorities, *CD*, 651

Nonaligned countries, 115, 117, 121, 866: and Falklands war, 115, 117, 121, 122

Nongovernmental organizations, 858, 908: and UN Sub-Commission on Minorities, 651, 652, 654, 655, 656, 657, 662
Non-self-governing territories, 120
Nordic states, 59
Norms of international law, *LA,* 413: dilution of, 422, 430–40; graduated, 421, 423–30; and international relations, 413, 418–21, 441–2; normativity threshold, 415–8, 421; "soft" law, 414–5, 416, 418. *See also* Human Dignity as a Normative Concept
North Atlantic Treaty Organization (NATO), 493: individual rights under Status of Forces Agreement, *Corr.* on, 134; 880
Northern Mariana Islands, 118, 622
Norway, 899: declarations by diplomat as binding agreement, 268
Nossal, Kim Richard, Robert Spencer, & John Kirton (eds.). The International Joint Commission Seventy Years On, *BR,* 714
Nuclear Material, Convention on the Physical Protection of (1980), 665
Nuclear Weapons, Treaty on the Non-Proliferation of (1968), and Israeli 1981 raid on Iraq, 587
Nuclear Weapons Tests in the Atmosphere, in Outer Space and Under Water, Treaty Banning (1963): and "instant custom," 435; soft law in, 414
Nun, Yenny, & Albert S. Golbert. Latin American Laws and Institutions, *BR,* 388

Oda, Shigeru. Fisheries under the United Nations Convention on the Law of the Sea, *LA,* 739; on ICJ Tunisia-Libya decision, 224, 235–6, 237–8
Odle, Maurice A. Multinational Banks and Underdevelopment, *BR,* 390
Official Documents, 733
Oliver, Covey T. *BN* of Wood, 403
Olson, Robert K. U.S. Foreign Policy and the New International Economic Order: Negotiating Global Problems, 1974–1981, *BR,* 186
On the Degradation of the Constitutional Environment of the United Nations, *Ed.,* 569
On the Inadequate Reach of Humanitarian and Human Rights Law and the Need for a New Instrument, *NC,* 589
Opsahl, Torkel. *BR* of Henkin, 347
Organisation for Economic Co-operation and Development (OECD), 478: and GATT Tokyo Round, 57, 64, 68, 73
Organization of African Unity (OAU), 45, 866: and African Human Rights Charter, 904, 907–8, 909, 910, 912; attitude to human rights violations, 902–3
Organization of American States (OAS), 115, 138, 139, 638, 641, 910: Draft Convention on torture, 663, 665; and entry into force of Human Rights Convention, 640; proposed convention on terrorism, 664–8; resolution on Falklands war, 297
Organization of Petroleum Exporting Countries (OPEC), 581
Osieke, Ebere. The Legal Validity of Ultra Vires Decisions of International Organizations, *LA,* 239; *Corr.* on, 873
Overseas Private Investment Corporation (OPIC), protection against civil strife, 603

Package concept, of LOS Convention, 11–2, 281: and third states, 566–7, 568
Palestine Liberation Organization, 573–4
Panama, 657: Canal Treaty and jurisdiction of US courts, *CD,* 167; and Falklands war, 111, 115, 118–9; US Senate's conditioning consent to Canal Treaties, 259–60, 262, 266
(The) Panama Canal Treaty and Jurisdiction of U.S. Courts, *CD,* 167
Panico, Giuseppe. La Politica Commerciale Convenzionale della CEE nel sistema commerciale internazionale, *BN,* 723
Papua New Guinea, 796
Paraguay, 652, 653
Parry, Clive (ed.). The Consolidated Treaty Series, 1648–1919. Vols. 1–231 + index vol., *BR,* 922
Partsch, Karl Josef. *BR* of Gnesa, 703
———, Michael Bothe, & Waldemar A. Solf. New Rules for Victims of Armed Conflicts: Commentary on the Two 1977 Protocols Additional to the Geneva Conventions of 1949, *BR,* 377

Peace and Security of Mankind, Draft Code of Offences against, 660: at ILC 34th session, 324–5, 338
Pericles, 809
Permanent Court of Arbitration, 788
Permanent Court of International Justice (PCIJ), 420, 820: and admission of aliens, 842; and binding force of unilateral declarations, 268
Peru, 547, 638, 657: exchange control regulations and IMF Agreement, *JD*, 155–7
Péteri, Zoltán, & Vanda Lamm (eds.). General Reports to the 10th International Congress of Comparative Law, *BR*, 962
Peterson, M. J. *BR* of Quigg, 372; Recognition of Governments Should Not Be Abolished, *LA*, 31: *Corr.* on, 615
Petrovskij, V. F. (ed.). Organizatsija Obedinennykh Natsij. Kratkij Spravochnik (3d ed.), *BR*, 712
Phegan, Colin. *BR* of Lipstein, 699
Philippines, Republic of the, 304, 577, 657: diplomatic privileges and immunities of consular officers in US, *CP*, 302–3; suggestion of President's immunity in US courts, *CP*, 305–7
Phillimore, Robert, on admission of aliens, 826
Phillips, Leo H., Jr. *BR* of Newman & Wypyski, 704
Plaia, Paul, Jr., Harvey Kaye, & Michael A. Hertzberg. International Trade Practice. Vols. 1–2, *BR*, 707
Plato, 809
Plischke, Elmer. *BR* of Foreign Relations of the United States, 1950, Vol. IV: Central and Eastern Europe; The Soviet Union, 394; *BR* of Foreign Relations of the United States, 1951, Vol. III: European Security and the German Question, 397
Poland, 569, 626, 653, 654, 867, 870: diplomatic privileges and immunities of consular officers in US, *CP*, 302–3
Polish Yearbook of International Law, Vol. X, 1979–1980, *BR*, 205
Pollution, transboundary. *See* International liability for lawful acts
Pomerance, Michla. Self-Determination in Law and Practice: The New Doctrine in the United Nations, *BR*, 669
Pooley, James. Trade Secrets: How to Protect Your Ideas and Assets, *BR*, 970
Portugal, 120, 570, 616, 902: and recognition of governments, 32, 43, 45
Positivism, and admission of aliens, 808, 811–5, 823
Postlewaite, Philip F., & Michael P. Collins. International Individual Taxation, *BR*, 708
Power Sharing in the Law of the Sea, *LA*, 1
Procedural Aspects of International Law Institute: 1980 report on teaching of human rights law, 855–8, 860; 1983 survey, 855, 858–61
Proceedings of the Twenty-Third Colloquium on the Law of Outer Space, *BR*, 194
Property rights, private, and FRG antitrust, 777, 778
Proposed Amendment of the Foreign Corrupt Practices Act of 1977, *CD*, 340
(The) Proposed Iran Claims Act of the United States, *CD*, 166
Puerto Rico, 118, 122, 622
Pufendorf, Samuel, on admission of aliens, 811, 812

Quadruple Alliance (1815–1830), 32, 37
Quentin-Baxter, Robert Q., 334, 335
Questiaux, Nicole, report on states of siege, 600–1, 659
Quigg, Philip W. A Pole Apart: The Emerging Issue of Antarctica, *BR*, 372

Rajan, M. S. The Expanding Jurisdiction of the United Nations, *BR*, 365: *Corr.* on, 984
Rambouillet Declaration and summit conference (1975), 452, 467, 468, 479
Reagan, Ronald, 281: exchange rate policy, 469–70; on Falklands war, 112, 123–4; on SALT II Treaty, 272–3, 278–9; statement and proclamation of EEZ, 552; *CP*, 619–23
Recognition, 27: of Governments Should Not Be Abolished, *LA*, 31; *Corr.* on, 615: democratic legitimism, 37–8; effectivist rule, 37, 39–40, 42, 44, 46, 48–50
Recognition and Enforcement of Foreign Arbitral Awards, Convention on, enforcement under, *JD*, 308–10

Recognition of Governments Should Not Be Abolished, *LA*, 31; *Corr.* on, 615
Recueil des Cours de l'Académie de droit international de La Haye, 1979. Vols. 1–3, *BR*, 353
Refugees, admission of, 806, 810–1, 815, 831, 834, 839–40, 846
Refugees, Convention relating to the Status of (1951), and Protocol to (1967), 839–40
Rehbinder, E., on FRG antitrust law, 763
Reinhard, Hans. Rechtsgleichheit und Selbstbestimmung der Völker in wirtschaftlicher Hinsicht, *BR*, 368
Reisman, W. Michael. *BR* of Morrisson, 345; *Corr.* on *LA* by, 295; on straits passage, 99, 100, 499, 559–60
Reservations, 440, 668: and applicability of UN Convention on Contracts for the International Sale of Goods, 529, 533, 535, 536, 537–9; to LOS Convention, 12, 20, 428, 548; US practice, 259–66. *See also* American Convention on Human Rights
Restatement of Foreign Relations Law of the United States (Revised), 272: on customary human rights norms, 592, 601; on nonbinding agreements, 270; on Senate reservations to treaties, 260–3; on Vienna Convention on Treaties as codification, 554
Restatement (Second) of Foreign Relations Law of the United States, 145, 168, 306
Restatement (Second) of the Law of Judgments, on second action on same claim, 299
Reuter, Paul, 323, 325
Review Essay: Good Faith in Public International Law, *NC*, 130
Rey Caro, Ernesto J. Estudios de Derecho Internacional, *BR*, 697
Riesenfeld, Stefan A. *BN* of Langen, 722; *BN* of Panico, 723
Rights and Responsibilities. International, Social, and Individual Dimensions, *BR*, 201
Riphagen, Willem, 332–3
Rivier, Alphonse, on recognition of governments, 41
Roach, J. Ashley. *BR* of Byrne, 198
Roberts, Adam, & Richard Guelff (eds.). Documents on the Laws of War, *BR*, 383: *Corr.* on, 982
Rode, Zvonko R. *BR* of Sukijasović, 969
Rogers, John M. *BR* of Smith, 385
Röhm, Eberhard H. *BR* of Jalles, 682
Roman Empire, and admission of aliens, 809–10, 826
Romania, US court on prejudgment attachment against state agency, *JD*, 880–2
Roosevelt, Theodore, 841
Rostow, Eugene V., on legal effect of treaty reservations, 264
Rousseau, J.-J., on the "general will" and law, 5
Rowles, James. El Conflicto Honduras-El Salvador y el orden jurídico internacional, *BN*, 208
Rubin, Alfred P. *BR* of Recueil des Cours de l'Académie de droit international de La Haye, 1979. Vols. 1–3, 353; response to *Corr.* on *BR* by, 406
Rubin, Seymour J. *BN* of Finger & Harbert, 207
Ruggie, John Gerard. *BR* of Jütte & Grosse-Jütte, 172
Rumpf, Helmut. Der internationale Schutz der Menschenrechte und das Interventionsverbot, *BN*, 208
Rusk, Dean. *BR* of Catudal, 671
Ryan, Hewson A. *BN* of Rowles, 208

Safire, William, on US breach of obligations under IMF Articles, 449
Sanctions, 447, 465: against Argentina in Falklands war, 111; re Israeli participation in international organizations, 573–4, 575–6
Sandstrom, Mark Roy. *BR* of Kaye, Plaia, & Hertzberg, 707
Sanford, Jonathan E. U.S. Foreign Policy and Multilateral Development Banks, *BN*, 725
San Francisco Conference (establishing the UN, 1945), 112, 113: and revision of international law, 287–8
Saudi Arabia, 796: and recognition of governments, 43; and regime for Gulf of Aqaba, 85, 90, 102
Sauvant, Karl P. (ed.). The Collected Documents of the Group of 77, *BR*, 192; The Group of 77. Evolution, Structure, Organization, *BR*, 192
Schachter, Oscar: *Ed.* on Alwyn Freeman, 285; Human Dignity as a Normative Concept, *Ed.*, 848; on states' right to reject decisions of international organizations, 255

Schanze, Erich, Günther Jaenicke, & Wolfgang Hauser. A Joint Venture Agreement for Seabed Mining, *BR*, 373
Schechter, Michael G. *BR* of Atimomo, 968
Schermers, H. G., P. J. G. Kapteyn, P. H. Kooijmans, R. H. Lauwaars, & M. van Leeuwen Boomkamp (eds.). International Organization and Integration: Annotated Basic Documents and Descriptive Directory of International Organizations and Arrangements. Vols. I.A. & II.A (2d rev. ed.), *BR*, 359
Schoenblum, Jeffrey A. Multistate and Multinational Estate Planning. Vols. I & II, *BR*, 948
Schwartz, I., on FRG antitrust law, 763, 765
Schwarz-Liebermann von Wahlendorf, H. A. The Forms of Action at International Law, *BR*, 942
Schwebel, Stephen, 324: on ICJ Tunisia-Libya decision, 237
Schwelb, Egon, 855, 860
Scientific research, marine. *See* Law of the sea
Seidl-Hohenveldern, Ignaz. *BR* of Courbe, 701; on economic "soft" law, 443, 444
Self-defense, 27, 333, 612: by coastal states, 500, 517–8, 519, 520; and Israeli 1981 raid on Iraq, 584–5, 587–8
Self-determination, 598: and Falklands war, 116, 118, 120–2, 608–9, 614; as justifying exclusion of aliens, 816, 822; and recognition of governments, 32; Soviet theory on, 864, 865–6, 869; under OAU and African Human Rights Charters, 902, 905, 907; and UN Sub-Commission on Minorities, 652, 653, 656, 657, 660
(The) Senate Role in Treaty Ratification, *LA*, 257
Senegal, 906, 912
Settlement of Investment Disputes Between States and Nationals of Other States, Convention on the (1966), 784: and immunity from execution, 799–802, 803; meaning of investment under, 795–6; recognition and enforcement by domestic courts, 785–6, 791, 796–800, 802; rule of abstention, 785–96, 802
Shafeiei, Shafie, 648
Shusterich, Kurt Michael. Resource Management and the Oceans: The Political Economy of Deep Seabed Mining, *BR*, 693
Siazon, Domingo, ruling on IAEA vote re Israel, 577–8
Sierra Leone, 800
Silard, Stephen A. *BR* of Mann, 676
Simons, Thad W., Jr. *BN* of Casad, 724; *BR* of Guy & Leigh, 360
Singh, Elen C. The Spitsbergen (Svalbard) Question: United States Foreign Policy, 1907–1935, *BR*, 177
Sinha, S. Prakash. *BR* of Maneli, 199
Slusser, Robert M., & George Ginsburgs. A Calendar of Soviet Treaties 1958–1973, *BN*, 982
Smith, Adam, 5
Smith, Bradley F. The American Road to Nuremberg: The Documentary Record, 1944–1945, *BR*, 385
Smith, Brian, on LOS Convention and customary law, 567
Smith, Myron J., Jr. The Secret Wars: A Guide to Sources in English: Vol. I: Intelligence, Propaganda and Psychological Warfare, Resistance Movements, and Secret Operations, 1939–1945; Vol. II: Intelligence, Propaganda and Psychological Warfare, Covert Operations, 1945–1980; Vol. III: International Terrorism, 1968–1980, *BR*, 717
Soft law: of exchange arrangements, *LA*, 443; and international normative system, 414–5, 416, 418
Sohn, Louis B. Broadening the Advisory Jurisdiction of the International Court of Justice, *Ed.*, 124
Sohn/Buergenthal, human rights course book, 858
Solf, Waldemar A., Michael Bothe, & Karl Josef Partsch. New Rules for Victims of Armed Conflicts: Commentary on the Two 1977 Protocols Additional to the Geneva Conventions of 1949, *BR*, 377
Somalia, 117
South Africa, 902: expulsion from UNGA, 570–2, 576; and FRG merger control case, 776, 777,

778; legal validity of UN decisions on, 243, 250, 252, 874; and UN Sub-Commission on Minorities, 653–4, 660
South African Yearbook of International Law, Vol. 6, 1980, *BR,* 393
Southern Rhodesia, 902
South West Africa People's Organization (SWAPO). *See* Namibia
Sovereign immunity, 496, 499: defense, in PRC courts, 316–7; in French courts, 797–9; of heads of foreign states in US courts, *CP,* 305–7; and prejudgment garnishment in FRG, *JD,* 159–60; ILC progress on codification, 324, 328–30, 338; of unrecognized governments, 35–6; whether applicable to Marshall Islands, *JD,* 158–9. *See also* Settlement of Investment Disputes Between States and Nationals of Other States, Convention on the; United States: Foreign Sovereign Immunities Act
Sovereignty and "inherent powers," as justifying exclusion of aliens, 816–9, 822, 823, 826, 831, 832, 840–1
Soviet Association of International Law, 862
Soviet bloc, 581, 582. *See also* East European states
Soviet Theory of International Law for the Seventies, *NC,* 862
Soviet Yearbook of International Law, 1977, 864
Soviet Year-book of International Law, 1980, *BR,* 203
Soviet Year-Book of International Law, 1981, *BR,* 971
Space law, UNGA resolution on principles governing television broadcasting by satellites, *OD,* 733
Spain, 118, 609: and recognition of governments, 42, 43; Senate's conditioning consent to US treaty with, 258–9; and transit passage of aircraft, 495, 501. *See also* Gibraltar
Spencer, Robert, John Kirton, & Kim Richard Nossal (eds.). The International Joint Commission Seventy Years On, *BR,* 714
Stateless persons, admission of, 806, 839–40
State responsibility, 296: contribution of Alwyn Freeman, 285; graduated norms, 423–30; ILC progress on codification, 324, 331–3, 338; subjects of norms, 430–40; for transiting aircraft, 496–7, 499; for treatment of aliens, revision of international law on, *NC,* 286. *See also* International liability for lawful acts
State succession, 290: liability of PRC for 1911 railway bonds, *JD,* 146–8
Stein, Eric. *BR* of Kapteyn, Kooijmans, Lauwaars, Schermers, & Boomkamp, 359
Stein, Ted L. *BR* of Elkind, 673; *Corr.* on *LA* by Reisman & Freedman, 295; recipient of Deák Prize, 615
Stockwell, A. J. *Corr.* on *BR* by Alfred P. Rubin, 404
Stone, Julius. *Corr.* on *BR* by Kirgis, 727; on UN Charter Art. 2(4), 584–5
Strabo, 810
Strait of Magellan, 96
Strait of Tiran, regime under Egyptian-Israeli Peace Treaty, *LA,* 84
(The) Strait of Tiran, the Gulf of Aqaba, and the 1979 Treaty of Peace between Egypt and Israel, *LA,* 84
Strategic Arms Limitation Talks (SALT): legal effect of Reagan declaration on SALT II Treaty, 272–3, 278–9; US and Soviet unilateral declarations on SALT I Treaty, 267, 268–70, 272, 278; US Senate conditions to SALT II Treaty, 263–4, 266
Strauss, Robert, 64–5, 71, 75
Streinz, Rudolf. Meinungs- und Informationsfreiheit zwischen Ost und West: Möglichkeiten und Grenzen intersystemarer völkerrechtlicher Garantien in einem systemkonstituierenden Bereich, *BR,* 963
Strengthening the Soft International Law of Exchange Arrangements, *LA,* 443
Sucharitkul, Sompong, 328
Sukijasović, Miodrag. Multinacionalno Preduzeće: Pravni Aspekti, *BR,* 969
Sumner, Colin (ed.). Crime, Justice and Underdevelopment, *BR,* 965
Suy, Eric, on regime of bays, 86
Swacker, Frank W. *BR* of Chatterjee, 956
Sweden, 616
Switzerland, 469, 616, 635, 745, 790, 794, 901: and GATT Tokyo Round, 59, 68; and recognition of governments, 38, 43; treaty establishing permanent neutrality, 565

Sybesma-Knol, R. G. The Status of Observers in the United Nations, *BR,* 935
Szawlowski, Richard. *BR* of Petrovskij, 712; *BR* of Vorotnikov & Lebin, 711

Taiwan. *See* China, Republic of
Tanzania, 111, 912: intervention in Uganda, 903
Tay, Alice Erh-Soon (ed.), in collaboration with Graeme Connelly & Roger Wilkins. Teaching Human Rights, *BR,* 349
(The) Teaching of International Human Rights Law in U.S. Law Schools, *NC,* 855
Telecommunications, UNGA resolution on principles governing television broadcasting by satellites, *OD,* 733
Territorial sea. *See* Law of the sea
Territorial sovereignty: and cultural property, *JD,* 631–4; and exclusion of aliens, 804, 806–7, 812, 816, 817. *See also* Falkland Islands
Terrorism, Model American Convention on the Prevention and Punishment of Serious Forms of Violence, *CD,* 662
Terrorism Taking the Form of Crimes against Persons and Related Extortion that Are of International Significance, Convention to Prevent and Punish the Acts of (1971), 664
Thatcher, Margaret, and Falklands war, 110, 112, 114, 118
Thiam, Doudou, 324
Third World, 572, 906: and Falklands war, 115, 121–2; and international legal norms, 422. *See also* Developing countries; Group of 77; New International Economic Order
(The) Thirty-fourth Session of the International Law Commission, *CD,* 323
Thomas, J. C., & D. M. McRae. The GATT and Multilateral Treaty Making: The Tokyo Round, *LA,* 51
Thomas, Peter A. *BR* of Hill, 376
Thoman, Roy E. *BR* of MacDonald, 694
Thorn, Gaston, on majority decisions of UN, 251
Tian Ruxuan, & Wang Tieya (comps.). Guoji Fa Ziliao Xuanpian, *BR,* 977
Togo, 118
Tokyo Declaration (1973), and GATT Tokyo Round, 54, 56–9, 60, 61, 62, 63, 68, 70, 77, 78, 81
Tongue, Susanne. *BR* of Charney, 940; *BR* of Johnston, 941
Touré, Sékou, 902–3
Towards Relative Normativity in International Law?, *LA,* 413
Transfer of Sentenced Persons, Convention on the. *See* Council of Europe
Transnational corporations, 660: jurisdiction over foreign incorporated subsidiaries of US companies, *JD,* 626–8; *JD,* 636–7. *See also* Antitrust
Treaties, 27: between states and international organizations, etc., at ILC 34th session, 324, 325–8; and compensation for expropriation, *CP,* 141–3; *JD,* 144–6; and creation of norms, 433, 434–40; The GATT and Multilateral Treaty Making: The Tokyo Round, *LA,* 51; and good faith, 130, 131, 132, 134; and ICJ's advisory jurisdiction, 127, 339–40; *jus cogens* and, 423–30; soft law in, 414; subject to Inter-American Court's advisory jurisdiction, *JD,* 637–9; supremacy over prior statute, *JD,* 161–2; and third states, 438, 543–55, 561–2, 563–6, 567–8; US Senate role in ratifying, *LA,* 257. *See also* Law of the sea; UN Convention; (The) Panama Canal Treaty and Jurisdiction of U.S. Courts; Reservations; Treaty of Peace between Egypt and Israel: Vienna Convention on the Law of Treaties; Warsaw Convention
Treaty of Paris (1928), 869
Treaty of Peace between Egypt and Israel: and general international law, 105–7; implementation of, 103–5; limitation of forces under, 97–9, 101, 103–4, 107; regime for Gulf of Aqaba and Strait of Tiran, *LA,* 84
Treaty of Rome (establishing the EEC, 1957), 7, 128: free movement of workers under, 837–8
Treaty of Versailles, 820
Trooboff, Peter D. Proposed Amendment of the Foreign Corrupt Practices Act of 1977, *CD,* 340
Truman Proclamation (1945), 22, 228, 622
Tunisia, ICJ delimitation of continental shelf with Libya, *LA,* 219; *Corr.* on, 872

(The) Tunisia-Libya Continental Shelf Case: Geographic Justice or Judicial Compromise?, *LA*, 219; *Corr.* on, 872
Tunkin, G. I., theory of international law, 862–3, 867–9, 871
Turkey, 39, 652, 653
Turkish Straits, 96

Uibopuu, Henn-Jüri. *BR* of Streinz, 963
Uganda, 111, 653, 911: Tanzanian intervention, 903
Umozurike, U. O. The African Charter on Human and Peoples' Rights, *CD*, 902
Union of Soviet Socialist Republics (USSR), 111, 125, 517, 533–4, 560, 588, 610, 612, 874: declaration on SALT I Treaty, 267, 268; expulsion from League of Nations, 569–70; international law theory for 1970's, *NC*, 862; and Reagan declaration on SALT II Treaty, 272, 278–9; and recognition of governments, 32, 35, 38, 39, 43; and UN Sub-Commission on Minorities, 652–3, 654, 659; US sanctions against exports to, *JD*, 626–8; *JD*, 636–7; and US Senate conditions to SALT II Treaty, 264, 266
United Kingdom, 160, 249, 274, 281, 551, 561, 569, 773, 776, 899–900: and admission of aliens, 815, 823, 826, 828–9, 834, 836–7; amicus brief to US court re antitrust litigation, *CP*, 136–7; attitudes towards Falklands war, 109–10, 113, 114, 123–4: Commonwealth attitudes, 119; court on currency conversion date in liquidation proceedings, *JD*, 635–6; court on territorial sovereignty and cultural property, *JD*, 631–4; enforcement of IMF Agreement and letters of credit, *JD*, 155–7; and exchange rates, 449, 452, 472; on IAEA procedure re Israel, 578, 579; and recognition of governments, 35, 38, 47, 615; sovereign immunity decisions, 158–9. *See also* Falkland Islands
United Nations. List of Treaty Collections, *BN*, 726
United Nations Administrative Tribunal, requests to ICJ for advisory opinions, 125–6
United Nations Centre for Human Rights, 651
United Nations Charter, 95, 113, 120, 241, 246, 253, 254, 333, 496, 518, 574, 575, 590, 592–3, 598, 667, 668, 741, 839, 841, 869, 902, 906–7, 912: and attempts to "unseat" Israel, 570, 580–3; and Falklands war, 115, 116, 117, 119, 607, 608, 610, 613, 614, 615; and good faith, 130, 131; on human dignity, 848, 849; and ICJ's advisory jurisdiction, 124, 125, 129; and international legal norms, 425; and Israeli 1981 raid on Iraq, *Ed.*, 584; and revision of international law, 287–8; and suspension and expulsion of South Africa, 570–2
United Nations Charter of Economic Rights and Duties of States, 293, 414
United Nations Commission of Inquiry on US hostages in Iran, *Corr.* on admission of evidence by, 296
United Nations Commission on Human Rights, 903–4, 907: 35th session of Sub-Commission on Discrimination and Protection of Minorities, *CD*, 651
United Nations Commission on International Trade Law (UNCITRAL), codification of law on international sale of goods, 522–3
United Nations Conference on the Law of the Sea (1958), 12, 57, 91, 517, 519, 551, 556, 739–40, 741
United Nations Conference on the Law of the Sea (1960), 12, 551, 740, 744
(Third) United Nations Conference on the Law of the Sea, 74, 75, 88, 91, 96, 623, 754–5: and aircraft, 494, 500, 504, 506, 515; and fisheries, 741, 743, 746, 747, 751; on third states' rights, 547–8, 552, 562–3, 564, 566, 568; and Tunisia-Libya ICJ decision, 222, 229, 235, 236. *See also* Law of the sea
United Nations Conference on the Law of Treaties, 325, 430
United Nations Conference on Trade and Development (UNCTAD), 59, 65, 251, 293
United Nations Convention on the Law of the Sea. *See* Law of the sea
United Nations Development Programme, 655
United Nations Economic and Social Council (ECOSOC), 651, 653, 655, 656, 658, 661
United Nations Educational, Scientific and Cultural Organization (UNESCO), 251, 634: exclusion of Israel, 573, 579
United Nations General Assembly, 51, 114, 115, 121, 287, 288, 586, 660, 907: attempts to "unseat" Israel, 580–3; Declaration on Principles concerning Friendly Relations, 115–6, 130, 419, 549, 598; Declaration on Territorial Asylum (1967), 839; and ICJ's advisory jurisdiction,

Ed., 124; 339; and ILC 34th session, 323, 324, 325, 328, 334–7; Resolution on Principles Governing the Use by States of Artificial Earth Satellites for International Direct Television Broadcasting, *OD*, 733; resolutions in Soviet theory, 866, 869; resolutions on colonialism, 607, 608; resolutions on Falklands, 121–2, 607–9, 613, 614
United Nations High Commissioner for Human Rights, proposed mandate for, 660
United Nations Human Rights Committee, 601
United Nations Sea-bed Committee, 740–1, 743, 754
United Nations Secretariat, 76, 522, 668
United Nations Secretary-General, 126, 652, 658–9, 660, 741, 904, 907: and Falklands war, 113; report on depositary practice re reservations, 139; report on treaty-making process, 51–2
United Nations Security Council, 27, 114, 117–8, 120, 124, 250, 580, 586, 660: Res. 487 (1981) on Israeli raid on Iraqi nuclear installation, 574–6, 584; resolutions and passage through Gulf of Aqaba, 84, 102, 106; resolutions on Falklands, 111, 115, 119, 297, 608, 613, 614–5
United Nations Trust Territories, location of sovereignty of, *JD*, 158–9. *See also* Northern Mariana Islands
United States
- and admission of aliens, 815–6, 823–8, 829, 834–6, 840–1
- and air defense identification zones, 515–6, 517
- and attempts to suspend or expel Israel from international organizations, 572–80, 583–4
- and broadening ICJ's advisory jurisdiction, 125, 126, 127–9
- Clayton Act, recovery of damages by foreign states under, *CP*, 303–5
- Consular Convention with Poland (1972), diplomatic privileges and immunities under, *CP*, 302–3
- Consular Convention with the Philippines (1947), diplomatic privileges and immunities under, *CP*, 302–3
- courts and ICSID arbitration, 785–94
- Deep Seabed Hard Mineral Resources Act (1980), revenue-sharing provisions, 283, 285
- discovery of evidence abroad, devices and practice, *CD*, 896
- and exchange arrangements: amendment of IMF Articles, 452–5, 457–8, 462, 466; on intervention in exchange market, 467–73; par value system, 445–52, 471; views on Art. IV of IMF Articles, 458–60, 477
- Export Administration Act (1979): constitutionality of antiboycott laws under, *JD*, 310–2; extraterritorial application of regulations under, *JD*, 626–8; *JD*, 636–7
- and Falklands war, 111–4, 608, 612
- Federal Arbitration Act, 318, 787: enforcement jurisdiction under, 309–10
- Federal Rules of Civil Procedure, 147, 307: on evidence taken abroad, 896–7, 898–9; on second action on same claim, 299
- Federal Tort Claims Act, 150, 158, 314, 317
- Fishery Conservation and Management Act (1976), 622
- Foreign Agents Registration Act (1938), private right of action under, *JD*, 628–30
- Foreign Corrupt Practices Act (1977), proposed amendments, *CD*, 340
- Foreign Sovereign Immunities Act (1976), 159, 328–9, 330, 625: applicability of exceptions re Mexican oil spill, *JD*, 149–51; and arbitral agreement not contemplating role for US courts, *JD*, 318–20; 787–92; and claims by former Iranian hostage, 313–4; immunity from prejudgment attachment, *JD*, 880–2; liability of PRC for 1911 railway bonds, *JD*, 146–8; practical application of immunity exceptions, *JD*, 888–91; and recovery of damages by foreign states, 304; and suits by alien plaintiffs against foreign sovereigns, *JD*, 885–8
- Freedom of Information Act, 448
- and GATT Kennedy Round, 53
- and GATT Tokyo Round, 55–6, 58, 61, 64–5, 68, 70, 71, 75
- Hostage Act (1868), 315
- Immigration Act (1891), 826
- Immigration and Nationality Act, 301, 836: and Mariel immigrants, 875, 876
- International Claims Settlement Act (1949), 166
- Iranian hostages crisis: *Corr.* on evidence in *Hostages* case, 295; President's authority to extinguish hostage's claims, *JD*, 312–5 (*see also* Iran-United States Claims Tribunal)

Judiciary Act (1789), 135
and LOS Convention: proclamation of EEZ, 552; *CP*, 619–23; proposal for alternative treaty, *Ed.*, 281; proposal re fishery conservation, 743, 751, 752–3; third states' rights and duties under, 541, 551–2, 559, 568
Marijuana on the High Seas Act (1980), jurisdictional reach, *JD*, 630–1
Nationality Act (1940), 301
National Stolen Property Act, 634
nonrecognition practice: in Central America, the Caribbean, and Mexico, 38–9; of PRC, 34–5, 46; legal effect of acts of unrecognized governments, 35, 46
Outer Continental Shelf Lands Act (1953), 622
Panama Canal Treaties: and jurisdiction of US courts, *CD*, 167; US Senate's conditioning consent, 259–60, 262, 266
and passage through Gulf of Aqaba, 90–1, 97, 104–5, 106–7
Public Vessels Act, access of Chinese nationals to US courts under reciprocity requirement, *JD*, 315–7
Sherman Act, 624
signature of Convention on transfer of offenders, *CP*, 616–9
Tax Equity and Fiscal Responsibility Act (1982), 344
teaching of international human rights law in law schools, *NC*, 855
Trade Act (1975), and GATT Tokyo Round, 61, 71
Treaty of Amity and Economic Relations with Ethiopia (1951), on compensation for expropriation, *CP*, 141–3; *JD*, 144–6
Treaty of Amity, Economic Relations and Consular Rights with Iran (1955), 892
Treaty of Friendship and Cooperation with Spain (1976), Senate's conditioning consent to, 258–9
Treaty of Friendship, Commerce and Navigation with the Netherlands (1957), 636–7
Tucker Act, remedy for taking of property in wrongful death claims, 154–5
Uniform Commercial Code: "reasonable" and "appropriate" relation tests, 526, 527–9, 537, 540; and UN Convention on Contracts for the International Sale of Goods, 524–6, 529, 535–40; and Uniform Law on the International Sale of Goods, 521–4, 525, 526
and UN Sub-Commission on Minorities, 654, 657
United States Civil Aeronautics Board, 322
United States Coast Guard: admissibility of evidence obtained in violation of international law, *JD*, 878–80; authority to arrest stateless vessels on high seas, *JD*, 630–1
United States Congress, 53, 58, 129, 166, 167, 283, 285, 322, 339, 573, 622, 625, 629, 759: air liability limitations not reviewable by courts, 153–4; intent re antiboycott laws, 311–2; intent re enforcement of foreign arbitral awards, 309–10; powers re alien admission, 824–6, 827; powers to vest jurisdiction in federal courts, 886–8; and President's authority to extinguish claims, 314–5; treaty-making role, 258, 262, 267, 279. *See also* United States House of Representatives; United States Senate
United States Constitution, 279, 280, 824, 835, 876: act of Congress and prior treaty provision under, 825; *Corr.* on rights of military personnel abroad, 134; exclusionary rule and international law, *JD*, 878–80; illegal aliens' entitlement to education under 14th Amendment, *JD*, 151–3; and international air liability limitations, *JD*, 153–5; President's treaty-making powers, 273, 276; on Senate consent to treaties, 258, 273; standing to sue under, 628–9; and suits by alien plaintiffs against foreign sovereigns, *JD*, 885–8; validity of antiboycott laws, *JD*, 310–2
United States Court of Claims, 154–5
United States Court of Military Appeals, constitutional and treaty rights of US military personnel abroad, *Corr.* on, 134; 880
United States Department of Commerce: antiboycott regulations, 311–2; sanctions against French pipeline exports to USSR, 626–7
United States Department of Justice, 137, 143, 342, 343, 875: Attorney General's Interpretation of *Afroyim*, 300–1; on broadening ICJ's advisory jurisdiction, 340; enforcement powers re registration of foreign agents, *JD*, 628–30; on jurisdiction of US courts in former Canal Zone, *CD*, 167; and procedural guarantees for Mariel detainees, 876; suggestion of immunity for Philippine President, *CP*, 305–7

United States Department of Labor, 574
United States Department of State, 44, 314, 573, 580, 616, 791, 886, 896: and adjudication of expropriation cases, *CP*, 141–3; on appeals and administrative relief re loss of nationality, *CP*, 298–302; and broadening ICJ's advisory jurisdiction, 129, 339–40; and Chinese railway bonds case, 147, 148; on Consular Conventions with Philippines and Poland, *CP*, 302–3; and Falklands war, 113; and federal jurisdiction based on alienage, *CP*, 135; on handling of settlements and "small" claims by US-Iran Tribunal, *CD*, 913; and immunity of heads of foreign states, 305–7; on Israeli participation in IAEA, 583; on jurisdiction of US courts in former Canal Zone, *CD*, 167; on notes from foreign governments to US courts, *CP*, 136–7; proposed law on "small" claims against Iran, *CD*, 166; 914; and ratification of treaties, 259; on recovery of damages amendment to Clayton Act, 304–5; representations to Cuba re hijackings, *CP*, 877; request for Cuban acceptance of ineligible Mariel immigrants, *CP*, 875–6; on Vienna Convention on Treaties as codification, 553–4
United States Department of the Treasury, 167: and exchange arrangements under IMF Articles, 448, 467, 469, 473, 481
United States Foreign Claims Settlement Commission, proposed authority to adjudicate "small" claims against Iran, *CD*, 166; 914
United States House of Representatives, 305: and amending Foreign Corrupt Practices Act, *CD*, 340; approval of proposal permitting ICJ to advise domestic courts, *CD*, 338. *See also* United States Congress
United States Internal Revenue Service, 913
United States President, 338–9: authority to extinguish former Iranian hostage's claims, *JD*, 312–5; 1971 breach of obligations under IMF Articles, 447–50; legal effect of executive agreements and unilateral declarations, 269, 270–2; and treaty ratification, 259–62, 264; and treaty signature, 272–8. *See also* Carter, Jimmy; Reagan, Ronald
United States Securities and Exchange Commission, 343, 645
United States Senate, 153, 304, 322, 340: and amending Foreign Corrupt Practices Act, *CD*, 340; Role in Treaty Ratification, *LA*, 257. *See also* United States Congress
United States Special Trade Representative, and GATT Tokyo Round, 64–5, 75
United States Supreme Court, 128, 137, 150, 155, 276, 310, 314–5, 320, 339, 417, 879, 880, 901: and admission of aliens, 808, 824–8, 829, 835; on illegal aliens' entitlement to education, *JD*, 151–3; on judicial abstention in expropriation cases, 142, 145, 146; on jurisdiction under Foreign Sovereign Immunities Act, *JD*, 885–8; nationality cases, 301–2; on recovery of damages by foreign states, 304; on second action on same claim, 299–300; on suggestions of immunity, 306
United States-Mexican General and Special Claims Conventions (1923), 649–50
Universal Declaration of Human Rights, 593, 842, 902, 904, 906, 912: applicability in wartime, 603–4; on human dignity, 848
Universal Postal Convention (1969), 665
Universal Postal Union, 874
Uruguay, 652, 653
Ushakov, Nikolai, 330

Vagts, Detlev F. *BR* of Horn, Kötz, & Leser, 386; *BR* of Péteri & Lamm, 962
Váli, Ferenc A. *BR* of Albinski, 715
van den Berghe, Guido. Political Rights for European Citizens, *BR*, 953
Van den Wijngaert, Christine. The Political Offence Exception to Extradition: The Delicate Problem of Balancing the Right of the Individual and the Public International Order, *BR*, 175
Vattel, Emmerich de, 420, 816: on admission of aliens, 807, 811–5, 823, 826–7, 845
Venezuela, 576: and Falklands war, 115, 117, 118
Versailles summit meeting (1982): exchange rate policy, 472, 479; study on intervention, 473, 486
Vienna Convention on Consular Relations (1963), 439
Vienna Convention on Diplomatic Relations (1961), 306, 439
Vienna Convention on the Law of Treaties, 21, 325, 439, 646–7: Art. 18 and signature by US President, 273–8; codification vs. development, 273–5, 428, 553–4; and devaluation of con-

ventional rules, 439–40; dispute settlement, 327–8; and good faith, 130, 131, 132–3; and *jus cogens,* 427, 430, 442; reservations and entry into force under, 138–41, 640–2; and third states, 543, 544–6, 549, 550–1, 561; *travaux préparatoires,* 7
Vietnam, Democratic People's Republic of (North), 111, 653
Vietnam War, US rationale, 114
Virally, Michel. Review Essay: Good Faith in Public International Law, *NC,* 130
Vitoria, Francisco de, 423: on admission of aliens, 811
Vitzthum, Wolfgang Graf (ed.). Die Plünderung der Meere: Ein Gemeinsames Erbe wird zerstückelt, *BR,* 691
Vlasic, Ivan A. *BR* of Proceedings of the Twenty-Third Colloquium on the Law of Outer Space, 194
Volcker, Paul, and 1971 breach of obligations under IMF Articles, 449
von Mehren, Robert B. *BR* of Wyatt & Dashwood, 188; Discovery of Documentary and Other Evidence in a Foreign Country, *CD,* 896
von Münch, Ingo (ed.). Festschrift für Hans-Jürgen Schlochauer zum 75. Geburtstag am 28. März 1981, *BR,* 685
Vorotnikov, V. V., & D. A. Lebin (eds.). Mezhdunarodnye Ekonomicheskije i Nauchno-tekhnicheskije Organizatsii Stran-chlenov SEV. Spravochnik, *BR,* 711

Wälde, Thomas W., with Peter Fischer (ed.). A Collection of International Concessions and Related Instruments, *BN,* 211
Walker, George K. *BR* of Anand and of Chen, 689
Walters, F. P., on expulsion of USSR from League of Nations, 569
Wang Tieya, & Tian Ruxuan (comps.). Guoji Fa Ziliao Xuanpian, *BR,* 977
———, & Wei Min (eds.). Guoji Fa, *BR,* 977
War, law of, and human rights law, on the inadequate reach of, *NC,* 589. *See also* Hague Conventions on laws of war
Warnke, Allan E. *BR* of Smith (3 vols.), 717
Warsaw Convention (1929): Hague Protocol (1955), 153; Montreal Agreement (1966), 153; Montreal Protocols, 155; preemption of California law on liability limitation, *JD,* 153–5; unit of conversion for liability under, *JD,* 320–2
Watercourses, international, at ILC 34th session, 324, 338
Weber, Ludwig. Die Zivilluftfahrt im Europäischen Gemeinschaftsrecht, *BR,* 196
Wei Min, & Wang Tieya (eds.). Guoji Fa, *BR,* 977
Weil, Prosper. Towards Relative Normativity in International Law?, *LA,* 413
Welch, Jane (ed.). The Regulation of Banks in the Member States of the EEC (2d ed.), *BR,* 950
Western Europe: and exchange arrangements, 451, 480–1; and Falklands war, 109, 110–1, 114
Western scholars, and revising international law, 291–2
Weston, Burns H., Richard A. Falk, & Anthony A. D'Amato. International Law and World Order: A Problem-Oriented Coursebook, *BR,* 350
Westphalia, Peace of (1648), 864
Wharton, Francis, 825, 826
Wiener, Alan D. *BN* of Katō, Kumamoto, & Matthews, 210
Wilkins, Roger. *See* Tay, Alice Ehr-Soon
Williams, John W. *BN* of Sanford, 725; *BR* of Chiswick, 716
Williamsburg summit meeting (1983), exchange rate policy, 486–7
Winiarski, Bohdan, on states' right to reject decisions of international organizations, 253
Wirth, Timothy, and amending Foreign Corrupt Practices Act, 341–3
Wiss, Marcia A. *BR* of Sauvant (2 works), 192
Wolff, Christian, on admission of aliens, 811
Wolfrum, C. Rüdiger. *BR* of Reinhard, 368
Wood, Philip. The Law and Practice of International Finance, *BN,* 403
World Health Organization (WHO), 253
World Meteorological Organization, 874
World Population Plan of Action (1974), and admission of aliens, 842–3
Wyatt, Derrick, & Alan Dashwood. The Substantive Law of the EEC, *BR,* 188

Wypyski, Eugene M., & Edwin S. Newman (eds.). United States International Trade Reports. Binder I, *BR,* 704

Yankov, Alexander, 336
Yemen Arab Republic, on passage through territorial sea and straits, 558
Yin, John. The Soviet Views on the Use of Force in International Law, *BR,* 687
Yom Kippur War, 493, 581
Young, Richard. *BN* of Amin, 721

Zagaris, Bruce. *BR* of Lillich, 173
Zambia, 903, 912
Zanotti, Isidoro. *BR* of Cavelier (2 works), 401; *BR* of Golbert & Nun, 388
Zartman, I. William, & Maureen R. Berman. The Practical Negotiator, *BR,* 670
Zhou Gengsheng. Guoji Fa. 2 vols., *BR,* 977
Zoller, Elisabeth. La Bonne Foi en droit international public, Review Essay on, *NC,* 130
Zuijdwijk, Ton J. M. Petitioning the United Nations: A Study in Human Rights, *BR,* 924

CHINESE YEARBOOK OF INTERNATIONAL LAW AND AFFAIRS

Volume 2 (1982)

Edited by Hungdah Chiu

Table of Contents

Articles

Ying-jeou Ma, The East Asian Seabed Controversy Revisited: Relevance (Or Irrelevance) of the Tiao-yu-t'ai (Senkaku) Islands Territorial Dispute

K.T. Chao, East China Sea: Boundary Problems Relating to the Tiao-yu-t'ai Islands

Lyu-shun Shen, The Washington-Peking Controversy Over United States Arms Sales to Taiwan: Diplomacy of Ambiguity and Escalation

Mitchell A. Silk, Imperial China and International Law: A Case Study of the 1895 Treaty of Shimonoseki

Recent Developments

David Simon, Legal Developments in the U.S.-ROC Trade from June 1, 1981 to July 1, 1983

Jyh-pin Fa, The 1982 Amendments to the Code of Criminal Procedure of the Republic of China (with text of Articles 27, 29, 30, 31, 33, 34, 77(a), 88(1), 150, 245, and 255 of the Code of Criminal Procedure as Amended—translated by Tzu-wen Lee)

Hungdah Chiu, Selected Documents Concerning United States Arms Sales to Taiwan

Contemporary Practice and Judicial Decisions of the Republic of China Relating to International Law, edited by Hungdah Chiu, Rong-jye Chen and Tzu-wen Lee

Book Reviews (edited by Hungdah Chiu, Jyh-pin Fa, and David I. Salem)

Bilateral Treaties/Agreements Concluded by the Republic of China, January 1, 1981 to December 31, 1982

Bilateral Official, Semi-Official or Unofficial Agreements Concluded between the Republic of China and Countries Without Diplomatic Relations, January 1, 1981 to December 31, 1982 (with text of Agreements between American Institute in Taiwan and Coordination Council for North American Affairs)

Republic of China's Diplomatic and Consular Missions Abroad

Republic of China's Official, Semi-Official or Unofficial Missions Abroad

Foreign Diplomatic/Consular Mission in the Republic of China

Foreign Semi-Official or Unofficial Missions in the Republic of China

Bibliography on Selected Books and Academic Articles Published in the Republic of China Relating to International Law, Relations and Foreign Policy January 1, 1981 to December 31, 1982. Compiled by Grace Y.D. Yu and Shaiw-chei Yin

Statistics in Brief of the Republic of China, 1972–1981

The American Society of International Law

2223 Massachusetts Ave., N.W., Washington, D.C. 20008 (202) 265-4313 CABLES "AMINTLAW"

1983 MEMBERSHIP APPLICATION

[ ] REGULAR MEMBERS . . . . $ 55

[ ] INTERMEDIATE MEMBERS (first 3 years of membership for *those under 30 years of age* at time of application) . . . . $ 25
Date of Birth ______________

[ ] STUDENT MEMBERS . . . Verification to be completed by a professor or administrative officer of your school: I hereby certify that the applicant is regularly registered in
(school) ______________________________
for academic year __________ Title ______________
Signature ______________________________ $ 15

[ ] SPECIAL CATEGORY (persons *not* resident in a member country of the OECD) . . . . $ 30

[ ] CONTRIBUTING MEMBERS . . . . $ 75

[ ] SUPPORTING MEMBERS . . . . $ 150

[ ] ANNUAL PATRON . . . . $ 500

[ ] LIFE (one-time dues) $1,000

[ ] PATRON (one-time dues) $5,000

($21 of membership fee is allotted to AJIL subscription)

[ ] Please send me *International Legal Materials* at member rate of $30, plus $5 if outside U.S.

Please enroll me as a member of the American Society of International Law for the calendar year starting January 1, 19____. My check, money order, UNESCO coupon, or payment in a convertible currency is enclosed $____________. I have checked membership category for which I am eligible.

(Please Print)

Name: . . . .

Address: . . . .

City: . . . .

State (or Country): . . . . Zip: . . . .

Member, U.S. Bar? . . . . State: . . . . Year: . . . .

Signature: . . . .

[ ] Check here if you would like to receive a list of Society publications, showing special reduced prices for members.

PLEASE MAKE CHECKS PAYABLE TO *The American Society of International Law*. Contributions above obligatory dues, and all dues if membership is related to your work or profession, are tax deductible in the United States.

NONMEMBER SUBSCRIPTIONS

[ ] *AJIL* incl. ASIL *Proceedings* (add $2.50 if outside U.S.) . . . . . $ 52

[ ] *International Legal Materials* (add $5.00 if outside U.S.) . . . . $ 65